Vol. 116 • No. 1 • February 2026

BSSA

Bulletin of the Seismological Society of America

Special Section
Earthquakes Hazards 25 Years After Chi-Chi

BSSA
Bulletin of the Seismological Society of America

Vol. 116 • No. 1 • February 2026

SPECIAL SECTION

Earthquake Hazards 25 Years after Chi-Chi: Learning from the Past to Prepare for the Future

Guest Editors: Tai-Lin Tseng, Kuo-Fong Ma, Jiun-Yee Yen, Domniki Asimaki, Yann Klinger, and P. Martin Mai

Introduction to the Special Section on Earthquake Hazards 25 Years After Chi-Chi: Learning from the Past to Prepare for the Future **1**
Tai-Lin Tseng, Kuo-Fong Ma, Jiun-Yee Yen, Domniki Asimaki, Yann Klinger, and P. Martin Mai

Neotectonic Framework of Eastern Taiwan: Insights from Coseismic Rupture Patterns of the 2022 Chihshang Earthquake and Paleoseismic Investigations **5**
I-Chin Yen, Jiun-Yee Yen, Shao-Yi Huang, Yi-Chun Hsu, Fajar Rizki Widiatmoko, Wen-Jeng Huang, Nai-Wun Shih, and Chung-Pai Chang

Seismogenic Structures Offshore Taiwan and Their Earthquake Potential from the Taiwan Earthquake Model (TEM) Project **26**
Cheng-Hung Chen and J. Bruce H. Shyu

Spatiotemporal Patterns of the 2 April 2024 Hualien Earthquake Sequence and Finite-Fault Solutions of Significant Aftershocks **52**
Mei Chien, Yopi Serhalawan, Po-Fei Chen, Wei-Li Chen, and Hsuan-Yu Kuo

Earthquake Directivity and Early Warning: The Response of *P*-Alert Network to the 2024 M_w 7.4 Hualien Event **68**
Benjamin M. Yang, Himanshu Mittal, and Yih-Min Wu

ON THE COVER

The cover image shows an aerial view of the ruins of Wuchanggong temple in Nantou, Jiji, that was damaged during the magnitude M 7.6 earthquake that struck Taiwan on Sept 21, 1999 (image taken by Chen Peng Guang). The Old Wuchang Temple ruins in Jiji Township (集集) became a recognized county-level heritage site in 2022. The ruins of the old shrine, located near a rebuilt Wuchang Temple, were left untouched after the collapse to commemorate this major historical event. This dramatic photo represents the topic of the Special Issue entitled, "Earthquake Hazards 25 Years after Chi-Chi: Learning from the Past to Prepare for the Future."

Image credit: *imageBROKER.com/Alamy Stock Photo*

A Comparative Analysis of the 14 November 1986 M_L 6.8, M_w 7.3 and 2 April 2024 M_L 7.1, M_w 7.4 Hualien, Taiwan, Earthquakes: Insights into Seismic Characteristics and Regional Impact **80**
Kuo-Fong Ma, Shiann-Jong Lee, Jolan Liao, and Shih-Nan Cheng

Surface Ruptures of the 2022 Guanshan–Chihshang Earthquake Sequence, Eastern Taiwan: Implications for Fault Behavior and Recurrence **94**
Ray Y. Chuang, Zixin Lee, Chao-Jung Chiang, Li-Chieh J. Lin, Lishiue Chen, You-Wei Jiang, Chuan-Min Chao, Geng-Pei Lin, and I-Ting Wang

Revisiting the 2010 Jiashian and 2016 Meinong Earthquakes in Taiwan: Geodetic Evidence for Shared Eastward-Dipping Ramp Fault **111**
Eric D. Szymanski, Eric A. Hetland, and Ping He

HVSR-Based Assessment of Soil Nonlinear Behavior During Strong Ground Motions: Insights from the 3 April 2024 Hualien Earthquake Sequence and Regional Comparisons **133**
Chun-Te Chen, Yi-Ying Wen, and Chien-Min Su

Mechanism of Dynamic Triggering for Slab-Related Fluid-Induced Tremors Occurred in Nanao, Taiwan **149**
Yi-Hsuan Wu, Wu-Cheng Chi, Liam Chai, Akiko Toh, M. Megawati, and Chin-Jen Lin

Leveraging Big Data for Earthquake Disaster Response: Insights from Taiwanese Decision-Support Systems from 1999 to 2024 **162**
Siao-Syun Ke, Chih-Hao Hsu, Ching-Yuan Yang, Carol C. Wu, and Ming-Wey Huang

Attributes of Resilience in Disaster Response and Preparedness: Public–Private Collaboration During the 2016 and 2018 Earthquakes in Taiwan **176**
Hsiang-Chieh Lee, Hui Hsuan Yang, Shyh-Yuan Maa, and Hongey Chen

MAILING & SUBSCRIPTION INFORMATION

Subscriptions to the *Bulletin of the Seismological Society of America (BSSA)*: Information regarding institutional subscriptions can be found at www.seismosoc.org/subscriptions. Eligible members of the Seismological Society of America receive online access to *BSSA*. Individuals may apply for membership or determine eligibility by visiting www.seismosoc.org.

Bulletin of the Seismological Society of America (BSSA) is the premier journal of advanced research in earthquake seismology and related disciplines. It first appeared in 1911. Each issue is composed of scientific papers on the various aspects of seismology, including investigation of specific earthquakes, theoretical and observational studies of seismic waves, inverse methods for determining the structure of the Earth or the dynamics of the earthquake source, seismometry, earthquake hazard and risk estimation, seismotectonics, and earthquake engineering. Special issues focus on important earthquakes or rapidly changing topics in seismology.

BSSA (ISSN 0037-1106) is published bimonthly in February, April, June, August, October, and December by the Seismological Society of America, 400 Evelyn Avenue, Suite 201, Albany, CA 94706- 1375. Periodicals postage paid at Berkeley, California and at additional mailing offices.

ARTICLES

Denoising Seismograms in the Time Domain Using a Deep Learning Model — 192
Chengping Chai, Derek Rose, Scott Stewart, Nathan Martindale, Mark Adams, Anibely Torres Polanco, Lisa Linville, Christopher Stanley, and Philip Bingham

Operator Learning for Earthquake Location: Methodology and Application to Out-of-Network Events in the Mendocino Triple Junction — 205
Hongyu Sun

The Role of "Equation Error" in Empirical Regressions for Seismic Magnitude Conversions — 225
Paolo Gasperini, Emanuele Biondini, and Barbara Lolli

Regional and Depth Variations in Source-Scaling Properties for Subduction Earthquakes — 238
Yujia Guo, Ken Miyakoshi, and Kojiro Irikura

Exploring the Feasibility of a Regional Earthquake Early Warning System in Utah — 249
Emily A. Morton, Keith D. Koper, Deborah L. Kilb, and Relu Burlacu

Complex Double-Event Rupture of the 2022 M_w 6.6 Luding Earthquake — 272
Hongbo Han, Sidao Ni, Qingjun Meng, Wangwang Gu, Zhe Jia, Baolong Zhang, Han Zhang, Yong Zhou, and Minhan Sheng

Estimating Moment Magnitudes of Moderate-to-Large Earthquakes in Western China Based on the Direct P Waves — 291
Guangjie Han, Dun Wang, and Li Sun

How the Cross-Faults Influence the Dynamic Rupture Process: Insights from the Littoral Fault Zone, China — 308
Chunjing Wang, Wenqiang Zhang, Houyun Yu, Xuping Feng, Duyuan Xu, and Xiaofei Chen

The 1912 M_s 7.2 Earthquake in the Denali Region of Central Alaska — 322
Carl Tape, Anthony Lomax, Sean P. Bemis, Peter J. Haeussler, and Jessalyn Ginnaty

Earthquake Magnitude and Source Parameter Estimation with a Distributed Acoustic Sensing Dataset in the Gorda Subduction Zone — 355
Andrew J. Barbour, Jeffrey J. McGuire, Martin Karrenbach, Robert C. McPherson, Mark A. Hemphill-Haley, and Connie Stewart

High-Precision Earthquake Catalog for Minto Flats Fault Zone, Central Alaska, Reveals Complex and Conjugate Faulting — 375
Nealey E. Sims, Carl Tape, Natalia A. Ruppert, and Michael E. West

Spatiotemporal Variation in Ambient Seismic Noise and Its Effect on the Microearthquake Monitoring Capability of the Pohang Community Seismograph Network (PCSN), South Korea — 397
Yujin Sohn, Kwang-Hee Kim, Tae-Seob Kang, Byung Seok Ahn, Dabeen Heo, and Hyungjin Jeon

Scaling and Variability of Broadband Earthquake Source Spectra in Japan **415**
Shota Shimmoto

Distinguishing Tapered and Non-Tapered Gutenberg–Richter Distributions **436**
Linxuan Li and Jean-Philippe Avouac

Near-Fault Amplification and Ground-Motion Variability During the 2019 Ridgecrest, California, Sequence **467**
Elizabeth S. Cochran, Grace A. Parker, Sarah E. Minson, and Annemarie S. Baltay

A Nonergodic Ground-Motion Model for Türkiye **482**
Chenying Liu, Jorge Macedo, Norman Abrahamson, and Albert Kottke

Nonergodic Probabilistic Fault-Displacement Hazard Analysis **498**
Irene Liou and Norman A. Abrahamson

Urban Attenuation Lengths in City-Like Environments: Insights from 3D Numerical Simulations of Site–City Interaction **515**
Malcon Celorio, Philippe Guéguen, Hideo Aochi, Florent de Martin, and Luis Fabian Bonilla

ERRATUM

Erratum to Enhancing V_{S30} Mapping in the Taipei Basin: Integrating New V_S Estimation Functions, Extrapolated V_S Profiles, and Kriging with Varying Local Means **532**
Stefan C. Nicholas, Linh Thi Mai Nguyen, Chun-Liang Kuo, Jia-Cian Gao, Chun-Hsiang Kuo, Duc-Huy Tran, Shih-Jung Wang, and Jia-Jyun Dong

Introduction to the Special Section on Earthquake Hazards 25 Years After Chi-Chi: Learning from the Past to Prepare for the Future

Tai-Lin Tseng[*1], Kuo-Fong Ma[2], Jiun-Yee Yen[3], Domniki Asimaki[4], Yann Klinger[5], and P. Martin Mai[6]

The 1999 M_w 7.6 Chi-Chi earthquake struck central Taiwan at 01:47 a.m. local time on 21 September 1999, as one of the most devastating natural disasters in Taiwan's history and the largest instrumentally recorded event in the country (Shin and Teng, 2001). Its intense ground shaking, extended surface rupture, and widespread damage provided an unprecedented dataset that has profoundly shaped our understanding of fault mechanics and earthquake hazards in active collision zones (e.g., Kao and Chen, 2000; Ma *et al.*, 2006).

Twenty-five years have passed, and large earthquakes have persisted to strike Taiwan (Fig. 1), resulting in collapses of buildings and bridges (e.g., Wu *et al.*, 2016; Lee *et al.*, 2023; Tang *et al.*, 2023) and pervasive landslides on a scale comparable to that induced by the Chi-Chi earthquake (Chang *et al.*, 2024). Yet, these events fortunately caused limited loss of life, primarily due to major advances in Taiwan in earthquake hazard assessment, changes in building codes, and established early warning systems (e.g., Chen *et al.*, 2015; Shyu *et al.*, 2016; Wu *et al.*, 2016; Chan *et al.*, 2020). However, challenges remain.

This special section contains twelve publications that build upon lessons learned from the 1999 Chi-Chi earthquake and focus on recent major seismic events in Taiwan. Most contributions address the destructive moment magnitude (M_w) 7.0 of 2022 and M_w 7.4 of 2024 earthquakes, presenting advances across a broad spectrum of topics, including fault-system neotectonics, strong ground motion observations, earthquake source modeling, engineering applications, and disaster-risk mitigation. Collectively, these studies illustrate how integrated earthquake system science contributes to improved preparedness and societal resilience. In what follows, we briefly summarize these contributions in the context of Taiwan's tectonics.

The 2 April 2024 M_w 7.4 Hualien earthquake is the largest event in Taiwan since the 1999 Chi-Chi earthquake (Fig. 1). The hypocenter is 22 km deep beneath the coastal region of northern Hualien, where the westernmost Ryukyu subduction terminated, and the plate convergence is significant. The seismogenic structures remain unclear due to limited seismic stations offshore and the nature of complexity. In this special issue, Chien *et al.* (2025) performed a series of analyses to constrain the ruptures and the spatial–temporal evolution of the aftershock sequence in high resolution, further illuminating the complicated conjugate fault system and aftershock–asperity relation. The interactions between the faults remain an intriguing question. In an area north of Hualien, Wu *et al.* (2025) investigated different types of tremors and found that the high dilation of triggered tremors can be explained by fluids associated with the dehydration melt near the edge of the subducting plate.

Although no surface rupture was identified for the 2024 earthquake, the maximum ground shaking of this event exceeded 0.8g near the epicenter. Even the Taipei metropolitan area, located ~100 km to the north, experienced light shaking due to rupture directivity. Using high-density seismic arrays and improved algorithms, Yang *et al.* (2025) show the effectiveness in improving early warning lead time near the epicentral region and better intensity estimation in the rupture propagation direction. The ground-motion effects due to this event can be compared with the 1986 M_w 7.3 earthquake that occurred offshore Hualien and also caused damage in Taipei. Using teleseismic and regional records at nearby sites but four decades apart, Ma *et al.* (2025) demonstrate that these two events exhibit high similarity in focal mechanism, spectral characteristics, and seismogenic process.

Aside from source directivity, site effects are also an important factor for building damage in large earthquakes. Using weak- and strong-motion data, Chen *et al.* (2025) show that the nonlinear behavior of ground motion of the 2024 earthquake is comparable with the 2018 temblor in Hualien, emphasizing the stability of nonlinear site response through time and a sharp threshold of strain proxy for the gravel-dominated site.

1. Department of Geosciences, National Taiwan University, Taipei, Taiwan, https://orcid.org/0000-0003-4918-6662 (T-LT); 2. Institute of Earth Sciences, Academia Sinica, Taipei, Taiwan, https://orcid.org/0000-0002-4500-8079 (K-FM); 3. Department of Natural Resources and Environmental Studies, National Dong Hwa University, Hualien, Taiwan, https://orcid.org/0000-0001-6942-9364 (J-YY); 4. Mechanical and Civil Engineering, California Institute of Technology, Pasadena, California, U.S.A., https://orcid.org/0000-0002-3008-8088 (DA); 5. Université Paris Cité, Institut de Physique du Globe de Paris, CNRS, Paris, France, https://orcid.org/0000-0003-2119-6391 (YK); 6. Division of Physical Sciences and Engineering, King Abdullah University of Science and Technology (KAUST), Thuwal, Saudi Arabia, https://orcid.org/0000-0002-9744-4964 (PMM)

*Corresponding author: tailintseng@ntu.edu.tw

Cite this article as Tseng, T.-L., K.-F. Ma, J.-Y. Yen, D. Asimaki, Y. Klinger, and P. M. Mai (2025). Introduction to the Special Section on Earthquake Hazards 25 Years After Chi-Chi: Learning from the Past to Prepare for the Future, *Bull. Seismol. Soc. Am.* **116**, 1–4, doi: 10.1785/0120250259

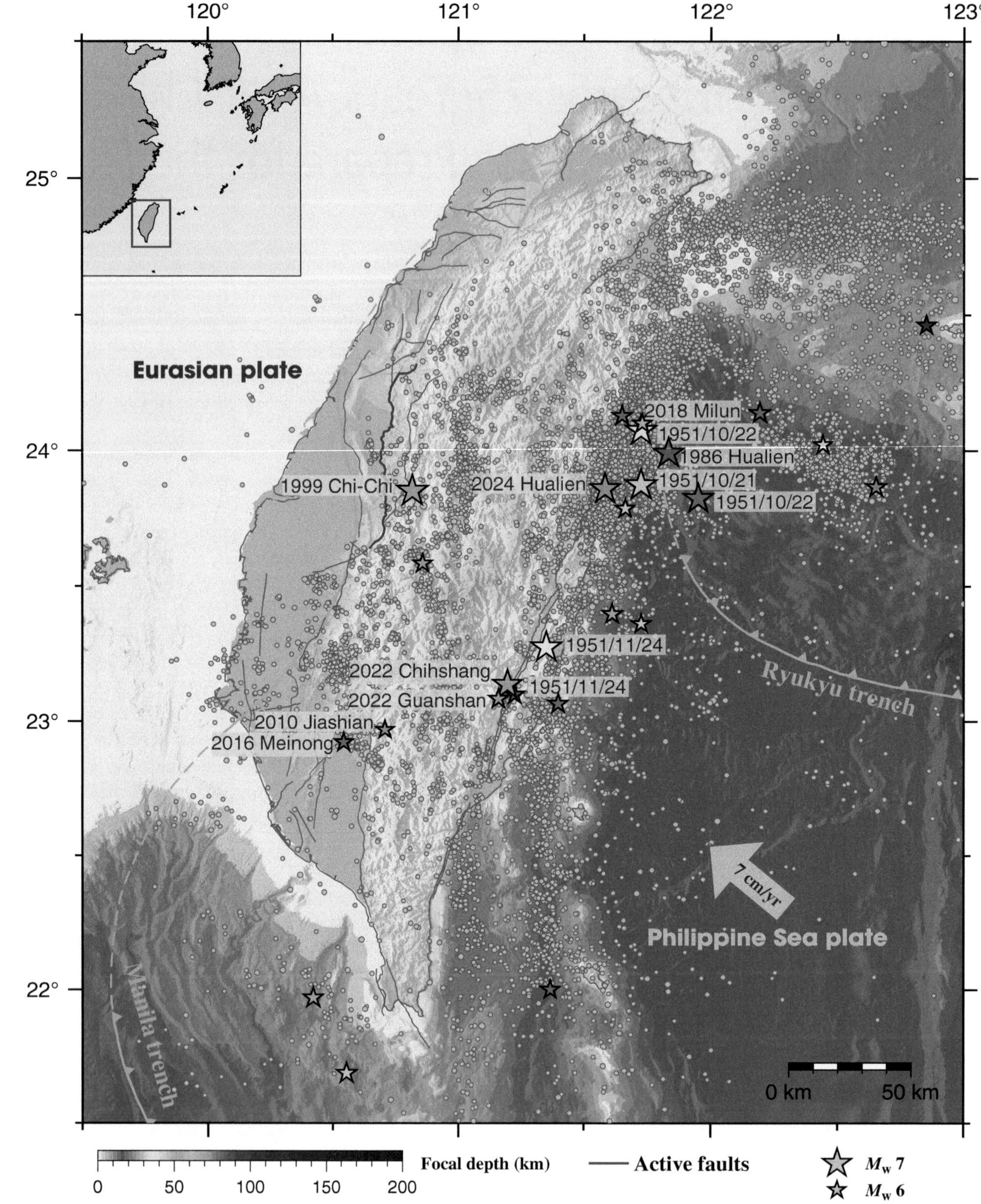

Figure 1. Map showing background tectonics, seismicity, and major large earthquakes in Taiwan. The gray small circles represent background seismicity from 1973 to 2025, based on the relocated earthquake catalog of the Central Weather Administration (CWA), Taiwan. Significant events with $M_w \geq 6.3$ are shown as stars, with colors indicating focal depth and symbol size scaled to M_w (Jian *et al.*, 2018; Shin and Teng, 2001). Labeled events correspond to those discussed in this Special Section. Hypocenters of the 1951 M_w 7 earthquake sequence are sourced from the CWA. The reddish-brown traces on land represent active seismogenic structures (Shyu *et al.*, 2020), with the Chelungpu fault highlighted by the red thick line. The red rectangle in the upper left inset map illustrates the Taiwan region within East Asia. The color version of this figure is available only in the electronic edition.

Another important earthquake sequence is the 2022 Guanshan–Chihshang doublet in southernmost Hualien, which consisted of an M_w 6.6 foreshock followed by an M_w 7.0 mainshock about 17 hr later (Fig. 1). Unlike the 2024 earthquake, this sequence resulted in discernible surface rupture in the Longitudinal Valley, which corresponds to the suture between Eurasian and Philippine Sea plates. The fault segments in the Yuli area clearly indicate left-lateral and reverse motion, the extent of which is well captured by unmanned aerial vehicle surveys and satellite images (Chuang *et al.*, 2025), offering new constraints on the complex geometry of fault systems formed by the suture zone. By combining field mapping and paleoseismic analysis, Yen *et al.* (2025) estimated the long-term slip rate and recurrence interval of the earthquakes for the past 600 yr. Considering the 1951 earthquake series, both studies highlighted the interacting behavior between the Central Range fault and the Longitudinal Valley fault, which are thought to coalesce at shallow depth.

In western Taiwan, two major earthquakes occurred in the past 25 yr with magnitudes above M_w 6.3, namely the 2010 Jiasian and 2016 Meinong earthquakes, both ruptured on blind faults at a depth of ~20 km in the crust (Fig. 1). Without a priori assumptions, Szymanski *et al.* (2025) re-estimated the slip distribution of the two events and discovered that they share a similar flat-ramp-fault geometry connecting to the detachment fault previously seen under the Chi-Chi rupture zone.

The earthquake potential of the onshore seismogenic structures is well documented in the database of the Taiwan earthquake model (Shyu *et al.*, 2020). However, faults offshore are also capable of producing large earthquakes. To further determine the potential magnitude of earthquakes offshore, Chen and Shyu (2025) investigated the disturbance of the seabed and the extent of fault structure in the offshore region using deep seismic refraction profiles, which will eventually be integrated into the current seismic hazard map in Taiwan.

Finally, rapid response and fast recovery are important for any natural disaster like the Chi-Chi earthquake. Ke *et al.* (2025) demonstrate how to integrate geoscience data (epicenter, intensity, geologic structures, and landslide risk) in real-time assessment to precisely locate affected facilities and trapped people during the 2024 Hualien earthquake and to help the government's response decision. In the scope of disaster management, Lee *et al.* (2025) discuss the resilience attributes and the relations between them (such as adaptability, connectivity, resourcefulness, agility, creativity, and diversity) based on the experiences learned in the 2016 and 2018 earthquakes.

DATA AND RESOURCES

Earthquake parameters for events occurring between 1973 and 2025 are available from the Taiwan Seismological and Geophysical Data Management System of the Central Weather Administration (CWA) (https://gdms.cwa.gov.tw/). Information on destructive earthquakes in Taiwan since 1900 can be downloaded from the CWA Seismic Center (https://scweb.cwa.gov.tw/zh-tw/page/disaster/5). Both websites were last accessed in October 2025.

DECLARATION OF COMPETING INTERESTS

The authors acknowledge that there are no conflicts of interest recorded.

ACKNOWLEDGMENTS

The authors would like to extend their sincere gratitude to the *BSSA* staff for their support throughout the Special Section. The authors also thank all authors who contributed their work to this Special Issue.

REFERENCES

Chan, C. H., K. F. Ma, J. B. H. Shyu, Y. T.Y. J. Lee, J. C. Gao, Y. T. Yen, and R. J. Rau (2020). Probabilistic seismic hazard assessment for Taiwan: TEM PSHA2020, *Earthq. Spectra* **36,** no. 1_Suppl, 137–159, doi: 10.1177/8755293020951587.

Chang, J. M., W. A. Chao, C. M. Yang, and M. W. Huang (2024). Coseismic and subsequent landslides of the 2024 Hualien earthquake (M 7.2) on April 3 in Taiwan, *Landslides* **21,** no. 10, 2591–2595, doi: 10.1007/s10346-024-02312-x.

Chen, C. H., and J. B. H. Shyu (2025). Seismogenic structures offshore Taiwan and their earthquake potential from the Taiwan earthquake model (TEM) project, *Bull. Seismol. Soc. Am.*, doi: 10.1785/0120250009.

Chen, C.-T., Y.-Y. Wen, and C.-M. Su (2025). HVSR-based assessment of soil nonlinear behavior during strong ground motions: Insights from the 3 April 2024 Hualien earthquake sequence and regional comparisons, *Bull. Seismol. Soc. Am.*, doi: 10.1785/0120250106.

Chen, D. Y., N. C. Hsiao, and Y. M. Wu (2015). The earthworm based earthquake alarm reporting system in Taiwan, *Bull. Seismol. Soc. Am.* **105,** no. 2a, 568–579, doi: 10.1785/0120140147.

Chien, M., Y. Serhalawan, P. F. Chen, W. L. Chen, and H. Y. Kuo (2025). Spatiotemporal patterns of the 2 April 2024 Hualien earthquake sequence and finite-fault solutions of significant aftershocks, *Bull. Seismol. Soc. Am.*, doi: 10.1785/0120250117.

Chuang, R. Y., Z. Lee, C.-J. Chiang, L.-C. J. Lin, L. Chen, Y.-W. Jiang, C.-M. Chao, G.-P. Lin, and I.-T. Wang (2025). Surface ruptures of the 2022 Guanshan-Chihshang earthquake sequence, eastern Taiwan: Implications for fault behavior and recurrence, *Bull. Seismol. Soc. Am.*, doi: 10.1785/0120250120.

Jian, P. R., T. L. Tseng, W. T. Liang, and P. H. Huang (2018). A new automatic full-waveform regional moment tensor inversion algorithm and its applications in the Taiwan area, *Bull. Seismol. Soc. Am.* **108,** no. 2, 573–587, doi: 10.1785/0120170231.

Kao, H., and W. P. Chen (2000). The Chi-Chi earthquake sequence: Active, out-of-sequence thrust faulting in Taiwan, *Science* **288,** no. 5475, 2346–2349, doi: 10.1126/science.288.5475.2346.

Ke, S.-S., C.-H. Hsu, C.-Y. Yang, C. C. Wu, and M.-W. Huang (2025). Leveraging big data for earthquake disaster response: Insights from Taiwanese decision support systems from 1999 to 2024, *Bull. Seismol. Soc. Am.*, doi: 10.1785/0120250188.

Lee, S. J., T. Y. Liu, and T. C. Lin (2023). The role of the west-dipping collision boundary fault in the Taiwan 2022 Chihshang earthquake sequence, *Sci. Rep.* **13,** no. 1, doi: 10.1038/s41598-023-30361-0.

Lee, H. C., H. H. Yang, S. Y. Maa, and H. Chen (2025). Attributes of resilience in disaster response and preparedness: Public–private collaboration during the 2016 and 2018 earthquakes in Taiwan, *Bull. Seismol. Soc. Am.*, doi: 10.1785/0120250069.

Ma, K. F., S. J. Lee, J. Liao, and S. N. Cheng (2025). A comparative analysis of the 14 November 1986 ML 6.8, M_w 7.3 and 2 April 2024 ML 7.1, M_w 7.4 Hualien, Taiwan, earthquakes: Insights into seismic characteristics and regional impact, *Bull. Seismol. Soc. Am.*, doi: 10.1785/0120250100.

Ma, K. F., H. Tanaka, S. R. Song, C. Y. Wang, J. H. Hung, Y. B. Tsai, J. Mori, Y. F. Song, E. C. Yeh, W. Soh, *et al.* (2006). Slip zone and energetics of a large earthquake from the Taiwan Chelungpu-fault drilling project, *Nature* **444,** no. 7118, 473–476, doi: 10.1038/nature05253.

Shin, T. C., and T. L. Teng (2001). An overview of the 1999 Chi-Chi, Taiwan, earthquake, *Bull. Seismol. Soc. Am.* **91,** no. 5, 895–913, doi: 10.1785/0120000738.

Shyu, J. B. H., Y. R. Chuang, Y. L. Chen, Y. R. Lee, and C. T. Cheng (2016). A new on-land seismogenic structure source database from the Taiwan earthquake model (TEM) project for seismic hazard analysis of Taiwan, *Terr. Atmos. Ocean. Sci.* **27,** no. 3, 311–323, doi: 10.3319/Tao.2015.11.27.02(Tem).

Shyu, J. B. H., Y. H. Yin, C. H. Chen, Y. R. Chuang, and S. C. Liu (2020). Updates to the on-land seismogenic structure source database by the Taiwan Earthquake Model (TEM) project for seismic hazard analysis of Taiwan, *Terr. Atmos. Ocean. Sci.* **31,** no. 4, 469–478, doi: 10.3319/Tao.2020.06.08.01.

Szymanski, E. D., E. A. Hetland, and P. He (2025). Revisiting the 2010 Jiashian and 2016 Meinong earthquakes in Taiwan: Geodetic evidence for shared eastward dipping ramp-fault, *Bull. Seismol. Soc. Am.*, doi: 10.1785/0120250050.

Tang, C. H., Y. N. Lin, H. Tung, Y. Wang, S. J. Lee, Y. J. Hsu, J. B. H. Shyu, Y. T. Kuo, and H. Y. Chen (2023). Nearby fault interaction within the double-vergence suture in eastern Taiwan during the 2022 Chihshang earthquake sequence, *Commun. Earth Environ.* **4,** no. 1, doi: 10.1038/s43247-023-00994-0.

Wu, Y. H., W. C. Chi, L. Chai, A. Toh, M. Megawati, and C. J. Lin (2025). Mechanism of dynamic triggering for slab-related fluid-induced tremors occurred in Nanao, Taiwan, *Bull. Seismol. Soc. Am.*, doi: 10.1785/0120240256.

Wu, Y. M., W. T. Liang, H. Mittal, W. A. Chao, C. H. Lin, B. S. Huang, and C. M. Lin (2016). Performance of a low-cost earthquake early warning system (P-alert) during the 2016 M6.4 Meinong (Taiwan) earthquake, *Seismol. Res. Lett.* **87,** no. 5, 1050–1059, doi: 10.1785/0220160058.

Yang, B. M., H. Mittal, and Y. M. Wu (2025). Earthquake directivity and early warning: The response of P-alert network to the 2024 M_w 7.4 Hualien event, *Bull. Seismol. Soc. Am.*, doi: 10.1785/0120250076.

Yen, I.-C., J.-Y. Yen, S.-Y. Huang, Y.-C. Hsu, F. R. Widiatmoko, W.-J. Huang, N.-W. Shih, and C.-P. Chang (2025). Neotectonic framework of eastern Taiwan: Insights from coseismic rupture patterns of the 2022 ML 6.9 Chihshang earthquake and paleoseismic investigations, *Bull. Seismol. Soc. Am.*, doi: 10.1785/0120250062.

Manuscript received 10 November 2025
Published online 17 December 2025

Neotectonic Framework of Eastern Taiwan: Insights from Coseismic Rupture Patterns of the 2022 Chihshang Earthquake and Paleoseismic Investigations

I-Chin Yen[1,2], Jiun-Yee Yen[*3], Shao-Yi Huang[4], Yi-Chun Hsu[5], Fajar Rizki Widiatmoko[3], Wen-Jeng Huang[1], Nai-Wun Shih[3], and Chung-Pai Chang[5]

ABSTRACT

OPEN ACCESS

The M_w 6.9 Chihshang earthquake on 18 September 2022 produced ∼65 km of surface ruptures in eastern Taiwan, marking the most extensive surface faulting since the 1999 M_w 7.6 Chi-Chi earthquake. Field and geophysical data reveal that the event ruptured the west-dipping Central Range fault system (CeRFS), rather than the traditionally dominant Longitudinal Valley fault system (LVFS). The rupture exhibited thrust motion with a significant left-lateral component, showing maximum vertical and horizontal offsets of ∼1.2 and 2.0 m, respectively. In the Changliang area, the 2022 Chihshang earthquake rupture reactivated a pre-existing scarp (∼1.7 m high), indicating cumulative displacements from past earthquakes. Paleoseismic trenching at Songpu identified five surface-rupturing events since ∼A.D. 1525, including the 1951 Longitudinal Valley earthquake sequence and 2022 Chihshang earthquake. Radiocarbon dating constrains three earlier events at A.D. 1658–1796, A.D. 1591–1689, and A.D. 1525–1611, yielding long-term vertical slip rates of 6.7–7.3 mm/yr and up to ∼11.5 mm/yr from stratigraphic reconstruction. The contrasting rupture geometries of the 1951 Longitudinal Valley earthquake sequence and 2022 Chihshang earthquake suggest mechanical interaction and stress transfer between the west-dipping CeRFS and the east-dipping LVFS. These findings redefine the fault architecture of the Longitudinal Valley and highlight the CeRFS as a critical but previously underappreciated source of seismic hazard in eastern Taiwan.

KEY POINTS

- Five paleoseismic events over 600 yr provide the first Yuli segment history with 140-year recurrence.
- Geomorphic and footwall data reveal sustained vertical slip of 6.7–11.5 mm/yr over the past 600 yr.
- Trenches reveal consistent west-up Central Range fault system ruptures in close proximity to the Longitudinal Valley fault system (LVFS) with minimal LVFS displacement.

INTRODUCTION

2022 Guanshan–Chihshang earthquake sequence

Taiwan has formed through the arc-continent collision between the Luzon arc and the Eurasian continental margin since approximately 6 Ma. This collision remains active today, generating high seismicity and rapid crustal deformation across the region (Biq, 1973; Tsai, 1986; Teng, 1990; Yu *et al.*, 1997; Wu, Chang, *et al.*, 2008). The Longitudinal Valley in eastern Taiwan, situated between the Ryukyu and Luzon arcs, marks the suture zone of this active collision, as evidenced by its intense seismic activity and tectonic features with an east-dipping geometry (Kuo-Chen *et al.*, 2023). On 18

1. Graduate Institute of Applied Geology, National Central University, Taoyuan, Taiwan, https://orcid.org/0000-0001-6360-300X (I-CY); https://orcid.org/0000-0001-7392-8027 (W-JH); 2. YIC Geological Office, Penghu, Taiwan; 3. Department of Natural Resources and Environmental Studies, National Dong Hwa University, Hualien, Taiwan, https://orcid.org/0000-0001-6942-9364 (J-YY); https://orcid.org/0000-0002-5107-1226 (FRW); https://orcid.org/0009-0000-7513-0107 (N-WS); 4. Science and Technology Research Institute for DE-Carbonization, National Taiwan University, Taipei, Taiwan, https://orcid.org/0000-0002-0305-3269 (S-YH); 5. Center for Space and Remote Sensing Research, National Central University, Taoyuan, Taiwan, https://orcid.org/0009-0003-1969-6749 (Y-CH)

*Corresponding author: jyyen@gms.ndhu.edu.tw

Cite this article as Yen, I.-C., J.-Y. Yen, S.-Y. Huang, Y.-C. Hsu, F. R. Widiatmoko, W.-J. Huang, N.-W. Shih, and C.-P. Chang (2025). Neotectonic Framework of Eastern Taiwan: Insights from Coseismic Rupture Patterns of the 2022 Chihshang Earthquake and Paleoseismic Investigations, *Bull. Seismol. Soc. Am.* **116**, 5–25, doi: 10.1785/0120250062

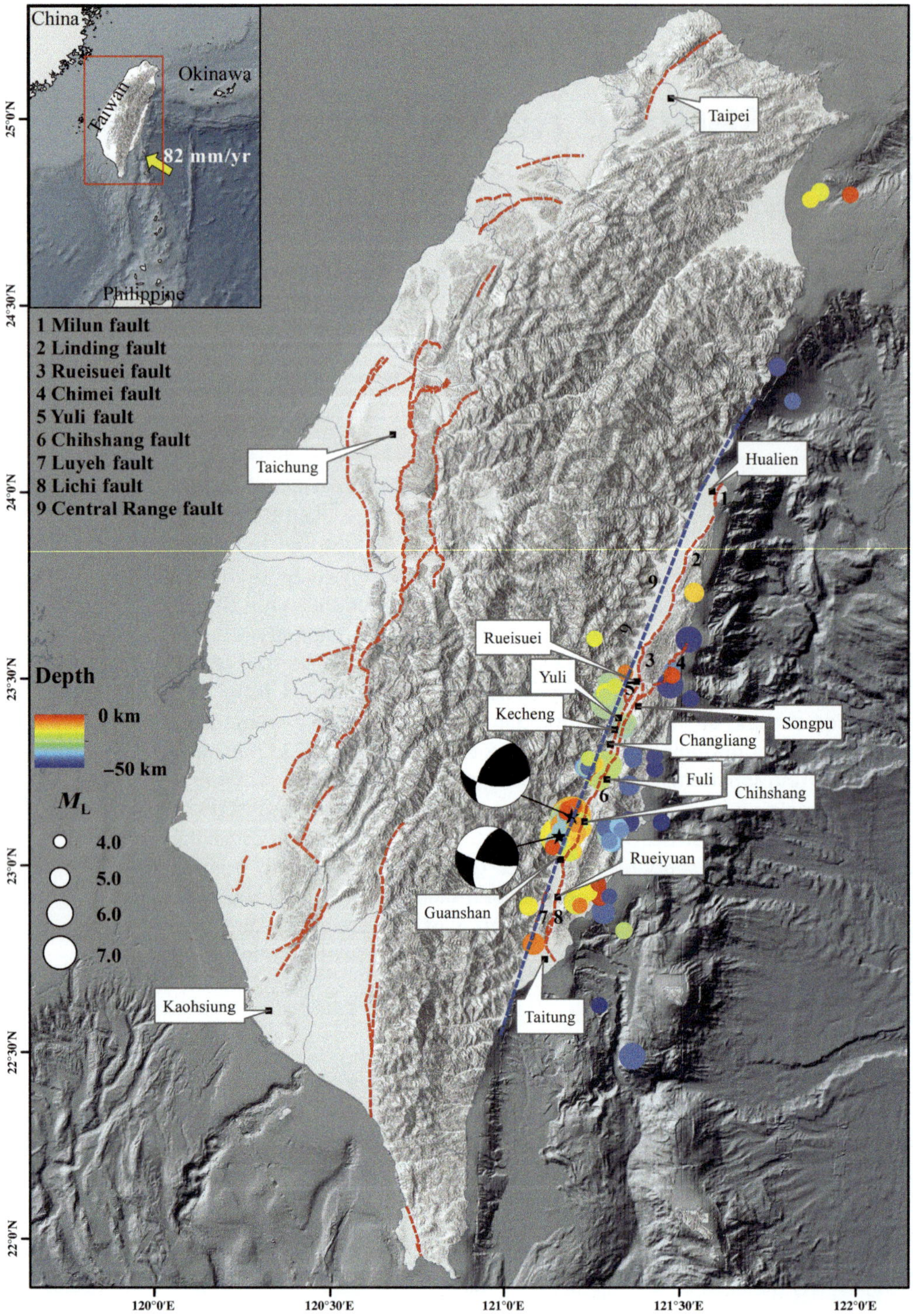

Figure 1. Distribution of earthquakes with magnitudes ≥ 4.0 in the Longitudinal Valley from September to October 2022, locations and focal mechanisms of the 17 and 18 September 2022 earthquakes are in Guanshan and Chihshang, respectively (Central Weather Administration [CWA], Taiwan, 2012). The red dashed lines indicate the locations of active faults issued by the Geological Survey and Mining Management Agency (GSMMA; see Data and Resources). Faults in eastern Taiwan are labeled with numbers and annotated in the map. The inset in the upper left corner shows the velocity vector of the Philippine Sea plate relative to the Penghu geodetic station S01R (Yu *et al.*, 1990).

September 2022 at 14:44 local time (UTC+8), a moment magnitude (M_w) of 6.9 earthquake occurred near Chihshang, eastern Taiwan, as reported by the Geophysical Database Management System (GDMS) of Taiwan's Central Weather Administration (Central Weather Administration [CWA], Taiwan, 2012). The mainshock, with a focal depth of 7.0 km (Fig. 1), followed an M_w 6.5 earthquake with a focal depth of 7.3 km that struck Guanshan on 17 September (Sun *et al.*, 2024). The earthquake caused substantial structural damage to critical infrastructure, including bridges, railroads, buildings, roads, tunnels, and utility networks (water, sewage, and electrical systems). Damage to transportation networks significantly hampered emergency response operations and left eastern Taiwan's rail system inoperable for several months after the event (Ko *et al.*, 2023; Lin *et al.*, 2024).

The earthquake, while resulting in no reported fatalities, triggered persistent aftershock sequences and caused significant structural damage across a wide area extending from Rueisuei Township in the north to Luyeh Township in the south, generating considerable anxiety among residents. Although Taiwan is situated in a highly seismically active region, visible surface ruptures have been relatively rare since the catastrophic 1999 M_w 7.6 Chi-Chi earthquake. The 6 February 2018 M_L 6.2 Hualien earthquake marked the first significant seismic event in eastern Taiwan to produce notable surface ruptures after the Chi-Chi earthquake, though with a relatively limited fault trace of approximately 7 km (Huang *et al.*, 2019). The September 2022 M_w 6.9 earthquake, however, far exceeded the 2018 event in magnitude and impact, ranking second only to the Chi-Chi earthquake in the recent seismic history of Taiwan. Our field

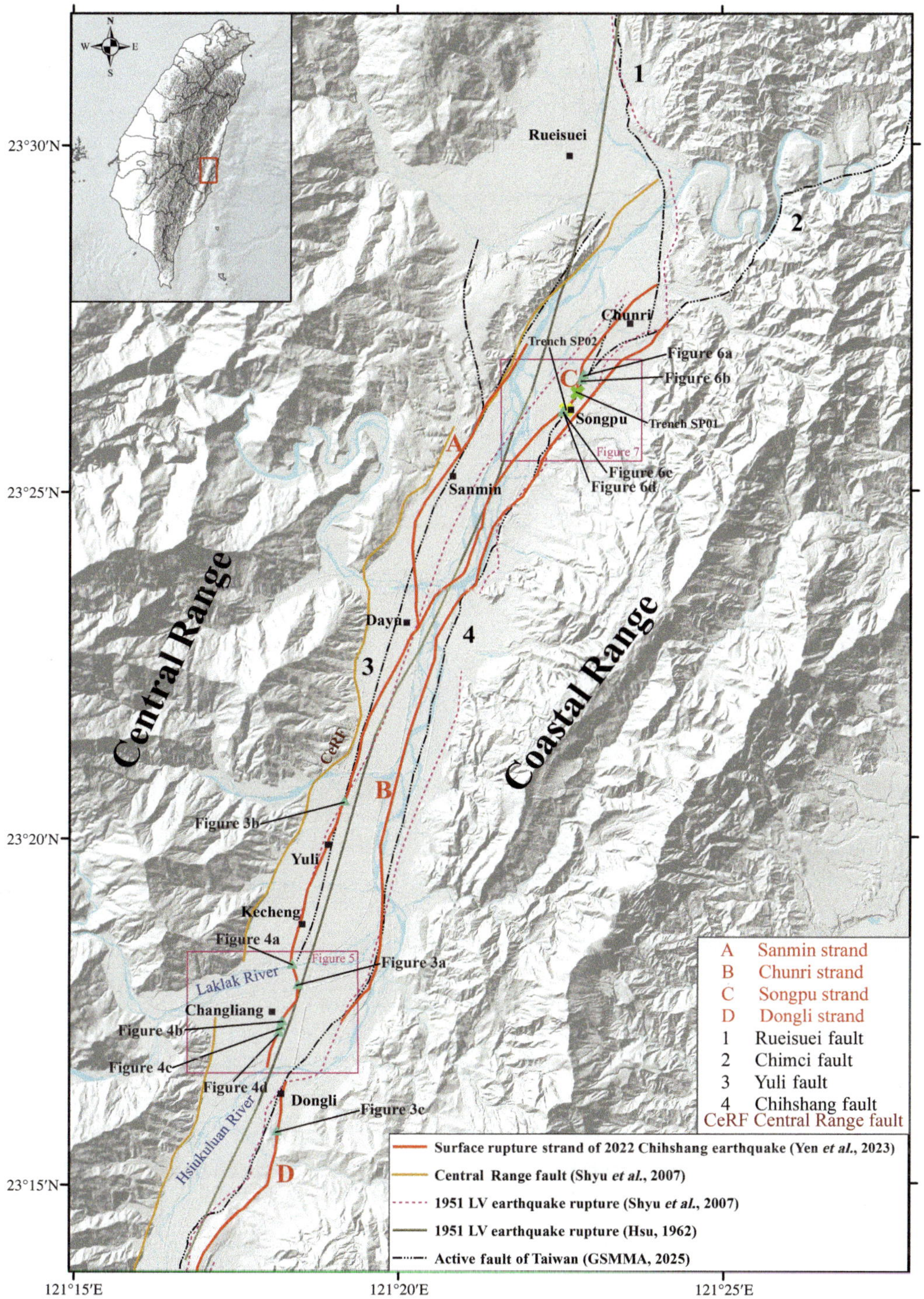

Figure 2. Close-up of main structures in the North-Central Longitudinal Valley, eastern Taiwan. The red line marks the surface rupture strand of the 2022 Chihshang earthquake (Yen *et al.*, 2023). The orange line represents the Central Range Fault (Shyu *et al.*, 2007). The pink dotted line shows the 1951 Longitudinal Valley earthquake rupture mapped by Shyu *et al.* (2007), while the yellow line indicates the 1951 rupture trace documented by Hsu (1962). The black dash-dotted line denotes active faults of Taiwan compiled by GSMMA (2005).

investigations revealed discontinuous surface ruptures extending from Rueiyuan in the south to Rueisuei in the north, with the cumulative length of all rupture strands exceeding 100 km when including discontinuous segments. This event now stands as the most significant earthquake event recorded in eastern Taiwan since the 1951 Longitudinal Valley earthquake sequence (hereafter 1951 LV earthquake sequence), raising concerns about extensive surface deformation comparable to these historic events.

The Longitudinal Valley of eastern Taiwan forms a prominent north-northeast-trending (N20°E) feature approximately 150 km long and 5–6 km wide at its maximum. The Longitudinal Valley Fault system (hereafter LVFS) separates it from the Coastal Range to the east. The LVFS, also known as the Coastal Range fault system, comprises several named segments from north to south: the Lingding fault, Rueisuei fault, Chihshang fault, Lichi fault, and Luyeh fault. Each segment belongs to the LVFS and exhibits distinct slip patterns (Chen *et al.*, 2007).

To the west of the Longitudinal Valley lies the Central Range, the eastern mountain front that descends to the valley floor; from Mt. Yushan (3952 m) to the valley, the relief is ~4 km within ~40 km (≈10% average grade). Biq (1965) proposed the existence of a Central Range fault along this mountain front, separating the Central Range from the Longitudinal Valley (Fig. 1). Over the subsequent ~30 yr, relatively few studies addressed the continuity or kinematics of this fault. Shyu, Sieh, Chen, and Chung (2006) later mapped fault⊠related geomorphic features along the mountain front and traced a Central Range fault from Rueisuei in the north to Chihshang in the south (Fig. 2), whereas in the same article, they treated the Yuli fault as a distinct structure within the Longitudinal Valley. In this study, we integrate these

TABLE 1
Summary of Major Active Fault Systems in Eastern Taiwan

Fault Name in This Article	Name in Previous Literature	Orientation/Movement	References
Central Range fault system (CeRFS)	Central Range fault (CeRF)	West-dipping, reverse fault	Biq (1965), Shyu, Sieh, Chen, and Chung (2006), and Wang *et al.* (2024)
Longitudinal Valley fault system (LVFS)	Longitudinal Valley fault (LVF)	East-dipping, reverse fault	Shyu, Sieh, Avouac, *et al.* (2006) and Chen *et al.* (2007, 2024)
Yuli segment	Yuli fault	Left-lateral fault	Shyu *et al.* (2007), Chen *et al.* (2007), Wang *et al.* (2024), Chen *et al.* (2024), and GSMMA (2005)
Rueisuei segment	Rueisuei fault	East-dipping, reverse fault	Shyu, Sieh, Avouac, *et al.* (2006), Chen *et al.* (2007), and GSMMA (2025; see Data and Resources)
Chihshang segment	Chihshang fault	East-dipping, reverse fault	Shyu, Sieh, Avouac, *et al.* (2006), Chen *et al.* (2007), and GSMMA (2005)
Sanmin strand	Dayu–Sanmin segment	Left-lateral fault	Yen *et al.* (2023)
Songpu strand	Changliang–Songpu segment	West-dipping, left-lateral reverse fault	Yen *et al.* (2023)
Chunri strand	Chuanzaishan–Chunri segment	East-dipping, left-lateral reverse fault	Yen *et al.* (2023)
Dongli strand	Luntian–Dongli segment	West-dipping, left-lateral reverse fault	Yen *et al.* (2023)
Zhutian strand	Dianguang–Zhutian segment	East-dipping, left-lateral reverse fault	Yen *et al.* (2023)

observations and refer to the combined structures as the Central Range fault system (hereafter CeRFS), comprising the Yuli segment and northern segments (Fig. 1). When citing other studies, we retain their original terminology (e.g., "CeRF," "LVF," and individual named faults; Table 1).

The 1951 LV earthquake sequence, which affected the city of Hualien and the central portion of the Longitudinal Valley, consisted of multiple seismic events with estimated magnitudes ranging from 7.3 to 7.8 (Cheng *et al.*, 1996; Shyu *et al.*, 2007; Lo *et al.*, 2012). This sequence extended approximately two months and produced maximum surface displacements of ~2 m, with ruptures exhibiting both vertical and left-lateral motion components. The 1951 LV earthquake sequence generated spatially discontinuous surface ruptures extending from Hualien City southward to Yuli (Fig. 2).

The 2022 Chihshang earthquake produced ~65 km of surface ruptures along the central Longitudinal Valley, partly overlapping the mapped traces of the Yuli fault and the Chihshang fault of the LVFS, while also generating several previously unrecognized faults. Field investigations by Yen *et al.* (2023) indicate that the 2022 Chihshang earthquake surface rupture composed six event-scale rupture strands, with maximum vertical displacement of ~1.2 m and horizontal displacement of ~2.0 m, consistent with renewed activity within the CeRFS and involvement of the Yuli fault as a subsidiary strand. Although portions of the 2022 Chihshang earthquake rupture trace locally coincide with mapped strands of the LVFS, detailed observations show that most surface breaks crosscut rather than reactivate the LVFS, and we find no compelling evidence for reactivation of the Chihshang fault during this event. Complementary observations by Wang *et al.* (2024), including left-lateral offsets up to ~1.4 m south of Yuli and an inferred steeply west-dipping geometry, further support interpreting the Yuli fault as a branch of the CeRFS. (Terminology note: hereafter, "segment" refers to structural partitions of the CeRFS, whereas "rupture strand" refers specifically to the 2022 Chihshang earthquake event-scale subdivisions; Table 1)

Building on this framework, Tung *et al.* (2025) analyzed deformation across the 2022 Chihshang earthquake using Global Navigation Satellite System (GNSS) and precise leveling data, resolving preseismic, coseismic, and early postseismic phases. Their results showed that coseismic slip was partitioned across a dual-vergence system involving the west-dipping CeRF and the east-dipping LVFS. Consistently, Tang *et al.* (2023), integrating GNSS, pixel-offset correlations, and Interferometric Synthetic Aperture Radar (InSAR) data, constrained the spatiotemporal slip evolution and proposed a conjugate, double-vergence geometry in which the CeRFS intersects the LVFS at depth, potentially accounting for the persistent seismic gap in the central Longitudinal Valley. Additional geodetic and field-based studies further refined the deformation field. Widiatmoko *et al.* (2023), based on the Real-Time Kinematic (RTK) GNSS surveys of nearly 200 benchmarks, documented distinct block movements and quantified displacements across the Central Range, Coastal Range, and different Longitudinal Valley blocks, thereby linking the Yuli fault to the CeRFS.

Overall, the 2022 Guanshan–Chihshang earthquake sequence exhibited lower magnitudes and smaller displacements than the 1951 LV earthquake sequence. However, our comparative analysis shows that although both sequences ruptured overlapping fault segments, they produced contrasting deformation styles, highlighting the complex kinematics and evolving structural architecture of the Longitudinal Valley.

Tectonic setting and previous work

The Longitudinal Valley represents one of the most seismically active plate boundaries in the world (Kim *et al.*, 2006; Wu *et al.*, 2006, 2007, 2014; Liang *et al.*, 2007; Wu, Chang, *et al.*, 2008; Wu, Zhao, Chang, and Hsu, 2008; Cheng 2009; Kuo-Chen *et al.*, 2023). As introduced earlier, the valley is bounded by two major fault systems: the west-dipping CeRFS and the east-dipping LVFS (or CoRF/LVF in earlier literature).

Geodetic surveys have demonstrated significant activity along the LVFS, characterized by differential horizontal velocities across various fault segments ranging from 5 mm/yr to exceeding 30 mm/yr (Liu and Yu, 1990; Yu *et al.*, 1990; Yu and Kuo, 2001; Peyret *et al.*, 2011; Yen *et al.*, 2018). InSAR analyses further indicate shallow creep along the Chihshang segment of the LVFS (Hsu and Bürgmann, 2006), consistent with geodetic measurements (Angelier *et al.*, 1997; Lee *et al.*, 2003; Murase *et al.*, 2013, 2024). The fault's high seismic potential is further evidenced by numerous large historical earthquakes producing substantial coseismic displacements (Cheng *et al.*, 1996; Shyu *et al.*, 2007). Seismic reflection studies have successfully imaged deformed strata in the shallow subsurface sediments of the Longitudinal Valley, revealing the LVFS along the western mountain front of the Coastal Range (Kuo-Chen *et al.*, 2023). Long-term slip rates of 22.7 mm/yr for the LVFS have been determined through analysis of geomorphic features (Shyu, Sieh, Chen, and Chung, 2006) and paleoseismic trenching investigations (Yen *et al.*, 2008), with the latter suggesting a recurrence interval of approximately 150 yr for major earthquakes along the north-central segment. These results suggest that aseismic creep accommodates a large portion of the near-surface slip, whereas a smaller component occurs seismically (Thomas *et al.*, 2014). The LVFS represents a critical tectonic structure accommodating significant deformation within the convergence boundary between the Eurasian and Philippine Sea plates.

In contrast to the LVFS, the Central Range fault system (CeRFS) presented a more enigmatic tectonic signature despite the pronounced topographic expression of the Central Range. Despite rising significantly higher than the Coastal Range, evidence for the CeRFS's precise location and activity remained largely inconclusive before the 2022 Chihshang earthquake. Geodetic leveling surveys conducted by Liu and Yu (1990) documented significant uplift of the Central Range relative to the Longitudinal Valley, revealing gradual elevation transitions rather than abrupt changes, suggesting the potential presence of a locked fault system between the Central Range and the Longitudinal Valley. Through detailed geomorphic analysis, Shyu, Sieh, Avouac, *et al.* (2006) proposed potential surface expressions of the CeRFS and calculated maximum slip rates of approximately 12.8 mm/yr. Nevertheless, the existence and exact configuration of the CeRFS remained debated. Alternative tectonic models, such as that proposed by Simoes *et al.* (2007), suggest that Taiwan's mountain-building processes could be adequately explained by an east-dipping backstop mechanism without necessitating a west-dipping fault to account for the topographic differential between the Central Range and the Longitudinal Valley. Chen *et al.* (2024) integrated seismic tomography, relocated seismicity, and field mapping of surface rupture to propose a cross-cutting relationship between the CeRFS and the LVFS, and suggested that the Yuli fault is a branch of the CeRFS.

Based on the surface rupture characteristics and their along-strike continuity, Yen *et al.* (2023) divided the 2022 Chihshang earthquake rupture into five strands: Zhutian, Dongli, Songpu, Chunri, and Sanmin. Overall, the ruptures display predominantly left-lateral strike-slip motion accompanied by localized compressional and extensional deformation. The Zhutian and Chunri strands are characterized by left-lateral motion with uplift on the eastern side, whereas the Dongli and Songpu strands exhibit similar left-lateral motion but with uplift on the western side. The Songpu strand shows the largest deformation, with horizontal offsets of 1–2 m and vertical uplift of 0.5–1.2 m. Northward along the Dongli strand, the rupture transitions to dominantly left-lateral extensional cracks. In contrast, the Sanmin strand mainly displays left-lateral motion, with minor local bulging near the Wuhe Terrace. These observations indicate systematic variations in rupture kinematics along strike, reflecting interactions between strike-slip motion and local compressional or extensional deformation within the Yuli segment of the CeRFS.

Outstanding questions

As described above (Fig. 3a–d; the coordinates of the photos as Appendix A), our field investigations following the 2022 Chihshang earthquake revealed complex patterns of surface deformation, with resident interviews indicating that some structural damage may have resulted from subsequent aftershocks. Despite the intricate distribution of surface ruptures, two predominant deformation styles were documented throughout the affected region (Yen *et al.*, 2023; Wang *et al.*, 2024). The first type consists of ruptures showing left-lateral displacement combined with reverse motion, where the western block represents the upthrown side. These ruptures mainly occurred along the western margin of the Longitudinal Valley, near the Central Range (Fig. 3a,b). The second type also displays left-lateral displacement with reverse motion, but with the eastern blocks as the upthrown side. These ruptures were primarily observed along the eastern margin of the Longitudinal Valley, adjacent to the Coastal Range (Fig. 3c,d). Importantly, these contrasting rupture types frequently occurred in close proximity to each other, with oppositely verging ruptures sometimes separated by distances of only tens of meters.

The occurrence of these two distinct rupture patterns aligns with the regional tectonic framework, wherein the Coastal Range develops along the east-dipping LVFS while the Central Range evolves along the previously enigmatic west-dipping CeRFS. The 2022 Chihshang earthquake has provided

Figure 3. Photos of surface ruptures by the 2022 Chihshang earthquake. The red markers and values in the photographs indicate the viewing directions and corresponding azimuth. (a) Rupture in the Laklak River bed located at the west side of the Longitudinal Valley, showing west-side-up scarp. (b) Left-lateral motion in the track field of Yuli Township, on the west side of the Longitudinal Valley. (c) Rupture across the track field of the Dongli Junior High school at the eastern part of the Longitudinal Valley, showing east-side-up ruptures. (d) Rupture in Fuli Township at the east side of the Longitudinal Valley, showing the left-lateral motion. Locations are labeled in Figure 2.

unprecedented documentation of surface deformation, offering the first definitive coseismic evidence validating the activity of the CeRFS. Most significantly, our field observations reveal a previously unrecognized phenomenon: ruptures associated with the CeRFS extend eastward, approaching very close to the Coastal Range fault traces, despite these two systems belonging to fundamentally different tectonic structures. This spatial convergence of opposing fault systems, now clearly exposed by the 2022 Chihshang earthquake, cannot be adequately explained by existing tectonic models of the region. This discovery raises critical questions that current frameworks fail to address: What controls the surface expression and subsurface geometry of both the Central Range fault and Longitudinal Valley fault systems? How do these contrasting fault systems interact at depth? And how can two tectonically distinct fault systems accommodate deformation in such close proximity? In this article, we present new data and interpretations that address these fundamental questions, offering insights into the complex fault interactions revealed by this significant seismic event.

Strategies

To investigate fault characteristics through the rupture patterns of the 2022 Chihshang earthquake and earlier seismic events, we implemented a multimethod approach combining surface mapping, high-precision topographic surveys using RTK GNSS, and

Figure 4. Photos of surface ruptures by the 2022 Chihshang earthquake at the Kecheng–Changliang area. The red markers and values in the photographs indicate the viewing directions and corresponding azimuth. (a) Ruptures by the northern bank of the Laklak riverbed. (b) Fault runs through the local watermelon field, stretching the plastic protective cover. (c) The irrigation waterway by the watermelon field is offset. (d) Farm roads and rice fields are offset by the fault. Locations are labeled in Figure 2.

paleoseismic trenching. Our investigations focused on two key sites: the Changliang area near the Central Range (Figs. 2 and 4) and the Songpu area adjacent to the Coastal Range (Figs. 2, 5, and 6). At the Changliang site, we conducted RTK GNSS topographic surveys in both 2015 and 2022, allowing us to quantify coseismic displacements by comparing pre-earthquake and post-earthquake topographic profiles. Importantly, the 2015 RTK profile revealed a pre-existing scarp that likely represents coseismic displacement from the 1951 LV earthquake sequence, potentially identifying the precise location of the elusive CeRFS. At the Songpu site, we excavated two trenches at locations exhibiting prominent surface offsets to examine the paleoseismic history of the region. These complementary datasets of deformed landscapes and disturbed strata provide valuable insights into the characteristics and activity patterns of the fault structures within the Longitudinal Valley.

RESULTS

Field observations of 2022 Chihshang earthquake surface rupture

Changliang site: Evidence for CeRFS activity. The Central Range rises immediately to the west of the Longitudinal Valley, exhibiting dramatic topographic relief that ascends from approximately 150 m above sea level (a.s.l.) to over 1500 m a.s.l. within a horizontal distance of roughly 10 km. This pronounced elevation differential has motivated researchers to investigate the previously constrained CeRFS along the mountain front, which has been hypothesized as a major structural feature in this region (Biq, 1965; Kuo-Chen *et al.*, 2023; Shyu, Sieh, Avouac, *et al.*, 2006; Huang and Wang, 2022; Kuo-Chen *et al.*, 2023). The ruptures observed in the western part of the valley display characteristics consistent with CeRFS activity—located at the mountain front and contributing to the increasing relief between the mountain range and the valley floor.

The 2022 Chihshang earthquake produced significant ruptures along the western margin of the Longitudinal Valley near

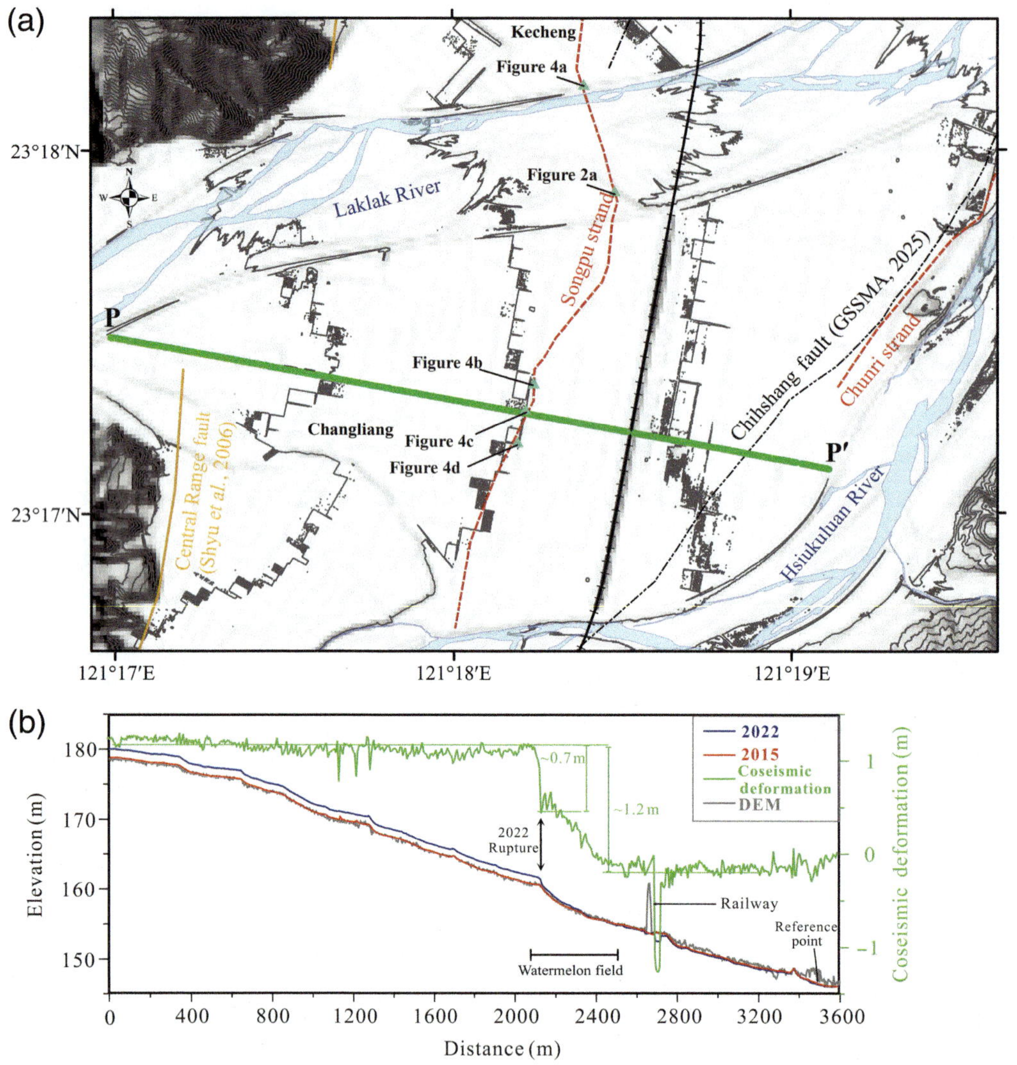

Figure 5. (a) Digital elevation model (1m DEM from this research) of the Changliang area showing the location of the repeated measurement profiles (green line); red dashed lines are surveyed surface fractures. (b) Repeated topographic surveys revealed pre-existing fault scarps before the 2022 Chihshang earthquake, as documented by the 2015 profiles (red). The post-earthquake profile (blue) was surveyed following the 2022 Chihshang earthquake; both profiles were aligned using reference points at the eastern end, with the green line representing the elevation difference between 2022 and 2015 measurements. The survey reveals 0.7 m of coseismic vertical displacement immediately at the scarp, increasing to approximately 1.2 m within a 300 m wide transition zone. West of the scarp, where no significant coseismic deformation occurred, elevation differences between the two surveys show minimal variation with a standard deviation of approximately 0.06 m.

the Central Range, most prominently from Yuli to the Changliang area. Field and unmanned aerial vehicle surveys conducted immediately after the event revealed that ruptures south of Yuli Township, between Kecheng and Changliang, strike in a north-northeast/south-southwest direction (Fig. 2). These ruptures extend from the bed of the Laklak River (Fig. 4a) to the now well-documented "watermelon field" in the Changliang area (Fig. 4b,c), where they display clear left-lateral and west-side-up coseismic deformation. Wang *et al.* (2024) estimated the vertical deformation could reach up to 40 cm, and the left-lateral displacement could be 86–140 cm in the watermelon field. The rupture zone continues southward through adjacent rice paddies (Fig. 4d) toward the Dongli area and beyond. Consistently, all these ruptures demonstrate coseismic uplift of the Central Range side.

The area between Kecheng and Changliang is characterized by an alluvial fan formed by the upper Laklak River. This fan accumulates sediment transported from the Central Range and deposits it at the mountain front, where the gradient gradually decreases, creating a gentle eastward slope toward the eastern portion of the Longitudinal Valley.

To clarify the temporal context of our topographic observation, the same RTK GNSS topographic profile across the mountain front of the Changliang area was surveyed both in 2015 (before the earthquake) and again after the 2022 Chihshang earthquake. The 2015 pre-earthquake survey revealed a generally eastward-sloping gradient of the Laklak River alluvial plain (Fig. 5a). Notably, at the site where the 18 September 2022 Chihshang earthquake later produced surface ruptures (~2100 on the x axis, Fig. 5b), a pre-existing scarp with a vertical offset of ~1.7 m was already present. This previously undocumented scarp most likely represents a surface expression of the CeRFS that primarily formed during the 1951 LV earthquake sequence, with possible minor contributions from earlier fault activities or seismic events. Although the 1951 LV earthquake sequence produced documented ruptures along the Yuli fault with predominantly strike-slip motion, the remote Changliang area likely remained unsurveyed due to its isolated location.

Following the 18 September 2022 Chihshang earthquake, we performed repeat RTK GNSS measurements along the same profile on 27–28 October 2022. Using a local topographic high at ~3600 m distance from the fault trace (Fig. 5b) as a

Figure 6. Photos of surface ruptures by the 2022 Chihshang earthquake at the Songpu area. The red markers and values in the photographs indicate the viewing directions and corresponding azimuth. (a,b) The rupture in the northern part of the Songpu area runs through the rice paddy and farm road, showing west-side-up motion, and in the southern part of the Songpu area. (c) The rupture bending the rice paddy and the irrigation canal. On the footwall side of the paddy field. (d) A complex surface rupture pattern in the rice paddy field. Locations are labeled in Figure 2.

stable reference point, we aligned the pre-earthquake and post-earthquake profiles to quantify coseismic displacement. Our measurements reveal that these ruptures display clear left-lateral and west-side-up coseismic deformation, with vertical displacement reaching up to 70 cm at the immediate scarp location (Fig. 5b), consistent with the 60–70 cm vertical uplift reported by Yen *et al.* (2023). This vertical offset increases to ~1.2 m when including the broader zone east of the scarp. The deformation is concentrated on the scarp and within a narrow transition zone approximately 300 m east of the main scarp. Our survey exclusively utilized fixed-solution RTK GNSS data, achieving reported accuracies of 1–2 cm horizontally and 3–5 cm vertically. West of the scarp, where coseismic deformation remains relatively constant at ~1.2 m relative to the reference point at the eastern profile end, we observed a standard deviation of 0.065 m (<6% of the mean value). This low variability confirms the high quality and consistency of our survey data. Although Wang *et al.* (2024) reported ~10 cm of postseismic displacement in the 3 months following the earthquake at several survey sites in Yuli Township, the topographic differences we measured between 2015 and 2022 (up to 1.2 m) significantly exceed these postseismic effects. The documented expression of the CeRFS with consistent west-side-up coseismic deformation provides compelling evidence for the mechanism responsible for the dramatic topographic relief between the Central Range and the Longitudinal Valley.

Songpu site: Deformation along the eastern valley margin. The Songpu area, situated along the eastern margin of the Longitudinal Valley and immediately west of the Coastal Range, was one of the most severely deformed areas where rice paddies and irrigation canals were deformed (Fig. 6a–d). This region represents a geomorphic transition zone that descends from the Coastal Range at ~140 m above sea level (a.s.l.) in the east, sloping westward toward the Hsiukuluan River at elevations below 80 m a.s.l. The landscape is characterized by converging alluvial fans from three mountain streams that slope westward, creating terraced rice fields west of Songpu Village and the county highway (Fig. 7a).

Several isolated north–south-trending ridges emerge within these terraced agricultural areas, with the majority of earthquake-induced fractures and deformation occurring on either side of these ridges, as illustrated by Figure 7a. Three topographic profiles P1–P3 (Fig. 7b) show that between the main 2022 Chihshang earthquake Songpu strand rupture (CeRFS, west-dipping) and the previously mapped LVFS trace (east-dipping, intersecting with the Songpu strand of the Yuli segment), there are west-facing topographic ridges that interrupt the westward sloping trend of the alluvial fan. Some of these topographic features can be seen as ridges in the area (Fig. 7c), whereas others are more prominently shown in the topographic profiles.

Surface ruptures traversing the rice fields show distinct patterns at two key locations. Near trench SP01 (Fig. 7a, green cross; Fig. 6a,b), fault traces exhibit west-side-up displacement evident in both the farm road and adjacent rice paddies. Farther south, near trench SP02 (Fig. 7a, yellow cross; Fig. 6c,d), the earthquake produced significant warping of rice fields and damaged irrigation infrastructure, resulting in the formation of a temporary sag pond in the immediate footwall (eastern side) of the fault.

Paleoseismic trenching at Songpu

Trench SP01: Coseismic displacement along a discrete shear plane. The SP01 trench (Fig. 8a,b) reveals two distinct stratigraphic units: an upper farming soil layer (BF) and an underlying conglomerate layer (Ga1). The BF unit comprises organic-rich soil containing sporadic gravel clasts and forms the uppermost stratum of the exposure. Because the SP01 trench is situated on an alluvial fan, the Ga1 unit exposed within the trench primarily consists of poorly sorted gravel, interbedded with well-sorted, thin, lens-shaped fine sand layers of approximately 2–5 cm thick. These lenticular sand layers exhibit flat upper or lower boundaries in some segments, but laterally pinch out, reflecting characteristics of localized overbank depositional events in alluvial fan environments. Because the trench walls are only 1.5–5 m apart, the distinctive geometry and sedimentological features of these sands make them reliable stratigraphic markers to assess fault-related displacements in the trench profile.

To estimate the amount of offset, we consider several important marker beds, such as the boundary between the BF and Ga1 units and the distinctive lenticular sand layer exposed on both walls. Analysis of the boundary between the BF and Ga1 units as a displacement indicator for the 2022 Chihshang earthquake revealed vertical offsets of 63 cm and ~50 cm along the north and south walls, respectively. East–west-shortening measurements yielded 125 cm of horizontal displacement along the north wall and 38 cm along the south wall, demonstrating significant spatial variability in deformation across the fault zone.

The lenticular sand layer within the conglomerate unit (Ga1) on the north wall exhibits pronounced folding, which developed across a distinct shear plane that correlates with the 2022 Chihshang earthquake (Fig. 8a). By correlating the subhorizontal sand layers on both limbs of the fold, we estimate 87 cm of vertical offset and 127 cm of horizontal shortening on the north wall. Meanwhile, the corresponding lenticular sand layer in the south wall reveals a more complex deformation due to the presence of two shear planes, with an estimated minimal vertical offset of 50 and 38 cm of horizontal shortening when accounting for the removal of surface soil during trench excavation. Integration of the two trench walls surface rupture indicates that the 2022 Chihshang earthquake coseismic shearing plane has an orientation of approximately north–south strike at the site.

If we look further to the western shear plane, the shallower sand layer exhibits a vertical displacement of 30 cm and a horizontal shortening of 12 cm, whereas the deeper lens-shaped sand layer shows a vertical displacement of 60 cm and a horizontal shortening of 71 cm. The shear deformation appears to decrease toward the surface. These phenomena can be attributed to the dissipation of frictional energy within the unconsolidated units (Rice, 2006; Reches and Lockner, 2010) or to variation in apparent offset related to left-lateral movement. However, because our trench walls are nearly perpendicular to the left-lateral slip sense, it is difficult to estimate the uncertainties associated with this.

Two distinct shear planes were observed on the south wall (Fig. 8b), and both are interpreted as products of the 2022 Chihshang earthquake. This interpretation is supported by the overlying conforming BF unit, which exhibits synchronous deformation across both shear planes, indicating coseismic activation rather than sequential movement. If only the western shear plane had been active during the event, the displacement associated with it should have been removed or truncated before deposition of the BF unit. From a regional strain perspective, the combined displacement accommodated by the two shear planes on the south wall is broadly comparable to the cumulative offset documented on the north wall. This strain balance further supports the interpretation that both shear planes were activated contemporaneously during the 2022 Chihshang earthquake.

If we consider that both shear planes contributed to the 2022 Chihshang earthquake, the range of displacement can be roughly estimated by combining the marker beds on both walls. For vertical displacement, the bottom of the soil layer above the western shear plane was 63–79 cm higher than that to the east of the eastern shear plane. As for horizontal displacement, the total displacement is estimated by summing the maximum horizontal displacement on the marker layer for both sides of the shear zone, yielding an approximate horizontal shortening of 109–127 cm.

Trench SP02: Deforming sediment layers revealing multiple events. The stratigraphic sequence exposed in

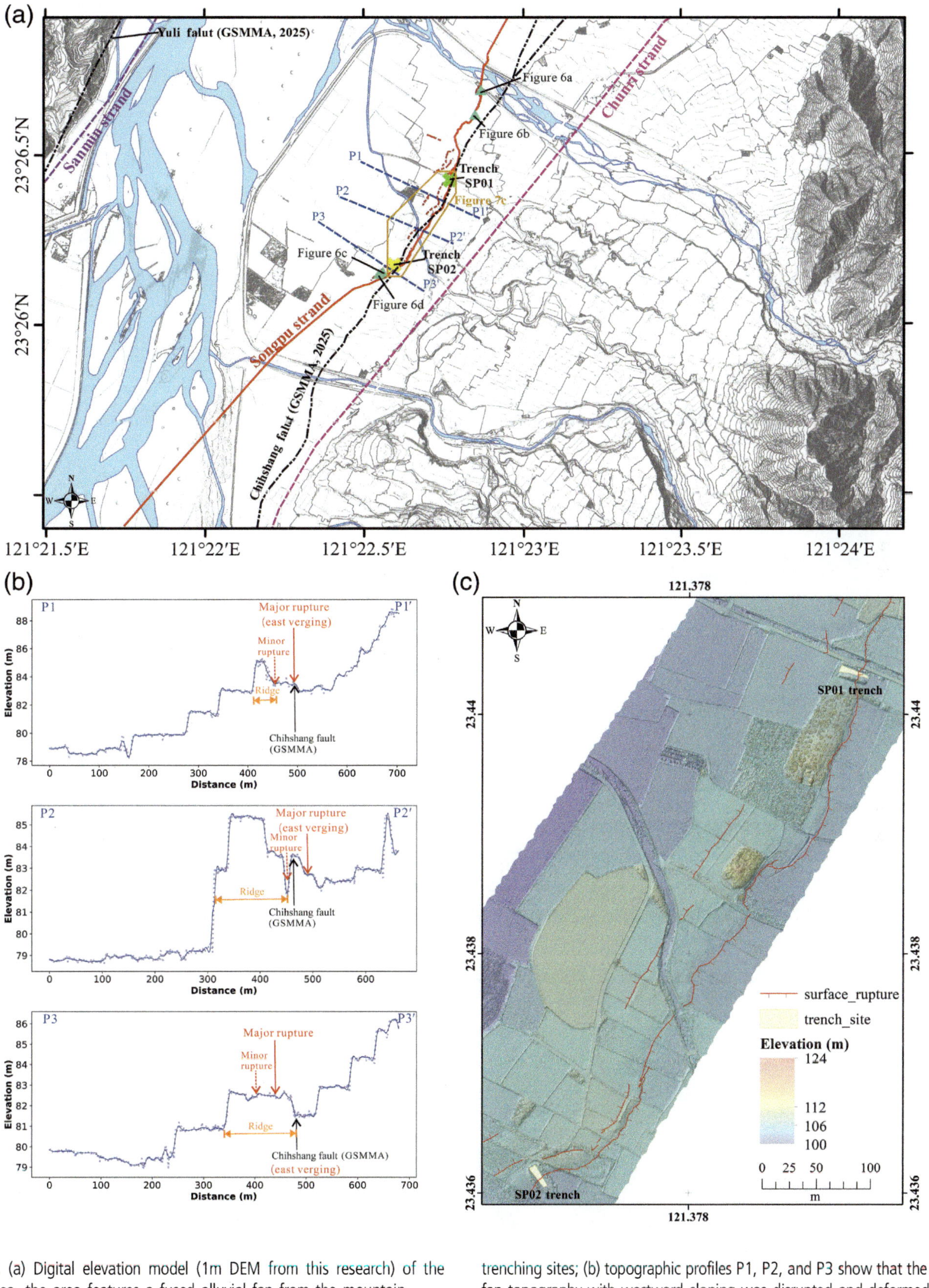

Figure 7. (a) Digital elevation model (1m DEM from this research) of the Songpu area, the area features a fused alluvial fan from the mountain streams in this area. The pink dashed line, purple dashed line, and red lines indicate surface ruptures strand of the Yuli segment, black dashed lines are the east-dipping LVFS from GSMMA (see Data and Resources) mapping, and blue dashed lines are topographic profiles. The green and yellow stars are trenching sites; (b) topographic profiles P1, P2, and P3 show that the alluvial fan topography with westward sloping was disrupted and deformed by the fault ruptures. (c) The distribution of surface ruptures near the trenches was mapped on the digital surface model (1m DSM from this research) map, with the trench location labeled by the yellow polygons.

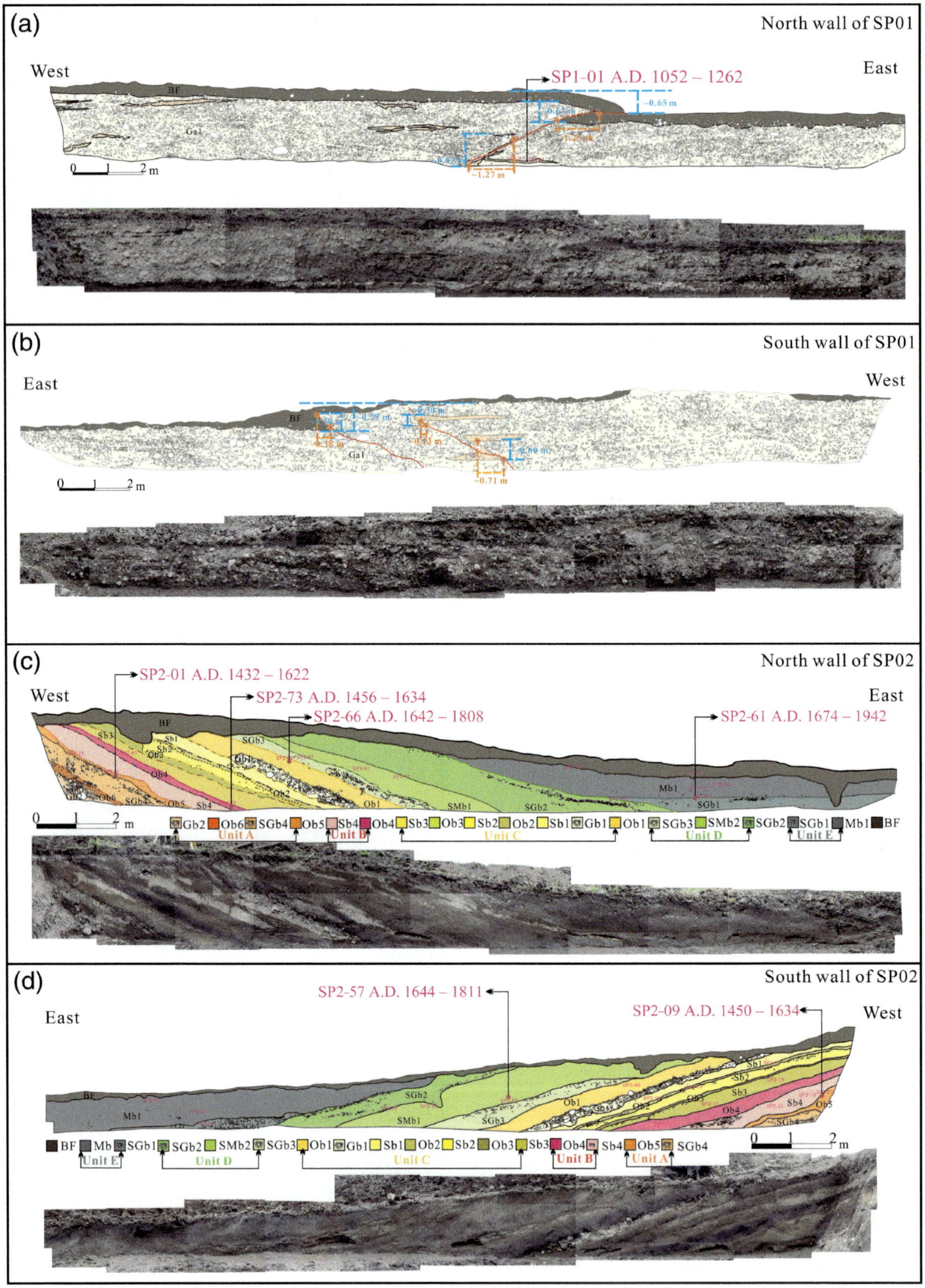

Figure 8. Panoramic view and schematic profiles of the Songpu SP01 and SP02 trenches excavated across the Songpu strand of the Yuli segment. (a, b) The north and south walls of trench SP01, respectively. The trench is an irregular tetragon with the west side of approximately 5 m and the east side narrows to about 1.5 m. (c,d) The north and south walls of trench SP02, respectively, with the west side of approximately 5 m and the east side of 3 m. The stratigraphic boundaries illustrated in (c) were used in the event reconstruction diagram shown in Figure 10.

trench SP02 comprises 19 distinct lithological units (Fig. 8c,d), from surface to base: cultivated soil (BF), mud (Mb1), sandy-gravel units 1–3 (SGb1–SGb3), sandy-mud (SMb1), organic soil units 1–6 (Ob1–Ob6), conglomerate units 1–2 (Gb1–Gb2), sand units 1–4 (Sb1–Sb4), and a basal sandy-gravel unit (SGb4).

The uppermost BF unit consists of organic-rich agricultural soil with occasional pebble clasts, representing the active rice cultivation horizon. The Mb1 unit is characterized by greenish-gray mud with dispersed pebbles. Sandy-gravel units (SGb1–SGb4) are sand-dominated with interbedded pebble/conglomerate horizons ranging from 1 to 10 cm in thickness. The SMb1 unit exhibits sandy-mud composition, likely representing mixtures between sand and organic-rich deposits. Conglomerate units (Gb1–Gb2) consist of poorly sorted gravels typically exceeding 20 cm in thickness, often displaying lenticular geometry. Sand units (Sb1–Sb4) are primarily composed of fine sand, occasionally containing pebble clasts or primary sedimentary structures. The organic soil units (Ob1–Ob6) comprise sandy mud with elevated organic content, interpreted as paleosol horizons representing former land surfaces.

Trench SP02 was strategically positioned across a fault scarp that lacked surface rupture expression. Although no discrete shear planes were identified on the surface and in the trench walls, the sedimentary units consistently dip eastward across the projected fault trace. The site is situated within terraced rice paddies where the natural alluvial fan morphology has been anthropogenically modified into a series of horizontal agricultural platforms that step down westward toward the Hsiukuluan River (Figs. 6c-d and 7a). Rice cultivation necessitates level surfaces for water management; therefore, the observed eastward tilting applies specifically to the uppermost cultivated soil horizon (BF), and is interpreted as deformation produced during the 2022 Chihshang earthquake. This BF layer exhibits ~1.2 m of vertical displacement (west-side-up) across the scarp (Fig. 8c).

Structural measurements along the north wall of the trench reveal a systematic increase in dip angle with stratigraphic depth, indicating progressive deformation over multiple events. Key structural attitudes include: the upper boundary of sandy-gravel unit SGb2 (N68°E/15°E), the upper boundary of organic soil unit Ob1 (N44°E/26°E), the upper boundary of organic soil unit Ob4 (N30°E/32°E), and the upper boundary of the lowermost organic soil unit Ob6 (N78°E/40°E).

Diagnostic stratigraphic features in trench SP02, including extensive onlapping relationships and progressively increasing dip angles with depth, exhibit the characteristic signature of growth strata, providing compelling evidence for recurrent seismic deformation (McCalpin, 1996). To establish a chronological framework for paleoseismic events and quantify recurrence intervals, we classified the stratigraphic sequence into five distinct depositional units: unit A (comprising layers Gb2, Ob6, SGb4, and Ob5), unit B (layers Sb4 and Ob4), unit C (layers Sb3, Ob3, Sb2, Ob2, Sb1, Gb1, and Ob1), unit D (layers SGb3, SMb1, and SGb2), and unit E (layers SGb1 and Mb1). The deformed cultivated soil horizon (BF) represents the most recent disturbance caused by the postseismic activity following the 1951 LV earthquake sequence, particularly the 2022 Chihshang earthquake.

We applied observation-based methods following McCalpin (2009) to identify paleoseismic events from cross-cutting relationships, fault-related folding, and onlap features. Detailed logs document sediment composition, layer attitudes, pinch-outs, and discontinuities (Fig. 8). Because the site is a leveled rice paddy, we assume the surface was horizontal before the 2022 Chihshang earthquake. The present ~6° dip of the shallowest layer, produced by the 2022 Chihshang earthquake, is used as a minimum deformation threshold for recognizing older events. Combining this criterion with onlap relationships, four pre-2022 Chihshang earthquake events (E1–E4) are identified.

Stratigraphic relations in the SP02 trench reveal distinct onlapping sequences and dip changes recording these events. E1 is marked by the onlap of the cultivated soil Mb1 and sandy-gravel layer SGb1 (unit E) onto SGb2 (unit D). In the south wall, gravel distribution within SGb3 and the oblique contact between the base of SMb1 and the top of Ob1 indicate E2, defined by the onlap of SGb3 (unit D) onto Ob1 (unit C). E3 is represented by the onlap of sand layer Sb3 (unit C) onto Ob4 (unit B). Although the limited exposure of unit A obscures clear onlap, disturbance within Ob1, and an ~8° dip difference between units A and B suggest E4, possibly represented by the onlap of Sb4 (unit B) onto Ob5 (unit A).

Notably, the uppermost cultivated soil horizon (BF), representing the most recent agricultural activity, displays an angular unconformity with the underlying mud (Mb1) and sandy-gravel (SGb1) units. This pronounced angular relationship strongly suggests that the previous major earthquake, the 1951 LV earthquake sequence, modified the local topography. This geological interpretation is corroborated by oral testimony from an elderly local farmer who recounted experiencing a significant earthquake in this area during his childhood, providing valuable historical context for our stratigraphic observations. Therefore, event E1 is interpreted as the 1951 LV earthquake sequence both chronologically and stratigraphically.

Geochronology: Radiocarbon dating and event timing. One organic sample from the SP01 trench and six samples from the SP02 trench were submitted to Beta Analytic for ^{14}C accelerator mass spectrometry (AMS) radiocarbon dating analysis. All results were calibrated using OxCal version 4.4 with the IntCal20 atmospheric calibration curve (see Appendix B for radiocarbon dates and calibrated ages).

The organic material recovered from the gravel layer (Ga1) in trench SP01 showed a calibrated age range with 2σ probability of A.D. 1052–1262. For trench SP02, six strategically collected samples provided chronological constraints on the depositional sequence. Initial calibration results indicated the following age ranges with 2σ probability: Unit A (Ob5 layer, basal unit) dated to A.D. 1432–1634; unit B (Ob4 layer) to A.D. 1456–1634; unit C (Ob1 layer) to A.D. 1642–1808; unit D (SMb1 layer) to A.D. 1644–1811; and unit E (SGb1 layer, uppermost dated unit) to A.D. 1674–1942 (Fig. 9).

To resolve the significant temporal overlap in the calibrated age distributions, we implemented Bayesian statistical modeling following methodologies established by Ramsey (2009, 2024) and Reimer *et al.* (2020), an approach widely adopted in paleoseismic investigations (Yen *et al.*, 2008; Lienkaemper and Ramsey, 2009; Kagan *et al.*, 2010). This analysis, incorporating stratigraphic constraints, refined the chronological framework and provided more precise age estimates with standard deviation of mean (see the circle and bar in Fig. 9). The modeled deposition ages for the sedimentary units in trench SP02 were summarized as follows: Unit A (A.D. 1437–1543), unit B (A.D. 1561–1629), unit C (A.D. 1640–1736), unit D (A.D. 1739–1909), and unit E (A.D. 1952–1958). The modeled age for the earthquake events in trench SP02 is as follows: event 2 (A.D. 1658–1796), event 3 (A.D. 1591–1689), and event 4 (A.D. 1525–1611).

DISCUSSIONS

Paleoearthquake and recurrence interval

Although repeated surface ruptures originate from the same underlying fault, temporal variations in the properties and thickness of overlying materials can result in either persistent rupture locations or spatial variability in surface deformation. In our study area, trench SP01 is situated within a geomorphic setting subject to active fluvial erosion and deposition. The stratigraphy within trench SP01 has likely been modified by erosional processes, and truncation relationships between shear surfaces and sedimentary units indicate that this trench preserves evidence of only the 2022 Chihshang earthquake surface-rupturing event. As a result, earthquake recurrence intervals cannot be reliably constrained from the trench SP01 dataset. In contrast, trench SP02, located within a floodplain depositional environment, preserves a more complete stratigraphic record of surface faulting events spanning the past ~600 yr.

Identifying paleoseismic events in trench SP02 presents methodological challenges common to sites where deformation occurs without surface rupture. We identified five events (the 2022 Chihshang earthquake and events E1–E4) from deformed but unfaulted sedimentary layers (Fig. 8c,d). Because of inherent fluctuations in the atmospheric radiocarbon calibration curve, multiple possible age ranges were considered for each sample. To resolve potential temporal overlaps between adjacent stratigraphic units, we prioritized stratigraphic relationships to refine their depositional ages. Radiocarbon dates were evaluated using the OxCal Bayesian statistical modeling framework (Yen *et al.*, 2008; Ramsey, 2009, 2024). The results (see Appendix B) indicate that, in addition to the 2022 Chihshang earthquake and event E1 associated with the 1951 LV earthquake sequence, three earlier seismic events can be identified from the stratigraphic record. These paleoearthquakes are dated as follows: event E2 occurred around A.D. 1727 ± 69, event E3 around A.D. 1640 ± 49, and event E4 around A.D. 1568 ± 43.

Based on the principle that earthquake events must occur between the deposition ages of bounding stratigraphic units, we refined the potential occurrence windows for each event. The 2022 Chihshang earthquake (E_2022) and the 1951 LV earthquake sequence (event E1) are constrained to the specific years. Event E2 is estimated to have occurred between A.D. 1736 and 1739, event E3 between A.D. 1629 and 1640, and event E4 between A.D. 1543 and 1561.

The temporal spacing between these five events reveals a series of recurrence intervals: 71 yr between the 2022 Chihshang earthquake and 1951 LV earthquake sequence, 212–215 yr (213 ± 2 yr) between events E1 and E2, 96–110 yr (103 ± 7 yr) between events E2 and E3, and 68–97 yr (82 ± 15 yr) between events E3 and E4. These four intervals suggest that paleoearthquake recurrence at this site ranges from approximately 70 to 210 yr. The mean recurrence interval is 140 ± 70 yr for the past 600 yr. This recurrence interval is similar to that of the Rueisuei segment of the LVFS, which exhibits an average recurrence interval of approximately 150 yr over the past 390 yr (Yen *et al.*, 2008). This similarity may reflect regional strain accumulation patterns affecting both fault systems in the central Longitudinal Valley.

Long-term vertical slip rate

The limited availability of datable material in trench SP01, along with the possibility that multiple events were eroded or not preserved, has introduced uncertainties and potential distortions in the estimation of the long-term slip rate. Therefore, this study does not further address the long-term vertical slip rate from trench SP01 (Fig. 8a,b).

In trench SP02, we estimate the vertical uplift associated with each paleoearthquake event based on the event reconstruction diagram (Fig. 10). Except for the 2022 Chihshang earthquake, which has completed pre- and post-deformation data allowing for accurate comparison, the remaining events were affected by erosion that removed surficial deposits in uplifted areas, preventing direct estimation of total displacement. Therefore, we infer the amount of vertical uplift for each of these events from the maximum relief between the top of the lowest preserved sedimentary unit and the overlying angular unconformity. The estimated displacements for events E1–E4 thus represent minimum values because erosion has removed part of the uplifted materials.

The 2022 Chihshang earthquake produced ~1.2 m of vertical uplift at trench SP02. In comparison, event E1 resulted in ~0.9 m of uplift, event E2 ~0.7 m, event E3 ~0.4 m, and event E4 ~0.6 m. Using these vertical displacements along with the estimated age ranges of paleoearthquake events, we constructed the diagram of slip history for the SP02 trench section

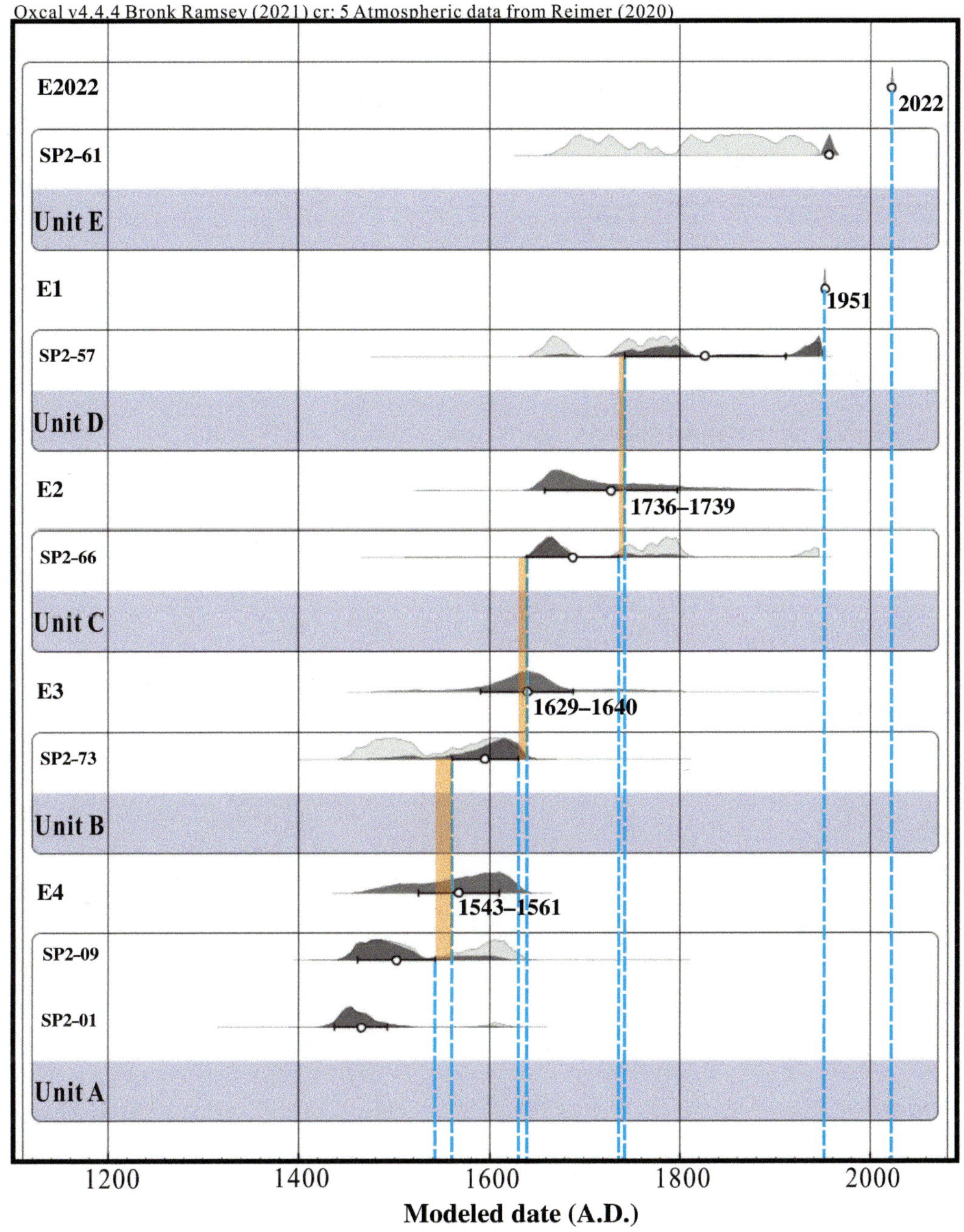

Figure 9. Modeled ages for each event and samples. The C14 result with 2σ probability is shown as a gray region, the modeled age as a black region, and the orange range shows the event time.

(Fig. 11). The cumulative vertical offsets and time intervals between events allow us to estimate the average vertical slip rate, represented as dashed trend lines in the diagram. These results suggest a long-term vertical slip rate ranging from 6.7 to 7.3 mm/yr over the past ~600 yr, calculated from the cumulative minimum displacements of individual events (E4 through 2022) divided by the elapsed time.

To provide an independent estimate of the vertical offset, we reconstructed the sediment thickness on the footwall side under the assumption of approximately constant sedimentation rate across the trench. This approach allows us to approximate the cumulative uplift by comparing the reconstructed predeformation stratigraphy. Figure 10d,f,h illustrates that the cumulative thickness of units B, C, and D is ~3.4 m. As shown in Figure 10a, the boundary between units B and A has been uplifted by at least 2.1 m relative to the top of unit D. Taken together, these observations indicate that since the deposition of unit A (post-A.D. 1543), the section has experienced a net uplift of ~5.5 m, corresponding to a minimum late Holocene vertical slip rate of ~11.5 mm/yr. This estimate is subject to the limitation that it assumes a constant rate of sediment accumulation across both sides of the fault.

Two independent vertical slip rates at the Songpu site were obtained: 6.7–7.3 mm/yr from offsets of dated horizons and ~11.5 mm/yr from footwall stratigraphic reconstruction. The lower value likely underestimates slip due to hanging-wall erosion, whereas the higher value assumes uniform sedimentation; thus, 6.7–7.3 mm/yr is a conservative lower bound and 11.5 mm/yr a more representative late Holocene rate. These two vertical slip rates are generally consistent with the vertical slip rate (3.5–12.0 mm/yr) converted from the dip-slip rate estimated for this area by Hsu and Bürgmann (2006). The lower rate (6.7–7.3 mm/yr) is roughly two-thirds of the vertical slip rate of the Rueisuei fault (12.2–16.0 mm/yr; Yen *et al.*, 2008; Chen *et al.*, 2007), whereas the higher rate (~11.5 mm/yr) is comparable to long-term rates for the LVFS (8–15 mm/yr; Shyu, Sieh, Avouac, *et al.*, 2006) and the ~8.1 mm/yr reported for the Chihshang fault (Yen *et al.*, 2014). This suggests that the Yuli fault at Songpu accommodates a deformation rate similar to the Chihshang fault. Because our estimates reflect the past few centuries, short-term deviations from millennial-scale averages may result from irregular earthquake recurrences.

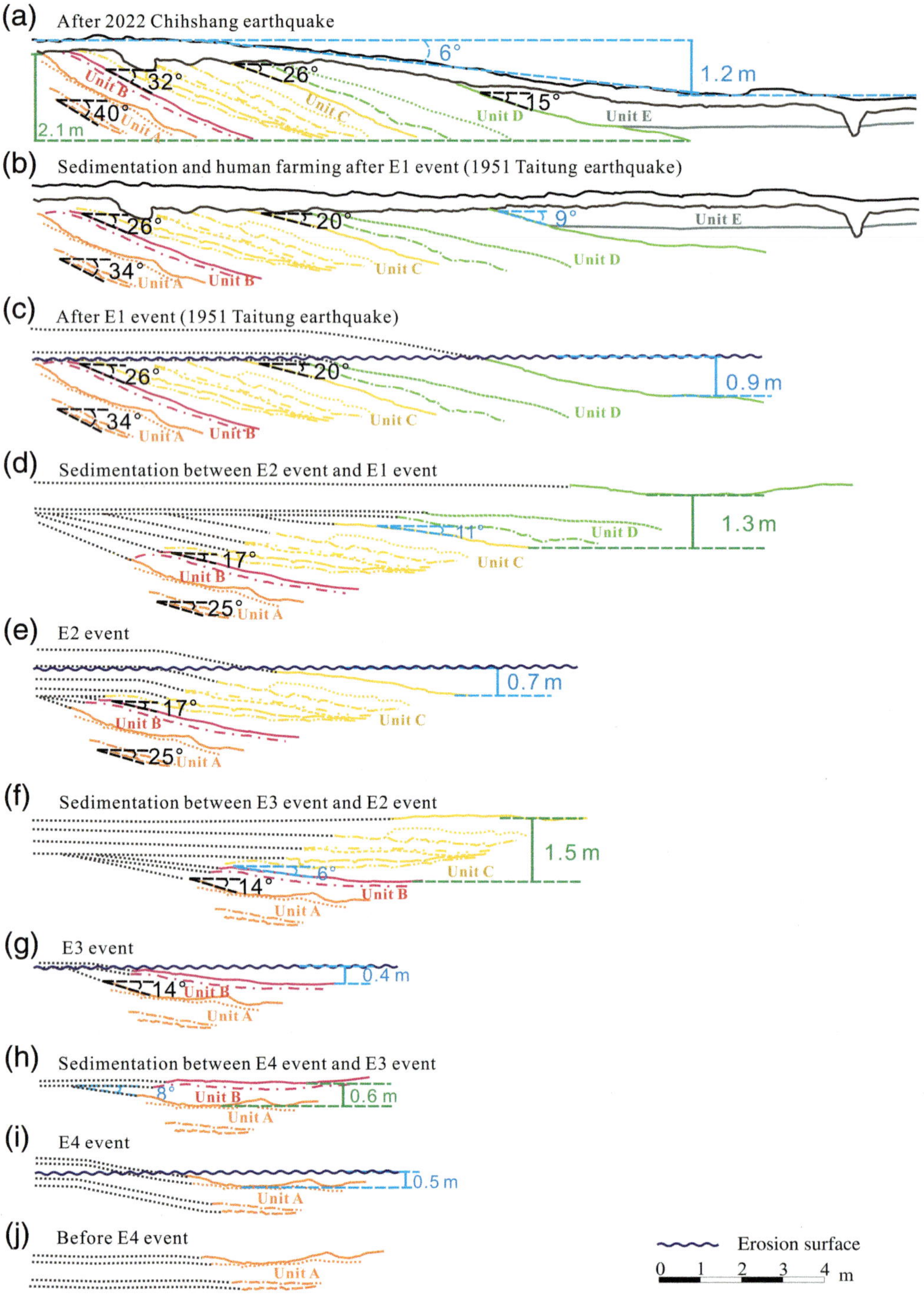

Figure 10. Restoration of paleoearthquake events on the north wall of the SP02 trench. The colored lines denote the basal contacts of stratigraphic units: orange indicates unit A, pink indicates unit B, yellow indicates unit C, green indicates unit D, dark green indicates unit E, and gray indicates the basal contact of the BF layer. The black line represents the present ground surface following the 2022 Chihshang earthquake. (a) The 2022 Chihshang earthquake generated ~1.2 m of vertical displacement with west-side uplift. (b) Reconstruction of the pre-2022 surface shows unit E overlapping unit D at ~9°. (c) Surface deformation following the event E1 (1951 LV earthquake sequence), with a minimum vertical displacement of ~0.9 m measured from undeformed unit D to the erosional surface. (d) Reconstruction of the pre-E1 surface shows unit D (~1.3 m thick) overlapping unit C at ~11°. (e) Surface deformation attributed to event E2, showing ~0.7 m of minimum vertical displacement from undeformed unit C to the erosional surface. (f) Reconstruction of the pre-E2 surface shows unit C (~1.5 m thick) overlapping unit B at ~6°. (g) Surface deformation attributed to event E3, with ~0.4 m of minimum vertical displacement from undeformed unit B to the erosional surface. (h) Reconstruction of the pre-E3 surface shows unit B (~0.6 m thick) overlying unit A at ~13°. (i) Surface deformation attributed to event E4, with ~0.5 m of minimum vertical displacement measured from undeformed unit A to the erosional surface. (j) Reconstruction of the pre-E4 surface.

Fault characteristics

Although the Songpu and Changliang sites are located on opposite sides of the Longitudinal Valley—adjacent to the Coastal Range in the east and the Central Range in the west, respectively—the 2022 Chihshang earthquake generated comparable west-side-up fault displacements at both locations. Multiple lines of evidence from the Songpu site, including surface ruptures and trench stratigraphy, demonstrate consistent west-side-up deformation consistent with west-dipping fault planes during coseismic events. This pattern contrasts markedly with the 1951 LV earthquake sequence, which produced predominantly left-lateral motion along the Yuli fault strand and sinistral slip on east-dipping fault planes within the Chihshang and Rueisuei segments of the LVFS (Cheng *et al.*, 1996; Shyu *et al.*, 2007; Chung *et al.*, 2008; Yen *et al.*, 2008; Chen *et al.*, 2010; Yen *et al.*, 2014).

The 2022 Chihshang earthquake demonstrates significantly stronger surface expression of the CeRFS compared to the 1951 LV earthquake sequence, producing more extensive and systematic surface deformation with rupture traces extending greater than 65 km (this study; Yen *et al.*, 2023) compared to the predominantly LVFS-affinity ruptures documented for the 1951 LV earthquake sequence (Cheng *et al.*, 1996; Shyu *et al.*, 2007). Notably, the 2022 Chihshang earthquake surface ruptures of the west-dipping CeRFS (the Songpu strand) occur within 50–100 m west of the previously

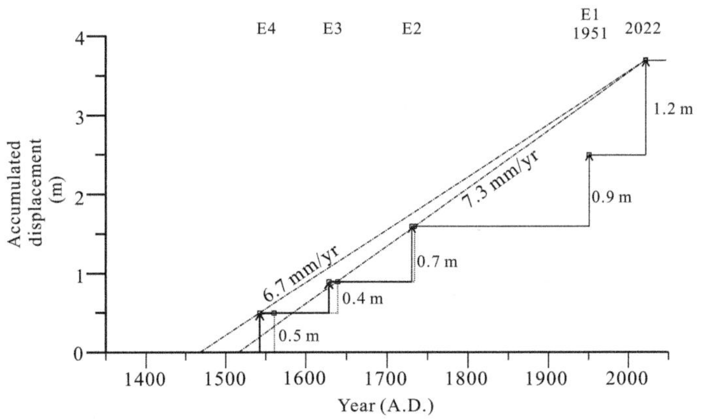

Figure 11. Slip history in the Songpu area. Accumulated vertical displacement in trench SP02 through time exhibits a slip-predictable pattern for the earthquake recurrence model. The dashed dot line is the long-term vertical slip rate, and the solid arrow line shows the coseismic uplift. The dotted line denotes the estimated age range of each earthquake event.

mapped east-dipping LVFS scarp in the Songpu area (Fig. 7a), indicating a dual-vergence fault system structure.

The relationship between cumulative vertical displacement and interevent intervals, as shown in Figure 11, indicates slip-predictable behavior (Shimazaki and Nakata, 1980) for this fault system. However, event E1—interpreted as the 1951 LV earthquake sequence—deviates from this established trend. Combined with the contrasting surface deformation patterns documented at both the Changliang and Songpu sites, this deviation indicates that the 2022 Chihshang earthquake and 1951 LV earthquake sequence represent fundamentally different fault kinematics and rupture styles.

We propose that the overlapping influence of both the CeRFS (exemplified by the 2022 Chihshang earthquake) and the LVFS (exemplified by the 1951 LV earthquake sequence) confirms their simultaneous activity in the Longitudinal Valley. This complex fault interaction represents a direct tectonic response to rapid convergence between the Philippine Sea and Eurasian plates along eastern Taiwan's plate boundary zone.

Neotectonic framework in the central segment of the Longitudinal Valley

Our 2015 RTK GNSS survey documented a fault scarp in the Changliang area. Following the 2022 Chihshang earthquake, analysis of our 2015 data revealed that this scarp was located precisely where the 2022 Chihshang earthquake surface rupture occurred, confirming it as a pre-existing expression of the CeRFS. Repeated topographic surveys demonstrated 70 cm of coseismic vertical displacement immediately adjacent to the rupture site of the 2022 Chihshang earthquake, with total vertical displacement reaching 1.2 m when including the broader transition zone (Fig. 5). The precise spatial coincidence of the 2022 Chihshang earthquake surface rupture with the pre-existing scarp at Changliang, combined with substantial coseismic vertical offsets and consistent west-side-up kinematics, provides compelling evidence that this feature represents an active expression of the CeRFS. The formation of scarps at Changliang by both the 2022 Chihshang earthquake and probably the 1951 LV earthquake sequence demonstrates recurrent fault activity that systematically contributes to topographic development. This pattern of recurrent deformation demonstrates that the CeRFS plays a fundamental role in the long-term geomorphological processes responsible for generating and sustaining the dramatic topographic relief between the Central Range and the Longitudinal Valley.

The spatial coincidence between the pre-existing scarp and the 2022 Chihshang earthquake surface rupture, together with the alignment of the 2022 Chihshang earthquake ruptures in Yuli Township with those documented in the 1951 LV earthquake sequence, strongly indicates that the CeRFS was responsible for surface rupture during the 2022 Chihshang earthquake. The rupture trace can be followed from Changliang northward to Yuli Township and further northeastward toward the Songpu area, where trench excavations have revealed evidence of five seismic events, including the 2022 Chihshang earthquake. These findings suggest that the CeRFS represents a persistently reactivated fault system, with repeated earthquake occurrences along the same structural feature over multiple seismic cycles.

Although both events produced surface ruptures in the Songpu area, the contrasting fault-slip kinematics observed between events indicate overlapping influence from both the CeRFS and LVFS in controlling deformation in this segment of the Longitudinal Valley. According to the field mapping results of Yen *et al.* (2023), five surface rupture strands were identified within the Longitudinal Valley following the 2022 Chihshang earthquake. Our trench site is located near the northern extend of the rupture strand along the Yuli fault. Lee *et al.* (2023) documented a west-dipping fault cropping out north of Chihshang and suggested that the CeRFS may intersect the LVFS at depth north of Rueisuei. Chen *et al.* (2024) also modeled CeRFS–LVFS intersection at depth in the Yuli and Fuli areas, though they characterized valley-floor fault strands as purely strike-slip structures. Our observations document significant west-side-up components, suggesting more complex fault kinematics across the region. Integrating field mapping (Chen *et al.*, 2024; Yen *et al.*, 2023), trenching results, RTK GNSS survey, and seismic data (Lee *et al.*, 2023; Sun *et al.*, 2024), we interpret the 2022 Chihshang earthquake as rupture along the Yuli segment of the CeRFS. Strike-slip motion along this segment produced several branch faults expressed as five distinct surface rupture strands. Some reactivated along the 1951 LV earthquake sequence surface rupture, whereas others intersected or slipped along the near-surface fault plane of the Chihshang segment of the LVFS (Fig. 12). Overall, the structural complexity observed in this region reflects the active and intricate deformation associated with the convergence between the Philippine Sea and Eurasian plates along the plate boundary zone in eastern Taiwan.

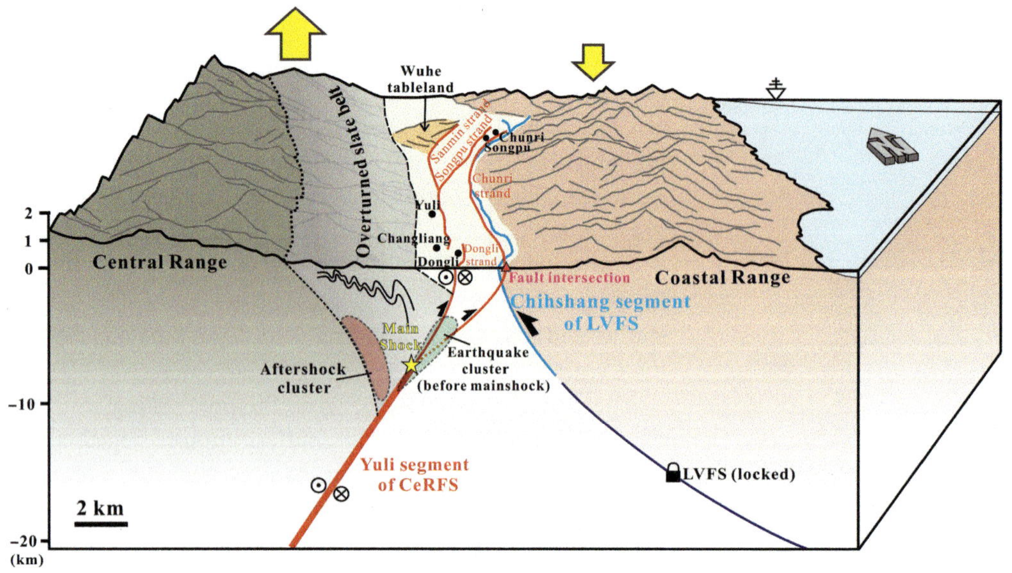

Figure 12. Schematic diagram showing the geological architecture of the Longitudinal Valley. The Yuli segment (red thick line) of the Central Range fault system (CeRFS) was activated during the 2022 Chihshang earthquake, exhibiting a left-lateral with reverse slip. Four fault strands emerged at the surface north of Changliang (red thin line). Premainshock seismicity was concentrated within the zone of this fault activation, whereas postseismic activity was predominantly distributed to the west of the activated fault plane. Schematic model showing that the east-dipping Longitudinal Valley fault system (LVFS) was locked at a depth of greater than 10 km (black line), whereas the shallow Chihshang segment (blue line) was intersected by the Yuli segment during the 2022 Chihshang earthquake.

CONCLUSIONS

1. The 2022 Guanshan–Chihshang earthquake sequence produced the most extensive surface ruptures in Taiwan since the devastating 1999 M_w 7.6 Chi-Chi earthquake and provided the first definitive coseismic evidence for the long-hypothesized Central Range fault.
2. Although previous tectonic models have emphasized the dominance of the west-verging Longitudinal Valley fault along the Coastal Range margin, the east-verging ruptures documented in both the Changliang and Songpu areas during the 2022 Guanshan–Chihshang earthquake sequence reveal a substantially more complex structural architecture, demonstrating that the west-dipping CeRFS plays a far more significant role within the Longitudinal Valley than previously recognized.
3. In the Changliang area, the 2022 Chihshang earthquake rupture trace precisely coincides with a pre-existing scarp that was initially identified and measured through RTK GNSS topographic surveys conducted in 2015 and 2022. This scarp, estimated at approximately 1.7 m in height prior to 2022, likely represents cumulative displacement from multiple previous seismic events, probably including the 1951 LV earthquake sequence. The 2022 Chihshang earthquake contributed an additional coseismic vertical offset of approximately up to 1.2 m to this feature.
4. Paleoseismic investigations in the Songpu area, including trench excavation, reveal truncated and tilted strata that record a history of recurrent surface deformation. Detailed analysis of cross-cutting relationships within trench SP02 identified evidence for five distinct seismic events, including the well-documented 2022 Chihshang earthquake and 1951 LV earthquake sequence. Bayesian statistical modeling of radiocarbon dates yielded central ages of A.D. 1658–1796, A.D. 1591–1689, and A.D. 1525–1611 for the three earlier events, indicating a long-term vertical slip rate of approximately 6.7–7.3-mm/yr based on offsets of dated horizons. An independent estimate of ~11.5-mm/yr derived from footwall stratigraphic reconstruction provides a more representative late Holocene rate, consistent with sustained vertical deformation of the Yuli segment over the past 600 yr.
5. Although the precise mechanical interaction between the CeRFS and the LVFS remains unresolved, evidence suggests that seismic activity along these two systems alternated and interacted within the Songpu area. This interaction likely produced the contrasting rupture patterns observed during the 1951 LV earthquake sequence and the 2022 Chihshang earthquake. We infer that the intersection of the west-dipping CeRFS and the east-dipping LVFS at depth promotes mechanical coupling between the two fault systems, enabling stress transfer and mutual influence during their seismic cycles within this structurally complex region.

DATA AND RESOURCES

The earthquake data of eastern Taiwan during September and October of 2022 are available at the Central Weather Administration of Taiwan (R.O.C.) website https://scweb.cwa.gov.tw/en-us/earthquake/data. The OxCal C14 calibration Program is available at https://c14.arch.ox.ac.uk/oxcal/OxCal.html. The 2025 active fault map of Taiwan is available at the Geological Survey and Mining Management Agency (GSMMA) website https://fault.gsmma.gov.tw/About/Fault_map. All websites were last accessed in November 2025.

DECLARATION OF COMPETING INTERESTS

The authors acknowledge that there are no conflicts of interest recorded.

ACKNOWLEDGMENTS

This research was partially funded by the Ministry of Science and Technology (MOST 110-2116-M-259-002-MY3) and the National Science and Technology Council (NSTC 112-2119-M-259-004) of Taiwan. The authors thank Yen-Chiu Liu and the 2022 Chihshang Earthquake Survey Group of the Central Geological Survey (MOEA, R.O.C.) for their field advice and discussions. The authors are also grateful for help in the field and trench excavations with Chih-Hao Chen, Ya-Chiu Tseng, and Yi-Chyun Tseng. The suggestions and comments from Associate Editor Yann Klinger and two anonymous reviewers, as well as the proofreading assistance from Wei-Fang Sun, greatly helped us improve this article.

REFERENCES

Angelier, J., H. T. Chu, and J. C. Lee (1997). Shear concentration in a collision zone: Kinematics of the active Chihshang fault, Longitudinal Valley, eastern Taiwan, *Tectonophysics* **274,** nos. 1/3, 117–143, doi: 10.1016/S0040-1951(96)00301-04.

Biq, C. (1965). The East Taiwan rift, *Petrol. Geol. Taiwan* **4,** 93–106.

Biq, C. (1973). Kinematic pattern of Taiwan as an example of actual continental-arc collision, *Rep. Seminar on Seismology, US-ROC Cooperative Science Program*, 21–26.

Central Weather Administration (CWA), Taiwan (2012). Central weather administration seismographic network [Data set], *International Federation of Digital Seismograph Networks*, doi: 10.7914/SN/T5.

Chen, W. S., Y. M. Wu, P. Y. Yeh, Y. X. Lai, S. S. Ke, M. C. Ke, and C. Y. Yang (2024). Insights into the seismogenic structures of the arc-continent convergent plate boundary in eastern Taiwan, *Terr. Atmos. Ocean. Sci.* **35,** no. 13, doi: 10.1007/s44195-024-00065-7.

Chen, W. S., I. C. Yen, K. P. Fengler, C. M. Rubin, C. C. Yang, H. C. Yang, H. C. Chang, C. W. Lin, W. H. Lin, Y. C. Liu, *et al.* (2007). Late Holocene paleoearthquake activity in the middle part of the Longitudinal Valley fault, eastern Taiwan, *Earth Planet. Sci. Lett.* **264,** nos. 3/4, 420–437, doi: 10.1016/j.epsl.2007.09.043.

Chen, W. S., I. C. Yen, C. C. Yang, H. C. Yang, Y. C. Chen, K. C. Tsai, N. W. Huang, Y. K. Chu, H. C. Chang, C. W. Lin, *et al.* (2010). Paleoseismic Study of the 1951 Hualien earthquake fault - AN DING Bridge trench, Hetsukang Village, Rueisuei Township, *Spec. Publ. Central Geol. Surv.*, Ministry of Economic Affairs, Vol. 15, 137–145 (in Chinese).

Cheng, W. B. (2009). Tomographic imaging of the convergent zone in Eastern Taiwan–subducting forearc sliver revealed? *Tectonophysics* **466,** nos. 3/4, 170–183, doi: 10.1016/j.tecto.2007.11.010.

Cheng, S. N., Y. T. Yeh, and M. S. Yu (1996). The 1951 Taitung earthquake in Taiwan, *J. Geol. Soc. China* **39,** no. 3, 267–286.

Chung, L. H., Y. G. Chen, Y. M. Wu, J. B. H. Shyu, and Y. T. Kuo (2008). Seismogenic faults along the major suture of the plate boundary deduced by dislocation modeling of coseismic displacements of the 1951 M7. 3 Hualien–Taitung earthquake, *Earth Planet. Sci. Lett.* **269,** nos. 3/4, 416–426, doi: 10.1016/j.epsl.2008.02.035.

Geological Survey and Mining Management Agency (GSMMA) (2005). Active fault map of Taiwan, available at https://fault.gsmma.gov.tw/ckfinder/connector?command=Proxy&type=Attach&currentFolder=/&fileName=2025%E5%B9%B4%20%E8%87%BA%E7%81%A3%E6%96%B7%E5%B1%A4%E5%88%86%E5%B8%83%E5%9C%96%EF%BC%88%E8%8B%B1%E6%96%87%E7%89%88%EF%BC%89.jpg&c=2&p=tblAbout_1&l=4 (last accessed November 2025).

Hsu, T. L. (1962). Recent faulting in the Longitudinal Valley of eastern Taiwan, *Mem. Geol. Soc. China* **1,** 95–102.

Hsu, L., and R. Bürgmann (2006). Surface creep along the Longitudinal Valley fault, Taiwan from InSAR measurements, *Geophys. Res. Lett.* **33,** L06312, doi: 10.1029/2005GL024624.

Huang, H. H., and Y. Wang (2022). Seismogenic structure beneath the northern Longitudinal Valley revealed by the 2018–2021 Hualien earthquake sequences and 3-D velocity model, *Terr. Atmos. Ocean. Sci.* **33,** no. 1, 17, doi: 10.1007/s44195-022-00017-z.

Huang, S. Y., J. Y. Yen, M. L. Wu, I. C. Yen, and R. Y. Chuang (2019). Investigating the Milun fault: The coseismic surface rupture zone of the 2018/02/06 M_L 6.2 Hualien earthquake, Taiwan, *Terr. Atmos. Ocean. Sci.* **30,** no. 3, 311–335, doi: 10.3319/tao.2018.12.09.03.

Kagan, E. J., M. Stein, A. Agnon, and C. B. Ramsey (2010). Paleoearthquakes as anchor points in Bayesian radiocarbon deposition models: A case study from the Dead Sea, *Radiocarbon* **52,** no. 3, 1018–1026.

Kim, K. H., J. M. Chiu, and K. C. Chen (2006). Polarity reversal of active plate boundary and elevated oceanic upper mantle beneath the collision suture in central eastern Taiwan. *Bull. Seism. Soc. Am.* **96,** no. 3, 796–806, doi: 10.1785/0120050106.

Ko, Y. Y., C. C. Tsai, J. H. Hwang, Y. W. Hwang, L. Ge, and M. C. Chu (2023). Failure of engineering structures and associated geotechnical problems during the 2022 M_L 6.8 Chihshang earthquake, Taiwan, *Nat. Hazards* **118,** 55–94, doi: 10.1007/s11069-023-05993-0.

Kuoc-Chen, H., Y. M. Wu, C. H. Chang, J. C. Hu, and W. S. Chen (2004). Relocation of the eastern Taiwan earthquakes and its tectonic implications, *Terr. Atmos. Ocean. Sci.* **15,** no. 4, 647–666, doi: 10.3319/tao.2004.15.4.647(t).

Kuo-Chen, H., D. Brown, S. Y. Lai, and Y. J. Chen (2023). Reflection seismic profiling along the Longitudinal Valley Basin, eastern Taiwan: In search of the Central Range fault, *Tectonophysics* **869,** 230,129, doi: 10.1016/j.tecto.2023.230129.

Lee, J. C., J. Angelier, H. T. Chu, J. C. Hu, F. S. Jeng, and R. J. Rau (2003). Active fault creep variations at Chihshang, Taiwan, revealed by creep meter monitoring, 1998–2001, *J. Geophys. Res.* **108,** no. B11, 2528, doi: 10.1029/2003JB002394.

Lee, S. J., T. Y. Liu, and T. C. Lin (2023). The role of the west-dipping collision boundary fault in the Taiwan 2022 Chihshang earthquake sequence, *Sci. Rep.* **13,** no. 1, 3552, doi: 10.1038/s41598-023-30361-0.

Liang, W. T., J. M. Chiu, and K. H. Kim (2007). Anomalous Pn waves observed in eastern Taiwan: Implications of a thin crust and elevated oceanic upper mantle beneath the active collision-zone suture, *Bull. Seismol. Soc. Am.* **97,** no. 4, 1370–1377, doi: 10.1785/0120060226.

Lienkaemper, J. J., and C. B. Ramsey (2009). OxCal: Versatile tool for developing paleoearthquake chronologies—A primer, *Seismol. Res. Lett.* **80,** no. 3, 431–434, doi: 10.1785/gssrl.80.3.431.

Lin, C. M., Y. W. Chang, C. C. Chou, M. Erri, S. J. Jhuang, Z. K. Lee, C. L. Wu, S. H. Chao, J. Y. Huang, H. C. Yang, *et al.* (2024). Reconnaissance of the 2022 Guanshan and Chihshang earthquakes in eastern Taiwan, *Earthq. Spectra* **40,** no. 1, 531–565, doi: 10.1177/87552930231209102.

Liu, C. C., and S. B. Yu (1990). Vertical crustal movements in eastern Taiwan and their tectonic implications, *Tectonophysics* **183,** nos. 1/4, 111–119, doi: 10.1016/0040-1951(90)90191-a.

Lo, C. L., E. T. Chang, and B. F. Chao (2012). Relocating the historical 1951 Hualien earthquake in eastern Taiwan based on tide gauge record, *Geophys. J. Int.* **192,** no. 2, 854–860, doi: 10.1093/gji/ggs058.

McCalpin, J. P. (1996). *Paleoseismology*, Academic Press, New York, 588 pp.

McCalpin, J. P. (2009). *Paleoseismology*, Second Ed., Academic Press, New York, 800 pp.

Murase, M., N. Matta, T. Ishiyama, C. H. Lin, W. S. Chen, J. Y. Yen, J. B. H. Shyu, J. J. Lin, Y. Nishikawa, I. C. Yen, *et al.* (2024). Effects of the 2022 M_w 7.0 Chihshang earthquake on the shallow creeping of the Central Longitudinal Valley fault in eastern Taiwan: Insights from precise leveling measurements, *Seismol. Res. Lett.* **96,** no. 3, 1521–1531, doi: 10.1785/0220240133.

Murase, M., N. Matta, C. H. Lin, W. S. Chen, and N. Koizumi (2013). An episodic creep-slip event detected by precise levelling surveys in the central part of the Longitudinal Valley fault, eastern Taiwan, in 2011–2012, *Tectonophysics* **608,** 904–913, doi: 10.1016/j.tecto.2013.07.027.

Peyret, M., S. Dominguez, R. Cattin, J. Champenois, M. Leroy, and A. Zajac (2011). Present-day interseismic surface deformation along the Longitudinal Valley, eastern Taiwan, from a PS-InSAR analysis of the ERS satellite archives, *J. Geophys. Res.* **116,** no. B3, doi: 10.1029/2010jb007898.

Ramsey, C. B. (2009). Bayesian analysis of radiocarbon dates, *Radiocarbon* **51,** no. 1, 337–360, doi: 10.1017/S0033822200033865.

Ramsey, C. B. (2024). Radiocarbon calibration: From bane to blessing, *Radiocarbon* **66,** no. 6, 2036–2046, doi: 10.1017/rdc.2023.32.

Ramsey, C. B. (2025). OxCal 4.4 program, availabe at https://c14.arch.ox.ac.uk/oxcal.html (last accessed November 2025).

Reches, Z., and D. A. Lockner (2010). Fault weakening and earthquake instability by powder lubrication, *Nature* **467,** 452–455, doi: 10.1038/nature09348.

Reimer, P. J. (2020) Composition and consequences of the IntCal20 radiocarbon calibration curve, *Quat. Res.* **96,** 22–27, doi: 10.1017/qua.2020.42.

Reimer, P. J., W. E. N. Austin, E. Bard, A. Bayliss, P. G. Blackwell, C. B. Ramsey, M. Butzin, H. Cheng, R. L. Edwards, M. Friedrich, *et al.* (2020) The IntCal20 Northern Hemisphere radiocarbon calibration curve (0–55 cal kBP), *Radiocarbon* **62,** doi: 10.1017/RDC.2020.41.

Rice, J. R. (2006). Heating and weakening of faults during earthquake slip, *J. Geophys. Res.* **111,** no. B5, doi: 10.1029/2005JB004006.

Shimazaki, K., and T. Nakata (1980). Time-predictable recurrence model for large earthquakes, *Geophys. Res. Lett.* **7,** no. 4, 279–282, doi: 10.1029/GL007i004p00279.

Shyu, J. B. H., L. H. Chung, Y.G. Chen, J. C. Lee, and K. Sieh (2007). Re-evaluation of the surface ruptures of the November 1951 earthquake series in eastern Taiwan, and its neotectonic implications, *J. Asian Earth Sci.* **31,** no. 3, 317–331, doi: 10.1016/j.jseaes.2006.07.018.

Shyu, J. B. H., K. Sieh, J. P. Avouac, W. S. Chen, and Y. G. Chen (2006). Millennial slip rate of the Longitudinal Valley fault from river terraces: Implications for convergence across the active suture of eastern Taiwan, *J. Geophys. Res.* **111,** no. B8, doi: 10.1029/2005jb003971.

Shyu, J. B. H., K. Sieh, Y. G. Chen, and L. H. Chung (2006). Geomorphic analysis of the Central Range fault, the second major active structure of the Longitudinal Valley suture, eastern Taiwan, *Geol. Soc. Am. Bull.* **118,** nos. 11/12, 1447–1462, doi: 10.1130/b25905.1.

Simoes, M., J. P. Avouac, and Y. G. Chen (2007). Slip rates on the Chelungpu and Chushiang thrust faults inferred from a deformed strath terrace along the Dungpuna river, west central Taiwan. *J. Geophys. Res.* **112,** no. B3, S10–S17, doi: 10.1029/2005jb004200.

Sun, W. F., S. Y. Pan, C. M. Huang, Z. K. Guan, I. C. Yen, C. W. Ho, T. K. Chi, C. S. Ku, B. S. Huang, C. C. Fu, *et al.* (2024). Deep learning-based earthquake catalog reveals the seismogenic structures of the 2022 M_w 6.9 Chihshang earthquake sequence, *Terr. Atmos. Ocean. Sci.* **35,** no. 1, 5, doi: 10.1007/s44195-024-00063-9.

Tang, C. H., Y. Lin, S. J. Lee, Y. J. Hsu, J. B. H. Shyu, Y. T. Kuo, and H. Y. Chen (2023). Nearby fault interaction within the double-vergence suture in eastern Taiwan during the 2022 Chihshang earthquake sequence, *Commun. Earth Environ.* **4,** 333, doi: 10.1038/s43247-023-00994-0.

Teng, L. S. (1990). Geotectonic evolution of Late Cenozoic arc-continent collision in Taiwan, *Tectonophysics* **183,** nos. 1/4, 57–76, doi: 10.1016/0040-1951(90)90188-E.

Thomas, M. Y., J. P. Avouac, J. Champenois, J. C. Lee, and L. C. Kuo (2014). Spatiotemporal evolution of seismic and aseismic slip on the longitudinal Valley fault, Taiwan, *J. Geophys. Res.* **119,** 5114–5139, doi: 10.1002/2013JB010603.

Tsai, Y. B. (1986). Seismotectonics of Taiwan, *Tectonophysics* **125,** nos. 1/3, 17–37, doi: 10.1016/0040-1951(86)90005-3.

Tung, H., H. Y. Chen, Y. J. Hsu, C. H. Tang, J. C. Lee, Y. Wang, and H. K. Lee (2025). Geodetic constraints on the September 2022 Guanshan and Chihshang earthquakes, eastern Taiwan, *Tectonophysics* **895,** 230,600.

Wang, Y., S. H. Wu, H. L. B. Chou, Y. Y. Li, W. S. Cheng, A. Ho, J. M. Chen, S. C. Liu, C. Y. Hsieh, S. Duan, *et al.* (2024). Surface ruptures of the 2022 Guanshan -Chihshang earthquakes in central Longitudinal Valley area, eastern Taiwan, *Terr. Atmos. Ocean. Sci.* **35,** no. 16, 25, doi: 10.1007/s44195-024-00077-3.

Widiatmoko, F. R., J. Y. Yen, I. C. Yen, S. Y. Huang, and N. W. Shih (2023). Assessing the Yuli surface deformation from the 20220918 Chihshang earthquake: An integrated RTK GNSS network approach, *Terr. Atmos. Ocean. Sci.* **34,** no. 1, 25, doi: 10.1007/s44195-023-00058-y.

Wu, F. T., H. Kuo-Chen, and K. D. McIntosh (2014). Subsurface imaging, TAIGER experiments and tectonic models of Taiwan, *J. Asian Earth Sci.* **90,** 173–208, doi: 10.1016/j.jseaes.2014.03.024.

Wu, Y. M., C. H. Chang, L. Zhao, J. B. H. Shyu, Y. G. Chen, K. Sieh, and J. P. Avouac (2007). Seismic tomography of Taiwan: Improved constraints from a dense network of strong motion stations, *J. Geophys. Res.* **112,** no. B8, doi: 10.1029/2007JB004983.

Wu, Y. M., C. H. Chang, L. Zhao, T. L. Teng, and M. Nakamura (2008). A comprehensive relocation of earthquakes in Taiwan from 1991 to 2005, *Bull. Seismol. Soc. Am.* **98,** no. 3, 1471–1481, doi: 10.1785/0120070166.

Wu, Y. M., Y. G. Chen, C. H. Chang, L. H. Chung, T. L. Tang, F. T. Wu, and C. F. Wu (2006). Seismogenic structure in a tectonic suture zone: With new constraints from 2006 M_w 6.1 Taitung earthquake, *Geophys. Res. Lett.* **33,** L22305, doi: 10.1029/2006GL027572.

Wu, Y. M., L. Zhao, C. H. Chang, and Y. J. Hsu (2008). Focal mechanism determination in Taiwan by genetic algorithm, *Bull. Seismol. Soc. Am.* **98,** no. 2, 651–661, doi: 10.1785/0120070115.

Yen, I. C., W. S. Chen, S. H. Sung, N. W. Huang, C. C. B. Yang, Y. C. Liu, and C. W. Lin (2014). Paleoseismological study on the Chihshang segment of the Longitudinal Valley fault in eastern Taiwan, *Central Geol. Surv.* **28,** 43–70 (in Chinese with English abstract).

Yen, I. C., W. S. Chen, C. C. B. Yang, N. W. Huang, and C. W. Lin (2008). Paleoseismology of the Rueisuei segment of the Longitudinal Valley fault, eastern Taiwan, *Bull. Seismol. Soc. Am.* **98,** no. 4, 1737–1749, doi: 10.1785/0120070113.

Yen, I. C., W. S. Chen, J. Y. Yen, S. Y. Huang, Y. C. Hsu, N. W. Shih, C. H. Chen, Y. C. Tseng, and Y. G. Chu (2023). The preliminary tectonic study of Central Part of Longitudinal Valley with Guanshan-Chihshang earthquake surface rupture and subsurface geological data, *Sino-Geotech.* **176,** 15–24 (in Chinese with English abstract).

Yen, J., C. Lu, R. J. Dorsey, H. Kuo-Chen, C. Chang, C. Wang, R. Y. Chuang, Y. Kuo, C. Chiu, Y. Chang, *et al.* (2018). Insights into seismogenic deformation during the 2018 Hualien, Taiwan, earthquake sequence from InSAR, GPS, and modeling, *Seismol. Res. Lett.* **90,** no. 1, 78–87, doi: 10.1785/0220180228.

Yu, S. B., and L. C. Kuo (2001). Present-day crustal motion along the Longitudinal Valley fault, eastern Taiwan, *Tectonophysics* **333,** nos. 1/2, 199–217, doi: 10.1016/s0040-1951(00)00275-4.

Yu, S. B., H. Y. Chen, and L. C. Kuo (1997). Velocity field of GPS stations in the Taiwan area, *Tectonophysics* **274,** nos. 1/3, 41–59, doi: 10.1016/S0040-1951(96)00297-1.

Yu, S. B., D. D. Jackson, G. K. Yu, and C. C. Liu (1990). Dislocation model for crustal deformation in the Longitudinal Valley area, eastern Taiwan, *Tectonophysics* **183,** nos. 1-4, 97–109, doi: 10.1016/0040-1951(90)90190-j.

APPENDIX A

Table A1 describes the locations of the photographs in Figures 3, 4, and 6.

TABLE A1
Coordinates of Photos

Name	Longitude	Latitude
Figure 3a	121.3080	23.2981
Figure 3b	121.3198	23.3422
Figure 3c	121.3026	23.2629
Figure 3d	121.2476	23.1716
Figure 4a	121.3030	23.2982
Figure 4b	121.3040	23.2893
Figure 4c	121.3036	23.2881
Figure 4d	121.3032	23.2866
Figure 6a	121.3811	23.4448
Figure 6b	121.3808	23.4436
Figure 6c	121.3760	23.4359
Figure 6d	121.3758	23.4358

APPENDIX B

Table B1 lists carbon-14 dating results and calibration dates used in this paper.

Manuscript received 22 March 2025
Published online 5 December 2025

TABLE B1
List of Radiocarbon Dates and Calibrated Ages

Parameter Name	Laboratory Number	Stratigraphic Unit/Earthquake Event	Material	Conventional Age (yr B.P.)*	Calendar Calibration (yr A.D.)†	Modeled Mean Age with Standard Deviation (yr A.D.)‡	Modeled Age (yr A.D.)‡	Paleoearthquake Age (yr A.D.)‡	Recurrence Interval (yr)
E2022		2022 Chihshang earthquake (trench 2)		–	–	2022 ± 0	2022	2022	–
SP2-61	Beta-654163	SGb1 (trench 2 unit E)	Charred material	130 ± 30 B.P.	1674–1942	1955 ± 3	1952–1958	–	71
E1		1951 LV earthquake sequence (trench 2)		–	–	1951 ± 0	1951	1951	–
SP2-57	Beta-664203	SMb1 (trench 2 unit D)	Charred material	200 ± 30 B.P.	1644–1811	1824 ± 85	1739–1909	–	212–215
E2		E2 paleoearthquake (trench 2)		–	–	1727 ± 69	1658–1796	1736–1739	–
SP2-66	Beta-654160	Ob1 (trench 2 unit C)	Charred material	210 ± 30 B.P.	1642–1808	1688 ± 48	1640–1736	–	96–110
E3		E3 paleoearthquake (trench 2)		–	–	1640 ± 49	1591–1689	1629–1640	–
SP2-73	Beta-654158	Ob4 (trench 2 unit B)	Charred material	360 ± 30 B.P.	1456–1634	1595 ± 34	1561–1629	–	68–97
E4		E4 paleoearthquake (trench 2)		–	–	1568 ± 43	1525–1611	1543–1561	–
SP2-09	Beta-664189	Ob5 (trench 2 unit A)	Charred material	370 ± 30 B.P.	1450–1634	1502 ± 41	1461–1543	–	–
SP2-01	Beta-654156	Ob5 (trench 2 unit A)	Charred material	410 ± 30 B.P.	1432–1622	1465 ± 28	1437–1493	–	–
SP1-01	Beta-654155	Ga1 (trench 1)	Organic sediment	860 ± 30 B.P.	1052–1262	–	–	–	–

*Radiocarbon conventional ages were measured using accelerator mass spectrometry by Beta Analytic, Inc.
†Calendar age dendrochronologically calibrated by method A from the program of Reimer *et al.* (2020), with 2 standard deviation uncertainty.
‡Calibrated modelling using OxCal Program 4.4 (Ramsey, 2025), the code to calibrate carbon-14 ages is available from the author upon request. LV, Long Valley.

Seismogenic Structures Offshore Taiwan and Their Earthquake Potential from the Taiwan Earthquake Model (TEM) Project

Cheng-Hung Chen[1] and J. Bruce H. Shyu[*1]

ABSTRACT

OPEN ACCESS

Taiwan is an active orogenic belt characterized by numerous active structures and frequent earthquake activities. As a result, identifying the locations and seismic potential of these structures is essential for minimizing earthquake-related damages. Although a comprehensive on-land seismogenic structure database for the island has been constructed by the Taiwan Earthquake Model project team, and the database has already been widely used for disaster preparedness work, a similar database for offshore structures is lacking. With an integration of available geological and geophysical data, we identified 54 offshore structures across six neotectonic domains around Taiwan using two criteria that faulting in seismic reflection profiles disturbs the seabed, and structural lineaments on the seafloor need to be continuous. Subsurface geometries of the faults were reconstructed based on their cross-cutting relationships and the seismogenic depth data from previous studies, and we applied three regression equations to estimate the potential earthquake magnitude of the structures. The results show that these structures are capable of generating earthquakes exceeding magnitude 6.5, and some specific multifault rupture scenarios could produce earthquakes greater than magnitude 8.0. With future updates when new data becomes available, this offshore seismogenic structure database would significantly improve earthquake hazard assessments and marine resource management studies in Taiwan.

KEY POINTS

- 54 offshore seismogenic structures were identified with available geological and geophysical data.
- We proposed their structural parameters, such as fault type, subsurface geometry, and earthquake magnitude.
- All 54 structures can potentially generate earthquakes of M_w 6.5 or greater in multifault rupture scenarios.

Supplemental Material

INTRODUCTION

Taiwan is an active orogenic belt with numerous seismogenic structures and frequent earthquake activities (e.g., Chen *et al.*, 2016; Shyu *et al.*, 2020). In this dynamic setting, the multidisciplinary team of the Taiwan Earthquake Model (TEM) project, which is funded by the National Science and Technology Council of Taiwan, integrates seismology, geology, and earthquake engineering approaches to assess future seismic hazards and risks. By continuously refining methodologies and exploring innovative research techniques, the TEM Team has achieved some leading case studies in seismic hazard research that have largely enhanced our overall understanding of earthquake hazards. For example, the seismic hazard assessment results presented by Chan *et al.* (2017) identified eastern and southwestern Taiwan as regions with high seismic potential, consistent with subsequent earthquake events. Overall, these studies not only enhanced our insight into regional seismic risks but also provided valuable experiences for seismic hazard assessment practices worldwide.

Although there have been many efforts to study seismic hazards in Taiwan, most of these studies have focused on onshore faults and often overlooked the impact of offshore structures (e.g., Shyu *et al.*, 2016, 2020; Chan *et al.*, 2020). However, there have been reports that historical major earthquakes and active structures are indeed located offshore (e.g., Deffontaines *et al.*, 2001; Shyu *et al.*, 2005; Wang *et al.*, 2011).

1. Department of Geosciences, National Taiwan University, Taipei, Taiwan, https://orcid.org/0009-0005-2934-2033 (C-HC); https://orcid.org/0000-0002-2564-3702 (JBHS)

*Corresponding author: jbhs@ntu.edu.tw

Cite this article as Chen, C.-H., and J. B. H. Shyu (2025). Seismogenic Structures Offshore Taiwan and Their Earthquake Potential from the Taiwan Earthquake Model (TEM) Project, *Bull. Seismol. Soc. Am.* **116**, 26–51, doi: 10.1785/0120250009

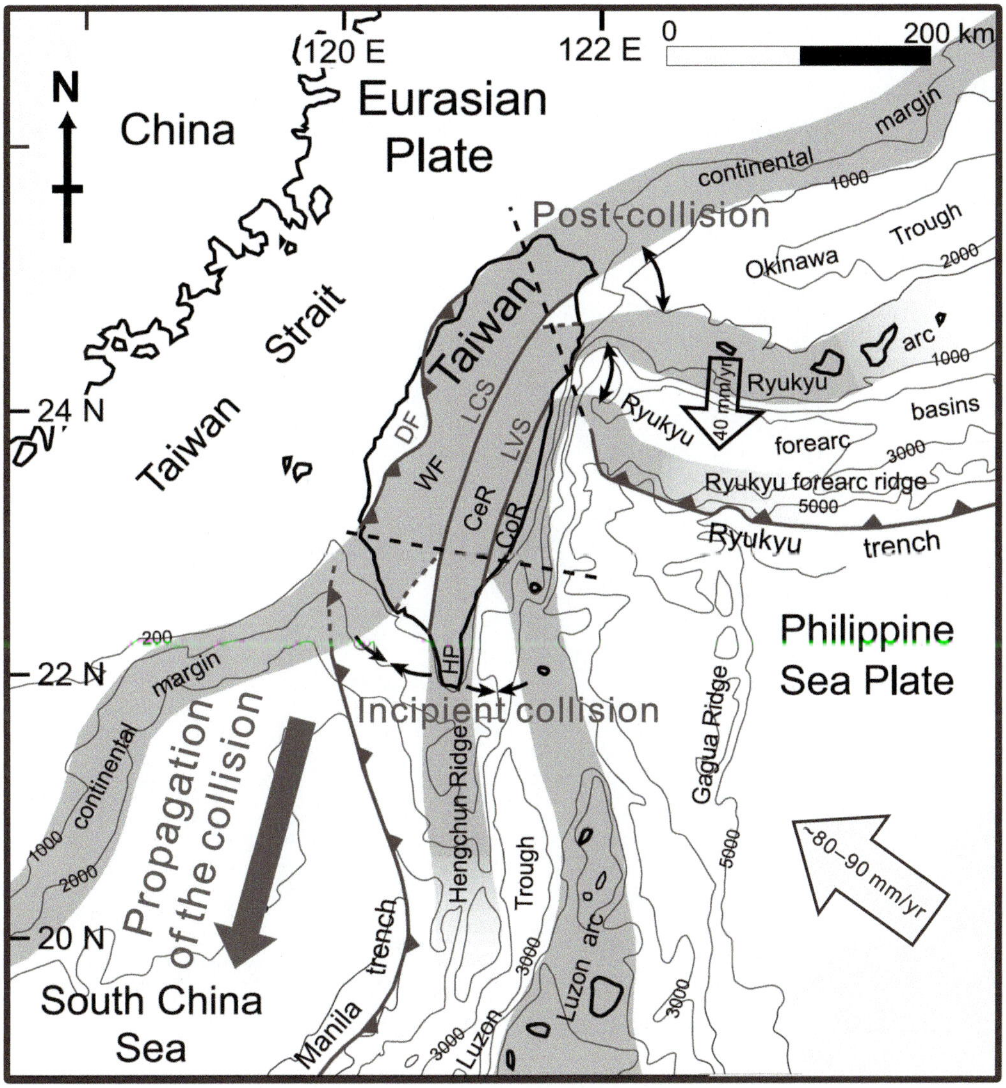

Figure 1. Tectonic setting of Taiwan (modified from Shyu *et al.*, 2005). Taiwan is located along a plate boundary where an oblique collision drives orogenic development from north to south (Suppe, 1981), resulting in various orogenic stages in offshore regions. For example, southern Taiwan is in the incipient collision stage, and northern Taiwan is in the post-collision stage. CeR, Central Range; CoR, Coastal Range; DF, deformation front; HP, Hengchun Peninsula; LCS, Lishan-Chaochou suture; LVS, Longitudinal Valley suture; WF, western Foothills. The color version of this figure is available only in the electronic edition.

Earthquakes generated by offshore seismogenic structures will produce significant impacts on both offshore and on-land areas. For example, the January 2024 Noto Peninsula earthquake in Japan triggered severe ground shaking and destruction (Suppasri *et al.*, 2024), and the April 2024 offshore Hualien earthquake in Taiwan caused road and bridge damage, utility disruptions, building collapses, and casualties (Kanwal, 2024). In both cases, the limited prior information on offshore seismic structures hindered effective earthquake impact assessments. To fill this gap, understanding the locations and seismic capacities of offshore structures is essential for disaster preparedness, as well as future exploration and development offshore.

Currently, several versions of active fault databases exist in Taiwan, including one developed by the Geological Survey and Mining Management Agency that identifies 36 active faults (Lin, Liu, *et al.*, 2021), and another by the TEM project, which includes 45 seismogenic structures (Shyu *et al.*, 2020). Offshore seismogenic structures, which also have the potential to generate significant earthquakes, are not included in these databases. Although Deffontaines *et al.* (2001) and Shyu *et al.* (2005) have mapped some offshore structures, their results only show structural locations, limiting their applicability for seismic hazard assessments.

Recent advances in geological and geophysical research in Taiwan's offshore regions, including bathymetry and seismic surveys, have substantially improved our ability to identify offshore seismogenic structures. As a result, we reassessed and integrated these new results to identify potential seismogenic structures in the offshore regions of Taiwan. In addition, the geometries of these offshore structures were analyzed using pre-existing datasets and earthquake hypocenter depths. By combining geometric parameters with empirical regression equations, we estimated potential earthquake magnitudes for these offshore faults. This study includes detailed information on the location, geometry, and earthquake potential of Taiwan's offshore structures, which will provide important references for future earthquake hazard assessment and marine resource management.

STUDY AREA AND GEOLOGICAL BACKGROUND

Taiwan is located at the boundary where the Philippine Sea Plate converges with the Eurasian Plate, moving northwest at a rate about 80–90 mm/yr (e.g., Yu *et al.*, 1997; Shyu *et al.*, 2006; Hsu *et al.*, 2016; Fig. 1). This convergence results in the collision between the Luzon volcanic arc and the Eurasian continental

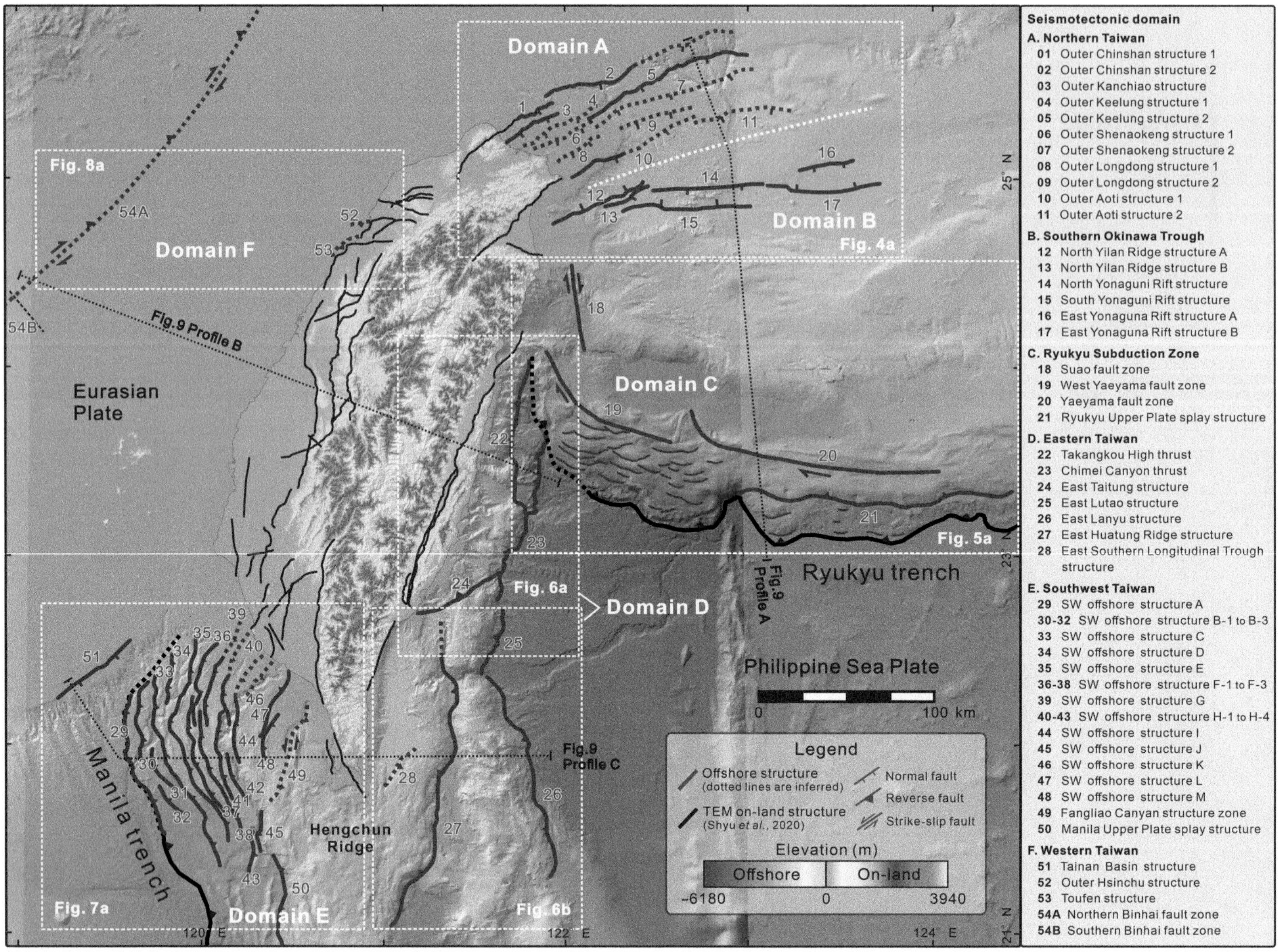

Figure 2. Seismogenic structure map of Taiwan. On-land seismogenic structures (black lines) are from the Taiwan Earthquake Model (TEM) project (Shyu *et al.*, 2020), and offshore structures (red lines) are identified in this study. The red solid lines mark structures with distinct seabed lineaments, and dashed lines represent less clear lineaments. Domains A to F correspond to the six marine neotectonic domains shown in Figures 4–8. The white dashed lines indicate the area shown in Figures 4–8, not the boundary between domains. Bathymetry data are divided at 123° E, with resolutions of 200 m to the west and 450 m to the east. The color version of this figure is available only in the electronic edition.

margin, forming Taiwan's north–south-trending orogenic belt and complex offshore topography (Yu and Song, 2000). In the Luzon subduction system south of Taiwan, the Eurasian Plate subducts beneath the Philippine Sea Plate, forming north–south-trending features such as the Manila Trench, fore-arc ridges, and the Luzon volcanic arc. In the Ryukyu subduction system east of Taiwan, the Philippine Sea Plate subducts beneath the Eurasian Plate, generating east–west-trending features and the Okinawa Trough.

According to the oblique collision model of Taiwan, the orogenic process propagates from north to south (Suppe, 1981, 1984), leading to distinct orogenic stages (Teng, 1996; Shyu *et al.*, 2005; Fig. 1). This progression, combined with varying regional stress conditions, results in different structural patterns and activities across the island. For instance, southern Taiwan, in the incipient stage of orogeny and under compressive stress, is more prone to the development of reverse faults, whereas northern Taiwan is in a post-collision environment and tends to develop normal faults.

The area of this study spans ~200 km offshore from Taiwan's coast, between 20° and 26° N and 119° and 124° E (Fig. 2). In the twenty-first century alone, this region has experienced several nearshore earthquakes that damaged buildings on-land and caused casualties, including the 26 December 2006 Hengchun offshore event, the 31 March 2002 earthquake offshore Hualien, and the 3 April 2024 Hualien earthquake. Although both the Manila Trench and the Ryukyu subduction zone are also primary seismic sources, both interplate and intraplate earthquake sources of the subduction zones have already been considered in previous seismic hazard assessment studies (e.g., Wang *et al.*, 2016; Chan *et al.*, 2020). Therefore, this study only focuses on crustal structures and excludes the subduction zones.

METHODS

Determining the location of offshore seismogenic structures

For the identification of offshore structures, direct methods such as outcrop and trenching surveys are generally not feasible, and it is necessary to rely on geophysical methods. Based on previous reports, Taiwan's seismogenic structures have recurrence intervals ranging from hundreds to tens of thousands of years (Shyu *et al.*, 2020). Although earthquake data from the past few decades can help identify some potential structures (e.g., Wu *et al.*, 2024), this timescale is too short to illustrate locked structures that have not produced recent seismicity. Therefore, this study investigates long-term structural deformation through the analysis of seismic reflection profiles and bathymetry data.

We integrated previously published geological and geophysical data from 1980 to 2024 to efficiently locate potential offshore seismogenic structures (Fig. S1, available in the supplemental material to this article). Structure names are based on prior studies; for unnamed structures, names were assigned based on nearby geographic features. Following the convention of the TEM project, for structures that have not been reported as faults in previous studies, we refer to them as just "structures." Different structures within the same system are distinguished by letter suffixes (e.g., A or B), and continuous segments by numbers (e.g., 1 or 2).

The credibility of these structural locations is ranked A, B, or C, from the highest to the lowest (Table S1), based on the resolution of the data using the following two criteria.

Criterion 1: Seismogenic structures need to disturb the seabed in seismic reflection profiles

Lateral discontinuities in seismic reflections commonly indicate faulting, and the disturbance of near-seafloor sediments is often interpreted as evidence of recent fault activity. The locations of such structures are identified based on existing interpretations of seismic reflection profiles and through the reinterpretation of original seismic data. Because of the differences in acquisition timing, methodologies, data processing, and resolution among the seismic reflection profiles, interpretations for any given structure are preferentially based on the highest-quality profile available.

Because of their limited penetration depth, seismic reflection profiles generally image only the upper few kilometers of the crust, restricting the detection of deeper seismogenic structures. Because deeper structures that do not yet reach the seafloor were excluded from this study, seismicity that occurred on them may be considered as areal sources in future probabilistic seismic hazard assessments.

Criterion 2: Seismogenic structures need to exhibit laterally extended seafloor lineaments in bathymetry

Criterion 1 provides point data for a structure's seafloor location, whereas criterion 2 defines its lateral extent. In the absence of significant erosion, active dip-slip faults typically display cumulative deformation with lateral extensions visible at surface exposures. Structures with dominant strike-slip components often form linear features due to topographic differences across the fault, particularly where the fault trace bends.

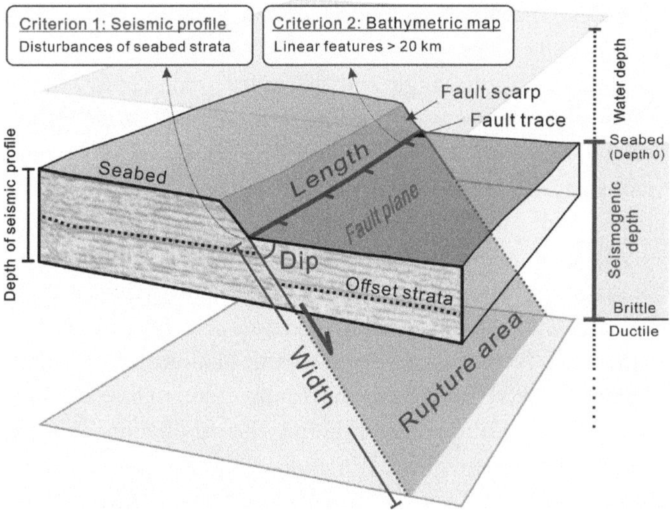

Figure 3. Geometric definition and identification standards for offshore seismogenic structures. The identification of offshore seismogenic structures in this study is based on two criteria: (1) discontinuous reflection signals in seismic reflection profiles extending near the seabed, and (2) laterally extending seabed lineaments visible on bathymetry maps. The seismogenic area is calculated by multiplying the structure's length by its width, which is derived from the dip angle and the seismogenic depth. The color version of this figure is available only in the electronic edition.

Faults with longer lengths tend to have a higher potential to generate large earthquakes (Wesnousky, 2008). As a result, this study focused on structures at least 20 km in length because such features are capable of generating magnitude 6.0 or greater earthquakes that may impact onshore areas.

We used ArcGIS software to analyze digital elevation models (DEMs; see Data and Resources for details), generating contour lines, shaded relief maps, and slope maps to identify seafloor lineaments. The solid lines represent structures with clear lineaments, and the dashed lines denote those inferred from seismic reflection profiles or other methods when lineaments are less distinct. DEMs for the offshore region surrounding Taiwan were obtained from the National Science and Technology Council's Oceanography Database (200 m resolution) and the GEBCO website (450 m resolution).

Determining the subsurface geometry of structures

Reconstructing the subsurface geometry of seismogenic structures is essential for estimating earthquake magnitudes, which is achieved by calculating the rupture area by multiplying the fault length and width (Fig. 3). The lengths were measured using ArcGIS, based on seabed lineaments. To determine fault width, we used two methods: when previous studies provided subsurface geometrical models, the published values were used. For structures without such data, the width was calculated using the fault's dip angle and the seismogenic depth (Fig. 3). When available, we used dip angles reported in prior studies. Otherwise, we applied Anderson (1905) theory, which assumes a constant dip angle with depth: 30° for reverse faults, 60° for normal faults, and 90° for strike-slip faults.

Seismogenic depth is defined as the vertical distance from the seabed to where brittle failure occurs in the crust (Fig. 3). We used 200 m resolution bathymetry data analyzed in ArcGIS to calculate average water depth (depth 0) along the fault lines (Appendix Excel Table). The maximum depth of historical and instrumental earthquakes, excluding the subduction zone and deeper source events (e.g., Wu *et al.*, 2017) serves as an initial proxy for brittle failure depth. The structural geometry is then adjusted based on the subsurface intersections of faults or the geometries of nearby on-land faults, assuming no variation in geometry along the strike direction of the structures.

For consistency with the assessments of on-land faults, we follow the error standards defined in the TEM project (Shyu *et al.*, 2016, 2020). Fault dip angles have an uncertainty of ±10° when estimated solely by Anderson's theory, and ±5° when supported by geological data. Seismogenic depth has a uniform uncertainty of ±2 km (Appendix Excel Table).

Determining the earthquake magnitude of structures

This study employed three methods to estimate the potential earthquake magnitude of each structure. Two regression methods used by Shyu *et al.* (2020) were also used to ensure comparability with on-land structures in Taiwan. The first method, based on Wells and Coppersmith (1994), estimates magnitudes using the structural movement type and rupture area, making it widely applicable in global and local studies (Shyu *et al.*, 2020). The second method, adapted from Yen and Ma (2011), incorporates parameters optimized for Taiwan's tectonic setting (Shyu *et al.*, 2020). The third method, following Stirling *et al.* (2013) and Wesnousky (2008), uses the fault's length and movement type to reduce uncertainties in rupture area estimation. Detailed results from all three approaches are compared in Table S2.

SEISMOGENIC STRUCTURES OFFSHORE TAIWAN

This study categorizes Taiwan's offshore region into six neotectonic domains (Figs. 2 and 4–8) based on their geologic settings, seafloor topography, and structural characteristics. These domains are: northern offshore Taiwan (domain A), the southern Okinawa Trough (domain B), the upper plate of the Ryukyu subduction zone (domain C), eastern offshore Taiwan (domain D), southwestern offshore Taiwan (domain E), and western offshore Taiwan (domain F). However, due to transitional geological features, the boundaries between some domains are not clearly defined. The geological background and structural features of each domain will be described in subsequent sections.

Domain A: Northern offshore Taiwan geological zone (located north of the Okinawa Trough)

Domain A is located in the northeastern offshore region of Taiwan, extending from the East China Sea Continental Shelf southeastward to the continental slope and the northern margin of the Okinawa Trough (Fig. 4a). The southwestward migration of the Taiwan orogeny (Teng, 1996) transformed the regional stress field from a compressional orogenic belt to an extensional environment during the late Pliocene to early Pleistocene. This change reactivated former reverse faults as normal faults (Emery *et al.*, 1970; Suppe, 1984; Hsiao *et al.*, 1998; Kong *et al.*, 2000; Shyu *et al.*, 2005; Shang *et al.*, 2017; Yang *et al.*, 2021; Nguyen *et al.*, 2022). Seismic reflection profiles show that deeper stratigraphic layers (Yang, 2017; green line in Fig. 4b) were deformed by early orogenic compressional folding, and younger unconformities (red line in Fig. 4b) show normal-faulting displacements (Hsiao *et al.*, 1998).

The northwestern boundary of this structural inversion zone is near the Shanchiao fault, which trends northeastward along its strike (Hsiao *et al.*, 1998; Nguyen *et al.*, 2022; Fig. 4a). West of this inversion boundary, the East China Sea Continental Shelf is a flat, shallow platform with no evidence of structural inversion. Seismic reflection profiles show faults with varying dip directions buried beneath thick, undeformed sedimentary deposits, suggesting that they are inactive (Sun, 1985; Chen and Watkins, 1994; Yang, 2017).

East of the structural reversal boundary lies a collapsed orogenic zone (Nguyen *et al.*, 2022), characterized by the Pliocene regional sequence boundary (PRSB; red line in Fig. 4b). The PRSB is offset by eleven northeast–southwest-oriented normal faults, dipping southeast and extending to the seabed (Hsiao *et al.*, 1998; Atomic Energy Council, 2016; Yang, 2017; Fig. 4b). The overlying Quaternary sequences thicken locally near the fault, indicating ongoing fault activity and rotation of the hanging wall during the deposition (Hsiao *et al.*, 1998). Seabed topographic maps reveal numerous northeast–southwest linear features that facilitate the identification of fault locations (Chung, 2021).

Apart from structure 1, structures 2 to 11 exhibit similar geometric properties. Vertical offsets typically decrease from the fault center toward its ends (Cowie and Roberts, 2001), so the offset variation of the PRSB is used to determine fault length. For example, the offset of the PRSB along a fault decreases from ~1 s in the middle of the fault to 0 s toward the southwest in the results of Yang (2017), allowing us to determine the length of the fault. This pattern also implies that normal faulting initiated in the northeast, with the reverse faults landward remaining unreactivated (Chen, 2014; Atomic Energy Council, 2016; Yang, 2017; Lai and Huang, 2023).

Structures in domain A

Outer Chinshan structure 1 (ST-I)(1), Outer Chinshan structure 2 (ST-III)(2), and Outer Kanchiao structure (ST-II)(3) (Fig. 4). Because of the safety assessments required for nearby nuclear power plants, this area has been extensively

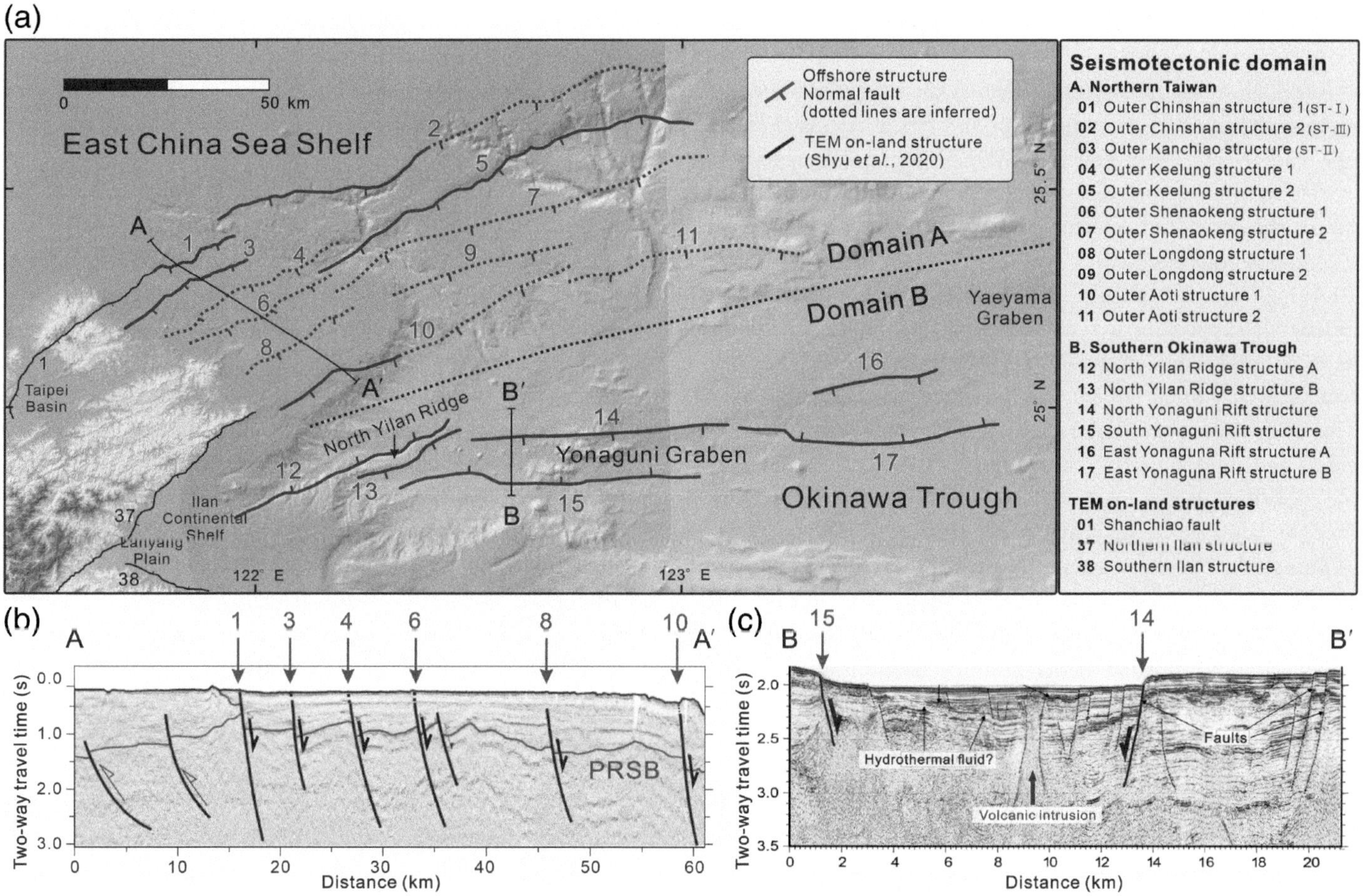

studied. The report of the Atomic Energy Council (2016) synthesized previous research, integrating multiple seismic reflection profiles and seabed topography to determine fault locations and activity for structures 1 to 3. Structure 1 in domain A serves as the master fault of a nearshore half-graben structure, which suggests a potential offshore extension of the on-land Shanchiao fault (Atomic Energy Council, 2016). For disaster prevention, this study compares the location of structure 1 with the Shanchiao fault based on the TEM database (Shyu *et al.*, 2020) and defines it as an extended segment of the fault.

Figure 4. Seismogenic structure map of offshore northern Taiwan for domains A and B. (a) On-land structures (black lines) are from Shyu *et al.* (2020), and offshore structures (red lines) are identified and numbered in this study. The solid lines with hachures indicate the downthrown side of faults. (b) A representative seismic reflection profile of domain A (location marked in panel a, modified from Yang, 2017) shows primary active normal faults east of the Outer Chinshan structures 1 and 2 (numbers 1 and 2). The green lines mark the Middle Miocene unconformity, revealing previous reverse faulting displacement along the Outer Chinshan structures. PRSB refers to the Pliocene regional sequence boundary, showing more recent normal-faulting displacements. (c) A seismic reflection profile of domain B (location marked in panel a, from Tsai *et al.*, 2021) shows boundary normal faults in the extensional system of the Okinawa Trough. The color version of this figure is available only in the electronic edition.

Northeast offshore structures 4 to 11 (Fig. 4). The locations of these structures are primarily based on the interpretations by Yang (2017, Fig. 4b), with minor adjustments in their locations using topographic maps (Chung, 2021).

The seismogenic depths of structures 1 to 11 are set at 10 km based on Atomic Energy Council (2016). This was constrained by seismic activity and studies of the on-land Shanchiao fault. For structure 1, we follow the published structural geometry, allowing its dip angle to vary with depth (see Appendix Excel Table). The dip angles for the remaining structures are assumed to be 60°, as is typical for normal faults.

Domain B: The southern Okinawa Trough geological zone

Domain B is located in the southern Okinawa Trough, stretching from west of 124° E to offshore the Lanyang Plain. The Okinawa Trough is a back-arc extensional basin formed above the Ryukyu subduction system, extending from southern Japan to northeastern Taiwan (Kimura, 1985; Sibuet *et al.*, 1998). The area near Taiwan features numerous submarine volcanoes and hydrothermal vents, indicating ongoing tectonic activity (Lee *et al.*, 1980; Sibuet *et al.*, 1998).

Since 0.1 Ma, the rifting direction in the southern Okinawa Trough has shifted to a nearly north–south orientation (Kimura, 1985; Hsiao *et al.*, 1998; Sibuet *et al.*, 1998; Tsai *et al.*, 2021), resulting in the formation of several east–west-oriented rift systems. Historical earthquake data revealed a normal-fault stress regime, with seismicity concentrated in the trough's center and distributed east–west (Sibuet *et al.*, 1998; Kubo and Fukuyama, 2003; Huang *et al.*, 2012).

Although it has been debated whether the extensional process in the southern Okinawa Trough is symmetrical at crustal scales (e.g., Park *et al.*, 1998; Arai *et al.*, 2017), the seismic reflection profiles show a series of east–west-striking normal faults dipping toward the spreading center, with no significant differences in structural geometry on either side (Sibuet *et al.*, 1998; Arai *et al.*, 2017; Fig. 4c). In addition, the overall strata appear nearly horizontal, supporting a symmetrical extension model during the recent extensional phase. Offsets of reflectors across boundary structures away from the center are generally larger (Klingelhoefer *et al.*, 2009; Arai *et al.*, 2017; Tsai *et al.*, 2021; Fig. 4c). Pronounced seabed cliffs indicate active boundary faults, when sedimentation rate variations across them indicate long-term tectonic activity since the late Pleistocene (Fang *et al.*, 2020).

This study focuses on structures west of the Yaeyama Graben for hazard studies and resource development in Taiwan (Fig. 4a). Six seismogenic structures have been identified in domain B: four normal faults in the Yonaguni Rift system (structures 14 to 17, Fig. 4a), and two normal faults on either side of the North Yilan Ridge (structures 12 and 13, Fig. 4a). Although normal faults may also develop on the Ilan Continental Shelf as the trough extends westward (Ku *et al.*, 2009), no seabed lineament was identified that meet the criteria of this study, possibly due to thick terrigenous sedimentation.

Structures in domain B

North Yilan Ridge structures A (12) and B (13) (Fig. 4). These two normal faults are located on either side of the North Yilan Ridge, with the northern fault dipping northwest and the southern fault dipping southeast (Sibuet *et al.*, 1998; Hsu, 1999; Tsai *et al.*, 2021). Seismic reflection profiles and bathymetry maps reveal basement offsets of up to 0.4–1.0 s (~600–1500 m) and clearly defined seabed lineaments. These structures may be influenced by both the formation of the Okinawa Trough and the orogenic collapse in northern Taiwan (Tsai *et al.*, 2021).

North Yonaguni Rift structure (14) and South Yonaguni Rift structure (15) (Fig. 4). These normal faults are located on the northern and southern sides of the Yonaguni Rift system, identified by the lateral extension of prominent seabed lineaments (Tsai *et al.*, 2021; Fig. 4c).

East Yonaguni Rift structures A (16) and B (17) (Fig. 4). Located east of the Yonaguni Rift system, these two normal faults dip toward the trough center and are identified by clear seabed lineaments (Arai *et al.*, 2017; Tsai *et al.*, 2021). The western endpoint of structure 17 is differentiated from the adjacent structure 14 by their opposite dip direction.

Seismogenic depths for structures 12 to 17 are set at 15 km based on earthquake distributions (Chen *et al.*, 2022) in the southern Okinawa Trough. Dip angles for these structures are assumed to be 60°, as for normal faults. Structures 14 and 15 dip toward each other and intersect at 11.3 km. Thus, we adjusted their seismogenic depths to this value (Fig. 9, profile A).

Domain C: Upper plate of the Ryukyu subduction zone geological zone

Domain C is located on the overriding plate of the Ryukyu subduction system and is characterized by the northwestward subduction of the Philippine Sea Plate. This setting features the accretionary wedge, fore-arc basins, and the volcanic arc (Lallemand *et al.*, 1999; Fig. 5a). Because of the lack of recent high-resolution seismic reflection profiles, seabed lineaments were primarily used to interpret seismogenic structures. Four structures were identified in this domain: one on the eastern edge of the Hoping Basin and three within the accretionary wedge.

In the fore-arc basins south of the Ryukyu arc, the seabed lineaments of small-scale faults are largely obscured by sedimentation (Dominguez *et al.*, 1998; Font *et al.*, 2001; Hsiung *et al.*, 2017; Deng *et al.*, 2023). Only one structure on the eastern side of the Hoping Basin (structure 18) is observed to cut through the seabed in seismic reflection profiles, which meets our criteria.

Two right-lateral faults along the northern boundary of the accretionary wedge are defined by distinct seabed lineaments (19 and 20). In addition, several parallel seabed anticlines within the wedge suggest reverse faulting (Dominguez *et al.*, 1998; Lallemand *et al.*, 1999; Hsu *et al.*, 2013; Chen *et al.*, 2017; Fig. 5a), and structure 21 is a particularly large-scale reverse fault. Other faults in the region are unlikely to generate significant earthquakes due to their limited length and the loose material of the accretionary wedge (Theunissen *et al.*, 2010). As such, these smaller faults are not analyzed further in this study.

Structures in domain C

Suao fault zone (18) (Fig. 5). This north–south structure is identified by a scarp along the eastern Hoping Basin that is unrelated to submarine channel erosion, and exhibits a flower structure in seismic reflection profiles (Font *et al.*, 2001; Font and Lallemand, 2009; Wang, Hsu, and Yeh, 2019; Fig. 5b,c). Previous studies identified it as a right-lateral fault (Lallemand *et al.*, 1999; Font *et al.*, 2001; Font and Lallemand, 2009), with a 5.5 km offset of the shelf-slope boundary. The northwestern extension of this fault aligns with the western end of the Okinawa Trough, suggesting its activity is related to the opening of the trough.

A boundary structure in the area was suggested by gravity anomalies (Doo *et al.*, 2018), and Global Positioning System velocity data indicate right-lateral motion across this boundary between the Yilan nearshore and Yonaguni Island (Lallemand and Liu, 1998). Although these results represent an integrated pattern over a large spatial scale, such pattern is consistent with the existence of the proposed Suao fault zone in this area.

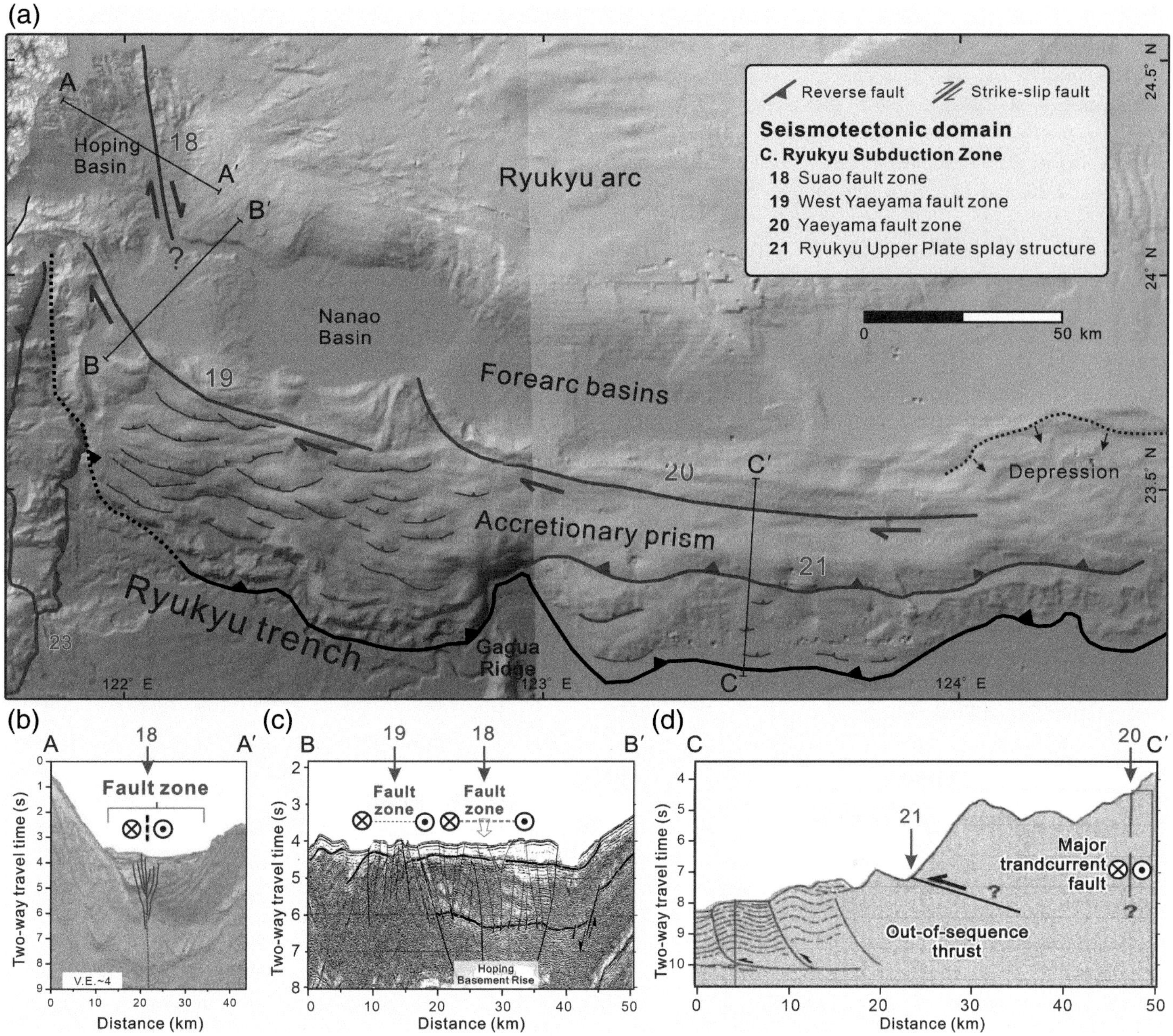

Figure 5. Seismogenic structure map of domain C, upper plate of the Ryukyu subduction system. (a) Offshore seismogenic structures in domain C are marked by red lines. (b–d) Representative seismic reflection profiles of domain C, with locations marked in panel (a), are adapted from Wang, Hsu, and Yeh (2019; A–A′ profile), Font *et al.* (2001; B–B′ profile), and Lallemand *et al.* (1999; C–C′ profile). The color version of this figure is available only in the electronic edition.

West Yaeyama fault zone (19) and Yaeyama fault zone (20) (Fig. 5). Two right-lateral structures near the northern boundary of the accretionary wedge were proposed and defined due to the oblique subduction (Dominguez *et al.*, 1998; Lallemand *et al.*, 1999; Font and Lallemand, 2009). Seismic reflection profiles show flower structures characteristic of strike-slip motion (Font *et al.*, 2001; Fig. 5b). The northern tip of the Gagua Ridge divides these structures into the West Yaeyama fault zone (19) and the Yaeyama fault zone (20). These faults have clear seabed lineaments, with the eastern side of structure 20 obscured by a submarine landslide (Okamura *et al.*, 2018). As a result, we used the western boundary of the landslide as the minimum eastern extension of the fault.

Ryukyu Upper Plate splay structure (21) (Fig. 5). A primary seabed lineament north of the Gagua Ridge represents the largest splay fault in this region (Lallemand *et al.*, 1999; Hsu *et al.*, 2013; Chen *et al.*, 2017).

The Suao fault zone (18) is assigned a dip angle of 90° as a strike-slip fault, with a depth reaching 25 km based on earthquake distributions (Wang, Hsu, and Yeh, 2019). The geometries of structures 19, 20, and 21 were constrained by the depth of their intersection with the subduction interface. Wu *et al.* (2009) suggested a 15° dip for the subduction interface beneath the accretionary wedge (Fig. 9, profile A; Fig. S2a). Structures 19 and 20 have dip angles of 90°, whereas structure 21 has a 30° dip, consistent with mega-splay fault characteristics (Strasser *et al.*, 2009; Conin *et al.*, 2012). Based on the depths at which these structures intersect with the subduction interface, the seismogenic depths for these structures are estimated at 17 km for structures 19 and 20, and 13 km for structure 21.

Domain D: Eastern offshore Taiwan geological zone

Domain D lies atop the Philippine Sea Plate, where topography and geological structures reflect the transition from subduction in the south to collision in the north (Hirtzel *et al.*, 2009; Huang *et al.*, 2018). The offshore Hengchun Ridge extends southward from the Central Range, representing the deformation zone above the Manila subduction zone (Fig. 2). To its east, the North Luzon Trough contains thick sediments in the forearc basin of the Luzon island arc (Fig. 6). Northward, plate convergence deforms these basin sediments, forming the Huatung Ridge, the South Longitudinal Trough, and the Taitung Trough (Huang *et al.*, 1992; Fig. 6b). Farther east lies the Luzon island arc, including the volcanic islands of Lanyu and Lutao. Northward, the region transitions into Taiwan's orogenic system, characterized by frequent seismic activity and seismogenic structures parallel to the mountain ranges (Deffontaines *et al.*, 2001; Malavieille and Trullenque, 2009; Wang *et al.*, 2011, 2024).

This study integrated various previous viewpoints and identified seven seismogenic structures (Deffontaines *et al.*, 2001; Malavieille *et al.*, 2002; Shyu *et al.*, 2005; Malavieille and Trullenque, 2009; Huang *et al.*, 2018; Fig. 6). Two west-dipping reverse faults (25 and 26) are located on the eastern side of the Luzon island arc, with another on the eastern side of the Huatung Ridge (27). To the west of these uplifted terrains, only the southeastern South Longitudinal Trough shows evidence of an east-dipping structure (28). Seismic reflection profiles do not support the presence of other westward thrusts proposed in some earlier studies (e.g., Chen *et al.*, 2019, 2024) at the junction between the western island arc and the Taitung Trough. Off the eastern coast of the Coastal Range, three west-dipping reverse faults (22, 23, and 24) deform the seabed. Farther east, seismic reflection profiles show no evidence of tectonic activity on buried Huatung Basin structures since at least 1.5 Ma (Hsiung *et al.*, 2017; Hsu *et al.*, 2021).

Structures in domain D

Takangkou High thrust (22) and Chimei Canyon thrust (23) (Fig. 6). Seismic reflection profiles reveal two west-dipping thrust faults deforming the strata off Taiwan's eastern coast (Malavieille *et al.*, 2002; Hsieh *et al.*, 2020). The northern part of these structures may have subducted beneath the Eurasian Plate; thus, we drew their ends at the trench. The Chimei Canyon thrust (23) features more prominent fault scarps than the Takangkou High thrust (22), suggesting higher activity. Historical earthquake hypocenters align with these west-dipping fault planes (Huang and Wang, 2022). The M_L 7.2 Hualien earthquake on 3 April 2024 occurred near this structural zone and may have been produced by one of these two structures.

East Taitung structure (24) (Fig. 6, Fig. S3). This southeastward-thrusting fault cuts through the seabed with a topographic scarp (Malavieille *et al.*, 2002; Lin, 2010; Fig. 6d). Possible left-lateral motion on this structure during the northwestward collision of the Luzon arc with Taiwan is consistent with paleomagnetic records that indicate clockwise rotations (Lee *et al.*, 1991). However, left-lateral motion may have ceased around 1.2 Ma (Chen *et al.*, 2015), indicating that its current activity is primarily thrust faulting.

East Lutao structure (25) and East Lanyu structure (26) (Fig. 6). Seismic reflection profiles show eastward-thrusting faults on the eastern side of the Luzon island arc (Lin, 2010; 25 and 26). Strata east of the island arc are deformed by folding, with long-term uplift of the hanging-wall block illustrated by marine terraces on the Lutao and Lanyu islands (Inoue *et al.*, 2011). Structures 23, 25, and 26 may belong to the same structural system; however, this study distinguishes them based on the differences in their surface features and the trends of their fault traces.

East Huatung Ridge structure (27) (Fig. 6). Seismic reflection profiles indicate a major thrust on the eastern side of the Huatung Ridge, cutting through and deforming the seabed (Malavieille *et al.*, 2002; McIntosh *et al.*, 2005; Hirtzel *et al.*, 2009; Malavieille and Trullenque, 2009; Chen *et al.*, 2015; Huang, 2018). Growth strata on the eastern flank of the South Longitudinal Trough indicate continued movement of this structure (Huang, 2018). Some minor seabed lineaments atop the ridge represent small-scale fault systems (Malavieille *et al.*, 2002), but these were not included in our database due to their limited length.

East Southern Longitudinal Trough structure (28) (Fig. 6; Fig. S4). Seismic reflection profiles from the west of the southern Huatung Ridge reveal an anticlinal structure with a small-scale, eastward-dipping reverse fault (Malavieille *et al.*, 2002; Malavieille and Trullenque, 2009; Huang, 2018; Fig. 6e). Shyu *et al.* (2005) mapped a structure there based on submarine topography, with a distinct straight scarp. The lack of evidence for channel erosion suggests it may be a structural scarp (about 90–150 m high from ArcGIS analysis, Fig. S4).

For structures 22 and 23, two geometric interpretations are considered. Hsieh *et al.* (2020) proposed a 25° fault dip transitioning to nearly horizontal at the depth of 6.0–6.1 km, but Malavieille *et al.* (2002) suggested a continuous 25° dip until they intersect with the on-land Longitudinal Valley fault system (Fig. 9, profile B). The coseismic coastal uplift observed during the M_L 7.2 earthquake near Hualien on 3 April 2024

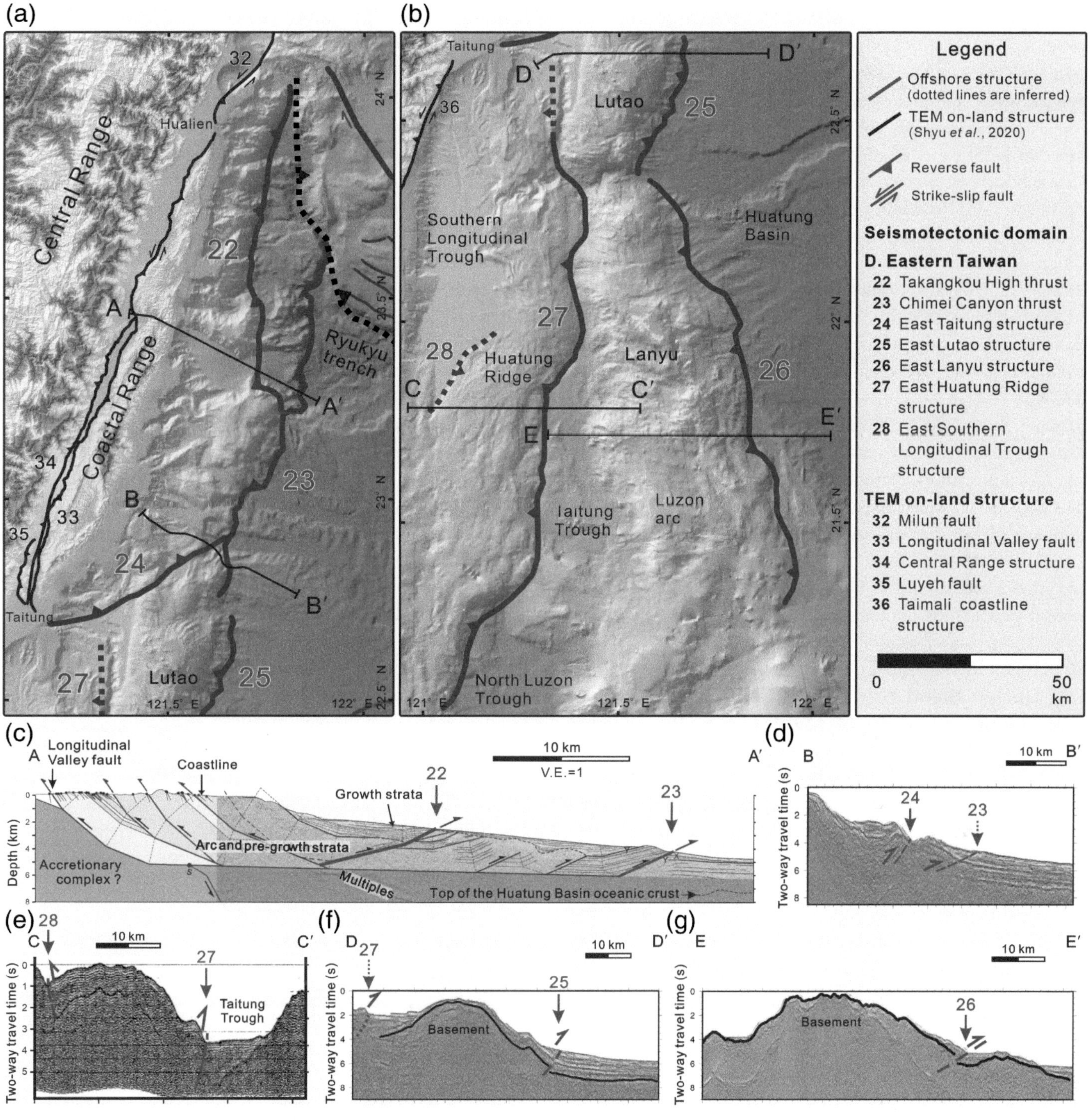

Figure 6. Seismogenic structures in domain D, offshore eastern Taiwan. (a,b) Maps of northern and southern domain D, showing seismogenic structures as red lines. (c–g) Representative seismic reflection profiles of domain D, with locations marked in panels (a) and (b), are adapted from Hsieh *et al.* (2020; A–A′ profile), Lin (2010; B–B′ profile), Malavieille *et al.* (2002; C–C′ profile), Lin (2010; D–D′ profile), and Lin (2010; E–E′ profile). The color version of this figure is available only in the electronic edition.

and its deeper focal depth support the latter model. Thus, we include both geometric assumptions but prefer the second interpretation.

Structure 24 shows reverse faulting with potential horizontal components. The fault dip angle thus ranges from 30° for reverse faults to 60° for faults with both reverse and strike-slip characteristics. The seismogenic depth is set at 14 km, where it intersects with the Longitudinal Valley fault (Fig. S3). Structures 25 and 26 have dip angles of 30°, with seismogenic depths set at 25 km (Chen *et al.*, 2016, 2018, 2019). Structures 27 and 28 are also assigned 30° dip angles, with depths of 20 and 10 km, respectively, based on their relationships with the Manila subduction system (Fig. 9, profile C).

Domain E: Southwestern offshore Taiwan geological zone

Domain E is located on the upper plate of the Luzon subduction system, where the processes of subduction and the transition into Taiwan's incipient collision stage dominate the tectonic framework (Shyu *et al.*, 2005; Fig. 1). Because the Eurasian Plate subducts eastward, deformed sediments accumulate, forming north–south-trending ridges and canyons.

Some studies related the area's topographic highs to late Pliocene to recent mud diapirism (e.g., Sun and Liu, 1993). However, high-gravity values suggest that compressional stress, rather than buoyant mud diapirism, plays a key role in the formation of topographic highs (Doo *et al.*, 2015). Seismic reflection profiles show that asymmetric landforms are more likely associated with reverse faults that deform the seabed (Liu *et al.*, 1997, 2004; Lin *et al.*, 2008, 2022; Hsiung *et al.*, 2018; Dirgantara *et al.*, 2020). Moreover, recent studies indicate that some chaotic seismic facies previously attributed to diapirism may also contain stratified signals (Ko, 2022). As a result, we attribute the topographic highs in this area mainly to reverse faulting.

We also identified the Fangliao Canyon structure zone (49) and the Manila Upper Plate splay structure (50) in the eastern part of this domain.

Structures in domain E

East Liuchiu Island structure (47) and Southwest offshore structures A to M (29–48) (Fig. 7). The Small Liuchiu is the only island above sea level in this region. The East Liuchiu Island structure (47), located east of the island, accounts for the uplift that forms the marine terraces on the island (Wang *et al.*, 2022). Other structures, identified by Lin *et al.* (2008), lie west of each anticlinal axis and are roughly parallel to the Manila Trench. Seismic reflection profiles show that these east-dipping reverse faults are spaced 5–10 km apart, and that their dip angles gradually decrease toward the west. Their distribution pattern follows the typical westward propagation of thrust faults in western Taiwan's fold-and-thrust belt. Although this region experiences fewer instrumental earthquakes than other parts of Taiwan (Wang *et al.*, 2011), seismic reflection profiles show these structures deformed seabed sediments with growth strata in their footwalls, indicating their ongoing activity (Chiang *et al.*, 2004; Lin *et al.*, 2008).

Fangliao Canyan structure zone (49) (Fig. 7). Seismic reflection profiles reveal two structures in the submarine Fangliao Canyon (Deffontaines *et al.*, 2016), though canyon erosion partially obscures the structural scarp. This study combined the two structures into a single fault zone located at the western edge of the west-facing scarp. Previous studies suggest both thrust and strike-slip components for this fault (Deffontaines *et al.*, 2016). We interpret it as a left-lateral fault with a thrust component, similar to the nearby Chaochou fault on land (Shyu *et al.*, 2020).

Manila Upper Plate splay structure (50) (Fig. 7, Fig. S5). Seismic reflection profiles show several thrust faults beneath the Hengchun Ridge off southern Taiwan (Lin *et al.*, 2009; Zhang *et al.*, 2022). Structure 50, a major westward-thrusting fault, is characterized by topographic features and their lateral continuity. This structure likely branches out from the subduction system and divides the accretionary wedge into a lower slope region with fold-and-thrust belts and a highly deformed upper slope region.

Seabed lineaments and seismic reflection profiles suggest this fault terminates near northern Luzon Island (Fig. S5; Liu *et al.*, 2006; Chen, 2015), where the interaction of subducting seamounts with the Manila Trench changes the geometry of the overlying accretionary complex (Zhu *et al.*, 2013). Other westward-thrusting structures between this fault and the trench (Lin *et al.*, 2009) were excluded from this study due to their shorter length and long distance from Taiwan.

Structure 47 off Small Liuchiu has a fault dip ranging from 60° at shallow depths to horizontal at around 4 km based on previous results (Wang *et al.*, 2022). For other structures, seismogenic depths are estimated based on the fault dip angles and the depth of the subduction interface (Tan, 2020; Tan *et al.*, 2022; Fig. 9, profile C; Figs. S2b and S6). Assuming the structural evolution follows the east-to-west pattern as in the on-land fold-and-thrust belt, the fault dip angles are set to decrease westward (Lin *et al.*, 2008, 2022), ranging from 30° to 40° (Fig. S6; Appendix Excel Table).

The Fangliao Canyon structure zone (49) is suggested as a high-angle strike-slip fault (Deffontaines *et al.*, 2016). Shyu *et al.* (2016) provided geometric data for the on-land Chaochou fault, with dip angles of 70°–80°. Hence, this study assumes a dip range of 70°–90° and a seismogenic depth of 9 km (Fig. 9, profile C). For the Manila Upper Plate splay structure (50), the fault dip is assigned at 40° and a seismogenic depth of 15 km, where it intersects with the subducting plate.

Domain F: Western offshore Taiwan geological zone

Domain F is part of the Eurasian Plate, extending from the shallow Taiwan Strait, with an average water depth of 60 m, to the deeper South China Sea Basin, where depths reach 3000 m. Before the Miocene, this region experienced extensional tectonics, forming northeast–southwest-striking normal faults and related grabens (Lin and Watts, 2002; Teng and Lin, 2004; Zhang *et al.*, 2020; Fig. S5). Since the Miocene, the collision between the Luzon arc and the continental margin resulted in the development of a foreland basin on the eastern side of the Taiwan Strait. Although many normal faults that formed earlier have become inactive, some on the eastern side were reactivated as reverse faults (Yu and Chou, 2001; Lin and Watts, 2002; Lacombe *et al.*, 2003; Lin *et al.*, 2003; Yang *et al.*, 2016, 2021).

In domain F, we mapped four seismogenic structures. Among them, two structures are related to the deformation front in western Taiwan that extends offshore in the vicinity

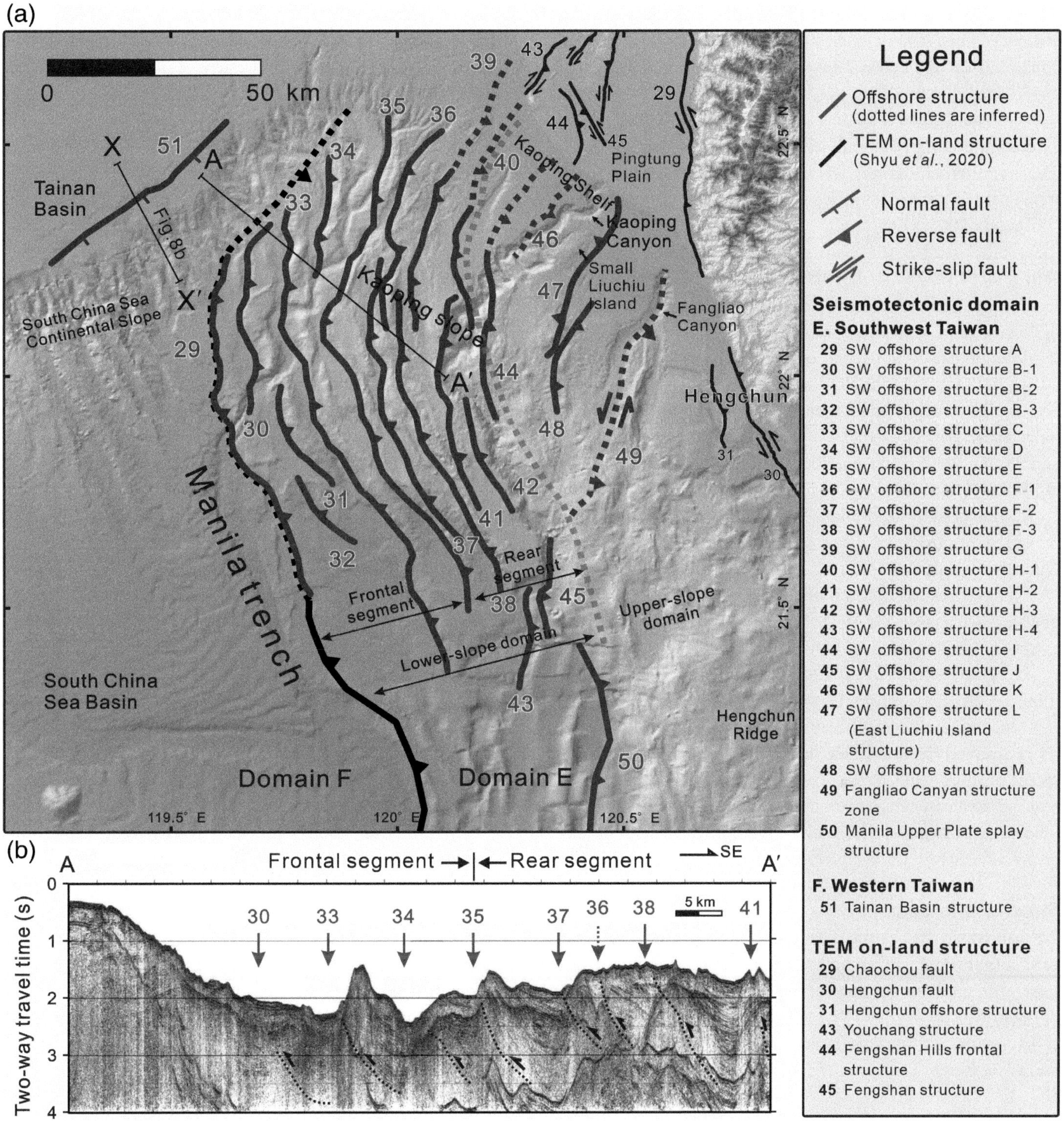

Figure 7. Seismogenic structure map of domain E, southwestern offshore Taiwan. (a) Seismogenic structures in domain E are represented by red solid lines for those with clear seabed lineaments and dashed lines for those with less distinct features. The purple dashed line marks the boundary between the upper- and lower-slope domains (Lin *et al.*, 2008). (b) A seismic reflection profile (location shown in panel a, modified from Lin *et al.*, 2008) displays westward-thrusting reverse faults in this domain. The color version of this figure is available only in the electronic edition.

of Hsinchu and Miaoli (Yu, 2004), where the stress conditions are favorable for the development of reverse faults (Lacombe *et al.*, 2003; Chiang, 2016; Yang *et al.*, 2016). Data from older oil and gas prospecting and recent offshore wind energy project assessments have enabled us to map structures 52 and 53 in this area. West of the deformation front, the fold-and-thrust belt is absent, and the seafloor topography is primarily shaped by terrigenous sedimentation and ocean currents (Lin and Watts, 2002; Yu, 2004; Yang, 2010; Chang *et al.*, 2015).

Only the Binhai fault zone (54) cuts through the seabed, as evidenced by seismic reflection profiles (Lin and Watts, 2002; Lin *et al.*, 2003; Teng and Lin, 2004; Chang *et al.*, 2015; Zhang *et al.*, 2020; Lin, Yang, *et al.*, 2021).

The Tainan Basin in the south of the strait has not yet entered the compressional stress field (Huang *et al.*, 2004). The continental margin features east-northeast–west-southwest-striking normal faults formed by earlier extensional stress (Lin *et al.*, 2005; Ding *et al.*, 2008; Yang *et al.*, 2016). Among these, one structure (51) shows significant seafloor lineaments (Liu *et al.*, 1997, 2004; Lin *et al.*, 2008; Fig. 7a).

Farther south, there is no clear evidence of active structures in the South China Sea Continental Slope, except for some local faults that do not seem to cut the seabed (e.g., Han *et al.*, 2019, 2021; Fig. 7a). The slope transitions into the South China Sea Basin, which remains unaffected by compression with older structures covered by at least 2 km of sediments (Lin and Watts, 2002; Li *et al.*, 2007; McIntosh *et al.*, 2013; Han *et al.*, 2019; Fig. 7a).

Seismic activity in domain F is relatively low compared to other regions around Taiwan. Notable events include the 1604 Quanzhou earthquake (M_w 7.5–8.1, Lee *et al.*, 1976; Yen *et al.*, 2021), likely related to the Binhai fault zone (54). Other earthquakes, such as those in 1994 (M_w 6.4–6.7; Kao and Wu, 1996; Huang *et al.*, 1999; Fig. S5) and 2018 (M_w 5.7–6.2; Wang, Ye, *et al.*, 2019; Wang *et al.*, 2021; Tang *et al.*, 2023; Fig. S5), had minimal impact onshore Taiwan due to their locations.

Domain F lacks detailed survey data compared to other offshore regions. However, new data are becoming available from recent offshore wind farm surveys led by the Geological Survey and the Mining Management Agency. Because more high-resolution data becomes available, they will improve the identification of potential seismogenic structures off Taiwan's western coast.

Structures in domain F

Tainan Basin structure (51) (Figs. 7a and 8b). This structure cuts through the seabed, forming a clear lineament near the continental margin that corresponds to the central segment of the previously mapped Yichu fault (Liu *et al.*, 1997, 2004; Lin *et al.*, 2003, 2008). This fault may also be associated with seabed sediment slumping (Ding *et al.*, 2008).

Outer Hsinchu structure (52) (Fig. 8). Seismic reflection profiles show that folded strata east of this structure are slightly elevated than those to the west (Chiang, 2016; Wu, 2017; Chen, 2019; Fig. 8d). This structure aligns with the onshore Hsinchu structure (6) described by Shyu *et al.* (2020), suggesting a combined length over 20 km, meeting the criteria of this study (Lacombe *et al.*, 2003; Chen, 2019).

Toufen structure (53) (Fig. 8). Seismic reflection profiles reveal that this fault cuts other structures, indicating that it is a relatively young structure in the area. The location of this structure is defined by the western edge of the anticline that deforms the Toukoshan Formation, the youngest late Pleistocene strata on land in western Taiwan (Huang *et al.*, 2020; Fig. 8e).

Binhai fault zone (54) (Fig. 8, Fig. S5). The Binhai fault zone is located on the western side of the Taiwan Strait and is likely related to multiple earthquake events (Wen and Xu, 2005; Yen *et al.*, 2021). Seismic reflection profiles and earthquake data reveal a 30–60 km wide structural zone cutting through the seabed, forming a right-lateral flower structure with branches that connect at depth (Zhang *et al.*, 2020; Fig. 8c).

Gravity, magnetic, and ambient noise tomography surveys have identified a primary structure along the proposed Binhai fault zone, marked by distinct geophysical anomalies parallel to the orientation of the Taiwan Strait (Huang and Wang, 2006; Zhang *et al.*, 2018). Because of the lack of clear fault trace evidence, the fault's approximate location is mapped as a dashed line, with a total length of about 500 km. Seismic reflection profiles show variations in basement depth, leading to the division of the fault into the northern Binhai fault zone (54A) and the southern Binhai fault zone (54B).

Besides strike-slip motion, the fault likely also exhibits a reverse component, with the northwestern side as the hanging-wall block, as evidenced by uplifted coastal features along the southeast Chinese coast (Zhang *et al.*, 1982; Huang and Wang, 2006). Thinner Quaternary sediments on the fault's western side also indicate ongoing relative uplift since the Quaternary (Huang and Wang, 2006).

The Tainan Basin structure (51) has a dip angle of 60° for the shallow part (0.2–4.5 km) and 20° for the deeper part (4.5–7.5 km) (Lin *et al.*, 2008; Fig. S7, Appendix Excel Table). The Outer Hsinchu structure (52) is suggested as a reverse fault that dips 45° to the south, following the on-land Hsinchu structure's geometry (Shyu *et al.*, 2020). The Toufen structure (53) is suggested as a reverse fault that dips 40° to the southeast, based on cross-section interpretations (Huang *et al.*, 2020).

The Binhai fault zone (54) has a seismogenic depth of 20 km, derived from earthquake depths and ambient noise tomography results (Zhang *et al.*, 2020, 2018). The fault is divided into two parts (Fig. S8): a deep basement part with a 60° dip and a sediment layer part with dips between 50° and 90°. Seismic reflection profiles suggest sediment thicknesses of 1.5 and 2 km for structures 54A and 54B, respectively (Zhang *et al.*, 2020).

DISCUSSION

Limitations in the identification of seismogenic structures

The accuracy of our seismogenic structure identification is primarily determined by the availability and quality of seismic reflection profiles offshore. In this study, we have integrated the literature about offshore Taiwan as comprehensively as

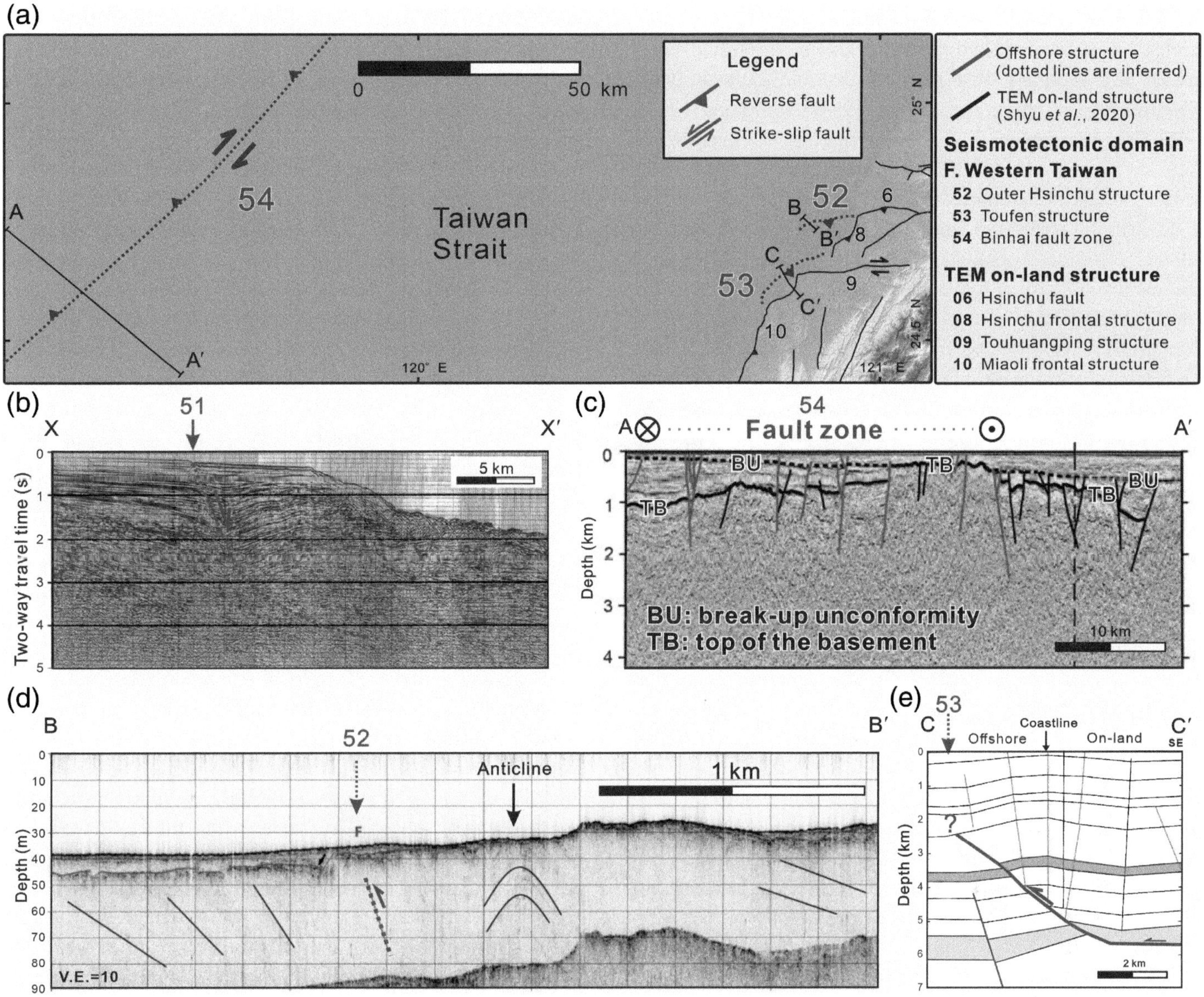

Figure 8. Seismogenic structure map of domain F, offshore western Taiwan. (a) Seismogenic structures in domain F are represented by dashed lines due to unclear seabed lineaments. (b) A representative seismic reflection profile of the Tainan Basin structure (modified from Lin *et al.*, 2008), with the profile location marked in Figure 7a. (c–e) Seismic reflection profiles show the Binhai fault zone (modified from Zhang *et al.*, 2020; A–A′ profile), Outer Hsinchu structures (modified from Chen, 2019; B–B′ profile), and Toufen structure (modified from Huang *et al.*, 2020; C–C′ profile). The color version of this figure is available only in the electronic edition.

possible (Fig. S1). However, there are still many regions with only limited seismic reflection profile data, such as the East China Sea Continental Shelf, the Ryukyu arc, the Huatung Basin, and some parts of Taiwan's coast. In these areas, it is difficult to conduct detailed structural mapping.

Another challenge comes from the resolution of the available DEMs. Because the grid resolution of the DEMs is between 200 and 450 m, it would be difficult to map the location of the offshore structural scarps with a higher accuracy than these numbers. To enhance the identification of offshore seismogenic structures in the future, it is necessary to obtain higher-resolution bathymetry maps and more seismic survey data.

Seafloor erosion and sedimentation can obscure topographic features formed by tectonic activities. Indeed, most structures identified in this study are not parallel to offshore channels, where erosion rates are generally high. For instance, the Chimei Canyon thrust (23) was traced via scarps outside the canyon. In domain E, some structures are parallel to submarine channels but are located in the footwall of reverse faults, making them less likely to be affected by erosion. Therefore, it is possible that some structures were not identified in this study due to their topographic features being eroded.

Sedimentation rates around Taiwan vary based on the proximity to sediment sources and ocean currents (e.g., Liu *et al.*, 2008; Huh *et al.*, 2011; Hsiung *et al.*, 2017). Although the slip rates of offshore structures remain highly uncertain, if we assume that offshore tectonic activity rates are comparable to those on land (~0.5–10 mm/yr; Shyu *et al.*, 2020), such rates would largely exceed the reported offshore sedimentation rates of 0.01–0.5 mm/yr (e.g., Hung and Chung, 1994; Chung and Chang, 1995; Dirgantara *et al.*, 2020; Hsu *et al.*, 2021). Therefore, we suggest that our identification of structures using topographic features is less likely affected by seafloor sedimentation.

Identifying strike-slip components in offshore faults using seismic reflection profiles is more challenging. Some faults may also exhibit horizontal movement, particularly when their orientations are oblique to the compressional stress field. In domain D, for example, we infer that some structures may have a left-lateral component due to the oblique collision that forms the Taiwan orogen, and this is also consistent with stress patterns inferred from historical seismicity (e.g., Fuh and Liu, 1998; Kao *et al.*, 1998; Wu *et al.*, 2010; Hsu *et al.*, 2016; Hui *et al.*, 2018; Wang *et al.*, 2024).

Although we have collected and integrated all available data to identify and characterize offshore structures in this study, the information on these structures is by no means complete. Further studies of these structures are essential for improving the structural locations and parameters. For example, estimation of fault-slip rates and earthquake recurrence intervals would enable more comprehensive seismic hazard assessments, albeit this would require much more data and assumptions than those currently available. To accurately calculate the earthquake recurrence intervals for each fault, their long-term slip rates need to be determined, a key objective for future offshore fault studies. For instance, direct age data of the offset seabed sediments would provide much better constraints for the long-term slip rates of the structures.

Single fault rupture model and earthquake magnitude

In this study, we utilized three empirical regression equations to estimate earthquake magnitudes for rupture events, based on the subsurface geometries of reconstructed structures (Table 1, Fig. 10). Structures 1, 52, and 53 were identified as possible offshore extensions of on-land faults, so magnitudes for scenarios involving simultaneous rupture of both on-land and offshore segments were also calculated.

A comparison of results from the three equations revealed that most structures yield similar magnitude ranges. Discrepancies were likely attributed to geometric uncertainties in this study (seismogenic depth ±2 km, fault dip ±10°), resulting in magnitude uncertainties of ±0.11 when using Wells and Coppersmith (1994) and ±0.13 when using Yen and Ma (2011). For larger reverse fault earthquakes (e.g., structures 23, 26, 27, and 50), calculations using Wells and Coppersmith (1994) yielded lower magnitudes compared to those using Yen and Ma (2011) and Wesnousky (2008). This is likely due to differences in the regression datasets used in these studies. For such cases, we recommend using the results from Yen and Ma (2011) and Wesnousky (2008) because they have included more complete datasets in their regressions.

In domains C and E, we found that some structures may intersect with other structures at depth. To prevent this, we have set the seismogenic depths of these structures shallower, thus their widths become narrower. In these cases, length-based magnitude estimates by Wesnousky (2008) sometimes exceed those based on fault area. Therefore, we recommend the use of Wells and Coppersmith (1994) and Yen and Ma (2011) for structures with shallow seismogenic depths.

Because of the limitation of data currently available, we modeled the fault geometry as a simple planar surface for most of the structures. Future studies may identify changes in fault dip with depth, and this would increase the estimated fault area. For example, the simplified geometry of Outer Chinshan structure 1 yielded a fault area of 261 km^2, corresponding to a potential earthquake magnitude of 6.4. However, data from the Atomic Energy Council (2016) suggest a dip angle variation for this structure, and the fault area could increase to 926 km^2 considering such variation, raising the estimated magnitude to 7.0 (Appendix Excel Table). Further offshore investigations are needed to refine these fault geometries and to improve the magnitude estimates.

It is possible that the empirical regression relationships for the geometries of offshore faults and their associated seismic events are different from on-land structures. However, because most previous studies have focused on on-land events, data for offshore structures are scarce. Because more offshore earthquake data will become available in the future, it would be important to develop regression models that are more appropriate for offshore regions.

Fault segmentation and multifault rupture scenario

Earthquake magnitudes were estimated in this study under the assumption that the entire fault would rupture simultaneously. However, it is recognized that longer structures may rupture in segments (e.g., structure 54), as evidenced by historical seismic events (Wen and Xu, 2005). For example, the 1604 Quanzhou earthquake was attributed to the rupture of the southern segment of structure 54A (Huang and Wang, 2006; Yen *et al.*, 2021; Fig. S5). Unfortunately, it is difficult to propose reasonable segmentation scenarios for most structures included in this study, due to the limitation of currently available data.

In addition to segmented ruptures, scenarios involving multifault ruptures were also evaluated because these can generate larger earthquakes than those occurred on a single fault, and are critical for seismic hazard assessments (e.g., Gómez-Novell *et al.*, 2020; Chang *et al.*, 2023). Potential multifault rupture scenarios between offshore and on-land structures were identified based on fault types, geometries, and the spacing of two faults that is less than 6 km (Cheng, 2023; Table 2). For instance, in domain A, many normal faults exhibit a lateral continuity and have the potential to be connected laterally or at depth (Fossen and Rotevatn, 2016; Chang *et al.*, 2021).

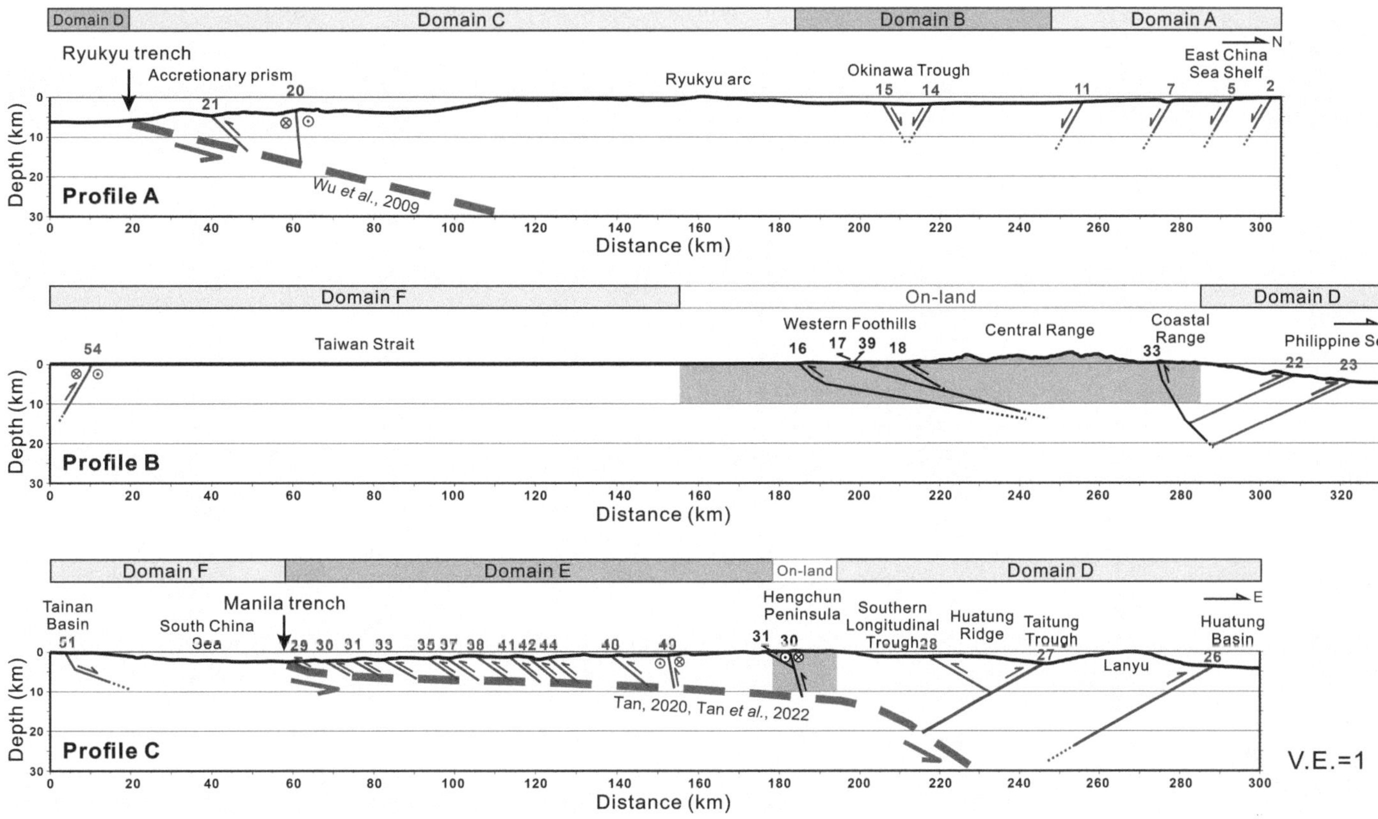

Figure 9. Geological cross-section of seismogenic structures in Taiwan. This cross-section shows the subsurface geometry of on-land seismogenic structures (black lines, Shyu *et al.*, 2020) and offshore structures (red lines, this study). The locations of the cross sections are indicated in Figure 2. The gray dotted lines represent the geometry of the subducting interface, based on Wu *et al.* (2009), Tan (2020), and Tan *et al.* (2022). The gray boxes in the cross sections indicate the land area of Taiwan. No vertical exaggeration. The color version of this figure is available only in the electronic edition.

In domain D, several closely spaced reverse faults on the eastern side of the island arc appear to display lateral continuity (structures 23, 25, and 26). In domain E, some structures may be offshore extensions from on-land faults (e.g., Chiang *et al.*, 2004; Wu *et al.*, 2024). In addition, many faults in domain E may connect at depth to a common detachment (Fig. 9, profile C). Multifault ruptures involving the underlying plate boundary fault were also considered in this region.

The magnitudes of earthquakes resulting from these multifault rupture scenarios were estimated (Table 2). Calculations were performed using the method by Yen and Ma (2011), with the seismic moment (M_0) determined with the formula $M_w = 2/3 \log M_0 - 10.73$. The combined seismic moment from both offshore and on-land faults, as estimated by Shyu *et al.* (2020), was used to calculate the total magnitude. If we consider multifault rupture scenarios, all 54 offshore structures may rupture longer than 20 km and have the potential to generate earthquakes of magnitude 6.5 or greater (Fig. 10b; Tables 1 and 2).

Historical earthquakes of offshore seismogenic structures

An understanding of historical earthquakes that may have occurred on the offshore seismogenic structures can provide additional constraints for these structures, as well as information needed for time-dependent seismic hazard assessments (Chan *et al.*, 2020). Among the 54 offshore seismogenic structures identified in this study, only the Binhai fault zone (54A) has been discussed as the likely source of the 1604 Quanzhou earthquake in previous studies (e.g., Lee *et al.*, 1976; Yen *et al.*, 2021). No other earthquakes have been proposed to have occurred on the other offshore structures.

We searched historical and instrumental earthquake events in an integrated catalog covering the time period from 1900 to 2023 to explore potential correlations between major earthquakes and the offshore faults identified in this study. This catalog combined earthquake data from multiple sources and agencies (see details in Data and Resources). In this catalog, there are 12 earthquakes with magnitudes of 7.0 or greater located offshore Taiwan (Fig. S5). We compared the location, magnitude, and focal mechanism of these events with the offshore structures and their parameters identified and proposed in this study. For the earthquake locations, we used the standard location error proposed by Wu *et al.* (2013), which is ~6 km in longitude, 3 km in latitude, and 10 km in depth.

Our results suggest that only two earthquake events may be related to the identified offshore structures: the 1915 M 7.2 earthquake in the hanging wall of the Ryukyu subduction

TABLE 1
Geometric and Magnitude Parameters of Offshore Seismogenic Structures in Taiwan

ID*	Fault Name	Type	Length (km)	Width (km)	Area (km^2)†	M_w (W&C)‡	M_w (Y&M)§	M_w (Wes)‖	Displacement (m)#	Reliability of Location**
1	Outer Chinshan structure 1 (ST-I)	N	23.1	11.3	261.2	6.4	6.4	6.8	0.67	A
1-2	Outer Chinshan structure 1 + Shanchiao fault	N	77.2		1312.9	7.1	7.1	7.0	1.56	
2	Outer Chinshan structure 2	N	120.0	11.3	1357.9	7.1	7.2	7.1	1.61	A
3	Outer Kanchiao structure (ST-II)	N	35.2	11.4	402.4	6.6	6.6	6.9	0.83	A
4	Outer Keelung structure 1	N	50.7	11.3	573.7	6.7	6.8	6.9	0.99	A
5	Outer Keelung structure 2	N	102.8	10.7	1104.0	7.0	7.0	7.1	1.38	A
6	Outer Shenaokeng structure 1	N	40.0	11.3	452.7	6.6	6.7	6.9	0.88	A
7	Outer Shenaokeng structure 2	N	98.2	10.7	1054.5	7.0	7.0	7.1	1.35	B
8	Outer Longdong structure 1	N	31.8	11.3	359.3	6.5	6.6	6.8	0.79	A
9	Outer Longdong structure 2	N	45.2	10.7	485.7	6.7	6.7	6.9	0.91	B
10	Outer Aoti structure 1	N	80.7	10.6	857.1	6.9	6.9	7.0	1.21	A
11	Outer Aoti structure 2	N	58.1	10.2	590.2	6.8	6.8	7.0	1.01	B
12	North Yilan Ridge structure	N	58.7	16.4	962.6	7.0	7.0	7.0	1.29	A
13	South Yilan Ridge structure	N	28.0	15.9	446.2	6.6	6.7	6.8	0.88	A
14	North Yonaguni Rift structure	N	62.0	13.0	809.5	6.9	6.9	7.0	1.18	A
15	South Yonaguni Rift structure	N	73.8	13.0	962.8	7.0	7.0	7.0	1.29	A
16	East Yonaguni Rift structure A	N	30.8	15.0	462.0	6.7	6.7	6.8	0.89	A
17	East Yonaguni Rift structure B	N	64.9	15.0	974.2	7.0	7.0	7.0	1.29	A
18	Suao fault zone	RL	49.3	22.1	1088.7	7.1	7.0	7.0	1.37	B
19	West Yaeyama fault zone	RL	93.9	14.2	1328.8	7.2	7.1	7.3	1.57	A
20	Yaeyama fault zone	RL	152.1	13.5	2046.3	7.4	7.4	7.5	2.43	A
21	Ryukyu Upper Plate splay structure	R	161.3	16.0	2580.8	7.4	7.5	8.3	3.06	A
22	Takangkou High thrust	R	95.8	10.0	1113.2	7.0	7.0	7.8	1.28	A
23	Chimei Canyon thrust	R	115.8	37.6	3210.2	7.6	7.8	8.0	5.16	A
24	East Taitung structure	R(LL?)	53.3	17.7	942.9	7.0	7.0	7.4	1.27	B
25	East Lutao structure	R	41.6	42.6	1770.8	7.3	7.3	7.2	2.10	A
26	East Lanyu structure	R	129.5	42.6	5516.7	7.7	8.0	8.1	6.54	B
27	East Huatung Ridge structure	R	193.5	22.0	4257.1	7.6	7.8	8.4	5.05	A
28	East Southern Longitudinal Trough structure	R	29.3	17.4	509.6	6.8	6.7	6.9	0.94	C
29	Southwest offshore structure A	R	88.2	13.0	1146.6	7.3	7.4	7.8	2.61	A
30	Southwest offshore structure B-1	R	48.0	13.0	624.0	7.1	7.0	7.3	1.35	A
31	Southwest offshore structure B-2	R	27.7	13.6	376.7	6.8	6.7	6.8	0.98	A
32	Southwest offshore structure B-3	R	20.4	13.8	281.5	6.7	6.7	6.6	0.90	A
33	Southwest offshore structure C	R	121.9	14.0	1706.6	7.4	7.5	8.0	3.18	A
34	Southwest offshore structure D	R	28.8	14.5	417.6	6.8	6.7	6.9	0.97	A
35	Southwest offshore structure E	R	131.3	13.0	1707.4	7.4	7.6	8.1	3.30	A
36	Southwest offshore structure F-1	R	52.7	14.6	769.4	7.1	7.1	7.4	1.43	A
37	Southwest offshore structure F-2	R	73.5	13.6	997.7	7.2	7.2	7.6	1.75	A
38	Southwest offshore structure F-3	R	76.0	14.9	1136.0	7.2	7.2	7.7	1.89	A

(continued)

TABLE 1 (*Continued*)

ID*	Fault Name	Type	Length (km)	Width (km)	Area (km^2)†	M_w (W&C)‡	M_w (Y&M)§	M_w (Wes)‖	Displacement (m)#	Reliability of Location**
39	Southwest offshore structure G	R	69.9	15.3	1068.7	7.2	7.3	7.6	1.93	B
40	Southwest offshore structure H-1	R	57.9	15.3	885.0	7.2	7.1	7.4	1.60	B
41	Southwest offshore structure H-2	R	53.5	13.6	725.3	7.1	7.1	7.4	1.42	A
42	Southwest offshore structure H-3	R	28.9	14.7	425.5	6.9	7.9	6.9	1.10	A
43	Southwest offshore structure H-4	R	24.0	13.4	322.7	6.7	6.7	6.7	0.90	A
44	Southwest offshore structure I	R	67.8	15.2	1031.7	7.2	7.3	7.6	2.03	B
45	Southwest offshore structure J	R	24.0	15.2	365.4	6.8	6.8	6.7	1.02	A
46	Southwest offshore structure K	R	25.0	15.0	375.0	6.8	6.7	6.7	0.95	C
47	Southwest offshore structure L (East Liuchiu Island structure)	R	41.8	11.3	471.2	6.7	6.7	7.2	0.90	A
48	Southwest offshore structure M	R	28.2	19.0	535.8	6.9	6.8	6.8	1.08	A
49	Fangliao Canyan structure zone	LL/R	63.9	9.1	583.8	6.8	6.8	7.1	1.00	C
50	Manila Upper Plate splay structure	R	284.8	23.3	6646.0	7.8	8.1	8.7	7.88	B
51	Tainan Basin structure	N	53.4	20.5	1094.2	7.0	7.0	6.9	1.37	A
52	Outer Hsinchu structure	R	13.5	14.1	190.9	6.4	6.3	6.2	0.57	B
52-2	Outer Hsinchu structure + Hsinchu fault	R	28.0		395.9	6.7	6.6	6.8	0.83	
53	Toufen structure	R	20.1	9.3	188.0	6.4	6.3	6.6	0.57	C
53-2	Toufen structure + Hsinchu frontal structure	R	32.2		430.0	6.7	6.6	7.0	0.86	
54A	Northern Binhai fault zone	RL/R	236.9	23.9	5651.7	7.8	8.0	7.6	6.70	B
54B	Southern Binhai fault zone	RL/R	220.4	23.9	5258.1	7.8	7.9	7.6	6.23	B
54-2	Northern Binhai fault zone + Southern Binhai fault zone	RL/R	457.3		10909.7	8.1	8.3	7.9	11.29	

This table provides a summarized version of the results. For the complete calculation process for all parameters, please refer to Text S1. For detailed parameters with maximum, minimum, and mean values, please refer to Appendix Excel Table. Appendix Excel Table also includes information such as the structure's average strike and dip direction, the upthrown side, seafloor depth, dip angles, seismogenic depth, magnitude estimated from three different equations, last earthquake event, and data sources for location and geometry. LL, a left-lateral strike-slip fault; LL/R, a reverse fault with a left-lateral component; N, a normal fault; R, a reverse fault; and RL, a right-lateral strike-slip fault; RL/R, a reverse fault with a right-lateral component. The "?" symbol denotes that the structure may exhibit the corresponding style of motion. Notes to this table are described subsequently.

*Structure numbers suffixed by "-2" represent calculated results for parameters where the structure ruptures simultaneously with other structures.

†The mean seismogenic area is calculated by multiplying the length and mean width values.

‡Wells and Coppersmith (1994) provide regression equations to calculate earthquake magnitude (M_w) based on fault type and rupture area. For normal faults, the equation is $M_w = 3.93 + 1.02 * \log A$, for reverse faults, $M_w = 4.33 + 0.90 * \log A$, and for strike-slip faults, $M_w = 3.98 + 1.02 * \log A$. In these equations, A represents the rupture area of the seismogenic structure.

§Yen and Ma (2011) provide regression equations to calculate earthquake magnitude (M_w) based on rupture area,

$$M = \log A + \frac{2}{3}\log\frac{\max\left(1, \sqrt{\frac{A}{H^2}}\right)}{\left[1 + \max\left(1, \frac{A}{H^2\beta}\right)\right]/2} + \text{const.}$$

in which A is the rupture area, H is set to 35 km for the Taiwan region, β is 6.9, and the constant value is 4.

‖Wesnousky (2008) provides regression equations to calculate earthquake magnitude (M_w) based on rupture length (L). For normal faults, $M_w = 6.12 + 0.47 * \log L$, for reverse faults, $M_w = 4.11 + 1.88 * \log L$, and for strike-slip faults, $M_w = 5.56 + 0.87 * \log L$.

#The average displacement (D) per event was calculated using the equation $M_0 = \mu AD$, in which μ equals 3×10^{11} dyn $\cdot$ cm^{-2}, A is the rupture area in dagger (†) footnote, and M_0 was derived from M_w using the equation: $M_w = 2/3 \log M_0 - 10.73$. The M_w-values presented in this table are based on the results from Y&M (section, §, footnote).

**Structures are classified based on reliability, with grades A, B, and C, from highest to lowest reliability. For more details, see Table S1.

system (possibly related to structure 20, or a subduction zone event) and the 1925 M 7.1 earthquake southeast of Taiwan (potentially linked to structure 27). Because these two events occurred long ago, detailed information such as their focal mechanisms is lacking, making it not feasible to further verify their seismogenic faults. The recorded magnitudes of these events are slightly lower than our estimates, possibly indicating partial ruptures of the structures. In short, only structures 20, 27, and 54 may have possible historical earthquake records, and we have included this information in the "Last event" column of the Appendix Excel Table.

Our comparison result shows that most recorded seismic events do not correlate with the structures we identified in this study. Instead, they are more likely associated with the subduction zone or deeper, subsurface seismic sources (Fig. S9). This is expected because most of the structures identified in this study may have not produced any major earthquake over the past few decades, similar to the situation for on-land seismogenic structures. This observation illustrates that it is not appropriate to rely solely on the instrumentally recorded seismic data to identify active structures because this may largely overlook the structures that have not ruptured in the time period of the instrumental record and are still accumulating strain.

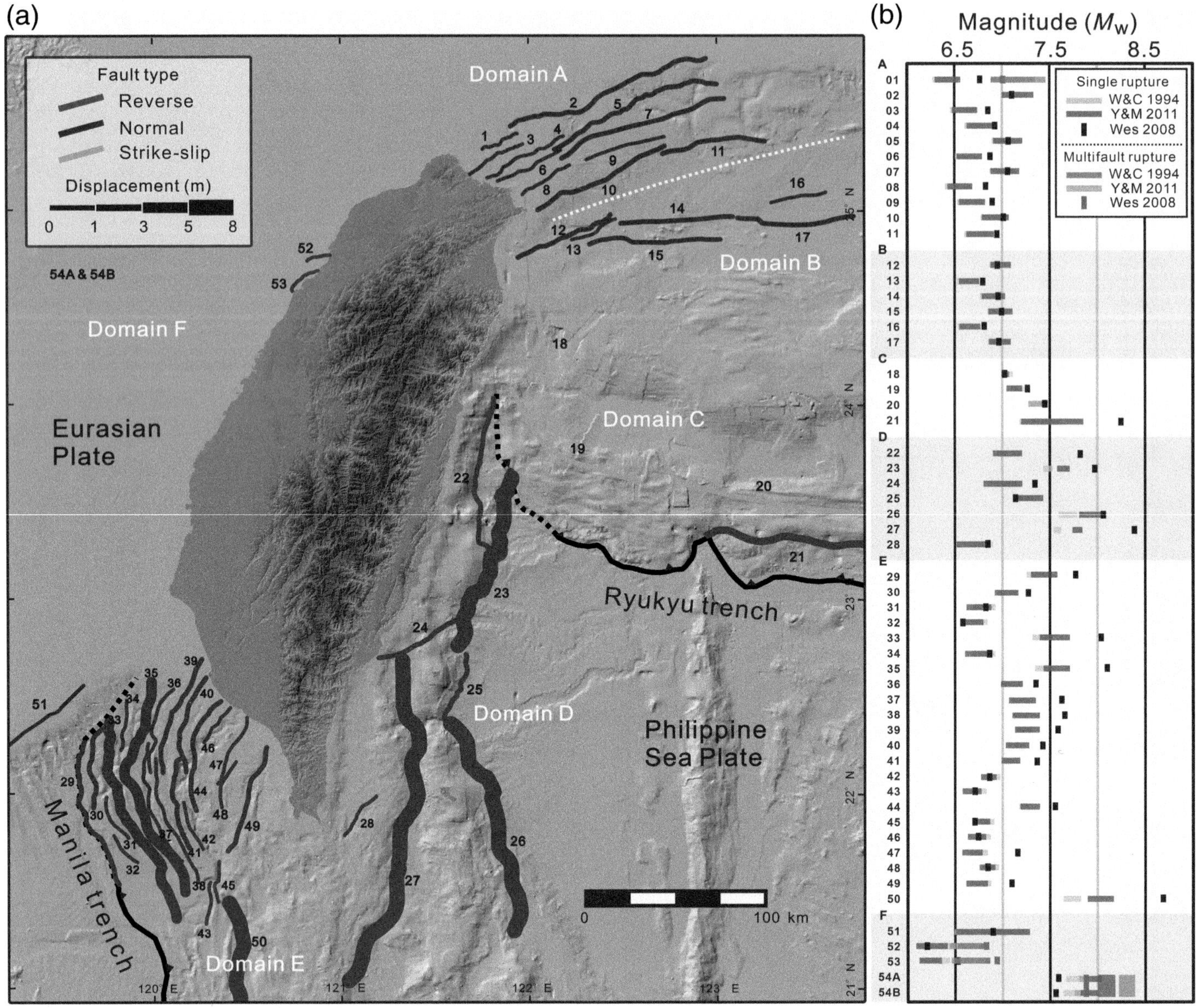

Figure 10. Characteristics of offshore seismogenic structures and potential earthquake magnitudes. (a) Offshore structures showing their average slip per earthquake. The thicker lines indicate greater displacement per event. The colors correspond to the fault types: reverse faults in red, strike-slip faults in orange, and normal faults in blue. The red, thicker lines (reverse faults) would suggest a higher potential for tsunami generation. (b) Potential earthquake magnitudes for offshore structures, derived from three empirical equations. Multifault rupture scenarios are included for structures 1, 52, 53, and 54. The color version of this figure is available only in the electronic edition.

TABLE 2
Multifault Rupture Scenarios and Potential Earthquake Magnitudes of Seismogenic Structures Offshore and On-Land Taiwan

Domain	Offshore Structure Number (This Study)	On-Land Structure Number (Shyu *et al.*, 2020)	Magnitude of Multifault Rupture	
			Wesnousky (2008)	Yen and Ma (2011)
A	1 + 2	1	7.2	7.3 (7.2–7.6)
	4 + 5		7.2	7.1 (7.0–7.3)
	5 + 6		7.1	7.1 (7.0–7.3)
	6 + 7		7.1	7.1 (7.0–7.3)
	7 + 8		7.1	7.1 (6.9–7.2)
	10 + 11		7.1	7.1 (6.9–7.2)
	10 + 11	37	7.2	7.2 (7.1–7.3)
B	13 + 14		7.0	7.0 (6.9–7.1)
C	19 + 20*		7.6	7.5 (7.4–7.6)
D	22 + 23 + 24		8.7	7.7 (7.6–7.8)
	23 + 25 + 26		8.7	8.1 (8.0–8.2)
E	40 + 41	43	8.1	7.3 (7.2–7.4)
	46	44	7.2	7.0 (6.8–7.3)
	49*	29	7.5	7.3 (7.3–7.5)
	Detachment fault†		8.1	8.4 (8.4–8.4)
F	54A + 54B		7.9	8.2 (8.0–8.3)

The offshore structures were based on this study, and on-land structures were referenced from Shyu *et al.* (2020). Their specific locations are indicated in Figures 4–8 of this article. Notes to this table are described subsequently
*Although these structures are separated by distances exceeding 6 km, we consider the possibility of multifault ruptures due to their geometries that may provide the continuation.
†Earthquake magnitudes of the detachment fault are calculated under the assumption of a multifault rupture along the décollement beneath structures 29 to 49 (see Fig. 9, profile C).

Applicability and future prospects of offshore seismogenic structure database

This study presents the first comprehensive offshore seismogenic structure database of Taiwan, which includes detailed information on structural locations, fault types, subsurface geometries, and potential earthquake magnitudes (Table 1, Appendix Excel Table). We envision that this database to be applied to studies of future earthquake disaster prevention, offshore infrastructure planning, resource development, and general tectonics of Taiwan.

In the event of an offshore earthquake, this database may provide some initial insights into the focal mechanism and seismogenic structure of the event, enabling rapid preliminary risk assessments. For example, all the identified structures have the potential to generate earthquakes of magnitude 6.5 or greater, which may result in the rupture of the seabed (Wu and Hu, 2024). Based on the earthquake magnitudes and structural geometries, some structures may have average displacements exceeding 3 m in an earthquake (Fig. 10a), enough to trigger tsunamis if the seabed is ruptured. Furthermore, some offshore earthquakes can cause ground shaking of intensity 6 or higher on land if they occur on structures closer to the coastline, as illustrated in historical records.

Most structures capable of generating major earthquakes greater than magnitude 7.5 are located offshore eastern Taiwan (Fig. 10). Assuming their long-term slip rates are similar to their on-land counterparts in eastern Taiwan (~7–15 mm/yr; Shyu *et al.*, 2020) and an ~3 m slip of the fault in a magnitude 7.5 event (Table 1), the earthquake recurrence interval can be estimated in the range of 200–450 yr. Such a short interval suggests that further studies and enhanced preparedness measures are necessary for eastern Taiwan.

The complex tectonic processes of the Taiwan orogenic belt result in diverse stress fields and structural patterns in offshore regions, providing a valuable reference for similar geologic settings worldwide. For example, the structures in domain C are influenced by the oblique subduction of the Philippine Sea Plate, with both reverse faults and large right-lateral faults developed through strain partitioning in the overriding accretionary wedge (Chen *et al.*, 2022). This pattern resembles the prominent seismogenic right-lateral faults observed in the Sumatra subduction system (e.g., McCaffrey, 2009; Sørensen and Atakan, 2008). In contrast, the Manila subduction system in domain D is characterized by a relatively perpendicular subduction direction and exhibits a fold-and-thrust belt that propagates upward from a basal detachment. This is similar to the Japan Trench subduction system, where the detachment fault is a primary seismogenic structure (e.g., Nakata *et al.*, 2012).

Information on offshore seismogenic structures is crucial for the planning and design of offshore and coastal projects, including nuclear power plants, wind farms, submarine cables, and carbon dioxide storage facilities. Because offshore wind energy and carbon dioxide storage have become more important in Taiwan, we hope this offshore seismogenic structure database will provide important constraints for these projects. Furthermore, we also hope our results and findings will point to the directions of future offshore studies in Taiwan, to gather more high-resolution geological and geophysical information to better understand the offshore structures of this active orogenic belt.

CONCLUSIONS

In this study, we collected and analyzed all available geological and geophysical data to identify and map offshore seismogenic structures. A total of 54 potential offshore seismogenic structures were identified. We also calculated structural parameters for these structures, including their fault type, geometry, and possible earthquake magnitude. Most of these structures are capable of generating earthquakes exceeding magnitude 6.5. In cases of multifault ruptures, some events could reach magnitudes above 8.0. As the very first offshore seismogenic structure database of Taiwan, we hope our results will provide additional constraints for the earthquake hazard assessment studies of the island.

DATA AND RESOURCES

All the seismic reflection profiles used in this study are from published sources listed in the references (Fig. S1). Digital elevation models (DEMs) for the offshore region surrounding Taiwan (119°–123° E, 21°–26° N) with a resolution of 200 m were obtained from the National Science and Technology Council's Oceanography Database. DEMs beyond this range, with ~450 m resolution, were acquired from the GEBCO website (https://download.gebco.net/, last accessed September 2021). Historical earthquake data were compiled from Broadband Array in Taiwan for Seismology (BATS), Central Weather Administration (CWA), Global Centroid Moment Tensor (Global CMT), USGS (U.S. Geological Survey), National Research Institute for Earth Science and Disaster Resilience (NIED), Japan Meteorological Agency (JMA), International Seismological Centre (ISC), and China Earthquake Networks Center (CENC) databases, covering the period from 1900 to 2023 (Taiwan Earthquake Model group, Gao *et al.*, in preparation). The supplemental material is provided as a separate document, including a detailed example of parameter calculations (Text S1), Tables S1 and S2, and Figures S1–S9, which contain supporting data for determining the locations and geometries of the structures. In addition, an independent excel table is included, presenting the complete parameter values for 54 seismogenic structures. This table includes information such as the average strike and dip direction of the structures, the upthrown side, seafloor depth, dip angles, seismogenic depth, and magnitudes estimated using three different equations.

DECLARATION OF COMPETING INTERESTS

The authors acknowledge that there are no conflicts of interest recorded.

ACKNOWLEDGMENTS

The authors sincerely thank C.-H. Chan, J.-H. Chang, L. Chen, W.-S. Chen, R. Y. Chuang, J.-C. Gao, W.-C. Han, Y.-H. Hsieh, Y.-J. Hsu, J.-C. Lee, L.-F. Lin, K.-F. Ma, H.-Y. Tang, L. S. Teng, Y. Wang, E. Y. Yang, and E.-C. Yeh for their valuable comments and insightful discussions. Comments and suggestions from Handling Editor T.-L. Tseng and three anonymous reviewers have significantly improved this article. This research is supported by the National Science and Technology Council (NSTC) of Taiwan (Project 110-2124-M-002-008, 111-2124-M-002-008, 112-2124-M-865-001, and 113-2124-M-865-001 as the TEM project, and 110-2116-M-002-019, 111-2116-M-002-044, 112-2116-M-002-030, and 113-2116-M-002-025-MY2 to J.B.H.S.).

REFERENCES

Anderson, E. M. (1905). The dynamics of faulting, *Trans. Edinb. Geol. Soc.* **8,** no. 3, 387–402.

Arai, R., S. Kodaira, K. Yuka, T. Takahashi, S. Miura, and Y. Kaneda (2017). Crustal structure of the southern Okinawa Trough: Symmetrical rifting, submarine volcano, and potential mantle accretion in the continental back-arc basin, *J. Geophys. Res.* **122,** no. 1, 622–641, doi: 10.1002/2016JB013448.

Atomic Energy Council (2016). Expanded Geological Survey results for the enhanced seismic safety re-evaluation of nuclear power plants, *AEC Safety Evaluation Rept. 109, NRD-SER-105-02* (in Chinese).

Chan, C.-H., K.-F. Ma, J. B. H. Shyu, Y.-T. Lee, Y.-J. Wang, J.-C. Gao, Y.-T. Yen, and R.-J. Rau (2020). Probabilistic seismic hazard assessment for Taiwan: TEM PSHA2020, *Earthq. Spectra.* **36,** no. S1, 137–159, doi: 10.1177/8755293020951587.

Chan, C.-H., Y. Wang, Y.-J. Wang, and Y.-T. Lee (2017). Seismic-hazard assessment over time: Modeling earthquakes in Taiwan, *Bull. Seismol. Soc. Am.* **107,** no. 5, 2342–2352, doi: 10.1785/0120160278.

Chang, C.-C., C.-Y. Chang, J.-C. Gao, and C.-H. Chan (2023). Quantifying the probability and uncertainty of multiple-structure rupture for Taiwan, *Terr. Atmos. Ocean.* **34,** 7, doi: 10.1007/s44195-023-00040-8.

Chang, J.-H., H.-H. Hsu, C.-C. Su, C.-S. Liu, H.-T. Hung, and S.-D. Chiu (2015). Tectono-sedimentary control on modern sand deposition on the forebulge of the western Taiwan Foreland basin, *Mar. Pet. Geol.* **66,** 970–977, doi: 10.1016/j.marpetgeo.2015.08.004.

Chang, J.-H., E. Y. C. Yang, H.-H. Hsu, T.-T. Chen, C.-S. Liu, and S.-D. Chiu (2021). Igneous activity and structural development of the Mianhua terrace, offshore North Taiwan, *Minerals* **11,** no. 3, 303, doi: 10.3390/min11030303.

Chen, K.-Y. (2014). A study on structural development from orogenic belt to extensional backarc setting in northern Taiwan and its offshore area, *Ph.D. Thesis*, Department of Earth Sciences, National Central University, 183 (in Chinese with English abstract).

Chen, S.-J. (2019). Preliminary study of shallow structure in the Miaoli offshore area, Taiwan, *Master's Thesis*, Institute of Oceanography, National Taiwan University, 88 (in Chinese with English abstract).

Chen, Y.-P. (2015). Combining seismic reflection and refraction data to investigate tectonic features of the Luzon subduction complex south of Taiwan (master's thesis), Institute of Oceanography, National Taiwan University, 107 (in Chinese with English abstract).

Chen, T.-T., and J. S. Watkins (1994). Structure and stratigraphy of south Pengchiahsu Basin northern offshore Taiwan, *Petrol. Geol. Taiwan.* **29,** 127–170.

Chen, H.-Y., Y.-J. Hsu, R. Ikuta, H. Tung, C.-H. Tang, C.-S. Ku, H.-H. Su, P.-R. Jian, M. Ando, and T. Tsujii (2022). Strain partitioning in the southern Ryukyu margin revealed by seafloor geodetic and seismological observations, *Geophys. Res. Lett.* **49,** no. 6, e2022GL098218, doi: 10.1029/2022GL098218.

Chen, W.-H., C.-Y. Huang, Y.-J. Lin, Q. Zhao, Y. Yan, D. Chen, X. Zhang, Q. Lan, and M. Yu (2015). Depleted deep South China Sea δ13C paleoceanographic events in response to tectonic evolution in Taiwan–Luzon Strait since Middle Miocene, *Deep Sea Res. Part II Top. Stud. Oceanogr.* **122,** 195–225, doi: 10.1016/j.dsr2.2015.02.005.

Chen, W.-S., Y.-M. Wu, Y.-X. Lai, P.-Y. Yeh, M.-C. Ke, S.-S. Ke, and Y.-K. Lin (2017). Seismotectonic analysis of Ryukyu subduction zone in the offshore northeastern Taiwan: Implications for the investigated tsunamigenic source zones, *Bull Central Geol Surv. MOEA.* **30,** 25–54 (in Chinese with English abstract).

Chen, W.-S., Y.-M. Wu, P.-Y. Yeh, Y.-X. Lai, M.-C. Ke, S.-S. Ke, and Y.-K. Lin (2018). Seismogenic structures of the eastern Taiwan collision zone, *Spec. Publ. Cent. Geol. Surv. MOEA.* **33,** 123–155 (in Chinese with English abstract).

Chen, W.-S., Y.-M. Wu, P.-Y. Yeh, Y.-X. Lai, M.-C. Ke, S.-S. Ke, and Y.-K. Lin (2019). Seismogenic structures of the subduction-collision transitional zone in southeastern Taiwan offshore, *Spec. Publ.*

Cent. Geol. Surv. MOEA. **34,** 125–140 (in Chinese with English abstract).

Chen, W.-S., Y.-M. Wu, P.-Y. Yeh, Y.-X. Lai, S.-S. Ke, M.-C. Ke, and C.-Y. Yang (2024). Insights into the seismogenic structures of the arc-continent convergent plate boundary in eastern Taiwan, *Terr. Atmos. Ocean.* **35,** no. 1, 13, doi: 10.1007/s44195-024-00065-7.

Chen, Y.-L., S.-H. Hung, J.-S. Jiang, and L.-Y. Chiao (2016). Systematic correlations of the earthquake frequency-magnitude distribution with the deformation and mechanical regimes in the Taiwan orogen, *Geophys. Res. Lett.* **43,** 5017–5025, doi: 10.1002/2016GL069020.

Cheng, W.-S. (2023). Applying multi-fault rupture scenario to Taiwan earthquake model, *Master's Thesis*, Department of Geosciences, National Taiwan University, 150.

Chiang, P.-S. (2016). Investigating occurrence of the deformation front offshore Miaoli, Taiwan,*Master's Thesis*, Institute of Oceanography, National Taiwan University, 81 (in Chinese with English abstract).

Chiang, C.-S., H.-S. Yu, and Y.-W. Chou (2004). Characteristics of the wedge-top depozone of the southern Taiwan foreland basin system, *Basin Res.* **16,** no. 1, 65–78, doi: 10.1111/j.1365-2117.2003.00222.x.

Chung, C.-C. (2021). Seafloor lineaments and volcanic features off northeastern Taiwan, *Master's Thesis*, Institute of Oceanography, National Taiwan University, 91 (in Chinese with English abstract).

Chung, Y., and W.-C. Chang (1995). Pb-210 fluxes and sedimentation rates on the lower continental slope between Taiwan and the South Okinawa Trough, *Cont. Shelf Res.* **15,** nos. 2/3, 149–164.

Conin, M., P. Henry, V. Godard, and S. Bourlange (2012). Splay fault slip in a subduction margin, a new model of evolution, *Earth Planet. Sci. Lett.* **341,** 170–175, doi: 10.1016/j.epsl.2012.06.003.

Cowie, P. A., and G. P. Roberts (2001). Constraining slip rates and spacings for active normal faults, *J. Struct. Geol.* **23,** 1901–1915, doi: 10.1016/S0191-8141(01)00036-0.

Deffontaines, B., C.-S. Liu, J. Angelier, C.-T. Lee, J.-C. Sibuet, Y.-B. Tsai, S. Lallemand, C.-Y. Lu, C.-S. Lee, S.-K. Hsu, *et al.* (2001). Preliminary neotectonic map of onshore-offshore Taiwan, *Terr. Atmos. Ocean. Sci. Sup. Issue.* 339–349, doi: 10.3319/TAO.2001.12.S.339(T).

Deffontaines, B., C.-S. Liu, and H.-H. Hsu (2016). Structure and deformation of the southern Taiwan accretionary prism: The active submarine Fangliao fault zone offshore west Hengchun Peninsula, *Tectonophysics* **692,** 227–240, doi: 10.1016/j.tecto.2016.11.007.

Deng, J.-M., T.-K. Wang, S. Wege, W.-T. Hu, and Y.-J. Deng (2023). A hypothesis of the obliquely subducted Gagua Ridge below Nanao Basin based on uplifted structures in Ryukyu forearc, *Terr. Atmos. Ocean.* **34,** no. 1, 6, doi: 10.1007/s44195-023-00039-1.

Ding, W.-W., J.-B. Li, M.-B. Li, X.-L. Qiu, Y.-X. Fang, and Y. Tang (2008). A Cenozoic tectono-sedimentary model of the Tainan Basin, the South China Sea: Evidence from multi-channel seismic profile, *J. Zhejiang Univ. Sci.* **9,** no. 5, 702–713, doi: 10.1631/jzus.A071572.

Dirgantara, F., H.-T. Chiang, A. T.-S. Lin, C.-S. Liu, and S.-C. Chen (2020). Depositional influence of submarine channel migration on thermal properties of the Lower Fangliao Basin, offshore southwestern Taiwan, *Mar. Geophys. Res.* **41,** no. 1, 1, doi: 10.1007/s11001-020-09401-1.

Dominguez, S., S. Lallemand, J. Malavieille, and P. Schnürle (1998). Oblique subduction of the Gagua Ridge beneath the Ryukyu accretionary wedge system: Insights from marine observations and sandbox experiments, *Mar. Geophys. Res.* **20,** 383–402.

Doo, W.-B., S.-K. Hsu, C.-L. Lo, S.-C. Chen, C.-H. Tsai, J.-Y. Lin, Y.-P. Huang, Y.-S. Huang, S.-D. Chiu, and Y.-F. Ma (2015). Gravity anomalies of the active mud diapirs off southwest Taiwan, *Geophys. J. Int.* **203,** no. 3, 2089–2098, doi: 10.1093/gji/ggv430.

Doo, W.-B., C.-L. Lo, W.-N. Wu, J.-Y. Lin, S.-K. Hsu, Y.-S. Huang, and H.-F. Wang (2018). Strength of plate coupling in the southern Ryukyu subduction zone, *Tectonophysics* **723,** 223–228, doi: 10.1016/j.tecto.2017.12.028.

Emery, K. O., Y. Hayoshi, T. W. C. Hilde, K. Kobayashi, J. H. Koo, C. Y. Meng, H. Niino, J. H. Osterhangen, L. M. Reynolds, J. M. Wangeman, *et al.* (1970). Geological structure and some water characteristics of the East China Sea and the Yellow Sea, *Petrol. Geol. Taiwan.* **7,** 243–279.

Fang, P., W. Ding, X. Lin, Z. Zhao, Y. Fang, and C. Li (2020). Neogene subsidence pattern in the multi-episodic extension systems: Insights from backstripping modelling of the Okinawa Trough, *Mar. Petrol. Geol.* **111,** 662–675, doi: 10.1016/j.marpetgeo.2019.08.051.

Font, Y., and S. Lallemand (2009). Subducting oceanic high causes compressional faulting in southernmost Ryukyu forearc as revealed by hypocentral determinations of earthquakes and reflection/refraction seismic data, *Tectonophysics* **466,** nos. 3/4, 255–267, doi: 10.1016/j.tecto.2007.11.018.

Font, Y., C.-S. Liu, P. Schnurle, and S. Lallemand (2001). Constraints on backstop geometry of the southwest Ryukyu subduction based on reflection seismic data, *Tectonophysics* **333,** nos. 1/2, 135–158.

Fossen, H., and A. Rotevatn (2016). Fault linkage and relay structures in extensional settings—A review, *Earth Sci. Rev.* **154,** 14–28, doi: 10.1016/j.earscirev.2015.11.014.

Fuh, S.-C., and C.-S. Liu (1998). Evolution of the Southern Longitudinal Trough in the incipient Taiwan arc-continent collision zone and its tectonic implication, *J. Geol. Soc. China.* **41,** no. 4, 497–516.

Gao, J.-C., C.-H. Chan, K.-F. Ma, J. B. H. Shyu, Y.-T. Lee, Y.-J. Wang, Y.-T. Yen, J.-C. Kao, and R.-J. Rau (in preparation). Probabilistic Seismic Hazard Assessment for Taiwan: TEM PSHA2025 (draft), *The 2024 Japan-New Zealand-Taiwan Seismic Hazard Workshop*, Kanazawa, Japan, 5–6 November 2024.

Gómez-Novell, O., T. Chartier, J. García-Mayordomo, M. Ortuño, E. Masana, J. M. Insua-Arévalo, and O. Scotti (2020). Modelling earthquake rupture rates in fault systems for seismic hazard assessment: The eastern Betics shear zone, *Eng. Geol.* **265,** 105452, doi: 10.1016/j.enggeo.2019.105452.

Han, W.-C., L. Chen, and C.-S. Liu (2021). Distribution and characteristics of gas chimneys in the passive margin offshore SW Taiwan, *Mar. Geophys. Res.* **42,** no. 3, 25, doi: 10.1007/s11001-021-09447-9.

Han, W.-C., L. Chen, C.-S. Liu, C. Berndt, and W.-C. Chi (2019). Seismic analysis of the gas hydrate system at Pointer Ridge offshore SW Taiwan, *Mar. Petrol. Geol.* **105,** 158–167, doi: 10.1016/j.marpetgeo.2019.04.028.

Hirtzel, J., W.-C. Chi, D. Reed, L. Chen, C.-S. Liu, and N. Lundberg (2009). Destruction of Luzon forearc basin from subduction to Taiwan arc–continent collision, *Tectonophysics* **479,** nos. 1/2, 43–51, doi: 10.1016/j.tecto.2009.01.032.

Hsiao, L.-Y., K.-A. Lin, S.-T. Huang, and L. S. Teng (1998). Structural characteristics of the southern Taiwan-Sinzi folded zone, *Petrol. Geol. Taiwan.* **32,** 133–153 (in Chinese with English abstract).

Hsieh, Y.-H., C.-S. Liu, J. Suppe, T. B. Byrne, and S. Lallemand (2020). The Chimei submarine canyon and fan: A record of Taiwan arc-continent collision on the rapidly deforming overriding plate, *Tectonics* **39,** no. 11, e2020TC006148, doi: 10.1029/2020TC006148.

Hsiung, K.-H., T. Kanamatsu, K. Ikehara, K. Shiraishi, C.-S. Horng, and K. Usami (2017). Morpho-sedimentary features and sediment dispersal systems of the southwest end of the Ryukyu Trench: A source-to-sink approach, *Geo-Mar. Lett.* **37,** 561–577, doi: 10.1007/s00367-017-0509-3.

Hsiung, K.-H., H.-S. Yu, and C.-S. Chiang (2018). The modern Kaoping transient fan offshore SW Taiwan: Morphotectonics and development, *Geomorphology* **300,** 151–163, doi: 10.1016/j.geomorph.2017.10.013.

Hsu, B.-H. (1999). Geological structure of south Okinawa Trough: A reflection seismic interpretation, *Master's Thesis*, Department of Earth Sciences, National Central University, 60 (in Chinese with English abstract).

Hsu, H.-H., C.-S. Liu, T.-T. Chen, and H.-T. Hung (2021). Stratigraphic framework and sediment wave fields associated with canyon-levee systems in the Huatung Basin offshore Taiwan orogen, *Mar. Geol.* **433,** 106408, doi: 10.1016/j.margeo.2020.106408.

Hsu, S.-K., Y.-C. Yeh, J.-C. Sibuet, W.-B. Doo, and C.-H. Tsai (2013). A mega-splay fault system and tsunami hazard in the southern Ryukyu subduction zone, *Earth Planet. Sci. Lett.* **362,** 99–107, doi: 10.1016/j.epsl.2012.11.053.

Hsu, Y.-J., S.-B. Yu, J. P. Loveless, T. Bacolcol, R. Solidum, A. Luis Jr, A. Pelicano, and J. Woessner (2016). Interseismic deformation and moment deficit along the Manila subduction zone and the Philippine fault system, *J. Geophys. Res.* **121,** no. 10, 7639–7665, doi: 10.1002/2016JB013082.

Huang, H.-H., and Y. Wang (2022). Seismogenic structure beneath the northern Longitudinal Valley revealed by the 2018–2021 Hualien earthquake sequences and 3-D velocity model, *Terr. Atmos. Ocean. Sci.* **33,** no. 1, 17, doi: 10.1007/s44195-022-00017-z.

Huang, J.-K. (2018). Morphology, structures and sedimentary processes of the Southern Longitudinal Trough, offshore southeast Taiwan (master's thesis), Institute of Oceanography, National Taiwan University, 84 (in Chinese with English abstract).

Huang, Z., and S. Wang (2006). Tectonic feature and activity of Binhai fault zone in Taiwan Strait, *J. Geodes.* **26,** no. 3, 16–22 (in Chinese with English abstract).

Huang, B.-S., K.-C. Chen, H.-Y. Yen, and Z.-X. Yao (1999). Re-examination of the epicenter of the 16 September 1994 Taiwan Strait earthquake using the beam-forming method, *Terr. Atmos. Ocean. Sci.* **10,** no. 3, 529–542.

Huang, C.-Y., W.-H. Chen, M.-H. Wang, C.-T. Lin, S. Yang, X. Li, M. Yu, X. Zhao, K.-M. Yang, C.-S. Liu, Y.-H. Hsieh, and R. Harris (2018). Juxtaposed sequence stratigraphy, temporal-spatial variations of sedimentation and development of modern-forming forearc Lichi Mélange in North Luzon Trough forearc basin onshore and offshore eastern Taiwan: An overview, *Earth Sci. Rev.* **182,** 102–140, doi: 10.1016/j.earscirev.2018.01.015.

Huang, C.-Y., C.-T. Shyu, S. B. Lin, T.-Q. Lee, and D. D. Sheu (1992). Marine geology in the arc-continent collision zone off southeastern Taiwan: Implications for Late Neogene evolution of the Coastal Range, *Mar. Geol.* **107,** no. 3, 183–212.

Huang, H.-H., J. B. H. Shyu, Y.-M. Wu, C.-H. Chang, and Y.-G. Chen (2012). Seismotectonics of northeastern Taiwan: Kinematics of the transition from waning collision to subduction and postcollisional extension, *J. Geophys. Res.* **117,** no. B1, doi: 10.1029/2011JB008852.

Huang, S.-T., T.-H. Huang, H.-H. Shih, and P.-J. Hsieh (2020). Orogenesis related to the reactivation of transtensional fault and hydrocarbon potential in Miaoli area: Retrospect and prospect, *Petrol. Geol. Taiwan.* **44,** 19–44.

Huang, S.-T., K.-M. Yang, J.-H. Hung, J.-C. Wu, H.-H. Ting, W.-W. Mei, S.-H. Hsu, and M. Lee (2004). Deformation front development at the northeast margin of the Tainan Basin, Tainan–Kaohsiung area, Taiwan, *Mar. Geophys. Res.* **25,** 139–156, doi: 10.1007/s11001-005-0739-z.

Huh, C.-A., W. Chen, F.-H. Hsu, C.-C. Su, J.-K. Chiu, S. Lin, C.-S. Liu, and B.-J. Huang (2011). Modern (< 100 years) sedimentation in the Taiwan Strait: Rates and source-to-sink pathways elucidated from radionuclides and particle size distribution, *Cont. Shelf Res.* **31,** no. 1, 47–63, doi: 10.1016/j.csr.2010.11.002.

Hui, G., S. Li, P. Wang, J. Zhu, L. Guo, Q. Wang, and I. D. Somerville (2018). Neotectonic implications and regional stress field constraints on mud volcanoes in offshore southwestern Taiwan, *Mar. Geol.* **403,** 109–122.

Hung, G. W., and Y.-C. Chung (1994). Sedimentation rates on the continental slope off eastern Taiwan, *Mar. Geol.* **119,** nos. 1/2, 99–109.

Inoue, S., H. Kayanne, N. Matta, W.-S. Chen, and Y. Ikeda (2011). Holocene uplifted coral reefs in Lanyu and Lutao Islands to the southeast of Taiwan, *Coral Reefs* **30,** 581–592, doi: 10.1007/s00338-011-0783-x.

Kanwal, M. (2024). Assessing the impact of the 2024 Hualien earthquake in Taiwan. Available at SSRN: https://ssrn.com/abstract=4786199 (last accessed November 2024).

Kao, H., and F. T. Wu (1996). The 16 September 1994 earthquake (m_b= 6.5) in the Taiwan Strait and its tectonic implications, *Terr. Atmos. Ocean. Sci.* **7,** no. 1, 13–29.

Kao, H., S.-S. J. Shen, and K.-F. Ma (1998). Transition from oblique subduction to collision: Earthquakes in the southernmost Ryukyu arc-Taiwan region, *J. Geophys. Res.* **103,** no. B4, 7211–7229.

Kimura, M. (1985). Back-arc rifting in the Okinawa Trough, *Mar. Pet. Geol.* **2,** no. 3, 222–240.

Klingelhoefer, F., C.-S. Lee, J.-Y. Lin, and J.-C. Sibuet (2009). Structure of the southernmost Okinawa Trough from reflection and wide-angle seismic data, *Tectonophysics* **466,** nos. 3/4, 281–288, doi: 10.1016/j.tecto.2007.11.031.

Ko, Y.-P. (2022). P-wave velocity analysis for the accretionary wedge offshore SW Taiwan, *Master's Thesis*), Institute of Oceanography, National Taiwan University, 102 (in Chinese with English abstract).

Kong, F., L. A. Lawver, and T.-Y. Lee (2000). Evolution of the southern Taiwan–Sinzi folded zone and opening of the southern Okinawa trough, *J. Asian Earth Sci.* **18,** no. 3, 325–341.

Ku, C.-Y., S.-K. Hsu, J.-C. Sibuet, and C.-H. Tsai (2009). The neo-tectonic structure of the south western tip of the Okinawa trough, *Terr. Atmos. Ocean. Sci.* **20,** no. 5, 749–759, doi: 10.3319/TAO.2008.09.01.01(Oc).

Kubo, A., and E. Fukuyama (2003). Stress field along the Ryukyu arc and the Okinawa trough inferred from moment tensors of shallow earthquakes, *Earth Planet. Sci. Lett.* **210,** nos. 1/2, 305–316.

Lacombe, O., F. Mouthereau, J. Angelier, H.-T. Chu, and J.-C. Lee (2003). Frontal belt curvature and oblique ramp development at an obliquely collided irregular margin: Geometry and kinematics of the NW Taiwan fold-thrust belt, *Tectonics* **22,** no. 3, doi: 10.1029/2002TC001436.

Lai, P.-W., and W.-J. Huang (2023). Normal fault in Bitou and Longdong areas, northeastern Taiwan, *Bull. Central Geol. Surv. MOEA.* **36,** 43–78 (in Chinese with English abstract).

Lallemand, S., and C.-S. Liu (1998). Geodynamic implications of present-day kinematics in the southern Ryukyus, *J. Geol. Soc. China* **41,** no. 4, 551–564.

Lallemand, S., C.-S. Liu, S. Dominguez, P. Schnürle, J. Malavieille, and , and ACT Scientific crew (1999). Trench-parallel stretching and folding of forearc basins and lateral migration of the accretionary wedge in the southern Ryukyus: A case of strain partition caused by oblique convergence, *Tectonics* **18,** no. 2, 231–247.

Lee, C.-S., G. G. Shor Jr, L. D. Bibee, R. S. Lu, and T. W. C. Hilde (1980). Okinawa Trough: Origin of a back-arc basin, *Mar. Geol.* **35,** nos. 1/3, 219–241.

Lee, T.-Q., C. Kissel, E. Barrier, C. Laj, and W.-R. Chi (1991). Paleomagnetic evidence for a diachronic clockwise rotation of the Coastal Range, eastern Taiwan, *Earth Planet. Sci. Lett.* **104,** nos. 2/4, 245–257.

Lee, W. H. K., F. T. Wu, and C. Jacobsen (1976). A catalog of historical earthquakes in China compiled from recent Chinese publications, *Bull. Seismol. Soc. Am.* **66,** no. 6, 2003–2016.

Li, C.-F., Z. Zhou, J. Li, H. Hao, and J. Geng (2007). Structures of the northeasternmost South China Sea continental margin and ocean basin: Geophysical constraints and tectonic implications, *Mar. Geophys. Res.* **28,** 59–79, doi: 10.1007/s11001-007-9014-9.

Lin, S.-H. (2010). Structural characteristics along the eastern Flank of the northern Luzon arc, *Master's Thesis*, Institute of Oceanography, National Taiwan University, 79 (in Chinese with English abstract).

Lin, A. T., and A. B. Watts (2002). Origin of the West Taiwan basin by orogenic loading and flexure of a rifted continental margin, *J. Geophys. Res.* **107,** no. B9, 2185, doi: 10.1029/2001JB000669.

Lin, A. T., C.-S. Liu, C.-C. Lin, P. Schnurle, G.-Y. Chen, W.-Z. Liao, L. S. Teng, H.-J. Chung, and M.-S. Wu (2008). Tectonic features associated with the overriding of an accretionary wedge on top of a rifted continental margin: An example from Taiwan, *Mar. Geol.* **255,** nos. 3/4, 186–203, doi: 10.1016/j.margeo.2008.10.002.

Lin, A. T., A. B. Watts, and S. P. Hesselbo (2003). Cenozoic stratigraphy and subsidence history of the South China Sea margin in the Taiwan region, *Basin Res.* **15,** no. 4, 453–478, doi: 10.1046/j.1365-2117.2003.00215.x.

Lin, A. T., C.-C. Yang, M.-H. Wang, and J.-C. Wu (2021). Oligocene-Miocene sequence stratigraphy in the northern margin of the South China Sea: An example from Taiwan, *J. Asian Earth Sci.* **213,** 104765, doi: 10.1016/j.jseaes.2021.104765.

Lin, A. T., B. Yao, S.-K. Hsu, C.-S. Liu, and C.-Y. Huang (2009). Tectonic features of the incipient arc-continent collision zone of Taiwan: Implications for seismicity, *Tectonophysics* **479,** nos. 1/2, 28–42, doi: 10.1016/j.tecto.2008.11.004.

Lin, C.-W., Y.-C. Liu, P.-S. Chou, and Y.-H. Lin (2021). Recent development of active fault investigations of Taiwan, *Bull. Central Geol. Surv. MOEA.* **34,** 1–40 (in Chinese with English abstract).

Lin, K.-A., K.-M. Yang, T.-H. Hsiuan, T.-Y. Chang, and S.-C. Liang (2005). Integrated assessment of hydrocarbon potentiality in the Tainan Basin, *Petrol. Geol. Taiwan.* **37,** 29–56 (in Chinese with English abstract).

Lin, L.-F., C.-S. Liu, C. Berndt, H.-H. Hsu, Y. Wang, and S.-C. Chen (2022). Gas hydrate and fluid-related seismic indicators across the passive and active margins off SW Taiwan, *World Atlas of Submarine Gas Hydrates in Continental Margins*, 173–181, doi: 10.1007/978-3-030-81186-0_14.

Liu, C.-S., B. Deffontaines, C.-Y. Lu, and S. Lallemand (2004). Deformation patterns of an accretionary wedge in the transition zone from subduction to collision offshore southwestern Taiwan, *Mar. Geophys. Res.* **25,** 123–137, doi: 10.1007/s11001-005-0738-0.

Liu, C.-S., I. L. Huang, and L. S. Teng (1997). Structural features off southwestern Taiwan, *Mar. Geol.* **137,** nos. 3/4, 305–319.

Liu, C.-S., P. Schnürle, Y. Wang, S.-H. Chung, S.-C. Chen, and T.-H. Hsiuan (2006). Distribution and characters of gas hydrate offshore of southwestern Taiwan, *Terr. Atmos. Ocean. Sci.* **17,** no. 4, 615.

Liu, J. P., C. S. Liu, K. H. Xu, J. D. Milliman, J. K. Chiu, S. J. Kao, and S. W. Lin (2008). Flux and fate of small mountainous rivers derived sediments into the Taiwan Strait, *Mar. Geol.* **256,** nos. 1/4, 65–76, doi: 10.1016/j.margeo.2008.09.007.

Malavieille, J., and G. Trullenque (2009). Consequences of continental subduction on forearc basin and accretionary wedge deformation in SE Taiwan: Insights from analogue modeling, *Tectonophysics* **466,** nos. 3/4, 377–394, doi: 10.1016/j.tecto.2007.11.016.

Malavieille, J., S. E. Lallemand, S. Dominguez, A. Deschamps, C.-Y. Lu, C.-S. Liu, P. Schnürle, and , and ACT Scientific Crew (2002). Arc-continent collision in Taiwan: New marine observations and tectonic evolution, *Spec. Pap. Geol. Soc. Am.* **358,** 189–213.

McCaffrey, R. (2009). The tectonic framework of the Sumatran subduction zone. *Annu. Rev. Earth Planet. Sci.* **37,** no. 1, 345–366.

McIntosh, K., Y. Nakamura, T.-K. Wang, R.-C. Shih, A. Chen, and C.-S. Liu (2005). Crustal-scale seismic profiles across Taiwan and the western Philippine Sea, *Tectonophysics* **401,** nos. 1/2, 23–54, doi: 10.1016/j.tecto.2005.02.015.

McIntosh, K., H. van Avendonk, L. Lavier, W. R. Lester, D. Eakin, F. Wu, C.-S. Liu, and C.-S. Lee (2013). Inversion of a hyper-extended rifted margin in the southern Central Range of Taiwan, *Geology* **41,** no. 8, 871–874, doi: 10.1130/G34402.1.

Nakata, T., H. Goto, M. Watanabe, Y. Suzuki, A. Nishizawa, N. Izumi, D. Horiuchi, and Y. Kido (2012). Active faults along Japan Trench and source faults of large earthquakes, *Proc. of the International Symposium on Engineering Lessons Learned from the 2011 Great East Japan Earthquake*, Tokyo, Japan, 1–4 March 2012, 254–262.

Nguyen, Q.-M., S.-K. Hsu, A. T.-S. Lin, and C.-C. Yang (2022). Sedimentary sequences offshore northeastern Taiwan and the offshore projection of the Shanjiao fault zone, *Tectonophysics* **826,** 229254, doi: 10.1016/j.tecto.2022.229254.

Okamura, Y., A. Nishizawa, Y. Fujii, and H. Yanagisawa (2018). Accretionary prism collapse: A new hypothesis on the source of the 1771 giant tsunami in the Ryukyu arc, SW Japan, *Sci. Rep.* **8,** no. 1, 13620, doi: 10.1038/s41598-018-31956-8.

Park, J.-O., H. Tokuyama, M. Shinohara, K. Suyehiro, and A. Taira (1998). Seismic record of tectonic evolution and backarc rifting in the southern Ryukyu island arc system, *Tectonophysics* **294,** 21–42.

Shang, L.-N., X.-H. Zhang, Y.-G. Jia, B. Han, C.-S. Yang, W. Geng, and Y.-M. Pang (2017). Late Cenozoic evolution of the East China continental margin: Insights from seismic, gravity, and magnetic analyses, *Tectonophysics* **698,** 1–15, doi: 10.1016/j.tecto.2017.01.003.

Shyu, J. B. H., Y.-R. Chuang, Y.-L. Chen, Y.-R. Lee, and C.-T. Cheng (2016). A new on-land seismogenic structure source database from the Taiwan earthquake model (TEM) project for seismic hazard analysis of Taiwan, *Terr. Atmos. Ocean. Sci.* **27,** no. 3, 311–323, doi: 10.3319/TAO.2015.11.27.02.

Shyu, J. B. H., K. Sieh, J. P. Avouac, W.-S. Chen, and Y.-G. Chen (2006). Millennial slip rate of the Longitudinal Valley fault from river terraces: Implications for convergence across the active suture of eastern Taiwan, *J. Geophys. Res.* **111,** B08403, doi: 10.1029/2005JB003971.

Shyu, J. B. H., K. Sieh, Y.-G. Chen, and C.-S. Liu (2005). Neotectonic architecture of Taiwan and its implications for future large earthquakes, *J. Geophys. Res.* **110,** B08402, doi: 10.1029/2004JB003251.

Shyu, J. B. H., Y.-H. Yin, C.-H. Chen, Y.-R. Chuang, and S.-C. Liu (2020). Updates to the on-land seismogenic structure source database by the Taiwan earthquake model (TEM) project for seismic hazard analysis of Taiwan, *Terr. Atmos. Ocean. Sci.* **31,** no. 4, 469–478, doi: 10.3319/TAO.2020.06.08.01.

Sibuet, J.-C., B. Deffontaines, S.-K. Hsu, N. Thareau, J.-P. Le Formal, C.-S. Liu, and , and ACT Party (1998). Okinawa Trough backarc basin: Early tectonic and magmatic evolution, *J. Geophys. Res.* **103,** no. B12, 30,245–30,267.

Sørensen, M. B., and K. Atakan (2008). Continued earthquake hazard in northern Sumatra, *Eos Trans. AGU* **89,** no. 14, 133–134.

Stirling, M., T. Goded, K. Berryman, and N. Litchfield (2013). Selection of earthquake scaling relationships for seismic-hazard analysis, *Bull. Seismol. Soc. Am.* **103,** no. 6, 2993–3011, doi: 10.1785/0120130052.

Strasser, M., G. F. Moore, G. Kimura, Y. Kitamura, A. J. Kopf, S. Lallemant, J.-O. Park, E. J. Screaton, X. Su, M. B. Underwood, and X. Zhao (2009). Origin and evolution of a splay fault in the Nankai accretionary wedge, *Nature Geosci.* **2,** no. 9, 648–652, doi: 10.1038/NGEO609.

Sun, S.-C. (1985). The Cenozoic tectonic evolution of offshore Taiwan, *Energy* 10, **nos.** 3/4, 421–432.

Sun, S.-C., and C.-S. Liu (1993). Mud diapirs and submarine channel deposits in offshore Kaohsiung-Hengchun, southwest Taiwan, *Petrol. Geol. Taiwan.* **28,** 1–14.

Suppasri, A., M. Kitamura, D. Alexander, S. Seto, and F. Imamura (2024). The 2024 Noto peninsula earthquake: Preliminary observations and lessons to be Learned, *Int. J. Disaster Risk Reduct.* **110,** 104611, doi: 10.1016/j.ijdrr.2024.104611.

Suppe, J. (1981). Mechanics of mountain building and metamorphism in Taiwan, *Mem. Geol. Soc. China.* **4,** 67–89.

Suppe, J. (1984). Kinematics of arc-continent collision, flipping of subduction and back-arc spreading near Taiwan, *Mem. Geol. Soc. China.* **6,** 21–33.

Tan, E. (2020). Subduction of transitional crust at the Manila Trench and its geophysical implications, *J. Asian Earth Sci.* **187,** 104100, doi: 10.1016/j.jseaes.2019.104100.

Tan, H., X. Gao, K. Wang, J. Gao, and J. He (2022). Hidden roughness of subducting seafloor and implications for megathrust seismogenesis: Example from northern Manila Trench, *Geophys. Res. Lett.* **49,** no. 17, e2022GL100146, doi: 10.1029/2022GL100146.

Tang, L., S. Wang, L. Xu, S. Liu, Y. Zhang, and D. Yao (2023). The aftershock sequences and seismogenic structure of the 2018 Taiwan Shoal M_w 5.7 earthquake, *Chin. J. Geophys.* **66,** no. 7, 2826–2842 (in Chinese with English abstract).

Teng, L. S. (1996). Extensional collapse of the northern Taiwan mountain belt, *Geology* **24,** no. 10, 949–952.

Teng, L. S., and A. T. Lin (2004). Cenozoic tectonics of the China continental margin: insights from Taiwan, *Geol. Soc. Lond., Spec. Publ.* **226,** no. 1, 313–332.

Theunissen, T., Y. Font, S. Lallemand, and W.-T. Liang (2010). The largest instrumentally recorded earthquake in Taiwan: Revised location and magnitude, and tectonic significance of the 1920 event, *Geophys. J. Int.* **183,** no. 3, 1119–1133, doi: 10.1111/j.1365-246X.2010.04813.x.

Tsai, C.-H., S.-K. Hsu, S.-C. Chen, S.-Y. Wang, L.-K. Lin, P.-C. Huang, K.-T. Chen, H.-S. Lin, C.-W. Liang, and Y.-Y. Cho (2021). Active tectonics and volcanism in the southernmost Okinawa Trough back-arc basin derived from deep-towed sonar surveys, *Tectonophysics* **817,** 229047, doi: 10.1016/j.tecto.2021.229047.

Wang, J.-P., C.-H. Chan, and Y.-M. Wu (2011). The distribution of annual maximum earthquake magnitude around Taiwan and its application in the estimation of catastrophic earthquake recurrence probability, *Nat. Hazards.* **59,** 553–570, doi: 10.1007/s11069-011-9776-x.

Wang, S., X. Zeng, M. Xu, Y. Zhang, Y. Zhou, X. Wei, and X. Lin (2021). Rupture directivity of the 25 November 2018 Taiwan Strait M_w 5.8 earthquake and its tectonic implications, *Tectonophysics* **809,** 228852, doi: 10.1016/j.tecto.2021.228852.

Wang, S.-Y., S.-K. Hsu, and Y.-C. Yeh (2019). Earthquake-related structures beneath the southernmost portion of the Ryukyu arc and forearc, *Geophys. Res. Lett.* **46,** no. 7, 3717–3725, doi: 10.1029/2019GL082121.

Wang, X., X. Ye, Y. Huang, and L. Wang (2019). Seismogenic structure of the M_s 6.2 Taiwan strait earthquake on 26 November, 2018, *Chin. J. Geophys.* **62,** no. 12, 4673–4683 (in Chinese with English abstract).

Wang, Y., Y. N. Lin, Y. Ota, L.-H. Chung, J. B. H. Shyu, H.-W. Chiang, Y.-G. Chen, H.-H. Hsu, and C.-C. Shen (2022). Mud diapir or fault-related fold? On the development of an active mud-cored anticline offshore southwestern Taiwan, *Tectonics* **41,** no. 9, e2022TC007234, doi: 10.1029/2022TC007234.

Wang, Y., S.-H. Wu, H. L. B. Chou, Y.-Y. Li, W. S. Cheng, A. Ho, J.-M. Chen, S.-C. Liu, C.-Y. Hsieh, S. Duan, *et al.* (2024). Surface ruptures of the 2022 Guanshan-Chihshang earthquakes in central Longitudinal Valley area, eastern Taiwan, *Terr. Atmos. Ocean.* **35,** no. 1, 16, doi: 10.1007/s44195-024-00077-3.

Wang, Y.-J., C.-H. Chan, Y.-T. Lee, K.-F. Ma, J. B. H. Shyu, R.-J. Rau, and C.-T. Cheng (2016). Probabilistic seismic hazard assessments for Taiwan, *Terr. Atmos. Ocean. Sci.* **27,** 325–340.

Wells, D. L., and K. J. Coppersmith (1994). New empirical relationships among magnitude, rupture length, rupture width, rupture area, and surface displacement, *Bull. Seismol. Soc. Am.* **84,** no. 4, 974–1002.

Wen, X., and X. Xu (2005). Analysis of the historical earthquakes of 1067 and 1574 in the southeast coastal region of China, *Seismol. Geol.* **27,** no. 1, 1–10 (in Chinese with English abstract).

Wesnousky, S. G. (2008). Displacement and geometrical characteristics of earthquake surface ruptures: Issues and implications for seismic-hazard analysis and the process of earthquake rupture, *Bull. Seismol. Soc. Am.* **98,** no. 4, 1609–1632, doi: 10.1785/0120070111.

Wu, Y.-S. (2017). A Preliminary study of the shallow structures in the Hsinchu offshore area, Taiwan, *Master's Thesis*, Institute of Oceanography, National Taiwan University, 87 (in Chinese with English abstract).

Wu, Z., and M. Hu (2024). Definitions, classification schemes for active faults, and their application, *Geosciences* **14,** 68, doi: 10.3390/geosciences14030068.

Wu, W.-N., H. Kao, S.-K. Hsu, C.-L. Lo, and H.-W. Chen (2010). Spatial variation of the crustal stress field along the Ryukyu-Taiwan-Luzon convergent boundary, *J. Geophys. Res.* **115,** B11401, doi: 10.1029/2009JB007080.

Wu, W.-N., J.-Y. Lin, W.-B. Doo, C.-L. Lo, and S.-K. Hsu (2024). Seismogenic structures along the deformation front from onshore to offshore SW Taiwan, *Geosci. Lett.* **11,** no. 1, 37, doi: 10.1186/s40562-024-00354-6.

Wu, W.-N., Y.-T. Yen, Y.-J. Hsu, Y.-M. Wu, J.-Y. Lin, and S.-K. Hsu (2017). Spatial variation of seismogenic depths of crustal earthquakes in the Taiwan region: Implications for seismic hazard assessment, *Tectonophysics* **708,** 81–95, doi: 10.1016/j.tecto.2017.04.028.

Wu, Y.-M., C.-H. Chang, H. Kuo-Chen, H.-H. Huang, and C.-Y. Wang (2013). On the use of explosion records for examining earthquake location uncertainty in Taiwan, *Terr. Atmos. Ocean. Sci.* **24,** no. 4, 685–694, doi: 10.3319/TAO.2013.01.31.01(T).

Wu, Y.-M., J. B. H. Shyu, C.-H. Chang, L. Zhao, M. Nakamura, and S.-K. Hsu (2009). Improved seismic tomography offshore northeastern Taiwan: Implications for subduction and collision processes between Taiwan and the southernmost Ryukyu, *Geophys. J. Int.* **178,** no. 2, 1042–1054, doi: 10.1111/j.1365-246X.2009.04180.x.

Yang, E. Y. (2017). The Neogene basin development offshore northern Taiwan, *Master's Thesis*, Institute of Oceanography, National Taiwan University, 96, doi: 10.6342/NTU201701534.

Yang, J.-N. (2010). Evaluation of CO2 storage capacity and storage sites in the Taoyuan Tableland, *Master's Thesis*, Department of Earth Sciences, National Central University, 75 (in Chinese with English abstract).

Yang, E. Y., J.-H. Chang, H.-H. Hsu, W.-C. Han, C.-S. Liu, and C.-C. Su (2021). Middle Miocene-Pleistocene foreland basin offshore northern Taiwan, *Petrol. Geol. Taiwan.* **45,** 29–54.

Yang, K.-M., R.-J. Rau, H.-Y. Chang, C.-Y. Hsieh, H.-H. Ting, S.-T. Huang, J.-C. Wu, and Y.-J. Tang (2016). The role of basement-involved normal faults in the recent tectonics of western Taiwan, *Geol. Mag.* **153,** nos. 5/6, 1166–1191, doi: 10.1017/S0016756816000637.

Yen, Y.-T., and K.-F. Ma (2011). Source-scaling relationship for M 4.6–8.9 earthquakes, specifically for earthquakes in the collision zone of Taiwan, *Bull. Seismol. Soc. Am.* **101,** no. 2, 464–481, doi: 10.1785/0120100046.

Yen, M.-H., Y.-W. M. Liao, K.-F. Ma, and Y.-C. Wu (2021). Investigation and hazard implication of 1604 Quanzhou earthquake using modern simulation with literature intensity, *Terr. Atmos. Ocean. Sci.* **32,** no. 2, 145–157, doi: 10.3319/TAO.2021.01.04.01.

Yu, H.-S. (2004). Nature and distribution of the deformation front in the Luzon Arc-Chinese continental margin collision zone at Taiwan, *Mar. Geophys. Res.* **25,** 109–122, doi: 10.1007/s11001-005-0737-1.

Yu, H.-S., and Y.-W. Chou (2001). Characteristics and development of the flexural forebulge and basal unconformity of western Taiwan Foreland basin, *Tectonophysics* **333,** 277–291.

Yu, H.-S., and G.-S. Song (2000). Submarine physiographic features in Taiwan region and their geological significance, *J. Geol. Soc. China.* **43,** no. 2, 267–286.

Yu, S.-B., H.-Y. Chen, and L.-C. Kuo (1997). Velocity field of GPS stations in the Taiwan area, *Tectonophysics* **274,** 41–59.

Zhang, J., G. Li, and X. Zhao (1982). Chronological studies on the Late Quaternary stratigraphy and neotectonics movement along the coastal area of south Fujian and east Guangdong, *Seismol. Geol.* **4,** no. 3, 27–37 (in Chinese with English abstract).

Zhang, R., S. Li, Y. Suo, J. Liu, X. Cao, J. Zhou, Z. Jiang, and X. Li (2022). A forearc pull-apart basin under oblique arc-continent collision: Insights from the North Luzon Trough, *Tectonophysics* **837,** 229461, doi: 10.1016/j.tecto.2022.229461.

Zhang, Y., H. Kuo-Chen, J. Alvarez-Marron, D. Brown, A. T.-S. Lin, Z. Xie, and X. Jin (2020). Imaging active faulting in the western Taiwan Strait, *Sci. Rep.* **10,** no. 1, 3703, doi: 10.1038/s41598-020-60666-3.

Zhang, Y., H. Yao, H.-Y. Yang, H.-T. Cai, H. Fang, J. Xu, X. Jin, H. Kuo-Chen, W.-T. Liang, and K.-X. Chen (2018). 3-D crustal shear-wave velocity structure of the Taiwan Strait and Fujian, SE China, revealed by ambient noise tomography, *J. Geophys. Res.* **123,** 8016–8031, doi: 10.1029/2018JB015938.

Zhu, J., Z. Sun, H. Kopp, X. Qiu, H. Xu, S. Li, and W. Zhan (2013). Segmentation of the Manila subduction system from migrated multichannel seismics and wedge taper analysis, *Mar. Geophys. Res.* **34,** 379–391, doi: 10.1007/s11001-013-9175-7.

Manuscript received 16 January 2025
Published online 5 June 2025

Spatiotemporal Patterns of the 2 April 2024 Hualien Earthquake Sequence and Finite-Fault Solutions of Significant Aftershocks

Mei Chien[1], Yopi Serhalawan[2,3,4], Po-Fei Chen*[3], Wei-Li Chen[3], and Hsuan-Yu Kuo[3]

ABSTRACT

The 2024 M_w 7.4 Hualien earthquake displayed a complex rupture process and an intricate aftershock (AF) sequence. In this study, we present a comprehensive analysis of the earthquake sequence, including finite-fault solutions for significant AFs. Using data from a dense temporary seismic network combined with automated phase-picking and earthquake location algorithms, we delineate the spatiotemporal evolution of the earthquake sequence. Using the Density-Based Spatial Clustering of Applications with Noise clustering algorithm, we group the seismicity into distinct clusters and identify two primary AF clusters. The first cluster is concentrated around the mainshock asperity, predominantly to the north, consistent with the northward rupture directivity observed in the mainshock. The second cluster, interpreted as a triggered swarm, began on 22 April and is localized within a confined shallow area to the south. The HypoDD catalog reveals a spatial pattern largely associated with significant AFs ($M_L > 5.8$), for which distributions are used to determine the corresponding fault planes based on moment tensor solutions. The results exhibit a clear spatial segmentation: whereas AFs to the north predominantly rupture on steeply east-dipping fault planes, those to the south, including the swarm events, rupture along a shallowly west-dipping plane. Finally, we revisit and assess prior investigations into the mainshock kinematics, drawing on insights from the spatiotemporal evolution of the AF sequence and the asperity distribution associated with significant AFs.

KEY POINTS

- The 2024 Hualien earthquake's complexity is revealed by seismic patterns and rupture faults of significant aftershocks (AFs).
- Steep east-dipping faults occurred to the north, and shallow west-dipping faults with swarm occurred to the south.
- AF studies help reveal the kinematics and dynamics of the mainshock.

Supplemental Material

INTRODUCTION

The 2024 M_w 7.4 Hualien earthquake occurred on 2 April at a depth of 22 km (according to the Central Weather Administration [CWA] catalog) beneath the coast of the northern Longitudinal Valley (LV) in eastern Taiwan. Among the ~8 cm/yr northwesterly convergence rate across Taiwan between the Philippine Sea plate and the Eurasian plate, about half is absorbed across the LV, making it capable of releasing a series of major earthquakes within a short period (Fig. 1). A well-known example is the 1951 series in LV, for which >10 major events were first triggered in the northern segment in late October and then leaped to the southern segment in late November (Chen *et al.*, 2008). More recently, another LV earthquake series, spanning a longer period, began with the 6 February 2018 M_w 6.4 Hualien earthquake (Lee *et al.*, 2019), followed by the 18 April 2019 M_w 6.4 Hualien earthquake (Lin *et al.*, 2022), 22 March 2022 M_w 6.8 Hualien-Taitung earthquake, the 17 September 2022 M_w 6.6 Guanshan earthquake, and 18 September 2022 M_w 7.0 Chihshang earthquake (Lee *et al.*, 2023). Unlike the 1951 series, in which most ruptures occurred on the east-dipping Longitudinal Valley fault (LVF), the majority of

1. Department of Earth, Environmental, and Planetary Sciences, Rice University, Houston, Texas, U.S.A., https://orcid.org/0000-0003-1768-216X (MC); 2. Taiwan International Graduate Program (TIGP)-Earth System Science Program (ESS), Academia Sinica and National Central University, Academia Sinica, Taipei, Taiwan, https://orcid.org/0000-0002-0188-0148 (YS); 3. Department of Earth Sciences, National Central University, Taoyuan, Taiwan, https://orcid.org/0000-0002-8523-3772 (P-FC); https://orcid.org/0009-0009-9128-7038 (W-LC); 4. The Indonesian Agency for Meteorological, Climatological and Geophysics, Jakarta, Indonesia

*Corresponding author: bob@ncu.edu.tw

Cite this article as Chien, M., Y. Serhalawan, P.-F. Chen, W.-L. Chen, and H.-Y. Kuo (2025). Spatiotemporal Patterns of the 2 April 2024 Hualien Earthquake Sequence and Finite-Fault Solutions of Significant Aftershocks, *Bull. Seismol. Soc. Am.* **116**, 52–67, doi: 10.1785/0120250117

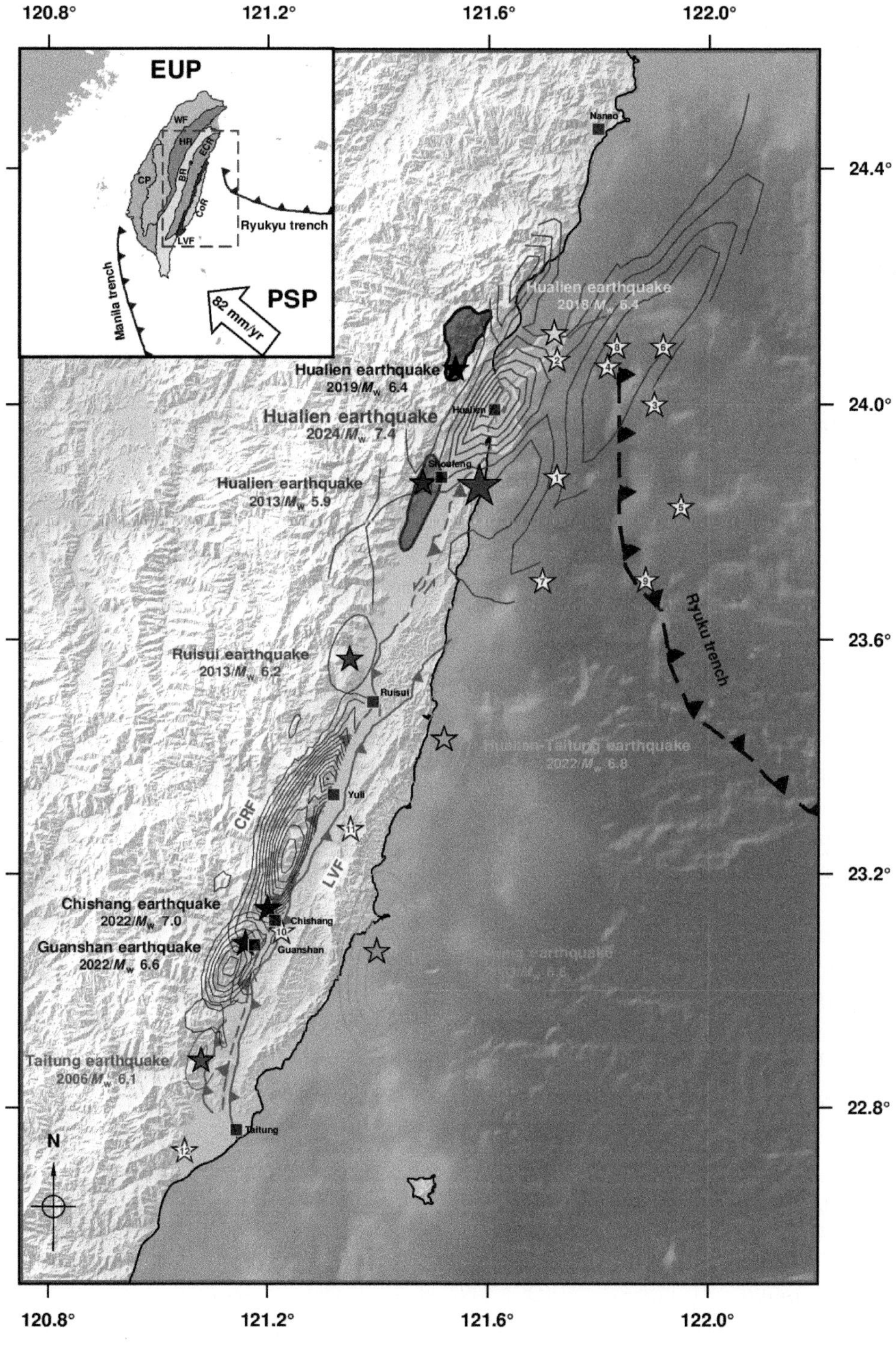

Figure 1. Tectonic setting and major earthquakes in eastern Taiwan. Colored contours show slip distributions projected vertically to the surface for the labeled events (contour interval = 0.2 m). Slip distributions are from our unpublished work, except for the 2013, 2018, and 2019 Hualien earthquakes (Lee *et al.*, 2023; Tang *et al.*, 2023). The white stars mark the 1951 Hualien–Taitung earthquake sequence (Chen *et al.*, 2008). The red star and contours correspond to those of the 2024 Hualien earthquake (east-dipping plane). The magenta lines show active faults: the Longitudinal Valley fault (LVF) on the east, with eastward triangles, and the Central Range fault (CRF) on the west, with westward triangles. The inset shows the study area (red-dashed box) and geological provinces defined by the Central Geological Survey (CGS): BR, Backbone range; CoR, Coastal range; CP, Coastal plain; ECR, East Central range; HR, Hsueshan range; LV, Longitudinal Valley; WF, Western Foothills. EUP and PSP represent the Eurasian plate and the Philippine Sea plate, respectively. The color version of this figure is available only in the electronic edition.

earthquakes in the recent series highlight seismic activity along the west-dipping Central Range fault (CRF; Tang *et al.*, 2023), which was initially identified through geological studies (Shyu *et al.*, 2006).

It is now widely accepted that both LVF and CRF play significant roles in seismic release, accommodating relative motion across the LV. The seismic interaction of double-vergent conjugate faults is an interesting and important issue to investigate and can be examined on different time scales. At one end of the spectrum, the long-term seismic moment budget of the LVF and CRF is assessed through the asperity distributions of major past earthquakes (Tang *et al.*, 2023). In this context, the 2024 Hualien earthquake, which effectively filled the seismic gap on the right side of the northern segment, symbolizes the culminating event of the modern series in the LV (Fig. 1). At the other end, the dynamically triggering of coseismic slip on secondary faults is investigated using finite-fault solutions (e.g., the 6 February 2018 Hualien earthquake, Lee *et al.*, 2019; the 2022 M_w 7.0 Chihshang earthquake, Lee *et al.*, 2023). In between, the triggering of events on the conjugate fault, likely caused by Coulomb stress changes, may manifest as a significant aftershock (AF) with its own AF sequence, as seen in cases such as the 2006 M_w 6.1 Taitung earthquake (Wu *et al.*, 2006).

For the 2024 Hualien earthquake, a composite fault model has been proposed for the mainshock (Cheloni *et al.*, 2024), involving a major segment of the CRF and a deeper segment of the LVF. This

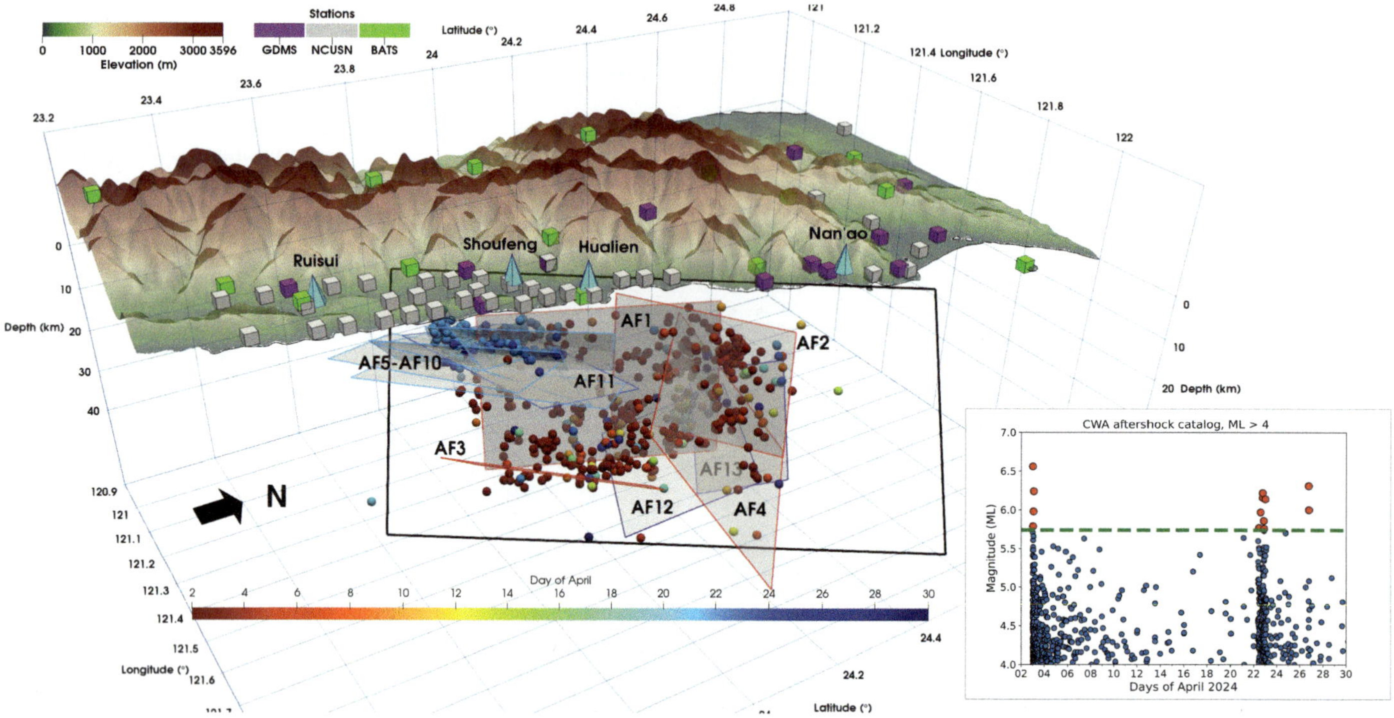

Figure 2. Cubes represent the distribution of stations used for spatiotemporal study of the earthquake sequence, with the seismic network marked by color. Circles indicate the distributions of aftershocks (AFs) in April with $M_L > 4.0$, based on the Central Weather Administration (CWA) catalog, and are color coded by the day of occurrence in April. The preferred fault planes of significant AFs ($M_L > 5.8$, labeled AF1–AF13) identified in this study are shown, with their sizes empirically determined by M_w and using the same color scheme. Cyan cones denote nearby cities. The east-dipping mainshock fault plane is outlined in black for reference. The inset shows the temporal distribution of earthquakes with $M_L > 4.0$, with significant AFs marked in red, based on the CWA catalog.

complexity may pose challenges for finite-fault studies. The earthquake sequence exhibited a distinct spatiotemporal pattern, characterized by two primary clusters. The first cluster comprised immediate AFs, predominantly located to the north, including a significant M_w 6.5 event that occurred 13 min later. The second cluster, likely a triggered swarm, was tightly confined in both space and time, occurring shallowly inland near offshore Shoufeng (121.6° E, 23.8° N; Fig. 2).

The purpose of this study is twofold. First, by integrating data from a temporary SmartSolo array and permanent local networks, we apply LOC-FLOW—end-to-end machine learning-based high-precision earthquake location workflow (Zhang *et al.*, 2022)—to comprehensively monitor the 2024 Hualien earthquake sequence through the end of April. Second, events with magnitudes greater than M_L 5.8 are considered significant and are labeled AF1–AF13 (Fig. 2; Table 1). The resulting AF catalog is used to determine the fault planes of AFs, followed by an analysis of their finite-fault solutions. The findings from the AF study, in turn, provide insights into the kinematics of the mainshock.

DATA AND METHODS

AF sequence monitoring

A SmartSolo array was deployed in Hualien immediately after the mainshock, and by 4 April, the network (hereafter referred to as NCUSN), comprising 42 stations, was fully installed. During initial data processing, it was noted that the SmartSolo sensors tended to clip during strong earthquakes, and the north–south alignment of the NCUSN lacked sufficient east–west constraints for accurate earthquake location determination. To address both issues, additional data from 19 stations in the CWA seismic network (downloaded from the Taiwan Seismological and Geophysical Data Management System [GDMS], primarily strong-motion sensors) and 18 stations from Broadband Array in Taiwan for Seismology (BATS, including mostly strong-motion sensors and some high-gain seismometers) were incorporated for the study. All stations operated with a sampling rate of 0.01 s (Fig. 2).

Our methodology follows the workflow of Liu *et al.* (2020), comprising four key stages: (1) phase detection using PhaseNet (Zhu and Beroza, 2019), (2) phase association and initial event location with REAL (Zhang *et al.*, 2019), (3) event relocation via VELEST (Kissling *et al.*, 1994), and (4) refinement of relocated events with HypoDD based on travel times (Waldhauser and Ellsworth, 2000).

PhaseNet is a deep neural network–based arrival-time picker (Zhu and Beroza, 2019) trained on >700,000 samples over three decades at the Northern California Earthquake Data Center with various instrument types. The robust application of the algorithm and generalization to other regions have been demonstrated by Liu *et al.* (2020) and Guan *et al.* (2024). For our analysis, we input three-component raw waveforms into the

TABLE 1
Mainshock and Significant AFs, CWA Source Parameters, and RMT Double-Couple Solution (Bold Texts for Fault Plane)

Number	Date and Time (yyyy/mm/dd hh:mm:ss.ss)	Latitude (°)	Longitude (°)	Depth (km)	Centroid Depth (km)	M_L	M_w (RMT)	Plane 1 Strike (°)	Plane 1 Dip (°)	Plane 1 Rake (°)	Plane 2 Strike (°)	Plane 2 Dip (°)	Plane 2 Rake (°)	Name_List
1	2024/04/02 23:58:09.89	23.8607	121.5837	22.52	42	7.2	7.3	**32**	**51**	**87**	218	40	94	Mainshock
2	2024/04/03 00:11:26.39	24.13	121.6513	13.44	22	6.6	6.5	**21**	**86**	**47**	287	42	174	AF1
3	2024/04/03 00:35:36.88	24.2005	121.7062	7.32	16	5.8	5.8	**52**	**85**	**61**	313	29	169	AF2
4	2024/04/03 01:39:48.60	23.7948	121.8143	13.85	16	6.0	5.8	26	55	81	**221**	**35**	**101**	AF3
5	2024/04/03 02:14:34.94	24.1468	121.9762	26.9	26	6.2	5.8	**313**	**50**	**−124**	180	50	−55	AF4
6	2024/04/22 10:50:31.52	23.75	121.545	6.8	12	5.8	5.6	19	72	78	**233**	**20**	**122**	AF5
7	2024/04/22 14:11:24.56	23.7752	121.502	8.58	10	6.0	5.7	59	56	104	**215**	**35**	**69**	AF6
8	2024/04/22 18:26:52.91	23.74	121.6127	9.2	8	6.2	6.2	17	69	81	**221**	**22**	**112**	AF7
9	2024/04/22 18:32:48.82	23.8482	121.5208	7.74	10	6.2	5.9	55	47	106	**212**	**45**	**73**	AF8
10	2024/04/22 20:49:58.06	23.736	121.5643	8.83	12	5.9	5.7	18	73	81	**225**	**18**	**116**	AF9
11	2024/04/22 21:31:39.47	23.8518	121.5408	7.7	16	5.8	5.3	15	83	60	**274**	**30**	**167**	AF10
12	2024/04/23 00:04:05.90	23.8352	121.5715	11.68	14	6.1	5.8	20	79	76	**252**	**17**	**140**	AF11
13	2024/04/26 18:21:24.09	24.1828	121.6748	35.54	45	6.3	5.8	**116**	**24**	**−12**	217	85	247	AF12
14	2024/04/26 18:49:29.32	24.2505	121.6865	29.43	33	6.0	5.4	**15**	**74**	**75**	239	21	132	AF13

AF, significant aftershocks; CWA, Central Weather Administration; RMT, Real-Time Moment Tensor Monitoring System.

model, which outputs probability distributions for *P*- and *S*-wave arrivals. We retained picks with probabilities >0.5, identifying 1,685,889 *P* picks and 1,406,015 *S* picks, spanning from 3 April at 00:00 to 30 April at 24:00 (UTC).

Next, REAL determines earthquake locations by evaluating 3D regions based on initial picks. Each grid cell is assessed primarily for the number of associated *P* and *S* picks within a specified time window and secondarily for the cumulative travel-time residuals (Zhang *et al.*, 2019). Our study targeted the Hualien earthquake series using a search area bounded by 121°–122.2° E and 23.5°–24.7° N with depths up to 30 km. Grid sizes were set to 0.04° horizontally and 2 km vertically. Events occurring within 2 s of each other or having nearest event-station distances >60 km were excluded. Minimum thresholds for picks were set at three *P* picks, two *S* picks, and six combined *P* and *S* picks, with at least two stations recording both types. Using theoretical travel-time tables derived from the East Taiwan 1D velocity model, REAL located 58,950 events.

As a benchmark catalog, the current CWA catalog is necessary but insufficient for comparison as human-picked events take a long time to complete during periods of intense seismic activity. Consequently, the recall rate serves as a reference to validate our resulting catalog. A CWA event is considered matched if a corresponding resulting event has an origin time difference within 3 s (Zhu *et al.*, 2022). Among the CWA events in the same region and period, 2984 of 3254 events are matched, yielding a recall rate of 92%. A comparison of spatial distribution between the REAL and CWA catalog is shown in Figure 3a. The matched CWA events are used to calibrate the magnitudes in our catalog (Shin, 1993), ensuring consistency with the M_L values reported in the CWA catalog (see the Supplementary I, available in the supplemental material to this article).

The REAL catalog results were further relocated using VELEST, a least-squares absolute location method, to produce the VELEST catalog. Initially, 1417 events were selected with station gaps <180°, travel-time residuals <0.35 s, and ≥45 *P* and *S* picks. These were used to update the 1D velocity model and obtain associated station corrections. The updated velocity model showed incremental increases in *P*-wave velocities with depth, rising by 0.2 km/s at 10 km and ≤0.6 km/s at 30 km. Using this updated model, events with station gaps <300° and residuals <0.5 s were relocated, resulting in 55,965 well-constrained events with an 88% recall rate (Fig. 3a). The VELEST catalog was further refined using HypoDD, a double-difference relocation method that minimizes residuals between paired events at each station (Waldhauser and Ellsworth, 2000). After refinement, 19,618 events were preserved with a 77% recall rate (Fig. 3a). Figure 3b shows distributions of CWA, REAL, VELEST, and HypoDD catalog.

Finite-fault solutions of significant aftershocks

We determined finite-fault solutions of AFs using the Wavelet- and Simulated-Annealing SliP (WASP) package (Goldberg

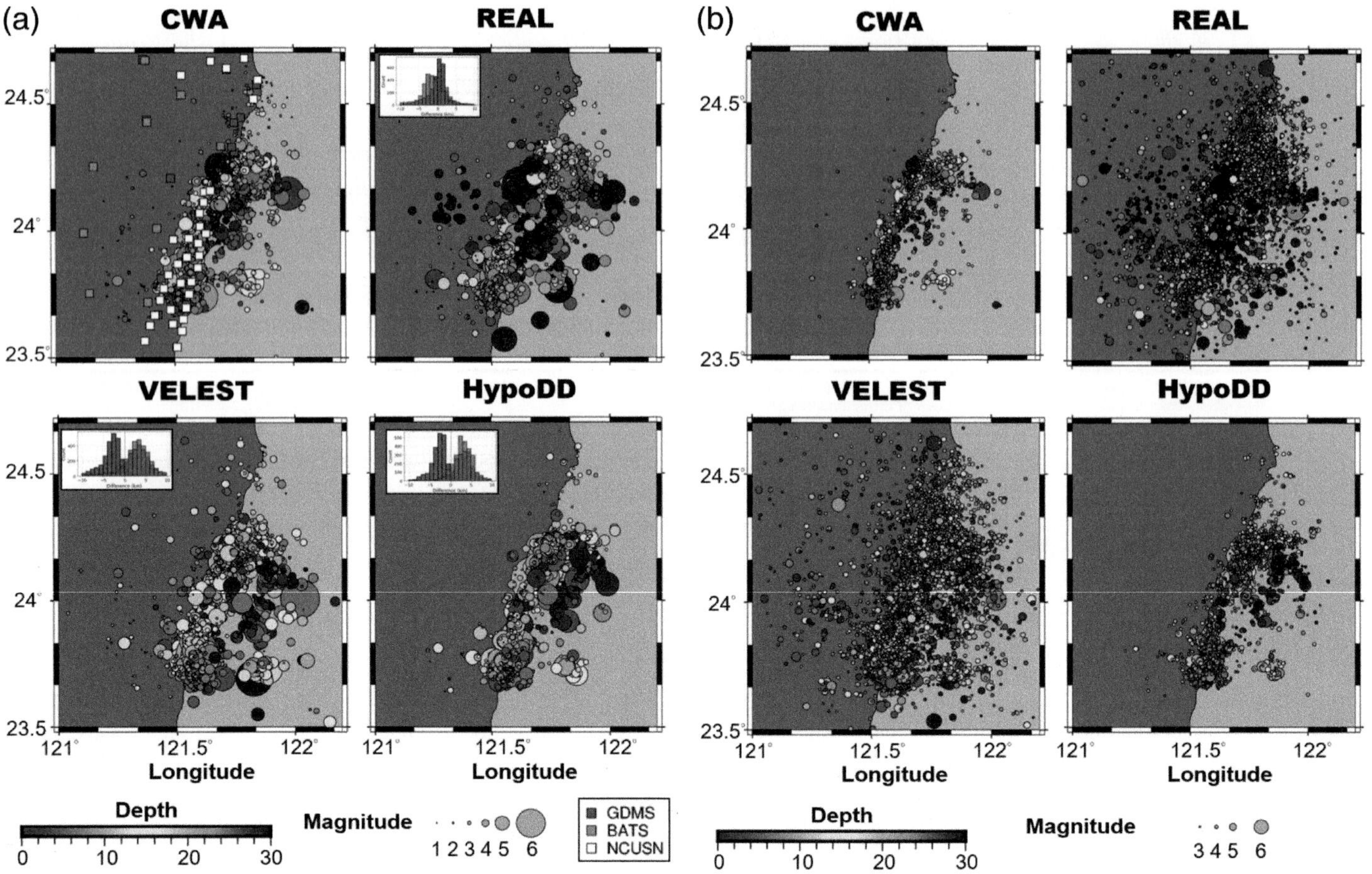

Figure 3. (a) Distribution of matched CWA events in the REAL, VELEST, and HypoDD catalogs. Circle size is scaled to earthquake magnitude, and color indicates event depth. The squares of the upper-left panel represent station locations. The location differences relative to CWA are shown as histograms in the upper-left corner for latitude (blue), longitude (green), and depth (brown). (b) Similar to panel (a) but showing the distribution of all earthquakes in the catalog. Note the reduced scale and the omission of events with $M_L < 3$. BATS, Broadband Array in Taiwan for Seismology; GDMS, Geophysical Data Management System. The color version of this figure is available only in the electronic edition.

et al., 2022), which simultaneously inverts for slip amplitude, rake, rupture-onset time, and an asymmetric-cosine rise function on a discretized fault mesh by minimizing a weighted wavelet-domain misfit via simulated annealing method (Ji *et al.*, 2002). For each event, we first attempted a joint inversion of teleseismic *P*- and *SH*-body waves together with near-field strong-motion data; if reliable teleseismic body-wave Green's functions could not be generated, we relied solely on local strong-motion data. Broadband teleseismic seismograms ($\Delta = 30°–90°$) were downloaded from the Incorporated Research Institutions for Seismology Data Management Center (IRIS-DMC), and strong-motion records within 80 km epicentral distance were obtained from the CWA's GDMS and Taiwan Strong Motion Instrumentation Program networks.

The parameters used for the finite-fault solutions are illustrated in Supplementary II. We follow the default approach of Goldberg *et al.* (2022) to determine the width and length of the fault area using the moment tensor solution provided by the Real-Time Moment Tensor Monitoring System (RMT; Lee *et al.*, 2014). The resulting HypoDD catalog is used to resolve the ambiguity of the fault plane as follows. (1) We divide the catalog into two subsets, separated by the occurrence time of AF5 (Table 1), corresponding to the two primary clusters. (2) We analyze AF1–AF4 and AF5–AF13 separately, with events counted from each significant AF's origin time to the end of its window (AF1–AF4: up to but not including AF5; AF5–AF13: until the end of April). For each significant AF and each candidate nodal plane, we retain only events for which hypocenters project within that plane's finite-fault along-strike length and down-dip width. (3) We adopt the Taiwan regional width–magnitude scaling relation proposed by Wu *et al.* (2013): $\log_{10} W = 0.52M_w - 1.68$, in which W is the full minor-axis width (in km) of the AF zone ellipse. (4) We define a perpendicular buffer zone as a fourth of the width ($W/4$) on each side of the fault and calculate the standard deviation (σ) of the hypocenters' signed normal distances to the plane for events within this buffer zone. (5) We count the number of events within the $\pm 2\sigma$ seismogenic thickness, and we identify the nodal plane with the greater number of events as the fault plane (Fig. 4).

Finally, the quality of each inversion is quantified by the average misfit error, which evaluates each channel's misfit in the

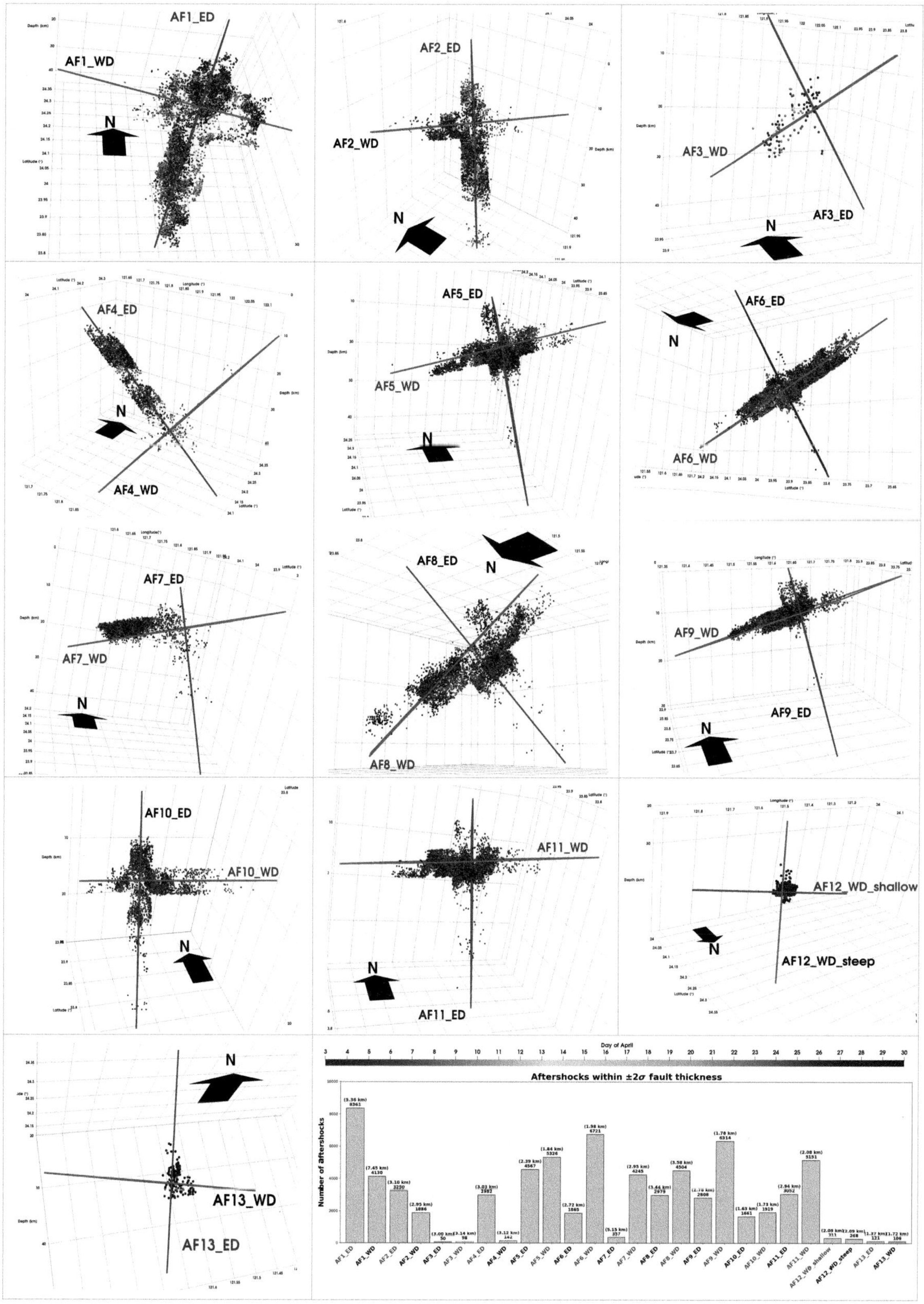

Figure 4. Projection of AF1–AF13, viewed along the intersection line of the two nodal planes. The HypoDD events within the seismogenic thickness of each nodal plane are shown as circles, color coded by their day of occurrence in April. The preferred fault planes are labeled in red text, with ED indicating east-dipping and WD indicating west-dipping orientations. The bottom histogram compares the seismogenic thickness and the number of events (noted above each bar) for each nodal plane of every significant AF. For each significant AF, the nodal plane with the higher event count is interpreted as the fault plane and is highlighted in red text. The color version of this figure is available only in the electronic edition.

wavelet domain using a hybrid L1 + L2 norm (Ji *et al.*, 2002), weighted by data type and averaged into a single scalar value. For joint inversions, we adopt the scheme of Goldberg *et al.* (2022): teleseismic *P*-wave traces are assigned unit weight, *SH* waves receive half that weight, and strong-motion records are given twice the *P*-wave weight. We successfully invert 11 of the 13 AFs; AF10 and AF13 were excluded, likely because of their small moment magnitudes, which may have prevented the generation of reliable Green's functions. For the completed inversions, the average misfit error ranged from ~0.13–0.43, a range typically considered indicative of a good fit in finite-fault studies (e.g., Zhang *et al.*, 2014; Zheng *et al.*, 2020; Sianipar *et al.*, 2022).

In addition to the WASP workflow, we apply a leave-one-out jackknife to quantify uncertainty in the finite-fault inversions (Chi and Dreger, 2004; Chen *et al.*, 2016; Sianipar *et al.*, 2022). For each significant AF, we remove one waveform at a time and rerun the inversion using the same fault geometry, parameterization, data weights, and regularization, retaining the corresponding jackknife model. This procedure is repeated until every usable seismogram has been omitted once, resulting in a set of jackknife models equal in number to the input waveforms. We summarize all jackknife models in space and time following Sianipar *et al.* (2022). Spatially, for each subfault, we compute the standard deviation of slip across the leave-one-out models and express it as a percentage of the slip in the full-data model at that subfault. Subfaults with relative uncertainty below 20% of the slip along the fault plane are considered well resolved and are highlighted on the maps. Temporally, we overlay the source time functions (STFs) from all jackknife models with that of the full-data model to provide a visual estimate of time-history uncertainty.

To evaluate sensitivity to dataset choice and weighting, we compare teleseismic-only, strong-motion-only, and joint inversions using AF7 as a representative case (highest moment among the joint inversions, with excellent coverage; Fig. 5). In the teleseismic-only inversion, slip is broad, forming a roughly circular high-slip patch near the hypocenter; the STF peaks at ~7.9 s and decays quickly, with only a small late bump near ~16 s. The strong-motion-only inversion yields a more concentrated high-slip patch in the deeper portion of the fault plane; its STF shows two prominent early peaks (~5.9 and ~7.4 s), followed by a secondary maximum at ~12.6 to 13 s and a minor late bump at ~17 to 19 s, giving the longest overall duration. Spatially, the joint model most closely resembles the strong-motion-only result: it retains the deep asperity and shows a weaker central–shallow asperity near the hypocenter, likely reflecting the teleseismic contribution. Temporally, the joint STF has a single dominant peak at ~6.4 s and a broad secondary pulse between ~11.7 and ~13.3 s. For the joint inversions, we adopt the Goldberg *et al.* (2022) dataset weights ($P = 1$, $SH = 0.5$, strong motion = 2). In a sensitivity run with the strong-motion weight set to 1, the spatial pattern is largely preserved: the deep high-slip patch remains but is broader and slightly lower in amplitude, and the up-dip extension is more diffuse; rupture-front contours and the overall geometry are maintained. The STF keeps the same qualitative shape (an early main peak with a modest late pulse), though the early portion splits into two closely spaced peaks.

RESULTS

AF sequence monitoring

The resulting REAL, VELEST, and HypoDD catalogs are evaluated for different purposes and presented here in order. Given the 92% recall rate of REAL, we examine the spatial distribution of matched events between the CWA and REAL catalogs. The overall spatial patterns are similar, with the average differences in latitude, longitude, and depth being 1, 2, and 3 km, respectively (Fig. 3a), validating the application of PhaseNet and REAL to the dataset used in this study. The number of REAL-detected events, nearly 10 times that of CWA events, significantly enhances the completeness of the earthquake catalog, reducing the magnitude of completeness (M_c) to ~1.2.

However, the investigation of the spatiotemporal pattern will be based on the results of the VELEST catalog rather than the REAL catalog for the following reasons. First, the empirically adopted depth range of 30 km—chosen to achieve a better recall rate compared to 40 km—results in the exclusion of events deeper than 30 km and introduces artificial clustering of events at that depth. Second, the REAL catalog may include poorly constrained events because of large station gaps and significant arrival-time residuals because its sole criterion for event inclusion is the number of *P*- and *S*-phase picks.

The VELEST catalog is relocated using an updated velocity model, excluding poorly constrained events, which results in a conceptually improved seismic distribution compared to the REAL catalog. In addition, the VELEST events, with an 88% recall rate, are generally deeper because of the higher velocities at depth in the updated model, enabling the inclusion of events deeper than 30 km (see histogram in Fig. 3a).

The spatiotemporal pattern of the Hualien earthquake sequence is analyzed based not on the evolution of individual events—an impractical approach—but rather on the evolution of event clusters. These clusters are defined as contiguous regions with high seismicity density. To group the seismicity in the VELEST catalog, we use the Density-Based Spatial Clustering of Applications with Noise (DBSCAN; Kriegel *et al.*, 2011) algorithm. Before clustering, we converted origin times to Unix epoch seconds (UTC) and standardized latitude, longitude, depth, and time with StandardScaler so that each dimension contributes equally to Euclidean distances. We then applied DBSCAN in 4D (x–y–z–t) with neighborhood radius $\varepsilon = 0.35$ and at least 200 neighboring earthquakes within ε to form a cluster using Euclidean metric. The resulting clusters are color coded by days in April, whereas noise events (those

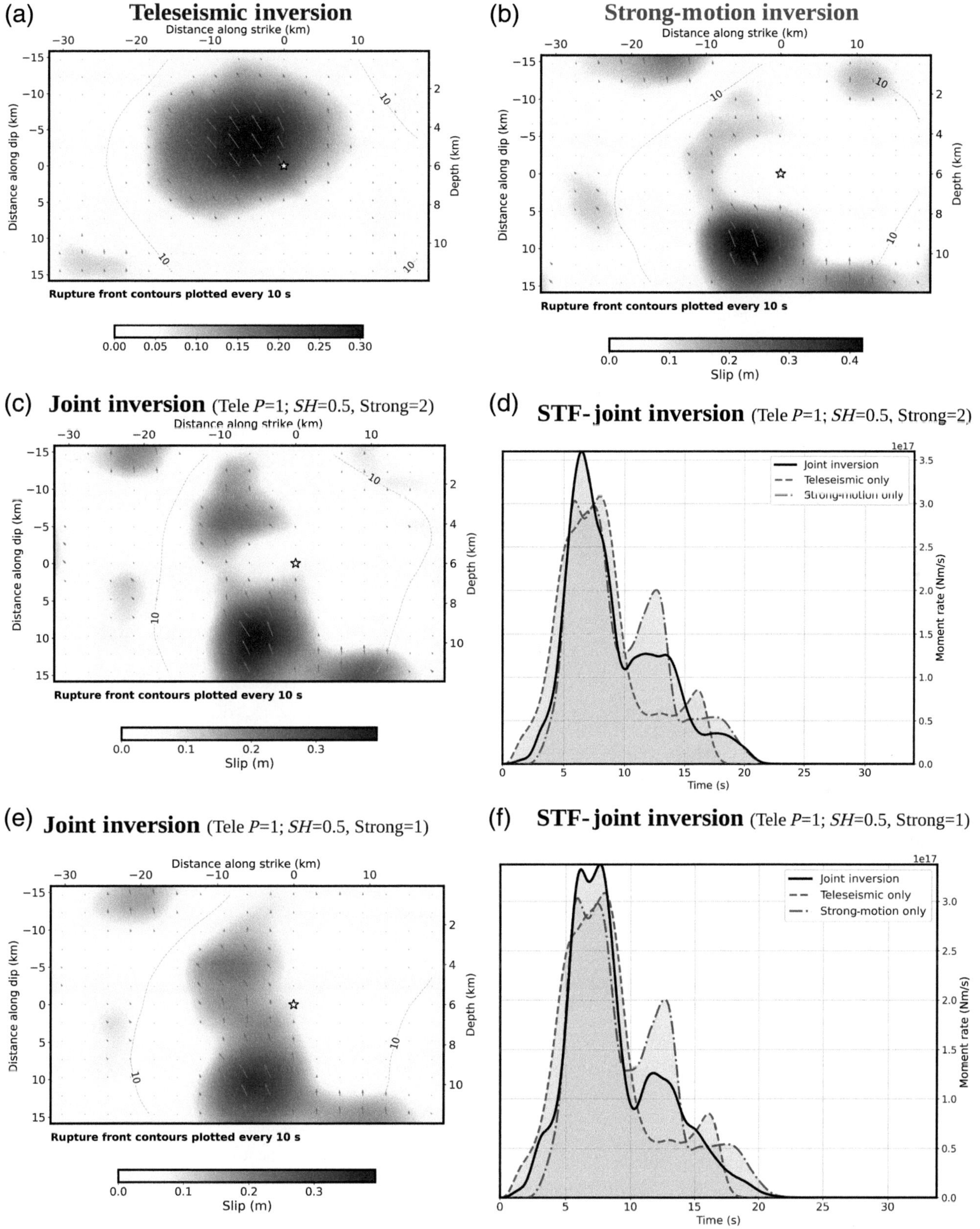

Figure 5. Sensitivity results of the AF7 finite-fault solution. (a) Teleseismic-only inversion. (b) Strong-motion-only inversion. (c) Joint inversion using Goldberg *et al.* (2022) weights (P = 1, SH = 0.5, strong = 2). (d) Source time functions (STFs) for panels (a–c): blue dashed = teleseismic-only, red dashed = strong-motion-only, black = joint. (e) Joint inversion with the strong-motion weight reduced to 1. (f) STFs for panel (e) shown together with the single-dataset results for reference (same color scheme as in panel d). The color version of this figure is available only in the electronic edition.

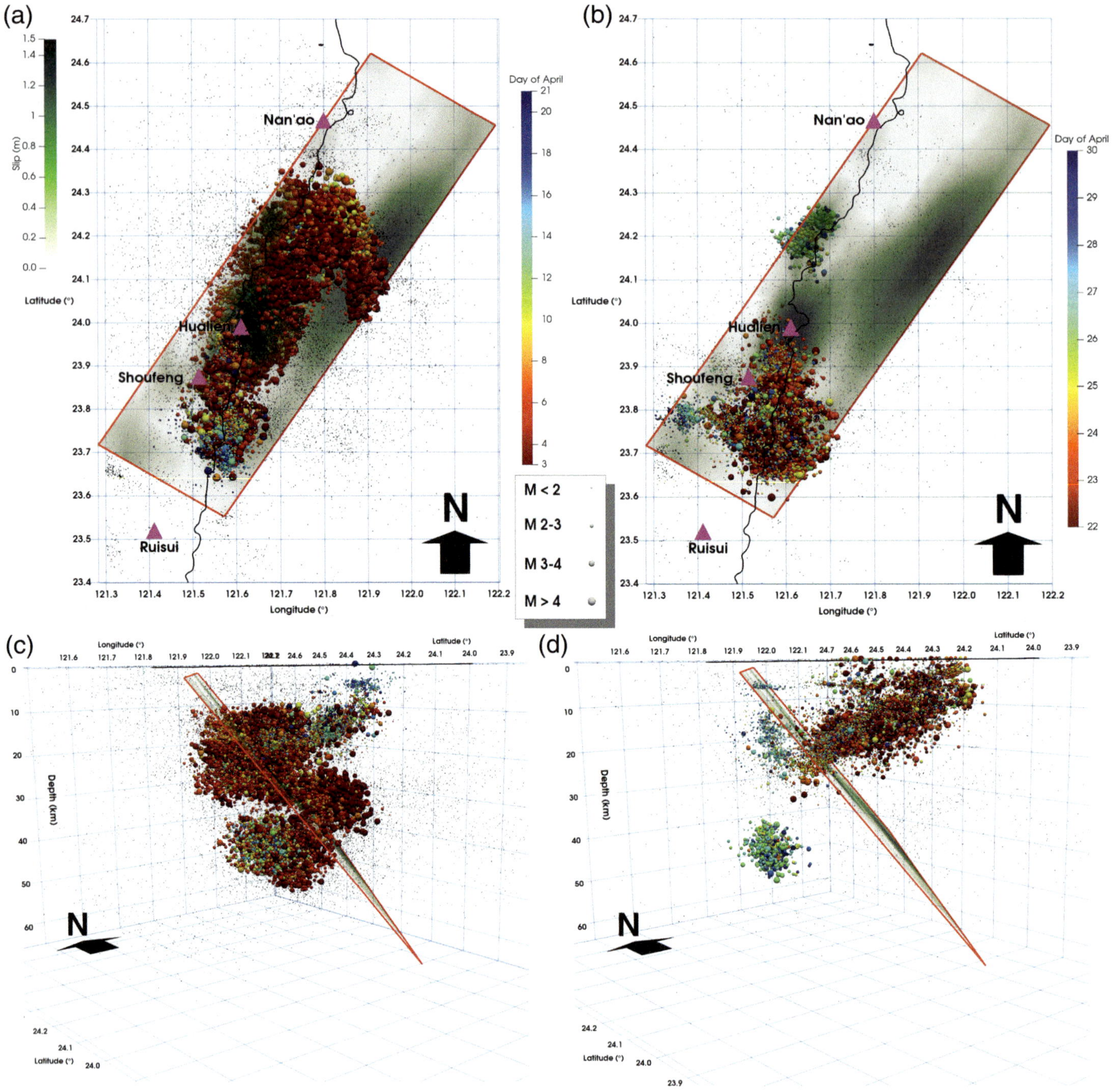

not assigned to clusters by DBSCAN) are displayed in black dots (Fig. 6).

The results reveal distinctive spatial distributions for two primary clusters: the immediate AFs of the 2 April mainshock (Fig. 6a,b) and those that began on 22 April (Fig. 6c,d). For reference, we also present our unpublished east-dipping finite-fault solution for the mainshock in Figure 6. In the first primary cluster, AFs initially appeared along the southern and northern boundaries of the asperity. Whereas the northern cluster continued propagating northward, the southern cluster ceased—consistent with the observed northward slip propagation. Around mid-April, additional events were observed propagating southward along both the upper and lower boundaries of the asperity. Notably, the main asperities correspond to regions devoid of clusters. In the second primary cluster, most events

Figure 6. Spatiotemporal distribution of clusters based on the VELEST catalog. (a) Map view and (c) northeastward vertical projection of the first primary clusters. Panels (b) and (d) same as panels (a) and (c) but for the second primary clusters, which began on 22 April. Circles represent clustered events with sizes indicating M_L and are color coded by the day of occurrence in April. The east-dipping finite-fault solution for the mainshock is shown for reference. Nonclustered events, considered noise, are shown as black dots. The magenta triangles denote nearby cities for reference.

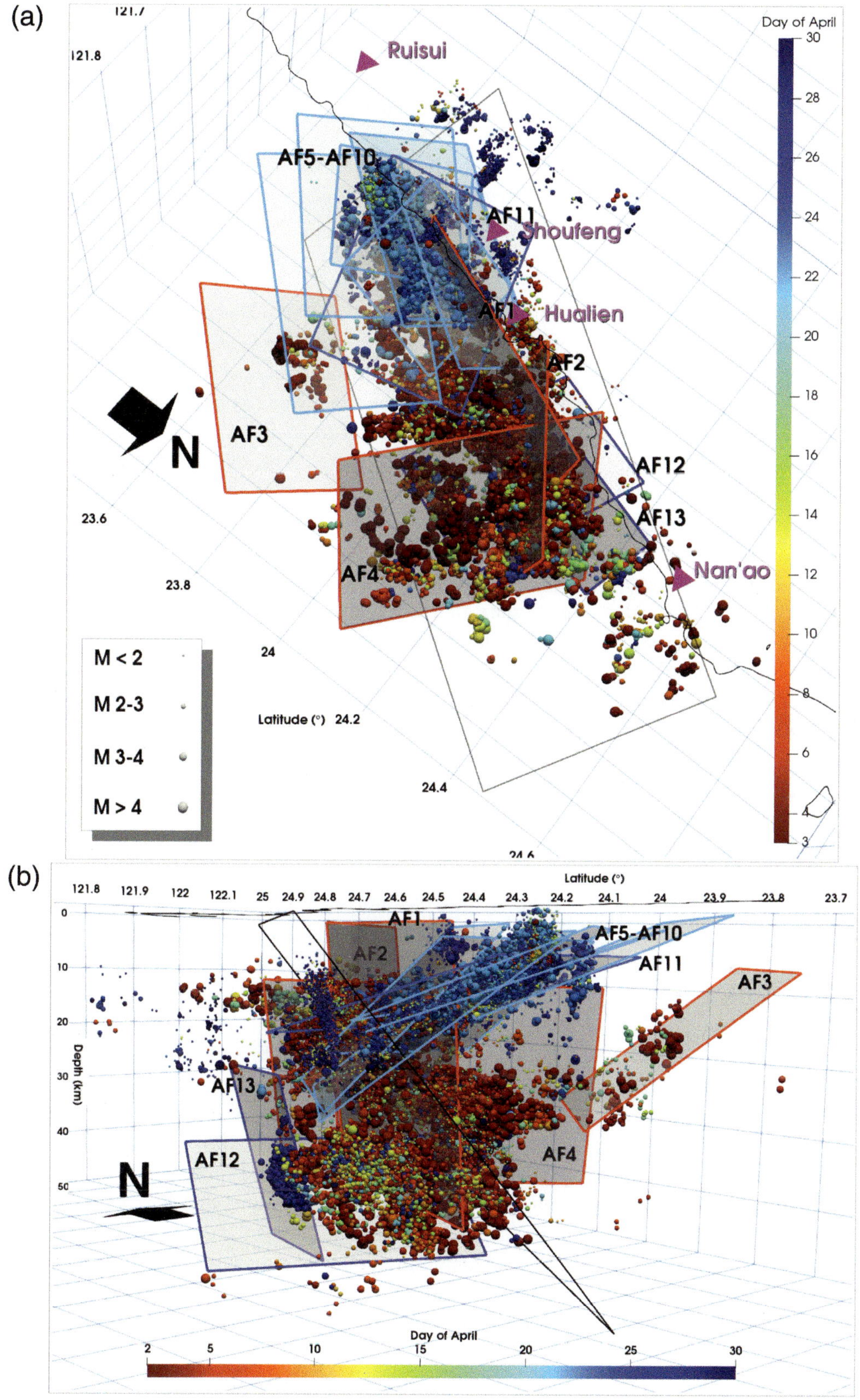

Figure 7. (a) 3D distribution of earthquakes in the HypoDD catalog. The circles represent earthquake events, with their sizes indicating local magnitude (M_L) as shown in the legend. Colors correspond to the day of occurrence in April. The determined fault planes of AFs are included for reference, with the borders of the boxes also color coded by day of occurrence in April. The magenta triangles denote nearby cities. The east-dipping mainshock fault plane is outlined in black for reference. (b) Same as panel (a), but viewed from a different perspective.

occurred within a confined area at depths shallower than 20 km and were tightly clustered in time. This spatiotemporal characteristic leads us to interpret the second primary cluster as a swarm activity triggered by the mainshock sequence. A smaller cluster also emerged to the north at greater depth (~40 km) near the end of April, hosting AF12 and AF13 (Fig. 6c,d and Table 1).

The HypoDD catalog exhibits a significant reduction in the number of events because only those associated with spatial clusters were retained. In addition, the distributions are highly concentrated, reflecting the use of relative travel times to ensure robust relative locations. By examining these distributions in 3D space, we found that most clusters are associated with the occurrence of AFs. The event distributions not only serve as proxies aligned along the determined fault planes but are also temporally correlated (Fig. 7). This finding provides valuable insights for determining the fault planes of AFs.

Finite-fault solutions of significant aftershocks

The determination of fault planes for the 13 significant AFs (Fig. 7) reveals a clear spatial pattern: steeply east-dipping faults are observed in significant AFs located to the north, either associated with the northern first primary cluster or the small cluster that emerged at the end of April, whereas shallowly west-dipping faults are observed in significant AFs to the south, associated with either the southern first primary cluster or the swarm cluster (Fig. 2). Notably, all significant AFs (AF5–AF11) in the second primary cluster (swarm) exhibit west-dipping faults. The result for AF12 is not well constrained because of its centroid depth of 45 km and the limited number of events within the seismogenic thickness that exhibit a concentrated distribution (Fig. 4).

After determining the fault planes, teleseismic body waves and near-field strong-motion data are used to invert the finite-fault solutions of the significant AFs. We present the results for the largest significant AFs from the first primary cluster (AF1) in Figure 8 and the second primary cluster (AF7) in Figure 9. Notably, the teleseismic body waves of significant AFs in the first primary cluster (AF1–AF4) are contaminated by surface waves from preceding events (Fig. 8) and are therefore excluded from the inversion. Finally, the spatial distribution of asperities for the significant AFs is illustrated in Figure 10.

Overall, the jackknife ensemble indicates low spatial and temporal uncertainties for the significant AFs. However, for AF3 and AF4, the jackknife STFs exhibit comparatively larger dispersion. Both events were inverted using strong-motion records only, with <25 waveforms, which weakened temporal constraints and led to greater variability in the STFs. By contrast, AF1 was inverted with 43 strong-motion records, yielding 43 jackknife models. The resulting STF ensemble is tightly clustered, with only minor variability near ~5 s, demonstrating that strong-motion-only inversions can provide robust temporal constraints when record counts are sufficient. Spatial resolution is also generally robust: across events, most high-slip subfaults are well resolved, with relative uncertainty below 20% of slip along the fault plane. For AF7, we performed a joint inversion of teleseismic body waves and strong-motion data, producing 103 jackknife models. The STF ensemble shows low overall dispersion with a slight increase near ~12 s, likely reflecting misfits in a subset of body-wave traces at that time. Spatially, the slip model remains stable, with high-slip subfaults again meeting the <20% criterion along the fault plane.

DISCUSSION

Both advancements in seismic instrument design (e.g., SmartSolo) and data analysis techniques (e.g., PhaseNet and REAL) have made the rapid deployment of comprehensive AF monitoring feasible, as demonstrated in this study. On the operational side, we can share some valuable experience for immediate earthquake response in the future. First, major earthquakes often exhibit rupture directivity, which influences the spatial distribution of AFs. For the 2024 Hualien earthquake, the primary AF cluster was located mostly to the north of the hypocenter, consistent with its northward rupture directivity. As a result, paying close attention to the location of early AFs and incorporating this information into the design of the temporary network can help optimize AF capture. Second, the geometry of the seismic network should ideally extend along two perpendicular lines to better constrain earthquake locations. In this study, the north–south linear configuration of the NCUSN reduced the east–west resolution for locating AFs, which partly motivated us to incorporate data from the GDMS and BATS networks. Another important factor was that SmartSolo instruments tended to clip during nearby strong earthquakes, limiting their effectiveness in certain scenarios. The lessons learned from these experiences significantly improved our response to the 2025 M_L 6.4 Dapu earthquake in southwest Taiwan (manuscript in preparation).

The 2024 Hualien earthquake sequence is complex in two aspects: (1) The seismic and geodetic data of the mainshock cannot be explained by rupture on a single fault plane. This is the main reason we do not report a finite-fault solution for the mainshock, although one is shown for reference. (2) The AF sequence is atypical because it does not follow the expected decay in magnitude and frequency over time. In this study, we do not attempt to analyze the rupture of the mainshock directly; instead, we focus on comprehensive monitoring of the AF sequence and the finite-fault solutions of significant AFs. The AF monitoring not only establishes the spatiotemporal characteristics of the first and second primary clusters (based on the VELEST catalog), but it also provides a dataset with more precise relative locations (based on the HypoDD catalog). Both datasets are validated by the recall rate and the spatial distribution resemblance of the CWA-matched events (Fig. 2). Furthermore, the HypoDD catalog allows us to distinguish the fault plane from the nodal planes by comparing the number and distribution of events within the seismogenic thickness. Given the stark contrasts observed in most AFs, we consider the results to be robust.

For the second aspect, we identify a swarm-like secondary cluster, consisting of significant earthquakes (AF5–AF11) that predominantly exhibit shallowly west-dipping fault planes. This cluster coincides spatially with the 2021 Shoufeng series in April, which began with M_L 5.8 and 6.2 events, followed by ~500 AFs that also indicate a west-dipping plane (Huang and Wang, 2022; Hwang *et al.*, 2022). Similarly, the CWA catalog records >500 monthly events within the same region in 1991, 2013, and 2020, suggesting that Shoufeng is prone to earthquake swarms and that such activity may be triggered by nearby significant earthquakes. During the 2024 Hualien earthquake sequence, the observed southward propagation of AFs in mid-April 2024 may have contributed to triggering the swarm in Shoufeng. Although the mechanisms and triggers of these swarms remain intriguing topics for further study, the observations support attributing the secondary cluster to swarm activity and justify its exclusion from discussions of the 2024 Hualien mainshock series.

For the first aspect, although there is consensus that the mainshock fault plane(s) cannot be represented by a single planar fault (Cheloni *et al.*, 2024; Zheng *et al.*, 2024), whether the main asperity should be attributed to the east-dipping or west-dipping nodal plane of the point-source solution remains an open question, largely because of its offshore location east of Taiwan and the predominantly northward rupture. Given

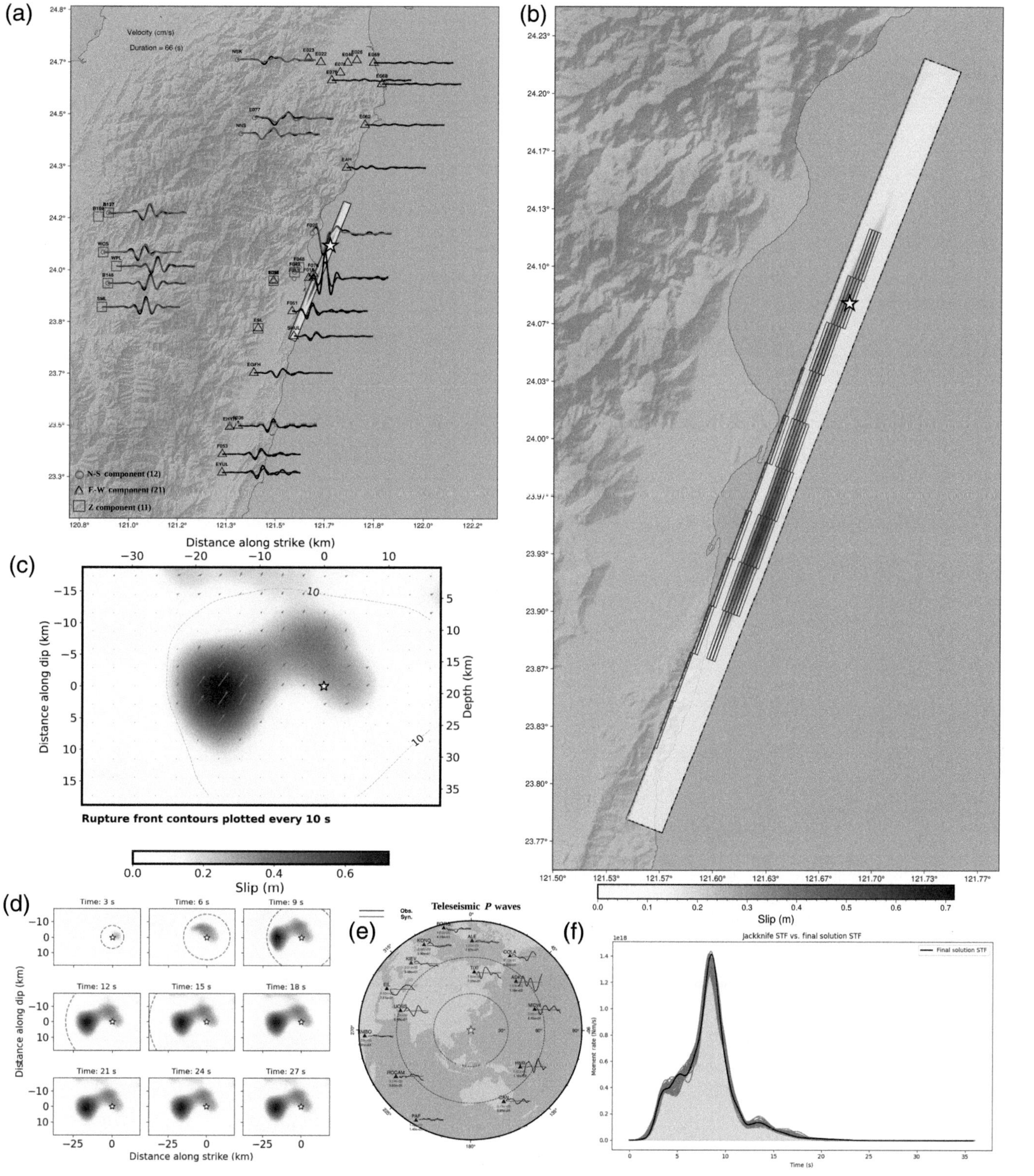

Figure 8. Finite-fault solution for the east-dipping plane of AF1. (a) Surface projection of the solution, including a comparison with strong-motion records: black lines denote observations; red, blue, and pink lines represent synthetic seismograms for the vertical (Z), east–west (E-W), and north–south (N-S) components, respectively. Symbols at station locations indicate the component(s) used. (b) Zoomed surface projection of the solution. Green rectangles outline subfaults with robust estimates, for which the jackknife uncertainty (standard deviation) is <20% of the slip on that subfault. (c) Slip distribution displayed on the fault plane. Whereas the y axis on the left corresponds to depth from the hypocenter, the right indicates depth from the surface. (d) Time evolution of propagating wavefronts and accumulated slip (scale in panel c). (e) Comparison between observed teleseismic P waves (black) and synthetics (red). Note that data are contaminated and were excluded from the inversion. (f) STF. The thick-black curve is the preferred solution using the complete dataset; gray curves are leave-one-out jackknife realizations ($n = 43$), showing temporal uncertainty. The color version of this figure is available only in the electronic edition.

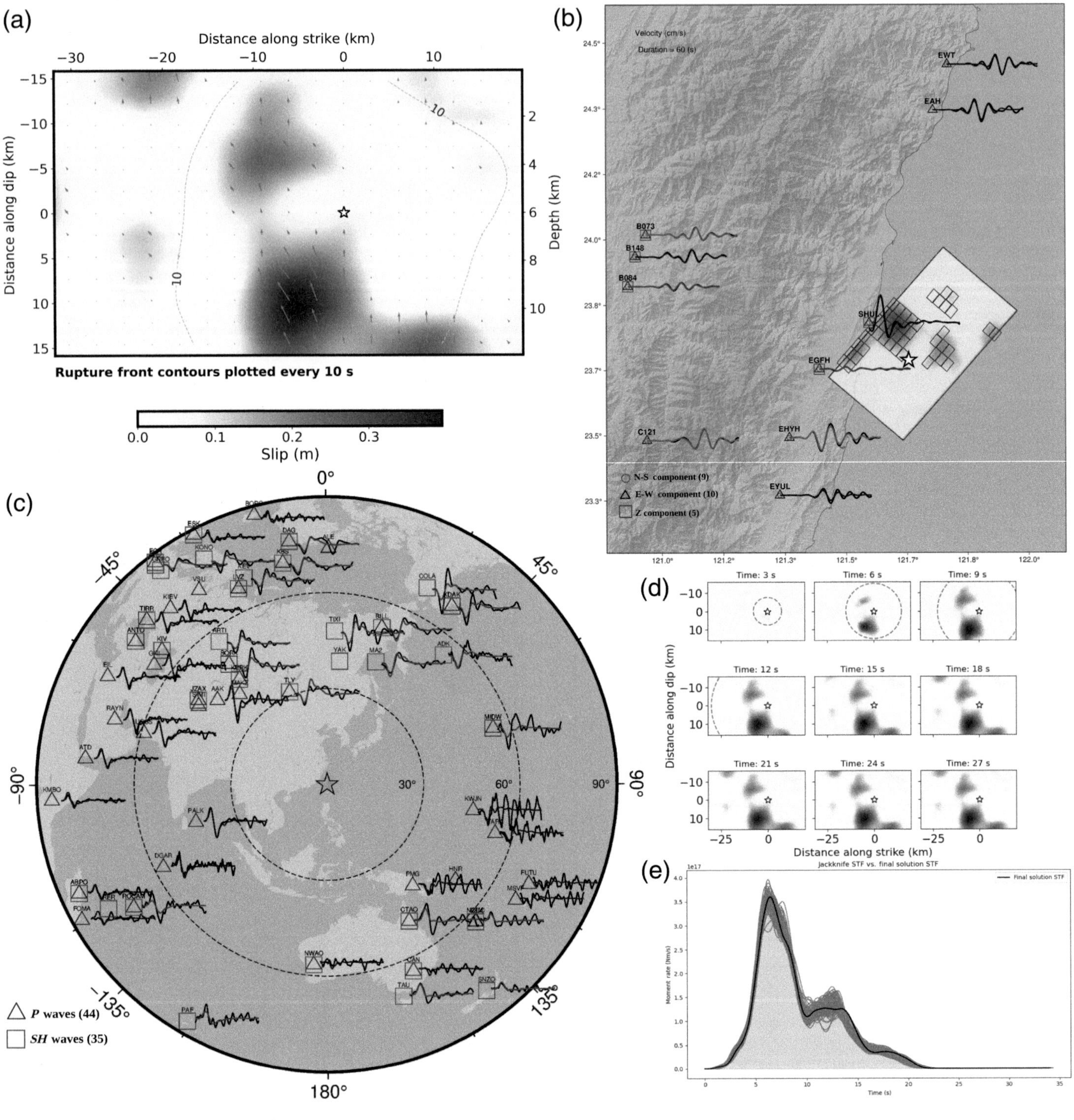

Figure 9. Finite-fault solution for the west-dipping plane of AF7. (a) Slip distribution displayed on the fault plane. The *y* axis on the left corresponds to depth from the hypocenter, whereas the right indicates depth from the surface. (b) Surface projection of the solution, including a comparison with strong-motion records: black lines denote observations; red, blue, and pink lines represent synthetic seismograms for the vertical (Z), east–west (E-W), and north–south (N-S) components, respectively. Symbols at station locations indicate the component(s) used. Green rectangles outline subfaults with robust estimates, for which the jackknife uncertainty (standard deviation) is <20% of the slip on that subfault. (c) Comparison between observed (black) teleseismic body waves and synthetics (colored by data type). (d) Time evolution of propagating wavefronts and accumulated slip (scale in panel a). (e) STF. The thick-black curve is the preferred solution using the complete dataset; gray curves are leave-one-out jackknife realizations ($n = 103$), showing temporal uncertainty. The color version of this figure is available only in the electronic edition.

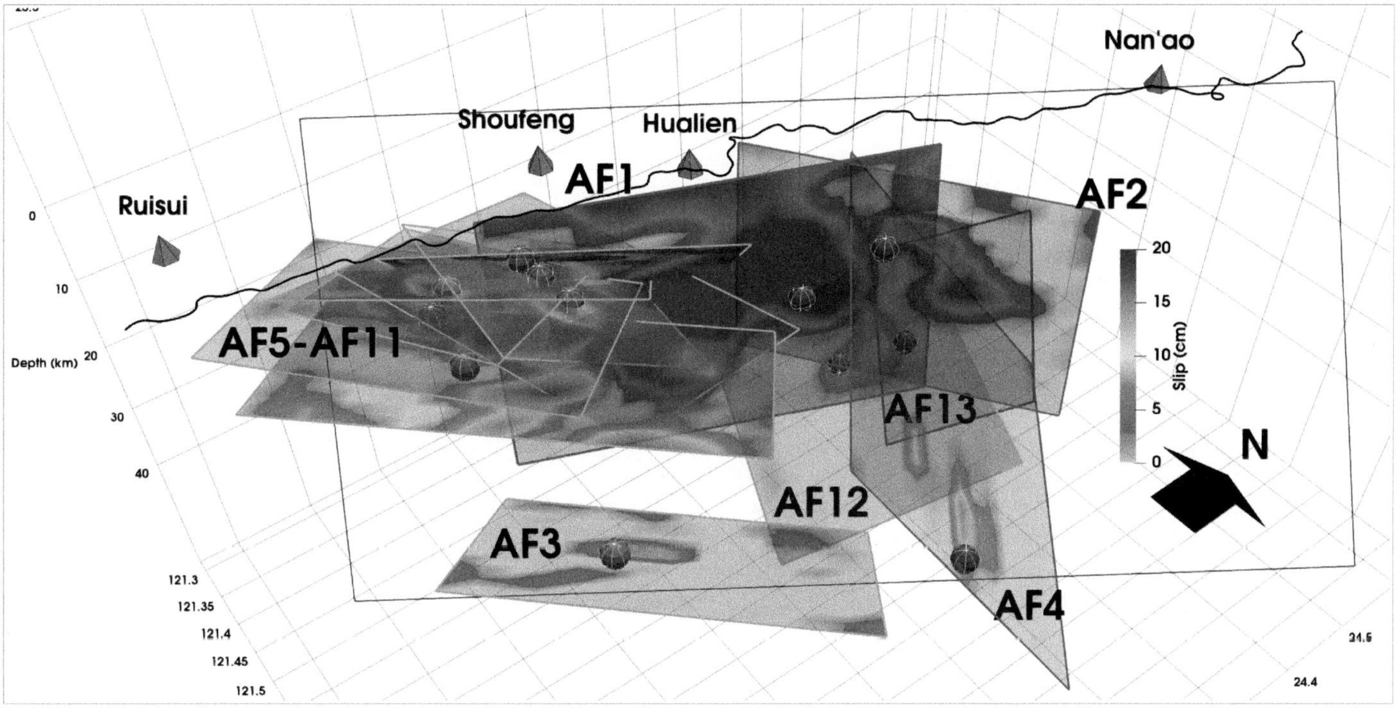

Figure 10. Spatial distribution of asperity of significant AFs. The east-dipping faults are outlined in magenta, and the west-dipping faults are outlined in green. For reference, the east-dipping mainshock fault plane is highlighted with a black border. The colored surface shows slip (cm). Spheres mark hypocenters of significant AFs, color coded to match their preferred fault plane. Cyan cones denote nearby cities for reference. The color version of this figure is available only in the electronic edition.

the steeply east-dipping fault plane of AF1 and AF2, we attribute the east-dipping nodal plane as the major fault plane of mainshock. The attribution is supported by the following observations. First, the east-dipping nodal plane spatially correspond to the Milun and Lingding segments of the east-dipping LVF (Chen *et al.*, 2007), for which structural features are inferred from an east-dipping seismicity plane at depths of 10–30 km depth (fig. 6 in Huang and Wang, 2022). Second, the steeply dipping fault planes of AF1 and AF2 at shallow depths are consistent with the listric geometry of an east-dipping fault. In any case, in relation to the recent LV earthquake sequence that occurred along the conjugated CRF and LVF (Fig. 1), the mainshock asperity coincides with, and effectively fills, a recognized seismic gap in the region.

Recent publications on the mainshock of the 2024 Hualien earthquake, such as that by Cheloni *et al.* (2024), have proposed a composite fault model involving a major segment of the CRF and a deeper segment of the LVF. In the development of their four-segment fault model, the location of the second primary cluster is interpreted as a 70° east-dipping fault (F2). However, our observations indicate a shallowly west-dipping fault for events AF5–AF11. Furthermore, if the second primary cluster indeed represents a triggered swarm activity, its inclusion in the inversion used to fit coseismic data may not be appropriate. Regarding the east-dipping blind listric fault proposed by Zheng *et al.* (2024), comparisons of AF distribution should exclude events from the second primary cluster. Analyzing the dip angle as a function of centroid depth for the immediate significant AFs (AF1, AF2, and AF4), we find that AF1 and AF2, which occurred at shallow depths, exhibit steep dip angles. However, the east-dipping listric feature likely does not extend south of the hypocenter because the AFs in that region rupture on a west-dipping fault.

CONCLUSIONS

By integrating data from the temporary SmartSolo array in Hualien with those from the permanent network and applying automated phase-picking and earthquake location algorithms, we are able to monitor the 2024 M_w 7.4 Hualien earthquake sequence more comprehensively. The resulting catalog contains an order of magnitude more events than the CWA catalog. Cluster analysis reveals distinctive spatiotemporal characteristics: whereas the first primary cluster is associated with immediate AFs of the mainshock, the second primary cluster is spatially and temporally confined, likely representing a triggered swarm activity. The double-difference relocated events exhibit highly concentrated patterns corresponding to the locations of the identified significant AFs and are therefore used to determine the respective fault planes for finite-fault solution inversions. The inferred fault planes show a clear spatial pattern: whereas east-dipping faults are predominantly located in the northern region and are steeply dipping, west-dipping faults are found to the south and exhibit shallower dips. Finally, we present the spatial distribution of asperities for the significant AFs and examine previously published studies on the mainshock kinematics in light of the insights gained from our AF analysis.

DATA AND RESOURCES

The hypocenters of the mainshock and aftershocks were obtained from the Recent Earthquake Report of the Central Weather Administration (CWA; https://www.cwa.gov.tw/V8/E/E/index.html), the Real-Time Moment Tensor Monitoring System (RMT) solutions from http://rmt.earth.sinica.edu.tw, and seismic waveform data from the Incorporated Research Institutions for Seismology Data Management Center (IRIS-DMC; http://www.iris.washington.edu). Please consult the corresponding author for the REAL, VELEST, and HypoDD catalogs. Some plots were created using the Generic Mapping Tools (GMT; Wessel *et al.*, 2019) and ParaView (Ayachit, 2015). All websites were last accessed in September 2024. The supplemental material includes procedures for magnitude calibration (Supplement I), waveform preprocessing and fault geometry setup for finite-fault inversions (Supplement II), and waveform fits and slip distributions for significant aftershocks (Supplement III).

DECLARATION OF COMPETING INTERESTS

The authors acknowledge that there are no conflicts of interest recorded.

ACKNOWLEDGMENTS

The authors thank Editor-in-Chief P. Martin Mai and the two anonymous reviewers for their constructive comments. The authors also appreciate the insightful discussions with Dimas S. J. Sianipar. The authors acknowledge the Central Weather Administration (CWA; Central Weather Administration [CWA, Taiwan] 2012) for providing Geophysical Data Management System (GDMS) data (https://gdms.cwa.gov.tw, last accessed September 2024) and the Institute of Earth Sciences, Academia Sinica, Taiwan (1996) for providing Broadband Array in Taiwan for Seismology (BATS) data (https://bats.earth.sinica.edu.tw, last accessed September 2024). This work was supported by the Taiwan Earthquake Research Center (TEC), funded through the National Science and Technology Council (NSTC) of Taiwan with Grant Number 114-2923-M-008-002. The TEC Contribution Number for this article is 00205. Additional support was provided by the Industrial Technology Research Institute in Taiwan under Grant Number FY114-4.

REFERENCES

Ayachit, U. (2015). *The Paraview Guide: A Parallel Visualization Application*, Vol. 303, Kitware, Clifton Park, New York.

Central Weather Administration (CWA, Taiwan) (2012). Central weather administration seismographic network [Data set], *International Federation of Digital Seismograph Networks*, doi: 10.7914/SN/T5.

Cheloni, D., N. A. Famiglietti, R. Caputo, C. Tolomei, and A. Vicari (2024). A composite Fault Model for the 2024 MW 7.4 Hualien earthquake sequence in Eastern Taiwan inferred from GNSS and InSAR data, *Geophys. Res. Lett.* **51,** no. 20, doi: 10.1029/2024GL110255.

Chen, K. H., I. Chen, and A. Kim (2016). Can slip heterogeneity be linked to earthquake recurrence? *Geophys. Res. Lett.* **43,** no. 13, 6916–6923, doi: 10.1002/2016gl069516.

Chen, K. H., S. Toda, and R. Rau (2008). A leaping, triggered sequence along a segmented fault: The 1951 ML 7.3 Hualien-Taitung earthquake sequence in Eastern Taiwan, *J. Geophys. Res.* **113,** no. B2, doi: 10.1029/2007JB005048.

Chen, W., I. Yen, K. Fengler, C. Rubin, C. Yang, H. Yang, H. Chang, C. Lin, W. Lin, and Y. Liu (2007). Late Holocene paleoearthquake activity in the middle part of the Longitudinal Valley fault, eastern Taiwan, *Earth Planet. Sci. Lett.* **264,** nos. 3/4, 420–437, doi: 10.1016/j.epsl.2007.09.043.

Chi, W., and D. Dreger (2004). Crustal deformation in Taiwan: Results from finite source inversions of six Mw > 5.8 Chi-Chi aftershocks, *J. Geophys. Res.* **109,** no. B7, doi: 10.1029/2003jb002606.

Goldberg, D. E., P. Koch, D. Melgar, S. Riquelme, and W. L. Yeck (2022). Beyond the teleseism: Introducing regional seismic and geodetic data into routine USGS finite-fault modeling, *Seismol. Res. Lett.* **93,** no. 6, doi: 10.1785/0220220047.

Guan, P., J. Lei, and D. Zhao (2024). Machine-learning based location of the 2021 MW 7.4 Maduo, Qinghai, China earthquake sequence: Insight into intraplate seismogenesis, *Tectonophysics* **888,** doi: 10.1016/j.tecto.2024.230458.

Huang, H., and Y. Wang (2022). Seismogenic structure beneath the northern Longitudinal Valley revealed by the 2018–2021 Hualien earthquake sequences and 3-D velocity model, *Terr. Atmos. Ocean. Sci.* **33,** no. 1, doi: 10.1007/s44195-022-00017-z.

Hwang, R., Y. Huang, W. Chang, C. Lin, C. Lin, S. Wang, J. Chan, J. Chang, and T. Lin (2022). Radiated seismic energy from the 2021 ML 5.8 and ML 6.2 Shoufeng (Hualien), Taiwan, earthquakes and their aftershocks, *Terres. Atmos. Ocean. Sci.* **33,** no. 1, doi: 10.1007/s44195-022-00020-4.

Institute of Earth Sciences, Academia Sinica, Taiwan (1996). *Broadband Array in Taiwan for Seismology*, Institute of Earth Sciences, Academia Sinica, Taipei, Taiwan, Other/Seismic Network, doi: 10.7914/SN/TW.

Ji, C., D. J. Wald, and D. V. Helmberger (2002). Source description of the 1999 Hector Mine, California, earthquake, part I: Wavelet domain inversion theory and resolution analysis, *Bull. Seismol. Soc. Am.* **92,** no. 4, 1192–1207, doi: 10.1785/0120000916.

Kissling, E., W. L. Ellsworth, D. Eberhart-Phillips, and U. Kradolfer (1994). Initial reference models in local earthquake tomography, *Seismology* **99,** no. B10, 19,635–19,646, doi: 10.1029/93JB03138.

Kriegel, H., P. Kröger, J. Sander, and A. Zimek (2011). Density-based clustering, *WIREs Data Min. Knowl. Discov.* **1,** no. 3, 231–240, doi: 10.1002/widm.30.

Lee, S., W. Liang, H. Cheng, F. Tu, K. Ma, H. Tsuruoka, H. Kawakatsu, B. Huang, and C. Liu (2014). Towards real-time regional earthquake simulation I: Real-time moment tensor monitoring (RMT) for regional events in Taiwan, *Geophys. J. Int.* **196,** no. 1, 432–446, doi: 10.1093/gji/ggt371.

Lee, S., T. Lin, T. Liu, and T. Wong (2019). Fault-to-fault jumping rupture of the 2018 Mw 6.4 Hualien earthquake in Eastern Taiwan, *Seismol. Res. Lett.* **90,** no. 1, doi: 10.1785/0220180182.

Lee, S., T. Liu, and T. Lin (2023). The role of the west-dipping collision Boundary Fault in the Taiwan 2022 Chihshang earthquake sequence, *Sci. Rep.* **13,** no. 3552, doi: 10.1038/s41598-023-30361-0.

Lin, Y., Y. Wen, and Y. Yen (2022). Source properties of the 2019 ML 6.3 Hualien, Taiwan, Earthquake, determined by the local strong motion networks, *Geophys. J. Int.* **229,** no. 3, 1665–1679, doi: 10.1093/gji/ggac003.

Liu, M., M. Zhang, W. Zhu, W. L. Ellsworth, and H. Li (2020). Rapid characterization of the July 2019 Ridgecrest, California, earthquake sequence from raw seismic data using machine-learning phase picker, *Geophys. Res. Lett.* **47,** no. 4, e2019GL086189, doi: 10.1029/2019gl086189.

Shin, T. (1993). The calculation of local magnitude from the simulated Wood-Anderson seismograms of the short-period seismograms in the Taiwan Area, *Terr. Atmos. Ocean. Sci.* **4,** no. 2, 155–170, doi: 10.3319/TAO.1993.4.2.155(T).

Shyu, J. B. H., K. Sieh, Y.-G. Chen, and L.-H. Chung (2006). Geomorphic analysis of the Central Range fault, the second major active structure of the Longitudinal Valley suture, eastern Taiwan, *Geol. Soc. Am. Bull.* **118,** nos. 11/12, 1447–1462, doi: 10.1130/b25905.1.

Sianipar, D., B. Huang, K.-F. Ma, M. Hsieh, and P. Chen (2022). Similarities in the rupture process and cascading asperities between neighboring fault patches and seismic implications: The 2002–2009 Sumbawa (Indonesia) earthquakes with moment magnitudes of 6.2–6.6, *J. Asian Earth Sci.* **229,** doi: 10.1016/j.jseaes.2022.105167.

Tang, C., Y. Lin, H. Tung, Y. Wang, S. Lee, Y. Hsu, J. B. H. Shyu, Y. Kuo, and H. Chen (2023). Nearby Fault interaction within the Double-Vergence Suture in Eastern Taiwan during the 2022 Chihshang earthquake, *Commun. Earth Environ.* **4,** no. 333, doi: 10.1038/s43247-023-00994-0.

Waldhauser, F., and W. L. Ellsworth (2000). A double-difference earthquake location algorithm: Method and application to the Northern Hayward Fault, California, *Bull. Seismol. Soc. Am.* **90,** no. 6, 1353–1368, doi: 10.1785/0120000006.

Wessel, P., J. F. Luis, L. Uieda, R. Scharroo, F. Wobbe, W. H. F. Smith, and D. Tian (2019). The generic mapping tools version 6, *Geochem. Geophys. Geosys.* **20,** no. 11, 5556–5564.

Wu, W., L. Zhao, and Y. Wu (2013). Empirical relationships between aftershock zone dimensions and moment magnitudes for plate boundary earthquakes in Taiwan, *Bull. Seismol. Soc. Am.* **103,** no. 1, 424–436, doi: 10.1785/0120120173.

Wu, Y., Y. Chen, C. Chang, L. Chung, T. Teng, F. T. Wu, and C. Wu (2006). Seismogenic structure in a tectonic suture zone: With new constraints from 2006 Mw 6.1 Taitung earthquake, *Geophys. Res. Lett.* **33,** no. 22, doi: 10.1029/2006GL027572.

Zhang, M., W. L. Ellsworth, and G. Beroza (2019). Rapid earthquake association and location, *Seismol. Res. Lett.* **90,** no. 6, 2276–2284, doi: 10.1785/0220190052.

Zhang, M., T. Feng, R. Wang, and W. Zhu (2022). LOC-FLOW: An end-to-end machine learning-based high-precision earthquake location workflow, *Seismol. Res. Lett.* **93,** no. 5, 2426–2438, doi: 10.1785/0220220019.

Zhang, Y., R. Wang, J. Zschau, Y. Chen, S. Parolai, and T. Dahm (2014). Automatic imaging of earthquake rupture processes by iterative deconvolution and stacking of high-rate GPS and strong motion seismograms, *J. Geophys. Res.* **119,** no. 7, 5633–5650, doi: 10.1002/2013JB010469.

Zheng, A., X. Yu, C. Bai, W. Xu, J. Qian, W. Zhang, and X. Chen (2024). Thrust-dominated unilateral rupture of a blind Listric Fault associated with the 2024 Hualien earthquake, *Sci. Rep.* **14,** doi: 10.1038/s41598-024-82971-x.

Zheng, X., Y. Zhang, R. Wang, L. Zhao, W. Li, and Q. Huang (2020). Automatic inversions of strong-motion records for finite-fault models of significant earthquakes in and around Japan, *J. Geophys. Res.* **125,** no. 9, doi: 10.1029/2020jb019992.

Zhu, W., and G. Beroza (2019). PhaseNet: A deep-neural-network-based seismic arrival-time picking method, *Geophys. J. Int.* **216,** no. 1, 261–273, doi: 10.1093/gji/ggy423.

Zhu, W., I. W. McBrearty, S. M. Mousavi, W. L. Ellsworth, and G. C. Beroza (2022). Earthquake phase association using a Bayesian Gaussian mixture model, *J. Geophys. Res.* **127,** no. 5, doi: 10.1029/2021jb023249.

Manuscript received 15 May 2025
Published online 15 October 2025

Earthquake Directivity and Early Warning: The Response of *P*-Alert Network to the 2024 M_W 7.4 Hualien Event

Benjamin M. Yang[1], Himanshu Mittal[2], and Yih-Min Wu[*1,3]

ABSTRACT

On 2 April 2024, a major earthquake with a moment magnitude (M_w) of 7.4 struck the Hualien area of eastern Taiwan. Because of a significant directivity effect, with the rupture propagating from the south-southwest to the north-northeast direction, the earthquake caused damage, including in the Taipei metropolitan area, which is located approximately 120 km north of the epicenter. The Central Weather Administration (CWA) earthquake early warning (EEW) system issued two Public Warning Service alerts at 8 and 14 s after the earthquake's origin. However, the system underestimated both the earthquake magnitude and ground-motion intensity in northern Taiwan, excluding the densely populated Taipei metropolitan area from the alerts. In contrast, the high-density *P*-Alert network, maintained by National Taiwan University, offered onsite EEW, delivering at least 3 s of lead time for areas near the epicenter and compensating for the missed warnings in the Taipei metropolitan area. The *P*-Alert network also generated detailed real-time shakemaps within 2.5 min, significantly aiding disaster response efforts and identifying the rupture's directivity. Finally, testing of the *ShakingAlarm* demonstrated its effectiveness in filling the gap left by the CWA regional EEW system, providing an additional warning for the Taipei metropolitan area. This research demonstrates the critical role of the *P*-Alert network in addressing the challenges posed by the earthquake's directivity effect and enhancing early warning effectiveness.

KEY POINTS

- This study addresses early warning challenges from the directivity effect of the 0403 Hualien earthquake.
- The *P*-Alert network provided onsite and ground-motion model-based warnings, compensating for missed alerts.
- A high-density seismic network could improve resource allocation and earthquake resilience.

INTRODUCTION

The earthquake early warning (EEW) system is critical for mitigating earthquake-related damage. By monitoring the initial seismic waves in real time, the system can quickly estimate the earthquake information and issue timely alerts to areas likely to be affected. This provides the public with valuable time to evacuate and take protective action, thereby significantly mitigating disaster-related losses. Taiwan is one of the leading countries in the world in implementing and operating a formal EEW system that issues public alerts (Wu *et al.*, 2021). Located at the junction of the Eurasian plate (EP) and the Philippine Sea plate (PSP), the geological structures of Taiwan are highly complex, making it vulnerable to frequent earthquakes (Fig. 1). The region experiences hundreds of earthquakes of varying magnitudes annually. Throughout recorded history, Taiwan has experienced numerous large earthquakes, resulting in significant casualties and property damage. The 15 November 1986 earthquake (M_w 7.4), despite its epicenter in the Hualien area, caused severe damage in the Taipei metropolitan area, 120 km away from the epicenter. This event further emphasized the need for a robust EEW system, prompting Taiwanese authorities to invest significantly in the development of EEW systems (Wu *et al.*, 1998, 1999).

Nearly 40 yrs later, on 2 April 2024 at 23:58:10 UTC, a major earthquake struck the Hualien area once again (hereafter referred to as the 0403 Hualien earthquake, according to the

1. Department of Geosciences, National Taiwan University, Taipei, Taiwan, https://orcid.org/0000-0003-2954-1997 (BMY); https://orcid.org/0000-0003-4542-1741 (Y-MW); 2. National Center for Seismology, Ministry of Earth Sciences, New Delhi, India, https://orcid.org/0000-0001-8836-2919 (HM); 3. Institute of Earth Sciences, Academia Sinica, Taipei, Taiwan

*Corresponding author: drymwu@ntu.edu.tw

Cite this article as Yang, B. M., H. Mittal, and Y.-M. Wu (2025). Earthquake Directivity and Early Warning: The Response of *P*-Alert Network to the 2024 M_w 7.4 Hualien Event, *Bull. Seismol. Soc. Am.* **116**, 68–79, doi: 10.1785/0120250076

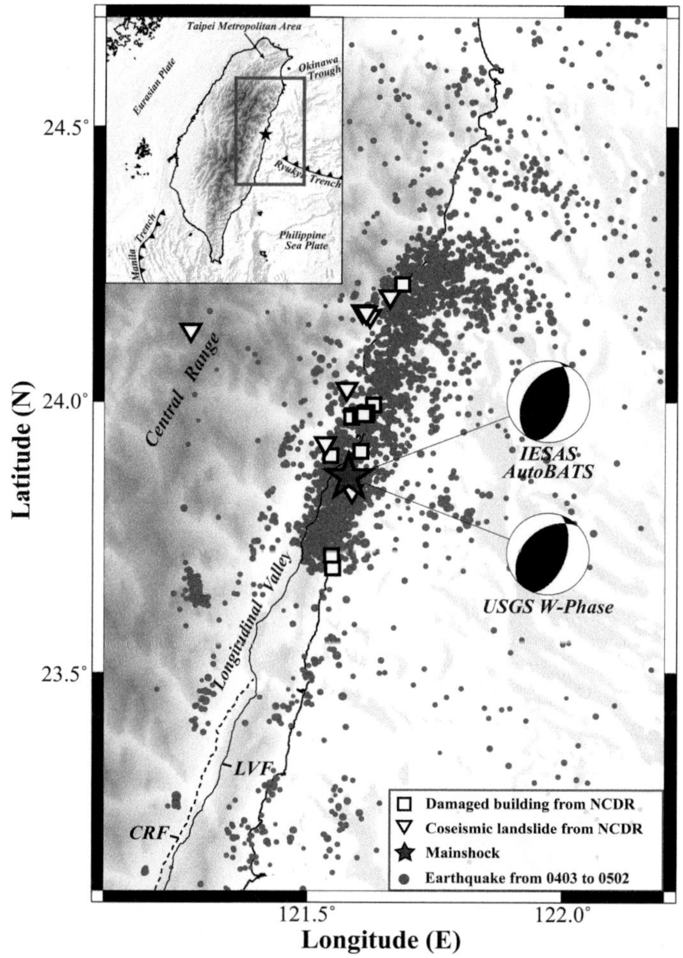

Figure 1. Tectonic setting of the Taiwan region (top-left inset map) and northern Longitudinal Valley (LV) area, with the star marking the epicenter of the 0403 Hualien earthquake. The black line represents the LV fault (LVF) and the black dashed line indicates the Central Range fault (CRF). Squares denote buildings that were damaged, as reported by the National Center for Disaster Reduction (NCDR), whereas inverted triangles represent landslides and rockfalls. Circles depict the aftershock sequence of the event. The focal mechanisms generated by the U.S. Geological Survey (USGS W-phase) and the Institute of Earth Sciences, Academia Sinica (IESAS AutoBATS) are also shown. The color version of this figure is available only in the electronic edition.

local time zone). According to a report released by the Central Weather Administration (CWA) of Taiwan, the epicenter of the earthquake was located 15 km south-southeast of the Hualien County Government, at a depth of approximately 20 km, with a magnitude of M_w 7.4. This event represents the largest earthquake in Taiwan in the past few decades. Latest reports indicated 19 deaths and 1155 injuries. The epicenter was located in the northernmost segment of the Longitudinal Valley (LV) in eastern Taiwan (Fig. 1), a tectonically active region where the converging relationship of the PSP and the EP alternates between collision and subduction. The geological structure beneath this region is highly complex, dominated by two intersecting fault systems: the west-dipping Central Range fault (CRF) system and the east-dipping LV fault (LVF) system (Shyu *et al.*, 2006; Huang and Wang, 2022).

The fault mechanism solutions (Fig. 1) provided by the Institute of Earth Sciences, Academia Sinica (IESAS) (Jian *et al.*, 2018) and the U.S. Geological Survey (USGS) (Hayes *et al.*, 2009) indicate that the earthquake was triggered by a reverse-fault rupture. Although there is some divergence in the interpretation of the fault dip based on available data (Cheloni *et al.*, 2024), regardless of the dip angle, the primary fault systems in the region align along a south-southwest to north-northeast trend (Shyu *et al.*, 2006; Huang and Wang, 2022). Furthermore, aftershock distributions (Fig. 1) and fault rupture models suggest that the rupture process initiated at a south-southwest point (the hypocenter) and propagated toward the north-northeast (Cheloni *et al.*, 2024; U.S. Geological Survey, 2024; Zheng *et al.*, 2024). Because of the extended rupture process, a distinct directivity effect was observed in the area north of the epicenter. The earthquake caused intense shaking and damage in the epicentral area, including Hualien City and Taroko Gorge, where the maximum recorded intensity reached CWA intensity level 6+ (peak ground acceleration [PGA] ≥ 80 gal; peak ground velocity [PGV] ≥ 80 cm/s and <140 cm/s). Similar to the Hualien earthquake that occurred 40 yr ago, strong ground motion was also felt in the Taipei metropolitan area, with a maximum recorded CWA intensity of 5− (PGA ≥ 80 gal; PGV ≥ 15 cm/s and <30 cm/s). In contrast, the southwestern and southeastern regions of Taiwan experienced weaker shaking, with a CWA intensity of 4 (PGA ≥ 25 gal and <80 gal; PGV < 15 cm/s).

During the 0403 Hualien earthquake, the EEW system of the CWA issued two Public Warning Service (PWS) alerts covering most of Taiwan. However, the system underestimated the earthquake's magnitude and ground-motion intensity in northern Taiwan, excluding Hsinchu City, Taoyuan City, and the Taipei metropolitan area—home to more than 10 million people, or 40% of Taiwan's population—from the alerts. Given that only a few seconds of initial *P*-wave data are available for analysis, accurately estimating the magnitude of large earthquakes remains inherently difficult, especially when the rupture process deviates from a point-source model (Rydelek and Horiuchi, 2006; Hoshiba and Iwakiri, 2011; Colombelli *et al.*, 2012; Chen *et al.*, 2015). Moreover, strong rupture directivity effects and the relatively distant location of the epicenter from densely populated regions posed additional challenges to the performance of the point-source model EEW system. These factors significantly affected the system's ability to provide timely and accurate intensity estimates and to issue effective alerts for northern Taiwan.

In addition to the system operated by the CWA, Taiwan also has several other EEW systems in operation (Wu *et al.*, 2021). Among them, the high-density *P*-Alert network, maintained by the team at National Taiwan University (NTU), plays

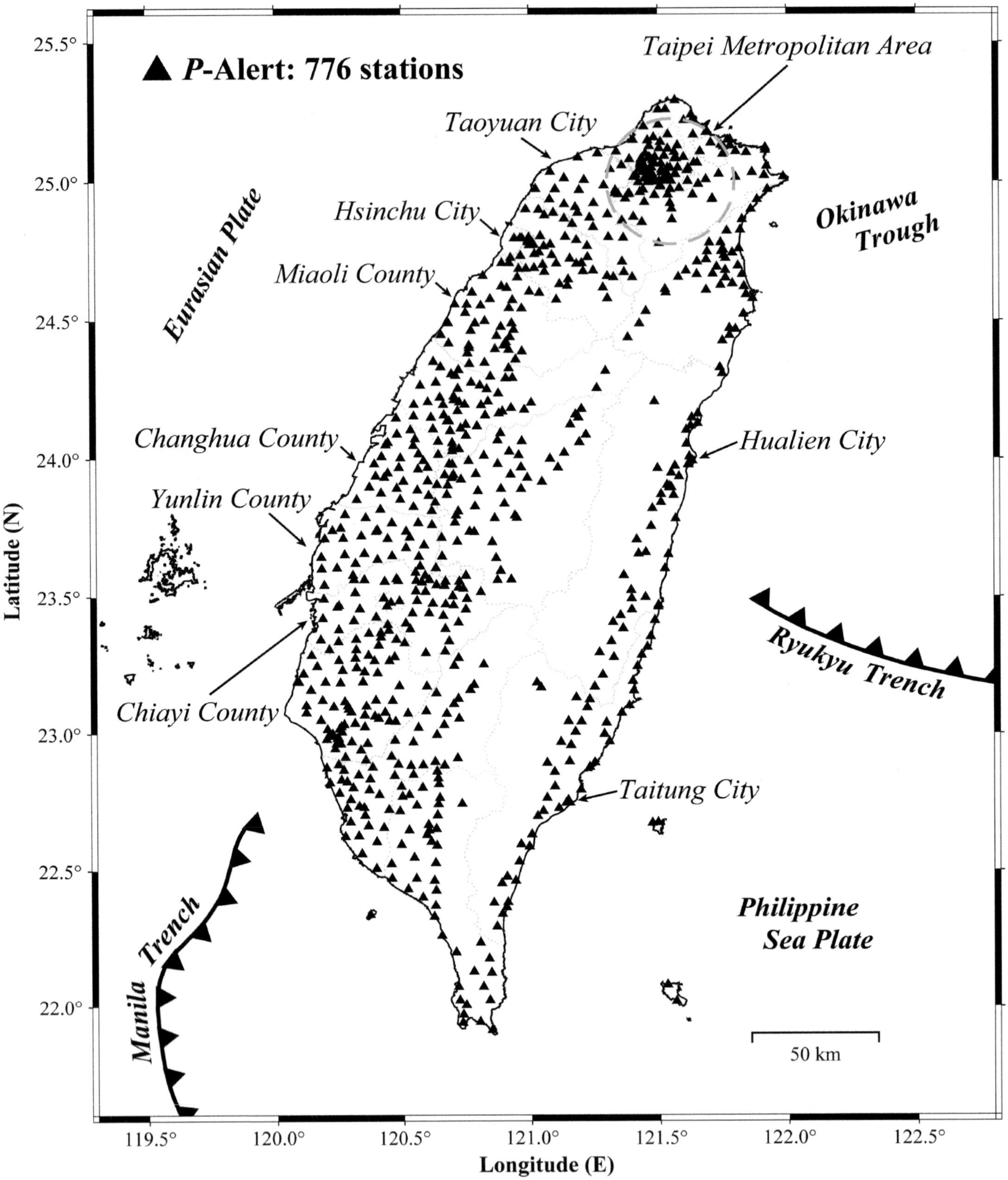

Figure 2. *P*-Alert network station distribution on 2 April 2024. The total number of stations is 776.

a key role in addressing the challenges mentioned earlier. The *P*-Alert network consists of a large number of stations (Fig. 2), designed for both regional and onsite EEW performance. Each *P*-Alert sensor can detect the arrival and peak amplitude of *P* waves to provide regional EEW systems with estimates of the earthquake's source location and magnitude and also offer onsite EEW. When the ground-motion values exceed a preset threshold, the sensor immediately issues an alert to nearby areas. This dual functionality ensures that even if the regional EEW system has not yet issued a warning, the local *P*-Alert sensor provides timely alerts, ensuring that residents still have sufficient time to respond to the impending shaking (Wu *et al.*, 2016, 2019; Wang *et al.*, 2018). Leveraging the high density of the *P*-Alert network, Yang *et al.* (2018) proposed a novel algorithm, *ShakingAlarm*, which takes directivity effects into account to predict the ground shaking without relying on earthquake source parameter calculations.

The magnitude and directivity effect of the 0403 Hualien earthquake posed significant challenges to the operation of EEW systems in Taiwan, surpassing those encountered in past earthquakes. Although previous studies (Wu and Lin, 2014; Wu *et al.*, 2016, 2019; Mittal *et al.*, 2021; Wu and Mittal, 2021; Yang *et al.*, 2023; Paurush *et al.*, 2024) extensively addressed the performance of the *P*-Alert network during moderate to large earthquakes, its performance during a strong earthquake with a moment magnitude greater than 7.0, especially one involving a directivity effect, has not been thoroughly explored. This study addresses this gap by analyzing the performance of the *P*-Alert network, focusing on how its high-density station coverage mitigates the warning challenges posed by directivity effects. The findings provide valuable validation data for future advancements in EEW technologies.

P-ALERT NETWORK

In 2010, the research team at NTU started pilot testing of the *P*-Alert network by installing 15 *P*-Alert sensors in eastern Taiwan (Wu and Lin, 2014), with Hualien as the first area to host *P*-Alert observation stations. By the time of the occurrence of the 0403 Hualien earthquake, the *P*-Alert network had expanded significantly, comprising nearly 780 self-established stations distributed across the main island of Taiwan and surrounding islands (Fig. 2). This network boasts the highest station density in Taiwan. In densely populated urban areas, the station density reaches up to one station every 5 km.

The *P*-Alert network employs cost-effective micro-electromechanical system sensors, facilitating large-scale installation. The monitoring data are transmitted in real time via the internet to central processing servers located at NTU and IESAS for immediate computation and data storage. Data processing at the central servers is performed using the Earthworm platform developed by the USGS (Johnson *et al.*, 1995; Chen *et al.*, 2015). The first-generation *P*-Alert sensors used in the *P*-Alert network provide three-axis (Z, north–south, and east–west) acceleration data with 16 bit resolution and a sampling rate of 100 samples per second. The horizontal dynamic range of the sensor is $\pm 2\ g$, whereas the vertical dynamic range is $+1g$ to $-3\ g$. To reduce high-frequency noise interference, the *P*-Alert sensors are equipped with selectable low-pass filters, with cutoff frequencies of either 10 or 20 Hz. In addition to the recording ground motion, the sensors also perform real-time computations, such as double integration combined with a high-pass filter at 0.075 Hz (Shieh *et al.*, 2008) and the short-term average/long-term average method (Allen, 1978). Using these embedded algorithms, the *P*-Alert sensor detects the arrival of *P* waves and calculates the vertical maximum displacement (P_d) within a defined time interval after the arrival of the *P* wave. Simultaneously, the sensors monitor PGA and PGV. If any of these parameters—P_d or PGA—exceed preset thresholds, the *P*-Alert sensor triggers an alarm. In the latest firmware version, the *P*-Alert sensors are also capable of using PGV as a threshold.

The *P*-Alert network provides both onsite EEW using individual stations and regional EEW using data from a few stations. Regional EEW is generated by the central server located at NTU, which receives raw acceleration data from various stations. These data are processed in real time to perform event detection, association, location, and magnitude estimation (Chen *et al.*, 2015). The CWA is the sole officially authorized organization in Taiwan to issue public warnings. Consequently, the regional EEW information generated by the *P*-Alert network is used exclusively for research purposes and is not publicly disseminated.

During the 0403 Hualien earthquake, the *P*-Alert network issued its first regional report 11 s after the earthquake's origin, with an estimated magnitude of 6.5. In comparison, the CWA system issued its first estimate of magnitude 6.2, only 8 s after the earthquake's origin. Given that both systems have similar station densities and utilize the same computational algorithms (Chen *et al.*, 2015; Wu *et al.*, 2021), this difference is reasonable. The additional 3 s delay allowed the *P*-Alert system to process a more complete waveform, resulting in a magnitude estimate closer to the final value. The CWA system revised its magnitude estimate to 6.8 in an updated report 14 s after the earthquake's origin, aligning more closely with the final result. However, despite further refinements, the system still underestimated the magnitude, likely due to the inherent challenge of estimating magnitude in the early stages of a large earthquake rupture (Rydelek and Horiuchi, 2006; Hoshiba and Iwakiri, 2011; Colombelli *et al.*, 2012; Chen *et al.*, 2015).

ONSITE EEW

Initially, the onsite EEW capability of the *P*-Alert sensors was designed to address blind zones in regional EEW systems without computation of the location and magnitude of an earthquake. Most regional EEW systems are capable of issuing alerts within 10–15 s after an earthquake occurs (Wu *et al.*, 2021), providing effective warnings for regions located more than 40 km from the epicenter. However, areas within this 40 km range cannot receive a warning, and these areas are known as blind zones.

The 0403 Hualien earthquake presented a considerable challenge to traditional regional EEW systems based on point-source

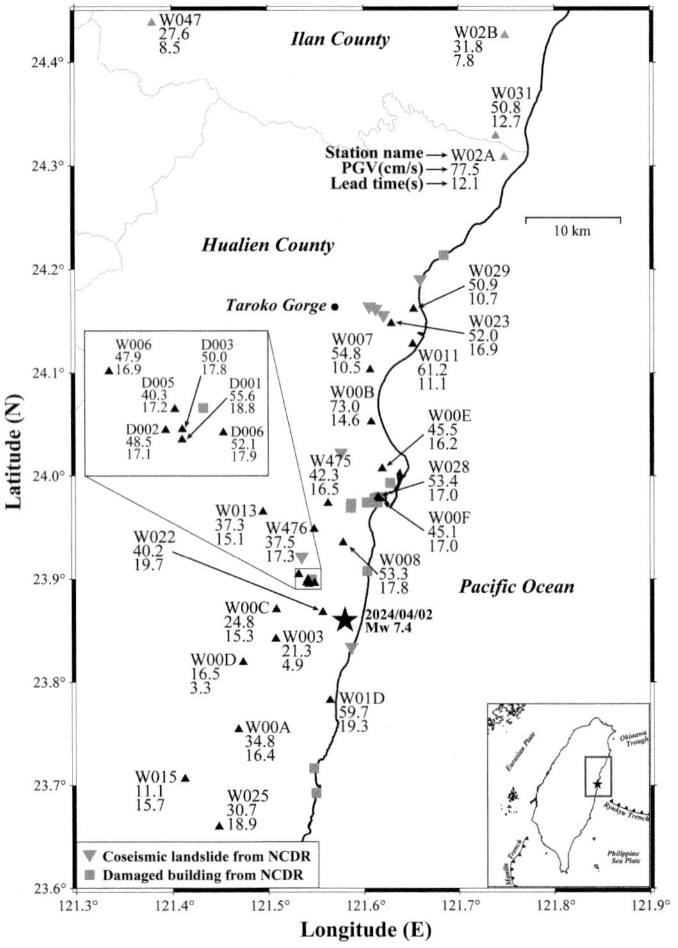

Figure 3. Distribution of onsite warning lead times based on peak ground velocity (PGV) for the *P*-Alert stations around the epicentral area during the 0403 Hualien earthquake. The stations marked as black triangles are used in Figure 7. The lower-right inset map shows the tectonic setting of Taiwan, with a rectangle indicating the study region. The color version of this figure is available only in the electronic edition.

models, which typically issue alerts based on point-source parameters such as earthquake location and magnitude due to the significant directivity effect. During the earthquake, the CWA system issued two PWS alerts. However, both alerts underestimated the magnitude of the earthquake and the ground-motion intensity in northern Taiwan, resulting in not issuing the alerts for the Taipei metropolitan area. In such a case, the onsite EEW capabilities of the *P*-Alert sensors become especially crucial. The *P*-Alert sensors' onsite EEW function alleviates these limitations with preset warning thresholds: a P_d greater than 0.35 cm and a PGA greater than 80 gal (Wu and Kanamori, 2005; Wu *et al.*, 2011; Hsieh *et al.*, 2015). Once these thresholds are exceeded, an alarm is triggered.

Figures 3 and 4 illustrate the performance of onsite EEW from *P*-Alert stations near the epicenter and in the Taipei metropolitan area during the 0403 Hualien earthquake, respectively. The key indicator used to evaluate the effectiveness of the onsite EEW function is the lead time, which is defined as the interval between the issuance of the warning and the arrival of the maximum ground motion (e.g., PGA or PGV). In this analysis, longer lead times indicate better system performance.

In the vicinity of the epicenter (Fig. 3), within the blind zone, such as Hualien City, the lead time ranged from a minimum of 3 s to exceeding 10 s in some cases. Stations near the Taroko Gorge, where most fatalities occurred, reported lead times exceeding 10 s. In the Taipei metropolitan area (Fig. 4), situated farther from the epicenter, the lead times were at least 6 s, with a maximum exceeding 10 s. Stations near the location of displacements in the box beams of the Metro Rapid Transit (MRT) Circular Line tracks (represented by the solid gray square in Fig. 4) also reported lead times exceeding 10 s. On average, the lead times for stations in the near-epicenter area and the Taipei metropolitan area were 14.7 ± 4.3 s and 11.3 ± 3.2 s, respectively.

Although this study defines lead time as the interval between the issuance of a warning and the arrival of maximum ground motion, an alternative approach considers the time difference between when the predicted and observed intensities exceed a damaging threshold, specifically the CWA intensity of 5−. According to this metric, effective lead times were still achieved, with 1.7 ± 1.7 s in the near-epicenter area and 8.6 ± 3.4 s in the Taipei metropolitan area. Overall, for blind zones and areas where the directivity effect prevented regional systems from issuing warnings, the onsite EEW function of the *P*-Alert sensors provided timely alerts, filling the gap, and enhancing overall earthquake preparedness.

SHAKEMAP

Generating real-time shakemaps is a core feature of the *P*-Alert network. Since 2014, the *P*-Alert network has been capable of generating detailed PGA shakemaps (Hsieh *et al.*, 2014) at 1 min intervals. By 2020, the system was upgraded (Yang *et al.*, 2021), expanding its capabilities to include the production of shakemaps for PGV, spectral acceleration (SA), and the intensity scales introduced by the CWA in 2020. The update also enhanced operational efficiency by reducing map production time from the original 1 min to 30 s.

The *P*-Alert network begins generating shakemaps once at least five stations are triggered. The optimal trigger conditions require the maximum acceleration at a referencing station to exceed 1.5 gal within 1 s, with at least two additional stations within a 30 km radius recording accelerations greater than 1.5 gal within 6 s. As long as new stations continue to trigger, the shakemaps are updated every 30 s. These maps are automatically emailed to relevant authorities, including the National Center for Disaster Reduction, to offer a clearer understanding of the affected areas and allow sufficient time for response and rescue operations (Mittal *et al.*, 2022). In addition, shakemaps are published on social media platforms such as Facebook and X (formerly Twitter), offering the public real-time information.

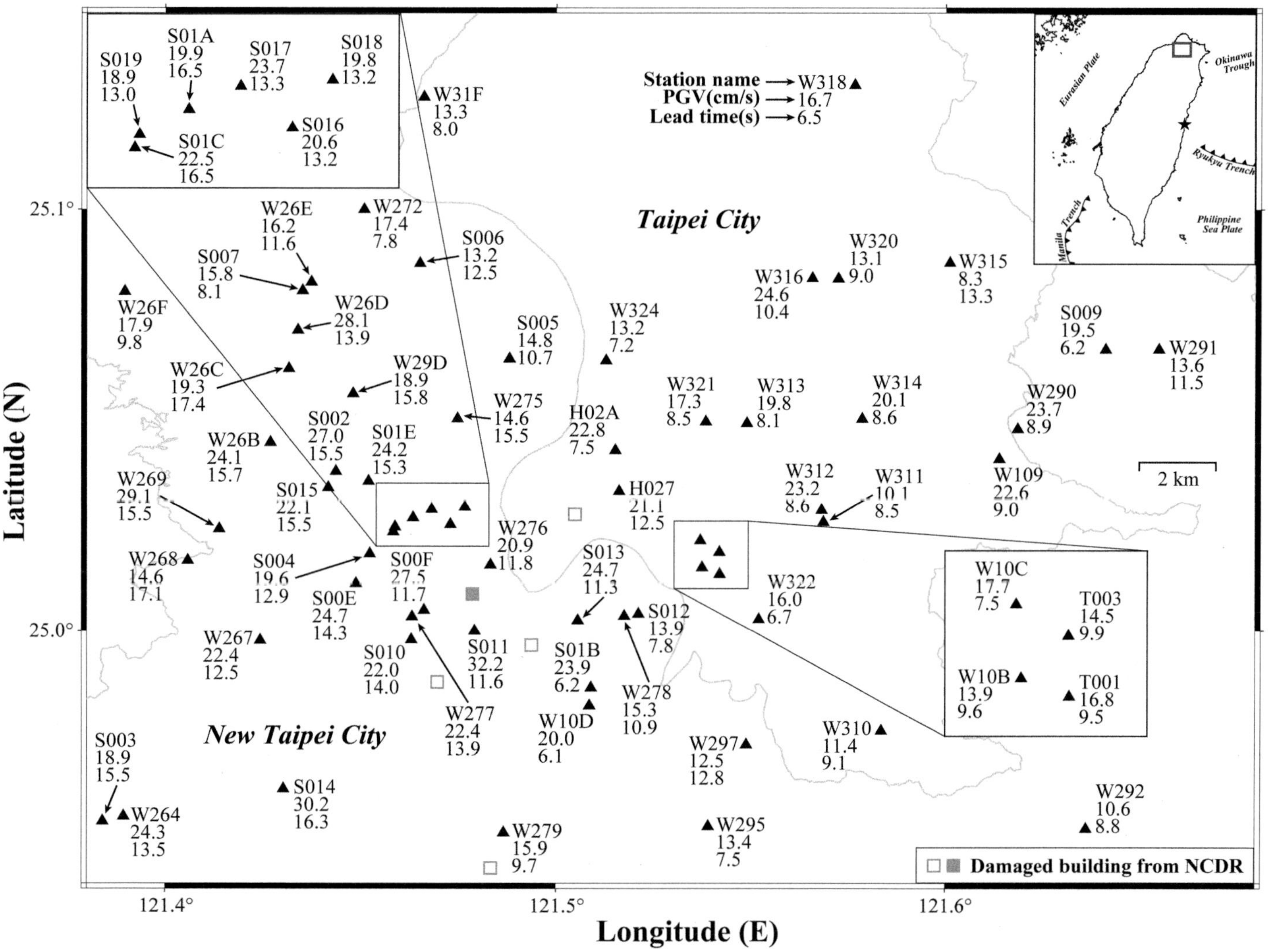

Figure 4. Distribution of onsite warning lead times based on PGV for the *P*-Alert stations in the Taipei metropolitan area during the 0403 Hualien earthquake. The solid gray square marks the location of displacements in the box beams of the Metro Rapid Transit Circular Line tracks. The top-right inset map shows the tectonic setting of Taiwan, with a rectangle indicating the study region. The color version of this figure is available only in the electronic edition.

During the 0403 Hualien earthquake, the *P*-Alert network posted its first shakemaps on social media platforms approximately 4 s after the earthquake's origin. The final shakemaps, incorporating observed data from 718 triggered stations, were completed around 2.5 min after the origin (Fig. 5a,b). According to the CWA earthquake report, the maximum ground motion was recorded at station EHP, located 51 km north of the epicenter. At this station, the single-component PGA was 363.72 gal, and the PGV was 76.37 cm/s. After vector summation, the PGA reached 374.06 gal, and the PGV increased to 84.00 cm/s, corresponding to a CWA intensity of 6+. Similarly, the *P*-Alert network recorded the maximum ground motion at station W02A, located approximately 250 m from station EHP. Here, the single-component PGA was 409.20 gal, and the PGV was 77.48 cm/s. After vector summation, the final PGA reached 431.28 gal, and the PGV was 85.38 cm/s, also indicating a CWA intensity of 6+, consistent with the CWA report. Overall, the *P*-Alert shakemap generation system operated smoothly, demonstrating stable performance comparable to that of the CWA network (Fig. 5c,d).

The distribution of damage (shown by squares and triangles in Fig. 5a,b) indicates that the 0403 Hualien earthquake caused the most significant damage to the north of the epicenter. In the Taipei metropolitan area, damage was concentrated in locations where PGA approached 150 gal and PGV approached 17 cm/s, corresponding to a CWA intensity of 5−. In contrast, regions such as Taitung and southwestern Taiwan experienced lower shaking intensities, with no significant damage reported.

Focusing on areas near the epicenter, damage—including coseismic landslides—was predominantly observed in locations where PGA exceeded 250 gal and PGV exceeded 31 cm/s, corresponding to a CWA intensity of 5+ (PGA $\geq$ 80 gal; PGV $\geq$ 30 cm/s and <50 cm/s), particularly north of the epicenter. In addition, higher PGA and PGV areas extended from the

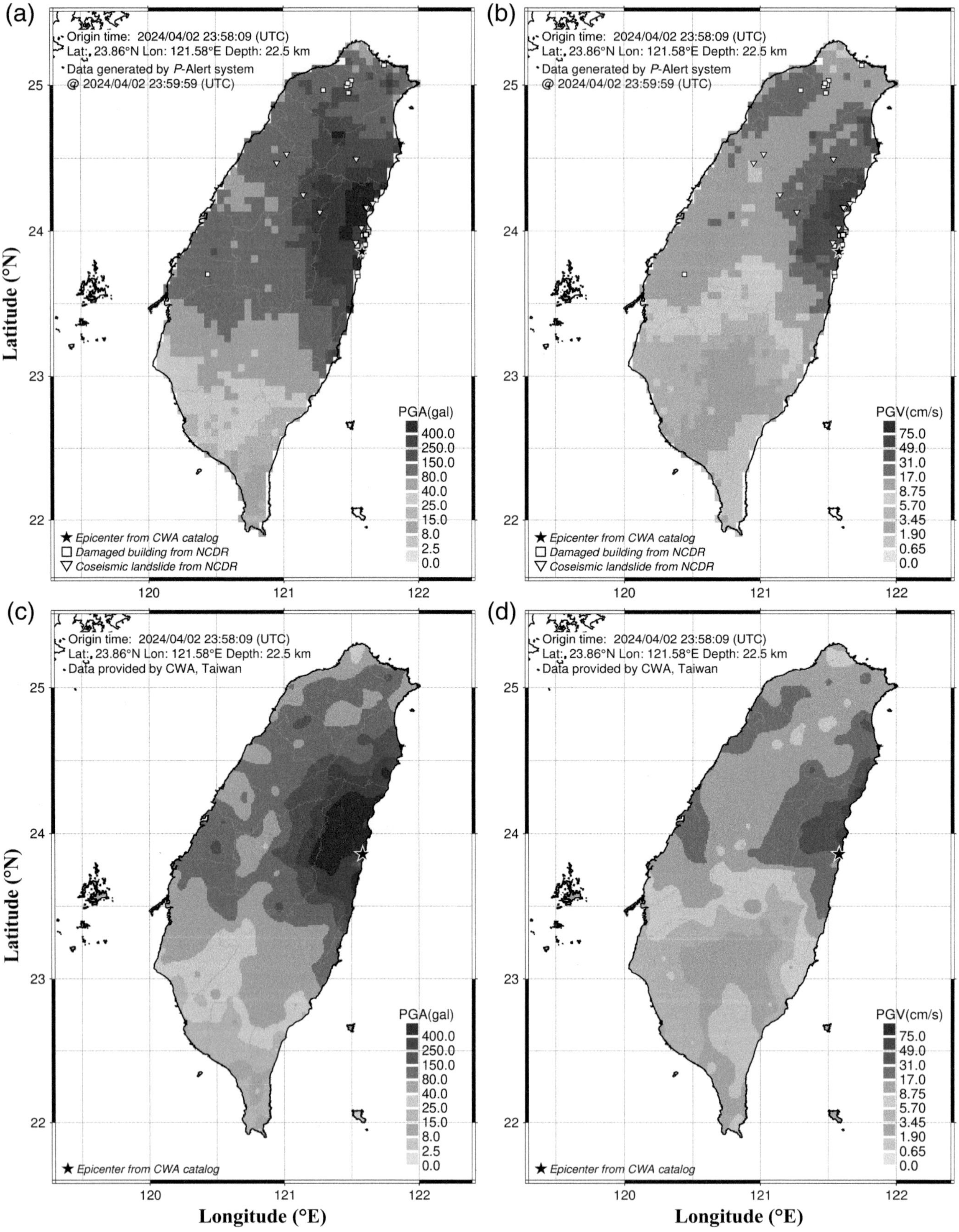

Figure 5. Shakemaps of the 0403 Hualien earthquake derived from real-time grid data produced by the *P*-Alert network after all available *P*-Alert stations were triggered, including (a) peak ground acceleration (PGA) and (b) PGV. These are compared to (c) PGA and (d) PGV shakemaps generated from grid data provided by the Central Weather Administration (CWA) network. The color version of this figure is available only in the electronic edition.

epicenter toward the north-northeast, whereas the south-southwest direction showed a distinct lack of extension, indicating that the rupture propagated in a north-northeast direction from the epicenter. High-resolution shakemaps from the *P*-Alert network effectively depict the fault rupture direction. By incorporating the directivity effect, these maps help identify disaster-prone areas. Had ground motion estimation relied solely on a point-source model, even with site effects considered, it would likely have underestimated the disaster impact in northern Taiwan, leading to ineffective response efforts.

SHAKINGALARM

Yang *et al.* (2018) proposed a potential EEW algorithm known as *ShakingAlarm* to address directivity effects in EEW systems. This algorithm aims to improve early warning effectiveness and accuracy by establishing an EEW system that does not rely on earthquake location or magnitude estimation. Instead, it leverages the exceptionally high station density of the *P*-Alert network to analyze real-time ground motion attenuation relationships in various directions during an earthquake. These attenuation relationships are then used to replace traditional, existing ground-motion prediction equations (GMPEs), enabling more accurate predictions of ground motion intensity. As such, this algorithm can be classified within ground-motion models (GMMs) (Allen and Melgar, 2019). *ShakingAlarm* accounts for directivity effects and mitigates errors in ground-motion intensity estimation caused by inaccuracies in magnitude estimation. Although initially designed for the *P*-Alert network, this algorithm can also be applied to other high-density seismic networks.

Testing the *ShakingAlarm* with data from the 0403 Hualien earthquake showed promising results, as illustrated in Figure 6. The algorithm provided an early estimate of ground-motion intensity for regions to the north and northwest of the epicenter, particularly in areas that did not receive PWS alerts. For comparison with the CWA system, the same intensity threshold (CWA intensity level 4) was applied, because the *ShakingAlarm* provides only ground-motion predictions. Although the available warning time before damaging ground motion arrived may not have been substantial, the *ShakingAlarm* provided an early estimate compared to the observed shakemap for northern Taiwan.

At 8 s after the earthquake's origin, when the CWA system issued its first warning to four counties (gray-shaded area in Fig. 6a), *ShakingAlarm*'s predictions in the Hsinchu and Miaoli areas had already reached CWA intensity level 4, surpassing the warning threshold (Fig. 6a). By 14 s, when the CWA system issued its second warning to 12 counties or cities (gray-shaded area in Fig. 6b), excluding Hsinchu and Taoyuan cities, *ShakingAlarm*'s predictions had also reached CWA intensity level 4 in those two cities (Fig. 6b). At 20 s after the origin, the CWA system did not issue a further update. However, *ShakingAlarm*'s predictions indicated that most of northern Taiwan had exceeded CWA intensity level 4 (Fig. 6c). These results suggest that the algorithm could have issued a warning for the Taipei metropolitan area at 20 s after the earthquake's origin, effectively filling the gaps left by the CWA system.

Figure 6d compares the predicted PGA with the observed real-time PGA at four stations. With the exception of station H01B, which will be discussed later, the predicted PGA values provided by the *ShakingAlarm* remained higher than the observed PGA values from the onset of ground motion until 15 s after the earthquake's origin. To assess the algorithm's performance, we consider the warning threshold of the CWA system. At station W028 in Hualien City, located only 12 km from the epicenter, the predicted PGA exceeded the threshold 5 s after the earthquake's origin, whereas the observed PGA surpassed it 2 s later. At station H002 in Hsinchu Science Park, the predicted PGA exceeded the threshold at 8 s after the earthquake's origin, whereas the observed PGA did not surpass it until 30 s after the origin. At station S011, near the displacements in the MRT Circular Line tracks, the predicted PGA exceeded the threshold at 11 s, compared to 29 s for the observed PGA. Notably, the warning provided by the CWA system, based on the predicted PGA values (marked with crosses in Fig. 6d) lagged behind *ShakingAlarm*'s predictions at all three stations. These findings suggest that *ShakingAlarm* is capable of providing advanced warning, particularly in northern Taiwan, where the system typically offers warnings approximately 20 s before the observed PGA reaches the threshold. Across the entire *P*-Alert network, *ShakingAlarm* provided advance estimates an average of 15.7 ± 8.2 s before the observed ground motion reached CWA intensity level 4. The corresponding false alarm rate was 0.6%, whereas the missed alarm rate was 55.8%.

Compared to the final observed shakemap (Fig. 5a), the predicted shakemap at 20 s after the origin shows a noticeable shrinkage in the PGA distribution across the Western Coastal Plain region, particularly in Changhua, Yunlin, and Chiayi counties. Most of the missed alarms were also located in this region. For example, at station H01B (Fig. 6d), the predicted PGA values closely matched the observed PGA values throughout the event. This discrepancy may be attributed to the insufficient number of stations on the western side of the epicenter, especially across the Central Range. This limited station density likely hindered the algorithm's ability to generate accurate predictions. Therefore, enhancing the station density in these gaps or integrating existing point-source model GMPEs could improve the overall accuracy and utility of the *ShakingAlarm*.

DISCUSSION

Although the *P*-Alert network's onsite EEW capability and high-density observations help mitigate challenges posed by the strong directivity effect, further improvements remain necessary. One potential improvement involves adjusting the

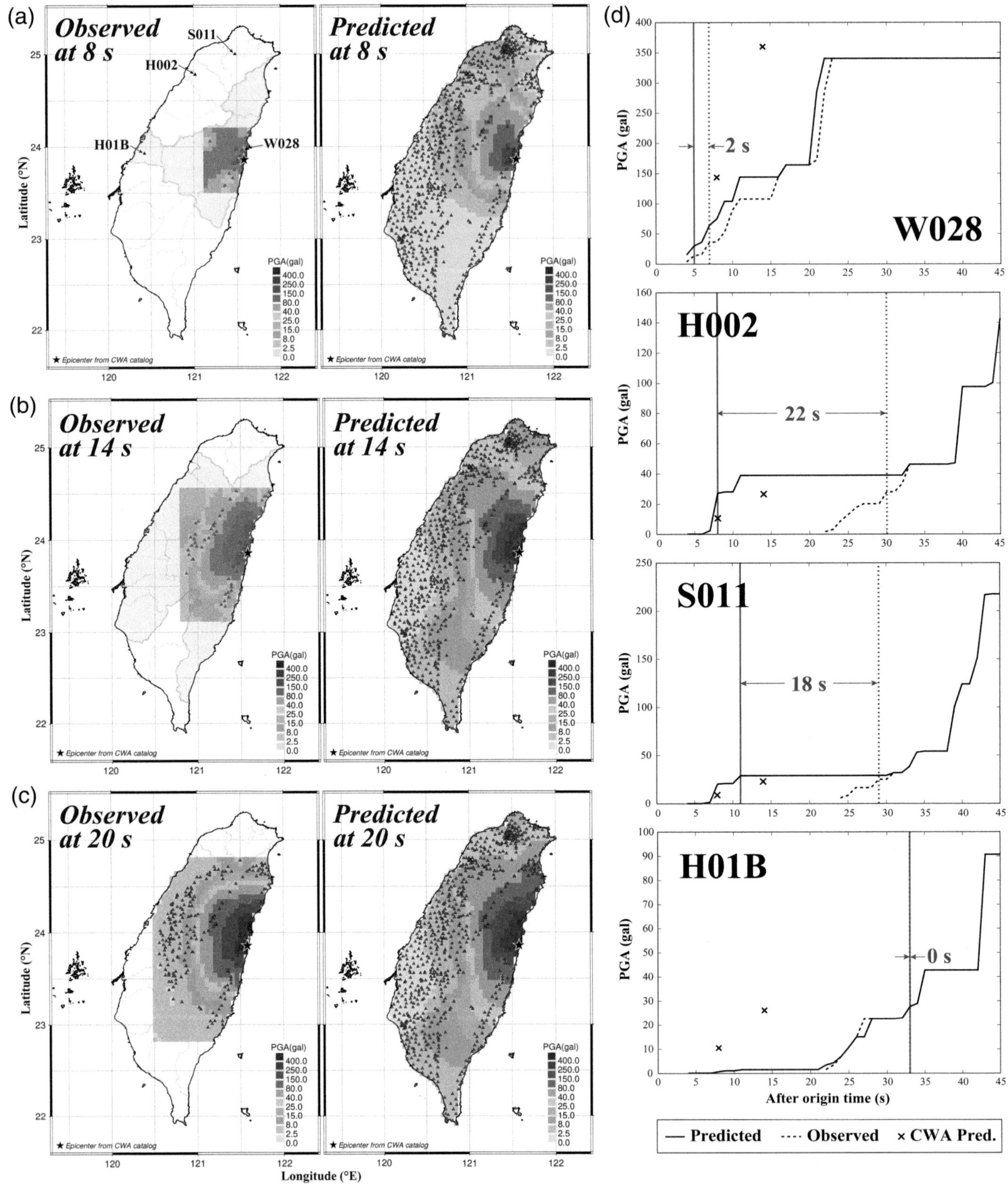

Figure 6. *ShakingAlarm* testing results for the 0403 Hualien earthquake. Comparison graphs illustrate the observed shakemap versus the *ShakingAlarm*-predicted shakemap at (a) 8 s, (b) 14 s, and (c) 20 s after the earthquake's origin. The black star marks the epicenter. Gray-shaded areas indicate regions that were able to receive CWA earthquake early warnings at 8 and 14 s. (d) Predicted and observed PGAs at four stations are shown. Cross symbols represent the PGAs predicted by the CWA system at 8 and 14 s. The red solid line indicates when *ShakingAlarm* predicts a CWA intensity of 4, whereas the red dashed line marks when observations reach the same level. The color version of this figure is available only in the electronic edition.

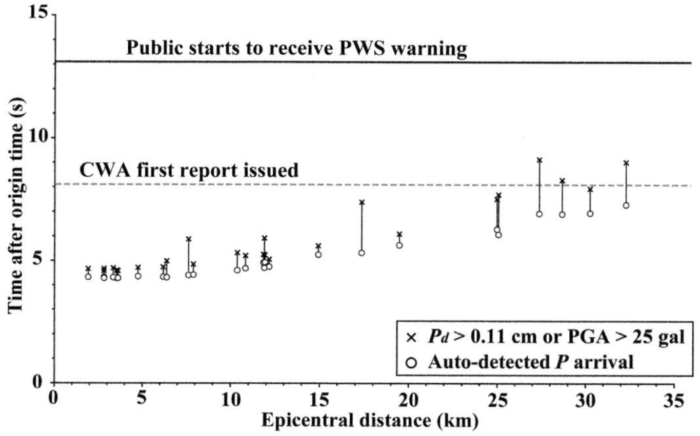

Figure 7. Effectiveness of *P*-Alert onsite warning based on CWA warning criteria. Open circles denote the automatic detection of *P*-wave arrivals, and crosses indicate the simulated onsite warninq activation at stations (marked with black triangles in Fig. 3) when $P_d > 0.11$ cm or PGA > 25 gal. The horizontal dashed line marks the time of the first CWA earthquake early warning, and the horizontal solid line represents the average time the public received the warning via the Public Warning System (PWS).

onsite warning threshold to align with the CWA system's criteria, specifically defining CWA intensity level 4. Using the following empirical relationships between P_d and PGV (Wu and Kanamori, 2008) and between PGA and PGV (Wu *et al.*, 2003), we updated the onsite EEW threshold to $P_d > 0.11$ cm and PGA > 25 gal:

$$\log(\mathrm{PGV}) = 1.642 + 0.920 \times \log(P_d), \quad (1)$$

$$\log(\mathrm{PGA}) = 0.595 + 1.069 \times \log(\mathrm{PGV}). \quad (2)$$

Figure 7 illustrates the automatic *P*-arrival detections and new alert issuance times for each station within 35 km of the epicenter. The CWA system issued its first warning at 23:58:18 UTC, just 8.1 s after the earthquake's origin (represented by the horizontal gray dashed line in Fig. 7). Because of transmission delays (Wu *et al.*, 2025), the first PWS alert reached the public approximately 13 s after the earthquake's origin (represented by the horizontal black line in Fig. 7). The results indicate that the updated threshold allowed most *P*-Alert stations to issue alerts earlier than the CWA regional system. Particularly, in the Taipei metropolitan area, most *P*-Alert stations with the updated threshold were able to deliver better lead times than existing results, enabling timely alerts before peak ground motion. This underscores the critical importance of the *P*-Alert onsite warning system, especially in regions not effectively covered by traditional regional systems.

Another key point is how the *ShakingAlarm* can estimate ground motion effectively in regions with sparse station coverage. One possible improvement involves integrating point-source information (e.g., epicenter and magnitude) with existing GMPEs to establish a baseline lower bound for intensity estimates. The *ShakingAlarm* intensity would then need to exceed this lower bound to be considered valid. This hybrid approach merges the traditional point-source model with *ShakingAlarm*'s directivity-sensitive predictions, resulting in more accurate and comprehensive ground motion estimations.

The 0403 Hualien earthquake, the largest event recorded since the establishment of the *P*-Alert network, provides strong evidence of the effectiveness of this system. The earthquake exhibited a significant directivity effect as the rupture propagated from the south-southwest to the north-northeast direction. The *P*-Alert network effectively played a crucial role by providing onsite EEW, real-time shakemaps, and GMM-based regional EEW, helping mitigate the challenges posed by the large event and the directivity effect.

The *P*-Alert network provided significant onsite EEW lead times across affected areas, including the Taipei metropolitan area, where the official CWA system failed to issue timely warnings. In the area close to the epicenter, the lead time ranged from 3 to 16 s. For the Taipei metropolitan area, the *P*-Alert network provided an average lead time of approximately 11 s. Moreover, the updated thresholds of the *P*-Alert system further enhanced lead times, including coverage of the blind zone (Fig. 7).

A comparative analysis of PGA and PGV shakemaps (Fig. 5a,b for *P*-Alert; Fig. 5c,d for CWA) shows consistency in overall ground-motion distribution patterns. Consistent with previous studies (Wu *et al.*, 2016, 2019; Yang *et al.*, 2023), the *P*-Alert's shakemaps effectively captured the primary rupture direction. Based on these shakemaps, higher intensities were distinctly observed extending north-northeast from the epicenter, whereas the opposite direction exhibited lower intensities. This pattern strongly suggests that the rupture propagated along an north-northeast–south-southwest fault plane, aligning with the regional fault system, including the LVF and CRF (Shyu *et al.*, 2006; Huang and Wang, 2022).

Fault mechanism solutions from IESAS and USGS (Fig. 1) further indicate that the two possible fault planes strike along the north-northeast–south-southwest axis. The aftershock distribution follows the same trend (Fig. 1), reinforcing the inferred rupture direction. The alignment between fault mechanism solutions, aftershock distribution, and shakemap data strongly supports a north-northeast–south-southwest rupture, consistent with observed damage patterns. The inversion models further corroborate this direction (Cheloni *et al.*, 2024; U.S. Geological Survey, 2024; Zheng *et al.*, 2024). The *ShakingAlarm*, leveraging the *P*-Alert network's ability to identify rupture direction, provided effective warnings in northern Taiwan (Fig. 6), enabling timely protective actions in regions not covered by the regional EEW system.

Overall, the 0403 Hualien earthquake underscores the value of integrating directivity-sensitive algorithm, updated thresholds, and hybrid modeling in EEW frameworks. The *P*-Alert network demonstrated its capability to compensate for blind zones and latency limitations in traditional systems, contributing significantly to timely hazard mitigation.

CONCLUSIONS

The 0403 Hualien earthquake validated the effectiveness of the *P*-Alert network in mitigating seismic risks through timely early warnings. The network successfully provided onsite EEW lead time ranging from 3 to 16 s in the near-epicentral area and approximately 11 s on average in the Taipei metropolitan area. These warnings were especially crucial in areas where the CWA system either failed to issue alerts or provided them too late.

With the adjustment of the onsite EEW threshold to $P_d >$ 0.11 cm and PGA > 25 gal, aligned with CWA criteria, *P*-Alert stations demonstrated improved coverage and extended lead times, including in previously under-alerted zones. The network's integration of high-resolution shakemaps, effective capture of rupture directivity, and its compatibility with advanced GMMs makes it an essential tool for real-time seismic monitoring and public safety.

Moving forward, the real-time data provided by the *P*-Alert network will serve as a valuable resource for emergency response agencies, enhancing disaster preparedness and response capabilities across Taiwan.

DATA AND RESOURCES

The strong-motion waveform records from the *P*-Alert network, used in this research, can be downloaded at https://palert.earth.sinica.edu.tw/database/. The official *P*-Alert shakemap pages are available at https://www.facebook.com/Palert. Shakemap/ and https://x.com/eew_p/. The earthquake reports and early warning data from Taiwan's CWA were obtained from https://www.cwa.gov.tw/. All websites were last accessed in April 2025. The Generic Mapping Tools (GMT) software from Wessel *et al.* (2019) was used in plotting part of the figures and is gratefully acknowledged. All focal mechanisms and fault rupture models referenced in this article came from published sources listed in the references.

DECLARATION OF COMPETING INTERESTS

The authors acknowledge that there are no conflicts of interest recorded.

ACKNOWLEDGMENTS

This study was supported by the National Science and Technology Council with Grant Numbers 113-2740-M-002-005, 113-2116-M-002-014, and 114-2116-M-002-011. The authors are profusely thankful to Editor Tai-Lin Tseng and two anonymous reviewers, whose constructive comments and suggestions helped in improving the article. The authors also thank the National Center for High-performance Computing for providing computational and storage resources. Author H. M. is thankful to O. P. Mishra, Director, National Centre for Seismology, India, for permitting participation in this research work.

REFERENCES

Allen, R. M., and D. Melgar (2019). Earthquake early warning: Advances, scientific challenges, and societal needs, *Annu. Rev. Earth Planet. Sci.* **47,** no. 1, 361–388, doi: 10.1146/annurev-earth-053018-060457.

Allen, R. V. (1978). Automatic earthquake recognition and timing from single traces, *Bull. Seismol. Soc. Am.* **68,** no. 5, 1521–1532, doi: 10.1785/BSSA0680051521.

Cheloni, D., N. A. Famiglietti, R. Caputo, C. Tolomei, and A. Vicari (2024). A composite fault model for the 2024 MW 7.4 Hualien earthquake sequence in Eastern Taiwan inferred from GNSS and InSAR data, *Geophys. Res. Lett.* **51,** no. 20, e2024GL110255, doi: 10.1029/2024GL110255.

Chen, D. Y., N. C. Hsiao, and Y. M. Wu (2015). The earthworm based earthquake alarm reporting system in Taiwan, *Bull. Seismol. Soc. Am.* **105,** no. 2A, 568–579, doi: 10.1785/0120140147.

Colombelli, S., A. Zollo, G. Festa, and H. Kanamori (2012). Early magnitude and potential damage zone estimates for the great Mw 9 Tohoku-Oki earthquake, *Geophys. Res. Lett.* **39,** no. 22, doi: 10.1029/2012GL053923.

Hayes, G. P., L. Rivera, and H. Kanamori (2009). Source inversion of the W-phase: Real-time implementation and extension to low magnitudes, *Seismol. Res. Lett.* **80,** no. 5, 817–822, doi: 10.1785/gssrl.80.5.817.

Hoshiba, M., and K. Iwakiri (2011). Initial 30 seconds of the 2011 off the Pacific coast of Tohoku Earthquake (Mw 9.0)—amplitude and τ c for magnitude estimation for earthquake early warning—7, *Earth Planets Space* **63,** no. 7, 553–557, doi: 10.5047/eps.2011.06.015.

Hsieh, C. Y., W. A. Chao, and Y. M. Wu (2015). An examination of the threshold-based earthquake early warning approach using a low-cost seismic network, *Seismol. Res. Lett.* **86,** no. 6, 1664–1667, doi: 10.1785/0220150073.

Hsieh, C. Y., Y. M. Wu, T. L. Chin, K. H. Kuo, D. Y. Chen, K. S. Wang, Y. T. Chan, W. Y. Chang, W. S. Li, and S. H. Ker (2014). Low cost seismic network practical applications for producing quick shaking maps in Taiwan, *Terr. Atmos. Ocean. Sci.* **25,** no. 5, 617, doi: 10.3319/TAO.2014.03.27.01(T).

Huang, H. H., and Y. Wang (2022). Seismogenic structure beneath the northern Longitudinal Valley revealed by the 2018–2021 Hualien earthquake sequences and 3-D velocity model, *Terr. Atmos. Ocean. Sci.* **33,** no. 1, 17, doi: 10.1007/s44195-022-00017-z.

Jian, P. R., T. L. Tseng, W. T. Liang, and P. H. Huang (2018). A new automatic full-waveform regional moment tensor inversion algorithm and its applications in the Taiwan area, *Bull. Seismol. Soc. Am.* **108,** no. 2, 573–587, doi: 10.1785/0120170231.

Johnson, C. E., A. Bittenbinder, B. Bogaert, L. Dietz, and W. Kohler (1995). Earthworm: A flexible approach to seismic network processing, *IRIS Newsl.* **14,** no. 2, 1–4.

Mittal, H., B. M. Yang, T. L. Tseng, and Y. M. Wu (2021). Importance of real-time PGV in terms of lead-time and shakemaps: Results using 2018 ML 6.2 & 2019 ML 6.3 Hualien, Taiwan earthquakes, *J. Asian Earth Sci.* **220,** 104936, doi: 10.1016/j.jseaes.2021.104936.

Mittal, H., B. M. Yang, and Y. M. Wu (2022). Progress on the earthquake early warning and shakemaps system using low-cost sensors in Taiwan, *Geosci. Lett.* **9,** no. 1, 42, doi: 10.1186/s40562-022-00251-w.

Paurush, P., K. Mohan, H. Mittal, Y. M. Wu, and O. P. Mishra (2024). Deciphering the cause of massive disaster during sept. 2022

Chihshang Taiwan earthquake of magnitude 6.8 using strong motion seismology, *Environ. Earth Sci.* **83,** no. 17, 520, doi: 10.1007/s12665-024-11826-5.

Rydelek, P., and S. Horiuchi (2006). Is earthquake rupture deterministic? 7100, *Nature* **442,** no. 7100, E5–E6, doi: 10.1038/nature04963.

Shieh, J. T., Y. M. Wu, and R. M. Allen (2008). A comparison of τc and τpmax for magnitude estimation in earthquake early warning, *Geophys. Res. Lett.* **35,** no. 20, doi: 10.1029/2008GL035611.

Shyu, J. B. H., K. Sieh, Y. G. Chen, and L. H. Chung (2006). Geomorphic analysis of the Central Range fault, the second major active structure of the Longitudinal Valley suture, eastern Taiwan, *GSA Bull.* **118,** nos. 11/12, 1447–1462, doi: 10.1130/B25905.1.

U.S. Geological Survey (2024). Earthquake hazards program, *U.S. Geological Survey.*

Wang, K. S., W. A. Chao, H. Mittal, and Y. M. Wu (2018). Building effects on the P-alert-based real-time shaking map determination, *Seismol. Res. Lett.* **89,** no. 6, 2314–2321, doi: 10.1785/0220170252.

Wessel, P., J. F. Luis, L. Uieda, R. Scharroo, F. Wobbe, W. H. F. Smith, and D. Tian (2019). The Generic Mapping Tools version 6, *Geochem. Geophys. Geosys.* **20,** no. 11, 5556–5564, doi: 10.1029/2019GC008515.

Wu, Y. M., J. K. Chung, T. C. Shin, N. C. Hsiao, Y. B. Tsai, W. H. K. Lee, and T. L. Teng (1999). Development of an integrated earthquake early warning system in Taiwan—Case for the Hualien area earthquakes, *Terr. Atmos. Ocean. Sci.* **10,** no. 4, 719, doi: 10.3319/TAO.1999.10.4.719(T).

Wu, Y. M., and H. Kanamori (2005). Rapid assessment of damage potential of earthquakes in Taiwan from the beginning of P waves, *Bull. Seismol. Soc. Am.* **95,** no. 3, 1181–1185, doi: 10.1785/0120040193.

Wu, Y. M., and H. Kanamori (2008). Development of an earthquake early warning system using real-time strong motion signals 1, *Sensors* **8,** no. 1, 1–9, doi: 10.3390/s8010001.

Wu, Y. M., T. liang Teng, T. C. Shin, and N. C. Hsiao (2003). Relationship between peak ground acceleration, peak ground velocity, and intensity in Taiwan, *Bull. Seismol. Soc. Am.* **93,** no. 1, 386–396, doi: 10.1785/0120020097.

Wu, Y. M., W. T. Liang, H. Mittal, W. A. Chao, C. H. Lin, B. S. Huang, and C. M. Lin (2016). Performance of a low-cost earthquake early warning system (P-alert) during the 2016 ML 6.4 Meinong (Taiwan) earthquake, *Seismol. Res. Lett.* **87,** no. 5, 1050–1059, doi: 10.1785/0220160058.

Wu, Y. M., and T. L. Lin (2014). A test of earthquake early warning system using low cost accelerometer in Hualien, Taiwan, in *Early Warning for Geological Disasters: Scientific Methods and Current Practice*, Advanced Technologies in Earth Sciences, Springer-Verlag, Berlin, Heidelberg, 253–261.

Wu, Y. M., T. L. Lin, W. A. Chao, H. H. Huang, N. C. Hsiao, and C. H. Chang (2011). Faster short-distance earthquake early warning using continued monitoring of filtered vertical displacement: A case study for the 2010 Jiasian, Taiwan, earthquake, *Bull. Seismol. Soc. Am.* **101,** no. 2, 701–709, doi: 10.1785/0120100153.

Wu, Y. M., Y. H. Lin, B. M. Yang, and S. S. Ke (2025). Performance of the P-alert real-time shakemaps system and onsite warning during the 2025 ML6.4 Dapu earthquake, *Terr. Atmos. Ocean. Sci.* **36,** no. 1, 3, doi: 10.1007/s44195-025-00086-w.

Wu, Y. M., and H. Mittal (2021). A review on the development of earthquake warning system using low-cost sensors in Taiwan 22, *Sensors* **21,** no. 22, 7649, doi: 10.3390/s21227649.

Wu, Y. M., H. Mittal, D. Y. Chen, T. Y. Hsu, and P. Y. Lin (2021). Earthquake early warning systems in Taiwan: Current status, *J. Geol. Soc. India* **97,** no. 12, 1525–1532, doi: 10.1007/s12594-021-1909-6.

Wu, Y. M., H. Mittal, T. C. Huang, B. M. Yang, J. C. Jan, and S. K. Chen (2019). Performance of a low-cost earthquake early warning system (P-alert) and shake map production during the 2018 Mw 6.4 Hualien, Taiwan, earthquake, *Seismol. Res. Lett.* **90,** no. 1, 19–29, doi: 10.1785/0220180170.

Wu, Y. M., T. C. Shin, and Y. B. Tsai (1998). Quick and reliable determination of magnitude for seismic early warning, *Bull. Seismol. Soc. Am.* **88,** no. 5, 1254–1259.

Yang, B. M., T. C. Huang, and Y. M. Wu (2018). ShakingAlarm: A nontraditional regional earthquake early warning system based on time-dependent anisotropic peak ground-motion attenuation relationships, *Bull. Seismol. Soc. Am.* **108,** no. 3A, 1219–1230, doi: 10.1785/0120170105.

Yang, B. M., H. Mittal, and Y. M. Wu (2021). Real-time production of PGA, PGV, intensity, and Sa Shakemaps using dense MEMS-based sensors in Taiwan 3, *Sensors* **21,** no. 3, 943, doi: 10.3390/s21030943.

Yang, B. M., H. Mittal, and Y. M. Wu (2023). P-Alert earthquake early warning system: Case study of the 2022 Chishang earthquake at Taitung, Taiwan, *Terr. Atmos. Ocean. Sci.* **34,** no. 1, 26, doi: 10.1007/s44195-023-00057-z.

Zheng, A., X. Yu, C. Bai, W. Xu, J. Qian, W. Zhang, and X. Chen (2024). Thrust-dominated unilateral rupture of a blind listric fault associated with the 2024 Hualien earthquake, *Sci. Rep.* **14,** no. 1, 31496, doi: 10.1038/s41598-024-82971-x.

Manuscript received 7 April 2025
Published online 29 July 2025

A Comparative Analysis of the 14 November 1986 M_L 6.8, M_w 7.3 and 2 April 2024 M_L 7.1, M_w 7.4 Hualien, Taiwan, Earthquakes: Insights into Seismic Characteristics and Regional Impact

Kuo-Fong Ma[*1,2,3], Shiann-Jong Lee[1], Jolan Liao[3], and Shih-Nan Cheng[4]

ABSTRACT

Offshore fault systems near northeastern Taiwan pose a significant seismic hazard, underscored by the damaging 14 November 1986 M_L 6.8, M_w 7.3 and 2 April 2024 M_L 7.1, M_w 7.4 Hualien earthquakes. Despite occurring nearly four decades apart and with epicenters over 120 km from Taipei, both events caused notable damage in the capital. The 1986 earthquake was recorded by a limited seismic network, leaving rupture details uncertain, whereas the 2024 event (M_w 7.4), Taiwan's largest since the devastating 1999 Chi-Chi earthquake, benefited from a modern, high-density seismic network, enabling precise relocation and detailed rupture analysis. Despite these differences, both earthquakes exhibited similar focal mechanisms and similar long-period (> 1 s) waveforms at Geophysical Data Management System (GDMS)/Incorporated Research Institutions for Seismology stations. Moreover, velocity records from a 1986 local strong-motion station (SMART1-C00) closely align with modern 2024 recordings (Taiwan Strong Motion Implementation Program [TSMIP]-E026), suggesting a shared underlying seismogenic mechanism. By applying analytical methods developed for the well-recorded 2024 earthquake to re-examine the 1986 event, we simulated synthetic waveforms at TSMIP-E026 using the 2024 source model and compared them with synthetics derived from source models of the 1986 earthquake. Although direct comparison using modern inversion standard is challenging, this qualitative agreement highlights a common concentration of energy releases around 30 s with similar duration in both earthquakes. Spectral analysis in both Hualien and the distant Taipei basin indicates comparable, and at times higher, ground motion in the southwestern Taipei basin, correlating with observed structural damage in both earthquake scenarios. Although enhanced building codes implemented post-1999 likely mitigated the impact of the 2024 event, the sustained strong shaking highlights persistent vulnerabilities. The striking similarities in waveforms and spectral characteristics imply that these Hualien earthquakes, despite their temporal separation, share not only comparable magnitudes and focal mechanisms but also a common seismogenic process.

KEY POINTS

- The 1986 and 2024 Hualien earthquakes share focal mechanisms and similar waveforms, and they caused strong motions in Taipei.
- Both earthquakes show similar energy release and Taipei basin amplification from offshore seismogenic structure.
- The 2024 losses lessened by codes, but offshore seismogenic structure needs study for hazard and risk.

INTRODUCTION

The damaging Hualien earthquake of 14 November 1986 M_L 6.8, M_w 7.3 (U.S. Geological Survey [USGS], 21:20 UTC) was a pivotal event in the evolution of Taiwan's seismic observation capabilities. Originating offshore near Hualien at 23.993° N, 121.810° E and a depth of 13.4 km (Chen

1. Institute of Earth Sciences, Academia Sinica, Taipei, Taiwan, https://orcid.org/0000-0002-4500-8079 (K-FM); https://orcid.org/0000-0002-3111-9675 (S-JL); 2. Earthquake-Disaster and Risk Evaluation and Management (E-DREaM) Center, National Central University, Taoyuan, Taiwan; 3. Department of Earth Sciences, National Central University, Taoyuan, Taiwan, https://orcid.org/0009-0004-7207-2772 (JL); 4. Department of Applied Geomatics, Chien Hsin University of Science and Technology, Taoyuan, Taiwan, https://orcid.org/0009-0009-9755-6630 (S-NC)

*Corresponding author: fong@earth.sinica.edu.tw

Cite this article as Ma, K.-F., S.-J. Lee, J. Liao, and S.-N. Cheng (2025). A Comparative Analysis of the 14 November 1986 M_L 6.8, M_w 7.3 and 2 April 2024 M_L 7.1, M_w 7.4 Hualien, Taiwan, Earthquakes: Insights into Seismic Characteristics and Regional Impact, *Bull. Seismol. Soc. Am.* **116**, 80–93, doi: 10.1785/0120250100

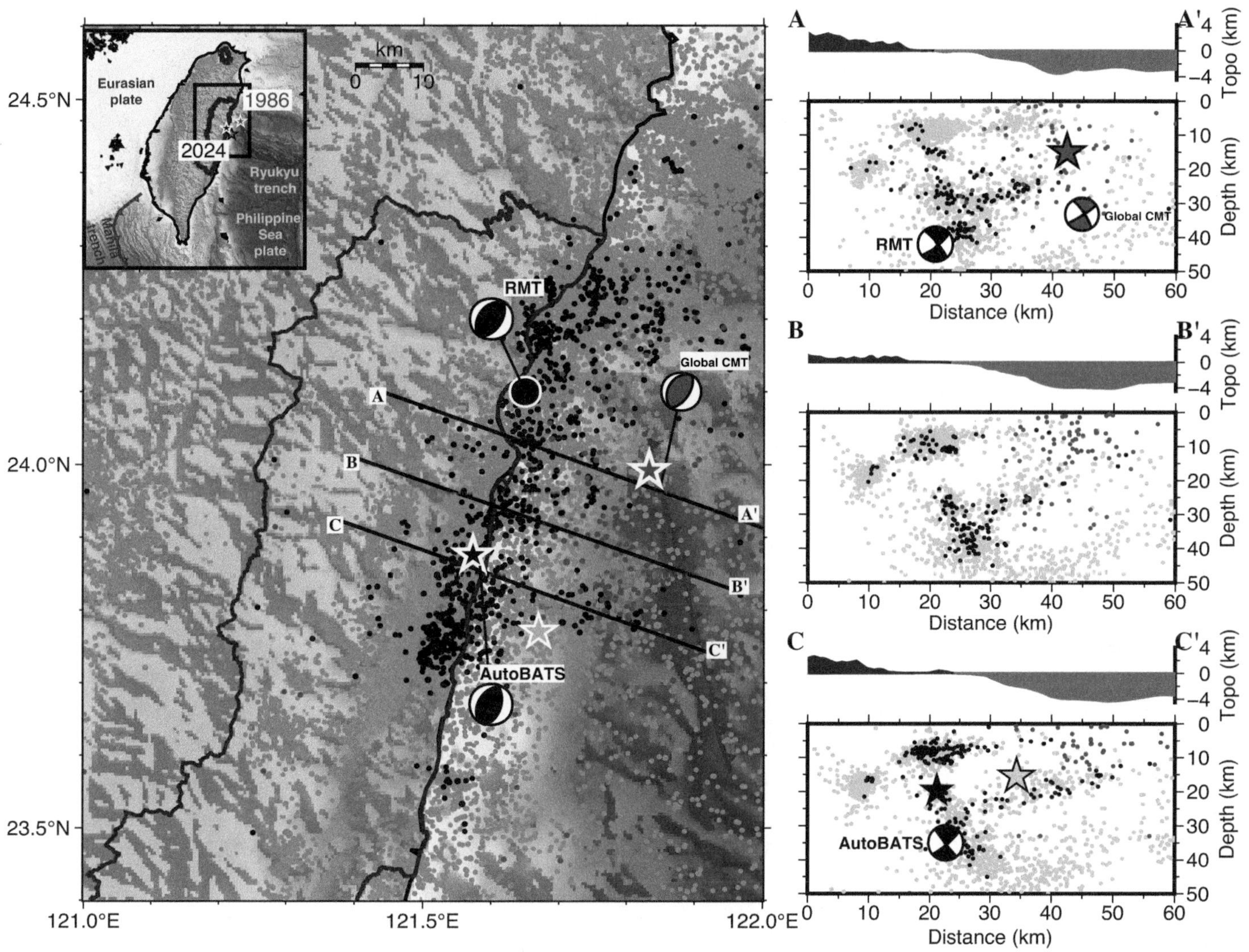

and Wang, 1986), according to records from the Taiwan Telemetered Seismographic Network (TTSN), the 1986 earthquake exhibited a first-motion focal mechanism with a strike of N33°E and dip of 58° to the southeast (Fig. 1a). Despite its epicenter being >120 km from Taipei, the event caused significant damage in the metropolitan area (Fig. 2a), leaving a lasting impact on public. Taiwan lies within a young, active orogenic belt at the complex junction of the Eurasian and Philippine Sea plates (Fig. 1a), where tectonic styles shift from collision along the Longitudinal Valley Fault to subduction at the offshore Ryukyu trench near Hualien. This structural transition, involving multiple interacting fault systems with poorly constrained offshore continuations, highlights the critical role of offshore seismogenic structures in controlling regional seismic hazard (Chen and Shyu, 2025). Similar to the 1985 Mexico City earthquake where significant damage occurred far from the epicenter (Anderson and Singh, 1989), the 1986 Taiwan earthquake highlighted the vulnerability of distant urban centers to offshore seismic events. This realization spurred the development of more advanced seismic networks in Taiwan (Fig. 2b). These enhanced networks proved crucial during the devastating

Figure 1. Tectonic setting of Taiwan at the complex junction of the Eurasian and Philippine Sea plates (inset), where tectonic regimes transition from arc-continent collision in central Taiwan to oceanic subduction at the offshore Ryukyu trench near Hualien. The administrative boundaries of Hualien County and Taipei City are outlined with bold lines. The 1986 Hualien earthquake is indicated by the Global Centroid Moment Tensor (Global CMT) solution (red focal mechanism plot) and its epicenter from the Taiwan Telemetered Seismographic Network (TTSN) catalog (red asterisk). For the 2024 Hualien earthquake, multiple epicentral locations are marked: a dark-gray asterisk (preliminary location by Central Weather Administration [CWA]), a black asterisk (CWA relocation), and a white-outlined black circle (real-time moment tensor [RMT] solution from Lee *et al.*, 2013). Corresponding focal mechanisms from AutoBATS and the RMT solution are also shown. Background seismicity (gray dots) includes events with M >3 recorded since 2000. Aftershock sequences are represented by red dots (1986 event, one-month window) and black dots (2024 event, one-month window). Seismic cross-sections AA′, BB′, and CC′, which are oriented approximately perpendicular to the strike of the focal mechanisms, are displayed with corresponding topography and bathymetry. Seismicity within ±8 km of each profile is projected, and focal mechanisms within the profiles are side projected for reference. The color version of this figure is available only in the electronic edition.

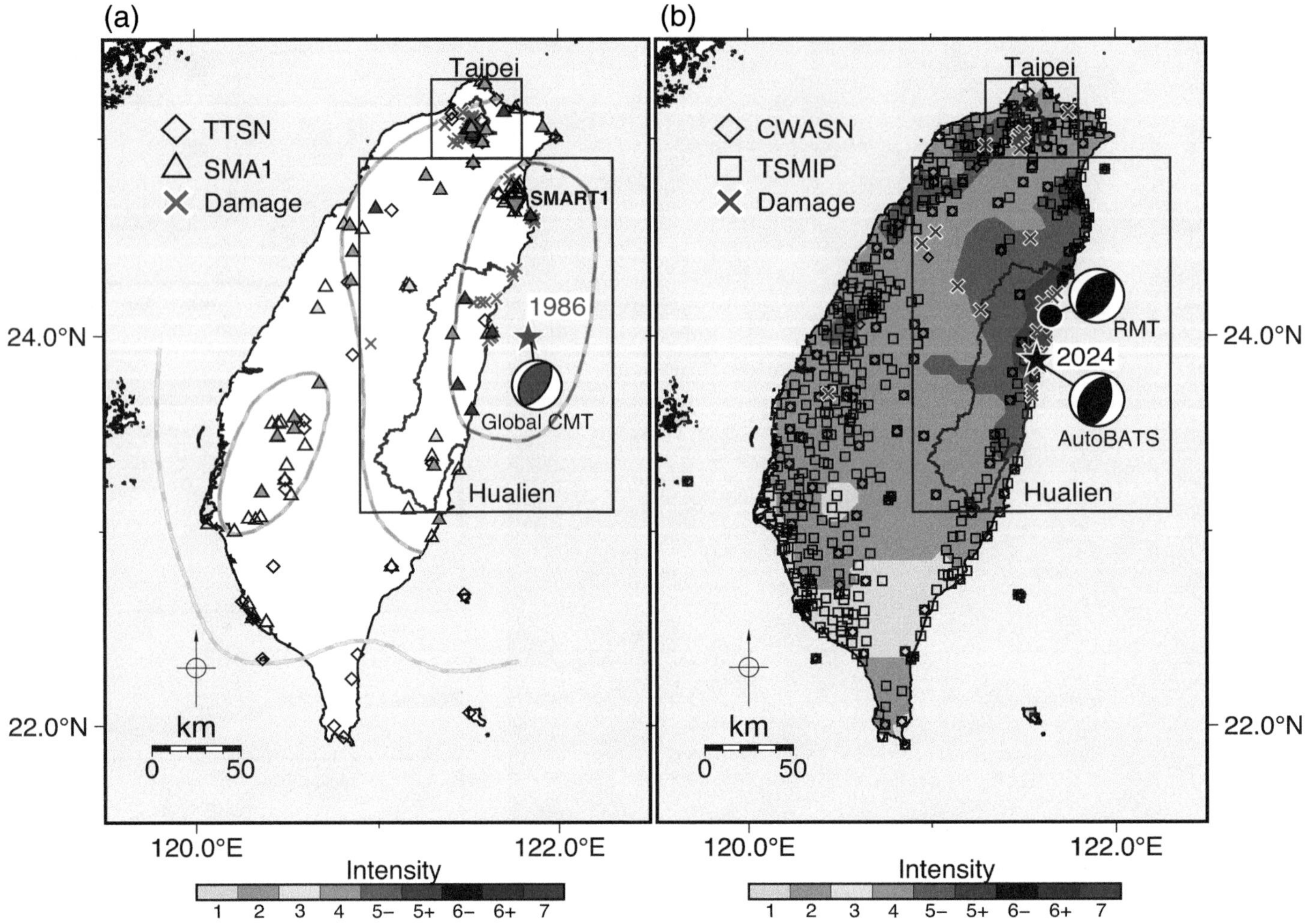

Figure 2. (a) Map showing the epicenter from TTSN, focal mechanism from Global CMT (Table 1) and seismic intensity distribution of the 14 November 1986 Hualien earthquake. Short-period stations from the TTSN (diamonds), strong-motion stations of strong-motion accelerograph (SMA; open triangles), and SMART1 (inverted triangles) networks are also shown. The color-coded SMA stations (solid triangles) represent the intensity derived from the recorded peak ground acceleration (PGA) values. Red crosses mark damage sites associated with the earthquake. Contour lines depict seismic intensity derived from the observed PGA at SMA stations. The Hualien region near the epicenter (asterisk) and the Taipei metropolitan area are highlighted with boxes. The damaged associated with the earthquake, including buildings, landslides, and rockfalls, are marked in the red crosses. (b) Map showing the epicenter (black asterisk), RMT location (white-outlined black circle), seismic intensity distribution (color-shaded contours), and station locations for the 2 April 2024 Hualien earthquake. CWA short-period stations are marked as diamonds and Taiwan Strong Motion Implementation Program (TSMIP) stations as squares. Blue crosses indicate damage sites, including buildings, bridges, landslide, and rockfalls. Boxes highlight the Hualien epicentral region and the Taipei area. The focal mechanism is from the Broadband Array in Taiwan for Seismology (BATS) CMT and RMT solutions. The corresponding color scale for the CWA intensity scale is shown at the bottom of the figure. The color version of this figure is available only in the electronic edition.

21 September 1999 M_w 7.6 Chi-Chi earthquake, yielding comprehensive datasets that significantly advanced global research on near-fault ground motion (Shin, 1993; Shin *et al.*, 2000).

The more recent 2 April 2024 M_L 7.1, M_w 7.4 earthquake (03:58:09 UTC), the largest in Taiwan since the 1999 Chi-Chi earthquake, was located by the Central Weather Administration (CWA) at 23.86° N, 121.58° E, depth 22.52 km, ~20 km southwest of the 1986 Hualien earthquake's epicenter (Fig. 1a). The focal mechanism, derived from the Broadband Array in Taiwan for Seismology (BATS; Institute of Earth Sciences, Academia Sinica, Taiwan, 1996), indicated a strike of N37.6° E, dip of 47.7°, and rake of 90.3° (Jian *et al.*, 2018), which is similar to the first-motion solution of the 1986 event (Fig. 1a). The real-time moment tensor (RMT) solution (Lee *et al.*, 2013) placed the centroid at 24.10° N, 121.65° E, depth 42 km, M_w 7.32, indicating a northward shift and deeper centroid moment release relative to the epicenter. Figure 1a shows the epicentral locations, aftershocks ($M_w \geq 3$) during the first month, and focal mechanisms of the 1986 and 2024 Hualien earthquakes, together with seismicity profiles along AA′, BB′, and CC′. Figure 1b–d shows the profiles perpendicular to the strikes of the focal mechanism. Because of advancements in Taiwan's seismic monitoring since 1999, the aftershock sequence of the 2024 earthquake was recorded with far greater density than that of 1986. The AA′–CC′ profiles reveal a complex inland-to-offshore structural transition. There are steeply east-dipping structures on land along with west-dipping offshore structures, suggesting multiple interacting fault systems with unclear offshore continuations (Huang and Wang, 2022). Improved earthquake preparedness meant casualties from the 2024 event were far lower than for the 1999 Chi-Chi earthquake, which caused >2000 deaths and extensive building damages. Nevertheless, some damages still occurred in Taipei (Fig. 2b, National Science and Technology Center for Disaster Reduction [NCDR], 2025), raising critical concerns about the potential for offshore earthquakes to impact not only nearby areas but also distant urban centers. Similar to the 1986 event, the 2024 earthquake underscores the enduring seismic risks posed by offshore fault structures near northeastern Taiwan, which have repeatedly caused significant damage in Taipei.

A key observation from the 2024 earthquake was the 10–20 km difference between the relocated epicenter from CWA location (Fig. 1a), underscoring the inherent challenges of precisely locating offshore events in regions with sparse eastward station coverage. This highlights the difficulties of accurately pinpointing earthquake sources in near-offshore settings. Similarly, the sparse instrumentation during the 1986 earthquake (Fig. 2a) limited investigation of the seismogenic structures responsible for damage observed in Taipei and Hualien, including landslides and rockfalls in Taroko Gorge (Chang *et al.*, 2024). As a result, the broader implications of the 1986 event, particularly its offshore origin, were not fully understood.

This study leverages the comprehensive instrumental recordings of the 2024 earthquake to compare regional and global datasets with those from the 1986 event, which were constrained by limited-bandwidth and triggered-mode analog recordings. Re-examining the sparse 1986 data allows us to evaluate the potential relationship between the seismogenic structures of the two earthquakes and the influence of offshore fault systems on metropolitan areas such as Taipei. The 2024 earthquake thus serves as a case study for evaluating interpretations of past seismic events and as a reminder of the need to investigate offshore seismogenic zones critical for hazard mitigation and risk management efforts in Taiwan.

REVISIT OF THE 14 NOVEMBER 1986 HUALIEN EARTHQUAKE

Teleseismic and local strong-motion data

In 1986, the Incorporated Research Institutions for Seismology (IRIS), now part of EarthScope, Inc., was in its nascent stages. The global seismic network was transitioning from the Worldwide Standardized Seismograph Network to the Global Digital Seismograph Network, a development that improved seismic data collection and archiving capabilities. The teleseismic records used in this study were primarily acquired from low-frequency, high-gain instruments (designated with the LH code), covering a frequency band of ~0.001–5 Hz.

During the 1980s, Taiwan significantly advanced its seismic monitoring infrastructure through the deployment of several strong-motion arrays, most notably the strong-motion accelerograph (SMA) network. This SMA network comprised numerous analog accelerographs (Fig. 2a) operating in triggered recording mode (Liu *et al.*, 1999), with data subsequently digitized using 12-bit analog-to-digital converters. These instruments were presumably activated when a preset acceleration threshold (typically between 0.01 and 0.05*g*, varying by instrument and location) was exceeded, recording for a fixed duration (e.g., 30–60 s) with a frequency band of 0.1–25 Hz. The SMART1 array, a circular array with a central reference station (Wen and Yeh, 1991), was established through collaborative effort between the Institute of Earth Sciences (IES); Academia Sinica; and the University of California, Berkeley. Unlike the SMA network, SMART1 used a more advanced clock and digital recording system for that era (Fig. 2a). These earlier networks were superseded by the modern Taiwan Strong Motion Implementation Program (TSMIP) starting in 1993 (Fig. 2b). Figure 2a,b shows the spatial distribution of the SMA and SMART1 arrays that recorded the 1986 Hualien earthquake, as well as the modern TSMIP network that recorded the 2024 Hualien earthquake, respectively.

Damaging patterns and PGA distribution from the SMA network

Damage data from the 1986 Hualien earthquake were compiled from the CWA of instrumental recoding disastrous earthquakes of 1898–1997 and manually georeferenced. The earthquake caused 13 fatalities and 45 injuries, resulting in 37 completely collapsed and 33 severely damaged buildings, along with numerous rockfalls and landslides as shown in Figure 2a. The spatial distribution of collapsed and damaged buildings, along with mapped rockfalls and landslides, is shown for the Hualien (Fig. 3a) and Taipei (Fig. 3b) regions. These are compared with the 2024 earthquake damage patterns (Fig. 2b). The strong-motion stations for the SMA in 1986 and TSMIP network in these two regions are also shown. Notable damage patterns included rockfalls and landslides along highways extending from the eastern coast toward Taroko National Park and significant building damage within the Taipei Metropolitan area, especially in the southwestern Taipei basin. Furthermore, Figure 2a displays the intensity map derived from the peak ground acceleration (PGA) distribution, calculated from the limited recordings of the SMA and SMART1 arrays (Chen and Wang, 1986). Despite the sparsity of instrumental data, the macroseismic intensity shows a strong correlation with the observed PGA distribution, particularly within the Taipei basin (Fig. 2a). Figure 2b shows the 2024 Hualien intensity map derived from modern

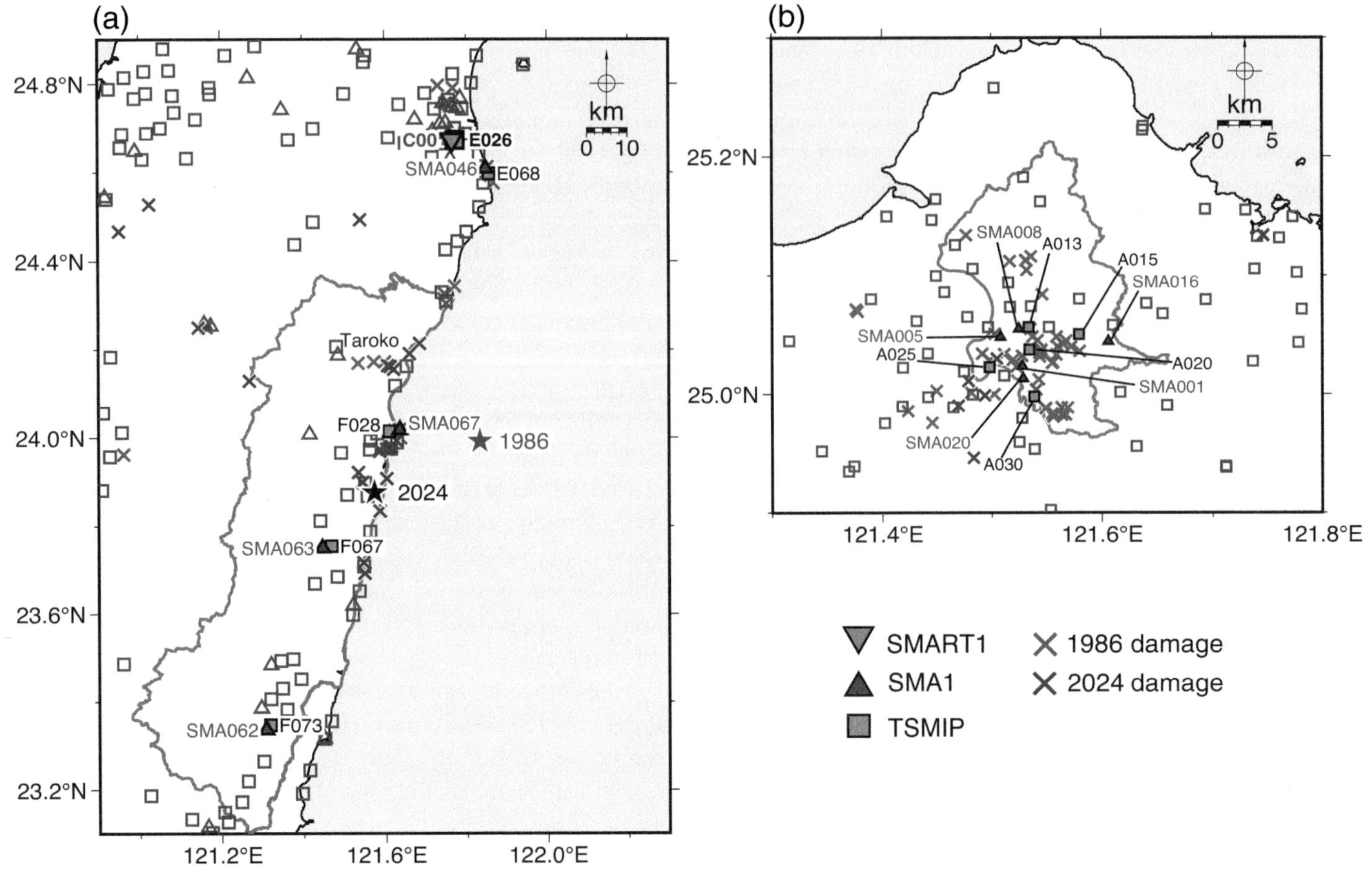

TSMIP data, plotted using the Taiwan CWA intensity scale. It reveals similar damage patterns but with much higher spatial resolution.

Spatial slip distribution inferred from teleseismic data

We employed advanced modern analytical techniques for finite-fault analysis, using teleseismic waveforms to map the spatial slip distribution of the 1986 Hualien earthquake. Deriving the slip distribution from local strong-motion stations proved challenging because of uncertainties in clock synchronization within the SMA array and its triggered recording mode. Consequently, our finite-fault inversion focused on teleseismic waveforms, excluding the strong-motion stations. Contemporary teleseismic inversion typically uses stations located 30°–90° from the epicenter to minimize the influence of regional low-velocity structures and shadow zones. However, the limited availability of stations in 1986 necessitated the inclusion of all available stations in our analysis, relying solely on long-period *P*-wave records for the inversion. The teleseismic velocity data were band-pass filtered between 0.01 and 0.5 Hz and then integrated to obtain displacements.

The teleseismic Green's functions were computed using the synthetic engines of the IRIS Data Management Center (DMC; Incorporated Research Institutions for Seismology Data Management Center [IRIS DMC], 2015). The inversion

Figure 3. Reported building damage, landslides, and rockfalls in (a) the Hualien region and (b) the Taipei region, corresponding to the areas highlighted in Figure 2a,b, are shown for the 1986 (red crosses) and 2024 (blue crosses) Hualien earthquakes. Strong-motion stations from the SMA network (triangles) and the TSMIP network (squares) are also indicated. Station pairs used in this study (listed in Table 2) are labeled with station names and color coded as follows: red station names with solid triangles for the SMA network and black station names with solid squares for the TSMIP network. The location of Taroko National Park in Hualien is also marked. In addition, the SMART1 station C00 (inverted blue triangle) and the TSMIP station E026 (blue square) are highlighted in bold. The color version of this figure is available only in the electronic edition.

modeled a finite fault with a 5 km grid spacing, incorporating the Global Centroid Moment Tensor (Global CMT) focal mechanism and location (Table 1), the preliminary reference Earth model global velocity model (Dziewonski and Anderson, 1981), and a multiple source time function of 1 s duration, consistent with the data bandwidth. It is noteworthy that the Global CMT determined a depth of 33.2 km for the 1986 Hualien earthquake, significantly deeper than the 15 km reported by the local TTSN network (Table 1). This discrepancy may be due to the fact that Global CMT locates the earthquake using its centroid moment tensor, whereas the local TTSN network determines the location from first arrivals, which were influenced by the initial ~5 s of foreshocks. However, the Global CMT focal depth

TABLE 1
Locations and Magnitude of the 14 November 1986 and 2 April 2024 Hualien Earthquakes from Different Agencies

Agency	Date and Time (yyyy/mm/dd hh:mm:ss.ss)	Latitude (°)	Longitude (°)	Depth (km)	Magnitude	Reference
CWB	1986/11/14 20:04.5	23.992	121.833	15	M_L 6.8	From TTSN (Chen and Wang, 1986)
Global CMT	1986/11/14 20:17.8	23.97	121.85	33.2	M_w 7.3	Global CMT
NEIC	1986/11/14 20:10.5	23.961	121.836	34	M_s 7.8	Hwang and Kanamori (1989)
USGS	1986/11/14 20:10.6	23.901	121.574	33.8	M_w 7.4	See Data and Resources
CWA	2024/04/02 23:58:09.94	23.8757	121.5735	19.72	M_L 7.19	CWA GDMS
CWA	2024/04/02 23:58:09.9	23.77	121.67	15.5	M_L 7.2	CWA initial report
IES	2024/04/02 23:58:09.89	23.8607	121.5837	35	M_w 7.3	AutoBATS
IES	2024/04/02 23.58:09	24.10	121.65	42	M_w 7.32	RMT

CWA, Central Weather Administration; Global CMT, Global Centroid Moment Tensor; IES, Institute of Earth Sciences; NEIC, National Earthquake Information Center; RMT, real-time moment tensor; TTSN, Taiwan Telemetered Seismographic Network; USGS, U.S. Geological Survey.

of the 1986 earthquake is comparable to the centroid depth obtained from the RMT of the 2024 earthquake (Fig. 2b), both reflecting the depth of centroid moment release. Nevertheless, the epicenters of the two earthquakes are separated by a distance on the order of 20–30 km.

Figure 4a,b shows the station distribution together with the observed and synthetic data for the assumed east- and west-dipping fault planes of the inverted slip distributions (Fig. 4c,d), respectively, considering the uncertainty in the involved rupture plane from the complex onshore–offshore fault system (Fig. 1b). However, the minimal misfit differences between the two models make it difficult to definitively identify the causative fault plane for the 1986 Hualien earthquake. The patterns in spatial slip distributions suggest a fault rupture extending ~60 km along strike and 30 km down-dip, with a maximum slip of ~3 m. The source time function (Fig. 4e) shows a primary concentration between 5 and 20 s, preceded by a quiet onset during the initial 5 s, potentially attributable to uncertainties in the earthquake's location and interference from a moderate foreshock 5 s before the mainshock (Hwang and Kanamori, 1989; Wang *et al.*, 1989). A secondary, smaller energy releases between 20 and 25 s. The derived spatial slip distribution is consistent with the findings of Hwang and Kanamori (1989), indicating a source duration primarily within the first 15 s, with bilateral rupture propagation extending 60 km along strike and 40 km down-dip. The moment release peaks between 5 and 14 s, followed by a prolonged, lower-amplitude release between 20 and 32 s.

COMPARISON WITH THE 2 APRIL 2024 HUALIEN EARTHQUAKE

Comparison of the observed teleseismic and strong-motion records

Although direct comparison of the 1986 and 2024 spatial slip distributions from the local strong-motion network is hindered by uncertainties in epicenter location, clock synchronization, and the limited frequency band of the instrumentation in 1986, a comparison of their observed teleseismic records at common stations offers valuable insights. Figure 5 presents a comparison of the original velocity waveforms for the vertical components: LHZ for the 1986 and 2024 earthquakes, recorded at stations COL (now COLA), CTAO, NWAO, and SNZO (as depicted in Fig. 4a). These records exhibit high cross-correlation values (CCVs), exceeding 0.9 at most stations within the initial 60 s, which aligns with the estimated source rupture duration. The highest CCV (~0.98) is observed at the COL(COLA) station across all three components. Despite differences in the instrumentation used in 1986 and 2024, the similarity in both phase and amplitude across all three components is striking. This direct comparison strongly suggests that the two earthquakes shared very similar source rupture processes. However, achieving these high CCVs required a 2.5 s shift of the 2024 earthquake records. Assuming an average global P-wave velocity of 8.5 km/s in the mantle, this temporal shift implies a potential separation of ~20 km between the source regions of the two earthquakes. Alternatively, this time difference could also be attributed to uncertainties in the determined locations of the 1986 and 2024 earthquakes.

In addition to the global teleseismic record comparison, we also compared more advanced digital recordings with improved clock accuracy from the SMART1 station C00 in 1986. We compared the three components of the 15 November 1986 records from SMART1 station C00 (Fig. 2a) with the corresponding records from the modern TSMIP station E026 for the 2 April 2024 earthquake (Fig. 2b). To ensure consistency with the 0.1–25 Hz instrument response range of the 1986 data, the acceleration records were band-pass filtered between 0.1 and 10 Hz and subsequently integrated to velocity for comparison. Notably, the 1986 C00 record required polarity correction to achieve better alignment with the 2024 data, indicating that polarity must be carefully considered when analyzing SMART1 station waveforms. The primary use of SMART1 array data for spectral analysis might explain why this polarity issue has not been previously documented in the literature. Following polarity correction, Figure 6a shows the strong correlation in both phase and amplitude of the initial 30 s of the waveforms, although peak

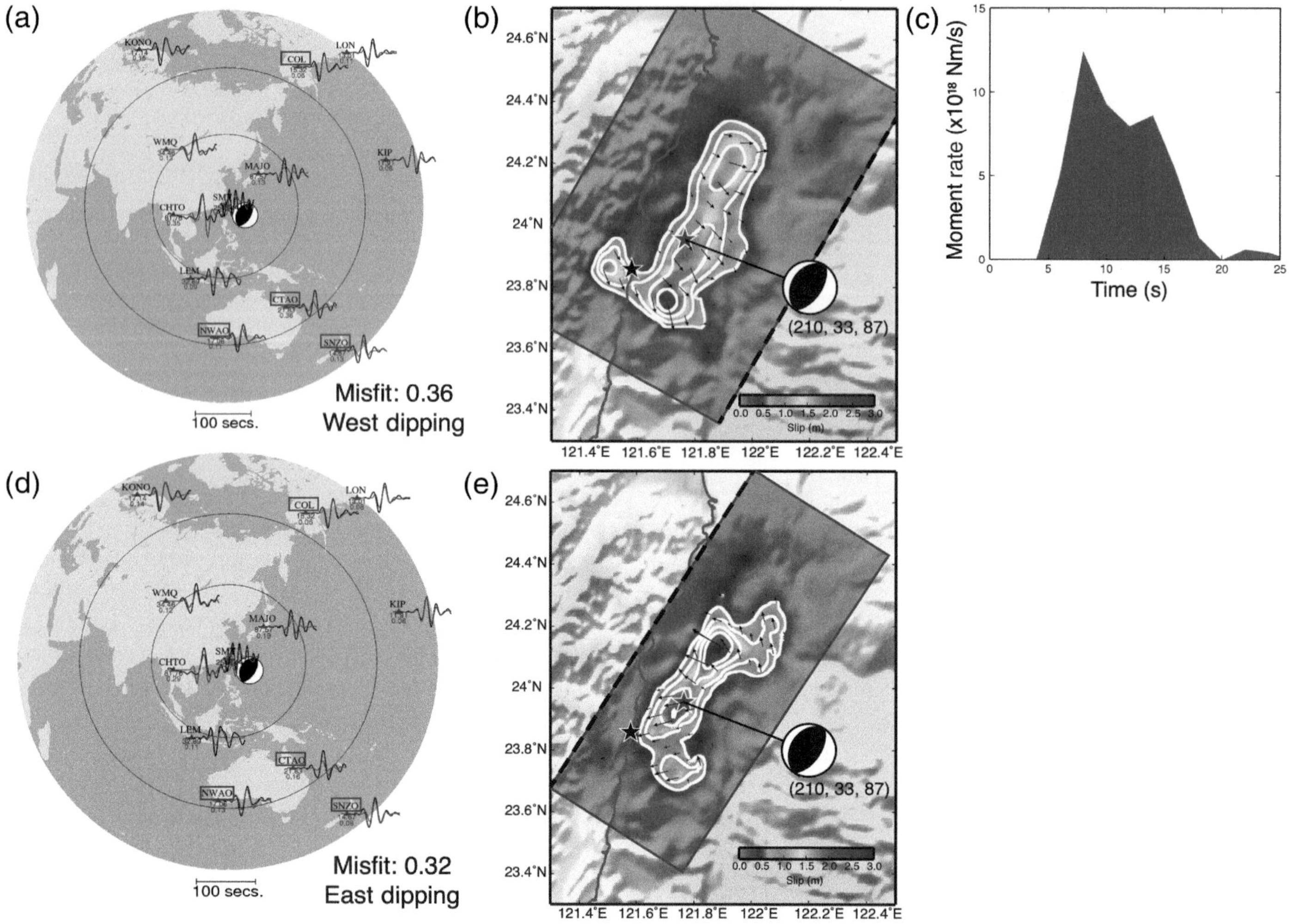

velocity at station E026 of 2024 earthquake is generally higher than that recorded at station C00 of 1986 earthquake. Discrepancies in the later phases may result from minor site differences between the 1986 location of station C00 and the relocated E026 station in 2024 (separated by a few hundred meters) or variations in the source rupture beyond the initial 30 s. Alternatively, consistent with the teleseismic comparison, the two earthquakes may have originated from slightly different locations despite their similar overall rupture processes. Figure 6b shows the corresponding three-component seismic spectra at station C00 for the 1986 earthquake and at station E026 for the 2024 earthquake, with their spectral ratio (E026/C00) presented in Figure 6c. The ratio is close to 1.0 across most of the frequency band, except for slightly larger values below 0.4 Hz, especially in north and vertical components, indicating overall similarity between the two events. The enhanced long-period amplitudes (<0.4 Hz) in 2024 may reflect its slightly larger magnitude relative to 1986 limitations in the dynamic range of the 1986 instrumentation. A more detailed comparison of the 2024 E026 strong-motion velocity records with forward modeling based on the aforementioned derived source model from the teleseismic waveforms of the 1986 earthquake is presented in a later section.

Figure 4. Teleseismic station distribution and observed and synthetic waveforms for the (a) west-dipping and (d) east-dipping fault planes are shown, along with their respective waveform misfit values. Stations marked with squares indicate the common teleseismic stations of the 14 November 1986 and the 2 April 2024 earthquakes. The corresponding finite-fault slip distributions are shown for the (b) west-dipping and (e) east-dipping fault planes. The color scale represents the spatial variation in slip, revealing bilateral rupture propagation and a peak slip of ~3 m. The focal mechanism and location (red asterisk) are also shown, along with the location of the 2024 earthquake (black asterisk). (c) The corresponding source time function, characterizing the rupture process of the 14 November 1986 earthquake. The color version of this figure is available only in the electronic edition.

Comparison of acceleration spectra in Hualien and the Taipei basin

Beyond the comparison of velocity records and spectra from SMART1, we also analyzed the acceleration spectra of the 1986 and 2024 earthquakes at near-co-site stations from the SMA and TSMIP networks in both Hualien and the Taipei Basin, regions where damage was reported (Fig. 3a,b). Our comparison focuses on station pairs located within a 3 km radius of each other near damaged areas. Table 2 lists these station pairs,

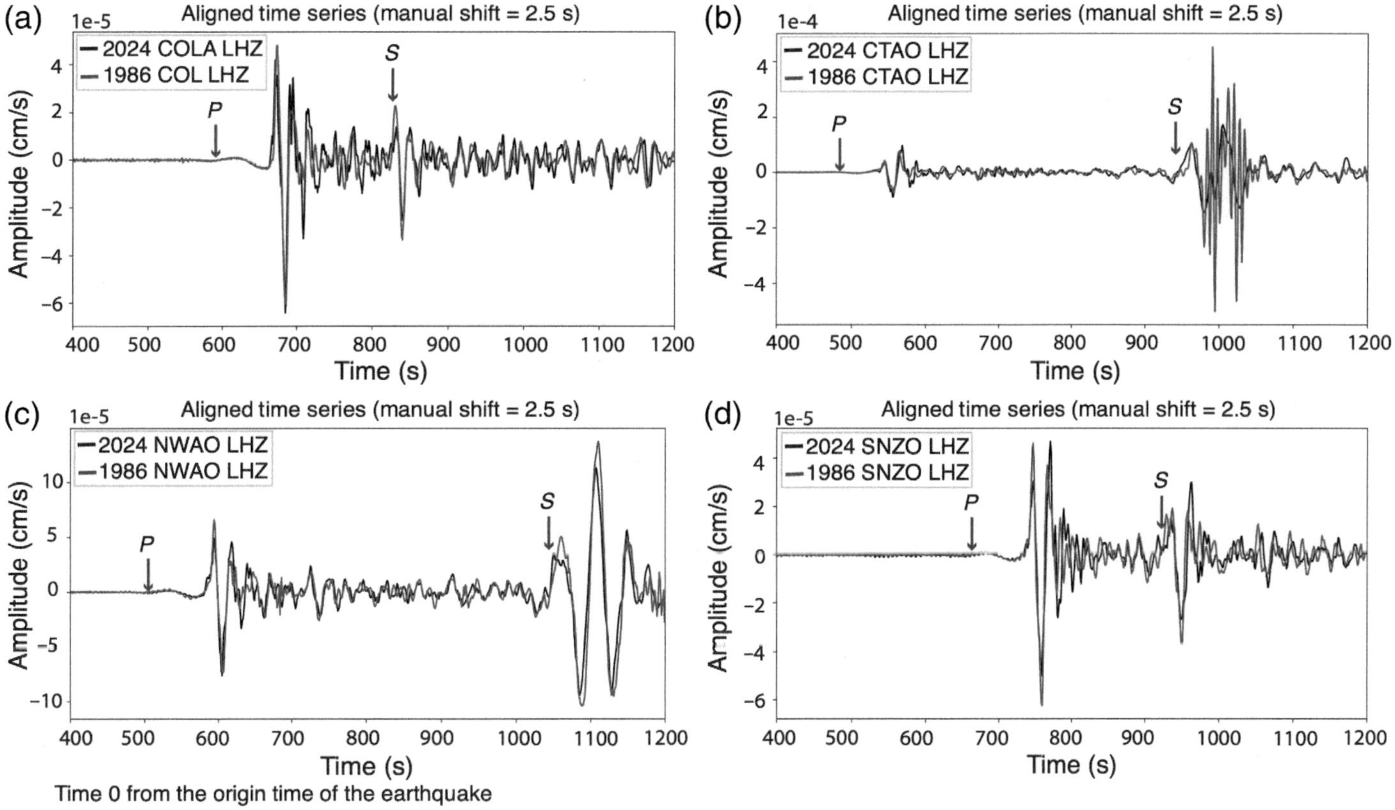

Figure 5. Comparison of teleseismic vertical component waveforms (LHZ) recorded at common Incorporated Research Institutions for Seismology (IRIS) stations for the 1986 (red) and 2024 (black) Hualien earthquakes, as shown in Figure 3a. The stations include (a) COL (now renamed COLA), (b) CTAO, (c) NWAO, and (d) SNZO. The waveforms are aligned by applying a 2.5 s time shift to achieve optimal correlation. Time is referenced from the origin time of each earthquake. The *P* and *S* arrivals are indicated on the time series are marked. The color version of this figure is available only in the electronic edition.

including four in the Hualien region and five in the Taipei basin. The pairs were chosen based on proximity to reported damage and record availability (Table 2). Because the 1986 SMA data were limited by trigger-mode recording and variable data availability, we used the SMA records as a reference to define the analysis window for the corresponding 2024 TSMIP records. Table 2 also lists the separation distance of each station pair and available recording durations used for spectral analysis. As expected, stations near damage zones often experience stronger shaking, which can lead to recording system interruptions. This poses a challenge in capturing signals associated with strong shaking using less resilient recording systems. Nevertheless, despite limitations in the analog time-series recordings of the triggered SMA array with its less precise timing, acceleration spectral comparisons still offer valuable insights into the similar damage patterns observed in Hualien and the Taipei basin.

The acceleration spectra for both the Hualien (Fig. 7a) and Taipei basin (Fig. 8a) regions show overall similarities between the 1986 and 2024 earthquakes, consistent with our time-series observations. To further evaluate the detail behavior in the station pairs, we applied a water-level deconvolution to derive the acceleration spectral ratios of the 2024 to 1986 earthquakes (Figs. 7b and 8b for Hualien and Taipei, respectively).

In the Hualien region (Fig. 7a,b), stations north of the epicenters exhibit higher acceleration spectra in the 0.2–1 Hz range for the 2024 event compared with the 1986 event, suggesting stronger source effects in 2024. In the 5–10 Hz band, the 2024 earthquake also shows larger amplitudes, which may explain the broader damage area observed in 2024 relative to 1986 as shown in Figure 3a. These results indicate that source effects, including directivity, played a more significant role in 2024 for the Hualien region. Station pairs analyzed are located 10–50 km from the epicenters, so the subtle source effects from the two earthquakes at short distances remains visible in the spectral ratios even though the high-frequency content might be influenced by the site effects. The larger long-period energy (≤ 0.4 Hz) in 2024 may reflect its slightly larger magnitude or subtle differences in locations of these two earthquakes despite restricting station pairs to within 3 km. Site conditions can still vary appreciably over such short distances.

In the Taipei basin, both earthquakes display consistently higher spectral amplitudes in the southwestern region (Fig. 8a), which experienced greater damage (Fig. 3b) and is underlain by thicker sedimentary deposits (Wang *et al.*, 2004). This is evident in the station pair A015–SMA016, located near the basin edge,

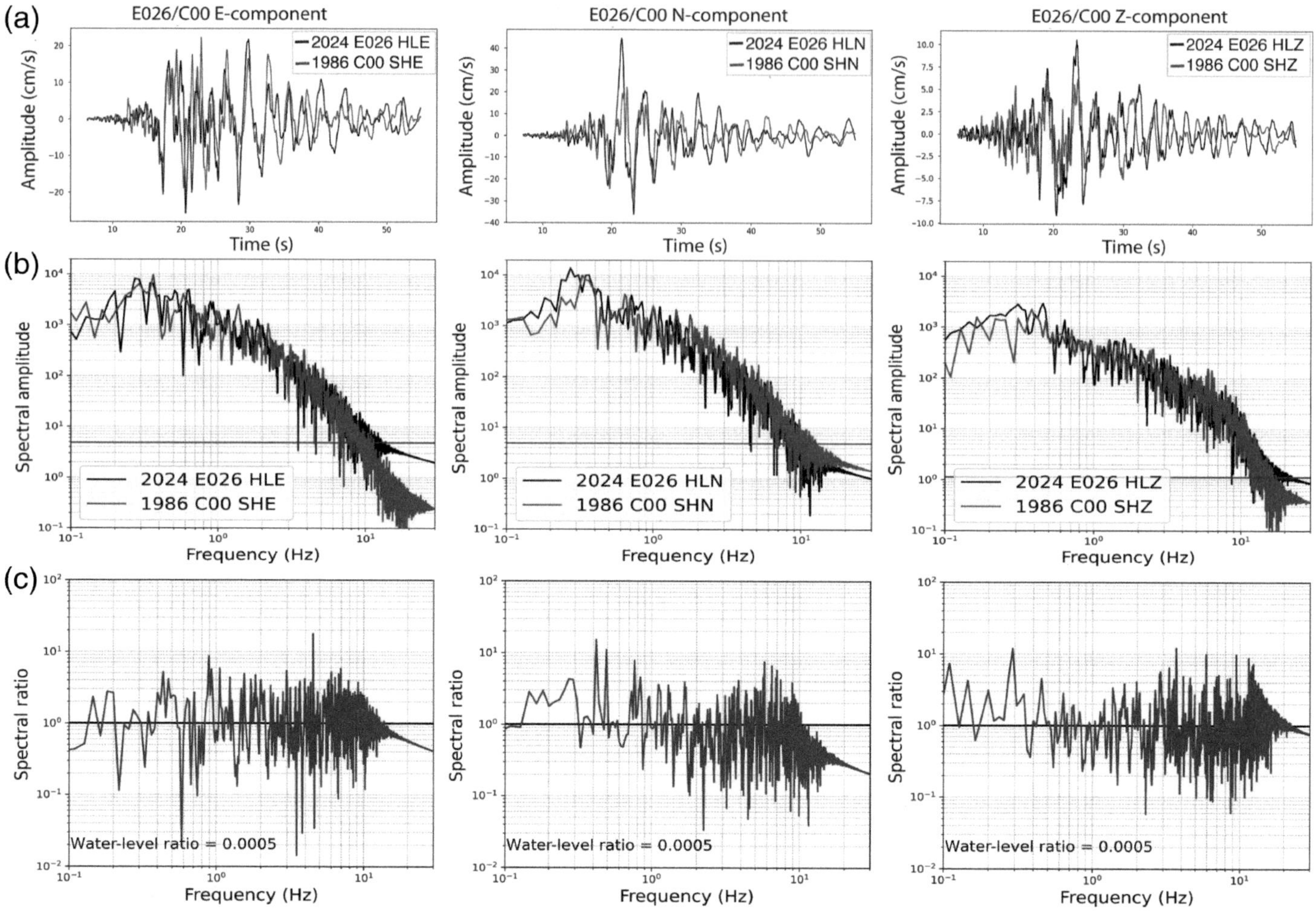

Figure 6. (a) Comparison of three-component velocity records (in cm/s) from station C00 (SMART1 array, 14 November 1986, shown in red) and station E026 (TSMIP, 2 April 2024, shown in black) for the Hualien earthquakes. Both datasets were band-pass filtered between 0.1 and 10 Hz and obtained by integrating the original acceleration records. The C00 records were time shifted to maximize cross correlation with the E026 records for each component. Time zero is defined as 15 s after the origin time of the 2 April 2024 earthquake. (b) Three-component seismic spectra at station C00 (red) for the 1986 earthquake and station E026 (black) for the 2024 earthquake. The water level used in the deconvolution analysis is indicated by the blue line. (c) Corresponding spectral ratio (E026/C00), with the reference ratio of 1 marked by the black line. The color version of this figure is available only in the electronic edition.

TABLE 2
Selected Station Pairs of the SMA Array in 1986 and TSMIP Network in 2024 for Hualien and Taipei Regions

Regions	TSMIP	Longitude (°)	Latitude (°)	SMA	Longitude (°)	Latitude (°)	Distance (km)*	Time Duration (s)†
Hualien	E068	121.8573	24.5972	SMA046	121.8488	24.6088	1.55	31.28
	F028	121.6094	24.0144	SMA067	121.6358	24.0178	2.71	50.38
	F067	121.4688	23.7545	SMA063	121.4467	23.75	2.31	51.02
	F073	121.3191	23.3472	SMA062	121.3088	23.3368	1.56	34.26
Taipei	A013	121.5337	25.0565	SMA008	121.5247	25.055	0.93	38.62
	A020	121.5344	25.0376	SMA001	121.528	25.0235	1.7	19.74
	A025	121.498	25.0228	SMA005	121.508	25.0482	3	35.34
	A030	121.5387	24.9979	SMA020	121.5287	25.0132	1.98	31.4
	A015	121.5794	25.0504	SMA016	121.6058	25.0443	2.75	10.3

*Distance: distance between the event pairs.
†Time duration: the length of time series used in the spectra analysis.
SMA, strong-motion accelerograph; TSMIP, Taiwan Strong Motion Implementation Program.

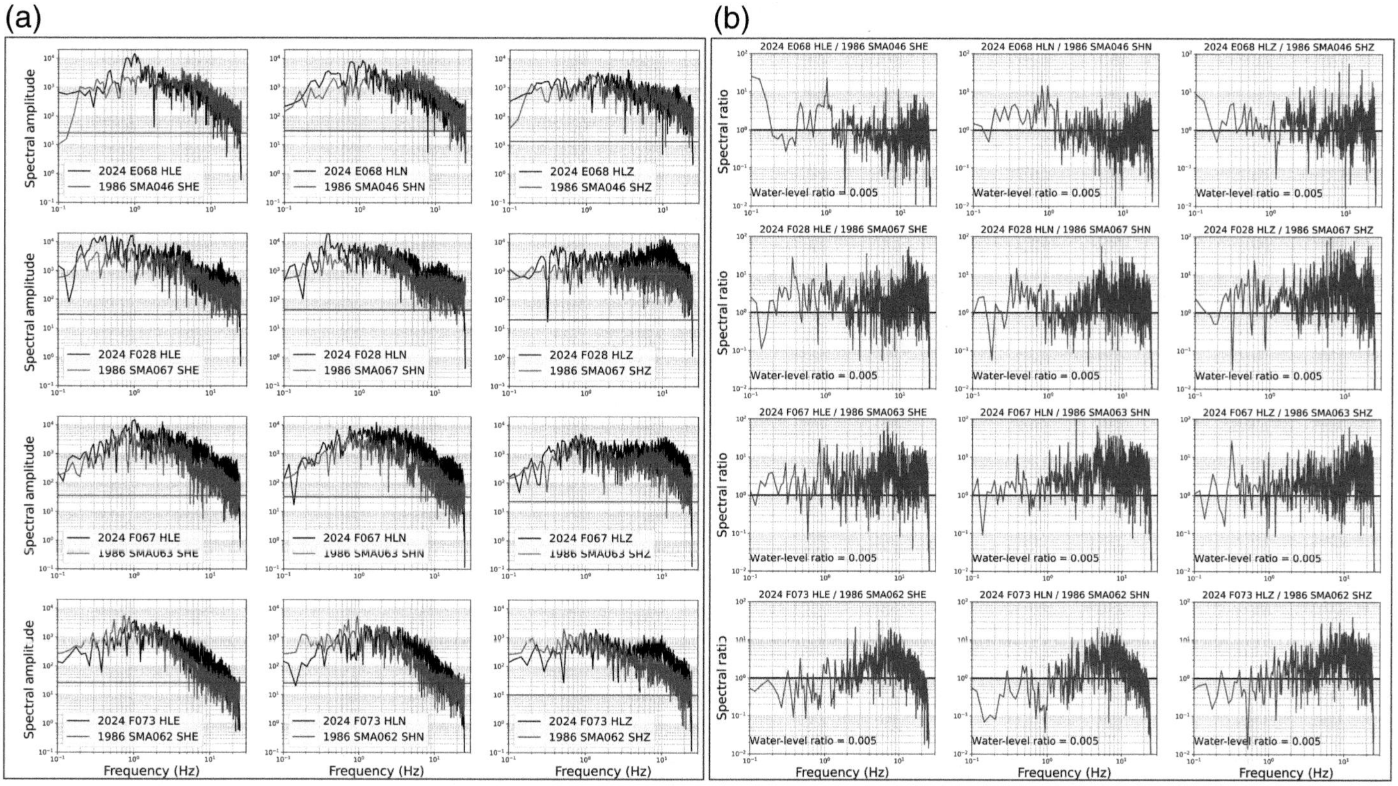

Figure 7. (a) Comparison of three-component acceleration spectra for four station pairs in the Hualien region. The water level used in the deconvolution analysis is indicated by the blue line. (b) Corresponding spectral ratios of the 2024–1986 Hualien earthquakes of reach station pair, with the reference ratio of 1 marked by the black line. The color version of this figure is available only in the electronic edition.

which contrarily have much smaller spectra amplitude. Overall, the spectral ratios of station pairs (Fig. 8b) remain close to unity across most frequencies, except for a slight increase at higher frequencies (6–10 Hz) in 2024. This pattern suggests weaker source effects in the Taipei basin, where site amplification dominates. Fortunately, despite the stronger high-frequency content of the 2024 event, the damage in the basin was less severe than in 1986, likely because of the stricter building regulations implemented after the 1999 Chi–Chi earthquake.

The comparison of acceleration spectra between Hualien and the Taipei basin reveals the seismic characteristics, for which the source effects are more prominent in Hualien, whereas site effects are the dominant factor in Taipei. The Hualien region exhibits larger acceleration spectral amplitudes in the ~0.2–1 Hz range for the 2024 earthquake, whereas the Taipei basin shows similar acceleration spectral amplitudes for both events in this frequency band. A study on site effects in the Taipei basin using amplitude spectra ratios (Wen and Peng, 1998) suggests a correlation with the structures of the tertiary basement shape and the overlying soft sediment layer (Lee *et al.*, 2008). For the higher frequency band (1–3 Hz), the primary amplification effects are observed near the northern, eastern, and southern edges of the basin, consistent with the basin structure described by Wang *et al.* (2004) and Chen *et al.* (2020).

DISCUSSION

The 1986 Hualien earthquake registered a local magnitude (M_L) of 6.8 according to the TTSN (Fig. 1), whereas teleseismic waveform inversion estimated its moment magnitude (M_w) to be ~7.3. In contrast, the 2 April 2024, Hualien earthquake had an M_L 7.1 reported by the CWA and M_w 7.4, determined using data from modern BATS broadband stations. The notable similarity in their waveforms, both in phase and amplitude, along with comparable spectral characteristics, strongly suggests that the two events may have originated from a similar seismogenic structure offshore eastern Taiwan.

Finite-fault analysis reveals that the majority of moment release in both earthquakes occurred within the initial 30 s. This temporal consistency implies a comparable seismogenic source mechanism during the early stages of rupture. However, despite the similar waveform patterns, the amplitude recorded at station E026 during the 2024 earthquake was generally higher than that at station C00 for the 1986 event, particularly in terms of peak ground motion. This suggests that although the initial rupture behavior was similar, the 2024 earthquake may have involved a larger overall rupture dimension than the 1986 event. These observations imply that the regional seismogenic structure might accommodate repeated rupture within specific segments but might also permit rupture propagation into adjacent areas, potentially leading to larger magnitude earthquakes.

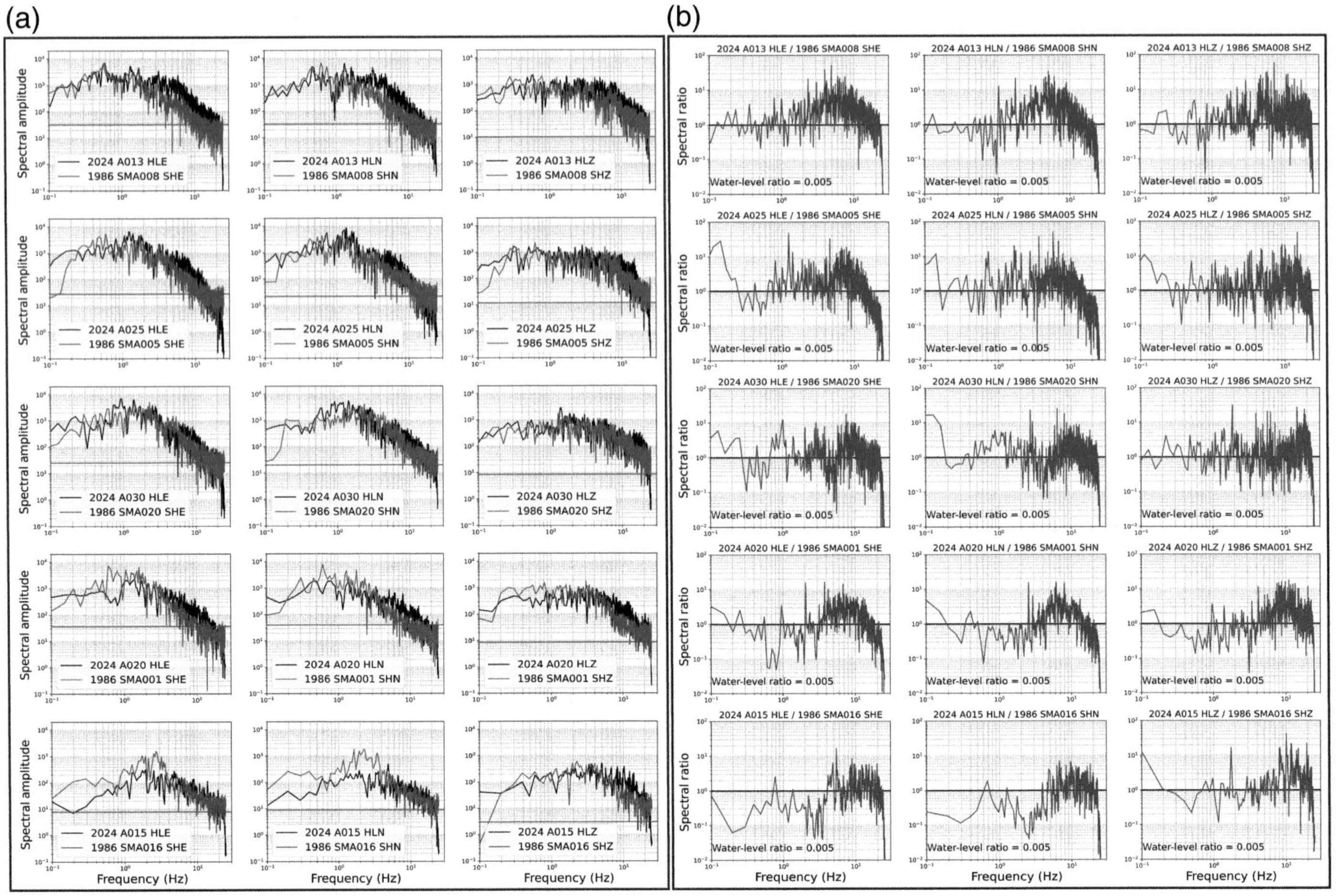

Figure 8. (a) Comparison of three-component acceleration spectra for five station pairs in the Taipei region. The water level used in the deconvolution analysis is indicated by the blue line. (b) Corresponding spectral ratios of the 2024–1986 Hualien earthquakes of each station pair, with the reference ratio of 1 marked by the black line. The color version of this figure is available only in the electronic edition.

To further examine the potential connection between the 1986 and 2024 Hualien earthquakes, we simulated synthetic waveforms at TSMIP station E026 using the 2024 source model and compared them with synthetics derived from source models of the 1986 earthquake. The 2 April 2024, earthquake source model of S.-J. Lee *et al.* (personal comm., 2025), which integrates teleseismic, local strong-motion, and Global Positioning System data, indicates a complex fault system composed of a steep east-dipping fault—suggested by the aftershock distribution (H.-Y. Yang *et al.*, personal comm., 2025)—and a west-dipping fault, with most of the seismic moment released on the latter. Despite differing tectonic interpretations (e.g., Fagan *et al.*, 2024; Xu *et al.*, 2025), all studies consistently identify a complex rupture sequence for the 2024 event. Figure 9 shows the observed vertical displacement waveform at station E026, obtained by double integration of the acceleration record within the 0.01 and 0.5 Hz frequency band (Fig. 9a); the forward-modeled synthetic vertical displacement waveforms (Fig. 9b) from the 2024 source model of S.-J. Lee *et al.* (personal comm., 2025); and the synthetics for the 1986 source models derived from teleseismic inversion for east-dipping (Fig. 9c) and west-dipping plane (Fig. 9d), each aligned by their peak amplitudes. It is worth noted that the observed waveform of station E026 was not used in the inversion of the 2024 source model of S.-J. Lee *et al.* (personal comm., 2025). The forward modeled synthetic displacement waveforms in Figure 9b shows similar pattern to the observation (Fig. 9a) with slightly smaller in amplitudes because of the resolution limit in the finite-fault modeling, which is often in the period of 0.01–0.5Hz. The forward-modeled synthetic displacement waveforms in Figure 9c,d from the teleseismic source model of 1986 earthquake show a similar waveforms in time-series duration of ~28 to 55 s to the observation (Fig. 9a) and synthetics from the 2024 source model (Fig. 9b). Although direct comparison using modern inversion standard is challenging, this qualitative agreement highlights a common concentration of energy releases around 30 s with similar duration in both earthquakes. This again points to a potentially similar complex seismogenic mechanism of these two earthquakes despite the epicenter differences reflected by ~5 s variation in the first arrivals of the 1986 and 2024 source model.

Although the limited quality and coverage of 1986 data preclude a definitive interpretation, the comparison nonetheless

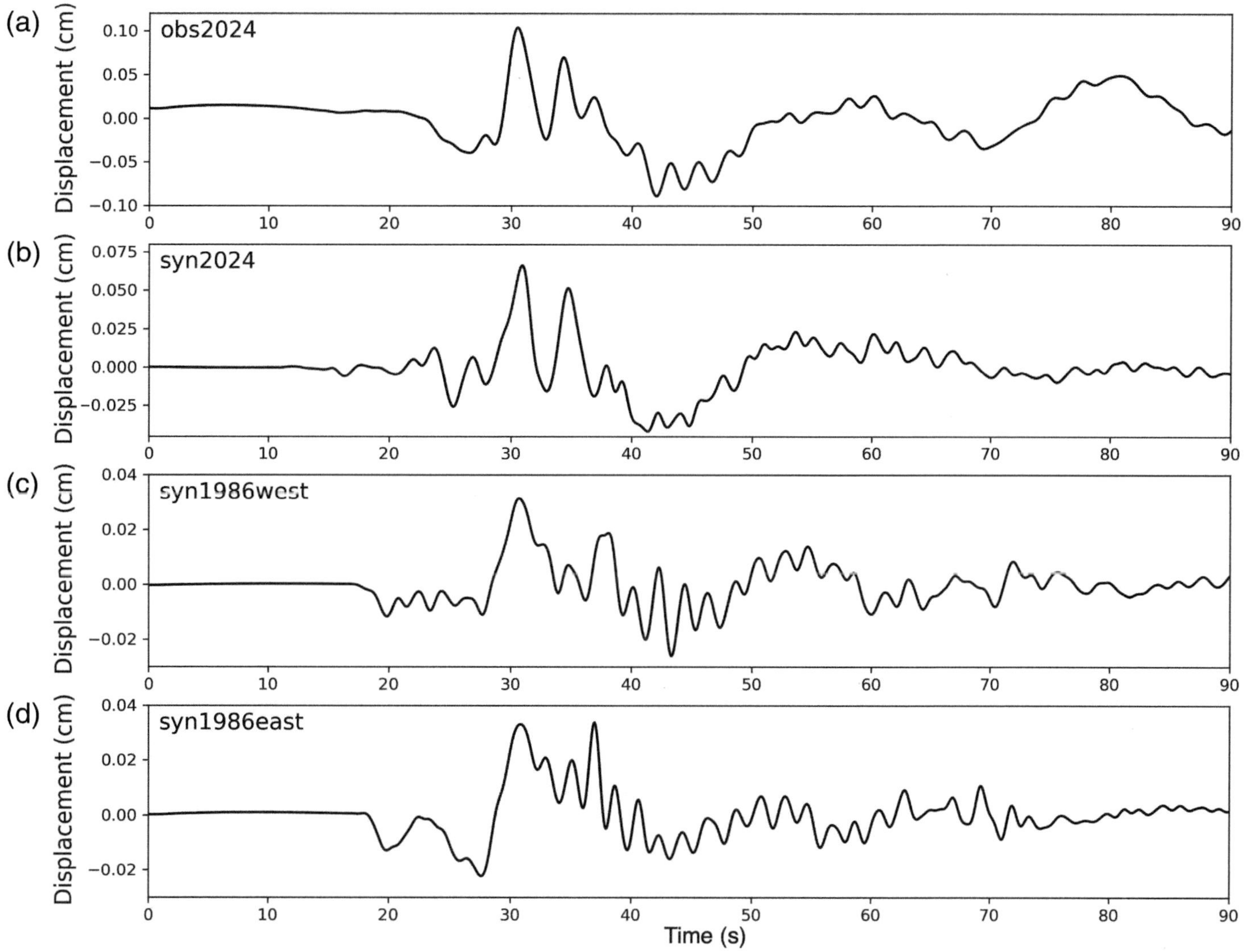

provides meaningful insight into shared rupture behavior between the two events. Taken together, the results suggest a possible link between the 1986 and 2024 earthquakes, with both influenced by the offshore fault systems near the Ryukyu subduction interface and their connections to inland tectonics in eastern Taiwan. The occurrence of two $M_w \sim 7.3$ to 7.4 earthquakes in this region within four decades underscores the seismic hazard posed by offshore ruptures, particularly given their potential to affect metropolitan areas such as Taipei, located >120 km away. Importantly, although the magnitudes were comparable, the extent of damage differed markedly between the two events. The substantially reduced damage in 2024 likely reflects the effectiveness of the stricter building codes implemented after the 1999 Chi-Chi earthquake, which have enhanced structural resilience and mitigated the impact of more recent large earthquakes.

Figure 9. (a) Observed vertical displacement waveform at station E026, obtained by double integration of the acceleration record within the 0.01 and 0.5 Hz frequency band; (b) Forward-modeled synthetic vertical displacement waveform based on the 2024 source model of S.-J. Lee *et al.* (personal comm., 2025). (c,d) Synthetics vertical displacement waveforms for the 1986 source models derived from teleseismic slip inversions for the west-dipping (Fig. 4c) and east-dipping plane (Fig. 4d), with all traces aligned by their peak amplitudes.

CONCLUSIONS

This study meticulously examined the seismic records of the 1986 and 2024 Hualien earthquakes, revealing both striking similarities and notable differences that underscore the complex seismic hazards posed by offshore fault structures near northeastern Taiwan. However, the 2024 earthquake exhibited generally larger ground-motion amplitudes at comparable distances, hinting at a potentially larger overall rupture dimension. Although direct comparison of detailed slip distributions is challenging because of data limitations from the 1986 event, the similarities in long-period waveforms and spectral characteristics further support the notion of a shared seismogenic origin.

The significantly reduced damage in Taipei during the 2024 earthquake compared with 1986 clearly highlights the effectiveness of updated building codes and seismic regulations implemented after the 1999 Chi-Chi earthquake. Nevertheless, the substantial destruction experienced in closer proximity to the source in Hualien City underscores the continued vulnerability of structures in geologically active regions and the necessity for targeted mitigation strategies, especially for high-rise buildings. Ultimately, this comparative study emphasizes the persistent seismic hazard from offshore tectonic features associated with the plate motion between Philippine Sea plate and Eurasian plate. The insights gained from the waveform comparisons and rupture analysis of these two significant earthquakes contribute valuable information for refining seismic hazard assessments and improving risk management strategies, particularly for urban areas such as Taipei. The remaining knowledge gaps regarding the intricacies of offshore rupture processes necessitate continued research and enhanced monitoring efforts in this tectonically active region.

DATA AND RESOURCES

Data processing and analysis were conducted using ObsPy. The strong-motion data from the strong-motion accelerograph (SMA) and SMART1 arrays for the 1986 Hualien earthquake and the Taiwan Strong Motion Implementation Program (TSMIP) data for the 2024 Hualien earthquake used in this study are available at the repository doi: 10.5281/zenodo.13318497. Teleseismic data were obtained from the EarthScope (Incorporated Research Institutions for Seismology [IRIS], https://www.iris.edu, last accessed January 2025). Damage data for both earthquakes were sourced from the Central Weather Administration (CWA), Taiwan, and the National Science and Technology Center for Disaster Reduction (https://scweb.cwa.gov.tw/en-US/page/disaster/55, last accessed September 2025). Seismic data analysis was conducted using Python and the Seismic Analysis Code (SAC). Data for the M_w 7.4 Hualien City, Taiwan, earthquake are available at https://earthquake.usgs.gov/earthquakes/eventpage/usp0003009/origin/detail (last accessed January 2025).

DECLARATION OF COMPETING INTERESTS

The authors acknowledge that there are no conflicts of interest recorded.

ACKNOWLEDGMENTS

This study was supported by the Ministry of Science and Technology in Taiwan under Grant Numbers MOST 113-2124-M-865-001, MOST 113-2740-M-001-003-, and MOST 113-2123-M-001-012. Additional financial support was provided by the Earthquake Disaster and Risk Evaluation and Management Center (E-DREaM) through the Featured Areas Research Center Program within the framework of the Higher Education Sprout Project of the Ministry of Education in Taiwan. The authors gratefully acknowledge the archiving of strong-motion accelerograph (SMA) and SMART1 array data since 1986 by Win-Gee Huang and currently by Chin-Shang Ku at the Institute of Earth Sciences (IES), Academia Sinica. The authors also thank the Central Weather Administration (CWA) for providing Taiwan Strong Motion Implementation Program (TSMIP) strong-motion data, and the National Science and Technology Center for Disaster Reduction (NCDR) for access to damage data. The authors sincerely appreciate the constructive comments and suggestions from the editor and two anonymous reviewers, which greatly improved the quality of this article.

REFERENCES

Anderson, J. G., and S. K. Singh (1989). Seismic risk and engineering decisions: The Mexico earthquake of September 19, 1985, *Earthq. Spectra* **5,** no. 4, 715–729.

Chang, J.-M., W.-A. Chao, C.-M. Yang, and M.-W. Huang (2024). Coseismic and subsequent landslides of the 2024 Hualien earthquake (M7.2) on April 3 in Taiwan, *Landslides* **21,** no. 10, 2591–2595, doi: 10.1007/s10346-024-02312-x.

Chen, C.-H., and J. B. H. Shyu (2025). Seismogenic structures offshore Taiwan and their earthquake potential from the Taiwan Earthquake Model (TEM) project, *Bull. Seismol. Soc. Am.* doi: 10.1785/0120250009.

Chen, C.-T., K.-L. Wen, and J.-Y. Huang (2020). Source location-dependency site response in the Taipei Basin of Taiwan by using HVSR analysis, *J. Asian Earth Sci.* **191,** 1104223, doi: 10.1016/j.jseaes.2019.104223.

Chen, K. C., and J. H. Wang (1986). The May 20, 1986 Hualien, Taiwan earthquake and its aftershocks, *Bull. Inst. Earth Sci. Acad. Sin.* **6,** 1–13.

Dziewonski, A. M., and D. L. Anderson (1981). Preliminary reference earth model (PREM), *Phys. Earth Planet. In.* **25,** no. 4, 297–356.

Fagan, C., M.-H. Huang, and H.-H. Huang (2024). Deciphering the multi-fault system of the 2024 Mw 7.4 Hualien, Taiwan earthquake using combined seismic and geodetic datasets, *AGU Fall Meeting Abstract*, NH31G-2179 pp.

Huang, H.-H., and Y. Wang (2022). Seismogenic structure beneath the northern Longitudinal Valley revealed by the 2018-2021 Hualien earthquake sequences, *Terr. Atmos. Oceanic Sci.* **33,** 17, doi: 10.1007/s44195-022-00017-z.

Hwang, L. J., and H. Kanamori (1989). Teleseismic and strong-motion source spectra from two earthquakes in Eastern Taiwan, *Bull. Seismol. Soc. Am.* **79,** no. 4, 935–944.

Institute of Earth Sciences, Academia Sinica, Taiwan (1996). Broadband array in Taiwan for seismology [Data set], *International Federation of Digital Seismograph Networks*, doi: 10.7914/SN/TW.

Incorporated Research Institutions for Seismology Data Management Center (IRIS DMC) (2015). Data services products: Synthetics engines, doi: 10.17611/DP/SYNGINE.1.

Jian, P.-R., T.-L. Tseng, W.-T. Liang, and P.-H. Huang (2018). A new automatic full-waveform regional moment tensor inversion algorithm and its applications in the Taiwan area, *Bull. Seismol. Soc. Am.* **108,** no. 2, 573–587, doi: 10.1785/0120170231.

Lee, S.-J., H.-W. Chen, and B.-S. Huang (2008). Simulations of strong ground motion and 3D amplification effect in the Taipei basin by using a composite grid finite-difference method, *Bull. Seismol. Soc. Am.* **98,** no. 3, 1229–1242, doi: 10.1785/0120060098.

Lee, S.-J., W.-T. Liang, H.-W. Cheng, F.-S. Tu, K.-F. Ma, H. Tsuruoka, H. Kawakatsu, B.-S. Huang, and C.-C. Liu (2013). Towards real-time regional earthquake simulation I: Real-time moment tensor monitoring (RMT) for regional events in Taiwan, *Geophys. J. Int.* **196,** no. 1, 432–446, doi: 10.1093/gji/ggt371.

Liu, K. S., B. S. Huang, K. L. Wen, and T. C. Shin (1999). A study on strong ground motion characteristics of SMART-1 array recordings, *Bull. Seismol. Soc. Am.* **89,** no. 3, 958–970.

National Science and Technology Center for Disaster Reduction (NCDR) (2025). 0403 Hualien earthquake response operations, geological characteristics, and disaster summary, *NCDR 113-A25.*

Shin, T. C. (1993). Progress summary of the Taiwan strong motion instrumentation program, *International Association of Seismology and Physics of the Earth's Interior (IASPEI) Proceedings*, 81–92.

Shin, T. C., T. L. Teng, Y. T. Yeh, and C. H. Chang (2000). A preliminary study of the Taiwan integrated seismic network, *Seismol. Res. Lett.* **71,** no. 4, 465–473.

Wang, C. Y., Y. H. Lee, M. L. Ger, and Y. L. Chen (2004). Investigating subsurface structures and P- and S-wave velocities in the Taipei basin, *Terr. Atmos. Ocean. Sci.* **15,** 222–250

Wang, J. H., T. C. Shin, and Y. T. Chen (1989). Analysis of the 1986 Hualien foreshock-mainshock sequence, *Bull. Inst. Earth Sci. Acad. Sin.* **9,** 1–20.

Wen, K. L., and H. Y. Peng (1998). Site effect analysis in the Taipei basin: Results from TSMIP network data, *Terr. Atmos. Ocean. Sci.* **9,** 691–704.

Wen, K.-L., and Y. T. Yeh (1991). Characteristics of strong motion durations in the SMART1 array area, *Terr. Atmos. Ocean. Sci.* **2,** 187–201, doi: 10.3319/TAO.1991.2.3.187(T).

Xu, L., L. Meng, W. Xu, Y.-Y. Lin, J. Geng, S. Mohanna, and G. Kawamoto (2025). Unzipping of the conjugate fault system during the 2024 Mw7.4 Hualien earthquake, *Geophys. Res. Lett.* **52,** e2025GL115218, doi: 10.1029/2025GL115218.

Manuscript received 2 May 2025
Published online 22 September 2025

Surface Ruptures of the 2022 Guanshan–Chihshang Earthquake Sequence, Eastern Taiwan: Implications for Fault Behavior and Recurrence

Ray Y. Chuang*[1], Zixin Lee[1], Chao-Jung Chiang[1], Li-Chieh J. Lin[1,2], Lishiue Chen[1], You-Wei Jiang[1], Chuan-Min Chao[1], Geng-Pei Lin[1,3], and I-Ting Wang[1]

ABSTRACT

The 2022 Guanshan–Chihshang earthquake sequence in eastern Taiwan, comprising an M_L 6.4 foreshock and an M_L 6.8 mainshock, produced widespread surface ruptures along both flanks of the Longitudinal Valley. Integrating field observations, unmanned aerial vehicle-based photogrammetry, and high-resolution satellite imagery, we delineated rupture distribution and fault displacement along the Yuli and Chihshang faults. The Yuli fault, a section of the Central Range fault located on the western margin of the valley, accommodated significant left-lateral and reverse motion, with a maximum offset of about 2 m in Changliang. The Chihshang fault, a part of the Longitudinal Valley fault on the eastern margin, displayed a more distributed rupture. These rupture patterns correspond well with geodetic slip inversion models and support the interpretation of the west-dipping Central Range fault as the main seismogenic source. Strain partitioning may occur along the northern Yuli fault, as the fault in the Sanmin area has dominant sinistral motion and the Songpu branch shows mainly vertical motion. We interpret the Yuli fault as the principal surface expression of the Central Range fault system, which may be partially blind near its southern extent beneath the Chihshang fault. Comparison with the 1951 Hualien–Taitung earthquake sequence demonstrates repeated, nearly full rupture of the Yuli fault in both events, suggesting its maturity and repeated seismic behavior. The characteristic rupture of the Yuli fault also implies the segmentation of the Central Range fault system. This study improves constraints on surface rupture recurrence, fault segmentation, and fault kinematics in one of the most seismically active suture zones in the world.

KEY POINTS

- We identified surface ruptures along the Yuli and Chihshang faults in the Longitudinal Valley suture.
- The Yuli fault shows strain partitioning in the north and may be a blind fault in the south.
- Recurrent faulting along the Yuli and Chihshang faults in 1951 and 2022 shows repeated seismic behavior.

Supplemental Material

INTRODUCTION

The characteristics of surface rupture play a critical role in understanding earthquake dynamics and fault behavior. Investigations of surface ruptures yield fundamental fault parameters that inform empirical scaling relationships used in seismic hazard assessments (e.g., Wells and Coppersmith, 1994; Wesnousky, 2008). For instance, the details of the collected data on surface rupture are critical in the perspective to improve the fault displacement hazard analyses (e.g., Youngs *et al.*, 2003; Petersen *et al.*, 2011; Nurminen *et al.*, 2022; Valentini *et al.*, 2025). In addition, comparative analyses of successive rupture events along individual fault systems

1. Department of Geography, National Taiwan University, Taipei, Taiwan, Republic of China, https://orcid.org/0000-0002-1071-9161 (RYC); https://orcid.org/0000-0001-5240-0055 (ZL); https://orcid.org/0009-0002-3165-4755 (Y-WJ); https://orcid.org/0000-0002-2612-2052 (G-PL); https://orcid.org/0009-0008-5771-9768 (I-TW); 2. Department of Earth and Planetary Sciences, University of California, Riverside, California, U.S.A.; 3. Department of Earth Sciences, National Central University, Taoyuan City, Taiwan

*Corresponding author: raychuang@ntu.edu.tw

Cite this article as Chuang, R. Y., Z. Lee, C.-J. Chiang, L.-C. J. Lin, L. Chen, Y.-W. Jiang, C.-M. Chao, G.-P. Lin, and I.-T. Wang (2025). Surface Ruptures of the 2022 Guanshan–Chihshang Earthquake Sequence, Eastern Taiwan: Implications for Fault Behavior and Recurrence, *Bull. Seismol. Soc. Am.* **116**, 94–110, doi: 10.1785/0120250120

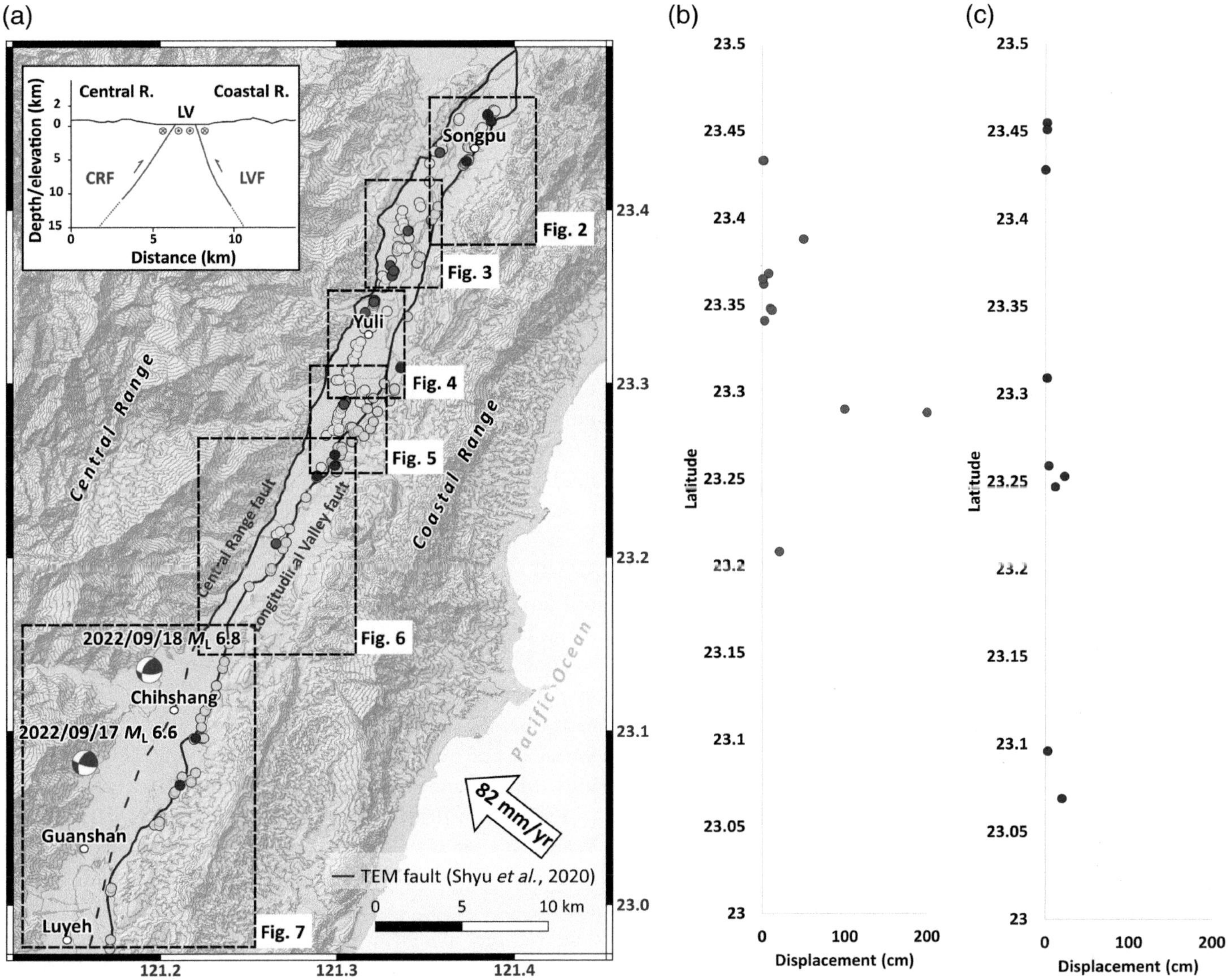

enhance constraints on fault segmentation and the development of robust earthquake recurrence models (e.g., Schwartz and Coppersmith, 1984; Rockwell *et al.*, 2001). Accurate characterization of fault behavior ideally requires detailed mapping of surface rupture from multiple past earthquakes. However, because the recurrence intervals of many active faults often exceed the temporal span of modern instrumental or historical records, investigations of repeated rupture on the same fault segment frequently rely on paleoseismic methods. Although indispensable, these approaches are inherently limited by potential sparse data coverage and associated uncertainties (e.g., Wang, Griffin, *et al.*, 2024).

The Longitudinal Valley suture in eastern Taiwan presents a compelling natural laboratory for the study of repeated surface-rupturing earthquakes along several active faults within recent decades. High level of seismicity is driven by the arc-continent collision resulting from the rapid convergence between the Eurasian and Philippine Sea plates (Suppe, 1981; Byrne *et al.*, 2011), with the majority of the convergence being accommodated by active fault systems across the island. Notably, the Longitudinal Valley is one of the most active suture zones globally (Yu and Kuo, 2001; Shyu, Sieh, and Chen, 2005; Shyu, Sieh, Chen, and Liu, 2005). The valley hosts two principal fault systems: the Longitudinal Valley fault system on the eastern side of the valley and the Central Range fault system on the western side (Shyu, Sieh, Chen, and Liu, 2005), which are also mapped in the Taiwan Earthquake Model (TEM) (Shyu *et al.*, 2016, 2020) (Fig. 1). The Longitudinal Valley fault is an east-dipping fault with fault dip of 54° (Kuochen *et al.*, 2004), and the Central

Figure 1. (a) Surface rupture area for the 2022 Guanshan–Chihshang earthquake sequence. Red stars denote the locations of the foreshock and mainshock. Yellow circles denote field survey locations with observed surface ruptures. Dark red lines are active fault traces based on the active structure map of the Taiwan Earthquake Model (Shyu *et al.*, 2020). This segment of the Longitudinal Valley fault is the Chihshang fault. The black box denotes the area for Figure S1. The boxes with dashed lines denote the areas for Figures 2–7. Panels (b) and (c) show measured horizontal offset in the field along the western (green) and eastern (purple) Longitudinal Valley, respectively. CRF, Central Range fault. The color version of this figure is available only in the electronic edition.

Range fault is a west-dipping fault with fault dip of ~45° (Chuang *et al.*, 2014; Shyu *et al.*, 2016). Collectively, these faults accommodate approximately 30 mm/yr of crustal shortening (Yu and Kuo, 2001; Hsu *et al.*, 2003)—a significant portion of the ~80 mm/yr plate convergence rate across the Taiwan orogen (Yu *et al.*, 1997). Although the geometry and kinematics of the Longitudinal Valley fault have been extensively documented through numerous geologic and geophysical studies (e.g., Angelier *et al.*, 2000; Kuochen *et al.*, 2004; Shyu, Sieh, Avouac, *et al.*, 2006; Kuochen *et al.*, 2007), the existence and structural characteristics of the Central Range fault have only been gradually revealed in the wake of recent moderate-to-large earthquakes, including the 2006 Peinan, 2014 Rueisui, and 2018 Hualien earthquakes (e.g., Wu, Chen, Chang, *et al.*, 2006; Chuang *et al.*, 2014; Lee *et al.*, 2019). Historically, the 1951 Hualien–Taitung earthquake sequence produced surface ruptures along several fault segments in the Longitudinal Valley, notably the Milun, Yuli, and Chihshang faults (Shyu, Sieh, Chen, and Liu, 2005; Shyu *et al.*, 2007). In more recent events, the 2003 Chengkung earthquake nucleated on the Chihshang fault and may have generated minor surface rupture (Lee *et al.*, 2006; Wu, Chen, Shin, *et al.*, 2006; Ching *et al.*, 2007), whereas the 2018 Hualien earthquake reactivated the Milun fault, producing significant surface deformation (Lin *et al.*, 2019; Yen *et al.*, 2019; Lin *et al.*, 2024). The most recent event, the 2022 Guanshan–Chihshang earthquake sequence, occurred on the west-dipping Central Range fault and produced prominent surface rupture along the Yuli fault (Lee *et al.*, 2023; Tang *et al.*, 2023; Wang, Wu, *et al.*, 2024).

The 2022 Guanshan–Chihshang earthquake sequence represents a critical opportunity for investigating repeated surface ruptures along active faults in eastern Taiwan. This sequence is composed of an M_w 6.6 Guanshan earthquake on 17 September and a subsequent M_w 7.0 Chihshang earthquake on 18 September (Lee *et al.*, 2023). Rapid field reconnaissance revealed that the earthquake sequence generated widespread surface ruptures along both margins of the Longitudinal Valley, especially along the Yuli fault to the west and the Chihshang fault (or the Chihshang segment of the Longitudinal Valley fault) to the east (Central Geological Survey [CGS], 2022; Lin *et al.*, 2023). Wang, Wu, *et al.* (2024) documented significant surface displacements along the Yuli fault in the western valley, whereas Hsu *et al.* (2024) reported minor surface ruptures near the southernmost extent of the valley. In this study, we present a comprehensive survey of surface ruptures derived from the integration of field investigations, unmanned aerial vehicle (UAV) surveys, and remote sensing imagery observed on both flanks of the valley to meticulously assess the spatial distribution and kinematics of the deformation associated with the 2022 earthquake sequence. A key objective is to elucidate the intricate relationship between surface ruptures and their corresponding seismogenic structures at depth. Furthermore, by comparing the 2022 rupture patterns with those documented from the 1951 Hualien–Taitung earthquake sequence (Hsu, 1962; Shyu *et al.*, 2007), we aim to explore the recurrence characteristics of surface faulting along the Yuli and Chihshang faults. Characterizing these surface ruptures is essential for understanding the seismogenic behavior of active faults within the complex Longitudinal Valley suture zone.

2022 GUANSHAN–CHIHSHANG EARTHQUAKES

Based on information from the Central Weather Administration, the 2022 Guanshan–Chihshang earthquake sequence was composed of an M_L 6.4 foreshock near Guanshan and an M_L 6.8 mainshock near Chihshang. The moment magnitude (M_w) of the foreshock and mainshock from the report of the real-time moment tensor monitoring system (RMT) (Lee *et al.*, 2013) is 6.6 and 7.0, respectively. The foreshock occurred at 21:41 local time on 17 September 2022, about 4.2 km northwest of Guanshan township, with a focal depth of 7.3 km. The mainshock occurred at 14:44 local time on 18 September 2022, 7.5 km southwest of the Chihshang township with a focal depth of 7 km. Both events occurred at the western side of the Central Range fault within the Central Range (Fig. 1a). Focal mechanism solutions and aftershock distributions suggest that the main rupture was along a west-dipping fault plane (Lee *et al.*, 2023; Lin *et al.*, 2023; Sun *et al.*, 2024). According to the RMT report, both foreshock and mainshock exhibited oblique mechanisms, involving left-lateral and reverse faulting components (Lee *et al.*, 2023).

Preliminary field investigations (CGS, 2022; Lin *et al.*, 2023; Wang, Wu, *et al.*, 2024), further supplemented by our own field surveys, revealed that surface ruptures largely follow the mapped traces of the Yuli and Chihshang faults (Fig. 1). The rupture along the Yuli fault extends ~16 km, from Sanmin in the north to Changliang in the south, with the most pronounced surface offsets observed near Changliang and diminishing in magnitude northward (Wang, Wu, *et al.*, 2024). In contrast, the rupture associated with the Chihshang fault extends for approximately 65 km, exhibiting a more distributed pattern with smaller surface displacements. Notably, the southernmost portion of this rupture zone, located south of Guanshan, may have been produced by the foreshock and coincides with the southern terminus of the Chihshang fault (e.g., Chuang *et al.*, 2012; CGS, 2022).

Beyond surface faulting, the earthquake sequence caused significant infrastructure damage, including building collapses, bridge failures, and landslides triggered by strong ground shaking (CGS, 2022; Ko *et al.*, 2023; Lin *et al.*, 2023; Paurush *et al.*, 2024; Chen *et al.*, 2025; Lin *et al.*, 2025). Fault-slip inversion results indicate that the majority of slip occurred north of the mainshock hypocenter along the west-dipping fault plane, whereas the east-dipping Chihshang fault (one segment of the Longitudinal Valley fault system) exhibited only minor shallow slip (Lee *et al.*, 2023; Tang *et al.*, 2023). These findings support the interpretation that the primary seismogenic source was on the deep portion west-dipping Central Range fault.

Prior to the 2022 earthquake sequence, the surface trace of the Central Range fault remained largely uncharacterized, despite its geometry being constrained by seismicity patterns. A prominent lineament along the frontal margin of the Central Range in the middle Longitudinal Valley suggests potential surface expression of this fault (Shyu, Sieh, Chen, and Chung, 2006). The only previously documented surface rupture in the western valley is associated with the 1951 Hualien–Taitung earthquake sequence, during which strike-slip displacements were recorded and later named as the Yuli fault (Hsu, 1962). However, the Yuli fault is not included in the active structure database of the TEM (Shyu *et al.*, 2020), and the tectonic interpretation of the Yuli fault remains debated. It has been regarded either as a subsidiary structure situated between the Chihshang and Central Range faults (Shyu *et al.*, 2007), or as a westward extension of the Chihshang fault, forming a segment of the broader Longitudinal Valley fault system (Lin *et al.*, 2021).

SURFACE RUPTURE INVESTIGATION

Field surveys

To document the surface deformation associated with the 2022 Guanshan–Chihshang earthquake sequence, we executed five systematic field campaigns aimed at characterizing the location, displacement, and spatial extent of surface ruptures. The initial reconnaissance began immediately following the M_L 6.4 Guanshan foreshock on 17 September. During this first survey conducted as a rapid response, we documented surface damages due to the foreshock south of Chihshang (see 4.6) and experienced the M_L 6.8 mainshock in the field on 18 September. In response to the mainshock, the field campaign was extended over the following week, followed by a second survey in early October. Subsequent fieldwork was carried out in March 2023, May 2023, and January 2024, constituting the third, fourth, and fifth surveys, respectively.

Because of the wide distribution of surface ruptures, we adopted a hybrid approach combining ground-based observations and remote sensing techniques. Estimating rupture zones immediately after an earthquake remains challenging and often requires iterative refinement as new data become available. To address this, our methodology incorporated both direct field measurements and UAV surveys. Concurrently, we compiled surface damage information from various sources, including news media, social media, and governmental or institutional reports, to strategically prioritize areas for detailed investigation. Satellite imagery analysis was also employed to delineate major displacement boundaries and to detect subtle surface ruptures not immediately discernible through ground-based reconnaissance alone. Our investigation covered both the eastern and western flanks of the Longitudinal Valley, extending from Rueisuei in the north to Luyeh in the south. At each observation site, we recorded precise geographic coordinates and documented displacement properties. Moreover, we utilized real-time kinematic (RTK) Global Navigation Satellite System (GNSS) to survey topographic profiles, enabling the measurement of vertical surface displacements across the fault traces in the Yuli and Kecheng areas.

UAV surveys

In recent years, the integration of UAV platforms with structure-from-motion (SfM) photogrammetry has significantly advanced post-earthquake field investigations (e.g., Westoby *et al.*, 2012; Bemis *et al.*, 2014; Johnson *et al.*, 2014; Anderson *et al.*, 2019). For example, UAV images were used to map surface ruptures for the 2018 Hualien earthquake in eastern Taiwan (Huang *et al.*, 2019; Lin *et al.*, 2019), and high-resolution images generated from UAV aerial photos were also used to map the 2019 Ridgecrest earthquake sequence (e.g., Donnellan *et al.*, 2020; Rodriguez Padilla, Quintana, *et al.*, 2022). The techniques enable the generation of high-resolution orthophotos and digital surface models (DSMs), and have been increasingly applied to both recent and historic earthquakes, as well as to long-term fault-slip quantification (e.g., Angster *et al.*, 2016; Gao *et al.*, 2017; Bi *et al.*, 2020; Pandey *et al.*, 2021; Li *et al.*, 2023). The use of UAV–SfM is particularly advantageous in post-disaster settings where satellite imagery may be hindered by cloud cover (Gomez and Purdie, 2016; Antoine *et al.*, 2020). These datasets have been utilized independently (e.g., Lin *et al.*, 2019; Ybañez *et al.*, 2021; Rodriguez Padilla, Quintana, *et al.*, 2022) or in combination with other geodetic observations such as Interferometric Synthetic Aperture Radar (InSAR) and GNSS (e.g., Pucci *et al.*, 2017; Luo *et al.*, 2020; Li *et al.*, 2021; Wu *et al.*, 2021; Pan *et al.*, 2022; Yuan *et al.*, 2022; Rodriguez Padilla, Quintana, *et al.*, 2022) to rapidly characterize surface ruptures and associated ground deformation.

In this study, flight planning followed established protocols for geological UAV surveys (e.g., Nex and Remondino, 2014; James, Robson, d'Oleire-Oltmanns, and Niethammer, 2017; Tziavou *et al.*, 2018; Giordan *et al.*, 2020), supplemented by operational experience from post-earthquake UAV deployments in Taiwan (e.g., Lin *et al.*, 2019). Following the mainshock on 18 September 2022, we identified nine target sites exhibiting prominent surface deformation: Songpu–Kuogailiang, Sanmin, Gaoliao Bridge, Dayu, Yuli, Kecheng, Changliang, Dongli, and Mingli. Across these sites, a total of 18,107 UAV images were collected, covering a combined area of approximately 10.1 km^2. Flight altitudes ranged between 50 and 120 m above ground level, resulting in ground sampling distances (GSDs) of approximately 1–2 cm. Please see the supplemental material for more details about UAV types, flight plans, and ground control point (GCP) surveys. We processed these images using the SfM technique to produce high-resolution orthophotos and DSMs, which were subsequently used to map fault ruptures in detail. The resulting orthoimages achieved spatial resolutions ranging from ~0.8 to 2.2 cm/pixel. We followed established best practices for UAV-based SfM workflows, including those outlined in James *et al.* (2019), to ensure the quality and geospatial accuracy of the products.

Imaging geodesy

We integrated high-resolution optical and radar satellite imagery to quantitatively assess coseismic surface displacements associated with the 2022 Guanshan–Chihshang earthquake sequence. Although several studies have produced the coseismic displacement field using GNSS and InSAR (Tang *et al.*, 2023; Yang *et al.*, 2024; Tung *et al.*, 2025), the spatial coverage and resolution are not good enough to resolve the near-field deformation pattern, which is important to identify the precise location of the surface rupture. Therefore, we used high-resolution optical and satellite images with a method of pixel tracking to find coseismic displacement boundaries. Optical imagery was used to detect horizontal displacements in the north–south direction, whereas radar imagery was used to resolve displacements in the range direction. The optical dataset consists of Pleiades imagery acquired by Airbus, featuring a native spatial resolution of 0.5 m. We selected the pre-event image acquired on 3 June 2022, and two post-event scenes acquired on 21 and 27 September 2022. Displacement fields were generated using the Coregistration of Optically Sensed Images and Correlation software (Leprince *et al.*, 2007). Various correlation window sizes and step lengths were tested to optimize signal clarity; a window size of 128×128 pixels with a subpixel step of 8 pixels yielded the most consistent results for this dataset. Radar data were obtained from the Advanced Land Observing Satellite (ALOS-2) Phased Array L-band Synthetic Aperture Radar-2 (PALSAR-2) sensor operated by the Japan Aerospace Exploration Agency, using StripMap mode imagery acquired along ascending orbits. We selected a pre-event acquisition dated 19 May 2022 and a post-event acquisition on 22 September 2022. Displacements were estimated using pixel offset tracking implemented in the InSAR Scientific Computing Environment (Rosen *et al.*, 2012).

To enhance the reliability of the displacement estimates, we applied filtering strategies tailored to each dataset. For optical imagery, we masked out pixels with signal-to-noise ratio (SNR) values below 0.94, which was determined based on the histogram of SNR following the method of Leprince *et al.* (2007). In both optical and radar datasets, water bodies and steep mountainous terrain, where correlation performance is typically degraded, were also masked out. To remove outliners, all displacement values were constrained within ± 2 m, corresponding to the maximum fault offset observed in the field following the method of Kuo *et al.* (2019). To validate and further constrain the remote sensing-derived displacements, we incorporated coseismic offsets recorded at GNSS stations maintained by the Geological Survey and Mining Management Agency. The GNSS measurements served as ground truth for assessing the accuracy of both the subpixel correlation and radar offset tracking results.

SURFACE RUPTURES

Based on our field investigations and UAV surveys, the surface ruptures associated with the 2022 Guanshan–Chihshang earthquake sequence are primarily distributed along two principal fault zones: the Yuli fault, extending ~16 km from Sanmin in the north to Dongli in the south, and the Chihshang fault, spanning ~60 km from Songpu in the north to Pingting in the south. In addition, a fault branch may be associated with the Central Range fault system distributed in the Songpu area west of the Chihshang fault trace. Surface ruptures in the Songpu and Changliang areas exhibit significant displacements, but most of the ruptures in the rest areas have small displacements with distributed fractures (Fig. 1). The north–south pixel offsets derived from the Pleaides images only show clear displacement discontinuity in limited areas of Yuli, Kecheng, and Changliang, which matches the mapped rupture traces and provides additional constraints on fault distributions (Fig. S1, available in the supplemental material to this article). The range offsets derived from the ALOS-2 images show blurry displacement discontinuity due to low resolution, and it is only used to roughly compare mapped rupture localities. In the following sections, we present detailed mapping and investigation results in six areas.

Kuokailiang–Songpu area

The northernmost surface ruptures of the 2022 Guanshan–Chihshang earthquake sequence are situated in the Songpu–Kuokailiang area, along the eastern bank of the Siouguluan River (Fig. 2a). The farthest rupture to the north identified in our surveys occurs near Kuokailiang—a small ridge previously deformed by the 1951 Hualien–Taitung earthquake sequence (Shyu *et al.*, 2007). Within this localized area, only scattered minor ground cracks were observed, and no prominent surface ruptures were identified along the adjacent hillslopes.

Between Kuokailiang and Songpu, the density of surface ruptures exhibits a noticeable increase toward the south (Fig. 2d). Both field observations and orthoimage analysis reveal clear evidence of vertical displacements but no discernible strike-slip motion. We identified two distinct types of vertical deformation: scarps with the eastern side up (Fig. 2f) and those with the western side up (Fig. 2g,h). To assess the dominant fault kinematics, we quantified the occurrence of each rupture type. The results show a significantly higher number of west-side-up scarps, which also display greater lateral continuity (Fig. 2b,c). Therefore, the west-side-up scarps should represent the main faulting in Songpu. Given that the ruptures are west of the Chihshang fault trace and the west-side-up motion is the opposite sense of the Chihshang fault, these ruptures are less likely to be associated with the Longitudinal Valley fault system. Instead, we interpret the Songpu–Kuokailiang ruptures as the surface expression of a west-dipping structure, possibly part of the west-dipping Central Range fault system, consistent with the interpretation of Wang, Wu, *et al.* (2024).

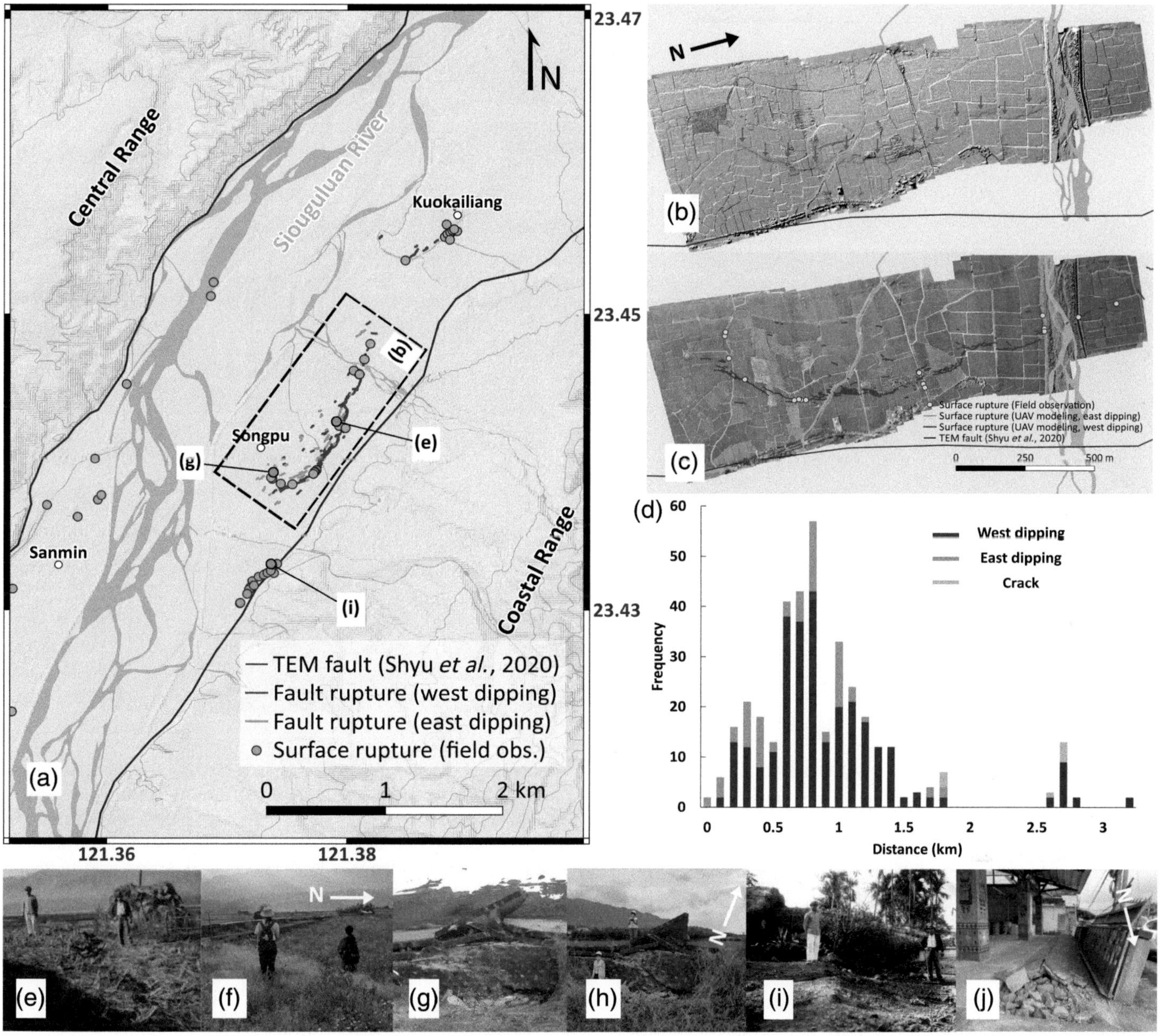

Figure 2. (a) Surface rupture in the Kuokailiang–Songpu area. The orange circles denote field survey locations with observed surface ruptures. The orange circles denote the locations with field photos. The dark red lines are active fault traces based on the active structure map of the TEM (Shyu *et al.*, 2020). The red lines denote surface rupture with the western side up, and the orange lines denote surface ruptures with the eastern side up. (b,c) Digital surface models (DSM) and orthoimage derived from the unmanned aerial vehicle (UAV) survey. The red arrows in (b) indicate the main fault trace. (d) Plot of the count of the surface ruptures along the main fault trace. The red bars indicate the count (frequency) of the surface ruptures with the western side up, the orange bars indicate the count of the surface ruptures with the eastern side up, and the yellow bars indicate the crack along the fault ruptures. (e) Historic photo of the 1951 earthquake showing the surface rupture with the eastern side up. (f) Field photo of the 2022 earthquake sequence showing the surface rupture with the eastern side up. (g,h) The destruction of an irrigation canal embankment of a 3D model derived from the UAV survey and a field photo, respectively. (i) Historic photo of the 1951 earthquake showing the surface rupture with the eastern side up along the main street in Songpu. (j) Field photo of the 2022 earthquake sequence showing the surface rupture with the eastern side up along the main street in Songpu. The color version of this figure is available only in the electronic edition.

South of Songpu village, along the main road, we observed a well-defined zone of surface ruptures coinciding with the mapped trace of the Chihshang fault (Fig. 2a). These ruptures exhibit tens of centimeters of vertical offset, with the eastern side up (Fig. 2j), and localized minor left-lateral displacement. Based on their geometry and kinematics, we infer that this segment of the Chihshang fault ruptured during the 2022 earthquake sequence. On the western bank of the Siouguluan River, minor surface cracks with negligible offset were observed north of Sanmin village. The lack of significant deformation

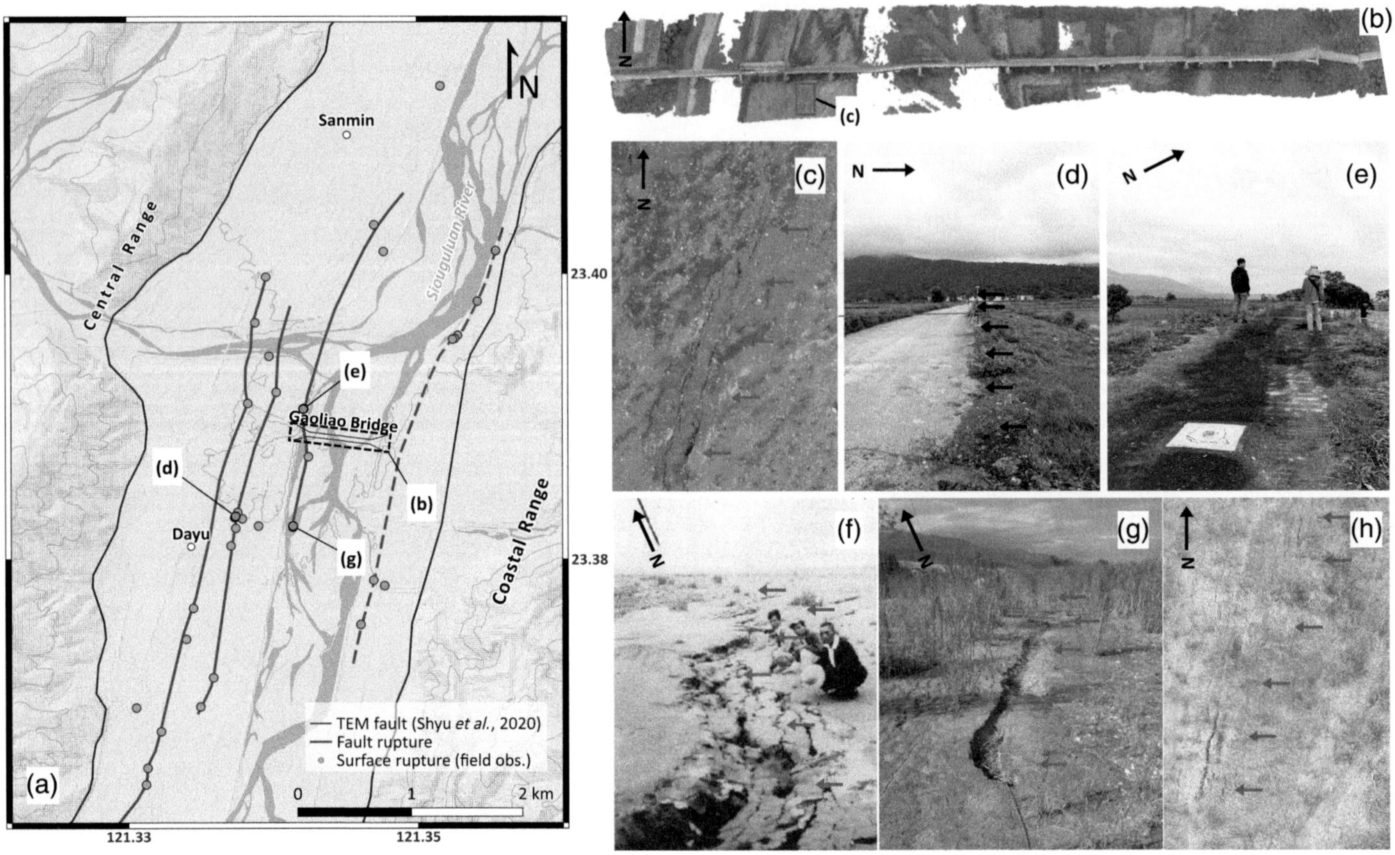

Figure 3. (a) Surface rupture in the Sanmin–Dayu area. The box with a dashed line indicates the area of panel (b). (b) UAV-based orthoimage of the Gaoliao Bridge. (c) Surface rupture close to the Gaoliao Bridge observed from the orthoimage in (b). (d) Road offset due to surface rupture. The red line indicates the fault location, and black arrows indicate the roadside for reference. (e) Damage to the river embankment on the western side. The red arrows denote the fault trace. (f) Historic photo of the 1951 earthquake showing the surface rupture within the Siouguluan River bed in the Sanmin area. (g) Field photo of the 2022 earthquake showing the surface rupture within the Siouguluan River bed. (h) UAV-derived orthoimage of the surface rupture in (g). The color version of this figure is available only in the electronic edition.

precludes the definitive identification of a coherent fault trace on the western side of the valley at this latitude.

Sanmin–Dayu areas

Surface ruptures in the Sanmin–Dayu area are distributed discontinuously across multiple fault zones (Fig. 3a). Sanmin and Dayu are situated on river terraces along the western bank of the Siouguluan River, with the Gaoliao Bridge spanning the river between the two townships. Our integrated analysis reveals that surface ruptures are more numerous and continuous in the Dayu area, whereas ruptures in the Sanmin area are relatively sparse and isolated. These observations are consistent with prior field investigations by the Central Geological Survey (CGS, 2022) and displacement field measurements (Fig. 3a).

At this latitude, the Yuli fault appears to bifurcate into three subparallel branches (Fig. 3a). The westernmost branch continues southward toward Yuli township and exhibits greater continuity in rupture distribution. The central branch displays minor left-lateral offsets of a few tens of centimeters (Fig. 3d). The eastern branch is primarily situated to the east of the river embankment. Within the Siouguluan River channel south of the Gaoliao Bridge, we observed several surface ruptures (Fig. 3b,c,e,g,h), suggesting that the eastern branch may extend northward across the northern embankment of the river. The surface rupture under the Gaoliao Bridge (Fig. 3b) may also have contributed to the bridge collapse in addition to strong shaking.

On the eastern bank of the Siouguluan River, sparse and minor surface ruptures were identified along the river levee (Fig. 3a). These ruptures exhibit limited offset and do not align precisely with the mapped trace of the Chihshang fault. Their orientation and location suggest that they may represent deformation along a previously unmapped western splay or branch of the Chihshang fault system.

Yuli–Kecheng areas

Surface ruptures in the Yuli–Kecheng area predominantly exhibit left-lateral strike-slip motion in several centimeters, as observed in the field, and provide strong constraints on the surface trace of the Yuli fault (Fig. 4a). Compared to the more scattered deformation observed in the Sanmin–Dayu region, the surface ruptures in Yuli township and the adjacent Kecheng area

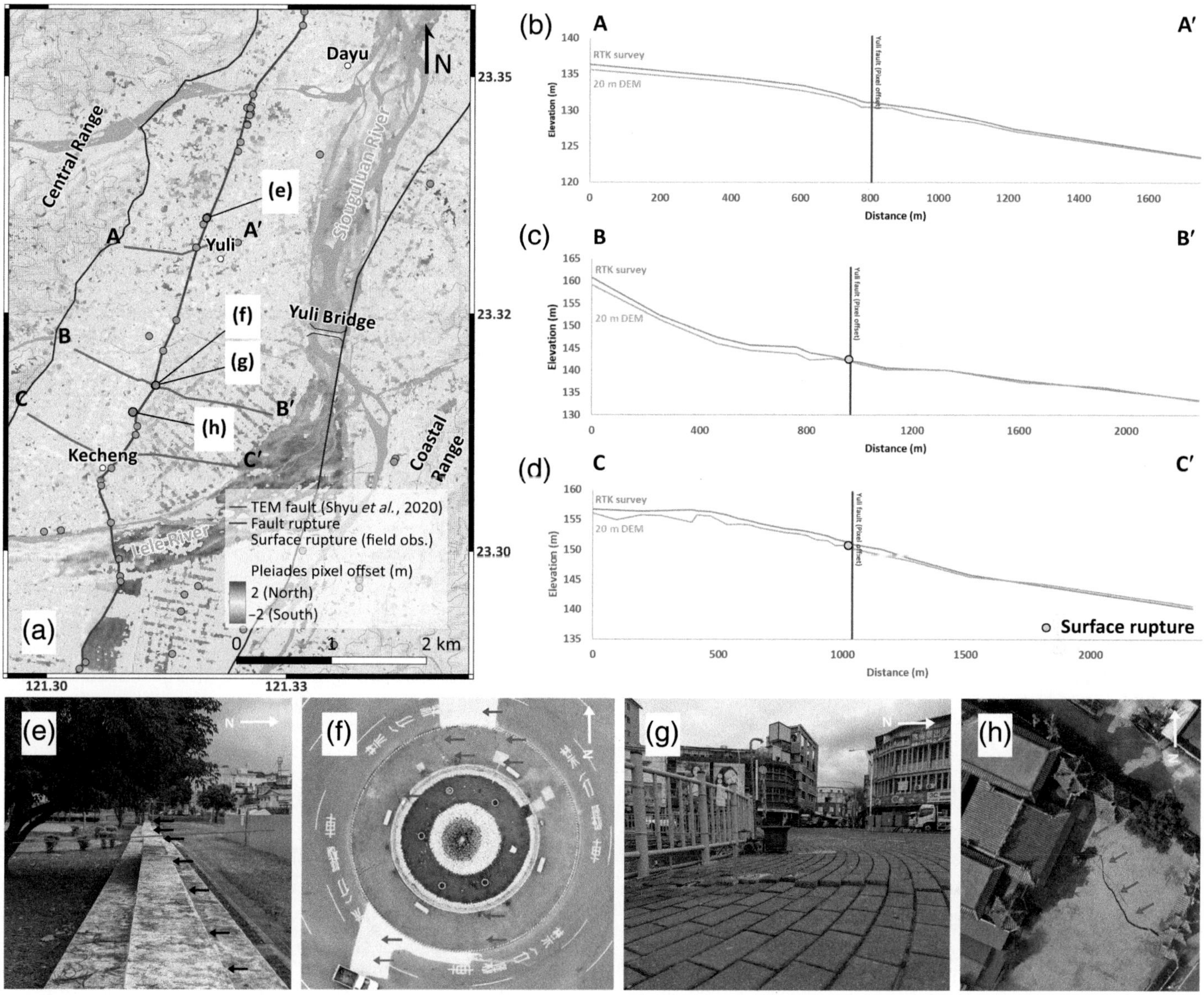

Figure 4. (a) Surface rupture in the Yuli–Kecheng area. The color bar shows the north–south displacements derived from the subpixel correlation for the Pleiades images. (b–d) Topographic profiles across the Yuli fault. The orange lines are topography based on our real-time kinematic (RTK)-GNSS surveys, and the grey lines are topography from a 20 m digital elevation model (DEM). (e) Field photo of one rupture trace crosses a stadium in Yuli. (f) UAV photo of surface rupture across the roundabout at the center of Yuli township. The UAV photo was taken after the road pavement. Light patches are the new pavement. (g) Close-up field photo of the surface rupture at the roundabout in (f). (h) UAV photo of surface rupture cutting across a temple in the Changliang area. The color version of this figure is available only in the electronic edition.

are more continuous, spatially aligned, and densely distributed. These characteristics are consistent with previous mapping results (CGS, 2022; Wang, Wu, *et al.*, 2024). Furthermore, the along-strike (north–south) displacement field derived from optical image correlation (Fig. S1) shows more pronounced displacement gradients south of Yuli (Fig. 4a), in agreement with the surface faulting pattern (Fig. 4e).

In addition to strike-slip movement, we also examined possible vertical motion. Although the surface ruptures did not seem to have obvious vertical movement, it is still plausible to detect dip-slip-related motion by considering the oblique focal mechanism and the east–west shortening across the fault from the range offset (Fig. S1). To quantify vertical deformation, we conducted RTK-GNSS surveys across the Yuli fault and compared the results with a pre-earthquake 20 m resolution digital elevation model. The comparison revealed localized uplift of several tens of centimeters, with the western side up. However, this vertical deformation appears to be distributed over a broad zone several hundred meters wide rather than sharply localized along the fault trace (Fig. 4b–d). Although some ruptures within the urbanized areas of Yuli township were rapidly modified or repaired after the earthquake, their locations remained identifiable based on repaired infrastructure (Fig. 4f), documented observations obtained before modification (Fig. 4g,h), and continuous postseismic deformation (e.g., Wang, Wu, *et al.*, 2024).

Changliang–Dongli area

The Changliang area exhibits the maximum observed surface offset associated with the 2022 Guanshan–Chihshang earthquake sequence. A prominent fault scarp with clear left-lateral strike-slip motion extends from the Lele River riverbed north of Changliang village to the southern margin of the Changliang terrace (Fig. 5a). Subpixel image correlation of Pleiades optical imagery also reveals significant left-lateral displacement consistent with the mapped rupture trace (Fig. 5a).

The fault scarp intersects multiple local roads, providing well-preserved geomorphic and anthropogenic markers of both vertical and horizontal displacement. Surface rupture mapping based on UAV-derived DSMs and orthoimages reveals a fault trace that closely aligns with the displacement boundary indicated in the optical correlation results (Fig. 5b,c). In the Changliang area, we measured an average left-lateral offset of 53.1 cm and a vertical offset of 27.6 cm using the UAV-derived DSMs and orthoimages, consistent with oblique-slip kinematics. The maximum recorded offsets from the UAV survey reach 200 cm (left-lateral) and 60 cm (vertical), creating a clear fault scarp displacing ridges and footpath in an agricultural field (Fig. 5d,f). Note that the positioning uncertainty for the UAV result is ~5 cm (Table S1), so the offset calculation could have uncertainties of ~7 cm based on error propagation.

Offset magnitudes peak near the center of the rupture zone and taper off toward both the northern and southern ends. In the Lele River riverbed to the north, UAV-based vertical offsets are approximately 15–20 cm, consistent with field measurements (Fig. 5e). The presence of west-side-up displacement and the relatively low sinuosity of the rupture trace suggest a high-angle, west-dipping fault with an oblique-slip component. Based on the UAV-derived orthoimage and DSM, we also found a secondary faulting ~300 m west of the main fault scarp (Fig. 5b). To the south, across the Siouguluan River, we identified scattered surface ruptures (Fig. 5g) that align with displacement boundaries observed in the optical correlation results (Fig. 5a). Thus, the Yuli fault should extend to the Dongli area and may be merged toward the Chihshang fault on the surface, which is not reported in previous field survey (Wang, Wu, *et al.*, 2024).

In addition, along the eastern Chihshang fault zone, several small cracks were observed (Fig. 5a). Some of these appear to be roughly parallel to the main trace of the Chihshang fault, potentially indicating minor slip along an eastern splay or secondary strand of the Longitudinal Valley fault system.

Dongli–Fuli area

In the Dongli–Fuli area, surface ruptures are predominantly aligned along the Chihshang fault (Fig. 6a) and exhibit vertical displacements with the eastern side up, consistent with previous characterizations of the fault's kinematics. One notable exception occurs near the Luntian area, where we identified three prominent scarps with western-side-up displacements across a rice paddy field (Fig. 6b–d). The longest scarp is about 90 m, and the maximum vertical offset is 40 cm, which does not fit the fault slip of the Chihshang fault. In addition, this scarp is located near the southern terminus of the displacement boundary in the range offsets associated (Fig. S1). Therefore, we interpret this feature as the surface expression of a subsidiary west-dipping fault branch belonging to the Central Range fault system.

At the structural junction between the Yuli and Chihshang faults in the Dongli area (Fig. 6a), we observed a well-defined fault scarp with the east side up in the sports field of Dongli Junior High School (Fig. 6e–g). UAV-derived DSMs reveal multiple fault scarps transecting the school's runway, with a cumulative vertical offset of approximately 56 cm and a maximum single-scarp vertical offset of 20 cm. Minor left-lateral offset is also evident along several cracks and scarps in this area. These fault traces are situated along the western margin of the Coastal Range, and the observed east-side-up displacement is consistent with the dominant dip-slip component of the Chihshang fault (e.g., Angelier *et al.*, 2000). Farther to the south, we traced additional surface ruptures that follow the known trace of the Chihshang fault (Fig. 6h–j), reinforcing the conclusion that this fault segment was reactivated during the 2022 Guanshan–Chihshang earthquake sequence.

Fuli–Luyeh area

Surface ruptures in the Fuli–Luyeh area are well aligned with the mapped trace of the Chihshang fault (Fig. 7a). Prior to the mainshock, we conducted reconnaissance along the southern segment of the Chihshang fault and observed a limited number of pre-existing surface ruptures, which should have been generated by the foreshock (Fig. 7b,c). Notably, we experienced the mainshock while positioned on the Baohwa Bridge and witnessed the occurrence of the bridge damage (Fig. 7a,e). After the mainshock, we found the presence of more surface ruptures from Chihshang to Baohwa Bridge, which means that this segment of the fault has ruptured during both the foreshock and mainshock, with larger displacements due to the mainshock.

Continuing our post-event field survey southward, we documented numerous distributed ruptures in the Pingding area consistent with Hsu *et al.* (2024), with the southernmost observed rupture located along the western bank of the Peinan River south of Pingding. The Pingding terrace has been interpreted as a geomorphic expression of multiple strands of the Peinan fault, which constitutes the southern segment of the Longitudinal Valley fault system (Shyu *et al.*, 2008; Chuang *et al.*, 2012). Given this structural configuration, we interpret the southern termination of surface ruptures associated with the 2022 Guanshan–Chihshang earthquake sequence to coincide with the Peinan River, marking the likely southern extent of rupture propagation.

To assess whether the Central Range fault or the Luyeh fault was reactivated during the sequence, we also conducted a systematic field investigation along the western flank of the valley,

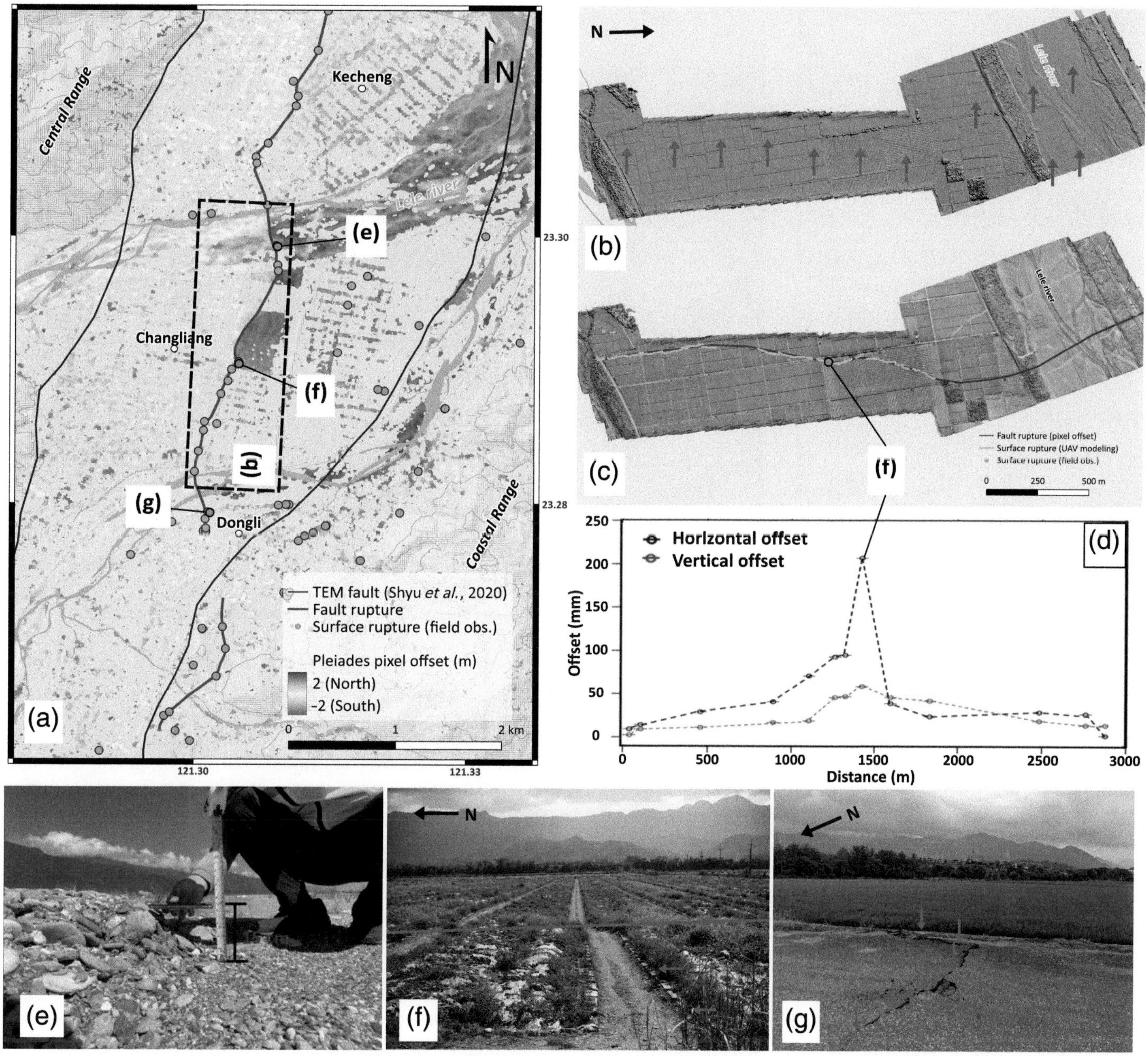

Figure 5. (a) Surface rupture in the Changliang–Dongli area. The box with dashed lines shows the area of the UAV survey in Changliang. The background color shows high relative displacement across the fault derived from the subpixel correlation result. (b,c) DSM and orthoimage derived from the UAV survey, respectively. (d) Measurements of vertical and horizontal offset along the fault in Changliang. We chose to measure the offset at the locations with a similar deformation pattern. (e) Field measurement of a 15 cm uplift observed in the Lele River bed. (f) Field photo of the largest surface rupture of maximum offset observed during the 2022 event. The offset agricultural manmade structures are modern ones after the 1951 earthquakes. (g) Field photo of surface ruptures extended southward across the Siouguluan River, continuing into the Dongli area. The color version of this figure is available only in the electronic edition.

from Chihshang to Luyeh. However, we did not observe any surface rupture along either the Central Range fault or the Luyeh fault (Fig. 7a). This absence of surface deformation indicates that these faults did not rupture on the surface.

DISCUSSION

Characteristics of the surface ruptures

The distribution of surface ruptures and measured fault offsets in this study is consistent with previous field observations and slip inversion results. In conjunction with field data and satellite image analysis, we delineated a well-defined fault trace along the Yuli fault and more distributed surface ruptures along the Chihshang fault (Fig. 1), consistent with previous investigations (CGS, 2022; Lin *et al.*, 2023; Wang, Wu, *et al.*, 2024). Our measurements indicate that the largest surface offset along the Yuli fault occurred in the Changliang area, with a maximum of ~2 m of sinistral motion and 60 cm of vertical displacement (Figs. 1b and 5d). In

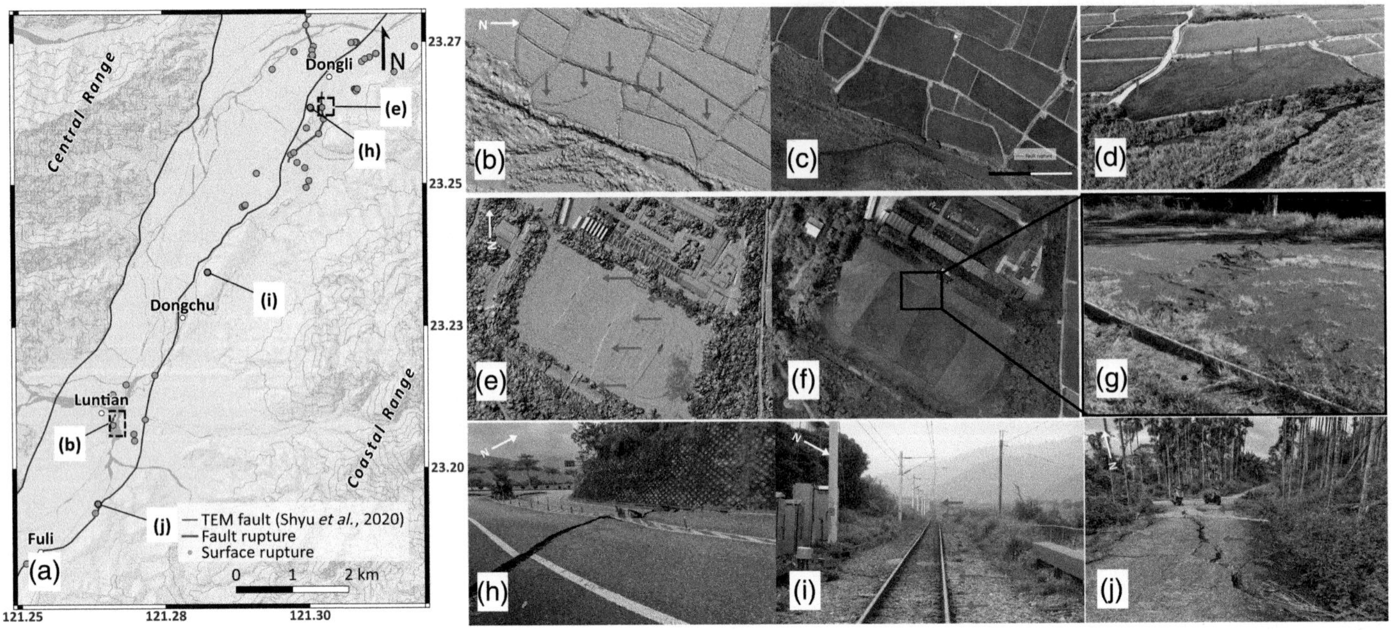

Figure 6. (a) Surface rupture in the Dongli–Fuli area. (b–d) DSM, orthoimage, and aerial photo of the UAV survey in Lungtian, respectively. The red arrows denote the fault trace. (e–g) UAV-derived DSM, UAV-derived orthoimages, and a field photo of surface rupture at the Dongli Junior High School. (h–j) Field photos of surface rupture along the Longitudinal Valley fault. The color version of this figure is available only in the electronic edition.

contrast, the largest offset associated with the Chihshang fault occurred in the Dongli area, exhibiting 56 cm of vertical displacement accompanied by minor left-lateral motion. The left-lateral motion at all rupture sites along the Chihshang fault is lower than 20 cm (Fig. 1c). These findings strongly suggest that the Yuli fault accommodated the majority of surface deformation during the 2022 Guanshan–Chihshang earthquake sequence, and the ruptures along the Chihshang fault were induced rather than seismogenic, consistent with geodetic and slip inversion studies (Lee *et al.*, 2023; Tang *et al.*, 2023; Yang *et al.*, 2024; Tung *et al.*, 2025).

Surface displacements observed along the Yuli fault are kinematically compatible with the geometry and motion of the seismogenic Central Range fault at depth. In general, sinistral strike-slip displacement dominates over vertical displacement along the Yuli fault, particularly in the Changliang area (Fig. 1b). Using the displacements in Changliang as an example, the average left-lateral offset is 53.1 cm and the average vertical offset is 27.6 cm, yielding a vertical-to-horizontal displacement ratio of approximately 0.52. This ratio closely matches the expected value of 0.54 derived from the mainshock's focal mechanism solution (dip ~70°, rake ~30°; Lee *et al.*, 2023). This agreement further supports the interpretation that the Yuli fault is the surface expression of the west-dipping Central Range fault system, consistent with the interpretation of Chen *et al.* (2024) and Wang, Wu, *et al.* (2024).

Although previous geomorphic interpretations have proposed the existence of the Central Range fault along the eastern margin of the Central Range (Shyu, Sieh, Chen, and Liu, 2005; Shyu *et al.*, 2007, 2020), our observations lead us to propose that the Yuli fault may represent the primary surface trace of this fault system. This interpretation is supported by the observation that the Yuli fault was the only fault to rupture at the surface during both the 1951 Hualien–Taitung and the 2022 Guanshan–Chihshang earthquake sequences. If the Yuli fault indeed represents the principal surface structure of the Central Range fault, then the topographic front between the eastern Central Range and the western Longitudinal Valley—often interpreted as a fault line—may instead be structurally insignificant or represent only a minor fault, in agreement with recent seismic imaging studies (Kuochen *et al.*, 2023).

Distribution of the Yuli fault trace

Our results indicate that the Yuli fault extends from the Kuokailiang and Sanmin areas in the north to Dongli in the south. The most prominent and continuous surface ruptures are observed between Yuli and Changliang, where a well-defined, throughgoing fault trace can be delineated (Figs. 4 and 5). North of Yuli, in the Sanmin–Dayu area, surface deformation becomes more diffuse, and the fault appears to bifurcate into three subparallel branches (Fig. 3). In this region, surface offsets are smaller and vertical displacement is negligible, particularly in the Sanmin area. At a similar latitude on the eastern side of the Siouguluan River, we observed west-dipping faulting near Songpu, west of the Chihshang fault trace (Fig. 2). The surface deformation here is characterized primarily by vertical uplift with little sinistral motion and may also be genetically related to the west-dipping Central Range fault system. Shyu *et al.* (2007) suggest that the Yuli fault may traverse the Siouguluan River north of Yuli town and was directly connected to the rupture in Kuokailiang. However,

Figure 7. (a) Surface rupture in the Fuli–Luyeh area. The cyan circles denote field survey locations with observed surface rupture before the mainshock. No surface rupture was found along the western flank of the valley and the Luyeh fault. (b,c) Surface ruptures crossing a north–south-oriented road, with a measured uplift of 6 cm in (c). Subsequent observations revealed more extensive damage in this area. (d) Surface rupture cutting across a roadway. (e) The Baohwa Bridge was tilted as a result of ground deformation during the mainshock. (f) Road cracking was observed close to the southernmost point of our survey area. The color version of this figure is available only in the electronic edition.

we found that the Yuli fault should extend consistently to the north along the western side of the Siouguluan River, and the faulting in Kuokailiang may act like a parallel structure to the Yuli fault in the Sanmin–Dayu area (Figs. 2 and 3). Thus, given that both the Sanmin and Songpu faulting zones are part of this west-dipping system, we suggest that strain partitioning may occur at this latitude, with the Yuli fault accommodating dominantly left-lateral motion in the Sanmin area and a Songpu branch accommodating reverse motion in the Songpu area.

Considering the entire extent from Sanmin in the north to Dongli in the south, the mapped surface trace of the Yuli fault spans approximately 16 km in length. If we consider the Songpu branch as a portion of the Yuli fault, the length of the Yuli fault is ~25 km. This is significantly shorter than the ~40 km rupture length inferred from geodetic slip inversion models (Lee *et al.*, 2023; Tang *et al.*, 2023). Although the surface ruptures along the Yuli fault become more scattered south of Changliang, the fault appears to intersect or underlie the Chihshang fault trace near Dongli (Fig. 5). Because the primary surface features south of Dongli follow the Chihshang fault, we propose that the Yuli fault may be blind in this region, underlying the Chihshang fault at depth. This interpretation is consistent with that of Chen *et al.* (2024), who suggest subsurface fault overlap in this area. Furthermore, if the west-side-up scarp observed near Lungtian (Fig. 6b–d) represents a southern surface expression associated with the Yuli fault, then the total rupture length would be consistent with the fault length derived from slip inversion models. This implies that the Yuli fault could extend farther south than indicated by surface rupture alone, and that the full length of the seismogenic structure may be obscured in areas where the fault is buried or structurally complex.

Comparison between 1951 and 2022 surface ruptures

Given that both the Yuli and Chihshang faults ruptured during the 1951 Hualien–Taitung earthquake sequence and the 2022 Guanshan–Chihshang earthquake sequence, it is valuable to examine the similarities and differences in their surface deformation patterns across these two events. Similar to the 2022 sequence, the 1951 Hualien–Taitung earthquake sequence included an M_w 6.2 foreshock and an M_w 7.0 mainshock (Cheng *et al.*, 1996), although the 1951 events were separated by only three minutes. Based on field investigations by Shyu *et al.* (2007), surface ruptures in 1951 occurred along the Yuli fault (from Kuokaikiang to Kecheng), the Chihshang fault (from Yuli to Chihshang), and the Rueisuei segment of the Longitudinal Valley fault. By comparing these 1951 rupture patterns with our observations from 2022, we can effectively examine the recurrence of surface deformation

In the northern Kuokailiang area, previous studies identified the deformation of the Kuokailiang ridge as a result of the 1951 earthquake (Shyu *et al.*, 2007). During the 2022 sequence, we also documented minor surface ruptures in the same area. Furthermore, a historical photograph from Songpu depicts a scarp with eastern-side-up vertical displacement (Fig. 2e). When compared with our 2022 observations, this scarp appears to align with the east-dipping minor faulting in the Songpu area (Fig. 2a), and we were able to match the viewing angle and location (Fig. 2f). These findings suggest that the Songpu branch of the Yuli fault in the Kuokailiang–Songpu area ruptured during both the 1951 and 2022 sequences.

West of the Siouguluan River, the Yuli fault also appears to have fully ruptured in both events. Although the 2022 surface ruptures in the Sanmin area are relatively diffuse, we identified similar deformation patterns in the riverbed (Fig. 3g,h) when compared with a historical photograph from 1951 (Fig. 3f). On the contrary, while surface ruptures in the Yuli–Kecheng area were well documented in 1951 and clearly observed again in 2022, the Changliang area where we measured the maximum fault offset in 2022 lacked any record of surface rupture in 1951 (Hsu, 1962; Shyu *et al.*, 2007). Therefore, we examined aerial photographs in 1956 (Fig. S2) and found that the Changliang area was then covered by an active alluvial fan. Thus, we suspect that the Yuli fault in Changliang may rupture in 1951, but the scarp was eroded by the fan lobe and could not able to be observed in the aerial photographs and later field investigation (Hsu, 1962).

Regarding the Chihshang fault, its surface rupture in 1951 may have extended farther north than previously recognized and may have matched the 2022 rupture extent. Shyu *et al.* (2007) proposed that the fault ruptured from Chihshang to the Yuli Bridge, though the segment between Songpu and the Yuli Bridge was interpreted as unruptured. However, our comparison of a historic photo from 1951 (Fig. 2i) with a 2022 field photo (Fig. 2j) reveals a strikingly similar fault scarp with the eastern side up along the same main street in Songpu. Thus, it suggests that this segment of the Chihshang fault likely also ruptured in 1951.

In contrast, rupture behavior along the Rueisuei segment of the Longitudinal Valley fault appears markedly different between the two sequences. In 1951, this segment experienced a significant uplift exceeding 1 m (Shyu *et al.*, 2007), whereas no surface rupture was observed during the 2022 sequence. Given that the Central Range fault is inferred to be buried beneath the Longitudinal Valley fault in the Rueisuei area (Shyu, Sieh, Chen, and Chung, 2006; Chuang *et al.*, 2014), it is possible that the pronounced surface deformation in 1951 along the Rueisuei segment of the Longitudinal Valley fault resulted from triggered slip along the deeper Central Range fault.

Insights into seismic hazards

Considering the primary surface trace of the Yuli fault from the Songpu–Sanmin area to the Dongli area, the Yuli fault ruptured along its entire length in both events, suggesting a relatively consistent rupture pattern and a characteristic earthquake behavior. The recurrent rupture behavior suggests the maturity of the Yuli fault itself. In addition, considering the Yuli fault is a portion of the Central Range fault system, the fault segmentation of the Central Range fault system is reflected by similar rupture extents and slip distributions (e.g., Lee *et al.*, 2023; Tang *et al.*, 2023). Furthermore, the repeated rupture behavior may be associated with a persistent asperity, as inferred from the seismic gap and fault coupling model (Peng *et al.*, 2023; Sun *et al.*, 2024). Because the relocation of the 1951 M_w 7.0 mainshock was within the Coastal Range with large uncertainty (Cheng *et al.*, 1996; Shyu *et al.*, 2007), the earthquake was thought to occur on the Longitudinal Valley fault. However, based on the high similarity of the surface ruptures in 1951 and 2022, it is possible that the 1951 mainshock occurred on the west-dipping Central Range fault system, similar to the 2022 mainshock.

On the other hand, the Chihshang fault also ruptured in both earthquake sequences with markedly different displacement magnitude. Although the rupture lengths are comparable, the 1951 earthquake sequence produced much greater surface offset along the Chihshang fault. For example, the maximum vertical offset in 1951 was 1–1.5 m in Dongli (Shyu *et al.*, 2007), whereas the 2022 sequence produced only 0.2 m at a similar location (Fig. 6g). The relocated hypocenter of the 1951 foreshock with small uncertainty suggests the earthquake occurred on the Longitudinal Valley fault (Cheng *et al.*, 1996; Shyu *et al.*, 2007). Therefore, the motion on the Chihshang fault should be seismogenic rather than induced during the 1951 earthquake sequence to produce a larger surface fault offset. On the contrary, accumulated strain on the Chihshang fault may have been significantly released by the 2003 Chengkung earthquake (e.g., Wu, Chen, Shin, *et al.*, 2006; Ching *et al.*, 2007) and therefore only relatively small deformation was induced during the 2022 earthquake sequence.

The contrasting rupture behavior of the Rueisuei segment of the Longitudinal Valley fault in 1951 and 2022 highlights the complex interplay between the Longitudinal Valley fault and the underlying Central Range fault. The significant uplift along the Rueisuei segment observed in 1951, potentially triggered by slip along the deeper Central Range fault, suggests that these two fault systems may interact in a complex and dynamic manner. Understanding why the 1951 rupture propagated beyond typical segmentation boundaries into the northern Central Range fault and Longitudinal Valley fault in Rueisuei requires more future studies.

In summary, our results support a rupture model governed by both structural segmentation and fault interaction in a tectonically compressed, obliquely convergent setting. Future research, including detailed paleoseismic studies and geodetic monitoring, is needed to further elucidate the recurrence behavior of these interacting fault systems.

CONCLUSION

The 2022 Guanshan–Chihshang earthquake sequence produced surface ruptures along both the Yuli and Chihshang faults, providing a rare opportunity to document the simultaneous rupture of two major faults in a plate suture zone and to observe repeated ruptures along the same faults. Field investigation and UAV survey with the assistance of satellite image correlation allowed for precise mapping of surface ruptures and quantification of strike-slip and vertical displacements. The centimeter-level resolution of UAV-derived DSM and orthoimages reveals maximum offsets of up to 2 m sinistral and 60 cm vertical along the Yuli fault. The Yuli fault exhibited surface rupture with dominant sinistral-reverse slip, strongly correlating with subsurface slip on the Central Range fault. South of Dongli, the Yuli fault may continue as a buried structure beneath the Chihshang fault. To the north, the Yuli fault may have strain partitioning. Comparison with the 1951 Hualien–Taitung earthquake sequence confirms that the Yuli fault ruptured repeatedly and nearly entirely in both events, suggesting high fault maturity of the Yuli fault itself, underscoring its maturity and persistence as the main surface trace of the Central Range fault. At a broader scale, the Central Range fault system possesses fault segmentation with distinct rupture behavior. These findings highlight that documenting repeated ruptures in arc-continent collision zones on both major and secondary faults is essential for understanding segmentation, fault interaction, and seismic hazard in tectonically complex regions.

DATA AND RESOURCES

The Advanced Land Observing Satellite (ALOS)-2 Phased Array L-band Synthetic Aperture Radar (PALSAR)-2 images used in this study were provided by Japan Aerospace Exploration Agency (JAXA), and access is restricted to authorized researchers within the project. The Pleiades satellite images were provided through the Center for Space and Remote Sensing Research. The Global Navigation Satellite System (GNSS) data used in this study were acquired through the Geological Survey and Mining Management Agency (GSMMA). Unmanned aerial vehicle (UAV) flight imagery, real-time kinematic (RTK)-Global Navigation Satellite System (GNSS) observations, and remote sensing analysis results are available by request. A 20 m digital elevation model (DEM) was created by the Ministry of Interior and is available at the Government Open Data Platform (https://data.gov.tw/en). The historic aerial photo was provided by the Center for GIS, Research Center for Humanities and Social Sciences, Academia Sinica. All maps were produced using QGIS version 3.34.4. The earthquake report of the Central Weather Administration is taken from its official website (https://www.cwa.gov.tw/V8/E/E/index.html). The moment magnitude (M_w) of the foreshock and mainshock from the report of the real-time moment tensor monitoring system (RMT) (https://rmt.earth.sinica.edu.tw). The authors present the details of the UAV flight plan and structure-from-motion (SfM) processing and a table of UAV parameters in the supplemental material. The authors also show the results of pixel correlation of optical and Synthetic Aperture Radar (SAR) images, and the comparison of a historic photo from 1956 to show the post-earthquake landscape of the 1951 Hualien–Taitung earthquake sequence. The authors provide a CSV file of rupture locations and representative measurements of fault offsets in our field investigation. The pixel correlation results from satellite imagery, the orthoimages, and digital surface models (DSMs) (10 cm resolution) derived from the UAVs, and mapped fault traces are shown in an open repository (https://osf.io/eagjs/overview?view_only=4d9e5ed1915041f3b93a8798503f97d7). Because of the large file size, higher resolution of orthoimages and DSMs (2-cm resolution), and original UAV aerial photos are available by request All websites were last accessed in August 2019.

DECLARATION OF COMPETING INTERESTS

The authors acknowledge that there are no conflicts of interest recorded.

ACKNOWLEDGMENTS

The authors thank Sheng-Wei Guo, Chin-Yi Lin, Yu-Hsuan Chen, Yu-Hsiu Lee, Yau-Hsuan Tsai, Guan-Zh Liao, and Min Lee for their help with field surveys and UAV flight missions. The authors thank Yu-Chang Chan, Kuo-Hsin Steven Tseng, and Chih-Yuan Chen for helping acquire data. This study is supported by the National Science and Technology Council (original Ministry of Science and Technology) with Grant Numbers 111-2116-M-002-044 and 111-2628-M-002-006-MY3. The Advanced Land Observing Satellite (ALOS-2) Phased Array L-band Synthetic Aperture Radar (PALSAR)-2 images were obtained through the EO-RA3 project of JAXA.

REFERENCES

Anderson, K., M. J. Westoby, and M. R. James (2019). Low-budget topographic surveying comes of age: Structure from motion photogrammetry in geography and the geosciences, *Progr. Phys. Geogr.* **43,** no. 2, 163–173.

Angelier, J., H. T. Chu, J. C. Lee, and J. C. Hu (2000). Active faulting and earthquake hazard: The case study of the Chihshang fault, Taiwan, *J. Geodynam.* **29,** 151–185.

Angster, S., S. Wesnousky, W. L. Huang, G. Kent, T. Nakata, and H. Goto (2016). Application of UAV photography to refine the slip rate on the Pyramid Lake fault zone, Nevada, *Bull. Seismol. Soc. Am.* **106,** no. 2, 785–798.

Antoine, R., T. Lopez, M. Tanguy, C. Lissak, L. Gailler, P. Labazuy, and C. Fauchard (2020). Geoscientists in the sky: Unmanned aerial vehicles responding to geohazards, *Surv. Geophys.* **41,** 1285–1321.

Bemis, S., S. Micklethwaite, D. Turner, M. R. James, S. Akciz, S. Thiele, and H. A. Bangash (2014). Ground-based and UAV-based photogrammetry: A multi-scale, high-resolution mapping tool for structural geology and paleoseismology, *J. Struct. Geol.* **69,** 163–178.

Bi, H., W. Zhang, Q. Lei, J. Zeng, P. Zhang, and G. Chen (2020). Surface slip distribution along the West Helanshan fault, northern China, and its implications for fault behavior, *J. Geophys. Res.* **125,** e2020JB019983, doi: 10.1029/2020JB019983.

Byrne, T., Y. C. Chan, R. J. Rau, C. Y. Lu, Y. H. Lee, and Y. J. Wang (2011). The arc-continent collision in Taiwan, in *Arc-Continent Collision*, D. Brown and P. D. Ryan (Editor), Springer, New York, 213–246.

CGS (2022). Field investigation report on 20220917 Guanshan earthquake and 0918 Chihshang earthquake, available at https://fault.gsmma.gov.tw/Reports/More/63cc5a4b2020403d9f79d3c33a7aba0c (last accessed October 2025).

Chen, C. W., L. W. Wei, R. Yamada, and T. Iida (2025). Spatial distribution of landslides triggered by the 2022 Taitung earthquakes in relation to active fault systems, topographic effects, and geological conditions, *Geomorphology* **473,** 109,615.

Chen, W. S., Y. M. Wu, P. Y. Yeh, Y. X. Lai, S. S. Ke, M. C. Ke, and C. Y. Yang (2024). Insights into the seismogenic structures of the arc-continent convergent plate boundary in eastern Taiwan, *Terr. Atmos. Ocean. Sci.* **35,** 13.

Cheng, S. N., Y. T. Yeh, and M. S. Yu (1996). The 1951 Taitung earthquake in Taiwan, *J. Geol. Soc. China* **39,** 267–285.

Ching, K. E., R. J. Rau, and Y. Zeng (2007). Coseismic source model of the 2003 M_w 6.8 Chengkung earthquake, Taiwan, determined from GPS measurements, *J. Geophys. Res.* **112,** no. B6, doi: 10.1029/2006JB004439.

Chuang, R. Y., K. M. Johnson, Y. T. Kuo, Y. M. Wu, C. H. Chang, and L. C. Kuo (2014). Active back thrust in the eastern Taiwan suture revealed by the 2013 Rueisuei earthquake: Evidence for a doubly Vergent orogenic wedge? *Geophys. Res. Lett.* **41,** no. 10, 3464–3470.

Chuang, R. Y., M. M. Miller, Y. G. Chen, H. Y. Chen, J. B. H. Shyu, S. B. Yu, C. M. Rubin, K. Sieh, and L. H. Chung (2012). Interseismic deformation and earthquake hazard along the southernmost Longitudinal Valley fault, eastern Taiwan, *Bull. Seismol. Soc. Am.* **102,** no. 4, 1569–1582.

Donnellan, A., G. Lyzenga, A. Ansar, C. Goulet, J. Wang, and M. Pierce (2020). Targeted high-resolution structure from motion observations over the M_w 6.4 and 7.1 ruptures of the Ridgecrest earthquake sequence, *Seismol. Res. Lett.* **91,** 2087–2095.

Gao, M., X. Xu, Y. Klinger, J. van der Woerd, and P. Tapponnier (2017). High-resolution mapping based on an unmanned aerial vehicle (UAV) to capture paleoseismic offsets along the Altyn-Tagh fault, China, *Sci. Rep.* **7,** 8281.

Giordan, D., M. S. Adams, I. Aicardi, M. Alicandro, P. Allasia, M. Baldo, P. D. Berardinis, D. Dominici, D. Godone, P. Hobbs, *et al.* (2020). The use of unmanned aerial vehicles (UAVs) for engineering geology applications, *Bull. Eng. Geol. Environ.* **79,** 3437–3481.

Gomez, C., and H. Purdie (2016). UAV-based photogrammetry and geocomputing for hazards and disaster risk monitoring—A review, *Geoenviron. Disasters* **3,** 23.

Huang, S. Y., J. Y. Yen, B. L. Wu, I. C. Yen, and R. Y. Chuang (2019). Investigating the Mulun fault: The coseismic surface rupture zone of the 2018/02/06 ML 6.2 Hualien earthquake, Taiwan, *Terr. Atmos. Oceanic Sci.* **30,** 311–335.

Hsu, T. L. (1962). Recent faulting in the Longitudinal Valley of eastern Taiwan, *Mem. Geol. Soc. China* **1,** 95–102.

Hsu, Y. C., C. P. Chang, I. C. Yen, S. Y. Huang, and J. Y. Yen (2024). Investigation of structure under the Pingting Terrace from the co-seismic surface rupture of the 2022 Guanshan earthquake, *Terr. Atmos. Ocean. Sci.* **35,** 3.

Hsu, Y. J., M. Simons, S. B. Yu, L. C. Kuo, and H. Y. Chen (2003). A two-dimensional dislocation model for interseismic deformation of the Taiwan mountain belt, *Earth Planet. Sci. Lett.* **211,** 287–294.

James, M. R., J. H. Chandler, A. Eltner, C. Fraser, P. E. Miller, J. P. Mills, T. Noble, S. Robson, and S. N. Lane (2019). Guidelines on the use of structure-from-motion photogrammetry in geomorphic research, *Earth Surf. Proc. Land.* **44,** no. 10, 2081–2084.

James, M. R., S. Robson, S. d'Oleire-Oltmanns, and U. Niethammer (2017). Optimising UAV topographic surveys processed with structure-from-motion: Ground control quality, quantity and bundle adjustment, *Geomorphology* **280,** no. 1, 51–66.

Johnson, K., E. Nissen, S. Saripalli, J. R. Arrowsmith, P. McGarey, K. Scharer, P. Williams, and B. Kimberley (2014). Rapid mapping of ultrafine fault zone topography with structure from motion, *Geosphere* **10,** no. 5, 969–986.

Ko, Y. Y., C. C. Tsai, J. H. Hwang, Y. W. Hwang, L. Ge, and M. C. Chu (2023). Failure of engineering structures and associated geotechnical problems during the 2022 M_L 6.8 Chihshang earthquake, Taiwan, *Nat. Hazards* **118,** 55–94.

Kuo, Y. T., Y. Wang, J. Hollingsworth, S. Y. Huang, R. Y. Chuang, C. H. Lu, Y. C. Hsu, H. Tung, J. Y. Yen, and C. P. Chang (2019). Shallow fault rupture of the Milun fault in the 2018 M_w 6.4 Hualien earthquake: A high-resolution approach from optical correlation of Pleiades Satellite Imagery, *Seismol. Res. Lett.* **90,** 97–107.

Kuochen, H., D. Brown, S. Y. Lai, and J. Y. Chen (2023). Reflection seismic profiling along the Longitudinal Valley basin, eastern Taiwan: In search of the Central Range fault, *Tectonophysics* **869,** 230,129.

Kuochen, H., Y. M. Wu, C. H. Chang, J. C. Hu, and W. S. Chen (2004). Relocation of eastern Taiwan earthquakes and tectonic implications, *Terr. Atmos. Ocean. Sci.* **15,** no. 4, 647–666.

Kuochen, H., Y. M. Wu, Y. G. Chen, and R. Y. Chen (2007). 2003 M_w 6.8 Chengkung earthquake and its related seismogenic structures, *J. Asian Earth Sci.* **31,** no. 3, 332–339.

Lee, J. C., H. T. Chu, J. Angelier, J. C. Hu, H. Y. Chen, and S. B. Yu (2006). Quantitative analysis of surface coseismic faulting and postseismic creep accompanying the 2003 $M_w = 6.5$, Chengkung earthquake in eastern Taiwan, *J. Geophys. Res.* **111,** no. B2, doi: 10.1029/2005JB003612.

Lee, S. J., W. T. Liang, H. W. Cheng, F. S. Tu, K. F. Ma, H. Tsuruoka, H. Kawakatsu, B. S. Huang, and C. C. Liu (2013). Towards real-time regional earthquake simulation I: real-time moment tensor monitoring (RMT) for regional events in Taiwan, *Geophys. J. Int.* **196,** 432–446.

Lee, S. J., T. C. Lin, Y. Y. Liu, and T. P. Wong (2019). Fault-to-fault jumping rupture of the 2018 M_w 6.4 Hualien earthquake in eastern Taiwan, *Seismol. Res. Lett.* **90,** no. 1, 30–39.

Lee, S. J., T. Y. Liu, and T. C. Lin (2023). The role of the west-dipping collision boundary fault in the Taiwan 2022 Chihshang earthquake sequence, *Sci. Rep.* **13,** 3552.

Leprince, S., S. Barbot, F. Ayoub, and J. P. Avouac (2007). Automatic and precise orthorectification, coregistration, and subpixel correlation of satellite images, application to ground deformation measurements, *IEEE Trans. Geosci. Remote Sens.* **45,** 1529–1558.

Li, K., Y. Li, P. Tapponnier, X. Xu, D. Li, and Z. He (2021). Joint InSAR and field constraints on faulting during the M_w 6.4, July 23, 2020, Nima/Rongma earthquake in central Tibet, *J. Geophys. Res.* **126,** e2021JB022212, doi: 10.1029/2021JB022212.

Li, K., P. Tapponnier, X. Xu, and W. Kang (2023). The 2022, *Ms* 6.9 Menyuan earthquake: Surface rupture, Paleozoic suture re-activation, slip-rate and seismic gap along the Haiyuan fault system, NE Tibet, *Earth Planet. Sci. Lett.* **622,** 118,412.

Lin, C. M., Y. W. Chang, C. C. Chou, S. J. Jhuang, Z. K. Lee, C. L. Wu, S. H. Chao, J. Y. Huang, H. C. Yang, C. Y. Chang, *et al.* (2023). Reconnaissance of the 2022 Guanshan and Chihshang earthquakes in eastern Taiwan, *Earthq. Spectra* doi: 10.1177/87552930231209102.

Lin, C. W., Y. C. Liu, P. S. Chou, and Y. H. Lin (2021). Recent development of active fault investigations of Taiwan, *Bull. Central Geol. Surv.* **34,** 1–40 (in Chinese).

Lin, L. C. J., R. Y. Chuang, C. H. Lu, K. E. Ching, and C. L. Chen (2024). Derivation of 3D coseismic displacement field from integrated azimuth and LOS displacements for the 2018 Hualien earthquake, *Remote Sens.* **16,** 1159.

Lin, Y. S., R. Y. Chuang, J. Y. Yen, Y. C. Chen, Y. T. Kuo, B. L. Wu, S. Y. Huang, and C. J. Yang (2019). Mapping surface breakages of the 2018 Hualien earthquake by using UAS photogrammetry, *Terr. Atmos. Ocean. Sci.* **30,** no. 3, 1–16.

Lin, Y. Y., Y. Y. Wen, C. T. Chen, and Y. T. Yen (2025). Strong-motion characteristics of two 2022 M 6.5+ disastrous earthquakes in the southern Longitudinal alley, Taiwan, *Earth Planet Space* **77,** 3.

Luo, J., S. G. Evans, X. Pei, R. Huang, M. Liu, and X. Dong (2020). Anomalous co-seismic surface effects produced by the 2014 M_w 6.2 Ludian earthquake, Yunnan, China: An example of complex faulting related to Riedel shear structures, *Eng. Geol.* **266,** 105,476.

Nex, F., and F. Remondino (2014). UAV for 3D mapping applications: A review, *Appl. Geomat.* **6,** 1–5.

Pan, J., H. Li, M.-C. Chevalier, P. Tapponnier, M. Bai, C. Li, F. Liu, D. Liu, K. Wu, P. Wang, *et al.* (2022). Co-seismic rupture of the 2021, M_w 7.4 Maduo earthquake (northern Tibet): Short-cutting of the Kunlun fault big bend, *Earth Planet. Sci. Lett.* **594,** 117,703.

Pandey, A., R. Jayangondaperumal, G. Hetényi, R. Singh Priyanka, I. Singh, P. Srivastava, and H. B. Srivastava (2021). Establishing primary surface rupture evidence and magnitude of the 1697 CE Sadiya earthquake at the Eastern Himalayan Frontal thrust, India, *Sci. Rep.* **11,** 879.

Paurush, P., K. Mohan, H. Mittal, Y. M. Wu, and O. P. Mishra (2024). Deciphering the cause of massive disaster during Sept. 2022 Chihshang Taiwan earthquake of magnitude 6.8 using strong motion seismology, *Environ. Earth Sci.* **83,** 520.

Peng, W., M. Radiguet, E. Pathier, and K. H. Chen (2023). Fault coupling on a creeping thrust fault: Joint inversion using geodetic data and repeating earthquakes, *J. Geophys. Res.* **128,** e2023JB026843, doi: 10.1029/2023JB026843.

Petersen, M. D., T. E. Dawson, R. Chen, T. Cao, C. J. Wills, D. P. Schwartz, and A. D. Frankel (2011). Fault displacement hazard for strike-slip faults, *Bull. Seismol. Soc. Am.* **101,** 805–825.

Pucci, S., P. M. De Martini, R. Civico, F. Villani, R. Nappi, T. Ricci, R. Azzaro, C. A. Brunori, M. Caciagli, F. R. Cinti, *et al.* (2017). Coseismic rupture of the 24 August 2016, M_w 6.0 Amatrice earthquake (Central Italy), *Geophys. Res. Lett.* **44,** 2138–2147.

Rockwell, T., A. Barka, T. Sawson, S. Akyuz, and K. Thorup (2001). Paleoseismology of the Gazikoy-Saros segment of the North Anatolia fault, northwestern Turkey: Comparison of the historical and paleoseismic records, implications of regional seismic hazard, and models of earthquake recurrence, *J. Seismol.* **5,** 433–448.

Rodriguez Padilla, A. M., M. E. Oskin, C. W. D. Milliner, and A. Plesch (2022). Accrual of widespread rock damage from the 2019 Ridgecrest earthquakes, *Nature Geosci.* **15,** 222–226.

Rodriguez Padilla, A. M., M. A. Quintana, R. M. Prado, B. J. Aguilar, T. A. Shea, M. E. Oskin, and L. Garcia (2022). Near-field high-resolution maps of the Ridgecrest earthquakes from aerial imagery, *Seismol. Res. Lett.* **93,** no. 1, 494–499.

Rosen, P. A., E. Gurrola, G. F. Sacco, and H. Zebker (2012). The InSAR scientific computing environment, *EUSAR 2012. 9th European Conference on Synthetic Aperture Radar, VDE*, 730–733.

Schwartz, D. P., and K. J. Coppersmith (1984). Fault behavior and characteristic earthquakes: Examples from the Wasatch and San Andreas fault zones, *J. Geophys. Res.* **89,** 5681–5698.

Shyu, J. B. H., Y. R. Chuang, Y. L. Chen, Y. R. Lee, and C. T. Cheng (2016). A new on-land seismogenic structure source database from the Taiwan Earthquake Model (TEM) project for seismic hazard analysis of Taiwan, *Terr. Atmos. Ocean. Sci.* **27,** 311–323.

Shyu, J. B. H., L. H. Chung, Y. G. Chen, J. C. Lee, and K. Sieh (2007). Re-evaluation of the surface ruptures of the November 1951 earthquake series in eastern Taiwan, and its neotectonic implications, *J. Asian Earth Sci.* **31,** no. 3, 317–331.

Shyu, J. B. H., K. Sieh, J. P. Avouac, W. S. Chen, and Y. G. Chen (2006). Millennial slip rate of the Longitudinal Valley fault from river terraces: Implications for convergence across the active suture of eastern Taiwan, *J. Geophys. Res.* **111,** no. B8, doi: 10.1029/2005JB003971.

Shyu, J. B. H., K. Sieh, and Y. G. Chen (2005). Tandem suturing and disarticulation of the Taiwan orogen revealed by its neotectonic elements, *Earth Planet. Sci. Lett.* **233,** 167–177.

Shyu, J. B. H., K. Sieh, Y. G. Chen, R. Y. Chuang, Y. Wang, and L. H. Chung (2008). Geomorphology of the southernmost Longitudinal Valley fault: Implications for evolution of the active suture of eastern Taiwan, *Tectonics* 27, TC1019, doi: 10.1029/2006TC002060.

Shyu, J. B. H., K. Sieh, Y. G. Chen, and L. H. Chung (2006). Geomorphic analysis of the Central Range fault, the second major active structure of the Longitudinal Valley suture, eastern Taiwan, *GSA Bull.* **118,** 1447–1462.

Shyu, J. B. H., K. Sieh, Y. G. Chen, and C. S. Liu (2005). Neotectonic architecture of Taiwan and its implications for future large earthquakes, *J. Geophys. Res.* **110,** no. B8, doi: 10.1029/2004JB003251.

Shyu, J. B. H., Y. H. Yin, C. H. Chen, Y. R. Chuang, and S. C. Liu (2020). Updates to the on-land seismogenic structure source database by the Taiwan Earthquake Model (TEM) project for seismic hazard analysis of Taiwan, *Terr. Atmos. Ocean. Sci.* **31,** 469–478.

Sun, W. F., S. Y. Pan, C. M. Huang, Z. K. Guan, I. C. Yen, C. W. Ho, T. C. Chi, C. S. Ku, B. S. Huang, C. C. Fu, *et al.* (2024). Deep learning-based earthquake catalog reveals the seismogenic structures of the 2022 M_w 6.9 Chihshang earthquake sequence, *Terr. Atmos. Ocean. Sci.* **35,** 5.

Suppe, J. (1981). Mechanics of mountain building and metamorphism in Taiwan, *Mem. Geol. Soc. China* **4,** 47–89.

Tang, C. H., Y. N. Lin, H. Tung, Y. Wang, S. J. Lee, Y. J. Hsu, J. B. H. Shyu, Y. T. Kuo, and H. Y. Chen (2023). Nearby fault interaction within the double-vergence suture in eastern Taiwan during the 2022

Chihshang earthquake sequence, *Commun. Earth Environ.* **4,** 333.

Tung, H., H. Y. Chen, Y. J. Hsu, C. H. Tang, J. C. Lee, Y. Wang, and H. K. Lee (2025). Geodetic constraints on the September 2022 Guanshan and Chihshang earthquakes, eastern Taiwan, *Tectonophysics* **895,** 230,600.

Tziavou, O., S. Pytharouli, and J. Souter (2018). Unmanned aerial vehicle (UAV) based mapping in engineering geological surveys: Considerations for optimum results, *Eng. Geol.* **232,** 12–21.

Valentini, A., F. Visini, P. Boncio, O. Scotti, and S. Baize (2025). Twenty-five years of probabilistic fault displacement hazard assessment, *Rev. Geophys.* **63,** e2024RG00875, doi: 10.1029/2024RG000875.

Wang, T., J. D. Griffin, M. Brenna, D. Fletcher, J. Zeng, M. Stirling, P. W. Dillingham, and J. Kang (2024). Earthquake forecasting from paleoseismic records, *Nat. Commun.* **15,** 1944.

Wang, Y., S. H. Wu, H. L. B. Chou, Y. Y. Li, W. S. Cheng, A. Ho, J. M. Chen, S. Z. Liu, C. Y. Hsieh, S. Duan, *et al.* (2024). Surface ruptures of the 2022 Guanshan-Chihshang earthquakes in central Longitudinal Valley area, eastern Taiwan, *Terr. Atmos. Ocean. Sci.* **35,** 16.

Wells, D. L., and K. J. Coppersmith (1994). New empirical relationships among magnitude, rupture length, rupture width, rupture area, and surface displacement, *Bull. Seismol. Soc. Am.* **84,** 974–1992.

Wesnousky, S. G. (2008). Displacement and geometrical characteristics of earthquake surface ruptures: Issues and implications for seismic-hazard analysis and the process of earthquake rupture, *Bull. Seismol. Soc. Am.* **98,** 1609–1632.

Westoby, M. J., J. Brasington, N. F. Glasser, M. J. Hambrey, and J. M. Reynolds (2012). "Structure-from-Motion" photogrammetry: A low-cost, effective tool for geoscience applications, *Geomorphology* **179,** 300–314.

Wu, D., Z. Ren, J. Liu, J. Chen, P. Guo, G. Yin, H. Ran, C. Li, and X. Yang (2021). Coseismic surface rupture during the 2018 M_w 7.5 Palu earthquake, Sulawesi Island, Indonesia, *GSA Bull.* **133,** nos. 5/6, 1157–1166.

Wu, Y. M., Y. G. Chen, C. H. Chang, L. H. Chung, T. L. Teng, F. T. Wu, and C. F. Wu (2006). Seismogenic structure in a tectonic suture zone: With new constraints from 2006 M_w 6.1 Taitung earthquake, *Geophys. Res. Lett.* **33,** L22305, doi: 10.1029/2006GL027572.

Wu, Y. M., Y. G. Chen, T. C. Shin, H. Kuochen, C. S. Hou, J. C. Hu, C. H. Chang, C. F. Wu, and T. L. Teng (2006). Coseismic versus interseismic ground deformations, fault rupture inversion and segmentation revealed by 2003 M_w 6.8 Chengkung earthquake in eastern Taiwan, *Geophys. Res. Lett.* **33,** L02312, doi: 10.1029/2005GL024711.

Yang, Y. H., L. Li, J. C. Hu, H. Tung, Q. Xu, X. Li, X. Fan, Z. Yao, Q. Xu, Q. Chen, *et al.* (2024). Double-vergent plate boundary faults and triggered coseismic rupture of the 2022 Chihshang doublet earthquake occurred in eastern Taiwan, *Seismol. Res. Lett.* **95,** 2081–2091.

Ybañez, R. L., A. A. B. Ybañez, A. M. F. A. Lagmay, and M. A. Aurelio (2021). Imaging ground surface deformations in post-disaster settings via small UAVs, *Geosci. Lett.* **8,** 23.

Yen, J. Y., C. H. Lu, R. J. Dorsey, H. Kuo-Chen, C. P. Chang, C. C. Wang, R. Y. Chuang, Y. T. Kuo, C. Y. Chiu, Y. H. Chang, *et al.* (2019). Insights into seismogenic deformation during the 2018 Hualien, Taiwan, earthquake sequence from InSAR, GPS, and Modeling, *Seismol. Res. Lett.* **90,** 78–87.

Youngs, R. R., W. J. Arabasz, R. E. Anderson, A. R. Ramelli, J. P. Ake, D. B. Slemmons, J. P. McCalpin, D. I. Doser, C. J. Fridrich, F. H. Swan III, *et al.* (2003). A methodology for probabilistic fault displacement hazard analysis (PFDHA), *Earthq. Spectra* **19,** 191–219.

Yu, S. B., and L. C. Kuo (2001). Present-day crustal motion along the Longitudinal Valley fault, eastern Taiwan, *Tectonophysics* **331,** nos. 1/2, 199–217.

Yu, S. B., H. Y. Chen, and L. C. Kuo (1997). Velocity field of GPS stations in the Taiwan area, *Tectonophysics* **274,** 41–59.

Yuan, Z., T. Li, P. Su, H. Sun, G. Ha, P. Guo, G. Chen, and J. T. Jobe (2022). Large surface-rupture gaps and low surface fault slip of the 2021 M_w 7.4 Maduo earthquake along a low-activity strike-slip fault, Tibetan plateau, *Geophys. Res. Lett.* 49, e2021GL096874, doi: 10.1029/2021GL096874.

Manuscript received 19 May 2025
Published online 15 December 2025

Revisiting the 2010 Jiashian and 2016 Meinong Earthquakes in Taiwan: Geodetic Evidence for Shared Eastward-Dipping Ramp Fault

Eric D. Szymanski[1,2], Eric A. Hetland[*1], and Ping He[3]

ABSTRACT

Coseismic surface deformation from the 4 March 2010 M_w 6.3 Jiashian and the 5 February 2016 M_w 6.4 Meinong earthquakes in southern Taiwan was measured by Global Navigation Satellite System for both events and Interferometric Synthetic Aperture Radar for the 2016 event. Several coseismic slip models for both events have been published, with those models developed using different estimation strategies and based on constrained a priori model parameter ranges. Here, we use a common estimation strategy to revisit coseismic slip models of the two earthquakes based on the geodetic observations, without constraining model parameters a priori. We employ a graph-guided fused LASSO inversion within a two-step, integrated estimation approach to infer fault geometry parameters and image coseismic slip. Our coseismic model for the 2010 Jiashian earthquake aligns well with the focal mechanisms and published models. In contrast, we find that the geodetic data suggest that the slip surface of the 2016 Meinong earthquake is more northerly oriented and shallower, with a more thrust slip component, than what is indicated by the focal mechanisms or previous coseismic slip models. We argue that constraints placed on fault geometry, particularly fault depth, biased the previous coseismic slip models. The similarity in fault strikes of our final coseismic models, combined with the proximity of the inferred fault-slip regions, indicates that these two earthquakes likely occurred on a single-fault structure with increasing dip to the east, evocative of a midcrustal flat–ramp–flat fault structure.

KEY POINTS

- Our fault-slip model for the Jiashian earthquake aligns with previously published models.
- The revised Meinong earthquake model reveals an eastward-dipping fault.
- Both earthquake source models indicate rupture on an east-dipping midcrustal flat–ramp structure.

Supplemental Material

INTRODUCTION

In 2010 and 2016, a pair of moderate magnitude yet extremely destructive earthquakes struck southern Taiwan: the 4 March 2010 M_w 6.3 Jiashian and the 5 February 2016 M_w 6.4 Meinong earthquakes. Coseismic slip in neither earthquake reached the surface (Hsu *et al.*, 2011, Jiashian; Huang *et al.*, 2016, Meinong; Qu *et al.*, 2017, Meinong; and Rau *et al.*, 2022, Meinong). Coseismic surface deformation of both earthquakes was captured by Global Navigation Satellite System (GNSS) data, and coseismic deformation in the 2016 event was captured by Interferometric Synthetic Aperture Radar (InSAR), allowing for the finite fault to be resolved. Coseismic slip in the Jiashian earthquake has been imaged on a northwest–southeast-striking fault plane, dipping to the northeast (Fig. 1; Ching *et al.*, 2011; Hsu *et al.*, 2011; Huang *et al.*, 2011; Lee *et al.*, 2013). The 2016 earthquake has been imaged to have occurred on a more east–west-trending and shallower dipping plane (Fig. 1; Huang *et al.*, 2016; Qu *et al.*, 2017; Rau *et al.*, 2022). In Figure 1, we show the surface projections of fault planes resolved by these authors, along with those of the 1999 M_w 7.6 ChiChi earthquake (e.g., Yoshioka, 2001), the 2013 M_w 6.2 and 6.5 Nantou earthquake pair, which occurred down-dip of the ChiChi earthquake (e.g., Lee *et al.*, 2015), and the 2012 M_w 5.9 Wutai

1. Department of Earth and Environmental Sciences, University of Michigan, Ann Arbor, Michigan, U.S.A., https://orcid.org/0009-0008-8971-1437 (EDS); https://orcid.org/0000-0002-8439-6465 (EAH); 2. Now at Oak Ridge National Laboratory, Oak Ridge, Tennessee, U.S.A.; 3. Hubei Subsurface Multi-scale Imaging Key Laboratory, Institute of Geophysics and Geomatics, China University of Geosciences, Wuhan, China, https://orcid.org/0000-0001-7691-8350 (PH)

*Corresponding author: ehetland@umich.edu

Cite this article as Szymanski, E. D., E. A. Hetland, and P. He (2025). Revisiting the 2010 Jiashian and 2016 Meinong Earthquakes in Taiwan: Geodetic Evidence for Shared Eastward-Dipping Ramp Fault, *Bull. Seismol. Soc. Am.* **116**, 111–132, doi: 10.1785/0120250050

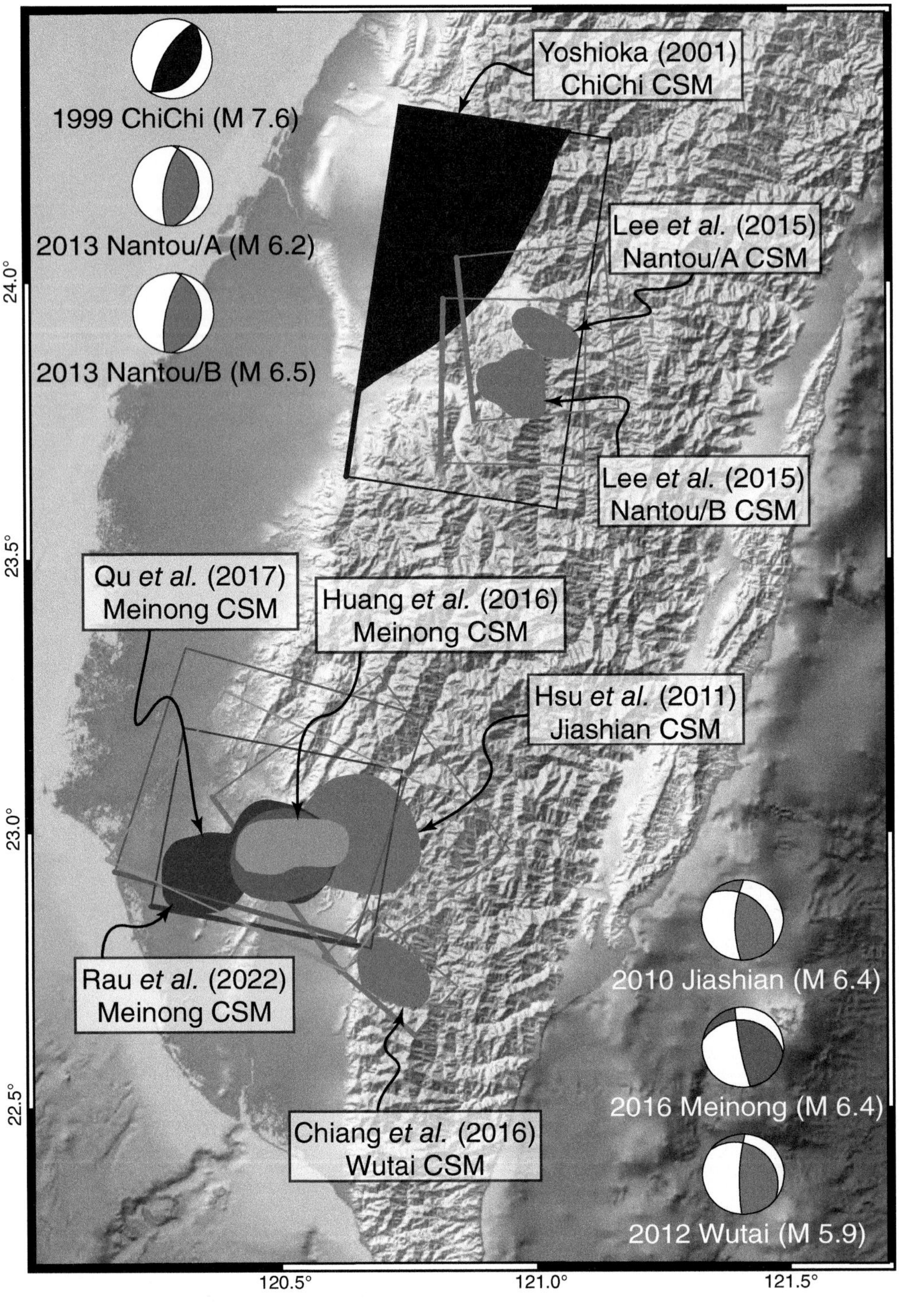

Figure 1. Focal mechanisms of several notable earthquakes in western Taiwan (double-couple solutions from the Global Centroid Moment Tensor Catalog, Global CMT), along with schematic representations of published coseismic slip models (CSMs) of those earthquakes; thick lines indicate the top edge of the fault in the CSMs, and filled areas are the approximate regions of sizable fault slip in those CSMs (regions are approximated from figures in the associated publications), with filled polygons roughly correspond to the regions where slip was larger than about 20% of the maximum slip and are just for illustration purposes, readers should see references for details of their CSMs; Yoshioka (2001; ChiChi), Hsu *et al.* (2011; Jiashian), Lee *et al.* (2015; Nantou events), Chiang *et al.* (2016; Wutai), Huang *et al.* (2016; Meinong), Qu *et al.* (2017; Meinong), and Rau *et al.* (2022; Meinong). The color version of this figure is available only in the electronic edition.

earthquake (Chiang *et al.*, 2016).

We re-examine the 2010 Jiashian and 2016 Meinong earthquakes, developing new coseismic source models from geodetic data. Our new models suggest that the earthquakes occurred on a single structure dipping to the east and steepening with depth, suggesting a flat–ramp–flat fault structure. We use GNSS data to constrain both the 2010 Jiashian (coseismic offsets from Hsu *et al.*, 2011) and the 2016 Meinong (offsets from Huang *et al.*, 2016) earthquakes, in addition to InSAR data for the 2016 Meinong event (data described below). We use the graph-guided, fused LASSO (GGFL) inversion method described in Szymanski *et al.* (2024), a compressed sensing-based inversion for which the objective function includes both Laplacian smoothing and sparsity constraints. We follow a two-step inversion process, initially performing a Monte Carlo search over fault strike, dip, location, depth, length, and width, assuming uniform fault slip. We then invert for distributed slip on the best 10,000 models found in the initial search, integrating the estimation of both fault geometry and slip distribution. This two-step process is a departure from our earlier work on the 2020 M_w 5.1 Sparta, North Carolina earthquake, where we fully integrated the inference of the fault dip and distributed slip in a single step. We use the two-step strategy here for computational tractability because the Sparta earthquake was surface breaking, allowing other fault geometry parameters to be estimated from the

TABLE 1

Ascending ("Asc") and Descending ("Des") Orbits and Dates of Synthetic Aperture Radar (SAR) Acquisitions (Year–Month–Day) Used to Produce Interferograms of the Meinong Coseismic Deformation

Orbit	Date 1 (yyyy/mm/dd)	Date 2 (yyyy/mm/dd)	Span (days)	Pre-eq Days	Post-eq Days	Role
Asc	2016/02/02	2016/02/14	12	3	9	Training
Asc	2016/01/09	2016/03/09	60	27	3	Testing
Des	2016/02/04	2016/02/28	24	1	23	Training
Des	2016/01/11	2016/03/23	72	25	47	Testing

The time span of each interferogram is indicated, along with number of days prior to ("Pre-eq") and following ("Post-eq") the earthquakes. The role of the interferograms in our inversion process, either being inverted to determine the coseismic slip model ("Training") or unseen data used to test the resulting coseismic slip model ("Testing"), is indicated.

earthquake trace. We do not impose any constraints on the slip rake.

The surface deformation due to the 2010 Jiashian earthquake was captured by GNSS observations, allowing for the development of coseismic slip models (Ching *et al.*, 2011; Hsu *et al.*, 2011; Lee *et al.*, 2013). Hsu *et al.* (2011) inverted for distributed slip using Laplacian smoothing and rake constraints, varying the slip plane strike from 290° to 330° and dip from 30° to 90°. The optimal fault strike and dip were found to be 324° and 40°, respectively, which is broadly consistent with aftershocks (Huang *et al.*, 2011) and the focal mechanisms (within 10° of one of the nodal planes of the Jiashian earthquake; Table 1). The oblique thrust slip was also quite consistent with Sh_{max} values (the azimuth of inferred slip rake in their model was in the range 245°–270°). Ching *et al.* (2011) developed a coseismic slip model in which the fault strike and dip were assumed to be 318° and 41°, respectively, taken from one of the nodal plane geometries of the Broadband Array in Taiwan for Seismology (BATS) focal mechanisms solution. They initially assumed unconstrained priors on the fault geometry, but found a more northerly strike and a shallower dip than the Centroid Moment Tensor (CMT) solutions. Upon constraining the fault strike and dip to be those from the BATS nodal plane corresponding to the slip surface, the estimated coseismic slip model of Ching *et al.* (2011) had the same reduced chi-square fit to the geodetic data as when all parameters were varied. Assuming the optimal planar slip surface determined by Hsu *et al.* (2011), Lee *et al.* (2013), subsequently determined a coseismic slip model from the same GNSS data, but adding in constraints from local seismic data. Their refined coseismic slip model had a slightly larger main slip patch, with some slip near the tip of the buried fault. In developing our coseismic slip model of the Jiashian earthquake, we only consider GNSS data and integrate the inference of the fault-plane geometry and distributed slip. As shown subsequently, our coseismic slip model is consistent with these three previously determined models. Our motivation for reconsidering the 2010 earthquake was that we wanted to consider a wider range of potential fault geometries, including geometries corresponding to the second nodal plane of the focal mechanism solutions, and to test whether our recovered solution was comparable to the published solutions.

The surface deformation due to the 2016 Meinong earthquake was captured by GNSS and InSAR data (e.g., Huang *et al.*, 2016). The coseismic deformation was also captured by leveling data (Rau *et al.*, 2022), although the data does not appear to be openly available. The study of Huang *et al.* (2016) used GNSS data and four InSAR interferograms, along with near-source seismic data, to develop a coseismic slip model of the 2016 Meinong earthquake. They searched planar fault geometries with strikes ranging from 280° to 320° and dips ranging from 0° to 40°, but at a fixed depth and location and with a uniform rake across the fault plane, ranging from 30° to 70°. They found that coseismic slip on a single planar fault (strike, dip, and rake, 299°, 15°, and 45°, respectively) was unable to explain all of the surface uplift, and proposed that the coseismic slip triggered aseismic slip on a smaller fault in the hanging wall. Qu *et al.* (2017) re-examined the Meinong earthquake, developing a coseismic slip model composed of a curved fault, with an initial dip of 30° at an assumed depth and then flattening to 10° dip at depth. Qu *et al.* (2017) assumed a fixed location of the fault, a strike of 288° (they state that the fault parameters were settled on through trial-and-error, although they do not give details on the strategy for that optimization), and a constant a priori unknown slip rake. They developed a coseismic slip model using two Sentinel-1A interferograms and the GNSS data, inferring coseismic slip with a rake of 24°. Similar to Huang *et al.* (2016), Qu *et al.* (2017) favored that there was aseismic slip induced on a shallow, north–south-striking fault in the hanging wall, based on residual uplift unexplained by the coseismic slip model and a pattern of aftershocks in the hanging wall that were delayed by 14 min. More recently, Rau *et al.* (2022) developed a finite-fault model constrained by local seismic data and high-rate GNSS data. They assumed a planar fault striking 288° and dipping 25°, with fixed location and at a depth of just over 10 km, inferring oblique thrust slip, with patches of substantial left-lateral slip (see fig. 4a of Rau *et al.*, 2022). Using that finite-fault model, Rau *et al.* (2022) forward modeled the observed geodetic offsets, finding that the finite-fault model underpredicted the large vertical offsets in the GNSS data. The lack of ability to capture the vertical offsets is a similar finding as that of Huang *et al.* (2016) and Qu *et al.* (2017), although Rau *et al.* (2022)

argued for inelastic deformation associated with mud diapirism rather than aseismic slip on a shallow fault. The latter followed that of Mai *et al.* (2021), who argued that stress changes predicted by the Lee *et al.* (2016) Meinong coseismic model were conducive to mud diapirism. Similarly, Lin *et al.* (2024) demonstrated that interferometric residuals from the Lee *et al.* (2016) model could be modeled by the opening of sills at 1.4 km depth, which they suggested were associated with diapirism.

All the Meinong coseismic slip models described earlier are largely consistent in their salient features, including the more east–west strike of the fault compared to the adjacent Jiashian fault plane (Fig. 1), the shallow dip of the fault, the large degree of left-lateral strike slip, and the inability to capture the observed vertical surface offsets by the seismic slip alone. All these models also share that they assumed some aspect of the geometry of the source fault a priori, and that the strikes and dips of the inferred fault plane were distinct from those resolved for the Jiashian earthquake. The difference in inferred fault planes is in contrast to the work of Jian (2021), who used teleseismic backprojection and relocated aftershocks to argue that the Jiashian and Meinong earthquakes occurred on a single fault, trending to the northwest and dipping to the northeast. Motivated by curiosity about the degree to which particular constraints on model geometry parameters affect the coseismic slip model, we develop a coseismic slip model of the 2016 Meinong earthquake, integrating the determination of all fault-plane geometry parameters with the determination of the coseismic slip. Faults nearer to the surface or with slip rake closer to pure thrust result in larger amplitude vertical deformation, and thus choosing to only consider deep fault planes may limit the ability to model large vertical offsets. There is also a strong trade-off between fault-plane strike and slip rake in coseismic slip models, with stronger thrust slip components resulting in more coseismic surface uplift. Finally, we wanted to test whether the geodetic constraint models are consistent with the single-fault conclusion of Jian (2021).

We use GNSS data and two interferograms to develop the Meinong coseismic slip model, reserving another two, fully independent, interferograms to test the resulting slip models. In contrast to the consistency between our new Jiashian coseismic slip model and published models, we find a Meinong coseismic model with a shallower, more northwest–southeast striking fault, and a larger thrust component than previously published coseismic slip models. The inferred strikes for each of the earthquakes is remarkably similar, with the top of the imaged coseismic slip in the Jiashian earthquake coincident with the bottom of the imaged slip in the Meinong earthquake. We interpret that these earthquakes occurred on a single fault, as argued for by Jian (2021), but that the Jiashian earthquake occurred on a steeper portion of the thrust fault at depth, likely stemming from a lower-crustal detachment fault as argued for by Ching *et al.* (2011), whereas the Meinong earthquake occurred on a more gently dipping thrust at shallower depths.

INTEGRATED ESTIMATION OF COSEISMIC SLIP MODELS

Geodetic data

To constrain the Jiashian and Meinong coseismic slip models, we invert the GNSS data from Hsu *et al.* (2011) and Huang *et al.* (2016), respectively (Fig. 2). Despite the similarity of the magnitudes of the two earthquakes, the coseismic surface offsets differ markedly. The maximum magnitude of the horizontal deformation in the Jiashian and Meinong earthquakes is 27.3 and 39.4 mm, respectively, with only 8 stations in the Jiashian coseismic data having offsets larger than 10 mm compared to 29 in the Meinong coseismic data (Fig. S1, available in the supplemental material to this article). The coseismic vertical offsets are even more contrasting, with a maximum uplift of 25.1 mm in the Jiashian earthquake, compared to 104.7 mm in the Meinong earthquake. Two GNSS stations recorded uplifts of over 70 mm in the Meinong earthquake, with 41 stations registering vertical deformation over 10 mm. In contrast, there are only 10 stations for which GNSS-derived offsets during the Jiashian earthquake were over 10 mm. The large vertical offsets in the Meinong earthquake were similarly discussed by Huang *et al.* (2016), Qu *et al.* (2017), and Rau *et al.* (2022). It is worth noting, however, that the ratio of the vertical offsets to the horizontal offsets is not drastically different for these two earthquakes (Fig. S1), and the Meinong produced a much larger magnitude of both horizontal and vertical deformation compared to the Jiashian earthquake (Fig. 2, Fig. S1).

For the Meinong earthquake, we additionally invert line-of-sight (LoS) offsets from two interferograms, derived from ascending or descending orbits of the European Space Agency's Sentinel-1A/B satellite, which we refer to as the "training" interferograms. The ascending interferogram is derived from radar scenes acquired on 2 and 14 February 2016, for a time span of 12 days, encompassing 3 days before the Meinong earthquake and 9 days of the postseismic period (Table 1; Fig. 3a). The descending interferogram is derived from scenes acquired on 4 and 28 February 2016, with a 24-day time span (Fig. 4a). We use LoS measurements from two independent interferograms to calculate the chi-square of the slip model resulting from the inversion of the training interferograms. These latter testing interferograms, unseen by the inversion and referred to as "testing" interferograms, are derived from Sentinel-1A/B radar scenes acquired on 9 January and 9 March 2016 in ascending orbit and 11 January and 23 March 2016 in descending orbit (Table 1; Figs. 3b and 4b). We choose to use the two interferograms for which time span closest brackets the Meinong earthquake for training, while using two fully independent interferograms with a longer temporal baseline for testing, as in general cleaner data should be used for model training to build a more precise understanding of the underlying signal, whereas use of noisier data for testing aids in selecting a robust model with more predictive power (Murphy, 2012). For both earthquakes, we use the GNSS

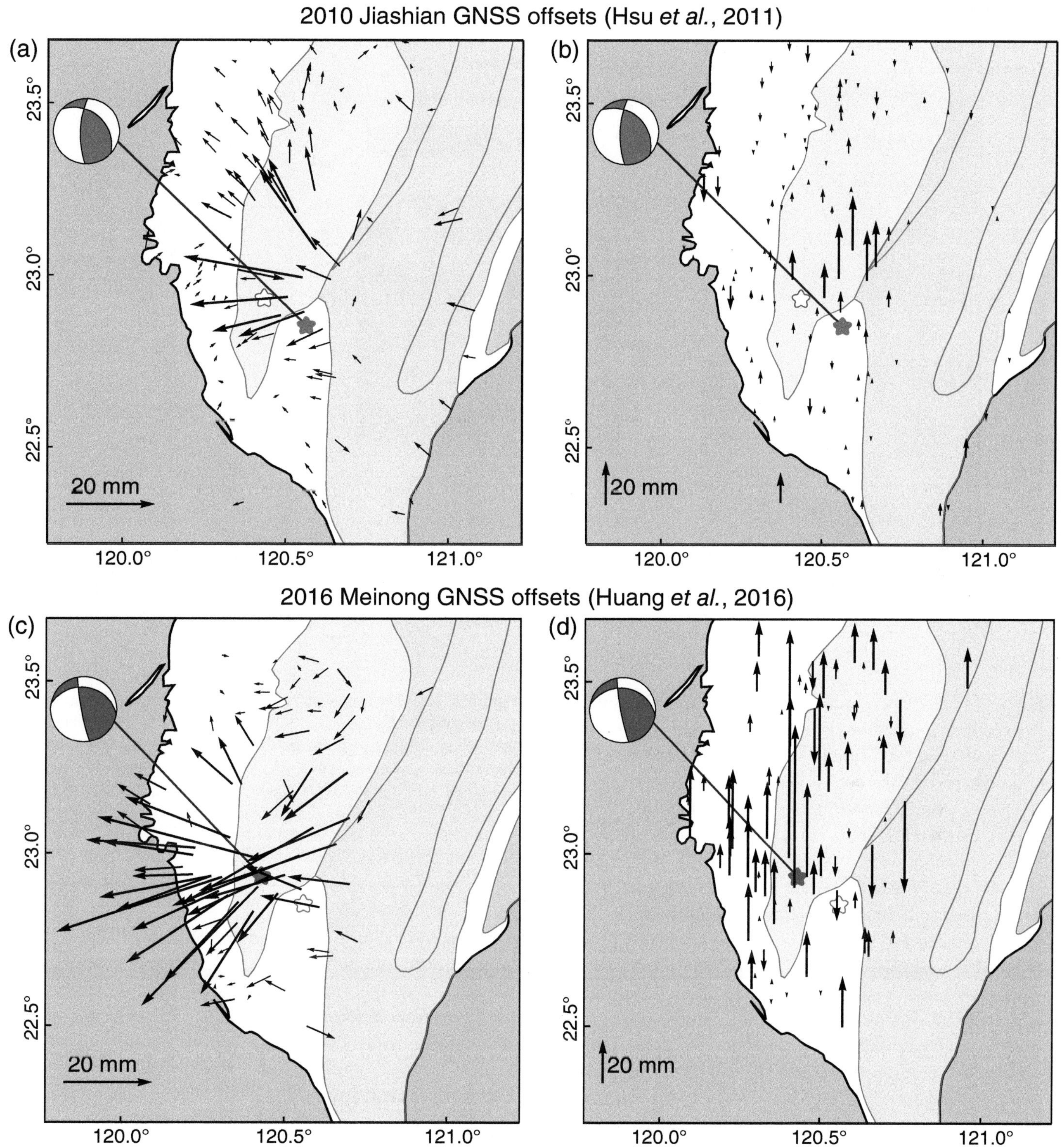

data both in the inversion and to rank the resulting model via chi-square.

To generate the interferograms, we use the open-source GMTSAR (Sandwell *et al.*, 2011). The wrapped scenes are first low-pass filtered with a 160-m wavelength Gaussian filter and then filtered a second time using a Goldstein adaptive filter (Goldstein and Werner, 1998) with an exponent of 0.6 and a patch size of 32×32 pixels. Once filtered, we unwrap phase

Figure 2. Global Navigation Satellite System (GNSS) coseismic offsets for the Jiashian (a and b; Hsu *et al.*, 2011) and Meinong (c and d; Huang *et al.*, 2016) earthquakes. Panels (a) and (c) are the horizontal deformation, and (b) and (d) are the vertical deformation. The purple and red stars indicate the Global CMT centroid locations for the Jiashian and Meinong earthquakes, respectively. The shaded regions are generalized geological regions of Taiwan: Western Foothills (tan); Hsueshan Range, Backbone Range, and Eastern Central Valley Range (yellow); and Coastal Range (green). The color version of this figure is available only in the electronic edition.

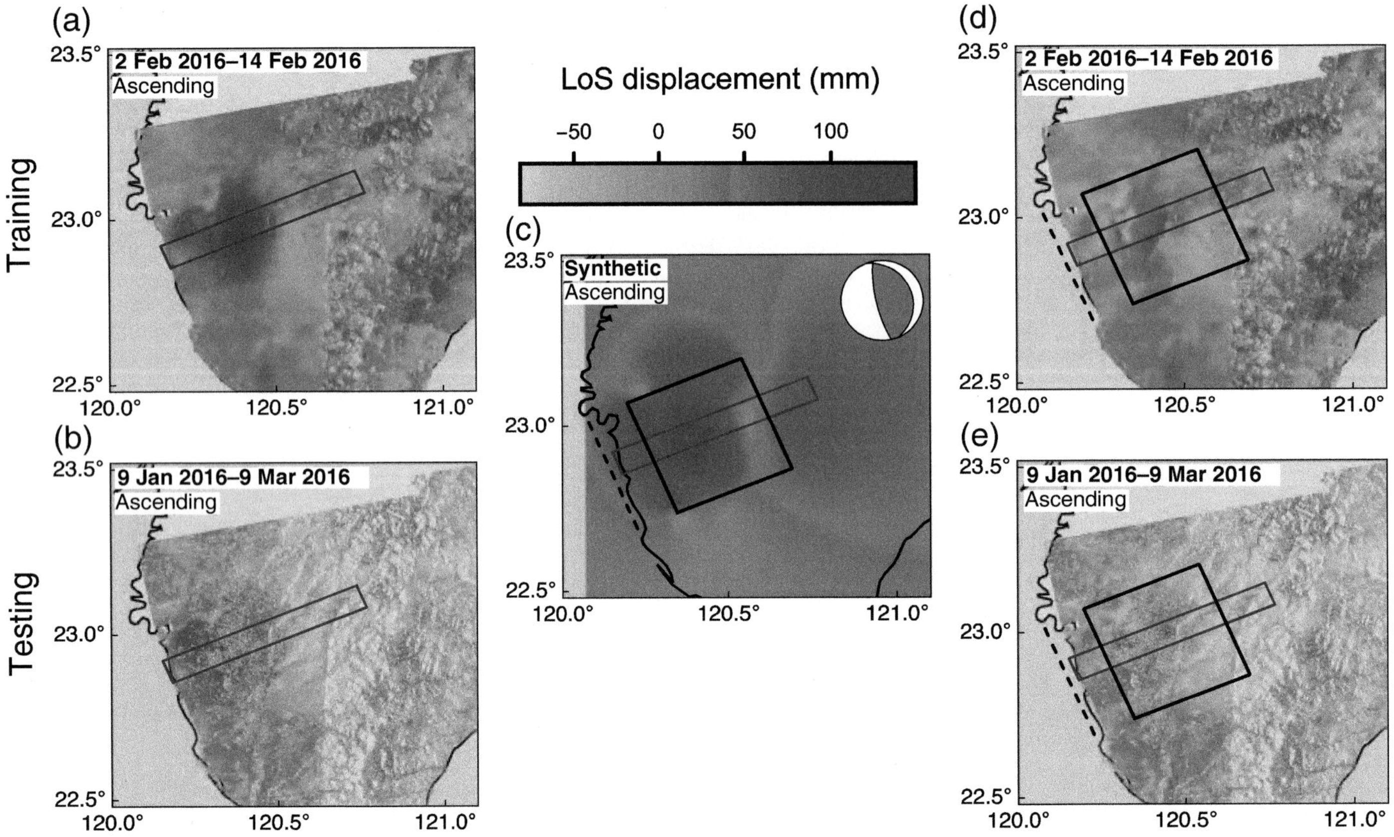

Figure 3. Ascending interferograms capturing the coseismic displacements of the Meinong earthquake (a and b), that are either inverted (training; a) or used to calculate the χ^2 of the resulting model (testing; b). The Burgundy line indicates a swath of line-of-sight (LoS) offsets in Figure 11. Synthetic LoS offsets resulting from slip in the best-fit Meinong coseismic model (c; with best-fit double couple of the model shown), and residual interferograms (d and e). The color version of this figure is available only in the electronic edition.

using SNAPHU (Chen and Zebker, 2002) for all resolution cells exceeding a coherence threshold of 0.1. We then estimate and remove residual orbital, topographic, tropostatic, and ionospheric phase contributions via a bicubic ramp containing an elevation term, fit to the interferograms using a robust least-squares algorithm (Xu *et al.*, 2014). The unwrapped, detrended scenes are then cropped to the box 120.0°–121.1° E longitude and 22.45°–23.53° N latitude, and then down-sampled using a saliency-based quad-tree sampling algorithm (Gao *et al.*, 2021). The mean LoS range change for each quad-tree node is retained as a sample, either inverted for slip (if from a training interferogram) or used to rank the resulting coseismic slip model (if from a testing interferogram). Sample sizes for the ascending and descending interferograms used for training are 210 and 196, respectively, and 387 and 229 for the testing ascending and descending interferograms, respectively. For the estimation of the InSAR noise covariance matrix, $\mathbf{C}_n$, we follow Lohman and Simons (2005) and use the structure function:

$$S(r) = E[(f(\mathbf{x}) - f(\mathbf{x} + \mathbf{r}))^2], \tag{1}$$

to calculate $\mathbf{C}_n$, as

$$C_n(r) = \sigma^2 - S(r)/2, \tag{2}$$

in which σ^2 is the noise variance for a given scene and r is the distance between two points. To estimate $S(r)$ and σ^2, we use variography. Following Lohman and Simons (2005), we use a large, uniform sampling from the interferograms, masking out the regions of the interferograms that are most expected to have coseismic deformation signal, to determine $S(r)$, taking the variogram sill value to be σ^2.

Estimation strategy

We follow a two-step process for developing the coseismic slip models, incorporating an initial step composed of a Monte Carlo search over all parameters describing the geometry of a planar fault, but assuming uniform coseismic slip. We follow this initial search with a secondary step integrating a search over fault geometry parameters with the inversion of distributed slip. Such a two-step search process is often used to determine coseismic slip models, allowing one to separate the estimation of the nonlinear parameters controlling the fault geometry from the linear inversion of distributed slip (e.g., Clarke *et al.*, 1997; Jónsson *et al.*, 2002). However, the most

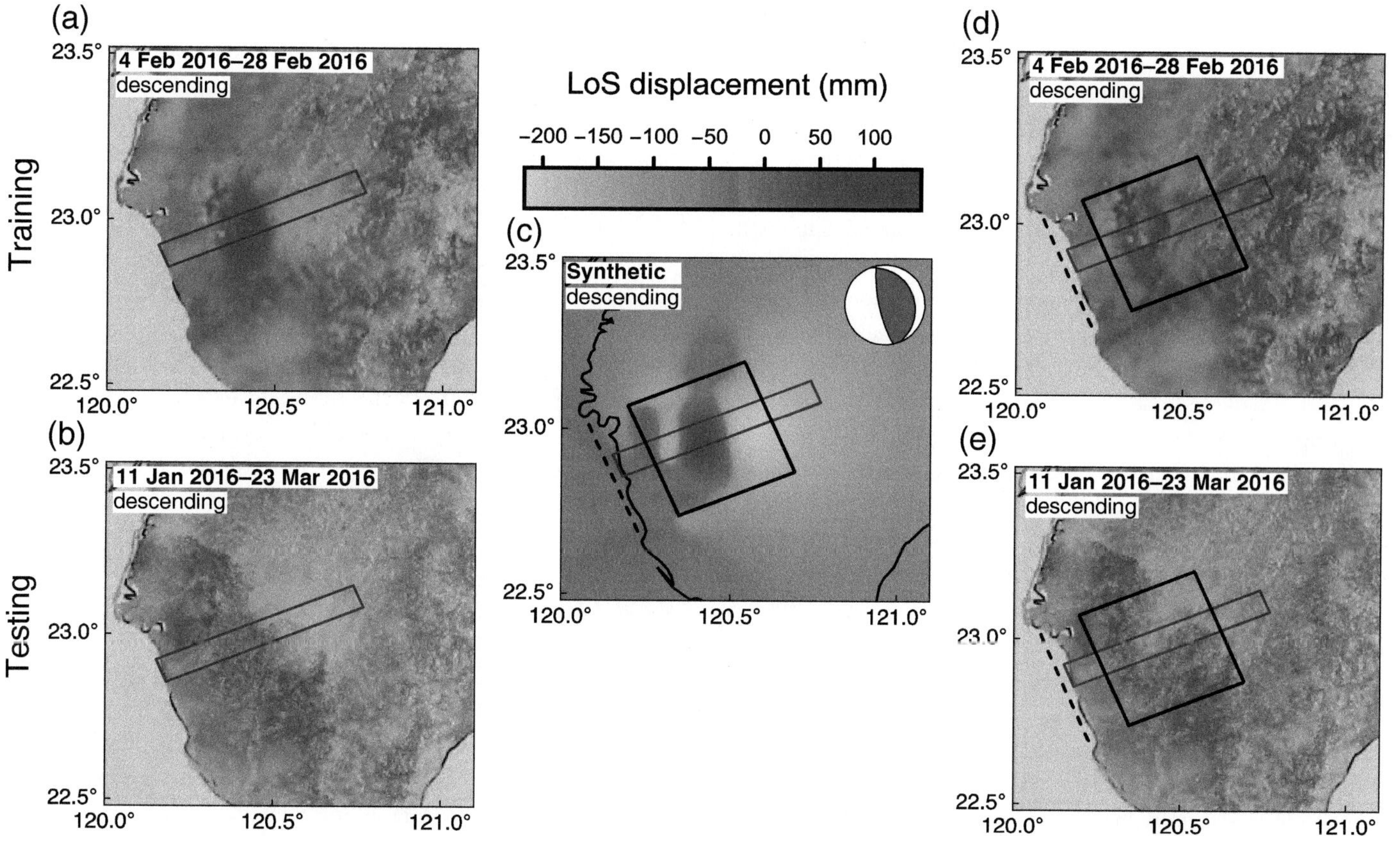

Figure 4. Descending interferograms capturing the coseismic displacements of the Meinong earthquake (a and b), that are either inverted (training; a) or used to calculate the χ^2 of the resulting model (testing; b). The Burgundy line indicates a swath of LoS offsets in Figure 11. Synthetic LoS offsets resulting from slip in the best-fit Meinong coseismic model (c; with best-fit double couple of the model shown), and residual interferograms (d and e). The color version of this figure is available only in the electronic edition.

optimal geometry determined assuming uniform slip is not necessarily the most optimal geometry for a model in which coseismic slip is nonuniform (e.g., Wicks *et al.*, 2013; He *et al.*, 2017; Szymanski *et al.*, 2024). Combining the estimation of the geometry parameters with slip distribution can range from a full estimation of all parameters simultaneously (e.g., Minson *et al.*, 2013) to using a parametric description of slip distribution (e.g., Wick and Chiu, 2022). For our work in the Sparta earthquake, we integrated a Monte Carlo search of the fault dip with the inversion for distributed slip into a single one-step process (Szymanski *et al.*, 2024), which included the determination of the inversion penalty parameters for each candidate slip surface (a full description of the penalty parameters is subsequently). This full integration was computationally tractable for the surface-breaking Sparta earthquake because the only nonlinear geometry parameter to be estimated was the fault dip. For the two blind-thrust earthquakes we consider here, we start from an assumption that none of the fault geometry parameters are a priori known, and thus fully integrating their estimation along with distributed slip is computationally burdensome. We, therefore, use a two-step estimation, taking the 10,000 best planar geometries out of more than four million trial models, in the initial uniform search as candidate geometries for which we determine distributed slip on. As we assume noninformative priors in our initial search, one may view our initial search as narrowing the priors on the fault geometry parameters, which are then used in a subsequent integrated estimation. To further reduce computational demands, we opt to use fixed penalty parameters, as discussed subsequently. The entire estimation process for a single coseismic slip model takes about 12 hr on a 2020 Intel Core i9 (3.7 GHz and 64 GB memory).

The initial search assumes uniform slip on a planar fault, parameterized by the location of the center of the top of the fault (c_x,c_y), the depth of the top of the fault (i.e., burial depth; d), the length and dip of the fault (L and W, respectively), and the strike and dip (ϕ and θ, respectively). We generate trial fault planes, assuming all parameters are equally likely, generating trial samples uniformly within the bounds of 5 km $\le L,W \le$ 12 km, c_x between 25 km west and 5 km east of the U.S. Geological Survey (USGS) epicenter, and c_y between 10 km south and 20 km north of the USGS epicenter. The range of c_x and c_y was chosen through iteration, so that the range fully encompassed the top 20,000 models. We assume any ϕ and θ are equally likely (*i.e.*, $-\pi < \phi \le \pi$ and $-\pi/2 \le \theta \le 0$) and generate near evenly spaced samples on a sphere defined by ϕ and θ, which ensures that we do not over-sample near horizontal faults relative to vertical faults. In total, we generated 4,050,080 and 4,051,420 trial fault planes for the Jiashian and Meinong coseismic slip models, respectively (note that the algorithm to sample the sphere is randomly seeded, and thus only a target number of samples can be specified, not the exact number). For each of the trial fault planes, we then invert for the strike- and dip-slip components of slip (U_s and U_d, respectively) via linear least squares, with no constraint on either the sign of slip or the slip rake.

We then take the fault geometries from the best 10,000 coseismic models found in the initial search for each earthquake, based on χ^2 fit. For both earthquakes, χ^2 includes the GNSS model residuals and the published data uncertainties. For the Meinong earthquake, χ^2 additionally includes the LoS model residuals and the uncertainties, as described above, for the testing data. From these coseismic models, we use c_x, c_y, ϕ, θ, and d to generate fault planes on which we solve for the distributed slip. We set each of the fault planes to 40 km by 40 km, and discretized them into 200 2×2 km^2 subfaults. We solve for the optimal distribution of slip on each trial fault plane using the GGFL inversion scheme we developed in Szymanski *et al.* (2024), which includes both sparsity and smoothness regularization terms. The sparsity constraint is imposed on the model vector in an L1 norm, and the constraint tends to decrease the number of subfaults with nonzero slip. The smoothness constraint is imposed via the L2 norm of the Laplacian on the slip across the fault surface, where the strike- and dip-slip components of slip are smoothed independently. Because the sparsity constraint is in terms of the L1 norm, we cast the estimation as a second-order cone program (SOCP; Boyd and Vandenberghe, 2004). Framing the optimization as an SOCP allows us to avoid approximating the absolute value contained in the L1 norm, as we did in our previous implementation (Szymanski *et al.*, 2024). To solve for the strike- and dip-slip offsets, we use a splitting-conic solver, which employs the alternating direction method of multipliers, and is a more efficient method than using other solvers, which typically employ less flexible interior point methods (O'Donoghue *et al.*, 2016). We do not add any constraint on allowable rake or sign of the strike- or dip-slip offsets.

In the GGFL estimation, there are two penalty parameters, λ_1 on the sparsity constraint and λ_2 on the Laplacian smoothness constraint. λ_1 can be related to a bound on the moment of the resulting coseismic slip model (Szymanski *et al.*, 2024), and we use the seismic moment along with the data errors to calculate it a priori. Using this approach allows us to both reduce computational burden and tie λ_1's value to observed physical attributes of the earthquake. λ_2 can be solved for using the L-curve criterion, an analytical method for determining the optimal trade-off point of a standard L-curve used to determine penalty parameters in least-squares problems (Hansen, 2000). For both earthquakes, we initially explored searches where the optimum λ_2 was solved for in each of the 10,000 sample fault geometries, finding two distinct populations, each associated with fault strikes and dips close to the nodal plane. The distributions of λ_2 for both earthquakes shared similar characteristics, with heavy right skew or symmetric distributions associated with north- or west-dipping faults. The median values for the north-dipping fault distributions were 0.12 and 0.1 for Meinong and Jiashian, respectively, with median values for the west-dipping fault distributions 0.23 and 0.13 for each of the earthquakes. For simplicity, we opted to set $\lambda_2 = 0.2$ and 0.1 for the Jiashian and Meinong coseismic models, respectively, which fell within the central regions of each of the distributions of λ_2. The higher λ_2 in the Jiashian coseismic model likely reflects the use of a much smaller data set compared to that for the Meinong earthquake. Inversion runs with different λ_2 values either resulted in noisy models (i.e., models with oscillations of normal and reverse dip-slip or left- and right-lateral strike slip), or overly smoothed models and associated degraded χ^2.

RESULTS

Initial uniform slip search

As described in the previous section, we initially invert for U_s and U_d on over four million trial fault-plane geometries for each of the earthquakes. Each of the trial fault planes is then ranked according to how well the associated coseismic slip model fits the GNSS data, along with the unseen InSAR data in the Meinong models. The locations, ϕ, and θ of the 20,000 best-fitting models are shown in Figure 5. As our goal with this initial search is to determine trial fault-plane geometries that are then used to determine distributed slip, we do not discuss the variations of L, W, U_s, and U_d here (the distribution of these parameters is discussed in the supplemental material, and is presented in Fig. S2), and save discussion of the fault slip for our discussion of the integrated search results subsequently. Likewise, we only discuss d in the context of the integrated search. From the initial search, we find that the fault location for steeply dipping planes is more tightly constrained than for shallow dipping planes, with the locations of the latter varying by 20–25 km (Fig. 5a,b).

The inferred dip of the fault planes in the initial search of both earthquakes is bimodal (Fig. 5c,d). The steeper dipping planes are associated with north–south-striking faults, whereas the shallower planes are associated with northeast–southwest strikes (Fig. 5e,f). For very shallow dipping planes, large variations in strike will result in minimal variation in the actual fault plane for these relatively compact planes (the dimensions of the uniform slip patches in these top 20,000 models are roughly 6–10 km; Fig. S02), which leads to a less well-constrained strike. Each of the clusters of ϕ and θ corresponds to one of the two nodal planes in the seismic moment tensors (Fig. 5e,f), although for these blind earthquakes, the geodetic data are fit better by the shallower dipping planes (Fig. 5d,e). Generally, the best-fitting coseismic models for the Meinong earthquake have strikes closer to north–south-trending than the associated nodal plane in the seismic moment tensor, an

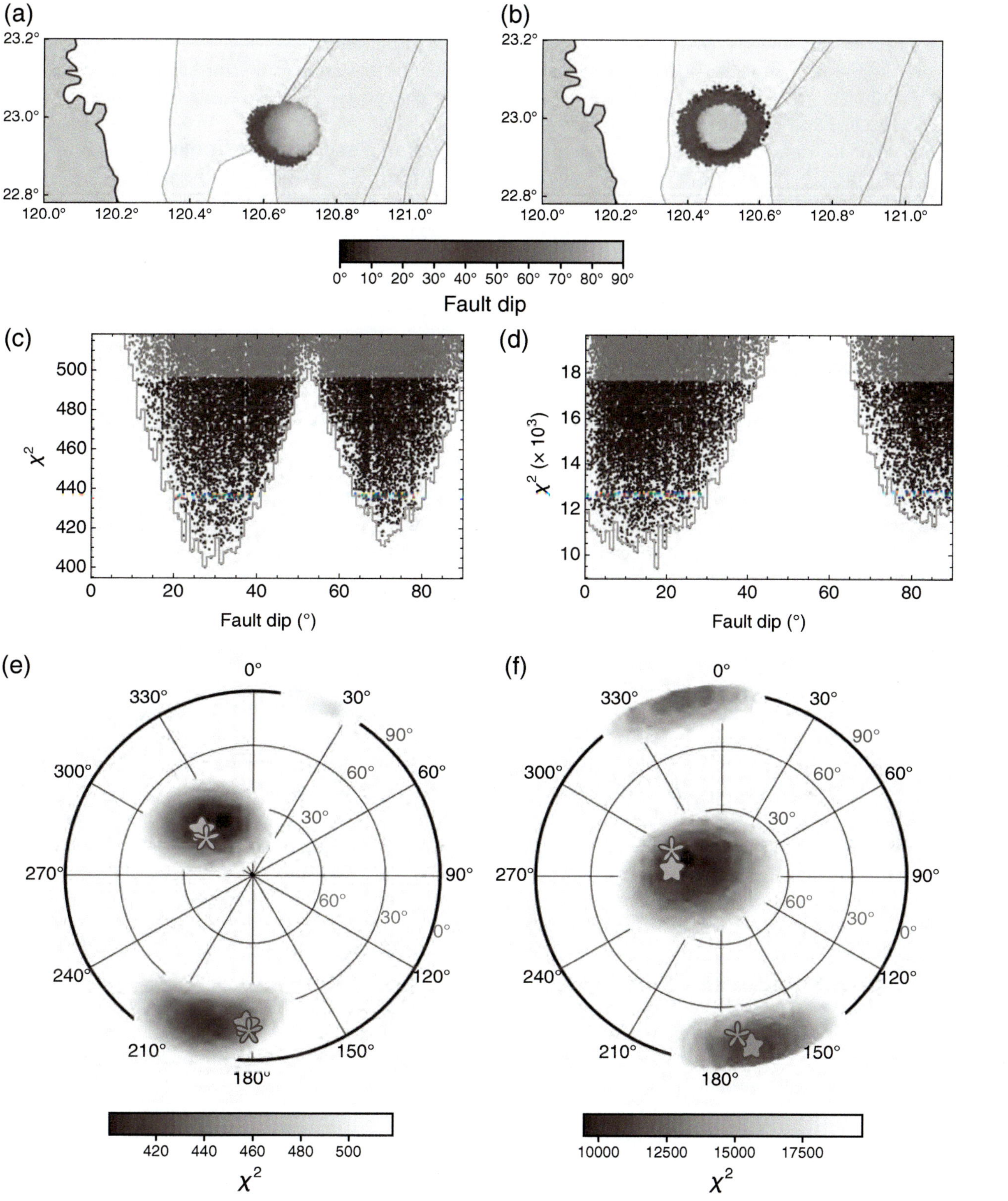

Figure 5. Location of the faults in the 20,000 best-fitting coseismic slip models found in the initial search for the Jiashian (a) or Meinong (b) earthquakes. The plotted point is the location of the center of the top of the fault plane, colored by the dip of the fault. Model fit versus fault dip in the top 20,000 initial Jiashian (c) or Meinong (d) coseismic slip models. The purple points depict the top 10,000 best-fitting models, and blue are the next 10,000; orange lines are the lowest χ^2 in 1° bins. Strike and dip of the fault planes in these 20,000 models for the Jiashian (e) or Meinong (f) earthquakes, shown in a Lambert projection and colored according to the fit of the coseismic slip model. Values along the outer circumference indicate the strike of the fault plane, and numbers in the interior circles indicate either dip (green text) or codip (blue text); stars and asterisks depict the two nodal planes in the Global CMT or U.S. Geological Survey (USGS) focal mechanisms, respectively. The color version of this figure is available only in the electronic edition.

issue we discuss further subsequently. Finally, the most successful Meinong coseismic models have faults with shallower dips compared to the Jiashian models (Fig. 5).

Integrated search: Fault geometries

We then invert for distributed slip on the fault geometries, including only location, ϕ, θ, and d, of the 10,000 best-fitting models found in the initial search. As before, the resulting coseismic slip models are ranked by the χ^2 fit to the GNSS data for each of the earthquakes, and the unseen InSAR data of the Meinong earthquake. We first discuss ϕ and θ in the context of the integrated search. We then discuss the location and d of the fault planes for the two earthquakes, and finally, we discuss the inferred slip distributions.

In the integrated search, the data fit increases over that in the initial search because more data features can be described by nonuniform distributions of slip. The trial values of ϕ and θ do not change from what was presented above, although the associated fit of these values does change, and hence the two clusters of ϕ and θ similar to each of the focal mechanism nodal plane persist; however, for both earthquakes fault geometries similar to the shallower of the nodal planes are even more favored by the data compared to in the uniform search (Fig. 6). Likewise, that the geodetic data of the Meinong earthquake are best fit by northwest–southeast-striking faults is more prominent in the integrated search (compare with Figs. 5f and 6d), an issue we address in the Discussion section.

The dips of the faults in the best-fitting Jiashian coseismic slip models are generally steeper than the dips in the best-fitting Meinong models (20°–40° in the Jiashian models, compared to less than about 20° in the Meinong models; Fig. 7). In contrast, the strikes of the faults in best-fitting Jiashian and Meinong coseismic models are quite similar, with the centroid of slip in the Meinong models almost directly west of the centroid of slip in the Jiashian models (Fig. 7a). The burial depths of the faults in the best-fitting Jiashian or Meinong earthquakes are similar (compare with Fig. 7b,c); although that does not indicate that the inferred slip in each earthquake is at the same depth because the dips of the fault planes are not the same for the two earthquakes. Rather, the shallower dip of the Meinong fault models results in shallower centroids (Table 2; Fig. S3). Note that the GGFL-based inversion of slip can indeed put the centroid of slip deep, corresponding to the lower part of the 20 km wide fault plane, and indeed of these 10,000 Meinong models many have inferred centroids that are up to 20 km deep (Fig. S3); however, overall most of the inferred centroids of the Jiashian earthquake are deeper than for the Meinong earthquake. Moreover, the Meinong models that best fit the geodetic data all have centroids closer to the surface than in the Jiashian models (Fig. S3). Taken together, the shallower slip in the Meinong earthquake directly to the west of the inferred Jiashian earthquake slip, on a more gently dipping fault plane with similar strike, suggests that the slip in these two earthquakes occurred on a single structure dipping to the east and steepening with depth, suggestive of a flat–ramp–flat structure. Before exploring this interpretation further, we present the inferred slip distributions for these two earthquakes.

Integrated search: Best-fit models

The inferred slip in each of the best-fitting coseismic slip models of the two earthquakes is relatively compact (Fig. 8). The average slip rake, weighted by the magnitude of slip in each subfault, is 44° and 80° for the Jiashian and Meinong earthquakes, respectively (Table 2). Although the average rake of the Jiashian coseismic slip model is comparable to rakes of both the USGS and Global CMT focal mechanisms (Fig. S6), our inferred slip rake of the Meinong earthquake is characterized by more thrust slip than resolved by the focal mechanism (Fig. 8), a point we come back to in the Discussion section. Slip in the Meinong earthquake is smoother and over a broader region than in the Jiashian earthquake, reflecting that the Laplacian smoothness regularization was dominant over the sparsity regularization in the Meinong coseismic slip models. This was likely a combined result of our choice of a lower penalty parameter on the sparsity constraint and additional data in the Meinong earthquake.

Both of the coseismic slip models contain slip at the edges of the fault-plane domain, which we take to be model noise. Indeed, we find that the slip at the fault edges in ensembles of all models is within 10% of the best-fit χ^2 for each event, varies to an appreciable degree (38 and 107 models for the Jiashian and Meinong earthquakes, respectively; Fig. 8). Both of the main slip patches are robust across the models in the ensembles of the two events. The ensemble varies less across most of the main fault for the Jiashian models compared to the Meinong models, due to the fact that the sparsity constraint dominates in the Jiashian model owing to the lower number of data.

The predicted offsets at the GNSS stations from best-fit coseismic slip models are quite close match to the observed GNSS velocities, both horizontal and vertical, for both earthquakes (Fig. 9; fit residuals are shown in Fig. S4). Likewise, the predicted LoS for each of the interferograms is also a close match to the observed (Figs. 3 and 4; a comparison between the predictions at the quad-tree samples for each of the interferograms is shown in Fig. S5).

DISCUSSION

The most surprising result of these inversions is that our best-fitting coseismic slip model of the 2016 Meinong earthquake is composed of a more northerly strike and larger thrust motion compared to focal mechanisms (Table 2) and previously determined coseismic slip models of this earthquake (compare with Figs. 1 and 7; Huang *et al.*, 2016; Qu *et al.*, 2017; Rau *et al.*, 2022). In contrast, our best-fit Jiashian model agrees well with the focal mechanisms (Table 1, Fig. S6), as well as compares

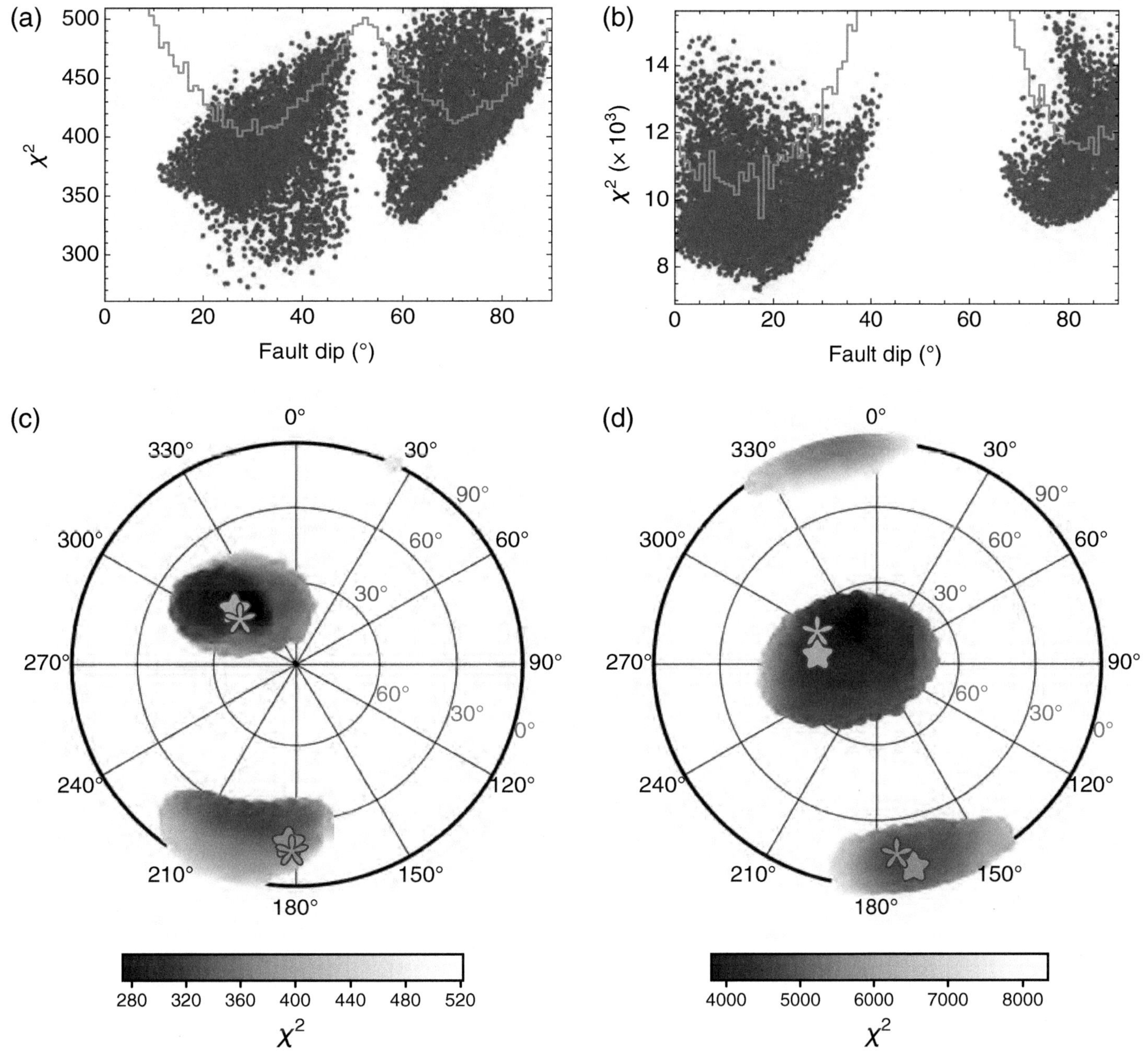

Figure 6. Model fit versus fault dip in the 10,000 trial faults in the integrated search for the Jiashian (a) or Meinong (b) coseismic slip models; orange lines in panels (c) and (d) are from Figure 5a,b, respectively. Strike and dip of the fault planes in the trial models for the Jiashian (c) or Meinong (d) earthquakes in the integrated search. Strike and dip are shown in a Lambert projection and colored according to the fit of the coseismic slip model. Values along the outer circumference indicate the strike of the fault plane, and numbers in the interior circles indicate either dip (green text) or codip (blue text); stars and asterisks depict the two nodal planes in the Global CMT or USGS focal mechanisms, respectively. The color version of this figure is available only in the electronic edition.

favorably to the coseismic slip models proposed by Ching *et al.* (2011) and Hsu *et al.* (2011). That our best Jiashian coseismic model is not a large deviation from prior models of this earthquake, indicates that it is not our estimation scheme which is the cause of our inferred Meinong coseismic model differing from prior models. In the following subsections, we first explore the relative support of our preferred Meinong model over a model that is closer to the seismic focal mechanisms or previously determined models. Second, we assess our Jiashian model in light of previous models. Third, we propose a connection between our Meinong and Jiashian models, suggesting that these two earthquakes occurred on the same fault structure. Fourth, we discuss robustness of our inversion strategy to potential interferometric noise in light of recognized ionospheric anomalies in the training ascending interferogram.

Geodetic support of a more north striking, and largely thrust Meinong coseismic model

In comparing our Meinong model to past models, it is important to recognize potential biases that can arise due to incompletely

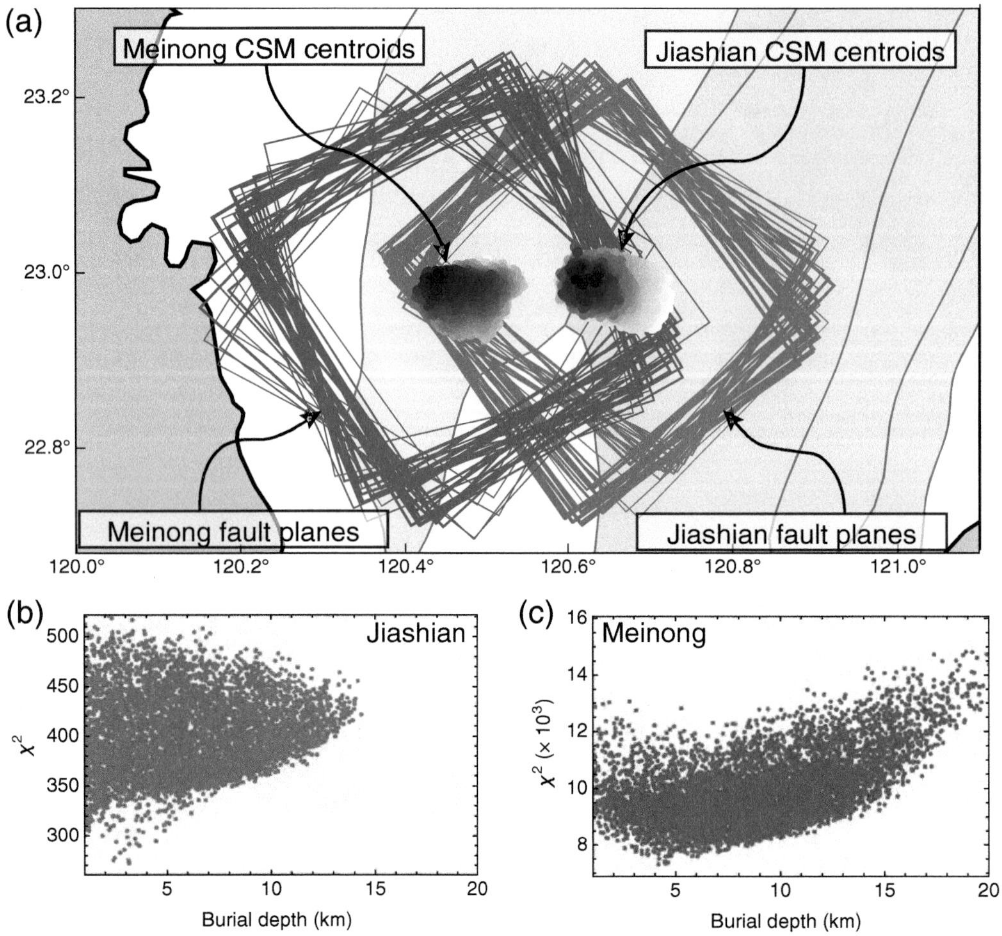

Figure 7. (a) Surface projections of the fault planes in the Jiashian (blue) and Meinong (red) coseismic slip models with χ^2 within 10% of the best-fitting model (38 and 107 models for Jiashian and Meinong coseismic models, respectively; line thickness scales with χ^2). Also shown are the centroid locations of all 10,000 of the models in the integrated search, colored by χ^2 (coloring of Jiashian and Meinong centroids as in Fig. 6a,b, respectively). Model fit versus burial depths of all 10,000 trial models in the integrated search for the Jiashian (b) and Meinong (c) earthquakes. The color version of this figure is available only in the electronic edition.

searching model space. This incomplete search might be due to limiting ranges of parameters searched over, or result from a decoupling the determination of different sets of parameters. The result of these biases might be a preference for some model features that are not the globally optimum.

Illustrating that decoupling estimation of different parameters can result in a bias, in our initial search over all fault geometry parameters assuming uniform fault slip, we find that a deeper fault with a more easterly strike and oblique slip provides the best fit to the geodetic data (Table 1). Indeed, the strike we resolve in this best-fit uniform search model (−63°) is quite similar to the strikes determined by Huang *et al.* (2016) (−61°) and Qu *et al.* (2017) (−72°), as well as strikes of the nodal plane most associated with the slip surface (Fig. 10). Moreover, the depth we find in the initial search (10.9 km) is comparable to the assumed depths of the faults in past coseismic models (Huang *et al.*, 2016; Qu *et al.*, 2017; Rau *et al.*, 2022) and focal depths (Table 1). We note that when using only the testing InSAR to rank the model misfit, the best model found in the uniform slip search is a north–south-striking fault (5°), but still at about the same depth (11.0 km). If we had fixed the fault geometry parameters based on an initial search assuming uniform slip, following standard practice in developing coseismic slip models (e.g.; Clarke *et al.*, 1997), we would have determined a much different coseismic slip model than the best-fitting model we present.

In our integrated search, our optimal solution is composed of a much shallower fault (4.1 km to the top of the fault plane) with almost pure thrust motion (rake of 80°; Table 1). Shallow faults and those with more thrust slip than strike slip both result in larger vertical deformation. In that, we posit that allowing the search to encompass more shallow faults results in a coseismic slip model that fits the large vertical deformation to a better degree (Fig. 9c,d). Our preferred Meinong coseismic model also provides a good fit to the InSAR data, including the interferograms that were not visible in the inversion (Figs. 3, 4, and 11).

To further demonstrate that allowing a shallower fault results in a more complete description of the geodetic data, we extract an alternative solution from the cloud of the 10,000 tested models. This alternative model has a strike, dip, and average rake close to the primary nodal plane of the Global CMT focal mechanism (strike, dip, and weighted average rake are −83°, 20°, and 20°, respectively, all within 2° of the nodal plane of the Global CMT solution). In addition, the centroid depth of this alternative fault is 16.3 km, just slightly shallower than the Global CMT centroid depth (Table 2). This alternative model, with a northeasterly fault dip, has a χ^2 about 40% larger than the best fit (it is the 4524th best-fit model). The fit to the horizontal GNSS observations is degraded compared to the best-fit model, and there are quite large vertical GNSS residuals over the hanging wall of the fault (Fig. S7). Likewise, the InSAR

TABLE 2
Nodal-Plane Orientations of the Global Centroid Moment Tensor (Global CMT) and U.S. Geological Survey (USGS) *W* Phase Focal Mechanisms Most Closely Associated With the Slip Surfaces Resolved Here, Along With Location and Depth of the Centroid

		Fault Plane				Centroid		
Event	**Solution**	**Depth (km)**	**Strike**	**Dip**	λ	**Latitude**	**Longitude**	**Depth (km)**
Jiashian	Global CMT	N/A	−47°	30°	45°	22.86°	120.56°	29.1
	USGS	N/A	−50°	26°	42°	22.92°*	120.80°*	35.0
	Uniform	14.3	−28°	27.5°	46°	22.90°	120.50°	18.8
	Best int.	3.1	−35°	29°	44°	22.99°	120.62°	13.5
	Ensemble	1.3	8°	6°	10°	0.01	0.01	1.2
Meinong	Global CMT	N/A	−81°	22°	21°	22.94°	120.43°	17.3
	USGS	N/A	−61°	25°	38°	22.94°*	120.60°*	25.5
	Uniform	10.9	−63°	18°	40°	22.90°	120.50°	16.0
	Best int.	4.1	−23	17°	80°	22.99°	120.44°	10.1
	Ensemble	1.4	15°	4°	14°	0.01	0.01	0.5

Parameters of the fault plane and centroid location for the model with the lowest χ^2 in the initial search with uniform fault slip, and the best model from the integrated search. Also given are the standard deviations of the parameters from an ensemble of all models within 10% of the best-fit χ^2 for each earthquake (38 and 107 models for Jiashian and Meinong coseismic models, respectively). Depth is to the top of the fault plane; λ is either slip rake or the average slip rake in the subfaults, weighted by the slip magnitude in that subfault, for the uniform or the integrated best/ensemble, respectively. For the uniform model, centroid depth is the depth of the center of the fault plane.
*USGS location is the epicenter.

observations are underpredicted by this alternate model (Fig. S8).

The previous coseismic models of the Meinong earthquake were unable to explain all the vertical deformation with coseismic slip on a single-fault plane alone (Huang *et al.*, 2016, Qu *et al.*, 2017; Rau *et al.*, 2022). In contrast, here we find little unexplained vertical deformation. To be clear, there are some vertical GNSS residuals (because the data errors on the vertical offsets are larger, the estimation favors explanation of the horizontal components), but there is no clear pattern of these residuals relative to the fault plane (Fig. S4d). Indeed, the vertical residuals at stations over the hanging wall are generally smaller than the far-field residuals (compare with Fig. 9b and Fig. S4d). We also note that the peak LoS offsets in the ascending interferogram used to test the model (Fig. 10c) are underpredicted by the best-fitting coseismic model (the full residual is shown in Fig. 3e); however, an underprediction of the peak LoS offsets is not apparent in the other three interferograms nor the vertical GNSS offsets (Fig. S4d). We surmise that the underprediction of the testing ascending interferogram is due to noise that is unique to that interferogram. We concede that there may be some component of aseismic deformation coincident with the Meinong earthquake (e.g., Mai *et al.*, 2021), but in our view, using a misfit between our coseismic slip model and the geodetic data alone is insufficient to argue for that additional deformation.

Although we contend that the differences between our best Meinong coseismic model and previously published models arise from those earlier models constraining the allowable ranges of model parameters—most notably by assuming a given depth—the discrepancy between our Meinong model and seismic focal mechanisms remains (Fig. 10). That the inferred double-couple mechanism trades off with depth, as well as that depth itself trades off with the moment magnitude and is sensitive to the assumed velocity model, are well established in the literature (e.g., Chang *et al.*, 2019). The depth of the centroid in our preferred Meinong model is about half the depths given by both the USGS and Global CMT (Table 2; it is interesting to note that the centroid depth of our preferred Jiashian coseismic model is also appreciably shallower than the seismically determined depths). On the other hand, Jian *et al.* (2017) found that a hypocentral depth of about 16 km was most consistent with teleseismic depth phases, which is more comparable to the depths we find, albeit still deeper than the depths of our best-fitting models (Fig. S3b). Jian *et al.* (2017) used seislmological data to show that the Meinong earthquake occurred on fault striking −40° and dipping northeast, a finding also quite distinct from the focal mechanisms (we discuss the model of Jian, 2021, further subsequently), which indicates that that our best-fitting Meinong model has such a stark mismatch to the focal mechanisms is not because we only consider geodetic data.

Assessment of the best-fit Jiashian model

Our best-fit Jiashian model agrees well with both the USGS *W* phase and Global CMT focal mechanisms (Table 2, Fig. S6). It is, however, important to note that the USGS and Global CMT moment tensors have 17% and 11% non-double-couple (non-DC) components, respectively. As our coseismic model is composed only of planar fault slip, it is by definition is a pure double couple, as are the previously published coseismic slip models (Ching *et al.*, 2011; Hsu *et al.*, 2011; Lee *et al.*, 2013). We are unsure if the non-DC components in the moment tensors are due to uncertainties in their determination, or if they indicate that coseismic slip in the Jiashian earthquake occurred on a nonplanar fault surface. Although there is some coherence

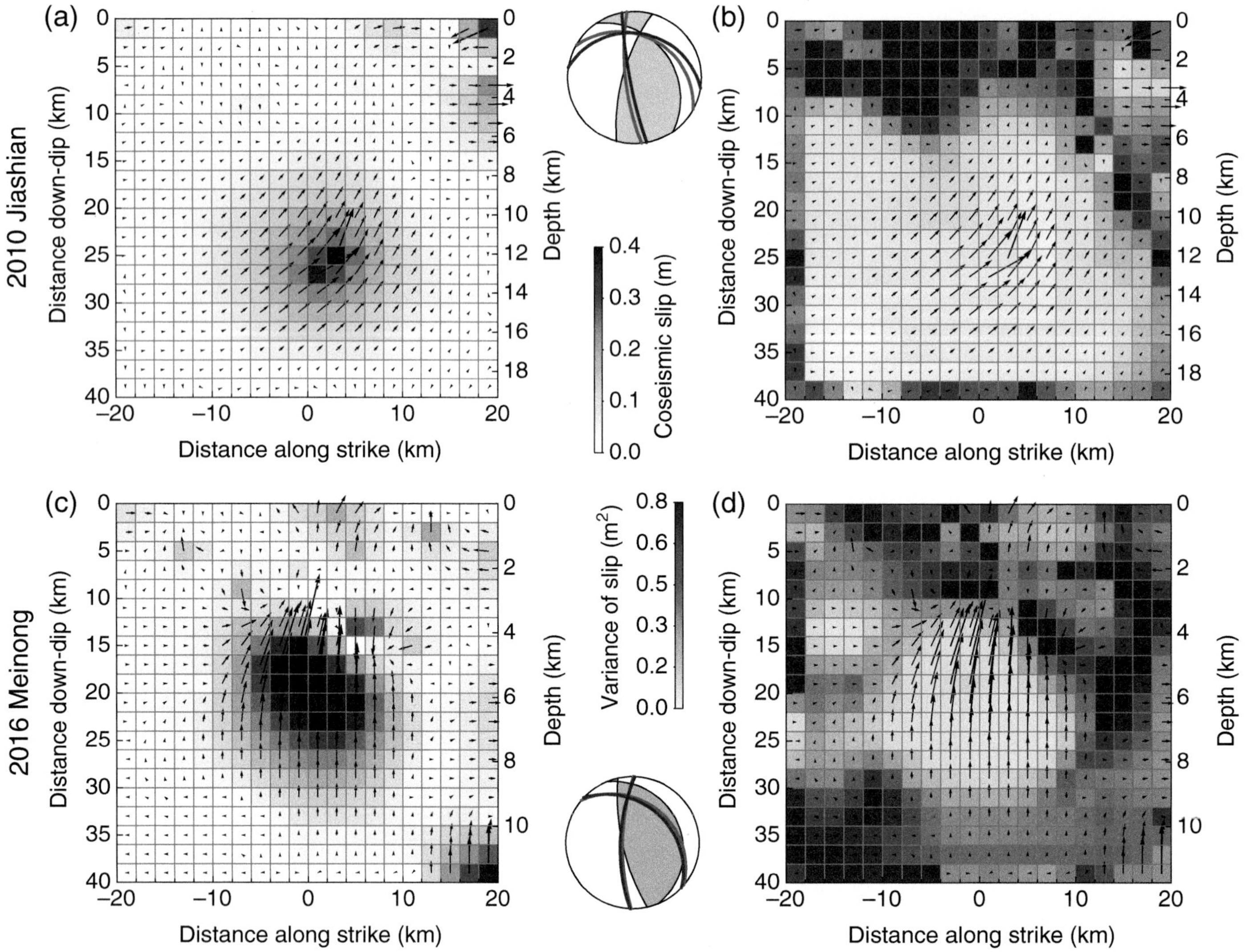

Figure 8. Slip distributions of the best-fitting Jiashian (a) and Meinong (c) coseismic slip models. To assess the degree to which the features of the slip are resolved, we plot the variance of the subfault slip in the coseismic models with χ^2 within 10% of the lowest χ^2 for the Jiashian (b; 38 models) and Meinong (d; 107 models) earthquakes (all models used to compute the variance have strikes and dips similar to the best-fit models; Fig. 7). The focal mechanism plots depict the double-couple focal mechanisms derived from the fault strike and dip, along with the weighted average slip rake, for each earthquake. The green and purple lines on the focal mechanism plots are the nodal planes from the U.S. Geological Survey (USGS) *W* phase and Global CMT focal mechanisms, respectively. The color version of this figure is available only in the electronic edition.

in residual GNSS horizontal offsets over the tip of the fault plane (Fig. 9a, Fig. S4a), the vertical offsets are well fit (Fig. 9b, Fig. S4b). Given the moderate magnitude of the Jiashian earthquake and the paucity of the GNSS data, we do not explore more complicated models.

The fault in our best-fit Jiashian model is consistently shallower than the relocated aftershocks determined by Huang *et al.* (2011); although it roughly follows the same dip (Fig. 12). That the Jiashian fault we infer is consistently shallower than the aftershocks, along with the depths determined by the constrained inversions of Ching *et al.* (2011) or Hsu *et al.* (2011) and the fact that our best-fit Meinong model is shallower than the depth of that earthquake inferred by Jian *et al.* (2017), indicates that there may be a bias toward shallower faults in our fully unconstrained inversions. This bias likely arises due to the assumption of an elastic half-space. Indeed, Du *et al.* (1994) and Simons *et al.* (2002) demonstrated that the assumption of an elastic half-space results in shallower inferred depths of slip compared to those when elastic heterogeneity is accounted for. It is also interesting to note that Ching *et al.* (2011) initially performed a completely unconstrained search for their Jiashian model, inferring slip at shallower depths than they did after constraining the search.

The optimal dip of 29° of the Jiashian fault is lower than either the 41° dip assumed by Ching *et al.* (2011) or the 40° dip inferred by Hsu *et al.* (2011). In contrast, the fault dips in the ensemble of our best-fitting Jiashian models are in line with the dips of the nodal planes in the focal mechanisms (25° and 30°; Table 2). The optimal dip we find is just 3° larger than

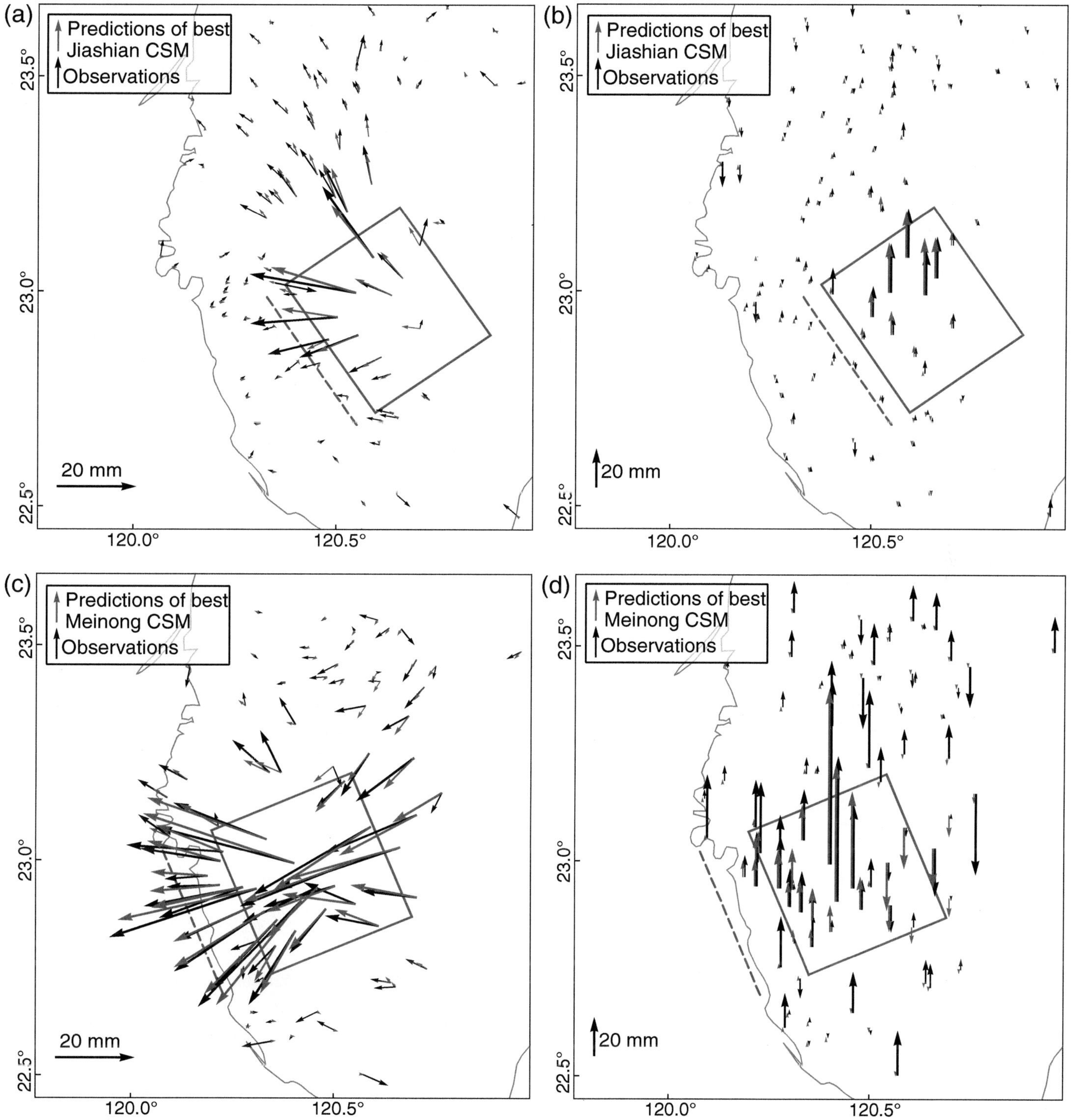

the 26° dip found in the unconstrained search of Ching *et al.* (2011). Hsu *et al.* (2011) only considered fault dips of 30°–70°, also constraining strike, so their search did not consider dips in the range we infer. In our estimation, coseismic models with fault dips close to 40° have only nominally higher χ^2 (Fig. 6a), and may suggest that the GNSS data alone are not able to provide an accurate constraint on fault dip for this earthquake. On the other hand, our optimal Jiashian fault strike is 1° of that inferred in the constrained search of Hsu *et al.* (2011),

Figure 9. Predicted horizontal (a and c) and vertical (b and d) displacements for the best coseismic slip models determined for the Jiashian (a and b) and Meinong (c and d) earthquakes. Vectors showing the model vertical displacements are slightly offset from the observed for clarity. The observed GNSS solutions are shown in black and are from Hsu *et al.* (2011) (Jiashian; a and b) or Huang *et al.* (2016) (Meinong; c and d). The green rectangle is the surface projection of the fault planes, and the green dashed line is the surface projection of the top of the fault along the constant fault dip. The color version of this figure is available only in the electronic edition.

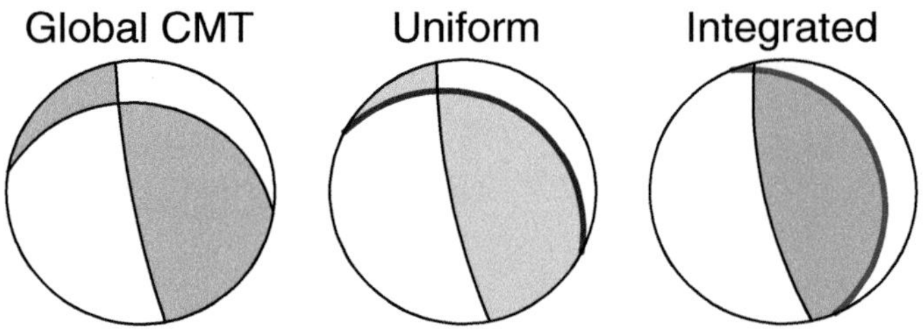

Figure 10. Global CMT focal mechanism of the Meinong earthquake compared to the focal mechanisms for the best model found from the initial search, assuming uniform slip, and from the integrated search (the slip surface is highlighted). The color version of this figure is available only in the electronic edition.

indicating that these geodetic data are well able to constrain the strike, regardless of whether the search is constrained or not. Even if the dip is not as well constrained, the dips we infer in the Jiashian earthquake are generally consistent with the dip of the Jiashian aftershocks (Fig. 12f–h) and the focal mechanisms solution (Table 2), and are consistently lower than for the Meinong earthquake (Fig. 6a,b).

Connecting the 2010 Jiashian and 2016 Meinong earthquakes

Neglecting the imaged slip at the edges of the fault domains in each model, both of the final Jiashian and Meinong coseismic models are composed well-defined patches of slip (Fig. 8). Within the regions where slip is significant, there are differences between the imaged slip in the two models, but that difference is largely driven by differences in the relative constraints on sparsity versus smoothness for these two earthquakes that are

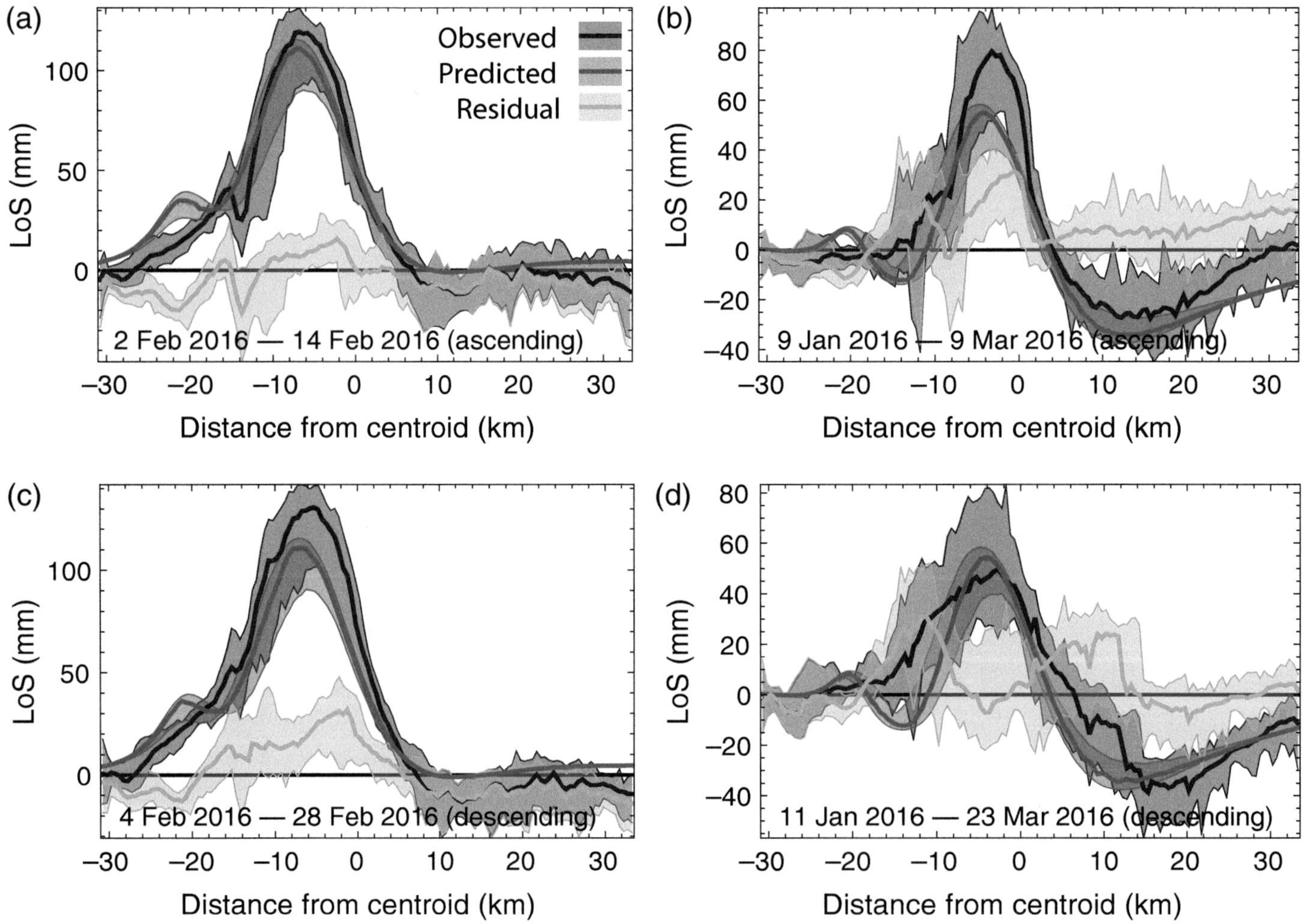

Figure 11. Line-of-sight (LoS) coseismic offsets for the Meinong earthquake along the swath shown in Figures 3 and 4, from southwest to northeast: profiles in (a) and (c) are from the training interferograms, either ascending or descending, respectively, and (b) and (d) are from the testing interferograms. The solid lines show the median LoS offset within the swath, and the shaded regions depict the range in which 90% of the LoS is along the swath (defined by the 5th to 95th percentiles). The color version of this figure is available only in the electronic edition.

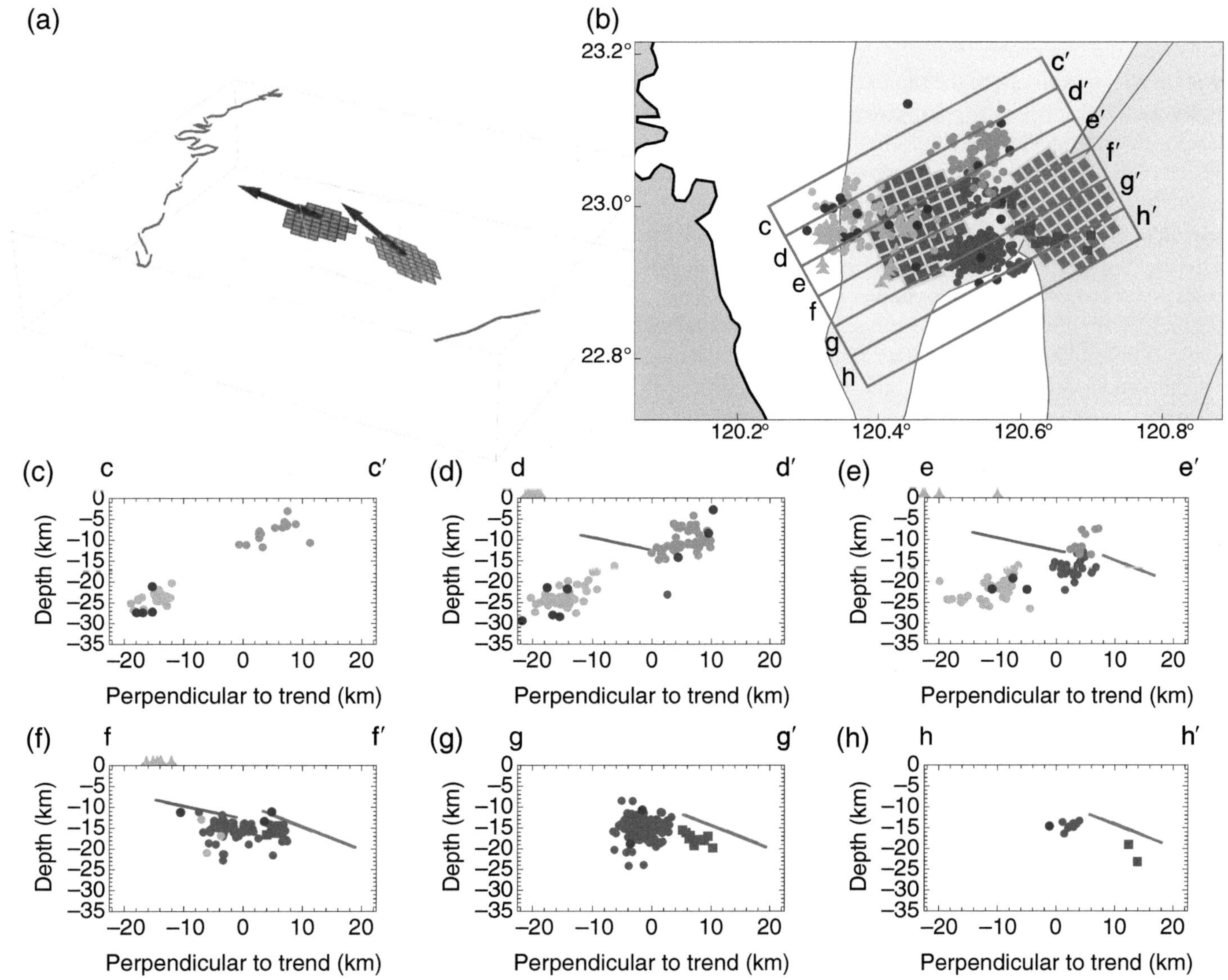

imaged by quite different data. The main slip patch of our Meinong preferred model is adjacent to the main slip patch in the Jiashian model (Fig. 12a), with similar strikes of the faults (Fig. 7a). In addition, the bottom edge of the Meinong slip patch is roughly at the same depth as the top edge of the Jiashian slip patch (Fig. 12). The proximity of the slip patches suggests that these two earthquakes occurred on a single, structure dipping to the east and steepening with depth. The oblique thrust-slip rake in the Jiashian is close to the slip direction that would be expected from the background stress (Hsu *et al.*, 2011). The slip direction we resolve in our Meinong earthquake is rotated toward pure thrust, suggesting that coseismic stress changes in the Jiashian earthquake perturbed the stress field at the Meinong slip.

Comparing our Meinong cosiesmic model with the aftershocks from Hsu *et al.* (2020), who located 524 aftershocks, is not directly clear (Fig. 12). When considered collectively, those aftershocks describe a westward-dipping plane of about 30°, quite contrary to our preferred Meinong model, but also published coseismic slip models (Huang *et al.*, 2016; Qu *et al.*, 2017; Rau *et al.*, 2022). However, Hsu *et al.* (2020) noted that

Figure 12. (a) Main slip patch of the Jiashian (blue) and Meinong (red) coseismic slip models (defined as subfaults with slip ≥20% of the maximum slip in each model, excluding subfaults at the edges of the fault domain, compare with Fig. 8a,c); arrows are the weighted average slip direction of each coseismic slip model. (b) Map view of slip patches with epicenters of aftershocks determined by Huang *et al.* (2011; green squares, Jiashian aftershocks), Wen *et al.* (2017; dark red circles, Meinong aftershocks), and Hsu *et al.* (2020; purple, orange, and gold circles, Meinong aftershocks); pink triangles are locations where ground fissures were observed by Yi *et al.* (2023). (c–h) Cross sections indicated in (b), symbols are aftershocks as in (b), and blue or red lines are the main slip patch of the Jiashian or Meinong coseismic models, respectively, in the transects. The color version of this figure is available only in the electronic edition.

aftershocks do not simply delineate a planar feature, but rather fall into three general clusters. Here, we slightly modify their clustering by considering the depth of the aftershocks relative to the slip surfaces we infer in our coseismic models. The first two groups of Meinong aftershocks are at the down-dip edge of the main slip patch we image, one to the south and in the footwall, and one to the north in the headwall (Fig. 12). The third group of aftershocks is located deeper in the footwall, and align into a west-dipping cluster (Fig. 12c–e). Based on the proximity of the first two groups to the slip in our Meinong coseismic model, we feel that these are relatively typical aftershocks associated with faulting. The aftershocks in these two groups, either individually or taken together, follow typical Omori–Utsu decays (Fig. S9). In contrast, the aftershocks in the deeper, west-dipping group do not have such a simple relationship to the faulting. The heightened frequency of aftershocks in that group is delayed, with the peak number of aftershocks occurring one day after the Meinong mainshock, and does not follow a typical Omori–Utsu decay (Fig. S9c). Hsu *et al.* (2020) argued that the aftershocks in this group are related to fluid processes following coseismic stress changes in the Meinong earthquake.

Interpreted together, these two earthquakes are evocative of a midcrustal flat–ramp–flat structure beneath southeastern Taiwan. This interpretation is quite similar to that of Jian (2021), who used a teleseismic backprojection, in conjunction with relocated aftershocks, to conclude that both the Jiashian and Meinong earthquakes occurred on a single-fault plane, which they coined the JSMN fault. Jian (2021) inferred that the strike of their inferred fault was −40° and dipping northeast. Our ensembles of the best-fitting models include strikes of the Jiashian and Meinong earthquakes of −35° ± 8° and −23° ± 15°, respectively (Table 2; the ± range is the standard deviation of the best-fit ensemble), and the −40° strike of Jian (2021) is within these ranges. Jian (2021) imaged a gap between the Jiashian and Meinong ruptures and that the Jiashian earthquake occurred down-dip of the Meinong earthquake, as in our findings. Based on the fault dips we infer, we argue that the fault proposed by Jian (2021) increases dip with depth. Ching *et al.* (2011) interpreted their Jiashian coseismic model in terms of a ramp–flat fault geometry, with the Jiashian earthquake occurring on a ramp fault stemming from a lower crustal detachment. The inset of Figure 13 shows a diagrammatic interpretation of the flat–ramp–flat structure we hypothesize from our coseismic slip models. In this interpretation, the Jiashian earthquake occurs on a ramp between two relatively flat, or low-angle faults: a detachment in the lower crust argued for by Ching *et al.* (2011) and a low-angle thrust in the midcrust illuminated by our Meinong coseismic slip model. We remark on how that structure might connect to the surface in the following paragraph.

Our interpretation that the Jiashian and Meinong earthquake illuminate a flat–ramp–flat structure is strikingly similar to interpretations of the Nantou earthquakes in central Taiwan by Chuang *et al.* (2013) and Lee *et al.* (2015). They argued that the Nantou earthquakes occurred on a ramp fault connecting an upper crustal thrust system that the Chi-Chi earthquake occurred on to a presumed midcrustal detachment under the central range of Taiwan. The dip of the Jiashian earthquake we infer (29°) is consistent with the eastward dips of the Nantou earthquakes, 25° and 29° (Lee *et al.*, 2015), suggesting a similarity in the midcrustal ramp fault. We infer a 17° dip of the Meinong source fault, suggestive of that earthquake occurring on a relatively flatter, shallower fault. The fault may then step up into a shallowly dipping thrust fault near the surface, as the Chi-Chi earthquake illuminated to the north (Yoshioka, 2001; Fig. 13) or may be accommodated by near-surface folding, potentially related to the actively deforming pop-up structure revealed by Huang *et al.* (2006; Fig. 13). Alternatively, near-surface deformation may be accommodated by back thrusting, as proposed by Le Béon *et al.* (2017). Both Mouthereau *et al.* (2002) and Huang *et al.* (2004) have interpreted shallow fault structures with ramp–flat geometries, overlaying and extending eastward of the Meinong source fault we interpret here (see inset of Fig. 13).

The similarities of the midcrustal ramp faults illuminated by the Nantou and Jiashian earthquakes are notable, given the differences in deformation styles between central and southwestern Taiwan (e.g., Lee *et al.*, 2023). Nevertheless, the average topographic profile across a 20-km-wide transect from east to west across the Jiashian and Meinong earthquakes is quite similar to that across the Nantou earthquakes, except slightly larger topography in the Western Foothills in central Taiwan (Fig. 13; the zero reference point of the distance scale in the northern transect is 31 km east of that in the southern transect). In addition, the eastward component of the GNSS velocities from Tsai *et al.* (2015) have a similar character across each of the transects, accounting for the 31 km westward offset of the profile across the Nantou earthquakes (Fig. 13). To illustrate the similarity of the GNSS velocities, Figure 13 shows the velocities predicted by a 2D, infinitely deep, buried reverse-fault dipping under the Central Range. These simple dislocation models are equivalent to the back-slip model proposed by Savage (1983; here we use the dislocation solution of Okada, 1985) to approximate strain accumulation of a subduction megathrust. This back-slip model is also used to model interseismic strain accumulation of reverse faults (e.g., Hsu *et al.*, 2003). The GNSS velocities across both transects are fairly well described by dislocations with remarkably similar geometries, with the southern dislocation coinciding with the slip surfaces of both the Jiashian and Meinong earthquakes we image (Fig. 13).

Finally, it is noteworthy that the average slip direction we resolved in the Jiashian earthquake is consistent with the orientations of the most compressive horizontal component of stress, $Sh_{\max}$, from the World Stress Map (Heidbach *et al.*, 2018; Fig. 13). In contrast, the slip direction in the Meinong earthquake is more southwestwardly directed, at an acute angle to the $Sh_{\max}$ orientation (Fig. 13). The slip directions in neither of the earthquakes are perfectly coincident with the GNSS velocities, but are consistent with the more southwestwardly directed velocities seen at some of the monuments near the coast relative to over the Western Foothills and Central Range (Fig. 13). The rotation of the slip rake in the Meinong earthquake relative to the Jiashian earthquake might be due to the

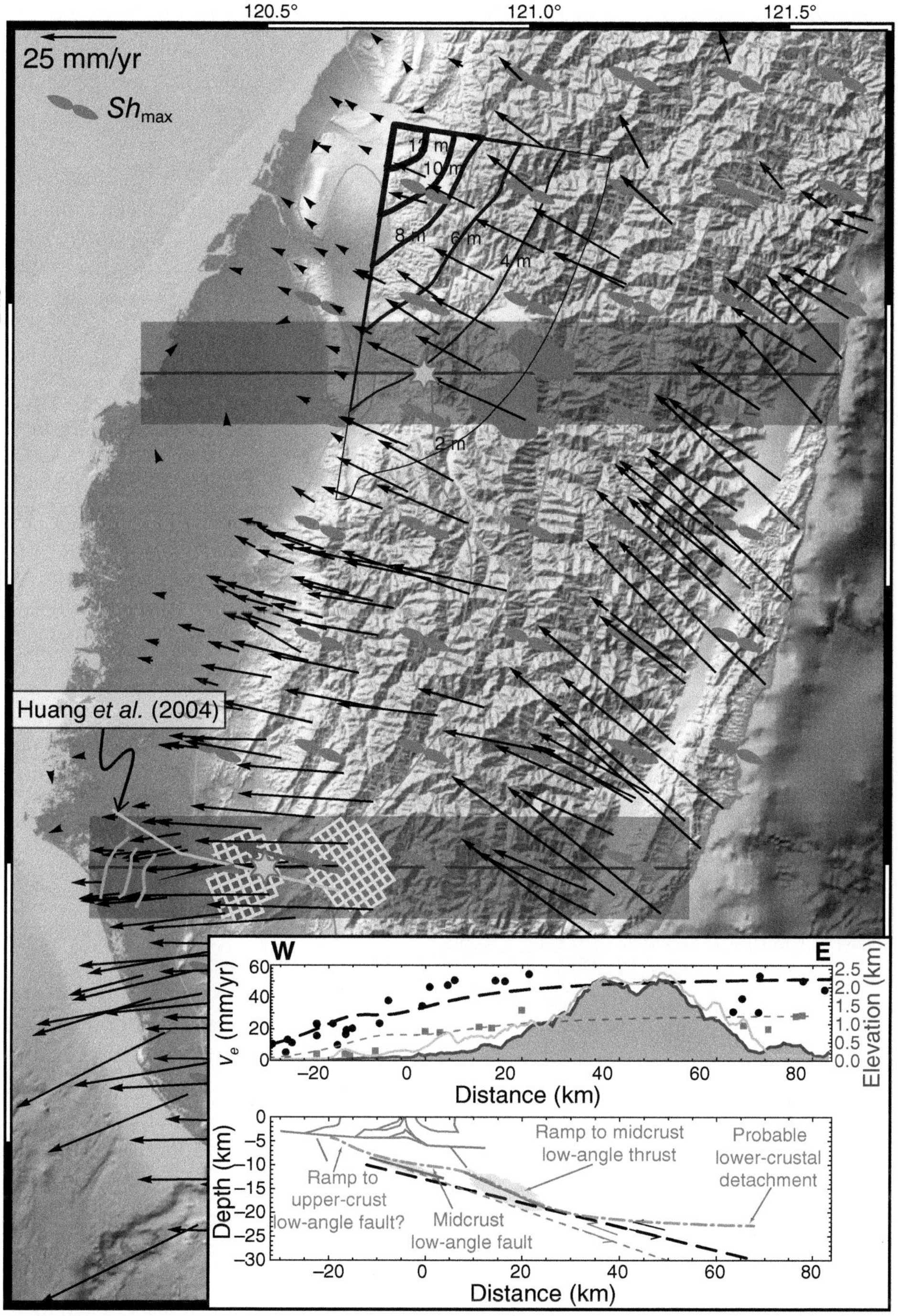

Figure 13. GNSS velocities (Tsai *et al.*, 2015) and orientations of the maximum compressive horizontal stress (Sh_{max}; Heidbach *et al.*, 2018), along with Chi Chi coseismic slip contours (blue; Yoshioka, 2001), the slip patches of the Nantou earthquakes (purple; Lee *et al.*, 2015), the Jiashian (red) and Meinong (blue) fault patches and average slip rakes from Figure 12, and the locations of faults from Huang *et al.* (2006; cyan). The red rectangles depict swaths ±10 km of the transects (red lines). Top panel of the inset shows the eastward GNSS velocity at all stations in each swath (black circles and gray squares are velocities in the southern and northern swaths, respectively; the zero distance point along each transect is indicated by the star) and the average elevation along the two transects (elevation is the average for constant longitude over the 20 km swaths; dark brown and tan lines are the southern and northern transects, respectively). Bottom panel shows the imaged Jiashian and Meinong coseismic slip surfaces along the southern transect, along with shallow interpretive faults from Huang *et al.* (2004; gray lines) and a diagrammatic interpretation of the flat–ramp–flat structure (brown dashed line). Also shown in the inset upper panel are the velocities predicted by the 2D reverse faults shown in the lower panel. The color version of this figure is available only in the electronic edition.

more western region affected by the proposed tectonic escape of southwestern Taiwan (e.g., Lu and Malavieille, 1994; Lacombe *et al.*, 2001; Ching *et al.*, 2007; Hu *et al.* 2007), although the rake change might have also been affected by the coseismic stress changes in the Jiashian earthquake.

Robustness to interferometric noise

The ascending training interferogram we use is formed from the same Synthetic Aperture Radar (SAR) acquisitions as used by Huang *et al.* (2016). This interferogram was shown by Gomba *et al.* (2017) to have a large level of corruption due to an ionospheric anomaly extending over Southeast Asia on 2 February 2016, with total electron count (TEC) exceeding 60 over Taiwan (Fig. S10). The anomaly resulted in a long-wavelength interferometric signal across Taiwan (see fig. 4 in Gomba *et al.*, 2017). Although much of that long-wavelength noise can be absorbed by the bicubic ramp, some of the ionospheric noise is likely preserved in the ascending interferogram we invert. However, we emphasize that because we test coseismic slip models against an independent ascending interferogram, coseismic slip models that overly fit interferometric signal that might be affected by the ionosphere would be penalized unless the ionospheric error was consistent between the training and testing ascending interferograms (TEC over Taiwan during either of the SAR acquisitions used to form the testing ascending interferogram were lower; Fig. S10). Moreover, TEC at the time of the SAR acquisitions used to form both the training and testing descending interferograms was lower (TEC values <12), and GNSS can correct for ionospheric path delays owing to the dual frequency transmitted by the GNSS satellites (e.g., Bevis *et al.*, 1992). We contend that our inversion strategy is robust against any interferometric noise that may be present in the ascending interferogram we invert. In general, we contend that our strategy is robust against any interferometric noise, as long as that noise does not produce a consistent interferometric signal across all four of the interferograms.

CONCLUSIONS

We develop coseismic slip models of the 2010 Jiashian and 2016 Meinong earthquakes in southwestern Taiwan, constrained by geodetic data and using the same estimation methodology. We find a Jiashian coseismic model that is broadly consistent with seismologically determined focal mechanisms, as well as previously published coseismic models of Ching *et al.* (2011) and Hsu *et al.* (2011). In contrast, we find a Meinong coseismic model consisting of a more northerly striking and shallower fault, as well as a larger degree of thrust slip, than was resolved by the focal mechanisms or in previously published coseismic slip models (Huang *et al.*, 2016; Qu *et al.*, 2017; Rau *et al.*, 2022). The previous studies of the Meinong earthquake constrained aspects of the fault geometry a priori, most notably the depth of the fault. We demonstrate that the assumption of a deep fault likely led to biases in the final inferred coseismic slip model. We also demonstrate that constraining fault geometry parameters using an assumption of uniform fault slip can also result in biases in the final coseismic slip model. We do not find systematic vertical residuals in our final Meinong model large enough to warrant appealing to aseismic processes concurrent with the earthquake. We find fault strikes of the Jiashian and Meinong coseismic models of $-35° \pm 8°$ and $-35° \pm 15°$, respectively, where the uncertainty range is determined from ensembles of models fitting within 10% of the best-fit models. We find fault dips of the Jiashian and Meinong earthquakes of $29° \pm 6°$ and $17° \pm 4°$, respectively. Finally, we find centroid depths of the Jiashian and Meinong earthquakes of 13.5 ± 1.2 km and 10.1 ± 0.5 km, respectively; however, we suspect that our inferences of depth might be biased to shallower depths owing to our assumption of an elastic half-space (e.g., Du *et al.*, 1994; Simons *et al.*, 2002).

The similarity of the fault strikes in our final coseismic models, along with the proximity of the inferred regions of fault slip, suggests that these two earthquakes occurred on a single-fault structure, dipping to the east. This unitary fault interpretation is similar to that of Jian (2021), but we posit that the fault is a flat–ramp fault structure. We propose that the Jiashian earthquake occurred on a ramp fault stemming from a lower crustal detachment, as also suggested by Ching *et al.* (2011), and connecting to a midcrust low-angle thrust fault on which the Meinong earthquake occurred. We find that a large number of the Meinong aftershocks, along with many of the Jiashian aftershocks, occurred at the gap between the Jiashian and Meinong coseismic slip patches, coincident with the bend from the ramp to the upper-crustal low-angle thrust fault.

DATA AND RESOURCES

The Sentinel-1 data are publicly available from the European Space Agency. All figures were rendered in Mathematica (Wolfram Research, Inc.). Focal mechanism solutions are from the U.S. Geological Survey (Jiashian: https://earthquake.usgs.gov/earthquakes/eventpage/usp000h8nd/moment-tensor; Meinong: https://earthquake.usgs.gov/earthquakes/eventpage/us20004y6h/moment-tensor) and the Global Centroid Moment Tensor project (https://www.globalcmt.org/CMTsearch.html; Jiashian event name 201003040018A; Meinong event name 201602051957A) (last accessed July 2024). The Synthetic Aperture Radar (SAR) data used to produce the interferograms in this research are publicly available from the European Space Agency (scihub.copernicus.eu/dhus/#/home; last accessed June 2021), with interferograms processed using GMTSAR (github.com/gmtsar, last accessed May 2020; Sandwell *et al.*, 2011). The coseismic slip models of the Jiashian and Meinong earthquakes are archived at https://zenodo.org/records/15636671 (last accessed May 2020). The supplemental material includes additional figures supporting the analysis in the main text, along with a description of those figures.

DECLARATION OF COMPETING INTERESTS

The authors acknowledge that there are no conflicts of interest recorded.

ACKNOWLEDGMENTS

Partial funding for this research was provided by the Department of Defense (DoD) through the Department of Defense Science and Engineering Fellowship (NDSEG) awarded to E. Szymanski. The authors thank N. Niemi for discussion pertaining to the structural implications of the coseismic slip models, as well as Guest Editor J.-Y. Yen and two anonymous reviewers, their comments improved this article.

REFERENCES

Bevis, M., S. Businger, T. A. Herring, C. Rocken, R. A. Anthes, and R. H. Ware (1992). GPS meteorology: Remote sensing of atmospheric water vapor using the Global Positioning System*J. Geophys. Res.* **97**, no. D14, 15,787–15,801, doi: 10.1029/92JD01517.

Boyd, S., and L. Vandenberghe (2004). *Convex Optimization*, Cambridge University Press.

Chang, Y., L. M. Warren, L. Zhu, and G. A. Prieto (2019). Earthquake focal mechanisms and stress field for the intermediate-depth Cauca cluster, Colombia, *J. Geophys. Res.* **124,** no. 1, 822–836, doi: 10.1029/2018JB016804.

Chen, C., and H. Zebker (2002). Phase unwrapping for large SAR interferograms: Statistical segmentation and generalized network models, *IEEE Trans. Geosci. Remote Sens.* **40,** no. 8, 1709–1719, doi: 10.1109/TGRS.2002.802453.

Chiang, P. H., Y.-J. Hsu, and W.-L. Chang (2016). Fault modeling of the 2012 Wutai, Taiwan earthquake and its tectonic implications, *Tectonophysics* **666,** 66–75, doi: 10.1016/j.tecto.2015.10.015.

Ching, K.-E., K. M. Johnson, R.-J. Rau, R. Y. Chuang, L.-C. Kuo, and P.-L. Leu (2011). Inferred fault geometry and slip distribution of the 2010 Jiashian, Taiwan, earthquake is consistent with a thick-skinned deformation model, *Earth Planet. Sci. Lett.* **301,** 78–86, doi: 10.1016/j.epsl.2010.10.021.

Ching, K.-E., R.-J. Rau, J.-C. Lee, and J.-C. Hu (2007). Contemporary deformation of tectonic escape in SW Taiwan from GPS observations, 1995–2005, *Earth Planet. Sci. Lett.* **262,** 601–619, doi: 10.1016/j.epsl.2007.08.017.

Chuang, R. Y., K.M. Johnson, Y.-M. Wu, K.-E. Ching, and L.-C. Kuo (2013). A midcrustal ramp-fault structure beneath the Taiwan tectonic wedge illuminated by the 2013 Nantou earthquake series, *Geophys. Res. Lett.* **40,** 5080–5084, doi: 10.1002/grl.51005.

Clarke, P. J., D. Paradissis, P. Briole, P. C. England, B. E. Parsons, H. Billiris, G. Veis, and J.-C. Ruegg (1997). Geodetic investigation of the 13 May 1995 Kozani-Grevena (Greece) earthquake, *Geophys. Res. Lett.* **24,** no. 6, 707–710, doi: 10.1029/97GL00430.

Du, Y. J., P. Segall, and H. J. Gao (1994). Dislocations in inhomogeneous-media via a moduli perturbation approach: General formulation and two-dimensional solutions, *J. Geophys. Res.* **99,** 13,767–13,779, doi: 10.1029/94JB00339.

Gao, H., M. Liao, and G. Feng (2021). An improved quadtree sampling method for InSAR seismic deformation inversion, *Remote Sens.* **13,** 1678, doi: 10.3390/rs13091678.

Goldstein, R. M., and C. L. Werner (1998). Radar interferogram filtering for geophysical applications, *Geophys. Res. Lett.* **25,** no. 21, 4035–4038, doi: 10.1029/1998GL900033.

Gomba, G., F. R. González, and F. De Zan (2017). Ionospheric phase screen compensation for the Sentinel-1 TOPS and ALOS-2 ScanSAR modes, *IEEE Trans. Geosci. Rem. Sens.* **55,** no. 1, doi: 10.1109/TGRS.2016.2604461.

Hansen, P. (2000). The L-curve and its use in the numerical treatment of inverse problems, in *Computational Inverse Problems in Electrocardiology*, Vol. 4, 119–142.

He, P., E. A. Hetland, Q. Wang, K. Ding, Y. Wen, and R. Zou (2017). Coseismic slip in the 2016 M_w 7.8 Ecuador earthquake imaged from Sentinel-1A radar interferometry, *Seismol. Res. Lett.* **88,** no. 2A, 277–286, doi: 10.1785/0220160151.

Heidbach, O., M. Rajabi, X. Cui, K. Fuchs, B. Müller, J. Reinecker, K. Reiter, M. Tingay, F. Wenzel, F. Xie, *et al.* (2018). The World Stress Map database release 2016: Crustal stress pattern across scales, *Tectonophysics* **744,** 484–498, doi: 10.1016/j.tecto.2018.07.007.

Hsu, Y.-F., H.-H. Huang, M.-H. Huang, V. C. Tsai, R. Y. Chuang, K.-F. Feng, and S.-H. Lin (2020). Evidence for fluid migration during the 2016 Meinong, Taiwan, aftershock sequence, *J. Geophys. Res.* **125,** no. 9, e2020JB019994, doi: 10.1029/2020JB019994.

Hsu, Y.-J., M. Simons, S.-B. Yu, L.-C. Kuo, and H.-Y. Chen (2003). A two-dimensional dislocation model for interseismic deformation of the Taiwan mountain belt, *Earth Planet. Sci. Lett.* **211,** 287–294, doi: 10.1016/S0012-821X(03)00203-6.

Hsu, Y.-J., S.-B. Yu, L. C. Kuo, Y. C. Tsai, and H. Y. Chen (2011). Coseismic deformation of the 2010 Jiashian, Taiwan earthquake and implications for fault activities in southwestern Taiwan, *Tectonophysics* **502,** nos. 3/4, 328–335, doi: 10.1016/j.tecto.2011.02.005.

Hu, J.-C., C.-S. Hou, L.-C. Shen, Y.-C. Chan, R.-F. Chen, C. Huang, R.-J. Rau, K. H.-H. Chen, C.-W. Lin, M.-H. Huang, *et al.* (2007). Fault activity and lateral extrusion inferred from velocity field revealed by GPS measurements in the Pingtung area of southwestern Taiwan, *J. Asian Earth Sci.* **31,** 287–302, doi: 10.1016/j.jseaes.2006.07.020.

Huang, H. H., W. Yih-Min, L. Ting-Li, C. Wei-An, J. B. H. Shyu, C. Chung-Han, and C. H. Chang (2011). The preliminary study of the 4 March 2010 M_w 6.3 Jiasian, Taiwan earthquake sequence, *Terr. Atmos. Ocean. Sci.* **22,** no. 3, 283–290, doi: 10.3319/TAO.2010.12.13.01(T).

Huang, M.-H., J.-C. Hu, C.-S. Hsieh, K.-E. Ching, R.-J. Rau, E. Pathier, B. Fruneau, and B. Deffontaines (2006) A growing structure near the deformation front in SW Taiwan as deduced from SAR interferometry and geodetic observation, *Geophys. Res. Lett.* **33,** L12305, doi: 10.1029/2005GL025613.

Huang, M.-H., H. Tung, E. J. Fielding, H.-H. Huang, C. Liang, C. Huang, and J.-C. Hu (2016) Multiple fault slip triggered above the 2016 M_w 6.4 Meinong earthquake in Taiwan, *Geophys. Res. Lett.* **43,** 7459–7467, doi: 10.1002/2016GL069351.

Huang, S.-T., K.-M. Yang, J.-H. Hung, J.-C. Wu, H.-H. Ting, W.-W. Mei, S.-H. Hsu, and M. Lee (2004). Deformation front development at the northeast margin of the Tainan basin, Tainan–Kaohsiung area, Taiwan, *Mar. Geophys. Res.* **25,** 139–156, doi: 10.1007/s11001-005-0739-z.

Jian, P. R. (2021). The 2010 Jiashian and 2016 Meinong earthquakes: Doublet ruptures interact across two strong asperities, in *AutoBATS and 3D MUSIC: New Approaches to Imaging Earthquake Rupture Behaviors*, Springer, Singapore, 59–72, doi: 10.1007/978-981-16-5584-5.

Jian, P.-R., S.-H. Hung, L. Meng, and D. Sun (2017). Rupture characteristics of the 2016 Meinong earthquake revealed by the back projection and directivity analysis of teleseismic broadband waveforms, *Geophys. Res. Lett.* **44,** 3545–3553, 10.1002/2017GL072552.

Jónsson, S., H. Zebker, P. Segall, and F. Amelung (2002). Fault slip distribution of the 1999 M_w 7.1 Hector Mine, California, earthquake, estimated from satellite radar and GPS measurements, *Bull. Seismol. Soc. Am.* **92,** no. 4, 1377–1389, doi: 10.1785/0120000922.

Lacombe, O., F. Mouthereau, J. Angelier, and B. Deffontaines (2001). Structural, geodetic and seismological evidence for tectonic escape in SW Taiwan, *Tectonophysics* **333,** 323–345, doi: 10.1016/S0040-1951(00)00281-X.

Le Béon, M., M.-H. Huang, J. Suppe, S.-T. Huang, E. Pathier, W.-J. Huang, C. L. Chen, B. Fruneau, S. Baize, K.-E. Ching, and J.-C. Hu (2017). Shallow geological structures triggered during the M_w 6.4 Meinong earthquake, southwestern Taiwan, *Terr. Atmos. Ocean. Sci.* doi: 10.3319/TAO.2017.03.20.02.

Lee, F.-Y., E. Tan, and E. T.-Y. Chang (2023). Escape mechanism with shallow ramp and décollements in southwest Taiwan, *Geosciences* **13,** 41, doi: 10.3390/geosciences13020041.

Lee, S.-J., L. Mozziconacci, W.-T. Liang, Y.-J. Hsu, W.-G. Huang, and B.-S. Huang (2013). Source complexity of the 4 March 2010 Jiashian, Taiwan, earthquake determined by joint inversion of teleseismic and near field data, *J. Asian Earth Sci.* **64,** 14–26, doi: 10.1016/j.jseaes.2012.11.018.

Lee, S.-J., T.-Y. Yeh, H.-H. Huang, and C.-H. Lin (2015). Numerical earthquake models of the 2013 Nantou, Taiwan, earthquake series: Characteristics of source rupture processes, strong ground motions and their tectonic implication, *J. Asian Earth Sci.* **111,** 365–372, doi: 10.1016/j.jseaes.2015.06.031.

Lee, S.-J., T.-Y. Yeh, and Y.-Y. Lin (2016). Anomalously large ground motion in the 2016 ML 6.6 Meinong, Taiwan, earthquake: A synergy effect of source rupture and site amplification, *Seismol. Res. Lett.* **87,** no. 6, 1319–1326, doi: 10.1785/0220160082.

Lin, G.-P., W.-L. Chang, and C.-Y. Chiu (2024). Unraveling the role played by a buried mud diapir: Alternative model for 2016 M_w 6.4 MeiNong earthquake in southwestern Taiwan, *Geosci. Lett.* **11,** 1–13, doi: 10.1186/s40562-024-00335-9.

Lohman, R. B., and M. Simons (2005). Some thoughts on the use of InSAR data to constrain models of surface deformation, *Geochem. Geophys. Geosys.* **6,** Q01007, doi: 10.1029/2004GC000841.

Lu, C.-Y., and J. Malavieille (1994). Oblique convergence, indentation and rotation tectonics in the Taiwan Mountain belt: Insights from experimental modelling, *Earth Planet. Sci. Lett.* **121,** 477–494, doi: 10.1016/0012-821X(94)90085-X.

Mai, H. A., J.-C. Lee, K. H. Chen, and K.-L. Wen (2021). Coulomb stress changes triggering surface pop-up during the 2016 M_w 6.4 Meinong earthquake with implications for earthquake-induced mud diapiring in SW Taiwan, *J. Asian Earth Sci.* **218,** doi: 10.1016/j.jseaes.2021.104847.

Minson, S. E., M. Simons, and J. L. Beck (2013). Bayesian inversion for finite fault earthquake source models I—Theory and algorithm, *Geophys. J. Int.* **194,** no. 3, 1701–1726, doi: 10.1093/gji/ggt180.

Mouthereau, F., B. Deffontaines, O. Lacombe, and J. Angelier (2002). Variations along the strike of the Taiwan thrust belt: Basement control on structural style, wedge geometry, and kinematics, in *Geology and Geophysics of an Arc-Continent Collision, Taiwan*, T. B. Byrne and C.-S. Liu (Editors), 35–58, doi: 10.1130/0-8137-2358-2.31.

Murphy, K. P. (2012). *Machine Learning: A Probabilistic Perspective*, MIT Press, Cambridge, Massachusetts, 1104 pp.

O'Donoghue, B., E. Chu, N. Parikh, and S. Boyd (2016). Conic optimization via operator splitting and homogeneous self-dual embedding, *J. Optim. Theory Appl.* **169,** 1042–1068, doi: 10.1007/s10957-016-0892-3.

Okada, Y. (1985). Surface deformation due to shear and tensile faults in a half-space, *Bull. Seismol. Soc. Am.* **75,** 1135–1154, doi: 10.1785/BSSA0750041135.

Qu, C., R. Zuo, X. Shan, J.-C. Hu, and G. Zhang (2017). Coseismic deformation of the 2016 Taiwan M_w 6.3 earthquake using InSAR data and source slip inversion, *J. Asian Earth Sci.* **148,** 96–104, doi: 10.1016/j.jseaes.2017.08.027.

Rau, R.-J., Y.-Y. Wen, K.-E. Ching, M.-C. Hsieh, Y.-T. Lo, C.-Y. Chiu, and M. Hashimoto (2022). Origin of coseismic anelastic deformation during the 2016 M_w 6.4 Meinong earthquake, Taiwan, *Tectonophysics* **836,** 229,428, doi: 10.1016/j.tecto.2022.229428.

Sandwell, D., R. Mellors, X. Tong, M. Wei, and P. Wessel (2011). Open radar interferometry software for mapping surface deformation, *Eos* **92,** no. 28, 234–234, doi: 10.1029/2011EO280002.

Savage, J. (1983). A dislocation model of strain accumulation and release at a subduction zone, *J. Geophys. Res.* **88,** 4984–4996, doi: 10.1029/JB088iB06p04984.

Simons, M., Y. Fialko, and L. Rivera (2002). Coseismic deformation from the 1999 M_w 7.1 Hector Mine, California, earthquake as inferred from InSAR and GPS observations, *Bull. Seismol. Soc. Am.* **92,** 1390–1402, 10.1785/0120000933.

Szymanski, E. D., E. A. Hetland, and P. M. Figueiredo (2024). Imaging left-lateral and reverse near-surface slip of the 2020 M_w 5.1 Sparta, North Carolina, earthquake, *Bull. Seismol. Soc. Am.* **114,** no. 4, 1870–1883, doi: 10.1785/0120230126.

Tsai, M.-C., S.-B. Yu, T.-C. Shin, K.-W. Kuo, P.-L. Leu, C.-H. Chang, and M.-Y. Ho (2015). Velocity field derived from Taiwan continuous GPS array (2007-2013), *Terr. Atmos. Ocean. Sci.* **26,** no. 5, 527–556, doi: 10.3319/TAO.2015.05.21.01(T).

Wen, S., Y.-L. Yeh, Y.-Z. Chang, and C.-H. Chen (2017). The seismogenic process of the 2016 Meinong earthquake, southwest Taiwan, *Terr. Atmos. Ocean. Sci.* **28,** no. 5, 651–662, doi: 10.3319/TAO.2017.02.17.01.

Wick, C. W. J., and J.-M. Chiu (2022). Surface rupture on a secondary fault associated with the 8 August 2020 Mw 5.1 Sparta North Carolina earthquake, *Seismic Rec.* **2,** no. 1, 59–67, doi: 10.1785/0320210044.

Wicks, C., C. Weaver, P. Bodin, and B. Sherrod (2013). InSAR Evidence for an active shallow thrust fault beneath the city of Spokane Washington, USA, *J. Geophys. Res.* **118,** 1268–1276, doi: 10.1002/jgrb.50118.

Xu, B., Z. W. Li, Q. J. Wang, M. Jiang, J.-J. Zhu, and X.-L. Ding (2014). A Refined strategy for removing composite errors of SAR interferogram, *IEEE Geosci. Remote Sens. Lett.* **11,** no. 1, 143–147, doi: 10.1109/LGRS.2013.2250903.

Yi, D.-C., R.-Y. Chuang, L.-H. Chung, C.-W. Lin, and R.-J. Rau (2023). Surface deformation induced by the 2016 Meinong earthquake and its implications to active folds, *Terr. Atmos. Ocean. Sci.* **34,** no. 1, 21, doi: 10.1007/s44195-023-00053-3.

Yoshioka, S. (2001). Coseismic slip distribution of the 1999 Chi-Chi, Taiwan, earthquake deduced from inversion analysis of GPS data, *Bull. Seismol. Soc. Am.* **91,** no. 5, 1182–1189, doi: 10.1785/0120000710.

Manuscript received 13 March 2025
Published online 31 October 2025

HVSR-Based Assessment of Soil Nonlinear Behavior During Strong Ground Motions: Insights from the 3 April 2024 Hualien Earthquake Sequence and Regional Comparisons

Chun-Te Chen[1], Yi-Ying Wen[*2,3], and Chien-Min Su[2,3]

ABSTRACT

In this study, a horizontal-to-vertical spectral ratio (HVSR)–based degree of nonlinearity (DNL) analysis was applied to investigate nonlinear soil behavior during the 2024 Hualien earthquake sequence in eastern Taiwan, including the 3 April mainshock (M_w 7.3) and two significant aftershocks (M_w 6.6 on 3 April and M_w 6.0 on 23 April). By comparing HVSRs from weak and strong motions, DNL values were computed for 18 stations and regressed against peak ground acceleration (PGA), peak ground velocity (PGV), and a strain proxy (PGV/V_{S30}). All three regressions showed clear piecewise linear trends with identified nonlinear thresholds: 111 cm/s^2 (PGA), 9.77 cm/s (PGV), and 0.0283% (strain proxy), with the last one showing the strongest correlation with DNL (correlation coefficient = 0.81). DNL–strain relationships from the 2018 M_w 6.4 Hualien earthquake generally fall within the regression model derived from the 2024 Hualien earthquake sequence, indicating similar nonlinear site behavior across events through a period of six years. In contrast, sites on the ChiaNan Plain, which are underlain by fine-grained sediments, exhibited more gradual nonlinear trends without a clear threshold, highlighting the influence of sediment composition. Variations in the vertical-to-horizontal ratios of the PGA and PGV further underscore the role of site conditions. These results offer empirical constraints that can improve the modeling of nonlinear site responses and contribute to applications in seismic microzonation, hazard assessment, and ground-motion prediction.

KEY POINTS

- We investigate the nonlinear site response using the horizontal-to-vertical spectral ratio and degree of nonlinearity for the 2024 Hualien earthquake sequence.
- Peak ground acceleration threshold of 111 cm/s^2 and peak ground velocity (PGV) threshold of 9.77 cm/s were identified for the onset of nonlinearity.
- A strain proxy (PGV/V_{S30}) threshold of 0.0283% shows the strongest correlation with the nonlinear response.

Supplemental Material

INTRODUCTION

On 3 April 2024, at 07:58 local time (UTC + 8; 23:58 UTC on 2 April), a moment magnitude (M_w) of 7.3 earthquake struck Shoufeng Township, Hualien County, Taiwan. Since the 1999 M_w 7.6 Chi-Chi earthquake, the Central Weather Administration (CWA) reported this 2024 M_w 7.3 Hualien event as the largest earthquake in Taiwan, with a focal depth of 19.7 km. Within the first month, seven $M_w \geq 6.0$ aftershocks occurred; the largest one (M_w 6.6) struck Xiulin Township 13 min after the mainshock. The distributions of the mainshock and aftershocks are shown in Figure 1, which also illustrates the focal mechanisms derived from the Automatic Broadband Array in Taiwan for Seismology (AutoBATS; Jian *et al.*, 2018) and Real-time Moment Tensor (RMT) monitoring system (Lee, Liang, *et al.*, 2014; Lee, Liu, *et al.*, 2014). The Hualien region experienced an intensity level of 6 upper (6+) on the CWA intensity scale, with peak ground acceleration (PGA) >500 cm/s^2 at Yuemei

1. Disaster Prevention Technology Research Center, Sinotech Engineering Consultants Inc., Taipei, Taiwan, https://orcid.org/0000-0003-3735-1317 (C-TC);
2. Department of Earth and Environmental Sciences, National Chung Cheng University, Chia-Yi County, Taiwan, https://orcid.org/0000-0002-0579-0676 (Y-YW); https://orcid.org/0000-0003-3806-1207 (C-MS); 3. Southern Taiwan Earthquake Center, National Chung Cheng University, Chia-Yi County, Taiwan
*Corresponding author: yiyingwen@gmail.com

Cite this article as Chen, C.-T., Y.-Y. Wen, and C.-M. Su (2025). HVSR-Based Assessment of Soil Nonlinear Behavior During Strong Ground Motions: Insights from the 3 April 2024 Hualien Earthquake Sequence and Regional Comparisons, *Bull. Seismol. Soc. Am.* **116**, 133–148, doi: 10.1785/0120250106

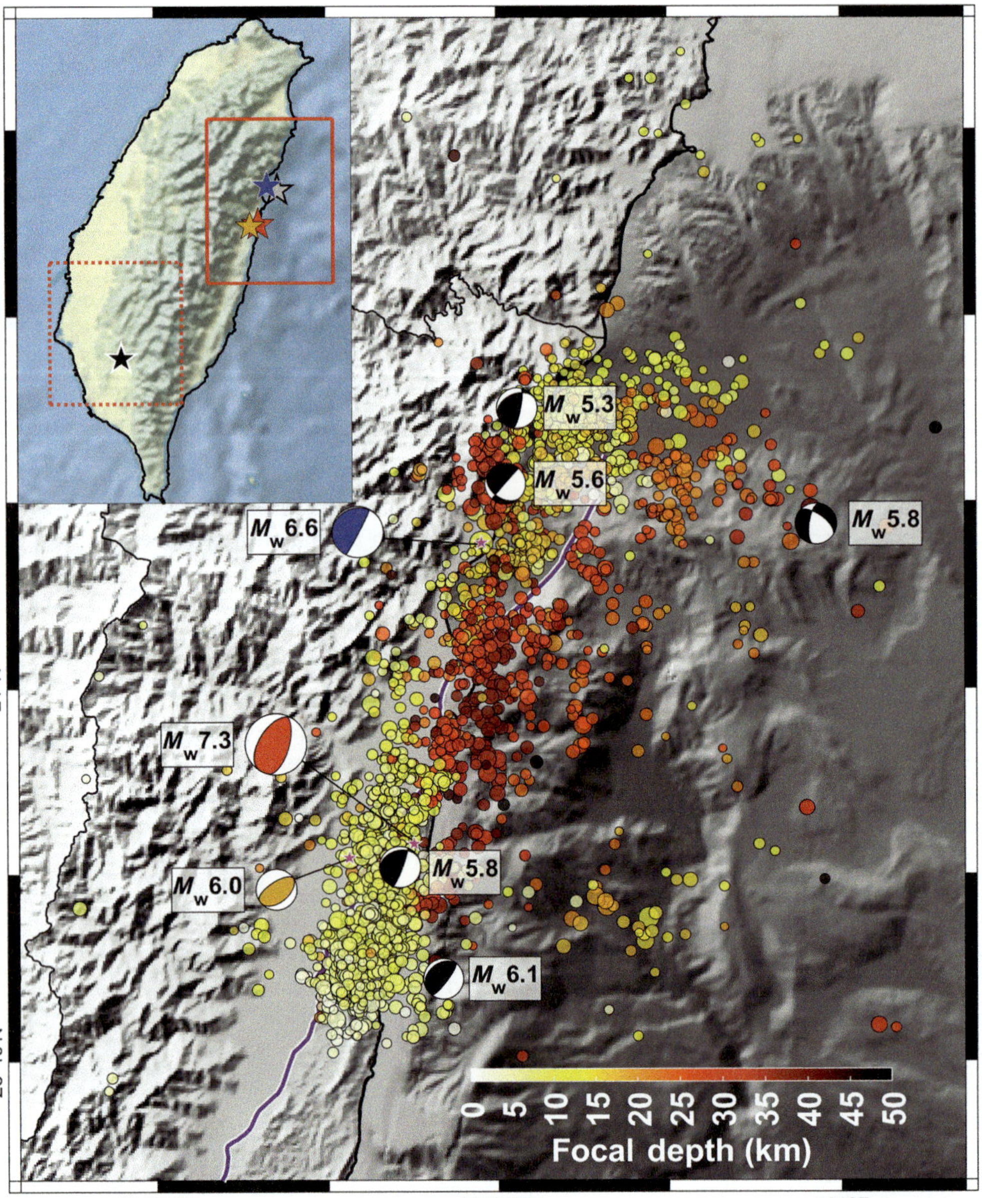

Figure 1. Seismicity map of the 2024 Hualien earthquake sequence. The mainshock (M_w 7.3) and major aftershocks that occurred within one month are shown with focal mechanism solutions from Broadband Array in Taiwan for Seismology (BATS) and Real-time Moment Tensor (RMT). The area outlined by the solid-red box in the inset map (Hualien region) corresponds to the region illustrated in the main figure. Other aftershocks with M >3 are plotted as colored circles, with the color indicating the focal depth. The inset map outlines the Hualien region in eastern Taiwan and the ChiaNan Plain region in southwestern Taiwan. Epicenters of the 2016 M_w 6.4 Meinong (black star) and 2018 M_w 6.4 Hualien (gray star) earthquakes, as well as the 2024 sequence (red, blue, and orange stars for the M_w 7.3, 6.6, and 6.0 events, respectively), are also shown.

Elementary School (F051) near the epicenter and approaching 1.5*g* at the Taroko (ETL) station. In Taipei, the intensity level reached 5 lower (5−), and several stations recorded PGA values >200 cm/s^2. The earthquake caused building collapses in Hualien, minor structural damage in Taipei, and transportation disruptions in several areas, which resulted in 21 fatalities, including 20 deaths caused by landslides and falling rocks, for a total of 1155 injuries. The Hualien region has long been recognized as seismically active, with high hazard potential identified by the Taiwan earthquake model (TEM; Chan *et al.*, 2020; Shyu *et al.*, 2020). In 2018, an M_w 6.4 earthquake with an epicenter north of Hualien (gray star in Fig. 1) generated strong ground motions in the region, with the PGA approaching 600 cm/s^2 and the peak ground velocity (PGV) reaching 146 cm/s. Kuo *et al.* (2019) reported significant nonlinear soil effects during this event. In contrast, the 2024 M_w 7.3 earthquake originated in southern Hualien but also produced intense shaking across the region. The occurrence of these two large earthquakes within six years of each other provides a rare opportunity to examine nonlinear site effects in Hualien and conduct an interevent comparison of local soil behavior.

Nonlinear soil behavior, characterized by shear modulus reduction and increasing damping with strain, has been extensively documented through laboratory testing and theoretical models. Seed and Idriss (1970) integrated laboratory and field data to produce reference curves for modulus reduction and damping increase. Hardin and Drnevich (1972) developed normalized relationships for design applications, whereas Vucetic and Dobry (1991) demonstrated the influence of soil plasticity and introduced plasticity index-dependent curves, which are now widely adopted in practice. Although nonlinear soil behavior has long been accepted on the basis of laboratory evidence, convincing observations from strong-motion earthquake records have been lacking for many years. This gap was addressed by Wen *et al.* (1994) and Beresnev and Wen (1996), who analyzed downhole array data from the Lotung large-scale seismic test site in Taiwan. Comparing surface-to-borehole spectral ratios for weak and strong motions, they reported intermediate-frequency deamplification, downward shifts in resonance frequency, and occasional high-frequency overamplification when the PGA exceeded ~0.1 to 0.2*g*. These results matched the hysteretic soil behavior predicted by theory and earlier laboratory findings. Subsequent studies worldwide using surface-to-borehole spectral ratios have confirmed that such nonlinear effects occur recurrently under strong shaking (Bonilla *et al.*, 2011; Kaklamanos *et al.*, 2013; Shi and Asimaki, 2017; Castro-Cruz *et al.*, 2020; Loviknes *et al.*, 2025).

Analyzing downhole array recordings through surface-to-borehole spectral ratios remains the most direct observational approach for identifying nonlinear soil behavior during strong shaking because they effectively isolate site response by minimizing source and path effects. However, their spatial coverage is limited. The horizontal-to-vertical spectral ratio (HVSR) method, originally proposed by Nakamura (1989) for microtremor measurements and later adapted for *S*-wave analysis by Lermo and Chávez-García (1993), offers a practical alternative using only surface records. Dimitriu *et al.* (1999) first demonstrated its ability to detect nonlinear site responses by analyzing near-field earthquake data from soft-sediment sites in Greece and reported a negative correlation between predominant frequency and ground-motion intensity measures. Dimitriu *et al.* (2000) extended this approach to Taiwan's SMART1 array, identifying high-frequency deamplification and frequency shifts consistent with standard spectral ratio results. Wen *et al.* (2006) validated the method using borehole array data and reported that HVSRs from weak- and strong-motion windows at the same station reliably reproduce nonlinear signatures. Noguchi and Sasatani (2008, 2011) advanced this methodology by introducing the degree of nonlinearity (DNL) index, which quantifies the downward shift in the predominant HVSR frequency and the reduction in amplification observed during strong shaking through direct comparison of HVSRs from weak- and strong-motion records. They proposed an empirical threshold of DNL ≈ 4 as an indicator of significant nonlinearity. This framework has been applied globally to quantify earthquake-induced nonlinear site responses across diverse tectonic and geological settings.

The HVSR–DNL approach was also adopted by Dhakal *et al.* (2017), who analyzed ocean-bottom seismograph data in Sagami Bay, Japan, and identified nonlinear behavior when surface accelerations exceeded 50–150 cm/s^2. Chen *et al.* (2017) examined the 2016 M_w 6.4 Meinong earthquake, which occurred in southwestern Taiwan (the epicenter is indicated by the black star in the inset of Fig. 1), and reported that the DNL was positively correlated with ground-motion intensity. They also reported that soft soils (National Earthquake Hazards Reduction Program [NEHRP] site class E; Building Seismic Safety Council [BSSC], 2020) exhibited stronger nonlinear effects and that the PGA reduction patterns matched the observed liquefaction areas. Dhakal *et al.* (2025) recently demonstrated a nonlinear site response using HVSR analysis during the 2024 M_w 7.5 Noto Peninsula earthquake, with 22 of 44 K-NET sites showing DNL > 4.0 at PGA levels of 50–2000 cm/s^2. In China, Ren *et al.* (2017) analyzed strong-motion and aftershock records from the 2008 M_w 7.9 Wenchuan earthquake to quantify soil nonlinear behavior and identified empirical thresholds for significant nonlinearity (PGA > 200 cm/s^2 or PGV > 15 cm/s). Previous studies have established a range of nonlinear triggering thresholds through various methodological approaches. Beresnev and Wen (1996) reported that soils tend to exhibit nonlinear behavior at PGAs ranging from 100 to 200 cm/s^2, whereas Wu *et al.* (2010) suggested that strong nonlinear effects are likely observed when the PGA exceeds 100 cm/s^2. Régnier *et al.* (2013) reported a high probability of nonlinearity with a PGA > 75 cm/s^2 on the basis of KiK-net data analysis, and more recently, systematic assessments of 350 KiK-net sites have shown that 68% of stations have PGA thresholds ranging between 33 and 115 cm/s^2 on the basis of amplitude change measurements (Loviknes *et al.*, 2025). With respect to PGV thresholds, Wu *et al.* (2009) reported predominant frequency reduction at PGV levels >~5 cm/s, whereas Ren *et al.* (2017) reported significant nonlinear effects at a PGV > 15 cm/s on the basis of an analysis of 2008 M_w 7.9 Wenchuan earthquake data. On the basis of DONET1 seafloor seismic records, Kubo *et al.* (2019) reported, using *S*-wave HVSRs, that seafloor stations can exhibit a nonlinear soil response (DNL > 4) at PGA levels <100 cm/s^2, indicating that compared with typical onshore sites, seafloor soft sediments are significantly more sensitive. These empirical thresholds provide important benchmarks for assessing the onset of soil nonlinearity across different geological and geotechnical conditions. Later studies have applied the HVSR–DNL approach to broader spatial assessments, such as regional-scale evaluations of nonlinear site effects (Dhakal *et al.*, 2019; Zhou *et al.*, 2020; Zhu *et al.*, 2020). In subsequent research, empirical correction functions were developed to transform linear-case HVSRs into nonlinear counterparts and to estimate horizontal site amplification factors without the need for detailed subsurface models (Wang *et al.*, 2023). More broadly, the HVSR–DNL approach has also been used to examine stations for linear response in empirical Green's function simulations (Lin *et al.*, 2025; Su *et al.*, 2025).

In this study, the HVSR–DNL method was applied to strong-motion records from the 2024 Hualien earthquake sequence, including the M_w 7.3 mainshock and two large aftershocks (M_w 6.6 and 6.0), and the results were compared with those from the 2018 M_w 6.4 Hualien earthquake. Empirical relationships were developed between DNL and ground-motion parameters (PGA, PGV, and a strain proxy), and their validity was assessed through comparison with the 2018 M_w 6.4 Hualien earthquake. The results of direct interevent comparisons demonstrate that nonlinear response characteristics tend to recur under comparable strong-motion conditions in the same region. We further contrasted the gravel- and coarse-sand-dominated

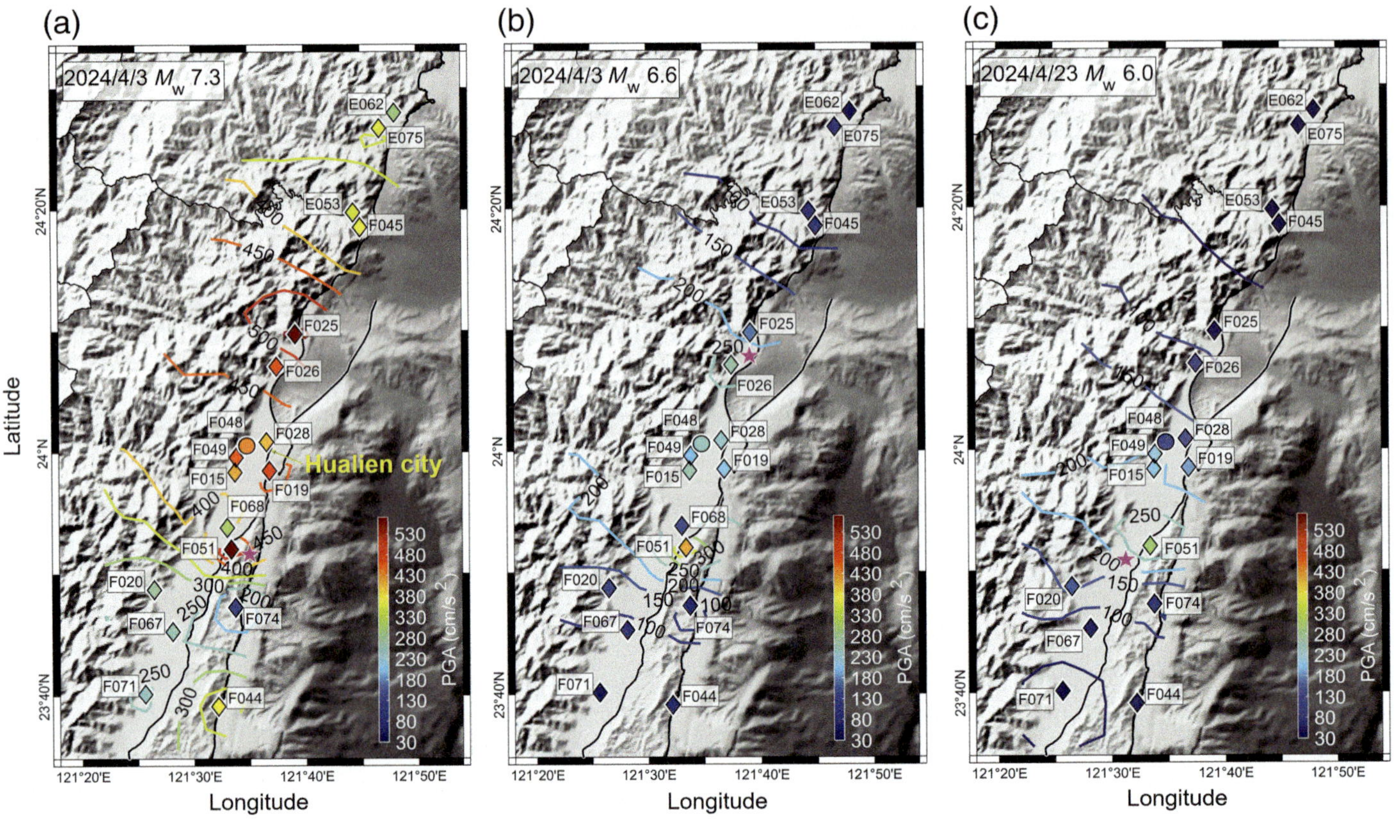

Figure 2. Distribution of the peak ground acceleration (PGA) vectors (PGA_{vec}, cm/s^2) for three major Hualien earthquakes in April 2024 (marked as pink stars): (a) M_w 7.3 mainshock, (b) M_w 6.6 aftershock, and (c) M_w 6.0 aftershock. Both the contour lines and the station marker colors indicate the spatial variation in PGA_{vec}. Diamond-shaped markers denote National Earthquake Hazards Reduction Program (NEHRP) site class C stations, and circular markers represent site class D stations (BSSC, 2020), as summarized in Table S1. The black lines indicate mapped fault traces from the Taiwan earthquake model (TEM; Shyu *et al.*, 2020).

deposits of Hualien with the fine-grained sediments of the ChiaNan Plain (red-dashed box in Fig. 1) to evaluate the role of soil composition. By applying the HVSR–DNL method to extensive strong- and weak-motion datasets and combining the results with statistical regression, this study provides a systematic characterization of nonlinear soil behavior in two geologically distinct regions of Taiwan. These findings enhance the understanding of both site-specific nonlinear behavior and strong ground-motion characteristics, providing empirical thresholds and regression relationships that can support site response characterization and the refinement of seismic hazard models in Taiwan.

STRONG-MOTION RECORDS AND SITE CHARACTERIZATION

The seismic waveform data used in this study were obtained from the Taiwan Strong-Motion Instrumentation Program (TSMIP) network, which was described by Liu *et al.* (1999) and is maintained by the CWA (Central Weather Administration [CWA], 2012). The monitoring network includes >700 force balance acceleration sensors, whose resolution was upgraded from 16 to 24 bits, significantly improving seismic motion detection. Since 2020, the CWA has begun equipping strong-motion instruments with real-time transmission capabilities, enabling immediate access to seismic waveforms through the Taiwan Geophysical Database Management System (GDMS). As of April 2025, more than 500 strong-motion instruments had been equipped with real-time transmission capabilities. We analyzed data from three major earthquakes in the April 2024 Hualien earthquake sequence (with magnitudes of M_w 7.3, 6.6, and 6.0), as well as reference weak-motion data (PGAs $\leq$ 20 cm/s^2), all obtained through the GDMS. We analyzed 18 strong-motion stations in the vicinity of the 2024 Hualien earthquake region (the station distributions are shown in Fig. 2), with a total of 568 weak-motion records. In addition, data from the 2018 M_w 6.4 offshore Hualien earthquake were collected for comparison with the strong-motion characteristics of the 2024 Hualien earthquake sequence. However, owing to changes in station configuration over the past six years, only 13 stations had complete records for all investigated Hualien events. Data from these common stations provide a valuable basis for comparing seismic event characteristics from different periods in comparable regions, facilitating the investigation of spatiotemporal variations in regional seismic response patterns. All strong-motion data underwent instrument response correction, mean and trend removal processing, and band-pass filtering between 0.075 and 20 Hz, which provided the processed waveforms subsequently used in the 0.5–20 Hz analyses of nonlinear site response.

The PGA for each station in this study was calculated on the basis of three orthogonal components of earthquake records: east–west (EW), north–south (NS), and up–down (UD). First, acceleration time series in three directions: $a_{EW}(t)$, $a_{NS}(t)$, and $a_{UD}(t)$, were obtained from the strong-motion instruments. At each time point, the composite acceleration was calculated by taking the square root of the sum of squares of the three components, and the maximum value throughout the entire time record was taken as the PGA:

$$PGA_{vec} = \max \sqrt{a_{EW}(t)^2 + a_{NS}(t)^2 + a_{UD}(t)^2}. \quad (1)$$

This method accounts for the composite effect of the 3D components, providing a more accurate representation of the maximum seismic intensity experienced at the site.

The PGA_{vec} contour maps for the three major earthquakes analyzed in this study are shown in Figure 2. It is evident that all three earthquakes generated significant seismic responses in the Hualien area, although their spatial distribution characteristics exhibit notable differences. The M_w 7.3 mainshock of 3 April 2024 produced the most intense ground response (Fig. 2a), with a maximum PGA_{vec} value of ~569 cm/s^2 recorded at station F051, whereas station F025 also recorded ~564 cm/s^2, forming a strong-motion zone of 400–460 cm/s^2 in Hualien city. The seismic intensity reached 350 cm/s^2 as far as station E075 in Yilan County, with the contour pattern clearly indicating stronger motion to the north of the epicenter than to the south, suggesting northward rupture propagation during faulting. With respect to the M_w 6.6 aftershock (Fig. 2b), which occurred 13 min later, a maximum PGA_{vec} value of ~410 cm/s^2 was recorded at station F051, whereas the PGA_{vec} values in Hualien city ranged between ~200 and 245 cm/s^2. Compared with the mainshock, its area of influence was more limited. The M_w 6.0 earthquake that occurred on 23 April (Fig. 2c) had relatively low-PGA_{vec} values, with a maximum value of ~298 cm/s^2, which was also recorded at station F051. PGA_{vec} values in Hualien city ranged between ~187 and 221 cm/s^2. The seismic motion distribution of this M_w 6.0 earthquake was more concentrated in Hualien city, with significantly diminished effects in other regions. Notably, station F051 recorded relatively high-PGA_{vec} values for all three earthquakes. Although these observations suggest that specific local factors may have controlled the amplification at this site, the detailed mechanisms are beyond the scope of this study. We tentatively attribute this phenomenon to site conditions and the installation environment, but the underlying cause cannot be confirmed at this stage.

For each station, we collected V_{S30} information (the time-averaged shear-wave velocity in the upper 30 m) to support subsequent analyses. V_{S30} data were primarily obtained from the Engineering Geological Database for TSMIP (Kuo *et al.*, 2012). For stations not covered by the database, we referenced V_{S30} information derived from microtremor analyses by Chen *et al.* (2022). The median V_{S30} in the Hualien area is ~500 m/s, with most station sites classified as class C according to NEHRP provisions (BSSC, 2020). Only one station, F048, is classified as site class D, as summarized in Table S1, available in the supplemental material to this article.

METHODOLOGY

To establish the basis for quantifying nonlinear site responses using differences between weak- and strong-motion HVSRs, we first noted the key physical characteristics of soil nonlinearity. During strong ground motion, the soil response may transition from linear to nonlinear behavior, typically involving reduced high-frequency amplification and a downward shift in predominant frequency (Wen *et al.*, 1994). This behavior arises from the nonlinear stress–strain relationship and hysteretic damping of soil, in which the shear modulus decreases and the damping ratio increases once the strain exceeds critical thresholds (Beresnev and Wen, 1996). Such characteristics have been recognized for decades from strong-motion records worldwide (Sato *et al.*, 1996; Trifunac and Todorovska, 1996; Dimitriu *et al.*, 1999; Frankel *et al.*, 2002; Bonilla *et al.*, 2011) and have been confirmed by recent observational studies with various tectonic and geological conditions (e.g., Chen *et al.*, 2017; Ren *et al.*, 2017; Dhakal *et al.*, 2019; Kuo *et al.*, 2019; Thornley *et al.*, 2021).

Although HVSR is widely used to infer site response, it relies on the assumption that source and path effects are reduced when taking the spectral ratio of horizontal to vertical components (Nakamura, 1989; Lermo and Chávez-García, 1993). This assumption may not fully hold for earthquakes with different azimuths, mechanisms, or incidence angles; thus, individual-event HVSRs may still contain variability unrelated to site response. In this study, interpretations of HVSR differences are therefore based on consistent patterns across multiple events rather than single-event behavior.

On the basis of the established understanding of nonlinear site effects from previous observational studies, we selected weak- and strong-motion records following criteria that ensure that the weak-motion set represents a linear site response and applied the DNL index proposed by Noguchi and Sasatani (2008) to quantify spectral differences. In this study, weak motion was defined as a PGA ≤ 20 cm/s, with at least one component ≥10 cm/s^2 to ensure signal quality. In addition, only events with magnitudes <5 were considered. A minimum of 10 weak-motion records were collected for each station, with earthquake magnitudes ranging from 2.02 to 4.99 and focal depths between 1.05 and 33.47 km (mean depth ≈ 13.6 km), and the average HVSR was calculated to establish the characteristic weak-motion spectral ratio. The HVSR computation procedure in this study follows the approach described by Chen *et al.* (2017), with the following steps.

1. The mean and trend are removed from the original waveform data.
2. Shear-wave (S wave) time windows are manually selected.
3. Mean and trend removal are again performed on the selected time windows.
4. A 5% cosine-tapered window is applied to minimize spectral leakage.
5. A fast Fourier transform is conducted on three-component signals to obtain the amplitude spectra.
6. Fivefold spectral smoothing is applied using a nine-point Hanning window in the frequency domain.
7. A root-mean-square combination of EW- and NS-component amplitude spectra is calculated to represent the horizontal component.
8. The HVSR is computed by dividing the combined horizontal component by the vertical component (UD).
9. Fivefold smoothing is applied to the HVSR curve using a nine-point Hanning window to reduce fluctuations and improve clarity.

To further quantify the DNL, the following DNL index formula was employed:

$$\mathrm{DNL} = \sum_{i=1}^{n} \left| \log_{10}\left(\frac{\mathrm{HVSR}_{\mathrm{event}}(f_i)}{\mathrm{HVSR}_{\mathrm{mean}}(f_i)}\right) \right| \times \Delta f_i, \quad (2)$$

in which $\mathrm{HVSR}_{\mathrm{event}}(f_i)$ represents the HVSR value of the investigated strong-motion event and $\mathrm{HVSR}_{\mathrm{mean}}(f_i)$ is the characteristic weak-motion HVSR value at the same station. Δf_i is the frequency interval, and n is the number of frequency points considered. Considering the typical distribution of resonant frequencies between the surface and bedrock layers, the frequency range in this analysis was set at 0.5–20 Hz, which is also consistent with the analytical range of Noguchi and Sasatani (2008) to ensure the comparability and representativeness of the results.

Soil's nonlinear effects are closely related to the shear strain induced by earthquakes. Because direct measurement of shear strain in the field is impractical, this study used PGV/V_{S30} as a strain proxy indicator (Idriss, 2011). The physical significance of this ratio is based on wave propagation theory, in which the ratio of ground surface particle velocity to shear-wave velocity approximates the displacement gradient or strain magnitude:

$$\gamma \propto \frac{v}{V_S}, \quad (3)$$

in which γ is the shear strain, v is the transient ground surface particle velocity induced by seismic shaking, and V_S is the shear-wave velocity of the near-surface material. PGV reflects ground-motion intensity, and V_{S30} represents the stiffness of the near-surface soil layers; thus, their ratio is positively correlated with soil shear strain (Idriss, 2011). In this study, the strain proxy is therefore defined as follows:

$$\gamma_{\mathrm{proxy}} = \frac{\mathrm{PGV}_{\mathrm{vec}}}{V_{S30}}, \quad (4)$$

in which $\mathrm{PGV}_{\mathrm{vec}}$ is computed as the peak vector sum of three-component velocity waveforms as follows:

$$\mathrm{PGV}_{\mathrm{vec}} = \max \sqrt{v_{\mathrm{EW}}(t)^2 + v_{\mathrm{NS}}(t)^2 + v_{\mathrm{UD}}(t)^2}, \quad (5)$$

in which $v_{\mathrm{EW}}(t)$, $v_{\mathrm{NS}}(t)$, and $v_{\mathrm{UD}}(t)$ represent the EW, NS, and vertical velocity time series, respectively, derived from integrated acceleration records. Through an analysis of γ_{proxy} and comparisons with other ground-motion intensity measures, such as the PGA and PGV, this study investigated the relationship between the DNL index and seismic loading characteristics to identify the primary controlling factors and critical thresholds for the onset of nonlinear soil behavior. The HVSR and DNL values calculated using the aforementioned methods were further subjected to regression analysis with various intensity measures and strain proxies to better understand the nonlinear response mechanisms.

RESULTS

On the basis of the analytical framework described in the previous section, the HVSRs of the S-wave windows at each station for three representative strong-motion events in the 2024 Hualien earthquake sequence were computed. These were then compared with the average HVSRs from weak-motion records (black lines in Fig. 3) at the same stations. The HVSR results from four representative stations are summarized in Figure 3, with additional stations provided in Figure S1, illustrating the nonlinear site response characteristics observed during the mainshock and subsequent large aftershocks. The corresponding PGA and DNL for each event and the representative site parameter V_{S30} are also presented for each station. Overall, several stations exhibited significant shifts in predominant frequency and reductions in high-frequency amplification during strong shaking, indicating a pronounced nonlinear site response. For example, at station F028 (Fig. 3d), the 2024 mainshock (M_w 7.3) and two aftershocks (M_w 6.6 and 6.0) recorded progressively decreasing PGAs of 407.2,235.2, and 142.0 cm/s^2, respectively. The corresponding DNL values also tended to decrease (12.57, 9.20, and 6.87, respectively), suggesting a positive correlation between the PGA and DNL. This phenomenon can also be observed at the other stations shown in Figure 3. For clearer visualization, the HVSR curves in Figure 3 were smoothed using a Gaussian-weighted moving average (full width at half-maximum ≈ 0.30 Hz, data resolution 0.0244 Hz). This smoothing was applied solely to improve the readability of the plotted spectra and was not applied to the HVSR data used in the DNL calculations. In addition, stations with higher V_{S30} values (e.g., E062 and F020 in Fig. S1) tended to exhibit relatively low-DNL values even under high-PGA conditions, suggesting that site stiffness may influence

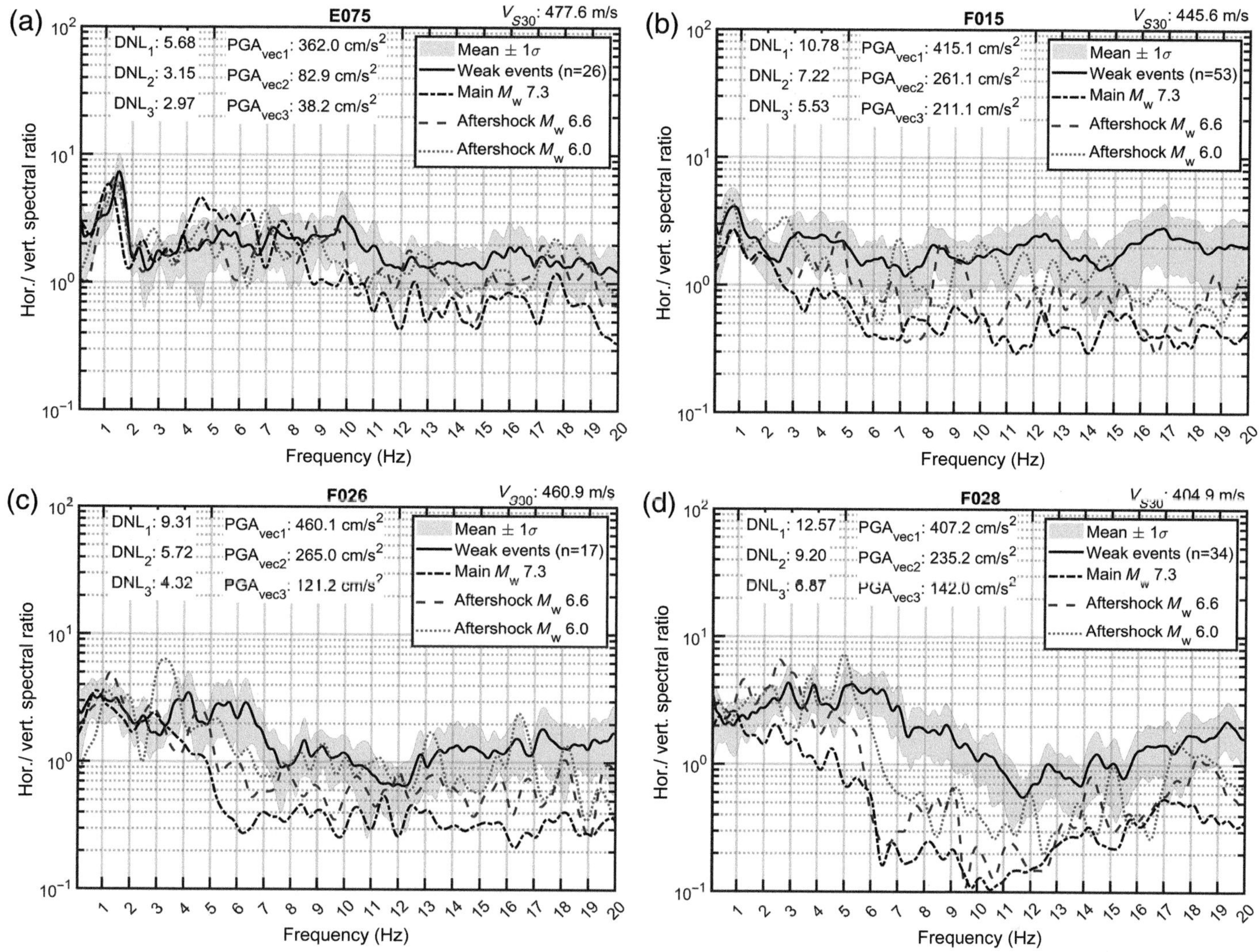

Figure 3. Horizontal-to-vertical spectral ratio (HVSR) results for four selected Taiwan Strong-Motion Instrumentation Program (TSMIP) stations during the 2024 Hualien earthquake sequence, including the mainshock (M_w 7.3) and two large aftershocks (M_w 6.6 and 6.0). The strong-motion HVSRs for these three events are shown using different line styles, and the black line and gray shading represent the mean and $\pm 1\sigma$ range, respectively, of weak events. PGA_{vec} and degree of nonlinearity (DNL) values for each event are listed in the upper left corner of each panel. The results from additional stations are provided in Figure S1. Panels (a)–(d) correspond to stations E075, F015, F026, and F028, respectively, with E075 located in southern Yilan and the F-series stations located within Hualien County.

the DNL response. Collectively, these findings indicate that although the PGA is a primary trigger for nonlinear site behavior, site conditions such as V_{S30} can also be important contributing factors. To further quantify the relationships between the DNL and ground-motion parameters, statistical correlation analyses were conducted, followed by the formulation of empirical regression models that characterize the nonlinear response.

In this study, we investigated the correlation between DNL and seismic intensity measures from the three strong-motion events, and Figure 4a reveals a clear increasing trend of DNL with increasing PGA, with a Pearson correlation coefficient of 0.70, confirming a statistically significant positive relationship. However, the DNL–PGA relationship was not purely linear. Instead, a two-phase trend was observed: when the PGA was below a certain threshold, the DNL values remained relatively stable, suggesting linear site behavior. When the PGA exceeded this threshold, the DNL increased markedly, indicating a transition to a nonlinear response. This behavioral shift implies the existence of a triggering threshold for a nonlinear site response.

Given the staged nature of this relationship, a simple linear regression model would be insufficient to capture the transition dynamics. Therefore, a piecewise regression model was adopted to describe the statistical relationship between the DNL and the PGA. To determine the optimal breakpoint, a grid-search approach was implemented across a plausible range of threshold values (excluding extreme outliers). For each candidate threshold, the model parameters were estimated by minimizing the root mean squared error (RMSE), and the one yielding the lowest RMSE was selected as the optimal model. For the Hualien region, the RMSE values were 1.776 for the linear model and 1.785 for the piecewise model, indicating that the statistical performance

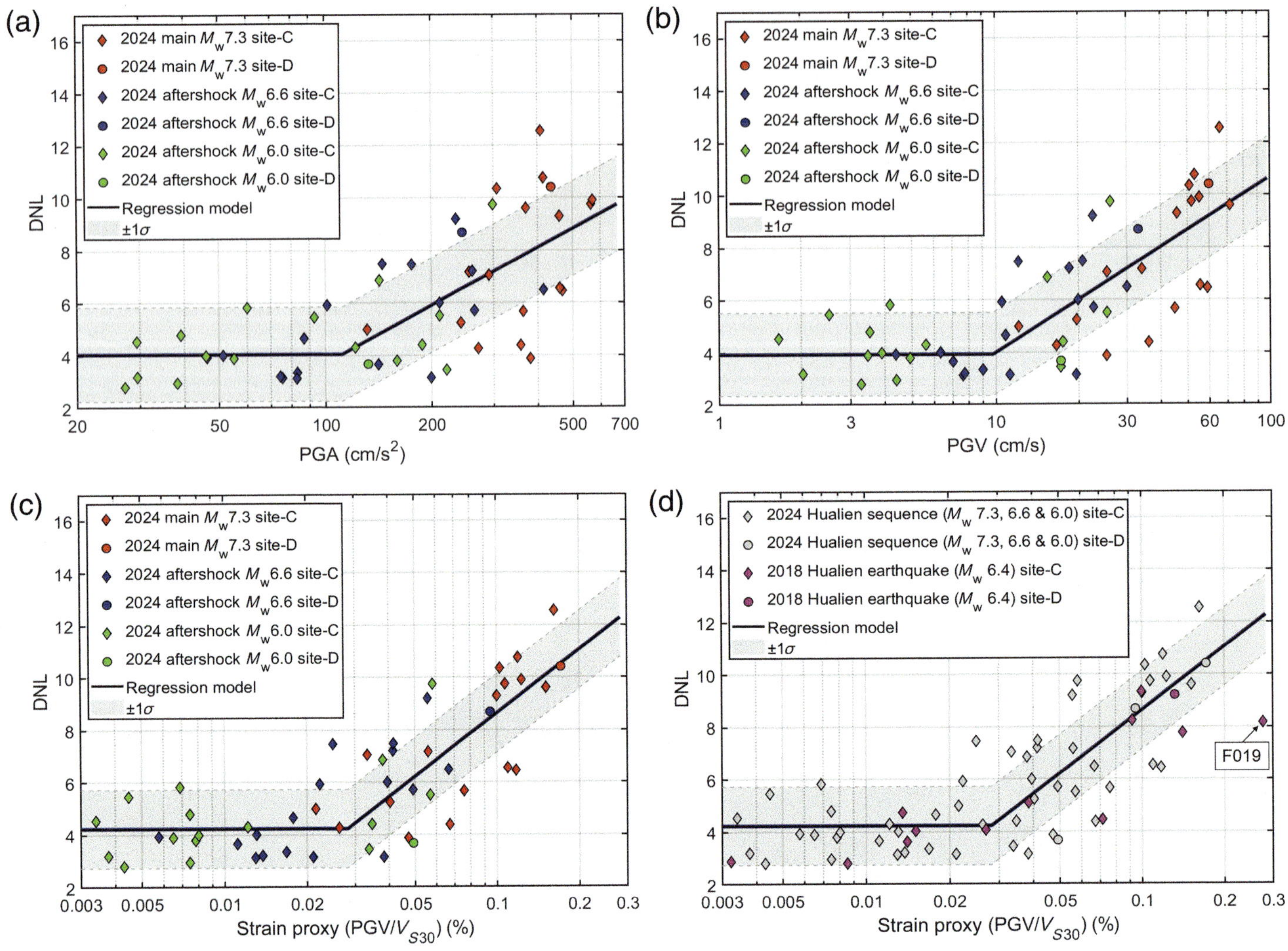

Figure 4. Correlations between the DNL and ground-motion parameters for the 2024 Hualien earthquake sequence. (a) DNL versus vector PGA (PGA_{vec}, cm/s^2), with a two-segment piecewise regression model showing a threshold at 111 cm/s^2. (b) DNL versus vector peak ground velocity (PGV) (PGV_{vec}, cm/s), with the regression model indicating a threshold at 9.77 cm/s. (c) DNL versus strain proxy γ_{proxy} (PGV/V_{S30}), in which the piecewise regression model identifies a nonlinear threshold at 0.0283%. (d) Comparison of DNL versus the strain proxy γ_{proxy} (PGV/V_{S30}) between the 2024 Hualien earthquake sequence (gray) and the 2018 Hualien earthquake (pink). The regression model and $\pm 1\sigma$ bounds are based on 2024 data points. Outlier station F019 is labeled. In all panels, the shaded regions represent the $\pm 1\sigma$ range of the regression model. Different markers denote NEHRP site classifications C and D based on V_{S30}.

of both models was nearly equivalent. Although the linear regression provided a slightly smaller error, the piecewise model was preferred because it allowed us to objectively identify a threshold associated with the onset of a nonlinear response and to quantify site behavior beyond that threshold. This interpretive value makes the piecewise form particularly useful in the context of nonlinear site response analysis. The resulting model is as follows:

$$\mathrm{DNL}(\mathrm{PGA_{vec}}) = \begin{cases} 4.05 \pm 1.802, & \mathrm{PGA_{vec}} < 111\ \mathrm{cm/s^2} \\ 4.05 + 3.173 \ln\left(\frac{\mathrm{PGA_{vec}}}{111}\right) \pm 1.802, & \mathrm{PGA_{vec}} \geq 111\ \mathrm{cm/s^2} \end{cases}, \quad (6)$$

in which 111 cm/s^2 is identified as the threshold triggering nonlinear behavior; 4.05 represents the average DNL under low-shaking intensity (linear) conditions; 3.173 is the logarithmic coefficient for the high-shaking intensity regime, reflecting the increasing rate of DNL with PGA_{vec}; and 1.802 is the global standard deviation.

On the other hand, the PGV is another commonly used intensity measure that better captures ground-motion energy and surface velocity, which are closely related to induced strain. Therefore, a regression analysis between DNL and PGV was further conducted using the same set of strong-motion data (Fig. 4b). The results indicate a significant positive correlation, with a Pearson correlation coefficient of 0.78, which is slightly greater than that of the PGA–DNL relationship and suggests that the PGV may better explain the observed variability in the nonlinear site response. A similar segmented trend was also observed in the DNL–PGV relationship. Applying the same grid-search method, the following piecewise regression model was developed:

$$\mathrm{DNL}(\mathrm{PGV_{vec}}) = \begin{cases} 3.94 \pm 1.587, & \mathrm{PGV_{vec}} < 9.77\ \mathrm{cm/s} \\ 3.94 + 2.898 \ln(\frac{\mathrm{PGV_{vec}}}{9.77}) \pm 1.587, & \mathrm{PGV_{vec}} \geq 9.77\ \mathrm{cm/s} \end{cases}, \quad (7)$$

in which 9.77 cm/s is identified as the critical PGV threshold triggering a nonlinear response. The DNL values remained stable when $\mathrm{PGV_{vec}}$ was <~9.77 cm/s but increased logarithmically as the PGV exceeded this threshold. Compared with the PGA-based model, the PGV-based model exhibited a clearer and more consistent relationship with DNL, supporting its suitability as a key predictor variable of nonlinear site behavior.

In addition to the PGA and PGV, a strain proxy defined as PGV/V_{S30} (γ_{proxy}) was used to better approximate shear strain levels at a site. The DNL–γ_{proxy} correlation was analyzed across the same dataset, and the results revealed a strong positive correlation (Fig. 4c), with a Pearson correlation coefficient of 0.81, which is higher than those for the PGA and PGV and demonstrates that γ_{proxy} is a more effective indicator for assessing nonlinear site response. The following piecewise model explains the relationship:

$$\mathrm{DNL}(\gamma_{\mathrm{proxy}}) = \begin{cases} 4.24 \pm 1.492, & \gamma_{\mathrm{proxy}} < 0.0283\% \\ 4.24 + 3.489 \ln\left(\frac{\gamma_{\mathrm{proxy}}}{0.0283\%}\right) \pm 1.492, & \gamma_{\mathrm{proxy}} \geq 0.0283\% \end{cases}. \quad (8)$$

This two-phase trend regression model suggests that when γ_{proxy} is <~0.0283%, DNL remains stable, with an average value of 4.24. When this threshold is exceeded, DNL increases logarithmically with γ_{proxy}. The coefficient 3.489 represents the logarithmic slope in the high-strain domain, and 1.492 denotes the global standard deviation. To validate the robustness and generalizability of the proposed models, observational data from the 2018 M_{w} 6.4 Hualien earthquake were incorporated. As shown in Figure 4d, the majority of DNL values from the 2018 M_{w} 6.4 Hualien event (marked as pink symbols) fell within the predicted bounds of the 2024-derived regression model, demonstrating the model's predictive capability and regional representativeness for nonlinear site response in Hualien.

One notable outlier in Figure 4d, station F019, has a large γ_{proxy} value (0.2753%) but a relatively low DNL (8.2), deviating beyond the $\pm 1\sigma$ prediction interval. Station F019 corresponds to the Hualien Weather Station operated by the CWA. In accordance with the station metadata documented in the GDMS (CWA, 2012; see Data and Resources), the strong-motion instrument was installed on a reinforced-concrete pedestal in the basement of a two-story reinforced concrete building. Although the site's V_{S30} and $Z1.0$ values are listed in Table S1, these installation conditions clearly indicate that F019 does not represent a free-field station. It is therefore plausible that soil-structure interaction and structural filtering during the earthquake produced the observed discrepancy, explaining why this outlier deviates significantly from the regression prediction.

To further assess regional applicability, this study incorporated DNL results from the 2016 M_{w} 6.4 Meinong earthquake, which occurred in southwestern Taiwan on 6 February 2016 and was originally computed by Chen *et al.* (2017) using the same methodology adopted in this study. The epicenter of this event is also shown in Figure 1. The strain proxy values were recalculated to ensure consistency with the processing applied to the 2024 Hualien dataset. The 2016 M_{w} 6.4 Meinong results are overlain onto the 2024 Hualien-derived regression model (marked as pink symbols) in Figure 5. Most stations on the ChiaNan Plain deviate from the Hualien trend, particularly under high-strain conditions in which DNL does not increase significantly. This suggests substantial regional differences in nonlinear site behavior. In Hualien, the alluvial deposits are dominated by gravels and coarse sands, which exhibit high-initial stiffness but undergo abrupt modulus reduction and increase in damping once the strain exceeds the threshold. In contrast, the ChiaNan Plain is characterized by fine-grained silts and clays with lower stiffness and higher damping, leading to a more gradual nonlinear response.

Given the absence of a distinct breakpoint in the ChiaNan dataset, the use of a piecewise regression model was less justified. Instead, a power-law regression was adopted (Fig. 6), which provided slightly better statistical performance (RMSE of 1.417 vs. 1.420 for piecewise) and more effectively represented the gradual progression of nonlinear behavior on the ChiaNan Plain, expressed as follows:

$$\mathrm{DNL}(\gamma_{\mathrm{proxy}}) = 3.6 + 0.456\left(\frac{\gamma_{\mathrm{proxy}}}{0.0979}\right)^{1.944} \pm 1.155. \quad (9)$$

This empirical model may serve as a useful framework for estimating DNL on the ChiaNan Plain and provides a foundation for subsequent regional comparisons of nonlinear site response characteristics and their physical interpretations.

DISCUSSION

Here, we conduct an integrated discussion of the physical significance and regional differences associated with the regression models of DNL and ground-motion parameters (PGA, PGV, and strain proxy) developed in this study. By comparing the derived nonlinear thresholds and triggering conditions with those proposed in previous studies, we evaluate the reasonableness of the models. In addition, we explore the possible causes of the discrepancies between the models for the Hualien and ChiaNan Plain regions and investigate the relationships between

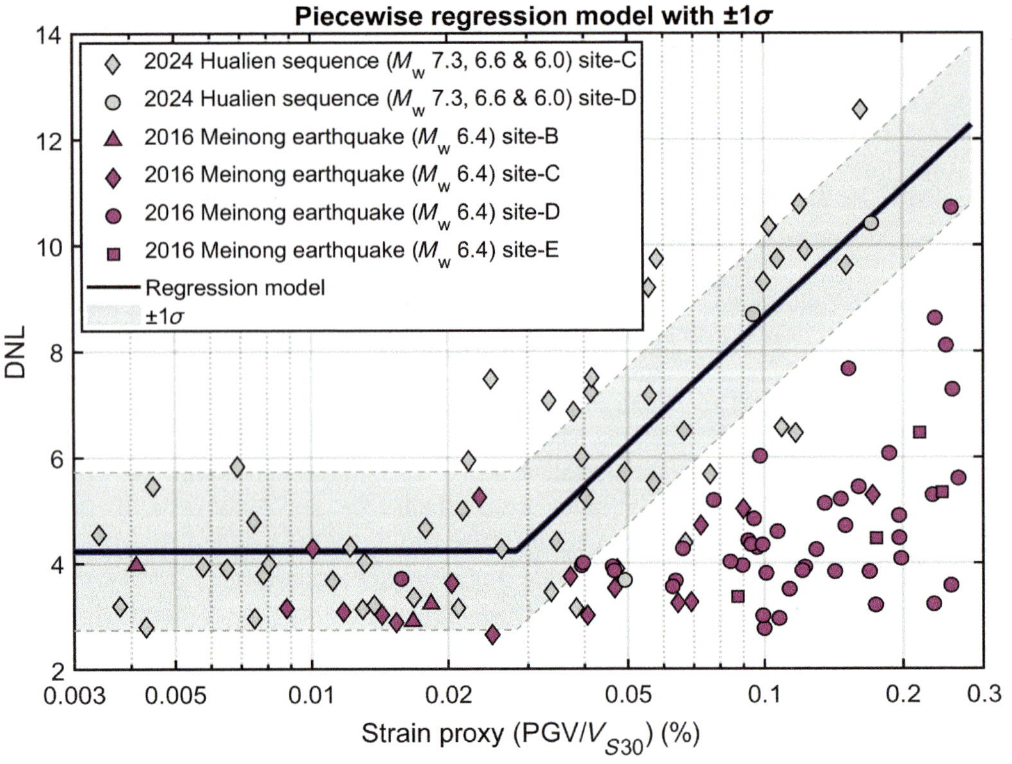

Figure 5. DNL versus strain proxy γ_{proxy} (PGV/V_{S30}) for the 2016 M_w 6.4 Meinong earthquake (pink symbols) is shown against the 2024 Hualien (gray symbols) regression model with $\pm 1\sigma$ bounds. Different markers indicate site classification (B, C, D, or E) based on V_{S30}.

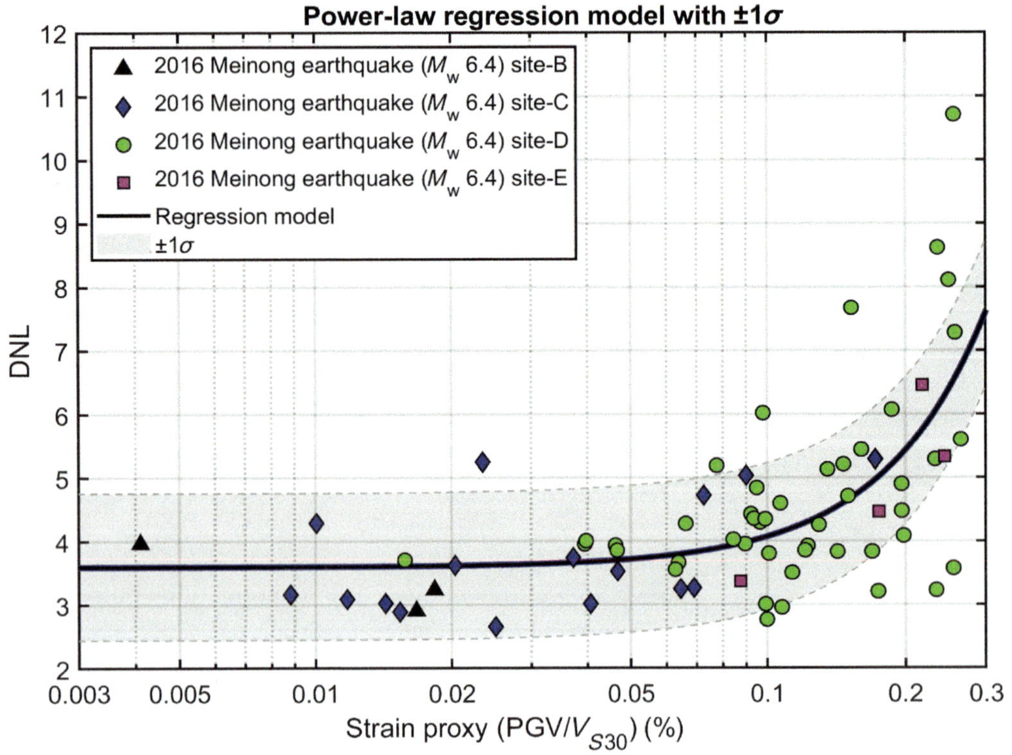

Figure 6. Power-law regression between DNL and the strain proxy γ_{proxy} (PGV/V_{S30}) for the 2016 M_w 6.4 Meinong earthquake. The shaded area represents the $\pm 1\sigma$ prediction interval. Different markers indicate site classification (B, C, D, or E) based on V_{S30}.

the vertical-to-horizontal (V/H) ratios of the PGA and PGV and their connections to nonlinear site responses to improve the understanding of nonlinear soil behavior under different geological conditions.

In the segmented regression models based on the PGA, PGV, and strain proxy, the plateau values in the first-stage regressions are 4.05, 3.94, and 4.24, respectively. These values are all close to 4, with a maximum difference of only 0.3. The plateau indicates a regime for which pronounced nonlinear behavior has not yet emerged. These findings are consistent with the DNL $\approx$ 4 threshold proposed by Noguchi and Sasatani (2011) for identifying nonlinear site responses, supporting the physical basis and validity of the regression models developed in our study.

The estimated nonlinear triggering thresholds derived from the regression analyses in this study are as follows: PGA = 111 cm/s^2, PGV = 9.77 cm/s, and strain proxy = 0.0283%. With respect to the PGA threshold, Beresnev and Wen (1996) reported that soils tend to exhibit nonlinear behavior at PGA levels ranging from 100 to 200 cm/s^2. Wu *et al.* (2010) suggested that strong nonlinear effects are likely observed when the PGA exceeds 100 cm/s^2. Régnier *et al.* (2013) reported a high probability of nonlinearity with a PGA > 75 cm/s^2, whereas Ren *et al.* (2017) reported a threshold of 200 cm/s^2 on the basis of data from the 2008 M_w 7.9 Wenchuan earthquake. Dhakal *et al.* (2017), who analyzed ocean-bottom seismograph data in Sagami Bay, concluded that a nonlinear response is evident when the PGA exceeds 50–150 cm/s^2. The PGA threshold derived for the Hualien region in this study fits well with the range reported in these previous studies. With respect to PGVs, Wu *et al.* (2009) reported a predominant frequency reduction at PGVs >~5 cm/s, whereas Ren *et al.* (2017) reported significant nonlinear effects at PGVs >15 cm/s. The PGV threshold of 9.77 cm/s identified in this study aligns with these findings, but the difference may also reflect potential variability caused by regional and site-specific conditions.

In terms of strain thresholds, Seed and Idriss (1970) reported a strong correlation between soil nonlinearity and shear strain, with pronounced nonlinear behavior beginning at ~10^{-3}% to 10^{-2}%. More recent studies using large datasets of downhole recordings have provided additional insights into these thresholds. Kaklamanos *et al.* (2013) reported that the peak shear strains beyond which linear analyses become inaccurate in predicting surface pseudospectral accelerations are a function of the vibration period and are between 0.01% and 0.1% for periods <0.5 s, with equivalent linear analyses becoming inaccurate at peak strains of ~0.4% over this range of periods. Shi and Asimaki (2017) reported that 0.04% is the threshold strain beyond which the performance of all the other methods deteriorate except for their proposed hybrid hyperbolic model; this value is lower than that reported by Kaklamanos *et al.* (2013) (0.1%) and only slightly lower than that reported by Kaklamanos *et al.* (2015) (0.05%). These shear strain ranges are dependent on the spectral period, with nonlinear effects manifesting at lower strains for higher frequencies. By applying an analysis of shallow materials for the 2016 Kumamoto earthquake sequence, Esfahani *et al.* (2024) reported that shear modulus degradation became evident with strains of 0.02%–0.03%, and 10%–20% degradation occurred with a strain of ~0.03%. The strain proxy threshold of 0.0283% derived in this study corresponds closely with previous findings and falls within a range of 0.015%–0.04%, which was identified by Shi and Asimaki (2017) for different frequency bands. In summary, the threshold values estimated in this study are consistent with those reported in the literature using the maximum shear strain computed from site response analyses, further supporting the reliability of our regression models.

Beyond the general threshold validation, this study reveals significant differences in nonlinear behavior between the DNL–strain proxy regression models for the Hualien and ChiaNan Plain regions, which are inferred to be related to differences in sedimentary composition. Geophysical imaging and borehole data indicate that Hualien's alluvial deposits primarily consist of sandy gravels, representing loosely consolidated fluvial sediments of late Pleistocene age (Chang *et al.*, 2023). The Meilun terrace in northern Hualien is dominated by conglomerates and sandy layers, indicating coarse-grained surface deposits (Hsu *et al.*, 2019). With respect to the Hualien model (solid line in Fig. 7), the DNL remains nearly flat under low-strain conditions, indicating a linear site response. However, when the strain exceeds a certain threshold, the nonlinearity increases sharply. This suggests that although coarse gravel sites may resist nonlinearity under small to moderate earthquakes, they can exhibit pronounced nonlinear behavior under strong ground motion. In contrast, the ChiaNan Plain is characterized by widespread fine-grained sediments. Borehole investigations in the Tainan area have revealed shallow mudstone layers (Wu *et al.*, 2025) and extensive deposits of high-plasticity clay (Lee *et al.*, 2007). Wu (1999) described the formation of the ChiaNan coastal plain as influenced by tidal flats and lagoonal environments, which promoted the accumulation of fine particles. Yang *et al.* (2007) also reported the prevalence of soft surface sediments. High-plasticity clay tends to behave linearly at small strains, but its modulus reduction curve is relatively gradual as strain increases (Vucetic and Dobry, 1991). The regression model for the ChiaNan region (red-dashed line in Fig. 7) reflects this behavior, with DNL increasing more gradually with strain. However, we should mention that the seismic stations selected for the analysis of the 2016 M_w 6.4 Meinong earthquake span a wide area across the ChiaNan region, including Kaohsiung, Tainan, and Chiayi, encompassing both plain and foothill terrains. The geological heterogeneity within this area could explain the relatively scattered DNL distribution under high-strain conditions. This study characterizes the ChiaNan Plain as dominated by fine-grained deposits, although this simplification may not fully represent the true variability in subsurface conditions. Overall, the coarse gravel deposits in the Hualien area and fine-grained sediments on the ChiaNan Plain exhibit distinct nonlinear response characteristics, resulting in different regression model behaviors (Fig. 7). The Hualien area tends to exhibit a higher threshold and sharper nonlinear transition, whereas the ChiaNan Plain shows no clear threshold and a more gradual increase in nonlinearity. This regional contrast is also consistent with the difference in depth to bedrock. As summarized in Table S1 (Hualien) and Table S2 (ChiaNan) and on the basis of $Z1.0$ values (Lin *et al.*, 2009; Kuo *et al.*, 2016; Chen *et al.*, 2022), the Hualien stations are typically underlain by much shallower bedrock (~100 m scale), whereas the ChiaNan Plain features considerably thicker sedimentary cover (~250 to 300 m scale). This basin-depth contrast may partly contribute, in addition to differences in sediment composition, to the observed sharper nonlinear transition in Hualien and the more gradual response on the ChiaNan Plain.

On the other hand, to further explore the manifestation of nonlinearity, it is important to note that elevated PGA V/H ratios during strong shaking can result from several factors, including source radiation patterns, path effects, site amplification characteristics, and component-specific site responses. Bozorgnia and Campbell (2016) reported that in near-fault regions, the most common cause of the vertical PGA exceeding the horizontal PGA is the reduction in high-frequency horizontal-motion amplitudes caused by soil nonlinearity.

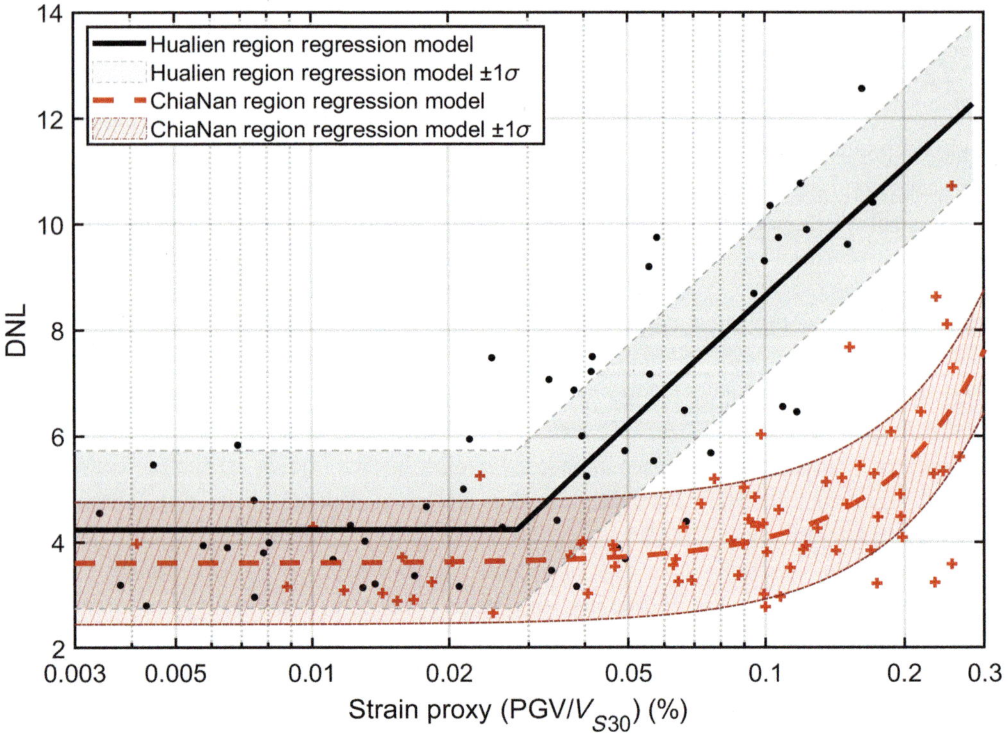

Figure 7. Comparison of regression models of DNL versus the strain proxy γ_{proxy} (PGV/V_{S30}) for the Hualien (solid-black line) and ChiaNan Plain (red-dashed line) regions. The black dots represent station data from the Hualien region, and the red crosses represent station data from the ChiaNan Plain region. Whereas the Hualien model is represented by a piecewise regression, the ChiaNan Plain model is represented by a power-law regression. The shaded areas denote the $\pm 1\sigma$ ranges of the respective models.

Among these, nonlinear soil behavior is often the dominant cause of intense ground motion and is typically characterized by a downward shift in predominant frequency and reduced amplification. The vertical component is generally less sensitive to nonlinearity (Tsai and Liu, 2017). The increase in the PGA V/H ratios observed in this study primarily reflects the suppression of high-frequency horizontal ground motion caused by shear modulus degradation rather than substantial amplification of the vertical component (Kuo *et al.*, 2019). Recent observations in Taiwan further confirm that nonlinear effects on the vertical component are present but significantly less pronounced than those on the horizontal component, which explains why high-PGA V/H ratios during strong shaking are dominated by a reduction in horizontal-motion amplitude (Chao *et al.*, 2023). Here, the PGA V/H ratios for five strong earthquake events were analyzed, including three from the 2024 Hualien earthquake sequence (M_w 7.3, 6.6, and 6.0), the 2018 M_w 6.4 Hualien earthquake, and the 2016 M_w 6.4 Meinong earthquake. As shown in Figure 8a, the median PGA V/H ratios for the three 2024 Hualien earthquakes were 0.67, 0.49, and 0.52, respectively. The ratio for the 2018 M_w 6.4 Hualien event was 0.56, with four outliers exceeding 1.0. In contrast, the 2016 M_w 6.4 Meinong earthquake had a median V/H ratio of 0.27, which was substantially lower than that of the Hualien events, and its outliers were also below the upper-quartile range of the Hualien distribution. The boxplots also incorporate V_{S30} values, showing that surface shear-wave velocities on the ChiaNan Plain are generally lower than those in the Hualien area.

For the PGV-based analysis (Fig. 8c), the changes in V/H with shaking intensity are much smaller than those observed in the PGA-based results. This finding indicates that nonlinear effects predominantly affect high-frequency ground motions, whereas their influence on long-period components is relatively limited, which is consistent with the findings of Kuo *et al.* (2019). This frequency-dependent behavior aligns with the expectation that shear modulus degradation has a more pronounced effect on short-period waves, leading to significant attenuation of the horizontal PGA but only minor changes in the horizontal PGV.

In the PGA V/H ratio versus PGA plots (Fig. 8b), stations in Hualien (marked as squares) show a clear upward trend in V/H ratios when the PGA exceeds ~0.1–0.2*g*. This is consistent with the onset of strong nonlinear effects that cause attenuation of high-frequency horizontal motion. However, the site-to-site variability in V/H remains substantial in the high-PGA range, indicating that although nonlinear attenuation of the horizontal component is common, local geological conditions and the potential occurrence of vertical-component nonlinearity (Chao *et al.*, 2023) can further modulate the extent and complexity of V/H changes during strong shaking. In contrast, stations on the ChiaNan Plain (marked as triangles) generally exhibit lower V/H ratios and a weaker upward trend with increasing PGA, reflecting the more gradual nonlinear transition inferred from the DNL–strain proxy regression analysis.

The PGV V/H ratio versus PGV plots (Fig. 8d) reveal that long-period components are less affected by nonlinearity, with V/H ratios showing only limited changes even under strong shaking, which is consistent with the conclusions of Kuo *et al.* (2019). The boxplots in Figure 8a,c reinforce these observations. For the PGA, the median V/H ratios are significantly higher in Hualien than on the ChiaNan Plain for comparable earthquake magnitudes, whereas for the PGV, the interregional

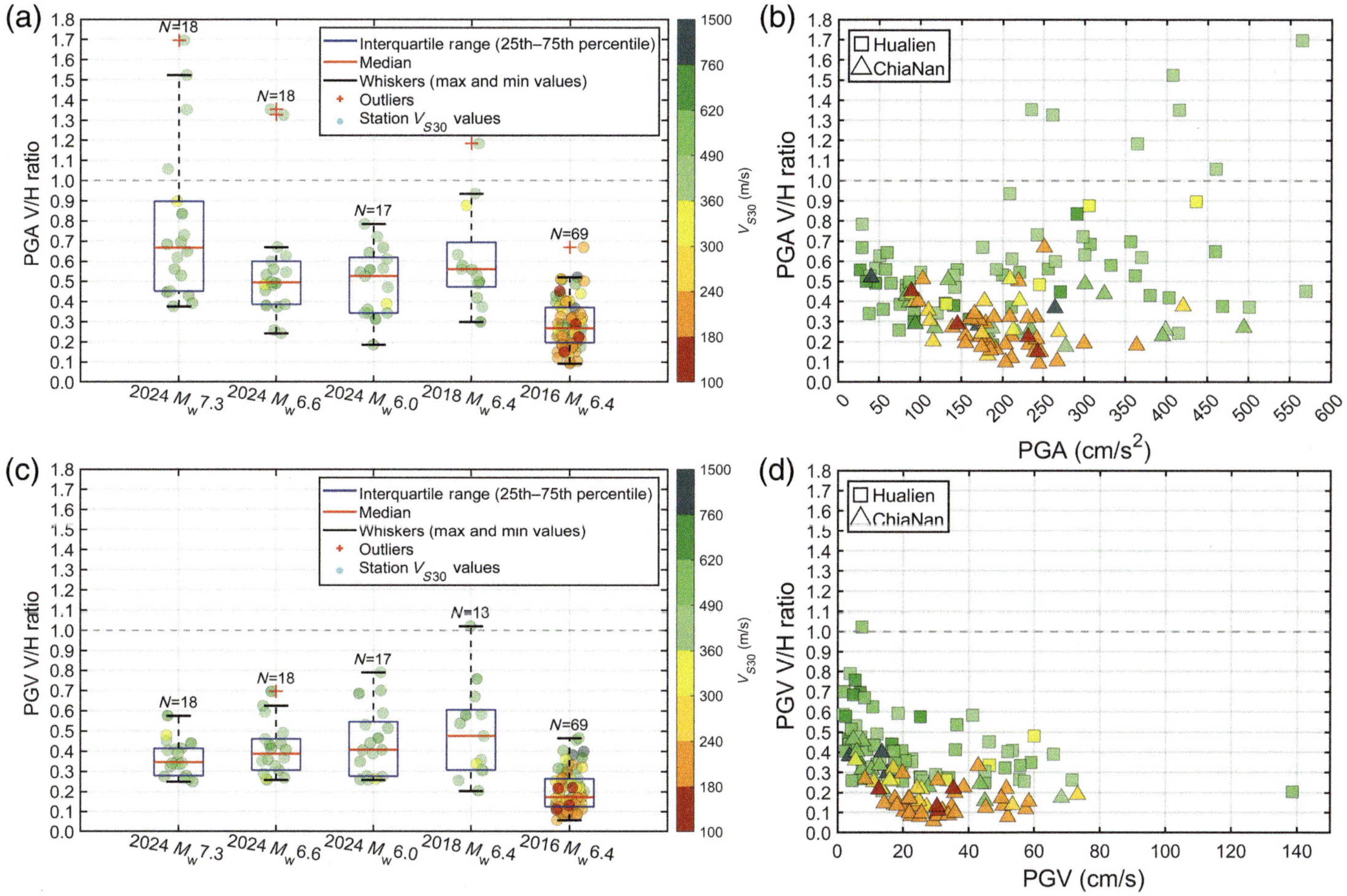

Figure 8. Vertical-to-horizontal (V/H) ratios of the PGA and PGV for five strong earthquake events, including three from the 2024 Hualien sequence (M_w 7.3, 6.6, and 6.0), the 2018 M_w 6.4 Hualien earthquake, and the 2016 M_w 6.4 Meinong earthquake. (a) Boxplots of the PGA V/H ratios, showing the interquartile range (25th–75th percentile, blue boxes), median (red line), whiskers (within 1.5 times the interquartile range), and outliers (red crosses). Station data are overlaid as colored circles scaled by V_{S30}, with the number of stations (*N*) labeled for each event. (b) Scatter plots of PGA V/H ratios versus PGA. (c) Boxplots of the PGV V/H ratios with the same format as in panel (a). The dashed line at V/H = 1.0 denotes the balance between horizontal and vertical amplification. (d) PGV V/H ratios versus PGV, with symbols distinguishing stations in Hualien (squares) and on the ChiaNan Plain (triangles).

contrast is less pronounced. Collectively, these results demonstrate that nonlinear site effects in Hualien are stronger and more abrupt at high frequencies, whereas on the ChiaNan Plain, the response is more gradual and less frequency dependent.

CONCLUSIONS

In this study, HVSR-based DNL analysis was applied to quantify nonlinear soil behavior during the 2024 Hualien earthquake sequence (M_w 7.3, 6.6, and 6.0), and the findings were compared with those of the 2018 M_w 6.4 Hualien and 2016 M_w 6.4 Meinong earthquakes. This method effectively captures changes in soil dynamic properties during seismic events, and the results provide new perspectives for earthquake hazard assessment. Regression models using DNL along with PGA, PGV, and the strain proxy (PGV/V_{S30}) successfully identified nonlinear response thresholds at 111 cm/s^2, 9.77 cm/s, and 0.0283%, respectively. The results revealed a strong correlation between DNL and these parameters, with the strain proxy demonstrating the highest predictive ability.

A significant contrast was found between the gravel-dominated Hualien sites and the fine-grained ChiaNan Plain, reflecting differences in dynamic soil properties. Hualien sites exhibited sharp transitions into nonlinearity beyond threshold values, whereas ChiaNan sites showed more gradual nonlinear behavior. The V/H analysis further supported these regional distinctions. With respect to the PGA, the median values of the Hualien sites were higher and clearly tended to increase under strong shaking, whereas the ChiaNan Plain sites exhibited lower ratios and weaker increases. In contrast, the PGV V/H results showed only limited changes even under strong shaking, indicating that nonlinear effects predominantly affect high-frequency ground motions, whereas long-period components remain less affected. Predictive consistency between models from the 2018 and 2024 Hualien earthquakes indicates stable nonlinear site response characteristics across different seismic events over a six-year period. However, further investigations are needed to determine whether similar behavior is observed in older events and whether changes in soil moisture during strong shaking affect the DNL. These findings enhance the understanding of regional soil dynamics and provide a valuable basis for seismic microzonation, hazard assessment, and earthquake-resilient engineering in Taiwan. Future research should expand observation networks to validate these models across different geological settings.

The regression models and thresholds presented here are region specific to eastern and southwestern Taiwan and reflect the distinct geological conditions of these areas. Although the absolute parameter values should not be directly transferred to other regions, the HVSR–DNL procedure is broadly applicable. With sufficient strong-motion recordings and site characterization, the same workflow can be employed to establish region-specific models elsewhere, enabling meaningful cross-regional comparisons of nonlinear soil responses.

DATA AND RESOURCES

Strong-motion data were obtained from Geophysical Database Management System (GDMS; CWA, 2012; https://gdms.cwa.gov.tw/index.php, last accessed April 2025). Fault-plane solutions and seismic moments were determined by Automatic Broadband Array in Taiwan for Seismology (AutoBATS; Jian *et al.*, 2018) and Real-time Moment Tensor (RMT; Lee, Liang, *et al.*, 2014; Lee, Liu, *et al.*, 2014). The supplemental material contains additional horizontal-to-vertical spectral ratio (HVSR) results for other selected Taiwan Strong-Motion Instrumentation Program (TSMIP) stations during the 2024 Hualien earthquake sequence, including the mainshock (M_w 7.3) and two large aftershocks (M_w 6.6 and 6.0). In addition, site parameters and DNL values at each station, used for the 2024 Hualien earthquake sequence (Hualien region) and for the 2016 M_w 6.4 Meinong earthquake (ChiaNan Plain region), are also listed. The supplemental material includes Figure S1 and Tables S1 and S2.

DECLARATION OF COMPETING INTERESTS

The authors acknowledge that there are no conflicts of interests recorded.

ACKNOWLEDGMENTS

The authors gratefully acknowledge the Geophysical Database Management System (GDMS), developed by the Central Weather Administration (CWA) of Taiwan, the Automatic Broadband Array in Taiwan for Seismology (AutoBATS), and the Real-time Moment Tensor (RMT) monitoring system for providing high-quality seismic data and focal mechanisms. The authors sincerely thank the editors and the two anonymous reviewers for their constructive and insightful comments, which have substantially improved the clarity and quality of this article. This research has been supported by the National Science and Technology Council, Taiwan (Grant Number NSTC 113-2116-M-194-012 and NSTC 114-2116-M-194-012). The contribution number of the Taiwan Earthquake Center (TEC) for this article is 00206.

REFERENCES

Beresnev, I. A., and K. L. Wen (1996). Nonlinear soil response—A reality? *Bull. Seismol. Soc. Am.* **86,** no. 6, 1964–1978, doi: 10.1785/BSSA0860061964.

Bonilla, L. F., K. Tsuda, N. Pulido, J. Régnier, and A. Laurendeau (2011). Nonlinear site response evidence of K-NET and KiK-net records from the 2011 off the Pacific coast of Tohoku earthquake, *Earth Planets Space* **63,** no. 7, 785–789, doi: 10.5047/eps.2011.06.012.

Bozorgnia, Y., and K. W. Campbell (2016). Ground motion model for the vertical-to-horizontal (V/H) ratios of PGA, PGV, and response spectra, *Earthq. Spectra* **32,** no. 2, 951–978, doi: 10.1193/100614eqs151m.

Building Seismic Safety Council (BSSC) (2020). NEHRP Recommended Seismic Provisions for New Buildings and Other Structures (FEMA P-2082-1): Volume 1: Part 1 Provisions, Part 2 Commentary, Federal Emergency Management Agency, Washington, D.C., 593 pp.

Castro-Cruz, D., J. Regnier, E. Bertrand, and F. Courboulex (2020). A new parameter to empirically describe and predict the non-linear seismic response of sites derived from the analysis of Kik-Net database, *Soil Dynam. Earthq. Eng.* **128,** 105833, doi: 10.1016/j.soildyn.2019.105833.

Central Weather Administration (CWA) (2012). Central Weather Administration Seismographic Network, *International Federation of Digital Seismograph Networks*, doi: 10.7914/SN/T5.

Chan, C. H., K. F. Ma, J. B. H. Shyu, Y. T. Lee, Y. J. Wang, J. C. Gao, Y. Y. Yen, and R. J. Rau (2020). Probabilistic seismic hazard assessment for Taiwan: TEM PSHA2020, *Earthq. Spectra* **36,** no. 1_suppl, 137–159, doi: 10.1177/8755293020951587.

Chang, P. Y., H. H. Amania, A. Fikri, J. M. Puntu, D. J. Lin, C. H. Kuo, C. Y. Wang, and W. Y. Chang (2023). Probing shallow subsurface structures in the arc-continent collision suture zone near Hualien in Eastern Taiwan with magnetotelluric methods, *Geosci. Lett.* **10,** no. 1, 29, doi: 10.1186/s40562-023-00283-w.

Chao, S. H., C. H. Kuo, C. M. Lin, J. Y. Huang, E. Rathje, and N. Abrahamson (2023). Observed nonlinear site amplification of vertical ground motion in Taiwan, *Earthq. Spectra* **39,** no. 4, 2379–2405, doi: 10.1177/87552930231190985.

Chen, C. T., S. C. Chang, and K. L. Wen (2017). Stochastic ground motion simulation of the 2016 Meinong, Taiwan earthquake, *Earth Planets Space* **69,** 1–15, doi: 10.1186/s40623-017-0645-z.

Chen, C. T., C. H. Kuo, C. M. Lin, J. Y. Huang, and K. L. Wen (2022). Investigation of shallow S-wave velocity structure and site response parameters in Taiwan by using high-density microtremor measurements, *Eng. Geol.* **297,** 106498, doi: 10.1016/j.enggeo.2021.106498.

Dhakal, Y. P., S. Aoi, T. Kunugi, W. Suzuki, and T. Kimura (2017). Assessment of nonlinear site response at ocean bottom seismograph sites based on S-wave horizontal-to-vertical spectral ratios: A study at the Sagami Bay area K-NET sites in Japan, *Earth Planets Space* **69,** 1–7, doi: 10.1186/s40623-017-0615-5.

Dhakal, Y. P., T. Kunugi, T. Kimura, W. Suzuki, and S. Aoi (2019). Peak ground motions and characteristics of nonlinear site response during the 2018 Mw 6.6 Hokkaido eastern Iburi earthquake, *Earth Planets Space* **71,** 1–26, doi: 10.1186/s40623-019-1038-2.

Dhakal, Y. P., T. Kunugi, H. Kubo, W. Suzuki, N. Shohei, S. Senna, and S. Aoi (2025). Characteristics of peak ground motions and nonlinear site response during the 2024 Mw 7.5 Noto Peninsula earthquake, *Earth Planets Space* **77,** no. 1, 93, doi: 10.1186/s40623-025-02212-x.

Dimitriu, P., I. Kalogeras, and N. Theodulidis (1999). Evidence of nonlinear site response in horizontal-to-vertical spectral ratio from near-field earthquakes, *Soil Dynam. Earthq. Eng.* **18,** no. 6, 423–435, doi: 10.1016/S0267-7261(99)00014-7.

Dimitriu, P., N. Theodulidis, and P. Y. Bard (2000). Evidence of nonlinear site response in HVSR from SMART1 (Taiwan) data, *Soil Dynam. Earthq. Eng.* **20,** no. 1/4, 155–165, doi: 10.1016/S0267-7261(00)00047-6.

Esfahani, R., F. Cotton, and L. F. Bonilla (2024). Temporal variations of the 'in-situ' nonlinear behaviour of shallow sediments during the 2016 Kumamoto earthquake sequence, *Geophys. J. Int.* **238,** no. 3, 1626–1637, doi: 10.1093/gji/ggae222.

Frankel, A. D., D. L. Carver, and R. A. Williams (2002). Nonlinear and linear site response and basin effects in Seattle for the M 6.8 Nisqually, Washington, earthquake, *Bull. Seismol. Soc. Am.* **92,** no. 6, 2090–2109, doi: 10.1785/0120010254.

Hardin, B. O., and V. P. Drnevich (1972). Shear modulus and damping in soils: Design equations and curves, *J. Soil Mech. Found. Div.* **98,** no. 7, 667–692, doi: 10.1061/JSFEAQ.0001760.

Hsu, Y. C., C. P. Chang, J. Y. Yen, H. Kuo-Chen, and C. C. Wang (2019). Investigating the structure of the Milun fault from surface ruptures of the 2018 Hualien earthquake, *Terr. Atmos. Ocean. Sci.* **30,** 337–350, doi: 10.3319/TAO.2018.09.28.01.

Idriss, I. M. (2011). Use of Vs30 to represent local site condition, *Proc. of the 4th IASPEI/IAEE International Symposium, Effects of Source Geology on Seismic Motion*, U.C. Santa Barbara, California, 23–26 August.

Jian, P. R., T. L. Tseng, W. T. Liang, and P. H. Huang (2018). A new automatic full-waveform regional moment tensor inversion algorithm and its applications in the Taiwan area, *Bull. Seismol. Soc. Am.* **108,** no. 2, 573–587, doi: 10.1785/0120170231.

Kaklamanos, J., L. G. Baise, E. M. Thompson, and L. Dorfmann (2015). Comparison of 1D linear, equivalent-linear, and nonlinear site response models at six KiK-net validation sites, *Soil Dynam. Earthq. Eng.* **69,** 207–219, doi: 10.1016/j.soildyn.2014.10.016.

Kaklamanos, J., B. A. Bradley, E. M. Thompson, and L. G. Baise (2013). Critical parameters affecting bias and variability in site-response analyses using KiK-net downhole array data, *Bull. Seismol. Soc. Am.* **103,** no. 3, 1733–1749, doi: 10.1785/0120120166.

Kubo, H., T. Nakamura, W. Suzuki, Y. P. Dhakal, T. Kimura, T. Kunugi, N. Takahashi, and S. Aoi (2019). Ground-motion characteristics and nonlinear soil response observed by DONET1 seafloor observation network during the 2016 southeast off-Mie, Japan, earthquake, *Bull. Seismol. Soc. Am.* **109,** no. 3, 976–986, doi: 10.1785/0120170296.

Kuo, C. H., C. T. Chen, C. M. Lin, K. L. Wen, J. Y. Huang, and S. C. Chang (2016). S-wave velocity structure and site effect parameters derived by microtremor arrays in the Western Plain of Taiwan, *J. Asian Earth Sci.* **128,** 27–41, doi: 10.1016/j.jseaes.2016.07.012.

Kuo, C. H., J. Y. Huang, C. M. Lin, T. Y. Hsu, S. H. Chao, and K. L. Wen (2019). Strong ground motion and pulse-like velocity observations in the near-fault region of the 2018 Mw 6.4 Hualien, Taiwan, earthquake, *Seismol. Res. Lett.* **90,** no. 1, 40–50, doi: 10.1785/0220180195.

Kuo, C. H., K. L. Wen, H. H. Hsieh, C. M. Lin, T. M. Chang, and K. W. Kuo (2012). Site classification and Vs30 estimation of free-field TSMIP stations using the logging data of EGDT, *Eng. Geol.* **129,** 68–75, doi: 10.1016/j.enggeo.2012.01.013.

Lee, D. H., H. M. Lin, and J. H. Wu (2007). The basic properties of mudstone slopes in southwestern Taiwan, *J. GeoEng.* **2,** no. 3, 81–95, doi: 10.6310/jog.2007.2(3).1.

Lee, S. J., W. T. Liang, H. W. Cheng, F. S. Tu, K. F. Ma, H. Tsuruoka, H. Kawakatsu, B. S. Huang, and C. C. Liu (2014). Towards real-time regional earthquake simulation I: Real-time moment tensor monitoring (RMT) for regional events in Taiwan, *Geophys. J. Int.* **196,** no. 1, 432–446, doi: 10.1093/gji/ggt371.

Lee, S. J., Q. Liu, J. Tromp, D. Komatitsch, W. T. Liang, and B. S. Huang (2014). Toward real-time regional earthquake simulation II: Real-time Online earthquake Simulation (ROS) of Taiwan earthquakes, *J. Asian Earth Sci.* **87,** 56–68, doi: 10.1016/j.jseaes.2014.02.009.

Lermo, J., and F. J. Chávez-García (1993). Site effect evaluation using spectral ratios with only one station, *Bull. Seismol. Soc. Am.* **83,** no. 5, 1574–1594, doi: 10.1785/BSSA0830051574.

Lin, C. M., T. M. Chang, K. L. Wen, Y. C. Huang, H. J. Chiang, and C. H. Kuo (2009). Shallow S-wave Velocity Structures in the Western Coastal Plain of Taiwan, *Terr. Atmos. Ocean. Sci.* **20,** no. 2, 299–308, doi: 10.3319/TAO.2007.12.10.01(T).

Lin, Y. Y., Y. Y. Wen, C. T. Chen, and Y. T. Yen (2025). Strong-motion characteristics of two 2022 M 6.5+ disastrous earthquakes in the southern longitudinal valley, Taiwan, *Earth Planets Space* **77,** no. 1, 33, doi: 10.1186/s40623-024-02128-y.

Liu, K. S., T. C. Shin, and Y. B. Tsai (1999). A free-field strong motion network in Taiwan: TSMIP, *Terr. Atmos. Ocean. Sci.* **10,** no. 2, 377–396, doi: 10.3319/TAO.1999.10.2.377(T).

Loviknes, K., P. Bergamo, D. Fäh, and F. Cotton (2025). Systematic assessment of nonlinear soil behavior at KiK-net sites in Japan: Thresholds and controlling site factors, *Earthq. Spectra* **41,** no. 3, 2278–2310, doi: 10.1177/87552930251325729.

Nakamura, Y. (1989). A method for dynamic characteristics estimation of subsurface using microtremor on the ground surface, *Q. Rep. Railway Tech. Res. Inst.* **30,** no. 1, 25–33.

Noguchi, S., and T. Sasatani (2008). Quantification of degree of nonlinear site response, *14th World Conference on Earthquake Engineering*, Beijing, China, paper ID: 03-03-0049.

Noguchi, S., and T. Sasatani (2011). Nonlinear soil response and its effects on strong ground motions during the 2003 Miyagi-Oki intraslab earthquake, *Zisin* **63,** 165–187.

Régnier, J., H. Cadet, L. F. Bonilla, E. Bertrand, and J. F. Semblat (2013). Assessing nonlinear behavior of soils in seismic site response: Statistical analysis on KiK-net strong-motion data, *Bull. Seismol. Soc. Am.* **103,** no. 3, 1750–1770, doi: 10.1785/0120120240.

Ren, Y., R. Wen, X. Yao, and K. Ji (2017). Five parameters for the evaluation of the soil nonlinearity during the Ms8.0 Wenchuan earthquake using the HVSR method, *Earth Planets Space* **69,** 1–17, doi: 10.1186/s40623-017-0702-7.

Sato, K., T. Kokusho, M. Matsumoto, and E. Yamada (1996). Nonlinear seismic response and soil property during strong motion, *Soils Found.* **36,** 41–52, doi: 10.3208/sandf.36.Special_41.

Seed, H. B., and I. M. Idriss (1970). Soil moduli and damping factors for dynamic response analysis, *Report No. EERC 70-10*, Earthquake Engineering Research Center, University of California, Berkeley, California.

Shi, J., and D. Asimaki (2017). From stiffness to strength: Formulation and validation of a hybrid hyperbolic nonlinear soil model for site-response analyses, *Bull. Seismol. Soc. Am.* **107,** no. 3, 1336–1355, doi: 10.1785/0120150287.

Shyu, J. B. H., Y. H. Yin, C. H. Chen, Y. R. Chuang, and S. C. Liu (2020). Updates to the on-land seismogenic structure source database by the Taiwan Earthquake Model (TEM) project for seismic hazard analysis of Taiwan, *Terr. Atmos. Ocean Sci.* **31,** no. 4, 469–478, doi: 10.3319/TAO.2020.06.08.01.

Su, C. M., Y. Y. Wen, and C. T. Chen (2025). Fast report: Strong-motion characteristics of 2025 ML 6.4 Dapu earthquake, Taiwan, *Terr. Atmos. Ocean. Sci.* **36,** no. 1, 8, doi: 10.1007/s44195-025-00094-w.

Thornley, J. D., U. Dutta, J. Douglas, and Z. J. Yang (2021). Nonlinear site effects from the 30 November 2018 Anchorage, Alaska, earthquake, *Bull. Seismol. Soc. Am.* **111,** no. 4, 2112–2120, doi: 10.1785/0120200347.

Trifunac, M. D., and M. I. Todorovska (1996). Nonlinear soil response —1994 Northridge, California, earthquake, *J. Geotech. Eng.* **122,** no. 9, 725–735, doi: 10.1061/(ASCE)0733-9410(1996)122:9(725).

Tsai, C. C., and H. W. Liu (2017). Site response analysis of vertical ground motion in consideration of soil nonlinearity, *Soil Dynam. Earthq. Eng.* **102,** 124–136, doi: 10.1016/j.soildyn.2017.08.024.

Vucetic, M., and R. Dobry (1991). Effect of soil plasticity on cyclic response, *J. Geotech. Eng.* **117,** no. 1, 89–107, doi: 10.1061/(ASCE)0733-9410(1991)117:1(89).

Wang, Z., J. Sun, E. Ito, H. Kawase, and S. Matsushima (2023). Empirical method for deriving horizontal site amplification factors considering nonlinear soil behaviors based on K-NET and KiK-net records throughout Japan, *Bull. Earthq. Eng.* **21,** no. 9, 4191–4216, doi: 10.1007/s10518-023-01712-z.

Wen, K. L., I. A. Beresnev, and Y. T. Yeh (1994). Nonlinear soil amplification inferred from downhole strong seismic motion data, *Geophys. Res. Lett.* **21,** no. 24, 2625–2628, doi: 10.1029/94GL02407.

Wen, K. L., T. M. Chang, C. M. Lin, and H. J. Chiang (2006). Identification of nonlinear site response using the H/V spectral ratio method, *Terr. Atmos. Ocean. Sci.* **17,** no. 3, 533, doi: 10.3319/TAO.2006.17.3.533(T).

Wu, C., Z. Peng, and D. Assimaki (2009). Temporal changes in site response associated with the strong ground motion of the 2004 M w 6.6 Mid-Niigata earthquake sequences in Japan, *Bull. Seismol. Soc. Am.* **99,** no. 6, 3487–3495, doi: 10.1785/0120090108.

Wu, C., Z. Peng, and Y. Ben-Zion (2010). Refined thresholds for nonlinear ground motion and temporal changes of site response associated with medium-size earthquakes, *Geophys. J. Int.* **182,** no. 3, 1567–1576, doi: 10.1111/j.1365-246X.2010.04704.x.

Wu, H. Y., H. C. Liu, L. C. Kao, K. E. Ching, C. C. Chen, C. F. You, T. C. Yi, Y. H. Chen, B. L. Wu, and C. J. Chen (2025). Potential geological risks from mud diatremes in the orogen regime of Southwestern Taiwan, *Sci. Rep.* **15,** no. 1, 7666, doi: 10.1038/s41598-025-91915-y.

Wu, L. C. (1999). Sedimentary environment analysis and stratigraphic correlation in Chianan coastal plain (in Chinese), *Central Geol. Surv. Rept. 88-015*, 1–212.

Yang, C. C. B., W. S. Chen, L. C. Wu, and C. W. Lin (2007). Active deformation front delineated by drainage pattern analysis and vertical movement rates, southwestern Coastal Plain of Taiwan, *J. Asian Earth Sci.* **31,** no. 3, 251–264, doi: 10.1016/j.jseaes.2006.07.026.

Zhou, Y., H. Wang, R. Wen, Y. Ren, and K. Ji (2020). Insights on nonlinear soil behavior and its variation with time at strong-motion stations during the Mw7.8 Kaikōura, New Zealand earthquake, *Soil Dynam. Earthq. Eng.* **136,** 106215, doi: 10.1016/j.soildyn.2020.106215.

Zhu, C., M. Pilz, and F. Cotton (2020). Evaluation of a novel application of earthquake HVSR in site-specific amplification estimation, *Soil Dynam. Earthq. Eng.* **139,** 106301, doi: 10.1016/j.soildyn.2020.106301.

Manuscript received 9 May 2025
Published online 17 December 2025

Mechanism of Dynamic Triggering for Slab-Related Fluid-Induced Tremors Occurred in Nanao, Taiwan

Yi-Hsuan Wu[*1,2], Wu-Cheng Chi[1], Liam Chai[3], Akiko Toh[4], M. Megawati[1], and Chin-Jen Lin[1]

ABSTRACT

The origin of nonvolcanic tremors has been linked to different ways the crust slips on a fault in the presence of fluids. We collected the tremors recorded by a seismic array in Nanao, Taiwan, and found a class of high-frequency tremors among ambient tremors and triggered tremors. The *f-k* analysis results and the large moveout implied that the triggered tremors originated from moving sources beneath the array. With seismogeodetic inversion, the triggered tremors occurred when dilation was larger than 10^{-8}, similar to the deep low-frequency fluid-related seismic tremors in the Nankai trough. Based on previous tomographic studies, the partial melting due to the dehydration of the subducting Ryukyu slab is distributed along the slab edge and migrates upward near Nanao. Such a partial melting at shallow depth can potentially elevate the pore-fluid temperature and the pressure. According to these findings, we proposed a scenario analogous to fluid-related acoustic emission lab experiments. Dehydration near the edge of a subducting slab provides fluid and heat, and the dilational strains from the teleseismic waves cause decompression and therefore the fluid motions. Teleseismically perturbed fluids helped create at least some of the triggered tremors. This could be among the first field examples of dynamically triggered tremors associated with moving fluids from a slab and its edge.

KEY POINTS

- The tectonic setting and potential fluids from subduction make Nanao ideal for tremor studies.
- We find a set of high-frequency tremors (HFTs) in Nanao with large moveout following the Tohoku earthquake.
- The mechanism of the tremors appears to be associated with decompression and fluid–rock interaction.

Supplemental Material

INTRODUCTION

Dynamic triggering of seismic events is an active research topic with broad implications for earthquake physics, seismic hazard mitigation, and the understanding of fault mechanics. Observational studies of dynamic triggering help uncover stresses, perturbations, and environmental conditions that facilitate the initiation of seismic events.

In Taiwan, triggered tremors have been documented in multiple regions, with particular concentration in the southern Central Range (Peng and Chao, 2008; Chao *et al.*, 2012). These tremors exhibit strong sensitivity to teleseismic surface waves, with small dynamic stress perturbations (≥2.86 kPa) capable of triggering events in critically stressed zones (Yeh, 2011). Beyond the well-known tremor zone beneath the southern Central Range, Ide and Chen (2024) identified ~7000 tremor events and discovered several new tremor zones along the mountain belt, including one extremely close to Nanao. These tremors occur at the termination of the subducting slabs and near the deep (25–50 km) extension of the Central Range fault, where repeating earthquakes cluster at a depth of 10–25 km near the termination of subducting slabs and deep faults (Ide and Chen, 2024).

Unlike the deep episodic tremors observed in Cascadia and Japan, tremors in Taiwan tend to occur at shallower depths (~15–35 km) and exhibit strong spatial clustering (Chuang *et al.*, 2014; Ide and Chen, 2024). In addition, tremor activity in the hotspots, such as the southern Central Range, is strongly

1. Institute of Earth Sciences, Academia Sinica, Taipei, Taiwan, https://orcid.org/0000-0002-8151-0592 (Y-HW); https://orcid.org/0000-0002-6111-6379 (W-CC); https://orcid.org/0009-0003-0965-6292 (MM); 2. Climate Change Research Center, National Environmental Research Academy, Taoyuan, Taiwan; 3. Taipei American School, Taipei, Taiwan, https://orcid.org/0000-0003-3195-6980 (LC); 4. Japan Agency for Marine-Earth Science and Technology (JAMSTEC), Yokosuka, Kanagawa, Japan, https://orcid.org/0000-0002-7800-9713 (AT)

*Corresponding author: maomaowyh@gmail.com

Cite this article as Wu, Y.-H., W.-C. Chi, L. Chai, A. Toh, M. Megawati, and C.-J. Lin (2025). Mechanism of Dynamic Triggering for Slab-Related Fluid-Induced Tremors Occurred in Nanao, Taiwan, *Bull. Seismol. Soc. Am.* **116**, 149–161, doi: 10.1785/0120240256

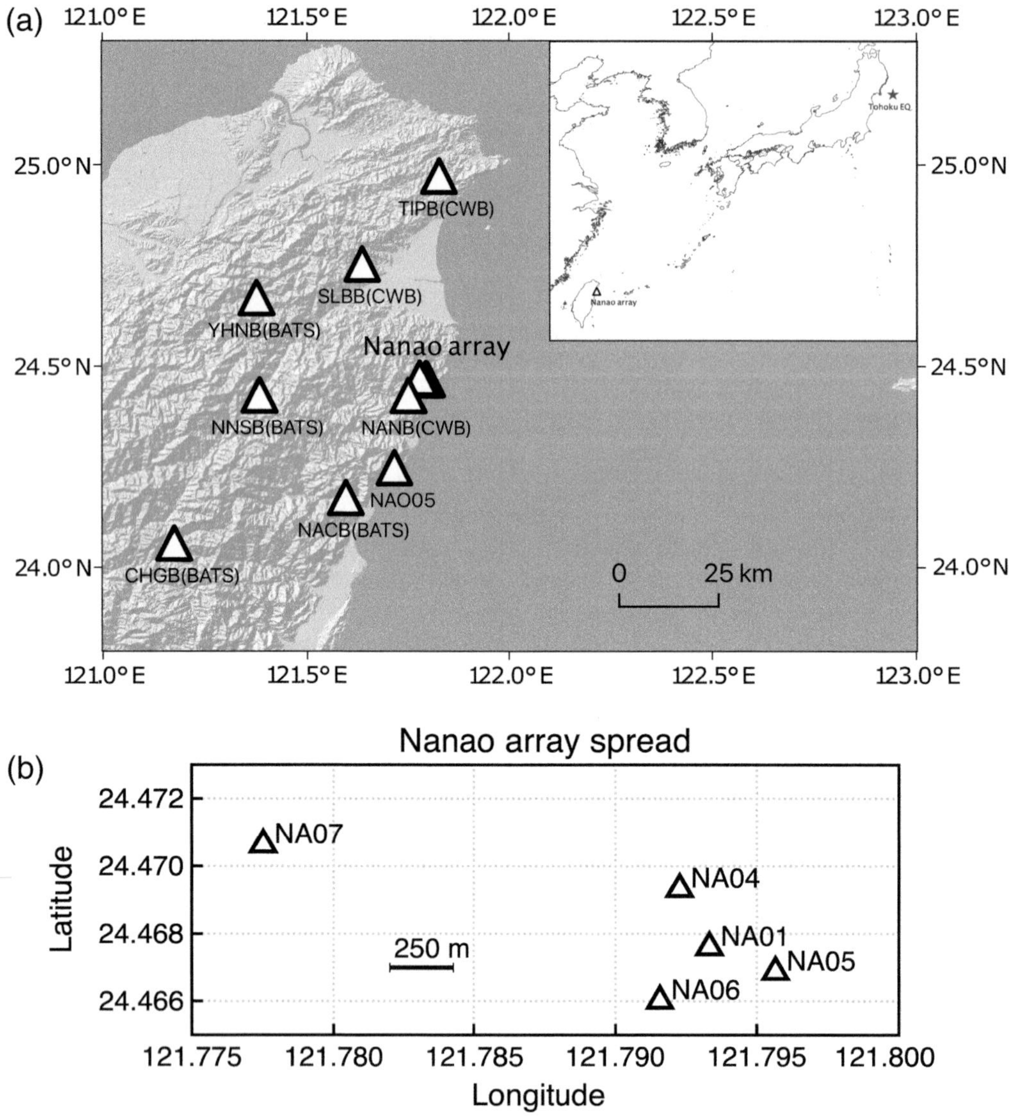

Figure 1. (a) The broadband stations in and around Nanao array. Some also equipped with collocated strong motion sensors. (Inset) Map showing the relative locations of the 11 March 2011 Tohoku earthquake epicenter (red star) and the Nanao array (black triangle) in northeastern Taiwan. This overview illustrates the distance and azimuth of the teleseismic source relative to the study area. (b) The Nanao array stations (NAO05 not included). The red star indicates the 11 March 2011 Tohoku earthquake epicenter. The coordinates of stations are listed in Table S1. The color version of this figure is available only in the electronic edition.

linked to high pore-fluid pressures and metamorphic dehydration reactions (Peng and Chao, 2008; Yeh, 2011; Ide and Chen, 2024). The role of high pore-fluid pressure and metamorphism was first proposed by Chuang *et al.* (2014) and further developed using a refined tectonic framework by Chen *et al.* (2018). More recently, Ide and Chen (2024) made significant observational contributions by detecting and locating ambient tremors in the same region. Nanao, however, is located at a tectonic transition zone where the edge of the Philippine Sea plate subducting slab subducts beneath the Eurasian plate. This setting introduces complex slab–fluid interactions, making Nanao a unique site for understanding fluid-driven tremor mechanisms.

Dynamic triggering can occur when teleseismic surface waves induce transient stress changes in the crust, as demonstrated by Velasco *et al.* (2008), who found that 12 out of 15 M_w 7.0+ earthquakes resulted in increased seismicity globally. Triggered earthquakes commonly occur in geothermal/volcanic regions associated with extensional and transtensional environment (Hill and Prejean, 2007), as well as in tectonically active plate boundaries, in which faults may be critically stressed and more susceptible to dynamic perturbation (Hill *et al.*, 1993; Hough *et al.*, 2003). Tremors, typically related to fluids near the fault zone, have also been dynamically triggered.

Several mechanisms have been proposed for dynamic triggering (Hill and Prejean, 2007), primarily Coulomb failure via different frictional laws (Gomberg *et al.*, 1998, 2005; Gomberg, 2001; Perfettini *et al.*, 2003; Gomberg and Johnson, 2005; Johnson and Jia, 2005; Hill, 2008), and the excitation of crustal fluids (Linde *et al.*, 1994; Brodsky *et al.*, 1998, 2003; Hill *et al.*, 2002). The tremors examined in this study are primarily interpreted as fluid related.

The 2011 M_w 9.0 Tohoku earthquake (11 March 2011 at 05:46:23 UTC) generated the largest teleseismic wavetrains (2 cm ground displacement at epicentral distance of ~2485 km) recorded by the six-element Nanao seismic array (NA01, NA04, NA05, NA06, NA07, and NAO05; see Table S1, available in the supplemental material to this article) in northeastern Taiwan (Fig. 1; note that NAO05 is not included due to its more distant aperture). Taiwan's active tectonics, due to the collision between Eurasian and Philippine Sea plates, provides a natural laboratory to study the dynamic triggering of tremors. The Nanao array, situated at a complex plate boundary with flipped subduction polarities, enables array-based analysis of crustal deformation during teleseismic wavetrains, even in the absence of direct strain meter measurements.

This study examines the seismic response of the Nanao seismic array to the Tohoku earthquake and explores whether the observed tremors following the Tohoku earthquake were triggered by fluids originating from the subducting slab, reaching the shallow crust beneath Nanao.

DATA DESCRIPTION: NANAO ARRAY AND THE HIGH-FREQUENCY TREMOR

The town of Nanao is located just to the north of the Coastal Range in eastern Taiwan, an accreted arc to the passive margin, near the juncture of two convergent boundaries at the western end of the Ryukyu arc, where uplift of Taiwan island is waning as a result of subduction polarity flip (e.g., Teng, 1996; Huang *et al.*, 2012; van Avendonk *et al.*, 2016). To the south, the Eurasian plate is subducting to the east underneath the Philippine Sea plate. To the east, the Philippine Sea plate is subducting northward underneath the Eurasian plate. The rollback of northward subduction results in both the opening of the Okinawa trough and the Yilan plain. The interactions between the plates cause active local seismicity and surface deformation.

The Nanao array is a semipermanent seismic array installed by the Institute of Earth Sciences (IES), Academia Sinica, of Taiwan (courtesy of Taiwan Earthquake Center Instrument Pool). It is located up-dip of the slab edge and therefore provides an opportunity to detect the tremors with low-amplitude ground motions that are typically masked by large earthquakes and potentially lead to a better understanding of small earthquakes and tremor triggering mechanisms. The sensors are located two meters below the surface in a vault-type station to reduce background noise. This array was partially operational in 2011; six stations equipped with accelerometer sensors were available at the time of the Tohoku earthquake (NA01, NA04, NA05, NA06, NA07, and NAO05; see Fig. 1 and Table S1), with three of them additionally collocated with broadband seismometers. The accelerometer (Kinemetrics EpiSensor) and the seismometer (Trillium Compact) feature wide-frequency responses from DC to 200 Hz and 120 s to 100 Hz, respectively.

The array consists of three arms with concentric circles geometry, covering a radius of ~250 m, and was designed for array-processing techniques such as *f-k* analysis and strain inversion. However, its small aperture and limited station coverage impose constraints on certain processing techniques, particularly for high-resolution strain estimation. In addition, because only six stations were operational during the Tohoku earthquake, strain inversion results must be interpreted with consideration of potential uncertainties introduced by station spacing and data resolution.

We studied the velocity seismograms using vertical components of Nanao array and compared their waveforms with the stations of the larger regional Broadband Array in Taiwan for Seismology (BATS, Institute of Earth Sciences, 1996) to examine the seismic characteristics (Fig. 2, Figs. S1–S9). Although the NNSB station was available during the 2011 Tohoku earthquake, no tremor signals were detected at this station during the study period, as shown in the supplementary material. In addition, the LATB station, which was important for later studies (e.g., Ide and Chen, 2024), was not installed until 2013, limiting the array coverage at the time of the 2011 events.

Intermittent high-frequency signals make the waveforms stand out from BATS records. Furthermore, the spectrograms of continuous wavelet transforms (CWTs) (Fig. 2b) show two prominent high-frequency bands, one at 2–8 Hz and the other at 10–30 Hz. In addition, there are two prominent low-frequency bands at 0.2–0.5 Hz and 0.03–0.06 Hz; the former overlaps microseism and is beyond the present scope. We applied different filters according to these frequency bands, except the 0.2–0.5 Hz one, in an attempt to identify and classify seismic events. We picked several time windows before (Figs. S1–S4), during (Fig. 2), and after (Figs. S5–S9) the Tohoku teleseismic waves had passed through Nanao to study their time-dependent characteristics. Each time window shows one-hour-long waveforms (Fig. 2a, Figs. S1a–S9a) and their CWTs (Fig. 2b, Figs. S1b–S9b).

We observed an abundance of high-frequency signals (2–8 Hz and 10–30 Hz) in the Nanao array, and some of them occurred in the company of those of the very low frequency (0.03–0.06 Hz) that can come from surface waves or very-low-frequency events. When local events or teleseismic events took place, the 2–8 Hz signals were usually observed across all the stations in northeastern Taiwan, but more of them were separately found in the Nanao array. The synchronous signals observed in the Nanao array before the Tohoku earthquake in the time interval 2500–3000 s of Figure S1 are likely coming from a broadband slow earthquake, a phenomenon that has been demonstrated by Masuda *et al.* (2020). The high-frequency signals of the tremor can be radiated from broadband slow earthquakes like this event. However, the accompanying >1 Hz tremor signals in Nanao are not only shown by 2–8 Hz signals that are usually observed in other regions, but also in 10–30 Hz. In addition, the filtered waveforms and the CWT show that the latter has stronger energy than the former by the plausible broadband slow earthquake (Fig. S1).

The signals with frequency >10 Hz are rarely discussed as usually attributed to noise or local and surface sources. Nanao array stations sat in a remote area with less traffic noise but with a train track nearby. For our Nanao data, to distinguish the tremors from the wind noise and train noise, we characterized the different signals from the sources. For the tremors with both 2–8 Hz and >10 Hz signals, hereafter called the high-frequency tremors (HFTs), the signals show the characteristics of nonvolcanic tremor: none impulsive onset and minutes-long duration recorded across the array without clear *P* and *S* phases (Obara, 2002; Beroza and Ide, 2011; Obara and Kato, 2016). They are different from the wind noise that has high-frequency

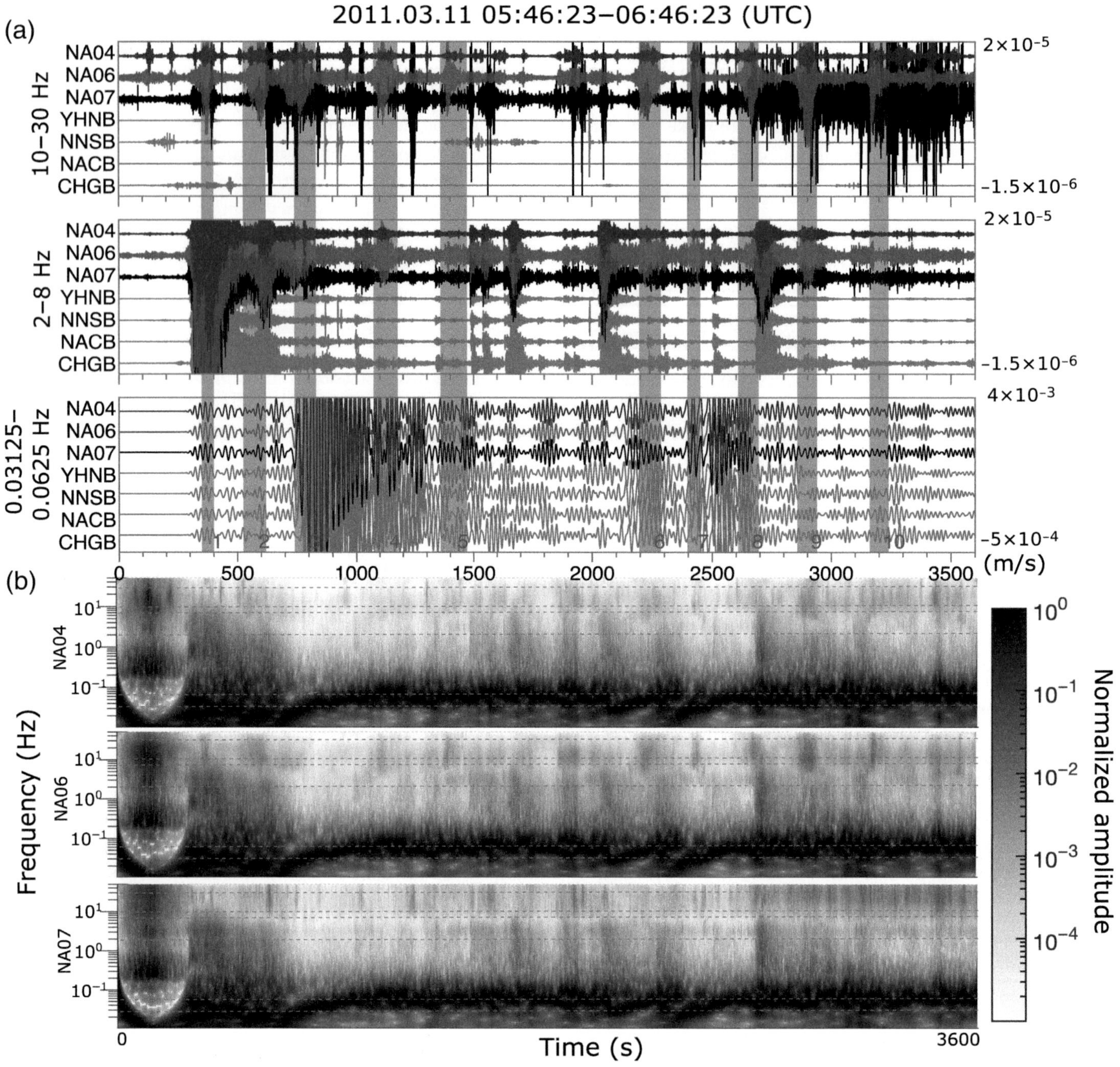

Figure 2. (a) The filtered velocity seismograms in the vertical component. The gray strips show the time windows of the triggered tremors, and the red numbers denote the triggered tremor sequence discovered within one hour after the Tohoku earthquake. (b) The continuous wavelet transform (CWT) spectrogram when the teleseismic wave of the Tohoku earthquake passes through (coseismic period). The dashed lines outline the frequency bands 10–30 Hz, 2–8 Hz, and 0.03125–0.0625 Hz (top to bottom). The color version of this figure is available only in the electronic edition.

signals produced by interaction with surface objects or vegetation but the frequency band drops to 1–8 Hz for borehole seismometers even during elevated wind condition (Johnson *et al.*, 2019). In the study by Johnson *et al.* (2019), a densely configured array with a nominal station spacing of ~30 m across a 350 × 300 m area (Sagebrush Flat site) was deployed to evaluate wind-generated signals. The high density of the array allowed for detailed analysis of the spatial variability and characteristics of wind-induced ground motion, as well as its interaction with surface structures. In contrast, the Nanao array's configuration, while effective for detecting seismic tremors, lacks such high density. Given the rapid attenuation of wind-generated signals over short distances, wind noise is unlikely to produce coherent tremor-like signals across our array setup. Besides, wind noise is more prominent on horizontals than on vertical components. The train track lies south of the Nanao array, having back azimuths ranging from ~120° to 240°. The train noise contributes some part of the high-frequency signal because the closest part of the track is only ~160 m from NA06. The train noise captured

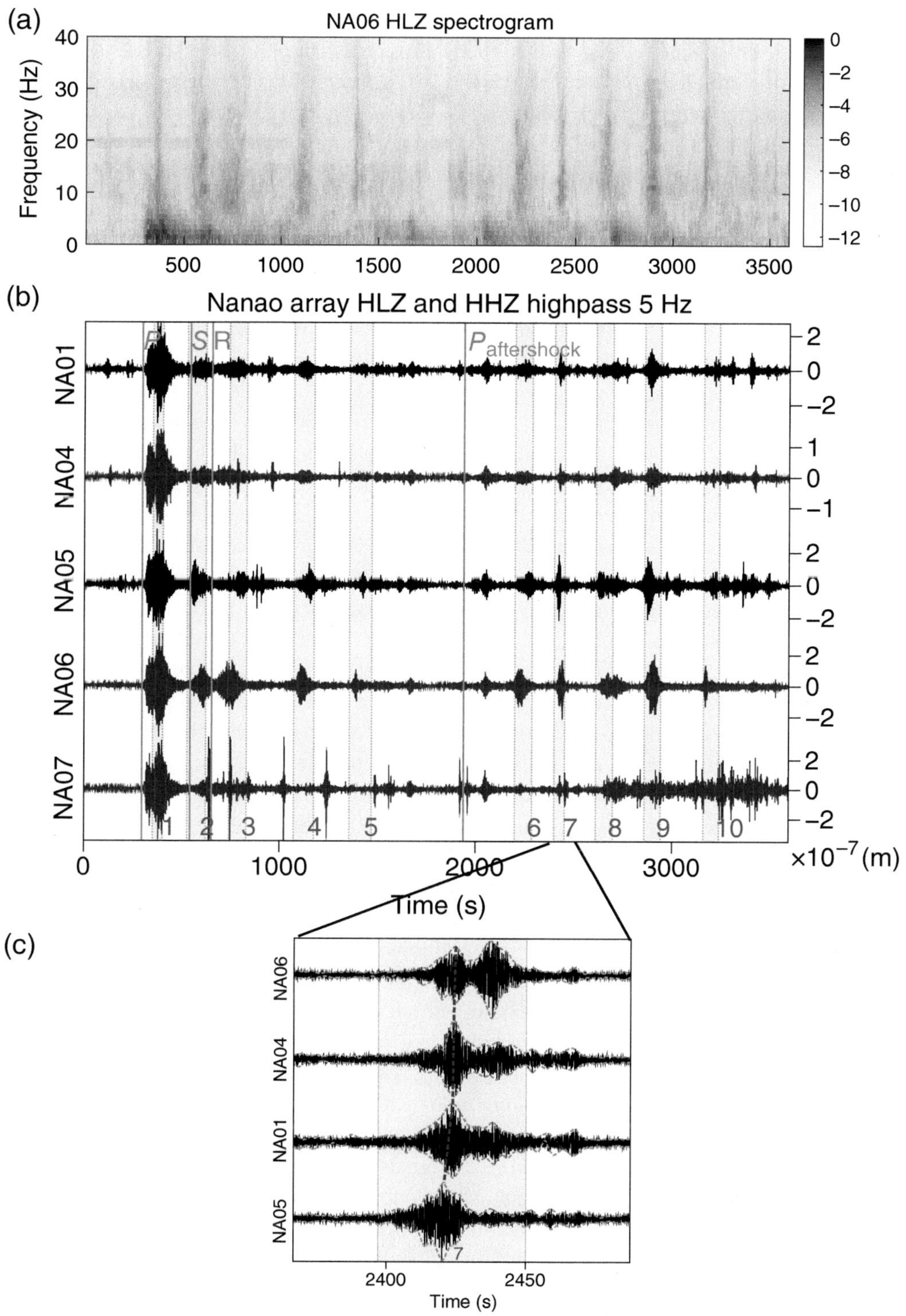

Figure 3. The (a) spectrogram and (b) waveform showing triggered tremor in one hour after the 2011 M_w 9.0 Tohoku earthquake. (b) The 5 Hz high-pass-filtered displacement waveform integrated from acceleration (HLZ, in black) and velocity (HHZ, in red). The gray strips show the time window of the triggered tremors identified by the visual inspection. (c) The zoomed-in window of tremor 7. The amplitudes of waveforms were normalized. The orange dashed lines are the envelopes of the waveforms, and the red dash line connects the maximum peaks of the envelopes and shows irregular moveout from one station to another. The color version of this figure is available only in the electronic edition.

by the Nanao array shows similar characteristics to the tremors, such as coherence signal throughout the stations (Fig. S10a,b) and high frequencies. However, they do show different time-dependent behavior from tremors: their energy first concentrates in the frequency band 2–5 Hz and then radiate to 20–30 Hz, the dispersion represents a chirped signal in the CWT spectrogram (e.g., Figs. S3b, S7b, S9b, and S10b). Furthermore, the train signal has a duration of about 10 min and a more impulsive onset distinguished from the tremors.

Excluding wind and train noises, there are still other high-frequency signals characterized by HFTs. Signals that occur most of the time and are not clearly associated with other seismic events are considered ambient tremors. Some tremors that coincide with larger teleseismic phases or local earthquakes are considered triggered tremors.

DATA PROCESSING: TRIGGERED TREMOR AND STRAIN INVERSION

We removed the instrument response and trend and transformed the waveform into displacement seismogram. To detect the triggered events hidden within the high-amplitude arrivals of the mainshock, we applied a 5 Hz high-pass filter following Gonzalez-Huizar and Velasco (2011) and Peng and Chao (2008). The primary reason for selecting a 5 Hz high-pass filter instead of a 1–10 Hz or 2–8 Hz band-pass filter is that mainshock waveforms exhibit unusually strong *P*- and *S*-coda signals extending up to 5 Hz. In addition, tremor signals in Nanao inherently contain energy above 10 Hz. After the high-pass filtering, we visually inspected both the seismogram and spectrogram (Fig. 3) to identify the events exhibiting characteristics of dynamically triggered tremors, as reported in previous studies (Jiang *et al.*, 2010; Chao *et al.*, 2013; Sun *et al.*, 2015; Velasco *et al.*, 2008).

To distinguish the tremor signals from teleseismic and train signals, we applied additional analysis techniques. Triggered tremors may be obscured by the strong *P*-wave coda. To address this, we decomposed the HHZ velocity waveforms into intrinsic mode functions (IMFs) (Fig. S11) using empirical mode decomposition, which captures oscillatory modes at different frequency scales within a signal. This decomposition technique allows for the analysis of components with varying frequency and energy over time, making it particularly useful for isolating tremor signals buried in noise.

In Figure S11,b, the extracted higher-order modes at stations NA06 and NANB are displayed, respectively. The IMFs from NA06 reveal distinct high-frequency components, while those from NANB exhibit significantly lower frequency content, highlighting the contrast between the local tremor signals and regional/teleseismic signals. IMF1, the first extracted mode, represents the highest frequency content. We applied Hilbert–Huang Transform (HHT) to analyze its instantaneous frequency and energy. In Figure S11c, IMF1 and the average instantaneous energy and frequency were derived from HHZ velocity waveform data for both Nanao array stations and the NANB station, with the instantaneous values smoothed using a 10 s moving window. The time series spans from 5000 s before the Tohoku earthquake to 8600 s after, including the coseismic period. The one-hour time window analyzed for the triggered tremor is represented by a black line in the left panel. The right panel presents a zoom-in of the 250–850 s window, highlighted in yellow in the left panel, and the gray strips within this window present the period of tremor 1 3.

During the 250–850 s window following the Tohoku earthquake (right panels of Fig. S11c), IMF1 from NANB exhibited a frequency drop and energy increase when the *P* wave arrived, gradually returning to high frequency and low energy about 500 s. In contrast, IMF1 from the Nanao array stations displayed several frequency peaks while the energy dropped during the tremor 1. The IMF1 from NANB, the closest seismic station outside the array, consistently showed low instantaneous frequency, never exceeding 3 Hz, unlike the signals in the Nanao array. The HHT results from the NANB waveform suggest that the *P* wave and its coda are not dominated by signals higher than 10 Hz. This is consistent with the common observations that typical teleseismic waves contain signals with frequencies less than 1 or 2 Hz (e.g., Oki *et al.*, 2004). Thus, we interpreted the >10 Hz signals following the *P* wave observed in array stations as locally triggered tremors.

The tremors 6, 8, 9, and 10 might coincide with train passages based on current timetables, and the signals may overlap. To investigate this, we performed frequency–wavenumber (*f-k*) analysis for the train signal (Fig. S12) using waveforms filtered between 0.5 and 20 Hz from 10 min of data starting from 20 July 2021 UTC 13:40, a time with confirmed train activity based on schedule data. This analysis showed that the back azimuth of the train signal shifts from ~240° to 120°, depending on the train's travel path. Although the train signal partially overlaps with tremor frequency bands, its significantly lower phase velocity (<1 km/s) distinguish it from tremor signals observed in the array. These findings led us to interpret that the train signals can be separated from the tremor signals.

Further *f-k* analysis (Fig. S13) on the triggered tremors using waveforms filtered in both the 10–30 Hz (Fig. S13a) and 2–8 Hz (Fig. S13b) bands revealed a consistent back azimuth of ~225°, suggesting that both HFTs and typical frequency tremors originate from the same region. However, the results of *f-k* analysis for the triggered tremors using waveforms filtered at 10–30 Hz show mixed back azimuths distinct from about 225° with lower velocity. The HFTs appear to be uniquely sensitive to specific environmental factors present at Nanao. The local geological and fluid conditions may facilitate HFT generation because they are not commonly observed outside this immediate region.

To better understand the behavior of the teleseismic waves and their impact on the triggered tremors, we applied a strain inversion method following Spudich *et al.* (1995) and Spudich and Fletcher (2008, 2009). This method assumes that the displacement gradient tensor is spatially uniform beneath the array, an assumption that holds best for long-wavelength teleseismic signals. To estimate the potential bias introduced by these assumptions, we performed strain inversions using multiple station configurations (Fig. 4). The resulting time series remain consistent across different subarrays, but inversions incorporating more distant stations (e.g., NAO05) showed reduced maximum strain values, suggesting that station spacing influences strain resolution and the larger station spacing might violate the assumption of rigid body rotation for high-frequency signals. As a measure of uncertainty, we calculated the misfit ratio for each inversion following Spudich *et al.* (1995), quantifying the proportion of total displacement unexplained by a rigid strain model. Across the different configurations, the misfit ratio ranged from 10% to 15%, implying that the inversion successfully captures first-order strain variations while potentially overlooking finer-scale deformation features.

We selected Spudich's method to calculate the shear strain and dilation because it is reliable for deriving vertical rotational synthetics using horizontal waveforms from array observations (e.g., Huang, 2003; Suryanto *et al.*, 2006; Chi *et al.*, 2011; Donner *et al.*, 2017; Yuan *et al.*, 2020). A detailed derivation is documented in appendix A of Spudich *et al.* (1995) and the text of Spudich and Fletcher (2009). A key assumption in this method is that the displacement gradient tensor is spatially uniform beneath the array, which is valid when the seismic

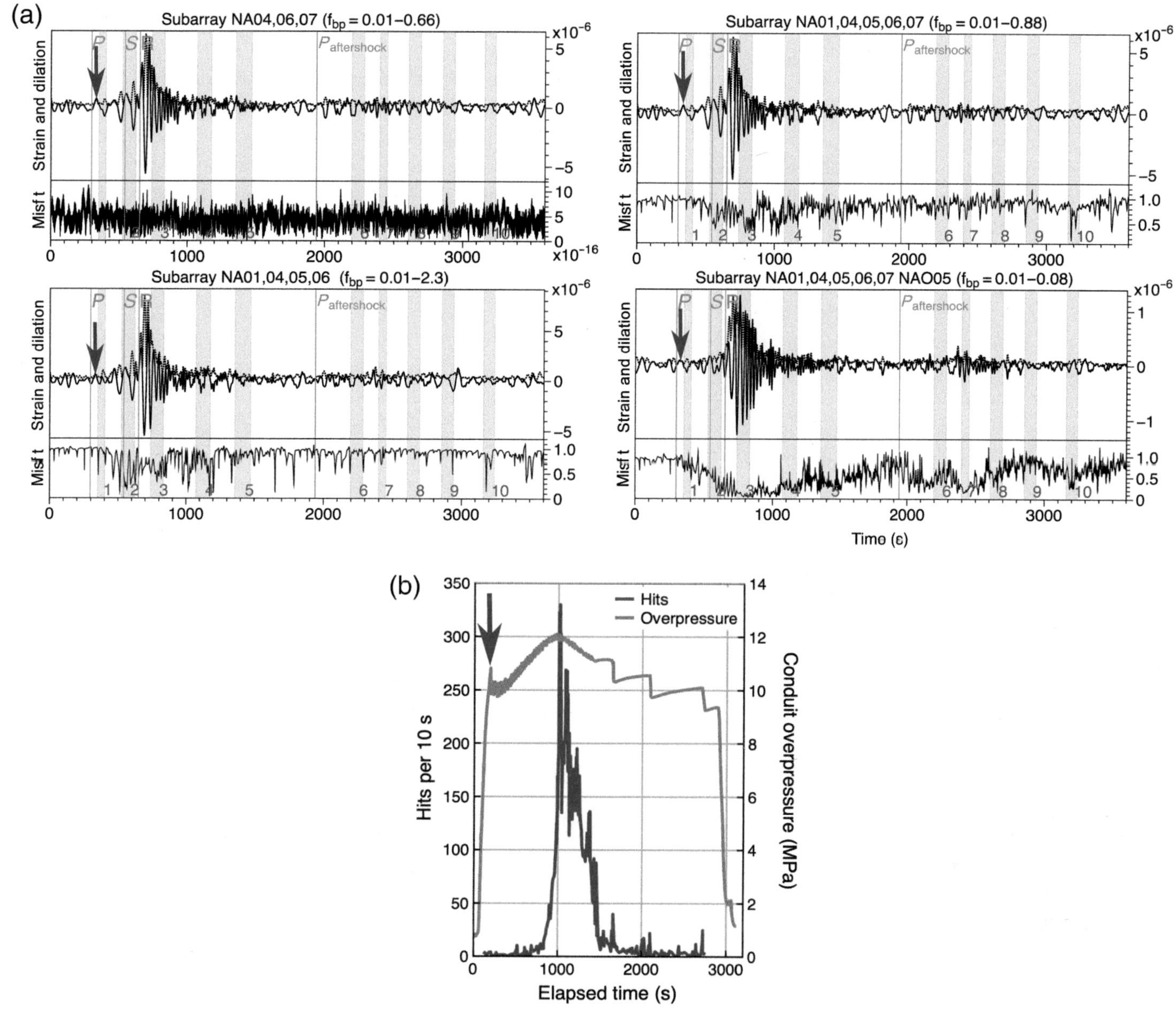

Figure 4. The comparison of the dilation in field and laboratory overpressure. (a) Time series of shear strains (dashed line), dilations, and misfits inverted using the method of Spudich *et al.* (1995) based on four different subarray configurations. The stations implemented in the inversion are [NA04, 06, 07], [NA01, 04, 05, 06], [NA01, 04, 05, 06, 07], and [NA01, 04, 05, 06, 07, NAO05] from the top to the bottom. The gray lines indicate the estimated arrival time of the *P*, *S*, and Rayleigh waves, and the light gray strips show the tremor durations. These inversion results show that the shear strain and dilation are strongly correlated with the arrival of the teleseismic wavetrain, with maximum values occurring shortly after the *P* and surface waves passed. (b) Results from the laboratory experiment showing the conduit overpressure and acoustic emission hit count during pressurization of a heated conduit filled with polymethyl methacrylate (PMMA), modified from Bakker *et al.* (2016). The red circles indicate the first large dilational strain observed in the field data (pointed out by the red arrow), which correlates with the initial drop in conduit overpressure and subsequent occurrence of measurable acoustic emission hits in the experiment. The simultaneous peak in teleseismic-induced dilation in the field data can be linked to the peak of conduit pressure and acoustic emission hit rate, associated with rock failure during the experiment. The color version of this figure is available only in the electronic edition.

source is distant and the incident wave can be approximated as a plane wave. Based on this assumption, seismic signals with wavelength (λ) shorter than four times the array's horizontal extent (h), that is, $\lambda < 4h$, must be filtered out. Given the relationship $\lambda = c/f$, in which c is phase velocity (3 km/s) and f is frequency, the maximum usable frequency is given by $f_{\max} = c/4h$. To ensure reliable inversion, we applied a band-pass filter to each subset of array containing three or more stations, limiting the frequency range to 0.01 Hz–$f_{\max}$ before calculating shear strain and dilation.

Figure S14 presents the filtered waveforms according to the constraints imposed by the strain inversion. The filtered waveforms across different frequency bands at NA06 (Fig. S14a) remained consistent with the raw waveform, whereas waveforms in the 0.01–0.08 Hz range at different stations (Fig. S14b) exhibited high coherence across the array, even at remote stations such as NAO05. This observation further confirms that low-frequency signals were primarily dominated by teleseismic waves, making them suitable for shear strain inversion.

RESULTS

The tremors triggered by the Tohoku earthquake and its M_w 7.9 aftershock are shown in Figure 3, identified as displacement waveforms with extended durations of higher-frequency signals with amplitudes of 10^{-7} m or greater when the teleseismic wavetrains passed by. The time windows of these tremors are listed in Table S2 and are indicated in Figure 3 by gray stripes. Notably, the tremor amplitude at station NA04 was the smallest, compared to the clearer tremor signals recorded at NA05 and NA06.

Although we obtained the back azimuth of the triggered tremor by *f-k* analysis, the large moveout between the stations made a further estimation of the source difficult. The envelope of tremor 7 (Fig. 3c) shows that the apparent velocity accelerated from 90 m/s (NA05–NA01), 220 m/s (NA01–NA04), to 380 m/s (NA04–NA06). The large moveout and the varying apparent velocity imply a moving source, or multiple sources, within the footprint of this array. However, the apparent velocity of tremor 7 exceeds the documented propagation speeds of the typical cultural surface sources, such as the traffic noise, wind, or river water. Seismic signals from traffic-induced vibrations generally exhibit velocities between 26 and 58 m/s, with larger trucks producing stronger vibrations around 50–58 m/s (Riahi and Gerstoft, 2015). Wind-induced seismic background noise is dominant for wind speeds above 3–4 m/s, but its coherence is limited to below 15 Hz, and it lacks consistent high-frequency components (Withers *et al.*, 1996). Given that the observed tremor apparent velocities significantly exceed these values, we interpret the signals as unlikely to originate from nearby cultural noise sources. Instead, we propose that the triggered tremors are generated by tremor sources.

Figure 4 presents the inverted time series of shear strain, dilation, and misfit ratio using different station configurations, as indicated at the top of each panel. The misfit ratio represents the proportion of the total array station displacements not explained by a rigid rotation and strain, as defined in Spudich *et al.* (1995). This ratio helps quantify how well the inversion fits the observed data across different station configurations.

The strain inversion (Fig. 4) showed that the crust beneath the array was strongly deformed during the teleseismic wave, especially the dilation component. The maximum dilation obtained during tremor 3 was almost 10^{-5}, and the maximum dilation during the other tremors was all larger than 10^{-7}. A strong correlation between the shear strain and dilation implied that the triggered tremors are associated with crustal fluid processes (e.g., Dreger *et al.*, 2000; Foulger *et al.*, 2004). Miyazawa and Mori (2006) found deep low-frequency seismic tremors beneath Japan triggered by the 2004 M_w 9.2 Sumatra–Andaman earthquake and demonstrated that volumetric dilation larger than $\sim 10^{-8}$ was the predominant factor for triggering caused by fluid.

The inversions performed with different subarray configurations yielded comparable time series, except for the configuration with six stations that had a very large footprint. Despite minor differences between subarrays, the maximum shear strain and dilation consistently occurred at approximately the same time, around 692 s, coinciding with the arrival of the teleseismic waves.

In this study, shear strain refers to the distortion or change in shape of the material without a volume change. It is a measure of how much deformation occurs in the horizontal plane due to seismic wave passage. Dilation, on the other hand, refers to the change in volume of the material, which can be either compressional (negative dilation) or extensional (positive dilation). Both components are important for understanding how the teleseismic waves deform the medium.

The results show that the trend of both dilation and shear strain is strongly correlated with the passing of the teleseismic wave train. Specifically, dilation began to increase after the *P* wave passed (e.g., during tremors 1 and 6), and it reached its maximum following the arrival of the surface waves (e.g., during tremors 3 and 7).

In the time windows of triggered tremors 1 to 5, the maximum shear strain observed during tremors 1 and 2 was primarily associated with compression (indicated by negative dilation), whereas in tremors 3–5, the shear strain was more influenced by extension (characterized by positive dilation). It is important to emphasize that after the surface waves passed, the shear strain and dilation values became inherently smaller, making it harder to distinguish them.

In addition, we observed that the value of maximum shear strain decreased as more remote stations, such as NA07 and NAO05, were added. This suggests that the increased station spacing affects the resolution of the strain inversion. Despite these variations, the core results remain consistent across different station configurations.

DISCUSSION AND CONCLUSIONS

The tremor activity in Nanao was notably active, with tremors occurring due to the triggering of teleseismic waves, local seismic waves, or being associated with very low-frequency events. The association with very-low-frequency events suggests a link between tremors and deep crustal processes. Observations of VLFEs occurring alongside tremors in subduction zones (Ito *et al.*, 2007; To *et al.*, 2015; Walter *et al.*, 2013) indicate that these events may be controlled by fluid-related stress changes and slow-slip deformation. A significant portion of the tremors were ambient tremors, occurring even during seismically quiet periods. We identified two types of tremors in Nanao: typical tremor with signal in the 2–8 Hz range, and HFTs exhibiting both 2–8 Hz and >10 Hz signals. These HFTs occurred as both ambient and triggered events. This suggests that environmental conditions, including the proximity to a shallow heat and fluid source, elevated pore-fluid pressures, and a highly stressed regime resulting from the tectonic transition between subduction and collision, predominantly control tremor occurrence and distinguish HFTs from typical tremors. External forces, including the teleseismic waves, local earthquakes, or plate motion, may then act as perturbations that further trigger tremor activity.

HFT signals were observed both during and before the Tohoku earthquake. This temporal distinction implies different mechanisms behind pre-Tohoku and teleseismically triggered tremors. The pre-Tohoku tremors are likely driven by continuous, localized subsurface processes, potentially involving fluid migration along fault zones or low-frequency fault-slip events. Such background processes are common in tectonically active regions and can generate tremor independently of external triggers. This type of activity is consistent with models of slow-slip events or localized fluid pressure fluctuations facilitating tremor without requiring large external seismic events (Obara *et al.*, 2010; Yang and Peng, 2013; Chen *et al.*, 2018; McGuire *et al.*, 2018; Martínez-Garzón *et al.*, 2023).

During the Tohoku mainshock, the passage of teleseismic waves introduced significant dynamic stress, likely altered the regional stress field and fluid pressure within the crust, thereby enhancing tremor activity. This interaction between teleseismic waves and subsurface fluids may have temporarily amplified fluid migration and pore-pressure changes, triggering additional tremors differently from background mechanisms. The increased tremor activity during the Tohoku earthquake reflects a combination of local fault conditions and enhanced fluid dynamics due to the large-amplitude teleseismic waves. Distinguishing between pre-Tohoku and Tohoku-induced tremors provides a comprehensive understanding of tremor generation in the study area and underscores the roles of both background tectonic processes and dynamic stress changes from distant earthquakes.

The HFTs are distinctive to the Nanao array because of its unique geological setting. Although the Nanao array's dense station coverage and high sampling rate improve their resolution, it is primarily the underlying tectonic and fluid conditions that make this region particularly prone to HFT generation. The mechanism of the moving source for the triggered tremors may relate to the localization of the HFTs in this region. The Nanao array is situated at the junction of the Philippine Sea plate and the Eurasian plate, in which long-term deformation transitions from contraction in the south to extension in the north. This interaction may create an environment with high-stress gradients and openings along pre-existing cracks or faults. Given this setting, fluids from slab dehydration and its edge could propagate along these pathways and trigger tremors.

The interpretation that these tremors originate from fluids is supported by multiple factors. First, the presence of active hot springs near Nanao suggests ongoing hydrothermal activity, a common indicator of deep fluid circulation. Second, previous studies (e.g., Shelly *et al.*, 2006; Chao *et al.*, 2013) have shown that tectonic tremors are often linked to fluid migration and high pore-fluid pressures in fault zones. Finally, seismic tomography studies indicate that tremor-generating regions in Taiwan frequently coincide with low-V_S and high-V_P/V_S anomalies, which are characteristic of fluid-saturated rock. These observations collectively support the hypothesis that crustal fluids play a significant role in tremor generation in the Nanao region.

A seismic tomographic study by Lin *et al.* (2004) identified a low V_S but high-V_P/V_S sausage-like body, interpreted as resulting from the dehydration process of the subducting Philippine Sea plate and its edge. The presence of a high-V_P/V_S anomaly in this region suggests a significant contribution of fluids or partial melt. H_2O-rich component and/or melt may migrate upward through veins or narrow conduits to very shallow depths. The sausage-like bodies identified by Lin *et al.* (2004) ranged from 20 to 100 km in depth, with shallowest extending to the shallow crust near Nanao (Fig. 5a). This alignment between tremor occurrence and documented deep fluid reservoirs further supports the role of fluid migration in tremor generation at Nanao.

Lin *et al.* (2004) suggested that slab dehydration could provide a fluid source (Seno *et al.*, 2001; Hacker *et al.*, 2003; Yamasaki and Seno, 2003), with fluids likely propagating upward along the slab until encountering the brittle–ductile transition (BDT) zone at ~20 km depth (Zhamaletdinov, 2019). This zone may control fluid circulation because decreasing permeability in the deeper ductile zone affects heat and fluid transfer along the propagation paths (Driesner and Geiger, 2007; Weis *et al.*, 2012; Violay *et al.*, 2015).

Further supporting this interpretation, Su *et al.* (2019) compared seismic structures in northeastern Taiwan with findings from Lin *et al.* (2004), Chou *et al.* (2009), and Huang *et al.* (2014). They consistently identified high-V_P anomalies of the subducted Philippine Sea plate slab and conspicuous low-V_P anomalies atop the slab, indicative of fluid presence. In addition, Su *et al.* (2019) identified high-V_P anomalies in regions where low-V_P anomalies typical of mantle wedges would generally be expected. These structural observations support the hypothesis that heat flow and fluid migration from slab dehydration contribute to the subsurface conditions conducive to tremor generation beneath the Nanao region.

Laboratory experiments of fluid-induced seismicity and hydraulic fracturing (Benson *et al.*, 2008, 2020; Bakker *et al.*, 2016) offer analogs to our findings. Benson *et al.* (2008) demonstrated that rapidly venting high-pressure pore fluids could induce turbulent fluid flow within damage zones, generating swarms of acoustic emissions (AEs). Although the experimental AEs were observed under controlled decompression conditions, the Nanao tremors exhibit similar waveform characteristics, suggesting that fluid movement and depressurization at depth may contribute to tremor generation.

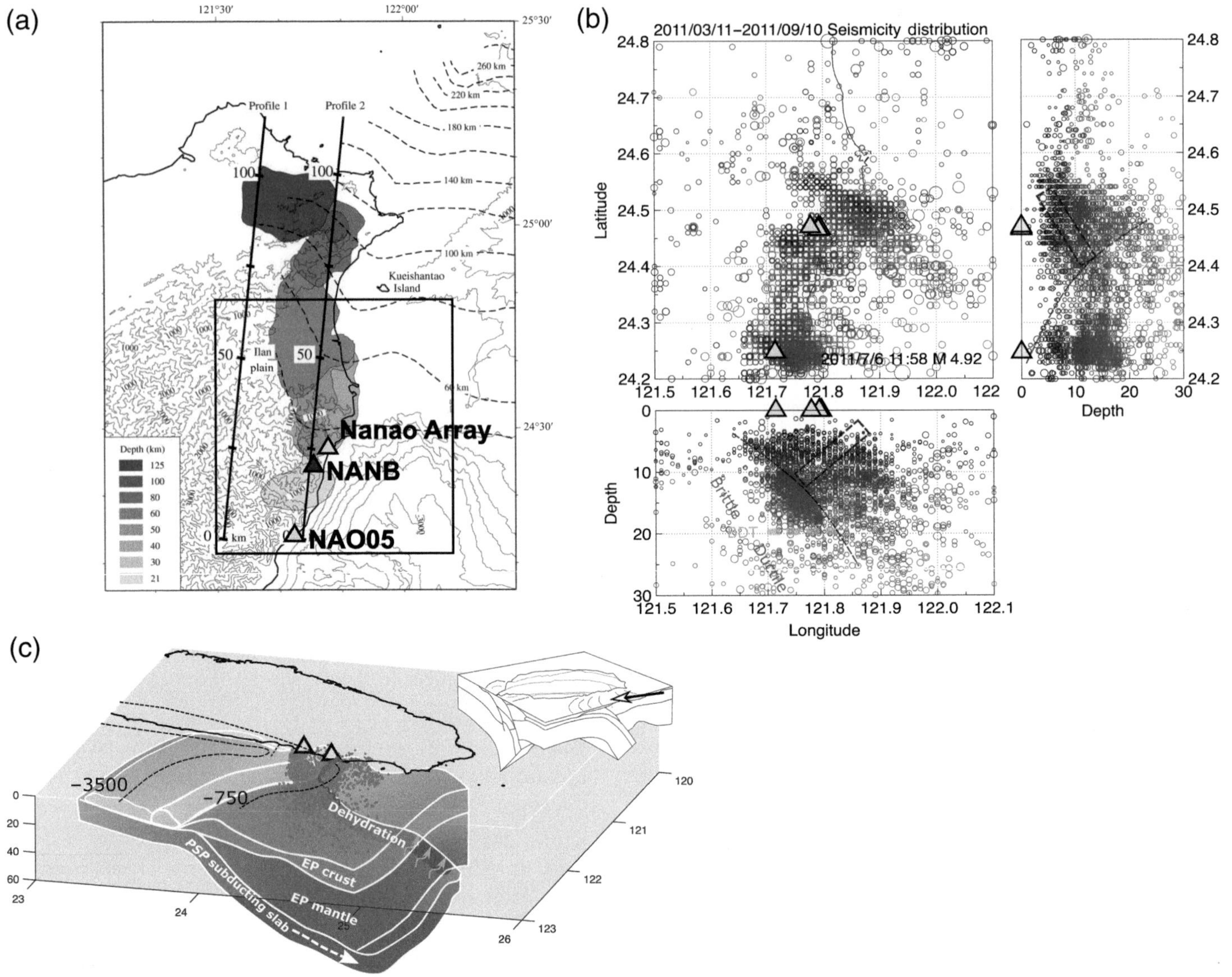

Figure 5. (a) Geographical distribution of higher V_P/V_S-values ranging from 21 km (light gray) to 125 km (dark gray), modified from Lin *et al.* (2004). The dashed lines are isobaths of the Wadati–Benioff zone (Font *et al.*, 1999). The areas of high-V_P/V_S anomalies are located above the western edge of the Ryukyu slab, and the stations of the Nanao array (yellow triangles) and NANB station (blue triangle) are located above the south end of high-V_P/V_S anomalies. The square shows the region of (b). (b) The post-seismicity occurred after the Tohoku earthquake around the array over six months. The yellow triangles represent the locations of the array stations. The southernmost one is station NAO05. The red star is the largest event that occurred during these 6 months. From the profile of the seismicity distribution, a northeast dip plane (gray dashed line) and a seismic gap (in blue dashed rectangular box) can be recognized at shallow depth. (c) Schematic of the tectonic setting for tremor triggering. The heat flow (red line) originated from dehydration of the subducting oceanic slab or mantle flow processes around the edge of the slab may provide additional fluid and heat to the shallow part when it propagated upward. The pore pressure may be elevated rapidly by the penetrating fluid, heat, and high strain caused by the teleseismic wave. High pore pressure may result in fractures (blue path) and activate rapid fluid flow under extreme conditions, that is, of high volume of fluid, high temperature, and high strain. The gray dots show the 6-month seismicity distribution, and the dashed lines are isobath lines along the high elevation of the accretion wedge and crust. The inset is the Taiwan tectonic setting modified from Angelier (1986), in which the arrow shows the view angle of our schematic diagram. The color version of this figure is available only in the electronic edition.

Bakker *et al.* (2016) demonstrated that a rapid increase in pore pressure, driven by applied stress and heat, can induce tensile fracturing, facilitating significant fluid movement over short timescales. The strain and dilation patterns observed in this study, derived from the teleseismic waveform (left panel of Fig. 4), show qualitative similarities to overpressure dynamics recorded in laboratory experiments (right panel of Fig. 4), suggesting comparable fluid-driven process may occur in natural tremor settings. The early-stage overpressure drop in experiments, leading to acoustic emissions and overpressure oscillations, correlates with crustal dilation following the *P* wave and preceding tremor occurrences.

The seismicity distribution over the six months following the Tohoku earthquake (Fig. 5b), revealed a seismic gap extending southwest from the Nanao array (blue dashed line in Fig. 5b), likely indicative of a fracture similar to those observed in laboratory experiments. We propose a model illustrated in Figure 5c, in which warm fluids from slab dehydration or mantle flow processes propagate upward, influencing local temperature and pressure conditions. This model aligns with previous studies indicating that pore-fluid pressure perturbations can dynamically trigger seismic events, particularly in regions with active fluid migration (Shelly *et al.*, 2006; Chao *et al.*, 2013). Dilation following the *P* wave likely caused transient pore-pressure changes, initiating rapid fluid flow, which correlates with the differential moveout observed in some Nanao tremors. The role of fluid migration in tremor triggering is further supported by similarities between our findings and laboratory experiments demonstrating fluid-induced seismicity under controlled conditions (Benson *et al.*, 2008; Bakker *et al.*, 2016). These observations suggest that fluid migration and associated pore-pressure changes played a significant role in the triggering of tremors at Nanao.

This represents one of the first documented example of fluid-related HFTs dynamically triggered by teleseismic waves above the edge of a subducted slab. Similar tremors may occur in comparable in tectonic settings globally. Further studies are necessary to better connect lab experiments with field observations like those presented here.

DATA AND RESOURCES

The data that support the findings of this study are available at doi: 10.7910/DVN/PNPEXA. Further data of the Nanao Array and the conditions for access will be available at the Taiwan Earthquake Research Center (TEC) Data center at http://tecdc.earth.sinica.edu.tw (last accessed December 2024). The supplemental material provides comprehensive figures and tables that support the study's findings on the triggered tremors at the Nanao Array. Figures S1–S9 display filtered velocity seismograms and continuous wavelet transform (CWT) spectrograms in relation to the Tohoku earthquake, emphasizing high-frequency tremor (HFT) signals. Figure S10 captures the characteristics of train signals observed at the Nanao array. Figure S11 uses Hilbert–Huang Transform (HHT) to display intrinsic mode functions (IMFs) for high-frequency signals, whereas Figure S12 presents the results of *f-k* analysis during train passage with waveforms filtered at 0.5–20 Hz. Figure S13 shows polar representations of back azimuth and slowness for the triggered tremors and for a separate time window, distinguishing tremor signals from potential sources. Figure S14 presents the waveforms applied in Spudich's strain inversion. Panel (a) shows the NA06 seismogram filtered with various upper corner frequencies, and panel (b) shows the seismograms filtered from 0.01 to 0.08 Hz at all six stations, illustrating waveform consistency across frequency bands and stations. Figure S15 compares filtered waveforms from a broader region, confirming that HFTs and triggered tremors are only observed at the Nanao array. Tables S1–S3 provide details on station locations, tremor timings, and subarray configurations for strain inversion, respectively.

DECLARATION OF COMPETING INTERESTS

The authors acknowledge that there are no conflicts of interest recorded.

ACKNOWLEDGMENTS

The authors thank the Taiwan Earthquake Center (TEC) for providing the instruments used in this study. The Nanao Array was designed and initiated by W.-C. Chi, and installed with the assistance of W. S. Liu. Chi also acknowledges the able support of engineers at the Institute of Earth Sciences (IES), Academia Sinica, initially led by C. C. Liu and later by C. J. Lin. We are grateful to T.-R. A. Song, F. B. Chao, and H.-H. Chen for their valuable suggestions and advice at the early stages of this work. This research was supported in part by the Institute of Earth Sciences, Academia Sinica, and the Ministry of Science and Technology of Taiwan. Additional support was provided by the National Environmental Research Academy (NERA). This article is a contribution of the Taiwan Earthquake Center (TEC Contribution Number 00200). Finally, the authors express our deep appreciation to the editor, the reviewers, and the *BSSA* Editorial Office for their constructive feedback and suggestions, which significantly improved the quality and clarity of this article.

REFERENCES

Angelier, J. (1986). Geodynamics of the Eurasia-Philippine Sea plate boundary: Preface, *Tectonophysics* **125,** IX–X, doi: 10.1016/0040-1951(86)90003-X.

Bakker, R. R., M. Fazio, P. M. Benson, K. U. Hess, and D. B. Dingwell (2016). The propagation and seismicity of dyke injection, new experimental evidence, *Geophys. Res. Lett.* **43,** 1876–1883, doi: 10.1002/2015GL066852.

Benson, P. M., D. C. Austria, S. Gehne, E. Butcher, C. E. Harnett, M. Fazio, P. Rowley, and R. Tomas (2020). Laboratory simulations of fluid-induced seismicity, hydraulic fracture, and fluid flow, *Geomech. Energy. Environ.* **24,** 100169, doi: 10.1016/j.gete.2019.100169.

Benson, P. M., S. Vinciguerra, P. Meredith, and R. Young (2008). Laboratory simulation of volcano seismicity, *Science* **322,** 249–252, doi: 10.1126/science.1161927.

Beroza, G. C., and S. Ide (2011). Slow earthquakes and nonvolcanic tremor, *Annu. Rev. Earth Planet. Sci.* **39,** 271–296, doi: 10.1146/annurev-earth-040809-152531.

Brodsky, E., B. Sturtevant, and H. Kanamori (1998). Earthquakes, volcanoes, and rectified diffusion, *J. Geophys. Res.* **103,** no. B10, 23,827–23,838, doi: 10.1029/98JB02130.

Brodsky, E. E., E. Roeloffs, D. Woodcock, I. Gall, and M. Manga (2003). A mechanism for sustained groundwater pressure changes induced by distant earthquakes, *J. Geophys. Res.* **108,** no. B8, 2390, doi: 10.1029/2002JB002321.

Chao, K., Z. Peng, H. Gonzalez-Huizar, C. Aiken, B. Enescu, H. Kao, A. A. Velasco, K. Obara, and T. Matsuzawa (2013). A global search for triggered tremor following the 2011 M_w 9.0 Tohoku earthquake, *Bull. Seismol. Soc. Am.* **103,** no. 2B, 1551–1571, doi: 10.1785/0120120171.

Chao, K., Z. Peng, C. Wu, C.-C. Tang, and C.-H. Lin (2012). Remote triggering of non-volcanic tremor around Taiwan, *Geophys. J. Int.* **188,** no. 1, 301–324, doi: 10.1111/j.1365-246X.2011.05261.x.

Chen, K. H., H.-J. Tai, S. Ide, T. B. Byrne, and C. W. Johnson (2018). Tidal modulation and tectonic implications of tremors in Taiwan, *J. Geophys. Res.* **123,** 5945–5964, doi: 10.1029/2018JB015663.

Chi, W.-C., W. H. K. Lee, J. A. D. Aston, C.-J. Lin, and C.-C. Liu (2011). Inversion of ground motion data from a seismometer array for rotation using a modification of Jeager's method, *Bull. Seismol. Soc. Am.* **101,** no. 6, 3105–3109, doi: 10.1785/0120100204.

Chou, H. C., B.-Y. Kuo, L.-Y. Chiao, D. Zhao, and S.-H. Hung (2009). Tomography of the westernmost Ryukyu subduction zone and the serpentinization of the fore-arc mantle, *J. Geophys. Res.* **114,** B12301, doi: 10.1029/2008JB006192.

Chuang, L. Y., K. H. Chen, A. Wech, T. Byrne, and W. Peng (2014). Ambient tremors in a collisional orogenic belt, *Geophys. Res. Lett.* **41,** 1485–1491, doi: 10.1002/2014GL059476.

Donner, S., C.-J. Lin, C. Hadziioannou, A. Gebauer, F. Vernon, D. C. Agnew, H. Igel, U. Schreiber, and J. Wassermann (2017). Comparing direct observation of strain, rotation, and displacement with array estimates at Piñon Flat observatory, California, *Seismol. Res. Lett.* **88,** no. 4, 1107–1116, doi: 10.1785/0220160216.

Dreger, D. S., H. Tkalčić, and M. Johnston (2000). Dilational processes accompanying earthquakes in the Long Valley Caldera, *Science* **288,** no. 5463, 122–125, doi: 10.1126/science.288.5463.122.

Driesner, T., and S. Geiger (2007). Numerical simulation of multiphase fluid flow in hydrothermal systems, in *Fluid-Fluid Interactions, Reviews in Mineralogy and Geochemistry*, A. Liebscher and C. A. Heinrich (Editors), Mineralogical Society of America, Chantilly, Virginia, 65**,** 187–212, doi: 10.2138/rmg.2007.65.6.

Font, Y., S. Lallemand, and J. Angelier (1999). Étude de la transition entre l'orogène actif de Taiwan et la subduction des Ryukyu—Apports de la sismicité, *Bull. Soc. Géol. Fr.* **170,** no. 3, 271–283 (in French).

Foulger, G. R., B. R. Julian, D. P. Hill, A. M. Pitt, P. E. Malin, and E. Shalev (2004). Non-double-couple microearthquakes at Long Valley caldera, California, provide evidence for hydraulic fracturing, *J. Volcanol. Geoth. Res.* **132,** no. 1, 45–71, doi: 10.1016/S0377-0273(03)00420-7.

Gomberg, J. (2001). The failure of earthquake failure models, *J. Geophys. Res.* **106,** no. B8, 16,253–16,263, doi: 10.1029/2000JB000003.

Gomberg, J., and P. Johnson (2005). Dynamic triggering of earthquakes, *Nature* **437,** 830, doi: 10.1038/437830a.

Gomberg, J., N. M. Beeler, M. L. Blanpied, and P. Bodin (1998). Earthquake triggering by transient and static deformation, *J. Geophys. Res.* **103,** no. B10, 24,411–24,426, doi: 10.1029/98JB01125.

Gomberg, J., P. A. Reasenberg, M. Cocco, and M. E. Belardinelli (2005). A frictional population model of seismicity rate change, *J. Geophys. Res.* **110,** no. B5, S03, doi: 10.1029/2004JB003404.

Gonzalez-Huizar, H., and A. A. Velasco (2011). Dynamic triggering: Stress modeling and a case study, *J. Geophys. Res.* **116,** B02304.

Hacker, B. R., S. M. Peacock, G. A. Abers, and S. D. Holloway (2003). Subduction factory 2. Are intermediate-depth earthquakes in subducting slabs linked to metamorphic dehydration reactions? *J. Geophys. Res.* **108,** no. B1, 2030, doi: 10.1029/2001JB001129.

Hill, D. P. (2008). Dynamic stresses, coulomb failure, and remote triggering, *Bull. Seismol. Soc. Am.* **98,** no. 1, 66–92, doi: 10.1785/0120070049.

Hill, D. P., and S. G. Prejean (2007). Dynamic triggering, in *Treatise on Geophysics*, Second Ed., G. Schubert (Editor), Amsterdam, Elsevier, Vol. 4, 273–304, doi: 10.1016/B978-0-444-53802-4.00078-6.

Hill, D. P., F. Pollitz, and C. Newhall (2002). Earthquake-volcano interactions, *Phys. Today* **55,** no. 11, 41–47, doi: 10.1063/1.1535006.

Hill, D. P., P. A. Reasenberg, A. Michael, W. J. Arabaz, G. Beroza, D. Brumbaugh, J. N. Brune, R. Castro, S. Davis, D. dePolo, W. L. Ellsworth, *et al.* (1993). Seismicity remotely triggered by the magnitude 7.3 Landers, California, earthquake, *Science* **260,** no. 5114, 1617–1623, doi: 10.1126/science.260.5114.1617.

Hough, S. E., L. Seeber, and J. G. Armbruster (2003). Intraplate triggered earthquakes: Observations and interpretation, *Bull. Seismol. Soc. Am.* **93,** no. 5, 2212–2221, doi: 10.1785/0120020055.

Huang, B. S. (2003). Ground rotational motions of the 1999 Chi-Chi, Taiwan, earthquake as inferred from dense array observations, *Geophys. Res. Lett.* **30,** no. 6, 1307, doi: 10.1029/2002GL015157.

Huang, H.-H., J. B. H. Shyu, Y.-M. Wu, C.-H. Chang, and Y.-G. Chen (2012). Seismotectonics of northeastern Taiwan: Kinematics of the transition from waning collision to subduction and postcollisional extension, *J. Geophys. Res.* **117,** B01313, doi: 10.1029/2011JB008852.

Huang, H.-H., Y.-M. Wu, X. Song, C.-H. Chang, S.-J. Lee, T.-M. Chang, and H.-H. Hsieh (2014). Joint V_P and V_S tomography of Taiwan: Implications for subduction-collision orogeny, *Earth Planet. Sci. Lett.* **392,** 177–191, doi: 10.1016/j.epsl.2014.02.026.

Ide, S., and K. H. Chen (2024). Spatiotemporal characteristics of tectonic tremors in the collisional orogen of Taiwan, *Geophys. Res. Lett.* **51,** e2023GL106759, doi: 10.1029/2023GL106759.

Institute of Earth Sciences, A. S. (1996). *Broadband Array in Taiwan for Seismology*. Institute of Earth Sciences, Academia Sinica, Taiwan, doi: 10.7914/SN/TW.

Ito, Y., K. Obara, K. Shiomi, S. Sekine, and H. Hirose (2007). Slow earthquakes coincident with episodic tremors and slow slip events, *Science* **315,** 503–506.

Jiang, T., Z. Peng, W. Wang, and Q.-F. Chen (2010). Remotely triggered seismicity in continental China following the 2008 M_w 7.9 Wenchuan earthquake, *Bull. Seismol. Soc. Am.* **100,** no. 5B, 2574–2589, doi: 10.1785/0120090286.

Johnson, C. W., H. Meng, F. Vernon, and Y. Ben-Zion (2019). Characteristics of ground motion generated by wind interaction with trees, structures, and other surface obstacles, *J. Geophys. Res.* **124,** 8519–8539, doi: 10.1029/2018JB017151.

Johnson, P., and X. Jia (2005). Nonlinear dynamic, granular media and dynamic earthquake triggering, *Nature* **437,** 871–874, doi: 10.1038/nature04015.

Lin, J.-Y., S.-K. Hsu, and J. C. Sibuet (2004). Melting features along the western Ryukyu slab edge (northeast Taiwan): Tomographic evidence, *J. Geophys. Res.* **109,** B12402, doi: 10.1029/2004JB003260.

Linde, A. T., I. S. Sacks, M. J. S. Johnston, D. P. Hill, and R. G. Billham (1994). Increased pressure from rising bubbles as a mechanism for remotely triggered seismicity, *Nature* **371,** 408–410, doi: 10.1038/371408a0.

Martínez-Garzón, P., G. Beroza, G. Bocchini, and M. Bohnhoff (2023). Sea level changes affect seismicity rates in a hydrothermal system near Istanbul, *Geophys. Res. Lett.* **50,** no. 3, doi: 10.1029/2022gl101258.

Masuda, K., S. Ide, K. Ohta, and T. Matsuzawa (2020). Bridging the gap between low-frequency and very-low-frequency earthquakes, *Earth Planets Space* **72,** no. 47, doi: 10.1186/s40623-020-01172-8.

McGuire, J. J., J. A. Collins, E. E. Davis, K. Becker, and M. Heesemann (2018). A lack of dynamic triggering of slow slip and tremor indicates that the shallow Cascadia megathrust offshore Vancouver Island is likely locked, *Geophys. Res. Lett.* **20,** no. 45, doi: 10.1029/2018gl079519.

Miyazawa, M., and J. Mori (2006). Evidence suggesting fluid flow beneath Japan due to periodic seismic triggering from the 2004

Sumatra-Andaman earthquake, *Geophys. Res. Lett.* **33,** L05303, doi: 10.1029/2005GL025087.

Obara, K. (2002). Nonvolcanic deep tremor associated with subduction in southwest Japan, *Science* **296,** no. 1679, doi: 10.1126/science.1070378.

Obara, K., and A. Kato (2016). Connecting slow earthquakes to huge earthquakes, *Science* **353,** no. 6296, 253–257, doi: 10.1126/science.aaf1512.

Obara, K., S. Tanaka, T. Maeda, and T. Matsuzawa (2010). Depth-dependent activity of non-volcanic tremor in southwest Japan. *Geophys. Res. Lett.* **37,** no. 13, 10.1029/2010gl043679.

Oki, S., Y. Fukao, and M. Obayashi (2004). Reference frequency of teleseismic body waves, *J. Geophys. Res.* **109,** B04304, doi: 10.1029/2003JB002821.

Peng, Z., and K. Chao (2008). Non-volcanic tremor beneath the Central Range in Taiwan triggered by the 2001 M_w 7.8 Kunlun earthquake, *Geophys. J. Int.* **175,** no. 2, 825–829, doi: 10.1111/j.1365-246X.2008.03886.x.

Perfettini, H., J. Schmittbuhl, and A. Cochard (2003). Shear and normal load perturbations on a two-dimensional continuous fault: 2. Dynamic triggering, *J. Geophys. Res.* **108,** no. B9, 2409, doi: 10.1029/2002JB001805.

Riahi, N., and P. Gerstoft (2015). The seismic traffic footprint: Tracking trains, aircraft, and cars seismically, *Geophys. Res. Lett.* **42,** 2674–2681, doi: 10.1002/2015GL063558.

Seno, T., D. Zhao, Y. Kobayashi, and M. Nakamura (2001). Dehydration of serpentinized slab mantle: Seismic evidence from southwest Japan, *Earth Planets Space* **53,** 861–871, doi: 10.1186/BF03351683.

Shelly, D., G. Beroza, S. Ide, and S. Nakamula (2006). Low-frequency earthquakes in Shikoku, Japan, and their relationship to episodic tremor and slip, *Nature* **442,** 188–191, doi: 10.1038/nature04931.

Spudich, P., and J. B. Fletcher (2008). Observation and prediction of dynamic ground strains, tilts, and torsions caused by the M 6.0 2004 Parkfield, California, earthquake and aftershocks derived from UPSAR array observations, *Bull. Seismol. Soc. Am.* **98,** 1898–1914, doi: 10.1785/0120070157.

Spudich, P., and J. B. Fletcher (2009). Software for inference of dynamic ground strains and rotations and their errors from short baseline array observations of ground motions, *Bull. Seismol. Soc. Am.* **99,** 1480–1482, doi: 10.1785/0120080230.

Spudich, P., L. K. Steck, M. Hellweg, J. B. Fletcher, and L. M. Baker (1995). Transient stresses at Parkfield, California, produced by the M 7.4 Landers earthquake of June 28, 1992: Observations from the UPSAR dense seismograph array, *J. Geophys. Res.* **100,** 675–690, doi: 10.1029/94JB02477.

Su, P.-L., P.-F. Chen, and C.-Y. Wang (2019). High-resolution 3D *P*-wave velocity structures under NE Taiwan and their tectonic implications, *J. Geophys. Res.* **124,** 11,601–11,614, doi: 10.1029/2019JB018697.

Sun, W.-F., Z. Peng, C.-H. Lin, and K. Chao (2015). Detecting deep tectonic tremor in Taiwan with a dense array, *Bull. Seismol. Soc. Am.* **105,** no. 3, 1349–1358, doi: 10.1785/0120140258.

Suryanto, W., H. Igel, J. Wassermann, A. Cochard, B. Schuberth, D. Vollmer, F. Scherbaum, U. Schreiber, and A. Velifoseltsev (2006). First comparison of array-derived rotational ground motions with direct ring laser measurements, *Bull. Seismol. Soc. Am.* **96,** 2059–2071, doi: 10.1785/0120060004.

Teng, L. S. (1996). Extensional collapse of the northern Taiwan mountain belt, *Geology* **24,** 949–952, doi: 10.1130/0091-7613(1996)024<0949:ECOTNT>2.3.CO;2.

To, A., K. Obana, H. Sugioka, E. Araki, N. Takahashi, and Y. Fukao (2015). Small size very low frequency earthquakes in the Nankai accretionary prism, following the 2011 Tohoku-Oki earthquake, *Phys. Earth Planet. Int.* **245,** 40–51.

Van Avendonk, H. J. A., K. D. McIntosh, H. Kuo-Chen, L. L. Lavier, D. A. Okaya, F. T. Wu, C.-Y. Wang, C.-S. Lee, and C.-S. Liu (2016). A lithospheric profile across northern Taiwan: from arc-continent collision to extension, *Geophys. J. Int.* **204,** 331–346, doi: 10.1093/gji/ggv468.

Velasco, A. A., S. Hernandez, T. Parson, and K. Pankow (2008). Global ubiquity of dynamic earthquake triggering, *Nature Geosci.* **1,** 375–379, doi: 10.1038/ngeo204.

Violay, M., B. Gibert, D. Mainprice, and J. P. Burg (2015). Brittle versus ductile deformation as the main control of the deep fluid circulation in oceanic crust, *Geophys. Res. Lett.* **42,** 2767–2773, doi: 10.1002/2015GL063437.

Walter, J. I., S. Y. Schwartz, M. Protti, and V. Gonzalez (2013). The synchronous occurrence of shallow tremor and very low frequency earthquakes offshore of the Nicoya Peninsula, Costa Rica, *Geophys. Res. Lett.* **40,** 1517–1522, doi: 10.1002/grl.50213.

Weis, J. P., T. Driesner, and C. A. Heinrich (2012). Porphyry-copper ore shells form at stable pressure-temperature fronts within dynamic fluid plumes, *Science* **338,** 1613–1616, doi: 10.1126/science.1225009.

Withers, M. M., R. C. Aster, C. J. Young, and E. P. Chael (1996). High-frequency analysis of seismic background noise as a function of wind speed and shallow depth, *Bull. Seismol. Soc. Am.* **86,** no. 5, 1507–1515.

Yamasaki, T., and T. Seno (2003). Double seismic zone and dehydration embrittlement of the subducting slab, *J. Geophys. Res.* **108,** no. B4, 2212, doi: 10.1029/2002JB001918.

Yang, H., and Z. Peng (2013). Lack of additional triggered tectonic tremor around the Simi Valley and the San Gabriel Mountain in southern California, *Bull. Seismol. Soc. Am.* **103,** no. 6, 3372–3378, doi: 10.1785/0120130117.

Yeh, T.-C. (2011). Dynamic triggering of earthquakes and tremors in Taiwan, *Master's Thesis*, National Taiwan University, Taipei, Taiwan, 101 pp. Available at https://scholars.lib.ntu.edu.tw/entities/publication/ca409192-00b2-4504-9e07-a105f5d46507 (last accessed March 2025).

Yuan, S., A. Simonelli, C.-J. Lin, F. Bernauer, S. Donner, T. Braun, J. Wassermann, and H. Igel (2020). Six degree-of-freedom broadband ground-motion observations with portable sensors: Validation, local earthquakes, and signal processing, *Bull. Seismol. Soc. Am.* **110,** no. 3, 953–969, doi: 10.1785/0120190277.

Zhamaletdinov, A. A. (2019). On the nature of the brittle-ductile transition zone in the Earth's crust (review), in *The Study of Continental Lithosphere Electrical Conductivity, Temperature and Rheology*, A. A. Zhamaletdinov and Y. L. Rebetsky (Editors), Springer, Cham, 13–21, doi: 10.1007/978-3-030-35906-5_3.

Manuscript received 3 November 2024
Published online 13 June 2025

Leveraging Big Data for Earthquake Disaster Response: Insights from Taiwanese Decision-Support Systems from 1999 to 2024

Siao-Syun Ke[1], Chih-Hao Hsu*[1], Ching-Yuan Yang[1,2], Carol C. Wu[1], and Ming-Wey Huang[1]

ABSTRACT

The 1999 M_w 7.6 Chi-Chi earthquake fundamentally transformed Taiwan's approach to earthquake disaster governance, prompting the establishment of the National Science and Technology Center for Disaster Reduction and the institutionalization of science-based decision support. Over the past 25 yr, Taiwan's earthquake decision-support framework has evolved into an integrated, grid-based system that synthesizes seismic, geological, landslide, and population data sets to generate rapid and reproducible postearthquake assessments. This study provides a comprehensive review of the development, methodological structure, and operational performance of this framework from 1999 to 2024, with a particular focus on its application during the 2024 M_w 7.4 Hualien earthquake. The case study demonstrates that the system enables near-real-time mapping of ground-shaking intensity, secondary landslide hazards, and population exposure, thereby enhancing situational awareness during emergency response. The incorporation of anonymized mobile-network data represents a major technological advancement, allowing dynamic estimation of population movement, and isolation in disaster-affected regions. Comparative analysis between the 1999 Chi-Chi and 2024 Hualien earthquakes further elucidates the role of cross-event calibration and data transparency in strengthening predictive capacity and reproducibility. Collectively, these findings underscore that Taiwan's institutionalized, data-driven framework constitutes a transferable model for integrating scientific research with decision-making in earthquake disaster management.

KEY POINTS

- Taiwan's integrated decision-support framework integrates multiple data for robust postearthquake assessment.
- Cross-event calibration from Chi-Chi (1999) to Hualien (2024) refines mapping of secondary hazards and infrastructure risks.
- Mobile-network data reveal near-real-time population movement and isolation, advancing earthquake response capability.

Supplemental Material

INTRODUCTION

At 01:47 local time on 21 September 1999, the M_w 7.6 Chi-Chi earthquake ruptured the Chelungpu fault in central Taiwan (Ma *et al.*, 1999, 2001), producing intense ground motion and widespread damage. More than 2400 lives were lost, over 100,000 buildings were destroyed, and massive landslides reshaped the landscape, making the Chi-Chi earthquake one the most devastating historical natural disasters in Taiwan (Shin and Teng, 2001; Tsai *et al.*, 2001; Shou and Wang, 2003; Khazai and Sitar, 2004). Scientifically, the event provided unprecedented strong-motion recordings that became a cornerstone for earthquake engineering and seismic hazard assessment (Yue *et al.*, 2005; Cheng *et al.*, 2007; Yang *et al.*, 2007; Wang *et al.*, 2016). Yet, from a disaster-response perspective, the Chi-Chi earthquake revealed critical limitations in situational awareness, coordination, and data availability. Early rescue efforts were hampered by the lack of timely and integrated information, underscoring the urgent need for a robust decision-support system.

1. National Science and Technology Center for Disaster Reduction, New Taipei City, Taiwan, https://orcid.org/0000-0001-7476-1396 (S-SK); https://orcid.org/0000-0001-7145-5780 (C-HH); https://orcid.org/0000-0002-5253-8422 (C-YY); https://orcid.org/0000-0001-5717-9521 (M-WH); 2. Department of Geosciences, National Taiwan University, Taipei, Taiwan

*Corresponding author: willie2567@ncdr.nat.gov.tw

Cite this article as Ke, S.-S., C.-H. Hsu, C.-Y. Yang, C. C. Wu, and M.-W. Huang (2025). Leveraging Big Data for Earthquake Disaster Response: Insights from Taiwanese Decision-Support Systems from 1999 to 2024, *Bull. Seismol. Soc. Am.* **116**, 162–175, doi: 10.1785/0120250188

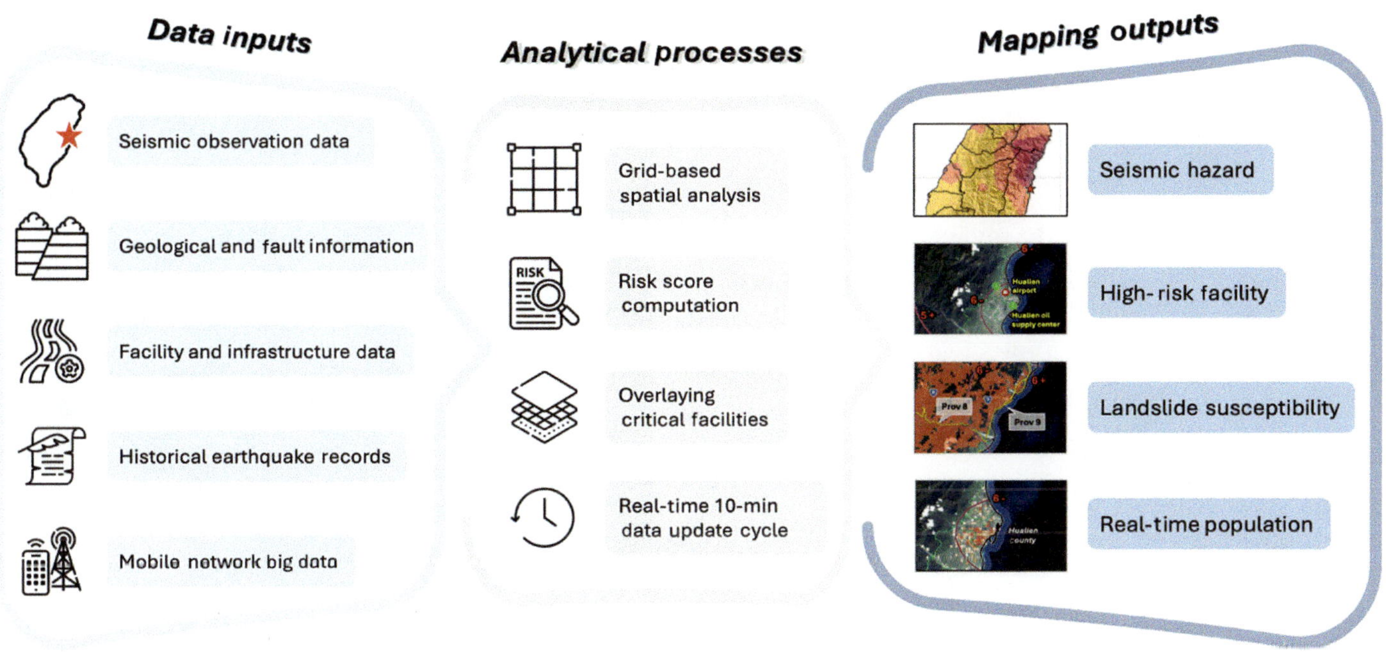

Figure 1. Conceptual workflow of the integrated earthquake disaster information system, showing the data inputs, analytical processes, and resulting mapping products used for the 2024 Hualien earthquake response.

In the aftermath, Taiwan launched a series of institutional and technological initiatives to strengthen its earthquake disaster management capacity. Following the promulgation of the Disaster Prevention and Protection Act, the establishment of the National Science and Technology Center for Disaster Reduction (NCDR) in 2003 reflected a broader commitment to integrating scientific knowledge into emergency operations. Over the following two decades, Taiwan progressively incorporated diverse data sets—seismic observations, geological maps, remote sensing imagery, historical earthquake archives, and, more recently, mobile network big data—into a unified framework for rapid earthquake disaster assessment. This evolution marked a paradigm shift from reactive rescue toward proactive, data-driven risk reduction.

The 2024 M_w 7.4 Hualien earthquake provided a timely test of these advances. Occurring 25 yr after Chi-Chi, the event struck eastern Taiwan with strong ground shaking that triggered widespread landslides (Chang *et al.*, 2024), disrupted transportation (Ministry of Transportation and Communications, 2024), and trapped hundreds of individuals in mountainous terrain (Central Emergency Operation Center, 2024). Unlike in 1999, response managers in the Central Emergency Operation Center (CEOC) had access to real-time hazard and exposure maps generated by an integrated decision-support system (National Science and Technology Center for Disaster Reduction, 2024). These maps combined seismic intensity, landslide risk, and mobile telecom-based population estimates, enabling rapid evaluation of disaster impact and prioritization of rescue efforts.

This study reviews the scientific foundations and operational performance of Taiwan's earthquake decision-support system between 1999 and 2024. We first describe the data sets that underpin the system, then present the methodological framework for integrating seismic, geological, remote-sensing, and telecom data into rapid mapping products. Using the 2024 Hualien earthquake as a case study, we evaluate the system's accuracy, highlight key scientific insights, and compare outcomes with those of the 1999 Chi-Chi earthquake. Finally, we discuss broader implications for earthquake hazard science and international disaster risk reduction.

DATA AND METHODOLOGY

Overall framework

The earthquake decision-support system developed in Taiwan integrates multisource data sets into a unified spatial framework designed to generate rapid hazard and exposure maps. This section outlines the data processing steps and methodological principles that support reproducibility. Figure 1 illustrates the overall framework, from multidisciplinary data inputs to mapping outputs. The system combines seismic observations, geological and fault data, remote sensing imagery, historical earthquake information, and mobile network big data. These inputs are integrated through a grid-based mapping approach, in which Taiwan is divided into 500 × 500 m cells (Liu *et al.*, 2016). For each grid cell, shaking parameters, landslide susceptibility, and population exposure are estimated, and the results are visualized as thematic maps. Compared with the fragmented approaches available in 1999, this framework enables rapid and reproducible assessment of hazard and impact within minutes of an earthquake. For a detailed description, including types and resources of the data combined in the system, please refer to Ke *et al.* (2023) and the supplemental material, available to this article.

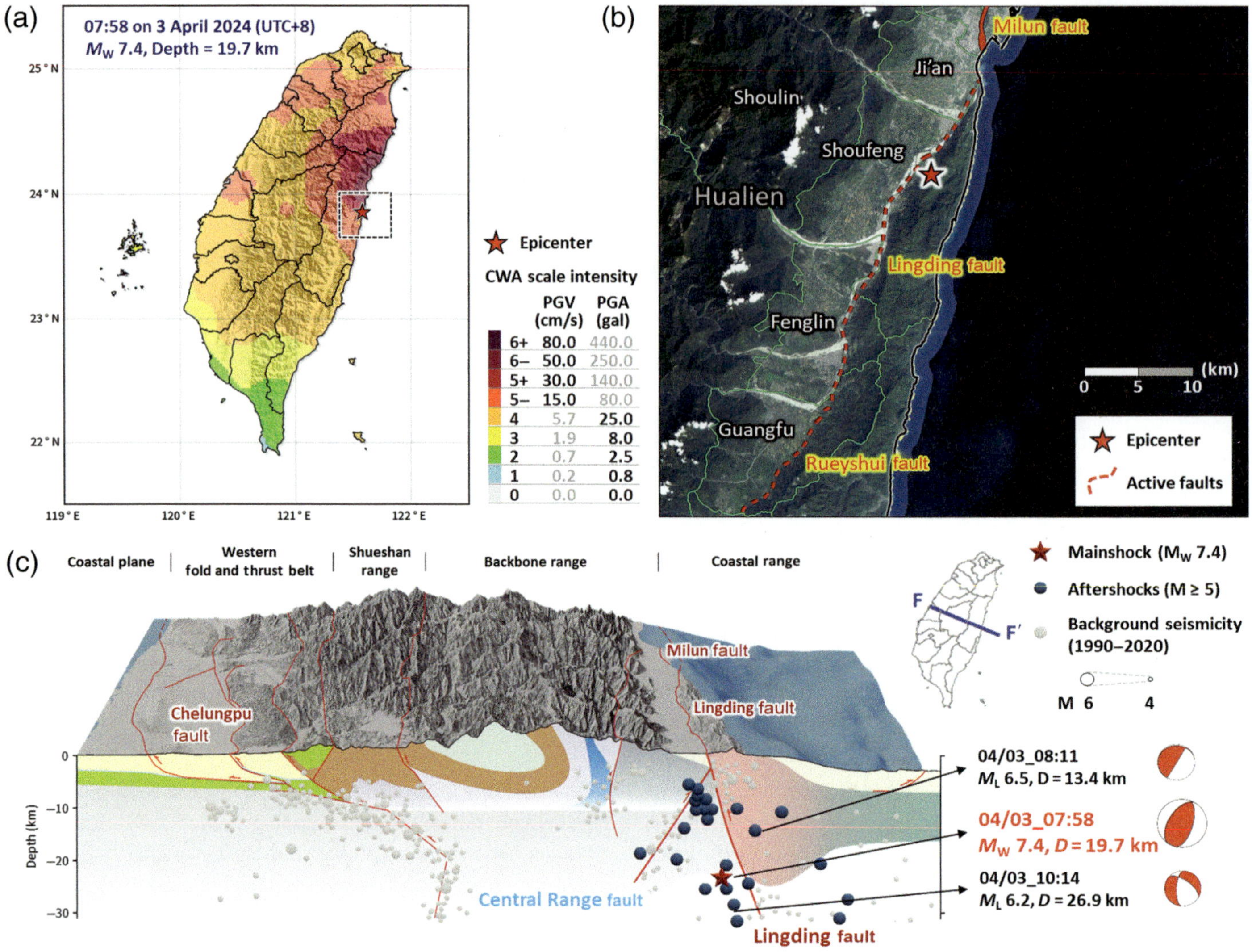

Figure 2. Seismic and geological information used to support the earthquake response mapping during the 2024 Hualien earthquake. (a) Distribution of seismic intensity across Taiwan. The red star marks the epicenter, and the color scale represents ground shaking intensity. The black rectangle indicates the area shown in panel (b). (b) Active faults surrounding the epicentral region. The solid lines denote surface fault traces, whereas dashed lines represent inferred or concealed segments. (c) Geological cross section nearest to the epicenter showing the spatial relationship between earthquake sequences and major fault systems. The mainshock (red star), aftershocks (blue circles), and background seismicity (gray circles) over the past 30 yr (Wu *et al.*, 2008) are projected vertically onto the section. Stratigraphic units and major fault geometries are shown to illustrate potential seismogenic structures controlling the 2024 rupture. PGA, peak ground acceleration. PGV, peak ground velocity.

Seismic and geological data integration

Immediately after an earthquake, seismic parameters from the Central Weather Administration (CWA)—including magnitude, hypocenter, and peak ground acceleration (PGA), peak ground velocity (PGV), and intensity values recorded at seismic stations—are automatically retrieved and processed. These parameters are interpolated onto the 500 m grid system using spatial weighting algorithms to construct continuous shaking fields (Fig. 2a). This procedure ensures that localized extremes in ground motion are captured while providing continuous coverage across the island.

Beyond shaking estimates, geological and fault data sets are used to provide structural context for interpreting the distribution of seismic energy (Fig. 2b,c). Active faults identified by the Geological Survey and Mining Management Agency (GSMMA; Lin *et al.*, 2021) and balanced cross sections (Suppe, 1980a,b; Yang *et al.*, 2002, 2006, 2007; Chen *et al.*, 2011; Chen, 2016) are integrated with aftershock distributions from the CWA. This integration helps constrain candidate rupture geometries within hours of the mainshock. The rapid overlay of aftershocks on known fault traces provides first-order constraints on which structures may have ruptured, whereas geological cross sections contextualize focal depths relative to major lithological and structural boundaries. In addition, by comparing observed shaking with expected

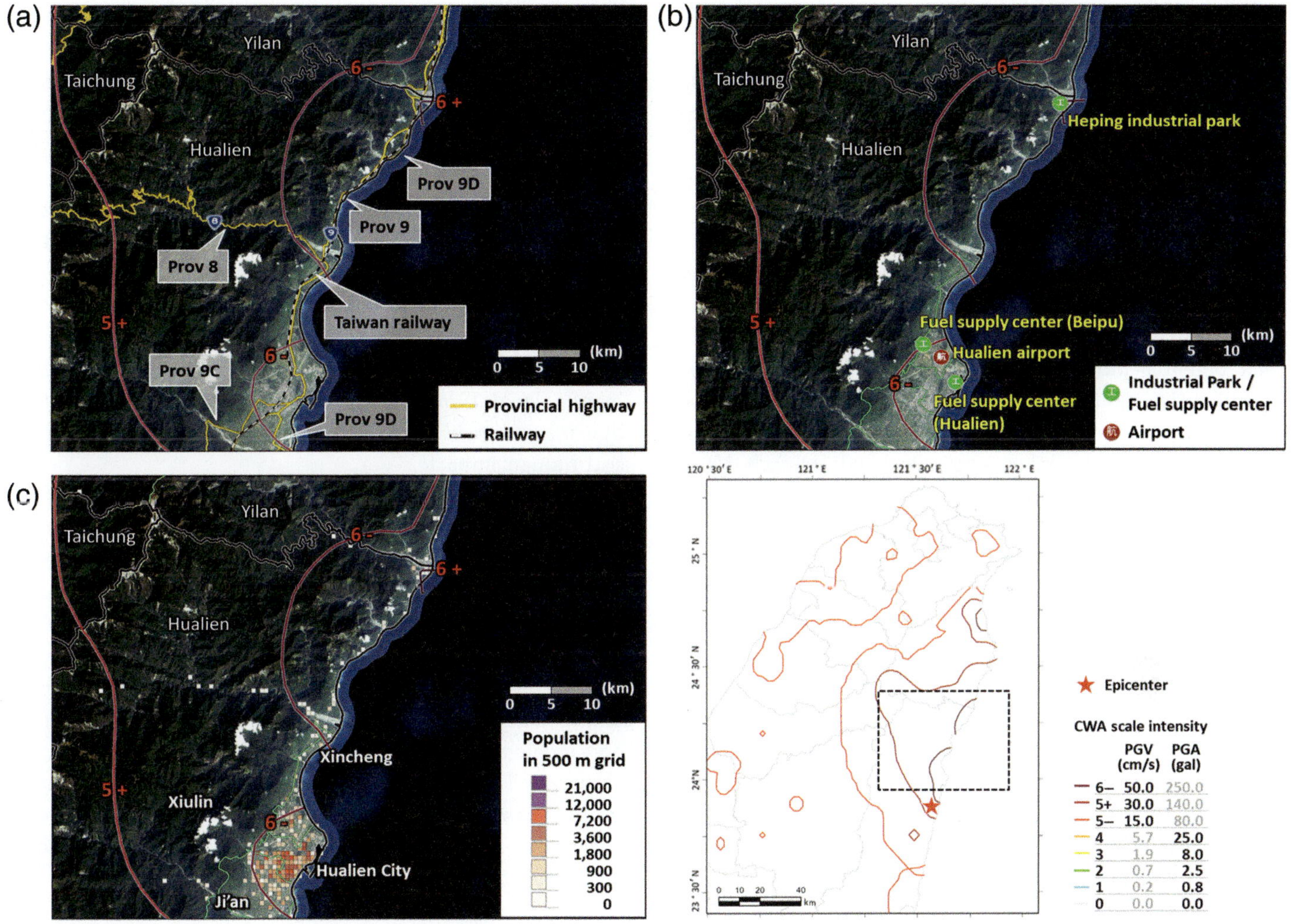

Figure 3. Earthquake impact maps illustrating areas of strong shaking during the 2024 Hualien earthquake. All three maps share the same spatial extent, indicated by the black-dashed rectangle in the index map at lower right, and display seismic intensity distribution derived from the Central Weather Administration's (CWA) data. The red star marks the epicenter, and colored contour lines represent intensity boundaries. (a) Transportation systems within high-intensity zones, including provincial highways and railway lines. (b) Major infrastructures located in the same zones, including industrial parks, fuel supply centers, and the regional airport. (c) Estimated population distribution in 500 × 500 m grids based on anonymized mobile-network data; grid colors correspond to the number of active users within each cell.

attenuation patterns from these faults, deviations can be used to identify possible blind or unmapped structures. This combination of ground-motion interpolation and geological integration therefore enables both rapid hazard assessment and preliminary seismotectonic interpretation.

Grid-based earthquake impact mapping

The core of the system is its grid-based approach to impact mapping. Taiwan is divided into more than 130,000 cells measuring 500 × 500 m (Liu *et al.*, 2016). For each grid cell, hazard intensity is classified according to intensity thresholds (considering both PGA and PGV), which are directly linked to observed levels of structural and nonstructural damage. Grids exceeding threshold values are assigned high risk, whereas those below the thresholds are considered medium to low risk. This classification is fully automated and can be updated within minutes of new seismic data becoming available.

Once hazard levels are assigned, the system overlays exposure layers including transportation corridors, power plants, reservoirs, industrial zones, and dense urban settlements (Fig. 3a,b). Facilities located within high-risk grids are automatically flagged for inspection, allowing authorities to prioritize limited engineering resources in the immediate aftermath. This procedure has the advantage of being reproducible and transparent: the same thresholds and overlay logic can be applied to any future event without modification.

Population exposure was initially estimated from census-based population density, spatially redistributed onto the same 500 m grid. Since 2018, this approach has been complemented by anonymized mobile network data, which are likewise resampled to the same grid, ensuring methodological consistency while enabling near-real-time monitoring of population dynamics (Fig. 3c). This provides response managers with a first-order picture of disaster scale before field data become available. Although relatively simple, the combination of hazard thresholds, infrastructure overlays, and population exposure in a uniform grid framework represents a methodological advance over purely descriptive postearthquake reports, enabling consistent and comparable impact assessments across multiple events.

Landslide risk modeling

Seismic-induced landslides represent one of the most critical secondary hazards in Taiwan, particularly in steep mountainous regions underlain by weak lithologies. To rapidly assess their potential during an earthquake, the system employs a multiplicative model that integrates geomorphological sensitivity with real-time ground-motion intensity. The geomorphological sensitivity index is precalculated for each 500 m grid cell based on slope, lithology, rock strength, the presence of weak layers, and drainage density (Ke *et al.*, 2016; Tanyaş *et al.*, 2017). These factors are weighted to yield a composite sensitivity score from 1 (low) to 5 (high). The ground-motion intensity index is event specific, derived from PGA observations, with thresholds calibrated using the extensive landslide catalog from the 1999 Chi-Chi earthquake (Ke *et al.*, 2016). Three PGA ranges—100–240 gal, 240–460 gal, and >460 gal—correspond, respectively, to the initiation, first rapid-accumulation, and second rapid-accumulation phases of coseismic landsliding. Scores of 1, 2, and 4 are assigned to these ranges, and the product of the two indices produces a composite landslide risk score for each grid cell.

During an event, only grids with composite scores ≥10 are displayed in the rapid impact maps as high-potential landslide zones, providing an efficient and concise data set for early decision making. These high-risk grids are subsequently overlaid with multiple exposure layers, including key transportation routes, mountain settlements, and high-voltage transmission towers, to identify areas requiring immediate inspection. Such integration allows the system to not only depict where landslides are most likely to occur but also highlight which infrastructures or communities are most vulnerable. The resulting maps (Fig. 4b–d) serve as rapid alerts to relevant agencies, supporting targeted safety checks and early-stage response operations. The scientific strength of this approach lies in its calibration against an extreme event (Chi-Chi), whereas validation against subsequent events (e.g., 2024 Hualien) allows refinement of region-specific thresholds. Importantly, the method links hazard (ground motion) with predisposition (geomorphology), producing a framework that is both reproducible and adaptable to different tectonic and geomorphic settings in Taiwan.

Mobile network data analysis

Since 2018, the system has incorporated anonymized mobile network data provided by Chunghwa Telecom. These data consist of aggregated counts of active mobile users per grid cell, available at both 500 and 50 m spatial resolutions and updated every 10 min (Fig. 5). Privacy is safeguarded by reporting only total counts, with no individual tracking possible (Huang *et al.*, 2019, 2021; Yeh *et al.*, 2022).

The methodological novelty lies in integrating these population data directly with seismic and landslide hazard grids. After an earthquake, population density maps are dynamically updated and intersected with high-shaking (Fig. 3c) or high-landslide-risk cells (Fig. 4c). This enables near-real-time estimation of the number and approximate demographics (e.g., elderly vs. general population) of individuals exposed or potentially trapped. Unlike census-based data, which are static, mobile signals capture postearthquake mobility and evacuation dynamics, thereby bridging the gap between hazard intensity and human impact.

Time-series decomposition techniques (Cleveland *et al.*, 1990) are applied to filter out long-term trends and seasonal variations, isolating the short-term anomalies that represent earthquake-induced displacements. For example, sudden declines in signal counts in high-risk grids may indicate evacuation, whereas stable counts in isolated grids may suggest trapped individuals. The advantages of this approach are speed and dynamic resolution; however, limitations include reliance on a single telecom operator, coarse temporal granularity, and absence of socioeconomic detail. Despite these challenges, telecom-based exposure mapping represents a methodological advance, complementing seismic intensity maps by providing real-time evidence of population-at-risk.

The framework outlined above provides a reproducible basis for integrating seismic, geological, and population data into hazard and exposure maps. To demonstrate its performance, we apply the system to the 2024 M_w 7.4 Hualien earthquake, which generated widespread shaking, extensive landslides, and detailed observational data sets. This case allows direct validation of rapid-response products against independent field and satellite observations, highlighting advances since the 1999 Chi-Chi earthquake.

CASE STUDY: 2024 HUALIEN EARTHQUAKE

Event overview

At 07:58 local time (UTC+8) on 3 April 2024, the M_w 7.4 Hualien earthquake struck eastern Taiwan, producing widespread strong shaking (Fig. 2a). The epicenter was in the eastern coast of Hualien, and PGV exceeded 80 cm/s in the county, corresponding to intensity level 6+ on the CWA scale. Shaking with an intensity of ≥5 was observed throughout northern and central Taiwan, including the most populous metropolitan areas such as Taipei, New Taipei, and Taichung. According to official emergency reports, the event resulted in 19 fatalities, 2 missing people, more than 1100 injuries, and over 700 individuals trapped in isolated mountainous areas (Central Emergency Operation Center, 2024; National Fire Agency, 2024). Infrastructure damage included nearly 300

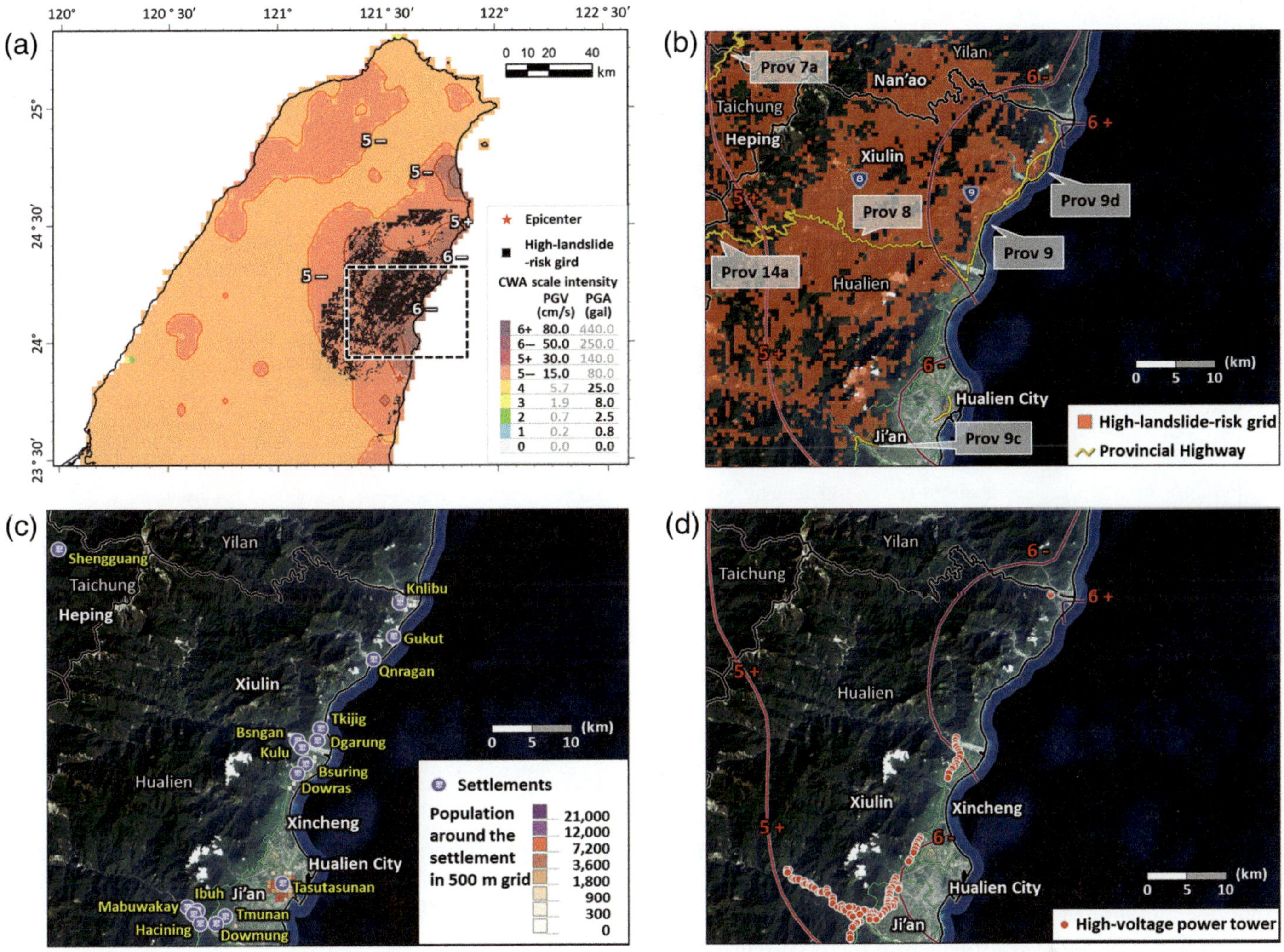

buildings tagged as unsafe and numerous slope failures that disrupted major transportation corridors (Ministry of Transportation and Communications, 2024; Yang *et al.*, 2024). In particular, landslides and rockfalls blocked multiple sections of Provincial Highways 8 and 9 within Taroko National Park (Fig. 4b), isolating hundreds of residents and tourists. The combination of severe shaking, rugged terrain, and aftershock-induced rockfalls created one of the most complex emergency situations in Taiwan since the 1999 Chi-Chi earthquake.

Figure 4. Maps illustrating areas of high potential for earthquake-induced landslides and associated facilities identified for safety inspection. (a) Intensity distribution and high-landslide-risk grids (500 × 500 m) computed by the rapid assessment system. The red star marks the epicenter, and the black rectangle indicates the extent of panels (b–d). (b) Enlarged view of the most severely affected region, showing high-risk grids and nearby transportation routes including provincial highways. The colored contour lines denote surface shaking intensity. (c) Settlements located within high-risk grids. Population estimates within each grid are derived from anonymized mobile-network data, with color shading representing the number of individuals per 500 × 500 m cell. (d) Locations of high-voltage power towers situated in high-landslide-risk grids that may be susceptible to slope failure.

Seismic and geological mapping

The seismic source parameters of the 2024 Hualien earthquake immediately suggested the potential for severe surface impacts. The mainshock occurred at the boundary between land and sea near Shoufeng Township, Hualien, at a shallow depth of only 19.7 km (Fig. 2a). Such a shallow focus implied that much of the released energy would reach the surface with limited attenuation, producing strong ground motion across a wide area. Intensity measurements confirmed this expectation: large parts of northern and central Taiwan experienced shaking of intensity level 5 or greater, whereas Hualien City recorded some of the most intense shaking nationwide (Fig. 2a). These early observations allowed rapid inference that severe structural damage would concentrate in Hualien City and extend into northern Taiwan. Subsequent building safety inspections, which identified clusters of red- and yellow-tagged buildings in precisely these regions, validated the initial assessment (Fig. 6).

The spatial distribution of aftershocks provided further constraints on the seismogenic structure (Fig. 2c). Hypocentral

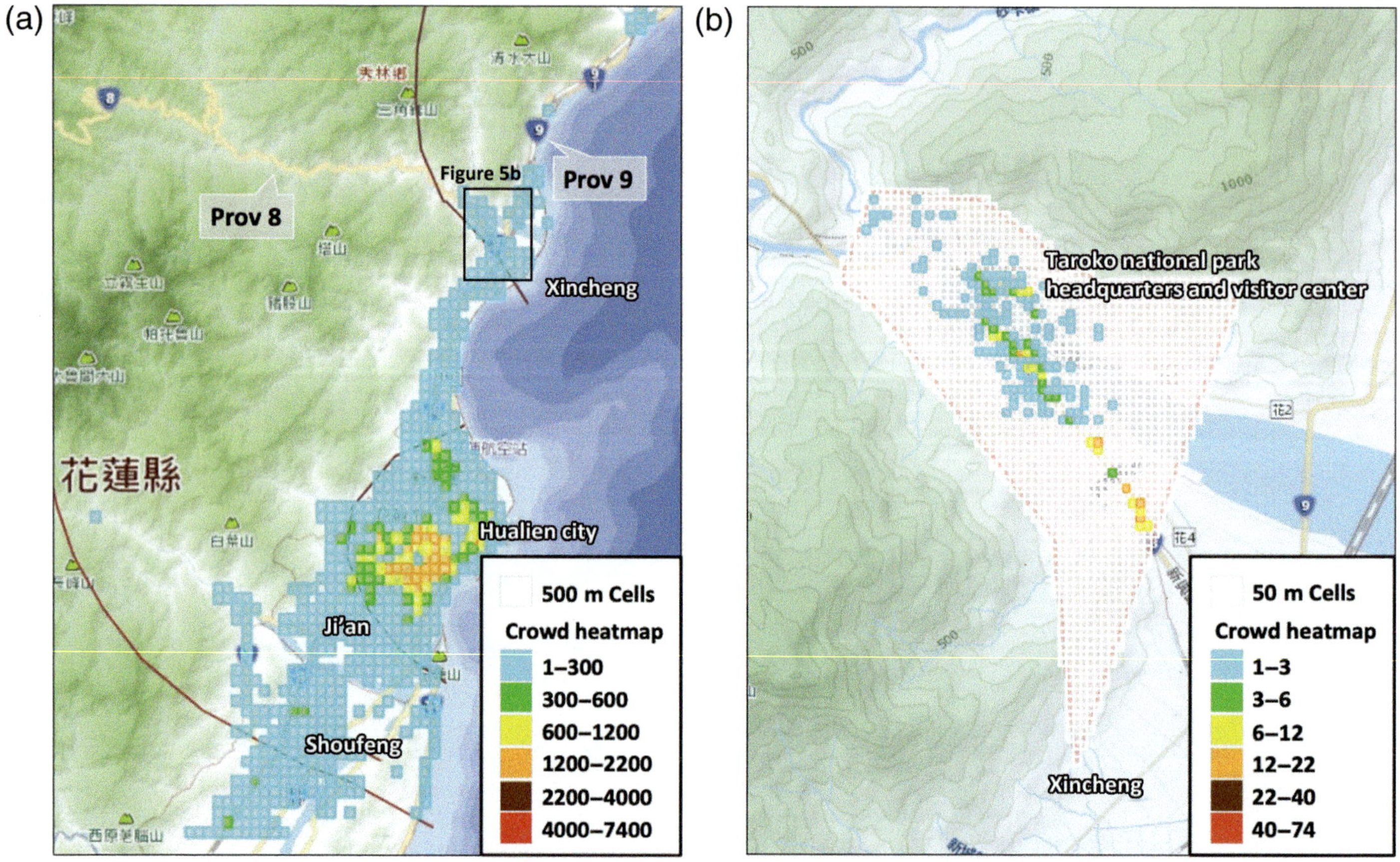

Figure 5. Population distribution estimated from anonymized mobile network data at 07:50 local time, the record closest to the 07:58 mainshock of the 2024 Hualien earthquake. The colors indicate the number of active mobile users derived from signal counts within each grid cell. (a) Population density mapped at a 500 × 500 m resolution for northern Hualien. The black-dashed rectangle marks the extent shown in panel (b). (b) Detailed population distribution in the vicinity of the Taroko National Park Headquarters and Visitor Center, mapped at a 50 × 50 m resolution.

clustering aligned closely with the Lingding fault, a segment of the Longitudinal Valley Fault system known for its high degree of locking and limited interseismic creep (Chen *et al.*, 2006). This tectonic behavior is consistent with the occurrence of a large mainshock and the expectation of abundant aftershocks released along the same structure. The aftershock cloud also extended into adjacent faults within the Central Range, suggesting a broader zone of stress redistribution and structural interaction (Shyu *et al.*, 2006; Lee *et al.*, 2023; Tang *et al.*, 2023; Chen *et al.*, 2024). This rapid correlation between seismicity and fault geometry provided near-real-time evidence for the controlling fault system, guiding both scientific interpretation and operational monitoring of ongoing seismic hazards.

Compared with the 1999 Chi-Chi earthquake, when rupture identification and fault association required weeks of field investigations and inversion analyses, the 2024 Hualien earthquake demonstrated the effectiveness of integrating epicentral data, intensity measurements, and aftershock distributions into a unified framework. These advances enabled scientists and decision-makers to infer likely impact zones and controlling faults within hours of the mainshock, representing a substantial improvement in situational awareness and response capability.

Assessment of critical infrastructure damage

Postevent assessments revealed that damage to critical infrastructure closely aligned with areas identified as high risk in the early-stage response maps (Figs. 3 and 4). In the power sector, although no high-voltage transmission towers collapsed, the Heping Power Plant in Hualien and the Taichung Power Plant in central Taiwan—both located within intensity level 4 or higher zones—reported damage to generation units and deformation of pipelines, leading to temporary reductions in power output (Fig. 6). Hualien Port experienced severe soil liquefaction and sand boils that caused ground subsidence and uplift, disrupting vessel operations.

Lifeline systems were also strongly affected, with widespread damage to power and water networks resulting in outages for roughly 370,000 households and water supply interruptions for more than 120,000 households. These facilities, situated within the strong-shaking zones, were prioritized for safety inspection during the initial response. Furthermore, several segments of Provincial Highways 8 and 9—highlighted in the system's early hazard maps as high-risk routes—sustained major slope failures and blockages (Fig. 4b,c). Settlements along Highway 8 reported trapped residents,

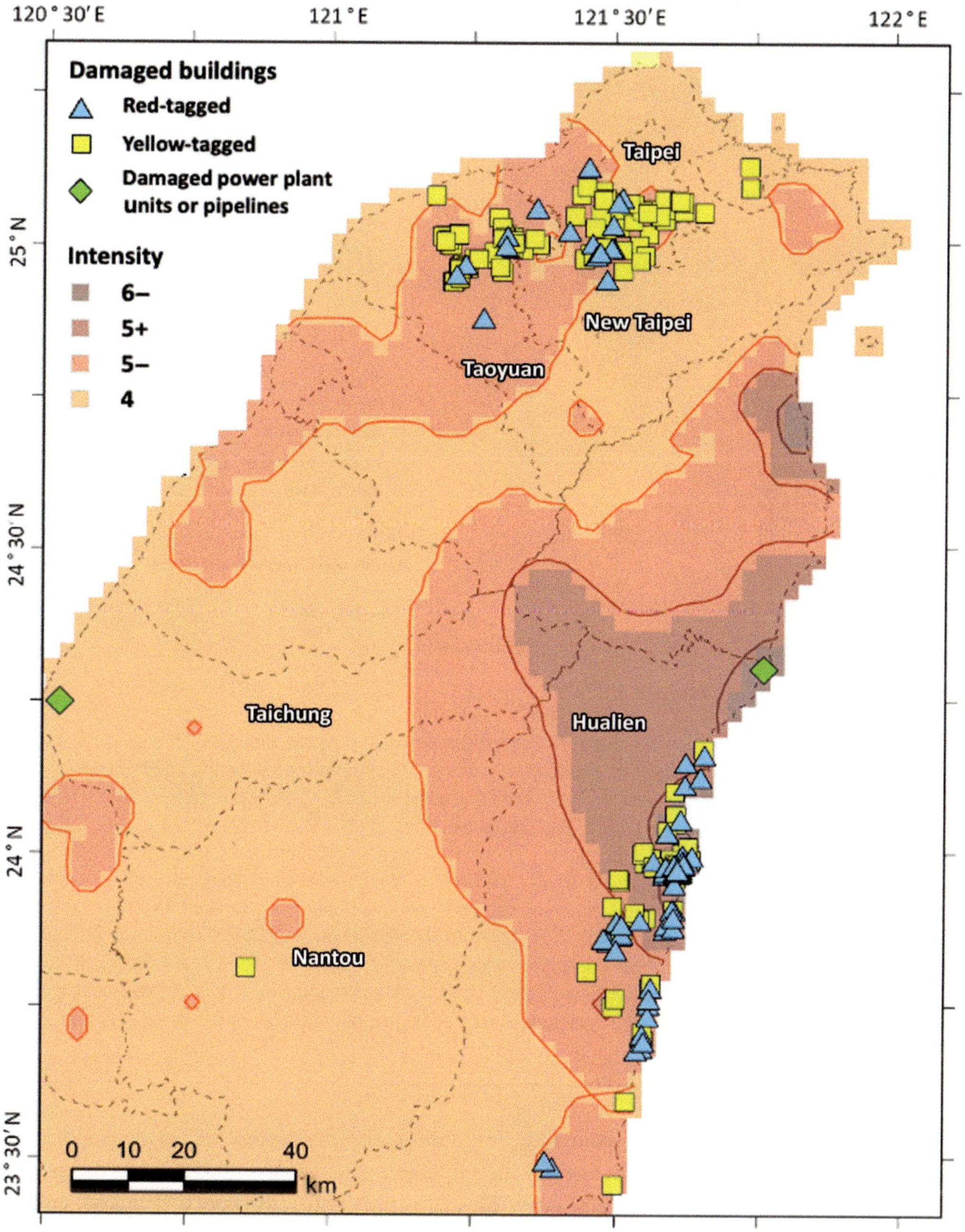

Figure 6. Distribution of damaged buildings and affected power facilities overlaid on the ground-shaking intensity map of the 2024 Hualien earthquake. The background shows seismic intensity derived from the CWA. The blue triangles represent buildings classified as red-tagged, yellow squares represent yellow-tagged buildings, and green diamonds denote power plants that sustained unit or line damage. Major cities are labeled for reference.

further confirming the predictive accuracy of the integrated framework in identifying vulnerable infrastructure corridors.

Landslide risk validation

The landslide risk model, calibrated with the 1999 Chi-Chi earthquake (Ke *et al.*, 2016), was applied to the 2024 Hualien event to test its predictive performance. Grids with scores above 10 were flagged as highly susceptible to slope failure and displayed in rapid impact maps within 15 min after the mainshock (Fig. 4). Comparison with the satellite-derived coseismic landslide catalog of Chang *et al.* (2024) demonstrates strong correspondence between predicted high-risk areas and observed slope failures (Fig. 7). Of the 3232 mapped landslide sites, 70% (2264) fell within high-risk grids, covering 82% of the total landslide-affected area (Fig. 6a). The model was particularly effective along Provincial Highways 8 and 9, where predicted hotspots aligned with actual blockages that disrupted access to Taroko National Park. These results confirm that a threshold-based approach can provide a scientifically robust first-order estimate of secondary hazards immediately after a major earthquake.

Nevertheless, discrepancies were observed (Fig. 7b). In northern Hualien and southern Yilan, where PGA exceeded 250 gal, the model overpredicted landslide occurrence in resistant terrains. By contrast, in southern Hualien, numerous slope failures occurred despite PGA values below 250 gal, leading to underprediction. These mismatches highlight the importance of local lithological and structural conditions in modulating slope response to ground shaking. Although the Chi-Chi-based thresholds remain valid as a national baseline, refinements through regional calibration will be necessary to improve accuracy across Taiwan's diverse geomorphic settings.

Mobile data and population exposure

Anonymized mobile network data provided near-real-time insights into population distribution during the 2024 Hualien earthquake. Within two hours of the mainshock, the system estimated that approximately 567 people were present in Tianxiang and 15 in the Heliu–Lushui camping area

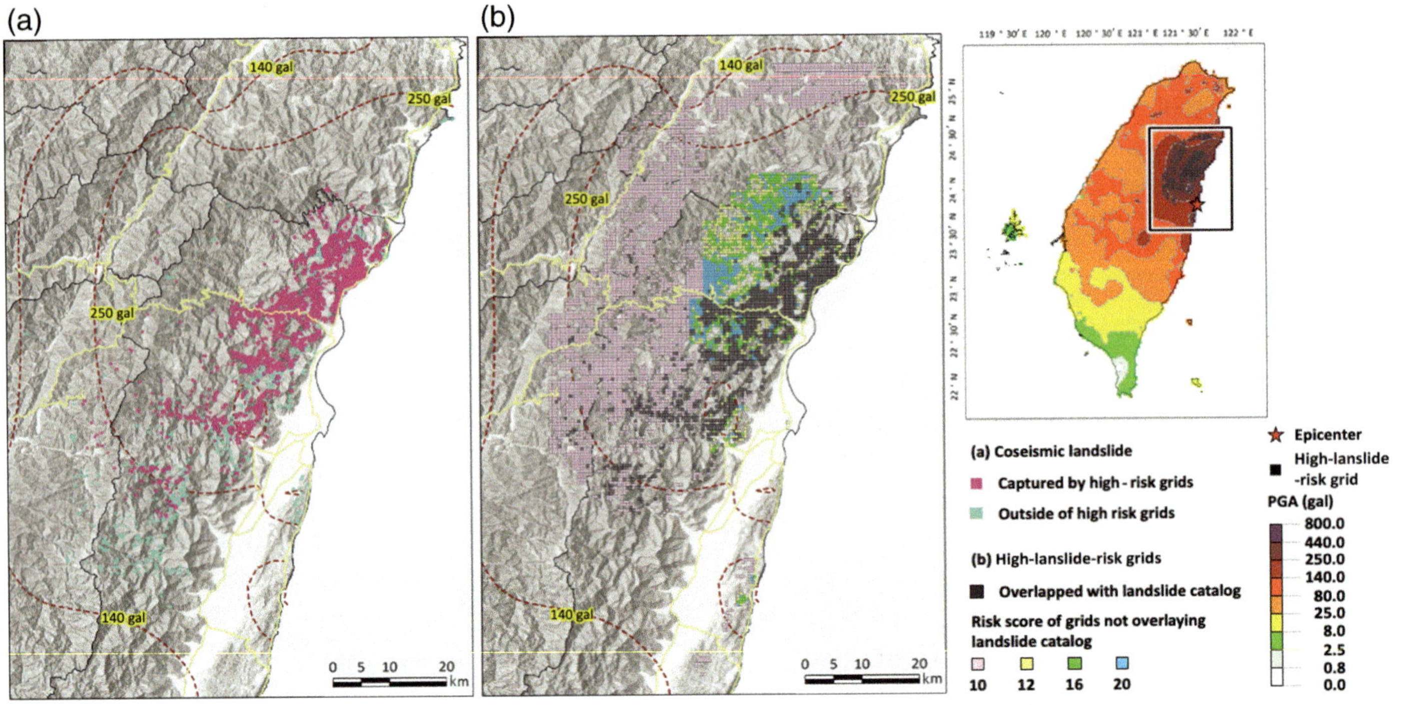

Figure 7. Comparison between modeled high-landslide-risk grids and the satellite-derived coseismic-landslide inventory for the 2024 Hualien earthquake. The right panel shows the distribution of PGA across Taiwan, with a black rectangle indicating the location of panels (a) and (b). (a) Coseismic landslides interpreted from postevent satellite images (Chang *et al.*, 2024). The hot-pink polygons indicate landslides located within modeled high-risk grids, and light-blue polygons mark landslides situated outside those grids. (b) Modeled high-landslide-risk grids. The black cells denote grids overlapping with mapped landslides, and colored cells (pink, yellow, light green, and blue) represent high-risk grids not overlapping with the inventory, corresponding to risk-score levels of 10, 12, 16, and 20, respectively.

along Provincial Highway 8 (Fig. 8). These estimates closely matched official CEOC reports compiled more than a day later (Central Emergency Operation Center, 2024), which documented 587 and 18 trapped individuals, respectively. The close correspondence demonstrates that telecom-based exposure mapping can rapidly capture both the scale and spatial concentration of isolated populations.

Beyond numerical accuracy, the mobile data highlighted critical features of the trapped population. Age-stratified signal counts indicated that more than 130 individuals in Tianxiang were over 60 years old, a demographic particularly vulnerable during prolonged isolation. This information provided actionable intelligence for prioritizing rescue operations and tailoring the delivery of medical support and supplies. Moreover, time-series trends in mobile signals revealed that most evacuees left the Taroko corridor in the hours immediately following the earthquake, whereas stable counts in blocked segments reflected individuals unable to leave. These dynamic patterns cannot be captured by static census data or delayed field surveys, underscoring the added value of telecom-based monitoring. This focus on dynamic movement provides maximum operational value in tourist hot zones (such as the Taroko corridor) where the exposed population is overwhelmingly transient rather than locally resident. In these critical areas, rapidly capturing the scale of dynamic exposure is more important than achieving an absolute, comprehensive total population count.

Despite its advantages, the approach has limitations. Coverage depends on a single telecom operator, temporal resolution is restricted to 10-min intervals, and demographic details are coarse. Nevertheless, integrating mobile signals into earthquake response mapping represents a methodological advance by directly linking hazard layers with human exposure in real time. This capability shortens reporting delays, enhances situational awareness, and improves the targeting of rescue operations—particularly in mountainous terrain where access is constrained and time is critical.

The application of Taiwan's integrated decision-support system to the 2024 Hualien earthquake demonstrates how multisource data integration advances rapid hazard assessment. Seismic and geological mapping constrained rupture structures in near-real time, impact mapping reliably identified hotspots of structural and infrastructural damage, the landslide model captured most observed slope failures while revealing regional discrepancies, and mobile telecom data provided accurate, population-sensitive estimates of trapped individuals. Collectively, these results show how situational awareness has shifted from descriptive reporting in the 1999 Chi-Chi earthquake to predictive, spatially explicit mapping in 2024, underscoring both the methodological robustness and operational

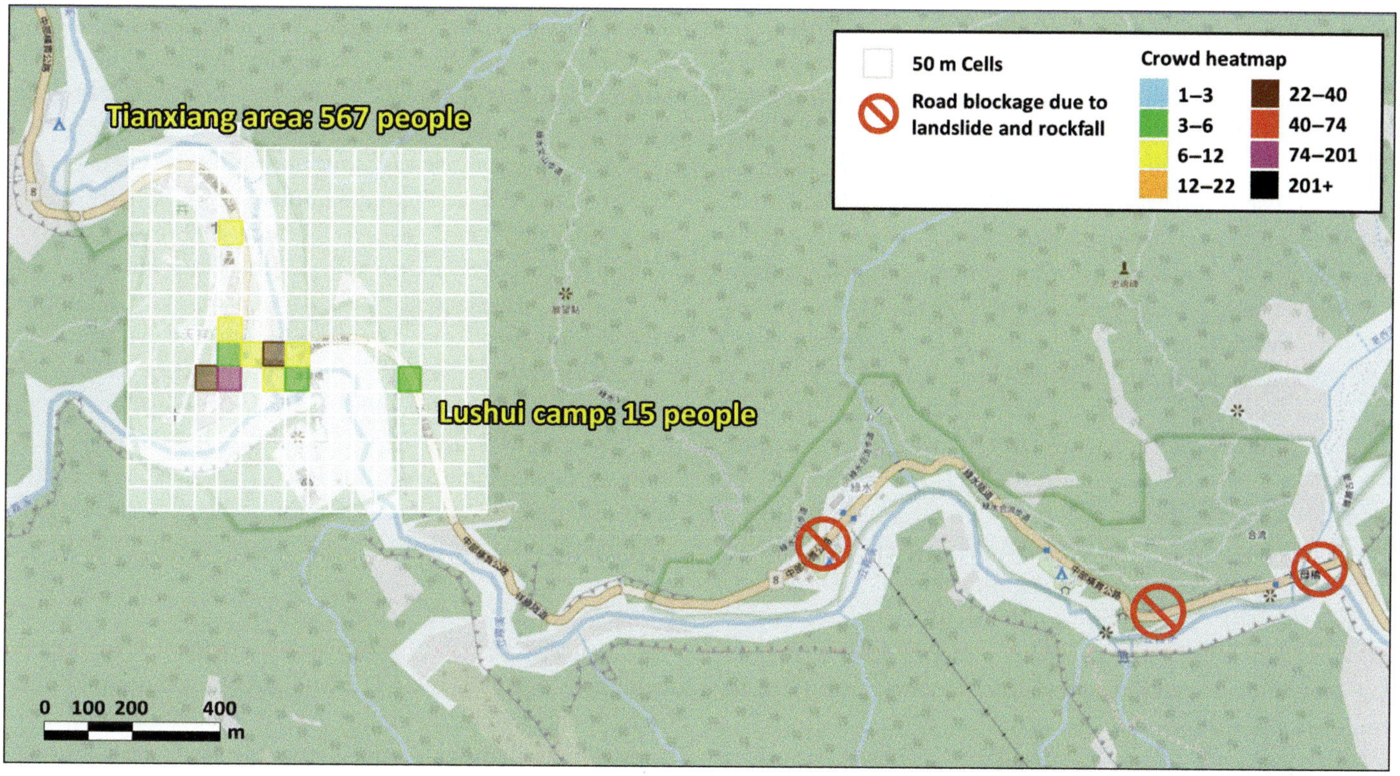

Figure 8. Estimated population distribution derived from anonymized mobile network data for the Tianxiang and Lushui areas along Provincial Highway 8, based on 50 × 50 m grids. Grid colors represent the number of active mobile users within each cell. The red symbols mark locations of road blockages reported due to landslides and rockfalls. The system estimated approximately 567 individuals in the Tianxiang area and 15 in the Lushui camp. The grid values correspond to direct signal counts, which were subsequently adjusted in the analysis using telecom market-share conversion.

value of the system and setting the stage for discussion of its broader scientific contributions and implications for disaster risk reduction.

DISCUSSIONS

Scientific contributions of the integrated framework

The integrated framework developed in Taiwan demonstrates how diverse data sets can be systematically combined to enhance the speed, transparency, and reproducibility of post-earthquake assessment. By embedding seismic, geological, landslide, and population data within a uniform 500 m × 500 m grid, the framework transforms primary observations into actionable hazard and exposure maps. This design enables consistent cross-event comparisons and rapid validation against observed outcomes, advancing both operational decision-making and earthquake science.

Several methodological contributions stand out. First, the grid-based hazard classification establishes a quantitative relationship between shaking thresholds and expected damage, providing a transparent and testable basis for rapid mapping. Second, integrating geomorphological sensitivity indices with PGA thresholds—calibrated using the 1999 Chi-Chi earthquake and validated by the 2024 Hualien event—offers a robust, data-driven approach for evaluating landslide potential. Third, the incorporation of anonymized mobile-network data introduces a population-sensitive dimension rarely available in traditional seismic analyses. By capturing short-term human mobility and isolation dynamics, this data set bridges the gap between physical hazard modeling and societal exposure.

Collectively, these methodological advances illustrate how a decision-support system can evolve into a reproducible research framework that benefits both emergency response operations and scientific understanding of earthquake processes.

Lessons from 1999 Chi-Chi versus 2024 Hualien

A direct comparison between the 1999 Chi-Chi and 2024 Hualien earthquakes illustrates how advances in data availability and methodological integration have transformed earthquake disaster assessment in Taiwan. In 1999, situational awareness was severely constrained. Rupture identification relied on weeks of field surveys and inversion analyses, damage mapping was compiled manually from scattered reports, and population exposure was inferred indirectly from census data or household registries. As a result, early response decisions were made with limited scientific support and considerable uncertainty.

By contrast, the 2024 Hualien earthquake highlighted the effectiveness of an integrated and automated framework. Within hours of the mainshock, seismic and geological data were combined to constrain rupture geometry, grid-based hazard maps identified hotspots of building and infrastructure risk, and telecom-derived population data provided near-real-time estimates of trapped individuals. These products were validated against independent observations—including building inspection records, road blockages, and satellite-derived landslide inventories—demonstrating that scientifically reliable insights could be generated rapidly and reproduced across events.

The contrast underscores two critical lessons. First, systematic integration of heterogeneous data sets enables predictive, spatially explicit mapping that is far more informative than descriptive reporting alone. Second, cross-event calibration, such as using Chi-Chi landslide data to refine PGA thresholds, ensures that historical earthquakes continue to inform present-day risk assessment. Together, these lessons show how Taiwan has moved from reactive, post hoc assessment in 1999 to proactive, data-driven disaster science in 2024.

Broader implications for science-based earthquake governance

The experience of Taiwan illustrates how the institutionalization of science-based decision-making can fundamentally transform national earthquake response capacity. Following the 1999 Chi-Chi earthquake, the establishment of the NCDR through formal legislation marked a critical shift from ad hoc coordination to a permanent, data-driven decision-support structure. By embedding scientific research directly into disaster assessment operations, the NCDR has become a central bridge between academic research institutions and government agencies. It consolidates scientific findings, provides modeled disaster scenarios and impact simulations before major events, and delivers rapid, evidence-based analyses immediately after an earthquake.

A key strength of Taiwan's framework lies in the transparency and accessibility of scientific data. The integration of data sets from multiple government agencies—including the CWA, GSMMA, the Ministry of Transportation and Communications, and the National Land Management Agency—enables comprehensive and multihazard evaluations of earthquake impacts. This open-data environment ensures that decision-support outputs are grounded in authoritative, cross-sectoral information, while also fostering trust and collaboration among agencies and researchers.

Equally important is the operation of the CEOC, which serves as a national coordination platform linking scientific assessments with emergency response. During the initial hours after a major earthquake, the CEOC convenes representatives from all relevant ministries to review model outputs generated by the decision-support system, identify the most probable high-impact areas, and prioritize field inspections by sectoral agencies. The inspection results are then fed back into CEOC meetings in near-real time, allowing continuous refinement of situational awareness and efficient allocation of response resources. This iterative exchange exemplifies a functional science-policy interface in which empirical data directly inform operational decisions.

Taiwan's experience demonstrates that integrating scientific institutions, transparent data systems, and centralized coordination mechanisms can create an effective ecosystem for disaster governance. Such a framework offers valuable lessons for other seismically active countries seeking to bridge the gap between scientific research and emergency management—showing how sustained investment in science-based institutions can translate into more adaptive, evidence-informed disaster response systems.

Limitations and future directions

Although the integrated framework demonstrated strong performance during the 2024 Hualien earthquake, several limitations remain. First, the landslide risk model relies on PGA thresholds calibrated primarily from the 1999 Chi-Chi earthquake. Although this baseline proved effective for central Hualien, discrepancies indicate that uniform thresholds cannot fully capture regional variations in slope conditions. Beyond seismic shaking from a single event, landslide occurrence is also strongly influenced by cumulative factors, including long-term slope degradation from repeated earthquakes (Keefer, 1994; Kuo and Brierley, 2014; Cui *et al.*, 2024), the thickness of weathered material accumulated on hillslopes (Duzgoren-Aydin and Aydin, 2006; Regmi *et al.*, 2013) and antecedent hydrological conditions such as heavy rainfall or typhoon-induced precipitation that predispose slopes to failure (Sassa *et al.*, 2007; Faris and Fawu, 2014). These factors may substantially alter slope stability and should therefore be systematically monitored. Regular field investigations and satellite-based remote sensing are needed to track the evolution of slope conditions, whereas new landslide inventories should be compiled following large earthquakes, typhoons, or extreme rainfall events to capture emergent failures. Dynamic adjustments to high-risk score thresholds may also be necessary, with higher values in regions with frequent slope failures and lower values in areas with little historical activity. Future work should thus pursue regional calibration using multiple inventories to refine susceptibility parameters for different geological provinces.

Second, reliance on a single telecom operator constrains the representativeness of population exposure estimates. Coverage gaps, network outages, and demographic biases may introduce systematic errors, whereas the 10-min update interval limits temporal resolution during highly dynamic evacuation phases. In the current framework, although the analysis relies solely on data from Chunghwa Telecom, this operator is the largest in

Taiwan, with a market share of approximately 40% and the widest base-station coverage nationwide. These characteristics provide a reasonable degree of representativeness in terms of both spatial distribution and user numbers. The credibility of this approach has been supported by previous applications, such as estimating attendance at a large concert event using telecom signals adjusted by market share, where results closely matched the known venue capacities (Wu *et al.*, 2022). Similarly, during the 2024 Hualien earthquake, estimates of trapped individuals in mountainous areas closely aligned with official reports, demonstrating the reliability of the current method. Nonetheless, incorporating data from multiple operators, as well as complementary mobility proxies such as Global Positioning System traces or social media geotags, would further mitigate these gaps and enhance robustness.

Third, issues of data governance and privacy remain critical. Although mobile data are anonymized, public trust and legal frameworks must be strengthened to ensure ethical use in disaster contexts. Developing clear protocols for data access, anonymization, and interagency sharing will be essential for broader adoption.

Looking forward, expanding data diversity and refining integration strategies will be central to advancing the framework. Potential directions include applying machine learning to detect landslide precursors from satellite imagery (Mohan *et al.*, 2020; Yi and Zhang, 2020), integrating real-time GNSS displacements with strong-motion data to improve shaking field estimation (Bock *et al.*, 2011; Dahmen *et al.*, 2020), and extending the methodology to international testbeds in seismically active mountain belts (Tanyaş *et al.*, 2017). Addressing these limitations will not only enhance Taiwan's resilience but also contribute to the global development of transparent, population-sensitive disaster information systems.

CONCLUSION

This study demonstrates how the integration of seismic, geological, landslide, and mobile data has transformed earthquake disaster assessment in Taiwan over the past 25 yr. Application of the framework to the 2024 Hualien earthquake showed that rapid mapping products could accurately delineate zones of strong shaking, validate damage hotspots, capture the majority of coseismic landslides, and estimate trapped populations with high fidelity. Together, these results highlight the system's ability to translate initial observations into spatially explicit, reproducible, and operationally useful hazard information within hours of a major earthquake.

Compared with the 1999 Chi-Chi earthquake, when rupture geometry, damage distribution, and population exposure were only understood after weeks of field investigation, the 2024 system provided scientifically validated insights in near-real time. This progress reflects methodological advances including grid-based hazard classification, cross-event calibration of landslide thresholds, and the incorporation of telecom-derived population dynamics. These contributions not only improved situational awareness during the Hualien event but also extend the scientific foundations of earthquake hazard assessment.

Looking forward, continued refinement will be necessary to address limitations such as the need for region-specific landslide calibration, expansion of telecom data sources, and the development of robust privacy frameworks. Nonetheless, Taiwan's integrated approach offers a reproducible template that bridges hazard science and operational response. By demonstrating how multisource data can be systematically combined to improve both accuracy and timeliness, this study provides lessons of broad relevance to other seismically active regions worldwide, where rapid, population-sensitive disaster information is essential for effective risk reduction.

DATA AND RESOURCES

The earthquake catalog used in this study was obtained from the Central Weather Administration of Taiwan. The data are publicly accessible through the Central Weather Administration (CWA) Earthquake Database (https://scweb.cwa.gov.tw/zh-tw/earthquake/data/). A relocated earthquake catalog covering events from 1990 to 2020 was provided by Yih-Min Wu and is available at http://seismology.gl.ntu.edu.tw/download.htm. Focal mechanism solutions were retrieved from the AutoBATS CMT catalog (https://tecdc.earth.sinica.edu.tw/FM/AutoBATS/). Active fault and lithological data were provided by the Geological Survey and Mining Management Agency, accessible at https://fault.gsmma.gov.tw/About/Fault_map and https://geomap.gsmma.gov.tw/gsb108-1/, respectively. Reports from each ministry presented during 2024 Hualien earthquake CEOC working meetings are publicly available through the official CEOC YouTube channel (https://www.youtube.com/channel/UCNj2vsaYzmxMZvyvfAX3tSQ). Icons used in Figure 1 were designed by various authors from Flaticon (https://www.flaticon.com/), used under the Free License with attribution. Geological profile in Figure 2 are published in the book *The Seismic Zones of Taiwan*, released by the National Science and Technology Center for Disaster Reduction (NCDR) in 2024, and can be accessed through NCDR's official website (https://www.ncdr.nat.gov.tw/Message/MessageView?itemid=6020&mid=70). All websites were last accessed in October 2025. The supplemental material to this article includes two primary components. The first provides a detailed description of the data sets used in this study, including data types, sources, and update frequencies. The second outlines how the Central Emergency Operation Center (CEOC) was activated and the corresponding phases of NCDR's response operations.

ACKNOWLEDGMENTS

The authors sincerely acknowledge the Central Weather Administration for providing real-time seismic observation data; the Geological Survey and Mining Management Agency for supplying geological and active fault data; the Ministry of Transportation and Communications for delivering essential road and infrastructure information; the National Land Management Agency for the damaged-building catalog; Che-Ming Yang for the earthquake-induced landslide catalog of the 2024 Hualien earthquake; and members of the Earthquake and Man-made disaster division of the National

Science and Technology Center for Disaster Reduction (NCDR) for supporting the earthquake emergency operations. The authors are also grateful to the editors and two anonymous reviewers for their constructive and insightful comments, which greatly improved the quality of this article.

REFERENCES

Bock, Y., D. Melgar, and B. W. Crowell (2011). Real-time strong-motion broadband displacements from collocated GPS and accelerometers, *Bull. Seismol. Soc. Am.* **101,** no. 6, 2904–2925, doi: 10.1785/0120110007.

Central Emergency Operation Center (2024). Official situation report No. 21 on the emergency response to the April 3 Hualien earthquake (in Chinese).

Chang, J. M., W. A. Chao, C. M. Yang, and M. W. Huang (2024). Coseismic and subsequent landslides of the 2024 Hualien earthquake (M7.2) on April 3 in Taiwan, *Landslides* **21,** 2591–2595, doi: 10.1007/s10346-024-02312-x.

Chen, W. S. (2016). An introduction to the geology of Taiwan, Geological Society located in Taipei, Taipei, Taiwan (in Chinese).

Chen, W. S., N. W. Huang, and C. C. Yang (2011). Pleistocene sequence stratigraphic characteristics and foreland basin evolution, southwestern Taiwan, *Spec. Publication Cent. Geol. Surv.* **25,** 1–38 (in Chinese).

Chen, W. S., Y. M. Wu, P. Y. Yeh, Y. X. Lai, S. S. Ke, M. C. Ke, and C. Y. Yang (2024). Insights into the seismogenic structures of the arc-continent convergent plate boundary in eastern Taiwan, *Terr. Atmos. Ocean. Sci.* **35,** no. 13, doi: 10.1007/s44195-024-00065-7.

Chen, W. S., I. C. Yen, K. P. Fengler, C. M. Rubin, C. C. Yang, H. C. Yang, H. C. Chang, C. W. Lin, W. H. Lin, Y. C. Liu, and Y. H. Lin (2006). Late Holocene paleoearthquake activity in the middle part of the Longitudinal Valley fault, eastern Taiwan, *Earth Planet. Sci. Lett.* **264,** nos. 3/4, 420–437, doi: 10.1016/j.epsl.2007.09.043.

Cheng, C. T., S. J. Chiou, and Y. B. Tsai (2007). Study on probabilistic seismic hazard maps of Taiwan after Chi-Chi earthquake, *J. GeoEng.* **2,** no. 1, 19–28, doi: 10.6310/jog.2007.2(1).3.

Cleveland, R. B., W. S. Cleveland, J. E. McRae, and I. Terpenning (1990). STL: A seasonal-trend decomposition procedure based on LOESS, *J. Off. Stat.* **6,** 3–73.

Cui, S., X. Pei, R. Huang, L. Zhu, H. Yang, Y. Liang, and C. Zhu (2024). The analysis of seismic induced progressive instability and failure mechanisms: A case study, *Int. J. Rock Mech. Min. Sci.* **174,** 105,646, doi: 10.1016/j.ijrmms.2024.105646.

Dahmen, N., R. Hohensinn, and J. Clinton (2020). Comparison and combination of GNSS and strong-motion observations: A case study of the 2016 M_W 7.0 Kumamoto earthquake, *Bull. Seismol. Soc. Am.* **110,** no. 6, 2647–2660, doi: 10.1785/0120200135.

Duzgoren-Aydin, N. S., and A. Aydin (2006). Chemical and mineralogical heterogeneities of weathered igneous profiles: Implications for landslide investigations, *Nat. Hazards Earth Syst. Sci.* **6,** 315–322, doi: 10.5194/nhess-6-315-2006.

Faris, F., and W. Fawu (2014). Investigation of the initiation mechanism of an earthquake- induced landslide during rainfall: A case study of the Tandikat landslide, West Sumatra, Indonesia, *Geoenviron. Disasters* **1,** 4, doi: 10.1186/s40677-014-0004-3.

Huang, M. W., M. C. Ke, and S. Y. Liu (2019). Mobile communication data for pedestrian flow information platform and applications, *Technical Rept. of the National Science and Technology Center for Disaster Reduction*, NCDR 107-A22, Taipei, Taiwan (in Chinese).

Huang, M. W., C. Wu, M. C. Ke, S. Y. Liu, and S. S. Ke (2021). The analysis of human dynamic and its application using mobile network data, *Technical Rept. of the National Science and Technology Center for Disaster Reduction*, NCDR 110-T19, Taipei, Taiwan (in Chinese).

Ke, M. C., M. W. Huang, and S. C. Lin (2016). Establishment and application of rapid potential assessment for earthquake-induced landslides, *Mag. Chin. Inst. Civil Hydraul. Eng.* **43,** no. 3, 17–26 (in Chinese).

Ke, S. S., C. H. Hsu, and C. Y. Yang (2023). Rapid crisis response in resilient cities: Emergency response to and reconnaissance of earthquake disasters in Taiwan, *J. Earthq. Tsunami* **18,** no. 4, 2,450,008, doi: 10.1142/S1793431124500088.

Keefer, D. K. (1994). The importance of earthquake-induced landslides to long-term slope erosion and slope-failure hazards in seismically active regions, in *Geomorphology and Natural Hazards*, Elsevier, 265–284, doi: 10.1016/0169-555X(94)90021-3.

Khazai, B., and N. Sitar (2004). Evaluation of factors controlling earthquake-induced landslides caused by Chi-Chi earthquake and comparison with the Northridge and Loma Prieta events, *Eng. Geol.* **7,** nos. 1/2, 79–95, doi: 10.1016/S0013-7952(03)00127-3.

Kuo, C. W., and G. Brierley (2014). The influence of landscape connectivity and landslide dynamics upon channel adjustments and sediment flux in the Liwu basin, Taiwan, *Earth Surf. Process. Landf.* **39,** no. 15, 2038–2055, doi: 10.1002/esp.3598.

Lee, S. J., T. Y. Liu, and T. C. Lin (2023). The role of the west-dipping collision boundary fault in the Taiwan 2022 Chihshang earthquake sequence, *Sci. Rep.* **13,** 3552, doi: 10.1038/s41598-023-30361-0.

Lin, C. W., Y. C. Liu, P. S. Chou, and Y. H. Lin (2021). Recent development of active fault investigations of Taiwan, *Bull. Cent Geol. Surv.* **34,** 1–40 (in Chinese).

Liu, S. Y., C. Wu, S. S. Ke, C. S. Lee, W. S. Li, and C. L. Chang (2016). Digital grid technology in seismic impact analysis and applications, *Mag. Chin. Inst. Civil Hydraul. Eng.* **43,** no. 3, 55–62 (in Chinese).

Ma, K. F., C. T. Lee, and Y. B. Tsai (1999). The Chi-Chi, Taiwan earthquake: Large surface displacements on an inland thrust fault, *Eos Trans. AGU* **80,** no. 50, 605–611, doi: 10.1029/99EO00405.

Ma, K. F., J. Mori, S. J. Lee, and S. B. Yu (2001). Spatial and temporal distribution of slip for the 1999 Chi-Chi, Taiwan, earthquake, *Bull. Seismol. Soc. Am.* **91,** no. 5, 1069–1087, doi: 10.1785/0120000728.

Ministry of Transportation and Communications (2024). *Report of 7th CEOC Working Meeting of the April 3rd Hualien Earthquake*, Central Emergency Operation Center, Taipei, Taiwan (in Chinese).

Mohan, A., A. K. Singh, B. Kumar, and R. Dwivedi (2020). Review on remote sensing methods for landslide detection using machine and deep learning, *Trans. Emerging Telecommun. Technol.* **32,** no. 7, e3998, doi: 10.1002/ett.3998.

National Fire Agency (2024). *Report of 7th CEOC Working Meeting of the April 3rd Hualien Earthquake*, Central Emergency Operation Center, Taipei, Taiwan (in Chinese).

National Science and Technology Center for Disaster Reduction (2024). *Report of 1st CEOC Working Meeting of the April 3rd Hualien Earthquake*, Central Emergency Operation Center, Taipei, Taiwan (in Chinese).

Regmi, A. D., K. Yoshida, M. R. Dhital, and K. Devkota (2013). Effect of rock weathering, clay mineralogy, and geological structures in the formation of large landslide, a case study from Dumre Bese landslide, Lesser Himalaya Nepal, *Landslides* **10,** no. 1, 1–13, doi: 10.1007/s10346-011-0311-7.

Sassa, K., H. Fukuoka, F. Wang, and G. Wang (2007). Landslides induced by a combined effect of earthquake and rainfall, in *Progress in Landslide Science*, Springer Berlin Heidelberg, Berlin, Heidelberg, 193–207, doi: 10.1007/978-3-540-70965-7_14.

Shin, T. C., and T. L. Teng (2001). An overview of the 1999 Chi-Chi, Taiwan, earthquake, *Bull. Seismol. Soc. Am.* **91,** no. 5, 895–913, doi: 10.1785/0120000738.

Shou, K. J., and C. F. Wang (2003). Analysis of the Chiufengershan landslide triggered by the 1999 Chi-Chi earthquake in Taiwan, *Eng. Geol.* **68,** nos. 3/4, 237–250, doi: 10.1016/S0013-7952(02)00230-2.

Shyu, J. B. H., K. Sieh, Y. G. Chen, and L. H. Chung (2006). Geomorphic analysis of the Central Range fault, the second major active structure of the Longitudinal Valley suture, eastern Taiwan, *Geol. Soc. Am. Bull.* **118,** nos. 11/12, 1447–1462, doi: 10.1130/B25905.1.

Suppe, J. (1980a). A retrodeformable cross section of northern Taiwan, *Proc. Geol. Soc. China* **23,** 46–55.

Suppe, J. (1980b). Imbricated structure of western foothills belt, south-central Taiwan, *Pet. Geol. Taiwan* **17,** 1–16.

Tang, C. H., Y. N. Lin, H. Tung, Y. Wang, S. J. Lee, Y. J. Hsu, J. B. H. Shyu, Y. T. Kuo, and H. Y. Chen (2023). Nearby fault interaction within the double-vergence suture in eastern Taiwan during the 2022 Chihshang earthquake sequence, *Commun. Earth Environ.* **4,** 333, doi: 10.1038/s43247-023-00994-0.

Tanyaş, H., C. J. van Westen, K. E. Allstadt, M. A. N. Jessee, T. Görüm, R. W. Jibson, J. W. Godt, H. P. Sato, R. G. Schmitt, O. Marc, and N. Hovius (2017). Presentation and analysis of a worldwide database of earthquake-induced landslide inventories, *J. Geophys. Res. Earth Surf.* **122,** 1991–2015, doi: 10.1002/2017JF004236.

Tsai, Y. B., T. M. Yu, H. L. Chao, and C. P. Lee (2001). Spatial distribution and age dependence of human-fatality rates from the Chi-Chi, Taiwan, earthquake of 21 September 1999, *Bull. Seismol. Soc. Am.* **91,** no. 5, 1298–1309, doi: 10.1785/0120000740.

Wang, Y. J., C. H. Chan, Y. T. Lee, K. F. Ma, J. B. H. Shyu, R. J. Rau, and C. T. Cheng (2016). Probabilistic seismic hazard assessment for Taiwan, *Terr. Atmos. Ocean. Sci.* **27,** no. 3, 325–340, doi: 10.3319/TAO.2016.05.03.01(TEM).

Wu, C., M. W. Huang, M. C. Ke, and S. Y. Liu (2022). Mobile communication crowd flow computation function and applications, *Technical Rept. of the National Science and Technology Center for Disaster Reduction*, NCDR 111-A27, Taipei, Taiwan (in Chinese).

Wu, Y. M., C. H. Chang, L. Zhao, T. L. Teng, and M. Nakamura (2008). A comprehensive relocation of earthquakes in Taiwan from 1991 to 2005, *Bull. Seismol. Soc. Am.* **98,** 1471–1481, doi: 10.1785/0120070166.

Yang, C. Y., K. T. Tu, M. C. Ke, M. W. Huang, T. S. Wu, C. Wu, B. R. Wu, C. Y. Lin, C. H. Hsu, S. Y. Liu, *et al.* (2024). Emergency operations, geological characteristics, and disaster information compilation of the April 3rd Hualien earthquake, *Technical Rept. of the National Science and Technology Center for Disaster Reduction*, NCDR 113-A25, Taipei, Taiwan (in Chinese).

Yang, K. M., S. T. Huang, J. C. Wu, H. H. Ting, and W. W. Mei (2006). Review and new insights on foreland tectonics in western Taiwan, *Int. Geol. Rev.* **48,** no. 10, 910–941, doi: 10.2747/0020-6814.48.10.910.

Yang, K. M., S. T. Huang, J. C. Wu, H. H. Ting, W. W. Mei, and H. H. Hsu (2002). Studies on geological structures and crustal deformation in the thrust belt onshore Taiwan (III)- northwesten areas (Hsincheng fault), *Rept. of Central Geological Survey*, 52 (in Chinese).

Yang, K. M., S. T. Huang, J. C. Wu, H. H. Ting, W. W. Mei, M. Lee, H. H. Hsu, and C. J. Lee (2007). 3D geometry of the Chelungpu thrust system in central Taiwan: Its implications for active tectonics, *Terr. Atmos. Ocean. Sci.* **18,** no. 2, 143–181, doi: 10.3319/TAO.2007.18.2.143(TCDP).

Yeh, E. H., P. Lin, and M. W. Huang (2022). ADPD: Anomaly detection for population distribution in geo-space using mobile networks data, *Internet Things J.* **9,** no. 22, 22,774–22,784, doi: 10.1109/JIOT.2022.3184072.

Yi, Y., and W. Zhang (2020). A new deep-learning-based approach for earthquake-triggered landslide detection from single-temporal RapidEye satellite imagery, *J. Sel. Topics Appl. Earth Obs. Remote Sens.* **13,** 6166–6176, doi: 10.1109/JSTARS.2020.3028855.

Yue, L. F., J. Suppe, and J. H. Hung (2005). Structural geology of a classic thrust belt earthquake: the 1999 Chi-Chi earthquake Taiwan (M_w 7.6), *J. Struct. Geol.* **27,** no. 11, 2058–2083, doi: 10.1016/j.jsg.2005.05.020.

Manuscript received 3 August 2025
Published online 18 November 2025

Attributes of Resilience in Disaster Response and Preparedness: Public–Private Collaboration During the 2016 and 2018 Earthquakes in Taiwan

Hsiang-Chieh Lee*[1], Hui Hsuan Yang[1], Shyh-Yuan Maa[2], and Hongey Chen[1,3]

ABSTRACT

Resilience has become a prominent concept in disaster management, yet empirical studies on its attributes remain scarce. This research has two main objectives: (1) to address this gap by examining the responses and related preparedness efforts of local governments to the earthquakes in Taiwan in 2016 and 2018, with a focus on collaboration between the public and private sectors, and (2) to further propose a conceptual diagram that illustrates the relationships among key attributes of resilience. Using interviews with key individuals and secondary data sources, the study identified five critical disaster response themes and 13 attributes of resilience. The conceptual diagram derived from the cases suggests that agility emerges as the overarching objective in the response phase and related preparedness phase; foresight capability and resourcefulness are key in the preparedness phase; creativity and connectivity are paramount in the response phase; and adaptive learning serves as a critical bridge between the two phases, fostering adaptation and evolution. Most attributes are anchored in the preparedness phase, reaffirming the principle that proactive measures are more effective than reactive ones. Furthermore, resourcefulness and inclusivity are crucial prerequisites for sustainability, and modularity is shown to be effectively applicable to organizational systems. This research contributes to a more nuanced understanding of the functional and operational aspects of resilience in seismic disaster contexts, emphasizing the need for balanced integration of all attributes for stronger disaster governance.

KEY POINTS

- This study discusses critical postearthquake response themes within the mitigation~response cycle.
- Attributes for success are adaptive learning, connectivity, resourcefulness, agility, creativity, and diversity.
- Public–private partnerships with local universities, nongovernmental organizations, and community groups are of great importance.

INTRODUCTION

Resilience has become a central concept in disaster management, referring to the capacity of systems, communities, and individuals to anticipate, prepare for, respond to, and recover from adversity (The National Academies, 2012). Because extreme weather events become normalized, the study of resilience has become crucial for informing effective policies and strategies for disaster management.

Despite its broad use, resilience often remains abstract within the disaster management literature, with limited attention to its real-world application. Few studies explore how specific resilience attributes contribute to different phases of disaster management and how they are related to one another.

This study addresses these gaps by analyzing two major earthquakes in Taiwan (2016 and 2018), focusing on local government collaboration with private sector actors during disaster response. The goals are to (1) identify how various resilience

1. National Science and Technology Center for Disaster Reduction, New Taipei City, Taiwan (R.O.C.), https://orcid.org/0000-0002-6101-4735 (H-CL); 2. Department of Urban Design and Sustainable Development, Ming Chuan University, Taoyuan, Taiwan (R.O.C.); 3. Department of Geosciences, National Taiwan University, Taipei, Taiwan (R.O.C.)

*Corresponding author: hchieh@ncdr.nat.gov.tw

Cite this article as Lee, H.-C., H. H. Yang, S.-Y. Maa, and H. Chen (2025). Attributes of Resilience in Disaster Response and Preparedness: Public–Private Collaboration During the 2016 and 2018 Earthquakes in Taiwan, *Bull. Seismol. Soc. Am.* **116**, 176–191, doi: 10.1785/0120250069 attributes were actualized in practice and (2) explore the relationships among these attributes. By grounding the analysis in empirical data, this study contributes to a more practical understanding of resilience in seismic disaster contexts.

LITERATURE REVIEWS

Evolution of resilience research

Resilience has gained significant interdisciplinary attention, evolving from its ecological origins (Holling, 1973) to encompass applications across sociology, psychology, and engineering (Adger, 2000; Bonanno, 2004; Manyena, 2006). Initially defined by Holling (1973) as the ability of an ecosystem to absorb disturbances while maintaining structure, this concept expanded to social systems, representing adaptive capacities in response to stressors. For instance, Bonanno (2004) demonstrated psychological resilience as a recovery process, challenging the inevitability of distress after trauma. Cutter *et al.* (2008) further developed community resilience frameworks, emphasizing not only recovery but also adaptation to future risks, influenced by social capital, economic resources, and governance.

More recently, resilience has intertwined with sustainability. Adger (2000) linked community resilience to social networks, institutions, and innovation in addressing environmental challenges, influencing policies for sustainable disaster management amid climate change. Furthermore, the importance of local contexts is increasingly recognized. For instance, Manyena (2006) highlights local knowledge, community involvement, and social networks as crucial for building resilience, especially in resource-constrained settings and advocating for context-specific strategies.

Disaster preparedness and response

In Taiwan, disaster management practitioners commonly adopt the four-phase disaster management cycle of mitigation, preparedness, response, and recovery. Within this framework, preparedness is traditionally viewed as a phase enables effective response. In contrast, U.S. federal policy treats preparedness as a foundational element supporting not only response but also mitigation and recovery (Fig. 1).

According to Homeland Security Presidential Directive/ HSPD-8 (2003), preparedness includes the plans, procedures, policies, training, and equipment necessary across all government levels to prevent, respond to, and recover from major events. This was reinforced by Presidential Policy Directive/ (PPD)-8 (2011), which emphasized building a national system to strengthen capabilities across all phases of disaster management.

According to the Homeland Security Presidential Directive/ HSPD-8 (2003, p. 1746), "The term 'Preparedness' refers to the existence of plans, procedures, policies, training, and equipment necessary at the Federal, State, and local level to maximize the ability to prevent, respond to, and recover from major events." This approach was reinforced by Presidential Policy Directive/

Figure 1. Phases of disaster management. The conceptual diagram illustrates the cyclical nature of disaster preparedness, encompassing direct postevent response measures, the recovery phase, and the subsequent implementation of mitigation strategies for future events.

PPD-8: National Preparedness (2011), which emphasized building a national preparedness system to improve the capabilities across all phases of disaster management. The 2022 National Preparedness Report reiterates this view and "summarizes [...] the capabilities needed to prevent, protect against, mitigate, respond to, and recover from the threats, hazards and incidents that pose the greatest risk to the nation" (FEMA, 2022, p. 3).

This study adopts this definition but narrows its focus to the response phase and preparedness activities that directly support response operations. Thus, the term *preparedness phase*, as used in this article, refers only to measures aimed at enhancing response effectiveness, not the full scope of preparedness functions in the disaster cycle.

Public–private cooperation in disaster management

Public–private cooperation refers to collaboration between governmental institutions and private sector entities to achieve shared goals. The public sector generally refers to government entities at various levels are responsible for policymaking, regulation, and public service delivery (Kapucu, 2006). It plays crucial roles in disaster management (Waugh and Streib, 2006). The private sector encompasses businesses, corporations, nongovernmental organizations (NGOs), and nonprofit organizations that operate independently of direct government control (Carter, 2008). These actors contribute specialized skills, resources, and innovation capabilities that complement governmental disaster management efforts (Comfort *et al.*, 2010).

Public–private cooperation has gained increasing attention due to complementary strengths each sector brings. During large-scale disasters, private companies often provide rapid logistical support, such as transportation, supply chain management, and communication infrastructure, more efficiently than public resources alone (Carter, 2008). Businesses also possess technical expertise and operational flexibility vital for innovative solutions in emergency medical services, telecommunications, and resource distribution (Comfort *et al.*, 2010).

Beyond response, public–private cooperation facilitates joint investment in risk assessments, early warning systems, and resilience building. Collaborations between governments and industries such as insurance, construction, and information technology have improved disaster risk modeling, resilient infrastructure design, and data-sharing frameworks (Boin and McConnell, 2007).

Effective public–private cooperation necessitates clearly defined roles, transparent communication, and mutual trust. Challenges such as conflicting priorities, unequal power dynamics, and data privacy concerns can impede collaboration (Olshansky and Chang, 2009). Addressing these issues requires formal agreements, shared training exercises, and integrated emergency management frameworks to strengthen partnerships (Kapucu and Garayev, 2011).

Attributes of resilience

This study reviewed resilience literature to examine how scholars have conceptualized its core attributes and to distinguish resilience from the traditional vulnerability approach. The resulting 14 attributes are as follows.

1. **Foresight capacity:** the capacity to anticipate and plan proactively for future uncertainties (Woods, 2005; Kuo *et al.*, 2022). The first step in the process resilience analysis framework is to identify potential risks that a process system might face and evaluate their impacts (Jain *et al.*, 2018).
2. **Robustness:** the ability to endure disturbances and adapt to new environments while maintaining core functions (Bruneau *et al.*, 2003; Klau and Weiskircher, 2005; Zolli and Healy, 2012; Kuo *et al.*, 2022). Often seen as an outcome, robustness can achieve through mechanisms such as modularity and redundancy (Csete and Doyle, 2002).
3. **Modularity:** characterized by semi-independent components, modularity enhances resilience by isolating failures and preventing systemic collapse (Zolli and Healy, 2012; Howe *et al.*, 2018; Kuo *et al.*, 2022).
4. **Redundancy:** the existence of multiple elements performing similar roles ensures functionality if one fails (Bruneau *et al.*, 2003). In ecology, systems with high species are more disturbances, or more tolerant (Biggs *et al.*, 2020). Similarly, system redundancy offers backup components or alternative pathways to ensure continued functionality (Zolli and Healy, 2012; Jain *et al.*, 2018; Kuo *et al.*, 2022).
5. **Flexibility:** in the current complex and uncertain world, flexibility becomes essential. Organizations that prioritize flexibility over strict adherence to standard operating procedures (SOPs) can better navigate uncertainty while upholding core goals (Zolli and Healy, 2012; Jain *et al.*, 2018).
6. **Adaptability learning:** often defined as the capacity to learn from disasters, acknowledge inherent vulnerabilities, and adjust to shocks (Folke *et al.*, 2003; Klein *et al.*, 2003; McAslan, 2010; Zolli and Healy, 2012; Kuo *et al.*, 2022). This concept often includes social learning, which emphasizes collective knowledge sharing (Djalante *et al.*, 2013; Choudhury *et al.*, 2021; Haque *et al.*, 2022). Small failures play a crucial role in releasing constraints and reorganizing systems for greater resilience (Jain *et al.*, 2018). However, some scholars contend that learning from experiences is not a necessary component of adaptability (Lengnick-Hall and Beck, 2005), thereby obscuring the conceptual boundary between adaptability and flexibility. To underscore the significance of experiential learning and to delineate it more clearly from flexibility, this study adopts the term *adaptive learning*.
7. **Sustainability:** the ability to maintain environmental, economic, and social systems in balance, ensuring long-term health and stability (Kuo *et al.*, 2022). Achieving sustainability requires a holistic perspective because overemphasis on one domain may lead to the decline of others, ultimately compromising the whole (Adger, 2000; Zolli and Healy, 2012). Although they are linked, sustainability and resilience differ: resilience enables a system to withstand and recover from disruptions, a fundamental prerequisite for achieving long-term sustainability (Prerna *et al.*, 2020). Some scholars stress equity-focused sustainability, particularly in underresourced settings. For example, Williams *et al.* (2023) argued that sustaining evidence-based health interventions requires attention to health equity in communities facing systemic barriers.
8. **Transformability:** the capacity of a system to fundamentally alter its structure and function in response to profound disturbances. Instead of merely withstanding disruptions, transformability enables systems to evolve amidst changing conditions. This challenges conventional management paradigms favoring stability, advocating adaptive strategies for which change and transformation as essential to sustaining resilience (Walker *et al.*, 2004).
9. **Inclusivity:** ensures active involvement of diverse stakeholders, fostering a comprehensive and equitable resilience approach (Kuo *et al.*, 2022). Inclusive strategies are vital for protecting marginalized communities (Remes and Horowitz, 2021), promoting fair resource distribution, and mitigating disparities. Neglecting inclusivity can inadvertently lead to unintended consequences: enhancing the resilience of one group increases the vulnerability of another (Zarnic *et al.*, 2017).

10. **Diversity:** encompasses varied solutions, technologies, approaches to address challenges, and reducing systemic failure risk (Folke *et al.*, 2003; Zolli and Healy, 2012; Kuo *et al.*, 2022). Scholars link diversity to inclusivity, noting inclusivity facilitate a more robust and equitable resilience (Remes and Horowitz, 2021). Although diverse perspectives foster innovation, their effectiveness relies on shared values and aligned goals within a team (McAslan, 2010; Zolli and Healy, 2012).
11. **Creativity:** fosters innovative approaches for addressing complex challenges (Adger, 2000; Kuo *et al.*, 2022). Continuous innovation thrives on the converging diverse perspectives and interdisciplinary collaboration (West *et al.*, 2009). Unlike sustainability, which prioritizes stability, resilience actively embraces innovation to prepare for and adapt to unpredictable disruptions, effectively navigating uncertainty (Zolli and Healy, 2012).
12. **Connectivity:** facilitates communication and information networks, enabling rapid response and effective coordination during crises (Manyena, 2006; Kuo *et al.*, 2022). Enhancing connectivity involves increasing nodes for shorter response times and local connections while reducing interdependencies to prevent system-wide failures (Zolli and Healy, 2012). However, increased connectivity also poses risks of environmental degradation and social inequalities, necessitating a balanced approach for sustainable resilience (Perz *et al.*, 2012).
13. **Agility:** the ability to swiftly respond to unexpected events (McAslan, 2010; Kuo *et al.*, 2022). Initially describing recovery speed (Bruneau *et al.*, 2003), resilience research in organizational and governance domains now emphasize both speed and response appropriateness. This shift led to "agility" replacing "rapidity" (Sambamurthy *et al.*, 2003; Lengnick-Hall and Beck, 2005).
14. **Resourcefulness:** refers to the availability and adequacy of resources practitioners can draw on for disaster management (Bruneau *et al.*, 2003; Kuo *et al.*, 2022). Emphasizing social agency, resourcefulness equips communities with the necessary skills, knowledge, and autonomy, fostering self-sufficiency over dependence on external support (MacKinnon and Derickson, 2013; Jain *et al.*, 2018).

Although various studies have identified attributes that contribute to system resilience, their relationships remain underexplored. A notable exception is the temporal perspective by Bruneau *et al.* (2003), who argued that robustness and redundancy primarily mitigate the initial impact of stressors, reducing damage rather than directly accelerating recovery. In contrast, resourcefulness facilitates recovery. Extending this temporal and functional differentiation, Cimellaro *et al.* (2010) applied similar reasoning in their studies on critical infrastructure. Given the limited discussion of these complex interdependencies, this article aims to clarify the relationships among resilience attributes through empirical case studies.

METHODOLOGY

Method of data triangulation

This study primarily used data triangulation to enhance the credibility and depth of the findings (Denzin, 1970). A widely recognized strategy in social science research, triangulation validates data by converging multiple perspectives, based on the premise that no single method fully captures the complexity of social phenomena; therefore, integrating different sources or approaches helps reduce potential biases and strengthens interpretive validity (Patton, 1999). Denzin (1970) identified four main types of triangulations: data triangulation (using data collected at different times, from varied contexts or participant groups), investigator triangulation (involving multiple researchers to limit individual bias), theory triangulation (applying different theoretical frameworks), and methodological triangulation (combining qualitative and quantitative methods).

In this study, data triangulation was achieved through following three primary strategies:

1. collecting data from two sources: in-depth interviews and secondary data
2. conducting in-depth interviews with stakeholders occupying diverse roles within the research context
3. analyzing secondary data drawn from multiple perspectives, including governmental reports, media coverage, and so forth

Cases

This study examines two major earthquakes in Taiwan: the earthquakes occurred on 6 February 2016, primarily affecting Tainan City, and on 6 February 2018, primarily affecting Hualien County. Hereafter, they are referred to as the 2016 Tainan earthquake and the 2018 Hualien earthquake, respectively.

The 2016 Tainan earthquake struck at 3:57 a.m. on 6 February, with a magnitude of 6.6. The epicenter was located in Meinong, Kaohsiung, at a shallow depth of 16.7 km (Fig. 2). The earthquake caused severe damage in Tainan, including the collapse of a building, the tilting of others, water outages affecting >400,000 households, power outages affecting >170,000 households, 117 deaths, and 551 injuries. This marked the deadliest disaster in Taiwan since the earthquake on 21 September 1999 (commonly referred to as the "921 earthquake") and resulted in the highest number of casualties from the collapse of a single building in the history of Taiwan (Central Weather Administration, n.d.; National Science and Technology Center for Disaster Reduction, n.d.a.).

The 2018 Hualien earthquake occurred at 11:50 p.m. on 6 February, with a magnitude of 6.2. The epicenter was located

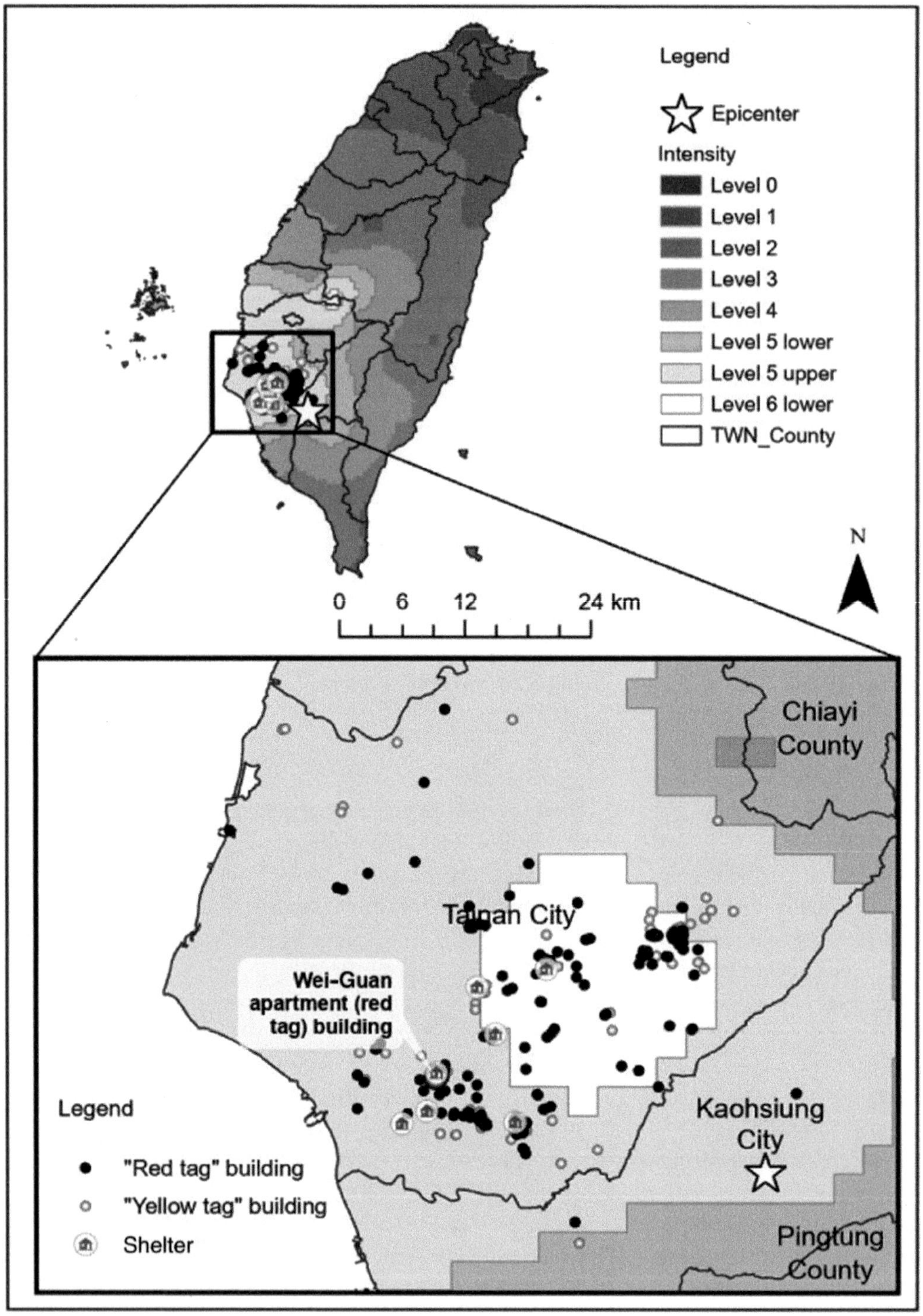

Figure 2. Epicenter and areas impacted by the 2016 Tainan earthquake. This map shows the recorded intensity levels based on the Central Weather Administration's seismic intensity scale. Most of the red- and yellow-tagged buildings were located in the southern part of Tainan City. The collapsed Wei-Guan apartment building, which caused >100 deaths, was in the city's southwestern part. As detailed in the Rescue operations section, a suggestion from the private sector prompted heavy machinery to enter the building in <72 hr to assist in the rescue, which altered existing standard operating procedures.

off the coast of Hualien County (Fig. 3). This earthquake caused several buildings to structural tilt or collapse, leading to 17 deaths and 291 injuries (National Science and Technology Center for Disaster Reduction, n.d.b.). Numerous aftershocks, each exceeding magnitudes of 5, followed. It was the largest to hit the region since the 1972 earthquake and occurred exactly two years after the 2016 Tainan earthquake.

Secondary data

The study analyzed various sources, including government reports, news articles, government websites, invited speeches, and relevant publications. We focused on official government documents (Central Emergency Operation Center, 2016, 2018; Tainan City Council, 2016) to understand governmental viewpoints. In addition, media reports and speeches by NGO leaders explored issues emphasized by the private sector.

For the news reports, this study first used integrated news search systems such as the United Daily News, the Liberty Times, and Central News Agency. This study also used the Google search engine to broaden the review of news coverage and related commentary on the two earthquakes.

This study also examines two invited speeches. The first was delivered in January 2025 by H. C. Lu, a director of Tzu Chi Foundation, who served the organization from 2004 until his retirement in 2024. Tzu Chi Foundation is a Taiwan-based international humanitarian organization renowned for its dedication to disaster relief and recovery. Founded in 1966, Tzu Chi has grown into a global network of volunteers who are often among the first responders on the ground. The second speech was given in March 2025 by Y. H. Huang, the founder and board member of the Union of

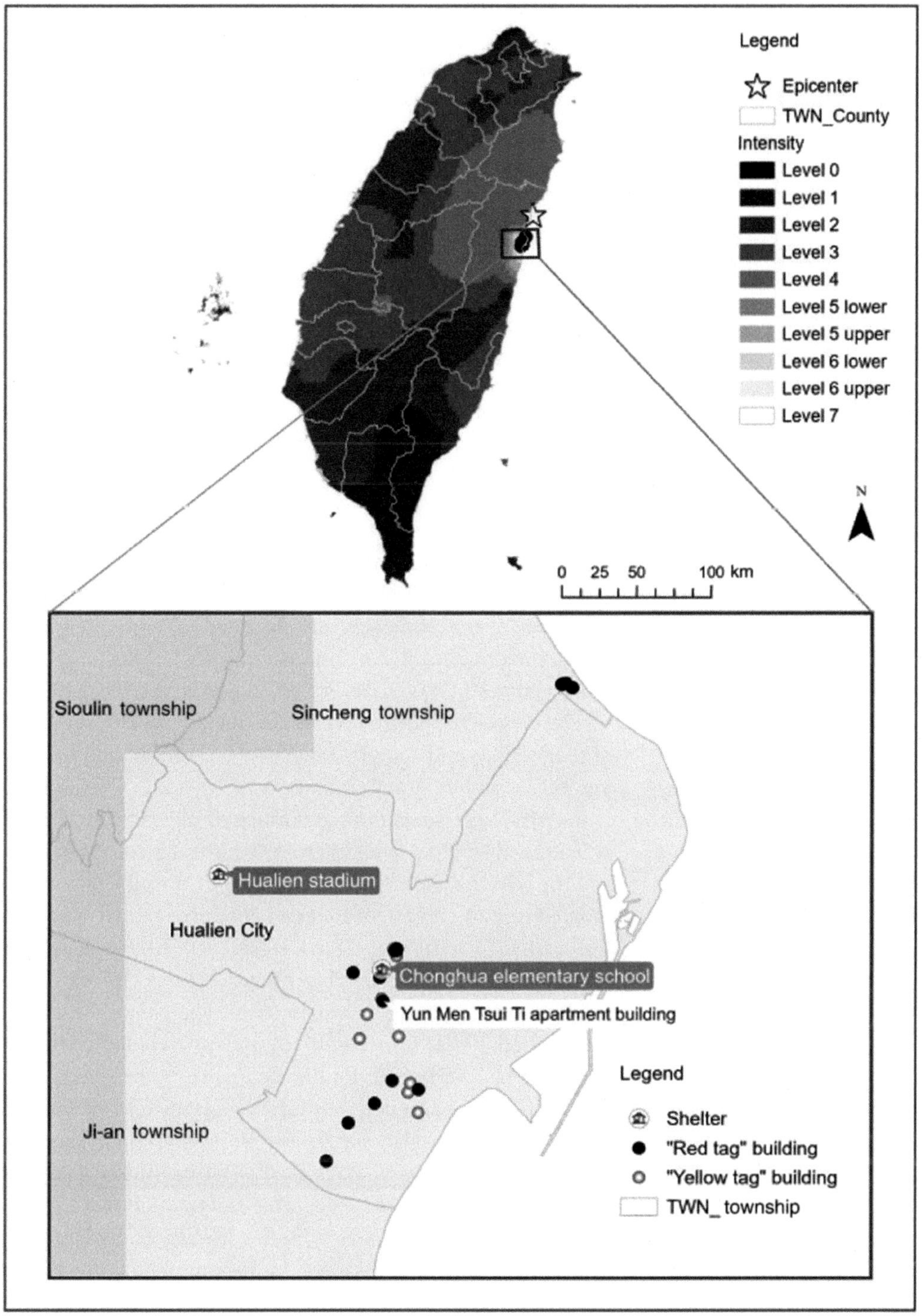

Figure 3. Epicenter and areas impacted by the 2018 Hualien earthquake. This map shows the recorded intensity levels based on the Central Weather Administration's seismic intensity scale. Most of the red- and yellow-tagged buildings were located in the southern part of Hualien City. The marked apartment building was the site where the most time was spent on search and rescue efforts. Chong Hua Elementary School, which served as the main shelter, is referenced in the Shelter management section for its exemplary public–private collaboration.

Hualien County Social Workers. Both speakers shared the experiences in shelter management during the 2018 Hualien earthquake. In the Results and Analyses section, they are referred to as Speakers Lu and Huang.

In-depth interviews

Interviewees were selected based on: (1) decision makers from emergency operation center (EOC) of the local governments and forward command posts because of their broad perspective and understanding of overall situation, (2) individuals frequently featured in news media, and (3) individuals recommended by the decision makers. The final list (Table 1) includes seven decision makers and implementers involved in the command system during the two earthquakes. All interviewees indicated that anonymity was unnecessary. In this article, they are referred to as Interviewee Chen and so forth.

The interviewees included key participants from the Fire Department, Construction Bureau, Disaster Management Office, and frontline workers from the private sectors. This diversity in roles aligns with the method of triangulation.

To capture the essence of resilience in disaster response, our interview protocol was meticulously designed to elicit reflections on the challenges and the resolution strategies during operations. The interview content was systematically divided into two main levels, organizational and operational, to guide participants in recalling diverse experiences.

At the organizational level, discussions focused on the division of labor and interorganizational conflicts or negotiations between the EOC and the forward command post and between the public sector and the private sector.

At the operational level, participants detailed difficulties executing SOPs and instances requiring improvised solutions where no pre-existing SOPs existed. Aligning with the Central Emergency Operations Center Operating Guidelines (Ministry

TABLE 1
List of Experts Interviewed

Disaster Events	Names	Job Titles at That Time	Main Roles
Both earthquakes	M. L. Chen	2016: Secretary General of Tainan City Government; 2018: Executive Yuan Minister, chairperson of the National Development Council	2016: deputy commander (at EOC and forward command post); 2018: Convener of the Disaster Relief and Reconstruction Task Force (the central government)
Both earthquakes	M. C. Cheng	Chairperson, Professional Civil Engineers Association	2016: commander of the oversized steel jaws (a type of excavator) plan; head of the Forensic Technician Team (forward command post)
2016 earthquake	C. Y. Ho	Disaster Management Office Advisor of the City	Commander (EOC)
2016 earthquake	M. F. Lee	Chief of Tainan City Fire Department	Deputy commander (forward command post)
2018 earthquake	W. R. Lin	Chief of the Hualien County Fire Department	Deputy commander (forward command post)
2018 earthquake	C. Y. Teng	Director of the County Construction Bureau	Building demolition and reconstruction (forward command post)
2018 earthquake	Y. S. Yen	Volunteer firefighter	Rescue, excavator operator (forward command post)

EOC, emergency operation center.

of the Interior, National Fire Agency, 2025) covering themes such as situation assessment, search, and rescue, the interview content was determined not only by the spontaneous recollections of the interviewees but also by references to issues identified in secondary data. The interviews were conducted in July and August 2023.

RESULTS AND ANALYSES

Given the operational themes outlined in the Central Emergency Operations Center Operating Guidelines (Ministry of the Interior, National Fire Agency, 2025), this study identified five key earthquake response themes involving public–private cooperation in the response phase, including situation assessment, rescue operations, rescue resource deployment, shelter management, and other supplies or services.

The following sections examine the disaster response subthemes under each of these themes, focusing on the role of civil society, and analyzed them through the lens of the resilience attributes outlined in the previous section. These subthemes were selected based on in-depth interviews, media reports, and speeches, as mentioned in the Methodology section. Selection emphasized cases that faced challenges or adopted new approaches, thus showcasing resilience. Government reports cited in the Secondary data section primarily served to confirm these subthemes and clarify responsibilities. To help readers identify how each part of the narrative relates to specific resilience attributes, the first letter of each attribute is capitalized.

Situation assessment

During the 2016 Tainan earthquake, the main disaster site was located along a major road, where the earthquake caused a water pipe rupture and led to road closures. As a result, alternative routes became critically important. At that time, the traffic bureau was unsure how to plan detours. It was only after National Cheng Kung University proposed a plan that it was handed over to the traffic bureau for implementation. The plan was finalized three days later, which, according to Interviewee Ho, resulted in a delay that affected disaster response. To date, only a few cities or counties have established principles for identifying alternative disaster routes in advance. Taipei is one of these, where the principles include avoiding potential disaster zones, proximity to EOCs, key medical institutions, and major thoroughfares (Taipei City Traffic Engineering Office, 2023).

The concept of "alternative routes" highlights the importance of redundancy and suggests the major transportation plan during this disaster lacked robustness. "National Cheng Kung University" represents the significance of diversity. In Taiwan, policies and funding support from the Ministry of the Interior and the National Science and Technology Council have enabled each county or city to collaborate with a designated university that assists in local disaster management. These policies and funding mechanisms exemplify resourcefulness and have contributed to the institutionalization of this form of public–private cooperation. These universities not only provide technical support to local governments for disaster management during noncrisis periods but also offer immediate assistance when disasters occur. Since 2005, National Cheng Kung University has been assisting Tainan City Government. The university possesses the capability to operate geographic information systems and conduct spatial data analysis, skills that are generally unavailable to public servants but are critical for disaster management, thus demonstrating diversity.

The phrase "in a delay that affected disaster response" implies there was insufficient foresight capacity because the principles for alternative routes were not planned in advance. As a result, during the disaster, it was difficult to demonstrate agility. To date, few counties and cities in Taiwan have established principles for predisaster alternative route planning, indicating a lack of adaptive learning in this regard.

Rescue operations

In the past, the fire departments believed that the first 72 hr following a disaster, known as the "golden 72 hr," were critical for saving lives and that large machinery should not be used during this period because of the potential risk of injuring survivors. Large machinery, such as oversized steel jaws, was typically deployed only after it was determined that further rescue of life was impossible and to proceed with demolishing collapsed buildings. However, the 2016 Tainan earthquake led to a shift in this approach. After 30 hr of rescue operations, relying solely on human effort reached its limit. Tainan Mayor Lai (currently the president of Taiwan) consulted with the director of Public Works and local experts and concluded that the simultaneous use of heavy machinery and human rescue efforts could significantly improve the efficiency of the rescue operations (Chen, 2019).

Forty-four hr after the building collapse, Mayor Lai appointed Interviewee Cheng as the commander of the oversized steel jaws operation, marking a pioneering move. This was the first instance when a civilian technician was appointed as the commander of a rescue operation; traditionally, such roles were filled by government officials. This change was made because Mayor Lai believed engineers are better equipped to assess the structural safety of buildings during demolition and can more effectively balance the use of heavy machinery with human rescue efforts. To reassure the families of the trapped victims, Interviewee Cheng drafted operational principles for the oversized steel jaws. These guidelines stipulated that demolition would begin in areas least likely to compromise the structural integrity of the building and that any detection of human lives or bodies would immediately halt the operation of heavy machinery.

The actual rescue operations began 64 hr after the disaster. The number of survivors or bodies recovered increased significantly. In hindsight, the Tainan City Fire Department acknowledged that the initiation of the oversized steel jaws rescue plan had a positive impact on accelerating the rescue of trapped individuals (Tainan City Fire Department, 2022).

Interviewees Yen, Teng, and Lin supported this approach, emphasizing that the success of this operation relied on the collaboration and division of labor between the excavator operator, structural engineer, and firefighters.

Since the 2016 Tainan earthquake, Interviewee Cheng and the Tainan City Fire Department have shared the experience of simultaneous use of human rescue efforts and heavy machinery with various counties and cities. This approach was also implemented during the 2018 Hualien earthquake, according to Interviewee Teng.

The "simultaneous use of heavy machinery and human rescue efforts" was considered "a pioneering move," which reflects the spirit of creativity. The situation revealed that waiting for 72 hr before allowing large machinery into the disaster area would miss critical opportunities to save lives. As a result, the rescue effort was adjusted based on the immediate needs, illustrating flexibility. The ultimate goal of the pioneering move was to improve the "efficiency of the rescue operations," which aligns with agility.

To implement this pioneering move, it was necessary to establish "operational principles" to guide current and future operators, representing resourcefulness. After the principles were defined, "collaboration and division of labor between the excavator operator, structural engineer, and firefighters" became essential, reflecting diversity. The practice of sharing the experience was used, making it an example of adaptive learning.

Rescue resource deployment

The Emergency Management Information Cloud of the Ministry of the Interior has established a disaster relief resource database of the governments for disaster support and coordination. The resource content includes general disaster rescue equipment, personnel, chemical disaster rescue equipment, vehicle and vessel information, specialized rescue machinery, and disaster relief supplies that can be mobilized by the government right after a disaster happens. Because the available mobilizable resources may be insufficient, several interviewees recommended that an additional list be created. Specific examples include oversized steel jaws, excavator specialists, wall drilling or stone crushing experts, and so forth.

During the 921 earthquake in 1999, the reconstruction committee requested the mobilization of 200 excavators (Institute of Taiwan History, Academia Sinica, 2012). The aforementioned oversized steel jaws plan also illustrates the importance of oversized steel jaws in search and rescue operations. However, according to Interviewee Yen, oversized steel jaws or other types of excavators are merely disaster relief tools, with the key focus being the skill required to operate the excavator. The oversized steel jaws plan was led by a civil engineer as the commander. However, as Yen pointed out, civil engineers are trained to construct buildings. Excavator operators, by contrast, are more knowledgeable about the safe dismantling of structures, highlighting the need for close cooperation between both parties.

In addition, Yen noted that unlike civil engineers, whose skills are supported by a rigorous licensing system, the skills of different excavator operators are more difficult to compare and largely depend on whether trust has been established. Consequently, Yen recommended that the fire department establish a platform involving local excavator operators during peacetime to share past disaster experiences, discuss rescue scenarios, and build mutual trust, ultimately enabling faster decision making during disasters.

Both the 2016 Tainan and 2018 Hualien experiences have also shown that when rescue efforts encounter bottlenecks, it is crucial to have someone on site who has connections with skilled wall drilling or stone crushing experts. These experts do not have certification or formal accreditation; their expertise is recognized through word of mouth or personal connections. When long-term drilling or crushing is required, the rescue teams often become exhausted, leaving them unable to continue rescue work. Wall drilling or stone crushing experts, on the other hand, have better skills to handle long-duration drilling or crushing without exhaustion.

The aforementioned narrative involves private sector participants such as excavator operators, drilling specialists, and stone crushing experts. These specialists possess expertise that addresses the gaps in government rescue personnel, reflecting diversity through public–private collaboration, with the goal of enhancing the efficiency of rescue operations (agility).

The government already maintains a disaster relief resource database (resourcefulness), with the objective of immediately identifying available resources in the aftermath of a disaster (agility). Since the 921 earthquake in 1999, although the government did not compile a comprehensive list of all excavators, it did include information on some excavators in the disaster relief resource database that could be immediately mobilized, marking progress (adaptive learning).

The establishment of platforms for excavator specialists and other relevant stakeholders to foster mutual understanding is an innovative approach (creativity) that has not yet been realized. The goals are to build trust during normal times (connectivity), facilitate discussions based on past disasters (adaptive learning), and achieve consensus quickly during a disaster, thus improving the timeliness of rescue efforts (agility).

Shelter management

Government-established shelters. The 2018 Hualien earthquake serves as a notable case in which civil society effectively collaborated in the operation of government-established shelters, representing an ideal scenario of public–private cooperation. On the night of the earthquake, Speaker Huang observed that the personnel from the Hualien County Office at the Chonghua Elementary School shelter were significantly understaffed. Meanwhile, several social welfare organizations and medical teams were already present but operated independently without coordination.

Because of his prior acquaintance with the relevant officials from the public health bureau, his independence from specific organizations or government agencies, his network in the Union of Hualien County Social Workers, and his disaster relief experiences, Huang assumed a pivotal role in facilitating collaboration among the various groups onsite and in formulating the interdisciplinary helping professionals support platform (NPOst, 2018).

Hung argued that prior disaster response experiences highlight the critical challenge of managing interorganizational dynamics. Ensuring effective division of labor among various responding entities is essential to optimizing service delivery for affected individuals. A specific example of this challenge was the redundancy in assessments, for which multiple organizations repeatedly asked survivors the same questions. Eventually, a division of labor emerged: the Tzu Chi Foundation, which mobilized the largest number of volunteers, took primary responsibility for nearly all logistics, maintenance, and spatial organization of public areas. According to Speaker Lu, the extensive experience of the Tzu Chi Foundation in resource management—acquired through its long-standing operation of recycling and environmental stations—has positioned the organization as a key agent in coordinating and organizing relief supplies during disaster events. Meanwhile, other social welfare organizations were tasked with assessing and addressing the individual needs of each disaster survivor.

This interdisciplinary helping professionals support platform required social welfare groups to conduct systematic visits of the disaster-affected individuals in the shelter at designated time slots each morning and afternoon and ensured an equitable distribution of responsibilities and visibilities across organizations. These visits involved social workers, mental health professionals, and volunteers working collaboratively to prevent excessive disruptions to survivors. Each survivor had an individual case file, and daily coordination meetings were held in the evening to facilitate intersectoral communication. These meetings served as a platform for public–private cooperation, enabling civil society groups and the city office to cross-check shelter occupancy records and assess the physical, psychological, and social needs of survivors.

During the 2024 Hualien earthquake, the county government proactively reached out to NGOs that had participated in the interdisciplinary helping professionals support platform in 2018. The efficient collaboration of these NGOs can be attributed to two key factors: (1) the operational experience gained from the 2018 Hualien earthquake and (2) the continued participation of some organizations in county- or township-level disaster preparedness drills between 2018 and 2024. Notably, in 2024, rather than convening meetings to delineate responsibilities, each organization was already aware of its designated role, thereby expediting the implementation of relief measures (Business Today, 2024; EToday, 2024).

Observations from the 2018 Hualien earthquake revealed that the lack of private spaces in the shelters often forced survivors to change clothes in public restrooms, highly inconvenient for mothers with infants or older adults with limited mobility. In response, the Tzu Chi Foundation initiated the design of partition tents for shelter in 2019 (Fig. 4). These partition tents were subsequently incorporated into disaster response drills across multiple counties and cities. The 2024 Hualien earthquake marked the first instance of their deployment in a real-world disaster scenario in Taiwan (Lin, 2024).

According to Speaker Huang, cases in the 2018 Hualien earthquake demonstrated how during shelter intake, the needs of vulnerable individuals were identified. For instance, military-grade emergency shower facilities, often installed in shelters, posed slip risks for older adults because of slippery surfaces. To mitigate this, chairs or nonslip mats were used. The foldable beds by the Tzu Chi Foundation were beneficial for people with

(a)
(b)
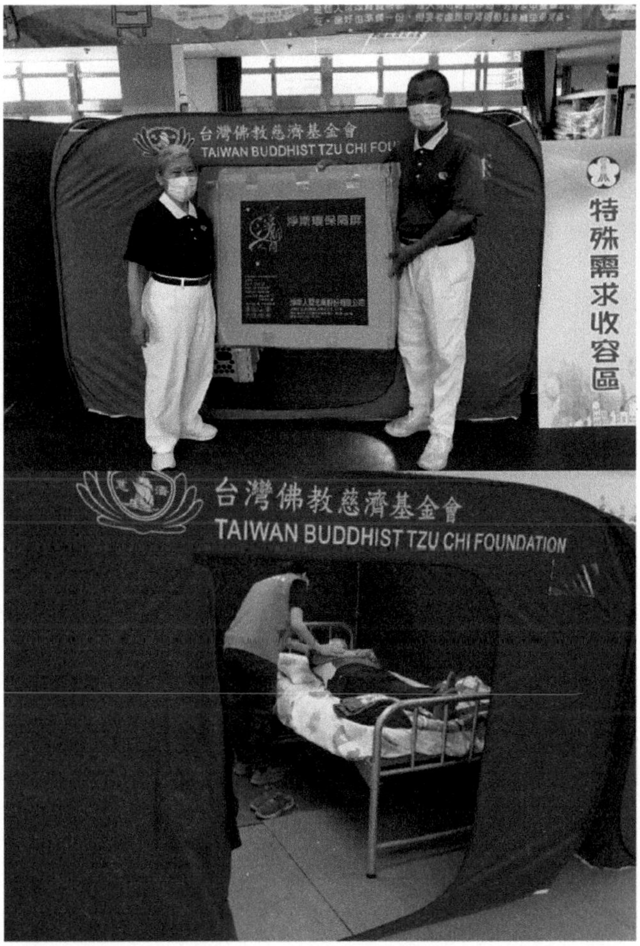

Figure 4. (a) The partition tents can be folded into a highly compact form. (b) The tents were used during a disaster preparedness drill in 2024. Since 2020, partition tents have frequently been seen in indoor disaster drills across Taiwan. These tents can be rapidly deployed to create individual spaces for two or three people in each tent, significantly increasing the efficiency of shelter operations while providing privacy for vulnerable groups. Developed by the Tzu Chi Foundation in collaboration with other partners based on past disaster experiences, this development exemplifies creativity and adaptive learning. The tents' design, which considers the privacy of vulnerable people, further demonstrates inclusivity. The foundation's ability to engage in collaborative research and integrate the product into government drills highlights its strong connectivity and resourcefulness. The color version of this figure is available only in the electronic edition.

limited mobility who could not lie on the floor (Fig. 5). For older adults who still found these beds too low, additional assistive devices were provided. A portable Child Friendly Center Toolbox of World Vision, when opened, transforms into a child-friendly area with play mats, children's books, drawing materials, and building blocks (Liberty Times, 2024).

In the aforementioned case of shelter management, key participants from the private sector included Speaker Huang, the Tzu Chi Foundation, various social welfare organizations, and other NGOs. The pre-existing social networks of Huang (connectivity), extensive experience in understanding the conditions in a shelter (adaptive learning), and professional background in social work (resourcefulness) enabled him to rapidly assume a central role in facilitating the efficient operation of the shelter.

Through a process of collaborative deliberation, a platform with a structured division of labor was created (creativity)—one that prioritized mutual coexistence and shared prosperity (sustainability), ensuring that interorganizational dynamics did not compromise the well-being of disaster survivors. This platform encompassed logistics management, sanitation, spatial organization, massage station, social work, psychological counseling, and physical health consultations, thereby facilitating a comprehensive and coordinated response (sustainability). Each civil organization leveraged its specialized expertise in coordination with public sector agencies, ensuring an optimized operational framework (diversity). This platform, which incorporates predefined roles and scheduled review meetings, allows one NGO to readily step in if another faces operational constraints or resource depletion (modularity). This modular setup inherently provides robustness. Furthermore, the daily coordination meetings facilitate real-time monitoring of needs, assessment of the performance of each module, and rapid adjustments to resource allocation or task assignments (agility). It also showcased the effectiveness of knowledge transmission between local governments and NGOs across subsequent disaster events (adaptive learning). This platform simultaneously developed various strategies for different vulnerable groups, exemplifying creativity and inclusivity.

Speakers Lu and Huang believed that the key factor behind the continued effectiveness of the platform in subsequent disaster events was that "the people were still here" (connectivity). However, whether the platform can continue to function effectively in future disasters still requires the test of time, and it remains uncertain whether this platform can be replicated in other regions. This article argues that their concerns stem from the fact that in this case, adaptive learning was transformed into resourcefulness primarily through training activities rather than through the institutionalization of the platform at the governmental level, which may represent a limitation of the case.

Despite the limitation at the platform level, some participating organizations continued to develop their own practices. Notably, the development of partition tents by the Tzu Chi Foundation (creativity) emerged from an evidence-based approach (adaptive learning), wherein the disaster experiences in 2018 identified the necessity for enhanced comfort and privacy of vulnerable people (inclusivity) within emergency shelters. Drawing on its existing capacity for collaborative research and development (connectivity), the Tzu Chi Foundation refined these partitions through disaster preparedness drills (resourcefulness). Ultimately, their successful deployment in actual disaster scenarios underscored the practical value of predisaster planning.

Figure 5. The foldable beds can be fully extended or configured with a backrest. Their elevated height makes seating easier, which is particularly beneficial for individuals with limited mobility. The idea for these beds originated after the 921 earthquake in 1999. They were first used in disaster drills across Taiwan starting in 2013 and were deployed in a shelter after the 2018 Hualien earthquake. Similar to the partition tents, these beds exemplify creativity, adaptive learning, inclusivity, connectivity, and resourcefulness. The color version of this figure is available only in the electronic edition.

Private shelter providers. Both earthquakes occurred during the Lunar New Year period. Because of the collapse or tilting of some buildings, affected residents had to be relocated and could not celebrate the Lunar New Year comfortably. According to Interviewee Chen and Ho, in 2016, some hotels in Tainan immediately provided free accommodation for disaster-affected residents, and this information was available on the Tainan City Government Open Data Platform website (Central Emergency Operation Center, 2016; Tainan City Council, 2016). As for the 2018 Hualien earthquake, >50 bed and breakfast (B&B) and hotel operators immediately mobilized, offering free washing and rest facilities. They announced this through Facebook and provided the services to those in need via online booking platforms. Three minutes after the collapse of a hotel, a member of the volunteer rescue team, also a member of the B&B association, quickly initiated disaster relief efforts in the social media group of the B&B association (Wu, 2018). Hualien is the county with the highest number of B&Bs in Taiwan, mostly operated by local residents. The quick mobilization was due to unity, which was key.

The aforementioned cases highlight the role of hotels and B&Bs in disaster response. In both events, these private actors demonstrated rapid mobilization (agility) and began to use online information platforms (creativity) to inform the public about available shelter locations. The Tainan case exemplifies a well-established practice, for which the open-data platform of the public sector (resourcefulness) was used as a consistent method for disaster communication, ensuring continued functionality in subsequent disaster events. The strength of the Hualien experience lies in the network of collaboration among B&B operators (connectivity).

Other supplies or services

Outdoor heating equipment. In Taiwan, it has become second nature for individuals and civil society organizations to provide financial donations and food supplies in the aftermath of major disasters, according to Interviewee Chen. However, what sets the Tzu Chi Foundation apart is its systematic approach to disaster response, which explicitly accounts for cold-weather conditions. Both the 2016 and 2018 earthquakes occurred during the Lunar New Year period, when temperatures were notably low. According to Speaker Lu and Interviewee Lin, during both earthquakes, the initial response of the Tzu Chi Foundation included the immediate distribution of hot ginger tea and small blankets to disaster survivors and the rescue team as a means of providing warmth. Furthermore, the Tzu Chi Foundation also deployed its collaboratively developed outdoor heating equipment (rocket stove) to disaster sites (EToday, 2015; ATA News, 2018). During the 2016 Tainan earthquake, search-and-rescue teams initially overlooked the need for heating provisions and ultimately relied on the Tzu Chi Foundation's heating devices. This incident prompted the Tainan Fire Department to recognize the necessity of outdoor heating equipment in disaster relief operations and made an adjustment, according to Interviewee Lee.

Notably, before governmental agencies identified the need, the Tzu Chi Foundation demonstrated flexibility by swiftly recognizing the critical importance of cold-weather relief goods. Beyond immediate response efforts, the organization leveraged its preestablished research and development collaborations (connectivity) to design and produce its own outdoor heating equipment (creativity). Through a hotwash, the governmental agency also incorporated outdoor heating equipment into emergency preparedness protocols (adaptive learning and resourcefulness).

Community-based disaster management. According to Interviewee Ho, in the 2016 Tainan earthquake, because the major collapsed building was located in Kunshan Village, the village chief immediately activated the community-based disaster management mechanism. Various community teams, including the patrol team, care centers, and volunteers, each played their role in disaster relief efforts (Tainan City Government, 2016). After the earthquake, power outages forced rescue operations to be carried out in near-total darkness. Fortunately, the community disaster management team had prepared headlamps in advance. The patrol team took charge of traffic control and maintaining order, and care center staff handled and distributed relief supplies onsite and guided people into the affected areas. Village volunteers assisted with paperwork, processed donation inquiries, and answered relief supply calls.

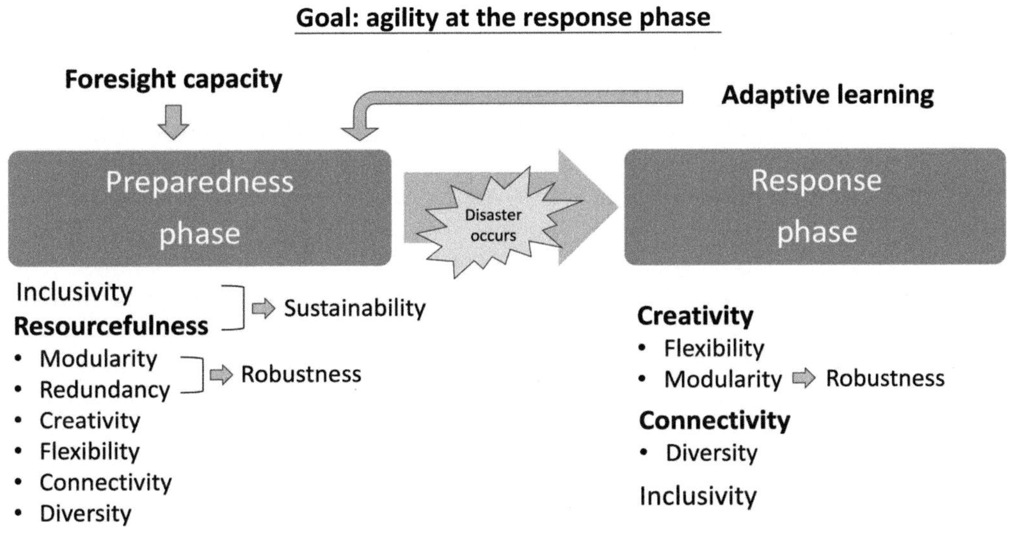

Figure 6. Resilience attributes: preparedness and response. This diagram presents the findings of this study on the relationships between various resilience attributes across the mitigation and response phases. Agility is identified as the overarching goal. Resourcefulness and foresight capability are central to the mitigation phase, and creativity and connectivity are crucial during the response phase. Adaptive learning serves to connect the response and mitigation phases. The concentration of most attributes in the mitigation phase underscores the widely recognized principle that proactive measures are more effective than reactive ones.

The preparation of community-based disaster management is a joint effort between the public and private sectors. Since 2000, the central and local government agencies have collaborated with university teams and NGOs to educate villages on how to operate community-based disaster management programs. In addition, the government provides subsidies for villages to purchase disaster management supplies they consider essential. As of 2024, 3091 community-based disaster management programs had received subsidies from the central government.

In this case, the central government provides funding and frameworks for disaster management initiatives (resourcefulness) to city and county governments, which collaborate with local universities (diversity) to support villages interested in implementing such programs. Proactive villages not only use government subsidies to procure disaster preparedness equipment but also develop context-specific operational strategies tailored to their own needs (flexibility). As highlighted in this case, community members established distinct roles, including patrol teams, care centers, and volunteers (diversity)—a structure that emerged through community-led discussions rather than external mandates. This decentralized decision-making process allowed the village to create a response mechanism suited to its local context, which proved effective in the actual disaster event.

DISCUSSION OF ATTRIBUTES AND THEIR RELATIONSHIPS

Among all 14 attributes mentioned in the Attributes of resilience section, only transformability was not addressed in the case analysis because its nature is closely related to disaster mitigation rather than disaster response. Building on the preceding case analysis, this section delves into a more profound discussion of the resilience attributes and their intricate relationships, offering extended insights and refined conceptualizations.

Agility: Prioritizing swift responsiveness

Agility embodies rapid and appropriate response, with all actions discussed in this study oriented toward this primary objective. Although the term encompasses other meanings, such as appropriateness, its predominant emphasis remains "speed." Given that the core purpose of the response phase is agile action and the preparedness phase aims to facilitate an even more agile response, this study considered agility to be the overarching goal for all other resilience attributes relevant to the response phase (Fig. 6).

Resourcefulness, creativity, connectivity, adaptive learning, and foresight capability

Based on the cases of this study, we propose that resourcefulness, creativity, connectivity, adaptive learning, and foresight capability are relatively important attributes when discussing the response phase and the related preparedness phase (as highlighted in bold in Fig. 6).

As mentioned, Bruneau *et al.* (2003) primarily discuss resourcefulness in the context of rapid resource deployment postdisaster. This study further posits that achieving the objective of rapid resource deployment necessitates predisaster preparation, thus closely linking resourcefulness with the preparedness phase. For instance, the case study illustrates that during peacetime, the Ministry of Interior and the National Science and Technology Council proactively established a mechanism for universities to assist various county and city governments in disaster management, which exemplifies resourcefulness.

In contrast, creativity and connectivity are particularly crucial in the response phase. If existing systems lack the necessary resources to respond to a situation, the resilience of a system heavily relies on the innovative capacity and social networks of relevant stakeholders at the immediate moment of disaster.

The coordinated deployment of heavy machinery alongside human rescuers was hailed as an innovative breakthrough, exemplifying creativity. The urgent search for stone masons and bricklayers discovered to be crucial only after a disaster is an example of connectivity.

Moreover, if creativity demonstrated in the response phase can be further adapted through adaptive learning, it may evolve into an element of resourcefulness. In this sense, adaptive learning serves as a critical attribute that links the response phase back to the preparedness phase. However, given the increasing uncertainties brought about by climate change and human-induced disasters, many challenges are no longer confined to past experiences. This is precisely why foresight capability has become equally essential.

Creativity and connectivity also appear in the preparedness phase; however, unlike in the response phase when they play a decisive role, in the preparedness phase, they serve more as contributing mechanisms that support the development of resourcefulness, which is the most essential capability. For instance, the development of various disaster relief equipment by the Tzu Chi Foundation, which was later used in subsequent disaster responses, exemplifies how creativity can be transformed into resourcefulness in the preparedness phase. Similarly, if the platform that would connect different types of stakeholders involved in rescue operations before disasters occur can be realized, it would illustrate how connectivity can be cultivated as a form of resourcefulness in the preparedness phase.

It is worth noting that the detailed meanings of connectivity vary across different phases. During the preparedness phase, connectivity refers to social networks intentionally built for disaster scenarios. In contrast, in the response phase, connectivity often involves realizing that the pre-established networks designed for disasters are insufficient, prompting the need to explore whether other existing social networks—originally developed for nondisaster purposes—can be repurposed for emergency response. In other words, although these networks were established in normal times, their relevance to disaster contexts was not previously recognized.

Sustainability, resourcefulness, and inclusivity: Beyond immediate benefit

The analysis categorized the interdisciplinary helping professionals support platform, which facilitates NGO-assisted shelters, as exhibiting sustainability because of its consideration of all participants' interests and comprehensive addressing of the needs of the displaced population. However, a critical aspect of sustainability is the capacity to sustain results rather than merely accommodating diverse interests. For long-term viability, institutionalization is paramount. Both Speakers Lu and Huang in this study indicated that the platform primarily relies on connectivity and has not yet achieved institutionalization, raising uncertainties about its longevity. Therefore, even if efforts are made to accommodate various interests in the present, the absence of subsequent institutionalization may prevent it from becoming an integral part of existing resources. Although training contributes to resourcefulness, it lacks the stability of institutionalized structures. Consequently, a causal relationship emerges: institutionalization of a strategy which seems to be sustainable in the response phase → resourcefulness → sustainability.

Inclusivity functions as a supporting attribute in both phases, as illustrated in Figure 6. The framework of the United Nations Sustainable Development Goals emphasizes that sustainable development must be socially just and participatory. As stated in official United Nations documentation: "Sustainable development cannot be achieved without ensuring that all voices are heard and all groups are included" (United Nations, n.d.). Based on this perspective, the present study identifies inclusivity in the preparedness phase as an attribute for achieving sustainability (Fig. 6). Inclusivity also plays a role in the response phase. Although flexibility and connectivity may contribute to responses, without considering inclusivity, such efforts may result in rapidity alone rather than true agility. Agility, by definition, requires not only speed but also responsiveness to diverse needs and equitable engagement.

Modularity: From physical to organizational systems

The interdisciplinary helping professionals support platform translates the concept of modularity, traditionally applied to physical systems, into an organizational and process-based framework. Each participating NGO functions as a distinct, yet interconnected, module. They possess specialized capacities, resources, and personnel, enabling them to operate with a degree of independence while contributing to the overarching mission of the shelter. Both resourcefulness and modularity serve as operational tools. The former emphasizes the accessibility and flexible use of existing resources. The latter, after it has been established, is very likely to become an integral part of the resources themselves.

Modularity, redundancy, and robustness

Modularity, redundancy, and robustness are interrelated but distinct concepts in system resilience. As mentioned in the Literature reviews section, robustness is typically understood as an outcome, achieved through mechanisms such as modularity and redundancy (Csete and Doyle, 2002). Although modularity and redundancy can contribute to robustness, they do so through different mechanisms. Modularity refers to the structural decomposition of a system into functionally independent units, which localizes failures. Redundancy involves the duplication of critical functions to ensure continuity in case of disruption.

Modularity is mainly designed to support preparedness-related functions. Yet, this study finds that with sufficient creativity in the response phase, it is possible to rapidly construct a functional modular system—even in the absence of pre-established structures. A case in point is the emergence of the interdisciplinary helping professionals support platform.

Flexibility, adaptive learning, and transformability: Degrees of systemic change

Flexibility represents the capacity for minor internal adjustments within an existing structure, often predisaster, to handle anticipated variations. Adaptive learning involves more significant modifications to structure or function to respond to major changes during and immediately after a disaster, without abandoning the core mission. Transformability, the most profound change, is the fundamental alteration of the form of a system in the long-term postdisaster phase, triggered by catastrophic events that render the old ways unsustainable. Essentially, they represent increasing degrees of systemic change.

Similar to modularity, the case study in this research reveals that with sufficient creativity, flexibility can also emerge post-disaster. The "simultaneous use of heavy machinery and human rescue efforts" was one such case. This case is categorized as a flexibility case because the operational principle was established based on adjusting the SOPs.

Diversity and resourcefulness: Difference between the private and public sectors

When the discussion centers on how the private sector assists the public sector in disaster response, diversity is the default assumption. If the diverse expertise of the private sector is understood during peacetime, it can be incorporated into resources (resourcefulness). Although the public sector also possesses diverse expertise, its division of labor is largely institutionalized. Consequently, the internal diversity within the public sector is generally not linked to the concept of resilient diversity but is more related to whether the users know how to apply it in a resilient manner (resourcefulness).

Most attributes are in the preparedness phase

The concentration of most attributes in the preparedness phase in Figure 6 underscores the widely recognized principle that proactive measures are more effective than reactive ones. This distribution highlights the strategic emphasis on proactive planning, risk reduction, and system readiness as foundational elements in building disaster resilience.

CONCLUSION

Through in-depth interviews with key individuals involved in the 2016 Tainan and 2018 Hualien earthquake responses, coupled with a comprehensive analysis of secondary sources, this study identified five critical disaster response themes associated with public–private cooperation: situation assessment, rescue operations, rescue resource deployment, shelter management, and other supplies or services. Private sector actors, integral to demonstrating resilience, included local universities, various experts assisting in search and rescue operations, diverse types of NGOs, hotels and B&Bs, and village-level community organizations.

To facilitate generalization to other case studies, this research also proposes a complex interplay of 13 resilience attributes and their varying significance across disaster phases. Most attributes are primarily anchored in the preparedness phase, thereby reaffirming the fundamental principle that preparedness is more effective than response. Notably, foresight capability and resourcefulness are identified because two key attributes in the preparedness phase; creativity and connectivity become paramount during the response phase. Adaptive learning serves as a critical bridge between these two phases, enabling systems to adapt rapidly and evolve over time. Resourcefulness and inclusivity are crucial prerequisites for achieving sustainability. Finally, this study highlights that modularity, traditionally applied to physical systems, can be applied within organizational systems to enhance their resilience.

DATA AND RESOURCES

All data used in this article were obtained from interviews and published sources listed in the references and footnotes. News reports were retrieved through search systems, including United Daily News, The Liberty Times, and the Central News Agency in Taiwan, as well as the Google search engine.

DECLARATION OF COMPETING INTERESTS

The authors acknowledge that there are no conflicts of interest recorded.

ACKNOWLEDGMENTS

This project was supported by funding from the Taiwan Foundation for Disaster Relief and the National Science and Technology Council. The authors also wish to thank the Guest Editor, and two anonymous reviewers for their valuable and constructive feedback, which significantly improved the quality of this article. ChatGPT and Gemini were used in the writing process to improve the readability and language of the article. The authors carefully reviewed and edited the result.

REFERENCES

Adger, W. N. (2000). Social and ecological resilience: Are they related? *Prog. Hum. Geogr.* **24,** no. 3, 347–364.

ATA News (2018). Tzu Chi's rocket stove provided heating at the disaster site in Hualien to help protect against the cold, available at https://www.atanews.net/?news=41205 (last accessed May 2025) (in Chinese).

Biggs, C. R., L. A. Yeager, D. G. Bolser, C. Bonsell, A. M. Dichiera, Z. Hou, S. R. Keyser, A. J. Khursigara, K. Lu, A. F. Muth, *et al.* (2020). Does functional redundancy affect ecological stability and resilience? A review and meta-analysis, *Ecosphere* **11,** no. 7, e03184, doi: 10.1002/ecs2.3184.

Boin, A., and A. McConnell (2007). Preparing for critical infrastructure breakdowns: The limits of crisis management and the need for resilience, *J. Contin. Crisis Manage.* **15,** no. 1, 50–59.

Bonanno, G. A. (2004). Loss, trauma, and human resilience: Have we underestimated the human capacity to thrive after extremely aversive events? *Am. Psychol.* **59,** no. 1, 20–28.

Bruneau, M., S. E. Chang, R. T. Eguchi, G. C. Lee, T. D. O'Rourke, A. M. Reinhorn, M. Shinozuka, K. Tierney, W. A. Wallace, and D. von Winterfeldt (2003). A framework to quantitatively assess and enhance the seismic resilience of communities, *Earthq. Spectra* **19,** no. 4, 733–752, doi: 10.1193/1.1623497.

Business Today (2024). The keyword "Taiwan's shelters" tops Japan's search rankings! Providing privacy for displaced survivors, Japanese netizens lament: "Japan falls behind", available at https://www.businesstoday.com.tw/article/category/183027/post/202404050004/ (last accessed April 2025) (in Chinese).

Carter, W. N. (2008). *Disaster Management: A Disaster Manager's Handbook*, Asian Development Bank, Mandaluyong City, Philippines.

Central Emergency Operation Center (2016). Summary report of the central emergency operation center for the 0206 earthquake in 2016 [Unpublished report], Central Emergency Operation Center, New Taipei City, Taiwan (in Chinese).

Central Emergency Operation Center (2018). Summary report of the central emergency operation center for the 0206 Hualien earthquake in 2018 [Unpublished report], Central Emergency Operation Center, New Taipei City, Taiwan (in Chinese).

Central Weather Administration (n.d.). List of destructive earthquakes since 1900, available at https://scweb.cwa.gov.tw/zh-tw/page/disaster/5 (last accessed May 2023) (in Chinese).

Chen, C. F. (2019). Disaster relief diary—Technician Cheng Mingchang: 0206 Meinong Century Earthquake Weiguan disaster area rescue documentary, Tainan Civil Engineering Technicians Association (TNCE), available at http://www.twtnce.org.tw/index.php/files/board/988e23c0-55ea-11e9-856c-525400fc6395 (last accessed February 2025) (in Chinese).

Choudhury, M.-U.-I., C. E. Haque, and B. Doberstein (2021). Adaptive governance and community resilience to cyclones in coastal Bangladesh, *Environ. Sci. Policy* **124,** 580–592, doi: 10.1016/j.envsci.2021.08.007.

Cimellaro, G. P., A. M. Reinhorn, and M. Bruneau (2010). Framework for analytical quantification of disaster resilience, *Eng. Struct.* **32,** no. 11, 3639–3649, doi: 10.1016/j.engstruct.2010.08.008.

Comfort, L. K., K. Ko, and A. Zagorecki (2010). Coordination in rapidly evolving disaster response systems: The role of information, *Am. Behav. Sci.* **48,** no. 3, 295–313.

Csete, M. E., and J. C. Doyle (2002). Reverse engineering of biological complexity, *Science* **295,** no. 5560, 1664–1669, doi: 10.1126/science.1069981.

Cutter, S. L., L. Barnes, M. Berry, C. Burton, E. Evans, E. Tate, and J. Webb (2008). A place-based model for understanding community resilience to natural disasters, *Global Environ. Change* **18,** no. 4, 598–606, doi: 10.1016/j.gloenvcha.2008.07.013.

Denzin, N. K. (1970). The Research Act: A Theoretical Introduction to Sociological Methods, Aldine Publ. Co., Chicago, Illinois.

Djalante, R., C. Holley, F. Thomalla, and M. Carnegie (2013). Pathways for adaptive and integrated disaster resilience, *Nat. Hazards* **69,** no. 3, 2105–2135, doi: 10.1007/11069-013-0797-5.

EToday (2015). Tzu Chi's 'Rocket Stove' used for the first time in aviation disaster response to provide warmth, available at https://www.ettoday.net/news/20150210/466043.htm (last accessed February 2025) (in Chinese).

EToday (2024). Hualien earthquake: Shelters established within two hours, gaining international praise; Japanese disaster prevention experts travel to learn from Taiwan, available at https://www.ettoday.net/news/20240517/2740611.htm#ixzz91Wr9Wgln (last accessed April 2025) (in Chinese).

FEMA (2022). National preparedness report, available at https://www.fema.gov/sites/default/files/documents/fema_2022-npr.pdf (last accessed May 2025).

Folke, C., S. R. Carpenter, B. Walker, M. Scheffer, T. Elmqvist, L. Gunderson, and C. S. Holling (2003). Resilience and sustainable development: Building adaptive capacity in a world of transformations, *Ambio* **32,** no. 5, 437–440.

Haque, C. E., M. A. K. Azad, and M.-U. Choudhury (2022). Social learning, innovative adaptation and community resilience to disasters, *Disaster Prev. Manage.* **31,** no. 5, 601–618, doi: 10.1108/DPM-12-2020-0373.

Holling, C. S. (1973). Resilience and stability of ecological systems, *Annu. Rev. Ecol. Syst.* **4,** no. 1, 1–23.

Homeland Security Presidential Directive/HSPD-8 (2003). National preparedness, available at https://www.govinfo.gov/content/pkg/PPP-2003-book2/pdf/PPP-2003-book2-doc-pg1745.pdf (last accessed May 2025).

Howe, G. A., I. T. Major, and A. J. Koo (2018). Modularity in Jasmonate signaling for multistress resilience, *Annu. Rev. Plant Biol.* **69,** 387–415, doi: 10.1146/annurev-arplant-042817-040047.

Institute of Taiwan History, Academia Sinica (2012). *Oral History of 921 Earthquake on Its Decennial*, Taiwan History Institute, Academia Sinica and National Science and Technology for Disaster Reduction, Taipei and New Taipei City, Taiwan (in Chinese).

Jain, P., H. J. Pasman, S. Waldram, E. N. Pistikopoulos, and M. S. Mannan (2018). Process Resilience Analysis Framework (PRAF): A systems approach for improved risk and safety management, *J. Loss Prev. Process Ind.* **53,** 61–73, doi: 10.1016/j.jlp.2017.08.006.

Kapucu, N. (2006). Interagency communication networks during emergencies, *Am. Rev. Public Adm.* **36,** no. 2, 207–225.

Kapucu, N., and V. Garayev (2011). Collaborative decision-making in emergency and disaster management, *Int. J. Public Adm.* **34,** no. 6, 366–375.

Klau, G. W., and R. Weiskircher (2005). Robustness and resilience, in *Network Analysis*, U. Brandes and T. Erlebach (Editors), Vol. 3418, Lecture Notes in Computer Science, Springer, Berlin, Heidelberg, 239–253, doi: 10.1007/978-3-540-31955-9_15.

Klein, R. J. T., R. J. Nicholls, and F. Thomalla (2003). Resilience to natural hazards: How useful is this concept? *Environ. Hazards* **5,** no. 1, 35–45.

Kuo, N. W., A. Sharifi, and C. E. Li (2022). Smart cities and urban resilience: Insights from a Delphi survey, in *Resilient Smart Cities: Theoretical and Empirical Insights*, A. Sharifi and P. Salehi (Editors), Springer Int. Publ., Cham, Switzerland, 119–138.

Lengnick-Hall, C. A., and T. E. Beck (2005). Adaptive fit versus robust transformation: How organizations respond to environmental change, *J. Manage.* **31,** no. 5, 738–757.

Liberty Times (2024). Hualien earthquake: Partitioned spaces in shelters impress Japanese netizens –On-site footage revealed, available at https://video.ltn.com.tw/article/f4TfZe8Acus/PLI7xntdRxhw0WAtjar8mbBJH6nFzOOxRb (last accessed June 2025) (in Chinese).

Lin, S. H. (2024). After the Hualien earthquake: Tzu Chi's swift 20-minute SOP for disaster relief, *Glob. Views Monthly*, available at https://www.gvm.com.tw/article/113452 (last accessed February 2025) (in Chinese).

MacKinnon, D., and K. D. Derickson (2013). From resilience to resourcefulness: A critique of resilience policy and activism, *Prog. Hum. Geogr.* **37,** no. 2, 253–270.

Manyena, S. B. (2006). The concept of resilience revisited, *Disasters* **30,** no. 4, 434–450.

McAslan, A. (2010). *The Concept of Resilience: Understanding Its Origins, Meaning, and Utility*, Torrens Resilience Inst., Adelaide, Australia.

Ministry of the Interior, National Fire Agency (2025). Central emergency operation center operational guidelines, available at https://www.nfa.gov.tw/ (last accessed February 2025) (in Chinese).

National Science and Technology Center for Disaster Reduction (n.d.a.). The 0206 Taiwan earthquake taught us an important lesson, available at https://drrstat.ncdr.nat.gov.tw/statistics/TainanEarthquake (last accessed May 2023) (in Chinese).

National Science and Technology Center for Disaster Reduction (n.d.b.). Things every Taiwanese living with earthquakes must know: the 0206 Hualien earthquake, available at https://drrstat.ncdr.nat.gov.tw/statistics/HualienEarthquake (last accessed May 2023) (in Chinese).

NPOst (2018). The flicker of light in the Hualien earthquake: This time, we finally made disaster relief different, available at https://npost.tw/archives/42608 (last accessed February 2025) (in Chinese).

Olshansky, R. B., and S. E. Chang (2009). Planning for disaster recovery: Emerging research needs and challenges, *Prog. Plan.* **72,** no. 4, 195–250.

Patton, M. Q. (1999). Enhancing the quality and credibility of qualitative analysis, *Health Serv. Res.* **34,** no. 5 Pt 2, 1189–1208.

Perz, S. G., A. Shenkin, G. Barnes, L. Cabrera, L. A. Carvalho, and J. Castillo (2012). Connectivity and resilience: A multidimensional analysis of infrastructure impacts in the Southwestern Amazon, *Soc. Indic. Res.* **106,** no. 2, 259–285.

Prerna, J., H. J. Pasman, and M. S. Mannan (2020). Process system resilience: From risk management to business continuity and sustainability, *Int. J. Bus. Contin. Risk Manage.* **10,** no. 1, 47–66, doi: 10.1504/IJBCRM.2020.105615.

Presidential Policy Directive/PPD-8 (2011). National preparedness, available at https://www.dhs.gov/presidential-policy-directive-8-national-preparedness (last accessed May 2025).

Remes, J. A. C., and A. Horowitz (Editors) (2021). *Critical Disaster Studies,* University of Pennsylvania Press, Philadelphia, Pennsylvania.

Sambamurthy, V., A. Bharadwaj, and V. Grover (2003). Shaping agility through digital options: Reconceptualizing the role of IT in contemporary firms, *MIS Q.* **27,** no. 2, 237–263.

Tainan City Council (2016). Special Report on the 0206 earthquake [Unpublished report], Tainan City Council, Tainan, Taiwan (in Chinese).

Tainan City Fire Department (2022). Analyzing disaster management issues from the rescue operations of the Weiguan Building collapse during the 2016 Tainan earthquake, available at https://odm.hsinchu.gov.tw/boxes/resume/20220707101728336Gk9w.pdf (last accessed February 2025) (in Chinese).

Tainan City Government (2016). During the 0206 earthquake, Kunshan Village in Yongkang District activated its community-based disaster management mechanism and voluntarily participated in rescue and relief efforts, earning widespread recognition and praise, *Tainan City Government Disaster Prevention Newsletter no. 42*, available at http://www.tainanfrc.com.tw/achievement/detail/38 (last accessed August 2025) (in Chinese).

Taipei City Traffic Engineering Office (2023). Taipei City's emergency rescue route plan for major disasters.

The National Academies (2012). Disaster Resilience: A National Imperative, Committee on Increasing National Resilience to Hazards and Disasters, Natl. Acad. Press, Washington, D.C.

United Nations (n.d.). Transforming our world: The 2030 Agenda for sustainable development, available at https://sdgs.un.org/2030agenda (last accessed May 2025).

Walker, B., C. S. Holling, S. R. Carpenter, and A. Kinzig (2004). Resilience, adaptability and transformability in social–ecological systems, *Ecol. Soc.* **9,** no. 2, 5, doi: 10.5751/ES-00650-090205.

Waugh, W. L., and G. Streib (2006). Collaboration and leadership for effective emergency management, *Public Adm. Rev.* **66,** 131–140.

West, G. B., L. M. A. Bettencourt, and J. Lobo (2009). A general model for the structure and dynamics of biological networks, *Nature* **446,** no. 7137, 168–172.

Williams, M. T., J. L. Smith, and R. Patel (2023). Making the connection between health equity and sustainability, *Front. Public Health* **11,** doi: 10.3389/fpubh.2023.10562663.

Woods, D. D. (2005). Creating foresight: Lessons for enhancing resilience from Columbia, in *Organization at the Limit: Lessons from the Columbia Disaster*, M. Farjoun and W. H. Starbuck (Editors), Blackwell, Malden, Massachusetts, 289–308.

Wu, F. C. (2018). Why were bed and breakfast and hotel operators able to mobilize immediately after the Hualien earthquake? *Common Wealth Mag.*, available at https://www.cw.com.tw/article/5088210 (last accessed February 2018) (in Chinese).

Zarnic, R., V. Rajcic, and B. Vodopivec (2017). Data collection for estimation of resilience of cultural heritage assets, in *Mixed Reality and Gamification for Cultural Heritage*, M. Ioannides, N. Magnenat-Thalmann, and G. Papagiannakis (Editors), Springer, Cham, Switzerland, 239–253, doi: 10.1007/978-3-319-49607-8_11.

Zolli, A., and A. M. Healy (2012). *Resilience: Why Things Bounce Back*, Free Press, New York, New York.

Manuscript received 1 April 2025
Published online 4 September 2025

Denoising Seismograms in the Time Domain Using a Deep Learning Model

Chengping Chai*[1], Derek Rose[1], Scott Stewart[1], Nathan Martindale[1], Mark Adams[1], Anibely Torres Polanco[1], Lisa Linville[2], Christopher Stanley[1], and Philip Bingham[1]

ABSTRACT

OPEN ACCESS

Deep learning has emerged as a transformative tool for enhancing the extraction of reliable information from seismograms, addressing the increasing demand for precise and efficient seismic data analysis. We introduce an innovative encoder–decoder deep learning model, named WaveDenoiser, designed for noise reduction in the time domain, thereby eliminating the need for spectrogram computations that have been used for existing deep learning tools and significantly improving processing speed. Utilizing the benchmark dataset that is Stanford Earthquake Dataset, we developed three models of varying sizes: base, medium, and large. Notably, the large (referred to as WaveDenoiser) model demonstrated superior performance, achieving a median signal-to-noise ratio improvement of 8.8 dB on in-distribution unseen data (in the same geographic region) and 7.7 dB on out-distribution unseen data (in a new geographic region), outpacing both the base and medium models. Further evaluation of the WaveDenoiser model revealed a reduction in median arrival-time errors by 0.02 s for *P* waves and 0.01 s for *S* waves when processing waveforms prior to phase picking using PhaseNet on in-distribution unseen data. When tested on out-distribution unseen data, the model also effectively reduced the *P*-wave median arrival-time error by 0.02 and 0.01 s in median arrival-time error for *S* waves. Importantly, the application of WaveDenoiser resulted in a significant reduction of phase picking outliers by 1.1% to 3.6% for both *P* and *S* waves. In addition, we achieved over five times acceleration in processing speed compared with the seisBench implementation of DeepDenoiser. Our findings underscore the potential of WaveDenoiser as a powerful tool for improving seismic data analysis and processing efficiency.

KEY POINTS

- Three deep learning models were developed and trained for noise reduction of seismograms in the time domain.
- Our WaveDenoiser model achieved a median improvement of 8 dB in signal-to-noise ratio.
- WaveDenoiser model improved phase picker performance and reduced time cost compared with an existing model.

Supplemental Material

INTRODUCTION

Seismic noise has various valuable applications (e.g., Shapiro *et al.*, 2005) in seismology, but it also interferes with earthquake signals, obscuring crucial features in seismic time series. To address this, statistic- and physics-based algorithms have been developed to reduce noise in earthquake seismograms. Parolai (2009) and Ditommaso *et al.* (2012) introduced effective signal denoising techniques based on the S-transform. Han and van der Baan (2015) developed a mode decomposition approach to reduce white noise in seismic data. Mousavi and Langston (2016) introduced a seismic data denoising technique utilizing the continuous wavelet transform. Chen (2018) implemented a least-square inversion method that enhances the signal-to-noise ratio (SNR) through waveform decomposition.

Recent advances in deep learning have significantly enhanced various seismic data processing tasks. For instance, several

1. Oak Ridge National Laboratory, Oak Ridge, Tennessee, U.S.A., https://orcid.org/0000-0002-6792-6014 (CC); https://orcid.org/0000-0002-5217-4374 (DR); https://orcid.org/0000-0003-4320-5818 (SS); https://orcid.org/0000-0002-5036-5433 (NM); https://orcid.org/0000-0002-5414-2800 (MA); https://orcid.org/0000-0001-5218-2174 (ATP); https://orcid.org/0000-0002-4226-7710 (CS); https://orcid.org/0000-0003-4616-6084 (PB); 2. Sandia National Laboratories, Albuquerque, New Mexico, U.S.A., https://orcid.org/0000-0003-1319-1056 (LL)

*Corresponding author: chaic@ornl.gov

Cite this article as Chai, C., D. Rose, S. Stewart, N. Martindale, M. Adams, A. Torres Polanco, L. Linville, C. Stanley, and P. Bingham (2025). Denoising Seismograms in the Time Domain Using a Deep Learning Model, *Bull. Seismol. Soc. Am.* **116**, 192–204, doi: 10.1785/0120250143 studies have reported improvements in seismic signal arrival-time picking (e.g., Ross *et al.*, 2018; Zhu and Beroza, 2019; Chai *et al.*, 2020; Mousavi *et al.*, 2020; Chai, Rose, Stewart, Martindale, Adams, Linville, *et al.*, 2025), earthquake parameter estimation (e.g., Mousavi and Beroza, 2020a,b), and source discrimination (e.g., Kong *et al.*, 2024; Maguire *et al.*, 2024). In the context of signal denoising, Zhu *et al.* (2019) developed a deep learning model that utilizes the short-time Fourier transform (STFT) and can effectively reduce background noise in seismic waveforms. More sophisticated deep learning models have been developed for earthquake data (Trappolini *et al.*, 2024). In this study, we explore the potential of a simple deep learning model for denoising seismograms directly in the time domain. This approach streamlines and accelerates the denoising workflow by eliminating the need for STFT and its inverse.

Training deep learning models typically requires extensive and well-organized datasets. The seismology benchmark collection (SeisBench; Woollam *et al.*, 2022) provides access to several datasets tailored for seismic applications. Among the available datasets, the Stanford Earthquake Dataset (STEAD, Mousavi *et al.*, 2019) features globally distributed earthquake signals recorded by local and regional seismic stations (within 350 km from the source) alongside noise traces. The Italian seismic dataset for machine learning (Michelini *et al.*, 2021) comprises ~43,000 hr of three-component waveforms and noise traces from the Italian region. Machine learning asset aggregation of the preliminary determination of epicenters (Cole *et al.*, 2023), compiled by U.S. Geological Survey, includes over 5.1 million global teleseismic waveforms and phase annotations. In addition, the Texas earthquake dataset (Chen *et al.*, 2024) consists of around 300,000 earthquake signals and 200,000 noise traces from Texas. We aim to develop a deep learning model adaptable to various geological settings at a local and regional scale. We selected STEAD for our research due to its global representation of seismic events and stations. To access the applicability of our trained model in scenarios that extend beyond the original training data, we divide the dataset both randomly and based on event and station locations, deviating from STEAD's original data partitioning.

Deep learning models with a greater number of parameters have consistently outperformed their smaller counterparts in both language and vision tasks (e.g., Villalobos *et al.*, 2022). In seismological applications, larger deep learning models have also demonstrated enhanced performance in picking signal arrival times compared with smaller models (Chai, Rose, Stewart, Martindale, Adams, Linville, *et al.*, 2025). Jin *et al.* (2024) illustrated that increasing the size of deep learning models improves the performance in data-driven full waveform inversion using a large-scale synthetic dataset. However, the effect of model size on performance in seismogram denoising remains unclear. To investigate this relationship, we trained three deep learning models with progressively increasing parameters to evaluate their performance in signal denoising.

The denoised seismograms produced by our deep learning model are anticipated to enhance the performance of subsequent data processing tasks. Because accurate measurement of *P*- and *S*-wave arrival times from seismograms is essential for effectively locating seismic events and probing subsurface structure, we assess the performance of arrival-time picking both before and after denoising to evaluate the impact of our denoising approach. Several deep learning-based arrival pickers (e.g., Ross *et al.*, 2018; Zhu and Beroza, 2019; Mousavi *et al.*, 2020) have shown superior performance compared with traditional methods. In this study, we employed Seisbench's implementation of PhaseNet (Zhu and Beroza, 2019) to conduct our downstream performance evaluation.

DATA

Our study utilized the STEAD benchmark dataset, which comprises over 1.2 million seismic signals captured by more than 2500 seismic stations worldwide. A band-pass filter was applied to seismograms in STEAD to preserve signals in the frequency range between 1 and 45 Hz. This extensive dataset included earthquake signals from ~450,000 seismic events along with background noise (see Fig. S1, available in the supplemental material to this article). The epicentral distances of the events ranged from 0 to 350 km, with magnitudes (a mix of 23 different magnitude scales) of seismic events spanning from −0.5 to 7.9. However, most events were below a magnitude of 2.5. The depths of these earthquakes varied from 0 to 350 km. We employed this benchmark dataset to train and evaluate our denoiser models. The seismic signals in STEAD were divided into three subsets: the training set (~950,000 earthquake signals and 220,000 noise waveforms), the development set (around 50,000 earthquake signals and 11,000 noise waveforms), and the test set (~30,000 earthquake signals and 2,000 noise waveforms). Notably, seismic events and stations from the Oklahoma region were excluded from both the training and development sets (see Fig. S1). The test set exclusively contained seismic signals recorded by stations in the Oklahoma region from seismic events occurred in the same region and background noise. Given that many seismic events in the Oklahoma region were induced by wastewater injection (Weingarten *et al.*, 2015), whereas most events in STEAD occurred naturally, the test set was considered data from a different study area. The training and the development sets were randomly split, with the development set designated for in-distribution evaluation. The spectral characteristics of noise waveforms differed significantly between the training and test sets (see Fig. S2). The test set showed a higher average noise spectral density compared with the training set.

METHODOLOGY

We initiated our data processing by generating noisy signals from 57-s-long earthquake seismograms (referred to as clean signals) and noise waveforms extracted from the STEAD. For

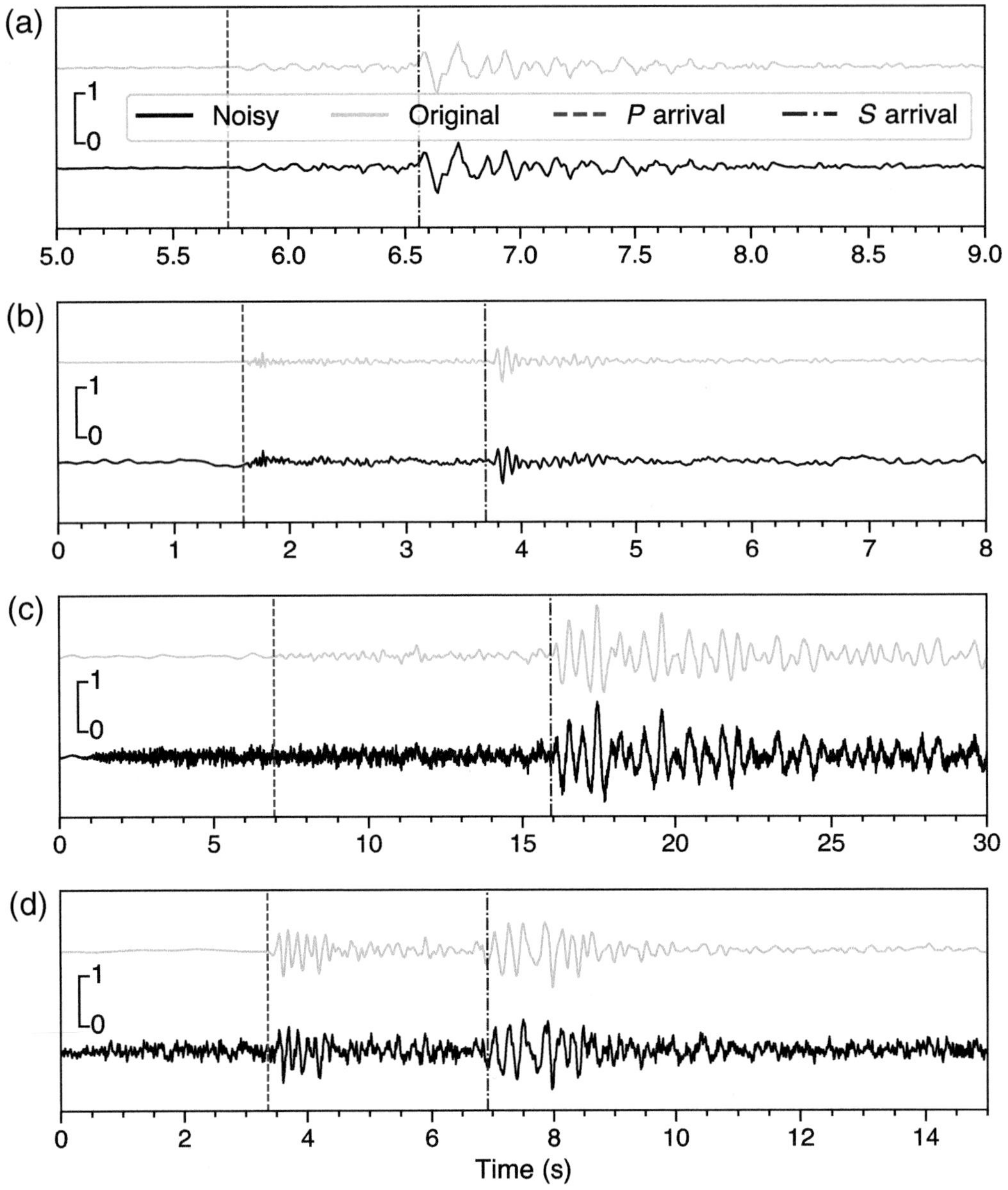

Figure 1. Example seismograms from the training set. (a–d) Four waveform pairs of clean and noisy signals. The amplitude of each waveform was normalized with the maximum amplitude of the associated three-component seismogram segment. The unit of the seismogram amplitudes is relative meters per second (or count) because the instrument response of seismic waveforms was not removed. The color version of this figure is available only in the electronic edition.

each earthquake or noise waveform, we randomly selected 21 noise waveforms from the same data subset (e.g., training), ensuring that only waveforms from the same subset were utilized. Each earthquake seismogram or noise waveform was normalized by its respective maximum amplitude. Next, we scaled the amplitude of each noise waveform by a random number between 0 and 0.5 before adding it to an earthquake seismogram, creating a noisy signal. To further reduce data bias, we introduced a random time shift to the earthquake seismogram. As a result, each earthquake seismogram generated 21 noisy signals. As illustrated in the four examples presented in Figure 1, our method effectively added noise of varying intensities to the clean signals. The resulting noisy signals were used as input for our deep learning model, whereas the clean signals served as the target during training. In addition to noisy signals, we also used pure noise waveforms as input for training.

We modified the architecture of SeisBench's PhaseNet implementation for our model by removing the softmax layer. The revised model architecture consists of an encoder and a decoder module (Fig. 2a). The encoder extracted an encoded representation from the input signals (noisy signals and pure noise), whereas the decoder reconstructed the representation features into the target outputs (clean signals and pure noise). We trained three deep learning models of varying sizes: a base model with ~268,000 trainable parameters, a medium model with around 1,071,000 trainable parameters, and a large model with around 4,278,000 trainable parameters. All models were trained using an Adam optimizer (Kingma and Ba, 2017) with a learning rate of 10^{-6}, a batch size of 256, and a total of 50 epochs. To evaluate model performance, we employed the SNR as our primary metric. The SNR was calculated in accordance with the methodology outlined by Mousavi *et al.* (2019). The improvement in SNR was determined by the difference between the SNR of a denoised signal and that of the input signal.

RESULTS

The training process converged after 50 epochs for all three models (see Fig. S3). Using the development set, our trained models achieved positive SNR improvements across a range of input signal SNRs (Fig. 3a). Notably, the large model exhibits a greater SNR improvement than both the base and medium

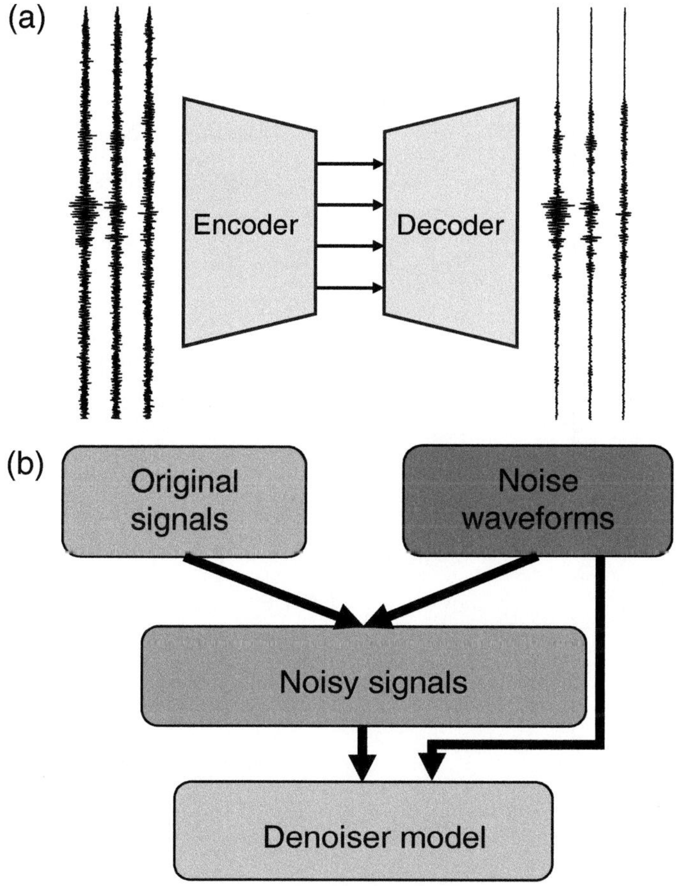

Figure 2. Schematic representation showing (a) the structure of the denoiser model and (b) its construction process. The color version of this figure is available only in the electronic edition.

models for the input signal with SNR values less than 31 dB. Conversely, the medium model showed slightly better SNR improvement for input signals with SNR values exceeding 31 dB. Given that denoising is particularly beneficial for signals with lower SNRs, we selected the large model as our preferred choice, referring to it as the WaveDenoiser model. When these three models were trained on a portion of the entire available waveform dataset, we found that the base model performed better when trained with fewer than 12 million waveforms (Fig. 3b). However, once the number of training waveforms exceeded 12 million, the large model outperformed the others. The trend suggests that additional training waveforms could lead to further improvements in model performance. Because of increasing computational demands, we opted not to implement additional data augmentation to expand the training dataset. Training on an NVIDIA A100 graphics processing unit (GPU) took 476 hr for the large model. The training times for the base and medium models are similar to those of the large model, likely due to high input/output usage. We observed that the hard disk's read/write operations nearly reached their maximum speed during model training. Employing a distributed computing system may alleviate this bottleneck and reduce overall training time.

For the development set, our base, medium, and large models produced median SNR improvements of 6.6, 8.0, and 8.8 dB, respectively (Fig. 4). The average SNR improvements were 8.0 ± 7.6 dB for the base model, 8.8 ± 6.0 dB for the medium model, and 9.7 ± 6.5 dB for the large model. We also computed the ground-truth SNR improvements by subtracting the SNR of the noisy signals from that of the clean signals, yielding median

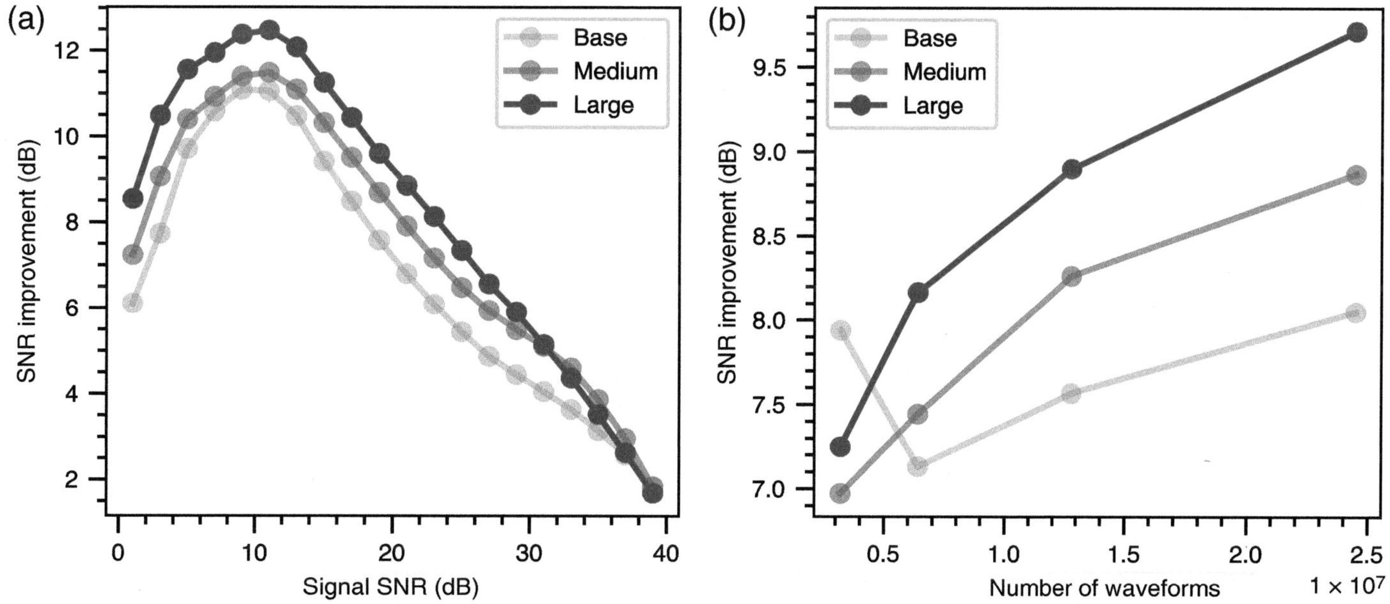

Figure 3. Signal-to-noise ratio (SNR) improvements on the development set. The SNR improvements were computed as the average difference in SNR between noisy waveforms and their denoised counterparts. (a) A comparison of SNR improvements achieved by our base, medium, and large models. (b) SNR improvement as a function of the number of training waveforms used to train the models. The color version of this figure is available only in the electronic edition.

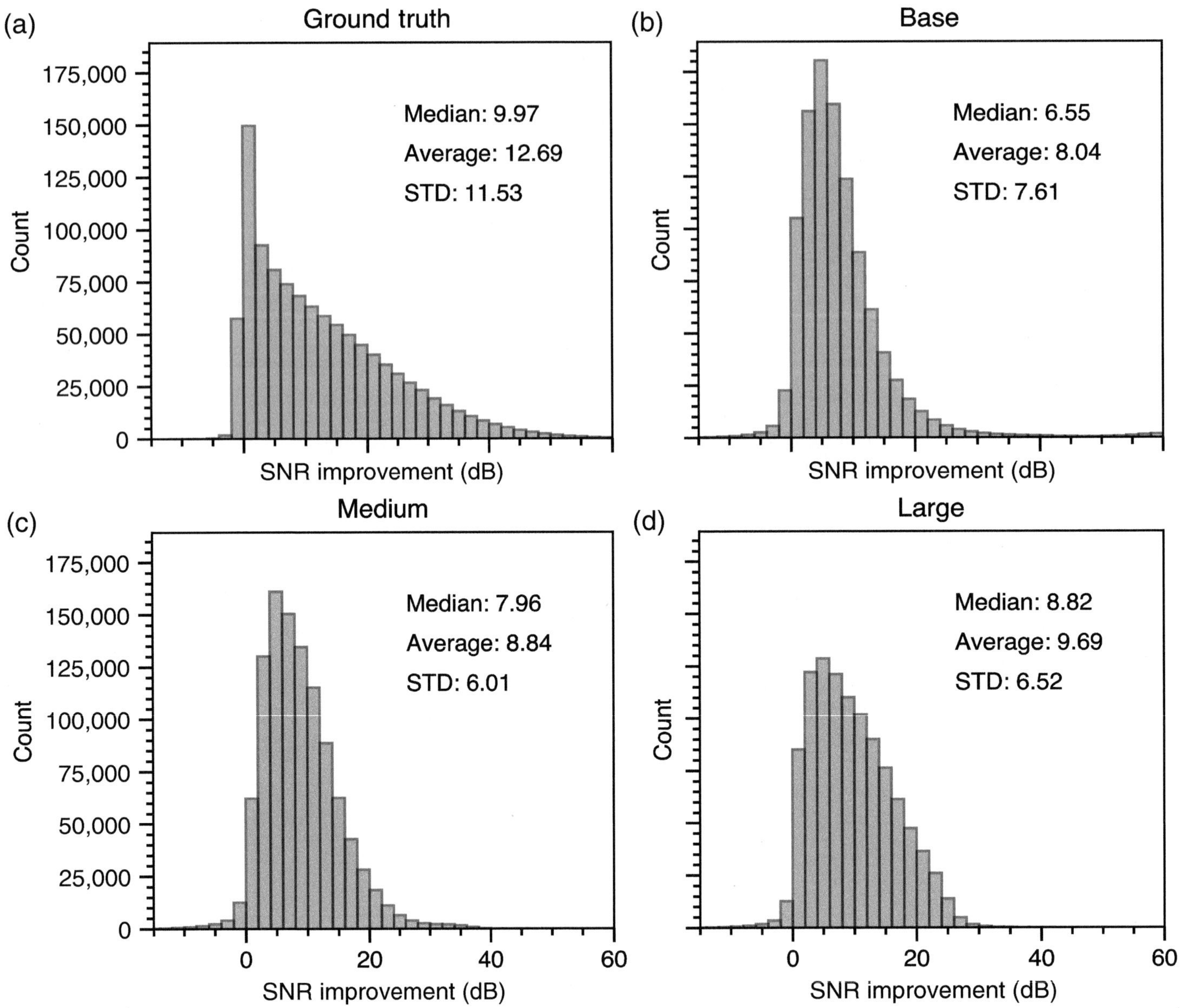

Figure 4. Histograms depicting SNR improvements for (a) the ground truth, (b) the base model, (c) the medium model, and (d) the large model, as evaluated on the development set. STD, standard deviation.

and average SNR improvements of 10.0 dB and 12.7 ± 11.5 dB, respectively. As shown in Figure 4, the SNR improvements from the base and medium models were relatively concentrated around their respective median values, whereas the improvements from the large model exhibited a slightly broader distribution. Waveform examples presented in Figure 5 (see Figs. S4–S7 for zoomed-in view) demonstrated that the denoised signals generated by the WaveDenoiser model closely resemble the clean signals. The WaveDenoiser model successfully reduced noise levels while preserving *P* and *S* waves. Furthermore, the WaveDenoiser model reduced spectral amplitudes across a wide range of frequencies in the noisy signals (see Fig. S8). Because the background noise added to the noisy signals spanned a wide range of frequencies, the WaveDenoiser model effectively reduced noise sacross a broad frequency bandwidth (see Fig. S9).

We compared the performance of and SeisBench's implementation of PhaseNet using noisy data from the development set against that of the denoised signal using our large model. As illustrated in Figure 6, the median *P*-wave arrival-time error for the noisy signals was −0.04 s, whereas the error for the denoised signals is −0.02 s. The absolute average error in *P*-wave arrival time for the noisy signals stood at 0.07 s, which is the same as the corresponding error for the denoised signals. We defined arrival-times errors larger than 0.5 s (or 50 time intervals) as outliers, which is consistent with the cutoff threshold that Mousavi *et al.* (2020) used. Our WaveDenoiser model successfully reduced the proportion of outliers from 18.9% to 15.3% for *P* waves. The median *S*-wave arrival-time error is −0.04 s for noisy signals and −0.03 s for denoised signals. Postdenoising,

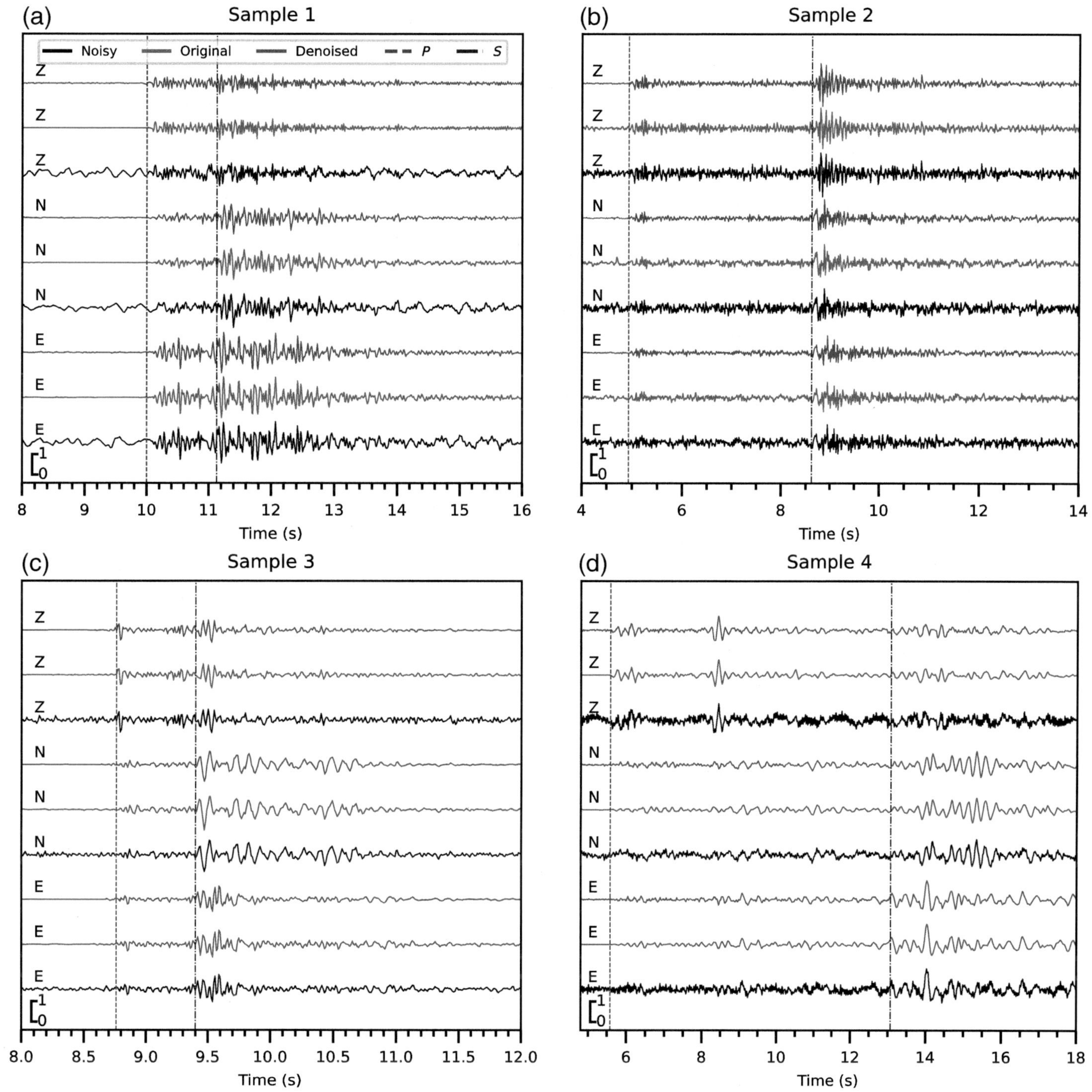

Figure 5. (a–d) Waveform examples from the development set, comparing clean, noisy, and denoised signals produced by the large model. The red and blue vertical lines indicate the arrival times of *P* and *S* waves, respectively. The unit of the seismogram amplitudes is relative meters per second (or count) because the instrument response of seismic waveforms was not removed. E, east–west; N, north–south; Z, vertical component. The color version of this figure is available only in the electronic edition.

we noted the absolute average error for *S* waves did not change, with arrival picking outliers decreasing from 8.6% to 7.1%. In addition, the standard deviation of arrival-time errors for both *P* and *S* waves remained unchanged after denoising.

For the test set, the median and average ground-truth SNR improvements were 14.2 dB and 15.7 ± 12.6 dB, respectively (Fig. 7). The base, medium, and large models resulted in median SNR improvements of 5.8, 7.5, and 7.7, respectively, with average SNR improvements of 6.2 ± 5.5 dB for the base model, 7.6 ± 5.1 dB for the medium model, and 8.3 ± 5.7 dB for the large model. As shown in Figure 8, we observed a 0.01 s

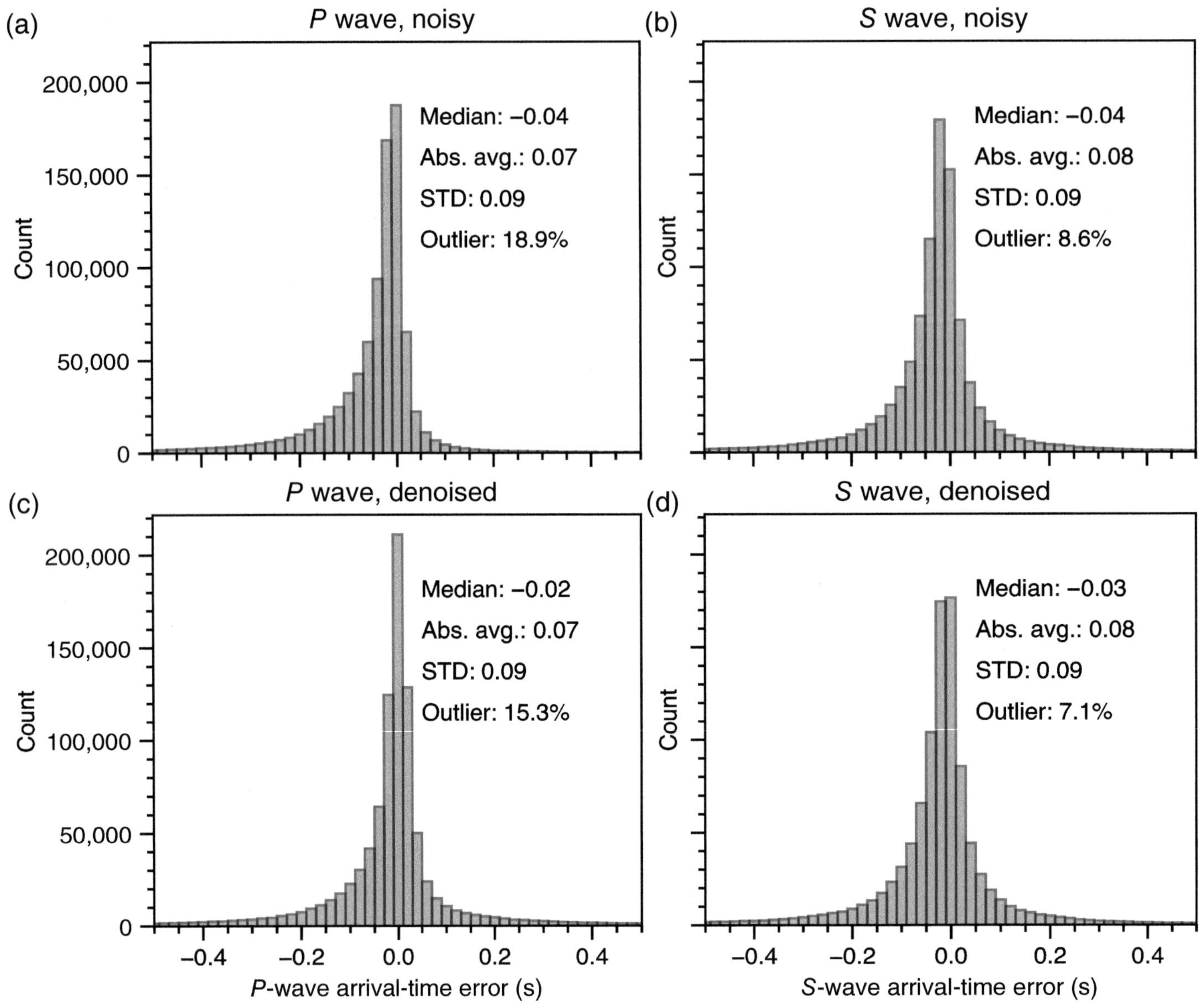

Figure 6. Performance of SeisBench's implementation of PhaseNet in estimating signal arrival times (a,b) before and (c,d) after denoising with our model, using noisy data from the development set. Arrival-time errors exceeding 1 s are classified as outliers. Abs. avg., absolute average; STD, standard deviation.

reduction in median *P*-wave arrival-time errors after using our large model for denoising. The median *S*-wave arrival-time errors decreased by 0.01 s postdenoising as well. The average arrival-time errors did not change for both *P* and *S* waves after denoising. Our WaveDenoiser model also achieved a reduction in outliers by 1.1% for *P* waves and 2.2% for *S* waves. Waveform examples indicate that our WaveDenoiser effectively reduced noise and recovered original signals in most instances (Fig. 9; Figs. S10–S13). Similar to in-distribution data, the reduction in spectral amplitudes for noisy signals was broadband for data from a different study area (see Fig. S14). The removed noise for the test set also covered a broad frequency range (see Fig. S15). However, the WaveDenoiser model did not effectively reduce noise at frequencies above 42 Hz, which can be addressed through additional frequency filtering. When comparing the noisy waveforms from the test set denoised by the base, medium, large models along with SeisBench's implementation of DeepDenoiser, we found the large model produced denoised waveforms that closely resemble clean signals and preserved the seismic waves. In contrast, SeisBench's implementation of DeepDenoiser effectively removed noise but sometimes altered seismic waves especially for later arriving ones (Fig. 10; Figs. S16–S19). Because the WaveDenoiser model was trained in the time domain, waveform integrity was the primary target metric, quantified by the mean square error between noisy and target waveforms. In contrast, DeepDenoiser was trained on the spectrogram, so it prioritized preserving the spectral content over enforcing waveform integrity. The WaveDenoiser model struggled to recover *P* waves from noisy waveforms when the *P*-wave

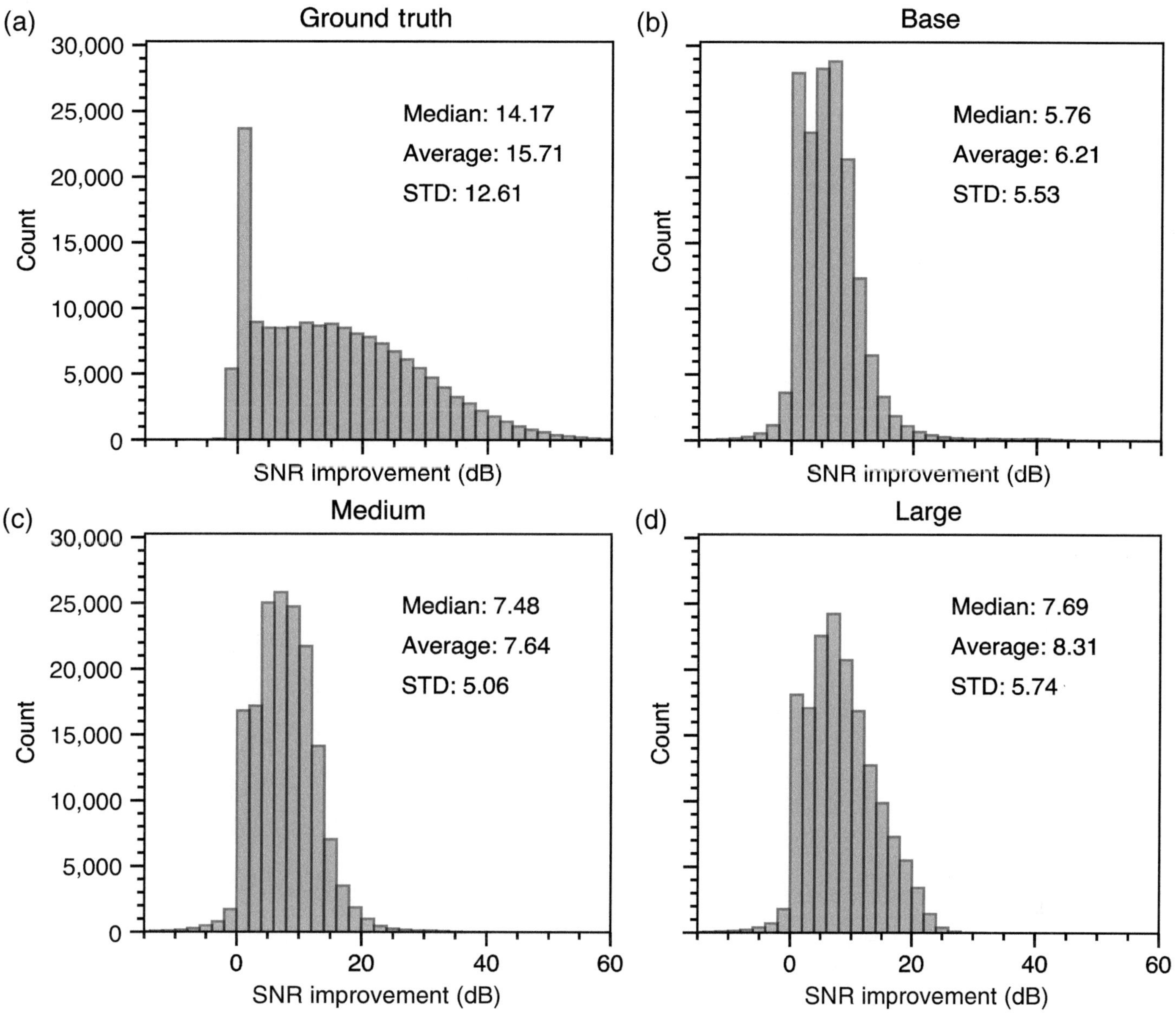

Figure 7. Histograms depicting SNR improvements for (a) the ground truth, (b) the base model, (c) the medium model, and (d) the large model, as evaluated on noisy data from the test set. STD, standard deviation.

amplitudes were very small or when the added noise exhibited similar characteristics as *P* waves (Fig. S20). Because each denoising method presents its own advantages and limitations, we recommend applying them with careful consideration of these constraints, and when possible, comparing results from multiple approaches.

We compared the processing time of our WaveDenoiser model against SeisBench's implementation of DeepDenoisor for 10,000 three-component waveforms. To ensure a fair comparison, the waveforms were converted to the respective input formats for both models and preloaded to computer memory: a NumPy array for WaveDenoiser and an ObsPy stream for DeepDenoiser. Both models were evaluated on a Tesla P40 GPU using the Pytorch environment. Initially, we assessed the processing time for handling individual waveforms. DeepDenoiser required 496.2 s to process 10,000 waveforms individually, whereas WaveDenoiser completed the same task in 40.4 s. When processing a batch of 256 waveforms at once, DeepDenoiser took 22.7 s, whereas WaveDenoiser finished in 3.7 s. Consequently, WaveDenoiser demonstrated an impressive processing rate of 2703 seismic waveforms per second, compared with SeisBench's DeepDenoiser, which processed 441 waveforms per second.

DISCUSSION AND SUMMARY

When evaluating with data from the same region as the training data (in-distribution data), our three deep learning models (base, medium, and large) effectively enhanced the SNR. The large model achieved greater SNR improvements compared

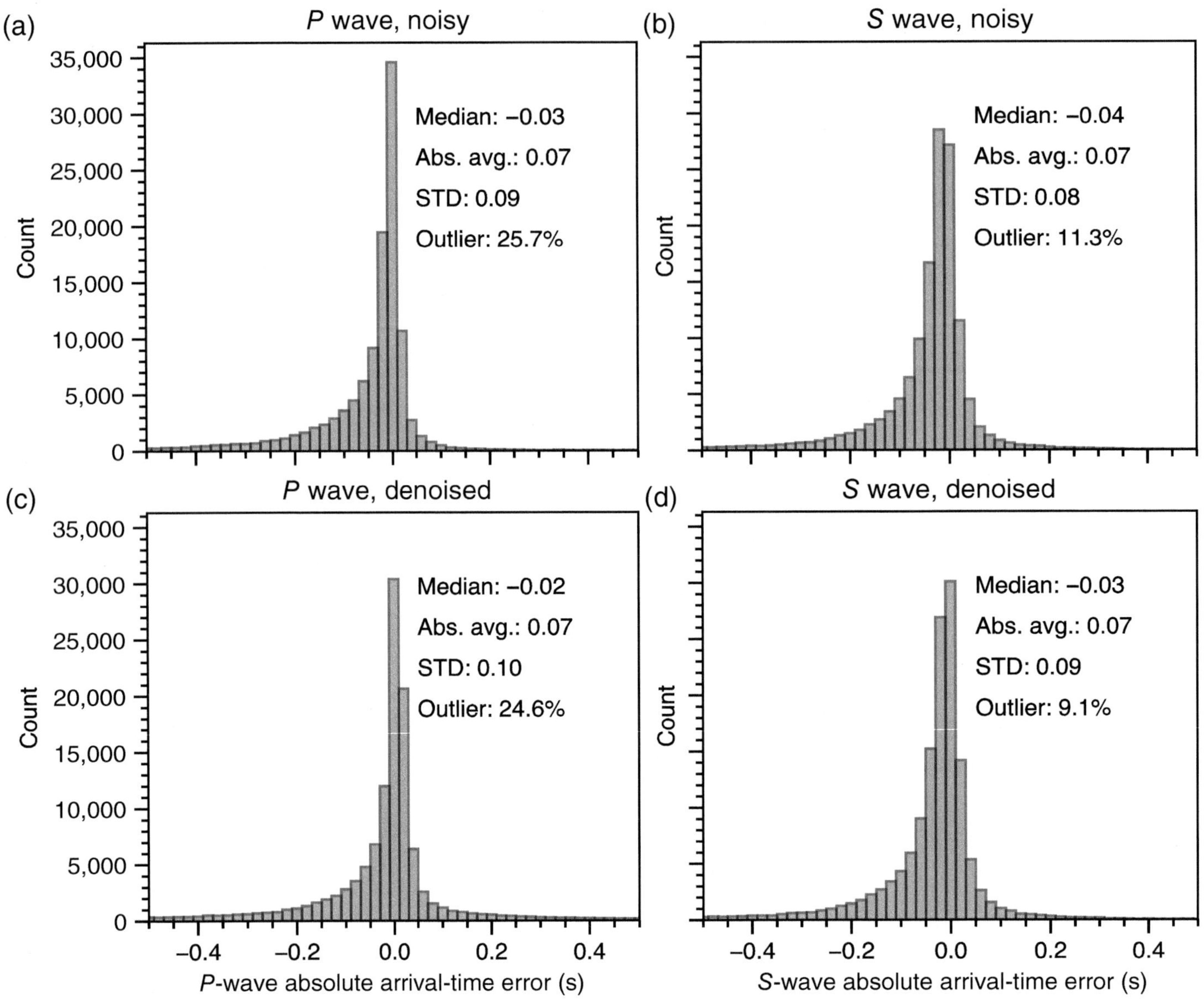

Figure 8. The performance of SeisBench's implementation of PhaseNet in estimating signal arrival times (a,b) before and (c,d) after denoising with our model, using noisy data from the test set. Arrival time errors exceeding 1 s are classified as outliers. Abs. avg., absolute average; STD, standard deviation.

with the base and medium models, consistent with findings from other deep learning studies for seismic data (e.g., Jin *et al.*, 2024; Chai, Rose, Stewart, Martindale, Adams, Linville, *et al.*, 2025). However, our models did not yield SNR improvements exceeding 35 dB, even though such SNR improvements were observed in the ground-truth data. The limitation maybe due to a fact that signals exhibiting significant SNR improvements (higher than 35 dB) were not predominant in the training data, leading our models to struggle with learning the characteristics of these signals. Potential future directions to address this limitation include exploring different data augmentation techniques tailored to generate training instances with higher SNR improvements, developing custom loss functions that specifically penalize errors to foster enhanced SNR improvements, and employing alternative model architectures. Our large or WaveDenoiser model demonstrated a median SNR improvement of 8.8 dB for in-distribution data and 7.7 dB for a new study area (out-distribution data). Furthermore, when comparing PhaseNet's arrival-time picking performance between noisy data and denoised data using our WaveDenoiser model, we found that denoising reduced arrival-time errors for both *P* and *S* waves. In addition, the number of arrival-time outliers decreased by 3.4% for *P* waves and 1.5% for *S* waves.

Our deep learning models also demonstrated the capability to enhance the SNR for data from study areas different from those of the training data. The large model consistently outperformed the base and medium models in terms of SNR improvements for data from a different study area. When denoising the data from a different study area (out-distribution) using our large model, we observed an enhancement in PhaseNet's performance for both *P* and *S* waves, with a reduction in median average arrival-time errors by 0.01 s. The

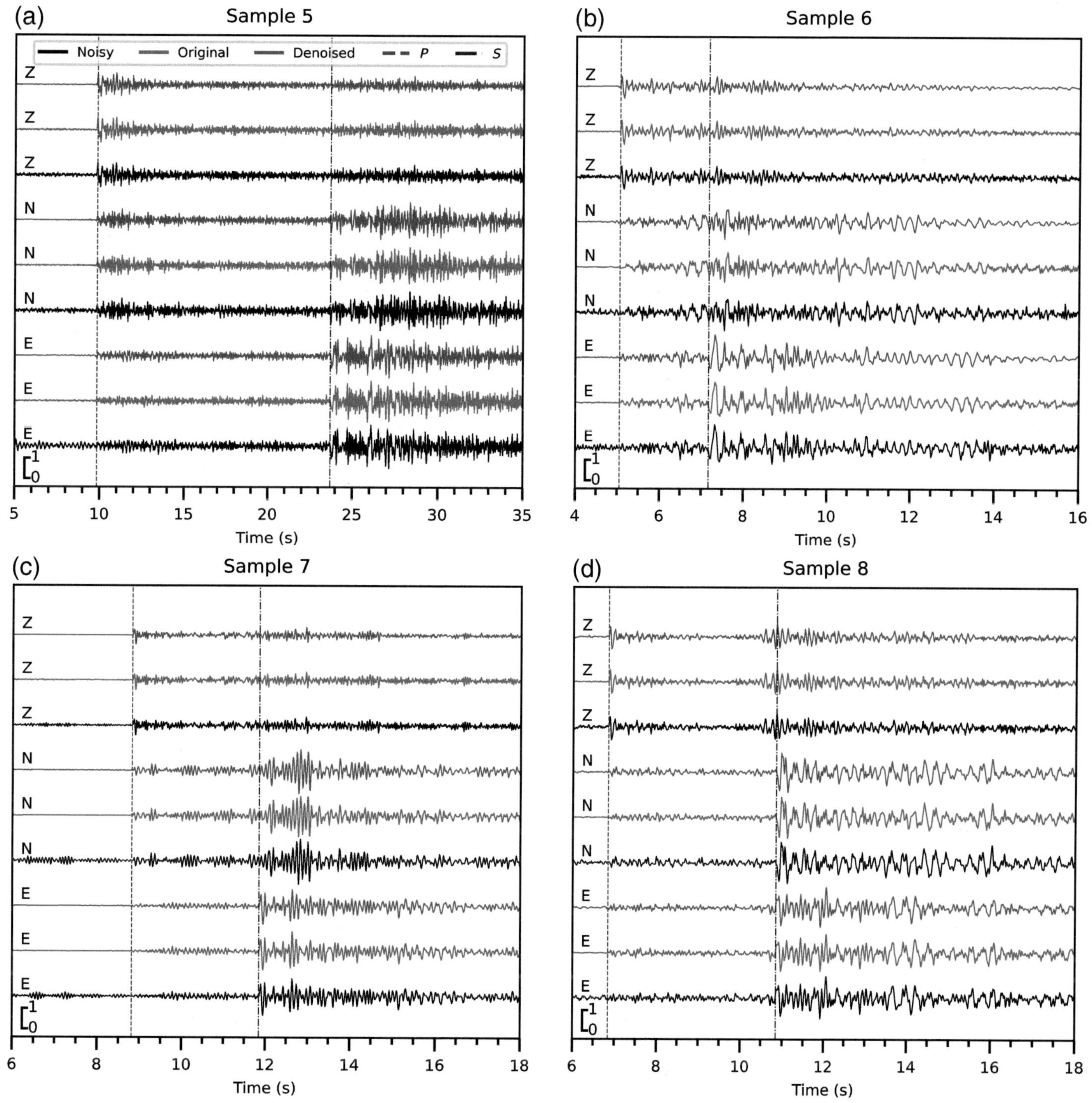

Figure 9. (a–d) Waveform examples from the test set, comparing clean, noisy, and denoised signals produced by the large model. Red and blue vertical lines indicate the arrival times of P and S waves, respectively. The unit of the seismogram amplitudes is relative meters per second (or count) because the instrument response of seismic waveforms was not removed. E, east–west; N, north–south; Z, vertical component. The color version of this figure is available only in the electronic edition.

absolute average arrival-time errors for *P* and *S* waves stayed the same. For data from a different study area, our WaveDenoiser effectively reduced phase picking outliers by 1.1% for *P* waves and 2.2% for *S* waves. Given that background noise is complex and varies from site to site, our deep learning model may not fully capture the characteristics of background noise. Implementing transfer learning with additional data (e.g., Chai *et al.*, 2020) from new sites could enhance the model's performance further. For instance, background noise and earthquake signals from a new site can be leveraged for transfer learning to fine-tune the model, thereby improving its performance on data from that location. In addition, because the original training dataset contained minimal instrument malfunction noise, applying transfer learning to nonstructural noise

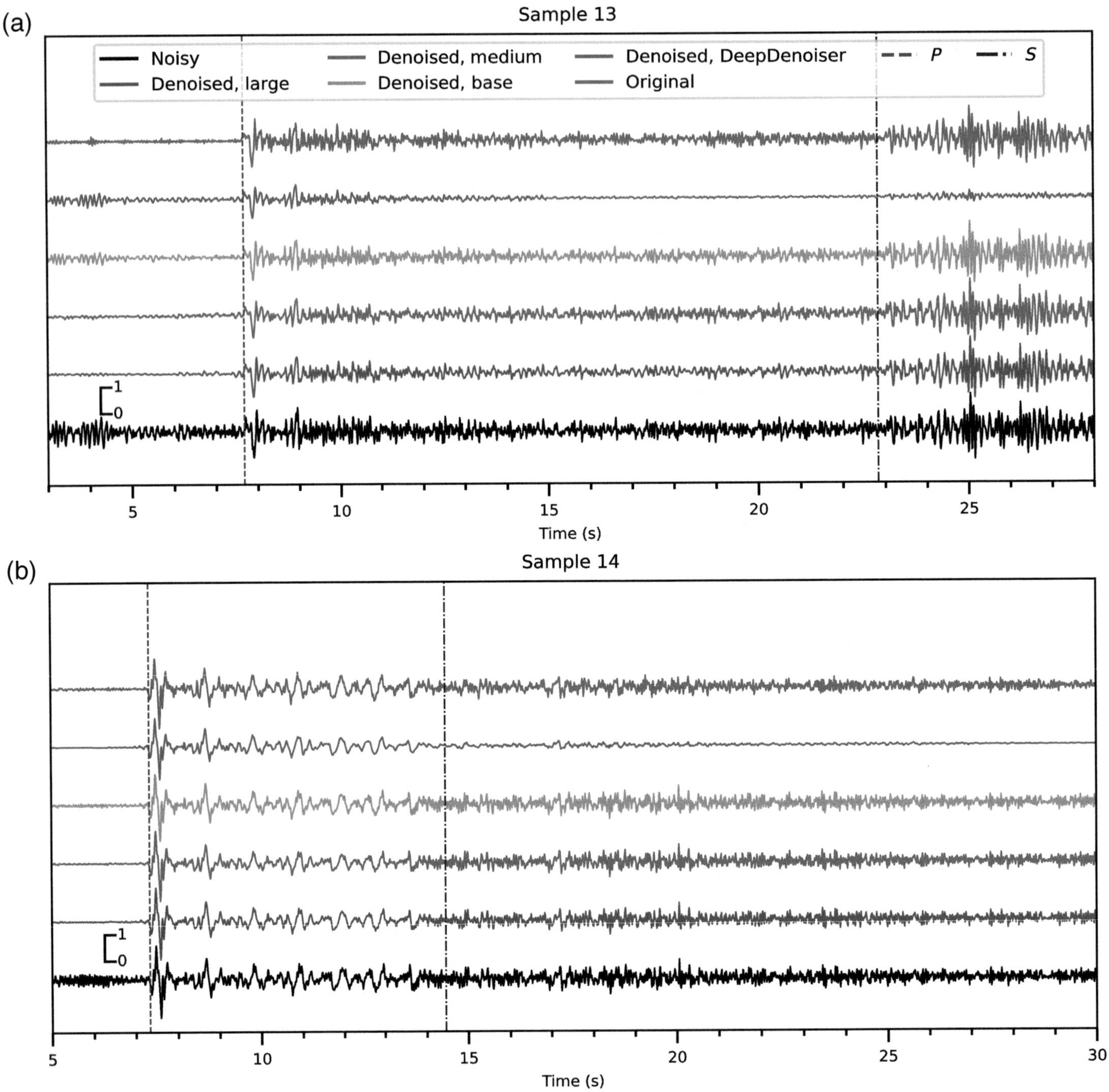

Figure 10. (a,b) Comparison of vertical-component noisy waveforms from the test set with clean waveforms and those denoised using the base, medium, large models, as well as SeisBench's implementation of DeepDenoiser. The unit of the seismogram amplitudes is relative meters per second (or count) because the instrument response of seismic waveforms was not removed. The color version of this figure is available only in the electronic edition.

could further enhance WaveDenoiser's denoising capacity. Because our deep learning model employed a denoising mechanism that differs from traditional methods such as frequency filtering, it serves as a complimentary approach to existing techniques and can be effectively integrated with established methods. Compared with an S-transform-based method (Parolai, 2009) with carefully optimized parameters (Text S1), the waveform denoised using WaveDenoiser demonstrated comparable results (Fig. S21). Although the S-transform method offers greater flexibility through tunable parameters, WaveDenoiser is more user-friendly because it requires no parameter tuning once the model is trained.

Our WaveDenoiser model outperformed SeisBench's implementation of DeepDenoiser significantly in terms of processing speed. Unlike DeepDenoiser, which used spectrogram masks as input, WaveDenoiser takes seismic time series as input directly. When processing 10,000 seismic waveforms,

WaveDenoiser model reduced the processing time by 92% for a batch size of 1 and by 84% for a batch size of 256. Overall, WaveDenoiser was over five times faster than SeisBench's DeepDenoiser implementation.

DATA AND RESOURCES

The seismic data and associated metadata were obtained from Mousavi *et al.* (2019). The figures were prepared with Matplotlib v. 3.9.2 (Hunter, 2007) and the Generic Mapping Tools v. 6.5.0 (Wessel *et al.*, 2019). NumPy v. 1.26.4 (Harris *et al.*, 2020), pandas v. 2.2.3 (The pandas development team, 2024) and ObsPy v. 1.4.1 (Beyreuther *et al.*, 2010; Megies *et al.*, 2011; Krischer *et al.*, 2015) were used to process the seismic data. The model architecture was modified from the SeisBench v. 0.8.2 (Woollam *et al.*, 2022) implementation of PhaseNet (Zhu and Beroza, 2019). Zarr v. 2.18.3 (Miles *et al.*, 2024) and H5py v. 3.12.1 (Collette, 2013) were used to store the seismic data. Pytorch v. 2.3.0 (Paszke *et al.*, 2019) and Lightning v. 2.4.0 (Falcon and Team, 2024) were used to train the convolutional neural network (CNN) models. Curifactory v. 0.17.1 (Martindale *et al.*, 2023) and Comet v. 3.47.3 (https://www.comet.com/, last accessed April 2025) were used for model management. The trained model (Chai, Rose, Stewart, Martindale, Adams, Torres Polanco, *et al.*, 2025) can be downloaded at https://github.com/ORNL/wave-denoiser (last accessed September 2025). The supplemental material includes details on the S-transform method (Text S1); two maps displaying the locations of seismic event and stations (Fig. S1); average power spectral densities (PSDs) of noise waveforms from training samples and the test set (Fig. S2); learning curves for the base, medium, and large models (Fig. S3); zoomed-in views of samples 1–4 (Figs. S4–S7); PSDs of original, noisy, and denoised waveforms for samples 1–4 (Fig. S8); PSDs of original waveforms, added noise, and removed noise for samples 1–4 (Fig. S9); zoomed-in views of samples 5–8 (Figs. S10–S13); PSDs of original, noisy, and denoised waveforms for samples 5–8 (Fig. S14); PSDs of original waveforms, added noise and removed noise for samples 5–8 (Fig. S15); addition samples showing the comparison of waveforms between our models and DeepDenoiser (Figs. S16–S19); additional denoising results from the test set (Fig. S20); and a comparison between the WaveDenoiser result against an S-transform method (Fig. S21).

DECLARATION OF COMPETING INTERESTS

The authors acknowledge that there are no conflicts of interest recorded.

ACKNOWLEDGMENTS

The authors would like to acknowledge the U.S. Department of Energy (DOE), National Nuclear Security Administration's Office of Defense Nuclear Nonproliferation Research and Development, for supporting this work. This work has been authored in part by UT-Battelle, LLC, under Contract DE-AC05-00OR22725 with the U.S. DOE. The U.S. Government retains, and the publisher, by accepting the article for publication, acknowledges that the U.S. Government retains a nonexclusive, paid-up, irrevocable, worldwide license to publish or reproduce the published form of this article, or allow others to do so, for U.S. Government purposes. The views and conclusions contained in this document are those of the authors and should not be interpreted as necessarily representing the official policies, either expressed or implied, of the U.S. Government. This research used resources of the Compute and Data Environment for Science (CADES) and Oak Ridge Leadership Computing Facility at Oak Ridge National Laboratory (ORNL), which is supported by the DOE Office of Science under Contract Number DE-AC05-00OR22725. DOE will provide public access to these results of federally sponsored research in accordance with the DOE Public Access Plan (http://energy.gov/downloads/doe-public-access-plan, last accessed April 2025). The authors thank Jason Hite for his contributions to an early version of the source code. The authors acknowledge helpful suggestions from Monica Maceira, Erin Cunningham, and Karl Pazdernik. The authors appreciate the support of Stefano Parolai for cross-checking the results of the S-transform denoised waveform in Figure S21. The authors thank Editor-in-Chief Martin Mai, Associate Editor Stefano Parolai, and two anonymous reviewers for their constructive comments that significantly improved the article.

REFERENCES

Beyreuther, M., R. Barsch, L. Krischer, T. Megies, Y. Behr, and J. Wassermann (2010). ObsPy: A Python toolbox for seismology, *Seismol. Res. Lett.* **81,** no. 3, 530–533, doi: 10.1785/gssrl.81.3.530.

Chai, C., M. Maceira, H. J. Santos-Villalobos, S. V. Venkatakrishnan, M. Schoenball, W. Zhu, G. C. Beroza, C. Thurber, and EGS Collab (2020). Using a deep neural network and transfer learning to bridge scales for seismic phase picking, *Geophys. Res. Lett.* **47,** no. 16, e2020GL088651, doi: 10.1029/2020GL088651.

Chai, C., D. Rose, S. Stewart, N. Martindale, M. Adams, L. Linville, C. Stanley, A. Torres Polanco, and P. Bingham (2025). PickerXL, a large deep learning model to measure arrival times from noisy seismic signals, *Seismol. Res. Lett.* **96,** no. 4, 2394–2404, doi: 10.1785/0220240353.

Chai, C., D. Rose, S. Stewart, N. Martindale, M. Adams, A. Torres Polanco, L. Linville, C. Stanley, and P. Bingham (2025). WaveDenoiser, doi: 10.11578/dc.20250915.4.

Chen, Y. (2018). Non-stationary least-squares complex decomposition for microseismic noise attenuation, *Geophys. J. Int.* **213,** no. 3, 1572–1585, doi: 10.1093/gji/ggy079.

Chen, Y., O. Savvaidis, O. M. Saad, G.-C. Dino Huang, D. Siervo, V. O'Sullivan, C. McCabe, B. Uku, P. Fleck, G. Burke, *et al.* (2024). TXED: The Texas earthquake dataset for AI, *Seismol. Res. Lett.* **95,** no. 3, 2013–2022, doi: 10.1785/0220230327.

Cole, H. M., W. L. Yeck, and H. M. Benz (2023). MLAAPDE: A machine learning dataset for determining global earthquake source parameters, *Seismol. Res. Lett.* **94,** no. 5, 2489–2499, doi: 10.1785/0220230021.

Collette, A. (2013). *Python and HDF5: Unlocking Scientific Data*, O'Reilly Media, Inc.

Ditommaso, R., M. Mucciarelli, and F. C. Ponzo (2012). Analysis of non-stationary structural systems by using a band-variable filter, *Bull. Earthq. Eng.* **10,** no. 3, 895–911, doi: 10.1007/s10518-012-9338-y.

Falcon, W., and The PyTorch Lightning (2024). PyTorch lightning, *Zenodo*, doi: 10.5281/zenodo.11100106.

Han, J., and M. van der Baan (2015). Microseismic and seismic denoising via ensemble empirical mode decomposition and adaptive thresholding, *Geophysics* **80,** no. 6, KS69–KS80, doi: 10.1190/geo2014-0423.1.

Harris, C. R., K. J. Millman, S. J. Van Der Walt, R. Gommers, P. Virtanen, D. Cournapeau, E. Wieser, J. Taylor, S. Berg, N. J.

Smith, *et al.* (2020). Array programming with NumPy, *Nature* **585,** no. 7825, 357–362, doi: 10.1038/s41586-020-2649-2.

Hunter, J. D. (2007). Matplotlib: A 2D graphics environment, *Comput. Sci. Eng.* **9,** no. 3, 90–95, doi: 10.1109/MCSE.2007.55.

Jin, P., Y. Feng, S. Feng, H. Wang, Y. Chen, B. Consolvo, Z. Liu, and Y. Lin (2024). An empirical study of large-scale data-driven full waveform inversion, *Sci. Rep.* **14,** no. 1, 20,034, doi: 10.1038/s41598-024-68573-7.

Kingma, D. P., and J. Ba (2017). Adam: A method for stochastic, *Optimization*, doi: 10.48550/arXiv.1412.6980.

Kong, Q., W. R. Walter, R. Wang, and B. Schmandt (2024). Evaluating physics-informed neural network performance for seismic discrimination between earthquakes and explosions, *Seismol. Res. Lett.* **96,** no. 1, 147–156, doi: 10.1785/0220240097.

Krischer, L., T. Megies, R. Barsch, M. Beyreuther, T. Lecocq, C. Caudron, and J. Wassermann (2015). ObsPy: A bridge for seismology into the scientific Python ecosystem, *Comput. Sci. Discov.* **8,** no. 1, 014003, doi: 10.1088/1749-4699/8/1/014003.

Maguire, R., B. Schmandt, R. Wang, Q. Kong, and P. Sanchez (2024). Generalization of deep-learning models for classification of local distance earthquakes and explosions across various geologic settings, *Seismol. Res. Lett.* **95,** no. 4, 2229–2238, doi: 10.1785/0220230267.

Martindale, N., S. L. Stewart, J. Hite, and M. B. Adams (2023). Curifactory: A research experiment manager, *J. Open Source Software* **8,** no. 90, 5793, doi: 10.21105/joss.05793.

Megies, T., M. Beyreuther, R. Barsch, L. Krischer, and J. Wassermann (2011). ObsPy - what can it do for data centers and observatories? *Ann. Geophys.* **54,** no. 1, 47–58, doi: 10.4401/ag-4838.

Michelini, A., S. Cianetti, S. Gaviano, C. Giunchi, D. Jozinović, and V. Lauciani (2021). INSTANCE—The Italian seismic dataset for machine learning, *Earth Syst. Sci. Data* **13,** no. 12, 5509–5544, doi: 10.5194/essd-13-5509-2021.

Miles, A., M. Bussonnier, J. Moore, D. Papadopoulos Orfanos, D. Bennett, J. Bourbeau, J. Hamman, D. Stansby, A. Fulton, G. Lee, *et al.* (2024). zarr-developers/zarr-python: v2.18.1, *Zenodo*, doi: 10.5281/zenodo.11206451.

Mousavi, S. M., and G. C. Beroza (2020a). A machine-learning approach for earthquake magnitude estimation, *Geophys. Res. Lett.* **47,** no. 1, e2019GL085976, doi: 10.1029/2019GL085976.

Mousavi, S. M., and G. C. Beroza (2020b). Bayesian-deep-learning estimation of earthquake location from single-station observations, *IEEE Trans. Geosci. Remote Sens.* **58,** no. 11, 8211–8224, doi: 10.1109/TGRS.2020.2988770.

Mousavi, S. M., and C. A. Langston (2016). Hybrid seismic denoising using higher-order statistics and improved wavelet block thresholding, *Bull. Seismol. Soc. Am.* **106,** no. 4, 1380–1393, doi: 10.1785/0120150345.

Mousavi, S. M., W. L. Ellsworth, W. Zhu, L. Y. Chuang, and G. C. Beroza (2020). Earthquake transformer—An attentive deep-learning model for simultaneous earthquake detection and phase picking, *Nat. Commun.* **11,** no. 1, 3952, doi: 10.1038/s41467-020-17591-w.

Mousavi, S. M., Y. Sheng, W. Zhu, and G. C. Beroza (2019). STanford EArthquake Dataset (STEAD): A global data set of seismic signals for AI, *IEEE Access* **7,** 179,464–179,476, doi: 10.1109/ACCESS.2019.2947848.

Parolai, S. (2009). Denoising of seismograms using the S transform, *Bull. Seismol. Soc. Am.* **99,** no. 1, 226–234, doi: 10.1785/0120080001.

Paszke, A., S. Gross, F. Massa, A. Lerer, J. Bradbury, G. Chanan, T. Killeen, Z. Lin, N. Gimelshein, L. Antiga, *et al.* (2019). PyTorch: An imperative style, high-performance deep learning library, doi: 10.48550/arXiv.1912.01703.

Ross, Z. E., M.-A. Meier, and E. Hauksson (2018). P wave arrival picking and first-motion polarity determination with deep learning, *J. Geophys. Res.* **123,** no. 6, 5120–5129, doi: 10.1029/2017JB015251.

Shapiro, N. M., M. Campillo, L. Stehly, and M. H. Ritzwoller (2005). High-resolution surface-wave tomography from ambient seismic noise, *Science* **307,** no. 5715, 1615–1618, doi: 10.1126/science.1108339.

The pandas development team (2024). pandas-dev/pandas: Pandas, *Zenodo*, doi: 10.5281/zenodo.10957263.

Trappolini, D., L. Laurenti, G. Poggiali, E. Tinti, F. Galasso, A. Michelini, and C. Marone (2024). Cold diffusion model for seismic denoising, *J. Geophys. Res.* **1,** no. 2, e2024JH000179, doi: 10.1029/2024JH000179.

Villalobos, P., J. Sevilla, T. Besiroglu, L. Heim, A. Ho, and M. Hobbhahn (2022). Machine learning model sizes and the parameter gap, doi: 10.48550/arXiv.2207.02852.

Weingarten, M., S. Ge, J. W. Godt, B. A. Bekins, and J. L. Rubinstein (2015). High-rate injection is associated with the increase in U.S. mid-continent seismicity, *Science* **348,** no. 6241, 1336–1340, doi: 10.1126/science.aab1345.

Wessel, P., J. F. Luis, L. Uieda, R. Scharroo, F. Wobbe, W. H. F. Smith, and D. Tian (2019). The Generic Mapping Tools version 6, *Geochem. Geophys. Geosys.* **20,** no. 11, 5556–5564, doi: 10.1029/2019GC008515.

Woollam, J., J. Münchmeyer, F. Tilmann, A. Rietbrock, D. Lange, T. Bornstein, T. Diehl, C. Giunchi, F. Haslinger, D. Jozinović, *et al.* (2022). SeisBench—A toolbox for machine learning in seismology, *Seismol. Res. Lett.* **93,** no. 3, 1695–1709, doi: 10.1785/0220210324.

Zhu, W., and G. C. Beroza (2019). PhaseNet: A deep-neural-network-based seismic arrival-time picking method, *Geophys. J. Int.* **216,** no. 1, 261–273, doi: 10.1093/gji/ggy423.

Zhu, W., S. M. Mousavi, and G. C. Beroza (2019). Seismic signal denoising and decomposition using deep neural networks, *IEEE Trans. Geosci. Remote Sens.* **57,** no. 11, 9476–9488, doi: 10.1109/TGRS.2019.2926772.

Manuscript received 6 June 2025
Published online 10 November 2025

Operator Learning for Earthquake Location: Methodology and Application to Out-of-Network Events in the Mendocino Triple Junction

Hongyu Sun*[1]

ABSTRACT

Accurate location of earthquakes outside the boundaries of seismic networks is a well-known challenge due to limited azimuthal coverage. Offshore earthquakes, particularly along the Mendocino Transform fault, pose considerable risks to nearby communities. However, the lack of permanent stations in marine environments hinders accurate earthquake location. This study investigates the feasibility of locating offshore earthquakes around the Mendocino Triple Junction (MTJ) using advanced deep learning techniques. We propose the location neural operator (LocNO), an innovative operator learning framework that directly estimates earthquake locations from full-waveform data, even under sparse and nonideal network conditions. The approach integrates the Fourier neural operator and graph neural operator to capture the intricate spatiotemporal dependencies of seismic wavefields across stations and to estimate a spatial pseudoprobability density function over earthquake source coordinates (easting, northing, and depth). Trained on historical seismicity and simulated sparse network scenarios, LocNO generalizes across varying network geometries and provides robust estimates for out-of-network events, with the mean absolute errors on the order of 10 km horizontally and 4 km in depth. A case study of the 2017 M_w 5.7 earthquake sequence, 218 km west of Ferndale, California, demonstrates that LocNO yields robust locations for out-of-network earthquakes newly detected by the phase neural operator, even when recorded by only a few stations with large azimuthal gaps. These results open a new avenue for investigating MTJ seismotectonics using deep-learning-enhanced earthquake catalogs.

KEY POINTS

- Sparse or nonideal seismic networks hinder the accurate location of offshore and out-of-network earthquakes.
- Location neural operator (LocNO) improves earthquake location by leveraging advanced operator learning to capture spatiotemporal dependencies.
- LocNO shows promise for improving earthquake monitoring in remote and under-instrumented regions.

INTRODUCTION

The Mendocino Triple Junction (MTJ) is one of the most seismically active regions in North America. This triple junction serves as a tectonic transition zone, linking the convergence of the Cascadia subduction zone with the translation of the San Andreas fault system. These complex interactions generate frequent offshore earthquakes concentrated along the Mendocino Transform fault. However, the lack of permanent seismic stations in the marine environments introduces substantial challenges to accurately locating these events.

Locating out-of-network earthquakes is a long-standing challenge (Ellsworth and Roecker, 1981) due to limited azimuthal coverage, unreliable phase arrival data, and low signal-to-noise ratios (SNRs). These challenges are worsened for offshore earthquakes by the attenuation of seismic signals over long distances and inaccuracies in the regional velocity models. Complex 3D geological structures can perturb ray paths and distort waveform characteristics, making accurate location even more difficult. Traditional methods often struggle with the nonlinear inversion processes required for earthquake location in such scenarios, resulting in high uncertainties, with location errors reaching up to 50 km in some cases (Cabieces *et al.*, 2020). For example, ShakeAlert, an earthquake early warning system (Burkett *et al.*, 2014; Given *et al.*, 2018;

1. Department of Earth, Environmental and Resource Sciences, The University of Texas at El Paso, El Paso, Texas, U.S.A., https://orcid.org/0000-0003-3828-1859 (HS)

*Corresponding author: hongyu-sun@outlook.com

Cite this article as Sun, H. (2025). Operator Learning for Earthquake Location: Methodology and Application to Out-of-Network Events in the Mendocino Triple Junction, *Bull. Seismol. Soc. Am.* **116**, 205–224, doi: 10.1785/0120250018

Kohler *et al.*, 2020), has located many offshore earthquakes near the MTJ with errors exceeding 50 km compared to U.S. Geological Survey (USGS) locations (Williamson *et al.*, 2023). This limitation creates significant uncertainties in the earthquake locations, hindering the development of accurate earthquake catalogs essential for seismic hazard assessment, early warning systems, and seismotectonic research.

Several approaches have been proposed to address these challenges and locate out-of-network earthquakes. Rubinstein and Beroza (2007) developed a relocation technique to improve earthquake locations for sparsely recorded earthquakes using full-waveform information. Array methods have shown promise in locating offshore and out-of-network earthquakes in earthquake early warning systems (Eisermann *et al.*, 2018; Nof *et al.*, 2019; Netanel *et al.*, 2021; Jung *et al.*, 2023; Ziv *et al.*, 2024). In addition, Bayesian frameworks have been applied to improve earthquake location in non-optimal network configurations. For example, Zollo *et al.* (2021) combined arrival times, amplitude ratios, and back azimuths to detect offshore seismicity. Williamson *et al.* (2023) proposed the bEPIC algorithm, which integrates historical seismicity into ShakeAlert's location procedure using a Bayesian framework. By incorporating prior seismic activity to downweight high-error solutions in regions with little or no past seismicity, bEPIC significantly reduced mean location errors offshore northern California from 58 to 14 km, especially improving performance for offshore and out-of-network events.

The emergence of machine learning in seismology offers additional opportunities to advance earthquake location. Some studies have shown that deep learning models can estimate earthquake locations from single-station waveforms, challenging the conventional notion that a minimum of three seismic stations is necessary for triangulating and locating a seismic source (Perol *et al.*, 2018; Mousavi and Beroza, 2020; Elsayed *et al.*, 2023; Castro *et al.*, 2024). Other studies follow the general use of earthquake location with multiple stations (Zhang *et al.*, 2020; Chen *et al.*, 2022; McBrearty and Beroza, 2022, 2025; Zhu, Tai, *et al.*, 2022; Kuang *et al.*, 2024; Si *et al.*, 2024). By incorporating geographic locations of stations as node features, graph neural networks (GNNs; Gilmer *et al.*, 2017) have been applied to explore spatiotemporal relationships within seismic networks (Van Den Ende and Ampuero, 2020; Zhang *et al.*, 2022), enabling more accurate earthquake location with adaptability to diverse station geometries using one trained GNN model. However, these methods are often optimized for well-instrumented seismic networks and may underperform for offshore or sparsely instrumented regions.

To overcome these limitations, this study investigates the feasibility of using deep learning to locate out-of-network earthquakes with sparse data, addressing the inherent challenges of locating offshore earthquakes with limited azimuthal coverage. We propose the location neural operator (LocNO), an operator learning framework (Kovachki *et al.*, 2023) designed to locate earthquakes directly from the full-waveform data recorded by seismic networks with arbitrary station geometries. Recent advancements in operator learning offer promising alternatives for processing the seismic data (Sun *et al.*, 2022, 2023; Aquib and Mai, 2024). Building on this progress, our approach adapts and extends classic operator learning frameworks (Li *et al.*, 2020, 2021) to enhance offshore earthquake location using the full-waveform seismic datasets from onshore stations.

To improve the offshore earthquake location accuracy in the MTJ region, we develop a training dataset by collecting historical seismicity data from the region and simulating sparse and nonideal station coverage scenarios. We randomly remove stations from cataloged earthquakes and generate an artificial out-of-network earthquake dataset for training purposes. By leveraging the spatiotemporal information of the seismic data recorded across multiple stations, LocNO is trained to directly estimate event locations, even under nonideal network conditions. The performance of the well-trained LocNO model demonstrates its capability to accurately locate offshore earthquakes beyond the boundaries of the onshore seismic network. LocNO provides locations for newly detected out-of-network earthquakes in the MTJ region that are recorded by only a few stations in the phase neural operator (PhaseNO)-detected catalog (Sun *et al.*, 2023), a setting that is challenging for travel-time-based location methods, as demonstrated by its application to an offshore sequence: the 22 September 2017 M_w 5.7 event located 218 km west of Ferndale, California. Incorporating LocNO into the standard seismic monitoring workflow has the potential to improve offshore location accuracy, thereby advancing our understanding of the seismotectonics in the MTJ region.

METHOD: LOCNO

We begin by introducing the fundamental principles underlying neural operators, which form the basis of the LocNO implemented in our public repository (Sun, 2025). For clarity, all notations are summarized in Table 1. Neural operators extend traditional neural networks by enabling mappings between functions defined over infinite-dimensional spaces. These models adhere to a version of the universal approximation theorem specifically formulated for operators (Kovachki *et al.*, 2023). One of the key applications of neural operators is solving partial differential equations (PDEs), which inspires their foundational design as approximations of inverse differential operators, typically represented by integral operators:

$$u(\mathbf{x}) = (\kappa * v)(\mathbf{x}) = \int \kappa(\mathbf{x},\mathbf{y}) v(\mathbf{y}) d\mathbf{y}, \quad (1)$$

in which v and u are input and output functions of one integral operator layer $\mathcal{K}$, and κ denotes the integration kernel. Here, $\mathbf{x}$

TABLE 1
Summary of Notations

Notation	Description
General Variables	
f	Input seismic waveform function
t	Time coordinate in the waveform input
C, L, N	Number of channels, discrete grid points, and stations, respectively
$i = 1, \ldots N$	Index of seismic station
$k = 1, 2, 3$	Index of spatial direction: $k = 1$ (easting), $k = 2$ (northing), and $k = 3$ (depth)
κ	Kernel for integral operator layer
v	Input of an operator layer
u	Output of an operator layer via integration with κ
σ	Activation function (e.g., GELU or sigmoid function for converting logits into probabilities)
$\mathcal{P}$	Lifting map to project f into a high-dimensional latent space
$\mathcal{U}$	U-shaped neural operator composed of FNO and GNO layers
h	Extracted spatiotemporal features via U-shaped neural operator $\mathcal{U}$
Fourier Neural Operator (FNO)	
$\mathcal{F}$, $\mathcal{F}^{-1}$	Fourier and inverse Fourier transforms
R_θ	Learnable spectral kernel in frequency domain parameterized by θ
W	Local linear transformation
M_l	Number of Fourier modes retained at FNO layer l
C_l,L_l	Number of channels and discretization points at FNO layer l
Graph Neural Operator (GNO)	
$\mathcal{N}(\mathbf{x}_i)$	Neighborhood of node $\mathbf{x}_i$
φ	Message function (e.g., two-layer MLP)
$m_{ij} = m(\mathbf{x}_i,\mathbf{x}_j)$	The edge features (message) computed using $\varphi(v(\mathbf{x}_i),v(\mathbf{x}_j))$ between the node $\mathbf{x}_i$ and $\mathbf{x}_j$, in which $\mathbf{x}_j \in \mathcal{N}(\mathbf{x}_i)$ is a neighboring node of the station i
$m_i = m(\mathbf{x}_i)$	The aggregated message at station i
ψ	Update function (e.g., two-layer MLP)
D	Radius threshold for defining graph edges
(a_0,b_0,c_0)	Geographical origin (longitude, latitude, and depth) used as the reference point for normalization
(a_i,b_i,c_i)	Geographical location of station i (longitude, latitude, and depth) in physical coordinates
(A,B,C)	Physical range in longitude, latitude, and depth used for normalization
$\mathbf{x}_i = (x_i,y_i,z_i)$	Input spatial coordinates of station i, normalized to the range [0,1]
Decoder and Output	
$g_i(t) \in \mathbb{R}^{C\times L}$	Spatiotemporal feature embedding at station i
$s_i(n) \in \mathbb{R}^{3\times L}$	Directional score from station i
$s(n) \in \mathbb{R}^{3\times L}$	Aggregated directional score over space
$\mathcal{Q}$	Station wise decoder mapping $g_i(t)$ to $s_i(n)$
n_k^ℓ	The ℓth discrete grid point along the kth spatial direction
$s_k^\ell = s(n_k^\ell)$	Logit score at discrete grid point ℓ in the spatial direction k
$p_k(n_k^\ell)$	Output probability at discrete grid point ℓ in the spatial direction k
$\mathcal{A}$	Probability aggregator across stations
α_i	Attention weight for station i, satisfying $\sum_i \alpha_i = 1$
Loss Function	
$p_k^*(n_k^\ell)$	Ground-truth probability at discrete grid point ℓ in the spatial direction k
w_k	Loss weight for direction k
$\mathcal{L}_{\mathrm{LocNO}}$	Total loss defined as weighted binary cross-entropy across all directions and grid points

and $\mathbf{y}$ denote coordinates (e.g., space, time, or other domain variables) in the output and input domains, respectively.

Our approach extends the applicability of neural operators beyond their traditional scope of solving PDEs by extracting features from seismic wavefields and predicting a pseudo-probabilistic function indicating the earthquake location. For seismic wavefields, both $\mathbf{x}$ and $\mathbf{y}$ are 4D vectors representing spatiotemporal sampling points, and $\kappa(\mathbf{x},\mathbf{y})$ is a learnable spatiotemporal kernel that governs the integration over neighboring points. Each spatiotemporal point $\mathbf{x} \in \mathbb{R}^4$ consists of three spatial coordinates and one time coordinate. For clarity, we treat time t separately from $\mathbf{x}$. At the ith station (in which $i = 1,\ldots,N$), the input waveform is expressed as $v_i(t) = v(\mathbf{x}_i,t)$, in which $\mathbf{x}_i$ represents the 3D spatial location of the station. In practice, $v_i(t)$ is not only the three-component ground-motion time series but also includes the spatial coordinates $\mathbf{x}_i$ concatenated as three additional channels, so that station location is explicitly embedded into the input

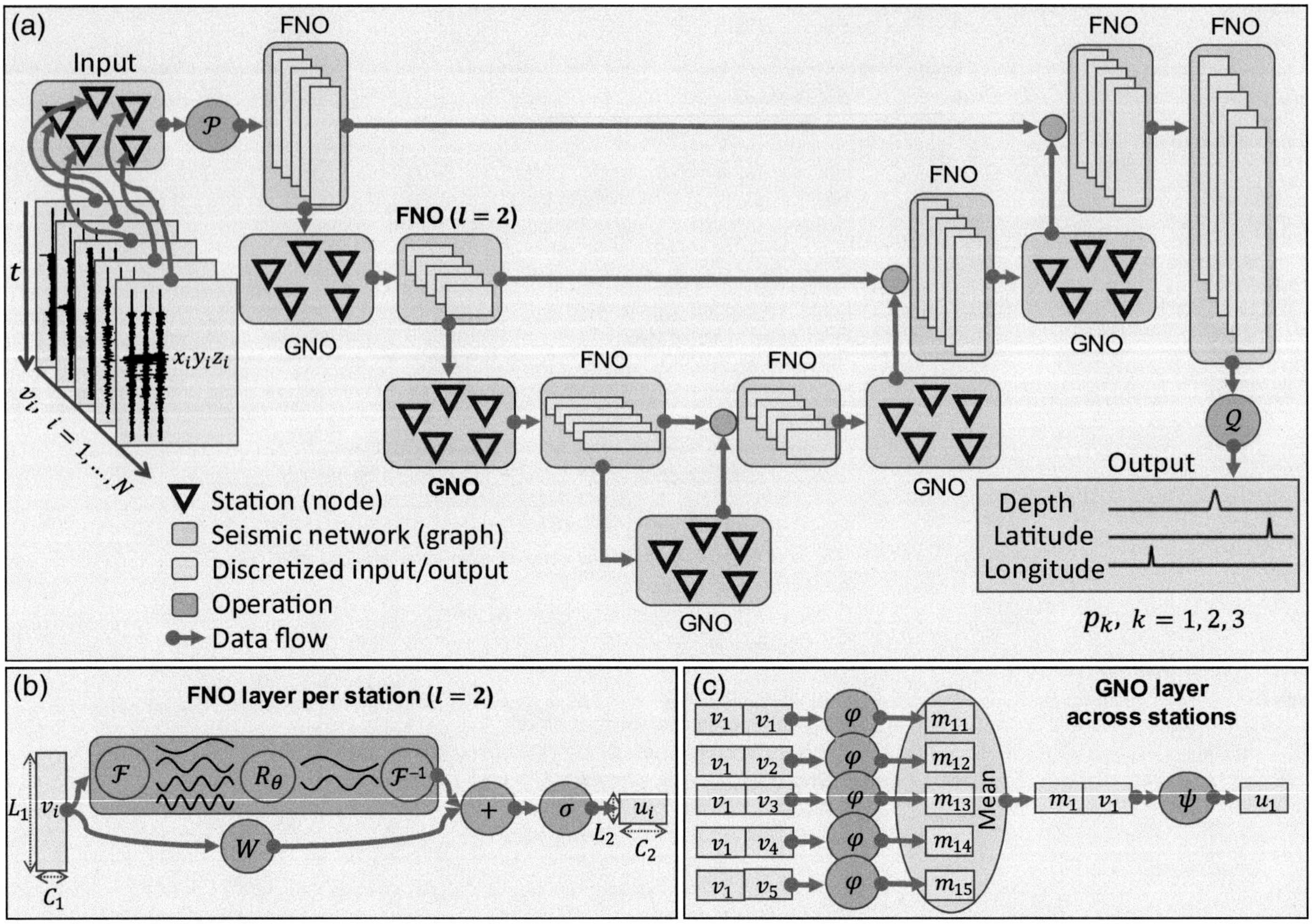

representation. This time-dependent function serves as the input representation for station i in a neural operator layer. The corresponding learned feature representation after a neural operator layer is denoted as $u_i(t) = u(\mathbf{x}_i, t)$.

Various methods can be employed to parameterize the kernel function κ and implement $\mathcal{K}$ (Kovachki *et al.*, 2023). Seismic data collected by a network of multiple stations can be viewed as a function discretized regularly in time at each station and irregularly in space due to the nonuniform distribution of station locations. Thus, we use graph neural operators (GNOs) to represent the spatially irregular discretization and Fourier neural operators (FNOs) to handle the temporally regular discretization. Moreover, applying a kernel integral fully over the 4D spatiotemporal domain is computationally inefficient and unnecessary because only a sparse set of seismic stations provides observed 1D time-series data. Therefore, we decouple temporal and spatial feature extraction: temporal features are modeled using 1D FNOs applied at individual stations, whereas spatial dependencies across stations are captured using GNOs, where the temporal signal at each station is considered as the node features in the computational graph. Consequently, LocNO integrates both FNO and GNO as the foundation of its architecture (Fig. 1). In addition, FNO and GNO layers are interleaved, allowing

Figure 1. Location neural operator (LocNO) architecture: (a) overview of the LocNO model. The feature update process in (b) the second Fourier neural operator (FNO) layer ($l = 2$), and (c) the following graph neural operator (GNO) layer. $\mathcal{P}$, lifting map; $\mathcal{Q}$, decoder map; $\mathcal{F}$, Fourier transform; $\mathcal{F}^{-1}$, inverse Fourier transform; R_θ, learnable spectral kernel; W, local linear transformation; σ, activation function; φ, message function; ψ, update function; v_i, input feature at station i to one layer; u_i, output feature at station i from one layer; $L_l \times C_l$, feature dimension at the lth FNO layer; m_{ij}, edge feature between stations i and j; m_i, aggregated message feature at station i; $\mathbf{x}_i = (x_i, y_i, z_i)$, spatial coordinates of station i; and p_k, pseudo-probability distribution of earthquake location. The model combines 1D FNOs to extract temporal features at each station and GNOs to capture spatial dependencies across stations. For clarity, only five stations are illustrated ($N = 5$). See Table 1 and main text for full descriptions. The color version of this figure is available only in the electronic edition.

temporal and spatial features to be progressively exchanged and jointly encoded through successive layers.

FNO

The FNO computes the kernel κ in the frequency domain by transforming the input into the frequency domain with fast Fourier transforms (FFT) (Li *et al.*, 2021). Because the FFT requires regular spacing, the FNO is best suited for inputs defined on regular grids, such as time series recorded at individual seismic stations. According to the convolution theorem:

$$u_i(t) = \mathcal{F}^{-1}(R_\theta \mathcal{F}(v_i))(t), \tag{2}$$

in which $\mathcal{F}$ and $\mathcal{F}^{-1}$ are the FFT and inverse Fourier transform, respectively, and R_θ is the Fourier-domain representation of the kernel, learned via parameters θ. During training, the model effectively learns the frequency spectrum of $u_i(t)$ through the multiplication in the Fourier domain. However, learning high-frequency components can be more challenging because high-frequency signals are often noisy. Therefore, in practice, only the first M lowest-frequency modes are retained and learned, whereas high-frequency modes are truncated (Li *et al.*, 2021). This strategy helps reduce overfitting risk, improve numerical stability, lower training difficulty, and decrease model complexity. Incorporating a local activation function σ, the output of one FNO layer becomes

$$u_i(t) = \sigma(W v_i(t) + \mathcal{F}^{-1}(R_\theta \mathcal{F}(v_i))(t)), \tag{3}$$

with W being a pointwise linear transformation. Each FNO layer includes two branches (Fig. 1): one performs the Fourier-based global convolution, whereas the other applies the local linear transformation W. The outputs are combined before the activation function. The purpose of introducing a nonlinear activation function after each integral operator is to enable the network to approximate complex, nonlinear mappings. Without such nonlinearities, the composition of multiple integral operators would collapse into a single linear operator, severely limiting the model's expressive power. The activation function σ used in LocNO is the Gaussian error linear unit (GELU; Hendrycks and Gimpel, 2016).

LocNO is structured as a U-shaped neural operator, in which changes in feature dimensions are governed by the FNO layers applied at each spatially sampled station. Each FNO layer models the long-range temporal dependencies present in seismic waveforms by performing 1D global convolution along the time dimension in the frequency domain. Specifically, the input sequence at each station is first transformed via the FFT, followed by a complex-valued multiplication with a learnable spectral kernel R_θ, and then mapped back via the inverse FFT. Operating in the Fourier domain allows the network to capture global temporal patterns efficiently, enabling it to integrate full-waveform information that is critical for improving the robustness and accuracy of hypocenter estimation. At station i, the learned feature representation u_i at layer l has shape $C_l \times L_l$, in which C_l denotes the number of channels and L_l represents the number of discretization points along the primary axis (e.g., input time). LocNO consists of seven FNO layers in total. The value of L_7 is related to the number of spatial bins in the predicted probability distribution and thus constrains the spatial resolution of the estimated source location along the easting, northing, and depth directions. Unless otherwise specified, we adopt the following parameter settings for the feature dimensions and the number of retained Fourier modes M_l across FNO layers:

$$\{L_l\}_{l=1}^{7} = \{3000,750,200,750,3000,3000,6000\}, \tag{4}$$

$$\{C_l\}_{l=1}^{7} = \{48,96,192,96,48,48,48\}, \tag{5}$$

$$\{M_l\}_{l=1}^{7} = \{24,12,8,8,12,24,24\}. \tag{6}$$

In this U-shaped neural operator architecture, the number of Fourier modes M_l is progressively reduced in proportion to the downsampling of the feature dimension along the primary axis. Concurrently, the number of channels is increased to compensate for the loss of feature resolution and to enrich the feature representation in deeper layers (Fig. 1).

GNO

The kernel integration κ in the spatial domain is computed through message-passing graph neural networks (GNNs) (Li *et al.*, 2020; McBrearty and Beroza, 2023). In our method, we treat the spatially irregular structure of the seismic data as a graph: seismic stations are nodes, and their connectivity forms the graph edges. Given node features $v(\mathbf{x}_i)$ computed by an FNO layer at individual stations, a GNO layer updates the value $v(\mathbf{x}_i)$ of node $\mathbf{x}_i$ to a new representation $u(\mathbf{x}_i)$ through an averaging aggregation:

$$u(\mathbf{x}_i) = \psi\left(v(\mathbf{x}_i), \frac{1}{|\mathcal{N}(\mathbf{x}_i)|} \sum_{\mathbf{x}_j \in \mathcal{N}(\mathbf{x}_i)} \varphi(v(\mathbf{x}_i), v(\mathbf{x}_j)) \right), \tag{7}$$

in which $\mathcal{N}(\mathbf{x}_i)$ denotes the set of neighboring nodes of $\mathbf{x}_i$. The edge features $m_{ij} = m(\mathbf{x}_i, \mathbf{x}_j)$ are computed using $\varphi(v(\mathbf{x}_i), v(\mathbf{x}_j))$, in which φ is a differentiable function that maps the node features from a pair of connected nodes concatenated along the channel axis to a latent edge representation. In LocNO, φ is implemented as a two-layer multilayer perceptron (MLP) with a hidden layer size of $4C_l$, in which C_l is the channel dimension of the node features produced by the lth FNO layer preceding the lth GNO layer (Fig. 1).

Once edge features are generated, each node aggregates messages from its neighbors by averaging, and then concatenates the aggregated message $m_i = m(\mathbf{x}_i)$ with its own original features $v(\mathbf{x}_i)$ along the channel axis. This concatenated tensor is passed through another differentiable function, $\psi(m(\mathbf{x}_i), v(\mathbf{x}_i))$, also implemented as a two-layer MLP with the same architecture as φ. The resulting $u(\mathbf{x}_i)$ is the updated node representation. This message-passing paradigm allows information to be exchanged across neighboring nodes and supports the learning of spatial correlations among seismic stations (Fig. 1).

GNO adopts a message-passing framework similar to GNNs, but is specifically designed for operator learning, enabling the approximation of the kernel integration and the generalization across different discretizations. In GNO, the graph is constructed based on a physical distance threshold D defined in the input physical space, to approximate integration over that domain. For any given node, its neighborhood set is composed of all discretized points located within a radius D centered at that node. In the context of spatial domains such as seismic networks, this means that the number of neighbors corresponds to the number of seismic stations located within that physical radius (geographic distance). Unlike radius-based graphs, k-NN graphs (Franceschi *et al.*, 2019) are not suitable for GNO layers because they may restrict connectivity to local clusters, which undermines the uniform spatial coverage needed to accurately approximate kernel integrals.

Within a specified threshold D, nodes are fully connected to form a graph, including self-loops where each node is connected to itself. This threshold serves as a tunable hyperparameter before training. Although seismic stations are irregularly distributed in physical space, increasing the distance allows more stations to be included within a single graph, which consequently increases computational cost due to the increased number of node-to-node communications. In this study, we use a distance threshold of 300 km to account for the long-range wave propagation from offshore earthquakes to onshore stations. This ensures that all stations can effectively exchange information to accurately determine hypocenter locations.

At each GNO layer, we concatenate the normalized node coordinates with the output from the preceding FNO layers to form the node attributes $v(\mathbf{x}_i)$. The geographical locations of all stations in the study area are normalized to the range [0, 1] before concatenation, assuming a geographical origin of (a_0,b_0,c_0) and a physical range of (A,B,C), representing longitude, latitude, and depth, respectively. If the geographic location and depth of one station is (a_i,b_i,c_i), the normalized node coordinates are computed as

$$x_i = \frac{a_i - a_0}{A}, \quad y_i = \frac{b_i - b_0}{B}, \quad z_i = \frac{c_i - c_0}{C}. \tag{8}$$

We use three channels to encode the node location information in both the input layer and the GNO layers (Fig. 1). In each channel, the corresponding normalized coordinate is repeated along the primary discretization dimension, allowing it to be concatenated with either the waveform input or the FNO output features. This strategy ensures consistent spatial encoding for all stations in the study area and enables the model to learn spatial relationships among seismic stations, which is crucial for accurate hypocenter location.

LOCNO

The LocNO is a hybrid architecture that combines the neural operator $\mathcal{U}$ to extract the spatiotemporal features from seismic wavefields with a decoding module $\mathcal{Q}$ to estimate earthquake locations (Fig. 1). The architecture of $\mathcal{U}$ integrates seven 1D FNO layers to extract temporal features at each station and five GNO layers to capture spatial dependencies across stations. The feature dimensions change across FNO layers but remain constant across GNO layers. These layers are sequentially connected; however, the input to deeper FNO layers is formed by concatenating the features from earlier FNO layers with the output of the corresponding deeper GNO layers, thereby introducing skip connections. Such skip connections help preserve low-level temporal information and facilitate gradient flow during training (He *et al.*, 2016). The model is capable of processing seismic data with an arbitrary number of stations and flexible station geometries. For clarity, Figure 1 illustrates only five stations. The bottom panels in Figure 1 depict the feature update process in the second FNO layer ($l = 2$) and the second GNO layer. In this figure, the five stations ($N = 5$) are fully connected in the computational graph of the GNO layer; however, the actual graph connectivity is determined by the interstation distances and the threshold D. The message aggregation and update process is illustrated for the station $i = 1$, but the same procedure is applied to all other stations. The output is a pseudoprobability distribution of the earthquake source location along the easting, northing, and depth directions, with the index of the highest probability corresponding to the ground truth in each direction.

After discretization, the input function f is represented as a tensor of shape $C \times L \times N$, in which C is the number of channels, L is the number of temporal samples, and N is the number of stations. Each station provides three-channel waveforms, either recorded along three orthogonal directions or repeated single-channel measurements. In addition, the spatial coordinates $\mathbf{x}_i = (x_i,y_i,z_i)$ of each station are repeated L times and concatenated to the time series as three additional channels, encoding positional information directly into the temporal feature input $v_i(t)$. The spatiotemporal feature $h \in \mathbb{R}^{C_7 \times L_7 \times N}$ extracted by the U-shaped neural operator $\mathcal{U}$ is given by

$$h = \mathcal{U}[\mathcal{P}(f)], \tag{9}$$

in which $\mathcal{P}$ is a lifting operator that maps the input function f into a higher-dimensional representation $\mathcal{P}(f) \in \mathbb{R}^{C_1 \times L_1 \times N}$. $\mathcal{P}$ in LocNO is a single fully connected layer, which maps the discretized input function to a latent space with C_1 channels. This lifting operation is applied locally at each spatial or temporal location, with shared parameters across the entire input domain. Such parameter sharing ensures that $\mathcal{P}$ behaves as a proper operator, independent of the discretization of the input function.

The architecture of $\mathcal{U}$ integrates FNO and GNO to leverage their complementary strengths. Similar to PhaseNO (Sun *et al.*, 2023), the FNO component establishes a U-shaped architecture, whereas the GNO facilitates information exchange among multiple stations. To enhance the exchange of features between the temporal and spatial domains, a GNO layer is strategically placed between two FNO layers.

We treat the output of the neural operator $h_i \in \mathbb{R}^{C_7 \times L_7}$ at the station i as a latent embedding that implicitly captures the station's spatiotemporal response to a seismic event. The following layer of the model is a shared decoder $\mathcal{Q}$ which maps the station-level latent features to directional score vectors over discretized spatial coordinates. Specifically, the latent embedding h_i is decoded into a three-channel output corresponding to the easting, northing, and depth directions:

$$s_i(n) = \mathcal{Q}(h_i) \in \mathbb{R}^{3 \times L}, \tag{10}$$

in which each channel of $s_i(n)$ represents a discrete score vector over one spatial axis, defined on L grid points $\{n_k^\ell\}_{\ell=1}^L$ for direction $k = 1,2,3$. $\mathcal{Q}$ in LocNO is implemented as a two-layer fully connected network with an input width (channel) of 48, a hidden layer of size 96, and an output layer with three channels.

To obtain the score vector $s(n)$ for all stations, we aggregate the station-wise estimates $\{s_i(n)\}_{i=1}^N$ using a structured attention pooling operator $\mathcal{A}$. Specifically, for each station i, a scalar attention weight is computed by applying a convolutional neural network (CNN) with a kernel size of one over the score $s_i(n)$. The resulting attention logits are averaged over the feature dimensions to yield a single scalar per station, and then normalized across stations via a softmax function to produce the attention weights. The total score is then given by

$$s(n) = \mathcal{A}(\{s_i(n)\}_{i=1}^N) = \sum_{i=1}^{N} \alpha_i s_i(n) \in \mathbb{R}^{3 \times L}, \tag{11}$$

in which $\alpha_i \in [0,1]$ is the normalized attention weight assigned to station i, satisfying $\sum_{i=1}^N \alpha_i = 1$. As a special case, uniform averaging corresponds to setting $\alpha_i = \frac{1}{N}$ for all i, which is equivalent to aggregating the station-level predictions via mean pooling.

Finally, for each direction k, the score $s_k^\ell = s(n_k^\ell)$ is transformed into a pseudoprobability distribution by applying the sigmoid function σ independently to each entry

$$p_k(n_k^\ell) = \sigma(s_k^\ell) = \frac{1}{1 + e^{-s_k^\ell}} \quad \text{for } \ell = 1,\ldots,L. \tag{12}$$

The loss function is defined as the sum of binary cross-entropy losses between the predicted and true probability distributions, applied independently to each spatial direction k and grid point ℓ. The ground-truth distribution in each direction $p_k^*(n_k) \in [0,1]$ is modeled as a truncated Gaussian centered at the true source coordinate, allowing the network to learn a continuous approximation over the discretized spatial grid. The loss is defined as

$$\mathcal{L}_{\text{LocNO}} = \sum_{k=1}^{3} w_k \sum_{\ell=1}^{L} [-p_k^*(n_k^\ell) \log p_k(n_k^\ell) - (1 - p_k^*(n_k^\ell)) \log(1 - p_k(n_k^\ell))], \tag{13}$$

in which w_k is a user-defined weight for direction k. This formulation treats each grid point as an independent binary classification task and supports soft target distributions, encouraging the model to produce accurate pseudoprobability densities over the discretized spatial grid in each direction.

The LocNO model is implemented using PyTorch, with custom modules for neural operator layers. Optimization is performed using the Adam optimizer with an initial learning rate of 1×10^{-4}. Adam adaptively adjusts learning rates for individual parameters using estimates of the first and second moments of the gradients, which improves convergence stability and efficiency. To further refine training, the learning rate is reduced by a factor of 0.1 when the validation loss does not improve for 10 consecutive epochs, where one epoch refers to a complete pass through the entire training dataset. This scheduler helps the model escape flat regions or suboptimal local minima during training. Model training and evaluation are conducted on a high-performance computing cluster equipped with NVIDIA graphics processing units, which enables efficient processing of large-scale seismic datasets.

DATA

To test the algorithm and to locate offshore earthquakes in the MTJ region, we use a dataset composed of earthquake waveforms and event catalogs around the MTJ region spanning three decades (Zhu *et al.*, 2025), sourced from the Northern California Earthquake Data Center (NCEDC). Many downloaded earthquake data based on the NCEDC catalog are in-network events, where seismic stations are distributed around the earthquake's location. The available out-of-network earthquakes are insufficient in quantity to create a large and diverse training dataset for deep learning models.

To enable the LocNO model to handle offshore and out-of-network earthquakes, we adopt a strategy to artificially generate additional out-of-network events from the existing in-network events. This is achieved by systematically removing selected seismic stations from the network surrounding an in-network earthquake. By strategically reducing the station coverage in specific areas, we simulate scenarios where the earthquake occurs outside the dense monitoring regions, effectively creating synthetic out-of-network events. These generated samples are then incorporated into the training dataset, enhancing the model's ability to generalize to real-world cases of out-of-network earthquakes.

Figure 2 illustrates the method for constructing an out-of-network earthquake sample from an in-network event. The process begins by positioning the earthquake's location at the center of an easting–northing coordinate system. A series of straight lines with slopes ranging from −1 to 1 is systematically drawn through this central point. For each line, the seismic stations are counted and grouped based on their positions relative to the line (either above or below). The line that minimizes the total number of seismic stations on one side is identified.

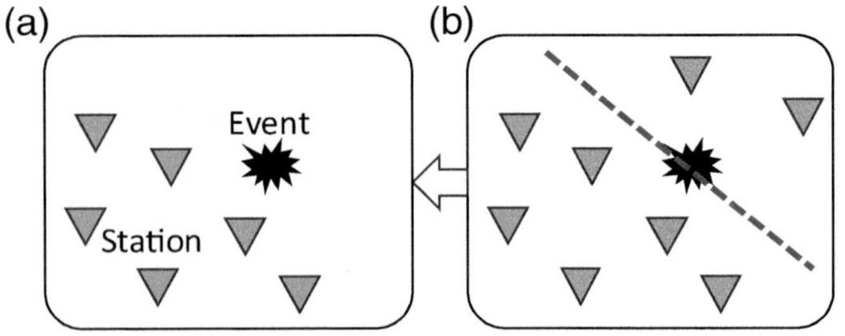

Figure 2. Diagram illustrating the procedure for generating (a) an out-of-network earthquake sample from (b) an in-network event. Starting at the earthquake's location in an easting–northing coordinate system, draw a straight line and count the seismic stations on each side. Repeat the process with lines of varying slopes from −1 to 1. Choose the line where one side has the fewest seismic stations and remove those stations. The remaining stations, all located on one side of the earthquake's position, form the out-of-network earthquake sample.

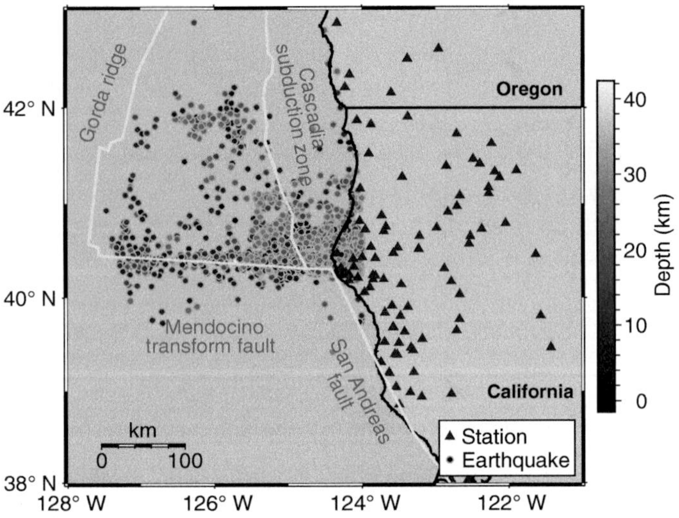

Figure 3. Earthquakes near the Mendocino Triple Junction (MTJ) region from 1987 to 2021. Plate boundaries are drawn following Bird (2003). The color version of this figure is available only in the electronic edition.

Stations on the less-populated side are excluded from further analysis. This approach ensures that the remaining seismic stations are all located on one side of the earthquake's position, effectively isolating the event from a portion of the seismic network and generating a well-defined out-of-network earthquake sample. Furthermore, we include the resulting earthquake sample in the training dataset only if the out-of-network earthquake is recorded by at least four stations.

Figure 3 shows the map of all out-of-network earthquakes and the remaining stations in the resulting dataset. All stations are onshore, whereas most earthquakes are offshore and classified as out-of-network earthquakes for these onshore stations. The dataset was split chronologically, with the events occurring before 2016 used for training, the events from 2016 for validation, and those from 2017 to 2021 for testing (Fig. 4). This resulted in 2486 training samples, 209 validation samples, and 911 test samples. We remove microseismicity below a magnitude of one from this dataset due to the large

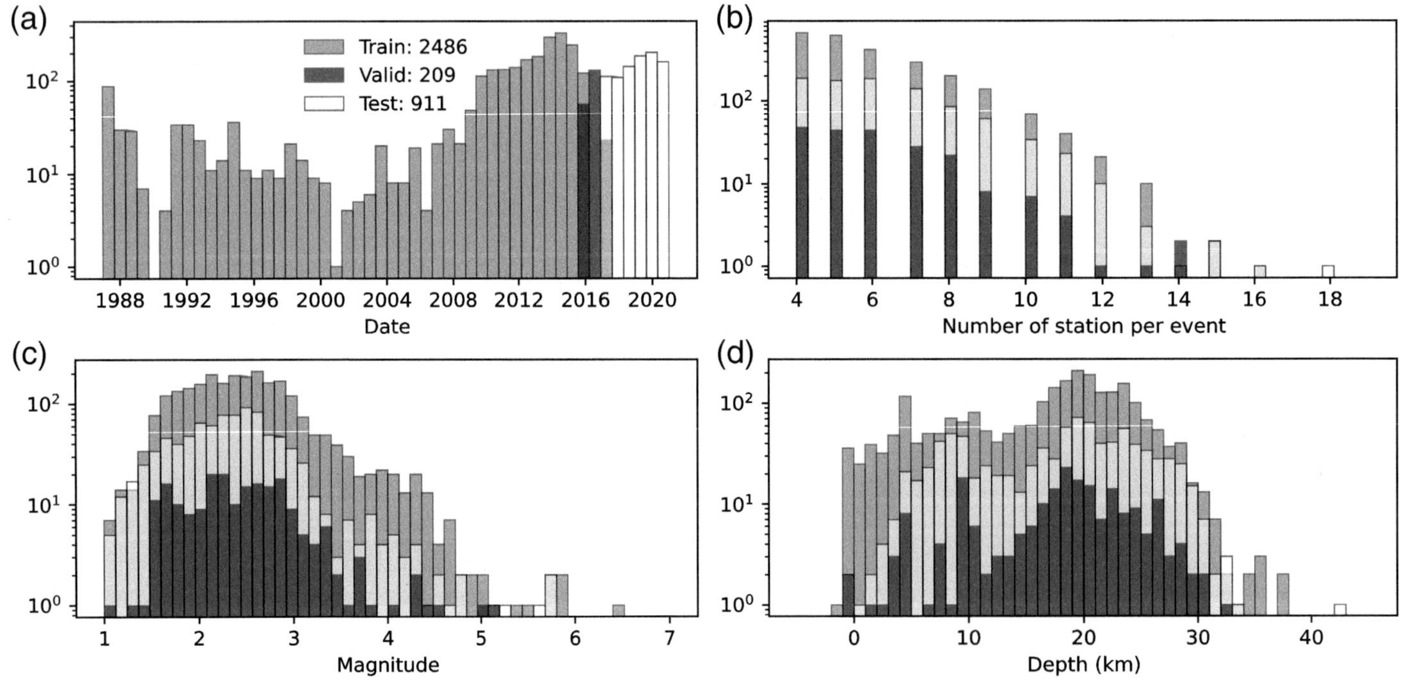

Figure 4. (a–d) Dataset of out-of-network earthquakes in the MTJ region for LocNO training and evaluation: We split the dataset based on their time: earthquakes before 2016, in 2016, and from 2017 to 2021, respectively, into the training, validation, and test datasets.

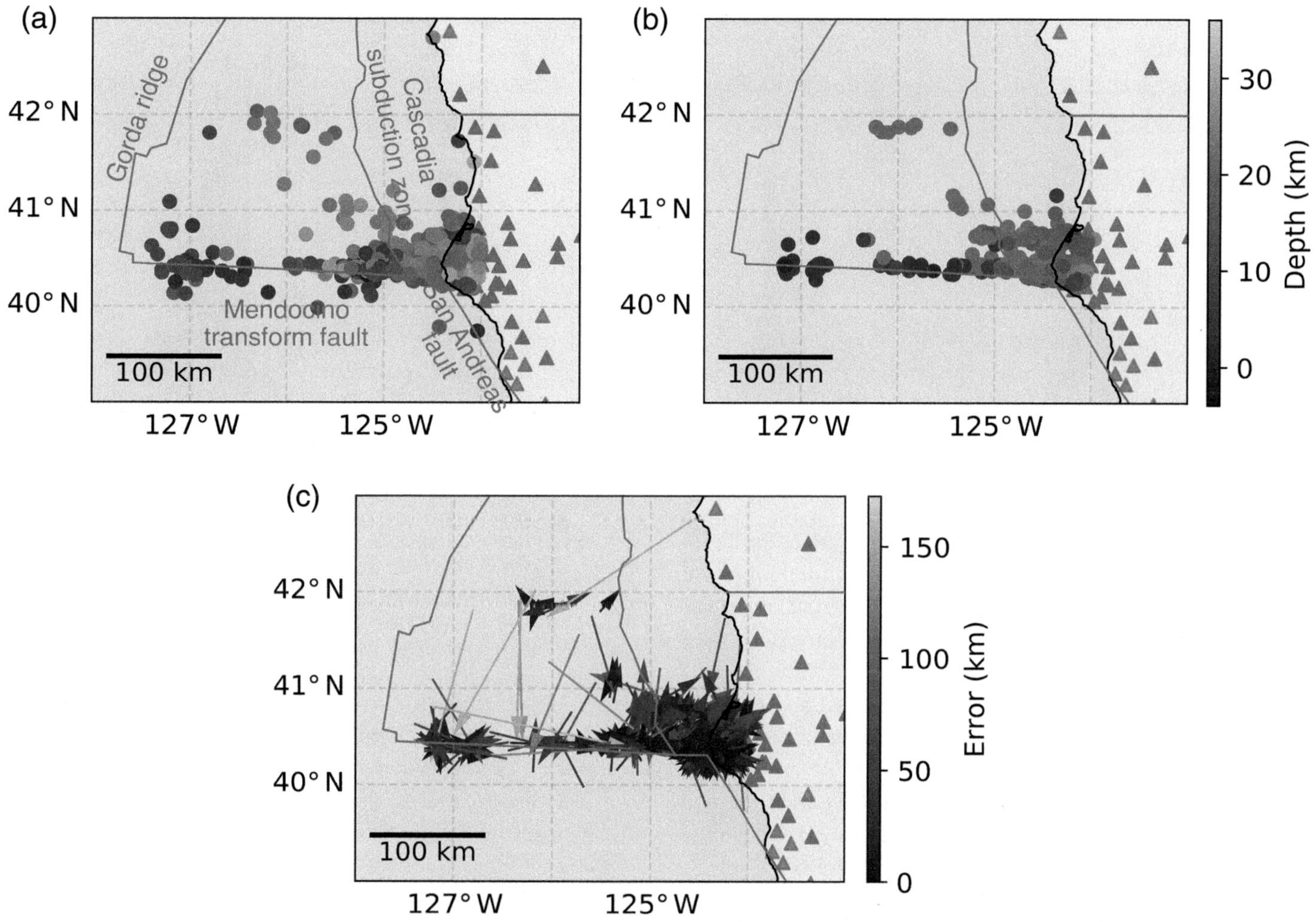

Figure 5. Comparison of earthquake locations between (a) the Northern California Earthquake Data Center (NCEDC) catalog and (b) the LocNO prediction in the out-of-network earthquake test dataset. (c) Epicentral location errors illustrated with arrows pointing from catalog locations to the corresponding LocNO-predicted locations. The color version of this figure is available only in the electronic edition.

offset between earthquake hypocenters and onshore stations. Both the training and test datasets cover a wide range of depth from surface to 40 km and magnitudes from 1 to 6 (Fig. 4). Most events have magnitudes between 1 and 5, at depths of 0–30 km, and were recorded by 4–13 stations.

LocNO is designed to be used in conjunction with external earthquake detection algorithms as part of a seismic monitoring workflow. Once an event is detected, LocNO is applied to estimate its location using waveforms from the stations where seismic signals have been identified. We use a waveform length of 30 s for all input stations, unless otherwise noted, where we study the impact of alternative lengths (5, 10, and 20 s) on performance. Because the input is event-based, the *P*-wave arrival exhibits moveout and therefore varies across stations. To prevent the model from relying on the absolute arrival time for location, we randomly place the earliest *P*-wave arrival within a window between 1 and 5 s from the beginning of the input waveform during training. During testing, the earliest arrival time is fixed at 1 s. In addition, in practical applications, it is common that a small subset of stations in a network may record clipped, low SNR, or otherwise unusable data. To improve the model's robustness, we explicitly simulated this condition during training by randomly including virtual stations that contain only noise in each training sample. This approach allows LocNO to learn to downweight or ignore stations with uninformative or misleading input. To simulate real-world scenarios where not all stations record high-quality earthquake signals, we augmented the dataset with up to two virtual stations placed randomly within the boundary of stations. Noise waveforms were randomly selected from the STanford EArthquake Dataset (Mousavi *et al.*, 2019), ensuring sample-specific variability. Note that in practical applications, the majority of associated stations for a detected earthquake are expected to contain meaningful signals. Therefore, it is not necessary to add many virtual stations, particularly in this dataset where many samples include only four stations (Fig. 4). All waveforms were preprocessed with trend removal, band-pass filtering (1–10 Hz), and normalization.

The study area for the MTJ region (Fig. 3) is defined as a geographical domain spanning 8° in both longitude and latitude. The longitude range extends from −128° to −120°, and

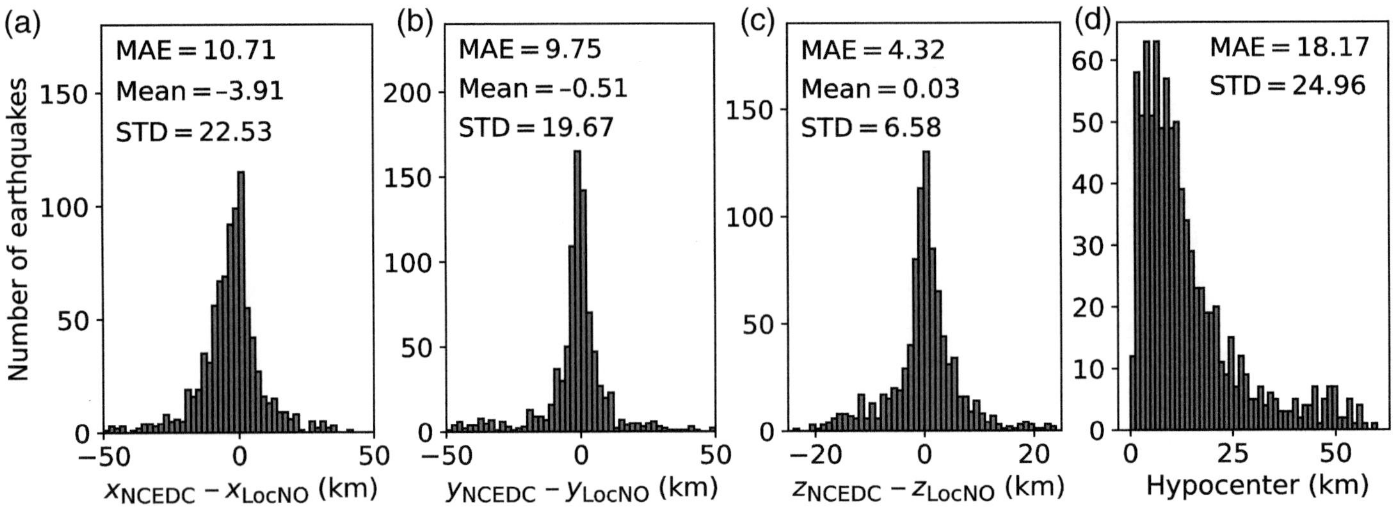

Figure 6. Histograms of location errors between LocNO and the NCEDC catalog for out-of-network earthquakes in the test dataset, shown separately for (a) easting (x), (b) northing (y), (c) depth (z), and (d) total hypocenter error. Evaluation metrics include mean absolute error (MAE), mean error (Mean), and standard deviation (STD), all in kilometers (km).

the latitude range covers from 35° to 43°. In addition, the depth ranges from −5 to 45 km, including the depth of stations above the sea level and the maximum depth of earthquakes in the dataset. The domain's coordinates in the three directions were independently normalized to [0,1] for compatibility with the learning process. Normalized positions of stations (x_i,y_i,z_i) are included in the node attributes along with three-component waveform data.

The sample label is generated based on catalog locations and consists of three channels, each representing a 1D probability function. These channels indicate the likelihood of the earthquake's occurrence along the easting, northing, and depth directions. Each channel is modeled as a truncated Gaussian function centered on the true location, where the real position has a maximum probability of one, gradually decaying to zero. For longitude and latitude, the probability function spans a width equal to 1/30 of the total range, whereas for depth, it spans a wider width of 1/12 of the total range. This broader Gaussian function for depth accounts for the greater uncertainty in determining earthquake depth using surface observations, particularly for out-of-network events.

RESULTS

Locating offshore earthquakes in the MTJ region

The LocNO model was evaluated after being trained for 20 epochs. Figure 5 compares the earthquake locations determined by the trained LocNO model with those from the NCEDC catalog using the out-of-network earthquakes in the test dataset. The results demonstrate that LocNO provides location estimates aligned with the NCEDC catalog. Notably, the model achieves higher accuracy for events near the Mendocino transform fault, showcasing its effectiveness in this tectonically active region.

However, larger discrepancies are observed for some events located farther from the Mendocino transform fault. These larger differences can be attributed to the limited number of prior seismic events in those areas available for training. As a supervised learning method, LocNO learns spatiotemporal features by capturing statistical relationships among multistation waveform patterns. Its generalization ability is, therefore, the strongest in regions where the training data are sufficiently dense and representative. In this study, the training catalog contains relatively few well-recorded events in the offshore region far from the fault, which limits the model's ability to learn reliable waveform–location relationships for those areas.

Figure 6 shows a quantitative comparison of location errors in easting, northing, and depth, evaluated using the metrics of mean absolute error (MAE), mean error (Mean), and standard deviation (STD). Location errors in degrees were converted to kilometers using a conversion factor of 111 km/° for latitude and ~85 km/° for longitude, consistent with the geographic position near the Mendocino transform fault. The MAE of the location errors is 10.71 km in easting, 9.75 km in northing, and 4.32 km in depth. LocNO provides location estimates within 20 km of the NCEDC catalog for 75% of the events in the test dataset (Fig. 6). These location errors are reasonable given that most events are located using only 4–6 stations (Fig. 4). The distribution of seismic stations, which is sparse along the easting direction but relatively uniform along the northing direction (Fig. 3), leads to larger location errors in easting than northing.

Figure 7 shows the epicenter errors between LocNO predictions and the NCEDC catalog for events located using 4–9 stations in the test dataset. Each panel corresponds to a fixed number of stations and presents epicenter errors as a function of the primary azimuthal gap. The minimum primary azimuthal gap is 180° for all samples due to the inclusion of out-of-network events. We bin the data into azimuthal gap ranges

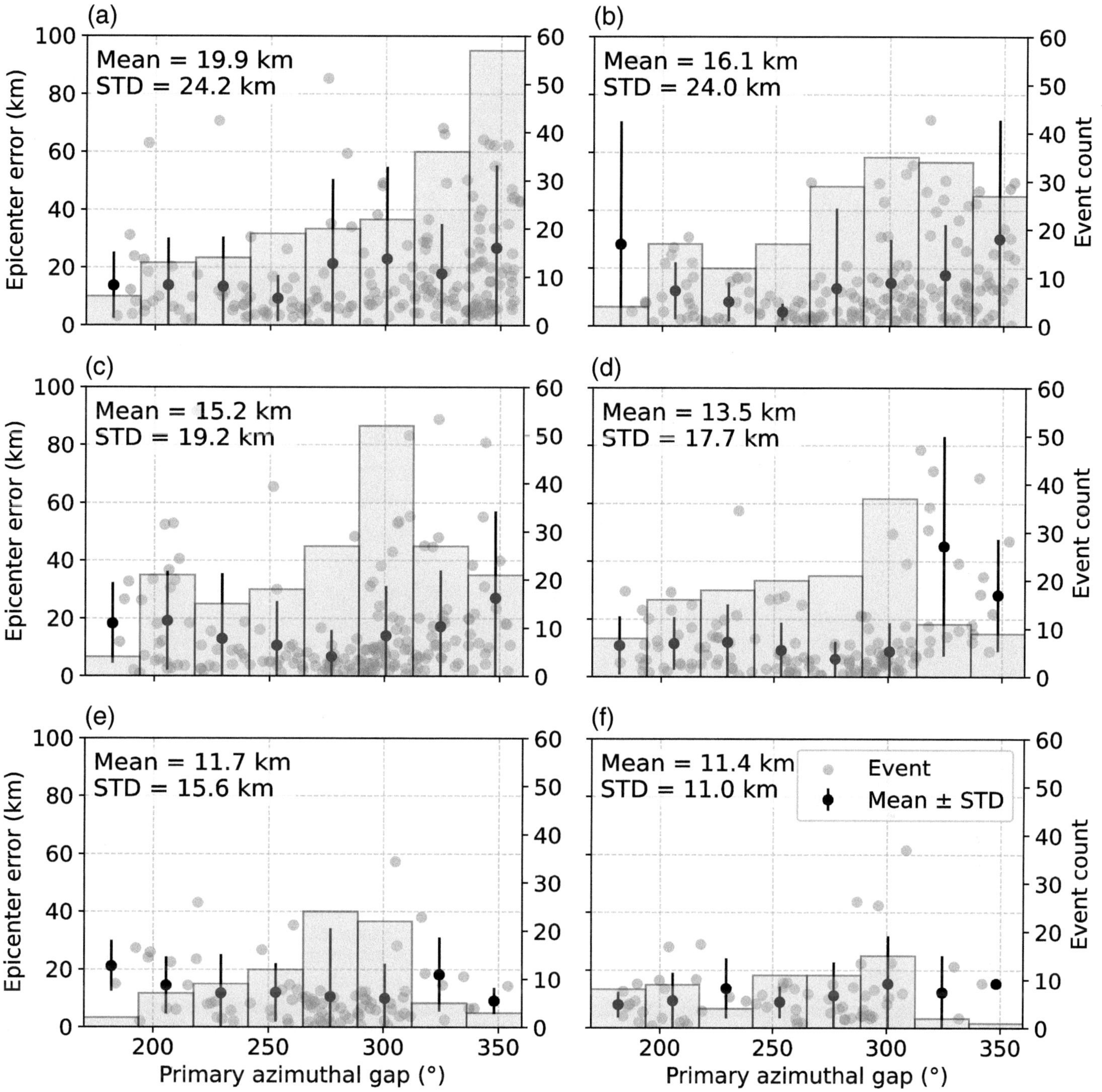

from 180° to 360° and compute the mean error (Mean) and standard deviation (STD) of epicenter errors in each bin. These statistics are most informative when sufficient samples exist in a bin. As described more fully subsequently, this figure demonstrates that increasing the number of stations and reducing the azimuthal gap improves the earthquake locations.

LocNO demonstrates the ability to handle out-of-network scenarios and maintains reliable performance even as the azimuthal gap increases. Although epicenter errors tend to increase slightly with larger azimuthal gaps, particularly when only a few stations are available, the overall performance

Figure 7. Epicenter errors as a function of the primary azimuthal gap, comparing LocNO predictions with the NCEDC catalog for events located using (a) 4, (b) 5, (c) 6, (d) 7, (e) 8, and (f) 9 stations in the test dataset. Histograms show the number of samples in each range of the primary azimuthal gap. The mean (Mean) and standard deviation (STD) of epicenter errors within each bin are labeled on the histograms. The overall Mean and STD for all samples in each panel are noted at the top of the corresponding subplot.

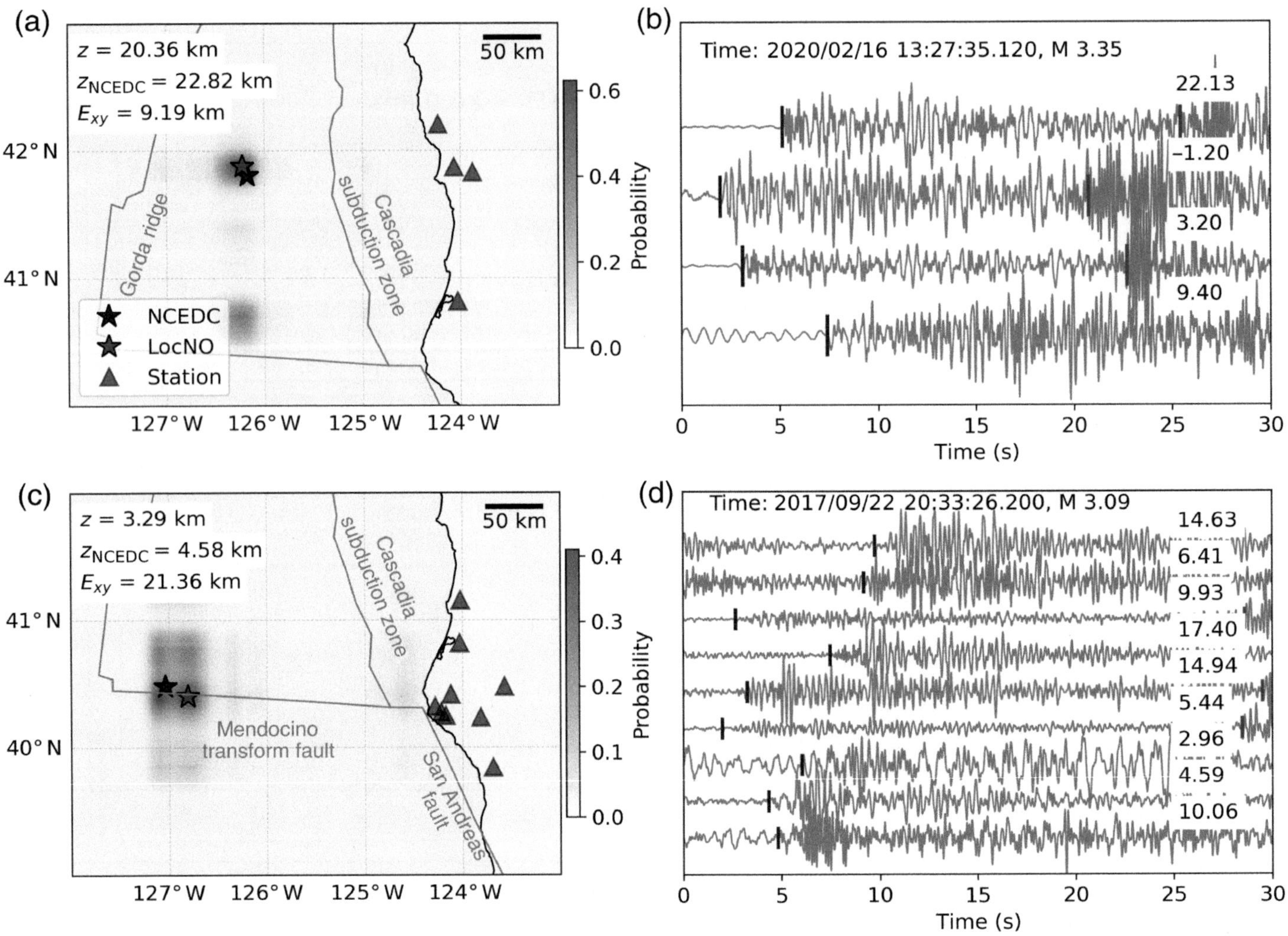

Figure 8. Examples of offshore earthquakes that are relatively well located by LocNO. The map annotates the epicentral error E_{xy}, the catalog depth z_{NCEDC}, and the LocNO-predicted depth z. For each event (row), the panels (a,c) show the earthquake and station locations, and the panels (b, d) present the waveform inputs to LocNO. The origin time and magnitude are labeled above the waveforms. The signal-to-noise ratio (SNR) (in dB) is labeled on each trace. The P-wave (blue) and S-wave (red) arrival times used for earthquake locations in the NCEDC catalog are labeled on the waveforms. The color version of this figure is available only in the electronic edition.

improves with more stations. Specifically: (1) for events located with nine stations, the overall mean and standard deviation of epicenter errors are 11.4 and 11.0 km, respectively, which are nearly half the values observed with only four stations; and (2) the number of outliers, defined as samples with unusually large epicenter errors relative to their bin mean, declines because the number of stations increases.

Figure 8 shows two examples of offshore earthquakes that are relatively well located by LocNO, with their origin times, magnitudes, and depths annotated on the figure. The seismic stations used by LocNO for locating these earthquakes are also highlighted. These examples demonstrate that, despite the challenges of having only several stations, large distances from the earthquake origin, and poor geometric coverage, the trained LocNO model accurately estimates the earthquake locations. This performance is achieved by effectively utilizing seismic records with relatively high SNR, which was estimated as the ratio of standard deviations between two five-second windows following and preceding the P-wave arrival. In contrast, offshore events with low SNR and clustered station configurations are poorly located by LocNO under these challenging monitoring conditions (Fig. 9).

The NCEDC catalog locations used as a reference point in these comparisons are also subject to significant uncertainties, especially for offshore events with poor station coverage. Figures 8 and 9 include the full spatial probability maps predicted by LocNO, which provide a more informative representation of location uncertainty. These maps allow readers to evaluate whether the catalog locations fall within high-probability regions of the LocNO's output. When comparing with NCEDC locations, we should keep in mind that both LocNO and the catalog locations are subject to uncertainty, and the observed differences do not necessarily imply error from a single source.

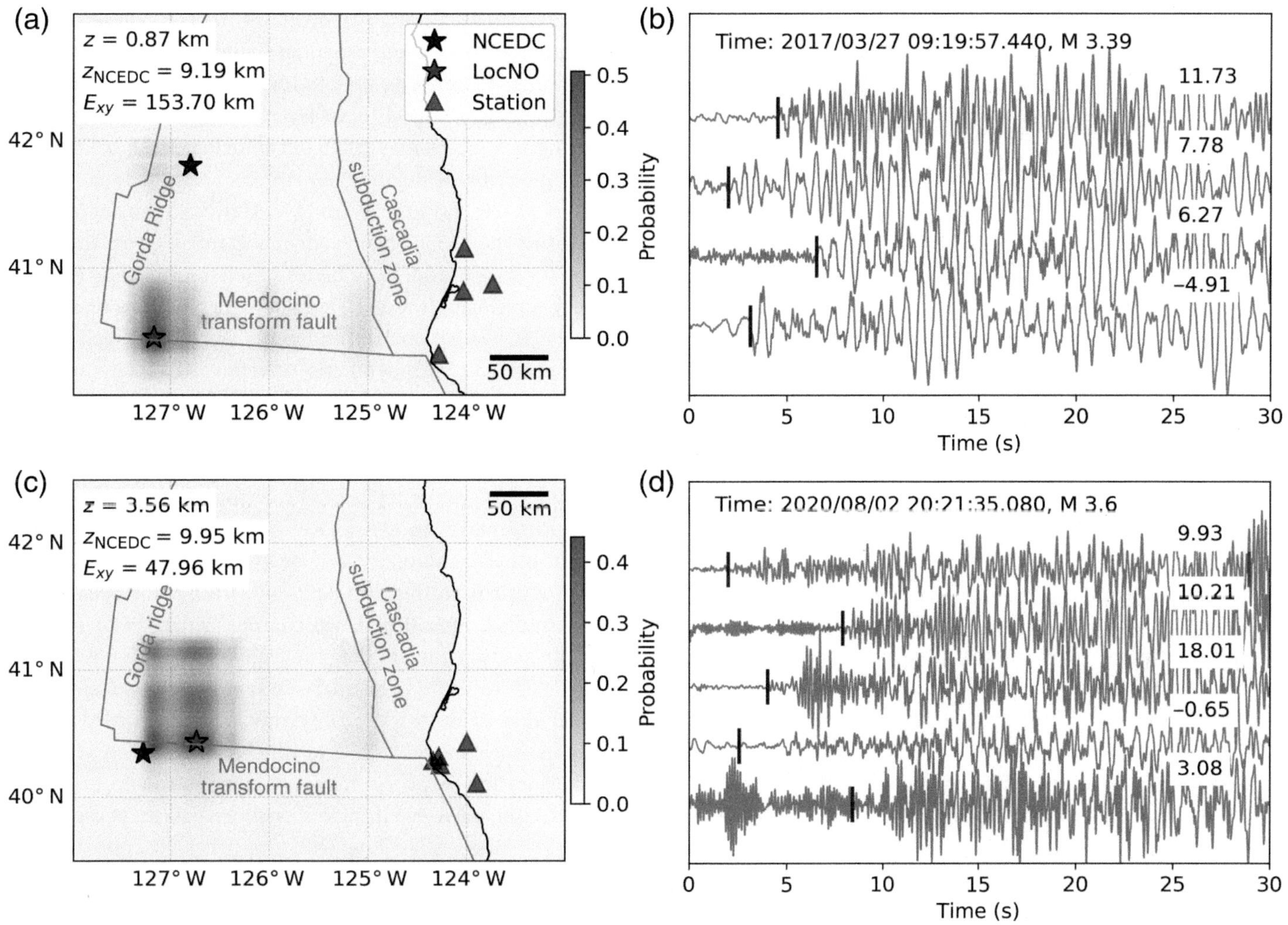

Figure 9. (a–d) Examples of offshore earthquakes poorly located by LocNO. The map annotates the epicentral error E_{xy}, the catalog depth z_{NCEDC}, and the LocNO-predicted depth z. The SNR (in decibels [dB]) is labeled on each trace. The blue lines mark the *P*-wave arrival times reported in the NCEDC catalog. In these cases, the lack of training data, the low SNR of the waveforms, and the cluster of stations impact the model's ability to accurately estimate earthquake locations. The color version of this figure is available only in the electronic edition.

Effect of waveform preprocessing settings

We investigate the impact of waveform preprocessing settings on the performance of LocNO. As a full-waveform location method, LocNO leverages all information contained in the input waveforms to infer earthquake hypocenters. Therefore, the preprocessing configuration may significantly influence the results. Under various waveform filtering bands and window lengths, Table 2 compares the location performance in terms of MAE between LocNO predictions and the catalog locations in the easting, northing, and depth directions for all test samples.

TABLE 2

Effect of Waveform Preprocessing Settings (Filtering and Waveform Length) on Location Performance, Measured by Mean Absolute Error (MAE)

Waveform Setting		MAE (Easting)	MAE (Northing)	MAE (Depth)
1–10 Hz	30 s	10.71 km	9.75 km	4.32 km
	20 s	12.61 km	9.02 km	4.02 km
	10 s	16.63 km	8.28 km	4.33 km
	5 s	23.18 km	9.87 km	4.77 km
30 s	1–20 Hz	10.98 km	11.40 km	4.18 km
	1–10 Hz	10.71 km	9.75 km	4.32 km
	1–5 Hz	12.47 km	10.20 km	4.50 km

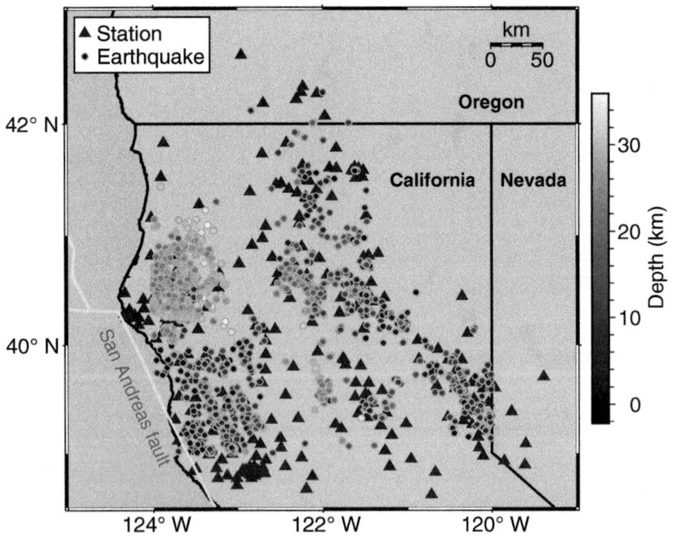

Figure 10. Dataset of in-network earthquakes near the MTJ region (1987–2021). This dataset serves as a benchmark for comparing LocNO with a baseline deep learning model for earthquake location using full-waveform data. The locations of these events are well determined by the onshore seismic network. The color version of this figure is available only in the electronic edition.

First, using waveforms filtered in the 1–10 Hz band, we evaluate the effect of different window lengths: 5, 10, 20, and 30 s. A clear trend is observed in the easting direction: location errors increase because the window length shortens. This may be attributed to the uneven station distribution because all stations are located east of the offshore earthquakes in the MTJ region. The full-waveform information preserved in longer time windows helps mitigate errors caused by this nonideal station geometry. In the northing direction, where stations are distributed more symmetrically, the effect of window length is less pronounced, with an average location error of around 10 km. Depth errors are relatively stable across all settings, likely due to the intrinsic difficulty of resolving depth using surface stations at large epicentral distances and limited azimuthal coverage.

Overall, waveform length shows a stronger influence on location accuracy, particularly in the easting direction due to the asymmetric station geometry. Notably, with a 5 s window (~4 s after *P*-wave arrival), the location error increases to 16.53 km (averaged over easting and northing), which is comparable to the performance of the bEPIC algorithm (14 km) in the MTJ region (Williamson *et al.*, 2023). This highlights the potential of LocNO for earthquake early warning applications in the MTJ area using short-window waveforms and only a few stations.

Next, fixing the waveform length at 30 s, we investigate the effect of applying band-pass filters at 1–5 Hz, 1–10 Hz, and 1–20 Hz to the observed waveform data before feeding it into LocNO. Among these, the 1–10 Hz band yields the best performance in the easting and northing directions, with an average MAE of 10.23 km, indicating that overly narrow filtering may remove useful high-frequency information needed for accurate location, whereas wider bands may retain noise. These trends are consistent with expectations: raising the upper frequency bound to 20 Hz may introduce noise, while lowering it to 5 Hz may filter out informative signal components. In terms of depth, the error increases gradually from 4.18 km (1–20 Hz) to 4.50 km (1–5 Hz). Still, the degradation from using the 1–5 Hz band is not substantial. Given that most regional velocity models are better suited for modeling low-frequency waveforms, the 1–5 Hz band may provide a reasonable trade-off between accuracy and generalizability, especially for training LocNO with synthetic waveform datasets simulated on a known velocity model.

Benchmark with SeismicGNN

In addition to evaluating LocNO's performance on out-of-network earthquake location, we benchmark its capabilities against other state-of-the-art deep learning models using well-monitored earthquake datasets, which have been extensively studied. Specifically, we compile a dataset of onshore earthquakes near the MTJ region (Fig. 10), covering the period from 1987 to 2021. This dataset provides an ideal testing ground due to the high-quality monitoring afforded by the dense onshore seismic network, which ensures relatively more reliable location data for comparison. Similar to the out-of-network dataset, each event in this onshore dataset is associated with 4–15 stations. In line with the previous approach, the dataset was split chronologically, with 1344 events recorded before 2016 used for training and 605 events from 2017 to 2021 reserved for testing.

Figure 11 presents a comparative analysis of the location performance between LocNO and SeismicGNN (Van Den Ende and Ampuero, 2020) on the in-network test dataset. SeismicGNN, a graph neural network framework, incorporates spatial information for seismic source characterization by facilitating information exchange between seismic stations. Node features at individual stations are processed using a CNN and an MLP to estimate earthquake locations. The baseline model was retrained on the same dataset as LocNO to ensure a fair comparison. However, the SeismicGNN model retrained with the NCEDC dataset compiled in this study performs worse than the original model reported in Van Den Ende and Ampuero (2020). The original model was trained on events with a minimum magnitude of 3 and at least 21 associated stations. In contrast, the dataset used here includes events with magnitudes as low as 1 and only 4–15 stations per event. This suggests that SeismicGNN may be less effective on more challenging datasets compared to high-quality training data.

The results demonstrate that LocNO outperforms SeismicGNN in geographic location accuracy, highlighting its ability to effectively leverage operator learning for earthquake location with full-waveform data (Fig. 11). LocNO achieves MAEs of 6.78 km (easting) and 5.52 km (northing),

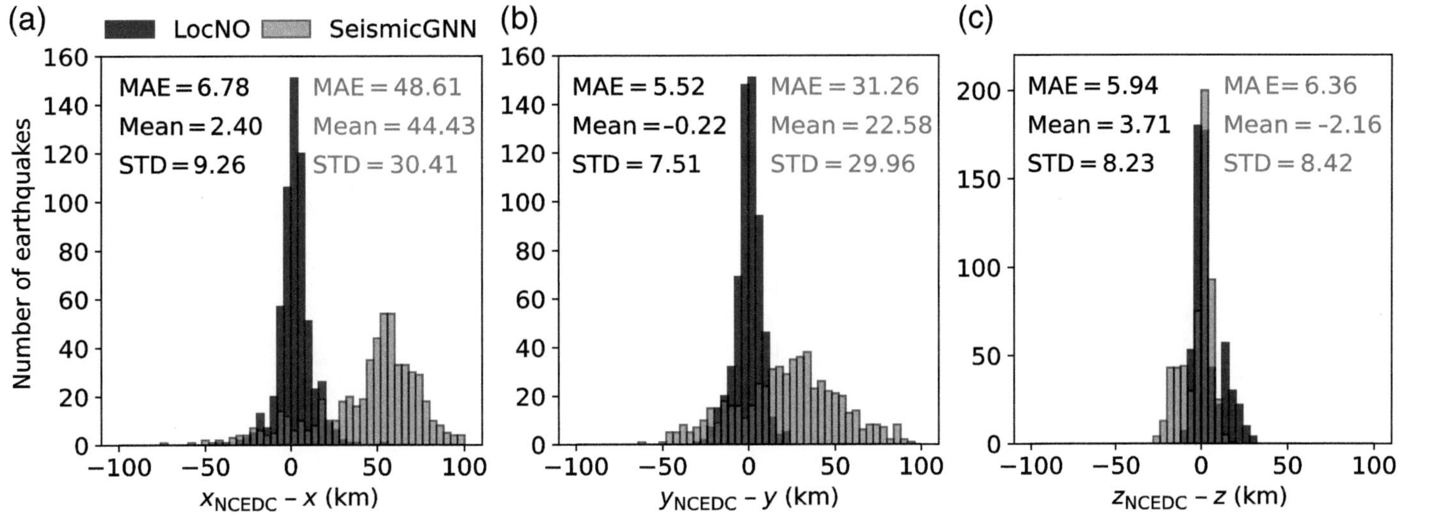

Figure 11. (a–c) Comparison of the locations determined by LocNO and SeismicGNN on the in-network test dataset in the MTJ. LocNO yielded mean absolute errors in horizontal locations that are less than 18% of the errors yielded by SeismicGNN. The errors in the determined depths were comparable between the two methods.

compared with 48.61 and 31.26 km for SeismicGNN, respectively, clearly showing LocNO's improvement in both directions. In addition, with a depth MAE of 5.94 km for LocNO compared to 6.36 km for SeismicGNN, LocNO shows comparable depth prediction, which is traditionally challenging when relying solely on surface observations.

Furthermore, a comparison of the histograms in Figures 6 and 11 reveals that LocNO achieves significantly lower location errors for in-network earthquakes compared to out-of-network earthquakes across all evaluation metrics. This finding aligns with the intuitive understanding that locating out-of-network earthquakes is inherently a more challenging problem due to limited station coverage. The complexity of this task underscores the necessity of training specialized deep-learning models tailored to out-of-network earthquake location.

Application to an offshore earthquake sequence: The 22 September 2017 M_w 5.7 event, 218 km west of Ferndale, California

A typical seismic monitoring workflow includes earthquake detection, seismic phase picking, initial location, and relocation. Traditional initial location methods rely on travel-time algorithms using picked phase arrivals, and they generally perform well when the seismic network has favorable geometry (see Yu *et al.*, 2025, for a benchmark study using synthetic controlled experiments). However, in regions with sparse or uneven station coverage, such as offshore settings, solutions to travel-time-based inverse problems are often unstable and can result in large location errors that are difficult to correct during relocation. In contrast, LocNO directly utilizes the spatiotemporal information contained in the multistation waveforms to infer earthquake hypocenters. As shown in Table 2, longer waveform segments better correct artifacts caused by uneven station distribution, confirming that waveform data provide additional constraints for mitigating such errors.

Since events before 2016 were used to construct the training dataset, we select an earthquake sequence that occurred after 2016 for this case study. According to the NCEDC catalog, an M_w 5.7 event occurred on 22 September 2017, ~218 km west of Ferndale, California. To analyze this earthquake sequence, we downloaded continuous waveform data from 25 onshore stations in Northern California (NC) and Plate Boundary Observatory Borehole (PB) networks via NCEDC, covering 21–28 September 2017. The selected seismic network consists of a combination of the three-component EH (high-gain short-period) channels, the three-component broadband HH (high-gain broadband) channels, and the one-component EH channels, as listed in Data and Resources.

LocNO can be applied after any detection algorithm, even when the method does not involve phase picking. In this study, however, we adopt a workflow that begins with phase picking using PhaseNO (Sun *et al.*, 2023), which performs both detection and picking directly on continuous seismic data. The resulting picks are then associated into events using GaMMA (Zhu, McBrearty, *et al.*, 2022), and LocNO is subsequently used to estimate the event locations based on the full-waveform information. For comparison, we also determine the locations of the earthquakes in the new catalog using HYPOINVERSE, a travel-time-based location algorithm that has been widely used for decades (Klein, 2002).

As a result, we construct an earthquake catalog for this offshore sequence containing 141 events over seven days. Each event is required to have at least eight associated phases, including both the *P*-wave and the *S*-wave arrivals. The number of earthquakes in this new catalog is nearly one order of magnitude greater than the 15 events reported by NCEDC for the same period (Fig. 12a). Figure 12b,d compares the locations

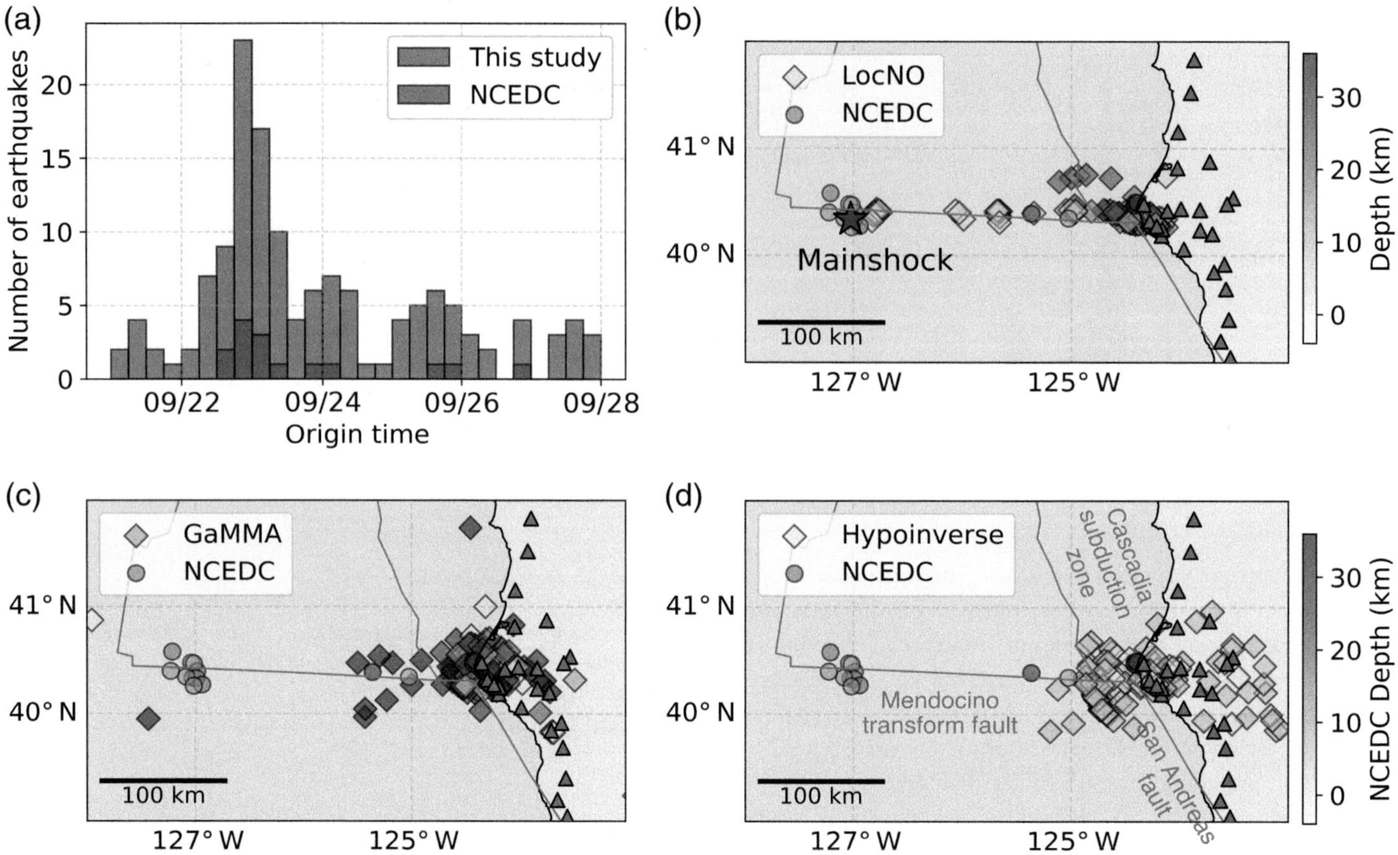

Figure 12. 22 September 2017 M_w 5.7 offshore earthquake sequence and their locations. (a) Comparison of earthquake counts between the newly detected catalog and the NCEDC catalog. Comparison of NCEDC catalog locations with earthquake locations determined by (b) the LocNO model, (c) GaMMA during phase association, and (d) HYPOINVERSE. The color version of this figure is available only in the electronic edition.

of these newly detected events with those in the NCEDC catalog. Figure 12c shows the locations estimated by GaMMA during phase association. For travel-time-based location, we use the 1D velocity model from Morton *et al.* (2023). Because of poor network geometry and a large primary azimuthal gap, events in the far western portion of the sequence, near the mainshock, are difficult to locate accurately using travel-time-based methods. In contrast, locations estimated by LocNO are closer to the Mendocino transform fault and to the NCEDC catalog events. In addition, several earthquakes near the mainshock hypocenter are incorrectly located by GaMMA and HYPOINVERSE, whereas LocNO provides locations that are more consistent with the mainshock's hypocenter.

DISCUSSION

This study introduces LocNO and an effective training strategy to address the challenges of earthquake location in regions with sparse station coverage and large azimuthal gaps. Advanced operator-learning techniques have proven highly adaptable to complex network geometries, establishing themselves as powerful tools to uncover the spatiotemporal patterns in seismic data for earthquake location. The architecture of LocNO is designed to leverage the waveform information directly, allowing it to mitigate artifacts even when the station coverage is sparse or the azimuthal gaps are large. This makes it highly applicable to offshore regions such as the MTJ, where traditional travel-time-based methods often struggle due to the lack of permanent stations in the marine environment. Quantitatively, LocNO achieves mean absolute errors of ~10 km in horizontal location and 4 km in depth when compared to the NCEDC catalog. Furthermore, LocNO can be integrated into deep-learning-based seismic monitoring workflows, where many of the detected small-magnitude events are recorded by only a few stations. In such cases, including additional distant stations may not meaningfully improve the azimuthal coverage because these stations often fail to record high-quality signals of small events. LocNO's ability to provide stable locations under these conditions demonstrates its potential as a standard component for modern catalog-building pipelines.

A training dataset designed for locating out-of-network earthquakes is particularly valuable for monitoring seismic activity in offshore regions. Using the MTJ region as an example, frequent offshore earthquakes near the Mendocino transform fault pose significant risks to surrounding communities. However, the inherent challenge of locating these out-of-network events stems from the limited number of stations in marine environments. Rather than incorporating historical seismicity as a prior in a Bayesian framework (Williamson *et al.*, 2023), we leverage past seismic data to construct a comprehensive training dataset and directly train a deep learning model to locate these offshore events using full-waveform information. Our results indicate that the challenge of locating out-of-network earthquakes can be effectively mitigated through advanced deep learning methods, provided that a sufficiently representative training dataset is available.

As a data-driven approach, LocNO relies on a well-curated training dataset with diverse earthquake locations across the monitoring region, ensuring comprehensive wavepath coverage in the MTJ area and enhancing the model's generalization ability to new earthquakes in this region. By leveraging this dataset, the model directly determines earthquake source locations from waveform data without an explicit velocity model. Although LocNO does not require an explicit velocity model during inference, the training labels come from catalog locations that were determined using a velocity model. As a result, the model is still influenced by the assumptions of that velocity model. For example, the deep learning model that directly maps waveforms to source parameters may encounter challenges when applied to regions with velocity distributions that significantly differ from those represented in the training dataset. This limitation highlights the critical need to construct training datasets that capture the geological and tectonic diversity of the target region. Therefore, leveraging historical seismicity data remains an effective strategy for accurately and efficiently locating newly detected earthquakes within the studied area.

Traditional template matching methods locate earthquakes by cross-correlating new waveforms against a library of known events, effectively detecting and refining the locations of repeating earthquakes with similar waveforms (Waldhauser and Ellsworth, 2000; Shelly *et al.*, 2006, 2007). In contrast, LocNO does not rely on waveform similarity between training and testing events. Although trained on catalog events, its goal is to learn a functional mapping from waveforms to source locations that generalizes to new events with previously unseen waveform characteristics. This generalization capability is analogous to deep learning-based phase pickers such as PhaseNet (Zhu and Beroza, 2019) and PhaseNO (Sun *et al.*, 2023), which can pick phases for earthquakes beyond the training sets. Moreover, while template matching is mainly used for event detection and relocation through cross correlation, LocNO directly infers absolute source locations from multistation waveforms. Unlike double-difference (DD) methods that require high waveform similarity, LocNO is not limited to repeated events and is thus applicable to general earthquake location tasks.

Despite the encouraging performance of LocNO in out-of-network earthquake location, significant errors are observed for events with poor station geometry, such as clusters of stations. Although the location errors for out-of-network events can be substantial, the results may still be useful for distinguishing between the in-network and the out-of-network events, as demonstrated in Annunziata *et al.* (2025). Furthermore, it is important to emphasize that simply increasing the number of stations does not necessarily improve location accuracy if the added stations do not enhance the overall station coverage by reducing the primary azimuthal gap (Fig. 7), particularly for out-of-network earthquakes.

To overcome the challenge of training the LocNO model in low seismicity areas, we may generate a synthetic training dataset to supplement the real-world dataset (Leong and Zhu, 2024). By sampling a known 3D velocity model with various earthquake locations, a comprehensive training dataset could be synthesized through seismic forward modeling to compensate for the scarcity of observed data. Moreover, the synthetic data may be further augmented using a generative model trained to map event locations to seismograms that exhibit the characteristics of the field data for a specific area (Spurio Mancini *et al.*, 2021).

The key question when training with synthetic data is how accurate and realistic the simulations must be to ensure that LocNO generalizes well to real-world observations. This strategy may be particularly effective in regions where a smooth velocity model sufficiently captures long-distance wave propagation. However, in local areas with significant scattering and small-scale heterogeneity, a high-resolution velocity model may be necessary to simulate seismic wavefields more accurately and ensure that the synthetic data can effectively enhance the model's performance. Because of the lack of high-resolution velocity models, synthetic data are typically inaccurate at higher frequencies. In this study, LocNO demonstrates the ability to infer earthquake source locations with an uncertainty of ~10 km in the MTJ region using data filtered in the 1–10 Hz frequency band. Although limiting the input to the 1–5 Hz band may exclude some informative high-frequency components, the resulting degradation in performance is relatively minor (Table 2). Most regional velocity models are better suited for simulating low-frequency waveforms, so simulating data in the 1–5 Hz band offers a practical compromise between accuracy and generalizability when training LocNO with synthetic waveform datasets.

Low SNR remains a significant challenge for accurate earthquake location. Traditional travel-time-based methods can sometimes provide reliable solutions for low SNR events when combined with robust phase pickers. In particular, deep-learning-based pickers such as PhaseNO have demonstrated their ability to extract *P*- and *S*-wave arrivals even from noisy waveforms, enabling subsequent location using conventional travel-time-based methods (Sun *et al.*, 2023). However, when the seismic network has poor geometry, such as sparse station coverage or large azimuthal gaps, these travel-time-based location methods may still produce unstable or biased estimates despite having accurate picks. This limitation is particularly evident for the out-of-network events, as demonstrated in the 22 September 2017 M_w 5.7 offshore earthquake sequence. In contrast, LocNO is trained on out-of-network examples that reflect these geometric challenges, allowing it to learn and correct for spatial biases using full-waveform information. To further improve LocNO's robustness for low SNR events, waveform denoising techniques could be incorporated before model inference. This approach could enhance the clarity of input signals, which is commonly employed in seismic full-waveform inversion. Overall, while travel-time-based methods remain effective in well-instrumented regions, waveform-based approaches like LocNO offer distinct advantages for events in challenging network settings.

The DD earthquake location is well known for achieving high relative accuracy and reduced sensitivity to the velocity model errors because it minimizes travel time differences between pairs of events recorded at common stations (Waldhauser and Ellsworth, 2000). However, its effectiveness is inherently constrained by the geometry of the seismic network (Waldhauser, 2001). In sparse or uneven station distributions, or when the azimuthal coverage is poor, DD methods cannot effectively constrain the absolute locations of event clusters, often resulting in systematic spatial drift. This limitation arises because DD techniques only update relative positions between events and cannot correct the initial absolute location of event clusters, which is typically determined before starting the DD relocation. Furthermore, constructing a sufficient number of strongly linked event pairs, typically defined by eight or more high-quality observations, is difficult in networks with limited station coverage. Consequently, the benefits of DD approaches diminish significantly for isolated earthquakes or in regions where stations are few and unevenly distributed.

In addition to algorithmic advancements such as the development of LocNO, a complementary strategy to improve the earthquake location accuracy in offshore or out-of-network regions is to enhance the seismic network by adding more stations and increasing the azimuthal coverage. The use of distributed acoustic sensing (DAS) on submarine fiber-optic cables (Gou *et al.*, 2025) and deployments of ocean-bottom seismometers (OBSs; Toomey *et al.*, 2014; Alongi *et al.*, 2021; Morton *et al.*, 2023) have shown promising results in extending the seismic monitoring capabilities into oceanic regions. These offshore instruments significantly improve the azimuthal coverage and reduce the path-length uncertainties, which are critical for accurate hypocenter determination. However, DAS deployment in the MTJ region is currently limited by the availability of dark fiber infrastructure, and OBS deployments are typically temporary, providing improved hypocenter constraints only during active recording periods. Integrating offshore deployments with LocNO may further improve location accuracy, but this requires careful evaluation in future studies.

CONCLUSION

This study proposes the LocNO, a deep learning framework for earthquake location using full waveforms recorded by multiple stations with arbitrary network geometry. Its application to offshore earthquakes in the MTJ region highlights the effectiveness of LocNO in addressing the persistent challenges of locating offshore events using onshore seismic stations. By utilizing operator learning frameworks and full-waveform seismic data, LocNO effectively captures spatiotemporal relationships in seismic signals, enabling robust performance even in regions with sparse monitoring networks. Quantitatively, LocNO achieves mean absolute errors of $\sim$10 km in horizontal location and 4 km in depth when compared to the NCEDC catalog. The combined use of PhaseNO for earthquake detection and LocNO for location provides a practical path to study MTJ seismotectonics with deep-learning-enhanced catalogs, permitting reliable locations of newly detected small offshore events even when only a few onshore stations record them. Future research could enhance the training dataset with synthetic data to address low-seismicity regions, extend LocNO's application to other tectonic settings, and integrate it into real-time monitoring systems. These efforts would further increase LocNO's potential for mitigating seismic risks and improving regional earthquake monitoring in poorly instrumented areas.

DATA AND RESOURCES

The Python package location neural operator (LocNO) is available at https://github.com/sun-hongyu/LocNO. Python code SeismicGNN is available at doi: 10.6084/m9.figshare.12231077. Detection of events for 22 September 2017 M_w 5.7 earthquake sequence, located 218 km west of Ferndale, California, was performed using the Python package phase neural operator (PhaseNO) (Sun *et al.*, 2023), available at https://github.com/sun-hongyu/PhaseNO. The case study used stations from the BK, NC, and PB networks. Station codes include BK.JCC.HH, NC.GHO.EH, NC.GNA.EH, NC.GTC.EH, NC.KBS.EH, NC.KCPB.HH, NC.KCR.EH, NC.KCS.EH, NC.KCT.HH, NC.KHMB.HH, NC.KMPB.HH, NC.KMR.HH, NC.KRMB.HH, NC.KRP.HH, NC.KSM.EH, NC.KSXB.HH, PB.B045.EH, PB.B046.EH, PB.B047.EH, PB.B049.EH, PB.B932.EH, PB.B933.EH, PB.B934.EH, and PB.B935.EH. Waveform data, metadata, and data products for this study were accessed through the Northern California Earthquake Data Center, doi: 10.7932/NCEDC. All websites were last accessed in September 2025.

DECLARATION OF COMPETING INTERESTS

The author acknowledges that there are no conflicts of interest recorded.

ACKNOWLEDGMENTS

The author thanks Associate Editor Thomas M. Brocher and the two anonymous reviewers for their thoughtful reviews, which greatly improved the article. This work was supported in part by the UTEP University Research Institute Grant, the UTEP Institute for Strategic and Sustainable Resources, and the UT System STARs Program. H.S. also acknowledges support during the revision of this article from the U.S. Department of Energy, Office of Science, Energy

Earthshots Initiative (Award Number DE-SC0024703). This work used Bridges-2 (Brown *et al.*, 2021) at Pittsburgh Supercomputing Center [EES240076] from the Advanced Cyberinfrastructure Coordination Ecosystem: Services and Support (ACCESS) program, which is supported by National Science Foundation Grant Numbers 2138259, 2138286, 2138307, 2137603, and 2138296.

REFERENCES

Alongi, T., S. Y. Schwartz, H. R. Shaddox, and D. T. Small (2021). Probing the southern Cascadia plate interface with the dense amphibious Cascadia initiative seismic array, *J. Geophys. Res.* **126,** e2021JB022180, doi: 10.1029/2021JB022180.

Annunziata, D., M. Savoia, C. Martino, F. Giampaolo, V. Convertito, F. Piccialli, and G. C. Beroza (2025). A robust and rapid grid-based machine learning approach for inside and off-network earthquakes classification in dynamically changing seismic networks, *Seismol. Res. Lett.* **96,** 933–948.

Aquib, T. A., and P. M. Mai (2024). Broadband ground-motion simulations with machine-learning-based high-frequency waves from Fourier neural operators, *Bull. Seismol. Soc. Am.* **114,** 2846–2868.

Bird, P. (2003). An updated digital model of plate boundaries, *Geochem. Geophys. Geosys.* **4,** 1–52.

Brown, S. T., P. Buitrago, E. Hanna, S. Sanielevici, R. Scibek, and N. A. Nystrom (2021). Bridges-2: A platform for rapidly-evolving and data intensive research, *Presented at the Practice and Experience in Advanced Research Computing 2021: Evolution Across All Dimensions*, Association for Computing Machinery.

Burkett, E. R., D. D. Given, and L. M. Jones (2014). ShakeAlert—An earthquake early warning system for the United States west coast, *Tech. Rept. US Geol. Surv.*, doi: 10.3133/fs20143083

Cabieces, R., E. Buforn, S. Cesca, and A. Pazos (2020). Focal parameters of earthquakes offshore Cape St. Vincent using an amphibious network, *Pure Appl. Geophys.* **177,** 1761–1780.

Castro, J. D., C. Meneses-Ponce, R. Ortega, J. Beltran-Gracia, and H. Gonzalez-Huizar (2024). Single station seismic event location with a neural-guided mixture model: Model-based weighting for improved accuracy, *J. Geophys. Res.* **1,** e2024JH000346, doi: 10.1029/2024JH000346.

Chen, Y., O. M. Saad, A. Savvaidis, Y. Chen, and S. Fomel (2022). 3D microseismic monitoring using machine learning, *J. Geophys. Res.* **127,** e2021JB023842, doi: 10.1029/2021JB023842.

Eisermann, A. S., A. Ziv, and H. G. Wust-Bloch (2018). Array-based earthquake location for regional earthquake early warning: Case studies from the Dead Sea transform, *Bull. Seismol. Soc. Am.* **108,** 2046–2053.

Ellsworth, W. L., and S. W. Roecker (1981). Sensitivity of the earthquake location problem to network geometry, in *Seismicity and Tectonics of the Pamir-Hindu Kush Region of Central Asia, Ph.D. Thesis*, Massachusetts Institute of Technology, 57–74 (Chapter in Ph.D. thesis by Steven W. Roecker).

Elsayed, H. S., O. M. Saad, M. S. Soliman, Y. Chen, and H. A. Youness (2023). EQConvMixer: A deep learning approach for earthquake location from single-station waveforms, *IEEE Geosci. Remote Sens. Lett.* **20,** doi: 10.1109/LGRS.2023.3312324.

Franceschi, L., M. Niepert, M. Pontil, and X. He (2019). Learning discrete structures for graph neural networks, *International Conf. on Machine Learning*, PMLR, 1972–1982.

Gilmer, J., S. S. Schoenholz, P. F. Riley, O. Vinyals, and G. E. Dahl (2017). Neural message passing for quantum chemistry, *International Conf. on Machine Learning (ICML)*, PMLR, 1263–1272.

Given, D. D., R. M. Allen, A. S. Baltay, P. Bodin, E. S. Cochran, K. Creager, R. M. de Groot, L. S. Gee, E. Hauksson, T. H. Heaton, *et al.* (2018). Revised technical implementation plan for the ShakeAlert system—An earthquake early warning system for the west coast of the United States, *U.S. Geol. Surv. Open-File Rept. 2018-1155.* (Supersedes USGS Open-File Report 2014–1097).

Gou, Y., R. M. Allen, W. Zhu, T. Taira, and L.-W. Chen (2025). Leveraging submarine DAS arrays for offshore earthquake early warning: A case study in Monterey Bay, California, *Bull. Seismol. Soc. Am.* **115,** 516–532.

He, K., X. Zhang, S. Ren, and J. Sun (2016). Deep residual learning for image recognition, *Proc. of the IEEE Conf. on Computer Vision and Pattern Recognition*, 770–778.

Hendrycks, D., and K. Gimpel (2016). Gaussian error linear units (GELUs), arXiv preprint arXiv:1606.08415.

Jung, S., J.-H. Park, Y. J. Seong, and D.-H. Sheen (2023). Automatic determination of back azimuth based on a single mini array for an earthquake early warning system, *Bull. Seismol. Soc. Am.* **113,** 1311–1323.

Klein, F. W. (2002). User's guide to HYPOINVERSE-2000, a Fortran program to solve for earthquake locations and magnitudes, *Tech. Rept. U.S. Geol. Surv. Open-File Rept. 2002-171.*

Kohler, M. D., D. E. Smith, J. Andrews, A. I. Chung, R. Hartog, I. Henson, D. D. Given, R. de Groot, and S. Guiwits (2020). Earthquake early warning ShakeAlert 2.0: Public rollout, *Seismol. Res. Lett.* **91,** 1763–1775.

Kovachki, N., Z. Li, B. Liu, K. Azizzadenesheli, K. Bhattacharya, A. Stuart, and A. Anandkumar (2023). Neural operator: Learning maps between function spaces with applications to PDEs, *J. Machine Learn. Res.* **24,** 1–97.

Kuang, W., C. Yuan, Z. Zou, J. Zhang, and W. Zhang (2024). Autonomous earthquake location via deep reinforcement learning, *Seismol. Res. Lett.* **95,** 367–377.

Leong, Z. X., and T. Zhu (2024). Machine learning-assisted microearthquake location workflow for monitoring the Newberry enhanced geothermal system, *J. Geophys. Res.* **1,** e2024JH000159, doi: 10.1029/2024JH000159.

Li, Z., N. Kovachki, K. Azizzadenesheli, B. Liu, K. Bhattacharya, A. Stuart, and A. Anandkumar (2020). Neural operator: Graph kernel network for partial differential equations, arXiv preprint arXiv:2003.03485.

Li, Z., N. B. Kovachki, K. Azizzadenesheli, B. Liu, K. Bhattacharya, A. Stuart, and A. Anandkumar (2021). Fourier neural operator for parametric partial differential equations, arXiv preprint, doi: 10.48550/arXiv.2010.08895.

McBrearty, I. W., and G. C. Beroza (2022). Earthquake location and magnitude estimation with graph neural networks, *2022 IEEE International Conf. on Image Processing (ICIP)*, IEEE, 3858–3862.

McBrearty, I. W., and G. C. Beroza (2023). Earthquake phase association with graph neural networks, *Bull. Seismol. Soc. Am.* **113,** 524–547.

McBrearty, I. W., and G. C. Beroza (2025). Double difference earthquake location with graph neural networks, *Earth Planets Space* **77,** 127.

Morton, E. A., S. L. Bilek, and C. A. Rowe (2023). Cascadia subduction zone fault heterogeneities from newly detected small magnitude earthquakes, *J. Geophys. Res.* **128,** e2023JB026607, doi: 10.1029/2023JB026607.

Mousavi, S. M., and G. C. Beroza (2020). Bayesian-deep-learning estimation of earthquake location from single-station observations, *IEEE Trans. Geosci. Remote Sens.* **58,** 8211–8224.

Mousavi, S. M., Y. Sheng, W. Zhu, and G. C. Beroza (2019). STanford EArthquake Dataset (STEAD): A global data set of seismic signals for AI, *IEEE Access* **7,** 179464–179476.

Netanel, M., A. S. Eisermann, and A. Ziv (2021). Off-network earthquake location by earthquake early warning systems: Methodology and validation, *Bull. Seismol. Soc. Am.* **111,** 3090–3102.

Nof, R. N., A. I. Chung, H. Rademacher, L. Dengler, and R. M. Allen (2019). MEMS accelerometer mini-array (MAMA): A low-cost implementation for earthquake early warning enhancement, *Earthq. Spectra* **35,** 21–38.

Perol, T., M. Gharbi, and M. Denolle (2018). Convolutional neural network for earthquake detection and location, *Sci. Adv.* **4,** e1700578, doi: 10.1126/sciadv.1700578.

Rubinstein, J. L., and G. C. Beroza (2007). Full waveform earthquake location: Application to seismic streaks on the Calaveras fault, California, *J. Geophys. Res.* **112,** doi: 10.1029/2006JB004463.

Shelly, D. R., G. C. Beroza, and S. Ide (2007). Non-volcanic tremor and low-frequency earthquake swarms, *Nature* **446,** 305–307.

Shelly, D. R., G. C. Beroza, S. Ide, and S. Nakamula (2006). Low-frequency earthquakes in Shikoku, Japan, and their relationship to episodic tremor and slip, *Nature* **442,** 188–191.

Si, X., X. Wu, Z. Li, S. Wang, and J. Zhu (2024). An all-in-one seismic phase picking, location, and association network for multi-task multi-station earthquake monitoring, *Commun. Earth Environ.* **5,** 22.

Spurio Mancini, A., D. Piras, A. M. G. Ferreira, M. P. Hobson, and B. Joachimi (2021). Accelerating Bayesian microseismic event location with deep learning, *Solid Earth* **12,** 1683–1705.

Sun, H. (2025). Location neural operator (LocNO): Source code, *GitHub*, available at https://github.com/sun-hongyu/LocNO (last accessed September 2025).

Sun, H., Z. E. Ross, W. Zhu, and K. Azizzadenesheli (2023). Phase neural operator for multi-station picking of seismic arrivals, *Geophys. Res. Lett.* **50,** e2023GL106434, doi: 10.1029/2023GL106434.

Sun, H., Y. Yang, K. Azizzadenesheli, R. W. Clayton, and Z. E. Ross (2022). Accelerating time-reversal imaging with neural operators for real-time earthquake locations, arXiv preprint arXiv:2210.06636.

Toomey, D. R., R. M. Allen, A. H. Barclay, S. W. Bell, P. D. Bromirski, R. L. Carlson, X. Chen, J. A. Collins, R. P. Dziak, B. Evers, *et al.* (2014). The Cascadia initiative: A sea change in seismological studies of subduction zones, *Oceanography* **27,** 138–150.

Van Den Ende, M. P. A., and J. Ampuero (2020). Automated seismic source characterization using deep graph neural networks, *Geophys. Res. Lett.* **47,** e2020GL088690, doi: 10.1029/2020GL088690.

Waldhauser, F. (2001). hypoDD-A program to compute double-difference hypocenter locations, *Tech. Rept. U.S. Geol. Surv. Open-File Rept. 2001-113.*

Waldhauser, F., and W. L. Ellsworth (2000). A double-difference earthquake location algorithm: Method and application to the northern Hayward fault, California, *Bull. Seismol. Soc. Am.* **90,** 1353–1368.

Williamson, A., A. Lux, and R. Allen (2023). Improving out of network earthquake locations using prior seismicity for use in earthquake early warning, *Bull. Seismol. Soc. Am.* **113,** 664–675.

Yu, Y., W. L. Ellsworth, and G. C. Beroza (2025). Accuracy and precision of earthquake location programs: Insights from a synthetic controlled experiment, *Seismol. Res. Lett.* **96,** 1860–1874.

Zhang, X., W. Reichard-Flynn, M. Zhang, M. Hirn, and Y. Lin (2022). Spatiotemporal graph convolutional networks for earthquake source characterization, *J. Geophys. Res.* **127,** e2022JB024401, doi: 10.1029/2022JB024401.

Zhang, X., J. Zhang, C. Yuan, S. Liu, Z. Chen, and W. Li (2020). Locating induced earthquakes with a network of seismic stations in Oklahoma via a deep learning method, *Sci. Rep.* **10,** 1941.

Zhu, W., and G. C. Beroza (2019). PhaseNet: A deep-neural-network-based seismic arrival-time picking method, *Geophys. J. Int.* **216,** 261–273.

Zhu, W., I. W. McBrearty, S. M. Mousavi, W. L. Ellsworth, and G. C. Beroza (2022). Earthquake phase association using a Bayesian Gaussian mixture model, *J. Geophys. Res.* **127,** e2021JB023249, doi: 10.1029/2021JB023249.

Zhu, W., K. S. Tai, S. M. Mousavi, P. Bailis, and G. C. Beroza (2022). An end-to-end earthquake detection method for joint phase picking and association using deep learning, *J. Geophys. Res.* **127,** e2021JB023283, doi: 10.1029/2021JB023283.

Zhu, W., H. Wang, B. Rong, E. Yu, S. Zuzlewski, G. Tepp, T. Taira, J. Marty, A. Husker, and R. M. Allen (2025). California earthquake dataset for machine learning and cloud computing, arXiv preprint arXiv:2502.11500.

Ziv, A., A. S. Eisermann, O. Volk, and I. Zbeda (2024). Introducing ViDA3, an earthquake early warning algorithm for offshore hypocenter determination using onshore seismic networks, *Bull. Seismol. Soc. Am.* **114,** 2446–2456.

Zollo, A., A. Caruso, G. De Landro, S. Colombelli, and L. Elia (2021). A Bayesian method for real-time earthquake location using multiparameter data, *J. Geophys. Res.* **126,** e2020JB020359, doi: 10.1029/2020JB020359.

Manuscript received 24 January 2025
Published online 15 October 2025

The Role of "Equation Error" in Empirical Regressions for Seismic Magnitude Conversions

Paolo Gasperini[1,2], Emanuele Biondini[1], and Barbara Lolli[*2]

ABSTRACT

In the last two decades, empirical regressions for the conversions of traditional magnitudes (e.g., M_L, M_s, and m_b) to moment magnitude M_w were mostly computed using error-in-variable (EIV) method, also known as general orthogonal regression, and not the ordinary least-squares (OLS) method because the uncertainties of traditional magnitudes are not negligible when compared to that of M_w. However, a few recent articles criticized such approaches based on the hypothesis that an error in the equation, that is, the epistemic uncertainty associated with the form of the regression equation, is present, and this is better accounted for by the OLS rather than by the EIV. In this work, we first discuss the problem theoretically and then make some analysis on real datasets. We find that the regression coefficients are strongly influenced by the assumption made about the sizes of the errors of traditional magnitudes. In particular, the role of equation error may be significant if the assumed errors of the traditional magnitudes are small (≤ 0.1 magnitude units) or may even be almost negligible if the errors are only slightly larger (> 0.12–0.15). In general, the EIV method has always to be preferred with respect to OLS, but it might require a small correction for equation error. These findings have significant implications for statistical forecasting and seismic hazard assessment.

KEY POINTS

- We analyze and compare regression methods to convert earthquake magnitudes.
- The most appropriate method must consider experimental errors in both variables.
- Our findings have significant implications for statistical forecasting and seismic hazard assessment.

INTRODUCTION

Seismic magnitude is an empirical estimate of the "size" of an earthquake based on the amplitudes of seismic waves recorded by seismic stations. Since the seminal work by Richter (1935) defined local magnitude M_L, other (teleseismic) definitions have been proposed to compute the magnitude at distances longer than 600 km, which is the maximum allowed for the original M_L definition. Successive definitions (e.g., Finetti and Morelli, 1972; Kim, 1998; Allen *et al.*, 2023) extended the maximum distance but usually not more than 1000 km. Teleseismic magnitudes that are currently computed are the long-period (20 s) surface-wave magnitude M_s (Gutenberg, 1945a; Karnik *et al.*, 1962) and the short-period (1 s) body-wave magnitude m_b (Gutenberg, 1945b; Engdahl and Gunst 1966).

Unfortunately, all traditional magnitudes revealed to saturate for large earthquakes, owing to the limited frequency passband sampled. To overcome such limitations, Kanamori (1977) defined the "work" magnitude M_w (defined literally "as a continuation of M_s for large earthquakes") based on scalar seismic moment M_0 determinations using very broadband recordings:

$$M_w = \frac{2}{3}(\log_{10} M_0 - 9.1) \quad (\text{with } M_0 \text{ in N} \cdot \text{m}). \qquad (1)$$

Subsequently, Hanks and Kanamori (1979), also considering the results of Thatcher and Hanks (1973) for M_L and of Purcaru and Berkeimer (1978) for M_s, defined the moment magnitude **M**, extending M_w over the whole range of measurable seismic moments. Because the definitions of **M** and M_w coincide with each other, both symbols are used to indicate the moment magnitude, with a certain preference for M_w in the most recent literature.

The methods developed by various authors (e.g., Dziewonski *et al.*, 1981; Arvidsson and Ekström, 1998; Dreger, 2003) to consistently compute the scalar seismic moment by the inversion of

1. Dipartimento di Fisica e Astronomia, Università di Bologna, Bologna, Italy, https://orcid.org/0000-0002-5314-0563 (PG); https://orcid.org/0000-0003-2305-9534 (EB); 2. Istituto Nazionale di Geofisica e Vulcanologia, Sezione di Bologna, Bologna, Italy, https://orcid.org/0000-0003-4186-9055 (BL)

*Corresponding author: barbara.lolli@ingv.it

Cite this article as Gasperini, P., E. Biondini, and B. Lolli (2025). The Role of "Equation Error" in Empirical Regressions for Seismic Magnitude Conversions, *Bull. Seismol. Soc. Am.* **116**, 225–237, doi: 10.1785/0120250007 the seismic moment tensor from broadband recordings are not feasible at magnitudes lower than about 3–3.5. Hence, the traditional magnitude definitions are still employed in areas where, and in epochs when, such modern instruments are not available and for small earthquakes.

Although all magnitude types (including M_w) were defined to coincide with the M_L defined by Richter (1935), they may differ within certain ranges of values because of the different frequency bands sampled. Hence, to obtain seismic catalogs with a homogeneous magnitude estimate for all earthquakes, some calibrations or conversions (e.g., Stromeyer *et al.*, 2004; Castellaro *et al.*, 2006) among different magnitude types are required. Because M_w does not saturate, it can be taken as a reference, and the other magnitude definitions can be converted to it using empirical regressions.

Deichmann (2006) argued that in theory M_L should coincide with M_w but in practice, differences between them might be observed due to inadequacies in the wave propagation model and/or to changes in stress drop or rupture velocity. Deichmann (2017) described some theoretical arguments for the breaking of the 1:1 scaling between M_L and M_w to 1:1.5 for low values. However, it is not clear what magnitude value is below which the 1:1.5 scaling starts to be effective. On the other hand, Malagnini and Munafò (2018) found that the slope of the linear relation between M_L and M_w is 1/1.28 above M_w 4 and 1.5 below, for the 2009 and 2016–2017 Central Italy sequences. However, using a larger Italian dataset of 682 earthquakes from 2005 to 2018 with M_w ranging from 3.1 to 6.6, Lolli *et al.* (2020) found a slope of 1/1.047 and no evidence of a slope change at M_w 4.0. The change of the slope of the M_L–M_w relation should be reflected by a change even of the slope (b value) of the frequency–magnitude distribution (FMD, Gutenberg and Richter, 1944). Lolli *et al.* (2020) also analyzed the FMD of an Italian dataset and did not find any change in b value down to about M_L 1.6. We can argue that the results of Malagnini and Munafò (2018) reflect the characteristics of the data of their Central Italy dataset; they cannot be generalized. Staudenmaier *et al.* (2018) found that the FMD around Parkfield, California, shows almost rectilinear behavior for duration magnitude M_d and M_w down to about magnitude 1.0, but it evidences a slope change for M_L below 2–2.5. This would imply a discrepancy in the M_L–M_w scaling of smaller events with a coefficient of 1.46 ± 0.02 for $M_w < 2$. Even in this case, the scale change must be confirmed using datasets recorded in wider areas.

Kanamori and Anderson (1975), based on theoretical considerations on the excitation of surface waves with a period of about 20 s, inferred that the scaling coefficient between M_s and $\log_{10} M_0$ should be 1 at low magnitudes, 1.5 at intermediate magnitudes, and 3 at high magnitudes (then the coefficients with M_w should be 2/3, 1, and 2 respectively). The transition between the slopes at intermediate and low magnitudes is estimated to be around $M_s \approx 6.2$ (Ekström and Dziewonski, 1988; Scordilis, 2006). The transition at high magnitudes is not precisely known, but it probably occurs for M_s around 8, where saturation begins to be observed.

A similar behavior should be observed for m_b but with transition points shifted down to lower magnitudes, owing to the shorter periods of seismic waves sampled (between 1 and 5 s). Gasperini *et al.* (2013a) showed that m_b provided by the International Seismological Centre (ISC) coincides with M_w at low values (m_b < 4–4.5), whereas it saturates for m_b > 5–5.5. Hence, the transitions between slopes 1 and 2 can be assumed around m_b 5. The transition point between slopes 1 and 2/3 is unknown, but according to Gasperini *et al.* (2013a) and Lolli *et al.* (2014), it is not observed above m_b 3.5, which is about the minimum m_b computed by ISC and other agencies.

Ekström and Dziewonski (1988) proposed a curvilinear relation between M_w and M_s in which two straight segments with slopes 1 and 2/3 at high and low M_s respectively are connected by a curved line. Following the same schema, Lolli *et al.* (2014) proposed a circularly connected bilinear model.

In the following, we will discuss first the various regression methods used in the literature for conversion between different types of magnitude to obtain homogeneous estimates for all the earthquakes of a seismic catalog. Then, we will consider various estimates of magnitude errors, and finally, we will test different regression methods on datasets of M_w and M_L from the standardized catalogue of New Zealand (Christophersen *et al.*, 2024) and from the Italian Horus catalog (Lolli *et al.*, 2020).

REGRESSION METHODS

The regression procedure can be described as the search for the functional model that best reproduces a dependent (response, predicted) variable y as a function of an independent (explanatory, predictor) variable x:

$$y = f(x). \tag{2}$$

Up to about two decades ago, the only regression method used for magnitude conversions (e.g., Johnston, 1996, Giardini *et al.*, 1997, Grünthal and Wahlström, 2003; Scordilis, 2006) was the ordinary least-squares (OLS) method, which minimizes the square Euclidean distance (SED) between observations and model predictions of the dependent variable:

$$\mathrm{SED} = \sum_{i=1}^{N}(y_i - f(x_i))^2. \tag{3}$$

This method implicitly assumes that only the dependent variable y is affected by measurement errors (stochastic or epistemic), whereas the independent variable x is known without error. Even if the latter assumption is never true (because the measurement error is never null), it can represent a reasonable approximation when the error of x is much smaller than that of y (for example, by an order of magnitude).

However, the error of x is not usually negligible for regressions between different magnitude types, in particular when x

is a traditional magnitude like M_L, M_s, or m_b and y is M_w because the latter is usually determined more accurately than other magnitude types. M_w is calculated indeed by modeling the entire recorded waveform and by considering the exact radiation pattern of seismic waves, through the simultaneous calculation of the earthquake moment tensor (e.g., Dziewonski *et al.*, 1981). Conversely, for other kinds of magnitude, only the amplitude of the maximum phase is measured, and a circularly isotropic attenuation pattern is assumed.

If the error of x is not negligible, the OLS method is not applicable, and error-in-variable (EIV) regression methods (Fuller, 1987; Stromeyer *et al.*, 2004; Castellaro *et al.*, 2006), considering the errors of both variables, must be used.

A simple demonstration of the latter assertion can be deduced by considering the likelihood of the regression equation with data, which is the total probability that the regression equation well reproduces a given dataset. It can be computed as the product of the probabilities that the single observations y_i are well described by the regression equation $f(x_i)$,

$$l = \prod_{i=1}^{n} p(f(x_i)|y_i). \tag{4}$$

For normally distributed continuous variables, p is the probability density function of the standardized normal distribution, so that l becomes

$$l = \prod_{i=1}^{n} \frac{1}{\sqrt{2\pi}} \exp\left(-\frac{Z_i^2}{2}\right), \tag{5}$$

in which

$$Z_i = \frac{y_i - f(x_i)}{\sigma}, \tag{6}$$

are the standardized residuals and σ is the standard deviation of the $y_i - f(x_i)$ differences (having zero mean).

Computing the logarithms, equation (5) becomes

$$L = -\frac{N}{2}\ln(2\pi) - \sum_{i=1}^{N} \frac{(y_i - f(x_i))^2}{2\sigma^2}, \tag{7}$$

L is usually indicated as the log-likelihood function. The best regression model is that one maximizing l (and thus even L). As the first term of equation (7) does not depend on the regression equation, it can be omitted, and thus the best model is the one that minimizes

$$\chi^2 = \sum_{i=1}^{N} \frac{(y_i - f(x_i))^2}{\sigma^2}, \tag{8}$$

which corresponds to the chi-square that Stromeyer *et al.* (2004) suggest minimizing to fit empirical regressions between different types of magnitude.

If the errors of the two variables are uncorrelated, the residual variance σ^2 can be computed, by the error propagation law, as (see Stromeyer *et al.*, 2004, and Lolli and Gasperini, 2012)

$$\sigma^2 = \left(\frac{\partial(y-f(x))}{\partial x}\right)^2 \sigma_x^2 + \left(\frac{\partial(y-f(x))}{\partial y}\right)^2 \sigma_y^2 = \left(\frac{\partial f(x)}{\partial x}\right)^2 \sigma_x^2 + \sigma_y^2, \tag{9}$$

in which σ_x^2 and σ_y^2 are the error variances of the independent and dependent variables, respectively.

If the error variance of the independent variable $\sigma_x^2 \approx 0$ and that of the dependent variable $\sigma_y^2 \neq 0$ and constant (as it is assumed by the direct OLS methods), then $\sigma^2 = \sigma_y^2$ is constant and the model maximizing the likelihood, and then minimizing the χ^2, is the one minimizing the numerator of equation (8), which exactly corresponds to the square Euclidean distance SED of equation (3), which is minimized by the OLS method. In all other cases, one must compute the derivative in equation (9) and minimize χ^2 of equation (8).

If the regression model is a straight line,

$$y = \beta_1 x + \beta_0, \tag{10}$$

then equation (8) becomes

$$\chi^2 = \sum_{i=1}^{N} \frac{(y_i - \beta_1 x_i - \beta_0)^2}{\beta_1^2 \sigma_x^2 + \sigma_y^2}. \tag{11}$$

If the errors of all the observations are equal (homoscedastic error), we can define the variance ratio $\eta = \sigma_y^2/\sigma_x^2$ and get

$$\chi^2 = \sum_{i=1}^{N} \frac{(y_i - \beta_1 x_i - \beta_0)^2}{\sigma_x^2(\beta_1^2 + \eta)}. \tag{12}$$

Lolli and Gasperini (2012) showed that minimizing such statistics yields the same expressions derived by Fuller (1987, note that here and elsewhere we refer to the integral reprint of such a textbook dated 2006) for computing regression parameters and related errors by the EIV method (reported in the Appendix).

Castellaro *et al.* (2006) showed that using the coefficients computed by the EIV method for converting magnitudes preserves the b value of the FMD (Gutenberg and Richter, 1944). Castellaro and Bormann (2007) demonstrated that "for $0.7 < \sqrt{\eta_{\text{true}}} < 1.8$ the orthogonal regression (GOR) under the $\eta = 1$ assumption performs better than standard regressions" (OLS).

Finally, if $\sigma_y^2 \approx 0$ and $\sigma_x^2 \neq 0$ and constant, equation (12) becomes

$$\chi^2 = \sum_{i=1}^{N} \frac{\left(\frac{y_i}{\beta_1} - x_i - \frac{\beta_0}{\beta_1}\right)^2}{\sigma_x^2}, \tag{13}$$

in which the numerator represents the square residual of the inverse OLS regression (x as a function of y) in which the regression error is fully attributed to the error of the variable x, which now becomes the dependent variable (whereas y becomes the independent variable),

$$x = \frac{1}{\beta_1} y - \frac{\beta_0}{\beta_1}. \tag{14}$$

Hence, equation (11) covers the entire range of possible linear regressions, from the direct OLS regression, when $\eta \gg \beta_1^2$, to the EIV, when $\eta \approx \beta_1^2$, and finally to the inverse OLS regression, when $\eta \ll \beta_1^2$.

Neglecting the error of the independent variable σ_x, as done by the OLS method, causes an underestimation of the regression slope β_1 called "attenuation" (Fuller, 1987; Carroll and Rupert, 1996) that must be "corrected" in some way (for example, using the EIV method).

In recent times, some criticisms of using the EIV method in magnitude regressions were raised by Das *et al.* (2018) and Christophersen *et al.* (2024). In particular, Christophersen *et al.* (2024) assert that "GOR method estimates the relation between the true (but unknown) values of Y and the true (but unknown) values of X based on the ratio of the variances of the observations of Y and X.". Hence, they argue that for this reason "it is unclear how to estimate Y from an observed value of X given that the true value of X is unknown." We disagree with this argument (already proposed by Das *et al.*, 2018, and already criticized by Gasperini *et al.*, 2023) because, as the unknown true values cannot be determined by any method, then they cannot be used for estimating the relation between them. What the EIV method described by Fuller (1987) does is not to compute the true values but instead to compute estimators of the true values that are closer to the true values than the observed values and then uses such estimators to compute more accurate regression coefficients. In this sense, even the observed values are estimators of the true values, and the relation estimated by the OLS methods is an approximation (less accurate than that obtained by the EIV method) of the (unknown) relation between the true values of the data.

Thus, for regression estimated by the EIV method, there are no problems in evaluating the Y from observed X. The only difference compared to relations computed using the OLS method is that the regression slope determined by the latter method is biased low, owing to the slope attenuation bias.

A second objection raised by Christophersen *et al.* (2024) is that "GOR assumes that only measurement error causes the scatter in the data and thus neglects equation error, which is present for most regressions due to further scatter in the data beyond pure measurement error (Carroll and Ruppert, 1996)," thus suggesting (although not explicitly affirming) that instead the OLS method they adopt appropriately accounts for the equation error. This argument is not exact because, as described subsequently, the GOR (or better the EIV) method can be corrected by including the actual contribution of the equation error to the total variance, as well as this can also be done for the OLS method.

Such a problem is discussed by Carroll and Ruppert (1996) for linear regressions. They state that if the variance ratio $\eta = \sigma_y^2/\sigma_x^2$ is correctly specified, the EIV method described by Fuller (1987) is an acceptable regression fitting method. Still, if it is incorrectly specified (in fact underestimated), the EIV method leads to an overestimation of the regression slope. To evidence such overestimation, they propose to apply the method of moments (MM), to compute a regression slope "corrected for attenuation" as

$$\beta_1(\mathrm{MM}) = \frac{s_{xx}}{s_{xx} - \sigma_x^2} \beta_1(\mathrm{OLS}), \tag{15}$$

in which

$$s_{xx} = \frac{1}{N-1} \sum_{i=1}^{N} (x_i - \bar{x})^2, \tag{16}$$

$$\bar{x} = \frac{1}{N} \sum_{i=1}^{N} x_i, \tag{17}$$

and compare it with the EIV regression slope $\beta_1(\mathrm{EIV})$.

Carroll and Ruppert (1996) affirm that such a method differs from the MM estimator used by Fuller (1987), but this is not exact because in section 1.2.1 (pp. 13–14) of the latter textbook, one can find the formula of the slope determined just by the MM for the case when the measurement variance of the independent variable σ_x^2 is known. When translated to the notation used here, it becomes

$$\beta_1(\mathrm{MM}) = \frac{s_{xy}}{s_{xx} - \sigma_x^2}, \tag{18}$$

in which

$$s_{xy} = \frac{1}{N-1} \sum_{i=1}^{N} (x_i - \bar{x})(y - \bar{y}), \tag{19}$$

$$\bar{y} = \frac{1}{N} \sum_{i=1}^{N} y_i. \tag{20}$$

As the estimator of the slope for the OLS method is (e.g., Fuller, 1987, pp. 2)

$$\beta_1(\mathrm{OLS}) = \frac{s_{xy}}{s_{xx}}. \tag{21}$$

Then equation (15) (equation 7 of Carroll and Ruppert, 1996) results from the trivial substitution of equation (21) in equation (18).

The same MM is also used in section 1.3.2 of Fuller (1987) (pp. 30–31) to derive the slope estimator of the classical EIV model (see the Appendix), in which the ratio of measurement error variances $\eta = \sigma_y^2/\sigma_x^2$ is known (corresponding to equation 6 of Carroll and Ruppert, 1996).

Carroll and Ruppert (1996) attribute the eventual difference between the MM and EIV estimates to "a missing component of variance" related to the (linear) form of the regression model. Their argument is: "the linear model states that in the absence of measurement errors only, the data would fall exactly on a straight line, but in practice, this is plausible only in rare circumstances." In support of such assertions, they only quote a sentence ("Real data almost never fall exactly on a straight line ...") taken from Weisberg (1985, p. 6), which is no longer present in the latest edition (fourth) of such a textbook (Weisberg, 2014). They also state that "Weisberg (1985) is talking about what Fuller (1987, p. 106) calls equation errors."

The discussion of Fuller (1987) about equation error can be found in section "2.2—The Model with an Error in the Equation" (pp. 103–124), but in the same chapter 2, one can also find section "2.3—The Model with no Error in the Equation" (pp. 124–148). Fuller (1987) does not provide a clear indication on how to choose among these two models; he only states that the latter is applicable when "the entire covariance structure is known or is known up to a scalar multiple" and the former when it is not. Note that chapter 2 of Fuller (1987) concerns regression models with multiple explanatory variables and not models with a single explanatory variable like those used for conversions among magnitudes and discussed in chapter 1 (ibidem).

In case an error in the equation is present, Carroll and Ruppert (1996) and Fuller (1987) suggest including in the regression equation (10) an additive random term q with zero mean and variance σ_q^2. This implies that the variance ratio used by EIV regression must be corrected as

$$\eta = \frac{\sigma_q^2 + \sigma_y^2}{\sigma_x^2}. \quad (22)$$

Without such a correction, the EIV regression might overestimate the slope β_1. Carroll and Ruppert (1996) also provide a method to estimate σ_q^2 as

$$\sigma_q^2 = s_v^2 - \sigma_y^2 - \beta_1(\mathrm{MM})\sigma_x^2, \quad (23)$$

in which

$$s_v^2 = \frac{\sum_{i=1}^{N}[y_i - \bar{y} - \beta_1(\mathrm{MM})(x_i - \bar{x})]^2}{N-2}, \quad (24)$$

even if, they also state that "There is no guarantee that $\sigma_q^2 \geq 0$.".

In any case, the presence of equation error is only a possibility and is not always true. For example, Cheng and Riu (2006) state that "the no-equation error model is frequently found in natural sciences, such as physics and chemistry, whereas the equation error model is more often found in econometrics and the medical sciences."

We can argue that an error in the equation might occur when the linear model is assumed tentatively without any real physical reason supporting it. It might instead be totally absent, or so small to be negligible, if physical considerations support the form of the relationship, as in the case of the regressions between different definitions of magnitude, for which there are physical reasons supporting the linear relation of M_w as a function of M_L (Deichmann, 2006), within given ranges at least, and the bilinear curved relation of M_w as a function of M_s and m_b (Kanamori and Anderson, 1975; Ekström and Dziewonski, 1988).

In the case of linear regressions, the above procedure to estimate σ_q^2, suggested by Carroll and Ruppert (1996), can be followed, and the coefficients of the three regression methods can be compared to each other.

DATA

We analyzed moment and local magnitudes from the New Zealand seismic catalog file re-evaluated by Christophersen *et al.* (2024) (see Data and Resources for details). Following Christophersen *et al.* (2024), we selected only earthquakes that occurred since 2004, located within the New Zealand testing center region (vertices taken from Gerstenberger and Rhoades, 2010). We considered only the records (2702) for which the magnitude type reported in column "Mpref.type" is "Mwnz" and took the value in column "Mpref" as M_{wNZ} to be regressed with respect to the local magnitude taken from column "ML". We assumed that the latter corresponds to M_{LNZ77} from 2004 to 2011, and to M_{LSC3} from 2012 to 2020.

Following the criteria indicated by Christophersen *et al.* (2024), we selected earthquakes with $4.55 < M_L < 6.5$ and depth < 40 km, excluding those within 4, 2, 1, and 0.5 hr following an earthquake of $M_{wNZ} > 7.0$, 6.0, 5.0, and ≤5.0, respectively. Christophersen *et al.* (2024) actually indicate 5 hr after an earthquake with $M_{wNZ} > 5.0$, but we guessed that it is a misprint and assumed 1 hr for coherence with other intervals. The number of earthquakes in the M_{LNZ77} and M_{LSC3} datasets result 200 and 213, respectively. They differ from those reported in table 5 of Christophersen *et al.* (2024), which are 166 and 193, respectively (the differences remain, even using 5 hr after $M_{wNZ} > 5.0$).

We also analyzed an Italian dataset built by Lolli *et al* (2020), which includes M_L taken from the INGV ISIDe webservices (M_{LISIDe}) and M_w from a comprehensive dataset combining various online sources available for the Italian area (see Data and Resources for details). We selected the data inside the Italian territory (with a star in column "Italia"), with $M_w > 0$ (column "Mw-MT"), $M_L \geq 3.0$ (column "ML") and depth < 40 km (column "Depth") from 16 April 2005 to 31 December 2023. For coherence with the New Zealand datasets, we applied the same exclusion rules in the first hours after strong shocks. The number of selected earthquakes is 599. In Figures 1–3, we plot the distribution of data points for datasets M_{LNZ77}, M_{LSC3}, and M_{LISIDe}, respectively, with regression lines obtained by different regression methods.

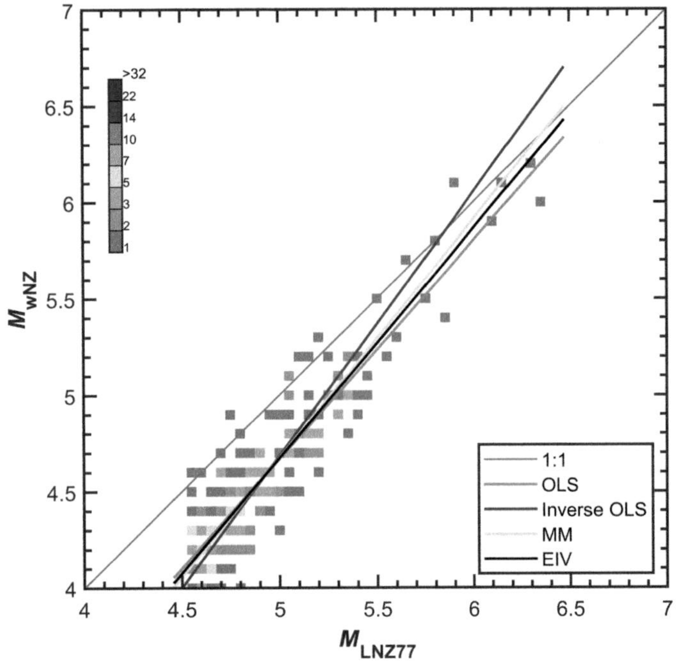

Figure 1. Data frequencies and regression lines (computed using $\sigma_x = 0.1$, $\sigma_y = 0.2$) for the dataset of M_{wNZ} with respect to M_{LNZ77}. EIV, error-in-variable; MM, method of moments; and OLS, ordinary least-squares. The color version of this figure is available only in the electronic edition.

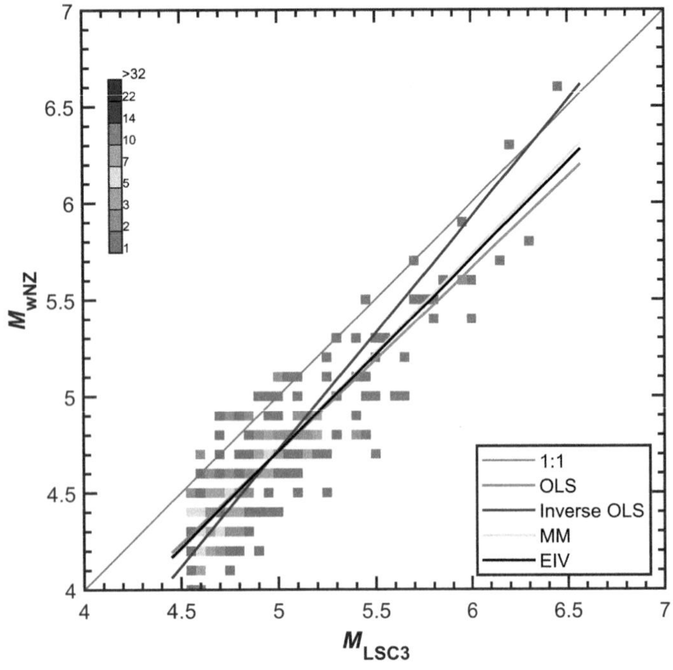

Figure 2. Same as Figure 1 for the dataset of M_{wNZ} with respect to M_{LSC3}. The color version of this figure is available only in the electronic edition.

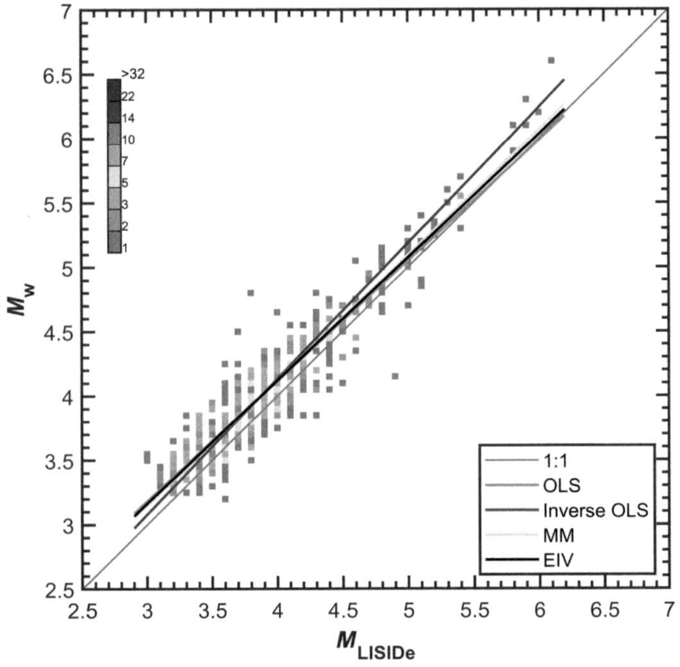

Figure 3. Same as Figure 1 for the dataset of M_w with respect to M_{LISIDe}. The color version of this figure is available only in the electronic edition.

MAGNITUDE ERRORS

The error of M_w, from global and regional moment tensor catalogs, was estimated to be 0.1 magnitude units (m.u.) or less by Helffrich (1997), Kagan (2002, 2003), and Lolli *et al.* (2014, 2023), whereas the errors of traditional magnitudes are usually estimated to be not less than 0.1 m.u. up to about 0.5 m.u. (Kagan, 2003; Gasperini *et al.*, 2013b; Lolli *et al.*, 2014, 2023).

Christophersen *et al.* (2024) argued that "it seems to be a general rule that the uncertainty on the seismic moment for regional solutions is approximately a factor of two, which translates to $\pm\sim 0.2$ in M_w." Unfortunately, they do not cite any evidence or reference in support of such an alleged "general rule."

Christophersen *et al.* (2024) estimated an error variance of 0.002 for all M_L datasets used by them, except one for which they estimated a variance of 0.0006, meaning that the corresponding errors of M_L (computed as the square roots of previous values) are 0.045 and 0.024 m.u., respectively. These values appear rather small when compared to the error of M_w that, as noted earlier, should be more accurate than that of traditional magnitudes because it is computed using the entire recorded waveforms rather than only from the amplitude of the maximum phase.

We may argue that among the possible reasons why Christophersen *et al.* (2024) estimated so small M_L errors is that they cut the 12.5% tails of the distribution of magnitudes. This tends to underestimate the error compared to considering the full dispersion of data. Moreover, in this way, Christophersen *et al.* (2024) evaluate only the stochastic error, based on the distribution of estimates made by different stations, whereas they neglect the epistemic error due, for example, to the calibration of seismic wave propagation properties. Hence, it is reasonable that, when considering the regression with M_w, the real error of M_L is definitely larger than that estimated by Christophersen *et al.* (2024).

We can note that, if the errors of the two variables are uncorrelated and the equation error is absent, the theoretical residual standard error of the linear regression, from the error propagation law (equation 9), is given by

$$s = \sqrt{\beta_1^2 \sigma_x^2 + \sigma_y^2}. \tag{25}$$

As the regression slope β_1 is very close to 1 for all the datasets of Christophersen *et al.* (2024), as reported in their table 5, then $s \approx \sqrt{\sigma_x^2 + \sigma_y^2}$. In the same table 5, we can also note that the residual standard errors s for regressions of M_{wNZ} with M_{LNZ77} and M_{LSC3} are both lower (0.166 and 0.181 m.u., respectively) than the error of M_{wNZ} (0.2 m.u.) assumed by Christophersen *et al.* (2024). But this is not possible because, according to equation (25), s must be larger than the error of both variables. So, we can argue that, for the earthquakes of such datasets, the real error of M_{wNZ} is probably definitely smaller than that assumed by Christophersen *et al.* (2024) and anyhow not larger than s. An alternative explanation of such a discrepancy, suggested by a reviewer, would imply the existence of a certain amount of correlation between the uncertainties of the two variables, which in turn would require that M_{wNZ} shares part of the information on which it is based with M_{LNZ77} and M_{LSC3}. But in our opinion, this explanation is rather unlikely because of the different procedures and seismic waveform data used for determining them.

Furthermore, in Christophersen *et al.* (2024), their table 5, the residual standard errors of the regressions of M_{LNZ20} with M_{LNZ77} and M_{LCS3} range from s = 0.079 to 0.233 while their expected values, based on the assumed values of variances of the two variables ($\sigma_x^2 = \sigma_y^2 = 0.002$) should be of the order of $\sqrt{1^2 \cdot 0.002 + 0.002} \approx 0.06$. Hence, we could argue that the true errors of M_{LNZ20}, M_{LNZ77}, and M_{LCS3} are probably larger than those assumed by Christophersen *et al.* (2024), and by corollary, not smaller than $s/\sqrt{2}$ (ranging from 0.06 to 0.16). An alternative explanation, suggested by a reviewer, is that the equation error significantly contributes to the total variance. In our opinion, this is plausible at the lower end of the range of s (for which it would result $\sigma_q = \sqrt{0.079^2 - 0.060^2} = 0.051$, that is of the same order of the stochastic error) but less plausible at the upper end (0.233, for which it would result $\sigma_q = \sqrt{0.233^2 - 0.060^2} = 0.225$, that is almost four times the stochastic error).

These arguments lead us to estimate variances of the same order of magnitude for M_w, M_{LNZ77}, and M_{LCS3}. Hence, in our opinion, the variances of the independent variables in Christophersen *et al.* (2024) regressions are not negligible with respect to the variances of the dependent variables. As noted

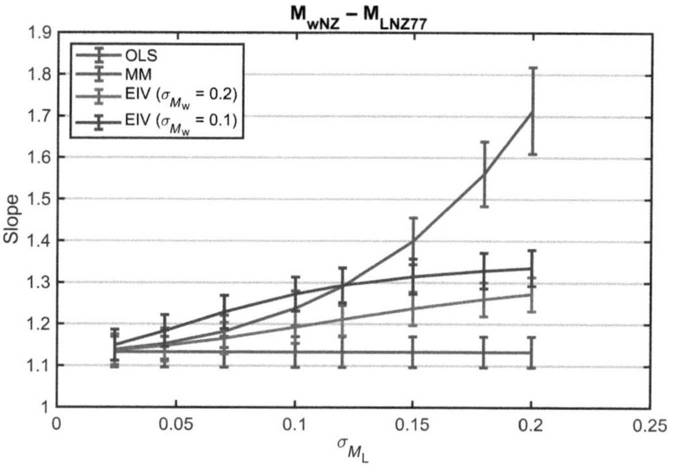

Figure 4. Behaviors, as a function of σ_x, of the slopes of the regressions of M_{wNZ} with respect to M_{LNZ77} computed using various methods (with numerical values reported in Table 1). With the green line β_1(OLS), with a gray line β_1(MM), and with red and blue lines, β_1(EIV) using $\sigma_y = 0.1$ and 0.2, respectively. The color version of this figure is available only in the electronic edition.

earlier, in such a case, the OLS method would not be applicable anymore, and EIV or MM regression methods would have to be used.

Gasperini *et al.* (2013b) estimated the error of M_L from the Italian ISIDe webservices after 16 April 2005 to be 0.18 m.u. by a comparison between M_L and M_d magnitude estimates.

REGRESSION RESULTS

According to the earlier discussion, for the error of M_{wNZ} we use both $\sigma_y = 0.2$, as assumed by Christophersen *et al.* (2024), and $\sigma_y = 0.1$, as suggested by other investigators (e.g., Helffrich, 1997; Kagan, 2002, 2003; Lolli *et al.*, 2014, 2023). Moreover, we vary the error of M_{LNZ77}, M_{LCS3}, and M_{LISIDe} from the minimum value assumed by Christophersen *et al.* (2024) of $\sigma_x = 0.024$ to $\sigma_x = 0.20$, commonly assumed for M_L by other investigators (e.g. Kagan, 2003; Gasperini *et al.*, 2013b; Lolli *et al.*, 2014, 2023).

In Figures 4–6, we show the behaviors, as a function of σ_x, of the slopes of the regressions of M_{wNZ} with respect to M_{LNZ77} and M_{LCS3} and of M_w with respect to M_{LISIDe}, respectively, computed using various methods (with values reported in Tables 1–3, respectively). With the green lines, we report the results of β_1(OLS). In this case, the estimated regression slope is independent of the a priori errors of the variables, and then it is a constant. Conversely, according to equation (18), β_1(MM) (gray lines) is independent of the error of the dependent variable σ_y but increases as the error of the independent variable σ_x increases. β_1(MM) is generally higher than β_1(OLS), owing to the slope attenuation bias affecting the OLS method. Finally, β_1(EIV) (computed without considering the correction for equation error of equation 22) depends on both σ_x and σ_y. For $\sigma_y = 0.2$ (blue lines), β_1(EIV) stays about

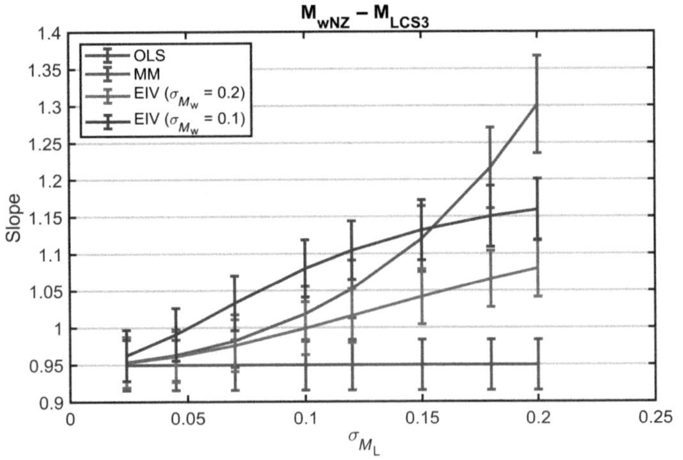

Figure 5. Same as Figure 4 for the regressions of M_{wNZ} with respect to M_{LCS3} (with numerical values reported in Table 2). The color version of this figure is available only in the electronic edition.

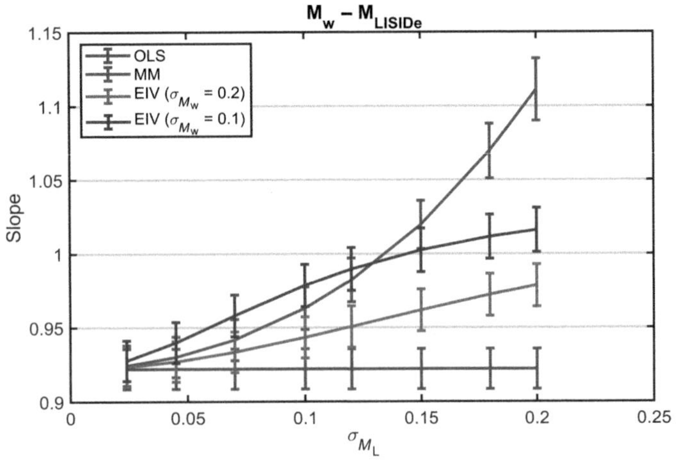

Figure 6. Same as Figure 4 for the regressions of M_w with respect to M_{LISIDe} (with numerical values reported in Table 3). The color version of this figure is available only in the electronic edition.

in the middle between β_1(MM) and β_1(OLS) and is very close to β_1(MM) at small σ_x (<0.1). For $\sigma_y = 0.1$ (red lines), β_1(EIV) is larger than β_1(MM) at small σ_x and become smaller for errors larger than 0.12, 0.15, and 0.12, for M_{LNZ77}, M_{LCS3}, and M_{LISIDe} datasets, respectively.

β_1(OLS) computed by Christophersen *et al.* (2024) is smaller than our one for M_{LNZ77} (1.094 ± 0.035 versus 1.133 ± 0.037) and larger for M_{LCS3} (1.043 ± 0.032 versus 0.950 ± 0.034). However, we must recall that the New Zealand datasets we analyzed do not have the same amount of data as those analyzed by Christophersen *et al.* (2024).

The ratios between β_1(MM) and β_1(OLS) for M_{LNZ77} and M_{LCS3} datasets computed by us, using the variances reported by Christophersen *et al.* (2024) ($\sigma_{Lx}^2 = 0.0006$ and $\sigma_{Lx}^2 = 0.002$, respectively), are 1.005 and 1.014, respectively, in reasonable agreement with those computed by them (1.004 and 1.012, respectively).

The equation error variance σ_q^2 estimated by equation (22) is negative for all σ_x, when $\sigma_y = 0.2$, as suggested by Christophersen *et al.* (2024). This is a further clue that such an error estimate is probably too large. If $\sigma_y = 0.1$, σ_q^2 is positive for $\sigma_x \leq 0.12$, ≤ 0.15, and ≤ 0.12 for M_{LNZ77}, M_{LCS3}, and M_{LISIDe}, respectively, and negative above such values. When σ_q^2 is negative, it does not make sense to apply the correction of equation (22) to the variance ratio η used by the EIV method, and we can infer that the equation error is so small as to be negligible. Alternative explanations suggested by a reviewer are that in such cases, the errors of the two variables may be correlated or not accurately specified. We already excluded in most cases that errors are correlated; we cannot exclude that errors are not accurate, and in fact, we test various possible error estimates.

In cases σ_q^2 is positive, applying the correction results in a slope estimated by the EIV method (indicated as $\mathrm{EIV_{corr}}$) very close (to the second/third decimal) to that estimated by the MM method (see Tables 1–3).

CONCLUSIONS

We analyzed the problem of the possible contribution of the equation error (that is, the epistemic uncertainty due to the poor knowledge of the true functional relation existing among regressed variables) to regressions between moment magnitude M_w and local magnitude M_L.

We studied the effects of equation error by comparing two regression methods used in magnitude conversions: the OLS method, considering the measurement error on the dependent variable M_w only, and the EIV method (Fuller, 1987), also known as general GOR, which considers instead the errors on both variables.

Ignoring the error of the independent variable (M_L), as done by the OLS method, produces a bias of the regressi on slope called "attenuation" (namely, an underestimation) (Fuller, 1987; Carroll and Ruppert, 1996). On the other hand, Carroll and Ruppert (1996) argued that the EIV method might overestimate the regression slope if the equation error is ignored and suggested using instead the regression MM (Fuller, 1987; Cheng and Van Ness, 1999).

We follow Carroll and Ruppert (1996) to estimate the equation error variance σ_q^2 by subtracting the contributions of the variances of the two variables from the regression variance (equation 23), using the regression slope computed by the MM method. As noted by Carroll and Ruppert (1996), there is no guarantee that such an estimate of σ_q^2 is positive.

We found that σ_q^2 strictly depends on the estimates of measurement errors of the two regressed variables. If the error of the dependent variable M_w is assumed relatively large (e.g., 0.2 m.u., as suggested by Christophersen *et al.*, 2024), σ_q^2 results are always negative, meaning that the equation error is substantially negligible. In such a case, the slope of the regression line

TABLE 1
Slopes and Corresponding Errors for Regression Between M_{wNZ} and M_{LNZ77}

σ_{M_w}	σ_{M_L}	β_1(OLS)	$\sigma_{\beta_1(OLS)}$	β_1(MM)	$\sigma_{\beta_1(MM)}$	β_1(EIV)	$\sigma_{\beta_1(EIV)}$	σ_q^2	$\beta_1(EIV_{corr})$	$\sigma_{\beta_1(EIV_{corr})}$
0.2	0.024	1.133	0.037	1.139	0.037	1.137	0.037	−0.009	–	–
0.2	0.045	1.133	0.037	1.153	0.037	1.148	0.037	−0.011	–	–
0.2	0.07	1.133	0.037	1.182	0.039	1.166	0.038	−0.015	–	–
0.2	0.10	1.133	0.037	1.238	0.042	1.193	0.039	−0.022	–	–
0.2	0.12	1.133	0.037	1.290	0.046	1.211	0.039	−0.029	–	–
0.2	0.15	1.133	0.037	1.400	0.056	1.237	0.040	−0.044	–	–
0.2	0.18	1.133	0.037	1.561	0.078	1.259	0.041	−0.065	–	–
0.2	0.20	1.133	0.037	1.713	0.104	1.272	0.041	−0.086	–	–
0.1	0.024	1.133	0.037	1.139	0.037	1.149	0.037	0.021	1.138	0.037
0.1	0.045	1.133	0.037	1.153	0.037	1.183	0.038	0.019	1.153	0.037
0.1	0.07	1.133	0.037	1.182	0.039	1.229	0.040	0.015	1.182	0.038
0.1	0.10	1.133	0.037	1.238	0.042	1.272	0.041	0.008	1.237	0.040
0.1	0.12	1.133	0.037	1.290	0.046	1.293	0.042	0.001	1.289	0.042
0.1	0.15	1.133	0.037	1.400	0.056	1.315	0.043	−0.014	–	–
0.1	0.18	1.133	0.037	1.561	0.078	1.329	0.043	−0.035	–	–
0.1	0.20	1.133	0.037	1.713	0.104	1.335	0.043	−0.056	–	–

σ_{M_w} and σ_{M_L} assumed errors of regressed variables, β_1 and σ_{β_1} computed values of regression slopes and relative standard errors for various models. EIV, not corrected error in variable method; EIV_{corr}, error-in-variable methods corrected for equation error according to equation (22); MM, methods of moments; OLS, ordinary least-squares method; and σ_q^2, equation error variance estimated by equation (23).

TABLE 2
Slopes and Corresponding Errors for Regression Between M_{wNZ} and M_{LSC3}

σ_{M_w}	σ_{M_L}	β_1(OLS)	$\sigma_{\beta_1(OLS)}$	β_1(MM)	$\sigma_{\beta_1(MM)}$	β_1(EIV)	$\sigma_{\beta_1(EIV)}$	σ_q^2	$\beta_1(EIV_{corr})$	$\sigma_{\beta_1(EIV_{corr})}$
0.2	0.024	0.950	0.034	0.953	0.034	0.953	0.034	−0.004	–	–
0.2	0.045	0.950	0.034	0.963	0.035	0.961	0.034	−0.006	–	–
0.2	0.07	0.950	0.034	0.982	0.035	0.976	0.035	−0.008	–	–
0.2	0.10	0.950	0.034	1.018	0.037	0.999	0.036	−0.013	–	–
0.2	0.12	0.950	0.034	1.052	0.039	1.016	0.036	−0.018	–	–
0.2	0.15	0.950	0.034	1.120	0.045	1.042	0.037	−0.028	–	–
0.2	0.18	0.950	0.034	1.216	0.055	1.066	0.038	−0.041	–	–
0.2	0.20	0.950	0.034	1.301	0.066	1.080	0.039	−0.053	–	–
0.1	0.024	0.950	0.034	0.953	0.034	0.963	0.034	0.026	0.953	0.034
0.1	0.045	0.950	0.034	0.963	0.035	0.991	0.036	0.024	0.963	0.034
0.1	0.07	0.950	0.034	0.982	0.035	1.033	0.037	0.022	0.982	0.035
0.1	0.10	0.950	0.034	1.018	0.037	1.080	0.039	0.017	1.018	0.036
0.1	0.12	0.950	0.034	1.052	0.039	1.104	0.040	0.012	1.051	0.038
0.1	0.15	0.950	0.034	1.120	0.045	1.132	0.041	0.002	1.119	0.040
0.1	0.18	0.950	0.034	1.216	0.055	1.150	0.041	−0.011	–	–
0.1	0.20	0.950	0.034	1.301	0.066	1.159	0.042	−0.023	–	–

Abbreviations as in Table 1.

computed by the MM is always larger than that computed by the EIV. Therefore, there is no risk of slope overestimation using the EIV, but rather using the MM.

If the error of the dependent variable M_w is smaller (e.g., 0.1 m.u. or less, as suggested by Helffrich, 1997; Kagan 2002, 2003; Lolli *et al.*, 2014, 2023), σ_q^2 is positive for any value of the error of M_L lower than about 0.12–0.15 m.u. and negative if the error is larger than that. In case σ_q^2 is positive, the application of the correction to the variance ratio η of equation (22), as suggested by Carroll and Ruppert (1996), makes the regression slope computed by the EIV and the MM methods almost exactly coincide with each other.

The error of M_L is estimated to be of the order of 0.024–0.045 m.u. by Christophersen *et al.* (2024) (computed as square roots of mean variances of M_{Lx} observations reported in their table 5) and of the order of 0.15–0.20 m.u. by Kagan (2003) and Gasperini *et al.* (2013b). The two error ranges have very different consequences because, assuming the former, the equation error might result in significant consequences, whereas with the latter, it is almost negligible in most cases.

TABLE 3
Slopes and Corresponding Errors for Regression Between M_w and M_{LIside}

σ_{M_w}	σ_{M_L}	β_1(OLS)	$\sigma_{\beta_1(OLS)}$	β_1(MM)	$\sigma_{\beta_1(MM)}$	β_1(EIV)	$\sigma_{\beta_1(EIV)}$	σ_q^2	$\beta_1(EIV_{corr})$	$\sigma_{\beta_1(EIV_{corr})}$
0.2	0.024	0.922	0.014	0.924	0.014	0.924	0.014	−0.015	–	–
0.2	0.045	0.922	0.014	0.930	0.014	0.927	0.014	−0.016	–	–
0.2	0.07	0.922	0.014	0.942	0.014	0.933	0.014	−0.018	–	–
0.2	0.10	0.922	0.014	0.963	0.014	0.943	0.014	−0.023	–	–
0.2	0.12	0.922	0.014	0.982	0.015	0.951	0.014	−0.027	–	–
0.2	0.15	0.922	0.014	1.020	0.016	0.962	0.014	−0.035	–	–
0.2	0.18	0.922	0.014	1.069	0.019	0.972	0.014	−0.046	–	–
0.2	0.20	0.922	0.014	1.111	0.021	0.979	0.014	−0.055	–	–
0.1	0.024	0.922	0.014	0.924	0.014	0.928	0.014	0.015	0.924	0.014
0.1	0.045	0.922	0.014	0.930	0.014	0.940	0.014	0.014	0.930	0.014
0.1	0.07	0.922	0.014	0.942	0.014	0.958	0.014	0.012	0.942	0.014
0.1	0.10	0.922	0.014	0.963	0.014	0.979	0.014	0.007	0.963	0.014
0.1	0.12	0.922	0.014	0.982	0.015	0.990	0.015	0.003	0.982	0.014
0.1	0.15	0.922	0.014	1.020	0.016	1.002	0.015	−0.005	–	–
0.1	0.18	0.922	0.014	1.069	0.019	1.012	0.015	−0.016	–	–
0.1	0.20	0.922	0.014	1.111	0.021	1.016	0.015	−0.025	–	–

Abbreviations as in Table 1.

Generally speaking, the error of M_w should be lower than that of M_L because the former is more strictly constrained by data because it is computed using the whole broadband recording and by considering a realistic propagation pattern from the seismic source by means of the simultaneous determination of the moment tensor (Dziewonski *et al.*, 1981; Arvidsson and Ekström, 1998; Dreger, 2003), whereas the latter is less constrained because it is computed only using the maximum recorded amplitude and assuming a circularly symmetric attenuation law. Hence, we believe that the errors estimated by Christophersen *et al.* (2024) are not fully appropriate.

In summary, we suggest not using the OLS regression method in magnitude conversions because it tends to underestimate the regression slope (Fuller, 1987; Carroll and Ruppert, 1996). The MM method suggested by Carroll and Ruppert (1996) might represent a valid alternative if the error of the independent variable (M_L) is relatively small (<0.12–0.15 m.u.) but provides unrealistically large slopes for larger errors. Hence, our preference goes to the EIV method because it provides realistic estimates in most cases, and eventually, when the error of M_L is demonstrated to be particularly small, it is possible to consistently account for the contribution of equation error using equations (21) and (22).

The use of the OLS in place of the EIV in magnitude conversions may have consequences on both seismic hazards assessment and statistical earthquake forecasting studies. In fact, Castellaro *et al.* (2006) demonstrated that the use of OLS biases upward the *b* value of the FMD (Gutenberg and Richter, 1944). The reason is that the slope attenuation (flattening) induced by the OLS method artificially reduces the proxy magnitude of large-magnitude earthquakes and correspondingly increases the proxy magnitude of small earthquakes, thus increasing the *b* value. This effect is clearly evidenced by comparing two versions of the reference seismic catalog used for seismic hazard assessment in Italy, named CPTI04 (CPTI Working Group, 2004) and CPTI15 (Rovida *et al.*, 2020) for which OLS and EIV regressions are used, respectively, for converting traditional magnitudes to M_w. The overall *b* value of CPTI04 resulted in about 1.3–1.5, with errors of the order of 0.1 (Rong *et al.*, 2011), well above the global *b* value average of about 1, while that of CPTI15 coincides with such global average within errors (Rovida *et al.*, 2020).

In hazard assessment, the overestimation of the *b* value would have the effect of underestimating the expected rates of the largest earthquakes. The *b* value is a key parameter even for earthquake forecasting studies because it was suggested to be a proxy of the state of stress within the Earth's crust; the smaller the *b* value, the larger the stress (Scholz, 1968, 2015; Amitrano, 2003). Accordingly, it was used in recent studies (e.g., Gulia and Wiemer, 2019; Gulia *et al.*, 2024; Biondini *et al.*, 2025) as a possible indicator of the state of preparation of a future strong earthquake.

DATA AND RESOURCES

The New Zealand seismic catalog file revalued by Christophersen *et al.* (2024) is available at the site doi: 10.21420/tap4-5s59 as data file "Cat_NSHM_magnitudes-revised_August22.csv." It contains the data of 452,848 earthquakes from 1460 to 31 December 2020. The Italian dataset built by Lolli *et al* (2020) is available at the website https://horus.bo.ingv.it as data file "HORUS_Ita_DataOrigin.txt." It contains the data of about 490,000 earthquakes from 1981 to the time the file is downloaded (it is updated hourly based on the data of the Istituto Nazionale di Geofisica e Vulcanologia [INGV] ISIDe webservices). The MATLAB scripts used to make all computations are freely available at https://github.com/Biondini/Empirical_regressions. All websites were last accessed in December 2024.

DECLARATION OF COMPETING INTERESTS

The authors acknowledge that there are no conflicts of interest recorded.

ACKNOWLEDGMENTS

The authors thank Associate Editor Silvia Castellaro, Trevor Allen, and four other anonymous reviewers for their thoughtful comments and suggestions, which helped much to improve the article. This article benefited from funding provided by the Istituto Nazionale di Geofisica e Vulcanologia, Italy, grant "Progetto INGV Pianeta Dinamico (NEMESIS)"—code CUP D53J19000170001—funded by the Italian Ministry MIUR and by the European Union, within the ambit of the H2020 project RISE (Number 821115), by the Eidgenössische Technische Hochschule Zürich (ETHZ), and by the Dipartimento di Fisica e Astronomia of the Università di Bologna, which partially financed the Postdoc grant of one of the authors (E. B.).

REFERENCES

Allen, T. I., J. D. Griffin, D. J. Clark, P. R. Cummins, H. Ghasemi, and R. Ebrahimi (2023). *The 2023 National Seismic Hazard Assessment for Australia: Model Overview, Record 2023/53*, Geoscience Australia, Canberra, doi: 10.26186/148969.

Amitrano, D. (2003). Brittle-ductile transition and associated seismicity: Experimental and numerical studies and relationship with the b value, *J. Geophys. Res.* **108,** no. B1, doi: 10.1029/2001JB000680.

Arvidsson, R., and G. Ekström (1998). Global CMT analysis of moderate earthquakes $M_w \geq 4.5$ using intermediate period surface waves, *Bull. Seismol. Soc. Am.* **88,** 1003–1013.

Biondini, E., F. D'Orazio, B. Lolli, and P. Gasperini (2025). Pseudo-prospective earthquake forecasting experiment in Italy based on temporal variation of the b-value of the Gutenberg–Richter law, *Geophys. J. Int.* **240,** no. 3, 1755–1772, doi: 10.1093/gji/ggaf005.

Carroll, R. J., and D. Ruppert (1996). The use and misuse of orthogonal regression in linear errors-in-variables models, *Am. Stat.* **5,** no. 1, 1–6.

Castellaro, S., and P. Bormann (2007). Performance of different regression procedures on the magnitude conversion problem, *Bull. Seismol. Soc. Am.* **97,** no. 4, 1167–1175, doi: 10.1785/0120060102.

Castellaro, S., F. Mulargia, and Y. Y. Kagan (2006). Regression problems for magnitudes, *Geophys. J. Int.* **165,** 913–930, doi: 10.1111/j.1365-246X.2006.02955.x.

Cheng, C., and J. Riu (2006). On estimating linear relationships when both variables are subject to heteroscedastic measurement errors, *Technometrics* **48,** no. 4, 511–519, doi: 10.1198/004017006000000237.

Cheng, C. L., and J. W. Van Ness (1999). *Statistical Regression With Measurement Error, London*, Arnold, New York, Oxford University Press.

Christophersen, A., S. Bourguignon, D. A. Rhoades, T. I. Allen, J. Ristau, J. Salichon, J. C. Rollins, J. Townend, and M. C. Gerstenberger (2024). Standardizing earthquake magnitudes for the 2022 revision of the Aotearoa New Zealand National Seismic Hazard Model, *Bull. Seismol. Soc. Am.* **114,** no. 1, 111–136, doi: 10.1785/0120230169.

CPTI Working Group (2004). Catalogo Parametrico dei Terremoti Italiani, versione 2004 (CPTI04), INGV, Bologna, available at http://emidius.mi.ingv.it/CPTI04/ (in Italian) (last accessed December 2024).

Das, R., H. R. Wason, G. Gonzalez, M. L. Sharma, D. Choudhury, C. Lindholm, N. Roy, and P. Salazar (2018). Earthquake magnitude conversion problem, *Bull. Seismol. Soc. Am.* doi: 10.1785/0120170157.

Deichmann, N. (2006). Local magnitude, a moment revisited, *Bull. Seismol. Soc. Am.* **96,** no. 4A, 1267–1277, doi: 10.1785/0120050115.

Deichmann, N. (2017). Theoretical basis for the observed break in ML/M_w scaling between small and large earthquakes, *Bull. Seismol. Soc. Am.* **107,** no. 2, 505–520, doi: 10.1785/0120160318.

Dreger, D. S. (2003). TDMT_INV: Time domain seismic moment tensor inversion, in *International Handbook of Earthquake and Engineering Seismology*, W. H. K. Lee, H. Kanamori, P. C. Jennings, and C. Kisslinger (Editors), Academic Press, London.

Dziewonski, A. M., T.-A. Chou, and J. Woodhouse (1981). Determination of earthquake source parameters from waveform data for studies of global and regional seismicity, *J. Geophys. Res.* **86,** 2825–2852.

Ekström, G., and A. M. Dziewonski (1988). Evidence of bias in estimation of earthquake size, *Nature* **332,** 319–323.

Engdahl, E. R., and R. H. Gunst (1966). Use of a high speed computer for the preliminary determination of earthquake hypocenters, *Bull. Seismol. Soc. Am.* **56,** 325–338, doi: 10.1785/BSSA0560020325.

Finetti, I., and C. Morelli (1972). Earthquake magnitude determination for Trieste WWSS station, *Boll. Geof. Teor. Appl.* **XIV,** 67–83.

Fuller, W. A. (1987). *Measurement Error Models*, Wiley, New York, New York, 440 pp. (note that we actually refer to the integral reprint dated 2006).

Gasperini, P., B. Lolli, and S. Castellaro (2023). Comment on "Earthquake Magnitude Conversion Problem" by Ranjit Das, H. R. Wason, Gabriel Gonzalez, M. L. Sharma, Deepankar Choudhury, Conrad Lindholm, Narayan Roy, and Pablo Salazar, *Bull. Seismol. Soc. Am.* **113,** 1366–1369, doi: 10.1785/0120180243.

Gasperini, P., B. Lolli, and G. Vannucci (2013a). Body-wave magnitude mb is a good proxy of moment magnitude M_w for small earthquakes (mb < 4.5–5.0), *Seismol. Res. Lett.* **84,** no. 6, 932–937, doi: 10.1785/0220130105.

Gasperini, P., B. Lolli, and G. Vannucci (2013b). Empirical calibration of local magnitude data sets versus moment magnitude in Italy, *Bull. Seismol. Soc. Am.* **103,** 2227–2246, doi: 10.1785/0120120356.

Gerstenberger, M. C., and D. A. Rhoades (2010). New Zealand earthquake forecast testing centre, *Pure Appl. Geophys.* **167,** 877–892, doi: 10.1007/s00024-010-0082-4.

Giardini, D., M. Di Donato, and E. Boschi (1997). Calibration of magnitude scales for earthquakes of the Mediterranean, *J. Seismol.* **1,** 161–180.

Grünthal, G., and R. Wahlström (2003). An M_W based earthquake catalogue for central, northern and northwestern Europe using a hierarchy of magnitude conversions, *J. Seismol.* **7,** no. 4, 507–531.

Gulia, L., and S. Wiemer (2019). Real-time discrimination of earthquake foreshocks and aftershocks, *Nature* **574,** 193–199, doi: 10.1038/s41586-019-1606-4.

Gulia, L., S. Wiemer, E. Biondini, B. Enescu, and G. Vannucci (2024). Improving the foreshock traffic light systems for real-time discrimination between foreshocks and aftershocks, *Seismol. Res. Lett.* **95,** no. 6, 3579–3592, doi: 10.1785/0220240163.

Gutenberg, B. (1945a). Amplitudes of surface waves and magnitudes of shallow earthquakes, *Bull. Seismol. Soc. Am.* **35,** 3–12, doi: 10.1785/BSSA0350010037.

Gutenberg, B. (1945b). Magnitude determination for deep-focus earthquakes, *Bull. Seismol. Soc. Am.* **35,** 117–130, doi: 10.1785/BSSA0350030117.

Gutenberg, B., and C. F. Richter (1944). Frequency of earthquakes in California, *Bull. Seismol. Soc. Am.* **34,** 185–188.

Hanks, T. C., and H. Kanamori (1979). A moment magnitude scale, *J. Geophys. Res.* **84,** 2348–2350.

Helffrich, G. R. (1997). How good are routinely determined focal mechanisms? Empirical statistics based on a comparison of Harvard, USGS and ERI moment tensors, *Geophys. J. Int.* **131,** 741–750.

Johnston, A. C. (1996). Seismic moment assessment of earthquakes in stable continental regions-I. Instrumental seismicity, *Geophys. J. Int.* **124,** 381–414.

Kagan, Y. Y. (2002). Seismic moment distribution revisited: I. Statistical results, *Geophys. J. Int.* **148,** 520–541.

Kagan, Y. Y. (2003). Accuracy of modem global earthquake catalogs, *Phys. Earth Planet. In.* **135,** nos. 2/3, 173–209.

Kanamori, H. (1977). The energy release in great earthquakes, *J. Geophys. Res.* **82,** 2981–2987.

Kanamori, H., and D. L. Anderson (1975). Theoretical basis of some empirical relations in seismology, *Bull. Seismol. Soc. Am.* **65,** no. 5, 1073–1095, doi: 10.1785/BSSA0650051073.

Karnik, V., N. V. Kondorskaya, Y. V. Riznichenko, Y. F. Savarensky, S. L. Soloviev, N. V. Shebalin, J. Vanek, and A. Zatopek (1962). Standardisation of the earthquake magnitude scales, *Stud. Geophys. Geod.* **6,** 41–48.

Kim, W.-Y. (1998). The M f scale in eastern North America, *Bull. Seismol. Soc. Am.* **88,** no. 4, 935–951, doi: 10.1785/BSSA0880040935.

Lolli, B., and P. Gasperini (2012). A comparison among general orthogonal regression methods applied to earthquakes magnitude conversions, *Geophys. J. Int.* **190,** 1135–1151, doi: 10.1111/j.1365-246X.2012.05530.x.

Lolli, B., P. Gasperini, and G. Vannucci (2014). Empirical conversion between teleseismic magnitudes (mb and Ms) and moment magnitude (M_w) at the Global, Euro-Mediterranean and Italian scale, *Geophys. J. Int.* **199,** 805–828, doi: 10.1093/gji/ggu264.

Lolli, B., D. Randazzo, G. Vannucci, E. Biondini, and P. Gasperini (2023). Homogenization of magnitudes of the ISC Bulletin, *Geophys. J. Int.* **234,** 1771–1785, doi: 10.1093/gji/ggad164.

Lolli, B., D. Randazzo, G. Vannucci, and P. Gasperini (2020). The homogenized instrumental seismic catalog (HORUS) of Italy from 1960 to present, *Seismol. Res. Lett.* **91,** 3208–3222, doi: 10.1785/0220200148.

Malagnini, L., and I. Munafò (2018). On the relationship between ML and M_w in a broad range: An example from the Apennines, Italy, *Bull. Seismol. Soc. Am.* **108,** no. 2, 1018–1024, doi: 10.1785/0120170303.

Purcaru, G., and H. Berckhemer (1978). A magnitude scale for very large earthquakes, *Tectonophysics* **49,** 189–198.

Richter, C. F. (1935). An instrumental earthquake magnitude scale, *Bull. Seismol. Soc. Am.* **25,** 1–31.

Rong, Y., M. Mahdyiar, B. Shen-Tu, and K. Shabestari (2011). Magnitude problems in historical earthquake catalogues and their impact on seismic hazard assessment, *Geophys. J. Int.* **187,** 1687–1698, doi: 10.1111/j.1365-246X.2011.05226.x.

Rovida, A., M. Locati, R. Camassi, B. Lolli, and P. Gasperini (2020). The Italian earthquake catalogue CPTI15, *Bull. Earthq. Eng.* **18,** 2953–2984, doi: 10.1007/s10518-020-00818-y.

Scholz, C. H. (1968). The frequency-magnitude relation of microfracturing in rock and its relation to earthquakes, *Bull. Seismol. Soc. Am.* **58,** 399–415, doi: 10.1785/BSSA0580010399.

Scholz, C. H. (2015). On the stress dependence of the earthquake b value, *Geophys. Res. Lett.* **42,** 1399–1402, doi: 10.1002/2014GL062863.

Scordilis, E. M. (2006). Empirical global relations converting MS and mb to moment magnitude, *J. Seismol.* **10,** 225–236.

Staudenmaier, N., T. Tormann, B. Edwards, N. Deichmann, and S. Wiemer (2018). Bilinearity in the Gutenberg-Richter relation based on ML for magnitudes above and below 2, from systematic magnitude assessments in Parkfield (California), *Geophys. Res. Lett.* **45,** 6887–6897, doi: 10.1029/2018GL078316.

Stromeyer, D., G. Grünthal, and R. Wahlström (2004). Chi-square regression for seismic strength parameter relations, and their uncertainties, with applications to an M_w based earthquake catalogue for central, northern and northwestern Europe, *J. Seismol.* **8,** no. 1, 143–153.

Thatcher, W., and T. H. Hanks (1973). Source parameters of southern California earthquakes, *J. Geophys. Res.* **78,** 8547–8576.

Weisberg, S. (1985). *Applied Linear Regression*, Second Ed., John Wiley, New York.

Weisberg, S. (2014). *Applied Linear Regression*, Fourth Ed., John Wiley & Sons Inc., Hoboken, New Jersey, 340 pp.

APPENDIX

Estimation of the regression parameters and of the corresponding errors by various regression methods

According to section 1.3.2 of Fuller (1987) (at pp.30–31), if the ratio $\eta = \sigma_y^2/\sigma_x^2$ between the measurement variances of the dependent (y) and independent (x) variables is known, the regression slope can be computed as

$$\beta_1(\mathrm{EIV}) = \frac{s_{yy} - \eta s_{xx} + \sqrt{(s_{yy} - \eta s_{xx})^2 + 4\eta s_{xy}^2}}{2s_{xy}}, \qquad \text{(A1)}$$

in which

$$s_{xx} = \frac{1}{N-1}\sum_{i=1}^{N}(x_i - \bar{x})^2, \qquad \text{(A2)}$$

$$s_{yy} = \frac{1}{N-1}\sum_{i=1}^{N}(y - \bar{y})^2, \qquad \text{(A3)}$$

$$s_{xy} = \frac{1}{N-1}\sum_{i=1}^{N}(x_i - \bar{x})(y - \bar{y}), \qquad \text{(A4)}$$

with

$$\bar{x} = \frac{1}{N}\sum_{i=1}^{N} x_i, \qquad \text{(A5)}$$

$$\bar{y} = \frac{1}{N}\sum_{i=1}^{N} y_i. \qquad \text{(A6)}$$

The standard error of β_1(EIV) can be computed as

$$\sigma_{\beta_1(\mathrm{EIV})} = \sqrt{\frac{s_{xx}\sigma_v^2(\mathrm{EIV}) - \beta_1^2(\mathrm{EIV})\sigma_{uu}}{\sigma_{xx}^2(N-1)}}, \quad \text{(A7)}$$

in which

$$\sigma_v^2(\mathrm{EIV}) = \frac{\sum_{i=1}^{N}[y_i - \bar{y} - \beta_1(\mathrm{EIV})(x_i - \bar{x})]^2}{N-2} = \frac{(N-1)[\eta + \beta_1^2(\mathrm{EIV})]\sigma_{uu}^2}{N-2}, \quad \text{(A8)}$$

$$\sigma_{xx} = \frac{\sqrt{(s_{yy} - \eta s_{xx})^2 + 4\eta s_{xy}^2} - (s_{yy} - \eta s_{xx})}{2\eta}, \quad \text{(A9)}$$

$$\sigma_{uu} = \frac{s_{yy} - \eta s_{xx} - \sqrt{(s_{yy} - \eta s_{xx})^2 + 4\eta s_{xy}^2}}{2\eta}. \quad \text{(A10)}$$

According to section 1.2.1 of Fuller (1987) (pp. 13–14), the slope derived by the MM for the case when the measurement variance of the independent variable σ_x^2 is known, is

$$\beta_1(\mathrm{MM}) = \frac{s_{xy}}{s_{xx} - \sigma_x^2}, \quad \text{(A11)}$$

the error of β_1(MM) can be computed as

$$\sigma_{\beta_1(\mathrm{MM})} = \sqrt{\frac{(s_{xx}\sigma_v^2 + \beta_1^2(\mathrm{MM})\sigma_x^4)}{(s_{xx} - \sigma_x^2)^2(N-1)}}, \quad \text{(A12)}$$

in which

$$\sigma_v^2 = \frac{\sum_{i=1}^{N}[y_i - \bar{y} - \beta_1(x_i - \bar{x})]^2}{N-2}. \quad \text{(A13)}$$

When the error variance of the independent variable is negligible ($\sigma_x^2 \approx 0$) the slope becomes

$$\beta_1(\mathrm{OLS}) = \frac{s_{xy}}{s_{xx}}, \quad \text{(A14)}$$

and the error

$$\sigma_{\beta_1(\mathrm{OLS})} = \sqrt{\frac{\sigma_v^2}{s_{xx}(N-1)}}. \quad \text{(A15)}$$

For all models, the intercept term can be computed as

$$\beta_0 = \bar{y} - \beta_1\bar{x}, \quad \text{(A16)}$$

and the corresponding error as

$$\sigma_{\beta_0} = \sqrt{\bar{x}^2\sigma_{\beta_1}^2 + \frac{\sigma_v^2}{N}}. \quad \text{(A17)}$$

The covariance of β_0 and β_1 can also be computed as

$$\mathrm{Cov}_{\beta_0,\beta_1} = -\bar{x}\sigma_{\beta_1}^2. \quad \text{(A18)}$$

Manuscript received 13 January 2025
Published online 28 October 2025

Regional and Depth Variations in Source-Scaling Properties for Subduction Earthquakes

Yujia Guo*[1], Ken Miyakoshi[1], and Kojiro Irikura[2]

ABSTRACT

Scaling relationships for earthquake source parameters provide fundamental information for characterizing source faults and simulating ground motions and/or tsunamis for scenario earthquakes. For subduction earthquakes, although variations in the physical properties of subducting oceanic plates, such as temperature, subduction velocity, and seismogenic zone depth, have been identified between subduction zones with different tectonic environments, whether variations in source-scaling relationships exist is still under debate. We investigated the regional variations in source parameters for subduction earthquakes by extracting these parameters from heterogeneous slip models for many events (M_w 6.7–9.1) in nine regions, based on source inversion analyses conducted by the U.S. Geological Survey. Regional differences were observed in the mean residuals of the extracted rupture areas with respect to the scaling relationship, although these differences were not substantial enough to reach statistical significance. Meanwhile, by investigating the depth of the source fault for each event, we found a depth-related variation indicating that the size of the rupture area correlates with the top depth of the source fault. This correlation leads to a magnitude-dependent scatter in rupture area and complicates the self-similar scaling model for events with M_w less than 8.4. For small magnitude ($M_w < 7.5$), the event for which rupture propagates upward and extends to the shallow part of the subduction zone has a larger rupture area, whereas the event propagating only downward has a smaller rupture area. The coexistence of these two event types for M_w less than 7.5 increases the scatter in the scaling relationship of rupture area. For large magnitude (M_w 7.5–8.4), most events extend ruptures to the shallow part of the subduction zone and have larger rupture areas, and thus the scatter is smaller than that for small M_w. The association between rupture propagation direction and rupture area may be useful for updating seismic hazard assessment for subduction earthquakes.

KEY POINTS

- We analyze the source scaling of global subduction earthquakes in terms of their location and depth.
- Some regional variation may exist, but the current dataset does not support definitive conclusions.
- For small M_w, coexistence of events with and without shallow rupture leads to a large scatter in rupture area.

Supplemental Material

INTRODUCTION

In characterizing source models for scenario subduction earthquakes expected in the future, source parameters should be set based on the source characteristics of past earthquakes, which are considered to depend on the regionality of subduction zones.

Estimating source parameters, such as the rupture area and the average slip, from a heterogeneous slip model obtained by source inversion analysis is efficient. For past subduction earthquakes, this approach has been widely utilized not only for developing empirical scaling relationships for source parameters (Murotani *et al.*, 2008, 2013; Tajima *et al.*, 2013; Goda *et al.*, 2016; Skarlatoudis *et al.*, 2016; Allen and Hayes, 2017; Thingbaijam *et al.*, 2017), but also for examining their regional variations (Allen and Hayes, 2017; Ogawa *et al.*, 2021). Thanks to these studies, there is currently a vast dataset of source parameters based on heterogeneous slip models. However, these source parameters were extracted using various procedures (Somerville *et al.*, 1999; Mai and Beroza, 2000; Murotani *et al.*, 2013; Thingbaijam and Mai, 2016; Allen

1. Ohsaki Research Institute, Inc., Tokyo, Japan, https://orcid.org/0000-0002-8850-1824 (YG); https://orcid.org/0000-0003-1526-8627 (KM); 2. Disaster Prevention Research Center, Aichi Institute of Technology, Aichi, Japan, https://orcid.org/0000-0001-8477-2478 (KI)

*Corresponding author: y.guo@ohsaki.co.jp

Cite this article as Guo, Y., K. Miyakoshi, and K. Irikura (2025). Regional and Depth Variations in Source-Scaling Properties for Subduction Earthquakes, *Bull. Seismol. Soc. Am.* **116**, 238–248, doi: 10.1785/0120250166

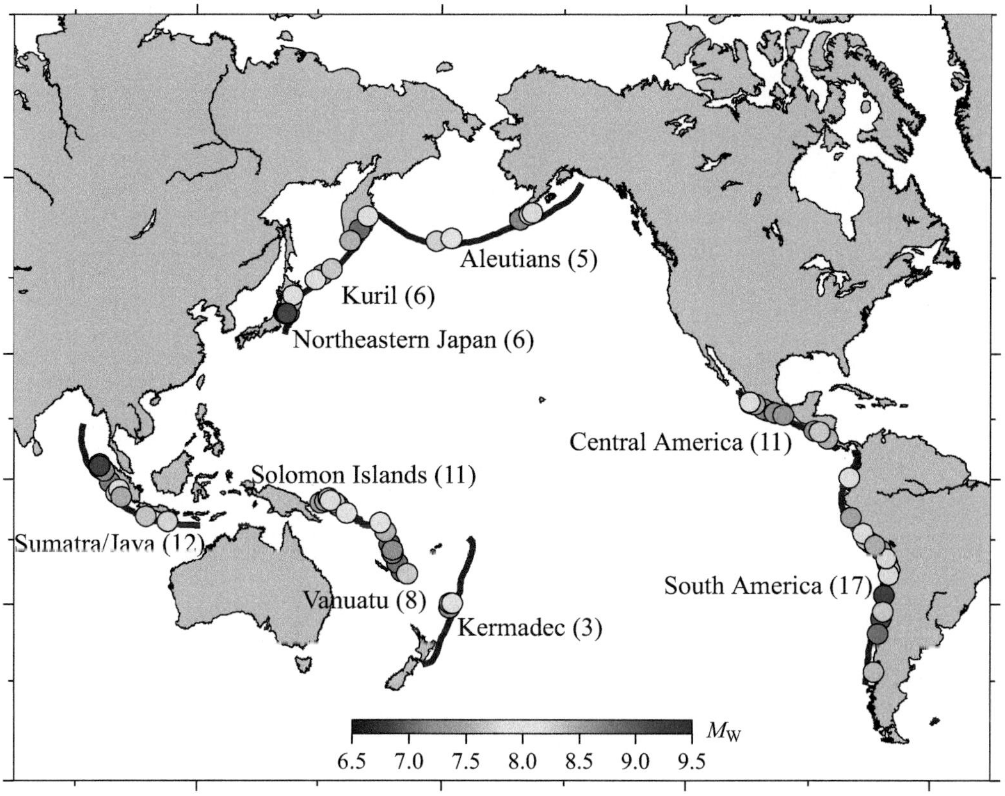

Figure 1. Epicenters of the collected 79 subduction earthquakes. The numbers in parentheses represent the number of earthquakes in each region. The color version of this figure is available only in the electronic edition.

and Hayes, 2017). Miyakoshi *et al.* (2020, 2021) showed the importance of using the source-parameter data estimated by the same procedure for validating scaling relationships or evaluating their regional variations. They focused on the dataset based on the fault trimming criteria of Somerville *et al.* (1999), which trim the edge rows or columns with less than 0.3 times the average slip of the entire slip model and define the "true" source fault as a rectangular area with an average slip of 0.3 times or more. Miyakoshi *et al.* (2021) confirmed that the scaling relationship proposed by Murotani *et al.* (2008) can adequately reproduce the rupture areas for subduction earthquakes in Japan.

In this study, using the fault length, fault width, rupture area, and average slip estimated from heterogeneous slip models of subduction earthquakes that occurred along major subduction zones, we evaluate regional variations in these parameters. These parameters are termed outer source parameters by Irikura and Miyake (2011) because they represent the overall characteristics of the source fault, in contrast to inner source parameters, such as asperity area, which describe the heterogeneity within the fault. One of our objectives is to determine whether differences in the outer source parameters exist between Japan and other regions. Thus, we follow the criteria of Somerville *et al.* (1999) in the same manner as Murotani *et al.* (2008). Furthermore, although the geometry of the seismogenic zone differs between subduction zones (Hayes *et al.*, 2018), a common feature among all subduction zones is that the depth range of their seismogenic zones is greater compared to that of inland crusts. Therefore, physical properties such as rigidity, temperature, and friction naturally have clear depth dependencies. The depth dependencies of the physical parameters are expected to correlate with those of source parameters (e.g., Bilek and Lay, 1999; Denolle and Shearer, 2016; Ye *et al.*, 2016). Therefore, we also investigate the depth dependence of the outer source parameters.

DATA AND METHOD

The heterogeneous slip models were published by the U.S. Geological Survey (USGS) (Hayes, 2017; Goldberg *et al.*, 2022), which has been conducting source inversion analyses for earthquakes worldwide with $M_w \sim 6.5$ and above since 1990. Consequently, there is a substantial number of earthquake slip models available.

We collected slip models for 79 M_w 6.7–9.1 subduction earthquakes that occurred from 1990 to 2024 in nine regions (Aleutians, Kuril, northeastern Japan, Sumatra/Java, Solomon Islands, Vanuatu, Kermadec, South America, and Central America; Fig. 1). These earthquakes did not include events that were likely intraslab earthquakes, with rake angles not within the range of 45°–135°, dip angles greater than 45°, and strikes that were obviously different from the trench axis. The seven regions, except northeastern Japan and Kuril, were based on the regional division by Hayes *et al.* (2018). Hayes *et al.* (2018) considered the Kamchatka–Kuril–Japan subduction zone as a single region, but this study divided it into two, defining the events in Japan as northeastern Japan and the others as Kuril, due to the variation in the dip angle of the subducting Pacific plate (Heuret *et al.*, 2011). The 79 events consisted of 36 events with M_w less than 7.5, 27 events with M_w between 7.5 and 7.9, and 16 events with M_w 8.0 and above. Most of the collected slip models were obtained using teleseismic waveform inversions, but the models for a few events were obtained using joint inversions of teleseismic waveforms and Global Navigation Satellite Systems (GNSS) data.

We applied the criteria of Somerville *et al.* (1999) to each slip model and trimmed the fault plane. We then compared the

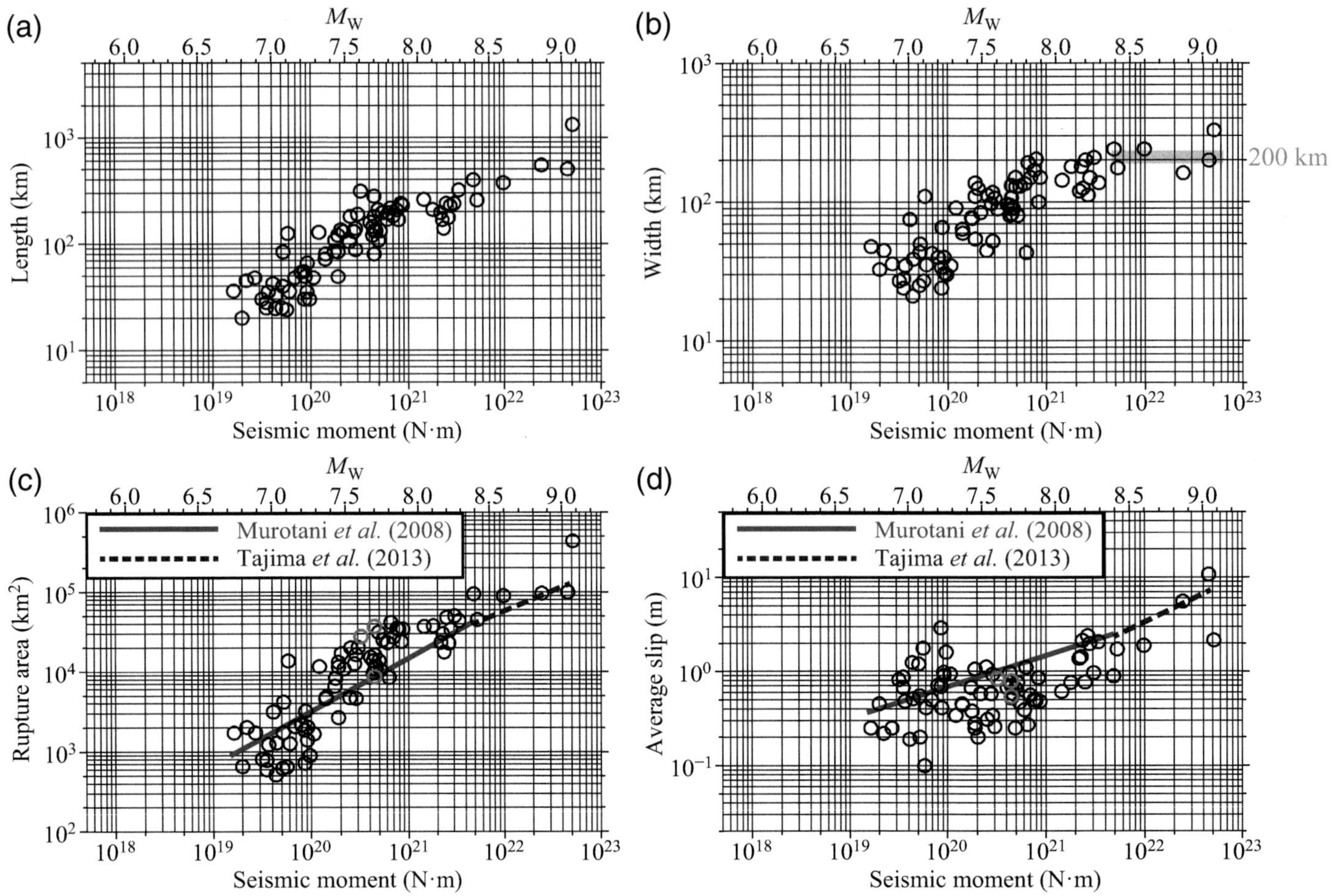

Figure 2. Scaling relationships between seismic moment and (a) fault length, (b) fault width, (c) rupture area, and (d) average slip. The gray thick line in (b) represents the saturation width. The red solid lines and blue dashed lines in (c) and (d) represent the scaling relationship of Murotani *et al.* (2008) and Tajima *et al.* (2013), respectively. The green circles in (c) and (d) represent the events classified as tsunami earthquakes based on the average slip duration in Table S1. The color version of this figure is available only in the electronic edition.

outer source parameters of the trimmed source faults with a two-stage scaling relationship (Murotani *et al.*, 2008; Tajima *et al.*, 2013). The first-stage scaling relationship proposed by Murotani *et al.* (2008), which is the standard scaling relationship for subduction earthquakes in Japan, was developed using 11 events with M_w ranging from 6.7 to 8.4. For events with M_w less than 8.4 (referred to as the "first-stage earthquakes"), the source parameters follow a self-similar scaling model with seismic moments. In other words, the rupture area (A) is proportional to the two-third power of the seismic moment (M_0) in terms of the common logarithm, while the average slip (D) is proportional to the one-third power of the seismic moment:

$$A \propto M_0^{2/3},\ D \propto M_0^{1/3}. \quad (1)$$

In contrast, for events with M_w 8.4 and above (referred to as the "second-stage earthquakes"), Tajima *et al.* (2013) proposed a non-self-similar model due to fault width saturation, based on their investigation of six events in Sumatra/Java, South America, and northeastern Japan. In this case, both the rupture area and average slip are proportional to the one-half power of the seismic moment:

$$A \propto M_0^{1/2},\ D \propto M_0^{1/2}. \quad (2)$$

GLOBAL SCALING RELATIONSHIPS BETWEEN SEISMIC MOMENT AND SOURCE PARAMETERS

Figure 2 shows the relationships between seismic moment and each source parameter (fault length, fault width, rupture area, and average slip) based on the criteria of Somerville *et al.* (1999) for the 79 events. Note that we use seismic moment values within the trimmed source faults.

The relationship between seismic moment and rupture area exhibits two distinct features (Fig. 2c). Data for M_w 7.5 and above are larger than the scaling relationship, whereas the data for M_w less than 7.5 are consistent with the scaling relationship but exhibit considerable scatter. Most of the events have smaller average slips compared to the scaling relationship, although the average slips for several events with M_w less than 7.5 exhibit large values (Fig. 2d). The fault widths reach a plateau at

~200 km (thick gray line in Fig. 2b), a value consistent with that reported by Tajima *et al.* (2013). The six events with M_w 8.4 and above in this study are the same as those studied by Tajima *et al.* (2013), although our slip models (from the USGS; primarily using teleseismic waveform data) differ from those compiled by Tajima *et al.* (2013), which were derived from published articles that inverted near-field waveform, teleseismic waveform, GNSS, and tsunami waveform data. Because similar results were obtained despite the differences in slip models, the potential bias due to model selection is likely small.

Among the 79 events analyzed in this study, three can be classified as textbook tsunami earthquakes (i.e., the 1992 M_w 7.6 Nicaragua earthquake in Central America, the 1994 M_w 7.7 Java earthquake in Sumatra/Java, and the 2006 M_w 7.7 Pangandaran earthquake in Sumatra/Java), based on their abnormally long source durations (Table S1, available in the supplemental material to this article). However, we cannot find any outlier plots corresponding to these events (green circles in Fig. 2c,d) in the relationships between seismic moment and rupture area, as well as between seismic moment and average slip. This implies that, at least for time-unrelated source parameters, tsunami earthquakes and non-tsunami earthquakes follow the same scaling relationship.

Because there is a complementary relationship between rupture area and average slip for a given seismic moment, we hereafter focus only on the rupture area. To perform a quantitative evaluation, we calculated the residuals in the common logarithm ($\log_{10}$(observation/prediction)) of the rupture-area data with respect to the scaling relationship of Murotani *et al.* (2008) and Tajima *et al.* (2013). The residuals have a mean of +0.10 for all 79 events (red diamond in Fig. 3), with a 95% confidence interval of +0.03 to +0.17 (red box in Fig. 3). Even when restricting the dataset to events with M_w less than 8.4, as targeted by Murotani *et al.* (2008), who focused only on the subduction earthquakes in Japan, the mean remains +0.10 (73 events). Furthermore, although the first-stage earthquakes are anticipated to follow the self-similar scaling model, the data distribution of the rupture area (Fig. 2c) clearly shows that there is some variation that cannot be fully explained by pure self-similarity. This leads us to conduct a more detailed investigation considering the locations where earthquakes occur (see the next section).

VARIATIONS OF SCALING RELATIONSHIP BETWEEN SEISMIC MOMENT AND RUPTURE AREA

Regional variation

First, we investigate the variation depicted in Figure 2c in terms of the difference in the subduction zone. Figure 4 shows the relationship between seismic moment and rupture area by region. It is clear that the M_w distribution of the data varies from region to region. Among the nine regions, the data for northeastern Japan, Sumatra/Java, and South America are evenly distributed from small ($M_w \sim 7$) to large ($M_w \sim 9$) magnitudes.

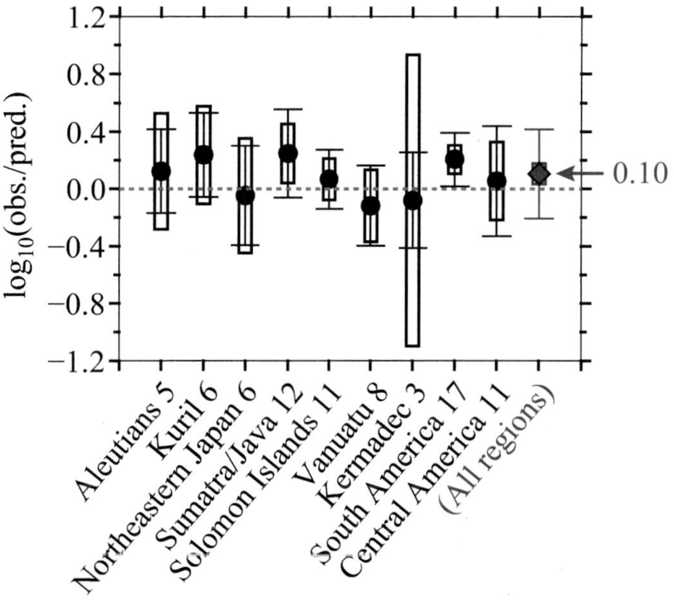

Figure 3. Means (solid circles), 95% confidence intervals (open boxes), and standard deviations (black bars) of residuals (common logarithm) of the rupture area with respect to the scaling relationship, shown for each region. The horizontal axis displays the region names along with the number of earthquake data. The red circle, box, and bar represent the mean (+0.10), 95% confidence interval, and standard deviation for all regions, respectively. The color version of this figure is available only in the electronic edition.

To identify regional variations, we calculated the mean (solid circles in Fig. 3) and the 95% confidence interval (open boxes in Fig. 3) by region for the residuals of the rupture area with respect to the scaling relationship of Murotani *et al.* (2008) and Tajima *et al.* (2013). Figure 3 shows no statistically significant differences, suggesting a lack of clear regional variations. This result is consistent with the findings of Allen and Hayes (2017), who investigated regional variations using a different fault trimming method from that employed in this study. Although some regional variations may exist in nature, the limited amount of data per region when divided into regions makes it difficult to detect such variations. To reach more definitive conclusions regarding regional variations, it is essential to conduct source inversion analyses for more earthquakes and accumulate data on source parameters.

For northeastern Japan, the mean is approximately zero, which means that the scaling relationship can reasonably predict the rupture area for the events in northeastern Japan. As a supplementary comparison, Figure 5 plots the Japanese data from this study, Murotani *et al.* (2008), and Tajima *et al.* (2013). Note that the dataset of Murotani *et al.* (2008) includes earthquake data not only for northeastern Japan (open circles in Fig. 5), but also for the Japanese regions not targeted in this study (open squares in Fig. 5), such as southwestern Japan (along the Nankai trough). Nevertheless, no clear differences are observed between northeastern Japan and the other

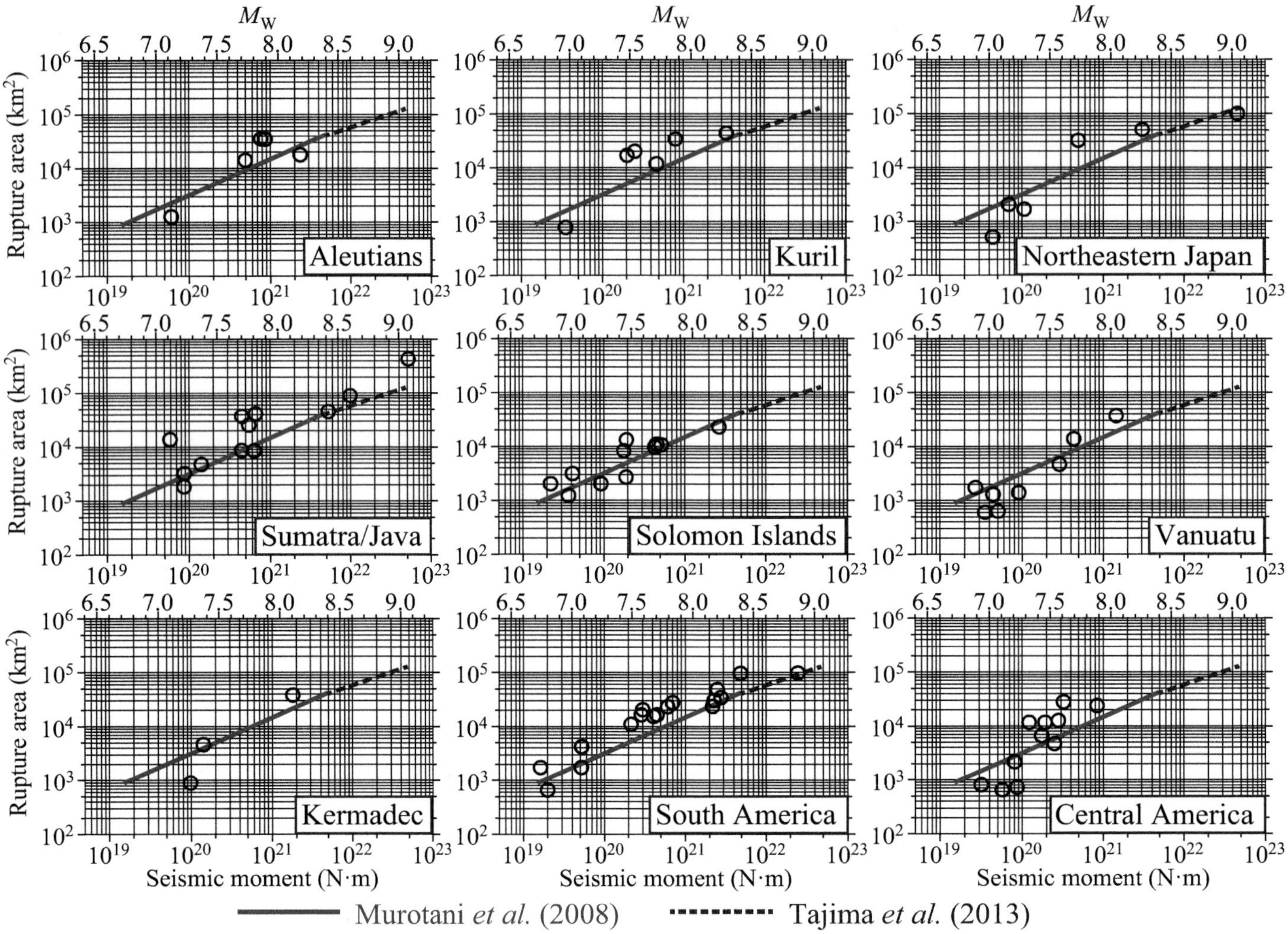

Japanese regions in this dataset, suggesting that the data for the events in Japan are consistent with this scaling relationship.

Although no significant regional variations are observed across regions, Figure 3 reveals an interesting feature common to multiple regions. The mean level and degree of standard deviation (black bars in Fig. 3) for northeastern Japan, Kermadec, and Central America are similar. In these regions, the existence of several small events ($M_w < 7.5$) with smaller rupture areas than the scaling relationship increases data scatter (Fig. 4). In the next section, we discuss this scatter in terms of the depth of source faults.

Depth variation

As depicted in Figure 2c, the rupture areas for events with M_w less than ~7.5 exhibited larger scatter compared to those for events with $M_w \sim 7.5$ and above. This characteristic is also observed in the fault-width data (Fig. 2b), but not visible in the fault-length data (Fig. 2a). Therefore, we speculate that this characteristic is likely associated with some characteristic along the fault dip direction (i.e., depth), rather than the fault strike direction.

Figure 6 shows the rupture-area data of Figure 2c color-coded by the trimmed source fault's top depth, bottom depth, and centroid depth based on the heterogeneous slip model. For

Figure 4. Relationship between seismic moment and rupture area for each region. The color version of this figure is available only in the electronic edition.

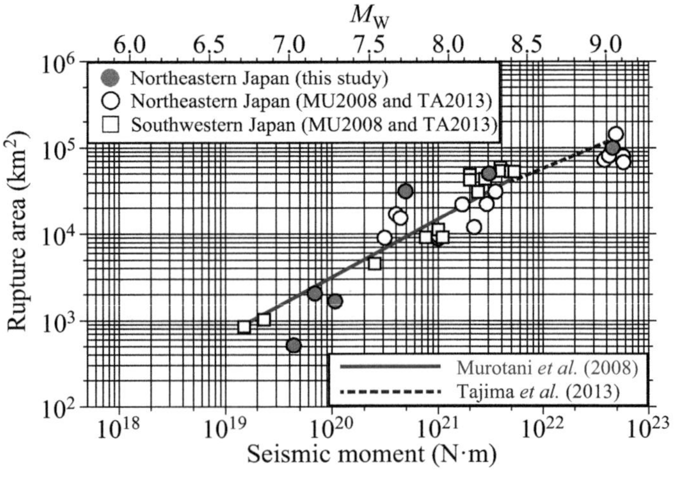

Figure 5. Relationship between seismic moment and rupture area for earthquakes in Japan (northeastern Japan and southwestern Japan). The data from Murotani *et al.* (2008) (MU2008) and Tajima *et al.* (2013) (TA2013) are also shown for comparison. The color version of this figure is available only in the electronic edition.

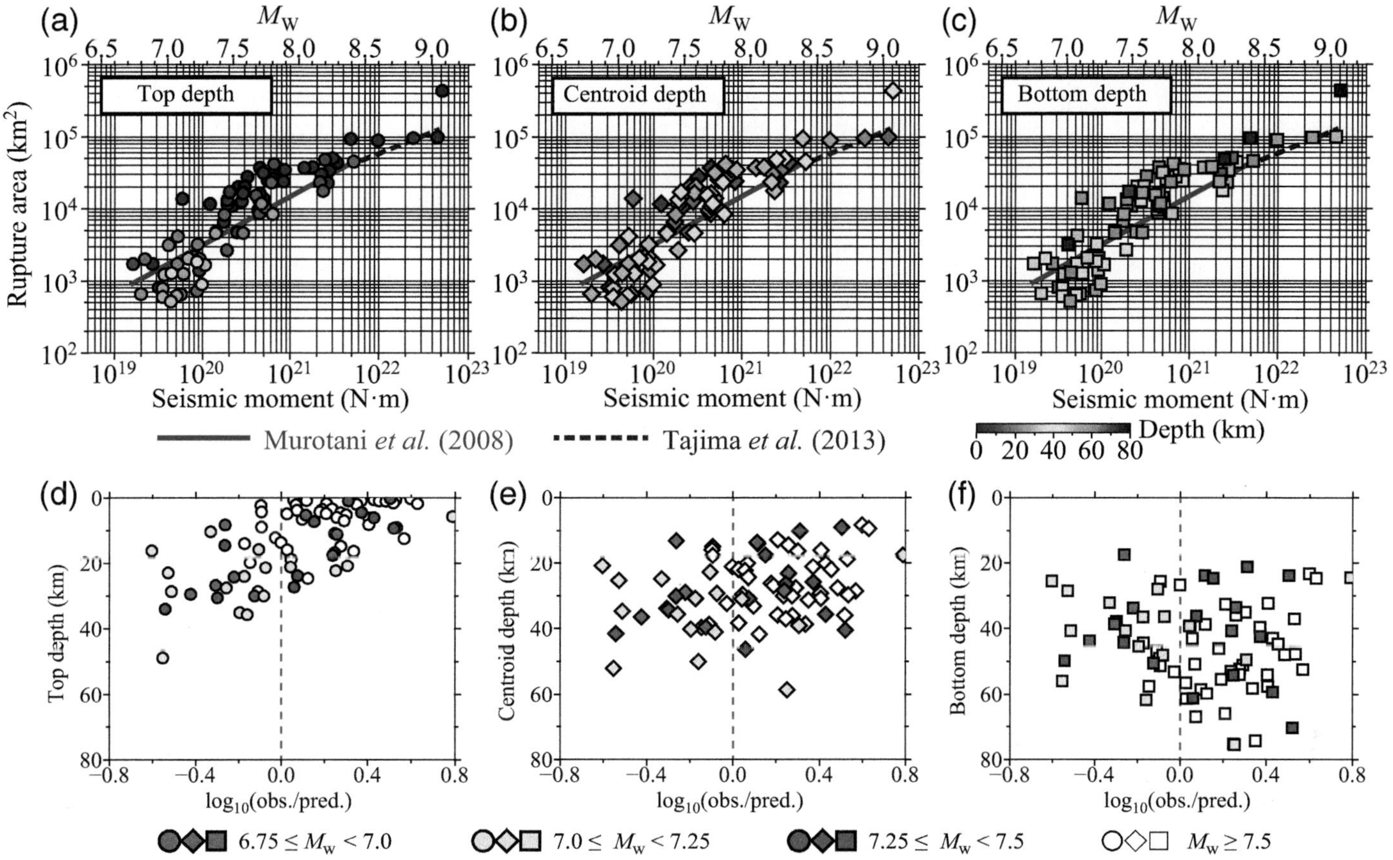

Figure 6. (a–c) Relationships for all earthquakes between seismic moment and rupture area (color coded by depth). (d–f) Relationships between the residuals (common logarithm) with respect to the scaling relationship and depth (color-coded by M_w). Panels (a,d), (b,e), and (c,f) correspond to the top (circle), centroid (diamond), and bottom (square) depths of the trimmed source fault, respectively. The color version of this figure is available only in the electronic edition.

larger events ($M_w > 7.5$), their top depths are generally shallower than ~20 km (Fig. 6a,d), indicating that fault ruptures extend to the shallow part of subduction zones (Domains B and sometimes A defined by Lay *et al.*, 2012). The rupture areas for most of these large events exceed those predicted by the scaling relationship of Murotani *et al.* (2008) and Tajima *et al.* (2013). In contrast, for smaller events ($M_w < 7.5$), in addition to the events where fault ruptures extend to shallow zones (e.g., the 2012 M_w 7.3 El Salvador earthquake in Fig. 7), there are also many events with top depths ranging from ~20 to 40 km (e.g., the 2017 M_w 6.9 Valparaiso, Chile, earthquake in Fig. 7). The data for M_w less than 7.5 show a larger scatter compared to M_w 7.5 and above. When focusing on data with similar M_w (plots with the same color in Fig. 6d), a trend is observed where the data are arranged from the bottom left to the top right. This trend means that the events with shallower top depths have larger rupture areas, whereas the events with deeper top depths have smaller rupture areas. This trend can also be observed, although weakly, in the case of the centroid depth (Fig. 6e). The correlation coefficients of the rupture area (its residual with respect to the scaling relationship of Murotani *et al.*, 2008, and Tajima *et al.*, 2013) with respect to the top and centroid depths are −0.65 and −0.24, respectively. In contrast, no depth-dependent trend is observed for bottom depth (Fig. 6f). The correlation coefficient between rupture area and bottom depth is 0.09.

Figure 8 shows the events with M_w less than 7.5 in Figure 6a, divided by region. Although the geometries of subduction zones along the dip direction vary from region to region, in all regions except Aleutians, where only one earthquake datum is available, the events with shallower top depths tend to have larger rupture areas than those with deeper top depths. Therefore, we suggest that this depth-dependent characteristic is a fundamental feature of subduction earthquakes, regardless of region.

DISCUSSION

To clarify which source depth or rupture propagation direction affects the rupture area more significantly, we show the top, hypocenter (rupture initiation point), bottom depths of each event (Fig. 9). Note that although the rupture process of each event is more complex, the rupture propagation direction we focus on here is the overall trend of rupture growth, which we assume is characterized by the relative positions of the upper and lower edges of the fault with respect to the hypocenter.

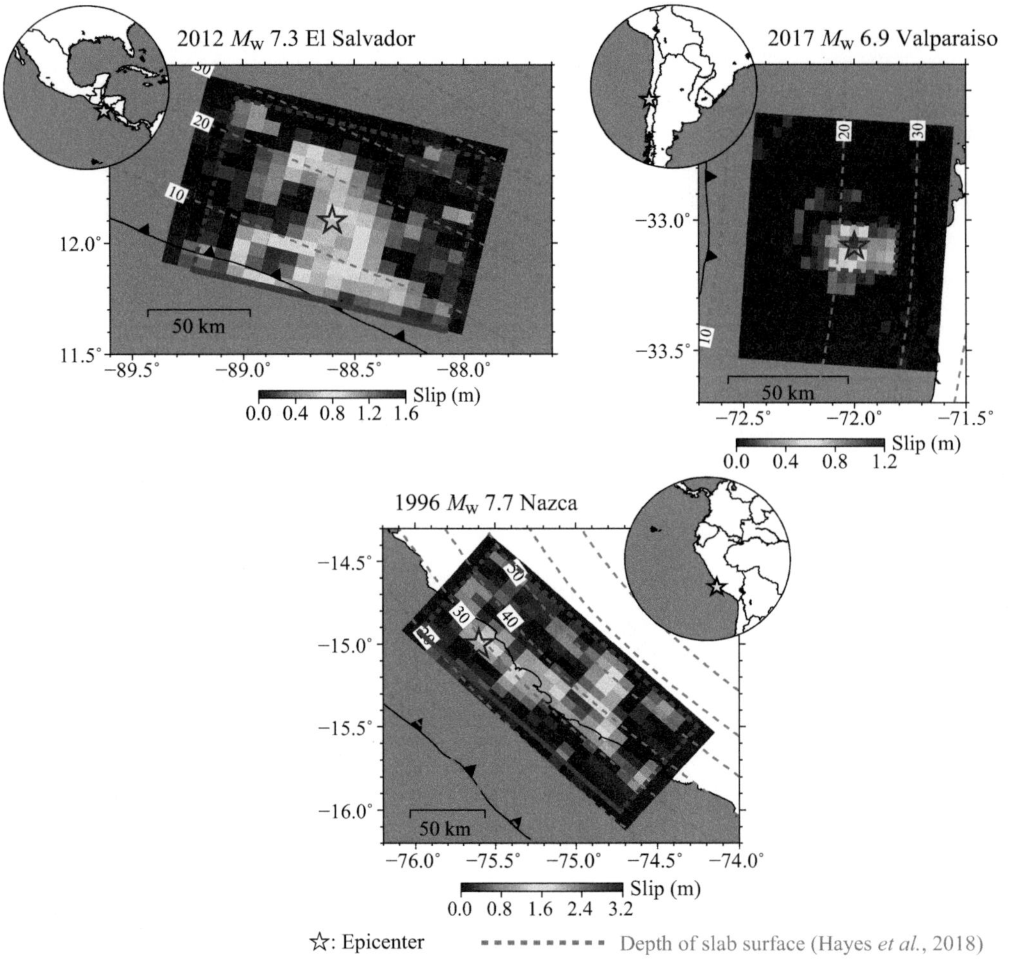

Figure 7. Heterogeneous slip models and trimmed source faults (red rectangles) for selected events. The stars and gray contours (contour interval: 10 km) represent the epicenters and the depths of subduction interfaces, respectively. The color version of this figure is available only in the electronic edition.

Figure 9a,b sorts the events by hypocenter depth, indicated by triangles, from shallow to deep. For M_w less than 7.5 (Fig. 9a), the distribution of plot colors (whether cool or warm) appears random, which means that the rupture area (its residual with respect to the scaling relationship of Murotani *et al.*, 2008, and Tajima *et al.*, 2013) does not depend on the hypocenter depth. Figure 10a shows the relationship between rupture area and hypocenter depth, revealing a random distribution. The correlation coefficient (R) is −0.09 (Fig. 10a), which is smaller in absolute value than those for top depth (−0.65) and centroid depth (−0.24). In contrast, when the events are rearranged in ascending order of the vertical distance from the top depth (indicated by circles) to the hypocenter depth, with the hypocenter depth plotted as zero (Fig. 9c,d), a clear separation between the cool-colored and warm-colored plots emerges for M_w less than 7.5 (Fig. 9c). This indicates that the events with less extent of the fault upper edge compared to the fault lower edge have smaller rupture areas (the left half of Fig. 9c), whereas those with greater extent have larger rupture areas (the right half of Fig. 9c). Figure 10b shows the relationship between the vertical distance from the top depth to the hypocenter depth and the rupture area, revealing a clear correlation (R = 0.56) between the two metrics. Therefore, we suggest that, for a given magnitude (M_w < 7.5), the size of the rupture area is primarily controlled by whether the rupture propagates upward.

The fact that the rupture area is small despite the presence of down-dip rupture propagation implies that the rupture does not spread extensively and instead halts prematurely. The consistently limited down-dip rupture propagation may be attributed to the low pore-fluid pressure and, consequently, high frictional strength (e.g., Das and Scholz, 1983; Moreno *et al.*, 2014), or to the subducting geometrical irregularity, such as bending (e.g., Wang and Bilek, 2014), in the deep part compared to the shallow part of the subduction zone. Although the observed relationship between rupture propagation direction and rupture area may reflect the depth-dependent frictional properties of subduction interfaces, clarifying the physical mechanisms that control rupture propagation direction requires further case studies, such as dynamic rupture simulations, which incorporate both depth-dependent and heterogeneous physical properties of subduction interfaces.

For M_w 7.5 and above, even the events with less extent of the fault upper edge compared to the fault lower edge exhibit slightly larger rupture areas compared to the scaling relationship (mainly in the left half of Fig. 9d), which is opposite to the characteristic observed for M_w less than 7.5 (the left half of Fig. 9c). Figure 9e,f shows the same plots as Figure 9c,d, but with different plot colors. The plot color in Figure 9e,f represents the fault aspect ratio (fault length divided by fault width), which tends to be large for the events with less extent of the fault upper edge (Fig. 9f). As M_w increases, fault ruptures become more complex. For the events with a modest extent of the fault upper edge, the ruptures spread along the fault strike direction as well as downward, resulting in larger rupture areas (e.g., the 1996 M_w 7.7 Nazca, Peru, earthquake in Fig. 7).

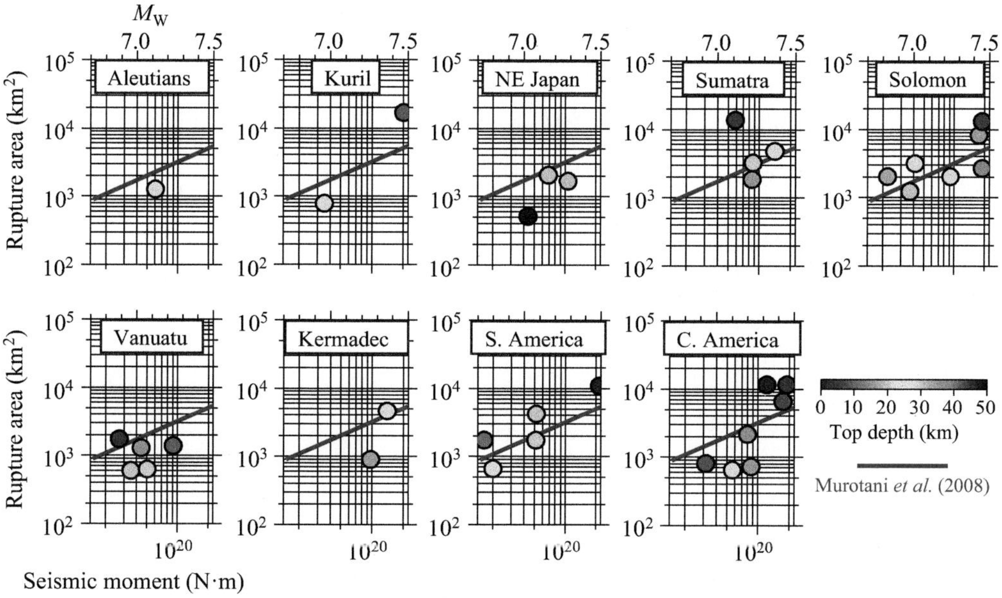

Figure 8. Relationships between seismic moment and rupture area for events with M_W less than 7.5 in each region. The plot color represents the top depth of the trimmed source fault. The color version of this figure is available only in the electronic edition.

and the overall mean level of the dataset appears to be roughly consistent with the scaling relationship. In contrast, for Sumatra/Java and South America, there are few events smaller than predicted by the scaling relationship, and the overall mean appears to be slightly larger than the scaling relationship. Our comparison, which relies on earthquake data, suggests only the possibility that there are differences in outer source parameters between Japan and the other two regions. Meanwhile, physical factors such as the heterogeneity (i.e., roughness and smoothness) and the slip deficit rate of subduction interfaces (e.g., van Rijsingen *et al.*, 2018; Graham *et al.*, 2021; Wirth *et al.*, 2022) are known to directly influence the spatial extent of source rupture (i.e., the size of the outer source parameters). Therefore, to reach more definitive conclusions regarding regional variations in outer source parameters, future studies should not only analyze past earthquake data but also investigate, through offshore geodetic and gravitational observations, whether such physical properties exhibit systematic regional differences in their spatial distribution.

Although the previous studies (Tajima *et al.*, 2013; Allen and Hayes, 2017) proposed the second stage of the scaling relationship for subduction earthquakes due to fault width saturation, our investigation of fault depth suggests that the first stage can be further divided into two substages with a threshold at $M_w \sim 7.5$. As mentioned earlier, in the substage with M_w 7.5 and above, most earthquakes extend their fault ruptures to shallow depths. Meanwhile, in the substage with M_w less than 7.5, there are events both with and without shallow ruptures, resulting in a large scatter in rupture area. If the rupture-area scaling relationship for the substage with M_w 7.5 and above, which is based on the two-third power of seismic moment, is directly extrapolated to the substage with M_w less than 7.5, there is a risk of overestimating the rupture areas and thus underestimating the average slips for the small events ($M_w < 7.5$) without shallow ruptures.

As mentioned in the Introduction, one of our objectives was to investigate whether source parameter differences exist between Japan and other regions. Here, we compare events with M_w 7.5 and above in three regions: Japan (Fig. 5), Sumatra/Java (Fig. 4), and South America (Fig. 4), each of which contains a relatively large amount of data. Note that this comparison excludes events with M_w less than 7.5 because the large scatter due to top depth obscures regional variations. Furthermore, we use Figure 5 for the Japanese data instead of Figure 4, because Figure 5 includes data from the previous studies (Murotani *et al.*, 2008; Tajima *et al.*, 2013), thereby increasing the total amount of data. For Japan, the dataset includes some events with rupture areas slightly smaller than those predicted by the scaling relationship of Murotani *et al.* (2008) and Tajima *et al.* (2013),

CONCLUSIONS

Using the criterion proposed by Somerville *et al.* (1999), we estimated the source parameters of global subduction earthquakes from the heterogeneous slip models obtained through source inversion analyses conducted by the USGS. The source parameters of all earthquakes are summarized in Table S1. The estimated rupture areas were used both for comparing with the standard scaling relationship for Japan (Murotani *et al.*, 2008; Tajima *et al.*, 2013) and for investigating regional variations in subduction earthquakes. It is likely that this scaling relationship slightly underestimates the mean rupture area of subduction earthquakes across the nine regions examined in this study. The total amount of data in this study was not small; however, it became limited when divided by region. This made it difficult to determine whether there are regional differences in source parameters between subduction zones. Nevertheless, our dataset may suggest that the rupture areas of events in Kuril, Sumatra/Java, and South America are slightly larger than the mean across the nine regions, whereas those in northeastern Japan and Vanuatu are slightly smaller. Beyond regional variation, we also focused on depth variation, a

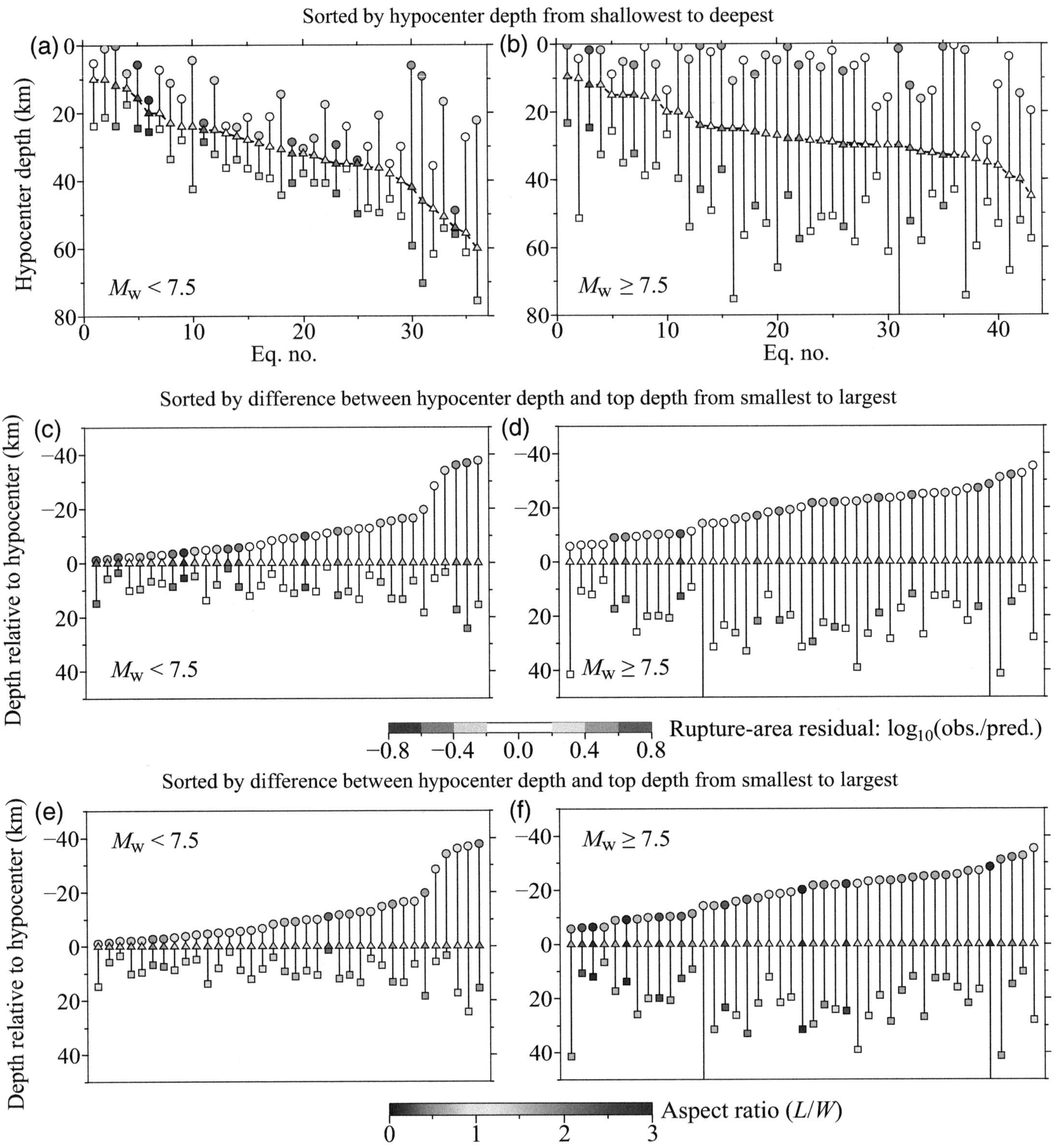

Figure 9. Top (circle), hypocenter (triangle), and bottom (square) depths of all earthquakes. Panels (a), (c), and (e) show data for M_W less than 7.5, and panels (b), (d), and (f) show data for M_W 7.5 and above. Panels (a) and (b) sort the events by hypocenter depth. Panels (c), (d), (e), and (f) sort the events by the top depth of the trimmed source fault relative to the hypocenter. The plot color in (a), (b), (c), and (d) represents the residual (common logarithm) with respect to the scaling relationship for the rupture area. The plot color in (e) and (f) represents the fault aspect ratio (fault length divided by fault width). The color version of this figure is available only in the electronic edition.

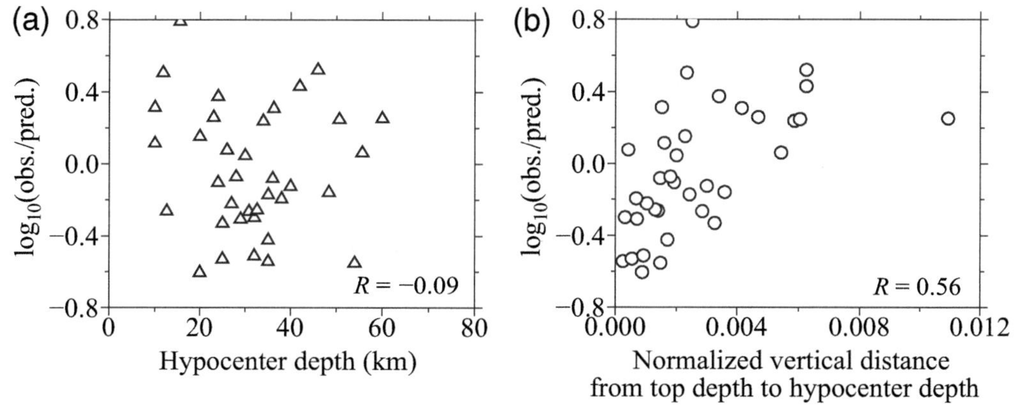

Figure 10. Residuals (common logarithm) with respect to the rupture-area scaling relationship for small events ($M_w < 7.5$), plotted against (a) hypocenter depth (triangle) and (b) normalized vertical distance from the top depth to the hypocenter depth (circle). The normalized vertical distance was calculated by dividing the vertical distance from the top depth to the hypocenter depth by the one third power of the seismic moment.

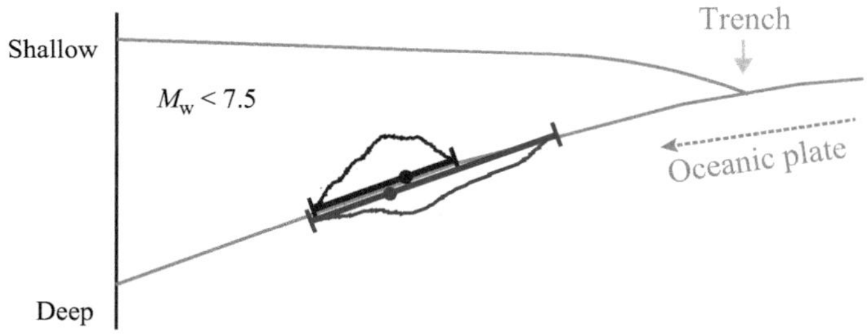

Figure 11. Schematic cross-section illustrating events for a given magnitude ($M_w < 7.5$). The blue and red lines represent events with rupture areas smaller and larger, respectively, than those predicted by the scaling relationship. For each line, the bars at both ends indicate the top and bottom depths, the circle represents the hypocenter, and the curves represent the slip distribution. The color version of this figure is available only in the electronic edition.

perspective that had not been addressed in the previous studies on global source-scaling relationships (e.g., Skarlatoudis *et al.*, 2016; Allen and Hayes, 2017; Thingbaijam *et al.*, 2017). We found a correlation between rupture area and depth of source faults: the events with M_w 7.5 and above typically have shallow top depths and large rupture areas with respect to the scaling relationship of Murotani *et al.* (2008) and Tajima *et al.* (2013); in contrast, for M_w less than 7.5, there is a coexistence of events with deep top depths and small rupture areas as well as events with shallow top depths and large rupture areas (Fig. 11), contributing to large scatter with respect to the scaling relationship. Because of this scatter, it appeared that the rupture-area data did not strictly follow the two-third power of the seismic moment in the first stage of the two-stage scaling relationship. We suggest that the larger rupture areas are associated with the ruptures that propagate upward and reach the shallow part (depths of less than ~20 km) of subduction zones.

From the perspective of seismic hazard assessment for future subduction earthquakes, our findings are expected to reduce the variability of predicted ground motions and/or tsunamis. As future work, the difference in scatter identified across the $M_w \sim 7.5$ threshold could be further validated by other approaches, such as estimating the static stress drop for each event through source spectral analyses.

DATA AND RESOURCES

The heterogeneous slip models by the U.S. Geological Survey for 79 earthquakes were downloaded from https://earthquake.usgs.gov/data/finitefault/. The supplemental material consists of an Excel file that provides digital data on the source parameters of the 79 earthquakes processed in this study, their residuals with respect to the scaling relationship of Murotani *et al.* (2008) and Tajima *et al.* (2013), and the depths of their source faults. Figures were made using the Generic Mapping Tools version 4.5.18 (http://www.soest.hawaii.edu/gmt/; Wessel and Smith, 1998). Both websites were last accessed in April 2025.

DECLARATION OF COMPETING INTERESTS

The authors acknowledge that there are no conflicts of interest recorded.

ACKNOWLEDGMENTS

The authors thank Mark Williamson Stirling and two anonymous reviewers for their helpful comments.

REFERENCES

Allen, T. I., and G. P. Hayes (2017). Alternative rupture-scaling relationships for subduction interface and other offshore environments, *Bull. Seismol. Soc. Am.* **107,** no. 3, 1240–1253.

Bilek, S. L., and T. Lay (1999). Rigidity variations with depth along interplate megathrust faults in subduction zones, *Nature* **400,** 443–446.

Das, S., and C. H. Scholz (1983). Why large earthquakes do not nucleate at shallow depths, *Nature* **305,** 621–623.

Denolle, M. A., and P. M. Shearer (2016). New perspectives on self-similarity for shallow thrust earthquakes, *J. Geophys. Res.* **121,** no. 9, 6533–6565.

Goda, K., T. Yasuda, N. Mori, and T. Maruyama (2016). New scaling relationships of earthquake source parameters for stochastic tsunami simulation, *Coast. Eng. J.* **58,** no. 3, 1,650,010.

Goldberg, D. E., P. Koch, D. Melgar, S. Riquelme, and W. L. Yeck (2022). Beyond the teleseism: Introducing regional seismic and geodetic data into routine USGS finite-fault modeling, *Seismol. Res. Lett.* **93,** no. 6, 3308–3323.

Graham, S. E., J. P. Loveless, and B. J. Meade (2021). A global set of subduction zone earthquake scenarios and recurrence intervals inferred from geodetically constrained block models of interseismic coupling distributions, *Geochem. Geophys. Geosys.* **22,** no. 11, doi: 10.1029/2021GC009802.

Hayes, G. P. (2017). The finite, kinematic rupture properties of great-sized earthquakes since 1990, *Earth Planet. Sci. Lett.* **468,** 94–100.

Hayes, G. P., G. L. Moore, D. E. Portner, M. Hearne, H. Flamme, M. Furtney, and G. M. Smoczyk (2018). Slab2, a comprehensive subduction zone geometry model, *Science* **362,** no. 6410, 58–61.

Heuret, A., S. Lallemand, F. Funiciello, C. Piromallo, and C. Paccenna (2011). Physical characteristics of subduction interface type seismogenic zones revisited, *Geochem. Geophys. Geosys.* **12,** no. 1, doi: 10.1029/2010GC003230.

Irikura, K., and H. Miyake (2011). Recipe for predicting strong ground motion from crustal earthquake scenarios, *Pure Appl. Geophys.* **168,** 85–104.

Lay, T., H. Kanamori, C. J. Ammon, K. D. Koper, A. R. Hutko, L. Ye, H. Yue, and T. M. Rushing (2012). Depth-varying rupture properties of subduction zone megathrust faults, *J. Geophys. Res.* **117,** no. B4, doi: 10.1029/2011JB009133.

Mai, P. M., and G. C. Beroza (2000). Source scaling properties from finite-fault-rupture models, *Bull. Seismol. Soc. Am.* **90,** no. 3, 604–615.

Miyakoshi, K., Y. Guo, K. Yoshida, and K. Irie (2021). Re-examination of scaling relationships of source parameters of the interplate earthquakes in Japan, *Abstracts of the Seismological Society of Japan 2021, Fall Meeting*, Online meeting, 14–16 October 2021, S15P-07 pp. (in Japanese).

Miyakoshi, K., K. Somei, K. Yoshida, S. Kurahashi, K. Irikura, and K. Kamae (2020). Scaling relationships of source parameters of inland crustal earthquakes in tectonically active regions, *Pure Appl. Geophys.* **177,** 1917–1929.

Moreno, M., C. Haberland, O. Oncken, A. Rietbrock, S. Angiboust, and O. Heidbach (2014). Locking of the Chile subduction zone controlled by fluid pressure before the 2010 earthquake, *Nature Geosci.* **7,** 292–296.

Murotani, S., H. Miyake, and K. Koketsu (2008). Scaling of characterized slip models for plate-boundary earthquakes, *Earth Planets Space* **60,** 987–991.

Murotani, S., K. Satake, and Y. Fujii (2013). Scaling relations of seismic moment, rupture area, average slip, and asperity size for $M{\sim}9$ subduction-zone earthquakes, *Geophys. Res. Lett.* **40,** no. 19, 5070–5074.

Ogawa, S., D. Ju, K. Dan, K. Irie, and H. Torita (2021). Regional characteristics of fault parameters for subduction inter-plate earthquakes, *Proc. of the 17th World Conf. on Earthq. Eng.*, Sendai, Japan, 27 September–2 October 2021, 1b-0013 pp.

Skarlatoudis, A. A., P. G. Somerville, and H. K. Thio (2016). Source-scaling relations of interface subduction earthquakes for strong ground motion and tsunami simulation, *Bull. Seismol. Soc. Am.* **106,** no. 4, 1652–1662.

Somerville, P., K. Irikura, R. Graves, S. Sawada, D. Wald, N. Abrahamson, Y. Iwasaki, T. Kagawa, N. Smith, and A. Kowada (1999). Characterizing crustal earthquake slip models for the prediction of strong ground motion, *Seismol. Res. Lett.* **70,** no. 1, 59–80.

Tajima, R., Y. Matsumoto, H. Si, and K. Irikura (2013). Comparative study on scaling relations of source parameters for great earthquakes in inland crusts and on subducting plate-boundaries, *Zisin* **66,** no. 3, 31–45 (in Japanese with English abstract).

Thingbaijam, K. K. S., and P. M. Mai (2016). Evidence for truncated exponential probability distribution of earthquake slip, *Bull. Seismol. Soc. Am.* **106,** no. 4, 1802–1816.

Thingbaijam, K. K. S., P. M. Mai, and K. Goda (2017). New empirical earthquake source-scaling laws, *Bull. Seismol. Soc. Am.* **107,** no. 5, 2225–2246.

van Rijsingen, E., S. Lallemand, M. Peyret, D. Arcay, A. Heuret, F. Funiciello, and F. Corbi (2018). How subduction interface roughness influences the occurrence of large interplate earthquakes, *Geochem. Geophys. Geosys.* **19,** no. 8, 2342–2370.

Wang, K., and S. L. Bilek (2014). Invited review paper: Fault creep caused by subduction of rough seafloor relief, *Tectonophysics* **610,** 1–24.

Wessel, P., and W. H. F. Smith (1998). New, improved version of Generic Mapping Tools released, *Eos Trans. AGU* **79,** 579.

Wirth, E. A., V. J. Sahakian, L. M. Wallace, and D. Melnick (2022). The occurrence and hazards of great subduction zone earthquakes, *Nat. Rev. Earth Environ.* **3,** 125–140.

Ye, L., T. Lay, H. Kanamori, and L. Rivera (2016). Rupture characteristics of major and great ($M_W \geq 7.0$) megathrust earthquakes from 1990 to 2015: 2. Depth dependence, *J. Geophys. Res.* **121,** no. 2, 845–863.

Manuscript received 3 July 2025
Published online 6 November 2025

Exploring the Feasibility of a Regional Earthquake Early Warning System in Utah

Emily A. Morton*[1], Keith D. Koper[1], Deborah L. Kilb[2], and Relu Burlacu[1]

ABSTRACT

In terms of annualized earthquake loss and casualties, Utah has the fourth-highest seismic risk among U.S. states, after California, Washington, and Oregon. Seismic hazard is highest in the urban corridor along the Wasatch fault zone, which has hosted ≥ 24 surface-rupturing earthquakes (*M* 6.75+) in the last 6500 yr. Motivated by the 2021 rollout of ShakeAlert along the U.S. West Coast—and the increasing popularity of earthquake early warning (EEW) systems worldwide—the Utah legislature commissioned a study on the feasibility of implementing EEW in the state. Here, we expand on the seismology component of that report, focusing on the required instrumentation upgrades to the existing network, the idealized warning times expected for six representative earthquake scenarios, and the frequency with which alerts would be issued. We investigate a regional EEW system, relying on the requirements of the existing West Coast ShakeAlert system. If the existing Utah seismograph stations were upgraded with low-latency recorders and improved telemetry, we find that a prototype EEW system could currently be operated along the Wasatch fault zone. Installation of 64 additional stations is required for EEW to be fully operational throughout the Wasatch Front, and another 117 stations for EEW to fully operate throughout the Utah Intermountain Seismic Belt. Areas expected to have damaging ground shaking (modified Mercalli intensity [MMI] ≥ 5.5) in the six earthquake scenarios would receive 0–10 s of warning to prepare for shaking, whereas areas expected to have noticeable ground shaking but little-to-no damage (MMI 1–5.5) would receive 10–55 s of warning. A fully operational Wasatch Front EEW system set to alert on *M* 4.5+ earthquakes, like the West Coast ShakeAlert system, would be expected to activate once every four years on average, although the alerts would strongly cluster in time, reflecting the natural patterns of earthquake activity.

KEY POINTS

- We evaluated early warning feasibility in Utah with warning time estimation and station requirements.
- The current network is at the desired density along the Wasatch fault zone and performs well in quality control metrics.
- Warnings would not be actionable for damaging shaking, but could be for felt shaking or very light damage.

Supplemental Material

INTRODUCTION

Motivated by the 2021 rollout of the ShakeAlert earthquake early warning (EEW) system along the U.S. West Coast (Kohler *et al.*, 2020; Lux *et al.*, 2024; McGuire *et al.*, 2025) and the increasing popularity of EEW systems globally (e.g., Allen *et al.*, 2009; Allen and Melgar, 2019), the Utah Geological Survey (UGS) led a state-sponsored study to evaluate the feasibility of EEW in Utah, particularly focusing on the densely populated Wasatch Front region (defined here as 39.65°–42.05° N, 111.30°–112.95° W). The study was a collaborative project between the UGS, the University of Utah Seismograph Stations (UUSS), and the Utah Division of Emergency Management to investigate how EEW could help protect people and critical infrastructure during large Utah earthquakes (Bowman *et al.*, 2024).

The Utah study (Bowman *et al.*, 2024) focused on evaluating a regional EEW system (e.g., ShakeAlert) that could leverage the existing Utah regional seismic network (Pankow *et al.*, 2020). It did not address on-site systems (Kanamori, 2005) or cellphone-based systems (Kong *et al.*, 2016; Allen *et al.*, 2025). On-site systems can provide warning in the epicentral area of a

1. Department of Geology and Geophysics, University of Utah Seismograph Stations, Salt Lake City, Utah, U.S.A., https://orcid.org/0000-0002-0156-2596 (EAM);
2. Scripps Institution of Oceanography, University of California San Diego, San Diego, California, U.S.A., https://orcid.org/0000-0002-7252-4167 (DLK)

*Corresponding author: emily.morton@utah.edu

Cite this article as Morton, E. A., K. D. Koper, D. L. Kilb, and R. Burlacu (2025). Exploring the Feasibility of a Regional Earthquake Early Warning System in Utah, *Bull. Seismol. Soc. Am.* **116**, 249–271, doi: 10.1785/0120250155

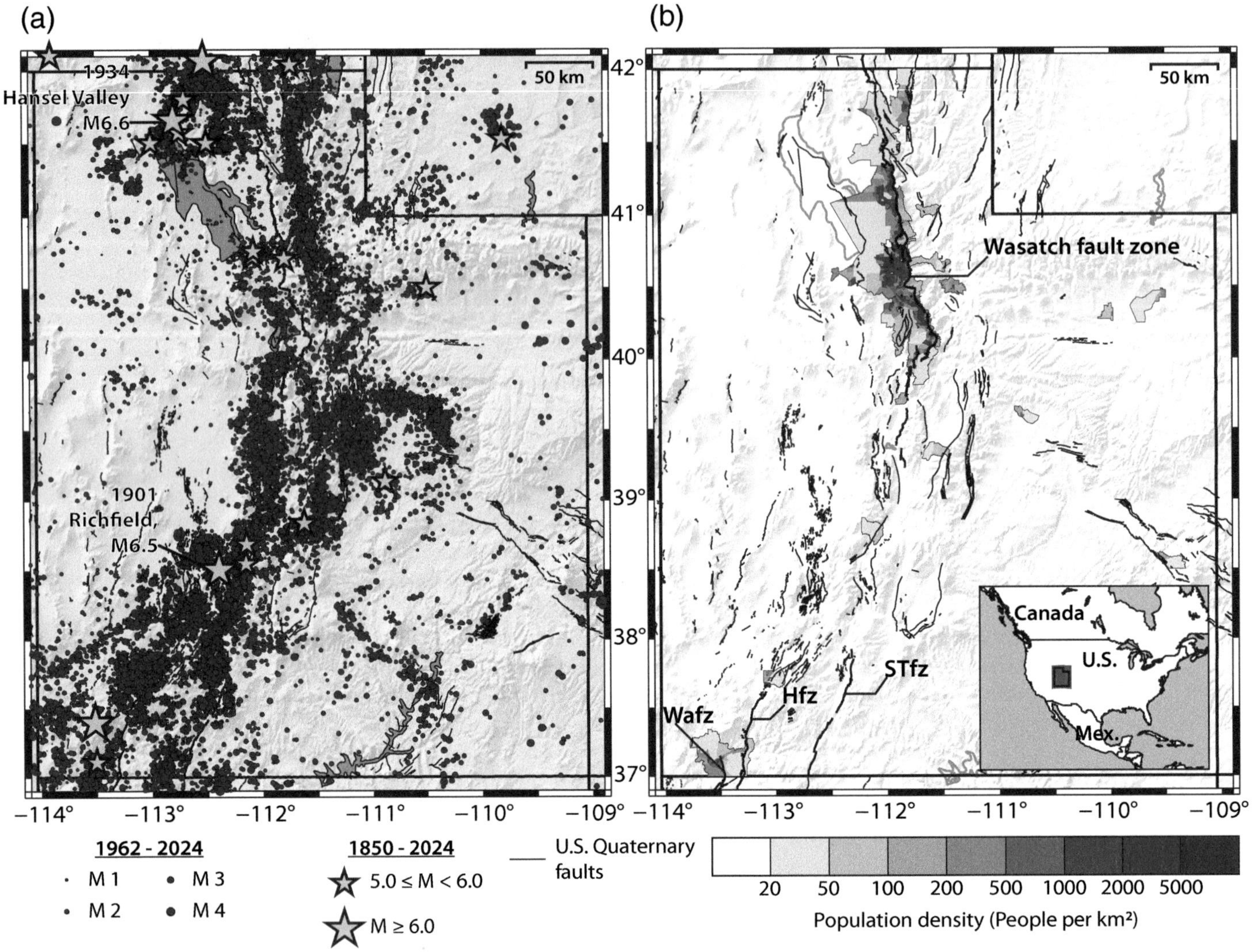

Figure 1. Utah seismicity and population density. (a) Seismicity 0 ≤ M < 5 during 1962–2024 (dots) and M ≥ 5 during 1850–2024 (stars), sized by magnitude. The two largest historical earthquakes, the 1901 *M* 6.5 Richfield, Utah, and the 1934 *M* 6.6 Hansel Valley, Utah, events, are highlighted. Scenario events are shown in Figure 6 and Figure S4, respectively, and are meant to mimic these historic events. (b) Utah population density in 2020 census tracts, colored by people per square kilometer (U.S. Census Bureau, 2024a). Labeled fault zones in the southwest corner of the state are as follows: Hfz, Hurricane fault zone; STfz, Sevier-Toroweap fault zone; and Wafz, Washington fault zone. The inset map shows the location of the study area (red box) in the context of North America. The color version of this figure is available only in the electronic edition.

large earthquake where a regional system would fail and so provide complementary capability (Wu *et al.*, 2021); however, on-site warning times at greater distances would generally be shorter than those from a regional system, and on-site systems may be more prone to false alarms (Satriano *et al.*, 2011). Analogous EEW feasibility studies using ShakeAlert-like methodologies have recently been conducted for Hawaii (Thelen *et al.*, 2016), the New Madrid Seismic Zone (Ogweno *et al.*, 2019), Alaska (Fozkos and West, 2025; Wolfe *et al.*, 2025), and Nevada (Kinkel and Trugman, 2025). Recent feasibility studies using regional but non-ShakeAlert EEW frameworks have been carried out in Italy (Picozzi *et al.*, 2015), Switzerland (Massin *et al.*, 2021), the whole of Europe (Cremen *et al.*, 2022), and Iran (Enferadi *et al.*, 2021). Most of the regional EEW studies, whether based on ShakeAlert or not, have focused on how existing and hypothetical station geometries impact potential warning times for various earthquake scenarios.

Utah has the fourth-highest seismic risk among U.S. states in terms of annualized earthquake loss and casualties, after ShakeAlert states California, Washington, and Oregon (Federal Emergency Management Agency [FEMA], 2023). Seismicity in Utah is concentrated in the Intermountain Seismic Belt (ISB), running north–south through the center of the state (Fig. 1a). The largest earthquake threat is within the Wasatch Front region, as more than 80% of the population is concentrated in the Ogden–Salt Lake City–Provo urban corridor (U.S. Census Bureau, 2024a), directly adjacent to the Wasatch fault zone where the seismic hazard is highest (Fig. 1b). Paleoseismic studies have reported 24 large-magnitude earthquakes (*M* 6.75+) on the five central segments of the Wasatch fault zone in the last 6500 yr, yielding an overall recurrence interval of ~300 yr for the central Wasatch, and individual segment recurrence intervals of ~900 to 1500 yr (DuRoss *et al.*, 2016). The most recent central Wasatch fault zone large earthquake was ~200 to 300 yr ago on the Nephi segment. The Salt Lake City and Brigham City segments of the fault last ruptured ~1300 and ~2400 yr ago (DuRoss *et al.*, 2016), respectively, and thus are typically considered "overdue" for a large earthquake.

In addition to characteristic surface-rupturing earthquakes, more frequent moderate-magnitude earthquakes (M ~5–6) can be damaging due to the large inventory of unreinforced masonry (URM) structures throughout the state. Twenty of Utah's 29 counties have at least one school campus with a URM building or addition, with a total of 119 school campuses, and >200 additional campuses with other types of vulnerable construction (Applied Technology Council, 2022). More than 140,000 URM buildings are estimated to exist in the Wasatch Front (Federal Emergency Management Agency [FEMA], Utah Division of Emergency Management [DEM], and Utah Seismic Safety Commission [USSC], 2021). This vulnerability was demonstrated during the 2020 M_w 5.7 Magna, Utah, earthquake, which occurred in a suburb close to Salt Lake City and caused a total economic loss of $629 million (Das, 2023). At least 145 historic buildings sustained damage (Utah State Historic Preservation Office, 2020), 48 mobile homes were destroyed or severely damaged in the Western Estates mobile homes park (Rascon, 2020), and the Granite School District reported 30 structures with damage, including West Lake Junior High which was deemed unrepairable and required a $55 million U.S. rebuild (Federal Emergency Management Agency [FEMA], Utah Division of Emergency Management [DEM], and Utah Seismic Safety Commission [USSC], 2021; Kirby, 2023). The damage from a large Wasatch fault earthquake will be substantially worse, with estimates for an M 7.0 event along the Salt Lake City segment on the order of thousands of casualties and tens of billions of dollars in short-term economic losses (Earthquake Engineering Research Institute, 2015).

Here, we expand on the UUSS contribution to the State of Utah EEW feasibility report (Bowman *et al.*, 2024) and address the following questions.

1. To what extent is the existing UUSS network prepared for integration into an EEW system, and what modifications are required to have a fully functional EEW system in Utah?
2. Would a fully functional EEW system provide sufficient warning for Utah residents, critical facilities, and infrastructure, given their proximity to the large earthquakes we expect?

First, we evaluated the existing UUSS network performance and geometry against the ShakeAlert station acceptance and spacing criteria currently used on the U.S. West Coast (Given *et al.*, 2018). Next, we evaluated the potential effectiveness of an EEW system in Utah by estimating the warning times (time between when an alert is received and strong shaking arrives) at surrounding cities for the large, damaging earthquakes likely to occur in Utah, and comparing them to modeled ground motion. We consider a warning to be "sufficient" if it allows enough time to take protective action, such as "Drop, Cover, Hold On" (DCHO) for people (5–10 s, Porter and Jones, 2018), or automatically slowing or shutting down vulnerable systems (≥10 s, see the Discussion section). We considered warnings for damaging shaking (modified Mercalli intensity [MMI] ≥ 5.5) and felt shaking (MMI ≥ 1.5). Finally, we examined the historic Utah earthquake catalog to estimate how often EEW alerts would be expected to be issued.

NEEDS FOR IMPLEMENTING EEW IN UTAH

Station performance

In assessing the current UUSS seismic network, we excluded the short period and NetQuake stations, which are unsuitable for EEW. Of the 209 seismic stations operating in or near Utah as of January 2024, 164 included either a broadband sensor or a strong-motion sensor, or both (Fig. 2). For these "EEW-Ready" stations we evaluated eight quality metrics using measurements and tools from the EarthScope Data Management Center (DMC), the University of Washington (the Seismic QUality Assessment Console [SQUAC]; Ulberg *et al.*, 2023), Earthworm software (Johnson *et al.*, 1995), and the UUSS internal database (Table 1 and Table S1, available in the supplemental material to this article). EarthScope and SQUAC sourced metrics were tested over multiple time periods to account for temporary outages and elevated noise levels. Four of the EarthScope DMC time periods examined correspond to those tested in SQUAC, with two additional, older time periods (Table 1). DC bias (metric 5; Table 1) was evaluated using SQUAC for four time periods and the EarthScope MUSTANG (the Modular Utility for STAtistical kNowledge Gathering system) webservice for two additional time periods; one overlapping two-week period was evaluated to ensure consistency between both sources. Metrics 6–8 were evaluated over a single time period.

We compared the network performance of metrics 1–6 (Table 1 and Table S1) to the station acceptance criteria of ShakeAlert (see Data and Resources) because the most likely implementation of EEW in Utah would be an expansion of the ShakeAlert system. Metrics 7 and 8 were compared to UUSS routine operating standards, in which P picks with uncertainty >0.3 s and station magnitude residuals >0.5 magnitude units are not used in origin and network magnitude estimation. Metrics 1–5 were computed for each channel, and the worst-performing channel was used to represent the corresponding sensor. Sensors were evaluated separately at stations where multiple EEW-compatible sensors existed for metrics 1–6. A sensor passed the test for metrics 1–5 if it met the station acceptance criteria for at least half of the time periods tested, for which

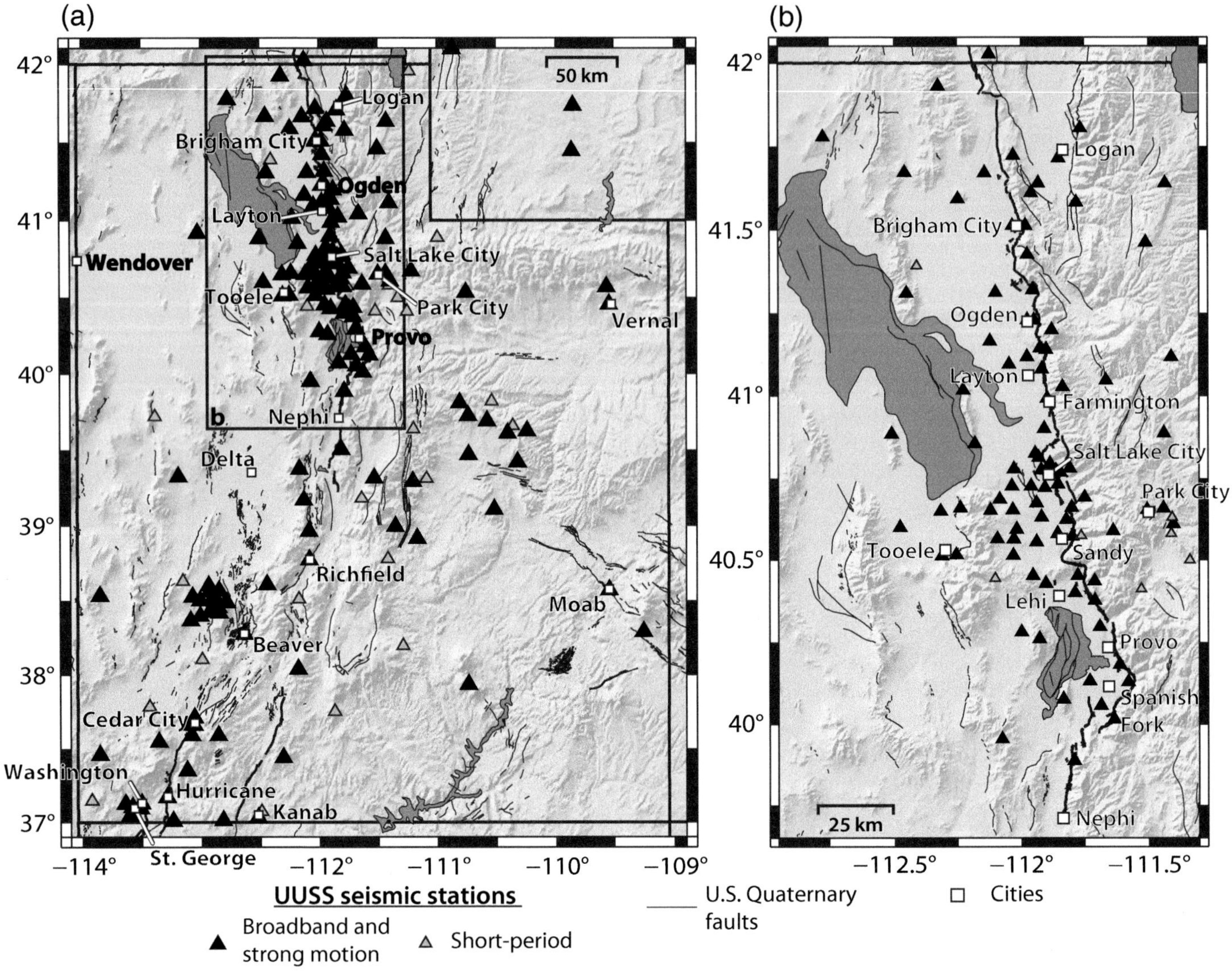

Figure 2. University of Utah Seismograph Stations (UUSS) in (a) Utah and (b) the Wasatch Front, colored by earthquake early warning (EEW) readiness (site has a broadband and/or strong-motion sensor) and sites with only short-period sensors. Bolded fault traces correspond to the Wasatch fault zone, Washington fault zone, Hurricane fault zone, and Sevier-Toroweap fault zone (see Fig. 1). The color version of this figure is available only in the electronic edition.

the sensor was operational (i.e., time periods before a station was installed or upgraded were not considered).

Of the 203 broadband and strong-motion sensors operational during the testing periods, 91% had at least 90% data availability for at least half of the six time periods tested (Table 2). Of the 19 sensors that failed the availability test, 13 (at 11 stations) had known interference, power, or cell coverage issues, and corrective actions are in progress. The network performs very well for metrics 2–5 (97%–99% pass rate) for sensors that have data available during at least one of the time periods examined. In addition, performance is high for automatic P arrivals and magnitudes (93%–98% pass rate) for stations with both automatic and reviewed P and/or amplitude picks (metrics 7 and 8). The only metric in which the network does not perform well is data latency (metric 6). Only one station shows <3.5 s latency for 90% of the packets received in a half-hour period. Over half (55%) of the sensors had average latencies <10 s, with the rest mostly averaging 10–100 s, and three sensors averaging >100 s. This level of latency is not unexpected because the Utah network was developed for conventional regional earthquake monitoring and not specifically for EEW. Overall, 142 of the 164 EEW-compatible stations (87%) have at least one sensor that passes metrics 1–5 and thus can be considered ShakeAlert compliant once data latency is improved (excluding metrics 7 and 8 because not all stations could be tested).

Station coverage

The UUSS network is concentrated along the ISB and is densest within the Wasatch Front region, particularly along the Wasatch fault zone (Fig. 2). We assessed the network coverage by comparing P-wave travel times to the nearest four stations

TABLE 1
Data Quality Metrics Evaluated to Assess UUSS for ShakeAlert Station Acceptance

Metric	Metric Source	Time Period(s) Tested (yyyy/mm/dd)
Data completeness Average gaps per hour	EarthScope DMC webservice*	2023/07/09–2023/07/23 2023/09/16–2023/09/30 2023/12/22–2024/01/05 2024/02/22–2024/03/07 2024/03/06–2024/03/20 2024/03/26–2024/04/09
Average data spikes per hour Average root mean square (RMS) noise duration per hour	SQUAC measurements†	2023/12/22–2024/01/05 2024/02/22–2024/03/07 2024/03/06–2024/03/20 2024/03/26–2024/04/09
DC bias	SQUAC measurements and EarthScope MUSTANG‡	2023/07/09–2023/07/23 (MUSTANG) 2023/09/16–2023/09/30 (MUSTANG) 2023/12/22–2024/01/05 (SQUAC) 2024/02/22–2024/03/07 (SQUAC) 2024/03/06–2024/03/20 (SQUAC) 2024/03/26–2024/04/09 (SQUAC)
Data latency	Sniffwave§	Individual 30 min periods between March and April 2024
P-arrival accuracy (average time difference between automatic and reviewed *P* picks) Station–magnitude accuracy (average difference between automatic and reviewed station-M_L estimates)	UUSS internal database	All finalized, local earthquakes in 2023

The metric source refers to where the metric measurement or data to estimate the measurement was accessed. Time periods cover two weeks of data for testing. See Data and Resources for more information on the metric sources used and Table S1 for more details on how the metrics are estimated. UUSS, University of Utah Seismograph Stations.
*EarthScope Data Management Center (DMC) International Federation of Digital Seismograph Networks (FDSN) availability webservice (see Data and Resources).
†University of Washington Seismic QUality Assessment Console (SQUAC; Ulberg *et al.*, 2023).
‡EarthScope Modular Utility for STAtistical kNowledge Gathering system (MUSTANG; Casey *et al.*, 2018).
§Earthworm (Johnson *et al.*, 1995) Sniffwave module.

TABLE 2
Performance of Existing Broadband and Strong-Motion Stations in the UUSS Network

Metric: Station Acceptance Criteria	Number of Sensors or Stations Evaluated	Pass Rate
Data completeness: at least 90% availability	203	91% of all broadband and strong-motion sensors
Gap rate: less than 1 gap per hour	200	99%
Spikes: less than 1 spike per hour	197	97%
RMS noise: exceeded for less than 1 min per hour	197	98%
DC bias: less than 10% of the instrument's full-scale range	200	99%
Data latency: less than 3.5s for 90% of the time	193	1%
P-pick time difference: less than 0.3 s	90	93%
Station–magnitude difference: less than 0.5 magnitude units	43	98%

Criteria that must be met for a given station to pass ShakeAlert station acceptance (metrics 1–6) and UUSS location requirements. The number of sensors or stations evaluated depends on whether data were available during the tested time periods and the way a metric is calculated. The pass rate is for the corresponding sensors or stations tested. RMS, root mean square; and UUSS, University of Utah Seismograph Stations.

with our current station geometry to that of a hypothetical EEW-optimal network with increased station density. The nearest four stations were used to be consistent with the currently implemented EPIC (Earthquake Point-source Integrated Code) algorithm, which requires at least four triggering stations to issue an alert (Chung *et al.*, 2019); other feasibility studies using alternative point-source algorithms similarly use four stations (e.g., Picozzi *et al.*, 2015; Enferadi *et al.*, 2021; Massin *et al.*, 2021). We defined the current network configuration as the 164 EEW-Ready UUSS stations, as of January 2024. We defined the EEW-optimal network as the current network (164 stations), plus all 26 short-period stations (assumed to be upgraded to be EEW compatible), and new stations installed across the state following ShakeAlert spacing criteria: 10 km in urban areas, 20 km in seismic source areas that endanger population centers, and 40 km in other areas (Given *et al.*, 2018). Along the West Coast, these spacing criteria called for 1675 EEW-capable seismic stations (1115 in California and 560 in the Pacific Northwest); Utah would require far fewer additional stations at 257 (Fig. S1a).

The 257 new stations include 125 at the 10 km urban spacing, 94 at the 20 km seismic source spacing, and 38 at the 40 km spacing. To define the urban and seismic source areas for smaller station spacing, we used 25 urban area polygons defined by the 2020 Census as areas of high population density and urban land use (U.S. Census Bureau, 2024b) and the ISB extent. For ease of design, we defined a box from the maximum longitudinal and latitudinal extent of the Census polygons, adding a 10 km outer buffer. As a proxy for ISB extent, we used the USGS 2018 National Seismic Hazard Map (NSHM) peak ground acceleration contour for which the 2% probability of exceedance (PE) in 50 yr is $\geq 0.2g$ (Rukstales and Petersen, 2019; Petersen *et al.*, 2020) and added a 20 km buffer to the eastern and western borders. The 2% PE in 50 yr version was used in the New Madrid EEW feasibility study (Ogweno *et al.*, 2019) because it is the basis for calculating design earthquake loads. We did not use the more recent 2023 NSHM (Petersen *et al.*, 2024) because it is currently being revised so that the hazard in central Utah will change (M. Petersen and J. Pechmann, personal comm., 2024).

The 125 new urban stations were added at 10 km spacing over the 25 urban area boxes. Similarly, 94 new seismic source area stations were added at 20 km spacing throughout the proxy-ISB, and the remaining areas of the state were filled with 38 stations spaced at 40 km (Fig. S1a). New stations were not included if an existing UUSS station or a previously placed new station was at a distance less than the spacing criteria. We did not account for the ease of installation, such as the presence of a body of water or an otherwise unreachable location. Actual station installations would be slightly shifted from grid points to accommodate telemetry line-of-sight, accessibility, and permitting limitations.

We computed *P*-wave travel times to the four closest stations for the two network configurations (i.e., the $N = 164$ current configuration and the $N = 447$ EEW-optimal network configuration), using a grid of hypothetical earthquake sources representing the ISB and historical seismicity. We assumed a 12 km source depth consistent with local seismicity, and a constant *P*-wave velocity of 5.9 km/s (Pechmann *et al.*, 2007; Holt *et al.*, 2021). We determined source locations by defining $0.05° \times 0.05°$ bins over the state and comparing them to the proxy-ISB defined earlier and earthquake density from the 1850–2024 UUSS catalog (University of Utah, 1962; Arabasz and McKee, 1979; Arabasz *et al.*, 2016, 2017; Bowman and Arabasz, 2017; Fig. S2). Earthquake sources selected for analysis included any bins inside the ISB polygon or those that contained five or more earthquakes (3756 bins total). This way, pockets of high earthquake density outside of the proxy boundary were also included (Fig. S2). Bins that met both criteria were used as an earthquake source only once. These criteria ensured that analysis of the network configuration was based only on realistic earthquake sources and would not include less seismically active areas of the state, where station density is intentionally lower.

The aforementioned procedures result in two maps of *P*-wave travel times for the earthquake source grid, corresponding to the current network and the EEW-optimal network configurations. These maps were differenced to determine how much faster a *P* wave could reach four stations with the EEW-optimal network. Here, we assumed the data latency, processing time, and alert delivery latency are constant between the two network configurations, such that the *P*-wave travel-time decrease results in a warning time increase.

In the Wasatch Front, the EEW-optimal network includes the upgrade of seven short-period stations and the installation of 64 new seismic stations. Along the mapped Wasatch fault zone, approximately from Logan to south of Payson, and from Park City to west of Tooele, the EEW-optimal network increases the amount of warning by less than 1 s (Fig. 3a). The EEW-optimal network would yield <2 s of increased warning time for earthquakes along the Oquirrh-Great Salt Lake fault zone from approximately 41.25° N to south of Tooele. The average gain in warning time in the Wasatch Front region is 1.6 s.

The EEW-optimal network would provide the largest increase in warning time for earthquake sources outside of the Wasatch fault zone, with up to a 7 s increase along the northwest shore of the Great Salt Lake and southwest of Tooele. Along the northern extent of the Oquirrh-Great Salt Lake fault zone, up to 4.7 s could be gained, and 2.1–3.5 s could be gained along the Stansbury fault zone. Though the Wasatch fault zone has the highest probability of hosting the next large earthquake, these additional fault zones contribute to the overall 43% probability of an *M* 6.75+ rupture in the Wasatch Front region in the coming decades (Wong *et al.*, 2017).

Beyond the Wasatch Front region, warning time could be improved by up to 10 s for earthquakes within the ISB (Fig. 3b) in the EEW-optimal network. The increase in warning time is greatest just south of Richfield (7.5 s) and along the eastern edge of the ISB between ~37.6° to 38.75° N and overlaps the source region of the 1901 *M* 6.5 Richfield earthquake (Fig. 1a) and the northern Sevier fault zone. In the southwest, the EEW-optimal network improves warning times ≤2.2 s around St. George, Hurricane, and Cedar City. Up to 4.2 s could be gained for earthquakes along the Utah–Nevada border, northwest of St. George.

Outside of the ISB, seismicity is infrequent and sparse, thus we did not evaluate many earthquake sources (~8% of the

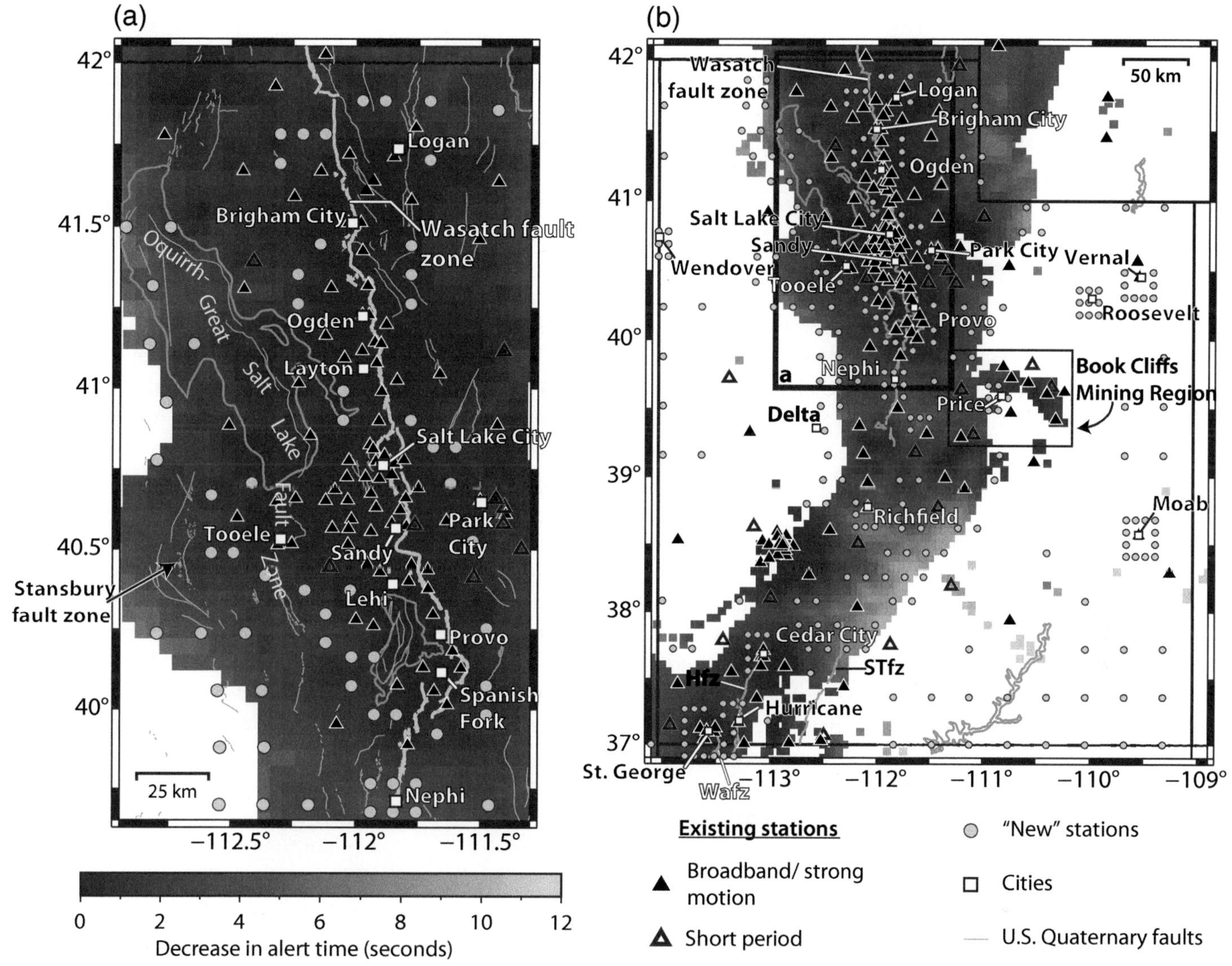

binned sources) for detection improvement (Fig. 3b and Fig. S2). Because of the lower seismic hazard, the 10 km urban spacing around Wendover, Vernal, Roosevelt, and Moab (38 stations) is likely unnecessary, and 10 stations at 40 km spacing would suffice (229 new stations total; Fig. S1b). Warning time increases by <1 s in the eastern Book Cliffs mining region—due to the existing enhanced coverage for monitoring mining-induced seismicity—to ~4.5 s in the western portion. The region along the Utah–Nevada border, west of Cedar City, could see a gain of up to 6.9 s in warning time, and earthquakes in a northwest–southeast-trending swath of elevated seismicity between 110.5° and 111.5° W and south of 38.25° N could see an improvement of 9–17 s.

Figure 3. Decrease in *P*-wave travel time to four stations due to increasing seismograph station density following ShakeAlert convention (a) in the Wasatch Front and (b) throughout the state. The bolded fault traces make up the Wasatch fault zone in panels (a) and (b), and highlight the Washington, Hurricane, and Sevier-Toroweap fault zones in panel (b). The denser network includes the upgrade of short-period sites (open triangles) to be EEW-compatible and the addition of 257 new stations (gray dots). Colors represent how much faster an earthquake at that location with a 12 km depth would be detected with the denser network. Assuming data latency, processing, and alert delivery times remain unchanged, the decrease in *P*-wave travel time to four stations translates to an increase in warning time; orange and yellow colors indicate the greatest subsequent increase in warning time for an earthquake at that location with the denser network. The color version of this figure is available only in the electronic edition.

POTENTIAL PERFORMANCE OF EEW IN UTAH

In Utah, most of the population is directly adjacent to mapped faults (Fig. 1b). Given this configuration, cities and people closest to the epicenter and experiencing the greatest shaking would not receive a shaking alert in time. To determine if sufficient warning could be achieved at other nearby areas expected to experience strong shaking, we estimated potential warning times for six hypothetical scenario earthquakes and examined the historical earthquake catalog to determine how often alerts are expected to be issued. The scenarios were taken from Pankow *et al.* (2013), which presented synthetic ShakeMaps (Worden *et al.*, 2020) that model ground motion for uniform slip on an input fault plane, based on characteristic fault models. Thus, we can compare our estimated warning times with the expected maximum shaking intensity for these hypothetical events, which is advantageous because the shaking distribution in Utah is highly variable with amplification in the valleys. The scenarios consist of *M* 7.0 ruptures on (1) the Salt Lake City and (2) Brigham City segments of the Wasatch fault zone, (3) an *M* 6.5 earthquake near Richfield, Utah, and (4) an *M* 6.7 earthquake on the Hurricane fault system in southwestern Utah. Two additional scenarios within the Wasatch Front region are presented in the supplement (Figs. S3, S4, and corresponding text): a scenario similar to the 1934 *M* 6.6 Hansel Valley earthquake—the largest historical earthquake in Utah (Fig. 1a; Doser, 1989)—and an *M* 7.0 on the Oquirrh-Great Salt Lake fault zone. We consider damaging shaking to be MMI ≥ 6, which, following the ShakeAlert convention, encompasses MMI ≥ 5.5 (Wald *et al.*, 1999; Chung *et al.*, 2020).

We defined the time to receive an alert in our Utah EEW system as the sum of (1) the *P*-wave travel time to four stations and the amount of time to (2) digitally record the ground motion at each site and transmit these data packets to the data center (data latency), (3) process and characterize the earthquake and determine whether to issue an alert, and (4) transmit the alert to users (alert delivery latency; e.g., figure 1 of Behr *et al.*, 2015). We calculated the *P*-wave travel time as discussed previously, assuming the EEW-optimal network geometry. We assumed all stations were operational in these scenarios, with no missing data. These assumptions allow us to gauge the best EEW performance we can expect in Utah.

For the six scenario earthquakes presented in the feasibility report (Bowman *et al.*, 2024; Figs. 4–7, Figs. S3–S4), the *P*-wave travel times to the four closest stations ranged from 2.1 to 5.1 s. The measured data latency and UUSS processing time would not be representative of an operational EEW system, so we refer to the performance times of the West Coast ShakeAlert system (Given *et al.*, 2014, 2018; Kohler *et al.*, 2020). In the ShakeAlert system, data latencies are typically 0–2 s (McGuire *et al.*, 2021) and are required to be <3.5 s at least 90% of the time for station acceptance (Table 2). Processing times can be less than a second to several seconds. Here, we assumed a combined data latency and processing time of 4 s, as used in other studies (Kuyuk and Allen, 2013; Ogweno *et al.*, 2019; Massin *et al.*, 2021; Cremen *et al.*, 2022; Fozkos and West, 2025; Kinkel and Trugman, 2025). Other studies have run offline playbacks of real-event data through EEW algorithms, therefore having variable processing times corresponding to actual offline processing (e.g., Picozzi *et al.*, 2015; Enferadi *et al.*, 2021).

The largest variability in estimating warning time performance is the time between when an alert is transmitted and when it is received by a person or machine (alert delivery latency). The ShakeAlert system provides an alert for established technical partners to distribute via smartphone apps, Google push notifications for Android OS, and wireless emergency alerts (WEAs; Kohler *et al.*, 2020; McGuire *et al.*, 2025). The alert delivery latency can be <1 s for internet-connected devices, 1–10 s for cellular delivery, and more than 10 s for WEAs (McGuire *et al.*, 2021). Tests of alert delivery latency found a median WEA delivery latency of 6–12 s (McBride *et al.*, 2023) and median MyShake app delivery latencies of ≤2.4–2.8 s in urban areas (Allen *et al.*, 2020; Patel and Allen, 2022). However, app-based alert latencies may increase when alerting large populations at once; recent surveys of ShakeAlert end users showed a consistent percentage of later-than-expected alerts across both alerting types (Saunders and Wald, 2025). Here, we focused on establishing maximum warning times, so we assumed alert delivery over the internet for machine-to-machine alerts and used an alert delivery latency of 1 s. Lux *et al.* (2024) do not include an alert delivery latency in their warning time estimations, but provide the caveat that they can be considered the maximum warning times of the system. Similarly, our 1 s assumption can be considered to contribute to a maximum potential-warning time, with decreases up to ~10 s depending on the delivery method. Previous feasibility studies have not included the alert delivery latency (Thelen *et al.*, 2016; Ogweno *et al.*, 2019) or have assumed it to be part of the 4 s processing time (Fozkos and West, 2025; Kinkel and Trugman, 2025).

Summing the four-station *P*-wave travel time, data latency and processing time, and alert delivery latency yields total alert times of 7.1–10.1 s after origin time (median 8.2 s) for the six scenario earthquakes. The average ShakeAlert alert time (which does not include alert delivery latency) for earthquakes *M* 3.5+ in 2020 to 30 September 2023 was 11.64 ± 7 s (E. Cochran, personal comm., 2023), and it has produced first alert times of 4–8 s in well-instrumented areas between 17 October 2019 and 1 September 2023 (Lux *et al.*, 2024). Our range of hypothetical alert times is easily within these ranges. Our alert timing estimation is necessarily simplified and does not account for earthquake rupture directivity or other complexities. In practice, the earliest EEW alerts may underpredict shaking or be based on an inaccurate location, with additional alerts being sent with updated information as more data are processed. These factors could add to the time for an alert to be received; however, our internal system performance has shown that automatic phase picks and magnitude estimations are usually very close to the final reviewed values (93% and 98%; Table 2).

We defined warning time as the amount of time between when the alert is received (7.1–10.1 s for our scenarios) and when the *S* waves arrive at a given location, using a constant *S*-wave velocity consistent with our region of 3.4 km/s (Pechmann *et al.*, 2007; Holt *et al.*, 2021). The no-alert zone represents the area traveled by the *S* waves by the time the alert is received; however, we acknowledge the possibility of damaging shaking (MMI ≥ 5.5) before or after the *S*-wave arrival. Using the *S*-wave timing for peak shaking is a common assumption in feasibility studies

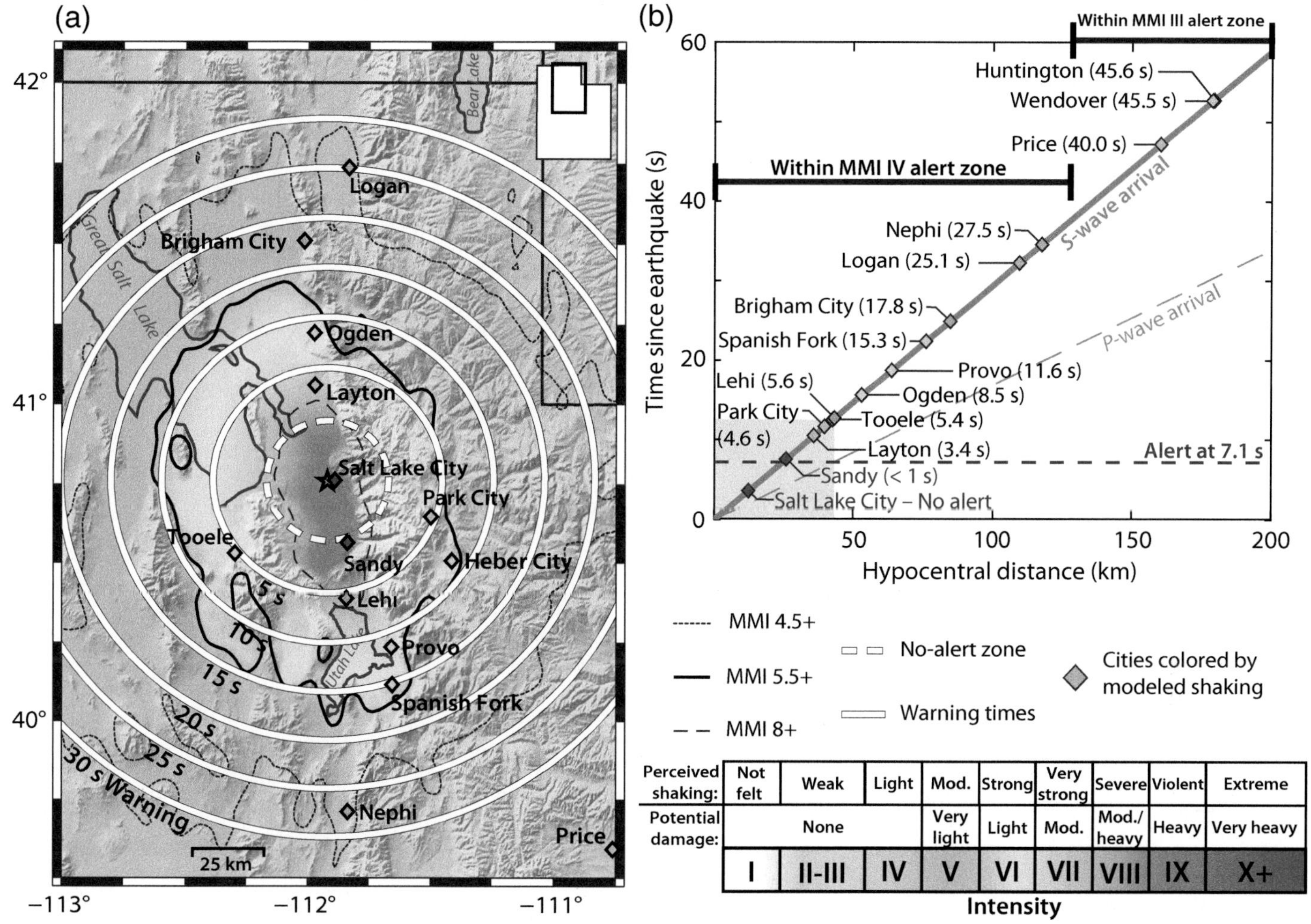

Figure 4. Maximum potential warning times for an *M* 7.0 earthquake scenario on the Salt Lake City segment of the Wasatch fault zone, modified from Bowman *et al.* (2024). The Salt Lake City scenario earthquake source is located at 40.76° N, 111.92° W, 12 km depth (star; Pankow *et al.*, 2013). Concentric white circles on the map (a) indicate the maximum potential warning time that could be provided at that location before the *S* wave arrives. The white-dashed circle is the no-alert zone for an alert that is received 7.1 s after the origin time. Colors indicate the maximum modified Mercalli intensity (MMI) of shaking modeled for the scenario earthquake (Pankow *et al.*, 2013). The black-dotted, black-solid, and black-dashed lines represent contours of MMI 4.5, 5.5, and 8, respectively, corresponding to regions of very light damage, light-to-moderate damage, and heavy damage. The inset map in the upper-right corner of (a) shows the location of the map area (box) in the state of Utah (white). (b) The upper-right panel summarizes the potential warning times and the expected MMI for select cities as a function of distance. The gray-shaded region encompasses the distances from the hypocenter where the *P* wave could be felt at or before the time the alert would be received. The color version of this figure is available only in the electronic edition.

(e.g., Picozzi *et al.*, 2015; Thelen *et al.*, 2016; Ogweno *et al.*, 2019; Enferadi *et al.*, 2021; Massin *et al.*, 2021; Kinkel and Trugman, 2025). One notable exception is in the Fozkos and West (2025) Alaskan warning time scenarios, for which they use a range of times between the *S*- and Love-wave arrivals, based on global moment rate functions.

M 7.0 scenario earthquake in Salt Lake City

Of the five most active, central segments of the Wasatch fault zone, the Salt Lake City segment is the second most "overdue" for a characteristic earthquake (Wong *et al.*, 2017). The last known paleoearthquake occurred ∼1300 yr ago, and recurrence on any given fault segment is ∼900 to 1500 yr. Potential warning times for an *M* 7.0 earthquake on the Salt Lake City segment are shown in Figure 4. The no-alert zone encompasses Salt Lake City and its nearest suburbs for an alert received 7.1 s after origin time, and ∼13% of the area that is expected to have damaging shaking. Cities such as Ogden, Provo, Spanish Fork, and Heber City have maximum potential-warning times of 8–15 s and are expected to experience shaking MMI ≥ 6. Cities with moderate shaking (MMI ∼ 4.5), such as Brigham City, Logan, and Nephi, would have up to 17–27 s warning and would be within the area that exceeds the MMI 4 threshold for alerting (e.g., McBride *et al.*, 2023; Lux *et al.*, 2024; McGuire *et al.*, 2025).

M 7.0 scenario earthquake in Brigham City

The Brigham City segment of the Wasatch fault zone is the segment most "overdue" for a large (*M* 6.75–7.0) earthquake,

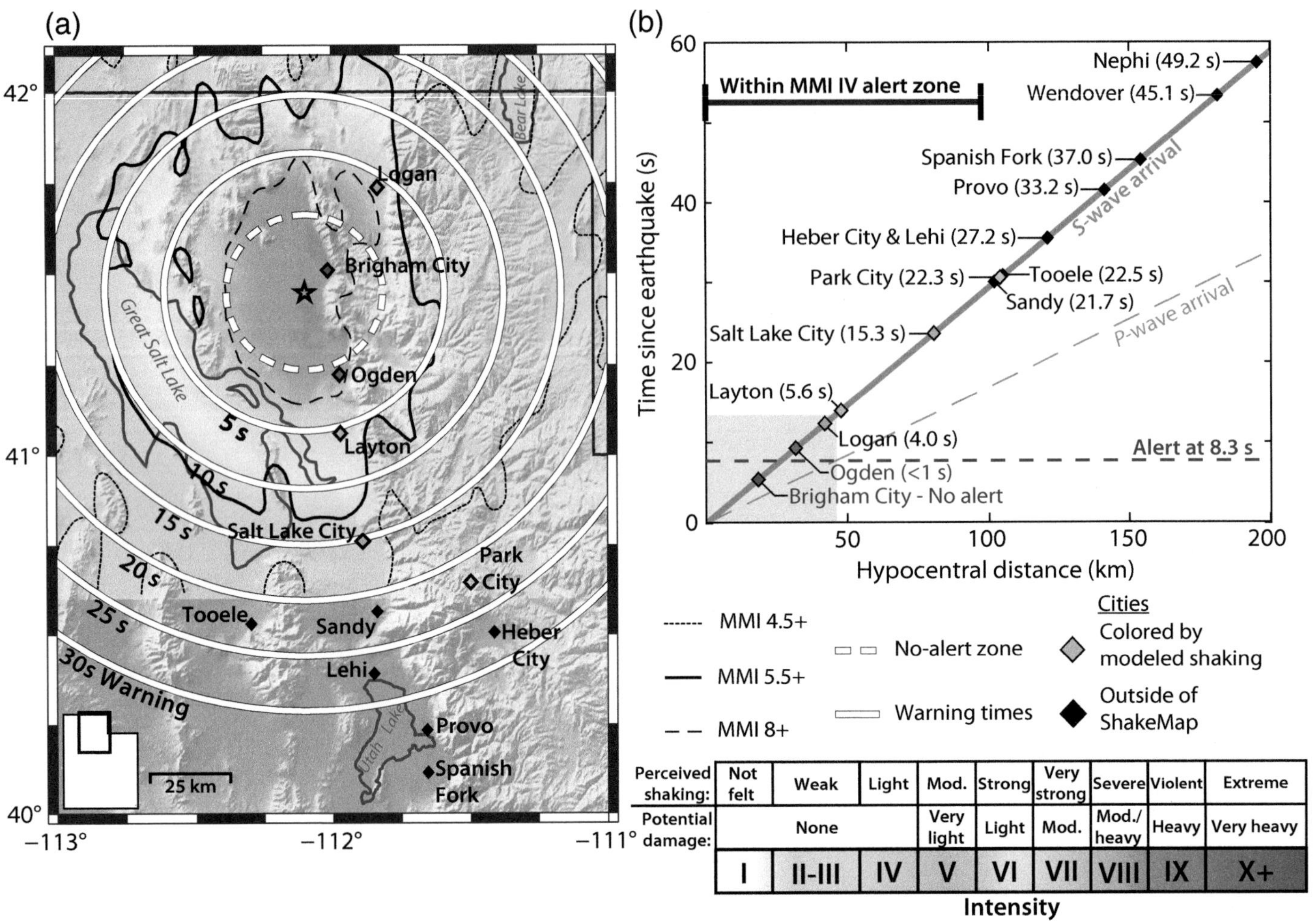

Figure 5. Maximum potential warning times for an M 7.0 earthquake scenario on the Brigham City segment of the Wasatch fault zone with an alert received at 8.3 s after origin time, modified from Bowman *et al.* (2024). The Brigham City scenario earthquake source is located at 41.45° N, 112.1° W, 15 km depth (Pankow *et al.*, 2013). Concentric white circles on the map (a) indicate the maximum potential warning time that could be provided at that location before the S wave arrives. The white-dashed circle is the no-alert zone for an alert that is received 8.3 s after origin time. Colors indicate the maximum modified Mercalli intensity (MMI) of shaking modeled for the scenario earthquake (Pankow *et al.*, 2013). The black-dotted, black-solid, and black-dashed lines represent contours of MMI 4.5, MMI 5.5, and MMI 8, respectively, corresponding to regions of very light damage, light-to-moderate damage, and heavy damage. The inset map in the lower-left corner of (a) shows the location of the map area (box) in the state of Utah (white). (b) The upper-right panel summarizes the potential warning times and the expected MMI for select cities as a function of distance. The gray-shaded region encompasses the distances from the hypocenter where the P wave could be felt at or before the time the alert would be received. Cities outside the modeled ShakeMap extent are still shown on (b) but are not colored by MMI. The color version of this figure is available only in the electronic edition.

as evidenced by paleoseismic studies which find that the most recent surface-rupturing earthquake occurred ~2400 yr ago (Swan *et al.*, 1980; Schwartz and Coppersmith, 1984; DuRoss *et al.*, 2016). Cities that are estimated to experience damaging shaking in the Brigham City scenario (Fig. 5) have lower maximum potential warning times outside the no-alert zone for an alert time of 8.3 s: Ogden (<1 s), Logan (4 s), and Layton (6 s) with MMI > 7. Salt Lake City could receive up to 15 s of warning with peak intensity MMI ~ 5. Additional cities are outside the modeled ShakeMap, but we expect some of these locations would be within the MMI 4 or MMI 3 alert thresholds, with more than 20 s of warning.

M 6.5 scenario earthquake near Richfield

In 1901, an M 6.5 earthquake occurred in central Utah near Richfield (Fig. 1a), with a felt area of 130,000 km^2 (Christenson and Nava, 1992). Structural damage occurred in multiple nearby cities, and some roads were rendered impassable by fallen rocks (O'Brien and Nava, 1997). We tested a scenario with a similar source, following Pankow *et al.* (2013; Fig. 6). The no-alert region for an 8.2 s alert time includes Richfield and other cities expected to experience MMI 7.2–8.2. Salina (MMI 6.8) and Fillmore (MMI 6.6) have maximum potential warning times ≤2 s. Gunnison and Loa could have up to 6 and 9 s, respectively, and these two cities are coincident with modeled MMI values of 4.9 and 5.6, just under and at what is likely to be damaging. Cities with larger potential warnings (14–22 s) correspond to

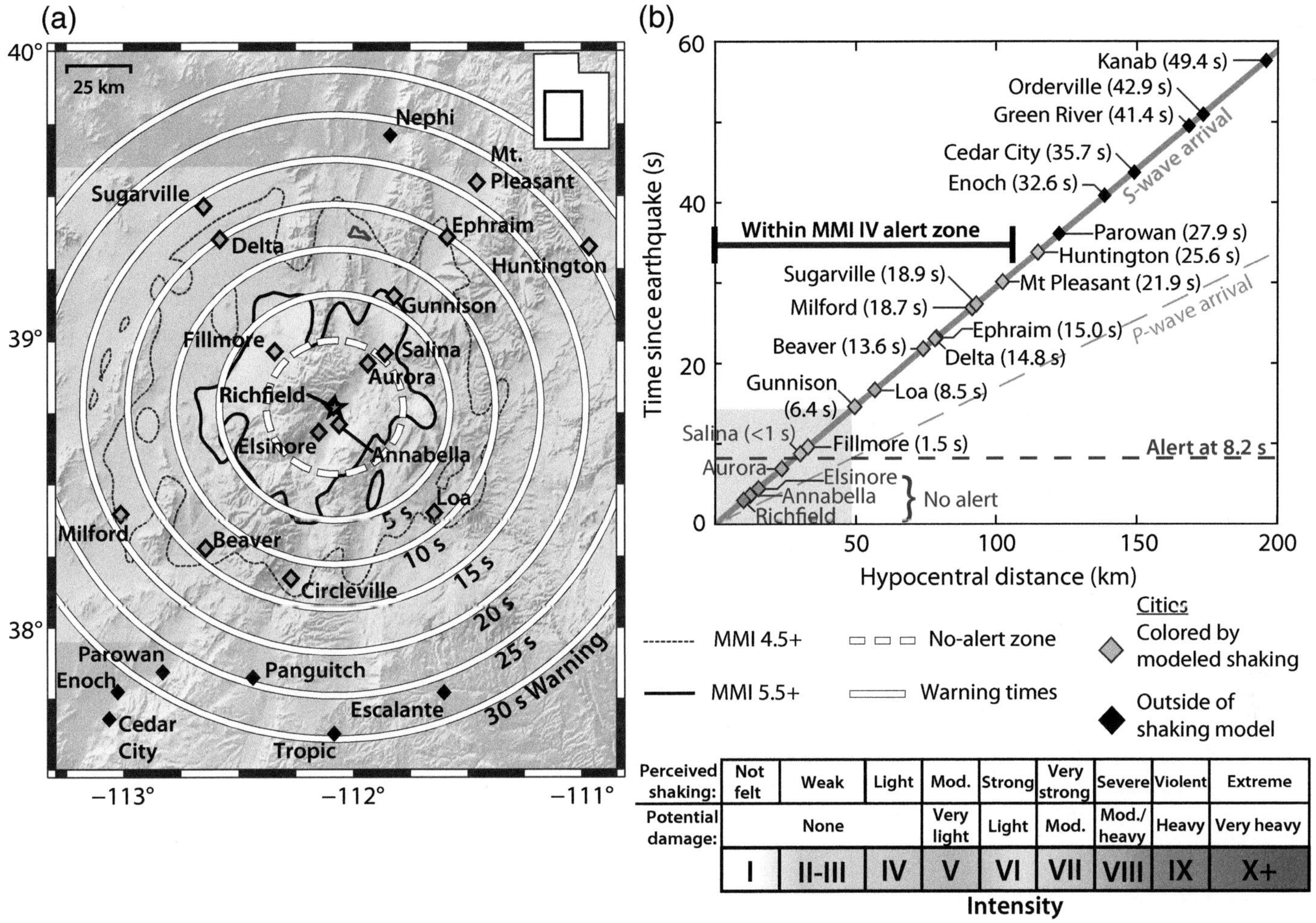

Figure 6. Maximum potential warning times for an *M* 6.5 earthquake scenario similar to the 1901 Richfield, Utah, earthquake, modified from Bowman *et al.* (2024). The Richfield scenario earthquake source is located at 38.77° N, 112.08° W, 10 km depth (star; Pankow *et al.*, 2013), and the alert would be received at 8.2 s after origin time. Concentric white circles on the map (a) indicate the maximum potential warning time that could be provided at that location before the *S* wave arrives. The white-dashed circle is the no-alert zone for an alert that is received 8.2 s after origin time. Colors indicate the maximum modified Mercalli intensity (MMI) of shaking modeled for the scenario earthquake (Pankow *et al.*, 2013). The black-dotted and black-solid lines represent contours of MMI 4.5 and MMI 5.5, respectively, corresponding to regions of very light damage and light-to-moderate damage. The inset map in the upper-right corner of (a) shows the location of the map area in the state of Utah (white). (b) The upper-right panel summarizes the potential warning times and the expected MMI for select cities as a function of distance. The gray-shaded region encompasses the distances from the hypocenter where the *P* wave could be felt at or before the time the alert would be received. Cities outside the modeled ShakeMap extent are still shown in plot (b) but are not colored by MMI. The color version of this figure is available only in the electronic edition.

predicted intensities of MMI 4.3–4.9 and thus would be within the MMI 4 alert region, where the shaking would not be expected to be damaging.

M 6.7 scenario earthquake on the Hurricane fault

Outside the Wasatch Front, the most populous area of the state is the southwestern corner, encompassing the rapidly growing cities of Cedar City, Hurricane, St. George, and Washington. Though it gets less attention than the Wasatch fault zone, the Hurricane fault zone and nearby Washington fault zone are thought to be capable of *M* 7+ earthquakes (Lund *et al.*, 2007, 2015). A 1992 *M* 5.8 earthquake on the Washington fault caused extensive structural damage in surrounding cities (O'Brien and Nava, 1997). We estimate warning times for an *M* 6.7 earthquake on the Anderson segment of the Hurricane fault zone with an alert time of 7.9 s (Pankow *et al.*, 2013; Fig. 7). Washington, Hurricane, and St. George are within the estimated no-alert zone, and the ShakeMap predicts MMI 7.2–8.7 within these cities. Enterprise and Cedar City are estimated to receive up to 10 and 13 s for this event with MMI values of 5.7 and 5.4, respectively. Farther cities could have up to 15–38 s of warning for felt but not damaging shaking (MMI 4.1–5).

EXPECTED FREQUENCY OF ALERTS FOR A UTAH EEW SYSTEM

Though an EEW system could be beneficial for large earthquakes such as the preserved paleoearthquakes, such events would not trigger an EEW system frequently. Paleoearthquakes on the

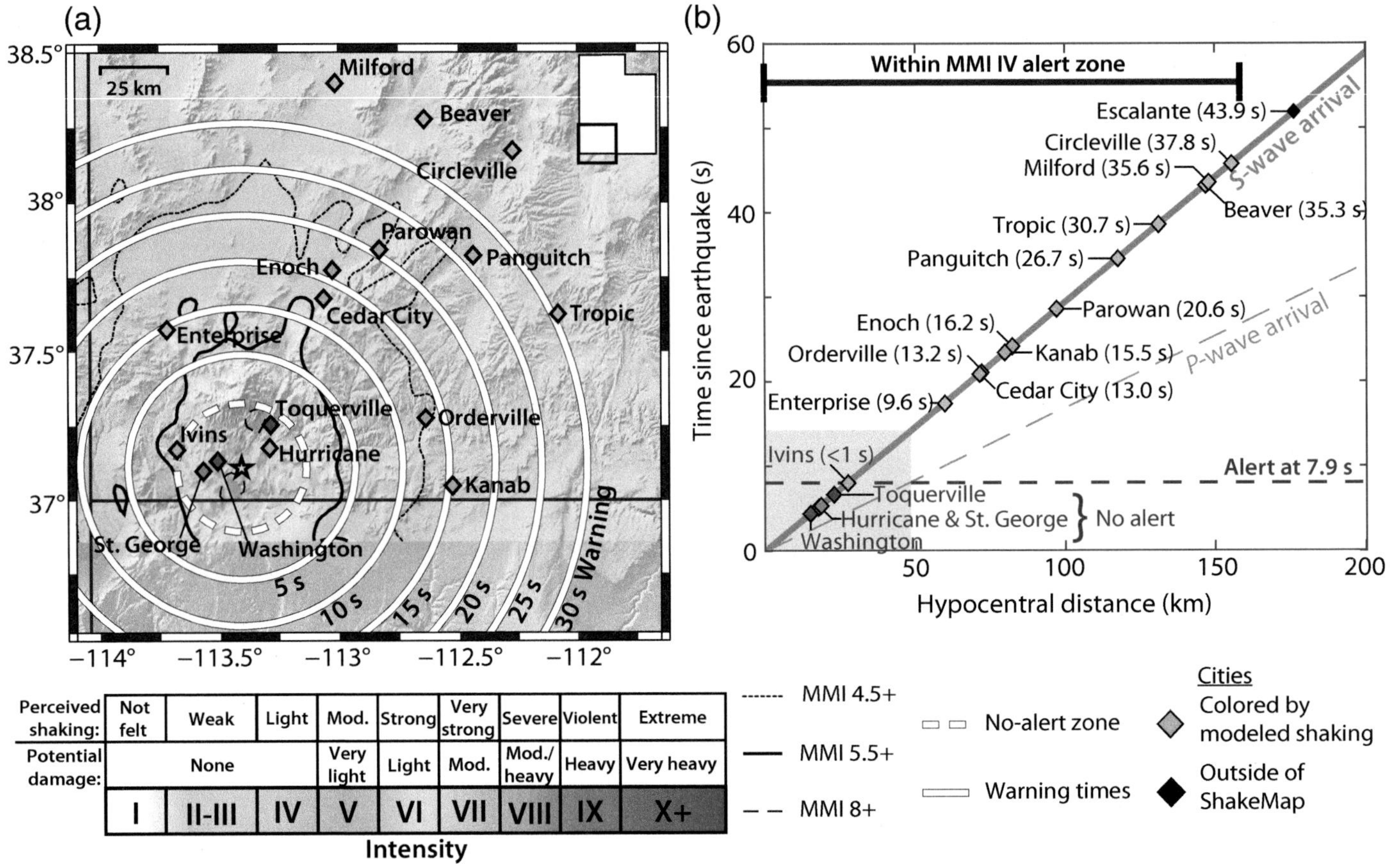

Figure 7. Maximum potential warning times for an M 6.7 earthquake scenario on the Anderson segment of the Hurricane fault zone in southwestern Utah, modified from Bowman *et al.* (2024). The Hurricane scenario earthquake source is located at 37.11° N, 113.41° W, 12 km depth (star; Pankow *et al.*, 2013), and the alert would be received at 7.9 s after origin time. Concentric white circles on the map (a) indicate the maximum potential warning time that could be provided at that location before the S wave arrives. The white-dashed circle is the no-alert zone for an alert that is received 7.9 s after origin time. Colors indicate the maximum modified Mercalli intensity (MMI) of shaking modeled for the scenario earthquake (Pankow *et al.*, 2013). The black-dotted, black-solid, and black-dashed lines represent contours of MMI 4.5, MMI 5.5, and MMI 8, respectively, corresponding to regions of very light damage, light-to-moderate damage, and heavy damage. The inset map in the upper-right corner of (a) shows the location of the map area (box) in the state of Utah (white). (b) The upper-right panel summarizes the potential warning times and the expected MMI for select cities as a function of distance. The gray-shaded region encompasses the distances from the hypocenter where the P wave could be felt at or before the time the alert would be received. Cities outside the modeled ShakeMap extent are still shown in plot (b) but are not colored by MMI. The color version of this figure is available only in the electronic edition.

central Wasatch fault zone suggest a recurrence interval of ~300 yr (DuRoss *et al.*, 2016; Utah Seismic Safety Commission, 2022), and in 2014, it was estimated there was a 43% chance of a large earthquake (M 6.75+) occurring in the Wasatch Front region within the next 50 yr (Wong *et al.*, 2017). Therefore, only a single use of an EEW system for a large, damaging earthquake would be expected within the next few decades. However, an EEW system could be triggered for smaller earthquakes that generate lesser amounts of damage. If a Utah EEW system—with the previously described timing assumptions—were in operation during the 2020 M_w 5.7 Magna, Utah, earthquake, some cities (Park City, Ogden) would have had up to 7–8 s of warning for peak shaking up to MMI 4.1 (Fig. 8), and would have been within the area that exceeds the MMI 4 intensity threshold for alerting (McBride *et al.*, 2023; Lux *et al.*, 2024; McGuire *et al.*, 2025). Cities that could have had up to 12–18 s of warning (Provo, Spanish Fork, and Brigham City) experienced peak shaking of MMI 3.1–3.9 and would have been within the MMI 3 alert region for cell phone apps, push notifications, and machine-to-machine actions (Lux *et al.*, 2024; McGuire *et al.*, 2025). Earthquakes with M ~5 occur roughly once a decade in Utah, thus they would infrequently trigger an EEW system; however, there is evidence that people desire warnings even if the shaking is not strong enough to cause significant damage (Allen, 2017; Allen *et al.*, 2018; Bostrom *et al.*, 2022). Because of their greater frequency, we can expect an EEW system to be activated more often for nondamaging earthquakes, although this is only feasible if the felt region (ShakeMap MMI 2 contour; Worden *et al.*, 2020) for such events is sufficiently larger than the no-alert zone.

We used the recent history of Wasatch Front earthquakes (University of Utah, 1962; Arabasz *et al.*, 2016, 2017; Bowman and Arabasz, 2017) and their ShakeMaps to estimate potential EEW activation frequency and to estimate if felt areas for relatively small earthquakes would receive timely alerts. We used the same methodology as before to estimate plausible warning times for four recent Wasatch Front earthquakes (M 3.6–4.6) with computed ShakeMaps. We determined warning times using the hypocentral distance between the event and nearby cities and compared these with the extent of the MMI 2 contour.

We estimated warning times for the following three felt earthquakes with available ShakeMaps (date, time, latitude, longitude, depth, magnitude, and location):

A:18 March 2020, 14:57:41, 40.755° N, 112.047° W, 8.3 km, M 3.6 near Magna

B:18 March 2020, 13:10:16, 40.748° N, 112.080° W, 6.9 km, M 4.0 near Magna

C:18 March 18, 19:12:23, 40.751° N, 112.059° W, 10.7 km, M 4.6 near Magna

to assess if the felt region (MMI 2+) extends beyond the no-alert zone such that meaningful alerts could be issued. All three

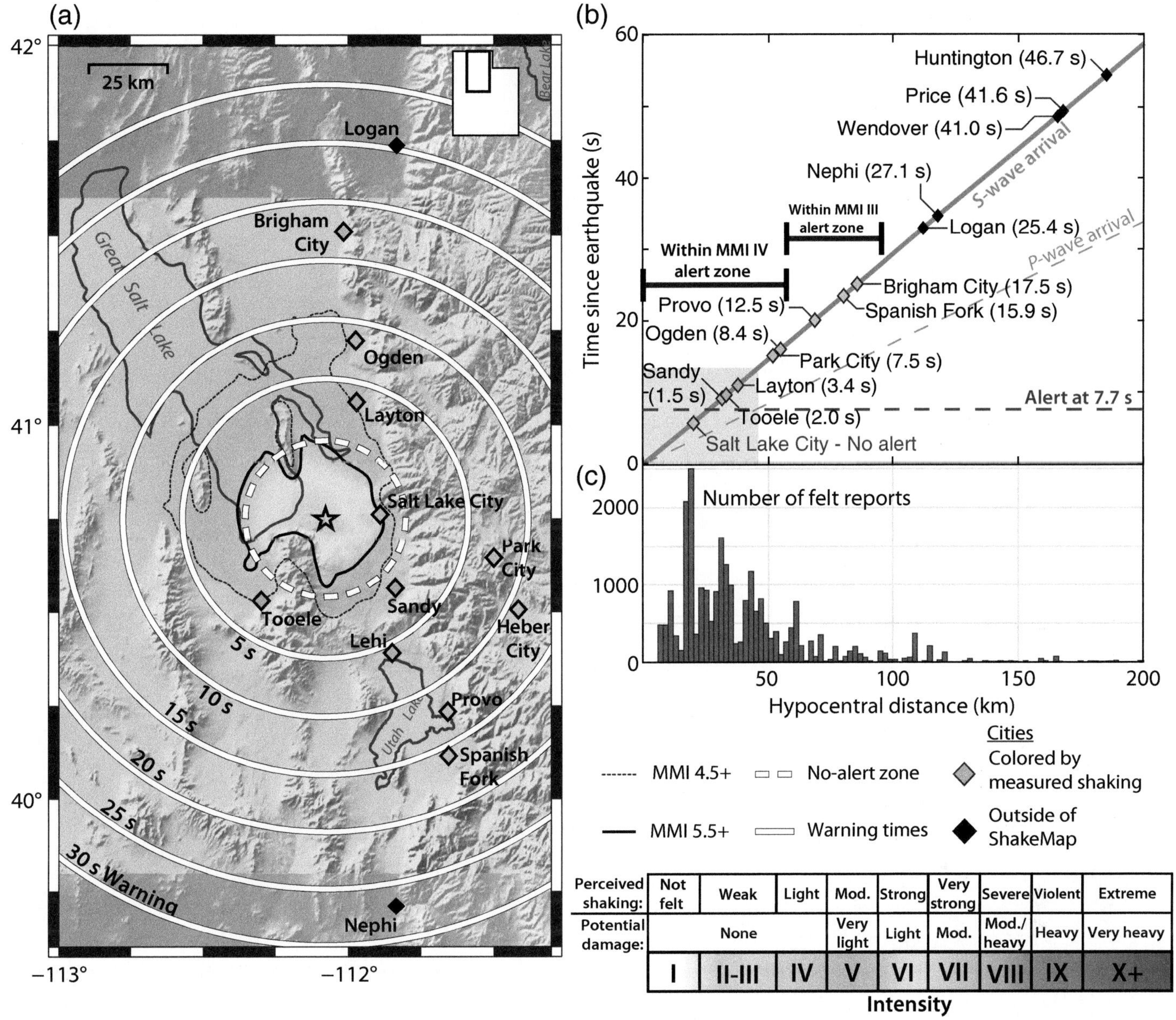

Figure 8. Maximum potential warning times for the 18 March 2020 M_w 5.7 Magna, Utah, earthquake, had an EEW system been operational with an ideally spaced seismic network, modified from Bowman *et al.* (2024). Concentric white circles on the map (a) indicate the maximum warning time that could have been provided at a given location before shaking associated with the *S* wave began. The white-dashed circle is the no-alert zone for an alert received 7.7 s after the earthquake origin time. Colors correspond to the authoritative MMI ShakeMap, generated for the event in routine operations (available through ComCat, evid uu60363602) and based on seismic measurements and felt reports. The black-dotted and black-solid lines represent contours of MMI 4.5 and MMI 5.5, respectively, corresponding to regions of very light damage and light-to-moderate damage. The inset map in the upper-right corner of (a) shows the location of the map area (box) in the state of Utah (white). (b) The upper-right panel summarizes the warning times and the shaking intensities for select cities. The gray-shaded region encompasses the distances from the hypocenter where the *P* wave could be felt at or before the time the alert would be received. (c) The corresponding number of felt reports logged at the U.S. Geological Survey (USGS) by distance from the earthquake. The color version of this figure is available only in the electronic edition.

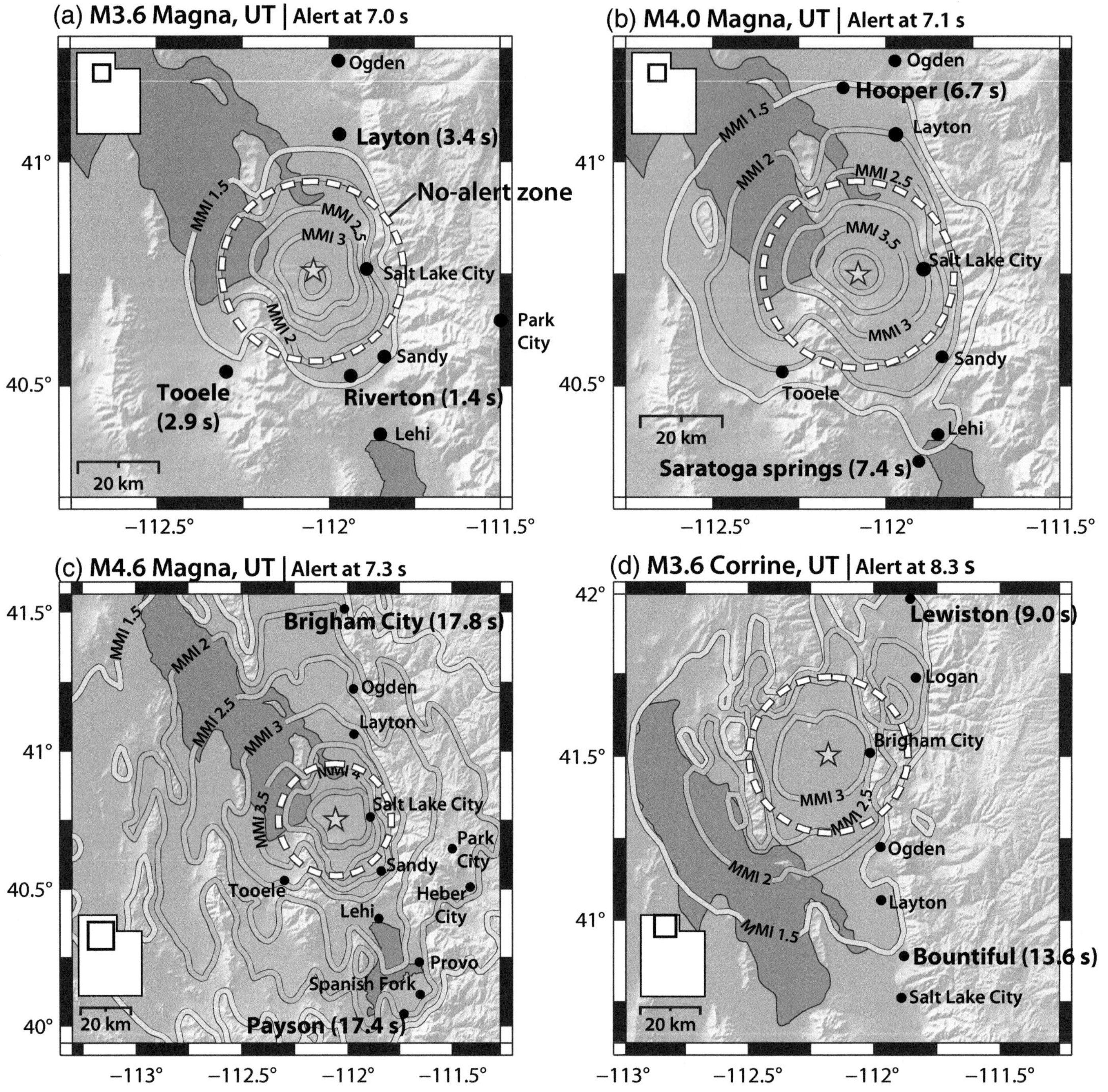

Figure 9. Comparison of the felt regions of four select Utah earthquakes (M 3.6+) with the no-alert zone following alerts received 7.0–8.3 s after earthquake origin time. Maps (a–d) correspond to earthquakes A–D in the Expected Frequency of Alerts for a Utah EEW System section with stars at their epicenters. Event maps show ShakeMap intensity contours, accessed via ComCat and colored and labeled by MMI. The extent of the no-alert zone is shown as a white-dashed circle. Bolded cities with corresponding warning times are discussed in the Expected Frequency of Alerts for a Utah EEW System section. The inset maps in the upper-left corner of (a) and (b) and lower-left corner of (c) and (d) show the locations of the corresponding map area (box) in the state of Utah (white). The color version of this figure is available only in the electronic edition.

earthquakes were part of the 2020 M_w 5.7 Magna aftershock sequence with epicenters about 10 km west of downtown Salt Lake City (Fig. 9a–c). Following the convention used by ShakeAlert (Wald *et al.*, 1999; Chung *et al.*, 2020), the MMI 2 region encompasses the range MMI 1.5–2.5; for earthquake A, the MMI 1.5 contour stretches as far south as Riverton and as far west as Tooele at hypocentral distances of 28.7 and 33.8 km, respectively. Warnings at these locations are up to 1.4 and 2.9 s before S-wave-related shaking begins. For earthquake B, the felt region extends to Saratoga Springs in the south (49.3 km) and as far north as Hooper (46.9 km), for which we could expect up to 7.4 and 6.7 s of warning,

TABLE 3
Average Recurrence of UUSS Catalog (1962–2024) Earthquakes by Region and Magnitude

Region	M ≥ 3.5 Recurrence (Yr)	M ≥ 4.0 Recurrence (Yr)	M ≥ 4.5 Recurrence (Yr)
Wasatch Front	0.91 (69 earthquakes)	2.25 (28 earthquakes)	4.5 (14 earthquakes)
Utah-Intermountain Seismic Belt (ISB; includes Wasatch Front)	0.40 (4.78 months; 158 earthquakes)	1.09 (58 earthquakes)	2.63 (24 earthquakes)
All earthquakes in and adjacent to Utah	0.27 (3.23 months; 234 earthquakes)	0.69 (8.31 months; 91 earthquakes)	1.58 (40 earthquakes)

UUSS, University of Utah Seismograph Stations.

respectively. For earthquake C, the felt region stretches as far south as Payson, 84.1 km, with up to 17.4 s of warning, and as far north as Brigham City, 85.2 km, yielding up to 17.8 s of warning.

Actual warning times may vary somewhat because felt areas are not solely a function of magnitude but also depend on rupture properties such as the fault orientation, the direction of rup ture, and the stress drop, as well as regional variations in propagation efficiency (attenuation) and geology (site effects). As an example, we analyzed another recent earthquake (date, time, latitude, longitude, depth, magnitude, and location):

D: 12 November 2022, 13:45:07, 41.513° N, 112.181° W, 10.1 km, *M* 3.6 near Corinne

that occurred about 13.8 km west of Brigham City (Fig. 9d). The MMI 1.5 contour stretches as far south as Bountiful, 74.4 km, and as far north as Lewiston, 59.0 km, for which we could expect 13.6 and 9.0 s warning, respectively. For comparison, it has the same magnitude as earthquake A, which yielded only 0–2 s of warning time in the MMI 2 region despite having a shorter alert time.

In the modern UUSS instrumental earthquake catalog spanning 1962–2024 (University of Utah, 1962; Arabasz *et al.*, 2016, 2017; Bowman and Arabasz, 2017), there have been 14, 28, and 69 earthquakes with magnitudes ≥4.5, 4.0, and 3.5, respectively, within or directly adjacent to the Wasatch Front, and 24, 58, and 158 earthquakes, respectively, throughout the ISB (including the Wasatch Front). Therefore, on average, there is an *M* 3.5+ earthquake every ~1 yr, an *M* 4.0+ earthquake every ~2 yr, and an *M* 4.5+ earthquake every ~4 yr in the Wasatch Front, and every ~5 months, ~1 yr, and ~3 yr, respectively, for the full ISB (Table 3). ShakeAlert publishes alert information for events *M* 3.5+ and issues public alerts for events *M* 4.5+ (Lux *et al.*, 2024). At the *M* 4.5+ alert threshold, during the time window of 17 October 2019 to 1 September 2023, ShakeAlert averaged 24 alerts per year along the West Coast (Lux *et al.*, 2024). This is 96 times higher than the rate estimated in this work of one alert every four years in the Wasatch Front, and 72 times higher than one alert every three years in the ISB. If the threshold was lowered in a Utah EEW system to include felt shaking, we estimate that an EEW system along the Wasatch Front would provide alerts in advance of noticeable ground shaking every 0.9–2.3 yr in the Wasatch Front, or 1–2 times a year throughout the entire ISB, corresponding to alerts at *M* 3.5+ and 4.0+ (Table 3).

It is important to note that EEW alerts would be heavily clustered in time during major earthquake sequences (Fig. S5). If we assume an EEW system had been in place for the last 63 yr (1962–2024), that it issued alerts for all 28 *M* 4+ earthquakes along and near the Wasatch Front, and that it did not issue alerts for any of the smaller earthquakes, then seven of the alerts (25%) would have been issued during one month associated with the 2020 M_w 5.7 Magna earthquake sequence. The longest "dry spell" with no alerts would have been 17 yr, corresponding to the time between an M_L 4.2 earthquake near Herriman in 1992 and an M_L 4.0 earthquake near Riverside in 2009. At the *M* 4.5+ alert threshold, the longest Wasatch Front dry spell would be ~31 yr, between an M_L 4.5 earthquake near Thatcher in 1989 and the 2020 Magna mainshock (M_w 5.7). In the ISB, the longest dry spells for *M* 4+ or 4.5+ alert thresholds would have been ~6 and ~18 yr.

DISCUSSION

The existing UUSS seismic network performs very well by the ShakeAlert station acceptance standards (Table 2), and station density along the Wasatch fault zone is within the optimal spacing for EEW (Fig. 3). Therefore, a prototype EEW system could be made operational along the Wasatch fault zone with no new station installations, only with reductions in data latency at the existing stations. The rest of the Wasatch Front region and ISB would need sensor upgrades and an additional 64 and 117 stations, respectively, to fully operate an EEW system (Fig. S1). An additional 48 stations spaced at 40 km throughout the remainder of the state would provide coverage outside of urban areas and the ISB, following the ShakeAlert convention. These additional stations could improve network detection time up to 7 s in the Wasatch Front, 10 s in the ISB, and 17 s in the state for common earthquake source regions. The 229 "new" stations (Fig. S1b) required to build a statewide EEW system in Utah are substantially lower than the installation of 1675 new stations needed to develop the West Coast

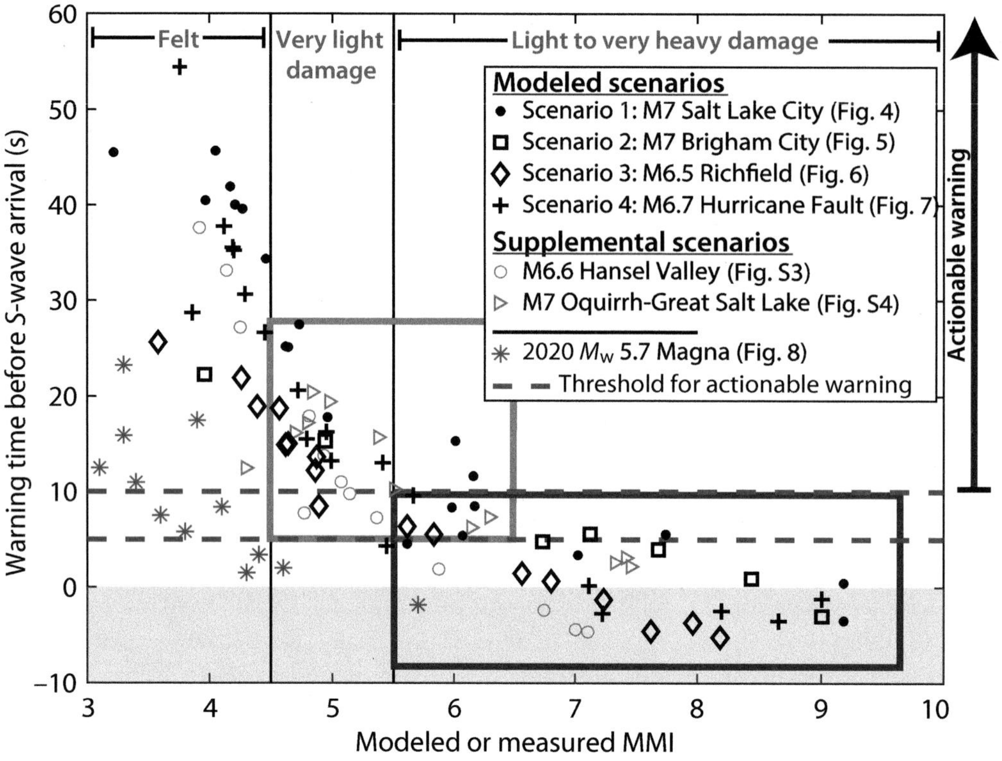

Figure 10. Estimated warning times for cities based on predicted MMI for the four scenarios presented in the Potential Performance of EEW in Utah section and the two supplemental scenarios, and measured MMI for the 2020 M_w 5.7 Magna earthquake. Red-dashed lines indicate warning times of 5 and 10 s as thresholds for potentially being able to act; 5–10 s is the proposed amount of time for a person to "Drop, Cover, Hold On" (DCHO), and automated actions require ≥10 s to be performed. The red box encompasses cities estimated to experience damaging shaking (MMI ≥ 5.5) but receiving less than 10 s warning. The blue box encompasses cities that would receive actionable warnings (≥5–10 s) and are expected to experience any amount of damage, including very light. Late warnings (≤0 s) are highlighted by the gray region. The color version of this figure is available only in the electronic edition.

ShakeAlert network because, in part, the most populated and highest seismic hazard areas of Utah (Wasatch Front and southwestern corner) are currently at or near the needed station density.

The estimated 7.1–10.1 s to receive an alert in the evaluated earthquake scenarios covers an area of nearly 1900 km^2 (24.1 km radius from the epicenter) to ~3700 km^2 (34.3 km radius), over which an alert would be received after the *S* wave arrived. In all six scenarios, potential warning times longer than 10 s could be provided in cities expected to experience shaking in the MMI 4–5 range, where little to no damage is expected (Fig. 10). For damaging shaking (MMI ≥ 5.5), potential warning times range from no alert to 14 s depending on the scenario, with all but two cities (Provo and Spanish Fork for the Salt Lake scenario) receiving less than 10 s possible warning.

Whether EEW could provide effective warnings depends on what is considered effective in the context of warning goals. Here, we considered three EEW goals: (1) providing actionable warnings to the public for strong, damaging shaking (MMI ≥ 5.5); (2) providing actionable warnings to the public for felt shaking (MMI ≥ 1.5); and (3) providing actionable warnings to automated systems for strong, damaging shaking.

Warning the public of strong, damaging shaking

The initial purpose of EEW was to alert ahead of strong shaking to save lives, property, and infrastructure (e.g., Given *et al.*, 2014, 2018). In the scenarios examined here, there is a "sweet spot" for successful warnings, for cities far enough from the epicenter to receive warnings longer than 5–10 s (proposed time for an able-bodied person to perform DCHO; Porter and Jones, 2018), but close enough to experience damaging shaking (Fig. 10). Here, the sweet spot is limited to cities experiencing light damage (MMI 4.5–6.3) during earthquakes of magnitude 6.5 or greater—83% of cities modeled to experience MMI 4.5–5.5 would receive 10 s or more of warning, and 93% would receive at least 5 s. Areas experiencing damaging shaking (MMI ≥ 5.5) would largely receive warnings that are late or too short to be useful (Fig. 10)—only 5% of cities experiencing damaging shaking could receive more than 10 s warning, and 25% could receive 5–10 s warning. No cities with MMI > 7.12 would receive an "actionable" warning. For moderate earthquakes, like the 2020 M_w 5.7 Magna event (Figs. 8, 10), warning times more than 5 s (7–17 s) could have been provided to cities where shaking was nondamaging (MMI ~3–4), whereas the peak shaking region MMI ~7 is within the no-alert zone. Thus, if the goal is to provide actionable alerts for damaging shaking, this can only be achieved during the infrequent *M* 6.75+ earthquakes, and only for those who will experience medium intensity shaking (MMI ~3.5 to 6.0). This finding is consistent with recent offline testing of ShakeAlert V3, for which ≥10 s of warning at sites experiencing MMI 5.5+ could be provided more frequently in the test suite of *M* 6+ crustal earthquakes than the test suite of smaller (moderate) magnitude earthquakes (86% of events M < 6.0; McGuire *et al.*, 2025).

We assumed our scenario ruptures were instantaneous, but realistically, the beginning waveforms of an earthquake, when an EEW system first estimates the earthquake location and size, are not always indicative of the eventual size. Thus, for large earthquakes, EEW can initially underestimate the magnitude and subsequently the expected ground motion, and warnings are shortened by the time it takes for the rupture to sufficiently grow such that the EEW system can accurately estimate the size (e.g., Meier, 2017; Wald, 2020). In the 2011 M_{ww} 9 Tohoku earthquake, some areas did not initially receive alerts despite eventually experiencing very strong shaking, which has been attributed to the rupture growing (Hoshiba *et al.*, 2011; Fujinawa and Noda, 2013). Minson *et al.* (2018) estimated warning times for which the only limitation was the time required for the earthquake to evolve and found that longer warning times could be achieved if the users are willing to be alerted for weak-to-light shaking when the size is initially underestimated. Following the underestimation of the magnitudes of the 2019 Ridgecrest earthquakes, ShakeAlert now incorporates a weighting scheme of initial *P*-wave data to allow the initial magnitude estimate to grow more quickly (Lux *et al.*, 2024; McGuire *et al.*, 2025). This change has conversely led to systematic overestimates of initial magnitude (McGuire *et al.*, 2025). Both the concept of lowering the alerting threshold to achieve longer warning times noted by Minson *et al.* (2018) and the initial overestimation of magnitudes with the newer weighting scheme would cause more frequent alerts for weak shaking or no shaking (false alerts). This might not necessarily be a bad thing because users are more tolerant to false alerts than missed alerts (e.g., Allen, 2017; Patchett, 2017; Nakayachi *et al.*, 2019).

There is potential for longer warning times for locations in the rupture direction of a propagating rupture, but this again requires a lower alerting threshold as the magnitude estimation updates with rupture growth (e.g., Meier, 2017; Minson *et al.*, 2018; Wald, 2020). For a >300 km long *M* 8.0 rupture propagating along the San Andreas fault (SAF), almost 90% of locations in the rupture direction would receive some warning for a 2%*g* alert threshold, and some warning times would exceed one minute (Minson *et al.*, 2018). Alternatively, for an alert threshold of 20%*g*, warnings are limited to ≤7 s, assuming a no-latency system. However, the Wasatch fault segments are relatively short, with lengths of ~40 km. Thus, an *M* 7.0 earthquake on the Wasatch would not lead to the same EEW benefit as an *M* 8.0 earthquake on the SAF.

Wald (2020) highlights that although Japan (Hoshiba *et al.*, 2008; Kamigaichi *et al.*, 2009) and Mexico City (Espinosa-Aranda *et al.*, 1995, 2009) EEW systems have had success in warning for offshore subduction zone events, the crustal earthquakes that occur inland can be too shallow for sufficient warning. For example, the 2018 M_{ww} 5.5 Osaka earthquake (~13 km depth) led to five casualties and more than 400 injuries, and "all of the impacts of the Osaka earthquake were well within the EEW [no-alert] zone" (Wald, 2020). Fujinawa and Noda (2013) noted that the only shortcomings that have not been mitigated for the Japanese EEW system were insufficient lead times for near-field earthquakes and initial underestimations of magnitude due to a growing rupture. In 2017, an M_{ww} 7.1 intermediate-depth (~50 km) intraplate event resulted in nearly 500 casualties in Mexico City. Though an EEW alert was issued ~20 s before the *S*-wave arrival, it was issued ~5 s after the *P* wave was already strongly felt, negating its effect (Allen *et al.*, 2018; Wald, 2020). Wald (2020) analyzed a scenario for the 1994 M_w 6.7 Northridge, California, earthquake, and found the *P* wave would have arrived before the warning and been strongly felt. He further states (p. 1423), "for nearly any S-wave shaking level that warrants a warning, the P-wave *should* be readily felt," dubbing the *P* wave "nature's built-in EEW system" (Wald, 2020).

Warning the public for felt but not damaging shaking

With more countries beginning to contemplate or implement EEW systems, information has pointed to public interest in receiving alerts for any felt earthquake, although this may be reflective of regions that infrequently experience damaging earthquakes (Bostrom *et al.*, 2022). For example, a survey of residents of Switzerland, where a damaging earthquake is expected every 50–150 yr, found that most participants preferred to receive alerts for earthquakes that might be or certainly will be felt (Dallo *et al.*, 2022). A survey of people within the ShakeAlert region (California, Washington, and Oregon) similarly reported interest in being alerted for any earthquake they may feel (Bostrom *et al.*, 2022). Notably, Los Angeles residents had the perception that they should have received an alert for felt shaking from the 2019 Ridgecrest, California, event, even though it was not damaging (Cochran and Husker, 2019; Bostrom *et al.*, 2022; Minson *et al.*, 2022). ShakeAlert originally aimed at alerting for strong, damaging shaking (MMI 6+), but subsequently lowered the alerting threshold to alert for felt shaking (MMI 4+; Cochran and Husker, 2019; Minson *et al.*, 2022). Conversely, residents in New Zealand preferred a higher intensity threshold (MMI 5–6), and the Japan EEW system alerts the public for MMI 7–8 (Kamigaichi *et al.*, 2009; Becker *et al.*, 2020), two places where damaging earthquakes are more frequent. However, even in Japan and Mexico City, the public likes and wants EEW alerts, even if the subsequent shaking is not damaging (Allen, 2017; Patchett, 2017; Allen *et al.*, 2018; Wald, 2020).

If Utah residents similarly wanted to be alerted for any felt shaking, our scenarios show locations experiencing MMI 3–4.5 could have ~10 to 55 s of warning in both large and moderate magnitude earthquakes (*M* 6+; Fig. 10). Warnings for felt shaking from the 2020 Magna earthquake could have been more than 20 s. For smaller felt earthquakes, warnings would depend on the location, depth, and magnitude of the event (Fig. 9). The frequency of use of an EEW system in Utah depends on the alerting threshold used. Based on the frequency of *M* 4.0+

of Utah earthquakes during 1962–2024, we could expect alerts for felt earthquakes to be issued every ~2.3 yr in the Wasatch Front or every ~1.1 yr in the ISB. This is significantly less than the average of 24 M 4.5+ alerts per year generated by ShakeAlert along the West Coast (2019–2023, Lux *et al.*, 2024).

Triggering automated actions for strong, damaging shaking

The effectiveness of EEW for automated actions depends on the amount of time needed to enact the safety actions, and there is relatively little information on such systems in practice. In Japan, use of EEW to halt machine operations or elevators has been lower than expected (Patchett, 2017), but there is anecdotal evidence of success. Following the 2011 M_{ww} 9.1 Tohoku earthquake, the East Japan Railway Co. issued a signal 12–22 s ahead of strong ground motions, safely slowing 27 trains (Yamamoto and Tomori, 2013), and the emergency brakes were automatically applied to all 33 Shinkansen ("Bullet") trains at least 9–12 s before the first felt shaking (Shimamura and Keyaki, 2013). More than 16,000 elevators with seismic detectors performed shutdown correctly with no one trapped or injured (Layne, 2011).

ShakeAlert highlights three case studies for which automation has been integrated, though there is currently no public information on them being enacted (ShakeAlert, see Data and Resources): slowing Southern California Regional Rail Authority Metrolink trains, closing water valves in Grants Pass, Oregon, to prevent water loss if pipes are damaged, and shutting off gas valves and opening garage doors at seven fire stations in Menlo Park, California. The Bay Area Rapid Transit (BART) was the first to adopt EEW in 2012 and has already slowed and stopped trains, albeit for nondamaging earthquakes (Gregory, 2018). The BART central computers "institute a normal service braking to slow trains down to 26 miles per hour" (Gregory, 2018). The Utah Transit Authority (UTA) light rail (TRAX) runs in the greater Salt Lake City region and has a maximum operational speed of 55 mph with a service brake rate of 3 mph/s (Hatch LTK, 2021). The FrontRunner, Utah's primary commuter rail line, runs 83 miles between Ogden and Provo, has a maximum speed of 79 mph, and a service brake rate of 2.5 mph/s (LTK Engineering Services *et al.*, 2018). The TRAX and Front Runner would need 10 and 21 s, respectively, to slow to 26 mph from full speed, and 18 and 32 s to stop completely. Fire station doors can open in as little as 7 or 14–21 s, depending on the type (e.g., Clear Fold fire station doors, see Data and Resources). Elevators only need ~10 s to halt at the closest floor or between floors (e.g., Patchett, 2017). We were unable to find time estimates for shutting off utilities or other vulnerable systems.

Assuming these automated actions would need to be performed for MMI 5.5+ shaking, the scenarios presented here largely show that cities in that shaking range have <10 s of warning, if any at all (Fig. 10). Only two cities in the Salt Lake City segment scenario (Figs. 4, 10) with expected shaking above MMI 5.5 could receive more than 10 s of warning: Provo (11.6 s) and Spanish Fork (15.3 s). If the FrontRunner is in Provo at the time of the alert, it could decelerate ~29 mph (to 50 mph if originally at top speed). Approximately 91% of the TRAX lines are within the no-alert region for this event, and the remainder could receive ≤2 s of warning, depending on where on the line the train is located. Elevators could potentially be halted, and fire station doors opened in the two cities. Two cities in one of six scenarios, four of which are in the targeted Wasatch Front, represent a relatively low success rate. Furthermore, it is worth reiterating that these are maximum potential warning times, and they could be shorter in practice.

Automated actions also depend on whether the cost to enact them is sufficiently lower than the cost of shaking damage. In practice, the alerting threshold in ShakeAlert is set lower than the damage threshold to minimize missed alerts due to variable ground motion and uncertainty in predictions, but if it is costly to perform the automated action during a false alert, then the warning would not be beneficial (Minson *et al.*, 2019). The cost of stopping trains and elevators and opening doors is low relative to the potential damage the shaking could cause, but turning off utilities during a false alert can have higher consequences. For example, an emergency shutdown of a nuclear power plant in Switzerland costs ~$250 million U.S. plus $1 million/day U.S. in lost revenue (Cauzzi *et al.*, 2016), and gas utility operators have expressed concern about shutdowns from false alerts in Utah. For such situations, EEW methods that use ground-motion observations over source parameter estimation, such as PLUM (Propagation of Local Undamped Motion) (Kodera *et al.*, 2018), or on-site-EEW methods would be more robust against rupture growth time and false alerts (Minson *et al.*, 2019, 2021).

CONCLUSIONS

Though the concept of EEW is not new, implementation and development have increased in recent years due to improvements in the speed and reliability of transmitting digital seismic data and advances in signal processing algorithms. We evaluated the potential efficacy of a regional, network-based EEW system in Utah as part of a collaborative EEW feasibility study (Bowman *et al.*, 2024), with specific focus on assessing (1) the extent to which the current UUSS network could be integrated into an EEW system; and (2) if, given the proximity of the source faults to the target areas for warning, even a best-case EEW system could provide actionable warning.

We evaluated the network's EEW readiness by assessing station performance in terms of data timing, quality, and availability, and comparing the station density with that of an optimal EEW system. We find that the current UUSS network performs in accordance with the ShakeAlert station acceptance criteria (91%–99% pass rate), except with respect to data latency (1% pass rate). This is due to the current network not being configured for faster data transfer and could be remediated by adjusting datalogger settings and telemetry improvements. Station coverage is sufficient for the detection of earthquakes on or near the surface expression of the Wasatch fault zone, and is near adequate spacing for much of the Wasatch Front. Thus, an EEW system could be implemented in the Wasatch Front region with telemetry upgrades to reduce data latency and relatively modest station build-out (64–117 new stations in the Wasatch Front and ISB, respectively; 229 total new stations for the full state).

We assessed if the geometry of the faults and population could allow for actionable warning by estimating theoretical warning times for six scenario earthquakes under an ideal EEW system configuration and examined the recorded history of Utah seismicity to determine how frequently such a system could be expected to send an alert. The six scenarios presented here indicate that 93% of the areas expected to experience damaging shaking (MMI ≥ 5.5) would receive 0–10 s of warning at best, and only 25% would receive between 5 and 10 s. This is hardly enough time to perform automated protective actions (requiring ≥10 s) where they are most needed, and only a quarter of these locations might have enough time for personal protective actions (DCHO) for able-bodied people. We emphasize that the warning estimates presented here are from a simplified exercise and represent maximum potential warning times. Thus, the warning times presented here would likely decrease in reality with more complex ruptures, delays due to inaccurate location and/or magnitude, and variations in alert delivery method. Our estimated alert times provide actionable warnings only for felt shaking associated with light damage (MMI ≤ 5.5), though even nondamaging, felt earthquakes (M 3.5+) would activate the EEW alert relatively infrequently at roughly once per year in the Wasatch Front or 2–3 times a year in the ISB. Thus, if the goal of EEW in Utah is to alert residents for felt and lightly damaging shaking, our warning time estimates show that this is possible. If the goal is to provide actionable time ahead of damaging shaking, however, these results suggest that the faults are too close to the target alert areas to provide enough time.

DATA AND RESOURCES

Waveform availability for data completeness and gap testing was accessed via the EarthScope Data Management Center (DMC) International Federation of Digital Seismograph Networks (FDSN) availability webservice (https://service.iris.edu/fdsnws/availability/1/, last accessed April 2024). Other data quality metrics were assessed using the University of Washington SQUAC measurements (Ulberg *et al.*, 2023) and EarthScope MUSTANG measurements (Casey *et al.*, 2018; https://service.iris.edu/mustang/measurements/1/, last accessed April 2024) on the University of Utah Seismograph Stations (UUSS) continuous data. Data latency was averaged over 30 min observation periods for all UUSS channels in the WAVE_RING on the UUSS data import server using the Sniffwave module in the Earthworm software (Johnson *et al.*, 1995). *P*-pick and amplitude-based magnitude quality were assessed using the initial automatic and final reviewed phase arrival picks and station magnitude estimations from the internal UUSS database for all 2023 Utah earthquakes. Final reviewed phase arrival times and station magnitudes can be accessed via the Advanced National Seismic System (ANSS) Comprehensive Catalog (ComCat, U.S. Geological Survey and Earthquake Hazards Program, 2017; https://earthquake.usgs.gov/data/comcat/). ShakeAlert station acceptance process and criteria are not publicly available and were provided to the authors by D. Croker on request. The Utah historical earthquake catalog 1850–1962 used in this article can be accessed from the UUSS webpage (https://quake.utah.edu/earthquake-information-products/earthquake-catalogs) and is sourced from Arabasz and McKee (1979), Arabasz *et al.* (2016), Arabasz *et al.* (2017), and Bowman and Arabasz (2017). The Utah instrumental earthquake catalog (1962–present; University of Utah, 1962) can be accessed from the UUSS webpage or ComCat under network code UU. UUSS and U.S. Geological Survey (USGS) ShakeMaps for the 18 March 2020 M_{ww} 5.7 Magna earthquake (Fig. 8) and example earthquakes A–D (Fig. 9) can be accessed from the corresponding USGS event pages: Magna mainshock: https://earthquake.usgs.gov/earthquakes/eventpage/uu60363602; A: https://earthquake.usgs.gov/earthquakes/eventpage/uu60364032; B: https://earthquake.usgs.gov/earthquakes/eventpage/uu60020264; C: https://earthquake.usgs.gov/earthquakes/eventpage/uu60364832; and D: https://earthquake.usgs.gov/earthquakes/eventpage/uu60524772 (all last accessed March 2025). Maps were created using the Generic Mapping Tools (GMT) software version 6.4.0 (https://docs.generic-mapping-tools.org/latest/index.html; Wessel and Smith, 1991; Wessel *et al.*, 2013). Mapped fault traces are from the Quaternary Fault and Fold Database of the United States (https://www.usgs.gov/natural-hazards/earthquake-hazards/faults; USGS and Utah Geological Survey [UGS], last downloaded January 2023). ShakeAlert case studies were accessed at https://shakealert.org/education-and-outreach/case-studies/ (last accessed March 2025). Example timing for fire station doors opening was found through a company, Clear Fold (https://clearfold.com/portfolio/fire-station-doors, last accessed March 2025). TRAX line locations for comparison to the Salt Lake City no-alert zone were downloaded from the Utah Geospatial Resource Center (https://opendata.gis.utah.gov/search?collection=dataset, last accessed May 2025; dataset: Utah Transit Authority [UTA] TRAX Light Rail Routes). The supplemental material for this article includes further details of data quality and network configuration testing, additional warning time scenarios, and details of potential alert frequency. Table S1 describes how the data quality metrics from Tables 1 and 2 were estimated. Figure S1 shows how hypothetical new stations were added to the UUSS network following ShakeAlert spacing convention, and Figure S2 illustrates the earthquake sources used to evaluate detection time improvement in Figure 3. Figures S3 and S4 and corresponding text detail two additional warning time scenarios for an M 6.6 earthquake in Hansel Valley and an M 7.0 earthquake on the Oquirrh-Great Salt Lake fault zone. Results from these scenarios are also shown in Figure 10. Figure S5 shows the UUSS catalog events M 3.5+ used in determining potential alert frequency for felt events in Table 3, as well as the corresponding distribution of alert frequency and "dry spells" between alerts.

DECLARATION OF COMPETING INTERESTS

The authors acknowledge that there are no conflicts of interest recorded.

ACKNOWLEDGMENTS

This work was funded by the State of Utah through the Utah Geological Survey (UGS). The authors thank Danielle Kinkel and an anonymous reviewer for their careful review and constructive comments, which have strengthened the article. The authors also thank the technical reviewers of the original state report for helpful comments and guidance: E. Cochran, S. Crane, D. Given, R. Hartog, E. Kleber, S. McGowan, K. Pankow, and B. Welliver.

REFERENCES

Allen, R., E. Cochran, T. Huggins, S. Miles, and D. Otegui (2018). Lessons from Mexico's earthquake early warning system, *Eos* **99,** doi: 10.1029/2018EO105095.

Allen, R. M. (2017). Quake warnings, seismic culture, *Science* **358,** no. 6367, 1111–1111, doi: 10.1126/science.aar4640.

Allen, R. M., and D. Melgar (2019). Earthquake early warning: Advances, scientific challenges, and societal needs, *Annu. Rev. Earth Planet. Sci.* **47,** 361–388, doi: 10.1146/annurev-earth-053018-060457.

Allen, R. M., P. Gasparini, O. Kamigaichi, and M. Böse (2009). The status of earthquake early warning around the World: An introductory overview, *Seismol. Res. Lett.* **80,** no. 5, 682–693, doi: 10.1785/gssrl.80.5.682.

Allen, R. M., Q. Kong, and R. Martin-Short (2020). The MyShake Platform: A global vision for earthquake early warning, *Pure Appl. Geophys.* **177,** no. 4, 1699–1712, doi: 10.1007/s00024-019-02337-7.

Allen, R. M., A. Barski, M. Berman, R. Bosch, Y. Cho, X. S. Jiang, Y. L. Lee, S. Malkos, S. M. Mousavi, P. Robertson, *et al.* (2025). Global earthquake detection and warning using Android phones, *Science* **389,** 254–259, doi: 10.1126/science.ads4779.

Applied Technology Council (2022). Utah K-12 public schools unreinforced masonry inventory: Methods, findings, and recommendations, Applied Technology Council, available at https://ussc.utah.gov/pages/view.php?ref=2082 (last accessed May 2025).

Arabasz, W. J., R. Burlacu, and J. C. Pechmann (2017). Earthquake database for Utah Geological Survey Map 277, *Utah Earthquakes (1850–2016) and Quaternary Faults.*

Arabasz, W. J., and M. E. McKee (1979). Utah earthquake catalog, 1850–June 1962, in *Earthquake Studies in Utah 1850 to 1978*, W. J. Arabasz, R. B. Smith, and W. D. Richins (Editors), University of Utah Seismograph Stations, Dept. of Geology and Geophysics, Salt Lake City, Utah, 119–143.

Arabasz, W. J., J. C. Pechmann, and R. Burlacu (2016). A uniform moment magnitude earthquake catalog and background seismicity rates for the Wasatch Front and surrounding Utah region, appendix E, in *Earthquake Probabilities for the Wasatch Front region in Utah, Idaho, and Wyoming*, Working Group on Earthquake Probabilities (Editor), Utah Geological Survey Miscellaneous Publication 16-3, E1–E126, Salt Lake City, Utah.

Becker, J. S., S. H. Potter, L. J. Vinnell, K. Nakayachi, S. K. McBride, and D. M. Johnston (2020). Earthquake early warning in Aotearoa New Zealand: A survey of public perspectives to guide warning system development, *Humanit. Soc. Sci. Commun.* **7,** no. 1, doi: 10.1057/s41599-020-00613-9.

Behr, Y., J. Clinton, P. Kästli, C. Cauzzi, R. Racine, and M. A. Meier (2015). Anatomy of an earthquake early warning (EEW) alert: Predicting time delays for an end-to-end EEW system, *Seismol. Res. Lett.* **86,** no. 3, 1–11, doi: 10.1785/0220140179.

Bostrom, A., S. K. McBride, J. S. Becker, J. D. Goltz, R. M. de Groot, L. Peek, B. Terbush, and M. Dixon (2022). Great expectations for earthquake early warnings on the United States West Coast, *Int. J. Disast. Risk Reduct.* **82,** doi: 10.1016/j.ijdrr.2022.103296.

Bowman, S., R. Burlacu, J. Crofts, D. Kilb, K. Koper, E. Morton, and D. Worthen (2024). On the feasibility of implementing an earthquake early warning (EEW) System in Utah, doi: 10.34191/EEW-2023.

Bowman, S. D., and W. J. Arabasz (2017). Utah earthquakes (1850–2016) and Quaternary faults, *Utah Geol. Surv. Map 277,* 1 plate, scale 1:500,000.

Casey, R., M. E. Templeton, G. Sharer, L. Keyson, B. R. Weertman, and T. Ahern (2018). Assuring the quality of IRIS Data with MUSTANG, *Seismol. Res. Lett.* **89,** no. 2A, 630–639, doi: 10.1785/0220170191.

Cauzzi, C., Y. Behr, T. Le Guenan, J. Douglas, S. Auclair, J. Woessner, J. Clinton, and S. Wiemer (2016). Earthquake early warning and operational earthquake forecasting as real-time hazard information to mitigate seismic risk at nuclear facilities, *Bull. Earthq. Eng.* **14,** no. 9, 2495–2512, doi: 10.1007/s10518-016-9864-0.

Christenson, G. E., and S. J. Nava (1992). Earthquake hazards of Southwestern Utah, in *Engineering and Environmental Geology of Southwestern Utah, 1992 Field Symposium*, K. M. Harty (Editor), Utah Geological Association Publication 21, Utah, U.S.A., 123–138.

Chung, A. I., I. Henson, and R. M. Allen (2019). Optimizing earthquake early warning performance: ElarmS-3, *Seismol. Res. Lett.* **90,** no. 2A, 727–743, doi: 10.1785/0220180192.

Chung, A. I., M. A. Meier, J. Andrews, M. Böse, B. W. Crowell, J. J. McGuire, and D. E. Smith (2020). ShakeAlert earthquake early warning system performance during the 2019 Ridgecrest earthquake sequence, *Bull. Seismol. Soc. Am.* **110,** no. 4, 1904–1923, doi: 10.1785/0120200032.

Cochran, E. S., and A. L. Husker (2019). How low should we go when warning for earthquakes? *Science* **366,** no. 6468, 957–958, doi: 10.1126/science.aaz6601.

Cremen, G., C. Galasso, and E. Zuccolo (2022). Investigating the potential effectiveness of earthquake early warning across Europe, *Nat. Commun.* **13,** 639, doi: 10.1038/s41467-021-27807-2.

Dallo, I., M. Marti, J. Clinton, M. Böse, F. Massin, and S. Zaugg (2022). Earthquake early warning in countries where damaging earthquakes only occur every 50 to 150 years – The societal perspective, *Int. J. Disast. Risk Reduct.* **83,** doi: 10.1016/j.ijdrr.2022.103441.

Das, M. (2023). Wasatch corridor in Utah prone to big quakes and shakes, *Temblor* doi: 10.32858/temblor.293.

Doser, D. I. (1989). Extensional tectonics in northern Utah-southern Idaho, U.S.A., and the 1934 Hansel Valley sequence, *Phys. Earth Planet. In.* **54,** nos. 1/2, 120–134, doi: 10.1016/0031-9201(89)90192-1.

DuRoss, C. B., S. F. Personius, A. J. Crone, S. S. Olig, M. D. Hylland, W. R. Lund, and D. P. Schwartz (2016). Fault segmentation: New concepts from the Wasatch Fault Zone, Utah, USA, *J. Geophys. Res.* **121,** no. 2, 1131–1157, doi: 10.1002/2015JB012519.

Earthquake Engineering Research Institute (2015). Scenario for a Magnitude 7.0 earthquake on the Wasatch Fault-Salt Lake City segment: Hazards and loss estimates, Salt Lake City, Utah, available at https://ussc.utah.gov/pages/help.php?section=EERI+Salt+Lake+City+M7+Earthquake+Scenario (last accessed January 2023).

Enferadi, S., Z. H. Shomali, and A. Niksejel (2021). Feasibility study of earthquake early warning in Tehran, Iran, *J. Seismol.* **25,** 1127–1140, doi: 10.1007/s10950-021-10014-3.

Espinosa Aranda, J. M., A. Jiménez, G. Ibarrola, F. Alcantar, A. Aguilar, M. Inostroza, and S. Maldonado (1995). Mexico city seismic alert system, *Seismol. Res. Lett.* **66,** no. 6, 42–53, doi: 10.1785/gssrl.66.6.42.

Espinosa-Aranda, J. M., A. Cuellar, A. Garcia, G. Ibarrola, R. Islas, S. Maldonado, and F. H. Rodriguez (2009). Evolution of the Mexican seismic alert system (SASMEX), *Seismol. Res. Lett.* **80,** no. 5, 694–706, doi: 10.1785/gssrl.80.5.694.

Federal Emergency Management Agency (FEMA) (2023). Hazus estimated annualized earthquake losses for the United States, *FEMA P-366,* available at https://www.fema.gov/sites/default/files/documents/fema_p-366-hazus-estimated-annualized-earthquake-losses-united-states.pdf (last accessed January 2024).

Federal Emergency Management Agency (FEMA), Utah Division of Emergency Management (DEM), and Utah Seismic Safety Commission (USSC) (2021). Wasatch front unreinforced masonry risk reduction strategy, available at https://www.fema.gov/sites/default/files/documents/fema_wasatch-front-urm-risk-reduction-strategy.pdf (last accessed May 2025).

Fozkos, A. M., and M. E. West (2025). Earthquake early warning scenarios for Alaska, *Bull. Seismol. Soc. Am.* **115,** no. 5, 2295–2312, doi: 10.1785/0120250051.

Fujinawa, Y., and Y. Noda (2013). Japan's earthquake early warning system on 11 March 2011: Performance, shortcomings, and changes, Earthquake Engineering Research Institute, doi: 10.1193/1.4000127.

Given, D. D., R. M. Allen, A. S. Baltay, P. Bodin, E. S. Cochran, K. Creager, R. M. deGroot, L. S. Gee, E. Hauksson, T. H. Heaton, *et al.* (2018). Revised technical implementation plan for the ShakeAlert system-an earthquake early warning system for the West Coast of the United States, *Open-File Rept. 2018-1155,* 1–54, doi: 10.3133/ofr20181155.

Given, D. D., E. S. Cochran, T. Heaton, E. Hauksson, R. Allen, P. Hellweg, J. Vidale, and P. Bodin (2014). Technical implementation plan for the ShakeAlert production system—An earthquake early warning system for the West Coast of the United States, doi: 10.3133/ofr20141097.

Gregory, M. (2018). BART successfully deploys early earthquake warning system, *The Daily Californian*, available at https://www.dailycal.org/archives/bart-successfully-deploys-early-earthquake-warning-system/article_7d929d85-d933-5a5e-9d4e-b86f97b63079.html (last accessed May 2025).

Hatch LTK (2021). UTA future of light rail, *Final Report to Utah Transit Authority, Document Number LTK.C5525.01,* 249 pp, available at https://www.rideuta.com/Current-Projects/Future-of-Light-Rail-Study (last accessed May 2025).

Holt, J., K. M. Whidden, K. D. Koper, K. L. Pankow, K. Mayeda, J. C. Pechmann, B. Edwards, R. Gök, and W. R. Walter (2021). Toward robust and routine determination of Mw for small earthquakes: Application to the 2020 M_w 5.7 Magna, Utah, Seismic sequence, *Seismol. Res. Lett.* **92,** no. 2A, 725–740, doi: 10.1785/0220200320.

Hoshiba, M., K. Iwakiri, N. Hayashimoto, T. Shimoyama, K. Hirano, Y. Yamada, Y. Ishigaki, and H. Kikuta (2011). Outline of the 2011 off the Pacific coast of Tohoku earthquake (M_w 9.0) -earthquake early warning and observed seismic intensity, *Earth Planets Space* **63,** no. 7, 547–551, doi: 10.5047/eps.2011.05.031.

Hoshiba, M., O. Kamigaichi, M. Saito, S. Tsukada, and N. Hamada (2008). Earthquake early warning starts nationwide in Japan, *Eos* **89,** no. 8, 73–74, doi: 10.1029/2008EO080001.

Johnson, C. E., A. Bittenbinder, B. Bogaert, L. Dietz, and W. Kohler (1995). Earthworm: A flexible approach to seismic network processing, *IRIS Newsletter* **14,** no. 2, 1–4.

Kamigaichi, O., M. Saito, K. Doi, T. Matsumori, S. Tsukada, K. Takeda, T. Shimoyama, K. Nakamura, M. Kiyomoto, and Y. Watanabe (2009). Earthquake early warning in Japan: Warning the general public and future prospects, *Seismol. Res. Lett.* **80,** no. 5, 717–726, doi: 10.1785/gssrl.80.5.717.

Kanamori, H. (2005). Real-time seismology and earthquake damage mitigation, *Annu. Rev. Earth Planet. Sci.* **33,** 195–214, doi: 10.1146/annurev.earth.33.092203.122626.

Kinkel, D., and D. T. Trugman (2025). Toward earthquake early warning in Nevada: Seismic network configuration and warning time analysis, *Bull. Seismol. Soc. Am.* **115,** no. 5, 2279–2294, doi: 10.1785/0120250048.

Kirby, D. (2023). Federal disaster funds to help pay for West Lake STEM Junior High School rebuild, *West Valley City Journal*, available at https://www.wvcjournal.com/2023/07/07/440813/federal-disaster-funds-to-help-pay-for-west-lake-stem-junior-high-school-rebuild (last accessed May 2025).

Kodera, Y., Y. Yamada, K. Hirano, K. Tamaribuchi, S. Adachi, N. Hayashimoto, M. Morimoto, M. Nakamura, and M. Hoshiba (2018). The propagation of local undamped motion (PLUM) method: A simple and robust seismic wavefield estimation approach for earthquake early warning, *Bull. Seismol. Soc. Am.* **108,** no. 2, 983–1003, doi: 10.1785/0120170085.

Kohler, M. D., D. E. Smith, J. Andrews, A. I. Chung, R. Hartog, I. Henson, D. D. Given, R. de Groot, and S. Guiwits (2020). Earthquake early warning Shakealert 2.0: Public rollout, *Seismol. Res. Lett.* **91,** no. 3, 1763–1775, doi: 10.1785/0220190245.

Kong, Q., R. M. Allen, L. Schreier, and Y. W. Kwon (2016). MyShake: A smartphone seismic network for earthquake early warning and beyond, *Sci. Adv.* **2,** no. 2, doi: 10.1126/sciadv.1501055.

Kuyuk, H. S., and R. M. Allen (2013). Optimal seismic network density for earthquake early warning: A case study from California, *Seismol. Res. Lett.* **84,** no. 6, 946–954, doi: 10.1785/0220130043.

Layne, R. (2011). Otis earthquake detectors take 16,700 Japan elevators to safety, *CT Insider*, available at https://www.ctinsider.com/business/article/Otis-earthquake-detectors-take-16-700-Japan-1307408.php (last accessed May 2025).

LTK Engineering Services, Fehr & Peers, and Jacobs Engineering (2018). Future of the FrontRunner Final Report, *Utah Transit Authority, Document Number LTK.C5016.02,* 389 pp., available at https://www.rideuta.com/-/media/Files/About-UTA/Reports/2019/C5016_UTA_Operations_Simulation_Tech_MemoV2_20190320.pdf (last accessed May 2025).

Lund, W. R., M. J. Hozik, and S. C. Hatfield (2007). *Paleoseismic investigation and long-term slip history of the Hurricane fault in Southwestern Utah*, Utah Geological Survey, Salt Lake City, Utah.

Lund, W. R., T. R. Knudsen, C. B. DuRoss, and G. N. McDonald (2015). Utah geological survey dutchman draw paleoseismic investigation, Fort Pearce Section, Washington Fault Zone, Mohave County, Arizona, in *Geologic Mapping and Paleoseismic Investigations of the Washington fault zone, Washington County, Utah, and Mohave County, Arizona*, W. R. Lund (Editor), Utah Geological Survey, Salt Lake City, Utah, 47–86.

Lux, A. I., D. Smith, M. Böse, J. J. McGuire, J. K. Saunders, M. Huynh, I. Stubailo, J. Andrews, G. Lotto, B. Crowell, *et al.* (2024). Status and performance of the ShakeAlert earthquake early warning system: 2019–2023, *Bull. Seismol. Soc. Am.* doi: 10.1785/0120230259.

Massin, F., J. Clinton, and M. Böse (2021). Status of earthquake early warning in Switzerland, *Front. Earth Sci.* **9,** 707654, doi: 10.3389/feart.2021.707654.

McBride, S. K., D. F. Sumy, A. L. Llenos, G. A. Parker, J. McGuire, J. K. Saunders, M. A. Meier, P. Schuback, D. Given, and R. de Groot (2023). Latency and geofence testing of wireless emergency alerts intended for the ShakeAlert® earthquake early warning system for the West Coast of the United States of America, *Saf. Sci.* **157,** doi: 10.1016/j.ssci.2022.105898.

McGuire, J. J., D. E. Smith, A. D. Frankel, E. A. Wirth, S. K. McBride, and R. M. de Groot (2021). Expected warning times from the ShakeAlert® earthquake early warning system for earthquakes in the Pacific Northwest, *U.S. Geol. Surv. Open-File Rept. 2021-1026*, 37, doi: 10.3133/ofr20211026.

McGuire, J. J., C. W. Ulberg, A. I. Lux, M. Böse, J. R. Andrews, D. E. Smith, B. W. Crowell, J. R. Murray, I. Henson, R. Hartog, *et al.* (2025). ShakeAlert® Version 3: Expected performance in large earthquakes, *Bull. Seismol. Soc. Am.* **115,** no. 2, doi: 10.1785/0120240189.

Meier, M. A. (2017). How "good" are real-time ground motion predictions from earthquake early warning systems? *J. Geophys. Res.* **122,** no. 7, 5561–5577, doi: 10.1002/2017JB014025.

Minson, S. E., A. S. Baltay, E. S. Cochran, T. C. Hanks, M. T. Page, S. K. McBride, K. R. Milner, and M. A. Meier (2019). The limits of earthquake early warning accuracy and best alerting strategy, *Sci. Rep.* **9,** no. 1, doi: 10.1038/s41598-019-39384-y.

Minson, S. E., E. S. Cochran, J. K. Saunders, S. K. McBride, S. Wu, A. S. Baltay, and K. R. Milner (2022). What to expect when you are expecting earthquake early warning, *Geophys. J. Int.* **231,** no. 2, 1386–1403, doi: 10.1093/gji/ggac246.

Minson, S. E., E. S. Cochran, S. Wu, and S. Noda (2021). A framework for evaluating earthquake early warning for an infrastructure network: An idealized case study of a Northern California rail system, *Front Earth Sci* **9,** doi: 10.3389/feart.2021.620467.

Minson, S. E., M.-A. Meier, A. S. Baltay, T. C. Hanks, and E. S. Cochran (2018). The limits of earthquake early warning: Timeliness of ground motion estimates, *Sci. Adv.* **4,** no. 3, eaaq0504, doi: 10.1126/sciadv.aaq0504.

Nakayachi, K., J. S. Becker, S. H. Potter, and M. Dixon (2019). Residents' reactions to earthquake early warnings in Japan, *Risk Anal.* **39,** no. 8, 1723–1740, doi: 10.1111/risa.13306.

O'Brien, E., and S. J. Nava (1997). Intermountain seismic belt historical earthquake project, available at https://quake.utah.edu/earthquake-information-products/historical-eq-project (last accessed February 2025).

Ogweno, L. P., M. M. Withers, and C. H. Cramer (2019). Earthquake early warning feasibility study for the New Madrid seismic zone, *Seismol. Res. Lett.* **90,** no. 3, 1377–1392, doi: 10.1785/0220180163.

Pankow, K., J. Rusho, M. Ellis, and B. Carey (2013). Integrating ShakeMap with ShakeCast for Earthquake Response in Utah, *Seismol. Res. Lett.* **84,** no. 2, 357, doi: 10.1785/0220130011.

Pankow, K. L., M. Stickney, J. Y. Ben-Horin, M. Litherland, S. Payne, K. D. Koper, S. L. Bilek, and K. Bogolub (2020). Regional seismic network monitoring in the Eastern Intermountain West, *Seismol. Res. Lett.* **91,** no. 2A, 631–646, doi: 10.1785/0220190209.

Patchett, M. (2017). *Best Practices in Rapid Alerting for Earthquake Early Warning*, Ocean Networks Canada, Victoria, Canada.

Patel, S. C., and R. M. Allen (2022). The MyShake app: User experience of early warning delivery and earthquake shaking, *Seismol. Res. Lett.* **93,** no. 6, 3324–3336, doi: 10.1785/0220220062.

Pechmann, J. C., S. J. Nava, F. M. Terra, and J. C. Bernier (2007). Local magnitude determinations for intermountain seismic belt earthquakes from broadband digital data, *Bull. Seismol. Soc. Am.* **97,** no. 2, 557–574, doi: 10.1785/0120060114.

Petersen, M. D., A. M. Shumway, P. M. Powers, E. H. Field, M. P. Moschetti, K. S. Jaiswal, K. R. Milner, S. Rezaeian, A. D. Frankel, A. L. Llenos, *et al.* (2024). The 2023 US 50-State National Seismic Hazard Model: Overview and implications, *Earthq. Spectra* **40,** no. 1, 5–88, doi: 10.1177/87552930231215428.

Petersen, M. D., A. M. Shumway, P. M. Powers, C. S. Mueller, M. P. Moschetti, A. D. Frankel, S. Rezaeian, D. E. McNamara, N. Luco, O. S. Boyd, *et al.* (2020). The 2018 update of the US National Seismic Hazard Model: Overview of model and implications, *Earthq. Spectra* **36,** no. 1, 5–41, doi: 10.1177/8755293019878199.

Picozzi, M., A. Zollo, P. Brondi, S. Colombelli, L. Elia, and C. Martino (2015). Exploring the feasibility of a nationwide earthquake early warning system in Italy, *J. Geophys. Res.* **120,** no. 4, 2446–2465, doi: 10.1002/2014JB011669.

Porter, K. A., and J. L. Jones (2018). How many injuries can be avoided in the HayWired scenario through earthquake early warning and drop, cover, and hold on? in *The HayWired Earthquake Scenario*, S. T. Detweiler and A. M. Wein (Editors), U.S. Geological Survey Scientific Investigations Report 2017-5013-I-Q, Reston, Virginia, 401–429.

Rascon, D. (2020). Dozens of west valley mobile homes destroyed, severely damaged by earthquake, *KSL-TV*, West Valley City, Utah, available at https://ksltv.com/earthquakes/west-valley-mobile-homes-destroyed-severely-damaged-by-earthquake/433412/ (last accessed May 2025).

Rukstales, K. S., and M. D. Petersen (2019). Data release for 2018 update of the U.S. national seismic hazard model, doi: 10.5066/P9WT5OVB.

Satriano, C., Y.-M. Wu, A. Zollo, and H. Kanamori (2011). Earthquake early warning: Concepts, methods and physical grounds, *Soil Dynam. Earthq. Eng.* **31,** no. 2, 106–118, doi: 10.1016/j.soildyn.2010.07.007.

Saunders, J. K., and D. J. Wald (2025). Quantitative evaluations of earthquake early warning performance using "Did You Feel It?" and post-alert surveys, *Seism. Record* **5,** no. 2, 239–249, doi: 10.1785/0320250018.

Schwartz, D. P., and K. J. Coppersmith (1984). Fault behavior and characteristic earthquakes: examples from the Wasatch and San Andreas fault zones (USA), *J. Geophys. Res.* **89,** no. B7, 5681–5698, doi: 10.1029/JB089iB07p05681.

Shimamura, M., and T. Keyaki (2013). How Japan's bullet trains survived the 2011 Great Tohoku earthquake, *Proc. of the Eastern Asia Society for Transportation Studies*, Vol. 9, Taipei, Taiwan, 9–12 September 2013.

Swan, F. H., D. P. Schwartz, and L. S. Cluff (1980). Recurrence of moderate to large magnitude earthquakes produced by surface faulting on the Wasatch fault zone, Utah, *Bull. Seismol. Soc. Am.* **70,** no. 5, 1431–1462.

Thelen, W. A., A. J. Hotovec-Ellis, and P. Bodin (2016). Feasibility study of earthquake early warning (EEW) in Hawaii, *U.S. Geol. Surv. Open-File Rept. No. 2016-1172*, doi: 10.3133/ofr20161172.

Ulberg, C. W., K. Marczewski, A. Hutko, and R. Hartog (2023). A one-stop shop for network status? Developing an application for a diverse set of users, *Seismol. Res. Lett.* **94,** no. 2B, 1223, doi: 10.1785/0220230054.

University of Utah (1962). University of Utah Regional Seismic Network [Data set], *International Federation of Digital Seismograph Networks*, doi: 10.7914/SN/UU.

U.S. Census Bureau (2024a). 2020 Census Tracts, "tl_2020_49_tabblock20" [data set], *TIGER/Line Shapefiles*, available at https://www2.census.gov/geo/tiger/TIGER2020/TABBLOCK20/ (last accessed July 2024).

U.S. Census Bureau (2024b). 2020 Census Urban Areas, "tl_2020_us_uac20" [data set], *TIGER/Line Shapefiles*, available at https://www2.census.gov/geo/tiger/TIGER2020/UAC/ (last accessed July 2024).

U.S. Geological Survey, and Earthquake Hazards Program (2017). Advanced National Seismic System (ANSS) comprehensive catalog of earthquake events and products, various, doi: 10.5066/F7MS3QZH.

Utah Seismic Safety Commission (2022). *Putting Down Roots in Earthquake Country: Your Handbook for Earthquakes in Utah*, Utah Geological Survey, Salt Lake City, Utah, doi: 10.1016/S0197-4572(80)80012-7.

Utah State Historic Preservation Office (2020). Magna earthquake historic building damage windshield survey, available at https://geodata.geology.utah.gov/pages/view.php?ref=63907 (last accessed May 2025).

Wald, D. J. (2020). Practical limitations of earthquake early warning, *Earthq. Spectra* **36,** no. 3, 1412–1447, doi: 10.1177/8755293020911388.

Wald, D. J., V. Quitoriano, T. H. Heaton, and H. Kanamori (1999). Relationships between peak ground acceleration, peak ground velocity, and modified Mercalli intensity in California, *Earthq. Spectra* **15,** no. 3, 557–564, doi: 10.1193/1.1586058.

Wessel, P., and W. H. F. Smith (1991). Free software helps map and display data, *Eos Trans. AGU* **72,** 441–446, doi: 10.1029/90EO00319.

Wessel, P., W. H. F. Smith, R. Scharroo, J. Luis, and F. Wobbe (2013). Generic Mapping Tools: Improved version released, *Eos Trans. AGU* **94,** 409–410, doi: 10.1002/2013EO450001.

Wolfe, C. J., N. A. Ruppert, D. G. Given, M. E. West, V. I. Thomas, J. R. Murray, and R. Grapenthin (2025). Phase 1 technical implementation plan for the expansion of the ShakeAlert earthquake early warning system to Alaska, *U.S. Geol. Surv. Open-File Rept. 2025-1003*, 32 pp., doi: 10.3133/ofr20251003.

Wong, I., W. Lund, C. Duross, P. Thomas, W. Arabasz, A. Crone, M. Hylland, N. Luco, S. Olig, J. Pechmann, *et al.* (2017). Estimating the probabilities of future large earthquakes along the Wasatch Front, *Utah Geological Association Publication 46*, 276–294.

Worden, C. B., E. M. Thompson, M. Hearne, and D. J. Wald (2020). ShakeMap manual online: Technical manual, user's guide, and software guide, doi: 10.5066/F7D21VPQ.

Wu, Y. M., H. Mittal, D. Y. Chen, T. Y. Hsu, and P. Y. Lin (2021). Earthquake early warning systems in Taiwan: Current status, *J. Geol. Soc. India* **97,** 1525–1532, doi: 10.1007/s12594-021-1909-6.

Yamamoto, S., and M. Tomori (2013). Earthquake early warning system for railways and its performance, *J. JSCE* **1,** no. 1, 322–328, doi: 10.2208/journalofjsce.1.1_322.

Manuscript received 24 June 2025
Published online 18 November 2025

Complex Double-Event Rupture of the 2022 M_w 6.6 Luding Earthquake

Hongbo Han[1], Sidao Ni[2], Qingjun Meng[*3], Wangwang Gu[2], Zhe Jia[4], Baolong Zhang[2], Han Zhang[2], Yong Zhou[5], and Minhan Sheng[2]

ABSTRACT

On 5 September 2022, a strong earthquake (M_w 6.6) struck Luding County, Sichuan, China, causing significant casualties and property damage and marking the deadliest earthquake in mainland China in eight years. Previous studies using seismologic and/or geodetic data estimated the centroid depth of the Luding earthquake, with results varying widely from 2 to 18.4 km depth. To investigate the cause of this discrepancy, this study first performed a single point–source moment tensor inversion and found that regional and teleseismic data prefer centroid depths of 6 and 17 km, respectively. This suggests that a single point–source model may not be adequate to characterize the rupture. We then used synthetic doublet models to test the sensitivity of regional and teleseismic data to subevent depths. The results support a model that the Luding earthquake comprises two subevents: a shallow event at 6 km depth (0.7×10^{19} N·m) and a deeper event at 17 km depth (0.3×10^{19} N·m), with the deeper one rupturing 7 s after the shallow one. A relocated hypocenter depth for the Luding earthquake, based on *Pn/Pg* relative location, also confirms a shallow nucleation. Furthermore, a multiple point–source inversion of the teleseismic data confirms the presence of two subevents. Although the deeper subevent had a smaller moment, it significantly influenced the single point–source centroid depth inversion. Our results suggest that the large variance in published centroid depth stems from different depth sensitivities of regional and teleseismic datasets to a complex source process with multiple subevents. Therefore, the multiple point–source inversion is crucial for accurately assessing seismic hazard and understanding the rupture processes of complex moderate events such as the Luding earthquake.

KEY POINTS

- The damaging 2022 Luding earthquake cannot be explained with a single point–source mechanism.
- We conducted synthetic tests and multiple point–source inversions considering several subevents.
- The Luding earthquake comprised two distinct subevents that initiated at different depths.

Supplemental Material

INTRODUCTION

On 5 September 2022, a strike-slip earthquake (U.S. Geological Survey [USGS]–National Earthquake Information Center parameters M_w 6.6; hypocenter: 29.679° N, 102.236° E, 12 km deep, 04:52:19 UTC) occurred in Luding County, Ganzi Tibetan Autonomous Prefecture, Sichuan, China. The earthquake caused 93 deaths and 25 missing persons in Luding and surrounding areas, making it the deadliest earthquake in mainland China in the previous eight years. Based on field geological investigations and strong-motion records, the maximum intensity reached IX in the most severely affected area (Qu *et al.*, 2023). The Luding earthquake occurred at the southernmost end of the Xianshuihe fault zone (the Moxi segment, Fig. 1a), which had been seismically quiet since the 1786 *M* 7.75 Kangding earthquake and had not experienced any earthquakes larger than *M* 6.5 since then (Yi *et al.*, 2023). The Luding earthquake filled in the seismic gap (Fig. 1a, dashed red circle) in the southern part of the Xianshuihe fault (Fig. 1a).

1. Laboratory of Seismology and Physics of Earth's Interior, School of Earth and Space Sciences, University of Science and Technology of China, Hefei, China, https://orcid.org/0009-0003-2730-3474 (HH); 2. State Key Laboratory of Precision Geodesy, Innovation Academy for Precision Measurement Science and Technology, Chinese Academy of Sciences, Wuhan, China, https://orcid.org/0000-0002-2577-8041 (WG); https://orcid.org/0000-0001-7068-707X (BZ); https://orcid.org/0000-0003-0362-433X (HZ); 3. University of California, Los Angeles, JIFRESSE, Los Angeles, California, U.S.A., https://orcid.org/0000-0001-9632-8518 (QM); 4. Institute for Geophysics, Jackson School of Geosciences, University of Texas at Austin, Austin, Texas, U.S.A.; 5. State Key Laboratory of Tropical Oceanography, South China Sea Institute of Oceanology, Chinese Academy of Sciences, Guangzhou, China, https://orcid.org/0000-0003-3155-3233 (YZ)

*Corresponding author: qingjun23@g.ucla.edu

Cite this article as Han, H., S. Ni, Q. Meng, W. Gu, Z. Jia, B. Zhang, H. Zhang, Y. Zhou, and M. Sheng (2025). Complex Double-Event Rupture of the 2022 M_w 6.6 Luding Earthquake, *Bull. Seismol. Soc. Am.* **116**, 272–290, doi: 10.1785/0120240278

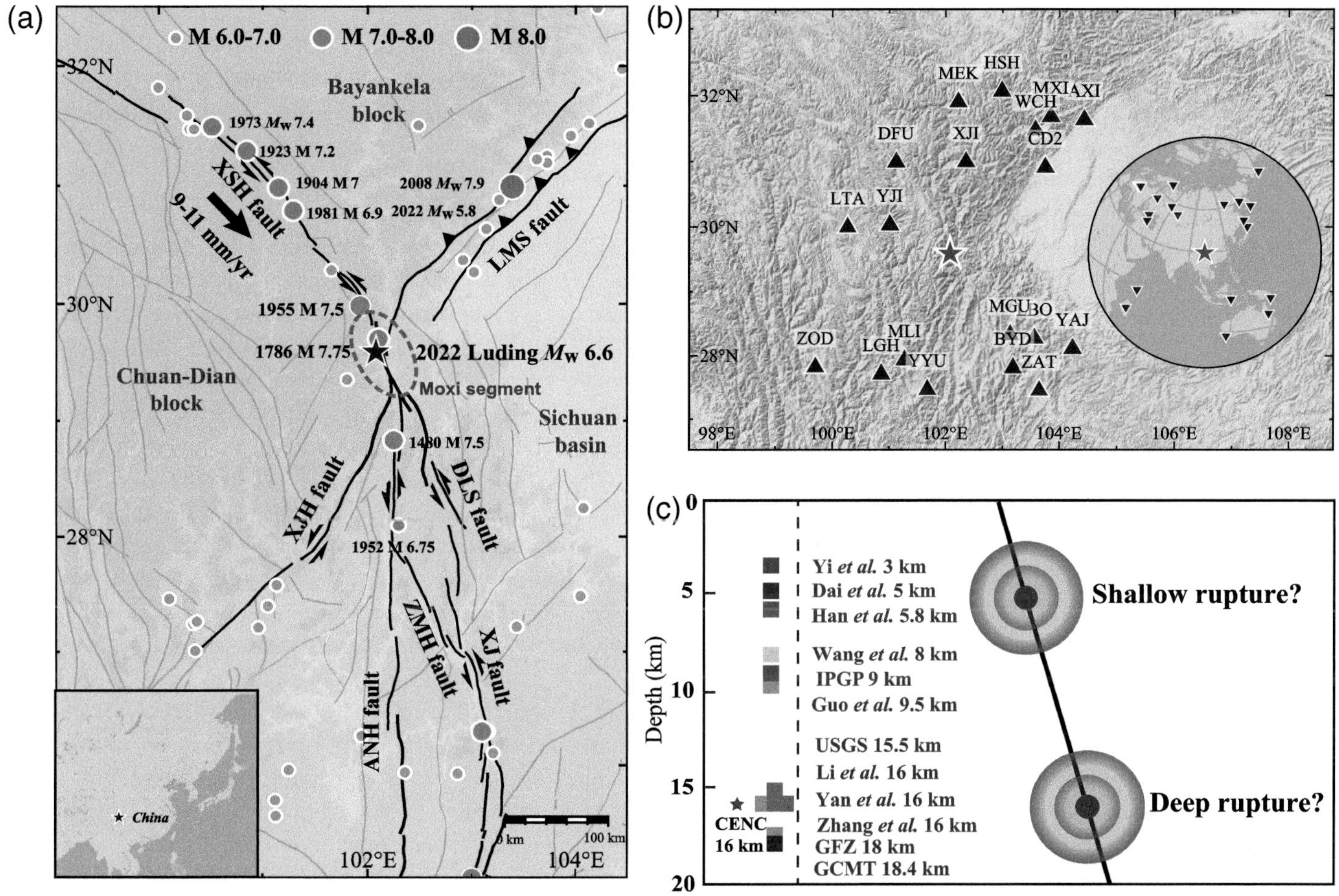

Figure 1. Tectonic background and distribution of regional and teleseismic stations around the Luding earthquake. (a) Map of regional tectonic background, in which the blue star indicates the epicenter of the Luding earthquake on 5 September 2022. The solid black line represents the main active block boundary faults associated with the Luding earthquake. The Luding earthquake locates on the Moxi segment on the southernmost end of the XSH (slip rate of 9–11 mm/yr). The dashed red circle represents the seismic gap around Moxi segment. The gray lines represent other active faults in the surrounding area. The circles indicate the distribution of historical earthquakes with magnitude $>M$ 6, with the earthquake catalog sourced from the International Seismological Centre (ISC) and Shan *et al.* (2023). The inset map displays the Luding earthquake within a larger regional context. (b) Distribution of regional and teleseismic (in inset map) stations, in which blue triangles represent regional stations, blue-inverted triangles represent teleseismic stations, and the red star indicates the epicenter. (c) Summary of previous results on the centroid depth of the Luding earthquake, from various scholars and institutions. CENC, China Earthquake Network Center. ANH, Anninghe fault; DLS, Daliangshan fault; LMS, Longmenshan fault; XJ, Xiaojiang fault; XJH, Xiaojinhe fault; XSH, Xianshuihe fault; ZMH, Zemuhe fault. The color version of this figure is available only in the electronic edition.

Accurate earthquake source parameters, such as focal depth, moment tensor, and fault-plane geometry, are essential for understanding earthquake nucleation, constraining crustal stress condition, and assessing seismic hazards (Luo *et al.*, 2013; Meng *et al.*, 2018). However, numerous studies have reported conflicting source depth of the Luding earthquake (Fig. 1c). Generally, studies based on teleseismic waveforms report a deep centroid depth. For example, the Global Centroid Moment Tensor (Global CMT) project (Ekström *et al.*, 2012) reported a centroid depth of 18.4 km. The USGS *W*-phase solution (Kanamori and Rivera, 2008; Duputel *et al.*, 2012) indicated a centroid depth of 15.5 km. The German Research Centre for Geosciences (GFZ) determined a centroid depth at 18 km. Other inversion results using global seismic records also found a deep centroid depth (>15 km, Li *et al.*, 2023; Zhang, Fang, and Xu, 2023). In contrast, studies using regional seismic data yielded much shallower estimates. Yi *et al.* (2023) estimated a centroid depth of 3 km using the cut-and-paste method to fit regional body and surface waveforms. Dai *et al.* (2022) inverted the rupture process of the Luding earthquake through an iterative deconvolution and stacking method and suggested the maximum slip occurred at a depth of ∼5 km. Other studies based on regional waveforms also reported shallow centroid depths (<10 km, Wang and Guo, 2022; Guo *et al.*, 2023).

Geodetic studies show similar variability. Yan *et al.* (2023) used Interferometric Synthetic Aperture Radar (InSAR) data to determine a deep centroid of 16 km depth, with slip distributed at depth range of 6–24 km. Conversely, Han *et al.* (2023), adopting Sentinel-1 and Advanced Land Observation

Satellite-2 satellite images and InSAR, found the slip distribution concentrated at shallow depth of 0–10 km, with maximum slip at 5.8 km. Xu *et al.* (2023), using 36 static near-field Global Navigation Satellite Systems (GNSS) stations, indicated the centroid depth did not exceed 6 km. Li *et al.* (2022), integrating seismic waveform, Global Positioning System, and InSAR data, resolved the coseismic deformation field and fault-slip distribution shallower than 10 km depth.

Previous results of the kinematic rupture of the Luding earthquake suggest this event may have involved complex process with at least two subevents (Zhang, Fang, and Xu, 2023; Liu *et al.*, 2024). We hypothesize that the large discrepancy of centroid depth estimates is caused by the oversimplified assumption of a single point–source, but the true rupture was complex. Different datasets (regional waveforms, teleseismic waveforms, InSAR, or near-field GNSS) are likely sensitive to subevents at different depths, leading to conflicting results. The potential of rupture complexity of the Luding earthquake is plausible given the region's complex tectonic environment at the boundary between the eastern Tibetan Plateau and the Sichuan basin, where the stress is heterogeneous and fluids are thought to be present (e.g., Wang *et al.*, 2007; Lei *et al.*, 2014; Liu and Wang, 2020; Liu *et al.*, 2021; Song *et al.* 2023). For example, Song *et al.* (2023), imaged the 3D *S*-wave velocity structure near Luding County, and the results show a pronounced low-velocity anomaly beneath the Sichuan basin at depths of 5–10 km and another low-velocity zone beneath the Chuan-Dian block at depths of 20–40 km, both of which may be related to fluid activities.

To test this hypothesis, we performed a series of inversions and tests. First, we conducted separate single point–source inversions using regional and teleseismic waveforms. Next, we ran a series of synthetic tests to assess how a composite source with two subevents affects the inverted centroid depth. Finally, we constrained the rupture process of the Luding earthquake using a multiple point–source inversion and a *Pn*/*Pg* relocated hypocenter depth.

REGIONAL TECTONIC SETTING

The epicenter of the Luding earthquake located on the Moxi segment at the southern end of the Xianshuihe fault, which is a major boundary between the Chuan-Dian block, South China continent, and the Bayankela block and exhibits complex tectonic deformation features with frequent seismic activity (Fig. 1a). The Xianshuihe fault (striking N40°W, dipping near vertical) is characterized by left-lateral strike-slip motion of 9–11 mm/yr, making it one of the most tectonically active fault zones in mainland China (Wen, Ma, *et al.*, 2008; Zhang, 2008). The Moxi segment marks an intersection of multiple active fault systems, with the Xianshuihe fault connecting to the southern end of the Longmenshan fault and the northern end of three left-lateral strike-slip faults: the Anninghe, Xiaojinhe, and Daliangshan faults (Allen *et al.*, 1991; Zhang, 2008). Thus, this region is crucial for studying tectonic behavior in the northern–southern seismic belt and along the Tibetan Plateau's periphery (Zhang *et al.*, 2003).

This region has long been a key focus for seismic hazard assessment. The Longmenshan fault zone has become one of the most seismically active regions in mainland China since 2008, highlighted by major events including the 2008 M_w 7.9 Wenchuan earthquake and the 2022 M_w 5.8 Lushan earthquake (Fig. 1a). The northern segment of the Anninghe fault experienced an *M* 7.5 earthquake in 1480 and an *M* 6.75 earthquake in 1952. The magnitudes of historical events prior to 1973 are from the China Earthquake Disaster Prevention Center and were estimated using an empirical relationship between maximum intensity and surface-wave magnitude; the same for the events discussed subsequently. In the 150 yr leading up to the 1973 Luhuo earthquake (M_w 7.4), >10 *M* 7+ events occurred along the Xianshuihe and Anninghe faults, but seismic activity significantly declined afterward, entering a period of relative quiescence. Over the past three decades, no *M* 7+ earthquakes have occurred on this fault system, except for the 2008 M_w 7.9 Wenchuan earthquake on the nearby Longmenshan fault (Wen, Fan, *et al.*, 2008; Zhang, 2008; Yi *et al.*, 2016). Since 1900, six *M* >6.5 earthquakes have ruptured segments along the Xianshuihe fault, covering nearly the entire fault length except the Moxi segment (Fig. 1a). The recent Luding earthquake is the first *M* >6.5 event occurring on the Moxi segment since the 1786 *M* 7.75 Kangding earthquake, filling a long-standing seismic gap (Yi *et al.*, 2023). This event underscores the potential seismic hazard on the Xianshuihe fault and other nearby faults, warranting further investigation into the fault dynamics and strain accumulation patterns in this tectonically active region.

SINGLE POINT–SOURCE INVERSION

We first conducted a single point–source inversion to examine the centroid depth of the Luding earthquake using regional and teleseismic waveforms separately. For the regional data, we selected, from Earth Science Data Center (see Data and Resources), waveforms on 20 seismic stations within 300 km from the epicenter (Fig. 1b). The *Pnl* waveforms were cut with a 60 s window, and the surface waves were cut with an 80 s window. For teleseismic data, waveforms on 20 stations within the epicentral distance of 30°–90° were obtained through the Incorporated Research Institutions for Seismology (IRIS; see Data and Resources), shown in Figure 1b. Afterward, *P* waves were extracted with a 70 s window and *SH* waves were extracted with a 100 s window. The velocity structure of the Chuan-Dian region has been explored extensively by previous studies (Zhao and Chen, 1995; Xie *et al.*, 2012; Yi *et al.*, 2020; Yi *et al.*, 2016, 2023). After comparison, we selected the 1D velocity model proposed by Yi *et al.* (2023) for the Luding area to calculate theoretical Green's functions.

Numerous techniques have been developed to invert single point–source parameters, including methods based on teleseismic body waves (Lay *et al.*, 1982; Dreger and Helmberger, 1993), long-period surface waves (Kanamori and Rivera, 2008; Ekström *et al.*, 2012), and regional datasets (Takeo, 1987; Zhao and Helmberger, 1994). This study used the generalized cut-and-paste (gCAP) inversion method to study the focal mechanism and centroid depth of the Luding earthquake. The gCAP method combines body and surface waveforms in a broad frequency range and enables the joint inversion of regional and teleseismic data to derive the moment tensor solution (Zhu and Helmberger, 1996; Zhu and Ben-Zion, 2013; Bai *et al.*, 2020).

Regional centroid moment tensor inversion

Before the regional single point–source inversion, we used the frequency–wavenumber integration method (*f-k*, Aki and Richards, 2002; Zhu and Rivera, 2002) to calculate Green's functions at each source depth between 1 and 30 km for near-field stations. We then applied the gCAP method to invert the source parameters, including centroid depth; strike, dip, and rake angles; and source duration. During inversion, the search interval for centroid depth is 1 km and for strike, dip, and rake angles is 5°. The body waves are filtered between 0.02 and 0.12 Hz, and the surface waves are filtered between 0.02 and 0.1 Hz. The time-shift windows for *Pnl* and surface waves are set at 5 and 10 s. Based on seismic scaling laws, the duration for magnitude 6–7 earthquake is ~3–30 s. Accordingly, we applied a series of source durations from 8 to 16 s during inversion. The minimum misfit residual occurs near centroid depth of 6 km with a source duration of 12 s and a magnitude of M_w 6.53 (Figs. 2a, 3a and Fig. S1, available in the supplemental material to this article). The optimal focal mechanism is left-lateral strike-slip yielding strike, dip, and rake angles of 161°/61°/−10° and 255°/81°/−150° on two conjugates fault planes (Fig. 2a). The regional *Pnl* and surface waves are well fitted under the optimal source parameters, with a waveform cross-correlation coefficient exceeding 80% across stations (Fig. 2a, Fig. S1).

Teleseismic centroid moment tensor inversion

Before the teleseismic single point–source inversion, we used the MultiTel3 method (Qian *et al.*, 2017), which accounts for reflections at the core–mantle boundary, to compute Green's functions at each depth (1–30 km) for far-field stations. We set the same searching intervals for depth and strike, dip, and rake angles as the regional inversion. We set the filter bands of 0.01–0.1 Hz for *P* waves and 0.01–0.05 Hz for *SH* waves and the time-shift window of 12 s for *P* wave and 15 s for *SH* wave. We tested source durations between 8 and 16 s and found the optimal duration at ~12 s (Fig. 3b), similar to the regional inversion. The optimal centroid depth is 17 km, and the inferred magnitude is M_w 6.72, with a left-lateral strike-slip focal mechanism: plane I (strike, dip, rake) = 157°/78°/−2° and plane II = 247°/88°/−167°. The *P*- and *SH*-wave records are generally well fitted, with a cross-correlation coefficient exceeding 80% on most stations (Fig. 2b, Fig. S1).

Centroid depth comparison: Regional versus teleseismic inversions

The comparison of centroid depth results from regional and teleseismic inversions shows a notable difference, for which the regional centroid depth is shallower (6 km) and the teleseismic centroid depth is much deeper (17 km). To assess the robustness of the source parameters, we conducted additional bootstrap tests involving 150 inversion iterations, each performed by randomly selecting 14 of the 20 available stations, using regional and teleseismic data. The results demonstrate good stability in the inverted parameters (strike, dip, rake, depth, and magnitude), indicating reliable and robust solutions (Figs. S2, S3). Our regional centroid depth is consistent with previous results using regional waveforms (Dai *et al.*, 2022; Yi *et al.*, 2023) and InSAR data (Han *et al.*, 2023). In addition, the teleseismic centroid depth agrees with the global solutions from Global CMT, GFZ, and other studies based on global network data (Li *et al.*, 2023; Zhang, Fang, and Xu, 2023). In this way, the Luding earthquake centroid depth discrepancy may indicate a complex rupture process, which likely involved both shallow and deep rupture sources. It also suggests that regional and teleseismic data are sensitive to different aspects of the rupture process, with the regional data primarily reflecting shallow rupture and the teleseismic data being more sensitive to deeper rupture.

We also conducted a joint inversion for the Luding earthquake using both regional and teleseismic waveforms (Figs. S4, S5). During the inversion process, we extracted 70 s of body waves and 100 s of surface waves and applied band-pass filters of 0.01–0.12 Hz for body waves and 0.01–0.1 Hz for surface waves. The source duration was set to 12 s, with time-shift windows of 10 s for body waves and 15 s for surface waves. The weight ratios of regional to teleseismic data were set to 5:1, 1:2, and 1:5. The inversion results demonstrate that as the weight of teleseismic data increases, the derived centroid depth progressively deepens from 5 km (regional to teleseismic ratio of 5:1) to 13 km (ratio of 1:2) and to 17 km (ratio of 1:5). This suggests that the centroid depth exhibits high sensitivity to the relative weighting between regional and teleseismic data, thus further implying source complexity.

SENSITIVITY TESTS OF DEPTH INVERSION

The teleseismic inversion presents a much deeper centroid depth than the regional inversion, as shown in the Single point–source inversion section, which inspires us to test whether the teleseismic waveforms are capable to reveal the actual depth for shallow earthquakes. We used the gCAP method to test the sensitivity of the teleseismic waveforms on the centroid depth of a synthetic shallow earthquake source (Figs. S6–S8). We found that teleseismic waveforms show good sensitivity to shallow source as well if the source is simple. Therefore, we highly suspect that the rupture process of the Luding earthquake is complex, leading to significant

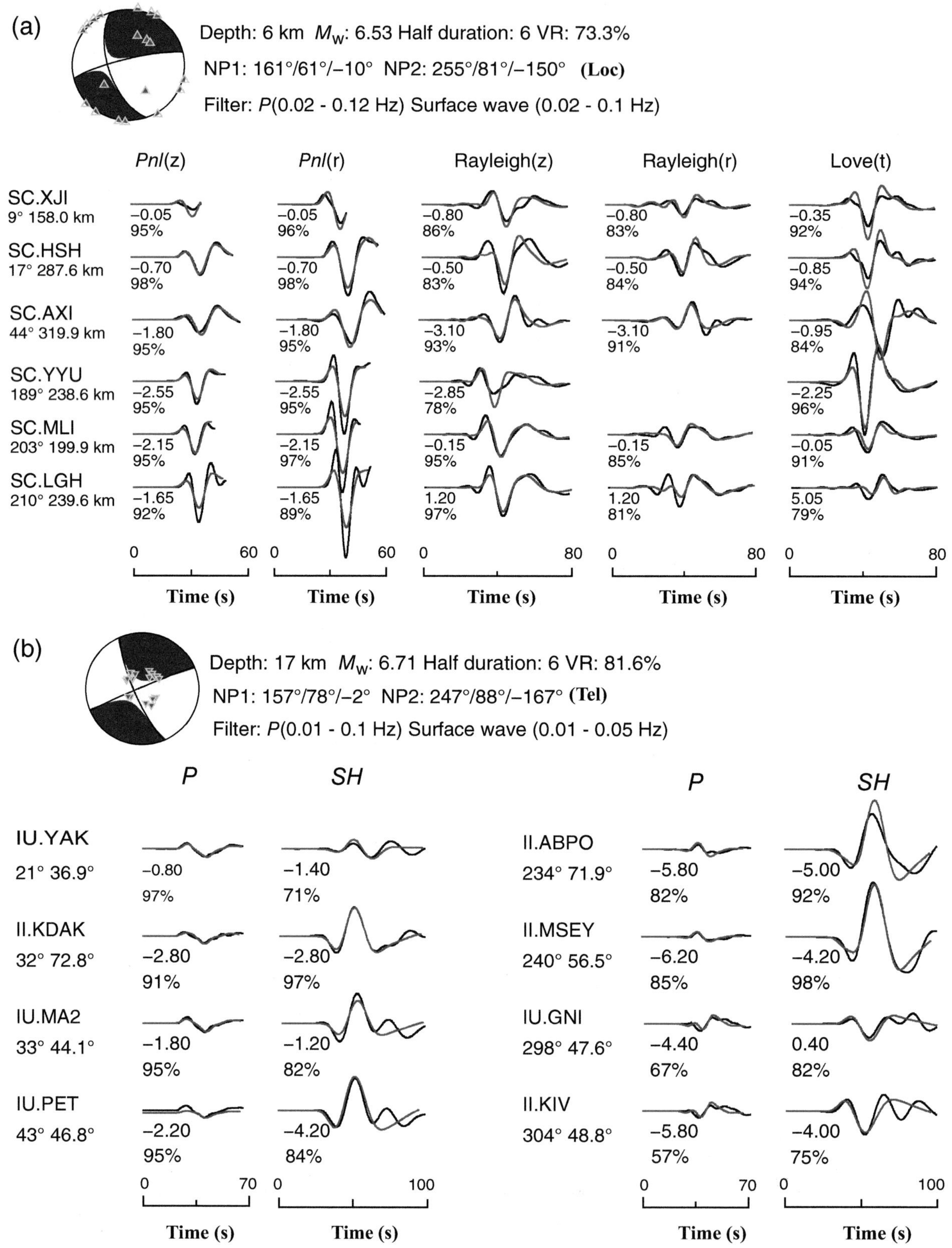

Figure 2. Single point–source inversion results of the Luding earthquake using regional and teleseismic waveforms. (a) The focal mechanism and waveform-fitting results obtained from regional inversion, with the red lines representing theoretical (predicted) waveforms and the black lines representing observed waveforms. (b) The focal mechanism and waveform-fitting results obtained from teleseismic inversion, with the red lines representing the theoretical (predicted) waveforms and the black lines representing observed waveforms. The degrees below the station name represent the azimuth and epicentral distance. More waveform-fitting results are shown in Figure S1. The color version of this figure is available only in the electronic edition.

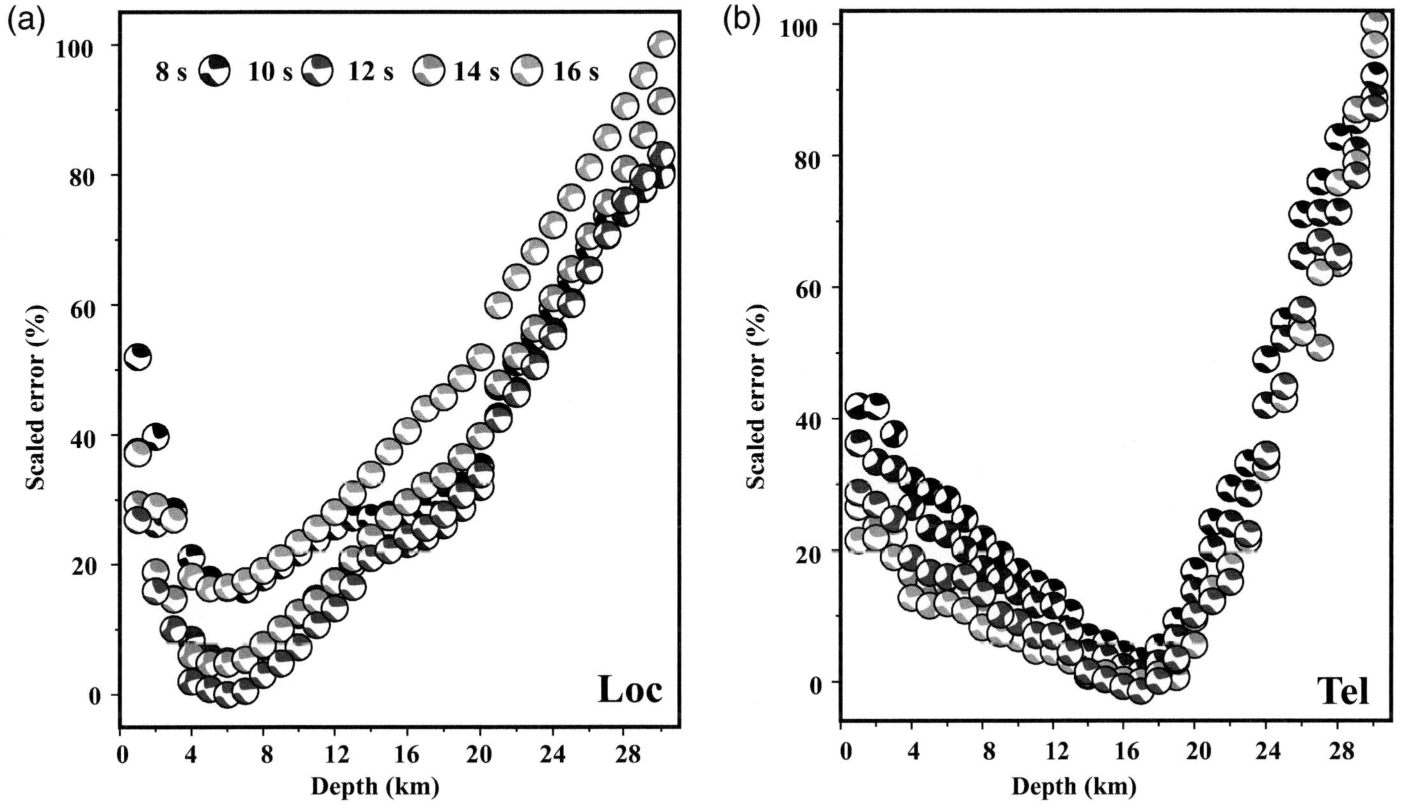

Figure 3. Depth–misfit curves for the (a) regional and (b) teleseismic single point–source inversions. The colored focal spheres illustrate the waveform misfits calculated for various assumed source durations. The horizontal axis indicates the centroid depth, and the vertical axis represents the normalized L2 norm of the waveform misfit computed across all stations. The color version of this figure is available only in the electronic edition.

discrepancy in centroid depth between the local and teleseismic inversions.

Subsequently, we tested the sensitivity of the regional and teleseismic inversion to the centroid depth using a synthetic doublet source as input while assuming a single point source during inversion. The synthetic doublet source model consists of two double-couple subevents locating at 6 and 17 km depth, with similar focal mechanisms as the Luding earthquake single point–source inversions (as shown in Fig. 2). Both synthetic subevents have a source duration of 12 s, and their total moment is 10^{19} N · m, referring to the moment of the Luding earthquake (0.926×10^{19} N · m). A series of moment ratios between the shallow and deep subevents was tested (e.g., 3:7, 4:6, 5:5, 6:4, 7:3, and 8:2), and multiple rupture time intervals (the time delay between the shallow and deep subevents) were also tested (e.g., 1, 3, 5, 7, and 9 s), yielding 30 distinct synthetic doublet source models.

Shallow subevent ruptures first

We first explored the case that the shallow subevent (6 km depth) triggers the rupture of the deep subevent (17 km depth) after a certain time interval. The gCAP inversion results indicate that regional and teleseismic waveforms exhibit different sensitivities to the centroid depth depending on the size of each subevent and the rupture time interval (Fig. 4). When the moment ratio of the shallow versus deep subevent is equal or smaller than 5:5 (i.e., 3:7, 4:6, and 5:5) and the rupture time interval increases, both regional and teleseismic inversions show a trend of getting deeper centroid depths (>10 km, Fig. 4a–c). However, when the rupture time interval reaches to 9 s, the regional centroid depth becomes unstable, for which the depth curve do not converge, especially for the case of moment ratio 5:5 (Fig. 4c). This may be because of the discrepancy between the synthetic source setup (a doublet) and the single point–source assumption used in the inversion. As the moment ratio between the shallow and deep subevents increases (from 6:4 to 8:2) and the rupture time interval becomes longer, the centroid depth derived from teleseismic inversion tends to deepen, and that from regional inversion becomes shallower (Fig. 4d–f). Specifically, when the moment ratio is 6:4 or 7:3 and the rupture time interval reaches to 7 s, the local and teleseismic inversions present a significant discrepancy in centroid depths. The regional inversion shows a shallower centroid depth (~5 km), and the teleseismic inversion yields a deeper centroid depth (~15 km), which is similar to the Luding earthquake centroid depth results (regional: 6 km, teleseismic: 17 km). However, when the moment ratio is as large as 8:2, centroid depths based on teleseismic inversion

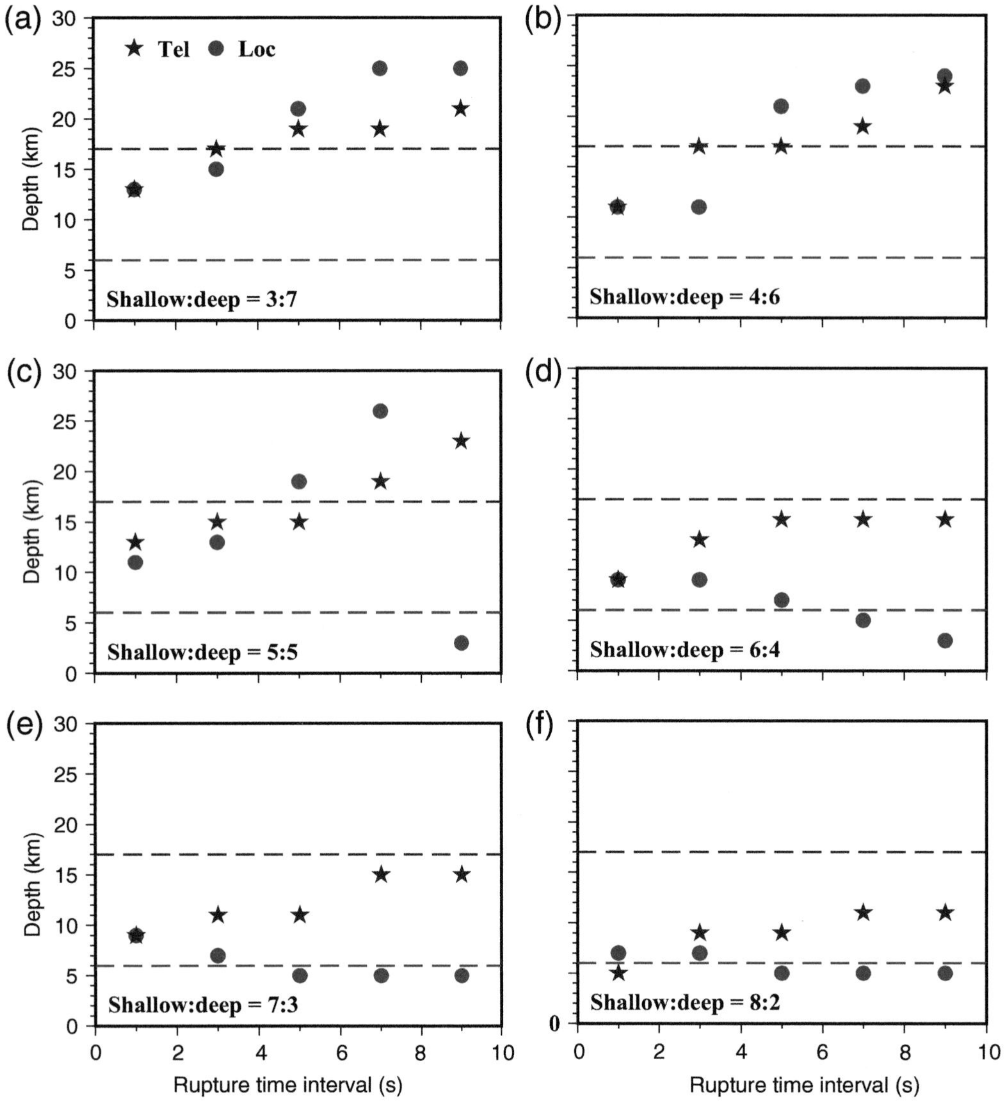

Figure 4. Testing the depth sensitivity of single point–source inversion using regional and teleseismic synthetic waveforms, generated by a synthetic doublet source model with initial rupture at "shallow" depth. The horizontal coordinate is the time interval between two synthetic point sources. The vertical coordinate is the inverted centroid depth, with red dots and blue stars representing the inversion using regional and teleseismic waveforms, respectively. The shallow:deep ratio is the prescribed seismic moment ratio between the shallow and the deep source when generating the synthetic waveforms. Panels (a–f) correspond to the shallow:deep moment ratios of 3:7, 4:6, 5:5:, 6:4, 7:3, and 8:2, respectively. The dashed blue line (17 km) is the centroid depth of the Luding earthquake obtained by teleseismic inversion (shown in Fig. 2b and Fig. 3b), and the dashed red line (6 km) is the centroid depth obtained by regional inversion (shown in Fig. 2a and Fig. 3a). The color version of this figure is available only in the electronic edition.

are generally shallow (<11 km), which does not align with the inversion results for the Luding earthquake.

Based on a series of tests, we found that the centroid depth inversion results best match those of the Luding earthquake when the synthetic doublet model includes a shallow and a deep subevent (at 6 and 17 km, respectively) with a moment ratio of 7:3 and a rupture time interval of 7 s, with the shallow subevent rupturing first. Under this synthetic doublet model, the waveform fittings of the regional and teleseismic synthetic data are both good, with cross-correlation coefficients >90% (Fig. 5, Fig. S9). The regional inverted mechanism is: 161°/63°/−11° versus 256°/80°/−152°, with a centroid depth of 5 km, and the teleseismic inverted focal mechanism is: 70°/90°/175° versus 160°/84°/0°, with a centroid depth of 17 km. The depth misfit curves for the doublet source synthetics and the Luding earthquake observations are consistent in both regional and teleseismic inversions (Fig. 6). This synthetic doublet source could serve as a useful proxy for the complex rupture process of the Luding earthquake.

Deep subevent ruptures first or simultaneously

We next tested the depth sensitivity assuming a synthetic doublet source model, within which the deep subevent (17 km) ruptures first and triggers the shallow subevent (6 km; Fig. 7). When the shallow-to-deep moment ratio is ≤5:5 (i.e., ratios of 3:7, 4:6, and 5:5) and the rupture time interval increases, both regional and teleseismic inversions show a trend of deeper centroid depths, with the depth range concentrated deeper than 10 km. Both local and teleseismic inversions are more sensitive to the deep subevent when the deep one is larger. When the shallow subevent has larger moment (i.e., for shallow-to-deep ratios of 6:4, 7:3, and 8:2), the centroid depth from regional inversion shallows with increasing rupture time interval, and the centroid depth from teleseismic inversion is concentrated between 5 and 11 km, indicating that both inversions are more sensitive to the shallow source. The results based on the doublet source model, for which the deep subevent ruptures first, do not exhibit the expected differences in sensitivity between regional and teleseismic inversions (i.e., regional

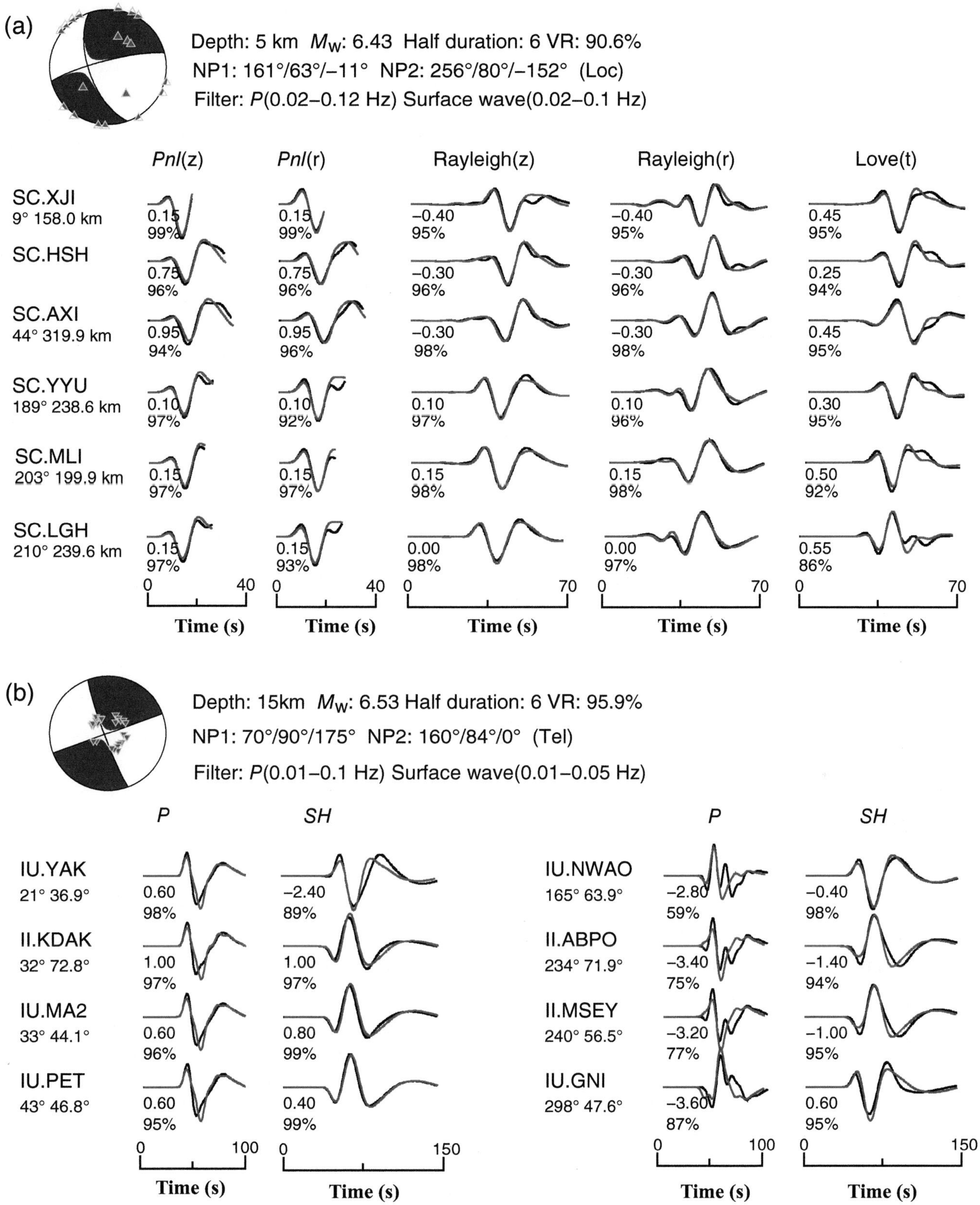

Figure 5. Single point–source inversion results based on synthetic regional and teleseismic waveforms generated from our preferred synthetic doublet source model, which consists of a shallow (6 km) and a deep (17 km) subevent with a moment ratio of 7:3 and a rupture time interval of 7 s. (The shallow subevent ruptures first.) (a) Inversion using synthetic regional waveforms. (b) Inversion using synthetic teleseismic waveforms. Red lines denote the predicted waveforms, and black lines denote the synthetic waveforms of the doublet source. More waveform-fitting results are shown in Figure S9. The color version of this figure is available only in the electronic edition.

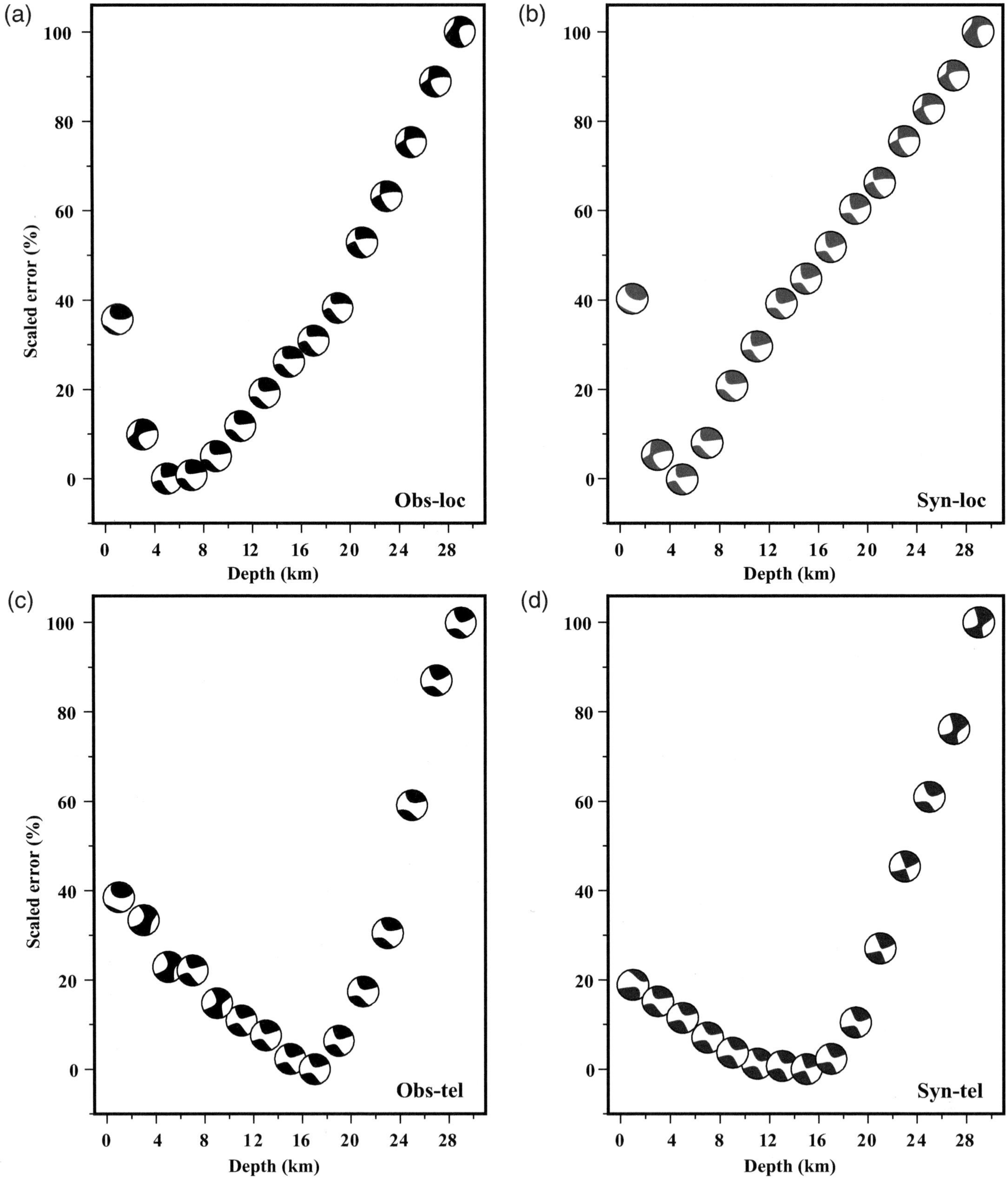

Figure 6. Comparison of waveform misfit curves between the inversion results using observed regional and teleseismic waveforms and the inversion results using synthetic regional and teleseismic waveforms (generated by our preferred model). Panels (a,c) are depth inversion misfit curves using observed regional and teleseismic waveforms, respectively. In panels (b,d), the red and blue curves demonstrate the inversion result using synthetic regional and teleseismic waveforms, respectively. During synthetic waveform generation, the moment ratio of the shallow and deep sources is set as 7:3, and the shallow source ruptures before the deep source with a rupture time interval of 7 s. The color version of this figure is available only in the electronic edition.

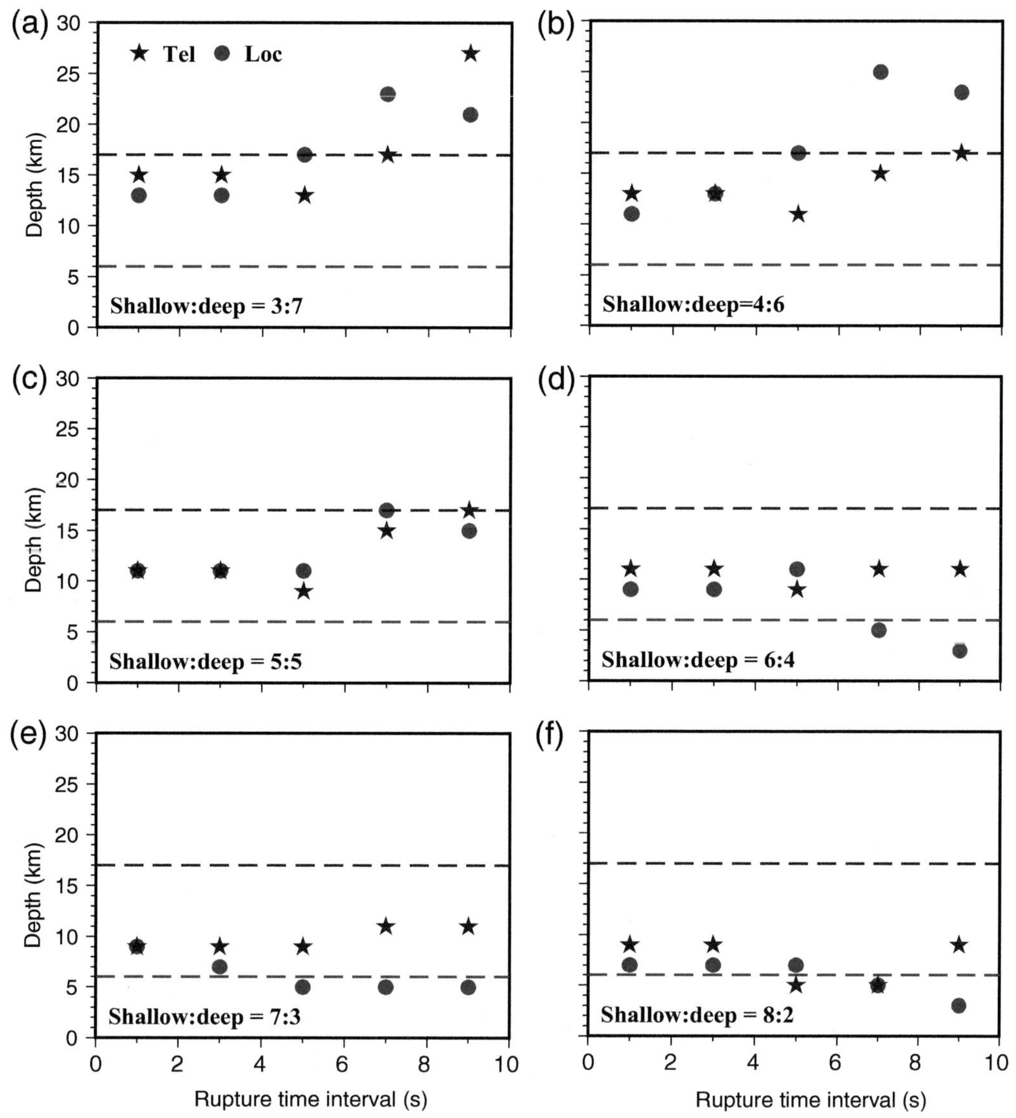

Figure 7. Testing the depth sensitivity for single point–source inversion using regional and teleseismic synthetic waveforms, generated by a synthetic doublet source model with initial rupture at "deep" depth, other features are similar to Figure 4. Panels (a–f) correspond to the shallow:deep moment ratios of 3:7, 4:6, 5:5:, 6:4, 7:3, and 8:2, respectively. The color version of this figure is available only in the electronic edition.

inversion sensitive to shallow source and teleseismic inversion sensitive to deep source). This suggests that the deep-rupture-first doublet source model is not suitable to represent the rupture process of the Luding earthquake.

In addition, we examined models assuming simultaneous rupture of the shallow and deep subevents. The results show that the local and teleseismic centroid depths are generally consistent (Fig. S10), with a depth discrepancy within 3 km. In general, the inverted centroid depths become shallower as the moment ratio of the shallow to deep subevent increases and become deeper when the ratio decreases. However, this does not match the actual centroid depth inversion results for the Luding earthquake, indicating that the rupture process likely did not involve simultaneous failure of shallow and deep sources. Overall, our analysis suggests that the Luding earthquake was more consistent with an initial rupture at a shallow depth (~6 km), followed by a deeper subevent (~17 km).

HYPOCENTER OF THE LUDING EARTHQUAKE

The sensitivity tests of depth inversion, in the Sensitivity tests of depth inversion section, indicate that the Luding earthquake likely initiated at a relatively shallow depth and propagated to deeper depth. This contrasts with the findings of Das and Scholz (1983), who analyzed earthquakes with magnitudes >5.5 in California and found that most moderate to large events nucleated at greater depths and ruptured upward from deep to shallow regions. To further verify whether the Luding earthquake nucleates in the shallow region, we used the *Pn*/*Pg* relative location method (Wang *et al.*, 2021) to determine the mainshock hypocenter depth through travel-time positioning. This method is primarily based on the arrival-time difference between a target and a reference event, for the *Pn* and *Pg* phases, to determine the relative location of the target event. The ray-path angles of these two seismic phases differ markedly: the *Pn* phase is more vertical, whereas the *Pg* phase is closer to horizontal (Fig. 8a). By combining these two phases, the *Pn* better constrains the depth, and the *Pg* more effectively constrains the horizontal position.

We select an *M* 4.5 aftershock (on 7 September 2022) of the Luding earthquake as the reference event. We inverted the focal mechanism and centroid depth of this event using the gCAP inversion method and regional waveforms (Fig. S11). The *Pn* waveforms are cut by a 30 s time window and then band-pass-filtered between 0.02 and 0.12 Hz. The surface waves are cut to 70 s and band-pass-filtered between 0.02 and 0.1 Hz. Based on earthquake scaling laws, the source duration is 0.3–

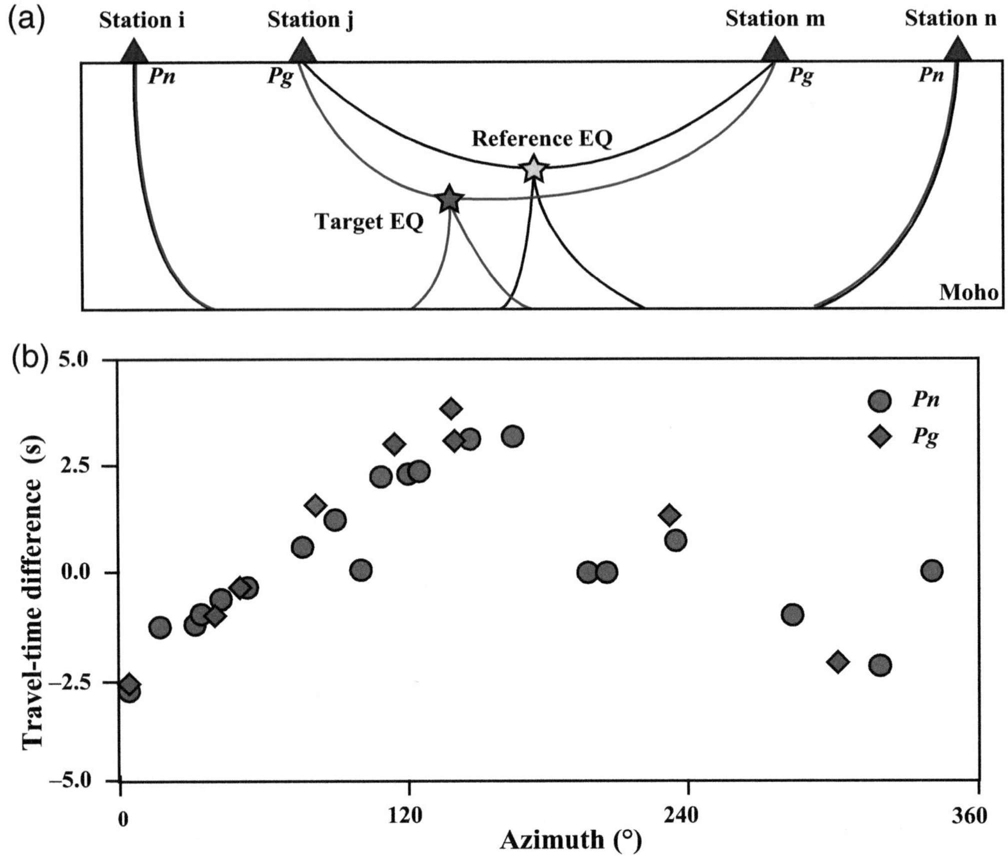

Figure 8. *Pn*/*Pg* relative location principle and results of *Pn*/*Pg* relative travel-time difference. (a) The principle of *Pn*/*Pg* relative location, where the red pentagram represents the target event; the yellow pentagram represents the reference event; and the solid red and black lines denote the ray paths of the target and the reference events, respectively. (b) The variation of *Pn*/*Pg* relative travel-time differences versus azimuths, in which the red circles represent the *Pn* phase relative travel-time differences (between two events) and the green diamonds represent the *Pg* phase relative travel-time differences. The color version of this figure is available only in the electronic edition.

1.0 s for an *M* 4–5 event, we set the duration of 0.8 s for this aftershock, after a series of tests. The inversion result of this aftershock yielded a centroid depth of 7 km (Fig. S11), consistent with the result from Yi *et al.* (2023). Using the velocity model near Luding (Yi *et al.*, 2023), we calculated the theoretical travel-time differences (between the mainshock and the reference event) for the *Pn* and *Pg* phases, to be compared with observed travel-time differences (Fig. 8b).We manually marked the *Pg* arrival times for stations within 150 km and the *Pn* arrival times for stations beyond 250 km, with an error margin of around ±0.1 s (Fig. 9a,c). The observed *Pn* and *Pg* travel-time differences show a sinusoidal trend versus azimuth, for which the peak corresponds to the azimuth of the Luding earthquake hypocenter (target event) relative to the reference event (Fig. 8b).

We applied the *Pn*/*Pg* relative location method to invert the hypocenter of the Luding mainshock. We used a horizontal step size of 0.01° and a depth step size of 0.5 km to search for the horizontal and vertical positions of the mainshock and found the optimal mainshock depth located near 7 km (Fig. 9b). This result agrees with our preferred synthetic doublet source (see the Shallow subevent ruptures first section), supporting the conclusion that the rupture process of the Luding earthquake propagated from shallow to deep depths.

MULTIPLE POINT–SOURCE INVERSION

We further applied the multiple point–source inversion method to investigate the rupture process of the Luding earthquake. Over the past few decades, rupture process studies have progressed from simple single point–source models (SPSMs; Zhu and Helmberger, 1996; Ekström *et al.*, 1998; Kanamori and Rivera, 2008) to more sophisticated finite-fault rupture models (Zhang *et al.*, 2009; Yue *et al.*, 2012; Yue and Lay, 2020). For large earthquakes (M >7), finite-fault models are typically used to infer the detailed rupture process. In contrast, for small earthquakes (M <5), the SPSM adequately captures the main source features because of the limited rupture scale. However, for moderate earthquakes (M_w 5–7), the SPSM tends to be overly simplistic, whereas finite-fault models often fail to provide robust rupture details because of the sparse regional station coverage and the limited resolution of teleseismic data at this magnitude range. The multiple point–source model, which bridges the gap between the two approaches (Tsai *et al.*, 2005; Shi *et al.*, 2018; Jia *et al.*, 2020, 2023; Shi and Wei, 2020; Yue and Lay, 2020), effectively compensates for their respective limitations and is particularly suitable for resolving the source parameters of moderate earthquakes.

This study used the subevent inversion method proposed by Jia *et al.* (2020), using teleseismic *P* displacement and velocity and *SH* displacement waveforms, to resolve the rupture process of the Luding earthquake. We obtained teleseismic waveform records from the IRIS (see Data and Resources) database, spanning epicentral distances between 30° and 90° from the Luding mainshock. After filtering, 26 *P*- and 29 *SH*-wave records, with a good signal-to-noise ratio, were selected for

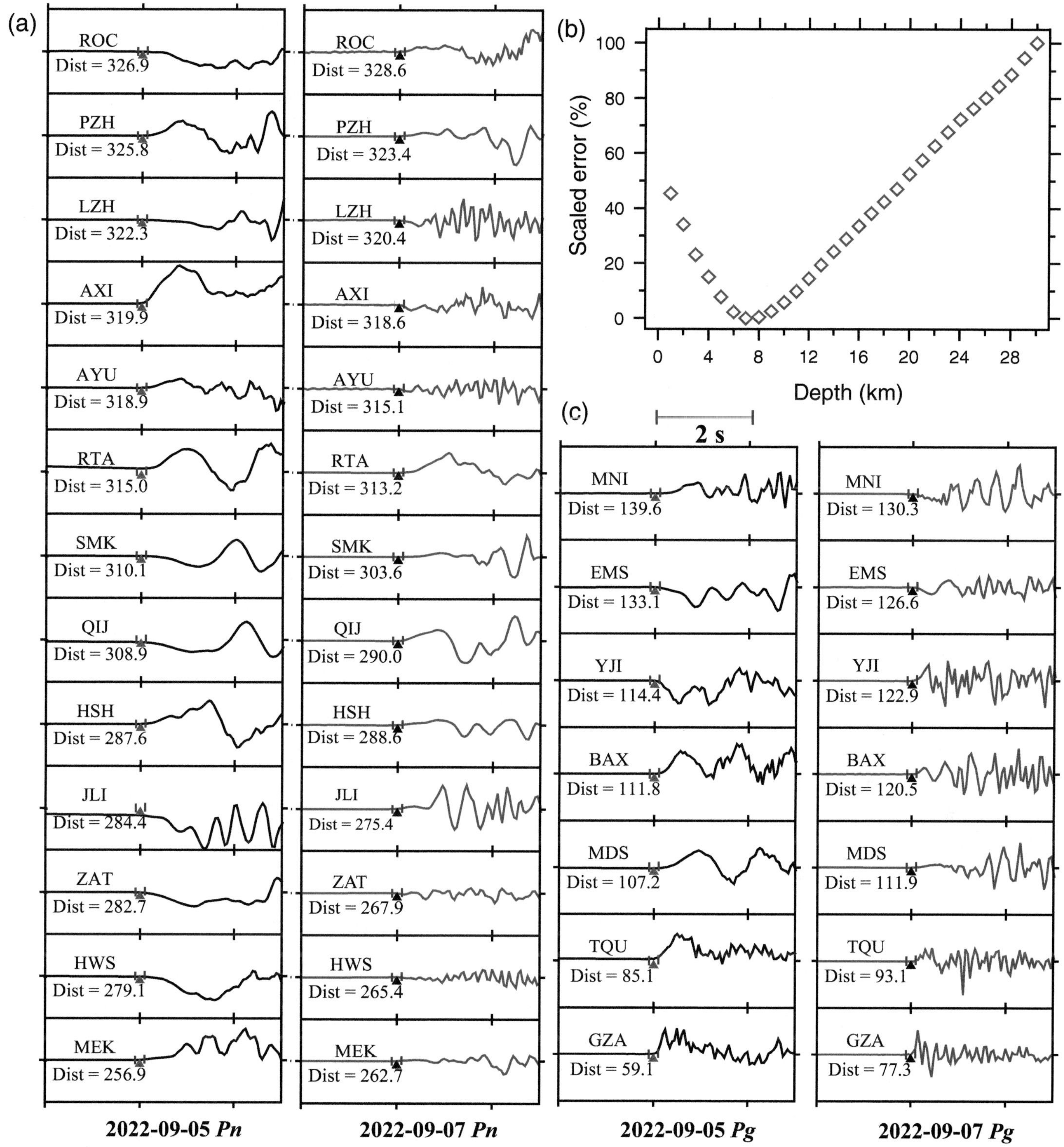

Figure 9. Relocation of the hypocenter depth of the Luding earthquake. (a) Manually picked *Pn*-wave arrival times for stations with epicentral > 250 km of the mainshock (left, red triangles) compared with those of the reference event (right, blue triangles). (b) The hypocenter depth versus the misfit of travel-time difference (normalized), with the minimum misfit near 7 km. (c) Manually picked *Pg*-wave arrival times for stations within 150 km range of the mainshock (left, red triangles) compared with those of the reference event (right, blue triangles). The triangles mark the *P*-wave arrival times we picked, and the blue short-vertical lines indicate the picking error of ±0.1 s. The color version of this figure is available only in the electronic edition.

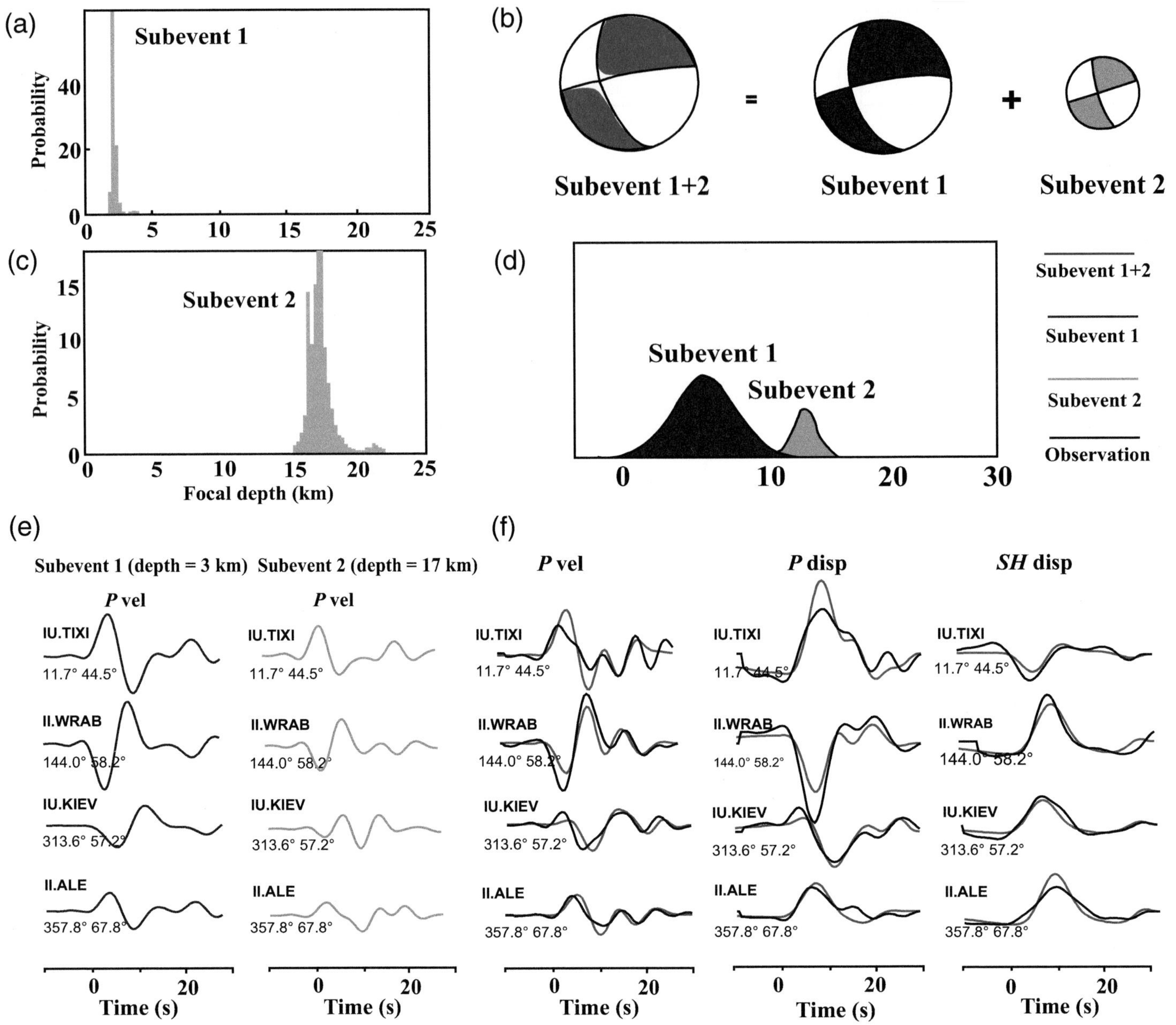

Figure 10. Two point-source inversion results based on multiple point–source method. (a) Probability density distribution of the centroid depth for subevent 1 (shallow). (b) Focal mechanism solutions for two subevents. (c) Probability density distribution of the centroid depth for subevent 2 (deep). (d) Source time functions for two subevents. (e) Theoretical *P*-velocity waveforms from two subevents, on four selected stations, with the blue lines for subevent 1 and orange lines for subevent 2. (f) Waveform fitting for *P*-wave velocity and displacement and *SH*-wave displacement waveforms for four selected stations. The red and black lines are the total theoretical waveforms (subevents 1 and 2) and observed waveforms, respectively. The color version of this figure is available only in the electronic edition.

inversion. In addition, both *P* and *SH* waveforms were bandpass filtered with a frequency range of 0.01–0.15 Hz, within the time windows of 40 and 50 s for the *P* and *SH* waveforms, respectively.

During inversion, we gradually increased the number of point sources. The results showed that when the number of point sources reached two or more, the observed waveforms were well fitted (Figs. 10, 11). Figure 10 shows the uncertainty in the centroid depth, source time function, focal mechanism, and waveform fitting for the optimal inversion result based on two point-source model. The waveform-fitting results indicate that both *P* and *SH* waves are well fitted, with cross-correlation coefficients >80%. The waveform-fitting situations, assuming one, two and three point sources, are compared in Figure 11, with more details are shown in Figures S12–S19. Multiple point–source inversion suggests that the Luding earthquake can be well explained by two subevents: the first subevent occurred at a shallow centroid depth of ~3 km, with a source duration of ~10 s, and the second subevent occurred 7 s later, with a centroid depth of ~17 km and a source duration of ~5 s.

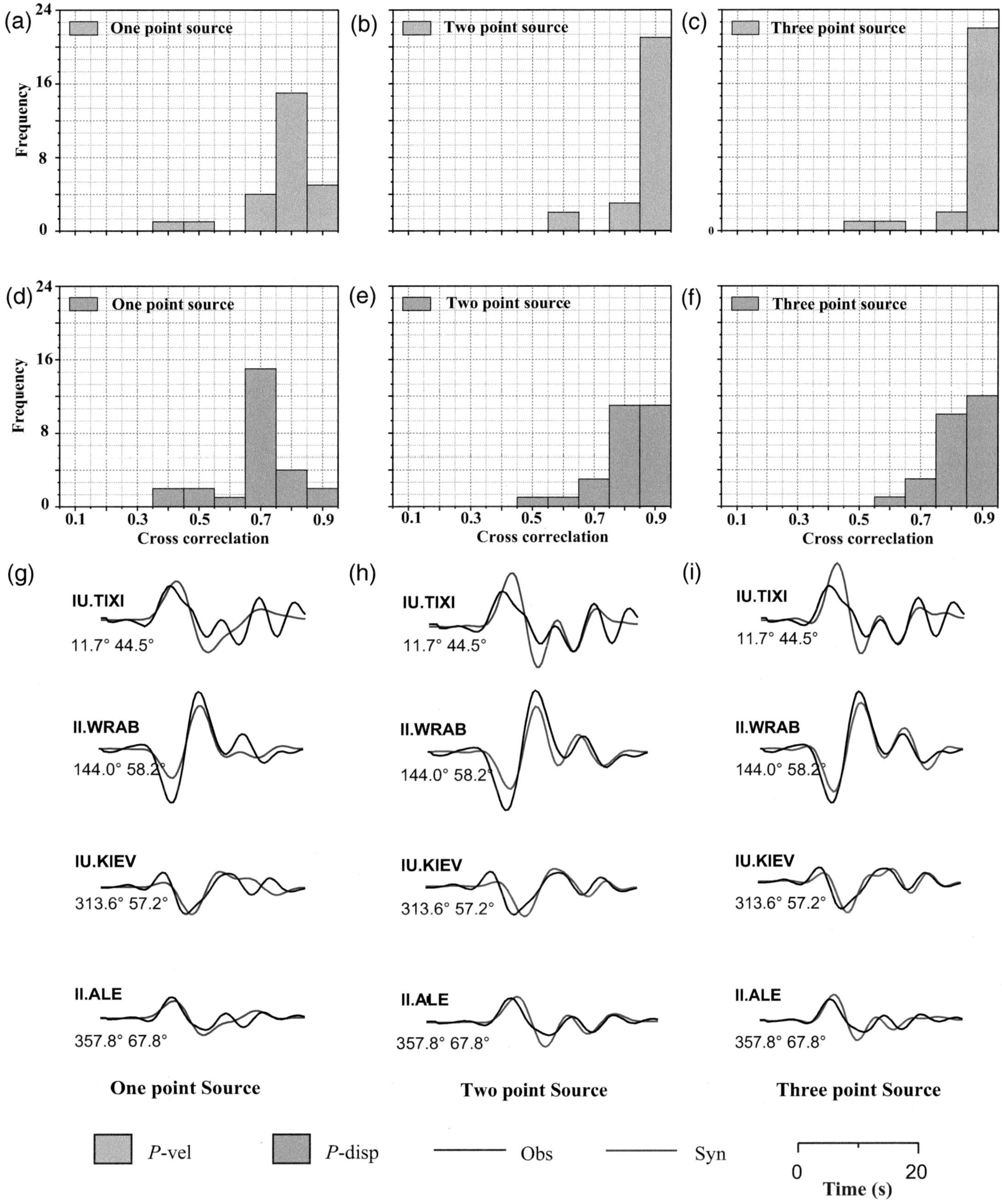

Figure 11. Comparison of results from multiple point–source inversions. (a–c) Histogram of the cross-correlation coefficients for the fitting of *P*-wave velocity waveforms, assuming one, two, and three point sources, respectively. (d–f) Histogram of the cross-correlation coefficients for *P*-wave displacement waveforms, assuming one, two, and three point sources, respectively. (g–i) Comparison of the fitting of *P*-wave velocity waveforms on four selected stations, considering different numbers of point sources. The color version of this figure is available only in the electronic edition.

DISCUSSION

This study first used an SPSM to invert the focal mechanism and centroid depth of the Luding mainshock based on regional and teleseismic seismograms. The inversion results indicate that the Luding earthquake was a left-lateral strike-slip event, but the centroid depth has a discrepancy between regional and teleseismic inversions. The regional inversion suggests a centroid depth of 6 km, whereas the teleseismic inversion indicates a depth of 17 km, differing by nearly 11 km. The joint inversion results demonstrate that the centroid depth of the Luding earthquake is dependent on the weighting ratio between local and teleseismic data (Figs. S4, S5). We further tested the sensitivity of regional and teleseismic data toward centroid depths using a series of synthetic doublet source models composed by two subevents (locating at 6 and 17 km depth) of varying moments and rupture time intervals. The testing results successfully reproduce the discrepancy between the locally and teleseismically inverted centroid depths of the Luding earthquake when the optimal synthetic doublet source model is adopted, consisting of a shallow subevent rupturing 7 s before a deep one (Fig. 12), with a moment ratio of 7:3. These inversions and tests collectively indicate the potential complexity of the Luding earthquake rupture process. Multiple point–source inversion based on teleseismic *P* and *SH* waves further supports this interpretation that the Luding earthquake consists of at least two subevents: a larger subevent at ~3 km and a smaller subevent at ~17 km, separated by a 7 s delay (Fig. 12). In addition, the *Pn*/*Pg* relative location analysis constraints the hypocenter depth to 7 km, yielding a consistent result that the initial rupture occurred at shallow depth.

The multiple point–source inversion results indicate that the Luding earthquake involved at least two subevents at both shallow and deep depth. To evaluate the effect of adding more sources, we further performed an inversion with three point sources (see Fig. 11, Figs. S13 and S16). The results show two point sources locate around 5 km depth, whereas the third lies at about 17 km depth (Fig. S13). Given their proximity, the first two point sources can effectively be treated as one source, implying that the earthquake rupture is dominated by two main subevents at 5 and 17 km depths (Fig. S20), respectively. For most small earthquakes, a single point source is generally sufficient to describe the rupture process. However, for moderate to large earthquakes, the rupture process can be more complex. When single point–source inversions from regional and teleseismic datasets yield consistent parameters and good waveforms fitting, the source process is likely simple. In contrast, when the results differ significantly between datasets, it strongly suggests a more complex rupture that requires a multiple point–source approach.

The multiple point–source inversion aims to get detailed information of the vertical and horizontal location, magnitude, and time of each subevent. However, the constraint on subevent horizontal location is not as good as the vertical location. Teleseismic body waves have nearly vertical take-off angle near the source side, making this method more sensitive to the relative depth than to the relative horizontal locations among different subevents. Specifically, when the number of point sources increases to three, for which the first two shallow subevents might be overfitted (Fig. 11, Figs. S17 and 18), the horizontal uncertainty of the third subevent (the deep one) reaches 20 km, shown in Figure S19. Generally, horizontal locations of more than two point sources cannot be considered as very reliable in this study within the frequency band up to 0.15 Hz/7 s. Future multiple point–source studies need to incorporate more accurate 3D velocity models and local seismic data to enhance the precision of horizontal positioning and avoid waveforms overfitting. Moreover, the centroid depth in this study was mainly obtained through seismic waveform inversion; future research could consider combining geological surveys to determine the horizontal rupture location and direction of the Luding earthquake.

Previous finite-fault inversion studies of the Luding earthquake have reported markedly different slip distributions at depth. Zhang, Zhou, *et al.* (2023) conducted a joint inversion using teleseismic *P* waves and local ground-motion data, identifying two subevents: the first with slip above 10 km and the second (to the southeast) extending from the surface to ~20 km depth. Guo *et al.* (2023) incorporated additional datasets—including teleseismic body waves, local strong motion, GNSS, and InSAR data—and obtained a major slip patch rupturing southeastward, with slip distributed over a broad depth range of 3–20 km. Li *et al.* (2022), using mainly InSAR, GNSS, and local ground-motion data, resolved three shallow asperities along the Moxi fault and one smaller asperity on the conjugate Mozigou fault, all confined above 10 km depth. Similarly, Zhang, Guo, *et al.* (2023), based on regional broadband seismograms and ground-motion data, derived a bilateral slip model with three rupture stages, most slip occurring above 12 km with a maximum slip at ~3.6 km depth. Although these models differ substantially, likely because of variations in dataset coverage and inversion strategies, a general trend emerges: slip distributions tend to extend deeper (to ~20 km) when both regional and teleseismic data are used (Guo *et al.*, 2023; Zhang, Zhou, *et al.*, 2023), but they remain shallower (<10–12 km) when only regional datasets are applied (Li *et al.*, 2022; Zhang, Guo, *et al.*, 2023). This observation is consistent with our synthetic tests, which show that regional datasets are more sensitive to shallow subevent depths, leading to shallower inverted centroid depths. Our multiple point–source inversion using teleseismic body waves further constrains the subevent depths and indicates that both shallow and deep slip zones were involved in the Luding earthquake.

For earthquake nucleation depth, Das and Scholz (1983) examined earthquakes with magnitudes >5.5 in California and found that their nucleation zones are commonly located at relatively deep levels, including the transition area between the seismogenic and creeping zones. These events frequently

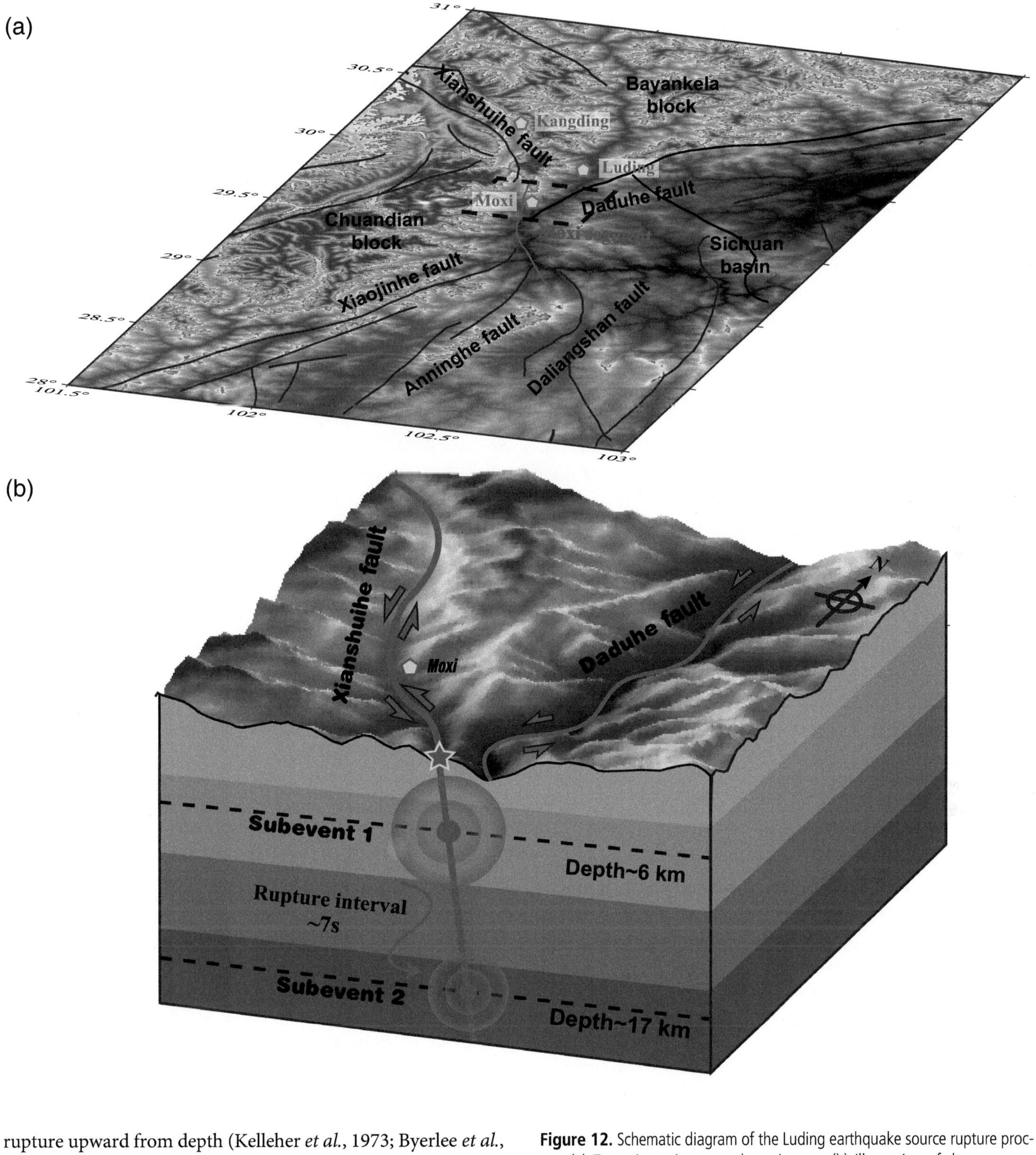

Figure 12. Schematic diagram of the Luding earthquake source rupture process. (a) Tectonic setting near the epicenter. (b) Illustration of the rupture process. The red circles mark two subevents at different depths, with centroid depths at 6 and 17 km, respectively. The red star denotes the epicenter (data from the China Earthquake Networks Center), and the red lines indicate active faults near the epicenter. The color version of this figure is available only in the electronic edition.

rupture upward from depth (Kelleher *et al.*, 1973; Byerlee *et al.*, 1978), likely because both fault strength and stress-drop increase with depth, enabling greater elastic energy release and longer rupture propagation, which in turn favor larger seismic events. Nevertheless, some moderate to large earthquakes have been observed to nucleate at shallow depths. For instance, Yue *et al.* (2021) analyzed the finite-fault rupture processes of the 2019 Ridgecrest sequence and found that the M_w 6.4 foreshock initiated at ~10 km, but the M_w 7.1

mainshock originated at a much shallower depth of ~3 km. Similarly, Hauksson *et al.* (1993) reported that the 1992 M_w 6.1 Landers foreshock nucleated at ~12 to 15 km depth, but the subsequent M_w 7.3 mainshock initiated at ~3 to 6 km depth. These cases illustrate that large earthquakes can also nucleate at shallow depths when deeper fault segments have already reached a critical stress state, as reflected by the deeper foreshock nucleation in both sequences. In this study, we inferred that the Luding earthquake initiated from a shallow region (3–6 km) and triggered a deeper subevent (~17 km). This pattern suggests that the deeper portion near the southern Xianshuihe fault zone may also be critically stressed, implying an elevated potential for future large earthquakes in this region.

Regarding the genesis of the Luding earthquake, prevailing academic consensus suggests that the Luding earthquake may be associated with tectonic activity on the seismic gap of the Xianshuihe fault (Moxi segment; e.g., Li *et al.*, 2023; Zhao *et al.*, 2023; Yi *et al.*, 2023; Zhang, Fang, and Xu, 2023). Several studies have also highlighted the possible involvement of deep fluid processes in this region. Song *et al.* (2023) showed that the mainshock and aftershocks occurred along the boundary between a shallow high-velocity zone (<15 km depth) versus a deeper low-velocity anomaly (>15 km depth), suggesting the presence of fluids likely associated with hot- and wet-mantle upwelling driven by the subduction of the India plate beneath the mantle transition zone. The fluids may have reduced frictional resistance by lowering both the friction coefficient and effective normal stress, thereby promoting strike-slip failure along the fault zone. Similarly, Dong *et al.* (2023) found that the Luding earthquake occurred at the margin of a low-velocity anomaly zone (>15 km depth), underlain by a distinct region characterized by low *S*-wave velocity, negative radial anisotropy ($V_{SH} < V_{SV}$), and high-Poisson's ratio anomalies, features indicative of fluid content. Our study further reveals two distinct rupture zones at different depths. The shallow subevent likely reflects tectonic stress accumulation in the seismic gap along the Xianshuihe fault. The deeper subevent may have been triggered on a preweakened fault zone influenced by long-term fluid migration from greater depth.

CONCLUSION

The 2022 M_w 6.6 Luding earthquake involved a complex composite rupture process that propagated from shallow to deep. Our analyses show the event consisted of at least two subevents: a major rupture at ~3 to 6 km depth followed ~7 s later by a smaller rupture at ~17 km depth. This multistage rupture process explains the substantial centroid depth discrepancy reported in previous studies. The rupture complexity may be related to the combined effects of tectonic stress heterogeneity and deeper crustal fluids near the southern end of the Xianshuihe fault. Our findings show that assuming a single point source for moderate to large earthquakes can be inadequate and highlight the importance of using multiple datasets and advanced source modeling techniques to accurately assess seismic hazards.

DATA AND RESOURCES

Waveform data were downloaded from the Data Management Center (DMC) of the China Earthquake Network Center (CENC) of the China Earthquake Administration (https://data.earthquake.cn, last accessed September 2024). The topography data used in this study are from ETOPO15 (https://www.ngdc.noaa.gov/mgg/global, last accessed October 2024), and the Seismic Analysis Code (SAC) were used in data processing. Most of figures were plotted by the Generic Mapping Tools (GMT). The Earth Science Data Center is available at esdc.ac.cn (last accessed September 2024). The Incorporated Research Institutions for Seismology (IRIS) data service website is available at ds.iris.edu (last accessed October 2024). The supplemental material for this article contains 20 figures (Figs. S1–S20), including bootstrap tests, joint inversion results, single point–source synthetic tests, single point–source inversion of the reference event, and more mainshock multiple point–source inversion results.

DECLARATION OF COMPETING INTERESTS

The authors acknowledge that there are no conflicts of interest recorded.

ACKNOWLEDGMENTS

This study is supported by the National Natural Science Foundation of China (Grant Numbers 42488301, L2424215, 42030311, and 42374077), the Project on Frontier and Interdisciplinary Research Assessment, Academic Divisions of the Chinese Academy of Sciences (Grant Number 5-XKC2015012), and the Hubei Province Science and Technology Innovation Talent Program (2022EJD015). The authors thank Editor-in-Chief Martin Mai and Associate Editor Shengji Wei for handling this article and two anonymous reviewers for their constructive comments.

REFERENCES

Aki, K., and P. G. Richards (2002). Quantitative Seismology, Second Ed., University Science Books, Sausalito, California, ISBN: 0-935702-96-2.

Allen, C. R., L. Zhuoli, Q. Hong, W. Xueze, Z. Huawei, and H. Weishi (1991). Field study of a highly active fault zone: The Xianshuihe fault of southwestern China, *Bull. Geol. Soc. Am.* **103,** no. 9, 1178–1199.

Bai, Q., S. Ni, R. Chu, and Z. Jia (2020). gCAPjoint: A software package for full moment tensor inversion of moderately strong earthquakes with local and teleseismic waveforms, *Seismol. Res. Lett.* **91,** 3550–3562, doi: 10.1785/0220200031.

Byerlee, J., V. Mjachkin, R. Summers, and O. Voevoda (1978). Structures developed in fault gouge during stable sliding and stick-slip, *Tectonophysics* **44,** nos. 1/4, 161–171.

Dai, D., L. Sun, and Z. Yang (2022). Rupture process of the 5 September 2022 Mw 6.6 Luding earthquake in Sichuan (in Chinese), *Earthq. Res. China* **43,** no. 05, 186–192.

Das, S., and C. H. Scholz (1983). Why large earthquakes do not nucleate at shallow depths? *Nature* **305,** no. 5935, 621–623.

Dong, X. P., D. H. Yang, and W. J. Meng (2023). Melt/fluid migration and the 2022 Luding M_s 6.8 earthquake (in Chinese), *Chin. Sci. Bull.* **68**, 2642–2647, doi: 10.1360/TB-2023-0015.

Dreger, D. S., and D. V. Helmberger (1993). Determination of source parameters at regional distances with three-component sparse network data. *J. Geophys. Res.* **98**, no. B5, 8107–8125.

Duputel, Z., L. Rivera, H. Kanamori, and G. Hayes (2012). W phase source inversion for moderate to large earthquakes (1990–2010), *Geophys. J. Int.* **189**, no. 2, 1125–1147.

Ekström, G., A. Morelli, E. Boschi, and A. M. Dziewonski (1998). Moment tensor analysis of the central Italy earthquake sequence of September–October 1997, *Geophys. Res. Lett.* **25**, no. 11, 1971–1974.

Ekström, G., M. Nettles, and A. M. Dziewoński (2012). The global CMT project 2004–2010: Centroid-moment tensors for 13,017 earthquakes, *Phys. Earth Planet. In.* **200**, 1–9.

Guo, R., L. Li, W. Zhang, Y. Zhang, X. Tang, K. Dai, Y. Li, L. Zhang, and J. Wang (2023). Kinematic slip evolution during the 2022 Ms 6.8 Luding, China, earthquake: Compatible with the preseismic locked patch, *Geophys. Res. Lett.* **50**, no. 5, e2023GL103164, doi: 10.1029/2023GL103164.

Han, B., Z. Liu, B. Chen, Z. Li, C. Yu, Y. Zhang, and J. Peng (2023). Coseismic deformation and slip distribution of the 2022 Luding Mw 6.6 earthquake revealed by InSAR observation, *Geomat. Inf. Sci. Wuhan Univ.* **48**, no. 1, 36–46.

Hauksson, E., L. M. Jones, K. Hutton, and D. Eberhart-Phillips (1993). The 1992 Landers earthquake sequence: Seismological observations, *J. Geophys. Res.* **98**, no. B11, 19,835–19,858.

Jia, Z., Z. Jin, M. Marchandon, T. Ulrich, A. A. Gabriel, W. Fan, and Y. Fialko (2023). The complex dynamics of the 2023 Kahramanmaraş, Turkey, Mw 7.8-7.7 earthquake doublet, *Science* **381**, no. 6661, 985–990.

Jia, Z., Z. Shen, Z. Zhan, C. Li, Z. Peng, and M. Gurnis (2020). The 2018 Fiji Mw 8.2 and 7.9 deep earthquakes: One doublet in two slabs, *Earth Planet. Sci. Lett.* **531**, 115997, doi: 10.1016/j.epsl.2019.115997

Kanamori, H., and L. Rivera (2008). Source inversion of W-phase: Speeding up seismic tsunami warning, *Geophys. J. Int.* **175**, no. 1, 222–238.

Kelleher, J., L. Sykes, and J. Oliver (1973). Possible criteria for predicting earthquake locations and their application to major plate boundaries of the Pacific and the Caribbean, *J. Geophys. Res.* **78**, no. 14, 2547–2585.

Lay, T., H. Kanamori, and L. Ruff (1982). The asperity model and the nature of large subduction zone earthquakes, *Earthq. Predict. Res.* **1**, 3–72.

Lei, J., Y. Li, F. Xie, J. Teng, G. Zhang, C. Sun, and X. Zha (2014). Pn anisotropic tomography and dynamics under eastern Tibetan plateau, *J. Geophys. Res.* **119**, 2174–2198.

Li, G., A. Wang, and Y. Gao (2023). Source rupture characteristics of the September 5, 2022 Luding MS 6.8 earthquake at the Xianshuihe fault zone in southwest China, *Earthq. Res. Adv.* **3**, no. 2, 100201, doi: 10.1016/j.eqrea.2022.100201.

Li, Y., D. Zhao, X. Shan, Z. Gao, X. Huang, and W. Gong (2022). Coseismic slip model of the 2022 Mw 6.7 Luding (Tibet) earthquake: Pre-and post-earthquake interactions with surrounding major faults, *Geophys. Res. Lett.* **49**, no. 24, doi: 10.1029/2022GL102043.

Liu, G., and Z. Wang (2020). Correlations of the deep structural characteristics, tidal stress variation and earthquake initiation along the Xianshuihe-Anninghe fault zone (in Chinese), *Chin. J. Geophys.* **63**, no. 3, 928–943.

Liu, G., B. Zhao, R. Xu, X. Qiao, C. Liu, Y. Li, and Q Wang (2024). GNSS-constrained rupture kinematics of the 2022 M w 6.7 Luding, China, earthquake: Directivity pulse during the asymmetrical bilateral rupture, *Seismol. Res. Lett.* **95**, no. 1, 264–276.

Liu, Y., H. Yao, H. Zhang, and H. Fang (2021). The community velocity model V1.0 of southwest China, constructed from joint body- and Surface-wave travel-time tomography. *Seismol. Res. Lett.* **92**, 2972–2987.

Luo, Y., X. Zeng, and S. Ni (2013). Progress on the determination of focal depth, *Prog. Geophys.* **28**, no. 5, 2309–2321.

Meng, Q., S. Ni, A. Guo, and Y. Zhou (2018). Ground surface deformation caused by the Mw 5.8 early strong aftershock following the 13 November 2016 Mw 7.8 Kaikōura mainshock, *Seismol. Res. Lett.* **89**, no. 6, 2214–2226, doi: 10.1785/0220180019.

Qian, Y., S. Ni, S. Wei, R. Almeida, and H. Zhang (2017). The effects of core-reflected waves on finite fault inversions with teleseismic body wave data, *Geophys. J. Int.* **211**, no. 2, 936–951.

Qu, Z., B. Zhu, Y. Cao, and H. Fu (2023). Rapid report of seismic damage to buildings in the 2022 M 6.8 Luding earthquake, China, *Earthq. Res. Adv.* **3**, no. 1, 100180, doi: 10.1016/j.eqrea.2022.100180.

Shan, X. J., Y. C. Li, Z. Y. Gao, J. Hua, X. Huang, W. Gong, C. Qu, D. Zhao, J. Chen, C. Huang, *et al.* (2023). Coseismic deformation of the 2022 Luding MS 6.8 earthquake and seismic potential along adjacent major faults (in Chinese), *Chin. Sci. Bull.* **68**, 944953, doi: 10.1360/TB-2022-0954.

Shi, Q., and S. Wei (2020). Highly heterogeneous pore fluid pressure enabled rupture of orthogonal faults during the 2019 Ridgecrest Mw7. 0 earthquake, *Geophys. Res. Lett.* **47**, no. 20, doi: 10.1029/2020GL089827.

Shi, Q., S. Wei, and M. Chen (2018). An MCMC multiple point sources inversion scheme and its application to the 2016 Kumamoto Mw 6.2 earthquake, *Geophys. J. Int.* **215**, no. 2, 737–752.

Song, X., J. Lei, and K. Zou (2023). The 2022 Luding, Sichuan, China, M 6.8 earthquake: A fluid-related earthquake? *J. Asian Earth Sci.* **258**, 105543, doi: 10.1016/j.jseaes.2023.105543.

Takeo, M. (1987). An inversion method to analyze the rupture processes of earthquakes using near-field seismograms. *Bull. Seismol. Soc. Am.* **77**, no. 2, 490–513.

Tsai, V. C., M. Nettles, G. Ekström, and A. M. Dziewonski (2005). Multiple CMT source analysis of the 2004 Sumatra earthquake, *Geophys. Res. Lett.* **32**, no. 17, doi: 10.1029/2005GL023813.

Wang, C., W. Han, J. Wu, H. Lou, and W. Chan (2007). Crustal structure beneath the eastern margin of the Tibetan plateau and its tectonic implications. *J. Geophys. Res.* **112**, no. B07307, 1–21.

Wang, X., Z. Li, J. Deng, J. Gao, H. Li, Z. Yao, and J. Li (2021). Hypocentral depth determination for moderate-magnitude shallow earthquakes in sedimentary basins with sparse network case studies of the 2013 Qainguo M_S 5.8 and the 2016 Fairview M_W 5.1 earthquake sequences, *Chin. J. Geophys.* **64**, no. 3, 851–863.

Wang, Z., and X. Guo (2022). The centroid moment tensor solution of 2022 Luding Ms 6.8 earthquake in Sichuan Province (in Chinese), *Prog. Earthq. Sci.* **52**, no. 10, 482–486.

Wen, X., J. Fan, G. Yi, Y. Deng, and F. Long (2008). A seismic gap on the Anninghe fault in western Sichuan, China, *Sci. China Earth Sci.* **51**, no. 10, 1375–1387.

Wen, X., S. Ma, and X. Xu (2008). Historical pattern and behavior of earthquake ruptures along the eastern boundary of the Sichuan-Yunnan faulted-block, southwestern China, *Phys. Earth Planet. In.* **168,** 16–36.

Xie, J., S. Ni, and X. Zeng (2012). 1D shear wave velocity structure of the shallow upper crust in central Sichuan Basin (in Chinese), *Earthq. Res. Sichuan* **02,** 20–24.

Xu, R, C. Chen, and T. Rao (2023). Interpretation of the 2022 Luding Mw6.6 earthquake based on GNSS data (in Chinese), *Chin. J. Geophys.* **66,** no. 4, 1409–1418.

Yan, B., H. Yin, and B. Feng (2023). Source parameters and slip distribution of the Luding Ms 6.8 earthquake in 2022 constrained by InSAR Data (in Chinese), *J. Geod. Geodyn.* **43,** no. 03, 221–225.

Yi, G., F. Lon, M. Liang, M. Zhao, H. Zhang, R. Zhou, Y. Li, H. Liu, P. Wu, S. Wang, *et al.* (2023). Seismogenic structure of the 5 September 2022 Sichuan Luding Ms6.8 earthquake sequence (in Chinese), *Chin J. Geophys.* **66,** no. 4, 1363–1384.

Yi, G., F. Long, M. Liang, M. Zhao, and S. Wang (2020). Geometry and tectonic deformation of seismogenic structures in the Rongxian-Weiyuan-Zizhong region, Sichuan basin: Insights from focal mechanism solutions (in Chinese), *Chin. J. Geophys.* **63,** no. 9, 3275–3291.

Yi, G., F. Long, A. Vallage, Y. Klinger, M. J. Liang, and S. W. Wang (2016). Focal mechanism and tectonic deformation in the seismogenic area of the 2013 Lushan earthquake sequence, southwestern China (in Chinese), *Chin J. Geophy.* **59,** no. 10, 3711–3731.

Yue, H., and T. Lay (2020). Resolving complicated faulting process using multi-point-source representation: Iterative inversion algorithm improvement and application to recent complex earthquakes, *J. Geophys. Res.* **125,** no. 2, doi: 10.1029/2019JB018601.

Yue, H., T. Lay, and K. D. Koper (2012). En échelon and orthogonal fault ruptures of the 11 April 2012 great intraplate earthquakes, *Nature* **490,** no. 7419, 245–249, doi: 10.1038/nature11492.

Yue, H., J. Sun, M. Wang, Z. Shen, M. Li, L. Xue, and T. Lay (2021). The 2019 Ridgecrest, California earthquake sequence: Evolution of seismic and aseismic slip on an orthogonal fault system, *Earth Planet. Sci. Lett.* **570,** 117066, doi: 10.1016/j.epsl.2021.117066.

Zhang, L., Y. Zhou, X. Zhang, A. Zhu, B. Li, S. Wang, and L. Fang (2023). 2022 Mw 6.6 Luding, China, earthquake: A strong continental event illuminating the Moxi seismic gap, *Seismol. Res. Lett.* **94,** no. 5, 2129–2142.

Zhang, P. (2008). A study on the present tectonic deformation, strain partitioning and deep dynamic process of west Sichuan region on eastern margin of Qinghai-Tibet Plateau, *Sci. China Earth Sci.* **38,** no. 9, 1041–1056.

Zhang, P., Q. Deng, and G. Zhang (2003). Active tectonic blocks and strong earthquakes in the continent of China, *Sci. China Earth Sci.* **46,** no. 2, 13–24.

Zhang, Y., W. Feng, L. Xu, C. Zhou, and Y. Chen (2009). Spatio-temporal rupture process of the 2008 great Wenchuan earthquake, *Sci. China Earth Sci.* **52,** no. 2, 145–154.

Zhang, Y., R. Guo, H. Sun, D. Liu, and J. Zahradník (2023). Asymmetric bilateral rupture of the 2022 Ms 6.8 Luding earthquake on a continental transform fault, Tibetan Border, China, *Seismol. Res. Lett.* **94,** no. 5, 2143–2153.

Zhang, Z., L. Fang, and L. Xu (2023). Primary source characteristics of the 2022 Sichuan Luding Ms 6.8 earthquake, *Chin. J. Geophys.* **66,** no. 4, 1397–1408.

Zhao, L. S., and D. V. Helmberger (1994). Source estimation from broadband regional seismograms, *Bull. Seismol. Soc. Am.* **84,** no. 1, 91–104.

Zhao, X., Z. Xiao, W. Wang, J. Li, M. Zhao, S. Chen, and L. Tang (2023). Fine seismogenic fault structures and complex rupture characteristics of the 2022 M6.8 Luding, Sichuan earthquake sequence revealed by deep learning and waveform modeling, *Geophys. Res. Lett.* **50,** no. 18, doi: 10.1029/2023GL102976.

Zhao, Z., and L. Chen (1995). Accuracy amendment of focal location along the Longmenshan fault in the North of Sichuan (in Chinese), *Sichuan Earthq.* **04,** 19–30.

Zhu, L., and Y. Ben-Zion (2013). Parametrization of general seismic potency and moment tensors for source inversion of seismic waveform data, *Geophys. J. Int.* **194,** no. 2, 839–843.

Zhu, L., and D. V. Helmberger (1996). Advancement in source estimation techniques using broadband regional seismograms, *Bull. Seismol. Soc. Am.* **86,** no. 5, 1634–1641.

Zhu, L., and L. Rivera (2002). A note on the dynamic and static displacements from a point source in multilayered media, *Geophys. J. Int.* **148,** no. 3, 619–627.

Manuscript received 18 December 2024
Published online 14 November 2025

Estimating Moment Magnitudes of Moderate-to-Large Earthquakes in Western China Based on the Direct *P* Waves

Guangjie Han[1], Dun Wang[*2,3], and Li Sun[1]

ABSTRACT

Timely and accurate estimation of earthquake moment magnitude (M_w) is crucial for damage assessment and emergency response. However, obtaining reliable M_w estimates within approximately 10 min of origin time remains challenging. In this study, we present a novel and robust algorithm for M_w estimation of moderate-to-large earthquakes using regional to teleseismic records. The method was applied to 22 earthquakes ($M_w \geq 6.5$, depth $\leq$ 60 km) in western China from 2008 to 2023. Magnitude estimates were obtained within ~6 to 11 min after origin time and agree with U.S. Geological Survey values, with a standard deviation of ~0.1. The estimates remain robust and stable despite variations in the number and spatial distribution of contributing stations. The algorithm mitigates contamination from reflected phases in regional data and uneven station distribution by employing adaptive time windows and spatial averaging of *P*-wave amplitudes in azimuth and take-off angle grids. Backprojection yields robust estimates of source durations even with relatively sparse seismic array coverage. However, larger events may require denser station spacing and wider apertures to suppress interfering phases in regional to teleseismic waveforms. Comparative analysis with widely used magnitude scales, such as broadband surface- and body-wave magnitude scales, further confirms the method's stability, demonstrating its potential as a rapid, reliable complement to existing real-time magnitude estimation techniques.

KEY POINTS

- We present a method for fast M_w estimation of events with $M_w \geq 6.5$ using direct *P* waves.
- The method minimizes interference from reflected phases and uneven station distribution for accurate results.
- M_w is obtained in ~6–11 min with ~0.1 standard deviation, matching U.S. Geological Survey values and stable across coverages.

Supplemental Material

INTRODUCTION

China's complex geological terrain, composed of cratonic blocks and orogenic belts, has been influenced by multiple episodes of amalgamation (Zheng *et al.*, 2013). Seismic activity is primarily concentrated in the Tibetan Plateau and its adjacent regions (Fig. 1). Over the past 15 yr, China has experienced six earthquakes with moment magnitude (M_w) greater than 7.0 and 16 with M_w 6.5–7 in this region (Han *et al.*, 2022). Among these, the 2008 M_w 7.9 Wenchuan earthquake was particularly devastating, resulting in nearly 69,000 fatalities and over $100 billion in damages. M_w serves as a paramount parameter for characterizing earthquake size because it directly reflects the energy released during rupture. Therefore, timely and accurate magnitude estimation is imperative for assessing shaking hazards, coordinating emergency responses, and estimating casualties (Chen *et al.*, 2023, G. J. Han *et al.*, unpublished manuscript, 2025).

Several magnitude scales have been developed, including local (Richter) magnitude (M_L; Richter, 1935) , body-wave magnitude (M_b; Gutenberg, 1945b), and surface-wave magnitude (M_s; Gutenberg, 1945a). Although widely used, these scales have inherent limitations, such as saturation for large earthquakes and inconsistent behavior across all magnitude ranges (Scordilis, 2006). M_w introduced by Kanamori (1977) and Hanks and Kanamori (1979), addresses these

1. China Earthquake Networks Center, Beijing, China, https://orcid.org/0000-0002-5558-6809 (LS); 2. School of Earth Sciences, China University of Geosciences, Wuhan, China; 3. State Key Laboratory of Geological Processes and Mineral Resources, China University of Geosciences, Wuhan, China

*Corresponding author: wangdun@cug.edu.cn

Cite this article as Han, G., D. Wang, and L. Sun (2025). Estimating Moment Magnitudes of Moderate-to-Large Earthquakes in Western China Based on the Direct *P* Waves, *Bull. Seismol. Soc. Am.* **116**, 291–307, doi: 10.1785/0120250079

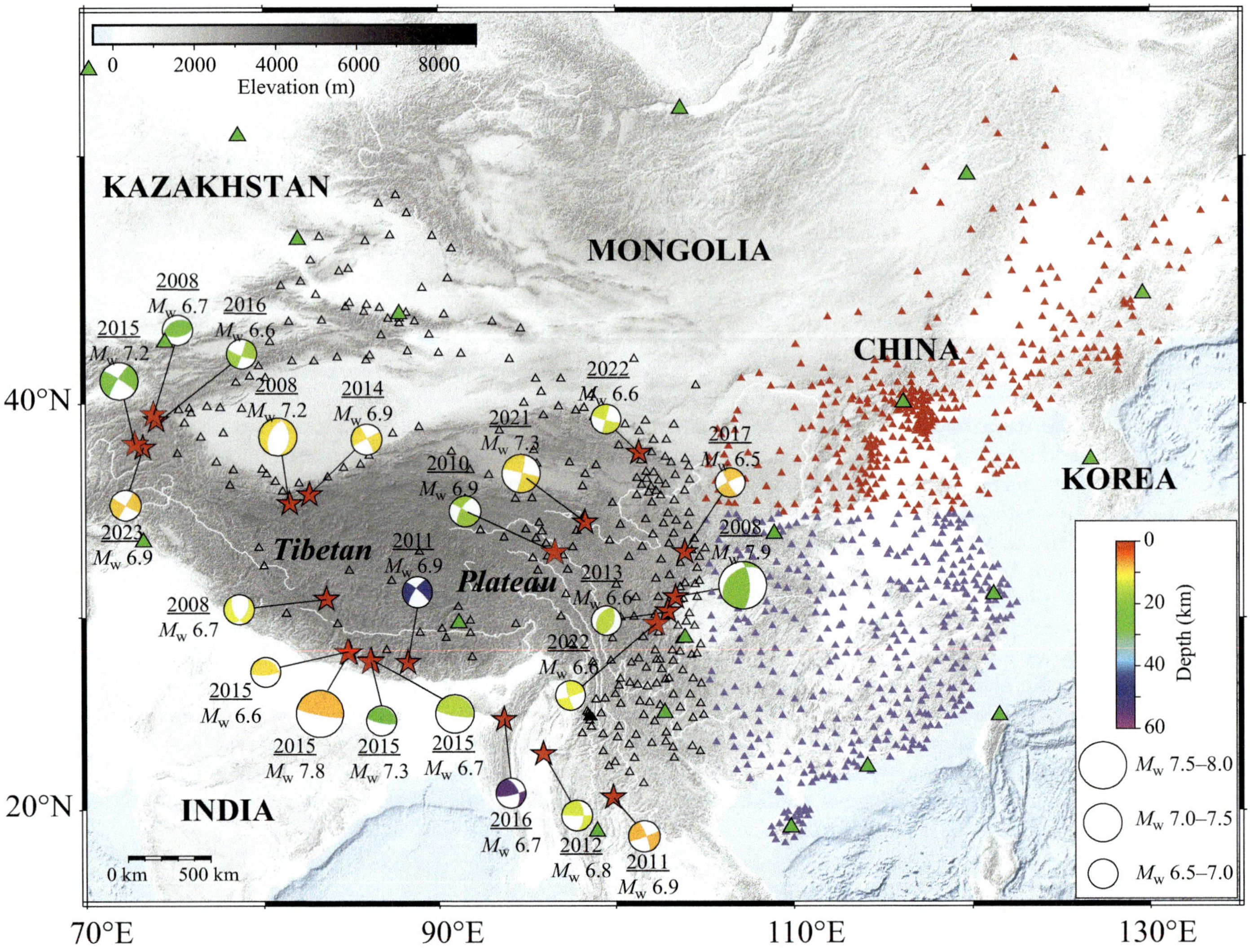

Figure 1. Location map of $M_w \geq 6.5$ shallow depth earthquakes (stars) and seismic stations. Colored focal mechanism plots represent the focal mechanisms of the 22 earthquakes, with colors indicating focal depth. Red and bluish-purple triangles denote the northeast and southeast seismic subarrays in China, respectively. Black hollow triangles indicate other China Digital Seismograph Network (CDSN) stations outside these subarrays. Green triangles represent the Global Seismological Network (GSN) stations.

shortcomings by being directly proportional to the logarithm of the seismic moment (M_0), physically linking it to fault size and dislocation. Unlike other scales, M_w does not exhibit saturation and is considered the most reliable descriptor of earthquake size, particularly for large and destructive events.

Various M_w estimation methods have been developed based on different seismic waveform characteristics. The *P*-wave moment magnitude (M_{wp}) estimates M_0 from the displacement records of the first arrival of *P* waves recorded by broadband seismometers and is widely used by agencies such as the Pacific Tsunami Warning Center (Tsuboi *et al.*, 1995; Hirshorn *et al.*, 2012). The *W*-phase moment magnitude (M_{ww}) derives M_0 through centroid moment tensor inversion based on modeling of the long-period *W* phase (Hanks and Kanamori, 1979; Kanamori, 1993; Duputel *et al.*, 2011, 2012). The duration-displacement magnitude (M_{dt}) estimates M_0 using the relationship between the maximum displacement of *P* waves and source duration (Hara, 2007, 2011; Wang *et al.*, 2017). The energy magnitude (M_E) is determined by evaluating the radiated seismic energy from the initial *P*-wave group recorded at near-teleseismic distances (Choy and Boatwright, 1995; Convers and Newman, 2011, 2013). Among these, methods based on *P* wave and *W*-phase signals are particularly well suited for rapid response because *P* waves are the earliest seismic arrivals, and the *W* phase begins before the *S* phase and is clearly visible on displacement seismograms.

Estimating M_w for moderate-to-large earthquakes within minutes remains challenging due to the complex rupture process, uneven station distribution, Earth model uncertainties, and interference from noisy signals. For example, following the 8 September 2017 M_w 8.2 Mexico earthquake, the Mexican National Seismological Service initially reported an M_{ww} 8.92 approximately 12 min after the event. This value was later

TABLE 1
All M_w ≥ 6.5 Earthquakes in the Western Region of China from 2008 to 2023

Number	Origin Time (yyyy/mm/ddThh:mm)	Latitude (°)	Longitude (°)	Depth (km)	M_w
1	2023/02/23T00:37	73.228 ±8.0 km	38.055	9 ± 1.7	6.9 ± 0.043
2	2022/09/05T04:52	102.236 ±8.2 km	29.678	12 ± 1.7	6.6 ± 0.04
3	2022/01/07T17:45	101.290 ±7.0 km	37.828	13 ± 1.7	6.6 ± 0.08
4	2021/05/21T18:04	98.251 ±3.0 km	34.598	10 ± 1.7	7.3 ± 0.037
5	2017/08/08T13:19	103.855 ±4.3 km	33.192	9 ± 1.7	6.5 ± 0.043
6	2016/11/25T14:24	73.977 ±5.9 km	39.273	17 ± 1.7	6.6
7	2016/01/03T23:05	93.650 ±4.5 km	24.803	55 ± 1.8	6.7
8	2015/12/07T07:50	72.779 ±5.5 km	38.210	22 ± 1.7	7.2
9	2015/05/12T07:05	86.065 ±7.4 km	27.808	15 ± 1.7	7.3
10	2015/04/26T07:09	86.017 ±6.6 km	27.771	22 ± 2.9	6.7
11	2015/04/25T06:45	84.821 ±7.4 km	28.224	10 ± 1.7	6.6
12	2015/04/25T06:11	84.731 ±7.3 km	28.230	8 ± 2.9	7.8
13	2014/02/12T09:19	82.586	35.905	10 ± 1.7	6.9
14	2013/04/20T00:02	102.888	30.308	14	6.6
15	2012/11/11T01:12	95.885	23.005	13 ± 3.7	6.8
16	2011/09/18T12:40	88.155	27.730	50	6.9
17	2011/03/24T13:55	99.822	20.687	8	6.9
18	2010/04/13T23:49	96.548	33.165	17	6.9
19	2008/10/05T15:52	73.824	39.533	27	6.7
20	2008/08/25T13:21	83.520	30.901	12	6.7
21	2008/05/12T06:28	103.322	31.002	19	7.9
22	2008/03/20T22:32	81.467	35.490	10	7.2

The origin times, locations, depths, and M_w are from the U.S. Geological Survey (USGS), with the associated uncertainties also reported where available.

revised to 8.36 after 55 min and subsequently adjusted to 8.26 about three hours later (Pérez-Campos *et al.*, 2020).

To address these challenges, Wang *et al.* (2017) proposed an algorithm that estimates M_w using the duration of high-frequency (0.5–2 Hz) energy radiation and maximum *P*-wave displacements recorded at teleseismic distances. Teleseismic waveforms are typically simpler, with coherent *P*-wave onsets, whereas regional waveforms are often complicated by upper-mantle triplications, reflected phases, and other factors. Yao *et al.* (2019) estimated magnitudes of earthquakes with $M \geq 7.0$ in Japan using recordings from seismic stations in China. Similarly, Song *et al.* (2019) demonstrated the feasibility of using local and regional seismic stations to estimate the magnitude of M_w 7.9 Alaska earthquake. These studies underscore the potential of incorporating regional data into magnitude estimation frameworks.

We developed a novel approach that employs backprojection of local to regional seismic data to constrain source duration and optimize *P*-wave amplitude extraction based on their density distribution on the focal sphere. After introducing the data and methodology, we present tests on 22 events ($M_w \geq 6.5$) in western China. Results demonstrate that the magnitude measurements are stable, reliable, and rapid, especially for moderate-to-large events (M_w 6.5–7.9). In the Discussion section, we systematically investigated the effects of regional phases and station density on magnitude determination. This method complements existing algorithms and provides an effective tool for enhancing the timeliness and robustness of earthquake magnitude estimation.

DATA

We analyzed all earthquakes (depth ≤ 60 km) with magnitudes greater than 6.5 that occurred in and around mainland China between 2008 and 2023, as documented in the U.S. Geological Survey (USGS) catalog (Table 1). To assess the lower

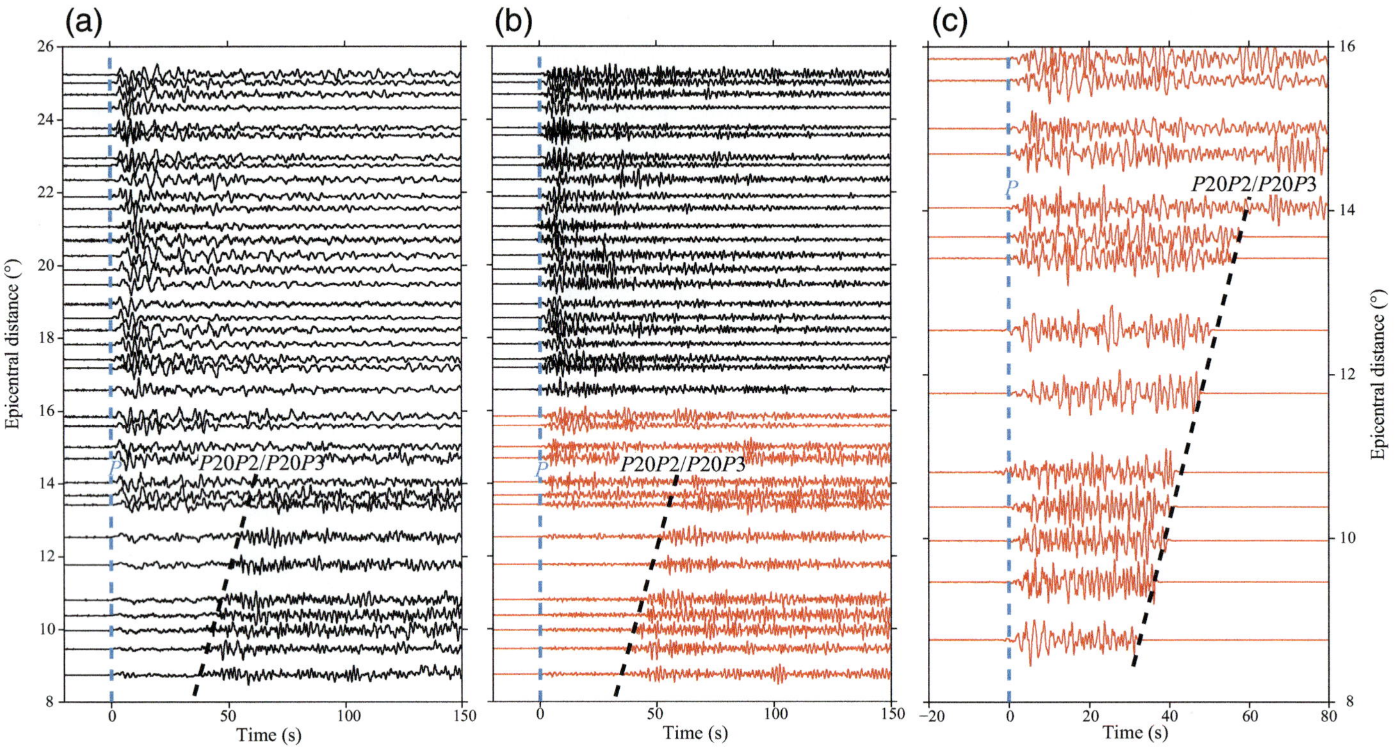

Figure 2. Vertical-component waveforms recorded by the northeast Chinese seismic subarray for the 2017 M_w 6.5 Jiuzhaigou earthquake. All waveforms were aligned by the *P*-wave onset of the geographical center of the northeast subarray. Time denotes the time difference relative to the direct *P* wave. The blue dashed line indicates the arrival time of the direct *P* wave, and the black-dashed line represents the arrival time of the *P20P2* and *P20P3* waves. (a) Original waveforms. (b) Waveforms band-pass filtered to 0.5–2 Hz. Waveforms from stations at epicentral distance of 8°–16° are highlighted in red, whereas others are shown in black. (c) Enlarged view of the red waveforms in panel (b), limited to epicentral distances less than 14°, with only the portion between the direct *P* wave and the *P20P2* or *P20P3* phases retained.

magnitude threshold of our method, we also evaluated its performance on moderate earthquakes with magnitudes ranging from 6.5 to 7.0.

For this analysis, we used vertical-component seismic records from the China Digital Seismograph Network (CDSN) and Global Seismological Network (GSN) to obtain distinct direct *P*-wave arrivals and to minimize site effects (e.g., near-surface geology and topography). In addition, the vertical component is not affected by sensor misorientation (Deng *et al.*, 2024). Based on station distribution and waveform characteristics, we divided the CDSN stations into two subarrays: northeast and southeast, which were used for backprojection analysis (Fig. 1). The epicentral distances of CDSN stations ranged from approximately 8° to 44° for the analyzed earthquakes. All stations within this range, from both the CDSN and GSN, were included to calculate the maximum displacement of *P* waves.

To evaluate the effectiveness of using local and regional stations for magnitude determination, we restricted the analysis to stations within 44° epicentral distance and excluded more distant stations from the GSN network. This criterion focused the analysis on the station range most critical for rapid and accurate magnitude estimation with the proposed method.

METHOD

We followed the seismic data processing procedures outlined by Wang *et al.* (2017) and Hara (2007) to estimate M_w. The process involved three main steps: (1) determining source duration by backprojecting waveforms recorded by the northeast and southeast subarrays, (2) calculating the maximum *P*-wave displacements at CDSN and GSN stations, and (3) integrating the source duration and maximum displacement of *P* waves to estimate the moment magnitude (M_{dt}). The following three subsections provide detailed descriptions of each step.

Source duration estimation

For teleseismic data, the *P*-wave onset typically exhibits notable coherence, whereas the later part of the *P*-wave train becomes more complex across different stations. Stacking procedures effectively reduce extraneous energy, enabling focused analysis of radiation from the target source point (Ishii *et al.*, 2005). This procedure supports the backprojection method in determining the source duration of high-frequency energy radiation emitted from the source (Hara, 2007).

In addition, seismic arrays tend to preserve similar waveform characteristics for earthquakes occurring at regional to teleseismic distances, suggesting that the backprojection method can also be applied to waveforms recorded at regional epicentral distances (Fig. 2).

For teleseismic waveforms, the direct P wave is the dominant phase, whereas reflected and refracted P waves are less prominent. However, for epicentral distances less than ~14°, later phases in the P-wave train can exceed the amplitude of the direct P wave. Their amplitudes decrease with increasing distance (Fig. 2). These phases likely originate from P-wave reflections at the Conrad and Moho discontinuities (Litak and Brown, 1989), which are commonly observed beneath most continents (Horiuchi *et al.*, 1982; Yang *et al.*, 2021). We denote multiple P-wave reflections from a discontinuity at depth d as $PdPN$, in which N is a positive integer. For example, $P20P2$ denotes a phase reflected twice at the 20 km discontinuity, corresponding to the full path sequence $P20PP20P$.

To address the influence of reflected P waves, we classified waveforms based on the amplitude ratio between the direct and reflected P waves, applying distinct parameter sets for each category. The source duration estimation procedure involved the following three steps.

First, we retrieved vertical-component waveforms, removed the mean, applied baseline correction and tapering. Because the backprojection method relies on normalized waveforms within a high-frequency band (0.5–2 Hz), it is not necessary to remove the instrument response. The theoretical travel times for the direct P wave and reflected P waves were calculated using the IASP91 model (Kennett and Engdahl, 1991). We defined time windows from −5 to 15 s relative to each predicted arrival to extract amplitudes, using a threshold of 1.5 for the amplitude ratio between the direct and reflected P waves.

If the amplitude ratio fell below 1.5, only the segment between the direct and reflected P waves was retained. Otherwise, data from 0 to 150 s relative to the direct P-wave arrival were retained (Fig. 2c). To ensure complete removal of the reflected P waves, the start of the time window was set 10 s earlier than the theoretical arrival time.

We excluded waveforms from stations with epicentral distances less than 8°. This exclusion is due to the typical time difference between the direct P and reflected P waves (~30 s), which corresponds to the source duration of most M_w 6.5–7.0 earthquakes (Yao *et al.*, 2019). For earthquakes in subduction zones with slower rupture rates, it is recommended to extend the time window appropriately. To assess the sensitivity of our results to the velocity model, we also tested the CRUST1.0 3D model to improve the accuracy of reflected phase arrival times. The differences were minimal, with less than ~0.3 s deviation for $P20PN$ phases, indicating a negligible impact on waveform truncation. Therefore, we adopted the IASP91 model in this study. However, when applying this method to other regions or networks, regional variations in lithospheric structure may require adjusting the amplitude ratio threshold or selecting a more appropriate velocity model.

Second, we applied cross-correlation to determine station corrections. The analysis was conducted in two frequency bands: 0.05–0.5 and 0.5–2.0 Hz. We cross-correlated the waveform at a reference station near the array's geographical center with waveforms from other stations. Normalized waveforms with correlation coefficients below 0.4 were excluded to improve data quality.

Third, we performed backprojection analysis using waveforms band-pass filtered between 0.5 and 2.0 Hz, with a 10 s window length and 1 s offset. Based on earthquake energy release characteristics and following Wang *et al.* (2017), source duration was derived from the energy–time plot obtained by backprojection (Wang *et al.*, 2017; Song *et al.*, 2019; Yao *et al.*, 2019).

Maximum displacement of *P* waves

Another crucial parameter is the maximum displacement of P waves, which depends on magnitude and epicentral distance. To compute this parameter, we first removed the instrument response and then determined the maximum displacement within the time window defined by the theoretical arrival times of P and S phases, calculated using the IASP91 model.

Because of the uneven azimuthal distribution of CDSN and GSN stations, primarily located east of the earthquakes (Fig. 1), the radiation pattern has a non-negligible influence on magnitude estimation (Kusumawati *et al.*, 2023). To address the resulting bias, we implemented a strategy to achieve a more uniform station sampling.

We identified azimuth and take-off angle as key parameters for station filtering. Stations used in the calculation had epicentral distances of 8°–44°, corresponding to take-off angles between 24° and 90°. Grid steps were set to 10° for azimuth and 5° for take-off angle. Within each grid, the median maximum P-wave amplitude was used to represent the grid's contribution, reducing the influence of anomalous amplitudes from instrument malfunction or site effects on magnitude estimation (Fig. 3). Utilizing the take-off angle as a criterion, instead of epicentral distance, ensures more uniform focal sphere coverage.

Moment magnitude calculation

The M_{dt} was calculated by combining the source duration and maximum displacement of P waves. Following the M_{dt} formula (see the supplemental material available to this article), an equation was developed based on the M_w formula (Hanks and Kanamori, 1979):

$$M_{dt} = \frac{2}{3}\frac{1}{N}\sum_{i=1}^{N}\left[\log_{10}(|u|^{P\max} R\,T)\right] + \delta(h,k), \qquad (1)$$

in which $|u|^{P\max}$ is the maximum displacement of P waves recorded at the ith station with epicentral distance R. N is the total number of stations used in the estimation. T is the source duration estimated from backprojection of northeast

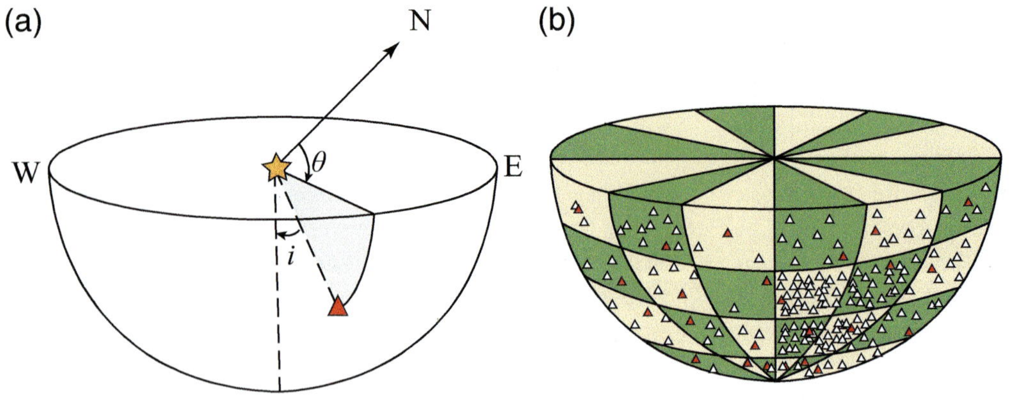

Figure 3. Schematic of the station filtering process. (a) Spherical geometry illustrating azimuth (θ) and take-off angle (i), with the yellow star denoting the source and the red triangle representing the station. (b) Station filtering process. The green and yellow shapes represent each grid, whereas the white and red triangles indicate all stations and the selected stations after filtering, respectively.

or southeast subarrays. For shallow earthquakes, $\delta(h,k)$ is a correction term related to the shape of the source time function and source depth, which can be expressed as

$$\delta(h,k) = \frac{2}{3}\left[\log_{10}(k\,4\pi\rho_s^{\frac{1}{2}}\rho_r^{\frac{1}{2}}\alpha_s^{\frac{5}{2}}\alpha_r^{\frac{1}{2}}) - 9.1\right], \quad (2)$$

in which ρ_s, ρ_r, α_s, and α_r are the density and P-wave velocity at the source and station, respectively. k is a constant that depends on the shape of the moment rate function. For calculating M_0, the source time function can be scaled to a triangle, with the best-fit value of k equal to 0.5. For shallow earthquakes, we adopt average values of $\alpha = 7.27$ km/s and $\rho = 3.12$ g/cm^3, yielding a representative δ of 4.49.

RESULTS

M_{dt} estimation for large shallow earthquakes in western China (2008–2023)

We established a real-time environment to systematically estimate M_{dt}, enabling continuous monitoring of M_{dt} over time. Using seismic data collected from northeast and southeast Chinese subarrays, we computed the source duration for 22 earthquakes (Fig. 1). The backprojection procedure is initiated when an event is recorded by at least 100 stations located at epicentral distances greater than ~8°.

The source durations of the 22 earthquakes are shown in Figure 4a. For earthquakes with magnitudes less than 7.5, source durations ranged from approximately 10 to 50 s, generally consistent with the scaling law proposed by Wells and Coppersmith (1994). For the 2008 M_w 7.9 Wenchuan earthquake, the source duration was determined to be ~84 s based on backprojection analysis using the northeast Chinese seismic subarray, consistent with durations of 70–100 s reported by finite-fault model (Zhang *et al.*, 2008), Rayleigh-wave inversion (Hwang *et al.*, 2011), and a previous backprojection study (Zhang and Ge, 2010). In contrast, the source duration of the 2015 M_w 7.8 Nepal event was ~53 s. Discrepancies in source duration between the 2008 Wenchuan and 2015 Nepal earthquakes may be influenced by various factors, including focal mechanism, rupture geometry, propagation velocity, rupture directivity, and the physical properties of the fault zone. Further investigation may help improve understanding of the complexities of seismic sources.

For all analyzed earthquakes, the maximum displacement of P waves recorded at CDSN and GSN stations within the epicentral distances of 8°–44°, ranged from 10^{-2} to 10^{-5} m. As indicated in equation (1), the value of M_{dt} varies across stations, influenced by the multiplication of maximum P-wave displacements and epicentral distance. Figure 4c shows the relationship between $\log_{10}(|u|^{P\max}R)$ and azimuth indicating that stations are predominantly located to the east and northwest of the epicenters. Through data screening, we achieved more uniform station sampling and eliminated anomalous data points. By combining source duration and maximum P-wave displacements, we estimated M_{dt} for the earthquakes. As illustrated in Figure 4b, M_{dt} estimates agree with M_w values reported by the USGS, with a standard deviation of 0.1. As the earthquake magnitude increases, the real-time estimation of M_{dt} becomes more stable, with smaller deviations from M_w.

The method also proved effective for aftershocks. For example, the 2015 M_w 6.6 Nepal earthquake (25 April 2015 06:45) occurred ~34 min after the M_w 7.9 mainshock (25 April 2015 06:11). Distorted by the mainshock coda waves, aftershock amplitudes became abnormally large, complicating magnitude estimation (Dhakal *et al.*, 2016). To mitigate this effect, we implemented a Butterworth band-pass filter with a frequency range of 0.1–10 Hz, instead of the typical 0.01–10 Hz range. The mean M_{dt} for the aftershock was 6.7, with a deviation of 0.1 from the M_w reported by the USGS.

12 May 2008 M_w 7.9 Wenchuan earthquake

On 12 May 2008, the M_w 7.9 earthquake struck Wenchuan, Beichuan, and Qingchuan counties in China (30.95° N, 103.57° E), with a depth of 14 km, as reported by the China Earthquake Networks Center (CENC). The event exhibited predominantly unilateral rupture spanning ~340 km in the northeast–southwest direction (Xu *et al.*, 2009; Zhang *et al.*, 2010; Wang *et al.*, 2011).

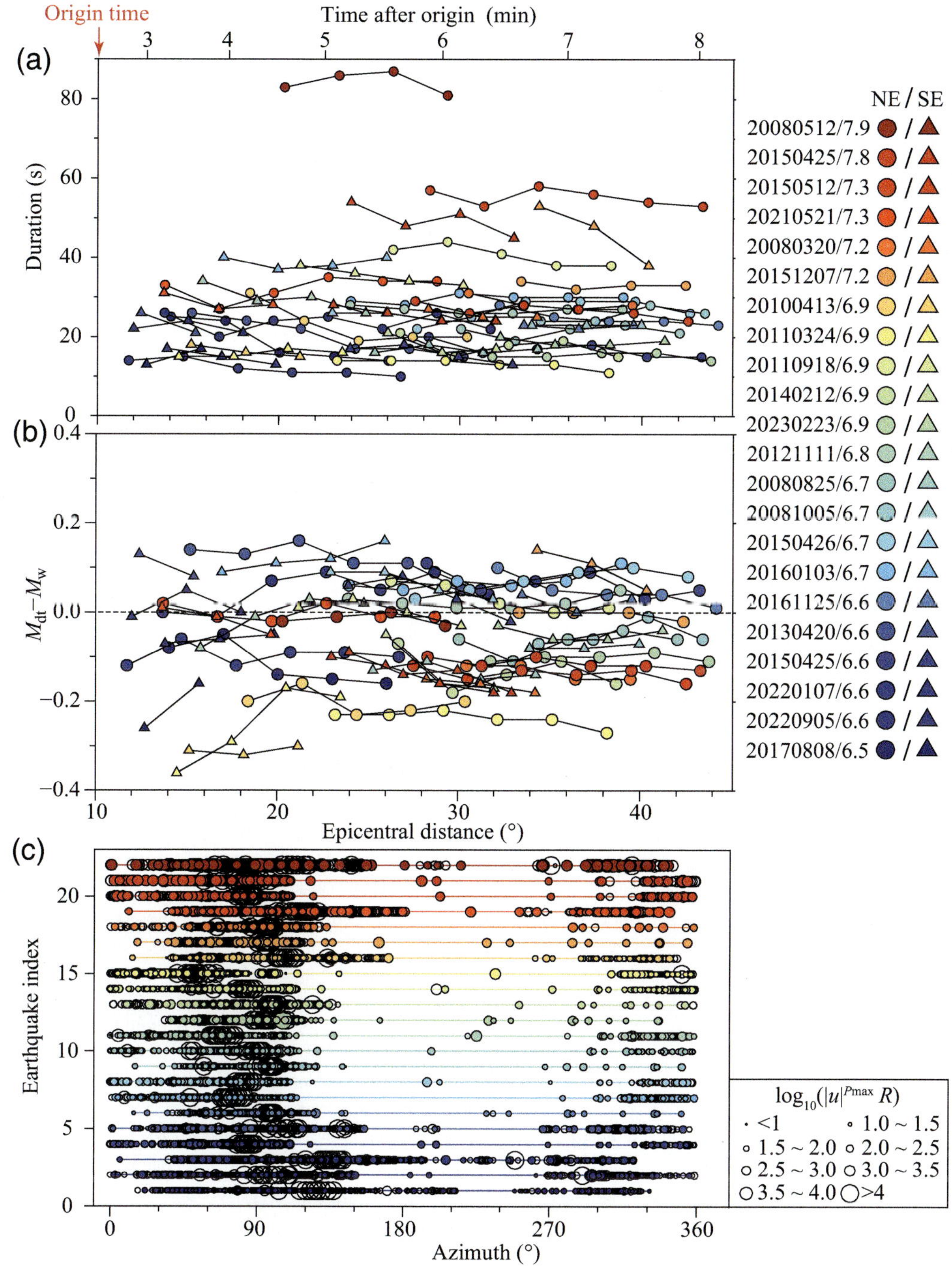

Figure 4. Real-time determination of M_{dt} for 22 earthquakes. (a) Time evolution of source duration derived from northeast and southeast Chinese seismic subarrays. Circles and triangles indicate the source durations estimated using northeast and southeast subarrays, respectively. (b) Statistical comparison of M_w (U.S. Geological Survey [USGS]) and our M_{dt} estimations over time. (c) Maximum P-wave displacements versus azimuth for all events recorded by CDSN and GSN stations. Black and colored circles represent all stations and the selected stations after filtering, respectively. Circle size corresponds to $log_{10}(|u|^{P\max} \cdot R)$.

We tested the algorithm on real-time waveform data to assess its performance. The backprojection was conducted ~4.5 min after the origin time, utilizing data from 128 stations in the northeast subarray (Fig. 5a). Waveforms from stations at 8° and 15° were extracted between the direct and reflected P waves, whereas for those beyond 15°, the 0–150 s window relative to the direct P arrival was retained. At this stage, the source duration was determined to be 83 s (Fig. 5b). Within the same epicentral distance range, 10 GSN and 389 CDSN seismic stations were available, and the maximum P-wave displacements ranged from $10^{-3}$to 10^{-2} m (Fig. 5c). Approximately 7.5 min after the event, we determined the M_{dt} to be 7.9, accounting for a 3 min delay due to source duration, network delay, and computation time (Fig. 5d).

As time progressed, the results were updated as more stations recorded this event, with additional stations added in 3° epicentral distance bins. By ~6 min after the origin time, all northeast subarray stations had recorded the event, and the source duration stabilized at ~81 s. Using maximum P-wave displacements from 472 CDSN and 15 GSN stations, the M_{dt} remained at 7.9. The estimated M_{dt} for the Wenchuan earthquake remained at ~7.9 (~7 to 9 min after the origin time), with minor fluctuations, aligning well with the M_s 8.0 from CENC and the German Research Centre for Geosciences, and the M_{ww} 7.9 from the USGS and Global Centroid Moment Tensor.

We also estimated the source duration using the southeast subarray, with the farthest station located 15.6° from the epicenter. For stations within the 8°–15° range, waveforms between the direct P and reflected P waves were used to minimize the influence of reflected P waves, for which arrival times were earlier than the end of the rupture process. As a result, the estimated source duration was only 61 s. A few stations recorded abnormally high or low

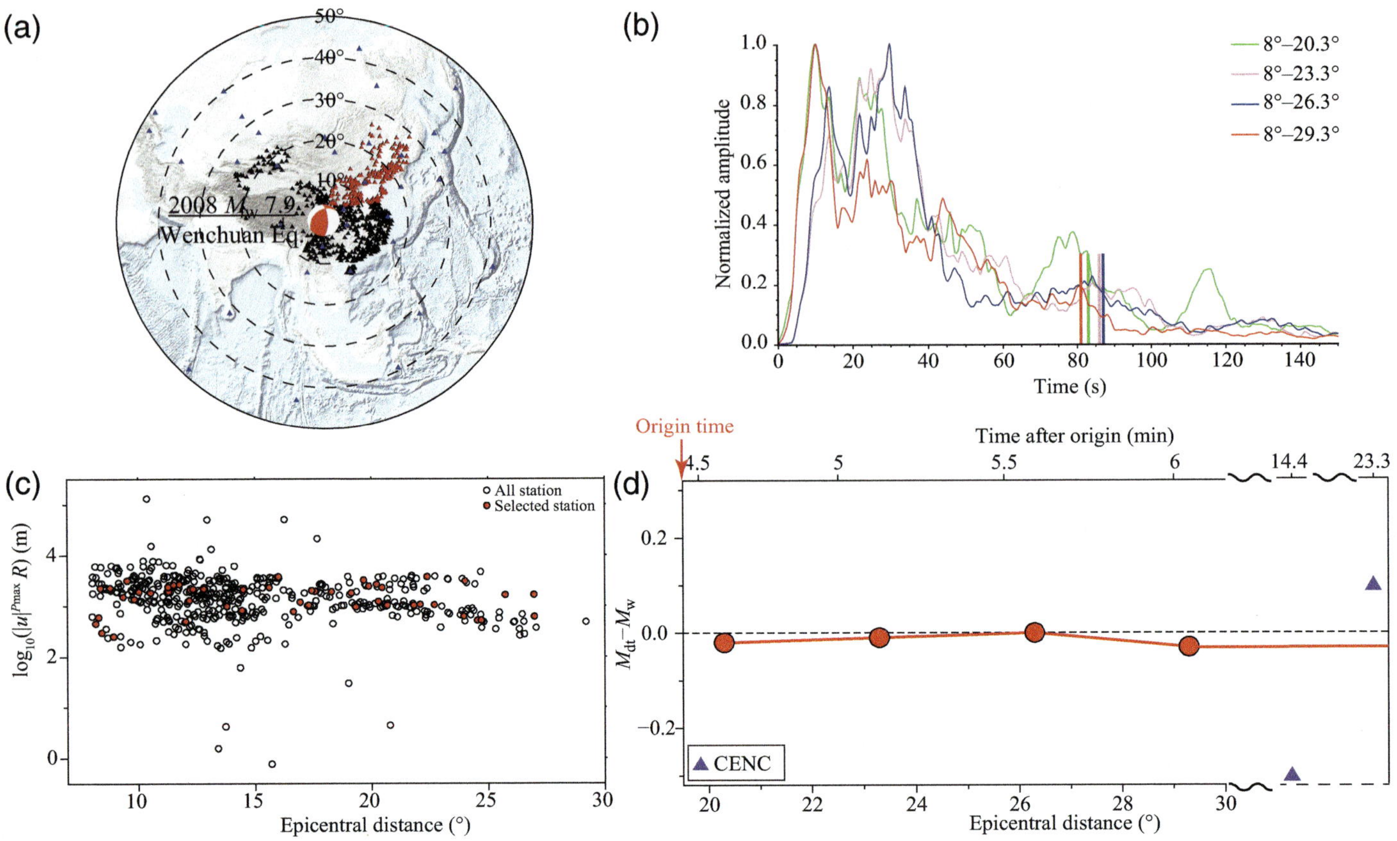

amplitudes, likely due to instrument sensitivity errors or other factors (Fig. 5c). These outliers were successfully removed using the station screening procedure, resulting in an M_{dt} estimate of 7.9 ± 0.1.

Figure 5. Real-time M_{dt} estimation of the 2008 M_w 7.9 Wenchuan earthquake. (a) Location of earthquake, CDSN (black hollow triangles) and GSN (blue triangles) seismic stations. Red triangles indicate the northeast Chinese subarray used for calculating the source duration. Black dashed concentric circles denote event equidistance contours. (b) Energy–time plots derived from backprojection using waveforms recorded at epicentral distances ranging from 8° to 20.3°, 8° to 23.3°, 8° to 26.3°, and 8° to 29.3°. The colored lines denote the determined end times of the seismic source. (c) Plot of $\log_{10}(|u|^{P\max} \cdot R)$ versus epicentral distance for all stations shown in panel (a). Red dots represent data used in the M_{dt} estimation after station screening, and the black dots represent data from all CDSN and GSN stations. (d) Time evolution of M_{dt} estimates. Purple triangles represent the magnitudes reported by the China Earthquake Networks Center (CENC).

DISCUSSION

Impact of various seismic phases on source duration estimation

In this study, we used seismic data from local to regional epicentral distance (8°–44°) to estimate the source durations for moderate-to-large (M_w 6.5–7.9) earthquakes. Within this range, the direct *P* wave is coherent across stations within a subarray. However, later parts of the *P*-wave train can be more complex due to overlapping phases and energy from multiple rupture points (Ishii *et al.*, 2005), such as the direct *S* wave, the reflection from the core–mantle boundary (*PcP*), and free-surface reflections (*PdPN*). Although variations in travel times help resolve some of these complexities, the influence of reflected phases persists at local to regional epicentral distances.

To assess the impact of these phases on the backprojection procedure, we analyzed the 2010 M_w 6.9 Qinghai earthquake, with a depth of 17 km. For stations within the 8°–19° epicentral distance range, the waveform window from 0 to 400 s relative to the direct *P* wave includes multiple phases, such as direct *P* and *S* waves, free-surface reflections of *P* waves (e.g., *PdPN*), and *PcP* waves. The travel-time differences between the direct *P* wave and the *S* and *PcP* waves are significant, exceeding the source duration for most earthquakes. For instance, the travel-time difference between the direct *P* and *S* waves ranges from 91 to 214 s, and the *P* to *PcP* travel-time difference decreases from 396 to 261 s (Fig. 6a), according to the IASP91 model.

To mitigate the influence of these phases, we selectively used time windows before the predicted arrival of the *S* wave to avoid the impact of *S* and *PcP* waves. In addition, within the frequency band of 0.05–2 Hz, *S*-wave energy is effectively suppressed. However, at epicentral distances closer than ~15°, we identified phases with unusually large amplitudes that exhibited travel-time differences of ~38 to 76 s relative to the direct *P* wave (Fig. 6b). These phases correspond to *P*-wave reflections off the 20 km discontinuity in the IASP91 model (*P20P2* and *P20P3*), and their travel-time differences relative

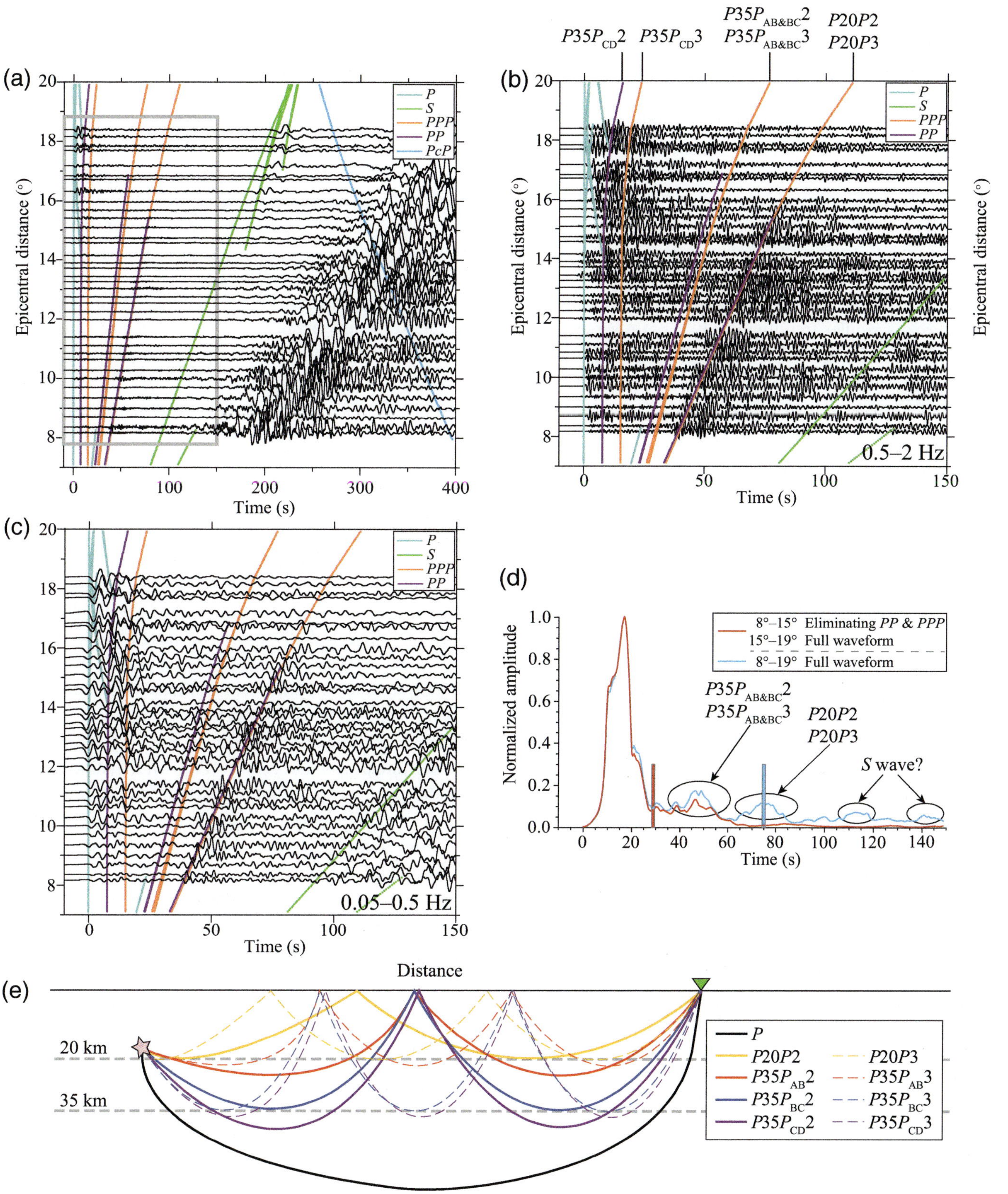

Figure 6. (a) Unfiltered waveforms recorded by the northeast Chinese subarray at epicentral distances of 8°–19°, with theoretical travel-time curves from the IASP91 model shown as colored lines. (b) Enlarged waveforms highlighted in the gray box in panel (a), filtered in the 0.5–2 Hz frequency band. (c) Same as (b), but filtered in the 0.05–0.5 Hz frequency band. (d) Energy–time plots derived from backprojection using waveforms recorded at epicentral distances of 8°–19°. Red- and blue-vertical lines indicate the estimated source durations from tests I and II, respectively. (e) Ray paths of the direct *P* wave and free-surface reflections of *P* waves. *P20P*2, *P* wave reflected off the 20 km discontinuity; $P35P_{AB}2$, *P* wave turning above the 35 km discontinuity; $P35P_{BC}2$, *P* wave reflected off the 35 km discontinuity; $P35P_{CD}2$: *P* wave diving below the 35 km discontinuity.

to the direct P wave are shorter than the typical source durations of many destructive earthquakes. Therefore, a detailed discussion of their effects on the backprojection analysis is necessary.

We conducted two tests to evaluate the influence of these reflected P waves on source duration estimation. In test I, we retained waveforms between the direct P and the $P20P2$($P20P3$) waves for stations within the 8°–15° range. For stations in the 15°–19° range, we used a window of 0–150 s relative to the direct P wave. In test II, we included waveforms from all stations within the 0–150 s time window relative to the direct P wave. The energy–time plots from both tests displayed a similar trend until ~30 s, but diverged more noticeably afterward, especially around ~75 s (Fig. 6d). In the period of ~60 to 90 s, the stacked energy reached 15% of the maximum stacked energy, corresponding to the appearance of the reflected P waves from the 20 km discontinuity. The difference in source duration estimations, 29 s for test I and 75 s for test II, highlights the significant impact of these reflected phases on the backprojection method (Fig. 6d).

Further analysis revealed an additional energy peak between 40 and 55 s, potentially associated with triplicated P waves from the 35 km discontinuity (IASP91 model, Fig. 6e). These include waves that turn above the discontinuity (AB), wide-angle reflect off it (BC), and dive below it (CD). However, following the methodology proposed by Wang *et al.* (2017), we defined the source duration as the shorter of the following two criteria: (1) the time window that contains 90% of the stacked energy, or (2) the time at which 80% of the stacked energy is reached and the subsequent stacked amplitude falls below 0.1 of the peak. This approach helps suppress interference from reflected phases originating at the 35 km discontinuity, improving the accuracy of magnitude determination. In addition, the $P35P_{AB\&BC}2$ and $P35P_{AB\&BC}3$ phases, which arrive nearly simultaneously with the direct P wave, have a negligible impact on the source duration due to the 10 s stacking window length.

In summary, our analysis indicates that reflections from the 20 km discontinuity have a significant impact on source duration estimation, whereas triplicated P waves from the 35 km discontinuity have minimal effect. This highlights the importance of carefully excluding reflected phases, particularly those from the 20 km discontinuity, to ensure accurate source duration and M_{dt} estimation. Moreover, it is essential to acknowledge that when the source duration exceeds the length of the available waveform window, there is a risk of underestimating the M_{dt} due to waveform truncation.

Assessment of the radiation pattern on M_{dt} estimation

One of the key advantages of the proposed approach is its independence from prerequisite constraints, such as fault geometry, focal mechanism, and initial stress. Instead, it relies solely on determining the potential rupture area. This independence allows backprojection to provide a relatively fast and stable estimation of source duration. In M_{dt} estimation, another crucial parameter is the maximum displacement of P waves. It is generally acknowledged that the spatial distribution of the observed maximum P-wave displacements is distorted by factors such as the geometrical spreading effects, radiation pattern, and variations in the regional velocity structure. Thus, establishing reliable methods for extracting this parameter is vital for accurate M_{dt} determination, warranting further discussion and comparison.

To explore these factors, we analyzed three representative earthquakes with distinct focal mechanisms and locations: the 2008 M_w 7.9 Wenchuan earthquake in Sichuan Province (reverse slip fault), the 2021 M_w 7.3 Maduo earthquake in Qinghai Province (strike-slip fault), and the 2008 M_w 7.2 Hotan earthquake in Xinjiang Province (normal slip fault).

Figure 7 depicts the spatial distribution of the maximum P-wave displacements. We removed the instrument response, filtered the data between 0.01 and 10 Hz, and extracted maximum displacements based on the theoretical travel time of P to S waves using the IASP91 model. Across all seismic stations, a consistent decrease in P-wave amplitudes with increasing epicentral distance is observed, primarily due to geometrical spreading effects. However, at the same epicentral distance, significant azimuthal variations in maximum P-wave displacements are evident (Takemura *et al.*, 2016). For strike-slip faults, the amplitude variations show a continuous four-lobe azimuthal variation pattern (Fig. 7e). Equation (2) initially included the P-wave radiation pattern term (see the supplemental material). However, due to the lack of precise focal mechanism and the complexities of local velocity structures, the impact of the radiation pattern can be neglected when utilizing data from evenly distributed stations.

To address the uneven station distribution and reduce the impact of radiation pattern variations, we grouped stations based on take-off angle and azimuth rather than epicentral distance. Compared to epicentral distance, the take-off angle allows for a more uniform sampling of the focal sphere. For ray paths with sufficiently similar take-off angles, differences in the radiation pattern can be effectively minimized.

Figure 8 illustrates the impact of this approach. When unfiltered data are used, the variation in M_{dt} estimates can be significant, with errors of up to ±0.5. The application of the proposed station screening strategy significantly reduces this variability. Moreover, this screening process helps eliminate abnormal data points, resulting in more accurate magnitude calculations compared to the prescreened dataset.

These findings underscore the critical importance of station screening, particularly in regions with uneven seismic station distribution. This screening method may also be applied in surface- and body-wave magnitude calculations to improve accuracy.

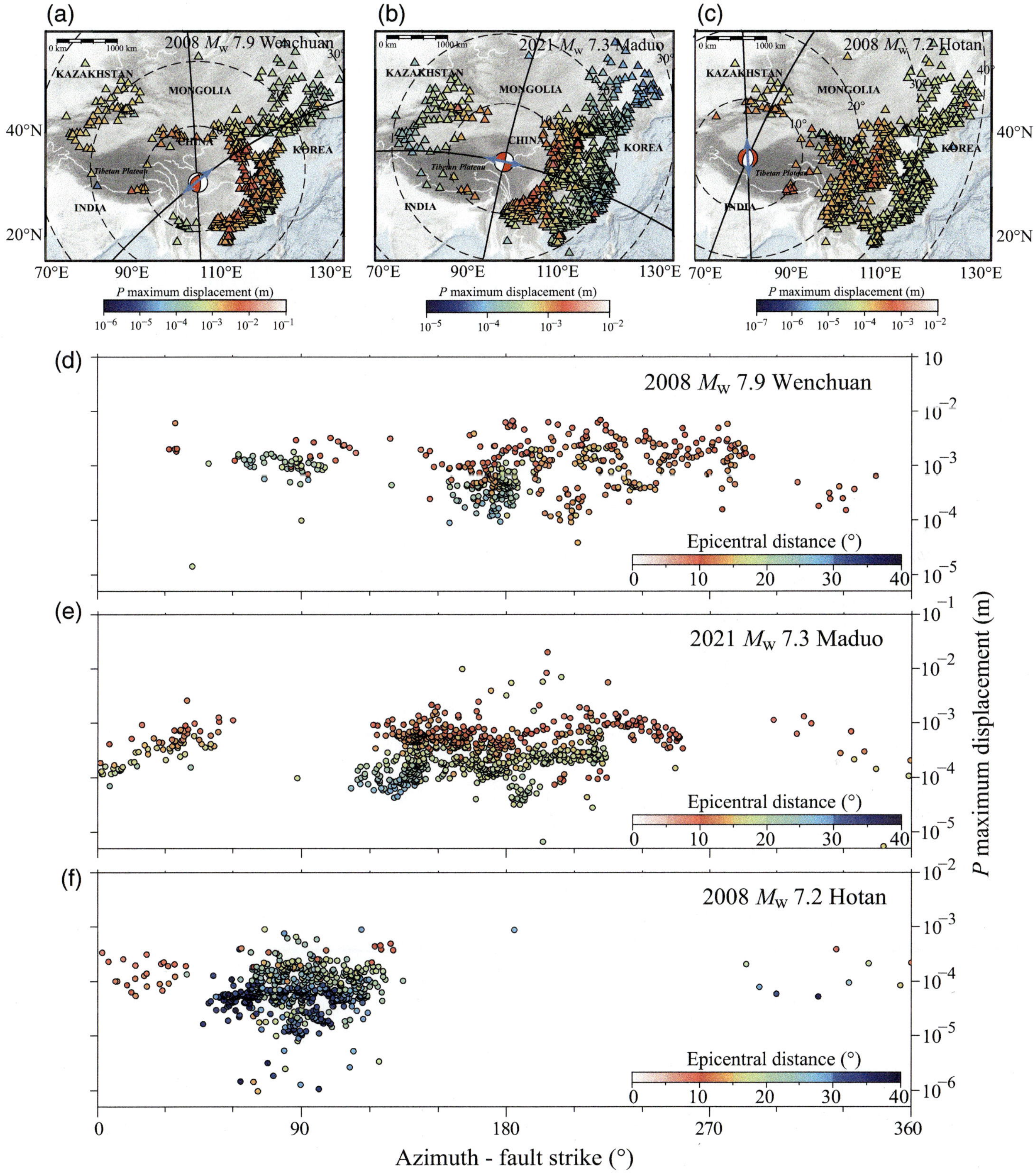

Figure 7. Azimuthal dependence of observed maximum *P*-wave displacements of three selected earthquakes. (a–c) Spatial distribution of the maximum *P*-wave displacements. Red focal mechanism plots denote focal mechanisms; solid and black dashed lines indicate the strikes of the nodal planes and event equidistance contours, respectively. Blue arrows mark the fault strike. (d–f) Maximum *P*-wave displacements versus fault strikes, with different colors representing seismic data at various epicentral distances.

Effects of station coverage on duration estimation

To evaluate the station coverage requirement for backprojection, we systematically reduced the number of stations and analyzed the resulting effects using the northeast subarray, focusing on two aspects: average station spacing and station aperture.

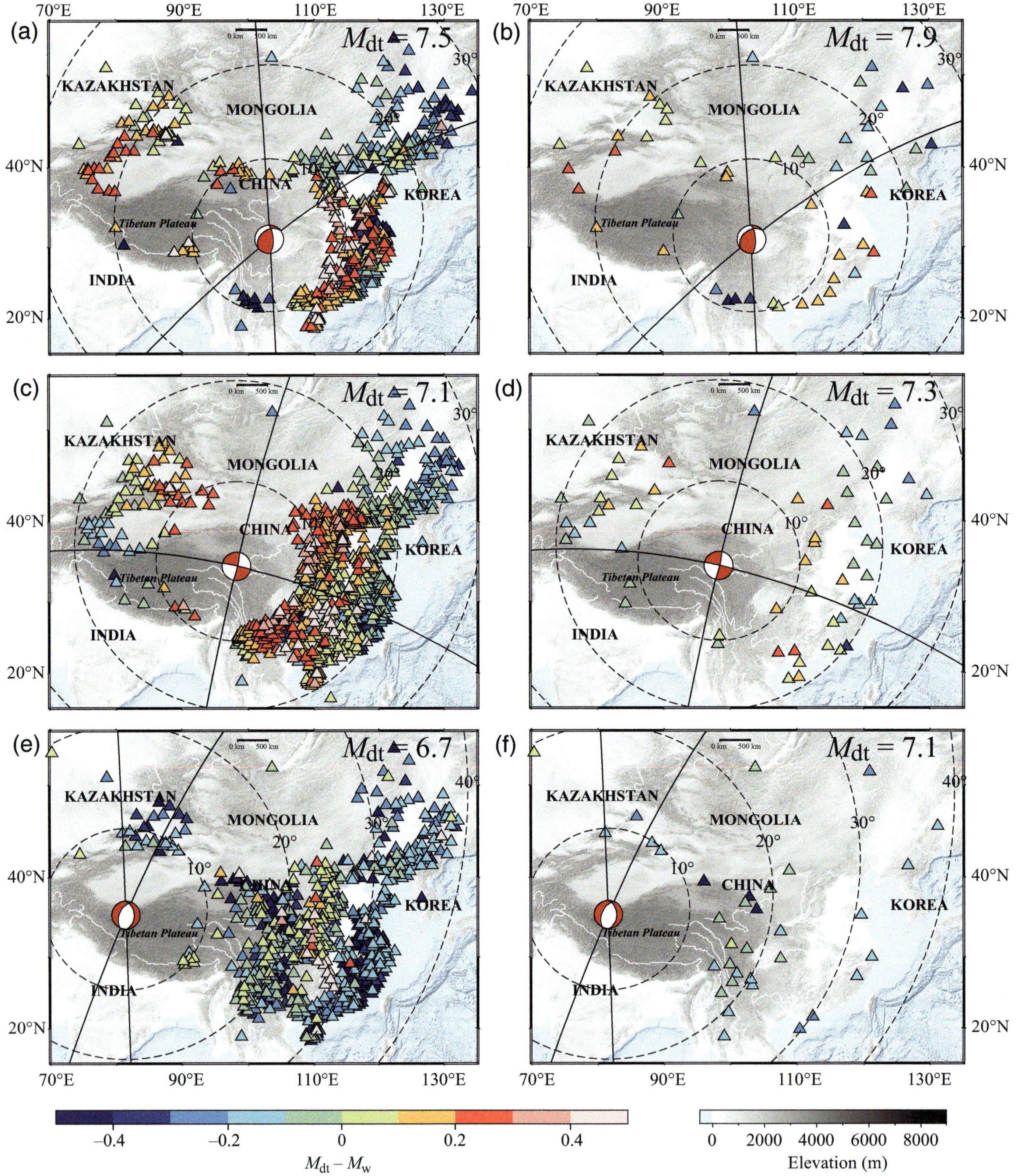

Figure 8. Differences between M_{dt} and M_w for the analyzed earthquakes. The left and right panels show results before and after data screening, respectively. (a,b) 2008 M_w 7.9 Wenchuan earthquake, (c,d) 2021 M_w 7.3 Maduo earthquake, (e,f) 2008 M_w 7.2 Hotan earthquake. Red focal mechanism plots denote focal mechanisms; solid and black dashed lines indicate the strikes of the nodal planes and event equidistance contours, respectively.

For the average station spacing tests, we began with the station closest to the epicenter and iteratively removed stations within a radius that increased from 20 to 360 km in 20 km steps. At each step, the nearest remaining station outside the exclusion zone was selected, and the process was repeated until all stations were considered.

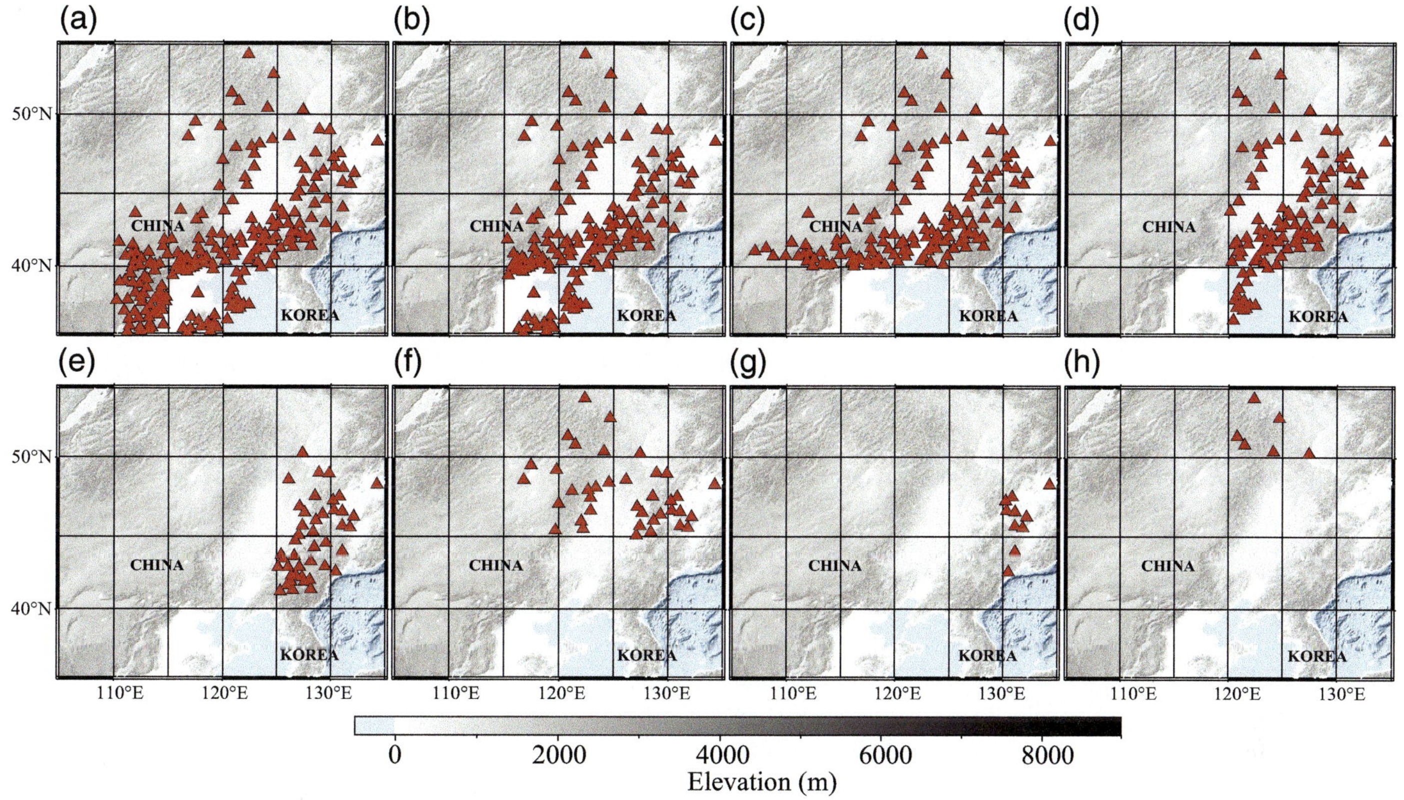

Figure 9. Station distributions for aperture tests. Red triangles denote stations. Panels (a–h) correspond to tests 1–8, respectively.

For the aperture tests, we progressively narrowed the station distribution in both longitude and latitude, reducing the longitude range from 110°–135° E to 130°–135° E and the latitude range from 40°–55° N to 50°–55° N in 5° increments (Fig. 9). Source durations were calculated for each resulting subarray.

Three earthquakes of varying magnitudes were analyzed. Reference source durations were obtained using all stations in the northeast subarray. A threshold was defined such that a deviation in magnitude greater than 0.1 was considered unacceptable. The acceptable duration ranges for the three events are 11–21, 20–40, and 58–113 s, respectively (Fig. 10). For the 2008 M_w 7.9 Wenchuan earthquake, duration estimates at 20–60 km spacing were consistent and in close agreement with the reference value. The actual average station spacing of the northeast subarray is 61 km. When the spacing exceeded ~160 km, the estimated durations approached 113 s, reaching the threshold. For the 2008 M_w 7.2 Hotan earthquake, the spacing requirement was less stringent, with acceptable durations observed up to a station spacing of 260 km. For the 2013 M_w 6.6 Lushan earthquake, durations remained within the acceptable range even at 360 km spacing.

The aperture tests exhibited similar patterns to the spacing tests. As aperture decreased, durations progressively deviated from the reference values. When fewer than 10 stations were distributed within an approximate 4° × 6° region, noticeable deviations were observed for all three events.

These results indicate that backprojection can resolve source durations using relatively sparse arrays for moderate-to-large earthquakes. However, larger events may require denser station coverage to mitigate interference from reflected phases in regional to teleseismic records. Because this study only included events up to M_w 7.9, further investigations are needed to assess station performance for even greater magnitudes.

Comparison with different magnitude scales

Accurate earthquake magnitude estimation is essential for evaluating the energy released during seismic events and guiding emergency responses. Traditional magnitude scales remain widely used by many institutions (e.g., CENC) for earthquake reporting and cataloging. The M_L was originally designed for moderate earthquakes recorded at local distances using the standard Wood–Anderson seismograph. It has an upper limit near magnitude 7 (Hanks and Kanamori, 1979; Deichmann, 2006) and is not well suited for estimating the magnitude of destructive earthquakes (Bormann and Dewey, 2014). According to the Chinese national standard (GB 17740-2017), the broadband surface-wave magnitude scale ($M_{S(BB)}$) is defined by the following equation:

$$M_{S(BB)} = \log_{10}\left(\frac{V_{max}}{2\pi}\right) + 1.66\log_{10}(\Delta) + 3.3, \quad (3)$$

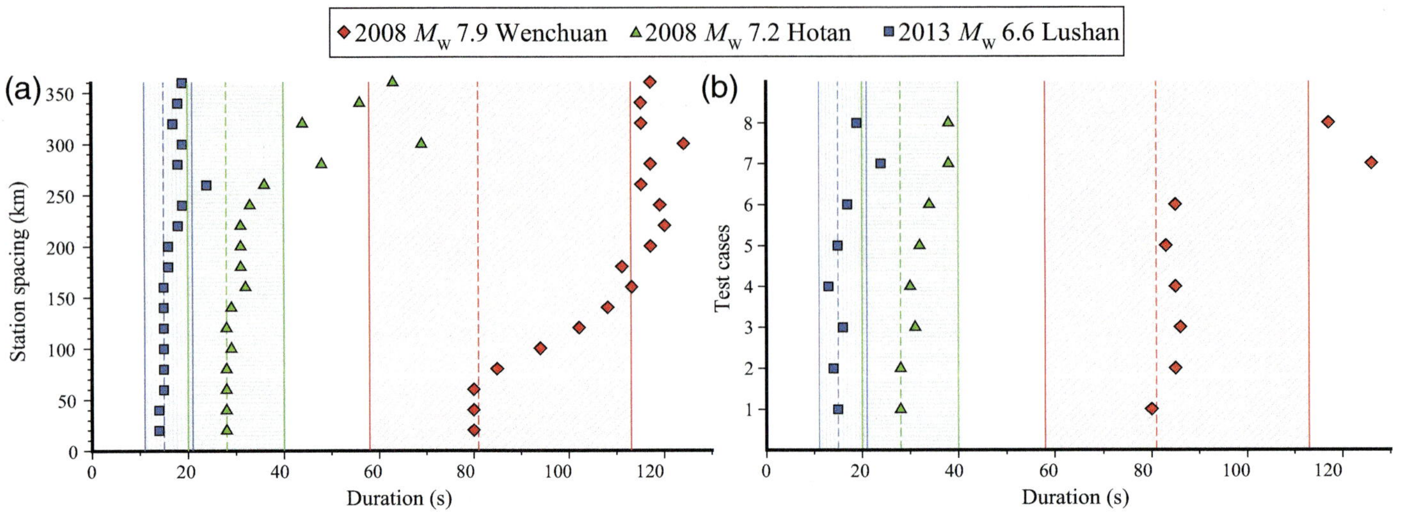

Figure 10. Source durations estimated using different (a) station spacing and (b) station aperture configurations for three earthquakes. The dashed lines represent the reference values obtained using all stations in the northeast subarray. Shaded regions denote the acceptable duration ranges corresponding to a magnitude deviation of ±0.1.

in which V_{max} is the maximum velocity of the surface wave in the vertical component (μm/s), and Δ is the epicentral distance in degrees (ranging from 2° to 160°).

Similarly, the broadband body-wave magnitude scale ($M_{B(BB)}$) can be estimated using the following equation:

$$M_{B(BB)} = \log_{10}\left(\frac{V_{max}}{2\pi}\right) + Q(\Delta,h), \tag{4}$$

in which V_{max} is the maximum velocity of the *P*-wave train for vertical-component waveforms (μm/s), Δ is the epicentral distance in degrees (ranging from 5° to 100°), h represents the focal depth in kilometers, $Q(\Delta,h)$ is the calibration function.

To compare the time efficiency and accuracy of $M_{S(BB)}$, $M_{B(BB)}$, and M_{dt}, we conducted real-time simulations using three earthquakes with magnitudes ranging from M_w 6.6 to 7.9. For each event, magnitudes were recalculated at every 3° increment in epicentral distance, ensuring that the original waveforms remained consistent across all magnitude scales.

The results showed significant variations in magnitude estimates with increasing earthquake magnitude. For events smaller than M_w 7.3, all three magnitude scales produced similar values. However, as the magnitude approached M_w 7.9, discrepancies between the scales became more pronounced, with magnitude estimates ranging from 7.5 to 8.0 (Fig. 11).

For M_w 7.9 Wenchuan earthquake, significant variations were observed in $M_{S(BB)}$ and $M_{B(BB)}$ scales. At local distances, surface waves do not fully develop, leading to a noticeable increase in $M_{S(BB)}$ values at greater epicentral distances, which affects the timeliness of magnitude determination. In contrast, the $M_{B(BB)}$ scale is less influenced by epicentral distance and

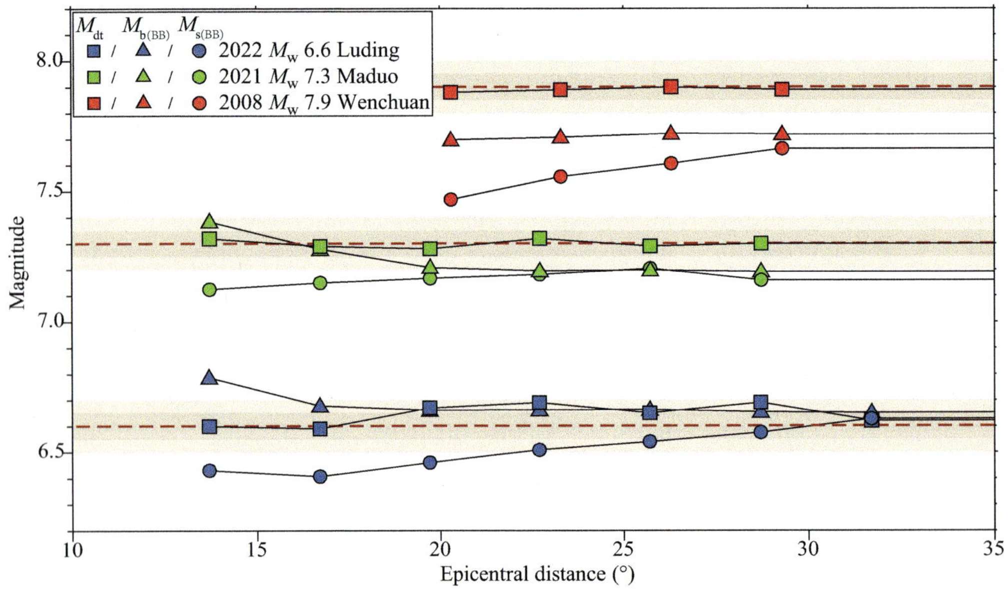

Figure 11. Comparison of different magnitude scales for the selected three earthquakes (colors). Squares, triangles, and circles represent M_{dt}, $M_{B(BB)}$, and $M_{S(BB)}$, respectively. The red dashed lines indicate the M_w published by USGS. Gray and flesh-colored shaded areas denote magnitude differences of ±0.05 and ±0.1, respectively.

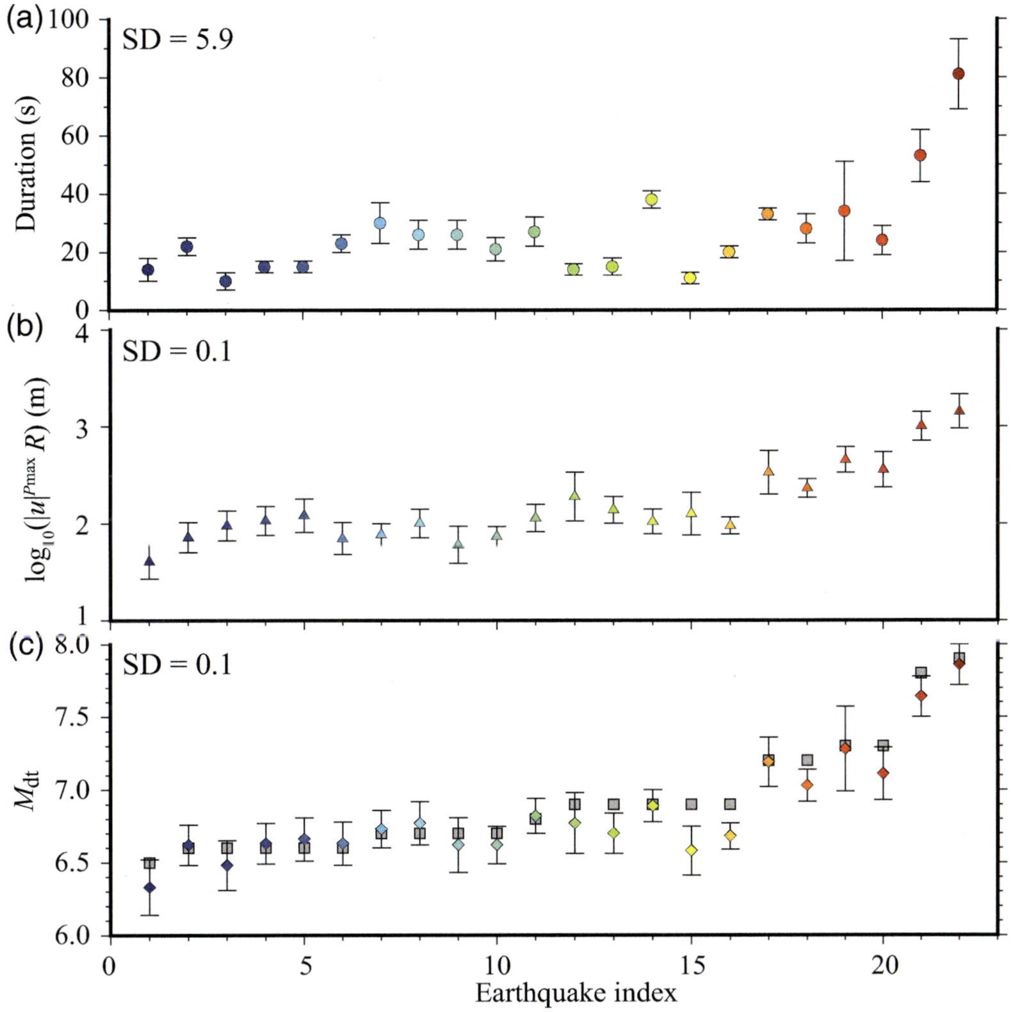

Figure 12. (a) Uncertainties in source duration, (b) maximum *P*-wave displacement, and (c) M_{dt} are shown for the 22 earthquakes. "SD" denotes the standard deviation. The earthquake color coding is consistent with that used in Figure 4. Gray squares indicate the M_{ww} values published by the USGS.

remains more stable. The final values for both $M_{S(BB)}$ and $M_{B(BB)}$ were 7.7, differing by 0.2 from the M_w reported by the USGS.

A primary limitation of traditional magnitude scales is their saturation effect for large earthquakes, resulting in inconsistent behavior across all magnitude ranges (Scordilis, 2006; Huang *et al.*, 2022). In contrast, M_{dt} can overcome these limitations and demonstrate notable stability over time, consistently yielding accurate estimates of around 7.9 for the Wenchuan earthquake (Fig. 11).

Uncertainty analysis of magnitude estimation

According to equation (1), M_{dt} is estimated based on both the source duration and maximum *P*-wave displacement. We therefore assessed the uncertainties in each component separately and used them to evaluate the overall precision of M_{dt}.

Uncertainty in source duration primarily arises from interference by other seismic phases. For shallow earthquakes, reflected *P* waves may closely follow the direct *P* wave, and improper waveform windowing may lead to over- or underestimation of the duration. To mitigate this uncertainty, we adopted a two-criterion approach based on the energy–time curve derived from backprojection (Wang *et al.*, 2017), with the reference duration defined as the shorter of the two. To estimate the uncertainty, we repeated the calculation using threshold pairs of 85% and 75% (as a lower bound) and 95% and 85% (as an upper bound), again selecting the shorter value in each case. The standard deviation of source duration across the 22 events was ±5.9 s (Fig. 12a).

To assess the uncertainty in maximum *P*-wave displacements, we calculated the average of the $\log_{10}(|u|^{P\max} R)$ values across all stations as the reference value. The values were ranked in descending order, and the central 40% (30th–70th percentiles) were used to estimate the standard deviation from the mean (Fig. 12b).

Combining these two components and applying equation (1), we obtained the uncertainty of M_{dt} for each earthquake. The overall standard deviation was ±0.1 (Fig. 12c).

CONCLUSION

We present a novel approach for determining the magnitudes of moderate-to-large earthquakes using regional to teleseismic waveform data. The method was tested in a simulated real-time environment by analyzing 22 earthquakes (M_w 6.5–7.9) that occurred in western China from 2008 to 2023, with data collected from CDSN and GSN stations. Magnitude estimates were obtained within 6–11 min after the origin time, with an uncertainty of ±0.1, and are consistent with M_w values published by the USGS (standard deviation ~0.1).

To improve the accuracy of source duration and magnitude estimates, we mitigated interference from reflected phases within the *P*-wave train by applying adaptive time windowing based on amplitude ratios between the direct and reflected P waves. Radiation pattern effects were reduced by spatially averaging maximum P-wave amplitudes within azimuth and take-off angle grids, enhancing sampling uniformity and reducing outliers caused by instrument or site effects.

Tests on station spacing and aperture size demonstrate that backprojection can resolve source durations of moderate-to-large earthquakes even with relatively sparse arrays. However, for larger events, effective suppression of interfering phases in regional to teleseismic waveforms requires denser station spacing and wider apertures. Notably, substantial deviations occur when spacing exceeds ~160 km or when fewer than 10 stations lie within an approximate $4° \times 6°$ region (e.g., M_w 7.9).

Finally, a quantitative evaluation of $M_{S(BB)}$, $M_{B(BB)}$, and M_{dt} underscores that this method can complement existing magnitude estimation techniques by providing rapid and reliable earthquake magnitude determinations.

DATA AND RESOURCES

The data are provided by the China Earthquake Networks Center (CENC) and the China Earthquake Administration Data Management Center (CEA DMC). Access is available through registration and application at https://data.earthquake.cn/datashare/website/data/contwave_csn.jsp (last accessed December 2024). Currently, this website is not directly accessible from regions outside mainland China. The Global Seismological Network (GSN) station data were obtained from the Incorporated Research Institutions for Seismology (IRIS) DMC at www.iris.edu (last accessed December 2024). The earthquake catalog was downloaded from the U.S Geological Survey (USGS) website (https://earthquake.usgs.gov/, last accessed January 2025). The focal mechanisms were from the Global Centroid Moment Tensor (Global CMT) website at http://www.globalcmt.org/CMTsearch.html (last accessed January 2025). Seismic Analysis Code (SAC; Goldstein *et al.*, 2003) and tauP (Crotwell *et al.*, 1999) were used for basic data analysis, and all figures were plotted with Generic Mapping Tools (GMT; Wessel *et al.*, 2013). The unpublished manuscript by G. J. Han *et al.*, 2025, "Estimating source parameters of the January 7, 2025 Ms 6.8 Dingri earthquake in Xizang, China," submitted to *J. Earth Sci.* The supplemental material for this article includes a detailed derivation of the formulas used in moment magnitude estimation.

DECLARATION OF COMPETING INTERESTS

The authors acknowledge that there are no conflicts of interest recorded.

ACKNOWLEDGMENTS

This study is funded by the National Natural Science Foundation of China (Grant Numbers 42304072, 41874062, and 41922025). The authors thank Zhifan Wan (China University of Geosciences) for valuable assistance with the backprojection code developed by Dun Wang. The authors also thank Editor-in-Chief Martin P. Mai, Deputy Editor-in-Chief Junghyun, Associate Editor Thomas M. Brocher, and two anonymous reviewers for their constructive comments and suggestions, which greatly improved the article.

REFERENCES

Bormann, P., and J. W. Dewey (2014). The new IASPEI standards for determining magnitudes from digital data and their relation to classical magnitudes, in *New Manual of Seismological Observatory Practice 2 (NMSOP-2)*, P. Bormann (Editor), Deutsches Geo ForschungsZentrum GFZ, Potsdam, Germany, 1–44, doi: 10.2312/GFZ.NMSOP-2_IS_3.3.

Chen, W., G. Rao, D. Kang, Z. Wan, and D. Wang (2023). Early report of the source characteristics, ground motions, and casualty estimates of the 2023 Mw 7.8 and 7.5 Turkey earthquakes, *J. Earth Sci.* **34,** no. 2, 297–303, doi: 10.1007/s12583-023-1316-6.

Choy, G. L., and J. L. Boatwright (1995). Global patterns of radiated seismic energy and apparent stress, *J. Geophys. Res.* **100,** no. B9, 18,205–18,228, doi: 10.1029/95jb01969.

Convers, J. A., and A. V. Newman (2011). Global evaluation of large earthquake energy from 1997 through mid-2010, *J. Geophys. Res.* **116,** no. B8, doi: 10.1029/2010jb007928.

Convers, J. A., and A. V. Newman (2013). Rapid earthquake rupture duration estimates from teleseismic energy rates, with application to real-time warning, *Geophys. Res. Lett.* **40,** no. 22, 5844–5848, doi: 10.1002/2013gl057664.

Crotwell, H. P., T. J. Owens, and J. Ritsema (1999). The TauP toolkit: Flexible seismic travel-time and ray-path utilities, *Seismol. Res. Lett.* **70,** no. 2, 154–160, doi: 10.1785/gssrl.70.2.154.

Deichmann, N. (2006). Local magnitude, a moment revisited, *Bull. Seismol. Soc. Am.* **96,** no. 4A, 1267–1277, doi: 10.1785/0120050115.

Deng, W., G. Han, J. Li, and L. Sun (2024). Seismometer orientation measurements of broadband seismic stations in the China Digital Seismograph Network, *Bull. Seismol. Soc. Am.* **115,** no. 1, 210–227, doi: 10.1785/0120240075.

Dhakal, Y. P., H. Kubo, W. Suzuki, T. Kunugi, S. Aoi, and H. Fujiwara (2016). Analysis of strong ground motions and site effects at Kantipath, Kathmandu, from 2015 Mw 7.8 Gorkha, Nepal, earthquake and its aftershocks, *Earth Planets Space* **68,** nos. 1/12, doi: 10.1186/s40623-016-0432-2.

Duputel, Z., L. Rivera, H. Kanamori, G. P. Hayes, B. Hirshorn, and S. Weinstein (2011). Real-time W phase inversion during the 2011 off the Pacific coast of Tohoku earthquake, *Earth Planets Space* **63,** no. 7, 535–539, doi: 10.5047/eps.2011.05.032.

Duputel, Z., L. Rivera, H. Kanamori, and G. P. Hayes (2012). W phase source inversion for moderate to large earthquakes (1990–2010), *Geophys. J. Int.* **189,** no. 2, 1125–1147.

Goldstein, P., D. Dodge, M. Firpo, and L. Minner (2003). SAC2000: Signal processing and analysis tools for seismologists and engineers, in *International Geophysics*, Vol. 81, Academic Press, 1613–1614, doi: 10.1016/S0074-6142(03)80284-X.

Gutenberg, B. (1945a). Amplitudes of P, PP, and S and magnitude of shallow earthquakes, *Bull. Seismol. Soc. Am.* **35,** no. 2, 57–69.

Gutenberg, B. (1945b). Magnitude determination for deep-focus earthquakes, *Bull. Seismol. Soc. Am.* **35,** no. 3, 117–130.

Han, Y., Y. Zang, L. Meng, Y. Wang, S. Deng, Y. Ma, and M. Xie (2022). A summary of seismic activities in and around China in 2021, *Earthq. Res. Adv.* **2,** no. 3, doi: 10.1016/j.eqrea.2022.100157.

Hanks, T. C., and H. Kanamori (1979). A moment magnitude scale, *J. Geophys. Res.* **84,** no. B5, 2348–2350, doi: 10.1029/JB084iB05p02348.

Hara, T. (2007). Magnitude determination using duration of high frequency energy radiation and displacement amplitude: Application to tsunami earthquakes, *Earth Planets Space* **59,** no. 6, 561–565.

Hara, T. (2011). Magnitude determination using duration of high frequency energy radiation and displacement amplitude: Application to the 2011 off the Pacific coast of Tohoku Earthquake, *Earth Planets Space* **63,** no. 7, 525–528, doi: 10.5047/eps.2011.05.014.

Hirshorn, B., S. Weinstein, and S. Tsuboi (2012). On the application of Mwp in the Near Field and the March 11, 2011 Tohoku earthquake, *Pure Appl. Geophys.* **170,** no. 6, 975–991, doi: 10.1007/s00024-012-0495-3.

Horiuchi, S., H. Ishii, and A. Takagi (1982). Two-dimensional depth structure of the crust beneath the Tohoku district, the northeastern Japan arc. Part I. method and Conrad-discontinuity, *J. Phys. Earth* **30,** no. 1, 47–69.

Huang, X., Y. Peng, C. Cheng, D. Wang, and Q. Yao (2022). Determination and comparison of M_L, M_{dt}, M_{S_BB}, m_B, M_{WP}, M_{WW}, and M(GNSS) for the 22 May 2021 M7.4 Madoi, Qianghai, China earthquake, *J. Earth Sci.* **33,** no. 4, 847–856.

Hwang, R. D., J. P. Chang, C. Y. Wang, J. Wu, C. Kuo, Y. Tsai, W. Chang, and T. Tin (2011). Rise time and source duration of the 2008 M_W 7.9 Wenchuan (China) earthquake as revealed by Rayleigh waves, *Earth Planets Space* **63,** no. 5, 427–434, doi: 10.5047/eps.2011.01.002.

Ishii, M., P. M. Shearer, H. Houston, and J. E. Vidale (2005). Extent, duration and speed of the 2004 Sumatra-Andaman earthquake imaged by the Hi-Net array, *Nature* **435,** no. 7044, 933–936, doi: 10.1038/nature03675.

Kanamori, H. (1977). The energy release in great earthquakes, *J. Geophys. Res.* **82,** no. 20, 2981–2987, doi: 10.1029/JB082i020p02981.

Kanamori, H. (1993). W-phase, *Geophys. Res. Lett.* **20,** no. 16, 1691–1694, doi: 10.1029/93gl01883.

Kennett, B. L. N., and E. R. Engdahl (1991). Traveltimes for global earthquake location and phase identification, *Geophys. J. Int.* **105,** no. 2, 429–465, doi: 10.1111/j.1365-246X.1991.tb06724.

Kusumawati, D., D. P. Sahara, A. D. Nugraha, N. T. Puspito, S. Widiyantoro, Z. Zulfakriza, S. Rosalia, H. A. Shiddiqi, A. Ardianto, A. W. Baskara, *et al.* (2023). Sensitivity analysis of moment magnitude (Mw) spectral fitting parameters based on orthogonal design: Using aftershocks of the 2019 Mw 6.5 Ambon, Indonesia earthquake, *Bull. Earthq. Eng.* **21,** no. 4, 1793–1819, doi: 10.1007/s10518-022-01606-6.

Litak, R. K., and L. D. Brown (1989). A modern perspective on the Conrad discontinuity, *Eos Trans. AGU* **70,** no. 29, 713–725, doi: 10.1029/89EO00223.

Pérez-Campos, X., V. H. Espíndola, J. Pérez, J. A. Estrada, C. C. Monroy, D. Bello, A. González-López, D. G. Ávila, R. Maldonado, E. Montoya-Quintanar, *et al.* (2020). Response of the Mexican National Seismological Service to significant earthquakes, under normal and COVID-19 pandemic circumstances, *Seismol. Res. Lett.* **92,** no. 1, 93–101, doi: 10.1785/0220200301.

Richter, C. F. (1935). An instrumental earthquake magnitude scale, *Bull. Seismol. Soc. Am.* **25,** no. 1, 1–32.

Scordilis, E. M. (2006). Empirical global relations converting M_S and m_b to moment magnitude, *J. Seismol.* **10,** no. 2, 225–236, doi: 10.1007/s10950-006-9012-4.

Song, C., Q. Yao, and D. Wang (2019). Magnitude of the 23 January 2018 M7.9 Alaska earthquake estimated from local dense seismic records in Alaska, *J. Earth Sci.* **30,** no. 5, 1005–1009, doi: 10.1007/s12583-019-1215-z.

Takemura, S., M. Kobayashi, and K. Yoshimoto (2016). Prediction of maximum P- and S-wave amplitude distributions incorporating frequency- and distance-dependent characteristics of the observed apparent radiation patterns, *Earth Planets Space* **68,** nos. 1/9, doi: 10.1186/s40623-016-0544-8.

Tsuboi, S., K. Abe, K. Takano, and Y. Yamanaka (1995). Rapid determination of Mw from broadband P waveforms, *Bull. Seismol. Soc. Am.* **85,** no. 2, 606–613.

Wang, D., H. Kawakatsu, J. Zhuang, J. Mori, T. Maeda, H. Tsuruoka, and X. Zhao (2017). Automated determination of magnitude and source length of large earthquakes using backprojection and P wave amplitudes, *Geophy. Res. Lett.* **44,** no. 11, 5447–5456, doi: 10.1002/2017gl073801.

Wang, Q., X. Qiao, Q. Lan, F. Jeffrey, S. Yang, C. Xu, Y. Yang, X. You, K. Tan, and G. Chen (2011). Rupture of deep faults in the 2008 Wenchuan earthquake and uplift of the Longmen Shan, *Nature Geosci.* **4,** no. 9, 634–640, doi: 10.1038/ngeo1210.

Wells, D. L., and K. J. Coppersmith (1994). New empirical relationships among magnitude, rupture length, rupture width, rupture area, and surface displacement, *Bull. Seismol. Soc. Am.* **84,** no. 4, 974–1002.

Wessel, P., W. H. Smith, R. Scharroo, J. Luis, and F. Wobbe (2013). Generic mapping tools: Improved version released, *Eos Trans. AGU* **94,** no. 45, 409–410, doi: 10.1002/2013EO450001.

Xu, X., X. Wen, G. Yu, G. Chen, Y. Klinger, J. Hubbard, and J. Shaw (2009). Coseismic reverse- and oblique-slip surface faulting generated by the 2008 Mw 7.9 Wenchuan earthquake, China, *Geology* **37,** no. 6, 515–518, doi: 10.1130/g25462a.1.

Yang, B., Y. Wang, L. Zhao, L. Yang, and C. Sha (2021). Depth variation of the Conrad discontinuity in the Qaidam Basin, northwestern China, and its crustal dynamic implications, *Earth Planet. Phys.* **5,** no. 3, 1–9, doi: 10.26464/epp2021030.

Yao, Q., D. Wang, L. Fang, and J. Mori (2019). Rapid estimation of magnitudes of large damaging earthquakes in and around Japan using dense seismic stations in China, *Bull. Seismol. Soc. Am.* **109,** no. 6, 2545–2555, doi: 10.1785/0120190107.

Zhang, H., and Z. Ge (2010). Tracking the rupture of the 2008 Wenchuan earthquake by using the relative back-projection method, *Bull. Seismol. Soc. Am.* **100,** no. 5B, 2551–2560, doi: 10.1785/0120090243.

Zhang, P. Z., X. Z. Wen, Z. K. Shen, and J. Chen (2010). Oblique, high-angle, listric-reverse faulting and associated development of strain: The Wenchuan earthquake of May 12, 2008, Sichuan, China, *Annu. Rev. Earth Planet. Sci.* **38,** no. 1, 353–382, doi: 10.1146/annurev-earth-040809-152602.

Zhang, Y., W. Feng, L. Xu, C. Zhou, and Y. Chen (2008). Spatio-temporal rupture process of the 2008 Great Wenchuan earthquake, *Sci. China Earth Sci.* **52,** no. 2, 145–154, doi: 10.1007/s11430-008-0148-7.

Zheng, Y. F., W. J. Xiao, and G. Zhao (2013). Introduction to tectonics of China, *Gondwana Res.* **23,** no. 4, 1189–1206, doi: 10.1016/j.gr.2012.10.001.

Manuscript received 4 April 2025
Published online 1 October 2025

How the Cross-Faults Influence the Dynamic Rupture Process: Insights from the Littoral Fault Zone, China

Chunjing Wang[1], Wenqiang Zhang[2], Houyun Yu[1], Xuping Feng[1], Duyuan Xu[3], and Xiaofei Chen[*1,4,5]

ABSTRACT

The Littoral fault zone (LFZ), located on the northern continental margin of the South China Sea, is a seismogenic structure controlling seismic hazard, having experienced multiple earthquakes with moment magnitudes of 7.5 along its eastern and western segments. However, despite sharing a similar tectonic environment, the central section of the LFZ at the Pearl River Estuary (PRE) is a seismic gap capable of large earthquakes. Therefore, the central section of LFZ (PRE) is considered to be a potential location for strong earthquakes. This fault segment is adjacent to the densely populated and economically developed Guangdong–Hong Kong–Macao Greater Bay area (GBA). Despite this, research on the seismic rupture process in the PRE section of LFZ is still scarce. This study utilizes dynamic rupture modeling to simulate M_w 7.5–8.0 scenario earthquakes of LFZ in the PRE and two northwest-trending cross-faults, the Xijiang fault and Qi'ao Guishan fault. By varying background stress, friction, and nucleation location assumptions, we simulate an earthquake rupture scenario and the associated ground motions. The results indicate that the Xijiang fault is more susceptible to being dynamically triggered than the Qi'ao Guishan fault. Among the six nucleation locations tested, three promote rupture on the Xijiang fault, with rupture patterns and trigger times varying with location. Other locations tend to rupture only the main northeast-strike faults of the LFZ without activating the cross-faults. Notably, the northwest-trending cross-faults extend onto land, potentially exacerbating the seismic hazard and risk to the neighboring regions compared to a rupture of the LFZ alone. This study provides a solid and reliable scientific basis for evaluating the regional seismic hazard and disaster reduction efforts.

KEYPOINTS

- We simulated seismic scenarios for six hypocenter locations along the Littoral fault zone (LFZ).
- A systematic investigation of scenario earthquakes reveals the Xijiang fault is more prone to be triggered.
- The nucleation and dip of the Xijiang fault can influence both the magnitude and direction of ruptures.

Supplemental Material

INTRODUCTION

The Littoral fault zone (LFZ) is a significant seismogenic structure along the northern margin of the South China Sea (SCS) (Liu, 1986). It was initially identified through anomalies in gravity and aeromagnetic data. The LFZ lies below 30–50 m of ocean and stretches over a thousand kilometers. It is located within the continental crust and is the boundary fault between the South China subplate and the thinned South China Sea subplate (Xu *et al.*, 2006). It trends in the northeast-east direction and is dominated by strike-slip movements.

Historically, multiple significant earthquakes have occurred near the LFZ (Chen and Huang, 1984), including the moment magnitude (M_w) 7.0 Nan'ao earthquake in 1600, the M_w 7.5

1. Department of Earth and Space Sciences, Southern University of Science and Technology, Shenzhen, China, https://orcid.org/0009-0005-1179-0428 (CW); https://orcid.org/0000-0002-4715-5654 (HY); https://orcid.org/0000-0003-3356-6644 (XF); https://orcid.org/0000-0002-0950-8121 (XC); 2. Department of Geophysics, Stanford University, Stanford, California, U.S.A., https://orcid.org/0000-0003-1568-1200 (WZ); 3. State Key Laboratory of Earthquake Dynamics and Forecasting, Institute of Geology, China Earthquake Administration, Beijing, China, https://orcid.org/0009-0000-2322-6641 (DX); 4. Guangdong Provincial Key Laboratory of Geophysical High-resolution Imaging Technology, Southern University of Science and Technology, Shenzhen, China; 5. Shenzhen Key Laboratory of Deep Offshore Oil and Gas Exploration Technology, Southern University of Science and Technology, Shenzhen, China

*Corresponding author: chenxf@sustech.edu.cn

Cite this article as Wang, C., W. Zhang, H. Yu, X. Feng, D. Xu, and X. Chen (2025). How the Cross-Faults Influence the Dynamic Rupture Process: Insights from the Littoral Fault Zone, China, *Bull. Seismol. Soc. Am.* **116**, 308–321, doi: 10.1785/0120250085

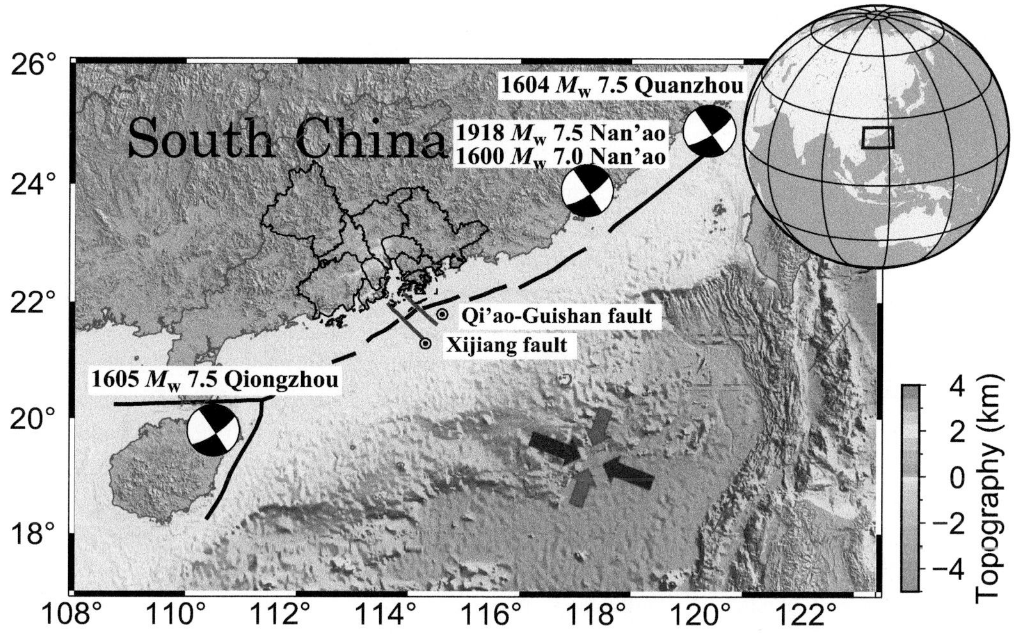

Figure 1. Map of the Littoral fault zone (LFZ) region. The black lines delineate the LFZ. The northwest-trending red lines, from west to east, represent the Xijiang fault (XJF) and the Qi'ao-Guishan fault (Xiong *et al.*, 2018; Zhang *et al.*, 2019). The Guangdong–Hong Kong–Macao Greater Bay area is outlined by the black boundary lines. The focal mechanisms (inferred from historical records) mark four historical earthquakes along the LFZ: the M_w 7.5 Qiongzhou earthquake in 1605, the M_w 7.0 Nan'ao earthquake in 1600, the M_w 7.5 Nan'ao earthquake in 1918, and the M_w 7.5 Quanzhou earthquake in 1604. The arrows indicate the orientation of the stress field. The red and blue arrows denote the maximum and the minimum horizontal compressive stresses, respectively. The color version of this figure is available only in the electronic edition.

Quanzhou earthquake in 1604, the M_w 7.5 Qiongzhou earthquake in 1605, and the M_w 7.5 Nan'ao earthquake in 1918 (Lei and Lv, 1985; Xia *et al.*, 2020; Jia *et al.*, 2023), as shown in Figure 1. These earthquakes were located in the eastern and western parts of the LFZ. In contrast, the PRE segment of the LFZ in the central part, which has similar tectonic conditions, is a seismic gap with a potential for major earthquakes. Thus, this earthquake gap zone is considered a potential source area for catastrophic earthquakes (Liu, 1986; Ding and Huang, 1998; Lv *et al.*, 2018; Xiong *et al.*, 2018). On the Seismic Intensity Zonation Map of China (1990), the PRE of the LFZ are classified as VIII-intensity zones.

The geometric characteristics of the LFZ exhibit significant variations from east to west, with numerous minor faults and a series of faults with obvious stepovers within the fault zone, some of which have different strikes (Xu *et al.*, 2010; Hui *et al.*, 2021; Liang *et al.*, 2023). Two relatively prominent northwest-trending cross-faults on the PRE segment of the LFZ are the Xijiang fault (XJF) and the Qiao-Guishan fault (QGF) (Zhang *et al.*, 2019).

Cross-faults are secondary structures intersecting primary fault systems, forming conjugate networks that accommodate complex strain. Their development depends on plate boundary geometry, basement heterogeneity, and strain localization (Powell *et al.*, 1993). In the 2019 Ridgecrest sequence, cross-faults result from fault rotation under prolonged shear, with right-lateral faults maintaining optimal orientations whereas left-lateral faults rotate unfavorably—consistent with simple shear models and global observations in shear zones (Fialko and Jin, 2021).

Earthquakes that occur on fault systems involving cross-faults are not unusual. For instance, during the 2019 Ridgecrest earthquake, an M_w 6.4 foreshock occurred, followed by an M_w 7.1 mainshock on a cross-fault 34 hr later (Ross *et al.*, 2019). The earthquake sequence ruptured numerous faults with complex orientations, demonstrating the complex interactions between cross-faults. Of course, cross-faults are not triggered in all cases. Notably, the 1992 Landers earthquake was also a complex earthquake sequence, and during this earthquake, the cross-faults such as Pinto Mountain fault and Blue Cut fault were not activated (Hauksson *et al.*, 1993). This indicates that many factors influence the triggering of cross-faults. Lozos (2022) concluded that multifault rupture on conjugate fault systems are primarily affected by the stress and nucleation locations through simulations of "T"-shaped and "+"-shaped conjugate fault ruptures. The presence of two cross-faults on the PRE of LFZ may also correspond to further rupture propagation or arrest. If the rupture further propagates in the northwest direction, its impact on important cities in the surrounding area will intensify.

To investigate the impact of cross-faults on the LFZ, this study employs rupture dynamics and the discontinuous Galerkin method (DGM, Zhang *et al.*, 2023), selects the cross-faults system of LFZ + XJF + QGF, and conducts a preliminary analysis of the rupture process and ground impact of potential large earthquakes in the LFZ. This research is of great significance for research on seismic hazards in the region.

METHOD

The fault geometry is a critical factor in simulating seismic rupture processes. In early dynamic simulations, isolated plane faults were commonly used as the subject of study (Andrews, 1976a,b; Madariaga, 1976; Das and Aki, 1977), despite the prevalence of complex fault geometries in nature.

With advancements in technology and enhancements in computer performance, simulations became increasingly more sophisticated, prompting researchers to seek models that can approximate actual fault geometries for a deeper understanding of source characteristics. The DGM combines geometric flexibility and local adaptability and represents an extension of the finite-element method. Since its introduction into seismology (Dumbser and Käser, 2006; Käser and Dumbser, 2006; de la Puente *et al.*, 2007), numerous researchers have applied DGM to dynamic and wavefield simulations (Wilcox *et al.*, 2010; Ye *et al.*, 2015; Möller and Friederich, 2019). SeisSol has emerged as a mature discontinuous Galerkin framework in seismology (Käser *et al.*, 2007; Pelties *et al.*, 2013), having achieved significant breakthroughs in high-performance computing (Heinecke *et al.*, 2014) and multiphysics coupling capabilities, for example, earthquake–tsunami wave interactions (Uphoff *et al.*, 2017). DGCrack is also a method that performs well in modeling seismic wave propagation and dynamic rupture processes, featuring hp-adaptive capabilities that allow it to flexibly handle complex fault geometries and heterogeneous media conditions (Tago *et al.*, 2012). Zhang *et al.* (2023) proposed a nodal-based DGM with a hybrid flux (upwind/central flux). This method develops the DGM based on Gauss–Lobatto–Legendre points (Hesthaven and Warburton, 2008). Numerical experiment results demonstrate that this method can suppress spatial spiking oscillations caused by the upwind flux, reduce dependence on mesh quality, and perform well in rupture process calculations.

The accuracy and flexibility of this method in simulating rupture dynamics were validated by comparing it with benchmark examples from the Southern California Earthquake Center/U.S. Geological Survey Spontaneous Rupture Code Verification Project (Harris *et al.*, 2009, 2018) (see Data and Resources). The favorable comparisons demonstrate the reliability of our approach.

Therefore, this method is adopted in this study. In the mesh generation process, this study utilizes the GMSH software (Geuzaine and Remacle, 2009).

In addition to numerical methods, several other key factors are involved in simulating seismic rupture processes:

Velocity structure

Wang *et al.* (2021) utilized data from the 2015 land–sea interaction survey conducted in the PRE to invert for a minimum 1D P-wave velocity model (with the smallest root mean square of travel-time residuals). Based on this 1D P-wave velocity (V_P) model, the present study employs the statistical empirical relationships proposed by Brocher (2005) to calculate the density (ρ) and S-wave velocity (V_S),

$$V_S(\text{km/s}) = 0.7858 - 1.234V_P + 0.7949V_P^2 - 0.1238V_P^3 + 0.0064V_P^4, \quad (1)$$

$$\rho(\text{g/cm}^3) = 1.6612V_P - 0.4721V_P^2 + 0.0671V_P^3 - 0.0043V_P^4 + 0.000106V_P^5. \quad (2)$$

Initial stress

As obtaining realistic in situ stress measurements along fault planes is virtually impossible, dynamic rupture simulations typically employ two established approaches for defining initial stress conditions. The first method directly prescribes traction forces, as implemented in actual earthquakes and theoretical studies (Olsen *et al.*, 1997; Brietzke *et al.*, 2007). In the second approach, which we have adopted in this study, the initial stress field is obtained by projecting the regional triaxial effective stress field onto the fault coordinate system, resulting in a triaxial stress tensor (Oglesby and Mai, 2012). In this study, the initial value of the relative intensity of the principal stresses R is selected as 0.6 (Kang *et al.*, 2008), and the initial value of the lateral pressure coefficient K_h is chosen as 0.67 (Wang *et al.*, 2012). The relevant equations are defined as follows in this study.

Generally, a form of background stress configuration that is uniform or increases with depth is used in dynamic rupture simulations. In this study, a stress model is employed where shallow stresses increase with depth but remain constant at greater depths to avoid excessive pressures at the base of the fault. The relationships among the three stress components are described as follows:

$$R = \frac{\sigma_v - \sigma_H}{\sigma_h - \sigma_H} = 0.6, \quad (3)$$

$$K_h = \frac{\sigma_h}{\sigma_v} = 0.67, \quad (4)$$

$$\sigma_v = (1 - \lambda)\rho g z. \quad (5)$$

Here, σ_H, σ_h, and σ_v represent the maximum horizontal principal stress, minimum horizontal principal stress, and vertical stress, respectively. The symbol ρ denotes density, g represents gravitational acceleration, and z represents depth. The parameter λ indicates the ratio of fluid pressure to rock stress, with a value of 0 corresponding to dry rock (Duan, 2010). The σ_H stress orientation adopted in this study is 20° (anticlockwise). By applying different values of λ to the equations above, the values of σ_H, σ_h, σ_v can be obtained. Taking $\lambda = 0.7$ as an example, at depths shallower than 5 km, stresses increase with depth (equation 3). Below 5 km, the stresses stabilize and remain constant. The magnitudes of the triaxial stresses are illustrated in Figure 2. C_0 is the cohesive strength, as shown in Figure 2c.

In addition, the radius of the nucleation zone is set to 2 km in this study, within which the shear force is slightly greater (0.5%) than the strength of the fault plane, enabling it to allow rupture nucleation.

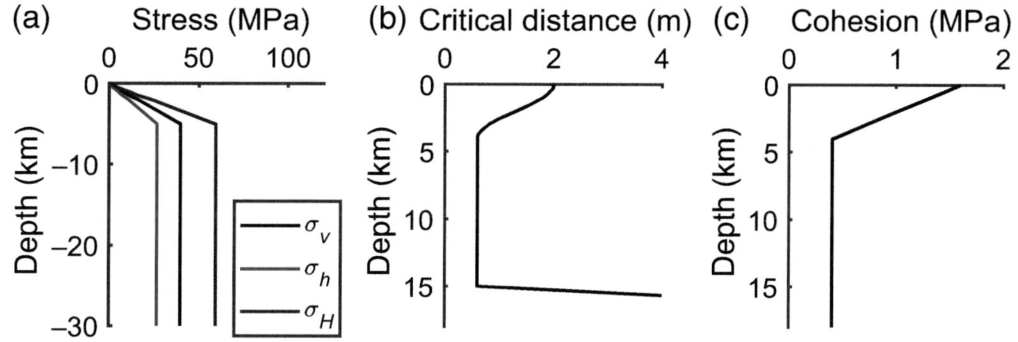

Figure 2. Distributions of (a) principal stresses, (b) the slip-weakening distance D_C, and (c) the cohesive strength C_0 varying with depth. The color version of this figure is available only in the electronic edition.

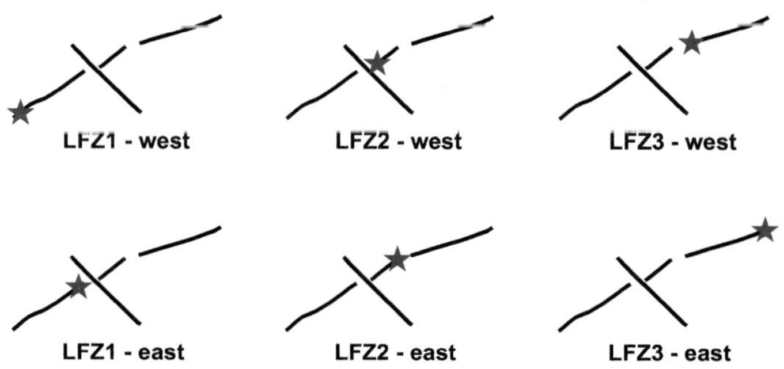

Figure 3. Black lines indicate the geometry of fault (LFZ + XJF). The six red stars indicate the assumed hypocenter locations. The color version of this figure is available only in the electronic edition.

Friction law

In our simulations, we utilize the slip-weakening friction law, which provides the relationship between stress and slip controlled by this friction law (Ida, 1972; Andrews, 1976a). This law states that the shear stress on the fault decreases linearly with increasing slip until it reaches a residual stress level beyond a critical slip-weakening distance (D_c). The fault strength can be obtained using the formula:

$$\tau_c = -\mu_f(s)\sigma_n. \quad (6)$$

Here, τ_c denotes the shear stress, μ_f is the friction coefficient, s is the fault slip, and σ_n is the effective normal stress.

Fault geometry

The submarine location of the LFZ prevents direct geological surveys and field outcrop studies and limits our understanding of its seismic potential. The most recent comprehensive survey was the 2015 onshore–offshore 3D deep seismic experiment in the PRE, led by the South China Sea Institute of Oceanology in collaboration with other institutions. Although these surveys have provided valuable constraints on velocity structure and regional tectonics, the fault geometry results are not well resolved due to limited spatial coverage and technical challenges (Lv *et al.*, 2018; Xiong *et al.*, 2018).

This study adopts the fault traces described in Zhang *et al.* (2019). The XJF and QGF, which are normal faults, dip southwest at ~75° and 45°, respectively. The LFZ is a right-lateral strike-slip fault trending southeast with a dip orientation of ~76° (Xu *et al.*, 2010). Its angle is not completely vertical, which seems to contradict Anderson's theory (Anderson, 1972), but similar cases do exist in reality. The southern San Andreas fault is the most extensively studied fault system in the world. Substantial evidence cited by Vavra *et al.* (2023) indicates that it is nonvertical and exhibits a distinct dip angle. The 2013 M_w 7.7 Balochistan earthquake also involved strike-slip activity on a thrust fault, one possible reason for which could be changes in the stress field (Avouac *et al.*, 2014). Observing the history of the LFZ, it is not difficult to see that it appears to have undergone stress field rotation during many tectonic periods. The nature of the fault was partially compressional shear in its early stages and tensile or tensile shear in its later stages (Zhong, 1987). It is precisely due to changes in the stress field that what was once a dip-slip fault has now evolved to favor strike-slip movement.

RESULTS

The primary objective of this study is to investigate the relationship between seismic rupture, epicenter location, and fault geometry. In the South China region, numerous intersecting faults are widely distributed, and the intersection points of these faults often serve as sites of seismicity (Xu *et al.*, 2006; Xia *et al.*, 2020). Thus, we set the epicenter locations at the intersection points, totaling six different positions, as illustrated in Figure 3.

Initially, we conducted separate analyses of the XJF and the QGF to ascertain the specific impacts of these two intersecting faults on the rupture patterns in the region. We employed multiple parameter sets (detailed in the supplemental material, available to this article) to model the fault systems of LFZ + XJF and LFZ + QGF. The results (Figs. S1 and S2) indicate that the hypocenter of the LFZ1 and LFZ2 easily triggers rupture of the XJF, whereas the QGF is relatively difficult to trigger. Even when rupture occurs in the QGF, it typically occurs under extreme conditions. The QGF is significantly less prone to rupture primarily due to its unfavorable geometric orientation within the current regional stress field. Our analysis shows that the QGF's dip angle results in substantially lower shear stress

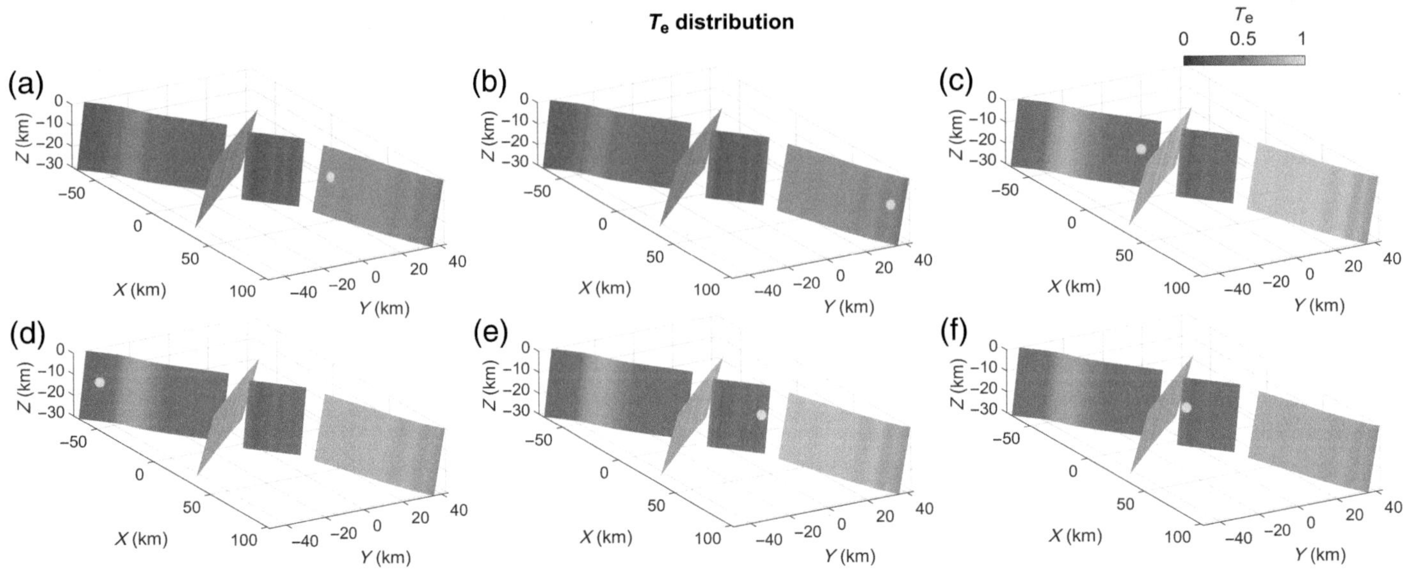

Figure 4. T_e spatial distribution of the six nucleation locations. (a,b) LFZ3 rupture under lower background stress. (c) LFZ1-east rupture under moderate background stress. (d–f) LFZ1-west, LFZ2-east, and LFZ2-west ruptures under higher background stress. The color version of this figure is available only in the electronic edition.

when projected from the regional stress tensor as shown in Figure S3. The difference in normal stress between the XJF and QGF is relatively small.

Herein, we introduce the shear stress ratio ($T_e = \frac{\tau_s - \tau_d}{\tau_p - \tau_d}$, τ_s is the initial shear stress, τ_d is the residual stress, and τ_p is the yielding stress), with a value range of 0–1, positively correlated with the likelihood of fault rupture. Specifically, the closer the T_e value is to 1, the more prone the fault is to rupture. It is primarily the lower resolved shear stress on the QGF (compared to the XJF) that leads to its lower T_e values, indicating reduced rupture potential. Therefore, the subsequent focus of this study will be on the interaction mechanisms between the LFZ and XJF.

By gradually decreasing the λ value, we enhance the magnitude of the regional effective triaxial stress field, further altering the shear stress on the fault plane. Simultaneously, we adjust the friction coefficient to change the fault strength, while keeping λ constant. These variations in μ_s do affect T_e values, though the changes remain relatively small. We observe the rupture conditions at the six nucleation locations. Each parameter set is listed in Table 1, along with the rupture status of its nucleation locations. Check marks denote the parameters of the events discussed in this study, whereas crosses represent instances where no rupture occurred or the magnitude was too small to be considered.

We also plotted six spatial distributions of T_e across the fault system in Figure 4, which facilitates further analysis of the rupture process. The T_e distribution clearly shows that LFZ3 and XJF have the highest T_e values compared to LFZ1 and LFZ2, making them most susceptible to rupture under appropriate conditions.

Lower background stress

Under the lower stress condition, we were able to initiate rupture only on LFZ3-west and LFZ3-east, as illustrated in Figure 5a,b, with no ruptures occurring at other locations. The T_e value on the LFZ3 fault is the highest within the fault system, rendering it most susceptible to triggering. Even with a relatively lower stress level, rupture can occur at the fault source. Consequently, this segment poses a higher seismic hazard.

TABLE 1
Nucleation, Stress (λ), and Friction (μ_s and μ_d): Assumptions and Parameter Choices

Stress Level	λ	μ_s	μ_d	LFZ1-West	LFZ1-East	LFZ2-West	LFZ2-East	LFZ3-West	LFZ3-East
Lower	0.7	0.5	0.2	✗	✗	✗	✗	✓	✓
Moderate	0.5	0.41	0.2	✗	✓	✗	✗		
Higher	0.4	0.43	0.2	✓		✗	✗		
		0.42	0.2			✗	✓		
		0.44	0.18			✓			

✓ denotes the parameter of the event discussed in this study, ✗ represents instance where no rupture occurred or the magnitude was too small to be considered.

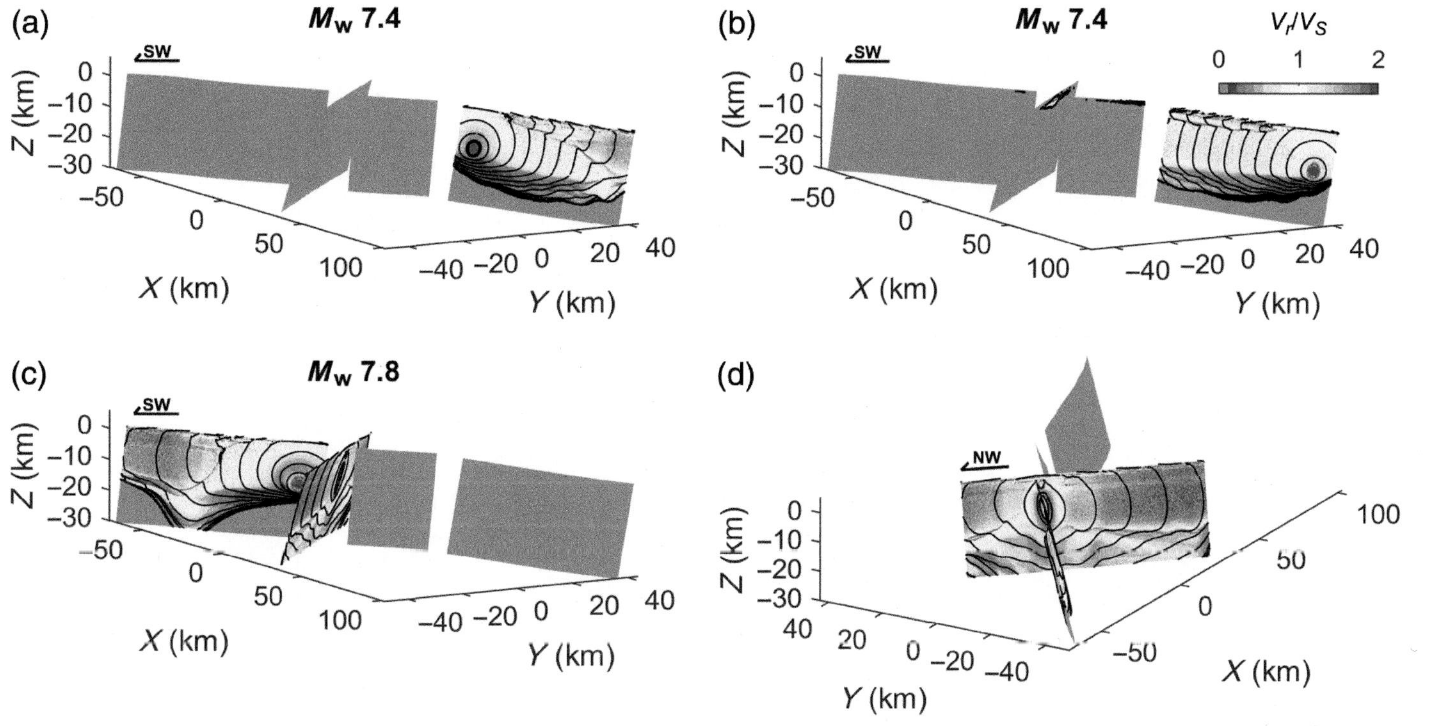

Figure 5. Under the lower stress condition, the rupture speed distribution, and rupture time contour every 2 s for earthquakes triggered by (a) LFZ3-west and (b) LFZ3-east. Under the moderate stress condition, the rupture speed distribution, and rupture time contour every 2 s for earthquakes triggered by LFZ1-east of (c) front view and (d) side view. The color version of this figure is available only in the electronic edition.

The red portions in the figures, where V_r (rupture velocity) $>V_S$ (*S*-wave velocity), indicate supershear rupture. In Figure 5a,b, one can see that some minor slip is present in other areas, particularly in the upper section of the XJF. However, fault sources on LFZ3 are less likely to trigger ruptures on XJF entirely.

Moderate background stress

Under the moderate background stress condition, rupture of LFZ1-east was observed, as shown in Figure 5c,d. Because of the relatively high T_e value on the XJF fault, XJF was also dynamically triggered to rupture at this time.

During the initial stage of LFZ1-east rupture, the free surface was highly susceptible to the induction of supershear phenomena. When the rupture propagated to the bend in LFZ1, this bent structure significantly facilitated the rupture propagation, causing the rupture to further extend into the lower part of the bent region.

Higher background stress

Under the higher background stress condition, we were able to nucleate rupture from three additional locations, each with distinct friction parameters as detailed in Table 1. Initially, rupture was observed in LFZ1-west, as illustrated in Figure 6a,b. Here, to compare the rupture processes between LFZ1-west and LFZ1-east, we simulated the rupture of LFZ1-east under identical stress conditions, with the results presented in Figure 6c,d.

During the rupture processes at both locations, XJF also ruptured due to secondary nucleation induced by a transient stop phase as the rupture propagated to the fault tips. LFZ1-west, located at the west boundary of the whole fault system, exhibited rupture propagation from west to east. Following the complete rupture of LFZ1, nucleation in XJF occurred almost immediately. In contrast, under the same stress conditions, the rupture in XJF initiated ~20 s after the complete rupture of LFZ1 in the case of LFZ1-east. This difference may manifest in actual earthquakes where the relative positions of the hypocenter and intersecting faults significantly influence the triggering time of rupture on the intersecting fault.

The peak ground velocity (PGV) distributions resulting from the two rupture models also exhibited differences, as illustrated in Figure 7. Specifically, Figure 7a represents the PGV distribution for LFZ1-west, with a more extensive radiation range and continuity between LFZ1 and XJF. In contrast, Figure 7b shows a segmented PGV distribution between LFZ1 and XJF, despite the high rupture velocity at the ends of XJF and LFZ1, with relatively limited area of strong ground motion. Therefore, the two rupture patterns also affect the continuity of PGV distribution.

In LFZ2-east, the reduction of the static friction coefficient (μ_s) weakens the fault's frictional strength (associated with an increased T_e value), thereby facilitating rupture initiation. In addition, compared to LFZ2-west, LFZ2-east has a longer acceleration distance (Hu *et al.*, 2016), which promotes higher energy accumulation and corresponds to a faster rupture rate,

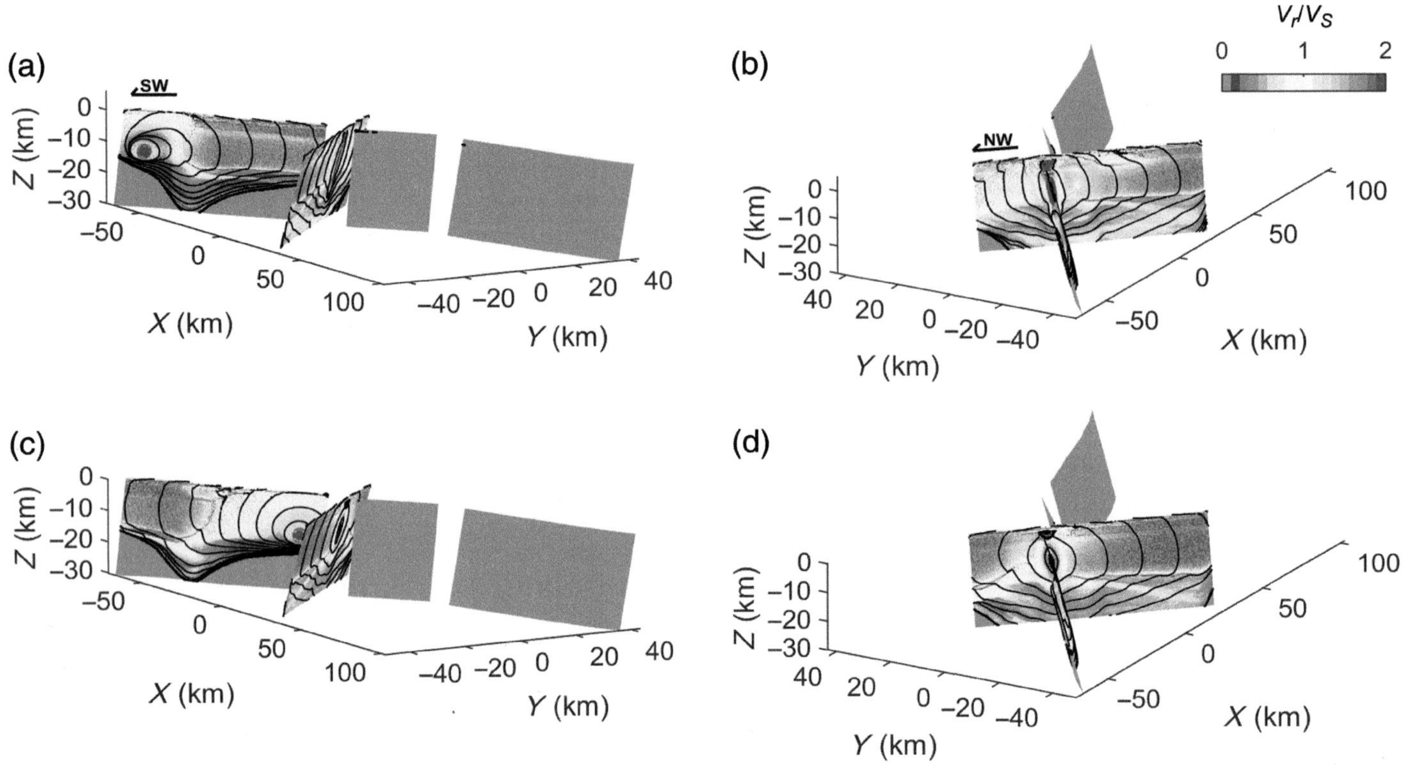

Figure 6. Under the higher stress condition ($\mu_s = 0.43$, $\mu_d = 0.2$), the rupture speed distribution, and rupture time contour every 2 s for earthquakes triggered by LFZ1-west of (a) front view and (b) side view and LFZ1-east of (c) front view and (d) side view. The color version of this figure is available only in the electronic edition.

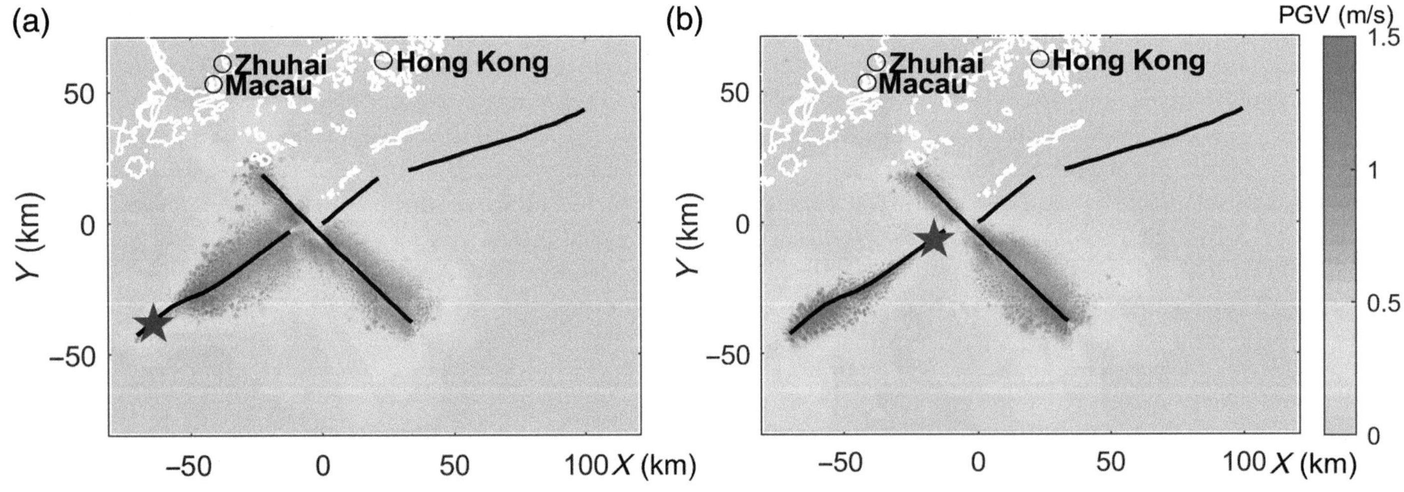

Figure 7. Map view of the PGV triggered by (a) LFZ1-west and (b) LFZ1-east. The white lines are coastlines. The color version of this figure is available only in the electronic edition.

potentially sufficient to trigger rupture along the XJF, as shown in Figure 8.

Under the same stress level, we also simulated the rupture scenario of LFZ1-west, with the results presented in Figure 9a. It is worth mentioning that when simulating the LFZ scenario without XJF, rupture was only observed to propagate on LFZ1, as shown in Figure 9b. In other words, including XJF and its stress modulation effect allowed the rupture to extend to LFZ3, increasing the rupture area. This further demonstrates the significant impact of intersecting faults during the rupture process. Their inclusion

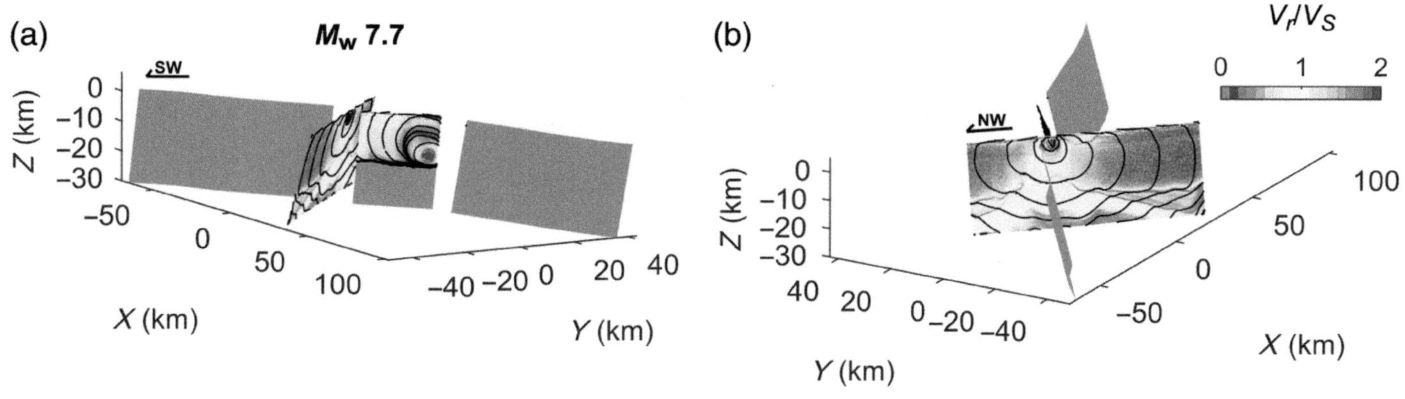

Figure 8. Under the higher stress condition ($\mu_s = 0.42$, $\mu_d = 0.2$), the rupture speed distribution, and rupture time contour every 2 s for earthquakes triggered by LFZ2-east of (a) front view and (b) side view. The color version of this figure is available only in the electronic edition.

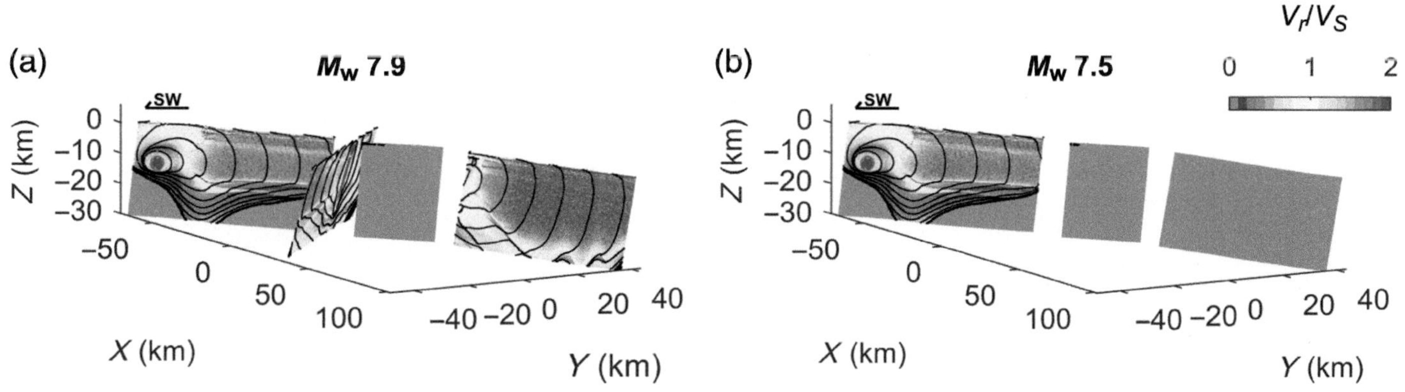

Figure 9. Under the higher stress condition ($\mu_s = 0.42$, $\mu_d = 0.2$), the rupture speed distribution, and rupture time contour every 2 s for earthquakes triggered by LFZ1-west of (a) LFZ + XJF and (b) LFZ. The color version of this figure is available only in the electronic edition.

facilitates rupture on the fault and enables further rupture on other faults. Therefore, identifying intersecting faults is crucial because they can connect distant stepover faults.

In contrast, LFZ2-west is relatively difficult to rupture due to its lower T_e value compared to other subfaults, requiring more favorable conditions. Consequently, LFZ2 is not only smaller in scale, but also less hazard prone compared to other faults. Even if rupture occurs at this location, it is unlikely to extend to the XJF. By altering the friction parameters to achieve a larger stress drop, the rupture was induced in LFZ2-west, but it remained confined to the fault itself, as shown in Figure S4.

DISCUSSION

Influence of fault-dip direction on the nucleation position (depth) of cross-faults

This study compares scenarios with different triggering locations of the XJF in Figures 5c,d and 8. The results indicate that the rupture initiated by the source location on LFZ1 nucleates at an intermediate depth of the XJF, whereas the rupture initiated by the seismic source location on LFZ2 nucleates in the shallow part of the XJF. In this study, the orientation of the XJF is set to southwest, but there is also literature indicating that its orientation may be northeast (Dong and Chen, 2017). Therefore, this study simulates the scenario earthquakes where the XJF is oriented northeast, as shown in Figure 10. Correspondingly, when the XJF is oriented northeast, the rupture initiated by the seismic source location on LFZ2 nucleates at an intermediate depth of the XJF, whereas the rupture initiated by the source location on LFZ1 nucleates in the shallow part of the XJF but fails to propagate fully. This result is opposite to the case when the XJF is oriented southwest. This is easily discernible, in summary, the rupture initiates at the location on the XJF that is proximal to LFZ1.

Comparing Figure 5c,d with Figure 10b, a significant difference is observed: the XJF oriented southwest undergoes complete rupture. In contrast, the XJF oriented northeast does not rupture, resulting in a huge difference in the rupture area.

Meanwhile, comparing Figure 8 with Figure 10a, although both undergo complete rupture on the XJF, the PGV results differ (see Fig. 11). The deeper nucleation position of the

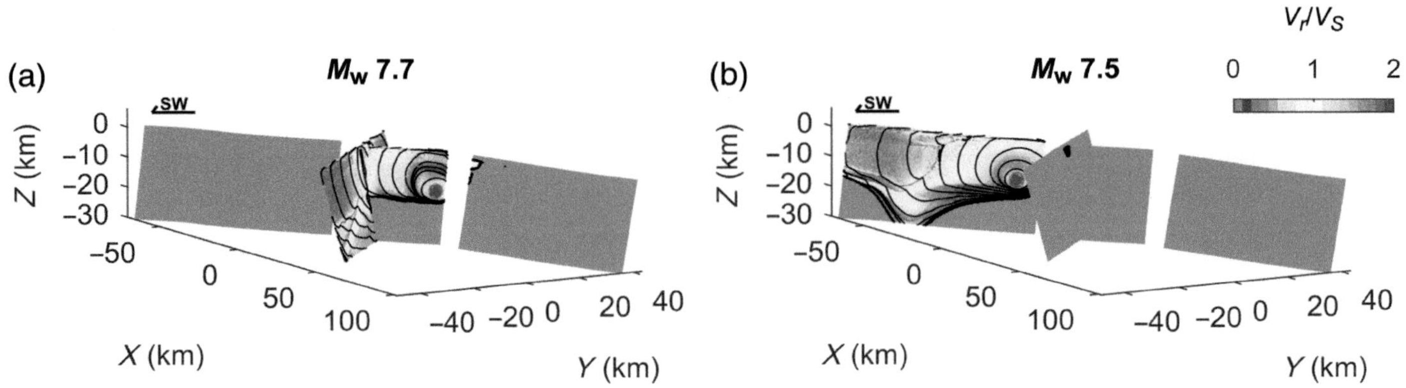

Figure 10. Rupture speed distribution and rupture time contour every 2 s for earthquakes triggered by (a) LFZ2-east (the higher background stress, corresponding to Fig. 8) and (b) LFZ1-east (the moderate background stress, corresponding to Fig. 5c,d). The XJF dips toward the northeast. The color version of this figure is available only in the electronic edition.

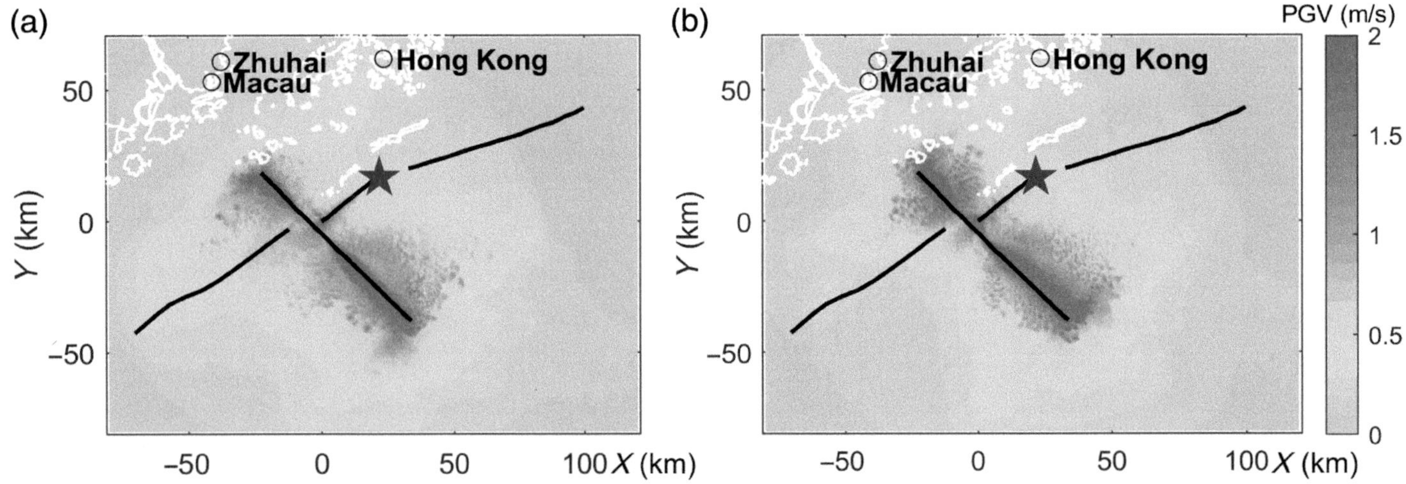

Figure 11. Map view of the PGV triggered by LFZ2-east from ground-motion simulation using rupture models in (a) the XJF dips toward the southwest (Fig. 9) and (b) the XJF dips toward the northeast (Fig. 11a). The white lines are coastlines. The color version of this figure is available only in the electronic edition.

XJF corresponds to a larger PGV value, indicating that the XJF oriented northeast poses a more severe hazard. Therefore, although determining the relative position between the seismic source and the cross-faults is important, the dip direction of the cross-faults also plays a decisive role in whether the cross-faults will rupture. Specifically, when the rupture initiation point on the receiving fault on the cross-faults is deeper, its impact range on the ground will be more extensive.

The dip direction of the intersecting faults affects the rupture process, influencing whether intersecting faults rupture and the strength of their rupture velocities after rupturing.

Effect of the distance of the nucleation location and cross-faults (XJF)

Rupture propagation onto the XJF requires that the shear stress exceeds its frictional strength. However, because the XJF is being dynamically triggered, the rupture process involves not only the background shear stress, but also the dynamic stress perturbations generated during the source rupture propagation. Consequently, in addition to being influenced by the background stress field and the fault's strength, rupture propagation onto the XJF is also affected by the hypocenter location. The XJF ruptures if the combined background and dynamic stresses surpass its strength.

The rupture sequences of LFZ1-west and LFZ1-east are different (Fig. 6). The rupture process associated with LFZ1-west begins at the west side of LFZ1, subsequently propagates toward the termination of the LFZ1 fault, and directly continues onto the XJF (Fig. 12a,b). The rupture process associated with LFZ1-east initiates at the east side of LFZ1 and propagates toward the west side of the LFZ1 fault. A delay of more than 20 s occurs before the XJF fully ruptures (Fig. 12c,d).

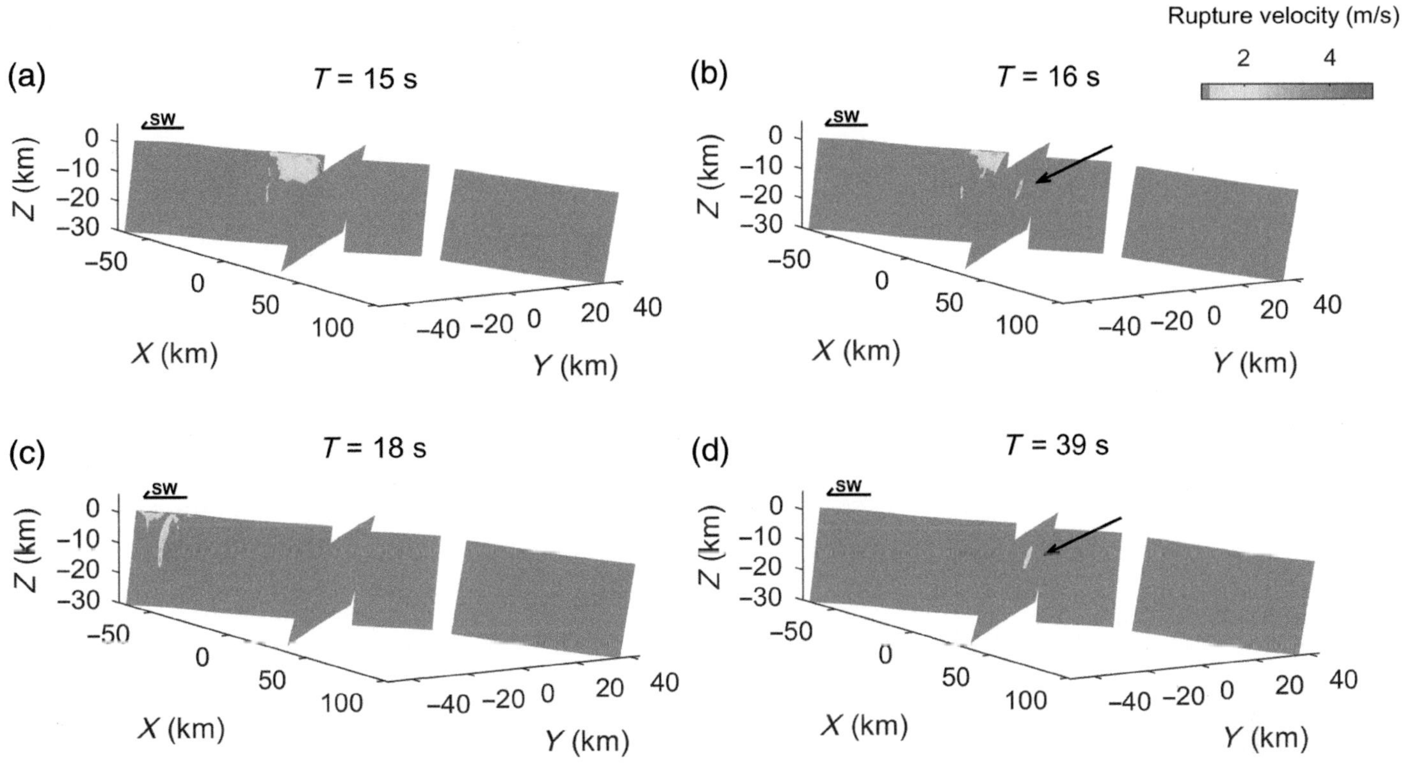

Figure 12. Snapshots of (a) LFZ1-west, T = 15 s, (b) LFZ1-west, T = 16 s, (c) LFZ1-east, T = 18 s, and (d) LFZ1-east, T = 39 s. The black arrows indicate the rupture nucleation point on the XJF. The color version of this figure is available only in the electronic edition.

We consider the observed 20 s delay in the LFZ1-east rupture scenario to be a physical phenomenon. To rule out numerical artifacts, we conducted high-resolution simulations by refining the mesh size from the original range (0.58–8 km, ~800,000 elements) to a finer resolution (0.3–4 km, ~5,800,000 elements). The results remained consistent, with the delay preserved (Fig. S5).

The delay arises from dynamic stress interactions between LFZ1-east and the cross-fault (XJF). Initially, LFZ1-east lacks sufficient energy to propagate unilaterally to the right. Upon reaching the fault edge, seismic waves reflect back to the opposite side, creating a stress perturbation. The XJF rupture initiates after ~20 s of stress wave propagation from LFZ1, with full nucleation achieved at ~40 s when the reflected wave energy generates sufficient transient stress perturbations. During this interval, the stress field undergoes gradual adjustments until shear stress exceeds locally shear strength at the XJF and rupture is triggered there (Fig. 13c,d). As can be observed in Figure 13, it corresponds to the initiation point of rupture on the XJF fault after being triggered. Near the 40 s mark, this location begins to exhibit clear rupture propagation and slip, accompanied by a sharp drop in shear stress following its release.

Furthermore, there were notable differences in the rupture patterns on XJF between LFZ1-west and LFZ1-east. The rupture in the XJF initiated by LFZ1-west was a direct propagation from LFZ1. Because the XJF is inclined relative to LFZ1, the rupture propagation on the XJF was asymmetric, exhibiting distinct rupture velocities on either side of the XJF, as shown in Figure 6b, with significant velocity differences observed between the west and east sides of the nucleation location of the XJF. This is primarily because the XJF is relatively far from the epicenter, resulting in an excessively long acceleration distance, and the angle between LFZ1 and the XJF plays a more significant role.

Conversely, the rupture on the XJF triggered by LFZ1-east occurred after the LFZ1 rupture completed, due to stress redistribution, and propagated without a preferred direction, as depicted in Figure 6d. Finally, it is evident that the rupture velocity is higher in LFZ1-east. When the epicenter is closer to the XJF, the energy imparted to the XJF is greater, leading to a correspondingly higher velocity. The initial rupture energy at the epicenter is insufficient to initiate rupture on the XJF. After the energy reflects back from LFZ1, rupture on the XJF begins, which is why the onset time of rupture on the XJF is almost twice the propagation time on LFZ1.

The rupture conditions on both sides of LFZ1 reveal the influence of the relationship between seismic sources and cross-faults locations on rupture patterns. Although ruptures occur on the XJF, there are differences in their trigger times and effects. The rupture propagates to the fault end and spreads to adjacent faults, and can cause a cascade of larger and more destructive earthquakes. Figure 14 illustrates the moment rate functions for LFZ1-west and LFZ1-east. In

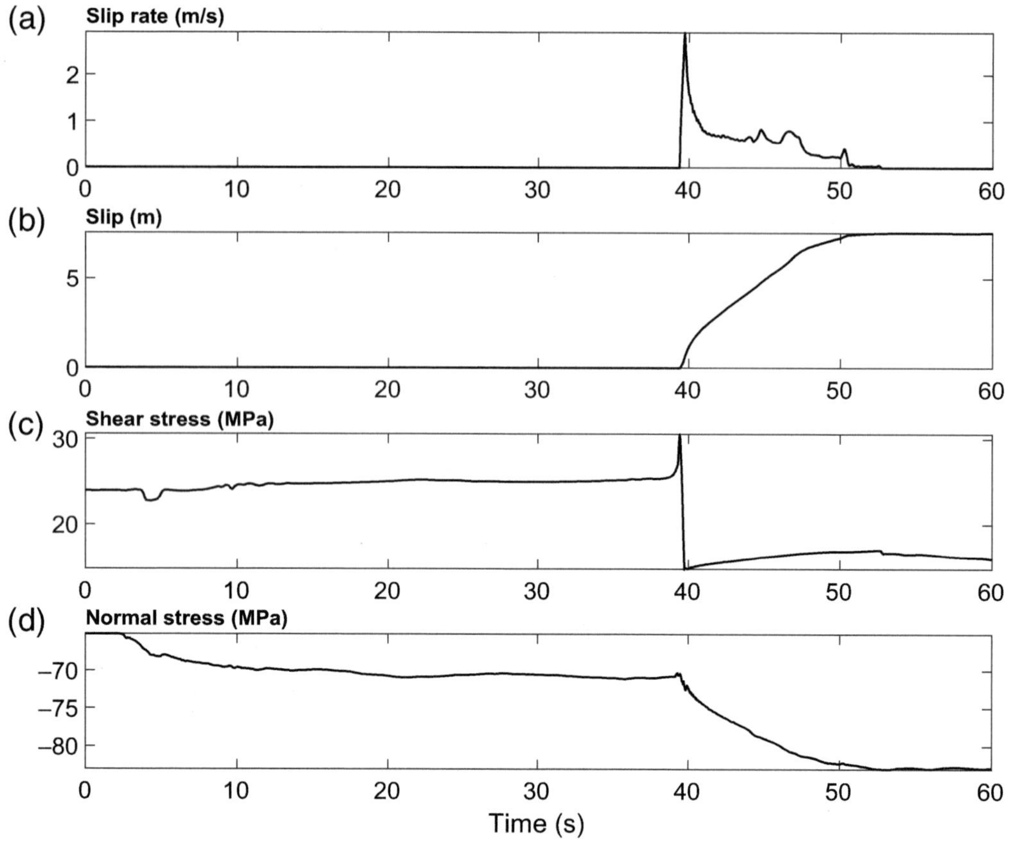

Figure 13. (a) Slip rate, (b) slip, (c) shear stress, and (d) normal stress at the rupture initiation point on the receiving fault of the XJF.

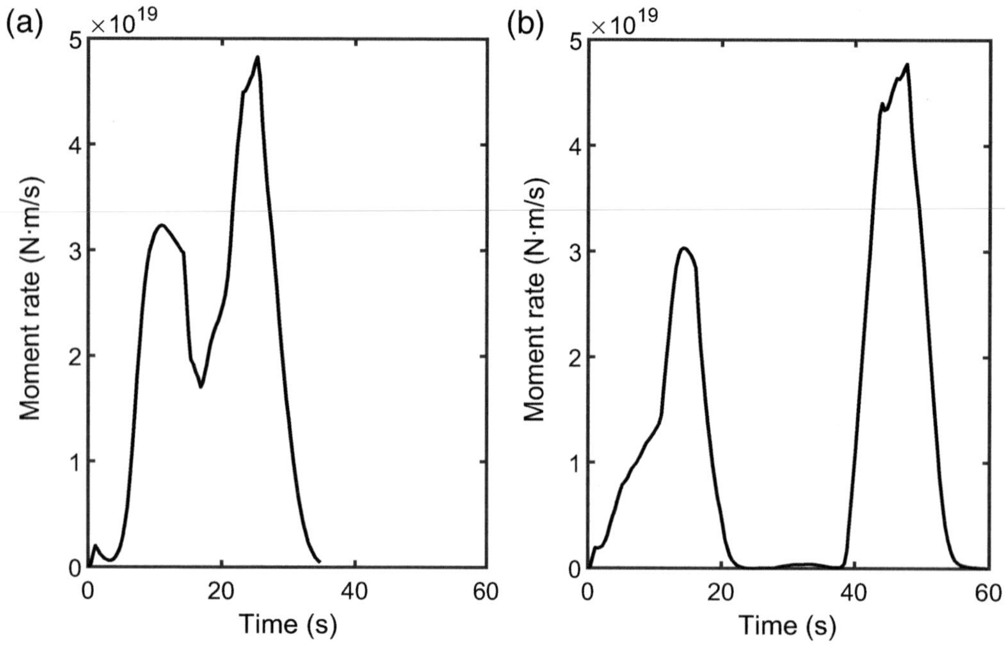

Figure 14. Moment rate function of (a) LFZ1-west (Fig. 6a,b) and (b) LFZ1-east (Fig. 6c,d).

other words, if the moment rate function indicates the presence of a cascade earthquake phenomenon, one should also consider the possibility of corresponding scenarios involving intersecting faults and their epicentral locations, as discussed in this study.

Analysis of nonintersecting and intersecting cross-faults characteristics and their impact on disaster propagation

The study mentions two types of cross-faults. Nonintersecting cross-faults (XJF) exhibit unique crossing and stepover characteristics. Specifically, the stepover distance acts as a physical barrier that hinders crack propagation.

On the other hand, the crossing characteristic involves a change in stress direction, which holds significant implications in geological structures. Taking the present study as an example, if only the LFZ, roughly parallel to the coastline, exists, its impact on coastal areas may be relatively limited. However, introducing nonintersecting cross-faults significantly affects the likelihood of rupture propagation, altering the area affected by strong ground shaking, thus highlighting the importance of monitoring and assessing such faults.

In contrast, the characteristics of intersecting cross-faults (QGF) differ. In these faults, the influence of the stepover distance is negligible, with the primary focus being on the rupture effects caused by the crossing action. Based on these differences, nonintersecting and intersecting cross-faults

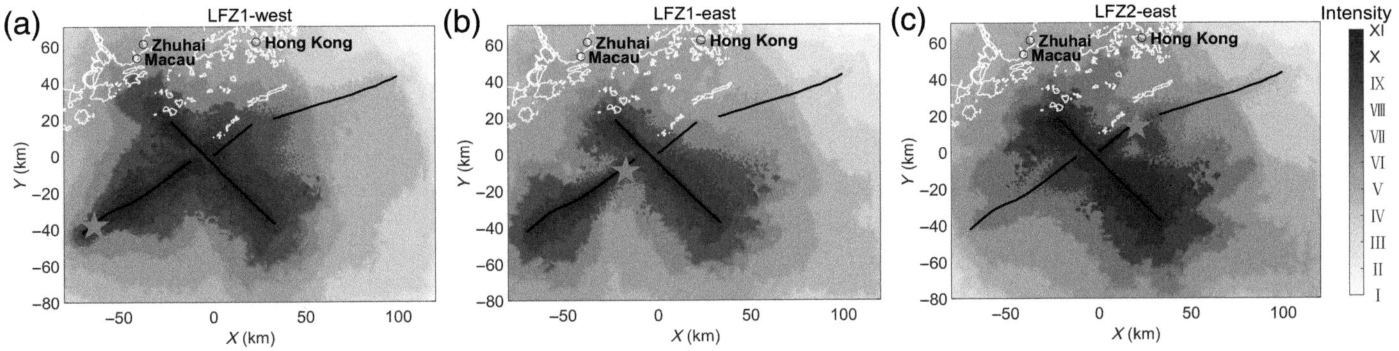

Figure 15. Intensity for the scenario earthquake triggered by (a) LFZ1-east, (b) LFZ1-east, and (c) LFZ2-east. The white lines are coastlines. The color version of this figure is available only in the electronic edition.

may be discussed separately as independent factors in numerical simulations of rupture dynamics.

This preliminary perspective guides subsequent research to further refine and validate the specific applications and impact mechanisms of the two cross-fault types in seismic hazard models.

Potential impact on land (intensity)

The XJF has a significant impact on the LFZ. Among the six simulated seismic source locations, LFZ1-west, LFZ1-east, and LFZ2-east all caused ruptures on the XJF, as shown in Figure 15. We convert PGV to intensity according to the 2020 Chinese seismic intensity scale (Text S1), which provides empirical relationships between PGV and intensity.

By observing the PGV in these three scenarios, it is evident that the coastal areas near Macao are significantly affected. Figure 15a corresponds to an intensity of VII near the coastal areas of Macao and Hong Kong, decreasing to intensity VI closer to the land. Figure 15b,c corresponds to an intensity of VI in the offshore areas, decreasing to intensity V closer to the land. It is noteworthy when the intensity reaches above V.

CONCLUSION

We present dynamic rupture simulations for six nucleation locations of LFZ. The potential for rupturing multiple faults varies among different source locations: LFZ3 can rupture under lower stress conditions, LFZ1 requires moderate to higher stress levels for rupture initiation, and LFZ2 poses more significant challenges, demanding the higher stress field. LFZ1 holds particular significance due to its large scale and proximity to the XJF.

The maximum earthquake magnitude recorded in the LFZ region has reached M_w 7.5. In this study, the simulated earthquake magnitudes range between M_w 7.5 and 8.0. In the simulated earthquake scenarios, the rupture magnitude reaches M_w 7.5 when LFZ1 ruptures alone completely, whereas the rupture magnitude for LFZ2 is M_w 7.2 and for LFZ3 is M_w 7.4. Therefore, in most cases, earthquakes exceeding M_w 7.5 typically involve the intersecting fault (XJF). This suggests that considering the influence of intersecting faults on the LFZ is crucial.

In addition to the two cross-faults (XJF and QGF) analyzed in this study, the surrounding area of the LFZ contains numerous secondary faults, including buried faults and minor cross-faults, complete geometries for which cannot be resolved. Stress concentrations at fault junctions enable rupture jumps between cross-faults, thereby facilitating the occurrence of multifault ruptures. Further investigation into the region's fault geometry and other large-scale intersecting faults is essential.

Given that the LFZ is located in shallow nearshore areas, its earthquake impacts will dominate the onshore seismic hazard compared to distant offshore faults in deeper waters. This study employs a source dynamics rupture process method to simulate several rupture possibilities and their impacts on LFZ + XJF. However, to investigate the potential impact of tsunami waves further, tsunami wave simulations will be conducted in subsequent work.

DATA AND RESOURCES

The Southern California Earthquake Center (SCEC)/U.S. Geological Survey (USGS) Spontaneous Rupture Code Verification Project website is available at http://strike.scec.org/cvws/. The fault surface traces are modified from Xiong *et al.* (2018) and Zhang *et al.* (2019). The *P*-wave velocity model is from Wang *et al.* (2021). The figures were generated using MATLAB (http://www.mathworks.com/products/matlab). Both websites were last accessed in October 2025. The supplemental material includes two texts and five figures. Text S1 summarizes the empirical relationships from the 2020 Chinese Seismic Intensity Scale used to convert peak ground velocity (PGV) to seismic intensity in this study. Text S2 details the methodology for estimating the maximum resolved frequency in the study, based on the mesh discretization and wave propagation criteria. Figure S1 displays the rupture speed distribution and rupture time contours for the Littoral fault zone (LFZ) + Xijiang fault (XJF) system under the parameters $\lambda = 0.2$, $\mu_s = 0.5$, $\mu_d = 0.2$. Figure S2 shows the corresponding rupture speed distribution and rupture time contours for the LFZ + QGF system under the same parameter set. Figure S3 presents the spatial distribution of T_e, shear stress, and normal stress across the combined fault system comprising the

LFZ, XJF, and Qiao-Guishan fault (QGF). Figure S4 illustrates the rupture speed distribution and rupture time contours every 2 s for earthquakes triggered by LFZ2-west. Figure S5 contains wavefield simulation snapshots using a refined mesh discretization.

DECLARATION OF COMPETING INTERESTS

The authors acknowledge that there are no conflicts of interest recorded.

ACKNOWLEDGMENTS

The authors thank Associate Editor Martin Galis and two reviewers for their careful reviews and constructive comments that improved the clarity and quality of this article. The authors sincerely thank the developers of the GMSH software (Geuzaine and Remacle, 2009) for their powerful support in generating 3D finite-element meshes, which greatly facilitated our research. The simulation is supported by the Center for Computational Science and Engineering at the Southern University of Science and Technology. This work is supported by the National Natural Science Foundation of China (Grant Number 42494864), National Key Research and Development Program of China (2022 YFC3003504), National Key R&D Program of China (2023YFC 3007404), Guangdong Provincial Key Laboratory of Geophysical High-resolution Imaging Technology (2022B1212010002), and Shenzhen Key Laboratory of Deep Offshore Oil and Gas Exploration Technology (Grant Number ZDSYS20190902093007855).

REFERENCES

Anderson, E. (1972). *The Dynamics of Faulting and Dyke Formation with Applications to Britain*, Hafner Publishing Company, New York, New York.

Andrews, D. J. (1976a). Rupture propagation with finite stress in antiplane strain, *J. Geophys. Res.* **81,** no. 20, 3575–3582.

Andrews, D. J. (1976b). Rupture velocity of plane strain shear cracks, *J. Geophys. Res.* **81,** no. 32, 5679–5687.

Avouac, J.-P., F. Ayoub, S. Wei, J.-P. Ampuero, L. Meng, S. Leprince, R. Jolivet, Z. Duputel, and D. Helmberger (2014). The 2013, m_w 7.7 Balochistan earthquake, energetic strike-slip reactivation of a thrust fault, *Earth Planet. Sci. Lett.* **391,** 128–134.

Brietzke, G. B., A. Cochard, and H. Igel (2007). Dynamic rupture along bimaterial interfaces in 3D, *Geophys. Res. Lett.* **34,** no. 11, doi: 10.1029/2007GL029908.

Brocher, T. M. (2005). Empirical relations between elastic wavespeeds and density in the earth's crust, *Bull. Seismol. Soc. Am.* **95,** no. 6, 2081–2092.

Chen, E., and Y. Huang (1984). An overview of nineteen major earthquakes in south china and the seismic zone along the northern continental margin of the south china sea, *South China J. Seismol.* **4,** no. 1, 11–32.

Das, S., and K. Aki (1977). A numerical study of two-dimensional spontaneous rupture propagation, *Geophys. J. Int.* **50,** no. 3, 643–668.

de la Puente, J., M. Käser, M. Dumbser, and H. Igel (2007). An arbitrary high-order discontinuous Galerkin method for elastic waves on unstructured meshes - IV. Anisotropy, *Geophys. J. Int.* **169,** no. 3, 1210–1228.

Ding, Y., and X. Huang (1998). Prediction of future seismic hazard in the pearl river delta region, *South China J. Seismol.* **18,** no. 1, 57–64.

Dong, H., and Y. Chen (2017). Re-visiting the quaternary activity of Xijiang fault from Sanshui to Modaomen, *J. Trop. Oceanogr.* **36,** no. 2, 26–32.

Duan, B. (2010). Role of initial stress rotations in rupture dynamics and ground motion: A case study with implications for the Wenchuan earthquake, *J. Geophys. Res.* **115,** no. B5, doi: 10.1029/2009JB006750.

Dumbser, M., and M. Käser (2006). An arbitrary high-order discontinuous Galerkin method for elastic waves on unstructured meshes —II. The three-dimensional isotropic case, *Geophys. J. Int.* **167,** no. 1, 319–336.

Fialko, Y., and Z. Jin (2021). Simple shear origin of the cross-faults ruptured in the 2019 Ridgecrest earthquake sequence, *Nature Geosci.* **14,** no. 7, 513–518.

Geuzaine, C., and J.-F. Remacle (2009). Gmsh: A 3-d finite element mesh generator with built-in pre- and post-processing facilities, *Int. J. Numer. Methods Eng.* **79,** no. 11, 1309–1331.

Harris, R. A., M. Barall, B. Aagaard, S. Ma, D. Roten, K. Olsen, B. Duan, D. Liu, B. Luo, K. Bai, *et al.* (2018). A suite of exercises for verifying dynamic earthquake rupture codes, *Seismol. Res. Lett.* **89,** no. 3, 1146–1162.

Harris, R. A., M. Barall, R. Archuleta, E. Dunham, B. Aagaard, J. P. Ampuero, H. Bhat, V. Cruz-Atienza, L. Dalguer, P. Dawson, *et al.* (2009). The SCEC/USGS dynamic earthquake rupture code verification exercise, *Seismol. Res. Lett.* **80,** no. 1, 119–126.

Hauksson, E., L. M. Jones, K. Hutton, and D. Eberhart-Phillips (1993). The 1992 landers earthquake sequence: Seismological observations, *J. Geophys. Res.* **98,** no. B11, 19,835–19,858.

Heinecke, A., A. Breuer, S. Rettenberger, M. Bader, A.-A. Gabriel, C. Pelties, A. Bode, W. Barth, X.-K. Liao, K. Vaidyanathan, *et al.* (2014). Petascale high order dynamic rupture earthquake simulations on heterogeneous supercomputers, *SC '14: Proc. of the International Conf. for High Performance Computing, Networking, Storage and Analysis*, pp. 3–14.

Hesthaven, J. S., and T. Warburton (2008). Nodal discontinuous Galerkin methods: Algorithms, analysis, and applications, Number 54 in *Texts in Applied Mathematics*, Springer, New York.

Hu, F., Z. Zhang, and X. Chen (2016). Investigation of earthquake jump distance for strike-slip step overs based on 3-d dynamic rupture simulations in an elastic half-space, *J. Geophys. Res.* **121,** no. 2, 994–1006.

Hui, G., S. Li, L. Guo, P. Wang, B. Liu, G. Wang, X. Li, and I. Somerville (2021). A review of geohazards on the northern continental margin of the south china sea, *Earth Sci. Rev.* **220,** 103,733.

Ida, Y. (1972). Cohesive force across the tip of a longitudinal-shear crack and griffith's specific surface energy, *J. Geophys. Res.* **77,** no. 20, 3796–3805.

Jia, L., X. Ma, J. Jiang, J. Lei, Y. Wei, J. Mao, and F. Hao (2023). Dynamic variation characteristics of in-situ stress in the 1605 Qiongshan m $7\frac{1}{2}$ earthquake area and its implications to the Dong Zhaigang subsidence, northeastern Hainan island, china, *J. Geomech.* **29,** no. 3, 339–354.

Kang, Y., X. Yang, X. Chen, G. Chen, and S. Zheng (2008). Inversion of stress field in Guangdong and its adjacent area, *Acta Seismol. Sinica* **30,** no. 1, 59–66.

Käser, M., and M. Dumbser (2006). An arbitrary high-order discontinuous Galerkin method for elastic waves on unstructured meshes - I. The two-dimensional isotropic case with external source terms, *Geophys. J. Int.* **166,** no. 2, 855–877.

Käser, M., M. Dumbser, J. de la Puente, and H. Igel (2007). An arbitrary high-order discontinuous Galerkin method for elastic waves on unstructured meshes - iii. Viscoelastic attenuation, *Geophys. J. Int.* **168,** no. 1, 224–242.

Lei, T., and H. Lv (1985). The seismogenic structure of the great overseas earthquake in Quanzhou in 1604, *J. Appl. Oceanogr.* **4,** no. 2, 171–178.

Liang, H., K. Zhang, Z. Li, Z. Chen, G. Hui, P. Huang, Q. Tian, Y. Tang, C. Chen, Y. Zhang, *et al.* (2023). Temporally varied coastal uplift rates north of the littoral fault zone since the late quaternary in the northern south china sea: Insights from the wave-cut platform and cosmogenic exposure dating, *Front. Earth Sci.* **10,** 1,026,181.

Liu, Y. (1986). Discussion on the basic characteristics and activity of the Nan'ao fault zone and the littoral fault zone, *South China J. Seismol.* **6,** no. 3, 1–8.

Lozos, J. C. (2022). Dynamic rupture modeling of coseismic interactions on orthogonal strike-slip faults, *Geophys. Res. Lett.* **49,** no. 5, e2021GL097585, doi: 10.1029/2021GL097585.

Lv, Z., X. Qiu, J. Lv, H. Huang, X. Ye, S. Wang, L. Wang, and X. Wang (2018). Crustal structure beneath the east side of pearl river estuary from onshore-offshore seismic experiment, *Int. Geol. Rev.* **60,** 1–13.

Madariaga, R. (1976). Dynamics of an expanding circular fault, *Bull. Seismol. Soc. Am.* **66,** no. 3, 639–666.

Möller, T., and W. Friederich (2019). Simulation of elastic wave propagation across fractures using a nodal discontinuous Galerkin method—Theory, implementation and validation, *Geophys. J. Int.* **219,** no. 3, 1900–1914.

Oglesby, D. D., and P. M. Mai (2012). Fault geometry, rupture dynamics and ground motion from potential earthquakes on the north Anatolian fault under the sea of Marmara: Rupture dynamics on the north Anatolian fault, *Geophys. J. Int.* **188,** no. 3, 1071–1087.

Olsen, K. B., R. Madariaga, and R. J. Archuleta (1997). Three-dimensional dynamic simulation of the 1992 landers earthquake, *Science* **278,** no. 5339, 834–838.

Pelties, C., A. Gabriel, and J. P. Ampuero (2013). Verification of an ader-dg method for complex dynamic rupture problems, *Geosci. Model Dev.* **7,** 847–866.

Powell, R. E., R. J. Weldon, and J. C. Matti (1993). *The San Andreas Fault System: Displacement, Palinspastic Reconstruction, and Geologic Evolution*, Geological Society of America, Boulder, Colorado.

Ross, Z. E., B. Idini, Z. Jia, O. L. Stephenson, M. Zhong, X. Wang, Z. Zhan, M. Simons, E. J. Fielding, S.-H. Yun, *et al.* (2019). Hierarchical interlocked orthogonal faulting in the 2019 Ridgecrest earthquake sequence, *Science* **366,** no. 6463, 346–351.

Tago, J., V. M. Cruz-Atienza, J. Virieux, V. Etienne, and F. J. Sánchez-Sesma (2012). A 3D hp-adaptive discontinuous Galerkin method for modeling earthquake dynamics, *J. Geophys. Res.* **117,** no. B9, doi: 10.1029/2012JB009313.

Uphoff, C., S. Rettenberger, M. Bader, E. H. Madden, T. Ulrich, S. Wollherr, and A.-A. Gabriel (2017). Extreme scale multi-physics simulations of the tsunamigenic 2004 Sumatra megathrust earthquake, *SC17: International Conf. for High Performance Computing, Networking, Storage and Analysis*, pp. 1–16.

Vavra, E. J., H. Qiu, B. Chi, P.-E. Share, A. Allam, M. Morzfeld, F. Vernon, Y. Ben-Zion, and Y. Fialko (2023). Active dipping interface of the southern San Andreas fault revealed by space geodetic and seismic imaging, *J. Geophys. Res.* **128,** no. 11, e2023JB026811, doi: 10.1029/2023JB026811.

Wang, L., B. Wang, X. Ye, Y. Zhang, X. Wang, and Z. Lv (2021). A high-order discontinuous Galerkin method for wave propagation through coupled elastic–acoustic media, *Seismol. Geol.* **43,** no. 1, 123–143.

Wang, Y., X. Cui, X. Hu, and F. Xie (2012). Study on the stress state in upper crust of china mainland based on in-situ stress measurements, *Chin. J. Geophys.* **55,** no. 9, 3016–3027.

Wilcox, L. C., G. Stadler, C. Burstedde, and O. Ghattas (2010). A high-order discontinuous Galerkin method for wave propagation through coupled elastic–acoustic media, *J. Comput. Phys.* **229,** no. 24, 9373–9396.

Xia, S., P. Zhou, D. Zhao, and J. Cao (2020). Seismogenic structure in the source zone of the 1918 m 7.5 Nanao earthquake in the northern south china sea, *Phys. Earth Planet. In.* **302,** 106,472.

Xiong, C., J. Cao, J. Sun, S. Xia, K. Wan, C. Fan, and B. Yang (2018). Variation characteristics along the strike of the littoral fault zone in offshore pearl river estuary, *Earth Sci.* **43,** no. 10, 3682–3697.

Xu, H., X. Qiu, M. Zhao, J. Sun, and J. Zhu (2006). Crustal structural characteristics and source tectonics of the epicentral region of the great Nan'ao earthquake (m=7.5) in the northeastern south china sea, *Chin. Sci. Bull.* **51,** no. S3, 83–91.

Xu, H., C. Ye, X. Qiu, J. Sun, and S. Xia (2010). Studies on the Binhai fault zone in the northern south china sea by the deep geophysical exploration and its seismogenic structure, *South China J. Seismol.* **30,** no. S1, 10–18.

Ye, R., M. de Hoop, C. Petrovitch, L. Pyrak-Nolte, and L. Wilcox (2015). A discontinuous Galerkin method with a modified penalty flux for the propagation and scattering of acousto-elastic waves, *Geophys. J. Int.* **205,** 1267–1289.

Zhang, W., Y. Liu, and X. Chen (2023). A mixed-flux-based nodal discontinuous Galerkin method for 3d dynamic rupture modeling, *J. Geophys. Res.* **128,** no. 6, e2022JB025817, doi: 10.1029/2022JB025817.

Zhang, X., J. Cao, F. Zhao, L. Wang, C. Xiong, and S. Xia (2019). Seismological features and geological implication of the NW faults in the pearl river estuary, *South China J. Seismol.* **39,** no. 4, 1–9.

Zhong, J. (1987). The location and activity of littoral fault zone, *South China J. Seismol.* **7,** no. 4, 4–10.

Manuscript received 8 April 2025
Published online 24 October 2025

The 1912 M_S 7.2 Earthquake in the Denali Region of Central Alaska

Carl Tape*[1], Anthony Lomax[2], Sean P. Bemis[3], Peter J. Haeussler[4], and Jessalyn Ginnaty[5]

ABSTRACT

OPEN ACCESS

The 2002 M_w 7.9 earthquake in central Alaska ruptured 340 km on three faults—Susitna Glacier thrust fault, Denali fault, Totschunda fault—crossing both the Richardson Highway and the Alaska Pipeline. Its occurrence prompted renewed interest in historical large earthquakes that possibly originated on the Denali fault. One of these earthquakes was a M_s 7.2 event on July 7, 1912, which we revisit with two approaches: (1) probabilistic relocation of the epicenter using globally recorded arrival times, and (2) compilation and reassessment of shaking intensity reports to estimate a macroseismic epicenter. Our preferred instrumental epicenter is west of the Parks Highway and in agreement with the maximum-reported shaking, which was from the Parker–Browne expedition of Denali. We also relocated a M_s 6.4 aftershock, whose epicenter is 11 km from the mainshock. Candidate faults for the 1912 earthquake include the Denali fault, the McLeod Creek thrust fault, and the Kantishna Hills thrust fault. Future analysis of active faults, paleoseismic results, 1912 instrumental data, and 1912 felt reports may help in interpreting the fault and mechanism of the 1912 earthquake.

KEY POINTS

- Felt reports and global arrival times indicate the 1912 earthquake occurred in the Denali region of Alaska.
- The 1912 epicenter is 163 km west of the 2002 M_W 7.9 earthquake that ruptured 340 km of thrust and strike-slip faults.
- Possible hosts for the 1912 earthquake include the Denali fault, McLeod Creek thrust, and Kantishna Hills thrust.

INTRODUCTION

On Saturday night, July 6, 1912, at about 10 p.m. local time (1912-07-07 08:00 UTC), earthquake shaking was felt across Alaska (Fig. 1), with the strongest effects reported from the gold-mining region of Fairbanks. The story was front-page news in the Sunday newspaper (Fig. 2), which reported the death of one man in a gold mine shaft, in addition to minimal damage and widespread alarm.

The location of the earthquake was unknown. Some reports, recognizing lesser shaking on the southern coasts, assumed an origin "not very far removed from Fairbanks" (*Alaska Daily Citizen*, 1912-07-08, p. 1), while other reports attributed the origin to Katmai volcano (Fig. 1), which had a massive eruption in southwestern Alaska a month earlier. Relevant news would arrive 16 days later (1912-07-24), after the Parker–Browne mountaineering expedition had returned from the heights of Denali and reported extreme shaking that they experienced during the earthquake. Their report, combined with others from across Alaska (Fig. 1), indicated that the earthquake originated from the Alaska Range region of central Alaska, not from the Fairbanks or Katmai regions. (Denali is the name recognized by the State of Alaska and used herein; it is federally recognized as Mount McKinley.)

The basic information about the 1912 earthquake was determined from globally recorded instrumental data. The earthquake was large enough to be included in the global compilation by Gutenberg and Richter (1949), who located its epicenter in central Alaska (−147°, 64°) (Appendix A and Table 1) and assigned a magnitude of 7.4 (Table 2). The magnitude was later estimated as M_s 7.2 within the global reassessment by Abe and Noguchi (1983b).

For decades following Gutenberg's epicentral estimate, the precise location for the 1912 earthquake remained unknown, leaving an opportunity for felt reports to provide constraints on the instrumentally derived epicentral estimates. The study

1. Geophysical Institute and Department of Geosciences, University of Alaska Fairbanks, Fairbanks, Alaska, U.S.A., https://orcid.org/0000-0003-2804-7137 (CT); 2. ALomax Scientific, Mouans-Sartoux, France, https://orcid.org/0000-0002-7747-5990 (AL); 3. Department of Geosciences, Virginia Tech, Blacksburg, Virginia, U.S.A., https://orcid.org/0000-0001-7854-6394 (SPB); 4. U.S. Geological Survey, Anchorage, Alaska, U.S.A., https://orcid.org/0000-0002-1503-6247 (PJH); 5. Elmer E. Rasmuson Library, University of Alaska Fairbanks, Fairbanks, Alaska, U.S.A.

*Corresponding author: ctape@alaska.edu

Cite this article as Tape, C., A. Lomax, S. P. Bemis, P. J. Haeussler, and J. Ginnaty (2025). The 1912 M_s 7.2 Earthquake in the Denali Region of Central Alaska, *Bull. Seismol. Soc. Am.* **116**, 322–354, doi: 10.1785/0120250150

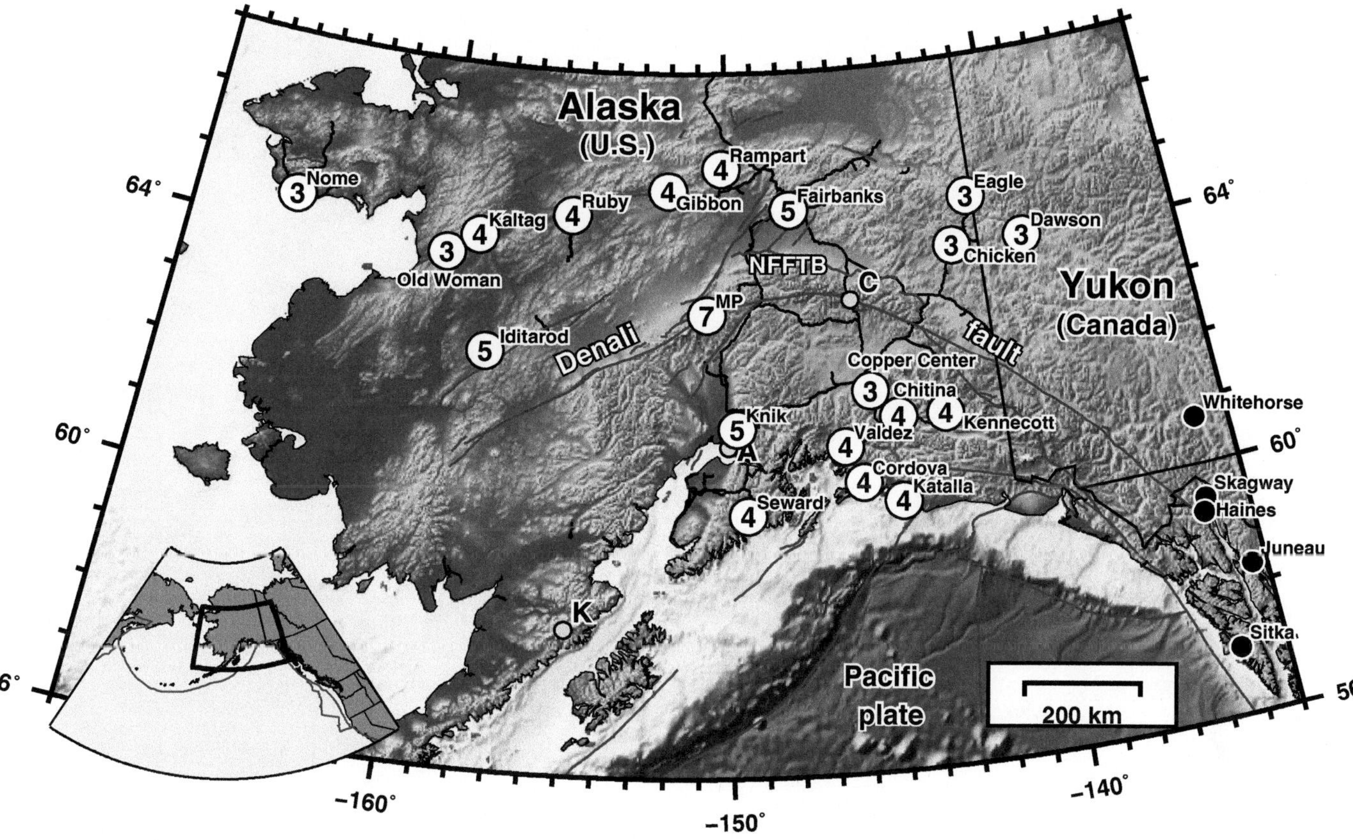

by Boyd and Lerner-Lam (1988) used arrival-time data from Gutenberg, combined with formal estimation methods, to relocate the 1912 earthquake, and they presented three felt reports from the compilation of Meyers *et al.* (1976). Their epicentral estimate was southeast of Gutenberg's by 112 km, with an uncertainty ellipse having semiaxes of 74 and 40 km.

The occurrence of the 2002-11-03 M_w 7.9 Denali fault earthquake led to renewed interest in the 1912 earthquake. The 2002 earthquake ruptured over a distance of 340 km (Eberhart-Phillips *et al.*, 2003; Haeussler *et al.*, 2004) and was exceptional for its magnitude (it is still the world's largest continental strike-slip earthquake in the modern era: 1960–2025), for its origin on the previously unknown Susitna Glacier thrust fault (Crone *et al.*, 2004), for its supershear rupture (Ellsworth *et al.*, 2004), and for its branching path to the Totschunda fault (Bhat *et al.*, 2004). In the aftermath of the 2002 earthquake, there was a new focus on the historical seismicity of central Alaska, with particular interest in the 1912-07-07 M_s 7.2 earthquake (Carver *et al.*, 2004; Doser, 2004, 2009). The 2002 earthquake also inspired several paleoseismic studies (Koehler and Carver, 2018, their fig. 12).

Carver *et al.* (2004) compiled felt reports of the 1912 earthquake, and they identified tree ring damage in the Delta River region. They attributed the tree damage to the 1912-07-07 earthquake. Their findings were enigmatic in that they placed the 1912 epicenter at the site of tree ring damage, which is 250 km east of the maximum-reporting shaking intensity, documented by the Parker–Browne expedition. To explain the strong shaking effects near Denali, west of the western extent of their assumed 1912 rupture, Carver *et al.* (2004) invoked an east-to-west unilateral rupture and also a larger magnitude (M_w 7.4).

Here we revisit macroseismic data (felt reports), instrumental data, tree ring damage, and paleoseismic studies to expand our understanding of the 1912 earthquake. First, we compile and reassess shaking intensity reports to estimate a macroseismic epicenter. Second, we perform a probabilistic relocation for the instrumental epicenter using globally recorded arrival

Figure 1. Shaking intensities derived from felt reports for the 1912-07-07 earthquake. The inset map shows the plate tectonic setting of the northern Pacific, where the Pacific plate subducts beneath Alaska. The 20 circles with numbers are a subset of the 32 shaking intensity values assigned to felt reports in this study (Table 3). MP, McGonagall Pass, where the Parker–Browne expedition experienced the earthquake following their descent from Denali. The black unnumbered circles are not-felt reports. Active faults of Haeussler *et al.* (2025) are plotted in red, with the Denali fault and Northern Foothills fold-and-thrust belt (NFFTB; Bemis and Wallace, 2007) labeled. The modern road system is plotted in black, but note that most of these roads were not established at the time of the earthquake. The label A is for Anchorage (south of Knik), which was founded three years after 1912. The label C is the 1912 epicenter assigned by Carver *et al.* (2004; C04M in Table 1), where the Denali fault crosses the modern Richardson Highway and Alaska Pipeline. This site is on the surface rupture of the 2002-11-03 M_w 7.9 earthquake. The label K is the location of the Katmai-Novarupta eruption on June 6–10, 1912 (Appendix B). The color version of this figure is available only in the electronic edition.

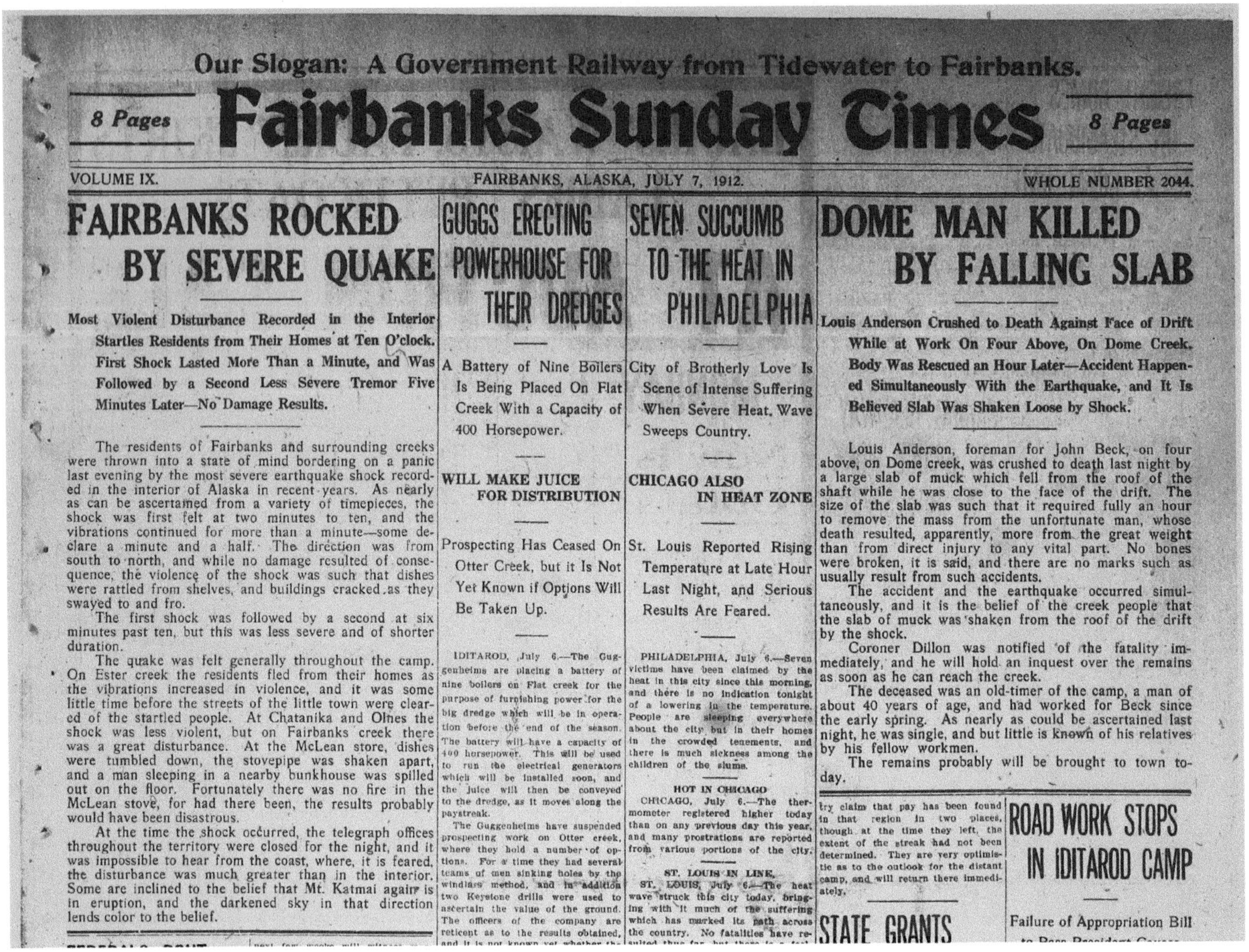

Our Slogan: A Government Railway from Tidewater to Fairbanks.

8 Pages **Fairbanks Sunday Times** 8 Pages

VOLUME IX. FAIRBANKS, ALASKA, JULY 7, 1912. WHOLE NUMBER 2044.

FAIRBANKS ROCKED BY SEVERE QUAKE

Most Violent Disturbance Recorded in the Interior Startles Residents from Their Homes at Ten O'clock. First Shock Lasted More Than a Minute, and Was Followed by a Second Less Severe Tremor Five Minutes Later—No Damage Results.

The residents of Fairbanks and surrounding creeks were thrown into a state of mind bordering on a panic last evening by the most severe earthquake shock recorded in the interior of Alaska in recent years. As nearly as can be ascertained from a variety of timepieces, the shock was first felt at two minutes to ten, and the vibrations continued for more than a minute—some declare a minute and a half. The direction was from south to north, and while no damage resulted of consequence, the violence of the shock was such that dishes were rattled from shelves, and buildings cracked as they swayed to and fro.

The first shock was followed by a second at six minutes past ten, but this was less severe and of shorter duration.

The quake was felt generally throughout the camp. On Ester creek the residents fled from their homes as the vibrations increased in violence, and it was some little time before the streets of the little town were cleared of the startled people. At Chatanika and Olnes the shock was less violent, but on Fairbanks creek there was a great disturbance. At the McLean store, dishes were tumbled down, the stovepipe was shaken apart, and a man sleeping in a nearby bunkhouse was spilled out on the floor. Fortunately there was no fire in the McLean stove, for had there been, the results probably would have been disastrous.

At the time the shock occurred, the telegraph offices throughout the territory were closed for the night, and it was impossible to hear from the coast, where, it is feared, the disturbance was much greater than in the interior. Some are inclined to the belief that Mt. Katmai again is in eruption, and the darkened sky in that direction lends color to the belief.

GUGGS ERECTING POWERHOUSE FOR THEIR DREDGES

A Battery of Nine Boilers Is Being Placed On Flat Creek With a Capacity of 400 Horsepower.

WILL MAKE JUICE FOR DISTRIBUTION

Prospecting Has Ceased On Otter Creek, but it Is Not Yet Known if Options Will Be Taken Up.

IDITAROD, July 6.—The Guggenheims are placing a battery of nine boilers on Flat creek for the purpose of furnishing power for the big dredge which will be in operation before the end of the season. The battery will have a capacity of 400 horsepower. This will be used to run the electrical generators which will be installed soon, and the juice will then be conveyed to the dredge, as it moves along the paystreak.

The Guggenheims have suspended prospecting work on Otter creek, where they hold a number of options. For a time they had several teams of men sinking holes by the windlass method, and in addition two Keystone drills were used to ascertain the value of the ground. The officers of the company are reticent as to the results obtained,

SEVEN SUCCUMB TO THE HEAT IN PHILADELPHIA

City of Brotherly Love Is Scene of Intense Suffering When Severe Heat Wave Sweeps Country.

CHICAGO ALSO IN HEAT ZONE

St. Louis Reported Rising Temperature at Late Hour Last Night, and Serious Results Are Feared.

PHILADELPHIA, July 6.—Seven victims have been claimed by the heat in this city since this morning, and there is no indication tonight of a lowering in the temperature. People are sleeping everywhere about the city but in their homes in the crowded tenements, and there is much sickness among the children of the slums.

HOT IN CHICAGO

CHICAGO, July 6.—The thermometer registered higher today than on any previous day this year, and many prostrations are reported from various portions of the city.

ST. LOUIS IN LINE.

ST. LOUIS, July 6.—The heat wave struck this city today, bringing with it much of the suffering which has marked its path across the country. No fatalities have re-

DOME MAN KILLED BY FALLING SLAB

Louis Anderson Crushed to Death Against Face of Drift While at Work On Four Above, On Dome Creek. Body Was Rescued an Hour Later—Accident Happened Simultaneously With the Earthquake, and It Is Believed Slab Was Shaken Loose by Shock.

Louis Anderson, foreman for John Beck, on four above, on Dome creek, was crushed to death last night by a large slab of muck which fell from the roof of the shaft while he was close to the face of the drift. The size of the slab was such that it required fully an hour to remove the mass from the unfortunate man, whose death resulted, apparently, more from the great weight than from direct injury to any vital part. No bones were broken, it is said, and there are no marks such as usually result from such accidents.

The accident and the earthquake occurred simultaneously, and it is the belief of the creek people that the slab of muck was shaken from the roof of the drift by the shock.

Coroner Dillon was notified of the fatality immediately, and he will hold an inquest over the remains as soon as he can reach the creek.

The deceased was an old-timer of the camp, a man of about 40 years of age, and had worked for Beck since the early spring. As nearly as could be ascertained last night, he was single, and but little is known of his relatives by his fellow workmen.

The remains probably will be brought to town today.

try claim that pay has been found in that region in two places, though at the time they left, the extent of the streak had not been determined. They are very optimistic as to the outlook for the distant camp, and will return there immediately.

STATE GRANTS

ROAD WORK STOPS IN IDITAROD CAMP

Failure of Appropriation Bill

Figure 2. *Fairbanks Sunday Times*, 1912-07-07, p. 1, featuring two stories about earthquake effects in the Fairbanks region: damage at McLean's Store on Fairbanks Creek and death of a miner in a gold mine shaft on Dome Creek, 22 km north of Fairbanks (Fig. 4). These are two among nine felt reports in the Fairbanks region, among 32 total felt reports in this study. Documentation of the felt reports is provided in Tape (2025).

times. We also estimate an epicenter for a newly documented M_s 6.4 aftershock that occurred 38 hr after the mainshock. The instrumental epicenters for the 1912 mainshock and aftershock are within 11 km of each other and near Denali, west of the Parks Highway. The two instrumental epicenters agree with the macroseismic epicenter.

Our preferred epicenter for the 1912 earthquake (25I in Table 1) lies in the Denali region, approximately 235 km west of the location assigned by Carver *et al.* (2004). We identify two fault systems as the most likely candidates for hosting the earthquake: the right-lateral strike-slip Denali fault and a thrust fault system situated north of it. Our study focuses on felt reports, global arrival-time data, and a review of paleoseismic evidence. Future investigations of recorded seismic waveforms and new paleoseismic studies in the epicentral region could help determine the responsible fault and provide estimates of magnitude and rupture length.

FELT REPORTS FOR THE 1912 EARTHQUAKE

We collected earthquake felt reports in two main categories: newspaper articles and monthly weather records. Because of the gold rush, there were many more newspapers across Alaska in 1912 than today. We performed an exhaustive search of newspaper archives for all newspaper articles published in Alaska and westernmost Canada in the 15 days following the 1912 earthquake (Tape, 2025). We also obtained all available monthly weather records from Alaska, following previous efforts (Tape *et al.*, 2017, 2021). For centuries, the U.S. government has aggregated weather data collected by a formal network of citizen weather observers. In 1912, this effort was run by the U.S. Weather Bureau under the Department of Agriculture, and the monthly records were compiled on the Voluntary Observers' Meteorological Record form, which

TABLE 1
Published Hypocenters and Origin Times for the 1912-07-07 Earthquake

Label	Date	Reference	Longitude (°)	Latitude (°)	Depth (km)	UTC Time	Δ_{25I} (km)
Historical and instrumental sources							
GR	1949	Gutenberg and Richter (1949, p. 119)	−147	64	"Shallow" (≤60)	7:57.6	185
BL88I	1988	Boyd and Lerner-Lam (1988, p. 639)	−146.14	63.07	33 (fixed)	–	218
C04M	2004	Carver *et al.* (2004, fig. 10)	−145.7328	63.3823	–	–	235
D04I	2004	Doser (2004, p. S135)	−147.18	63.56	–	–	164
D09M	2009	Doser (2009, p. 3450)	−149.70	63.00	–	–	53
ISCG	2018	International Seismological Centre (2018)	−148.030	63.604	10	07:57:39.75	123
Hypocenters from this study							
25I	2025	This study	−150.43	63.34	3	07:57:38	–
25M	2025	This study	−150.8	62.9	–	–	54
25IA	2025	This study	−150.50	63.44	0	21:53:50	11

Figure 7 displays several of these epicenters and their uncertainty ellipses, if known. In the labels, an I suffix refers to "instrumental," and an M refers to "macroseismic." UTC times are listed as hh:mm:ss for the day 1912-07-07. The final column lists the distance Δ_{25I} from each epicenter to the preferred epicenter 25I. See Table 2 for magnitudes associated with some of the hypocenters. The last row (25IA) is the 1912-07-08 aftershock. An entry of "–" means that it was either not estimated or not provided in the study. Gutenberg's time of 07:57.6 corresponds to 07:57:36 UTC. The longitude and latitude listed for C04M are determined from Google Earth based on the details in Carver *et al.* (2004).

included a "Miscellaneous Phenomena" section that provided space for reporting phenomena such as earthquakes. We did not perform an archival search for additional felt reports, as we did for the 1904 earthquake (Tape *et al.*, 2017), but we did obtain one additional 1912 felt report, from the diary of Orville Herning, who was in the Knik region. We then assigned modified Mercalli intensity (MMI) values to each felt report, and we estimated the macroseismic epicenter using previously established empirical relationships between magnitude, distance, and shaking intensity (Bakun and Wentworth, 1997).

Parker–Browne account of the earthquake

A mountaineering expedition team led by Herschel Parker and Belmore Browne happened to be in the epicentral region at the time the 1912 earthquake struck. Having descended from near the summit of Denali, the four-man party of Parker, Brown, Arthur Aten, and Merl La Voy was at McGonagall Pass when they experienced strong shaking from the earthquake (Figs. 1, 3). Parker–Browne's report of the shaking was published in front-page newspapers, with the full account appearing in 1913 in a magazine article (Browne, 1913b) and a book (Browne, 1913c). Their account is discussed in Appendix B and presented in full in Tape (2025).

One excerpt includes the following key observations of shaking effects at McGonagall Pass (Browne, 1913b, p. 388):

> *In front of me was a boulder weighing more than two hundred pounds. We had pulled it there with a sled and dog team to anchor our tent; it had sunk into the moss from its own weight, and as I watched, the boulder turned, broke loose from the earth, and moved several feet. Then came the crash of our falling caches, followed by another muffled crash as the front of our hill slid into the creek, and a lake nearby boiled as if it was hot.*

TABLE 2
Published Magnitudes for the 1912-07-07 Earthquake in Central Alaska

Label	Date	Reference	Magnitude
GR	1949	Gutenberg and Richter (1949)	M 7.4
–	1981	Abe (1981)	M_s 7.5, m_B 7.3
–	1983	Abe and Noguchi (1983a)	M_s 7.5
–	1983	Abe and Noguchi (1983b)	M_s 7.2
–	1992	Pacheco and Sykes (1992)	M_s 7.1
C04M	2004	Carver *et al.* (2004)	M_w 7.2–7.4
ISCG	2018	International Seismological Centre (2018)	M_w 7.27 ± 0.39
–	1965	Duda (1965)	M 7.1
–	1988	Brockman *et al.* (1988)	M_s 7.4
–	1991	Page *et al.* (1991)	M_s 7.2
–	1993	Stover and Coffman (1993)	M_s 7.2

The bottom four rows in the table are compilations based on previously published estimates. M, Gutenberg–Richter magnitude; M_s, surface-wave magnitude; m_b, body-wave magnitude; M_w, moment magnitude.

As explained later, we assign a shaking intensity of MMI 7 to the account from McGonagall Pass.

Previous compilations of felt reports

As detailed in Appendix B, the U.S. seismicity compilations (Heck and Eppley, 1958) included three felt reports via secondary sources: McGonagall Pass, Fairbanks, and Kennecott. The McGonagall Pass account was obtained from Fenner (1925) via Browne (1913c). The Fairbanks account was from BSSA (1912). The Kennecott report was apparently from the unpublished records of Harry Fielding Reid. These three accounts were assigned MMI values by Meyers *et al.* (1976; Table 3). The three MMI values were displayed in Boyd and Lerner-Lam (1988) and discussed in the context of their relocation study based on global arrival-time data.

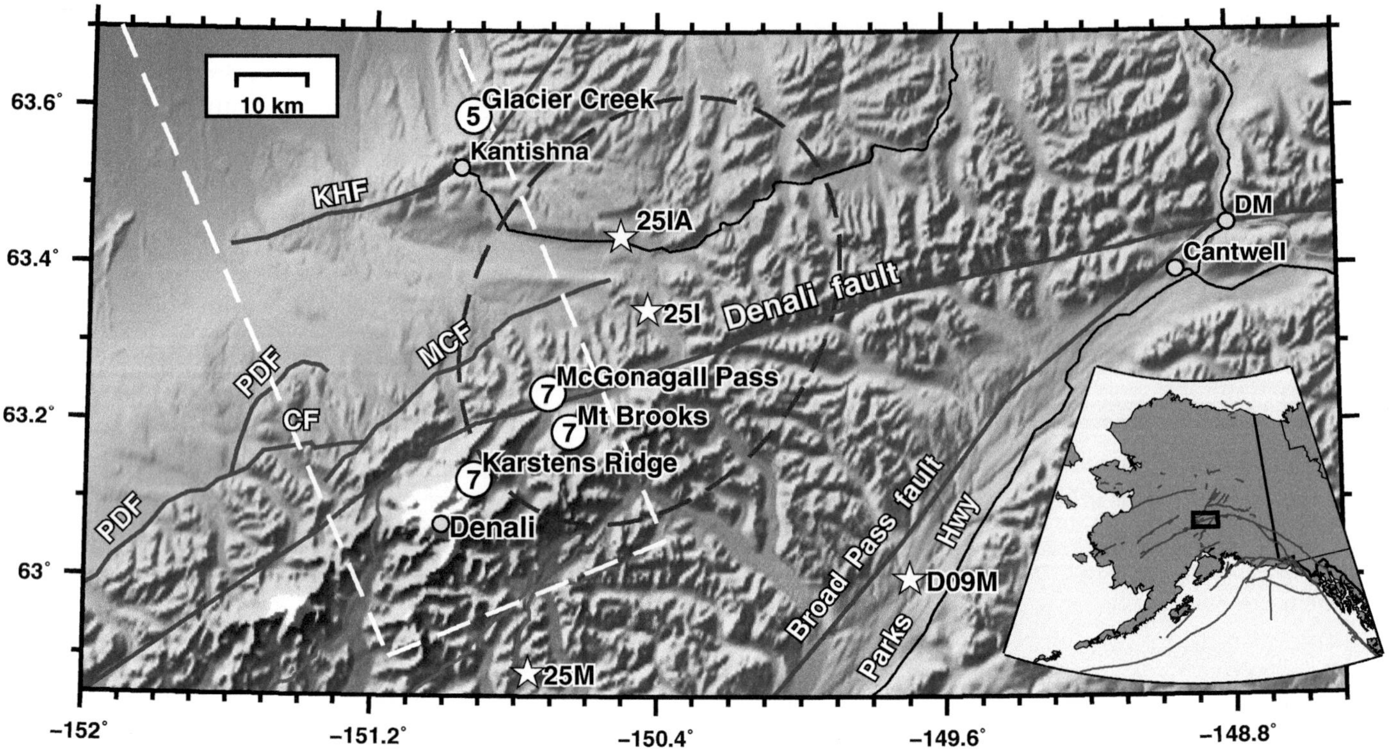

Figure 3. Map featuring four locations having felt reports in the Denali region (Table 3, column X): McGonagall Pass, Mt. Brooks, Karstens Ridge, and Glacier Creek. Also shown are epicenters from Table 1 (25I, 25IA, 25M, and D09M), as well as the uncertainty ellipse (68% confidence contour) for our preferred epicenter (25I). Active faults are plotted in red (Haeussler *et al.*, 2025) and include the Peters Dome–Chedotlothna–McLeod Creek (PDF–CF–MCF) thrust fault system (Burkett *et al.*, 2016) and the Kantisha Hills fault (KHF). The dashed box depicts the region containing the low-angle detachment fault proposed by Schulte-Pelkum *et al.* (2025). Primary bedrock faults of Haeussler (2008) are plotted in magenta. Modern roads are plotted in black and include the Parks Highway and the Denali Park Road, which ends in Kantishna. Yellow circles denote reference locations at the Denali summit, Cantwell, and the paleoseismic "Dead Mouse" (DM) site of Carlson *et al.* (2018). The inset map displays the active faults in red as well as a small black box depicting the region of the main plot. The color version of this figure is available only in the electronic edition.

The compilation by Brockman *et al.* (1988) lists MMI 6 for the 1912-07-07 earthquake, yet gives it the category of "no intensity data are currently available". They were familiar with Meyers *et al.* (1976), which is likely the source of the MMI 6 value. The 1912 earthquake is not featured in Espinosa *et al.* (1986), which includes several smaller events.

A major advancement came in 1980 with the publication of a seismological report commissioned by the Alaska Power Authority and pertaining to the possibility of hydroelectric dams installed on the Susitna River (Woodward-Clyde Consultants, 1980). The report included a map with 16 sites that were assigned MMI values inferred from historical newspaper reports (Tape, 2025). Unfortunately, the report contains no details on the felt reports, and the report itself, while now publicly available, does not seem to have entered into the seismological literature.

Two decades after the 1980 report, Carver *et al.* (2004) performed an archival search for newspaper reports of the 1912 earthquake, dramatically increasing the number of documented felt reports, from three to 19 (Table 3). We identified several minor and major corrections to the Carver *et al.* (2004) compilation; the minor ones are described in Tape (2025). The five major corrections are summarized here for sites listed in table 1 of Carver *et al.* (2004):

- **Tanana:** The article in *The Alaska Citizen* is referring to the Tanana district (Fairbanks and surroundings), not to the town of Tanana, which is 200 km west of Fairbanks.
- **Gibbon I:** The report from "Gibbon" is referring to Fort Gibbon, which is near the town of Tanana, central Alaska. Carver attributed "Gibbon" to Gibbon Anchorage, which is on the north side of Green Island in Prince William Sound, 600 km south of Fort Gibbon.
- **Galena:** There is no mention of Galena in the weekly *Ruby Record-Citizen* in the July 13th account about the earthquake or in the following publication on July 20th.
- **Skagway:** The earthquake is mentioned in *The Daily Alaskan*, but there is no mention of local shaking.
- **Sitka:** The Cordova newspaper mentioned that the earthquake was felt in Sitka, but the Sitka seismic station register did not (Hazard, 1914; Tape, 2025).

Furthermore, there are differences between the table of felt reports in Carver *et al.* (2004) and the map displayed in the

TABLE 3
Compilations of MMI Shaking Intensities from Meyers *et al.* (1976; M 76), Carver *et al.* (2004; C04), and This Study

	Previous Compilations			This Study†					Source	
Location	**M76**	**C04 Table**	**C04 Map**	**X**	**Q**	**Y**	**Longitude (°)**	**Latitude (°)**	**Reference**	**Details**
McGonagall Pass	6	9+	9+	7	A	7	−150.7082	63.2376	Browne (1913b)	p. 387
Mt. Brooks	–	–	–	7*	A	–	−150.6472	63.1878	Browne (1913b)	p. 389
Karstens Ridge	–	–	–	7*	B	–	−150.9157	63.1264	Stuck (1914)	p. 40
Glacier Creek	–	–	–	5*	B	–	−150.9265	63.5915	Browne (1912)	
Fairbanks	5	6	6	4	A	5	−147.7217	64.8438	*Fairbanks Sunday Times*	July 7, p. 1
Agriculture Exp.	–	–	–	4*	A	–	−147.8620	64.8568	Weather (Neal, 1912)	
Ester	–	–	–	4*	A	–	−148.0167	64.8472	*Fairbanks Sunday Times*	July 7, p. 1
Olnes	–	–	–	4*	B	–	−147.6694	65.0750	*Fairbanks Sunday Times*	July 7, p. 1
Dome	–	–	–	5*	A	–	−147.599	65.031	*Fairbanks Sunday Times*	July 7, p. 1
Gilmore	–	–	–	4*	B	–	−147.5375	64.9911	*Alaska Citizen*	July 8, p. 1
Golden	–	–	–	3*	B	–	−147.4792	65.0139	*Alaska Citizen*	July 8, p. 1
Fairbanks Creek	–	–	–	6*	A	–	−147.2135	65.0726	*Fairbanks Sunday Times*	July 7, p. 1
Chatanika	–	–	–	4*	B	–	−147.4722	65.1125	*Fairbanks Sunday Times*	July 7, p. 1
Rampart	–	–	–	4*	A	4	−150.15	65.51	Weather (Gasser, 1912)	
Tanana	–	4	4	–	–	–	−152.09	65.17	C04	
Gibbon	–			4*	C	4	−152.09	65.17	*Valdez Daily Prospector*	July 8, p. 1
Ruby	–	5	5	4	A	4	−155.49	64.74	*Ruby Record-Citizen*	July 13, p. 3
Galena	–	4	4	–	–	–	−156.87	64.74	C04	
Kaltag	–	–	4	4*	B	4	−158.73	64.33	*Iditarod Pioneer*	July 13, p. 1
Old Woman	–	4	4	3	B	3	−159.82	64.01	*Iditarod Pioneer*	July 13, p. 1
Nome	–	3	3	3	C	3	−165.41	64.50	*Dawson Daily News*	July 8, p. 4
Iditarod	–	5	5	5	A	5	−158.10	62.54	*Iditarod Pioneer*	July 13, p. 1
Flat	–	4	–	4	A	–	−158.01	62.45	*Iditarod Pioneer*	July 13, p. 1
Knik	–	–	–	5*	A	–	−149.7314	61.4560	Herning (1912)	
Seward	–	4	4	4	C	4	−149.44	60.10	*Ruby Record-Citizen*	July 13, p. 1
					A				Weather (McNeilly, 1912)	
Gibbon I.	–	5	5	–	–	–	−147.39	60.29	C04	
Valdez	–	5	5	4	A	4	−146.2663	61.1157	*Valdez Miner*	July 7, p. 1
Cordova	–	5	5	4	A	4	−145.75	60.54	*Cordova Daily Alaskan*	July 8, p. 1
Copper Center	–	–	–	3*	A	3	−145.30	61.95	Weather (Jones, 1912)	
Katalla	–	5	5	4	B	4	−144.53	60.20	*Cordova Daily Alaskan*	July 8, p. 1
Chitina	–	5	5	4	C	4	−144.44	61.52	*Cordova Daily Alaskan*	July 8, p. 1
Kennecott	5	5	5	4	B	4	−142.89	61.49	*Cordova Daily Alaskan*	July 8, p. 1
Skagway	–	2	3	–	–	–	−135.31	59.46	C04	
Juneau	–	–	2	–	–	–	−134.42	58.30	C04	
Sitka	–	3	2	–	–	–	−135.33	57.05	C04	
Fort Yukon	–	–	1–2	–	–	–	−145.25	66.56	C04	
Chicken	–	–	–	3*	A	3	−141.94	64.07	Weather (Davis, 1912)	
Eagle	–	–	2	3*	C	3	−141.20	64.79	*Dawson Daily News*	July 8, p. 4
Dawson	–	3	3	3	A	3	−139.43	64.06	*Dawson Daily News*	July 9, p. 4

The stations are ordered by region: epicentral, Fairbanks, northwest, west, southeast, southeast Alaska, and northeast. MMI, modified Mercalli intensity.
†This study has column X for the full set of 32 felt reports, column Y for the set of 20 felt reports used to estimate a macroseismic epicenter (Fig. 6), and column Q for a quality assignment of the felt report in column X. The starred values in column X denote the 18 reports that are new to this study.

same article; these differences are documented in Table 3. In addition, the coordinates for Old Woman and Chitina in table 1 of Carver *et al.* (2004) are incorrect, as are the plotted locations for Kennecott and Ruby in the map of Carver *et al.* (2004).

Our compilation of felt reports

We perform a search for new felt reports, as well as for previously identified felt reports. We assign an MMI value to each report following Wood and Neumann (1931) and the modifications by Stover and Coffman (1993). The results are displayed in Table 3 and Figure 1. Our pursuit is summarized in Tape (2025), with key items discussed here. In our discussion and in Table 3, we order the felt reports by geographical region, starting with the epicentral region (Parker–Browne near Denali), then followed by north (Fairbanks), northwest (Ruby), west (Iditarod), southeast (Valdez), southeast Alaska (Juneau), and northeast (Dawson). In some cases, we list the epicentral distances (Δ, in km) from the site to our preferred epicenter (25I in Table 1).

Epicentral region. Felt reports in the epicentral region of Denali exist because of the Parker–Browne expedition. From their written accounts, we identify four felt reports (Table 3) and use the MMI from McGonagall Pass in our formal estimation of the macroseismic epicenter. Figure 3 shows the epicentral region.

The Parker–Browne team experienced the 1912 earthquake from their camp at McGonagall Pass (Δ = 18 km). Carver *et al.* (2004) assigned MMI 9+ to the McGonagall Pass felt report written by Belmore Browne. We assign it MMI 7 based on three clauses (Wood and Neumann, 1931): "Damage… considerable in poorly built or badly designed buildings" (the temporary caches and tent), "Overturned heavy furniture" (the boulder that moved), and "Incaving to some extent of sand or gravel stream banks" (Browne: "the front of our hill slid into the creek"). In our view, the before-and-after photographs of the camp in Browne (1913b) do not provide evidence for any MMI above 7.

At McGonagall Pass during the earthquake, the Parker–Browne expedition witnessed massive avalanching of the Alaska Range, which caused clouds of ice dust to blast through their camp (Browne, 1913b). This is their description of Mt. Brooks (Δ = 21 km), observed from McGonagall Pass at a distance of only 6 km (p. 389):

> *… we saw that the whole extent of the wall that formed its buttress was avalanching. I have never seen a sight of such overpowering grandeur. The avalanche seemed to stretch along the range for a distance of several miles, like a huge wave, and like a huge wave it seemed to poise for an instant before it plunged downward to the ice fields thousands of feet below. The mountain was about ten miles away, and we waited breathlessly until the terrific thunder of the falling mass began to boom and rumble among the mountains.*

We assign MMI 7 to the site of Mt. Brooks for this eyewitness account (Table 3).

Another site in the Alaska Range that avalanched was Karstens Ridge (Δ = 35 km), 16 km southwest of McGonagall Pass and outside the direct view of the expedition. As described in Appendix B, the avalanche effects were encountered by the 1913 Denali expedition led by Hudson Stuck (Stuck, 1914). We agree with Stuck's inference that the jumbled ice at Karstens Ridge was caused by the 1912-07-07 earthquake, and we assign MMI 7 to this site (Table 3). We recognize that an MMI of 7 should be based on the shaking effects of manmade objects (Stover and Coffman, 1993), documented in near-real time, and there was neither a human witness nor manmade objects in the case of Karstens Ridge.

Following the earthquake, the Parker–Browne team proceeded north to Wonder Lake (Browne, 1913b, p. 393):

> *As we traveled toward the Clearwater, we were constantly reminded of the big earthquake. In every direction, we could see fissures looking like partly healed scars on the hillsides, and wherever the streams were bounded by bluffs, large slides had occurred that in some cases were partly damming the current.*

Just north of Wonder Lake, they reached gold prospectors in Kantishna on July 10th and then Glacier Creek (Δ = 37 km) on July 13th, 41 km from where they experienced the earthquake shaking at McGonagall Pass (Fig. 3). After speaking with the local prospectors, Browne wrote in his diary (Fig. B1b), "July 13th Earth quakes have been working steadily. The big shake was not as bad down this way as it was on the Clear Water. We are now at Quiggly's and Fanny McKenzie's." Lacking any details, we conclude that the earthquake was felt at Glacier Creek by the locals and that it would have MMI 4–6; we list MMI 5 for Glacier Creek in Table 3.

Fairbanks region. There were two damage reports from the Fairbanks region. The first was the collapse of a mining shaft at Dome Creek (Δ = 233 km), which killed a man (Fig. 2). The second was at a store on Fairbanks Creek (Δ = 248 km; *Fairbanks Sunday Times*, 1912-07-08, p. 1): "At the McLean store, dishes were tumbled down, the stovepipe was shaken apart, and a man sleeping on in a nearby bunkhouse was spilled out on the floor." Otherwise, "… while no damage resulted of consequence, the violence of the shock was such that dishes were rattled from shelves, and buildings cracked as they swayed to and fro."

Both damage reports occurred north of Fairbanks in the mining camps (Fig. 4). We assign MMI 6 to Fairbanks Creek based on the damaged stove pipe ("Damage slight in poorly built buildings."), but given that this is the only reported instance in the region of more than 7000 people, we consider it to be an outlier. Even the newspaper recognized extreme variability in local shaking effects—what modern seismologists would call "site effects" (*Alaska Citizen*, 1912-07-08, p. 1): "Gilmore experienced a good shock, but strangely enough at Golden and farther up the hill it was hardly felt. The shock at Olnes and Chatanika was the heaviest ever felt. Although apparently not as severe as on Fairbanks creek, due doubtless to a difference in formation which was not so well adapted to the transmission of the waves." (These locations are shown in Fig. 4.) We assign MMI 5 to the collapsed mine shaft at Dome Creek. Photographs show a hazardous work setting, especially during the summer, when the partially frozen ground would be subject to collapse, even without earthquake effects (Tape, 2025).

The town of Fairbanks had no reports of damage. Considering the nine felt reports in the Fairbanks region

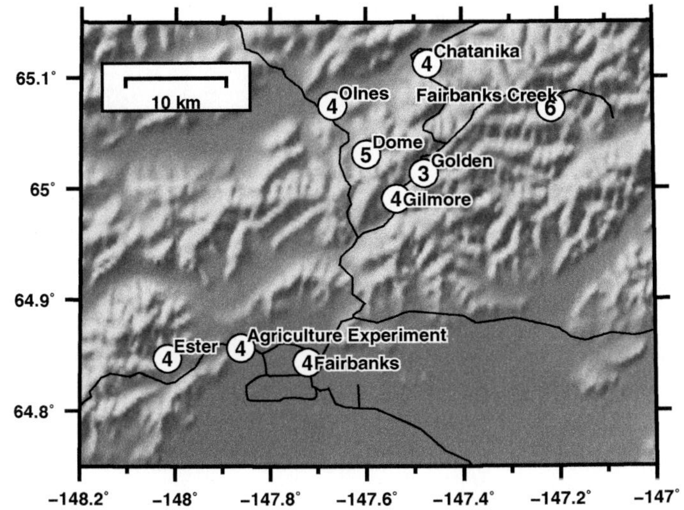

Figure 4. Map showing nine locations having felt reports in the Fairbanks region (Table 3, column X). Damage occurred at the McLean Store on Fairbanks Creek (modified Mercalli intensity [MMI] 6), and a prospector died in a mine collapse on Dome Creek (MMI 5; Fig. 2).

(Fig. 4), we assign a single value of MMI 5 to Fairbanks (Table 3) for the purpose of estimating a macroseismic epicenter.

Knik. Orville Herning lived in the upper Cook Inlet townsite of Knik, which predated the development of Wasilla and Palmer to the east. Herning's diary entries for July 6–8, 1912 can be seen in Figure 5, with annotated transcriptions in Tape (2025). The July 6th entry includes: "About 10 P.M. Heavy Earthquake Vibration lasted for 5 Minutes. Log buildings cracked under the shake." Then on July 7th: "Everybody talking Earthquake today." And then on July 8th: "At Noon another Quake."

We assign MMI 5 based on the merchant's assessment of five minutes of shaking, as well as the possibility of damaged log buildings ("cracking" probably refers to sound only). Knik and Fairbanks turn out to be the same distance from the preferred epicenter ($\Delta = 213$ km).

Iditarod. Newspapers reported shaking effects in Iditarod and the nearby site of Flat (Table 3). Iditarod reported: "Although no damage resulted, several people felt decidedly uneasy for a time." Heavy objects moved in both places. In Iditarod, "tables, chairs, and beds moved from their accustomed positions," and in Flat, "John Hanson, of the Idaho association, was thrown off his chair by last Saturday's earthquake." We assign MMI 5 based on the movements of these objects.

Additional felt reports. The remaining felt reports are presented and assessed in Tape (2025) and summarized in Table 3. Column X lists the MMI assignment for the complete set, with column Q providing a quality assessment of the corresponding felt report. A high-quality (A) assignment is for a definite primary source from a person who experienced the shaking. The weather reports are all quality A, even though they tend to have nothing more than the approximate time that the earthquake was felt. A newspaper report mentioning locally felt shaking, possibly by the writer himself, is quality A or B, depending on the details in the report. A quality C report is for a site that is outside the local region of the newspaper and also lacks any details of the shaking effects.

For a modern earthquake, especially in a densely populated region, there may be dozens or hundreds of reports for a single community, and there are formal methods that can be used to infer an MMI for a community, such as the Community Decimal Intensity scale of Dengler and Dewey (1998). In column Y in Table 3, we establish a declustered version of 20 MMI values based on the full set of 32 felt reports in column X. The nine felt reports in the Fairbanks region are reduced to one, the four from the Denali region are treated as one, and the Iditarod-Flat pair is treated as one. This reduction provides spatial balance of the data set and simplifies the presentation (Fig. 1).

Table 3 shows differences between our MMI assignments and those of Carver *et al.* (2004). Our MMI assignments are generally lower than those of Carver *et al.* (2004). Table 3 also shows newly discovered felt reports—such as the weather observers at Chicken, Rampart, and Copper Center—and reports that we assigned as not-felt, including Sitka, Juneau, and Skagway. Our compilation has no felt reports for southeastern Alaska, whereas Carver listed Sitka, Juneau, and Skagway in either his table or map (Table 3). In summary, we verify 14 of the 19 felt reports listed in table 1 of Carver *et al.* (2004), and we discredit five (Tanana, Galena, Gibbon Island, Skagway, and Sitka). Our compilation of 32 felt reports in Table 3 therefore adds 18 new felt reports, several of which (such as in Fairbanks) do not significantly broaden the geographic extent of felt shaking but are nevertheless valuable. The most important new felt report is from Knik.

EPICENTRAL ESTIMATION WITH SHAKING INTENSITIES

Carver *et al.* (2004) did not formally estimate a macroseismic epicenter using their compiled felt reports and MMI values. As discussed in the Introduction section, they assigned an epicenter to the site of tree damage (labeled C on the map in Fig. 1), thereby overruling the information provided in the felt reports.

The first formal approach to estimating a 1912 epicenter based on MMI values was performed by Doser (2009), who used a set of calibration events in central Alaska to determine coefficients for the empirical relationship between MMI and intensity magnitude derived by Bakun (2006). Then, using the shaking intensity data from Carver *et al.* (2004), Doser (2009) used the Alaska-specific coefficients to relocate the 1912 event following the method outlined in Bakun and

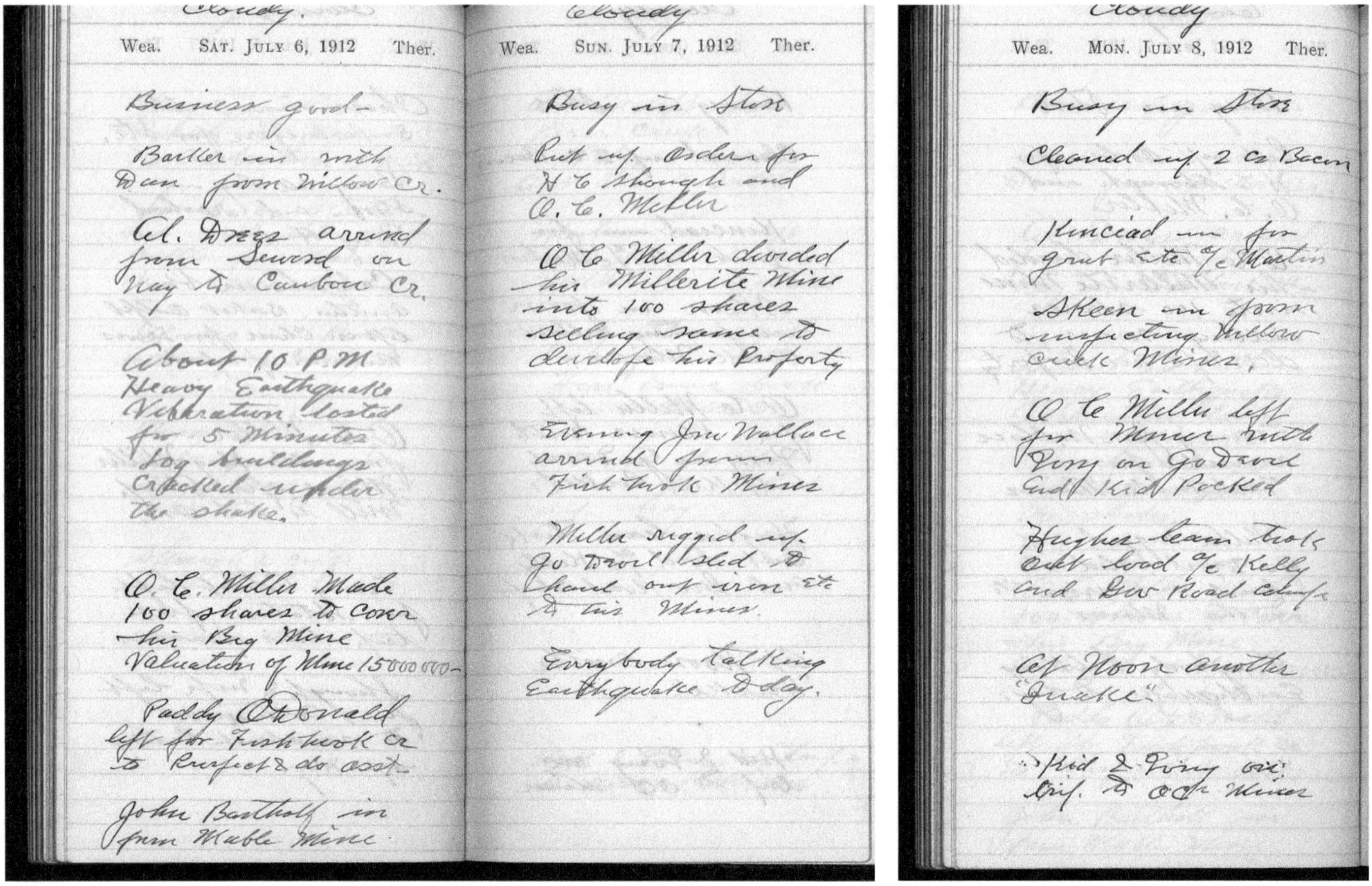

Wentworth (1997). The Doser (2009) estimated epicenter is close to the McGonagall Pass (Cache Creek) location and 204 km west of Carver's epicenter (Table 1). This discrepancy is because Doser's epicenter is based on the shaking intensity data, whereas Carver's epicenter is assigned to the site of observed tree ring damage.

Figure 5. Diary entries of Orville Herning from Knik, Alaska, in July 1912 (Herning, 1912). (Left) July 6th, with red text describing shaking from the M_s 7.2 mainshock. (Center) July 7th, ending with "Everybody talking Earthquake today." (Right) July 8th, ending with "At Noon another Quake." This is the only known felt report for the M_s 6.4 aftershock, which we locate using global arrival times (25IA in Table 1). Knik is 213 km from our preferred 1912 epicenter (25I in Table 1). All dates and times in the diary are (of course) local times, whereas the dates and times in Table 1 are UTC.

Following the approach in Tape *et al.* (2017, 2021), we use an empirical relationship (Bakun and Wentworth, 1997, their eq. 6) as follows:

$$\mathrm{MMI} = 5.07 + 1.09M - 3.69\log_{10}\Delta, \qquad (1)$$

where MMI is the predicted shaking intensity, M is the earthquake magnitude, and Δ is the epicentral distance in kilometers. We consider a large spatial grid of possible epicenters and, for each epicenter, calculate the misfit between the 20 observed MMI (column Y in Table 3) and the MMI predicted from equation (1). We assume a fixed magnitude of 7.2 (Abe and Noguchi, 1983b).

Figure 6 displays contours of the root mean square misfit in MMI values, with the lowest value defining the estimated epicenter 25M. Zooming into the epicentral region (Fig. 6b) reveals a U-shape to the innermost contour surrounding 25M. This suggests an epicentral uncertainty region west of the Parks Highway and described by an annulus centered on the MMI 7 at McGonagall Pass and having a radius of about 40 km and a width of about 20 km. This uncertainty region overlaps with the uncertainty region of D09M (Doser, 2009); the epicenters 25M and D09M are 55 km apart (Fig. 6b).

We considered several different choices in estimating the macroseismic epicenter: (1) using the empirical relationship of Doser (2009, her eq. 3), (2) using the distance-weighting function of Bakun and Wentworth (1997, their eq. 17), (3) using our full set of 32 MMI values (instead of the reduced subset of 20), (4) excluding the McGonagall Pass (MMI 7) observation, and (5) allowing the magnitude to vary (instead of fixing it to 7.2). These choices resulted in macroseismic epicenters that were all within the uncertainty region described earlier (Tape, 2025).

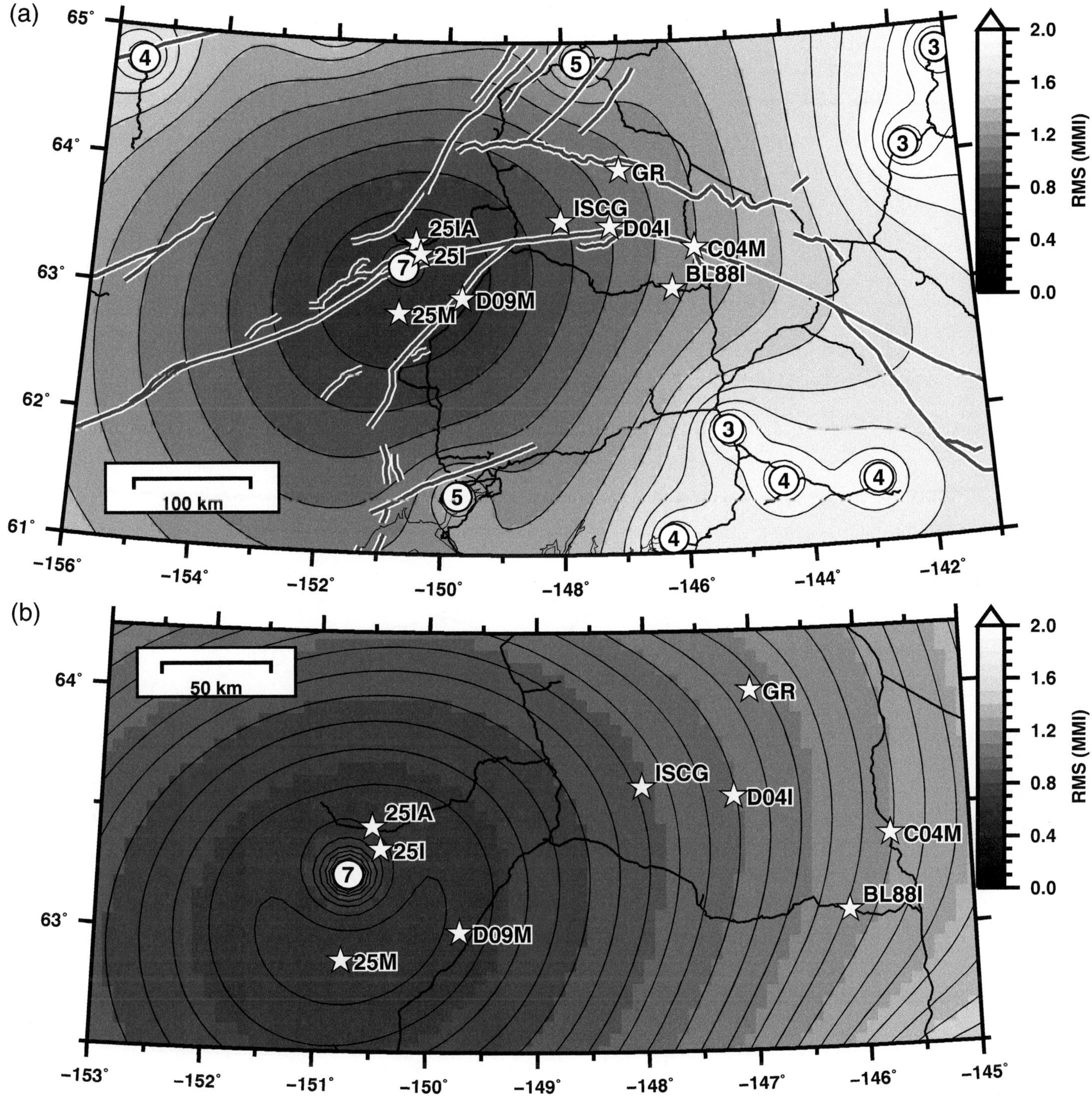

Figure 6. Epicentral estimation of the 1912-07-07 M_S 7.2 earthquake using the felt reports shown in Figure 1. (a) Root mean square (RMS) residuals of shaking intensity (units of MMI; contour interval 0.10), considering a grid of possible epicenters, a fixed magnitude, and the empirical formula of Bakun and Wentworth (1997). The minimum misfit occurs at the epicenter labeled 25M, south of the MMI 7 felt report (Table 3). Active faults of Haeussler *et al.* (2025) are plotted in red; the modern road system is plotted in black. Other epicenters and abbreviations are summarized in Table 1. (b) Zoom-in, revealing the shape of the misfit surface in the vicinity of the minimum; contour interval 0.04. The U-shaped region, defined by the contour value of 0.64, provides an approximation of the uncertainty region for epicenter 25M. The color version of this figure is available only in the electronic edition.

EPICENTRAL ESTIMATION WITH GLOBAL ARRIVAL TIMES

In the early 1900s, efforts to compile global arrival times and to determine earthquake locations were led by John Milne and the Seismology Committee of the British Association for the Advancement of Science. Milne compiled the Shide Circulars, which contained arrival times reported by several global seismic stations, including his own station at Shide on the Isle of Wight off the southern coast of England. The global arrival times were then used by British seismologists to produce compilations of earthquake epicenters, in tables and on maps.

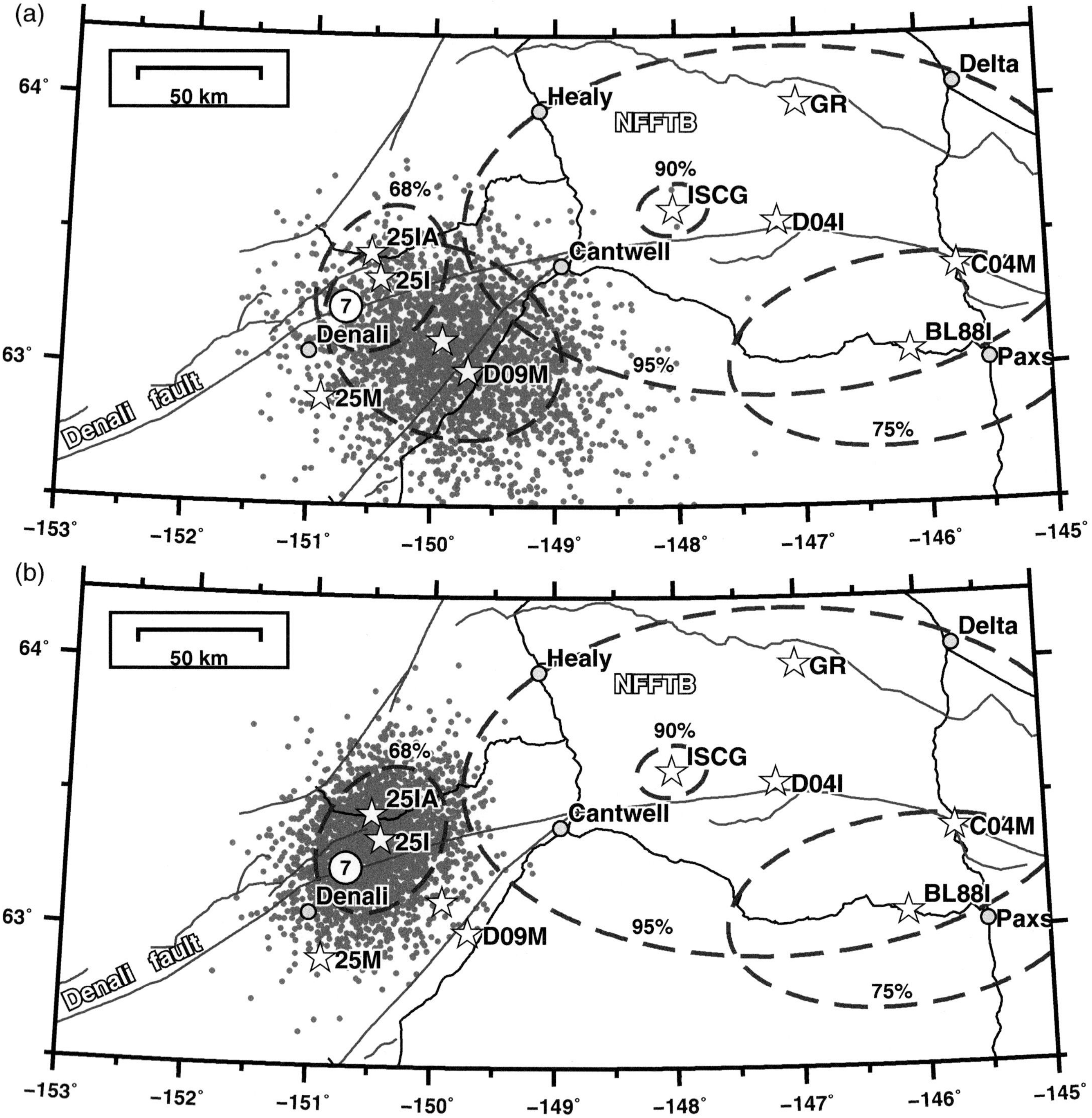

Figure 7. Summary of epicenters for the 1912 earthquake (Table 1) and featuring Run A and Run B from Table 4. (a) NonLinLoc (NLL) results for Run A using the original International Seismological Centre (ISC) data set of global arrival times. The cloud of points—centered on the unlabeled star—depicts the posterior density function for the epicenter; the dashed ellipse is the 68% confidence contour. The dashed ellipse surrounding the 25I epicenter is the 68% confidence ellipse for our preferred epicenter, featured in panel (b). Other ellipses are displayed for their published confidence contours: 75% for BL88I (Boyd and Lerner-Lam, 1988), 95% for D04I (Doser, 2004), and 90% for ISCG (International Seismological Centre, 2023). Active faults are plotted in red, with the Denali fault and NFFTB labeled. Roads are plotted in black, with the north–south highways of Parks (west) and Richardson (east) connected by the Denali Highway, from Cantwell to Paxson. (b) NLL results for Run B, our preferred epicenter (25I), using an expanded ISC data set of global arrival times. The color version of this figure is available only in the electronic edition.

TABLE 4
Summary of Instrumental Epicenters Estimated in This Study

Run	Epicenter	Longitude (°)	Latitude (°)	Depth (km)	UTC Time (hh:mm:ss)	Δ_B (km)	Δt_B (s)
A	all_ISC	−149.91	63.11	8	07:57:38	36	−1
B	all_ISC_new_SIT_S	−150.43	63.34	3	07:57:39	0	0
C	all_ISC_new_SIT_S_no_beyond_70	−150.37	63.42	2	07:57:39	9	0
D	all_ISC_new_SIT_S_no_beyond_65	−150.34	63.42	2	07:57:38	9	−1
E	all_ISC_new_SIT_S_no_beyond_60	−150.33	63.44	2	07:57:38	11	−1
F	all_ISC_new_SIT_S_no_beyond_55	−149.98	63.74	2	07:57:39	49	0
G	all_ISC_new_SIT_S_no_beyond_50	−149.91	63.81	2	07:57:39	58	0
H	all_ISC_new_SIT_S_no_beyond_47	−150.13	63.89	2	07:57:39	62	0
I	SIT_PandS	−158.71	55.50	92	07:56:28	991	−71
J	SIT_PandS_ashock	−160.85	62.90	78	–	528	–
K	all_ISC_new_ashock	−150.50	63.44	0	–	11	–

Each epicenter is obtained using a different subset of arrival-time data. UTC times are listed as hh:mm:ss for the day 1912-07-07. Δ_B is the distance from our preferred epicenter (Run B); $\Delta t_B = t_i - t_B$ is the difference (in seconds) between the estimated origin time t_i and our preferred origin time t_B. Runs J and K are for the aftershock.

The 1912-07-07 earthquake was the 3363rd event recorded by John Milne at Shide. It is listed in Shide Circular 27 as event 3363 with an arrival time of 08:08 UTC (Milne and Turner, 1912). Unfortunately, Milne died in 1913, and this was the final Shide Circular. Milne's death and the onset of World War I interrupted British seismological efforts. The Committee's final annual seismicity map was for the year 1910, which appeared posthumously in Milne *et al.* (1914). The British Association's seismological efforts were resumed years later, led by H. H. Turner and published as the International Seismological Summaries. Turner (1917) published 1913 seismicity and acknowledged the challenges associated with compiling seismicity for the years of 1911 and 1912, given the higher priority of keeping up with the current seismicity (Turner, 1923, 1924).

As far as we know, Gutenberg was the first to estimate an instrumental epicenter for the 1912-07-07 earthquake, whereas Matuzawa (1929) was the first to estimate an origin time (07:56:58 UTC). A summary of previous studies estimating the 1912 epicenter is shown in Table 1 and Figure 7. Gutenberg's epicenter (GR) is documented in Appendix A. Using Gutenberg's arrival times, Boyd and Lerner-Lam (1988) applied a formal inversion method to determine an epicenter BL88I that was south of the Denali fault and 112 km southeast of GR (Fig. 7). Doser (2004) estimated an epicenter D04I that was on the Denali fault and approximately between GR and BL88I. In 2018, the International Seismological Centre Global Instrumental Earthquake Catalogue (ISC-GEM) determined an epicenter ISCG that was just north of the Denali fault and 43 km west of D04I (International Seismological Centre, 2018).

Methods

NonLinLoc (NLL) is described in detail in Lomax *et al.* (2000, 2014); here, we review some key features. For a single earthquake, NLL thoroughly explores and maps the posterior density function for the hypocentral parameters, longitude, latitude, and depth, using tens of thousands of evaluations of a misfit function. This procedure is guided by an efficient cascading grid-search importance-sampling method called oct-tree (Lomax *et al.*, 2014). To aid in statistical calculations and for ease of visualization, posterior samples are drawn stochastically from the oct-tree posterior density function grid. These samples form a 3D cloud of points, which can be used to represent our confidence in the solution; for example, within the volume containing 90% of the posterior probability, there will be ~90% of the posterior samples. The NLL misfit function we use is based on the equal differential time (EDT) formulation (Zhou, 1994; Font *et al.*, 2004), which is more robust than standard location L2- or L1-norm misfit functions in the presence of outliers in the data. (An outlier observation has a residual much larger than its nominal uncertainty.) Travel times for *P*, *S*, and other phases used here are calculated using the TauP Toolkit (Crotwell *et al.*, 1999) with the spherical Earth model ak135 (Kennett *et al.*, 1995); uncertainties for all travel times are set to 2.0 s. (A larger assignment of travel-time errors—such as assuming that the Earth structure is significantly different from spherically symmetric—would result in larger estimated uncertainties of the epicenter.)

We primarily rely on the insensitivity of the NLL EDT formulation to outliers to effectively ignore observations with large errors. For more detail, see applications of NLL using historical data to the 1904 Alaska earthquake (Tape *et al.*, 2017), the 1900 Alaska earthquake (Tape *et al.*, 2021), and the 1906 San Francisco earthquake (Lomax, 2005, 2008).

For the 1912 Alaska earthquake, we performed the NLL EDT search over the volume bounded by longitudes −165° to −135° and latitudes 55° to 71°, and from the surface to 100 km depth.

Results

We perform 11 epicenter estimations using different subsets of the global arrival-time data. The results are summarized in Table 4. The single letter (A–K) provides an index for the run, with the longer text string providing basic information

No.	Date	Component	First P. T. begin	Second P. T. begin	Large waves begin	Maximum	End of principal portion	End	Maximum amplitude
	1912.		h m s	h m s	h m s	h m s	h m	h m	mm
301	June 24	N	.. .. ..	.. .. ..	10 37 00	.. .. ..	10 38	10 40	0. 1
		E	.. .. ..	10 36 40	10 36 54	10 36 57	10 38	10 41	0. 2
302	28	N	.. .. ..	.. .. ..	18 39 40	18 40 20	18 43	18 48	0. 2
		E	.. .. ..	.. .. ..	18 42 15	18 42 30	18 46	18 51	0. 1
303	July 7	N	7 59 29	.. .. ..	8 01 52	8 05 00	8 09	10 04	53. 8
		E	.. .. ..	.. .. ..	.. .. ..	8 03 ..	8 13	10 05	49+
304	8	N	21 56 12	.. .. ..	21 58 45	22 00 24	22 02	23 05	9. 0
		E	.. .. ..	.. .. ..	.. .. ..	.. .. ..	.. ..	.. ..	6. 0
305	25	E	23 29 20	.. .. ..	23 45 20	23 46 20	23 53	24 05	0. 2
306	Aug. 6	N	21 33 40	.. .. ..	21 45 50	21 46 30	.. ..	22 04	...

Figure 8. Excerpt from the Sitka, Alaska, seismic station register for July 1912 (Hazard, 1914). Times are listed in UTC. The 1912-07-07 mainshock is event 303, with the first detection at 07:59:29 UTC, which would be Saturday, 1912-07-06 21:59:29 local Alaska time. There is a significant aftershock recorded on 1912-07-08 21:56:12 UTC, which would be Monday, 1912-07-08 11:56:12 local Alaska time. The maximum amplitudes are 53.8 mm (N) and 49+ mm (E) for the mainshock and 9.0 mm (N) and 6.0 mm (E) for the aftershock.

on the run and corresponding to the output file names that are available (Lomax and Tape, 2025). For example, Run A is all_ISC, which refers to using all ISC data.

Our first relocation (Run A) is based on the data that are currently available from ISC and which we first retrieved in 2024. This data set includes arrival times from 58 global stations, including 49 *P* waves and 36 *S* waves. During the course of our study, we requested collaborative support from ISC for them to assemble arrival-time data for a specific event. The event was an aftershock that we inferred based on it (1) having a high-amplitude recording at Sitka (station code SIT), (2) occurring 38 hr after the mainshock, and (3) having a similar *S–P* differential time as the mainshock (Fig. 8). In the process of compiling arrival times for the aftershock, ISC discovered additional arrival times for the 1912-07-07 mainshock, and they also modified some phase assignments. Therefore, our preferred mainshock data set is an expanded version of ISC arrival times, with 85 stations, including 65 *P* waves and 50 *S* waves. We also include an *S*-arrival time for Sitka on the basis of the "Large waves begin" entry in the station register (Fig. 8). All of the arrival times used in this study for the 1912 mainshock and aftershock are available in Lomax and Tape (2025).

Table 4 summarizes a subset of relocations performed in this study. The first two runs, A and B, demonstrate the impact of the newly expanded data set of arrival times. The epicenter for Run A is in the Denali region, 55 km east of the summit, 42 km southeast of the MMI 7 shaking at McGonagall Pass, and west of the Parks Highway (Fig. 7a). Using the new data set, the epicenter shifts to the northwest by 36 km but still lies within the uncertainty ellipse of Run A (Fig. 7). Run B is our preferred epicenter, which we will discuss later.

Runs B–I demonstrate the influence of excluding distant stations from the full data set (Run B). This sequence was motivated by the clustering of data in Europe, as shown in Figure 9, as well as by high residuals encountered for certain North American stations. Starting with Run B, we progressively remove European stations (and others in the same epicentral range), to C, D, E, F, and then G, which contains no European stations. The last two columns of Table 4 list the difference in distance and origin time from the preferred epicenter. For Run G, the epicenter is 58 km northeast of the preferred epicenter (Table 4). For Run H, which uses all stations within North America, the epicenter is 62 km northeast of the preferred epicenter (Table 4). This northeastward shift from the preferred epicenter is much more pronounced for the original data set of arrival times than for the new expanded data set.

For illustrative purposes, we perform epicenter estimations using only the *P*- and *S*-arrival times at Sitka, for the mainshock (Run I) and for the largest aftershock (Run J). These single-station runs produce an expected annulus of epicenters, centered on Sitka and having an average radius corresponding to the *P–S* differential time. These runs result in epicenters in western Alaska, inconsistent with felt reports (Fig. 6), suggesting that either the *P* or *S* time (or both) at Sitka is not representative of the true arrival times.

Our preferred epicenter (25I in Table 1; Run B in Table 4) considers all ISC arrival times, including ones newly obtained for this study, in addition to SIT *S*. The global station coverage of *P* and *S* picks used in the relocation is displayed in Figure 9. Residuals are especially large (and negative) for three *P*-wave arrivals in North America (SIT, VIC, and SLM); these residuals remain high even when the distant stations are excluded, as in Run H (Tape, 2025). All epicenter locations were performed with station distribution weighting, which down-weights stations, such as in Europe, in our case, in proportion to the number and closeness of nearby stations. For the 1912 epicenter, this weighting results in a small reduction in epicenter uncertainty (semimajor axis 38 km to 33 km) and a small (7 km) shift in epicenter.

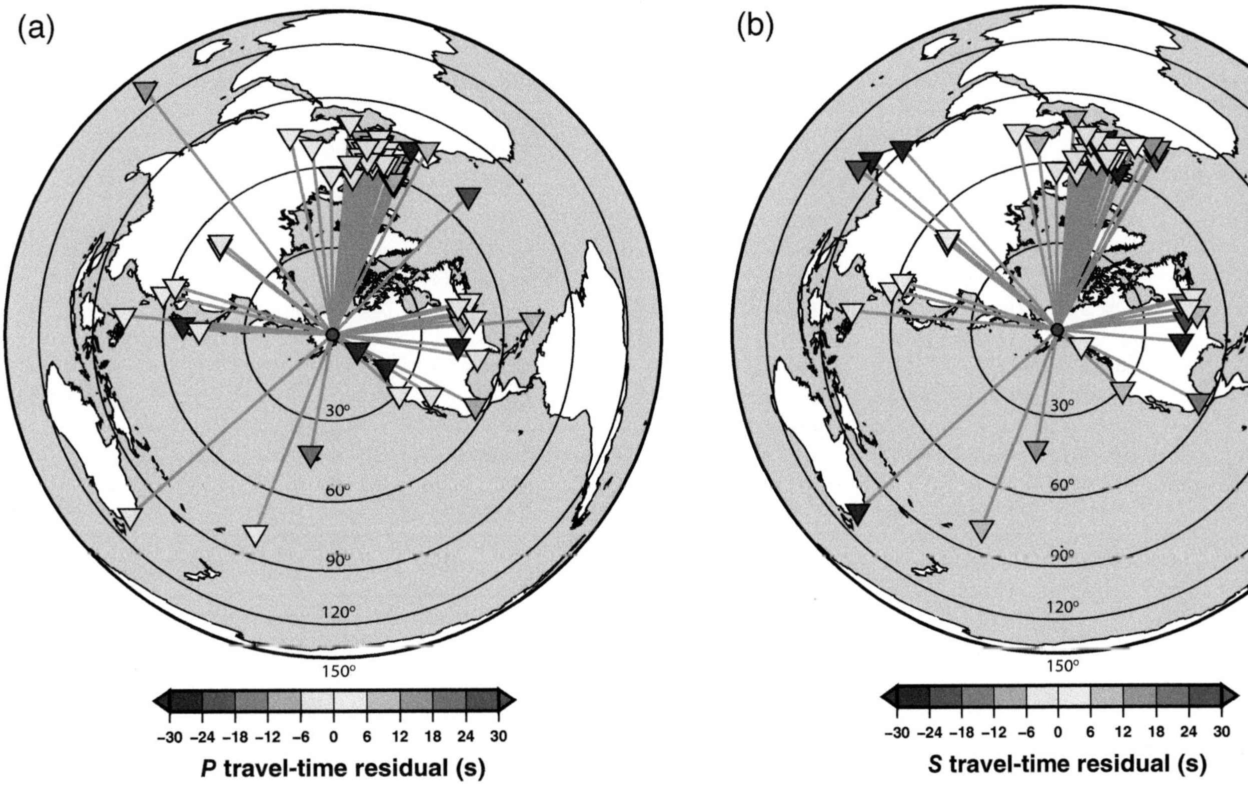

Figure 9. Global travel-time residuals, (a) *P* and (b) *S*, for our preferred epicenter (25I) for the 1912-07-07 earthquake (Table 1), which is at the center of the map. The residual values are tabulated in Lomax and Tape (2025). The color version of this figure is available only in the electronic edition.

Our preferred epicenter (25I) and its 68% confidence ellipse are near Denali and west of the Parks Highway (Fig. 7). Specifically, the maximum-likelihood epicenter is 42 km northeast of the summit and 18 km northeast of the MMI 7 shaking at McGonagall Pass. This epicenter is 235 km west of the epicenter assigned by Carver *et al.* (2004) at the site of reported tree damage near where the Richardson Highway crosses the Denali fault (C04M in Fig. 7). Epicenter 25I is also west of other instrumental epicenters: 218 km from BL88I, 185 km from GR, 164 km from D04I, and 123 km from ISCG (Fig. 7). It is important to note that these other studies used different arrival-time data and also different estimation methods. Further runs would be needed to demonstrate these influences. For example, the data used by Gutenberg are shown in Figure A1, and the data used by Boyd and Lerner-Lam (1988) are listed in Lomax and Tape (2025). It is probable that the data considered for the ISC-GEM location are the same as those used for our Run A, so the differences in those two epicenters (109 km) are mostly due to differences in methods. A previous study of a 1900 Alaska earthquake (Tape *et al.*, 2021) demonstrated that our epicenter differences from those of Gutenberg and Richter (1949), Boyd and Lerner-Lam (1988), and Doser (2006) were due to differences in methods.

Epicenter 25I is close to macroseismic-estimated epicenters: 54 km from our 25M and 53 km from D09M (Fig. 7b). Our two epicenters, estimated from instrumental data (25I) and macroseismic data (25M), agree with each other when considering their uncertainties.

SUMMARY OF AFTERSHOCKS

The locations of aftershocks help determine the mainshock epicentral region (Benioff, 1955; Sykes, 1971), and this was true for the 2002 rupture to the east of the 1912 earthquake (Haeussler *et al.*, 2004; Ratchkovski *et al.*, 2004). Detailed 1912 aftershock locations could provide an estimate of the rupture extent of the 1912 mainshock, and the sizes of the aftershocks would provide a proxy for the size of the mainshock (Båth's law). Nevertheless, it is also known that aftershocks can occur adjacent to, and on the margins of, the main slip areas (e.g., Doser and Kanamori, 1986; Hartzell and Heaton, 1986; Hsu *et al.*, 2006; Wetzler *et al.*, 2018).

In the days following the 1912 mainshock, there were many earthquakes felt at distances near and far from the epicenter. From the epicentral region, Browne wrote, "The earthquakes continued at regular intervals for about thirty-six hours. None of them could compare in strength with the first shock, but many of them were severe enough to wreck a modern city" (Browne, 1913b, p. 390). Belmore Browne's diary entry for July 13th included "Earthquakes have been working steadily." (Fig. B1b).

The aftershocks were also felt in Fairbanks, as reported by the newspapers (*Alaska Citizen*, 1912-07-08, p. 1: "repeated

TABLE 5
Seven Aftershocks (Labeled 1–7) of the 1912-07-07 Earthquake

Type	Index	Magnitude	Day	Local Time (yyyy/mm/dd hh:mm:ss)	Day	UTC Time (yyyy/mm/dd hh:mm:ss)	Felt or Recorded Location	Time Lag (hh:mm)	Distance (km)	Source
I	0	7.2	Saturday	1912/07/06 21:59:29	Sunday	1912/07/07 07:59:29	Sitka	–	–	Hazard (1914)
F	0	7.2	Saturday	1912/07/06 21:58	Sunday	1912/07/07 07:58	Fairbanks	–	213	FST, AC
F	0	7.2	Saturday	1912/07/06 21:53	Sunday	1912/07/07 07:53	Copper Center	–	305	Jones (1912)
F	1	–	Saturday	1912/07/06 22:06	Sunday	1912/07/07 08:06	Fairbanks	00:08	213	FST
F	1	–	Saturday	1912/07/06 22:0?	Sunday	1912/07/07 08:0?	Fairbanks	00:0?	213	AC
F	1	–	Saturday	1912/07/06 22:00	Sunday	1912/07/07 08:00	Copper Center	00:07	305	Jones (1912)
F	2	–	Sunday	1912/07/07 07:50	Sunday	1912/07/07 17:50	Fairbanks	09:52	213	AC
F	3, 4, 5	–	Sunday	1912/07/07 12:00	Sunday	1912/07/07 22:00	Fairbanks	14:02	213	AC
F	6	–	Monday	1912/07/08 05:10	Monday	1912/07/08 15:10	Fairbanks	31:12	213	AC
I	7	6.4	Monday	1912/07/08 11:56:12	Monday	1912/07/08 21:56:12	Sitka	37:57	–	Hazard (1914)
F	7	6.4	Monday	1912/07/08 12:00	Monday	1912/07/08 22:00	Knik	38:00	213	Herning (1912)

The first column denotes whether the data is from instrumental data at Sitka (I) or from a felt report (F). The index refers to the aftershock, with 0 representing the mainshock. The time lag is $t_i - t_0$, where t_0 is the mainshock time reported by the same literature source. The distance is listed for locally felt shaking; it is with respect to our preferred mainshock epicenter (−150.43°, 63.34°). The time lag entry "00:0?" represents the description "a few minutes later." The Sitka times listed are from the recorded seismic data (Fig. 8). AC, *Alaska Citizen*; FST, *Fairbanks Sunday Times*.

shakings of the earth's crust during the next 24 hours") and weather observer ("light tremors all night"). Fairbanks is 213 km from the instrumentally determined epicenter.

A summary of the seven felt aftershocks is shown in Table 5. We interpret the July 9 (local time) date of Sieberg (1920) to be mistaken for July 8; the event (Appendix A: "only slightly weaker than on the 6th" local time) is likely the aftershock that occurred at about noon local time on July 8, which we document next.

Aftershock at 1912-07-08 21:56 UTC

The closest-recording seismic station to the 1912 earthquake was Sitka, Alaska ($\Delta = 1087$ km; Fig. 1), which recorded an event with arrival time 1912-07-08 21:56:12 UTC having amplitudes that were about 15% of those recorded for the mainshock (Fig. 8). Assuming the same epicenter for the two events, this would suggest a magnitude of 6–7 for the aftershock. The aftershock interpretation is supported by the second event having a comparable *P–S* ("Large waves" minus "First P.T." = 153 s) to the mainshock (143 s). This aftershock event was listed in Somville (1925) and noted by Gutenberg, who may have mistaken the Somville entry to be the mainshock (Appendix A). A source of possible confusion is that the local origin time for the mainshock (21:58) is close to the UTC origin time of the aftershock (21:54).

Although this main aftershock does not currently appear in the ISC-GEM catalog or its supplement (International Seismological Centre, 2023), it does have globally recorded arrival times, such as the ones from Sitka (Fig. 8). Using a new collection of arrival times provided to us by ISC, we estimated the instrumental epicenter for the aftershock using NLL. The results are included as Run K (Table 4). The maximum-likelihood origin time is 21:53:50, the epicenter is at longitude −150.50°, latitude 63.44°, and the depth is 0 km. Its uncertainty ellipse is about twice the size of the mainshock uncertainty ellipse (Lomax and Tape, 2025).

The maximum-likelihood epicenter for the 1912-07-08 21:53:50 aftershock is 11 km from the mainshock epicenter, as shown in Figure 7a. Thus, both the mainshock and its largest aftershock occurred in the same region, just northeast of Denali.

The magnitude of the 1912-07-08 aftershock was estimated by ISC to be M_s 6.37 ± 0.16 using 25 stations (Domenico Di Giacomo, e-comm., 2025; see Lomax and Tape, 2025). We adopt these results and list M_s 6.4 for the event.

We found one felt report—Orville Herning in Knik (Fig. 5)—for the 1912-07-08 M_s 6.4 aftershock, which occurred at noon local time on Monday, July 8th (Table 5). The two times listed in Herning's diary (Herning, 1912) match the two events instrumentally recorded at Sitka (Fig. 8). We expect that the M_s 6.4 aftershock was felt in Fairbanks and recorded in the newspapers, but unfortunately there do not appear to be any preserved newspaper pages from Fairbanks for the key dates of July 9th and 10th (Tape, 2025). Belmore Browne does not mention any earthquake in his limited diary entry for July 8th, a day when the team trekked from McGonagall Pass to McKinley River (Browne, 1912).

REVIEW OF PALEOSEISMIC STUDIES IN CENTRAL ALASKA

The global instrumental record extends back to about 1900. Although some earthquakes in coastal Alaska were recorded during the Russian era starting in 1784 (Kisslinger, 1983; Lander, 1996), the written record in central Alaska began at about the time of the gold rush, in 1900. Therefore, identifying any pre-1900 ruptures in central Alaska requires paleoseismic studies. Furthermore, these same faults that record pre-1900 ruptures may also preserve evidence for instrumentally recorded ruptures, such as 2002. This section includes a review of paleoseismic studies within the 1912 epicentral region and extending to the Alaska Pipeline crossing of the Denali fault.

The paleoearthquake record of the Denali fault and adjacent portions of the Alaska Range has a limited spatial and temporal resolution due to the reconnaissance nature of most investigations in the region and practical constraints imposed by tectonics, geomorphology, and accessibility. For one, active glaciers cover ~40% of the 250 km of Denali fault trace between McGonagall Pass and the Alaska Pipeline, preventing preservation of paleoearthquake records for the subglacial portions of the fault. Furthermore, there are few faults with known or suspected Holocene activity within 30 km of the Denali fault (Bemis *et al.*, 2012; Koehler *et al.*, 2015; Koehler and Carver, 2018), and most of these are near Denali where several faults with morphologically youthful scarps occur between 5 and 10 km north of the Denali fault (Burkett *et al.*, 2016). Finally, most of the Alaska Range and Denali fault lie far from the road system, limiting access in general, and notably preventing access for mechanized excavation equipment often used to facilitate more comprehensive paleoseismic studies.

We summarize here the known constraints on the timing of the most recent earthquake occurring on the Denali fault between McGonagall Pass and the Alaska Pipeline, from west to east. Studies by Carlson *et al.* (2018) examine the Denali fault where it crosses the Nenana River, 98 km east of McGonagall Pass and 82 km east of the 1912 instrumental epicenter. (This is termed the "Dead Mouse [DM]" site; Fig. 3.) At this location, the fault offsets two fluvial terraces with sag ponds and shutter ridges along the surface trace (Carlson *et al.*, 2018). Excavations at this site revealed well-bedded sand and silty-sand deposits, with several brown–black organic-rich horizons representing buried soils. These bedded deposits are displaced and deformed across several fault zones; however, the earthquake-related deformation is capped by undeformed sediments that constrain the age of the youngest earthquake at this site to between 1510–1630 cal C.E. Immediately west of the study site, the fault crosses the Nenana River, and a broad low-relief floodplain formed between the Nenana and Jack rivers. This floodplain region exhibits well-developed fluvial morphology and, nearer to the Nenana River, a mature white spruce forest. Field surveys and analysis of lidar-derived topography provide no evidence of a surface rupture across the abandoned floodplain surfaces that span the projection of the Denali fault, nor any evidence of tree damage that could have occurred during a historic earthquake.

Personius *et al.* (2015) and Koehler *et al.* (2015) conducted paleoseismic studies on the Denali fault approximately 11 and 24 km east of the DM site. The Personius *et al.* (2015) study excavated two trenches across the Denali fault trace (the Schist Creek site), abandoning the first due to the absence of visible fault displacements. Their "Western" trench contained multiple fault strands that they map within 10–20 cm of the ground surface, overlain by a thin unfaulted sand layer and the modern tundra root mat. The radiocarbon sample analyzed for a minimum age for this youngest earthquake, collected from the unfaulted sand layer, resulted in a "modern" radiocarbon age. As a result, they interpret the timing of the most recent earthquake as between ~200 and 400 yr ago, based on the morphology of the fault scarp and the shallow depth of fault evidence. The Koehler *et al.* (2015) study excavated one trench at their site, documenting multiple fault traces that extend into the modern soil and correspond with tectonic geomorphic features of the landscape, including a steep facet at the base of the fault scarp and partially filled fissures. Unfortunately, all radiocarbon samples returned "modern" radiocarbon ages and thus the age of the most recent event is unconstrained.

Additional paleoseismic investigations have been conducted along the Denali fault between the Koehler *et al.* (2015) site and the Alaska Pipeline, but only studies on the intersecting Susitna Glacier fault are currently published. The rupture of this fault initiated the 2002 Denali fault earthquake, and paleoseismic investigations on the fault by Personius *et al.* (2017) document an age of 2210 ± 420 cal B.P. for the last earthquake before 2002.

REVIEW OF THE TREE DAMAGE ANALYSIS BY CARVER *et al.* (2004)

We examine the tree damage analysis by Carver *et al.* (2004), noting that we rely on the publication and a post-2002 field investigation of coauthor Haeussler at the field site of Carver *et al.* (2004). There are no data archives or data supplements pertaining to the study of Carver *et al.* (2004).

A critical part of the Carver *et al.* (2004) arguments for an eastern epicenter for the 1912 earthquake relates to observations of damaged trees in the Delta River valley. Specifically, they described evidence of tree damage associated with the surface rupture of the 2002 Denali fault earthquake, and then they made arguments that there was similar damage to older trees that occurred in 1912. We agree with the Carver *et al.* (2004) characterization of surface rupture and tree damage along the 2002 fault trace in the Delta River valley (see also Haeussler *et al.*, 2004). However, we find the Carver *et al.* (2004) evidence for linking older tree damage to the 1912 event is less robust and inconclusive.

Their arguments for 1912 damage to trees are in a section titled, "Evidence of Pre-2002 Tree Damage," which is summarized in the first paragraph (p. S60):

> *Many of the older trees damaged in the 2002 Denali fault earthquake have scars and deformities that record similar damage from the past. The old damage includes bent and deformed trunks, healed splits in the base of the trunks, trees lacking living lower branches, broken trees with multiple stump sprouts, dead trees, and trees with abrupt changes in the annual ring width coincident with past damage.*

Carver *et al.* (2004) argue that the trees on and near the 2002 fault trace have "bent or deformed trunks and few living branches on the lower part of the trunk" and they are "conspicuous because almost all other spruce trees in the forest have classic, straight vertical trunks and many living branches within a meter or two of the ground." An alternative interpretation is that bent trunks are common in spruce, typically no less than 25% of the population (Witkowska, 2008). Carver *et al.* (2004) also state that older trees near the fault generally lack low-to-the-ground branches, which alternatively could be interpreted as a feature of older trees (Millington and Chaney, 1973).

Carver *et al.* (2004) note the presence of trees with healed radial splits. "Trees with healed splits in the base of their trunks are present on the fault and absent in the rest of the forest." And that "The healed splits were found only in the larger (older) trees on the fault." Alternatively, commercial timber harvesters have found that cracks in trees can be attributed to: large size (Cameron *et al.*, 2017), fast growth (Valinger and Fridman, 1999), drought (Day, 1954; Persson, 1994; Schlyter *et al.*, 2006), wind (Valinger and Fridman, 1999; Schlyter *et al.*, 2006; Cameron *et al.*, 2017), snow damage (Nykänen *et al.*, 1997; Valinger and Fridman, 1999), cold (Cherubini *et al.*, 1997), and frost cracking (Kubler, 1983). Carver *et al.* (2004) note that it is the older trees that have evidence for radial cracks, consistent with the notion that older trees are more susceptible to cracking (e.g., Cameron *et al.*, 2017). Older trees would have more opportunities for splitting, due to the potential for rotting of the core of the trees, and more time for the trees to experience extreme wind and temperature events. Wind can have localized and devastating consequences. In one wind storm, a 160-yr-old stand of black spruce lost 28% of its stems (Van Cleve and Zasada, 1970).

Carver *et al.* (2004) observed that "A few trees growing on the fault had been broken off near their base in the past and have since regrown multiple trunks from stump sprouts (Coppice regrowth)." Although the regrowth of multiple trunks from a stump is a symptom of past tree breakage, breakage events are not diagnostic of fault rupture, and the Carver *et al.* (2004) assertion that trunks exhibiting coppice regrowth "are present along the fault but generally are absent in the remainder of the forest" is not demonstrated with data in their article.

To be more quantitative, Carver *et al.* (2004) conducted a tree damage survey of 76 trees along two ~120-m-long transects. One transect was along the fault trace (which was presumably focused on the damaged trees), and the other was about 300 m to the south. Their damage categories were: damage, leaning, part dead, dead, split, broken, multiple. Their statistics show 79% of trees were damaged along the fault. We suggest the study would have been improved by stating the on-fault and off-fault population sizes, and it would have benefited from examining a similar stand of trees 10–20+ km away from the fault trace.

Finally, Carver *et al.* (2004) examined the tree ring widths of trees damaged before the 2002 earthquake. Critical to their arguments is "Tree #12," which had a deep crack near the center of the tree, which was healed over. The tree died some number of years before 2002, but in the 2002 earthquake, the surface rupture went through the stump, and the tree fell over. They found that tree rings 79 and higher (older) were wider than rings 78 and younger. They infer that the change in ring width is related to fault-induced damage. However, they stated there is nothing to tie the change in ring width between rings 78 and 79 to the year 1912. In addition, if the change in ring width was related to surface faulting from the 1912-07-07 earthquake, it should occur in the middle of ring 79, but it is clear from figure 5(d) in Carver *et al.* (2004) that the change in ring width occurs during the winter after a wide ring 79 was laid down, which is inconsistent with the proposed timing of the formation of the crack. Alternatively, as outlined earlier, there are a multitude of possible causes for radial cracks in trees in the absence of earthquakes.

Carver *et al.* (2004) present tree ring-width data for five other trees: three that are along the fault, and two that are undamaged and "growing at a distance from the fault." The three trees along the fault show a progressive change in ring widths straddling 1912 that occurs over a span of 4–8 yr, with changes preceding 1912 by one or two years. The two off-fault trees show an increase in width for 1–3 yr around 1912. The fact that ring widths were changing before 1912 indicates that factors other than surface faulting were the cause of the change in growth rate. Alternative multiyear causes of changes in ring width are typically attributed to climate (Schweingruber, 1988; Davi *et al.*, 2003) or subsurface hydrology (Creutzfeldt *et al.*, 2015; Hunter *et al.*, 2020). Even the cyclic abundance of snowshoe hare has been found to drastically affect spruce seedlings and saplings and their growth rate in boreal forests (Hodges, 1999; Krebs *et al.*, 2001; Olnes *et al.*, 2017).

In summary, although the tree damage study of Carver *et al.* (2004) is intriguing, we infer that alternative interpretations are viable where damage may be consistent with a typical boreal forest. We suggest that additional studies could offer further insight.

DISCUSSION

Our new results provide a consistent picture of the 1912 earthquake, which occurred in the Denali region, west of the Parks Highway (Fig. 3), 163 km west of the western extent of the 2002 M_w 7.9 rupture (Fig. 10), and 235 km west of the 1912 epicenter assigned by Carver *et al.* (2004). The Denali region contains two independent epicentral estimates (25I, 25M) derived from the expanded data sets of global arrival times and felt reports. We locate a M_s 6.4 aftershock only 11 km from the instrumentally determined mainshock (25IA in Fig. 3), providing additional support for the mainshock epicenter estimate.

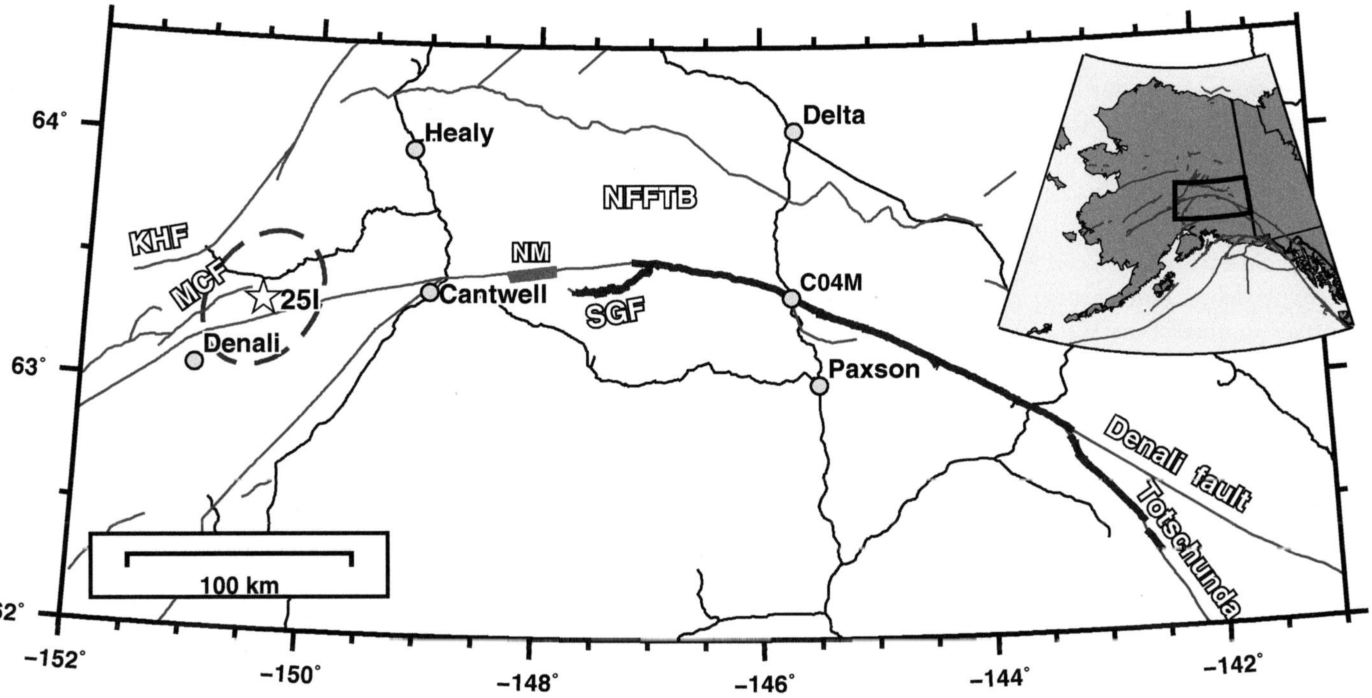

Candidate faults for the 1912 earthquake

We consider three possible fault sources for the 1912 earthquake (Fig. 3):

1. **Denali fault:** The Denali fault is a major right-lateral strike-slip fault extending from the Yukon Territory, Canada, into southwest Alaska (St. Amand, 1957; Grantz, 1966). It last ruptured in 2002 along a 226 km segment, plus 66 km on the Totschunda fault and 48 km on the Susitna Glacier thrust fault (Haeussler *et al.*, 2004). The Denali fault has a significant cumulative offset that decreases from east (~480 km since 52 Ma; Waldien *et al.*, 2021) to west (155 km since 37 Ma; Regan *et al.*, 2021). The fault trace forms a topographic trough in the Alaska Range, and this trough is occupied by active glaciers, recently deglaciated terrain, and young alluvial fans and talus slopes for a significant portion of its length. Near the 1912 epicentral region, the Denali fault trace makes an abrupt 17° bend to the southwest, forming a major restraining bend and driving uplift and regional deformation (e.g., Benowitz *et al.*, 2022). The surface trace of the Denali fault in the vicinity of the 1912 epicenter is obscured beneath the Muldrow Glacier, active talus slopes, and a smaller glacier that occupies the fault trace immediately to the east. Clear surface rupture-related geomorphology increases eastward from the eastern margin of the uncertainty ellipse in Figure 3, and consists of fault scarps, sag ponds, and displaced landforms. The DM paleoseismic site (Fig. 3; Carlson *et al.*, 2018) provides a limit on the potential extent for a rupture of this portion of the Denali fault in 1912 because the most recent surface rupture at that location on the Denali fault occurred between 1510 and 1630 C.E.

   Our preferred, relocated maximum-likelihood epicenter (251) is about 10 km from the Denali fault, and its uncertainty ellipse spans a ~50 km section of the Denali fault (Fig. 3). The maximum felt shaking from the 1912 earthquake occurred at McGonagall Pass, adjacent to the Muldrow Glacier, which overlies the Denali fault. One consideration is that the Parker–Browne team was therefore about 1–2 km from the Denali fault. Browne's descriptions from McGonagall Pass are dramatic, but they are not at the MMI 9–10 level that would be expected for an on-fault site of a M_s 7.2. Possibly the Denali fault ruptured further to the east or west than the site at McGonagall Pass—or on another fault altogether.
2. **McLeod Creek fault:** The McLeod Creek fault is an active, southeast-dipping thrust fault situated 10–15 km north of and subparallel to the Denali fault (Burkett *et al.*, 2016). It is characterized by a prominent fault scarp that is readily

Figure 10. Relationship between the 1912 M_s 7.2 epicentral region (251, with dashed ellipse), near Denali, and the 2002-11-03 M_w 7.9 earthquake. The 2002 earthquake ruptured 340 km (blue line) along the Susitna Glacier fault (SGF), the Denali fault, and the Totschunda fault (Haeussler *et al.*, 2004). Active faults are plotted in red and include Kantishna Hills (KHF), McLeod Creek (MCF), and the NFFTB. The rupture of the 2002-10-23 M_w 6.7 Nenana Mountain (NM) earthquake (Wright *et al.*, 2003) is plotted as a short gray segment on the Denali fault. C04M is the 1912 epicenter assigned by Carver *et al.* (2004). Inset map of Alaska shows a box of the expanded region. The color version of this figure is available only in the electronic edition.

traced in satellite imagery and high-resolution topographic data across late Pleistocene and Holocene surficial deposits continuously along the topographic range front. Burkett *et al.* (2016) highlight the youthfulness of recent surface rupture on the McLeod Creek fault based on radiocarbon dating of samples from a buried soil that is offset by the fault. This soil horizon was the ground surface at the time of a prehistoric debris flow, which buried the soil, and this soil and debris flow package was subsequently offset by a surface rupture of the McLeod Creek fault. The buried soil age of 630 cal B.P. indicates this fault ruptured sometime after 1320 C.E.

3. **Kantishna Hills fault:** The Kantishna Hills anticline (Lesh and Ridgway, 2007; Bemis *et al.*, 2012) was included as an active fold structure in Koehler *et al.* (2012), and it is listed as a two-section thrust fault in the latest compilation (Haeussler *et al.*, 2025). This modeling as a thrust fault is based on the receiver function analysis by Schulte-Pelkum *et al.* (2025) that inferred a gently south-dipping detachment fault at depth, extending from beneath the Kantishna Hills southward towards the Denali fault (Fig. 3). This structure appears to be a blind thrust, with no known surface fault trace associated with this fault and the up-dip termination of the fault at ~12 km depth in a zone of abundant seismicity (Ratchkovski and Hansen, 2002) and beneath the Kantishna Hills anticline. Bender *et al.* (2019) illustrate the latest Pleistocene and Holocene deformation associated with this fault based on the folding of fluvial terraces across the anticlinal axis.

Another set of faults—the East Fork faults (Plafker *et al.*, 1994)—occur as two subparallel, steeply south-dipping normal faults near the preferred epicenter 25I, 7 and 10 km north of the Denali fault. The fault traces are well defined by fresh-appearing fault scarps that traverse ridges, floodplains, and glacial moraines, forming uphill and up-valley facing scarps that increase in vertical separation with increasing surficial geology unit age. This normal-fault geometry is unexpected in this location because the McLeod Creek fault occurs as a thrust fault a few kilometers along strike to the west, and because the sense of displacement across the fault appears to be opposite to the long-term motion based on the juxtaposed geologic units (Burkett *et al.*, 2016). The East Fork faults are not included in the 2023 compilation (Haeussler *et al.*, 2025), due to their short lengths. We infer, based on the short map traces and out-of-place fault geometry, that these faults are not seismogenic sources themselves. Instead, these may occur as secondary, hanging-wall faults that slip during motion on an underlying fault—either the Kantishna Hills fault or the speculative eastward continuation of the McLeod Creek fault from Burkett *et al.* (2016). Although the East Fork faults may not be seismogenic themselves, the recent surface rupture indicated by the freshness of the scarps would support recent displacement on the primary fault.

We also discuss two sets of structures that are outside our uncertainty region (Fig. 3), making them lower-likelihood candidates for the 1912 earthquake.

- **South of Denali bedrock faults:** Haeussler (2008) described several reverse faults in bedrock south of the high peaks of the Alaska Range: the Foraker thrust (~40 km long), the Roosters Comb thrust (~30 km long), the Pittock Pass thrust (~30 km long), and related structures. These features exhibit large geologic offsets, are in a position to accommodate strain in the bend of the Denali fault system, and may be active. But activity can not be proven because there are no Quaternary sediments or landforms in this glacially mantled region that could provide a record of an earthquake surface rupture. The faults are not included within the 2023 compilation (Haeussler *et al.*, 2025).

  We consider these bedrock faults to be a lower likelihood possibility for the 1912 earthquake, due to their location outside of our uncertainty ellipse (Fig. 3) and due to their lack of evidence of active faulting.
- **Broad Pass fault:** The northwest-dipping Broad Pass thrust fault (Fig. 3) was proposed by Haeussler *et al.* (2017) to explain a Neogene terrestrial basin—Peters Hill basin—interpreted as a wedge-top basin that formed on top of an active, southeast vergent, thrust fault. Movement along this thrust raised a ridge of Jurassic and Cretaceous metasedimentary rocks, which then trapped Miocene and Pliocene sediments behind it that were derived from the growing Alaska Range. The presence of this thrust fault is consistent with regional structural, stratigraphic, seismicity, gravity, and aeromagnetic data (Haeussler *et al.*, 2017). The Peters Hills basin is no longer a depocenter, but if the Broad Pass thrust remains active, it would help explain the westward decrease in Quaternary slip rate along the Denali fault system.

  We consider the Broad Pass fault as a low-likelihood possibility for the 1912 earthquake. Projecting the fault to the northwest at its listed dip of 60° (Haeussler *et al.*, 2025) would reach a depth of 30 km at a lateral distance of about 17 km ($30/\sqrt{3}$) from the surface trace; this down-dip extent is outside of the uncertainty ellipse (Fig. 3). There are no Holocene scarps associated with this fault, and therefore if it hosted the 1912 earthquake, it would have been a blind-fault thrust rupture, lacking any surface expression.

Three rupture scenarios

Based on our two leading candidate faults—Denali and McLeod Creek (Fig. 3)—we propose three potential rupture scenarios: (1) a strike-slip rupture on the Denali fault, (2) a thrust rupture on the south-dipping McLeod Creek fault, and (3) a combined strike-slip and thrust rupture involving both faults. The McLeod Creek rupture, in turn, could occur with or without the rupture of the underlying proposed

Kantishna detachment (Schulte-Pelkum *et al.*, 2025). In discussing these scenarios, we are interested in identifying what kind of evidence, if any, would be left behind at the surface. Surface ruptures are most likely for large-magnitude ($M_w > 7$) and shallow (depths < 20 km) events, irrespective of mechanism (strike slip, thrust, or normal; Baize *et al.*, 2019).

Considering the 1912 epicentral region, the closest definitive evidence for surface-breaking earthquake ruptures comes from the 2002 M_w 7.9 earthquake, which initiated as a M_w 7.2 subevent on the Susitna Glacier thrust fault (rupturing 48 km) and then continued for 292 km as a strike-slip rupture on the Denali and Totschunda faults (Eberhart-Phillips *et al.*, 2003; Haeussler *et al.*, 2004; Fig. 10). About 30% (99/340) of the rupture occurred within glacier ice (Haeussler *et al.*, 2004).

For the strike-slip scenario of the 1912 earthquake, we might expect extensive surface rupture, as was the case in 2002 (Haeussler *et al.*, 2004). However, glaciers and the steep, unvegetated, talus-covered slopes obscure any record of recent displacement for ~120 km of the Denali fault in the 1912 epicentral region.

For a thrust earthquake of M_s 7.2, the possibility of surface rupture would depend on the depth of the rupturing fault. The documented youthful surface rupture of the McLeod Creek fault makes it a promising candidate fault for the 1912 earthquake, although a preinstrumental (pre-1900) rupture of this fault is also compatible with the 1320 C.E. maximum age constraint. The Kantishna Hills fault, as proposed, lies deeper beneath the McLeod Creek fault in the epicentral region, and it could potentially rupture without generating surface displacement. Smaller "blind thrust" events have produced no surface displacements, such as the 1983 M_w 6.3 Coalinga earthquake and the 1994 M_w 6.7 Northridge earthquake (Stein and King, 1984; USGS and SCEC, 1994).

The 2002 M_w 7.9 earthquake, which started 163 km east of the 1912 epicenter (Fig. 10), is a prime example of a combined thrust and strike-slip rupture. Potentially this same large-scale transpressive tectonic stress regime could have activated the McCleod Creek and Denali faults in the 1912 earthquake. Multiple factors might contribute to the occurrence of a multifault rupture: (1) the close proximity of the Denali fault, McLeod Creek fault, and Kantishna Hills fault; (2) their inferred connection at depth; and (3) the geometric complexity of the Denali fault restraining bend to the west. It is possible that the 1912 rupture initiated on one of the candidate faults and proceeded to another fault.

We acknowledge another earthquake scenario in the epicentral region—an intraslab earthquake—but we rule it out on the basis of seismic recordings. Based on the combined GCMT catalog (1976–2025; Ekstrom *et al.*, 2012) and the ISC-GEM catalog (1904–1976), the most common events in the 1912 epicentral region are within the underlying slab. Within the uncertainty ellipse of our preferred epicenter, all 11 events are intraslab, having depths of 97–155 km and magnitudes M_w 4.8–5.6. Within 150 km of our preferred epicenter, the largest intraslab events are 1991-05-01 M_w 6.3 (depth 118 km, distance 110 km), 2021-05-15 M_w 6.1 (depth 66 km, distance 134 km), and 1995-12-30 M_w 5.7 (depth 143 km, distance 32 km). As discussed in Tape *et al.* (2017), the global catalog of Gutenberg and Richter (1954) contained hundreds of deep events, including 1948-08-19 M 6.25, which is listed in the ISC-GEM supplemental catalog with undetermined magnitude and a high-quality depth of 89.5 ± 5.9 km.

Gutenberg categorized the 1912 earthquake as "shallow," which meant ≤60 km depth. The ISC-GEM catalog lists a depth of 10 ± 3.7 km along with the highest quality depth rating. Our own inversion results also place the depth near the surface (Table 1), with an estimated uncertainty of 8 km (Lomax and Tape, 2025). Therefore we believe that an intraslab origin for the 1912 earthquake is unlikely.

Possibility of foreshocks and aftershocks

The ISC-GEM catalog was originally complete for $M_s \geq 7.5$ for events between 1904 and 1917 (Di Giacomo, Bondár, *et al.*, 2015). This magnitude of completeness is expected to decrease as additional events are included. For example, the 1912 M_s 7.2 earthquake was included in the ISC-GEM catalog in 2018 (Table 1). Smaller events from this era, such as the M_s 6.4 aftershock, neither appear in the ISC-GEM catalog nor its supplement nor the more expansive ISC Bulletin. This reminds us that there are likely other $M_s \geq 6.0$ earthquakes that could improve our understanding of the M_s 7.2 mainshock. We found the M_s 6.4 aftershock from inspection of the Sitka station register (Fig. 8), but a more comprehensive analysis of global arrival-time data and amplitudes would be needed to identify the presence or absence of significant foreshocks and aftershocks.

The 2002 sequence of events included a key foreshock, with the 2002-10-23 M_w 6.7 Nenana Mountain earthquake rupturing the Denali fault 11 days prior to the 2002-11-03 M_w 7.9 earthquake. The M_w 6.7 was immediately west of the M_w 7.9, with 33 km separating the eastern extent of the uniform-slip model of Wright *et al.* (2003) from the westernmost inferred surface rupture on the Denali fault, at the West Fork glacier (Haeussler *et al.*, 2004). Wright *et al.* (2003) demonstrated that the M_w 6.7 earthquake "increased the Coulomb stress at the Denali Earthquake hypocenter by 30–60 kPa, encouraging the subsequent failure" (p. 4). If the 1912 earthquake had a foreshock hours to days earlier, then it would be expected to be in the vicinity of the mainshock, within the Denali region.

The large negative P-wave residuals at the two closest stations, SIT (Sitka, Alaska: −31 s) and VIC (Victoria, Canada; −34 s), indicate that the observed arrivals are early relative to the predictions of our preferred epicenter (Fig. 9; table B in Lomax and Tape, 2025). This raises the possibility of a smaller event occurring about 30 s before the mainshock.

An alternative explanation for the large residuals is just the typical timing and phase picking challenges that were common to seismic recordings of this era.

Magnitude and rupture length

The magnitude of an earthquake is an essential characteristic and also one that can be challenging to determine, especially for the largest earthquakes. Our study does not use recorded amplitudes or waveforms, and therefore we rely on previous efforts to ascribe a magnitude. Table 2 summarizes previously determined magnitude estimates for the 1912 earthquake. We adopt the surface-wave magnitude value of M_s 7.2 by Abe and Noguchi (1983b), recognizing the possibility of a higher (M_w 7.66) or lower (M_w 6.88) magnitude implied by the ISC-GEM estimate (M_w 7.27 ± 0.39).

Both Doser (2004) and Carver *et al.* (2004) invoke empirical scaling relations to infer a rupture length for the 1912 earthquake. From Wells and Coppersmith (1994), a magnitude of 7.2 for a strike-slip earthquake corresponds to a surface rupture of 60 km. We raise two issues with this application. First, the empirical relationship does not appear to work well for the nearby 2002 event: the predicted surface rupture for a 7.9 magnitude is 181 km, whereas the actual surface rupture length was 292 km on the Denali–Totschunda and 340 km if including the 48 km rupture of the Susitna Glacier thrust (Haeussler *et al.*, 2004). Second, the published uncertainties in the slope and intercept terms for the log-scaled empirical relationship lead to large uncertainties in the predicted rupture length. For example, for the magnitude 7.2, the predicted rupture length is 60 ± 110 km, and for the magnitude 7.9, the predicted rupture length is 181 ± 368 km.

Value of historical instrumental data

Our study is enabled by the continued archival and digitization of historical seismic data. Previous studies estimating the 1912 epicenter (Gutenberg and Richter, 1949; Boyd and Lerner-Lam, 1988; Doser, 2004) spent considerable effort trying to collect the globally available arrival-time data, and in all of these cases, those data sets were incomplete. The ISC continues to pursue this undertaking, resulting in the expansion of its database and catalog for historical earthquakes. The 1912 earthquake was added to the ISC-GEM catalog in 2018, and the arrival times are accessible from the computer command line.

The impact of an expanded data set of arrival times can be seen in Figure 7. The preferred epicenter, in Figure 7b, is shifted northwestward by 36 km and, importantly, its uncertainty ellipse is smaller. In addition, with the expanded dataset, the epicentral estimates are more stable for different data subsets (Table 4). Both the shift in epicenter and the reduction in uncertainty influence and substantiate our interpretation of the 1912 earthquake.

CONCLUSIONS

We conclude by listing some future opportunities for understanding the 1912 earthquake.

1. **New paleoseismic studies:** The unique correlation of a fault to the 1912 earthquake through paleoseismic methods would be challenging, with timing limitations due to radiocarbon dating uncertainties and site-specific conditions. Unfortunately, higher resolution age control that is possible through dendrochronologic studies is not suitable in the epicentral region (Fig. 3) because the fault zones there are primarily above treeline. However, examination of surface faulting records could further constrain potential source fault scenarios by determining if the age constraints for the most recent surface rupture are compatible with a 1912 earthquake or not. Paleoseismic investigations of the Denali fault in the epicentral area are limited to the ~60 km stretch of the fault trace from the easternmost extent of active glaciers to the location of the DM site (Fig. 3). Current efforts, expanding on Schwartz *et al.* (2005), may provide information on the potential for a surface rupture compatible with a 1912 earthquake for this portion of the fault. Improving the post-1320 C.E. surface rupture constraint for the McLeod Creek fault (Burkett *et al.*, 2016) should be feasible with focused paleoseismic investigations along this fault because the current age control is from a soil buried by a debris flow, and the faulting occurred an unknown amount of time after the debris flow. Excavating to expose soils and sediments directly buried by displacement of the McLeod Creek fault would directly limit the age of the surface rupture. Without a surface trace, the Kantishna Hills fault does not have a recognized target for directly dating the rupture of the fault. If displacement on the Kantishna Hills fault produced surface folding, a low abandoned floodplain surface could have formed along any stream that flows across the fold. With our current interpretation of the East Fork faults, paleoseismic investigations of them would produce surface rupture age constraints that represent displacement on the underlying Kantishna Hills or McLeod Creek fault.
2. **Comprehensive assessment of historical and active seismicity and mechanisms:** It has been over two decades since Ratchkovski and Hansen (2002) relocated seismicity and estimated source mechanisms in the Kantishna region. With the benefit of more seismicity, improved methods for estimating source mechanisms (Silwal and Tape, 2016), and improved methods for relocating seismicity (Shelly *et al.*, 2007; Ross *et al.*, 2019), it is time to revisit the seismotectonics of the Kantishna region and the proposed faulting model of Schulte-Pelkum *et al.* (2025).

3. **Analysis of globally recorded seismic waveforms:** There are a few known seismograms for the 1912 earthquake (e.g., Doser, 2004) that could potentially be used to understand the mechanism of the earthquake, as well as the rupture time history. A small number of historical seismograms can provide fundamental insights into large earthquakes (e.g., Kanamori *et al.*, 2010). Recorded seismograms could also be searched for foreshocks and aftershocks of the 1912 earthquake.
4. **Revisiting the trees damaged in 2002 M_w 7.9 earthquake:** Dendrochronological methods have improved in the past two decades since Carver *et al.* (2004). If the trees were not damaged during the 1912 rupture, then how (and when) were they damaged? It could also be interesting to document the healing of any 2002-damaged trees that survived.

The intraplate region of mainland Alaska is ideally suited for studies of historical earthquakes starting in about 1900. First, there are many faults (known and unknown) that appear to be capable of producing magnitude-7 earthquakes, yet the seismicity rate is relatively low on account of low strain rates (Koehler and Carver, 2018). It may be the case that centuries are needed to witness maximum-magnitude events on these faults. Examples of these events include 1904 M_s 7.3 Iditarod-Nixon (Tape *et al.*, 2017), 1958 M_s 7.3 Huslia (Davis, 1960), and the 1937 M_s 7.3 Salcha earthquake (Bramhall, 1938). Second, the rise in felt reports—associated with the Alaska Gold Rush—coincides with the dawn of the instrumental era, providing essential complementary information. The sparse global coverage of stations in the early 1900s increases the value of felt reports to help identify the epicentral region (e.g., Boyd and Lerner-Lam, 1988; Doser, 2009; Tape *et al.*, 2021). As shown in our study, archival records can provide valuable information on earthquake shaking in Alaska. Still, the cornerstone of our efforts is to estimate the epicenter using all available global arrival times.

For the 1912 M_s 7.2 earthquake, our findings have shifted the attention from the eastern section of the Denali fault, which ruptured in the 2002 M_w 7.9 earthquake, to a western section near the namesake mountain of the fault (Fig. 10). Whereas Carver *et al.* (2004) interpreted the 1912 rupture as coinciding with the western portion of the 2002 rupture on the Denali fault, we interpret the 1912 earthquake as occurring 163 km west of the western extent of the 2002 Denali fault rupture (Haeussler *et al.*, 2004) and 104 km west of the western extent of the 2002-10-23 M_w 6.7 foreshock rupture (Wright *et al.*, 2003). We also raise the possibility of a thrust fault hosting all or part of the 1912 earthquake rupture. Our results imply a gap of about 100 km between the 1912 and 2002 earthquakes (Fig. 10), raising questions about the past and future ruptures on the Denali fault and adjacent thrust faults in this gap region.

DATA AND RESOURCES

All the felt reports for the 1912 earthquake (Table 3) are documented in Tape (2025), which also contains details on our estimation of macroseismic epicenters using the felt reports. Arrival-time data were obtained from the International Seismological Centre (ISC; Run A of Table 4), with an enhanced data set provided from ISC by Domenico Di Giacomo (Run B of Table 4). The arrival times used for each run in Table 4 are provided in Lomax and Tape (2025). Published studies on the 1912 earthquake are listed in the ISC Event Bibliography (Di Giacomo *et al.*, 2014). We identified three additional publications (BSSA, 1912; Carver *et al.*, 2004; Doser, 2004), which have since been added to the ISC Event Bibliography. Generic Mapping Tools (GMT; https://www.generic-mapping-tools.org/) was used for plotting several figures (Wessel and Smith, 1991). NonLinLoc (NLL) is available at https://github.com/ut-beg-texnet/NonLinLoc. All epicentral location results from NLL are provided in Lomax and Tape (2025). The ISC-GEM catalog is available from the ISC website and is documented in Di Giacomo, Bondár, *et al.* (2015), Di Giacomo, Harris, *et al.* (2015), and Bondár *et al.* (2015). The active fault database for Alaska is available from Bender *et al.* (2021) and described in Haeussler *et al.* (2025). The 75% confidence ellipse for epicenter BL88I in Figure 7 was calculated from hard-copy computer code output sent from Thomas Boyd to Carl Tape in August 2017 (Lomax and Tape, 2025). All websites were last accessed in October 2025.

DECLARATION OF COMPETING INTERESTS

The authors acknowledge that there are no conflicts of interest recorded.

ACKNOWLEDGMENTS

The authors thank Editor Tom Brocher, Diane Doser, Natalia Ruppert, and an anonymous reviewer for providing thorough reviews that improved the article. This research was supported in part by the National Science Foundation (NSF; EAR 1250461 to Bemis) and by the U.S. Geological Survey (USGS), Department of the Interior, under USGS Award Numbers G23AP00293 (Tape, Lomax) and G14AP00134 (Bemis). Domenico Di Giacomo at the International Seismological Centre (ISC) provided a revised data set of arrival times for the M_s 7.2 mainshock, as well as a new collection of arrival times for the M_s 6.4 aftershock. The authors thank Thomas Boyd for providing detailed results from the study of Boyd and Lerner-Lam (1988). The authors acknowledge several contributions to their archival efforts. Caltech Archives digitized Beno Gutenberg's notepads (Fig. A1) and made them publicly accessible. The Rauner Special Collections Library at Dartmouth provided a scan of the Browne diary (Browne, 1912). Elizabeth Drewes-Todd searched the archive of USGS geologists' field notebooks at the USGS Alaska Science Center in Anchorage. Matthew Sturm provided expertise regarding the geography of the Denali region and the 1910 (Sturm, 2023), 1912, and 1913 expeditions. Kelly Taylor optimized the newspaper image in Figure 2. Ronni Grapenthin translated the German script in Sieberg (1920) (Fig. A2a), and Julien Thurin helped in reading the French text of Somville (1925). The authors are grateful for these contributions. Any use of trade, firm, or product names is for descriptive purposes only and does not imply endorsement by the U.S. Government.

REFERENCES

Abe, K. (1981). Magnitudes of large shallow earthquakes from 1904 to 1980, *Phys. Earth Planet. In.* **27,** 72–92.

Abe, K. (1992). Seismicity of the caldera-making eruption of Mount Katmai, Alaska in 1912, *Bull. Seismol. Soc. Am.* **82,** no. 1, 175–191.

Abe, K., and S. Noguchi (1983a). Determination of magnitude for large shallow earthquakes 1898–1917, *Phys. Earth Planet. In.* **32,** 45–59.

Abe, K., and S. Noguchi (1983b). Revision of magnitudes of large shallow earthquakes, 1897–1912, *Phys. Earth Planet. In.* **33,** 1–11.

Adkins, J. D. (1940). The Alaskan earthquake of July 22, 1937, *Bull. Seismol. Soc. Am.* **30,** no. 4, 353–376.

Baize, S., F. Nurminen, A. Sarmiento, T. Dawson, M. Takao, O. Scotti, T. Azuma, P. Boncio, J. Champenois, F. R. Cinti, *et al.* (2019). A worldwide and unified database of surface Ruptures (SURE) for fault displacement hazard analyses, *Seismol. Res. Lett.* **91,** 499–520.

Bakun, W. H. (2006). MMI attenuation and historical earthquakes in the Basin and Range province of western North America, *Bull. Seismol. Soc. Am.* **96,** no. 6, 2206–2220.

Bakun, W. H., and C. M. Wentworth (1997). Estimating earthquake location and magnitude from seismic intensity data, *Bull. Seismol. Soc. Am.* **87,** no. 6, 1502–1521.

Bemis, S. P., and W. K. Wallace (2007). Neotectonic framework of the north-central Alaska Range foothills, in *Tectonic Growth of a Collisional Continental Margin: Crustal Evolution of Southern Alaska*, K. D. Ridgway, J. M. Trop, J. M. G. Glen, and J. M. O'Neill (Editors), Geol. Soc. Am. Special Paper 431, Boulder, Colorado, 549–572.

Bemis, S. P., G. A. Carver, and R. D. Koehler (2012). The Quaternary thrust system of the northern Alaska Range, *Geosphere* **8,** no. 1, 1–10.

Bender, A. M., P. J. Haeussler, and P. M. Powers (2021). Geologic inputs for the 2023 Alaska update to the U.S. National Seismic Hazard Model (NSHM) (ver. 2.0, February 2023), *U.S. Geol. Surv. Data Release*, doi: 10.5066/P97NRR0F.

Bender, A. M., R. O. Lease, P. J. Haeussler, T. Rittenour, L. B. Corbett, P. R. Bierman, and M. W. Caffee (2019). Pace and process of active folding and fluvial incision across the Kantishna Hills anticline, central Alaska, *Geophys. Res. Lett.* **46,** 3235–3244.

Benioff, H. (1955). Mechanism and strain characteristics of the White Wolf fault as indicated by the aftershock sequence, in *Earthquakes in Kern County, California During 1952*, O. P. Jenkins and G. B. Oakeshott (Editors), State of California Natural Resources, Division of Mines, Bulletin 171, San Francisco, California, 199–202.

Benowitz, J. A., S. M. Roeske, S. P. Regan, T. S. Waldien, J. L. Elliott, and P. B. O'Sullivan (2022). Large-scale, crustal-block vertical extrusion between the Hines Creek and Denali faults coeval with slip localization on the Denali fault since ca, 45 Ma, Hayes Range, Alaska, USA, *Geosphere* **18,** no. 3, 1030–1054.

Bhat, H. S., R. Dmowska, J. R. Rice, and N. Kame (2004). Transfer from the Denali to Totschunda faults, Alaska: Testing theory for fault branching, *Bull. Seismol. Soc. Am.* **94,** no. 6B, S202–S213.

Bondár, I., E. R. Engdahl, A. Villaseñor, J. Harris, and D. Storchak (2015). ISC-GEM: Global Instrumental Earthquake Catalogue (1900–2009), II. Location and seismicity patterns, *Phys. Earth Planet. In.* **239,** 2–13.

Boyd, T. M., and A. L. Lerner-Lam (1988). Spatial distribution of turn-of-the-century seismicity along the Alaska-Aleutian Arc, *Bull. Seismol. Soc. Am.* **78,** no. 2, 636–650.

Bramhall, E. H. (1938). The central Alaska earthquake of July 22, 1937, *Bull. Seismol. Soc. Am.* **28,** 71–75.

Brockman, S. R., A. F. Espinosa, and J. A. Michael (1988). Catalog of intensities and magnitudes for earthquakes in Alaska and the Aleutian Islands—1786–1981, *U.S. Geol. Surv. Bull. 1840*.

Browne, B. (1912). Belmore Browne's Mt McKinley Diary: The Earthquake etc. 1912 Expedition Mt. McKinley, in *Belmore Browne Papers*, Dartmouth College, Rauner Library Archives and Manuscripts Repository, Box 3, Folder 5.

Browne, B. (1913a). Conquering Mt. McKinley, Part 3: Scaling America's highest peak, *Outing Mag.* **62,** no. 1, 3–23.

Browne, B. (1913b). Conquering Mt. McKinley, Part 4: Hitting the home trail from Mt. McKinley, *Outing Mag.* **62,** no. 1, 387–404.

Browne, B. (1913c). *The Conquest of Mount McKinley*, G. P. Putnam's Sons, New York, New York.

BSSA (1912). Seismological notes, *Bull. Seismol. Soc. Am.* **2,** no. 3, 209–212.

Burkett, C. A., S. P. Bemis, and J. A. Benowitz (2016). Along-fault migration of the Mount McKinley restraining bend of the Denali fault defined by late Quaternary fault patterns and seismicity, Denali National Park & Preserve, Alaska, *Tectonophysics* **693,** 489–506.

Cameron, A., D. Orr, and J. Clark (2017). Variation in the incidence and severity of drought crack in three conifer species in North East Scotland, *Scand. J. Forest Res.* **32,** no. 8, 658–662.

Carlson, J. K., S. P. Bemis, N. Toke, B. Bishop, and T. P. Taylor (2018). Documentation of seven earthquakes over the past ~7000 years on the west-central Denali fault at the Nenana River, Alaska, *Bull. Seismol. Soc. Am.* **108,** no. 1, 84–100.

Carver, G., G. Plafker, M. Metz, L. Cuff, B. Slemmons, E. Johnson, J. Roddick, and S. Sorensen (2004). Surface rupture on the Denali fault interpreted from tree damage during the 1912 Delta River M_w 7.2–7.4 earthquake: implications for the 2002 Denali fault earthquake slip distribution, *Bull. Seismol. Soc. Am.* **94,** no. 6B, S58–S71.

Cherubini, P., F. H. Schweingruber, and T. Forster (1997). Morphology and ecological significance of intra-annual radial cracks in living conifers, *Trees* **11,** 216–222.

Coffman, J. L., and C. A. von Hake (1973). Earthquake History of the United States, National Oceanic and Atmospheric Administration, Publication 41-1 Revised Edition (Through 1970).

Coffman, J. L., C. A. von Hake, and C. W. Stover (1982). Earthquake History of the United States, *National Oceanic and Atmospheric Administration and U.S. Geol. Survey*, Publication 41-1 Revised Edition (Through 1970), Reprinted 1982 With Supplement (1971-80).

Creutzfeldt, B., I. Heinrich, and B. Merz (2015). Total water storage dynamics derived from tree-ring records and terrestrial gravity observations, *J. Hydrol.* **529,** 640–649.

Crone, A. J., S. F. Personius, P. A. Craw, P. J. Haeussler, and L. A. Staft (2004). The Susitna Glacier thrust fault: characteristics of surface ruptures on the fault that initiated the 2002 Denali Fault earthquake, *Bull. Seismol. Soc. Am.* **94,** no. 6B, S5–S22.

Crotwell, H. P., T. J. Owens, and J. Ritsema (1999). The TauP Toolkit: flexible seismic travel-time and ray-path utilities, *Seismol. Res. Lett.* **70,** no. 2, 154–160.

Davi, N. K., G. C. Jacoby, and G. C. Wiles (2003). Boreal temperature variability inferred from maximum latewood density and tree-ring width data, Wrangell Mountain region, Alaska, *Quaternary Res.* **60,** no. 3, 252–262.

Davis, E. E. (1912). Voluntary Observers' Meteorological Record, July, 1912, Chicken, Alaska, National Ocean and Atmospheric Administration, National Centers for Environmental Information, Cooperative Observations online database at https://www.ncdc.noaa.gov/IPS/coop/coop.html (last accessed October 2025).

Davis, T. N. (1960). A field report on the Alaska earthquakes of April 7, 1958, *Bull. Seismol. Soc. Am.* **50,** no. 4, 489–510.

Day, W. R. (1954). Drought crack of conifers. Forest Record No. 26, Forest Commission, H.M. Stationary Office, London, United Kingdom, 40 pp.

Dengler, L. A., and J. W. Dewey (1998). An intensity survey of households affected by the Northridge, California, earthquake of 17 January 1994, *Bull. Seismol. Soc. Am.* **88,** no. 2, 441–462.

Di Giacomo, D., I. Bondár, D. A. Storchak, E. R. Engdahl, P. Bormann, and J. Harris (2015a). ISC-GEM: Global instrumental earthquake catalogue (1900–2009), III. Re-computed M_S and m_b, proxy M_W, final magnitude composition and completeness assessment, *Phys. Earth Planet. In.* **239,** 33–47.

Di Giacomo, D., J. Harris, A. Villaseñor, D. A. Storchak, E. R. Engdahl, W. H. K. Lee, and , and The Data Entry Team (2015b). ISC-GEM: Global Instrumental Earthquake Catalogue (1900–2009), I. Data collection from early instrumental seismological bulletins, *Phys. Earth Planet. In.* **239,** 14–24.

Di Giacomo, D., D. A. Storchak, N. Safronova, P. Ozgo, J. Harris, R. Verney, and I. Bondár (2014). A new ISC service: The bibliography of seismic events, *Seismol. Res. Lett.* **85,** no. 2, 354–360.

Doser, D. I. (2004). Seismicity of the Denali-Totschunda fault zone in central Alaska (1912–1988) and its relation to the 2002 Denali fault earthquake sequence, *Bull. Seismol. Soc. Am.* **94,** no. 6B, S132–S144.

Doser, D. I. (2006). Relocations of earthquakes (1899–1917) in south-central Alaska, *Pure App. Geophys.* **163,** 1461–1476.

Doser, D. I. (2009). Estimating magnitude and location of Alaskan earthquakes using intensity data, *Bull. Seismol. Soc. Am.* **99,** no. 6, 3430–3453.

Doser, D. I., and H. Kanamori (1986). Depth of seismicity in the Imperial Valley region (1977–1983) and its relationship to the heat flow, crustal structure, and the October 15, 1979, earthquake, *J. Geophys. Res.* **91,** no. B1, 675–688.

Duda, S. J. (1965). Secular seismic energy release in the circum-Pacific belt, *Tectonophysics* **2,** no. 5, 409–452.

Eberhart-Phillips, D., P. J. Haeussler, J. T. Freymueller, A. D. Frankel, C. M. Rubin, P. Craw, N. A. Ratchkovski, G. Anderson, G. A. Carver, A. J. Crone, *et al.* (2003). The 2002 Denali fault earthquake, Alaska: A large magnitude, slip-partitioned event, *Science* **300,** 1113–1118.

Ekström, G., M. Nettles, and A. M. Dziewoński (2012). The global GCMT project 2004-2010: Centroid-moment tensors for 13,017 earthquakes, *Phys. Earth Planet. Inter.* **200–201,** 1–9.

Ellsworth, W. L., M. Celebi, J. R. Evans, E. G. Jensen, R. Kayen, M. C. Metz, D. J. Nyman, J. W. Roddick, P. Spudich, and C. D. Stephens (2004). Near-field ground motion of the 2002 Denali fault, Alaska, earthquake recorded at Pump Station 10, *Earthq. Spectra* **20,** no. 3, 597–615.

Espinosa, A. F., S. R. Brockman, and J. A. Michael (1986). Modified Mercalli intensity distribution for the most significant earthquakes in Alaska, 1899–1981, *U.S. Geol. Surv. Open-File Rept. 86-203*, 1 sheet, scale 1:12,500,000.

Fenner, C. N. (1925). Earth movements accompanying the Katmai eruption, *J. Geol.* **33,** no. 2, 116–139.

Font, Y., H. Kao, S. Lallemand, C.-S. Liu, and L.-Y. Chiao (2004). Hypocentre determination offshore of eastern Taiwan using the Maximum Intersection method, *Geophys. J. Int.* **158,** 655–675.

Gasser, G. W. (1912). Voluntary Observers' Meteorological Record, July, 1912, Rampart, Alaska, *Meteorological Observation Rept. 1881-1924*, Division of Station Facilities & Meteorological Observations, Alaska, Records of the Weather Bureau, Record Group 27; National Archives at Seattle.

Grantz, A. (1966). Strike-slip faults in Alaska, *U.S. Geol. Surv. Open-File Rept. 66-53*, Washington, D.C.

Griggs, R. F. (1922). *The Valley of Ten Thousand Smokes*, National Geographic Society, Washington, D.C.

Gutenberg, B. (1962). 1912 July 7, in *The Papers of Beno Gutenberg*, California Institute of Technology, Notepad 78, p. 726.

Gutenberg, B., and C. F. Richter (1949). *Seismicity of the Earth and Associated Phenomena*, First Ed., Princeton University Press, Princeton, New Jersey.

Gutenberg, B., and C. F. Richter (1954). *Seismicity of the Earth and Associated Phenomena*, Second Ed., Princeton University Press, Princeton, New Jersey.

Haeussler, P. J. (2008). An overview of the neotectonics of interior Alaska: Far-field deformation from the Yakutat microplate collision, in *Active Tectonics and Seismic Potential of Alaska*, J. T. Freymueller, P. J. Haeussler, R. Wesson, and G. Ekström (Editors), Vol. 179, Geophysical Monograph, American Geophysical Union, Washington, D.C., 83–108.

Haeussler, P. J., A. M. Bender, P. M. Powers, R. D. Koehler, and D. S. Brothers (2025). Updating the crustal fault model for the 2023 National Seismic Hazard Model for Alaska, in *Tectonics and Seismic Structure of Alaska and Northwestern Canada: EarthScope and Beyond*, N. A. Ruppert, M. A. Jadamec, and J. T. Freymueller (Editors), Vol. 290, Geophysical Monograph, American Geophysical Union, Washington, D.C., 85–127.

Haeussler, P. J., R. W. Saltus, R. G. Stanley, N. Ruppert, K. Lewis, S. M. Karl, and A. Bender (2017). The Peters Hills basin, a Neogene wedge-top basin on the Broad Pass thrust fault, south-central Alaska, *Geosphere* **13,** no. 5, 1464–1488.

Haeussler, P. J., D. P. Schwartz, T. E. Dawson, H. D. Stenner, J. J. Lienkaemper, B. Sherrod, F. R. Cinti, P. Montone, P. A. Craw, A. J. Crone, *et al.* (2004). Surface rupture and slip distribution of the Denali and Totschunda faults in the 3 November 2002 **M** 7.9 earthquake, Alaska, *Bull. Seismol. Soc. Am.* **94,** no. 6B, S23–S52.

Hartzell, S. H., and T. H. Heaton (1986). Inversion of strong ground motion and teleseismic waveform data for the fault rupture history of the 1979 Imperioal Valley, California, earthquake, *Bull. Seismol. Soc. Am.* **73,** no. 6, 1553–1583.

Hazard, D. L. (1914). Earthquakes, in *Results of Observations Made at the United States Coast and Geodetic Survey Magnetic Observatory at Sitka, Alaska, 1911 and 1912*, U.S. Department of Commerce and Labor, Washington, D.C., U.S. Coast and Geodetic Surv. 96–100.

Heck, N. H. (1938). Earthquake History of the United States. Part I—Continental United States (Exclusive of California and Western Nevada) and Alaska, U.S. Dept. of Commerce, Coast and Geodetic Survey, Washington, D.C., Serial No. 609, 83 pp.

Heck, N. H. (1947). Earthquake History of the United States. Part I—Continental United States (Exclusive of California and Western Nevada) and Alaska, U.S. Dept. of Commerce, Coast and Geodetic Survey, Washington, D.C., Serial No. 609 Revised (1947) edition, 83 pp.

Heck, N. H., and R. A. Eppley (1958). Earthquake History of the United States. Part I—Continental United States and Alaska (Exclusive of California and Western Nevada), U.S. Dept. of Commerce, Coast and Geodetic Survey, Washington, D.C., No. 41-1 Revised (1956) edition, 80 pp.

Herning, O. G. (1912). Orville George Herning Papers 1898–1947, UAF Rasmuson Library, Alaska and Polar Regions Collections & Archives.

Hildreth, W., and J. Fierstein (2012). The Novarupta-Katmai Eruption of 1912—Largest Eruption of the Twentieth Century: Centennial Perspectives, *U.S. Geol. Surv. Profess. Pap. 1791*, Reston, Virginia.

Hodges, K. E. (1999). The ecology of snowshoe hares in northern boreal forests, in *Ecology and Conservation of Lynx in the United States*, Ruggiero, L. F., K. B. Aubry, S. W. Buskirk, G. M. Koehler, C. J. Krebs, K. S. McKelvey, and J. R. Squires (Editors), Gen. Tech. Rep. RMRS-GTR-30WWW, Chapter 6, 117–162. US Department of Agriculture, Forest Service, Rocky Mountain Research Station, Fort Collins, Colorado.

Hsu, Y.-J., M. Simons, J.-P. Avouac, J. Galetzka, K. Sieh, M. Chlieh, D. Natawidjaja, L. Prawirodirdjo, and Y. Bock (2006). Frictional afterslip following the 2005 Nias-Simeulue earthquake, Sumatra, *Science* **312,** 1921–1926.

Hunter, S. C., D. M. Allen, and K. E. Kohfeld (2020). Comparing approaches for reconstructing groundwater levels in the mountainous regions of interior British Columbia, Canada, using tree ring widths, *Atmosphere* **11,** no. 12, 1374.

International Seismological Centre (2018). ISC-GEM Global Instrumental Earthquake Catalogue, Version 5.0, Released on 2018-02-27.

International Seismological Centre (2023). ISC-GEM Global Instrumental Earthquake Catalogue. Version 10.0, Released on 2023-03-01.

Jones, L. A. (1912). Voluntary Observers' Meteorological Record, July, 1912, Copper Center, Alaska, *Meteorological Observation Rept. 1881-1924*, Division of Station Facilities & Meteorological Observations, Alaska; Records of the Weather Bureau, Record Group 27; National Archives at Seattle.

Kanamori, H., L. Rivera, and W. H. K. Lee (2010). Historical seismograms for unravelling a mysterious earthquake: The 1907 Sumatra earthquake, *Geophys. J. Int.* **183,** 358–374.

Kennett, B. L. N., E. R. Engdahl, and R. Buland (1995). Constraints on seismic velocities in the Earth from traveltimes, *Geophys. J. Int.* **122,** 108–124.

Kisslinger, J. B. (1983). "Some volcanoes, volcanic eruptions, and earthquakes in the former Russian America": Peter Doroshin's account of volcanic activity and earthquakes between 1840 and 1866, *Pacific Northwest Quart.* **74,** no. 2, 59–68, translated from an 1870 Russian publication by P. Doroshin.

Koehler, R., D. Schwartz, D. Rood, R. Reger, and G. Wolken (2015). Preliminary paleoseismic observations along the central Denali fault, Alaska, *Eos Trans. AGU Fall Meeting*, Suppl., Abstract #T23C-2598, San Francisco, California, 10 December 2013.

Koehler, R. D., and G. A. Carver (2018). Active faults and seismic hazards in Alaska, Alaska Div. Geol. Geophys. Surv., Miscellaneous Publication 160, 59 pp., doi: 10.14509/29705.

Koehler, R. D., R.-E. Farrell, P. A. C. Burns, and R. A. Combellick (2012). Quaternary faults and folds in Alaska: A digital database, Alaska Div. Geol. Geophys. Surv., Miscellaneous Publication 141, 31 pp., 1 sheet scale 1:3,700,000.

Krebs, C. J., R. Boonstra, S. Boutin, and A. R. Sinclair (2001). What drives the 10-year cycle of snowshoe hares? *BioScience* **51,** no. 1, 25–35.

Kubler, H. (1983). Mechanism of frost crack formation in trees—A review and synthesis, *Forest Sci.* **29,** no. 3, 559–568.

Lander, J. F. (1996). Tsunamis affecting Alaska, 1737–1996, NGDC Key to Geophysical Research Documentation No. 31, National Oceanic and Atmospheric Administration, National Environmental Satellite, Data, and Information Service, National Geophysical Data Center, Boulder, Colorado.

Lesh, M. E., and K. D. Ridgway (2007). Geomorphic evidence of active transpressional deformation in the Tanana foreland basin, south-central Alaska, in *Tectonic Growth of a Collisional Continental Margin: Crustal Evolution of Southern Alaska*, K. D. Ridgway, J. M. Trop, J. M. G. Glen, and J. M. O'Neill (Editors), Geol. Soc. Am. Special Paper 431, Boulder, Colorado, 573–592.

Lomax, A. (2005). A reanalysis of the hypocentral location and related observations for the great 1906 California earthquake, *Bull. Seismol. Soc. Am.* **95,** no. 3, 861–877.

Lomax, A. (2008). Location of the focus and tectonics of the focal region of the California earthquake of 18 April 1906, *Bull. Seismol. Soc. Am.* **98,** no. 2, 846–860.

Lomax, A., and C. Tape (2025). Relocation of the 1912-07-07 M_s 7.2 central Alaska earthquake using global arrival time data [Data set], *Zenodo*, doi: 10.5281/zenodo.15642448.

Lomax, A., A. Michelini, and A. Curtis (2014). Earthquake location, direct, global-search methods, in *Encyclopedia of Complexity and System Science*, Second Ed., R. A. Meyers (Ed.), Springer, New York, New York, 1–33, doi: 10.1007/978-3-642-27737-5_150-2.

Lomax, A., J. Virieux, P. Volant, and C. Berge (2000). Probabilistic earthquake location in 3D and layered models: Introduction of a Metropolis-Gibbs method and comparison with linear locations, in *Advances in Seismic Event Location*, C. H. Thurber and N. Rabinowitz (Editors), 101–134, Kluwer, Amsterdam, The Netherlands.

Matuzawa, T. (1929). Observation of some recent earthquake and their time-distance curves (Part IV.), *Bull. Earthq. Res. Inst.* **6,** 213–229.

McNeilly, W. (1912). Voluntary Observers' Meteorological Record, July, 1912, Seward, Alaska, *Meteorological Observation Rept. 1881-1924*, Division of Station Facilities & Meteorological Observations, Alaska; Records of the Weather Bureau, Record Group 27; National Archives at Seattle.

Meyers, H., R. J. Brazee, J. L. Coffmann, and S. R. Lessig (1976). An analysis of earthquake intensities and recurrence rates in and near Alaska, *NOAA Technical Memorandum EDS NGSDC-3*, 101 pp. and four sheets of microfiche.

Millington, W. F., and W. R. Chaney (1973). Shedding of shoots and branches, in *Shedding of Plant Parts*, T. T. Kozlowski (Editor), Academic Press, New York, 149–204.

Milne, J., and H. H. Turner (1912). British Association for the Advancement of Science, *Seismological Committee Circular No. 27*, Newport, Isle of Wight, Vol. 3, 229–280.

Milne, J., H. H. Turner, C. V. Boys, G. Darwin, H. Darwin, R. T. Glazebrook, M. H. Gray, R. K. Gray, J. W. Judd, C. G. Knott, *et al.* (1914). Seismological investigations, *Eighteenth Report of the Committee, Report of the Eighty-third Meeting of the British Association for the Advancement of Science*, Birmingham, United Kingdom, 10–17 September 1913, 69–103.

Neal, J. W. (1912). Voluntary Observers' Meteorological Record, July, 1912, Fairbanks, Alaska, *Meteorological Observation Rept. 1881-1924*, Division of Station Facilities & Meteorological Observations, Alaska; Records of the Weather Bureau, Record Group 27; National Archives at Seattle.

Nykänen, M. L., H. Peltola, C. Quine, S. Kellomäki, and M. Broadgate (1997). Factors affecting snow damage of trees with particular reference to European conditions, *Silva Fenn.* **31,** 193–213.

Olnes, J., K. Kielland, G. P. Juday, D. H. Mann, H. Genet, and R. W. Ruess (2017). Can snowshoe hares control treeline expansions? *Ecology* **98,** no. 10, 2506–2512.

Pacheco, J. F., and L. R. Sykes (1992). Seismic moment catalog of large shallow earthquakes, 1900 to 1989, *Bull. Seismol. Soc. Am.* **82,** 1306–1349.

Page, R. A., N. N. Biswas, J. C. Lahr, and H. Pulpan (1991). Seismicity of continental Alaska, in *Neotectonics of North America*, D. B. Slemmons, E. R. Engdahl, M. D. Zoback, and D. D. Blackwell (Editors), Vol. 1, The Geology of North America, Chapter 4, Geol. Soc. Am., Decade Map, Boulder, Colorado, 47–68.

Personius, S. F., A. J. Crone, P. A. Burns, and N. G. Reitman (2017). Recurrent Holocene movement on the Susitna Glacier thrust fault: the structure that initiated the M_w 7.9 Denali fault earthquake, central Alaska, *Bull. Seismol. Soc. Am.* **107,** no. 4, 1593–1609.

Personius, S. F., A. J. Crone, P. A. C. Burns, and N. Rozell (2015). Paleoseismology of the Denali fault system at the Schist Creek site, Central Alaska, *U.S. Geol. Surv. Open-File Rept. 2015-1225*, 15 pp., 1 oversize plate.

Persson, A. (1994). Stem cracks in Norway spruce in southern Scandinavia: Causes and consequences, *Ann. For. Sci.* **51,** no. 3, 315–327.

Plafker, G., L. M. Gilpin, and J. C. Lahr (1994). Neotectonic Map of Alaska, in *Geology of Alaska*, G. Plafker and H. C. Berg (Editors), Volume G-1 of The Geology of North America, Geol. Soc. Am., Boulder, Colorado, Plate 12.

Ratchkovski, N. A., and R. A. Hansen (2002). New constraints on tectonics of interior Alaska: Earthquake locations, source mechanisms, and stress regime, *Bull. Seismol. Soc. Am.* **92,** no. 3, 998–1014.

Ratchkovski, N. A., S. Wiemer, and R. A. Hansen (2004). Seismotectonics of the central Denali fault, Alaska, and the 2002 Denali fault earthquake sequence, *Bull. Seismol. Soc. Am.* **94,** no. 6B, S156–S174.

Regan, S. P., J. A. Benowitz, T. S. Waldien, M. E. Holland, S. M. Roeske, P. O'Sullivan, and P. Layer (2021). Long distance plutonic relationships demonstrate 33 million years of strain partitioning along the Denali fault, *Terra Nova* **33,** 630–640.

Ross, Z. E., D. T. Trugman, E. Hauksson, and P. M. Shearer (2019). Searching for hidden earthquakes in Southern California, *Science* **364,** 767–771.

Schlyter, P., I. Stjernquist, L. Bärring, A. M. Jönsson, and C. Nilsson (2006). Assessment of the impacts of climate change and weather extremes on boreal forests in northern Europe, focusing on Norway spruce, *Climate Res.* **31,** no. 1, 75–84.

Schulte-Pelkum, V., A. M. Bender, and N. A. Ruppert (2025). Seismicity and anisotropic imaging reveal an active detachment beneath the northern Alaska Range foothills, in *Tectonics and Seismic Structure of Alaska and Northwestern Canada: EarthScope and Beyond*, N. A. Ruppert, M. A. Jadamec, and J. T. Freymueller (Editors), Vol. 290, Geophysical Monograph, Am. Geophys. Union, Washington, D.C., 575–587.

Schwartz, D. P., P. J. Haeussler, G. G. Seitz, T. E. Dawson, H. D. Stenner, A. Matmon, A. J. Crone, S. Personius, P. B. Burns, A. Cadena, *et al.* (2005). Unraveling the earthquake history of the Denali fault system, Alaska: Filling a blank canvas with paleo earthquakes, *Eos Trans. AGU*, Vol. 86, Abstract U42A-06.

Schweingruber, F. H. (1988). *Tree Rings: Basics and Applications of Dendrochronology*, Kluwer, Dodrecht, The Netherlands.

Shelly, D. R., G. C. Beroza, and S. Ide (2007). Non-volcanic tremor and low-frequency earthquake swarms, *Nature* **446,** 305–307.

Sieberg, A. (1920). Mitteilungen über Erdbeben im Jahre 1912, Herausgegeben von der Hauptstation für Erdbebenforschung fruher in Straßburg, zurzeit in Jena, [Reports on earthquakes in 1912. Published by the main station for earthquake research, formerly in Strasbourg, now in Jena.].

Silwal, V., and C. Tape (2016). Seismic moment tensors and estimated uncertainties in southern Alaska, *J. Geophys. Res. Solid Earth* **121,** 2772–2797.

Somville, O. (1925). Sur la nature de l'onde initiale des téléséismes enregistrés à Uccle de 1910 à 1924, in *Union Géodésique et Géophysique Internationale*, Secion de Séismologie, Publications du Bureau Central Séismologique International Sous la direction de E. Rothé, Volume 2 of Series A: Travaux, Scientifiques, Les Presses Universitaires de France, Paris, France, 5–76.

St. Amand, P. (1957). Geological and geophysical synthesis of the tectonics of portions of British Columbia, the Yukon Territory, and Alaska, *Bull. Seismol. Soc. Am.* **68,** 1343–1370.

Stein, R. S., and G. C. P. King (1984). Seismic potential revealed by surface folding: 1983 Coalinga, California, earthquake, *Science* **224,** 869–872.

Stover, C. W., and J. L. Coffman (1993). Seismicity of the United States, 1568–1989 (Revised), *U.S. Geol. Surv. U.S. Geol. Surv. Profess. Pap. 1527*, Denver, Colorado.

Stuck, H. (1914). *The Ascent of Denali*, Charles Scribner's Sons, New York, New York.

Sturm, M. (2023). Shadows on the snow, *Alpinist* **84,** 93–100.

Sykes, L. R. (1971). Aftershock zones of great earthquakes, seismicity gaps, and earthquake prediction for Alaska and the Aleutians, *J. Geophys. Res.* **76,** no. 32, 8021–8041.

Tape, C. (2025). Felt reports for the 1912-07-07 M_s 7.2 central Alaska earthquake, [Data set], *Zenodo*, doi: 10.5281/zenodo.15642344.

Tape, C., A. Lomax, V. Silwal, J. D. Agnew, and B. Brettschneider (2017). The 1904 M_s 7.3 earthquake in central Alaska, *Bull. Seismol. Soc. Am.* **107,** no. 3, 1147–1174.

Tape, C., L. Sykes, and A. Lomax (2021). The 1900 M_w 7.6–8.0 earthquake offshore of Kodiak Island, Alaska, *Bull. Seismol. Soc. Am.* **111,** no. 2, 1080–1109.
Turner, H. H. (1917). *The Large Earthquakes of 1913. Epicentres, Dates and Times, and Residuals for P. and S*, British Association Seismology Committee, Isle of Wight County Press, Newport, 1–74.
Turner, H. H. (1923). *The International Seismological Summary for 1918*, University Observatory, Oxford, United Kingdom, 1–200.
Turner, H. H. (1924). *The International Seismological Summary for 1920 January, February, March*, University Observatory, Oxford, United Kingdom, 1–50.
USGS and SCEC (1994). The magnitude 6.7 Northridge, California, earthquake of 17 January 1994, *Science* **266,** 389–397.
Valinger, E., and J. Fridman (1999). Models to assess the risk of snow and wind damage in pine, spruce, and birch forests in Sweden, *Environ. Manage.* **24,** 209–217.
Van Cleve, K., and J. C. Zasada (1970). Snow breakage in black spruce and white spruce stands in interior Alaska, *J. Forest.* **68,** no. 2, 82–83.
Waldien, T. S., S. M. Roeske, and J. A. Benowitz (2021). Tectonic underplating and dismemberment of the Maclaren-Kluane schist records Late Cretaceous terrane accretion polarity and ~480 km of post-52 Ma dextral displacement on the Denali fault, *Tectonics* **40,** 1–35.
Wells, D. L., and K. J. Coppersmith (1994). New empirical relationships among magnitude, rupture length, rupture width, rupture area, and surface displacement, *Bull. Seismol. Soc. Am.* **84,** no. 4, 974–1002.
Wessel, P., and W. H. F. Smith (1991). Free software helps map and display data, *Eos Trans. AGU* **72,** no. 41, 441.
Wetzler, N., T. Lay, E. E. Brodsky, and H. Kanamori (2018). Systematic deficiency of aftershocks in areas of high coseismic slip for large subduction zone earthquakes, *Sci. Adv.* **4,** no. 2, 1–9.
Witkowska, I. (2008). Spruce quality in mixed stands, *M.Sc. Final Thesis* no. 104, Swedish University of Agricultural Sciences, Southern Swedish Forest Research Centre, Uppsala, Sweden.
Woodward-Clyde Consultants (1980). *Interim Report on Seismic Studies for Susitna Hydroelectric Project*, Acres American Incorporated, Buffalo, New York, 369 pp.
Wood, H. O., and F. Neumann (1931). Modified Mercalli intensity scale of 1931, *Bull. Seismol. Soc. Am.* **21,** no. 4, 277–283.
Wright, T. J., Z. Lu, and C. Wicks (2003). Source model for the M_w 6.7, 23 October 2002, Nenana Mountain earthquake (Alaska) from InSAR, *Geophys. Res. Lett.* **30,** no. 18, 1–4.
Zhou, H. (1994). Rapid three-dimensional hypocentral determination using a master station method, *J. Geophys. Res.* **99,** no. B8, 15,439–15,455.

APPENDIX A: GUTENBERG'S NOTEPAD

The notepads of Beno Gutenberg are preserved in hard copy, microfilm, and digital scans at the California Institute of Technology Archives. The notepads provide the details regarding the arrival-time data, amplitude data, and methods Gutenberg used to estimate the epicenters published in the seminal global catalog *Seismicity of the Earth* (Gutenberg and Richter, 1949). Gutenberg studied the 1912 Alaska earthquake, and his table of arrival times was used by subsequent authors studying the earthquake (Boyd and Lerner-Lam, 1988; Doser, 2004).

The notepad for the 1912-07-07 earthquake contains the following notes at upper left:

> *1912 July 7 7: Sieberg #24 felt Fairbanks, Kennecott, and "In fast allen Orten des Inneren verspuert" "sehr heftig".*
> *Landslides at Dome Creek; ice brake of glaciers*
> *Somville gives 63N 143W*
> *BSS. 30 p. 353 Adkins 64.7 N 146.6 W*

The origin day is 1912-07-07 UTC, and the mm:ss in the table are for the hour of 07:00 UTC ("7:"). The first two references are to Sieberg (1920) and Somville (1925), which are displayed in Figure A2. Interestingly, the listed earthquake in Somville (1925) (−143°, 63°) is an aftershock that occurred on 1912-07-08 22:00 UTC, about 38 hr after the mainshock. The "BSS. 30 p. 353" reference is to Adkins (1940) (v. 30), and the location (−146.6°, 64.7°) is Adkins's estimated epicenter for the 1937-07-22 M_s 7.3 earthquake. In summary, neither set of the coordinates listed in Gutenberg's header—via Somville (1925) and Adkins (1940)—is for the 1912-07-07 earthquake.

Sieberg's notes on the 1912 Alaska earthquake were the earliest ones noted by Gutenberg, though it is likely that earlier notes were written in the registers from the seismic stations recording the earthquake, such as Sitka (Fig. 8) and others. Here we provide a breakdown of Sieberg's notes for the Alaska earthquake in Figure A2a. The columns are as follows.

1. Ort [Location]. The three lines are: Schweres Erdbeben in Alaska [Large earthquake in Alaska].
2. Tag [Day]. This is the local date, not UTC date. The entry is 6 for the Alaska earthquake.
3. Zeit (0h = Mitternacht) der Quelle|Greenw [Time (0h = midnight) at the source|Greenwich] The entry is "23 –" for the local time (it was in fact 22:00) and "+ 8 –" for the UTC time, with the + indicating to add one day to the local time and 08:00 being the UTC time.
4. Art der Bewegung [Style of Motion].
5. Stärke [Strength] I–XII.
6. Dauer, Sek. [Duration, Sec.].
7. Richtung aus [Direction from].
8. Bemerkungen [Remarks]. The entry is: In fast allen Orten des Inneren verspuert - Reg.: Strassburg am 7. um 8 h 8 m 35 s, Jena 8 h 8 m 17 s. [felt in almost all places of the Interior - Reg.: Strasbourg on the 7th at 08:08:35, Jena 08:08:17.] These times are UTC.

The next two lines are for the same earthquake, but specific to two locations. The first is "Fairbanks am Tananafluß"

(a)

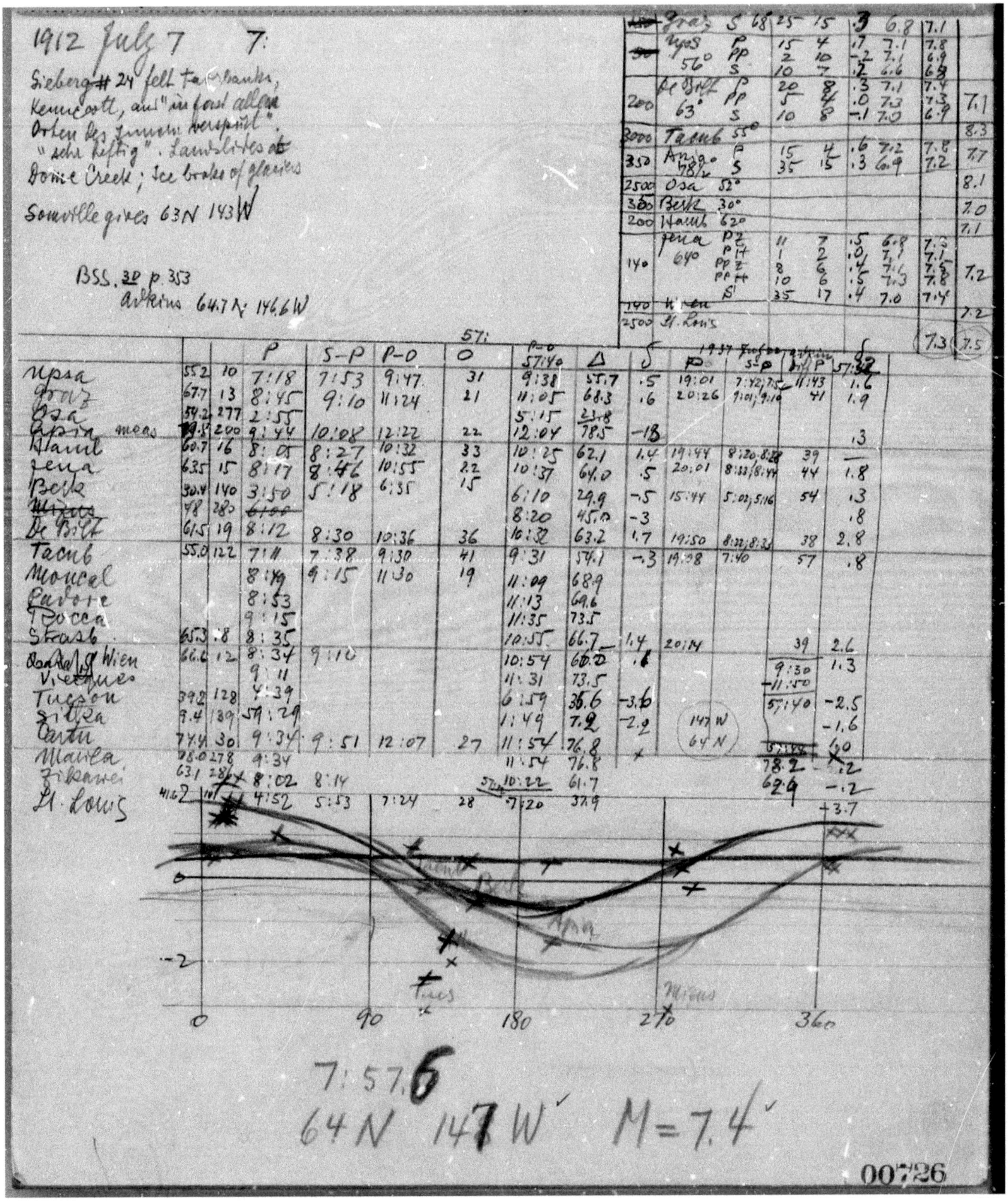

(b) 740 1912, July 7 07:57.6 64 N 147 W 7.4

Figure A1. (a) Notepad of Beno Gutenberg (Gutenberg, 1962), showing the work used to determine the magnitude, origin time, and epicentral estimate of (−147°,64°) published in Gutenberg and Richter (1949, p. 144), which is displayed in panel (b). See Appendix A for details.

(a)

12.

Ort	Tag	Zeit (Ob.-Mitternacht) der Quelle h m	Greenw. h m	Art der Bewegung	Stärke I–XII	Dauer Sek.	Richtung aus	Bemerkungen
Juli 1912								
Deißlingen (Württemberg)	1	10½ –	9½ –	Stoß	VI–VII	–	–	
Pfullingen	"	"	"	"	zieml. kräftig	einige	–	
Ebingen	"	"	"	"	–	–	–	
Schakalskuppe (Deutsch-Südwest-afrika)	3	10 01	9 01	–	–	–	–	Mit unterirdischem Donnern
Eduardsfelde (Deutsch-Südwest-afrika)	5	15 45	14 45	1 Stoß	–	1	W	Gleichzeitig schußartiger Donner
Mo-sü-yü (Yün-nan, China)	5	8 55	2 04	1 Stoß	VI	2	SE	
Mo-sü-yü	5	22 23	15 32	1 Stoß	–	–	–	
Schweres Erdbeben in Alaska	6	23 –	+8 –	–	–	–	–	In fast allen Orten des Innern verspürt. – Reg.: Straßburg am 7. um 8h 8m 35S, Jena 8h 8m 17S.
Fairbanks am Tananafluß	"	"	"	langdauerndes Rucken und Schütteln	sehr heftig	40	–	
Kennecott am Kupferfluß	"	"	"	Stöße	sehr schwer	–	–	
Guayaquil (Ecuador)	7	17 35	22 59	1 Stoß	V	35	E	
Olty (Gouv. Kars, Transkaukasien)	8	11 30	8 10	Häufiger Schwanken	–	–	–	
Ise-kü (Yün-nan, China)	8	22 15	15 24	–	IV–V	–	–	
Fairbanks (Alaska)	9	–	–	Stoß	Nur wenig geringer als am 6.			Auch in Städten des Innern gefühlt
Garapan (Marianeninsel Saipan)	9	8 10	–22 17	1 Stoß	ca. IV	–	–	

(b)

1	1912	4 I	15h58m54s	52° N	179°	E	iP	cond.
2		8 VII	22 04 24	63	143	W	iP	cond.
3		7 XI	7 51 31	57	155	W	iP	cond.
4	1913	30 IV	11 46 35	52	174	W	iP	cond.
5	1917	25 VII	22 44 33	54	159	W	iP	cond.
6	1922	2 IV	19 29 34	54	166	W	eP	cond.
7		2 VII	13 47 33	53,5	157,5	W	P	cond.
8	1923	3 II	16 13 15	50	168	E	P, iP	cond.
9		4 V	16 38 10	55	159	W	P	cond.
10		22 VII	14 29 54	52	174	E	eP	cond.

Figure A2. Two publications noted by Gutenberg in his analysis of the 1912-07-07 earthquake (Fig. A1). See Appendix A for details. (a) Excerpt from Sieberg (1920, p. 12) for earthquakes in July 1912. (b) Table from Somville (1925, p. 67) with the title "Alaska et Iles Aléoutiennes" [Alaska and the Aleutian Islands]. For our purposes, the relevant event is the one with onset time 1912-07-08 22:04:24, which is a major aftershock of the 1912-07-07 earthquake and is also recorded at Sitka (Fig. 8).

[Fairbanks on Tanana River], the style of motion is "langdauerndes Rucken und Schuetteln" [long-lasting jerks and shaking], the strength is "sehr heftig" [very severe; violent], and the duration is 40 s. The second location is "Kennecott am Kupferfluß" [Kennecott on Copper River], the style of motion is "Stoß" [shock], and the strength is "sehr schwer" [very strong].

There is also an aftershock entry listed for July 9th (local date; time not listed) for "Fairbanks (Alaska)" with style of motion "Stoß" [shock], strength "Nur wenig geringer als am 6." [only slightly weaker than on the 6th.], and having remarks "Auch in Städten des Innern gefuehlt" [Also felt in towns in the Interior].

Somville (1925) compiled tables of global earthquakes having recorded a clear P arrival at Uccle (Belgium). His list for the Aleutian–Alaska region includes 10 events between 1912-01-04 and 1923-07-22 (Fig. A2b). The list includes an aftershock (1912-07-08 22:04:24 UTC) but not the mainshock on 1912-07-07 at about 08:00 UTC.

APPENDIX B: PARKER–BROWNE ACCOUNT OF SHAKING

The Parker–Browne description of shaking (Browne, 1913b) is the most important account of the 1912-07-07 earthquake. Here we summarize a chronological sequence of events, intending to understand how this felt report was used (or not) in the press and in the scientific literature.

Published confusion between the earthquake and the Katmai eruption

Over the days of June 6–10, 1912, the volcano complex of Katmai–Novarupta erupted in the largest (by volume) eruption of the twentieth century (Hildreth and Fierstein, 2012). The eruption included 14 earthquakes with a magnitude $M_s \geq 6.0$ (Abe, 1992), it produced ashfall across much of Alaska, and it was also heard hundreds of kilometers away (Griggs, 1922). For example, many people in the Fairbanks region, 800 km from the volcano, reported hearing explosions starting on Friday, June 7th (*Fairbanks Daily News-Miner*, 1912-06-10, p. 1).

Meanwhile, near Denali and still 550 km from the volcano, the Parker–Browne expedition also heard the eruption (Browne, 1913a, p. 19):

> *Under June 8th there is an interesting entry in my diary: "The glacier has been very noisy all day; it has groaned and cracked, and at short intervals there have been deep, powerful reports, sounding for all the world like the boom of big guns at a distance. We have been talking about this queer noise, but are undecided as to its cause. It must be due to the settling of the great ice caverns under the tremendous weight of new snow." It was not until we reached civilization long afterwards that we found that the unusual booming sound had not come from the glacial caverns, but that it was made by Katmai in eruption 300 miles away—Katmai, the volcano whose eruption buried Kodiak Island in ashes. Later, we found these Katmai ashes in our teapot after we had melted snow, but again we accepted the easiest explanation and decided that the grit in our teacups was merely dust blown from the cliffs. After the snow ceased falling, we were held by good weather, for tons of snow hung poised on the steep cliffs, and the route over the seracs under these avalanche-polished slopes was out of the question.*

Parker–Browne spent the next month attempting to reach the summit of Denali, and then finally reached their base camp at

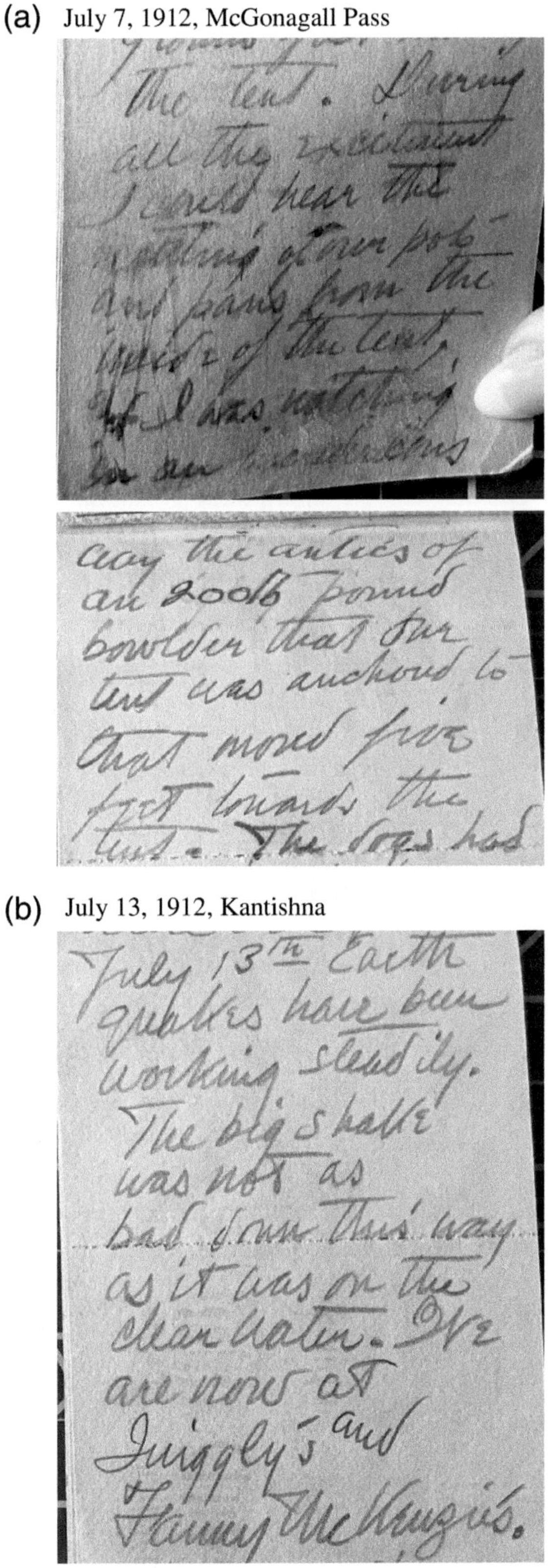

Figure B1. Excerpts from Belmore Browne's diary (Browne, 1912). (a) From July 7th, the day after experiencing the 1912 earthquake from their base camp at McGonagall Pass. Browne describes a boulder that moved during the earthquake. The word "200lb" is written on top of a mostly erased word that is likely "eighty." See Appendix B for details. (b) From July 13th at Kantishna. See "Felt reports" and Tape (2025).

McGonagall Pass on July 5th. One day later, at 22:00 local time, the earthquake struck, causing one death in Fairbanks and startling people throughout Alaska. This news reached global outlets, including the front page of *The New York Times* on 1912-07-08, one day after the Fairbanks coverage (Fig. 2). Included within several reports were speculative connections between Katmai and the July earthquake, for example, from Fairbanks (Tape, 2025):

> *At the time the shock occurred, the telegraph offices throughout the territory were closed for the night, and it was impossible to hear from the coast, where, it is feared, the disturbance was much greater than in the interior. Some are inclined to the belief that Mt. Katmai again is in eruption, and the darkened sky in that direction lends color to the belief.*

and from Cordova (Tape, 2025):

> *It is argued that renewed activity on the part of volcanoes to the westward will follow the underground disturbance, and it is not at all unlikely another fall of ashes will result, though much lighter than that following the blow-out of Mt. Katmai, which will cover a considerable extent of territory. It is also worthy of remark that there has been scarcely one day of sunshine since the Katmai eruption.*

Parker–Browne's experience with the earthquake did not reach news outlets until after they reached Tolovana, on the telegraph line, on July 22nd. Following the earthquake on July 6th, the Parker–Browne team continued north toward civilization. They reached the gold prospectors of Kantishna on July 10th and then eventually reached the Kantishna River, which they boated to its confluence with the Tanana River, reaching the Tolovana roadhouse on July 22nd.

Seeing the extreme remoteness today of the Tolovana roadhouse, at the confluence of the Tolovana and Tanana rivers, it is hard to believe that this was the site where the Parker–Browne accounts reached international news sources. The story of the expedition and earthquake broke in Fairbanks on Wednesday, July 24th, in the Fairbanks newspaper. As a testament to global interest, the short report from Tolovana was printed on the front page of *The New York Times* on July 25th.

The September 1912 issue of the nascent *Bulletin of the Seismological Society of America* included this entry within its quarterly "Seismological Notes" column (BSSA, 1912, p. 211):

> *Mt. Katmai, Alaska, July 6, 1912.—A month after the eruptions of Katmai began, a violent earthquake was felt at Fairbanks, Alaska, 10 p.m., July 6th. Other shocks occurred during the following night. At Prince William's Sound, four hundred or five hundred miles east of Mt. Katmai, the volcanic explosions of July 6th are said to have been heard. Volcanic ash fell for several days thereafter throughout the region. At Tanana, central Alaska, about six hundred miles from Katmai and at Prince William's Sound, the dust was noticed. At the latter place, it is also reported that falling rain on July 10th was stinging to the hand. Polished metal was rusted and corroded even under shelter. Vegetation was affected for several days by atmospheric conditions. Leaves turned yellow on the edges, and holes were eaten through them.*

The effects from the Katmai eruption are accurate—falling ash, acidic rain, rusted tools, heard from central Alaska—but these effects happened the month before, following the June 6–10 eruption. The July 1912 earthquake had no connection to the Katmai eruption, but many news sources, not knowing where the epicenter was, attributed the earthquake to Katmai. In the aforementioned excerpt, the first two sentences are correct, whereas the remaining sentences describe effects from the Katmai eruption a month earlier.

While the basic information of the Parker–Browne earthquake experience reached international media outlets on July 24th, via Tolovana, it was not until 1913 that the full account was published, both in a magazine article (Browne, 1913b) and a book (Browne, 1913c).

Parker–Browne account in the seismological literature

The Parker–Browne account was a key component of the study by Carver *et al.* (2004), who assigned it a shaking intensity of modified Mercalli intensity (MMI) 9+. As far as we know, the only publication prior to Carver *et al.* (2004) to treat shaking intensities for the 1912-07-07 earthquake was Boyd and Lerner-Lam (1988), who plotted three MMI values in their figure 3, citing Meyers *et al.* (1976). The three sites were (Table 3): Fairbanks (MMI 5), Kennecott (MMI 5), and "Mt. McKinley–North base" (MMI 6). ("Mt. McKinley–North base" is the McGonagall Pass site.) The U label to the right of each MMI number in Meyers *et al.* (1976) represented "unpublished intensity assigned for this study" (p. 25), indicating that although the felt reports were previously known, the MMI values had not been assigned prior to that study.

As described in Meyers *et al.* (1976), they used the official U.S. earthquake compilations as their basis for assembling the shaking intensity database for Alaska. Referring to *Earthquake History of the United States*, they wrote (p. 12):

> *This publication is the source for most of the intensity data for the 1786–1928 period. However, several of the earthquakes listed do not have published intensity evaluations, and the descriptions are not always sufficiently detailed for assigning an accurate intensity. Basically, all earthquakes listed in this publication were considered to be at least MM intensity V. Higher intensities (VI+) were assigned*

only if the text contained information to substantiate the intensity.

It is reasonable, then, to assume that the three 1912 felt reports in Meyers *et al.* (1976) (Fairbanks, Kennecott, and Mt. McKinley) were assigned based on the entry in the *Earthquake History* volumes, such as Coffman and von Hake (1973, pp. 112–113):

> *1912. July 6. Central Alaska. Violent at Fairbanks with other shocks lasting until the 9th. Felt strongly at Kennecott. It was reported that the earth heaved and rolled at the northern base of Mount McKinley, and the country far and near was scarred with landslides.*

The entry pertaining to Mount McKinley first appeared in the 1958 edition, which also includes explicit citations (Heck and Eppley, 1958, p. 75):

> *1912. July 6, 21:57. Violent at Fairbanks with other shocks lasting until the 9th. Felt strongly at Kennecott. At the northern base of Mount McKinley, it was reported that the earth heaved and rolled, and the country far and near was scarred with landslides. Probably felt over 200,000 square miles.*[3-2, 8, 31]

The first citation (3-2) refers to BSSA (1912) ("violent earthquake was felt at Fairbanks"). The second citation (8) refers to the "Unpublished records of Harry Fielding Reid," which we have never found (Tape *et al.*, 2017, 2021). Presumably Reid had newspaper clippings describing the Kennecott report, which appeared in the Cordova newspaper (Table 3), or perhaps he had seen Sieberg's report (Appendix A), which listed shaking at Fairbanks and Kennecott (only). The third citation (31) refers to Fenner (1925), who cited Browne (1913c) in his study of the Katmai eruption (Fenner, 1925, p. 120):

> *On July 6 the same party, then at the northern base of Mount McKinley, experienced an undoubted earthquake of great violence. The earth heaved and rolled, and the country far and near was scarred with landslides.*

Given that this Fenner (1925) passage was cited in future compilations (Stover and Coffman, 1993), it is worth attempting to extract the original phrases from Browne (1913c), which are likely these (p. 356):

> *Aten was yelling something that I could not understand and that the valley above us turned white—and then the earth began to heave and roll, and I forgot everything but the desire to stay upright.*

> *The Alaskan Range was still wrapped in the haze of avalanche dust, and the country far and near was scarred and stripped of vegetation where the earth had slid.*

The Parker–Browne account, via Fenner (1925), was absent from the 1912-07-07 entry in Heck (1938), the first U.S.-led compilation of Alaska earthquakes. It was absent in the revised 1947 edition (Heck, 1947), but was then discovered sometime between 1947 and 1958: it appeared in the 1958 edition (Heck and Eppley, 1958) and remained there through the major (and final) updates (Coffman *et al.*, 1982; Stover and Coffman, 1993). The appropriate reference to the Parker–Browne account of the 1912 earthquake is either Browne's diary (Browne, 1912), his magazine article (Browne, 1913b), or his book (Browne, 1913c).

Weight of the boulder

The movement of a large boulder is a key observation in assessing the shaking intensity at McGonagall Pass. The description in Browne (1913b, p. 388) is "a boulder weighing more than two hundred pounds." The diary of Browne contains this passage (Fig. B1):

> *During all the excitement I could hear the rattling of our pots and pans from the inside of the tent, and I was watching in an incredulous way the antics of an 200lb pound boulder that our tent was anchored to that moved five feet towards the tent.*

The phrase "an 200lb pound" clearly does not make sense. The word "200lb" is in a darker text and overprints a faint word that is very likely "eighty." (The dot of the i and the extensions of the g, h, t, y are faintly visible.) Our inference is that Browne's assessment of the weight of the boulder was 80 pounds at the time of his diary entry (Sunday, July 7th), and then this was later changed in the diary to 200 pounds, and then it was published as "more than two hundred pounds." Either Browne realized, after writing his diary entry, that 200 pounds was a better estimate of the boulder, or he embellished the story when he wrote the magazine article. In any case, the weakened men may have had a hard time moving it themselves. Browne's diary entry for July 10th, having reached Kantishna ("Clark's cabin on Moose Creek"), included this: "We are getting all food now and we need it. My waist when we hit base camp measured 23½ inches!" Whatever the weight of the boulder, it would have made sense to seek help from the dog team and sled to pull it into place, as they described (Browne, 1913b).

Carver *et al.* (2004) identified a boulder in a published photograph of the expedition team and their tent, taken prior to the earthquake: "The upper photo shows the large boulder (arrow) that was used as a tent tie down." To us, it is unclear if (1) the boulder was used to tie the tent down and (2) whether this was the boulder that moved and was described by Browne. There is no detail about the boulder in the caption of the originally published photograph (Browne, 1913b, p. 388).

Karstens Ridge in 1912 and 1913

Karstens Ridge is on the northeastern flank of Denali and is about 15 km southwest of McGonagall Pass. The ridge was photographed by Browne (1913a) and offered the Parker–Browne expedition their best-determined pathway to the summit (p. 17):

> *We finally reached a point where we could study the whole sweep of the great northeastern ridge [Karstens Ridge] and to our delight we saw a low col [Karstens Col], or break in the ridge, that could be reached easily from our glacier, and the ridge itself looked climbable all the way to the big basin [Thayer Basin] between the two highest peaks of the big mountain.*

The Parker–Browne photographs and descriptions of the ridge in 1912 were initially perplexing to what the Stuck–Karstens expedition encountered in 1913 (Stuck, 1914, p. 40):

> *To our surprise, the ridge offered no resemblance whatever to the description of the photograph. The upper one-third of it was indeed as described, but at that point there was a sudden sharp cleavage, and all below was a jumbled mass of blocks of ice and rock in all manner of positions, with here a pinnacle and there a great gap. Moreover, the floor of the glacier at its head was strewn with enormous icebergs that we could not understand at all. All at once, the explanation came to us—"the earthquake"!...*
>
> *The difficulty of our task was very greatly increased; that was plain at a glance. This ridge, that the pioneer climbers of 1910 went up at one march with climbing-irons strapped beneath their moccasins, carrying nothing but their flagpole, that the Parker-Browne party surmounted in a few days, relaying their camping stuff and supplies, was to occupy us for three weeks while we hewed a staircase three miles long in the shattered ice.*

These accounts form the basis for our inclusion of Karstens Ridge as a site of shaking intensity (Table 3).

Manuscript received 18 June 2025
Published online 20 November 2025

Earthquake Magnitude and Source Parameter Estimation with a Distributed Acoustic Sensing Dataset in the Gorda Subduction Zone

Andrew J. Barbour*[1], Jeffrey J. McGuire[2], Martin Karrenbach[3], Robert C. McPherson[4], Mark A. Hemphill-Haley[4], and Connie Stewart[4]

ABSTRACT

Distributed acoustic sensing (DAS) systems offer a cost-effective way to create large-scale strainmeter arrays for seismological applications using fiber-optic cables. DAS-based strain measurements are known to be influenced by various factors, bringing into question their general reliability for accurate earthquake characterization. A 15-km-long DAS deployment in northern California was operational within 3 days of the 2022 M_w 6.4 Ferndale earthquake and ran continuously throughout the aftershock sequence. We utilize these aftershock data to validate DAS-based strain measurements in two ways. We first test the accuracy of DAS-based magnitude estimates from peak dynamic strains by comparing them with magnitude and attenuation scaling relations derived independently from traditional borehole strainmeter (BSM) data. We demonstrate that DAS-based magnitudes are comparable to BSM-based magnitudes when corrections for variations in site response along the fiber-optic cable are properly made. Magnitude errors are spatially correlated, potentially because of factors such as finite-fault effects (e.g., stress drop) or more complex, unmodeled path attenuation or because of wave propagation effects in heterogeneous media. We then apply more advanced source characterization methodology to the DAS data using a time-domain empirical Green's function (EGF) deconvolution approach to measure details of the moment rate history. The EGF approach using DAS data depends on careful treatment of distorting factors such as anthropogenic sources of noise and optical phase wrapping but successfully isolates source spectra for moderate-magnitude earthquakes: source spectral ratios obtained from DAS data, broadband seismometer data, and BSM data in the same region show consistent results, revealing differences in directivity and spectral shape among earthquakes. Although further research is needed to refine source-time-function estimation techniques for DAS data, particularly for larger magnitude events, these case studies demonstrate the clear potential of DAS for earthquake source characterization.

OPEN ACCESS

KEY POINTS

- Distributed acoustic sensing (DAS) on dark telecom fiber can be used for local earthquake source characterization.
- Accuracy of amplitude-based magnitude depends on local amplification corrections.
- Source-time functions are faithfully recovered with a fraction of the fiber-optic array.

Supplemental Material

INTRODUCTION

Distributed acoustic sensing (DAS) is an increasingly popular technique in seismological applications for its ability to transform a single fiber-optic cable into a large-scale, high-frequency strainmeter array at a relatively low cost per sensor. Results from DAS deployments on both custom fiber and unlit (dark) fiber in telecom networks show repeatedly the potential for DAS to provide rich observations of the strain wavefield both in terrestrial settings and in more challenging offshore environments

1. U.S. Geological Survey, Vancouver, Washington, U.S.A., https://orcid.org/0000-0002-6890-2452 (AJB); 2. U.S. Geological Survey, Moffett Field, California, U.S.A., https://orcid.org/0000-0001-9235-2166 (JJMG); 3. Seismics Unusual, LLC., Fullerton, California, U.S.A., https://orcid.org/0000-0003-2190-8598 (MK); 4. California Polytechnic University, Arcata, California, U.S.A., https://orcid.org/0009-0009-4189-7735 (RCMP); https://orcid.org/0000-0002-2975-9083 (MAH-H); https://orcid.org/0009-0002-1641-4657 (CS)

*Corresponding author: abarbour@usgs.gov

Cite this article as Barbour, A. J., J. J. McGuire, M. Karrenbach, R. C. McPherson, M. A. Hemphill-Haley, and C. Stewart (2025). Earthquake Magnitude and Source Parameter Estimation with a Distributed Acoustic Sensing Dataset in the Gorda Subduction Zone, *Bull. Seismol. Soc. Am.* **116**, 355–374, doi: 10.1785/0120250077 (e.g., Lindsey *et al.*, 2019; Zhan, 2020; Lindsey and Martin, 2021; Viens *et al.*, 2022; Romanowicz *et al.*, 2023). Although fundamental earthquake research is possible with DAS data (e.g., Li, Taeho, *et al.*, 2023; Li, Zhu, *et al.*, 2023), the reliability of waveform amplitudes has been a general point of concern, primarily because DAS systems measure strains within the fiber that are not necessarily equivalent to true strains in the surrounding rock resulting from phenomena of interest (e.g., seismic wave propagation). Various physical and environmental factors may influence DAS strain amplitudes in ways that are difficult to generalize outside of laboratory settings, especially in telecom systems where fiber installation is not optimized for geophysical sensing.

Instruments for measuring seismic strains have existed for nearly a century (e.g., Benioff, 1935), with modern strainmeter designs providing reliable high-frequency data in the near field of complex ruptures (e.g., Canitano *et al.*, 2017; Cao *et al.*, 2018; Hirakawa and Barbour, 2020), for local earthquakes (Barbour *et al.*, 2021), and for teleseisms (e.g., Benioff *et al.*, 1961; Agnew and Wyatt, 2014). Earthquake data from DAS deployments have seen relatively limited testing against magnitude and attenuation scaling relations derived from strainmeter data, in part because long-term DAS datasets in high-hazard regions are limited. The most comprehensive DAS-based comparison so far (Yin *et al.*, 2023) shows that for local earthquakes, the path attenuation of peak strain rates recorded by DAS systems is consistent with path attenuation in peak strains recorded by borehole strainmeters cemented in crustal rock (Barbour *et al.*, 2021). This finding is critically important because fiber-optic cables are typically buried only a few meters deep, increasing their susceptibility to near-surface effects in shallow soils. However, unlike the borehole strainmeter (BSM) results, which show relatively small site terms, the accuracy of DAS-based results hinges on the corrections for localized site effects along the fiber, which can vary by an order of magnitude over scales of hundreds of meters. Furthermore, the source magnitude scaling terms in the Yin *et al.* (2023) equations were derived from strain-rate data, whereas the comparable terms in the Barbour *et al.* (2021) scaling were derived from dynamic strains directly. In other words, an additional comparison is needed to verify the consistency in the source magnitude scaling not only because the native output of a given DAS interrogator unit (IU) can be strain or strain rate, depending on the technology used in the IU but also because larger ruptures generate lower frequency signals that may not be fully represented in strain-rate records.

DAS datasets that contain on-scale recordings of moderate-magnitude earthquakes (M ~ 3–5.5) also suggest the possibility of resolving fundamental properties of the earthquake source beyond its magnitude. Seismograms from moderate-magnitude earthquakes with average network station spacing typically record only the far-field term of the displacement solution, which is proportional to the time history of moment rate during the earthquake (Aki and Richards, 2002). Thus, resolving the summary properties of the moment-rate function—often termed the source-time function (STF)—such as duration and scalar moment, is a standard practice in source seismology as are methods that look at finer scale subevent structure within the STF. Most STF studies work in the frequency domain where the shape of the displacement amplitude spectrum can be approximated by key source models of cracklike ruptures (Brune, 1970; Madariaga, 1976; Boatwright, 1980; Kaneko and Shearer, 2015). Measurements of low-frequency spectral amplitude are proportional to seismic moment M_0, and the corner frequency is a rough proxy for rupture duration; these are routinely made on large seismic datasets and interpreted in terms of the average static stress drop using the simplified crack model (e.g., Shearer *et al.*, 2019). Such results have been widely used to study earthquake self-similarity and scaling laws (Ide and Beroza, 2001). An alternate approach is to retrieve the moment-rate function in the time domain (Ammon *et al.*, 1993; Hough and Dreger, 1995), which allows for the isolation of duration, length, and directivity parameters (McGuire, 2004). Although the time-domain approach potentially provides more information, it usually requires some form of regularization to enforce positivity constraints on the moment-rate function (Ammon *et al.*, 1993; McGuire, 2004; Vallée *et al.*, 2011). Initial studies using DAS data have demonstrated success for M $\lesssim$ 4 earthquakes with frequency-domain methods (Chen, 2023; Lior, 2024; Nayak *et al.*, 2024; Strumia *et al.*, 2024), but time-domain approaches have not yet been applied to DAS data. DAS data present potential challenges to both approaches, particularly for larger magnitude events: they represent uniaxial strain along the path of the fiber, they may have relatively high-low-frequency noise levels (e.g., Chen, 2023), scattered surface waves may contaminate the body wavetrain, and there may be phase wrapping (e.g., Ajo-Franklin *et al.*, 2022) akin to dynamic range saturation with inertial sensors.

To help resolve these issues, we investigate time domain–based methods for resolving source properties using DAS data, particularly (1) whether the relationships for dynamic strain based on BSMs are applicable to DAS strain observations in telecom fiber, and (2) whether accurate estimates of moment-rate functions can be determined using standard methods. We use data from a continuous, dark-fiber DAS deployment with colocated nodal seismometers in northern California (see McGuire *et al.*, 2025); this DAS deployment sits above the actively subducting Gorda slab in southern Cascadia, using telecom fiber running from downtown Arcata to Eureka, California, with nodal seismometers colocated every few hundred meters along the surface projection of the fiber, and we can compare with multiple BSMs in the region. Our principal target is the abundant local seismicity related to the complex tectonics of the Mendocino Triple Junction, located just offshore Cape Mendocino in northern California (Fig. 1). Notably, the dataset includes the 2022 Ferndale aftershock sequence (e.g., Shelly *et al.*, 2024) that began with an

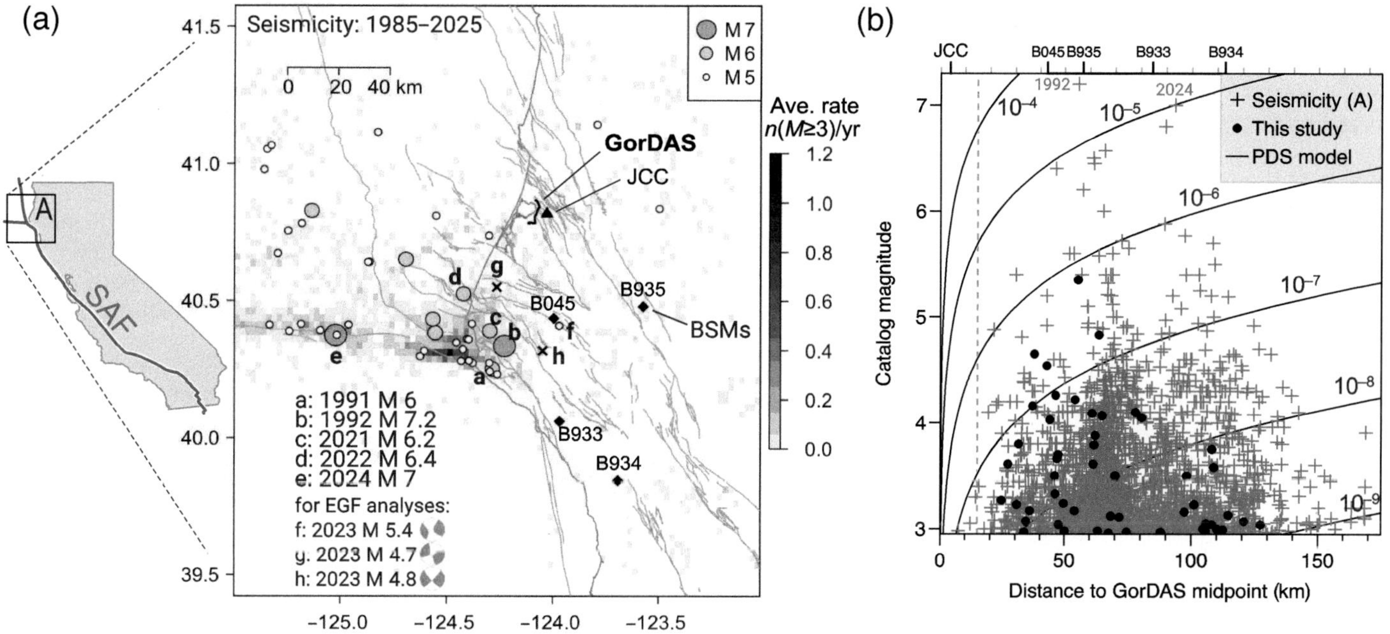

Figure 1. Study region in Humboldt County, northern California, at the Mendocino Triple Junction, and distributed acoustic sensing (DAS) data coverage. The context map shows where the study region is along the simplified plate boundary triple junction in California (SAF, San Andreas fault). (a) The location of the GorDAS array (black thick line) over a map of average seismicity rates for M ≥ 3 events between 1985 and 2025 in ComCat in 90 arcsec grid cells, notable events with M ≥ 5 (circles), and the events used in empirical Green's function (EGF) analyses: the M 5.4 (event "f"), and M 4.7 and 4.8 events (×). Quaternary active faults (gray lines), the four Network of the Americas (NOTA) borehole strainmeters (BSMs) in the region (diamonds), and the broadband seismometer JCC in the BK network. (b) Magnitude and distance coverage of seismicity in (a). The distance is calculated from the hypocenter to the midpoint of the GorDAS fiber-optic cable. Events used in this study are from McGuire *et al.* (2024), shown as black circles. The distances between the fiber midpoint and the seismometer JCC and NOTA BSMs are marked at the top, and the vertical dashed line shows the length of the GorDAS fiber (15 km), which also happens to represent the median depth of these events. Contours are of peak dynamic strain based on the attenuation model of Barbour *et al.* (2021). The color version of this figure is available only in the electronic edition.

M_w 6.4 earthquake on 21 December 2021. DAS and nodal data collection began within 3 days of the mainshock, capturing numerous M > 4 events, including the largest aftershock so far, the M 5.4 one on 1 January 2023.

MAGNITUDE AND SOURCE PROPERTY ESTIMATION

Dynamic strain data

We analyze dynamic strain signals associated with seismic waves emanating from local crustal earthquakes, specifically ones that occurred within 100 km of any point on the fiber-optic cable during the two phases of the GorDAS deployment (McGuire *et al.*, 2025). This dataset is composed of dynamic strain records from a DAS IU connected to an ~15-km-long fiber-optic cable (see Fig. 1). The IU (Quant-X model from Luna-OptaSense) was set to sample at 250 Hz with a channel spacing of 2 m and a gauge length of 8 m. The events in this dataset are primarily from the 2022 M 6.4 Ferndale aftershock sequence (McGuire *et al.*, 2024) but include events representing background seismicity from the first phase of the deployment in summer 2022 (McGuire, Barbour, Karrenbach, *et al.*, 2022; McGuire, Barbour, McPherson, *et al.*, 2022). We also use BSM waveforms from stations in the EarthScope Consortium's Network of the Americas (NOTA), from the four stations with codes B045, B933, B934, and B935. NOTA BSMs are all electromechanical systems that use differential capacitance to measure strain in a borehole (Gladwin, 1984); at each site they provide strain data from ~200 m deep, from four independent sensors oriented at known, precise angles to each other. Strains are sampled at 20 Hz and form the basis for obtaining time series of the full horizontal strain tensor at seismic frequencies for comparisons with the GorDAS data.

Amplitude-based source magnitudes

Our first test of the reliability of DAS strain amplitudes is the accuracy of earthquake magnitudes inferred from them compared with published catalog estimates. Our methodology for doing this is relatively simple. In summary, we first pass the raw DAS data through a set of preprocessing and quality control checks before calculating peak dynamic strain (PDS) for *S*-wave arrivals; we then correct for site amplification (or attenuation) effects at each sensing point along the fiber. Finally, the magnitude is estimated from the site-corrected, peak dynamic strains within the *S*-wave window, verified by visual inspection, and the catalog location for hypocentral distances at each peak strain measurement.

The raw DAS records come in the form of optical phase changes at a set of channels i along the fiber (Φ_i), which can be converted to uniaxial strains in the direction of the fiber at the same locations (ϵ_i). Assuming uniform strain over the gauge length L, the optical phase measured by the IU is related to strain by

$$\Phi_i = \frac{4\pi n L\xi}{\lambda_l}\epsilon_i, \tag{1}$$

in which λ_l is the wavelength of the laser source (1550 nm), n is the effective refractive index of the fiber core and cladding combined in single-mode fiber (1.468), and ξ is the photoelastic scale factor,

$$\xi = 1 - \frac{n^2}{2}[p_{12} - \nu(p_{11} + p_{12})], \tag{2}$$

in which p_{11} and p_{12} are isotropic photoelastic properties of the fiber and ν is its Poisson's ratio. The variable terms in the right side of equation (2) typically equal ~0.206 for common single-mode fiber ($p_{11} = 0.113$, $p_{12} = 0.253$, and $\nu = 0.17$; see Hartog, 2017, chapter 9), making $\xi \approx 0.794$.

Because the path of this DAS array goes along an active highway, vehicular traffic represents a nontrivial source of coherent signal (e.g., Lindsey, Yuan, *et al.*, 2020) with amplitudes that might bias magnitude estimates. However, because the propagation speed is far slower than seismic body waves, we use a frequency–wavenumber (*f-k*) filter to mask signal content unrelated to seismic waves. Specifically, signals with apparent speeds <63 m/s are masked out using a Gaussian taper in the *f-k* domain that is combined with a band-pass filter, yielding dynamic strain estimates in the 1–7 Hz band that are suitable for our time-domain earthquake source characterization methods (see Fig. S1, available in the supplemental material to this article).

We use the *f-k*-filtered strain records to identify PDS across the array for each event. Barbour *et al.* (2021) established an amplitude-based magnitude scale for PDS based on decades of data from the NOTA and U.S. Geological Survey (USGS) BSM networks, completely independent of any DAS data. They showed that distance-dependent decay of PDS from local crustal earthquakes from southern California, United States, to Vancouver Island, Canada, can be characterized by a 1D, distance-based attenuation correction as in the local magnitude (M_L) scale (e.g., Richter, 1935):

$$-\log_{10} A_0(R) = 1.45\log_{10} R + 0.00072\,R,\ R < 500\ \text{km}, \tag{3}$$

in which R is hypocentral distance. As with M_L, the source magnitude can be estimated by correcting the observed PDS A for these attenuation effects,

$$M \sim \log_{10} A - \log_{10} A_0. \tag{4}$$

With surface telecom fiber-optic systems, however, local site effects introduce potentially dramatic variations in the amplitudes A across the fiber-optic cable being interrogated, so removing them prior to assessing source magnitudes is critical (e.g., Yin *et al.*, 2023). Site effects in this context represent the convolution of ground motion–related effects (e.g., structural or basin effects) with cable installation and coupling effects.

Our approach to removing site effects from DAS data is to first calculate the ratio of A to A_0 from equation (3) at every DAS channel i:

$$S_i = \log_{10}[A_i/A_0(R_i)],\ i = 1,2,\ldots,c, \tag{5}$$

in which c is total number of DAS channels. Because S_i includes a constant related to earthquake source magnitude, we then subtract the mean ratio, $S_i^{'} = S_i - \langle S_i \rangle$, and compute the sample median of $S_i^{'}$ across the fiber for all events. In other words, these median values (S_i) represent a vector of "site" terms, in log space, with positive values indicating amplification relative to the general dynamic strain attenuation relation (equation 3) and negative values indicating relative attenuation. We calculate a set of $S_i^{'}$ for both the *P*- and *S*-wave windows, denoted as S_i^P and S_i^S, respectively, to compare the robustness and linearity of these site terms (discussed later). Finally, we correct the observations for these site effects by subtracting the median site amplifications from the observations in the *S*-wave window,

$$\log_{10} A_i^{'} = \log_{10} A_i - S_i^S, \tag{6}$$

and $\log_{10} A_i^{'}$ is used for magnitude estimation, in which magnitude is proportional to $\log_{10} A^{'} - \log_{10} A_0$ (e.g., equation 4).

One important aspect of the BSM and DAS-based magnitude scaling is that they do not depend on converting to inertial quantities: Barbour *et al.* (2021) and Yin *et al.* (2023) used attenuation-corrected dynamic strains and strain rates, respectively, to relate to catalog magnitude. For dynamic strain, the inferred magnitude (M_{DS}) is

$$M_{DS} = \log_{10} A^{'} - \log_{10} A_0 + \log_{10}(3 \times 10^{-9}), \tag{7}$$

in which A_0 is from equation (3) and $A^{'}$ is from equation (6), and the three nanostrain constant is from Barbour *et al.* (2021). Strain measurements are broadband and inherently linear up to a spatial aliasing limit set by the gauge length and the wavelength of the seismic wave, λ_w, as $\text{sinc}(2\pi L/\lambda_w)$. Barbour *et al.* (2021) showed that M_{DS} scales linearly with moment magnitude (M_w) as

$$M_{DS} \approx 0.92 M_w,\ 3.5 \le M_w \le 7.2, \tag{8}$$

in which M_w and seismic moment M_0 (N · m) scale as $\log_{10} M_0 = 1.5 M_w + 9.05$ (Hanks and Kanamori, 1979).

From this, we obtain the maximum-likelihood moment magnitude estimate based on dynamic strain data: $M_{\mathrm{wDS}} = M_{\mathrm{DS}}/0.92$. Importantly, M_{DS}-to-M_{w} scaling does not show an apparent break between low- and high-magnitude events as M_{L}-to-M_{w} scaling does (Barbour *et al.*, 2021), although this break might be more apparent below $M_{\mathrm{w}} \approx 2$ or 3 (e.g., Deichmann, 2017).

Far-field strain waveforms and empirical Green's functions

To further test waveform reliability, we move beyond simple attenuation distance corrections for amplitudes to results that characterize the source kinematics. DAS systems capture additional details of the seismic strain (or strain rate) wavefield compared with more standard inertial seismometer networks. BSM recordings of both near-field (Cao *et al.*, 2018; Hirakawa and Barbour, 2020) and far-field strain waveforms (Barbour *et al.*, 2021) place strong constraints on detailed earthquake kinematics and magnitude estimates, respectively, suggesting the potential utility of DAS-derived strain measurements. A few articles from the exploration seismology literature have explored this because of the presence of near- and intermediate-field strain terms in borehole DAS records of microearthquakes (Vera Rodriguez and Wuestefeld, 2020; Luo *et al.*, 2021; Lecoulant *et al.*, 2023). In particular, the standard expression for the wavefield resulting from a point source is considerably different for strain than for displacement. Following the notation of Luo *et al.* (2021) and Aki and Richards (2002), the expression for the axial strain wavefield in homogeneous and isotropic media from a point source is given by equation (3) of Luo *et al.* (2021):

$$\begin{aligned}\epsilon(r,t) = &\frac{1}{4\pi\rho}\frac{B^N}{r^5}\int_{\frac{r}{V_P}}^{\frac{r}{V_S}} \tau M(t-\tau)d\tau \\ &+\frac{1}{4\pi\rho r^3}\left[\frac{B^{\mathrm{INP}}}{V_P^2}M\left(t-\frac{r}{V_P}\right)+\frac{B^{\mathrm{INS}}}{V_S^2}M\left(t-\frac{r}{V_S}\right)\right] \\ &+\frac{1}{4\pi\rho r^2}\left[\frac{B^{\mathrm{IFP}}}{V_P^3}\dot{M}\left(t-\frac{r}{V_P}\right)+\frac{B^{\mathrm{IFS}}}{V_S^3}\dot{M}\left(t-\frac{r}{V_S}\right)\right] \\ &+\frac{1}{4\pi\rho r}\left[\frac{B^{\mathrm{FP}}}{V_P^4}\ddot{M}\left(t-\frac{r}{V_P}\right)+\frac{B^{\mathrm{FS}}}{V_S^4}\ddot{M}\left(t-\frac{r}{V_S}\right)\right], \end{aligned} \quad (9)$$

in which $M(t)$, $\dot{M}(t)$, and $\ddot{M}(t)$ are the moment release history of the earthquake and its first two time derivatives, respectively; ρ, V_P, and V_S are the density and compressional and shear-wave velocities of the medium, respectively; and r is the distance from the source to receiver. Subscripts on the moment tensor and radiation pattern terms have been omitted for clarity but are given by Luo *et al.* (2021). The $1/r^5$ term is analogous to the near-field term in the solution for the displacement field (Aki and Richards, 2002). The terms that decay as $1/r^3$ and $1/r^2$ are traveling wave terms that are analogous to the intermediate-field terms in displacement data. Similarly, the $1/r$ terms are analogous to the far-field terms and are expected to dominate the strain wavefield at significant distances from the source. The radiation pattern terms (B^N, B^{INP}, B^{INS},...) are given by Luo *et al.* (2021). In particular, the terms corresponding to the far-field P and S waves (e.g., the $1/r$ terms) correspond to

$$-\frac{1}{4\pi\rho r}\left[\frac{A^{\mathrm{FP}}}{V_P^3}\frac{\gamma}{V_P}\ddot{M}\left(t-\frac{r}{V_P}\right)+\frac{A^{FS}}{V_S^3}\frac{\gamma}{V_S}\ddot{M}\left(t-\frac{r}{V_S}\right)\right], \quad (10)$$

which comes from Luo *et al.* (2021, their equation A6); the prefactors γ/V_P or γ/V_S are the apparent slownesses along the local cable direction. Thus, we would expect the incoming, planar, far-field body waves to have a time history in strain that is proportional to the time derivative of the moment-rate function, rather than the standard STF, and with amplitudes that scale with the apparent slowness.

A standard technique for isolating the source amplitude spectrum from inertial seismic data involves spectral division of the seismograms from a moderate earthquake by a smaller, nearly colocated earthquake recorded at the same station. In this spectral ratio, the smaller event is used to correct for unknown propagation, site, and instrument effects. Most studies of this type use broadband seismograms that have a flat frequency response over the range of interest (~0.5–50 Hz) and are proportional to velocity. The fundamental assumption is that the larger earthquake seismogram results from the convolution of the moment-rate function with a Green's function for the velocity seismogram that is approximated by the seismograms of the smaller earthquake with a similar focal mechanism, termed an *empirical Green's function (EGF)*. This approach follows naturally from the equation for the far-field displacement and the well-known result that the derivative of a convolution integral is the convolution of one of the original time series with the derivative of the other. Although the expression for far-field terms in strain is more complex than the corresponding one for displacement, it does not theoretically affect the spectral-ratio calculation. Lior (2024) present similar expressions (their equations S1 and S2) to those in Luo *et al.* (2021) in terms of the prefactor depending on the apparent slowness of the wavefield along the cable direction, but Lior *et al.* (2023) also include the effect of measuring the strain along a finite gauge length. In the spectral domain, the additional time derivative of the moment-rate function (relative to the equations for displacement) results in factors of $2\pi f$ in both the mainshock and EGF, which cancel when the spectral ratio is taken (Lior *et al.*, 2023). Both Lior (2024) and Chen (2023) used this approach to isolate source spectra for moderate M 2–3 earthquakes in DAS data despite the extra time derivative applied to the moment-rate function in equation (10).

To retrieve the more complete description of the earthquake source specified by the moment-rate function (e.g., both the amplitude and phase information), the standard techniques

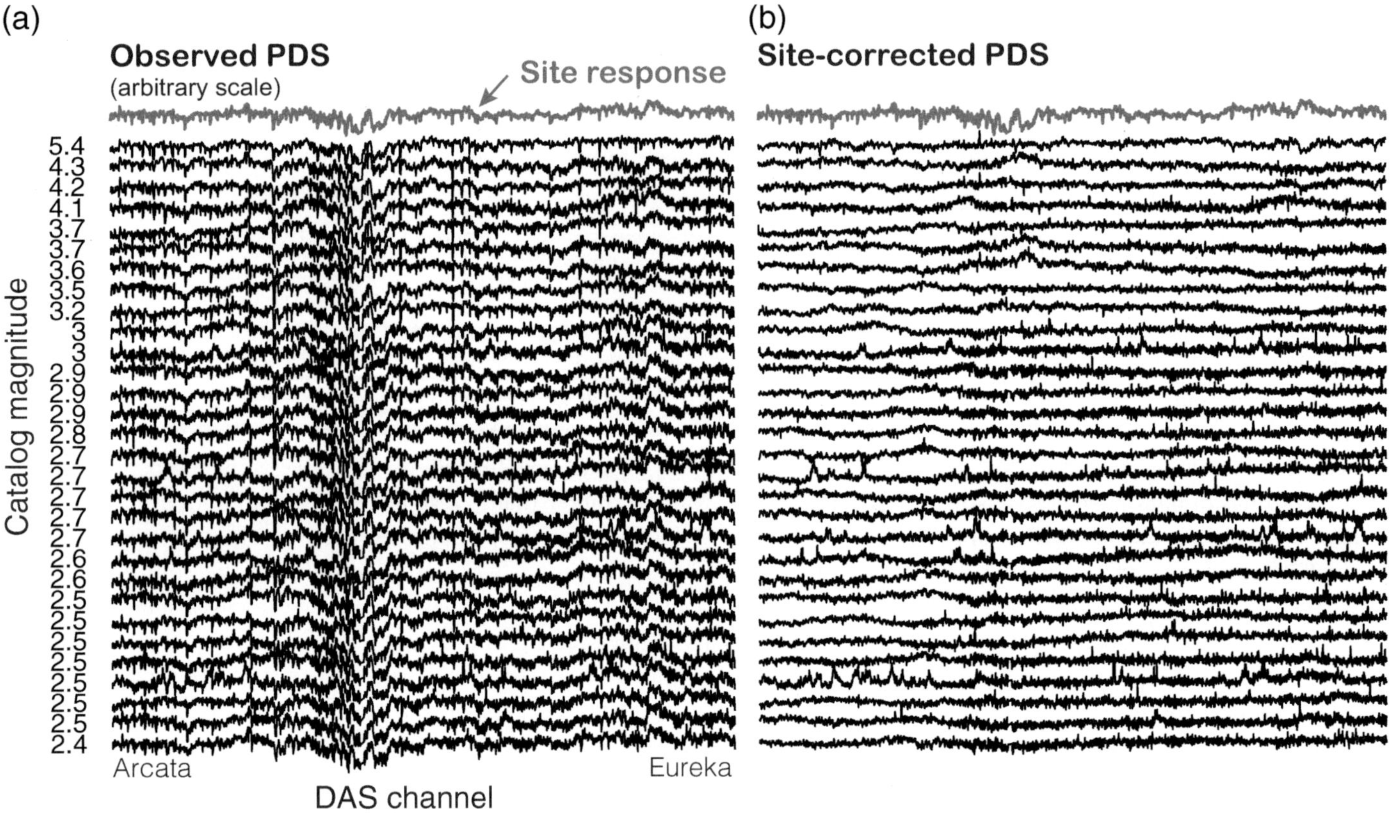

Figure 2. Efficacy of site-response correction factors applied to DAS-based peak dynamic strain (PDS). (a) Uncorrected PDS across the fiber, ordered by event magnitude and shifted on an arbitrary (logarithmic) scale for visualization; the median site response for all events (S_i^S, see the Magnitude and source property estimation section) is shown at the top. The horizontal scales run the full length of the cable. (b) PDS values corrected with the same S_i^S, shown on the same scale as the uncorrected PDS. Although site response is a dominant feature in DAS–PDS observations, it is highly repeatable and removed effectively by the application of S_i^S corrections. The color version of this figure is available only in the electronic edition.

require a slight modification (equation 10). Although performing an EGF deconvolution for the moment-rate function with seismic data is valid with either a velocity or acceleration record for the mainshock and EGF, more consistent results are produced using velocity time series. Hence, standard practice is to integrate accelerograms before doing the time-domain deconvolution (e.g., Meng *et al.*, 2020), which has the effect of emphasizing the lower frequencies in whatever objective function governs the deconvolution. Applying the same logic to strain data suggests that any time-domain EGF deconvolution method that enforces a positivity constraint on the moment-rate function would be inherently more stable when using integrated strain time series; this approach should ensure the data are directly proportional to moment rate, and the low-frequency component of the source spectrum is emphasized, assuming lower frequency signals are recorded at a sufficiently high signal-to-noise ratio (SNR).

MAGNITUDE ESTIMATION RESULTS

We found that one critical aspect of peak amplitude–based magnitude estimation is the removal of localized site effects along the fiber, which manifest in records of PDS as persistent, localized zones of attenuation or amplification relative to the median model (i.e., equation 3). The site-response correction factors applied to the PDS observations, S_i^S as described in the Magnitude and Source Property Estimation section, adequately remove the site effects without needing to include frequency-dependent terms: residual PDS distributions are largely uncorrelated across a wide range of sources from M 2.4 to 5.4 (Fig. 2), which suggests that considering frequency-dependent effects would lead to marginal reductions in residual variance.

For each of the 30 events we analyzed with DAS data, we calculated M_{wDS} for every channel in the array and their median value (Fig. 3a). Linear regression of the median estimates against the associated catalog magnitude indicates $M_{\mathrm{wDS}}^{(\mathrm{DAS})} \approx 0.97M^{(\mathrm{catalog})} + 0.14$, with standard errors in the coefficients of 0.05 and 0.16, respectively, and a standard deviation of the residuals of 0.53. In this regression, various magnitude types are in the catalog: 10% are M_{L}, 23% are M_{w}, and 67% are M_d (duration). Mixing scales is not ideal because they each relate to M_{w} differently, but not enough M_{w} events are available to obtain a stable regression for M_{w} events only; however, the error for M_{w} events ($M_{\mathrm{wDS}}^{(\mathrm{DAS})} - M_{\mathrm{w}}^{(\mathrm{catalog})}$) has a marginally nonzero mean of 0.07 and a standard deviation of 0.29.

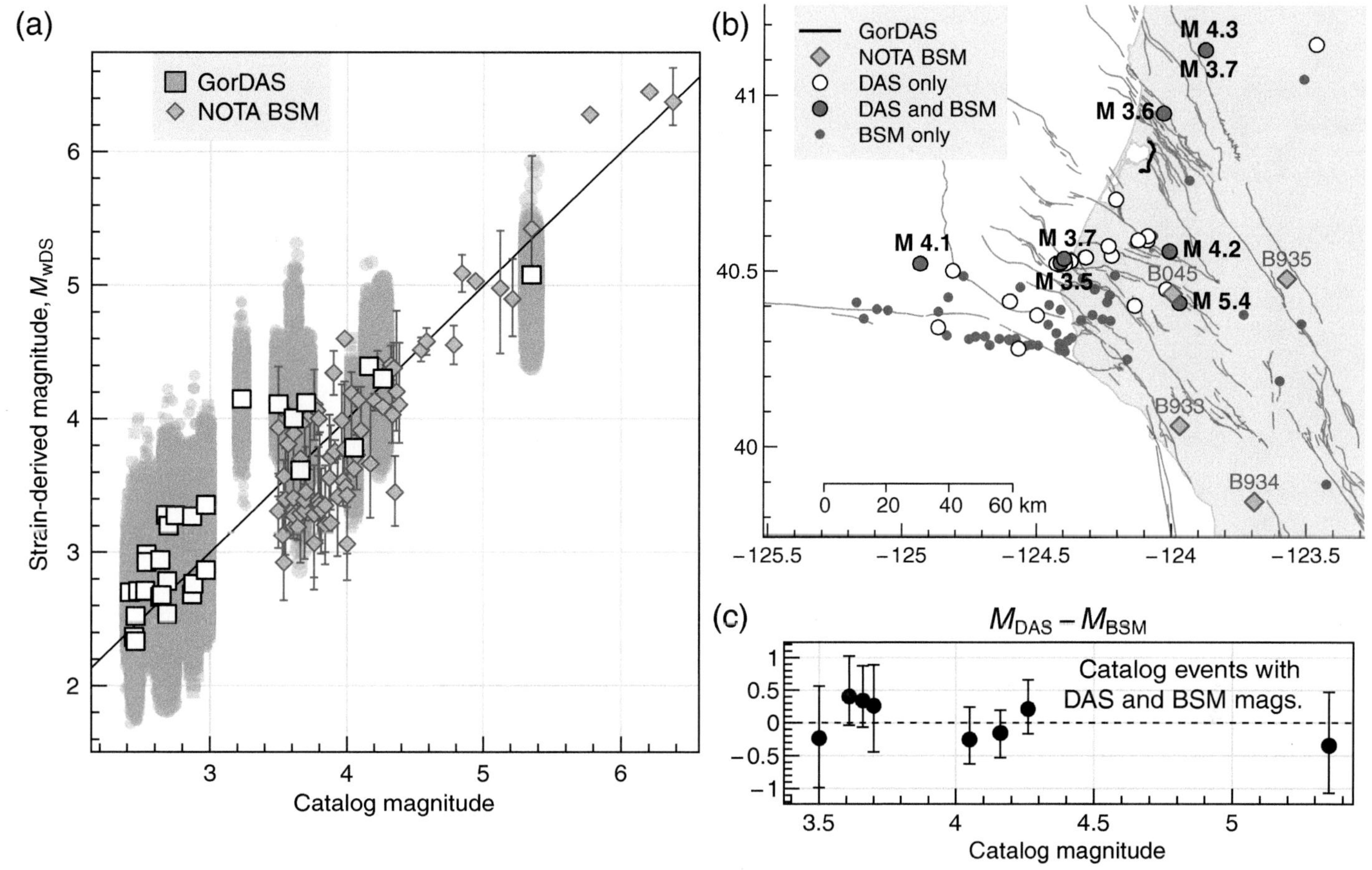

Figure 3. Comparison of moment magnitude estimates from DAS and BSM dynamic strain data. (a) Results from GorDAS data and NOTA BSM data. For the GorDAS results, the light gray points show the results for all DAS channels and the white squares show the median estimate; events analyzed are larger circles in the map. BSM results are from events with M ≥ 3.5, an origin time between 2 January 2020 and 4 July 2023, and a hypocenter located within 100 km [smaller blue dots in map (b)] of the stations (diamonds in the map); the bars show the range of estimates for all BSMs, and the diamonds show the mean. (c) Differences between the DAS- and BSM-based magnitudes for events where both DAS and BSM data are available (eight total, with their magnitudes labeled in the map). The variability and accuracy of GorDAS magnitudes are comparable to completely independent strain sensing systems. The color version of this figure is available only in the electronic edition.

We also processed NOTA BSM data for $M_w \geq 3.5$ events within 100 km of any of the four BSMs in the region going back to the start of 2020. Of the 72 events that meet these criteria and have viable BSM data, eight occurred during the DAS study period with both DAS and BSM dynamic strain data available (Fig. 3b). The distribution of residual magnitudes between the DAS and BSM results for these eight events has a marginally nonzero mean of 0.03 and a standard deviation of 0.30 (Fig. 3c). Thus, the site-corrected variability in these dark telecom-fiber DAS strain-derived magnitudes is comparable to that from a completely independent strain sensing system cemented to crystalline rock in deep boreholes.

One of the reasons for the relatively high residual standard deviation in the $M^{(\text{DAS})}$–$M^{(\text{catalog})}$ regression may be because some of the DAS-based magnitudes are systematically biased relative to the catalog, which affects the strain scaling coefficients (Barbour and Crowell, 2017). In these results, magnitude errors are spatially correlated (Fig. 4) in ways that suggest a physical explanation: conditions of the fault system that hosted the 2022 Ferndale sequence might have generated the anomalously strong radiation pattern, finite-fault effects, or unmodeled wave propagation effects in inhomogeneous subsurface or a combination of all factors.

SOURCE PROPERTY RESULTS

Isolating the properties of the moment-rate function using DAS is challenging. In this section, we demonstrate the extent to which the moment-rate function and derived quantities can be recovered from DAS data. The most straightforward calculations with DAS data are *S*-wave spectral ratios owing to the large amplitudes of *S* waves. First, we demonstrate this calculation between the M 5.4 and 4.8 earthquakes, which have similar focal mechanisms (events "f" and "h" in Fig. 1a) and source depths (~30 km) but differ by a factor of ~8 in seismic

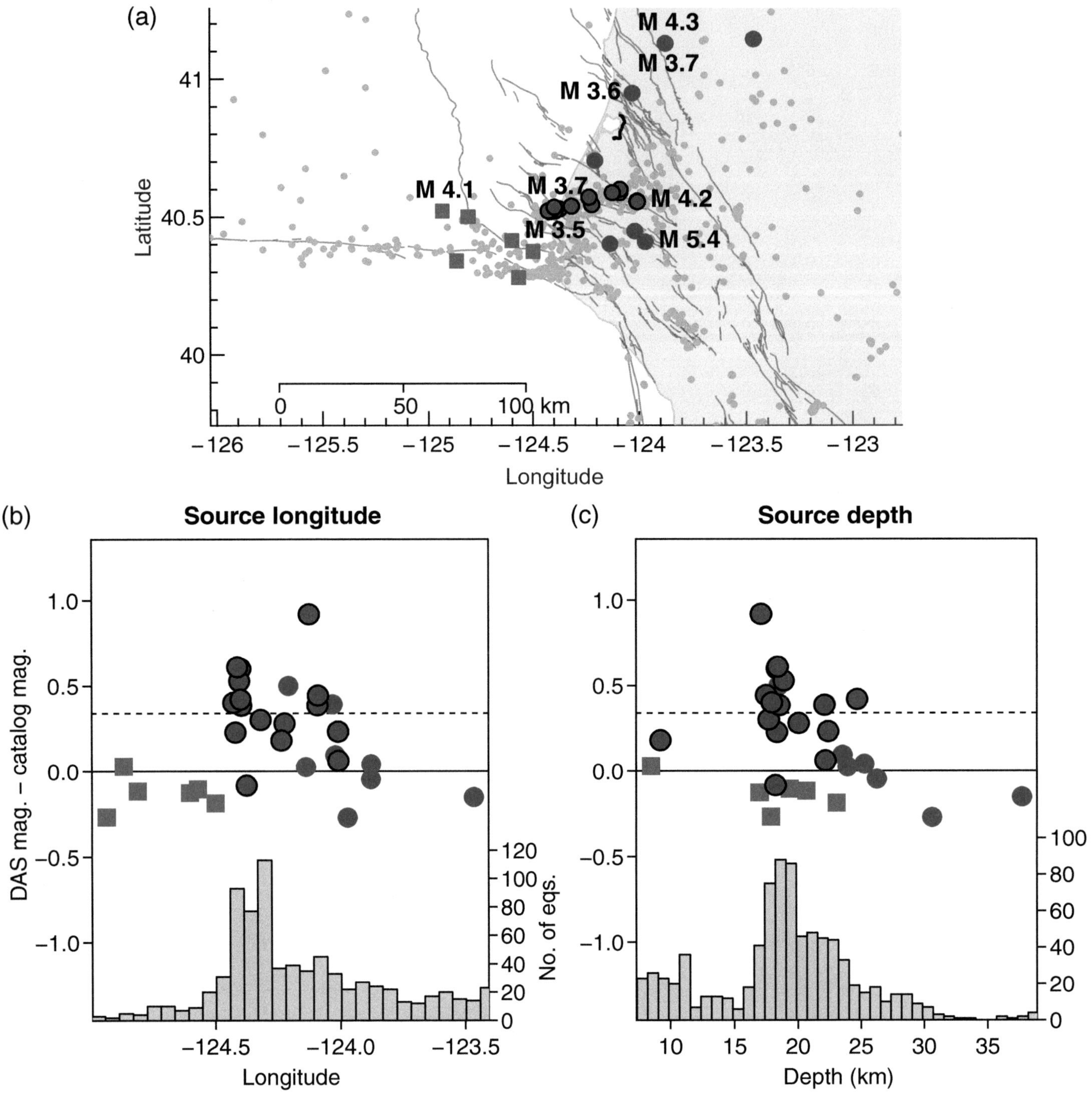

Figure 4. Spatial patterns in DAS-based magnitude errors. (a) Map of study region (as in Fig. 1) but with DAS-based event magnitude results colored according to their location relative to the −124.5° W meridian. The gray dots show cataloged seismicity with $M \geq 0$ in the study period. (b,c) Errors as a function of source longitude (b) and depth (c), with color schemes as in the map. The histograms below show the distributions of the same quantities for the crustal seismicity in the map. The dashed line shows the ad hoc correction suggested by Barbour *et al.* (2021) for events west of the same meridian. Events associated with the M 6.4 Ferndale fault system are shown with black outlines; nearly all these generated higher-than-average dynamic strains compared with other events in the region. The color version of this figure is available only in the electronic edition.

moment as estimated in the Advanced National Seismic System (ANSS) ComCat catalog. They are located ~12 km apart and 50 km from the southern end of the cable. Peak strains recorded by the DAS reach 10^{-6} in both earthquakes and vary by >2 orders of magnitude along the cable. Owing to the channel-to-channel variability in waveforms and the number of channels that do not appear to record ground deformation with high fidelity, we first estimate the spectral ratios on a channel-by-channel basis. To isolate channels that faithfully recorded the *S* wavefield, we have a multistep channel selection procedure. First, we manually pick *P*- and *S*-wave

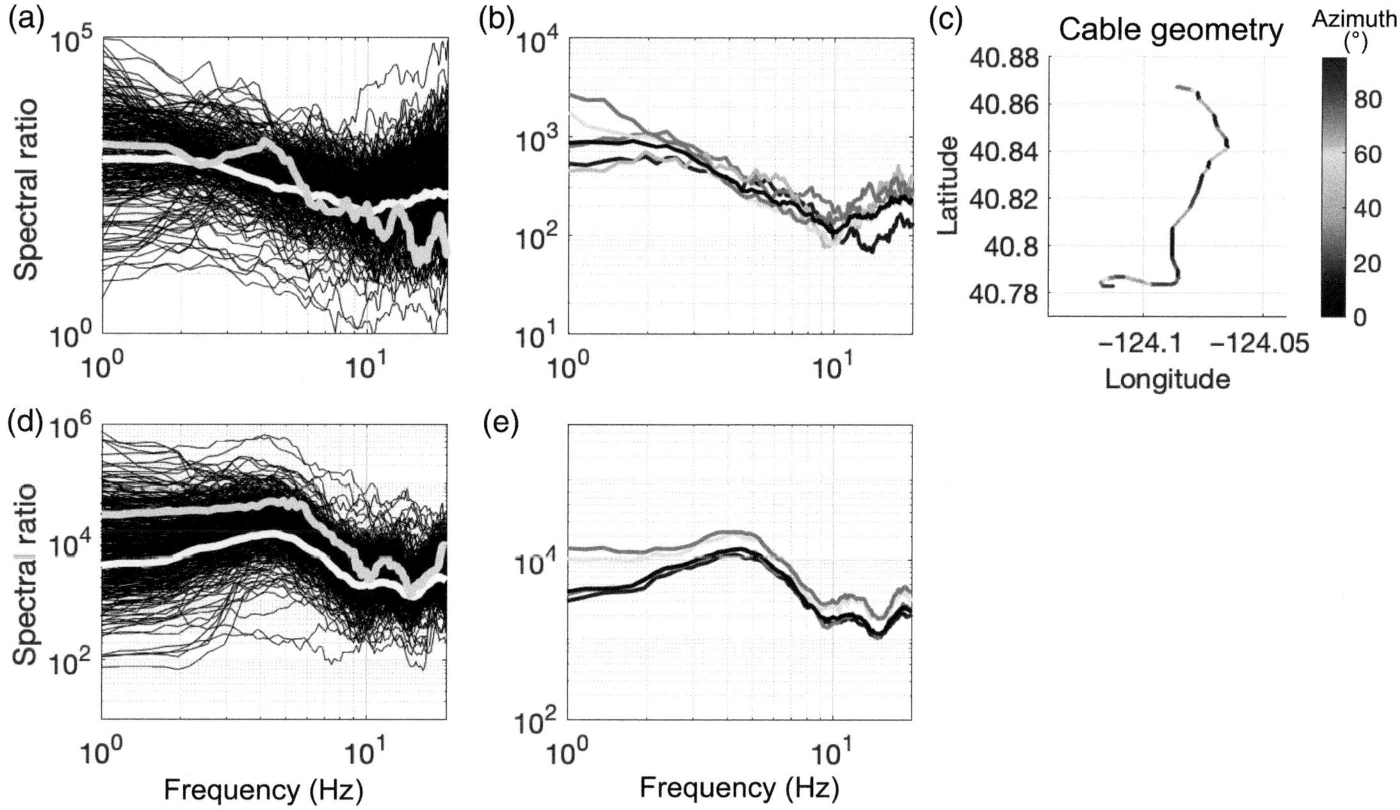

Figure 5. Comparison of spectral ratios for M 4.7 (a,b) and M 4.8 (d,e) mainshocks. (a and d) *S*-wave a) and *P*-wave (d) spectral ratios for individual DAS channels that passed the quality criteria (black lines), the median of all these DAS spectral ratios (white line), and the *S*-wave spectral ratio from nearby broadband station (yellow line, BK.JCC.HHN in a and BK.JCC.HHZ in d). (b,e) Spectral ratios in bins of cable azimuth. The individual channels are assigned an azimuth between 0° (north–south) and 90° (east–west) based on the approximate heading of the cable near their location, and then the median spectral-ratio value is calculated in 20° bins (e.g., 0°–20°, 20°–40°, ...). The overall median spectral ratio is shown as a black line for comparison. (c) Map of cable azimuth used in panels (b) and (e). The color version of this figure is available only in the electronic edition.

arrival times on the full record section using discrete linear fits to ~200 channel segments. The end points are then interpolated using a polynomial to capture the travel-time moveout across the record section (Fig. S2). We then isolate 512-sample-long windows starting 0.5 s before and extending 4.6 s after the *S*-arrival time on each individual channel. Individual traces are demeaned, detrended, and band-pass filtered between 0.1 and 15 Hz. We cross correlate the mainshock and EGF *S* waves (in this case, the M 5.4 and 4.8, respectively) and only keep channels where the correlation coefficient is >0.4. The time windows for the two earthquakes are aligned using the peak of the cross-correlation function. The power spectral densities are calculated using Slepian multitapers to minimize spectral leakage (Fig. S3). Similar processing is done on samples of the noise preceding the *P*-wave arrival time. The spectral ratio is computed at evenly spaced frequencies for all selected channels (Fig. S4). The spectral-ratio results are essentially insensitive to whether the power spectra are computed on strain or integrated strain time series because they resemble velocity and displacement spectra, respectively. The ability to recover the moment ratio between two moderate-magnitude earthquakes to well within a factor of 2 (the expected moment ratio is ~8, and spectral ratios give ~7.1) despite small differences in moment tensor and propagation distance demonstrates the fidelity of the DAS strain recordings at high levels of dynamic strain, approaching 10^{-6}.

To further demonstrate the reliability of the source spectrum estimation, we use more traditional mainshock–EGF pairs. We use the same M 4.8 earthquake (event "h" in Fig. 1a) as a mainshock, with a colocated M 3.0 event as the EGF, and a similar M 4.7 (event "g" in Fig. 1a) and M 3.1 pair (Fig. 5, Table S1). We were not able to find an EGF for the M 5.4 with suitably high SNR because its aftershock sequence mainly included M 2 events during daytime periods, when traffic noise is highest. A similar procedure was followed for the M 4.7 and 4.8 earthquakes except that the M 4.8 used *P*-wave time windows from 1 s before the *P* wave to 4.11 s after the *P* wave (see Fig. S5). These earthquakes were studied using the seismic network data by Guo *et al.* (2024) and show opposite directivity with the M 4.8 rupturing toward the DAS array and the M 4.7 rupturing away from the DAS array. For both earthquakes, we use the same EGF events as in Guo *et al.* (2024) and compare their spectral ratios and

STFs. We also compare the individual channel and median spectral ratios for the two events to the ratios obtained from the broadband S and P waves at nearby station of the Berkeley Seismic Network (BK.JCC, see Fig. 1). The median M 4.8 spectral ratio is flat up to about 4 Hz (Fig. 5d), and the M 4.7 ratio starts to decay at ~2 Hz (Fig. 5a). The relatively sharp corner at relatively high frequencies seen in the M 4.8 ratio is characteristic of stations in the forward rupture direction (Kaneko and Shearer, 2015; Fan and McGuire, 2018) and matches that seen on the broadband station (Fig. 5d). Similarly, the lower frequency corner and gentler fall-off for the M 4.7 ratio is characteristic of stations in the backward rupture direction and is comparable to the nearby broadband observations (Fig. 5a). The ability of DAS to not only match the general features of the source spectrum in nearby broadband recordings but also capture the difference in directivity and spectral shape between the M 4.8 and 4.7 ratios is encouraging for applications that require higher-order source information.

The raw spectra along the cable should vary with the apparent slowness of the wavefield, which for these epicentral distances is dependent primarily on the cable orientation (equation 10). However, this dependence, although key for mapping observed strains into magnitudes, should cancel in spectral-ratio calculations. The GorDAS cable has essentially orthogonal segments with most of the cable being in the north–south direction (Fig. 5c, blue) but ~25% being east–west (Fig. 5c, red). For earthquakes coming from due south, such as the M 4.8 and 4.7 mainshocks, the apparent velocity is much higher on the east–west portion of the cable compared with that on the north–south portion. Thus, one would expect higher average strains on the north–south sections, but these differences should cancel in the ratios, and in practice, local site effects are at least as influential on the peak strains (Fig. 2). When stacked in 20° azimuthal bins, similar differences in spectral ratios for the two mainshocks match our expectations for azimuthal dependence, but these arise only at lower frequencies ($\lesssim$2 Hz; Fig. 5b,e). Otherwise, from 2 to 20 Hz, the spectral ratios show no systematic azimuthal dependence.

Moment-rate function estimation

The far-field P and S waves recorded by a strainmeter should have time histories proportional to the moment–acceleration history of the rupture (equation 10; see also Luo *et al.*, 2021). Strain seismograms in the Earth (instead of a whole space) represent the convolution of a time-dependent Green's function that accounts for wave propagation complexities with the moment–acceleration function, which can be expected to be both positive and negative. Thus, to apply a deconvolution technique that enforces positivity constraints on the temporal function describing the moment release, it would be more robust to work with a time series of integrated strain rather than strain or strain rate. Guo *et al.* (2024) investigated this approach using borehole strainmeter data from the same region, and some aspects of that study are reproduced in more detail here.

For the M 4.7 and 4.8 mainshocks, we retrieve very similar estimates of the moment-rate function from broadband velocity seismograms, strong-motion seismograms, and borehole strainmeter records for closely located stations (see Fig. 6, Figs. S6 and Fig. S7). For the borehole strainmeter data, we performed deconvolutions for both the mainshock and EGF in two ways: (1) using both the strain records, which assumes that far-field strain is proportional to moment acceleration (e.g., equation 10), and (2) using the integrated strain records, which emphasizes lower-frequency signals in the record (e.g., far-field strain is more sensitive to moment rate). We use a deconvolution technique that enforces positivity of the moment-rate function (Lanza *et al.*, 1999); the duration of the resulting moment-rate function is calculated using the apparent characteristic duration (McGuire, 2004), which is twice the square root of the variance of the apparent source time function (ASTF). For reference, the apparent characteristic durations of different seismic stations range from 0.12 to 0.46 s for the M 4.7 mainshock and from 0.09 to 0.31 s for the M 4.8 mainshock (Guo *et al.*, 2024).

For the M 4.7 mainshock, the closest strainmeter is B045 (Fig. 1); the ASTF recovered from the integrated strain is smoother than the one directly from strain as expected, but both waveforms are fit well and result in nearly identical apparent durations (0.30 s for strain versus 0.31 s for integrated strain; Fig. 6a, Fig. S6). These duration estimates fall between those from the two nearest seismic stations (GHOP and KCR). Similarly, for the M 4.8 mainshock, two strainmeters are at similar distances (B933 and B934) and produce apparent durations from integrated strain that are very similar to those from nearby broadband seismic stations: 0.23 versus 0.21 s for B933 and PRDS, respectively, and 0.17 versus 0.24 s for B934 and HALS, respectively (Fig. 6c, Fig. S7). Furthermore, the ASTFs derived from the strain and integrated strain time series are consistent with those measured from nearby inertial sensors (Fig. 6a,c). In the frequency domain, the strain and integrated strain time series produce similar spectral ratios, as expected, and their low-frequency asymptotes and high-frequency decays are comparable to results from the nearby inertial sensors (Fig. 6b,d). In short, the ability to recover the ASTF of M 4 earthquakes from strain data is straightforward, and using either strain or integrated strain is effective in this range of earthquake magnitudes and frequency content. For the remainder of the article, we use strain records to keep the approach as simple as possible and to avoid any low-frequency noise amplification in the DAS data.

Having established that borehole strainmeter records can reliably recover time-domain ASTF estimates from seismometers for M ~4 earthquakes, we developed a semiautomated DAS data processing approach that results in estimates of the ASTF for groups of adjacent channels along the cable.

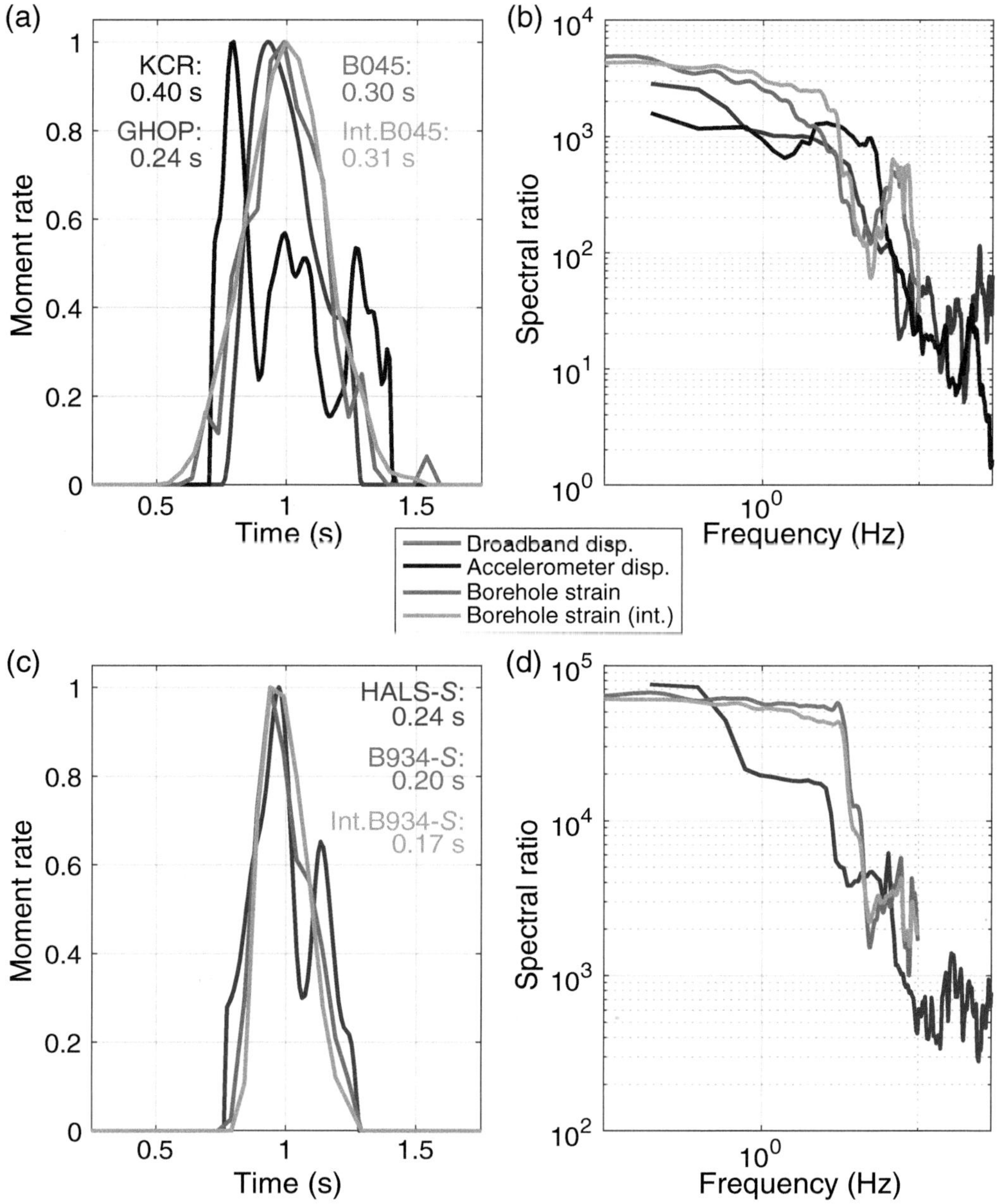

Figure 6. Comparison of *S*-wave derived apparent source time functions (ASTFs, a,c) and spectral ratios (b,d) for the M 4.7 (panels a and b) and M 4.8 (panels c and d) earthquakes. ASTFs are shown for NOTA strainmeter B045 compared with results from nearby broadband and strong-motion instruments. The same EGF events were used as in Guo *et al.* (2024). For the NOTA strainmeters, the spectral ratio and EGF deconvolution were done with both the raw record (magenta lines) and a time-domain integrated record ("Int strain," orange lines). In (a) and (c), the apparent characteristic duration, calculated following Guo *et al.* (2024), is labeled for each result. Some apparent differences in the ASTFs may relate to station separation between the strainmeter and seismometer, but the differences between using integrated strain and strain records from the same strainmeter led to marginal differences in duration estimates. The time axes in this figure are defined relative to the record start time in the deconvolution. Hence, the different ASTFs have been arbitrarily aligned for comparison purposes. The color version of this figure is available only in the electronic edition.

Because some channels are not reliable recordings of ground motion and the SNR of M 2–3 EGF earthquakes is often only moderate, we choose to implement a stacking-based approach that attempts to both isolate high-quality ground-motion recordings and improve the SNR of the EGFs. The goal of this preprocessing is to produce high-quality DAS waveforms that can be used with the same deconvolution techniques that are successful with borehole strainmeter records (e.g., Fig. 6). The processing steps are as follows:

1. Data are band-pass filtered between 3 and 20 Hz because of the low SNR of the EGF *P* waves below 3 Hz.
2. *P*- and *S*-wave arrival times are picked on record sections at an arbitrary set of points roughly every 100 channels, which are fit with piecewise continuous polynomial (e.g., Fig. S2). These picks are intentionally crude first-break picks with accuracies of 0.1–0.2 s. They are only used to initiate the alignment process subsequently.
3. An attempt is made to create a stacked waveform around the *P* (or *S*) wave using bins of adjacent channels. The bin size is arbitrary but set at 20 channels (corresponding to ~100 m of cable length) for the figures shown here.
4. For each channel, a 5.12 s (512 samples) window starting 1 s before the *P* pick is extracted and band-pass filtered with corners at 1 and 15 Hz.
5. Optionally, integrate the strain records; for these examples, we did not.
6. The filtered mainshock and EGF strain records for each channel are cross correlated. If the cross-correlation coefficient is ≥0.5, the channel is retained. The EGF waveforms are windowed based on the peak of the cross-correlation function to align them with the mainshock.
7. If at least two channels within a bin pass these criteria, a stack is created for that bin. For both the EGF and the

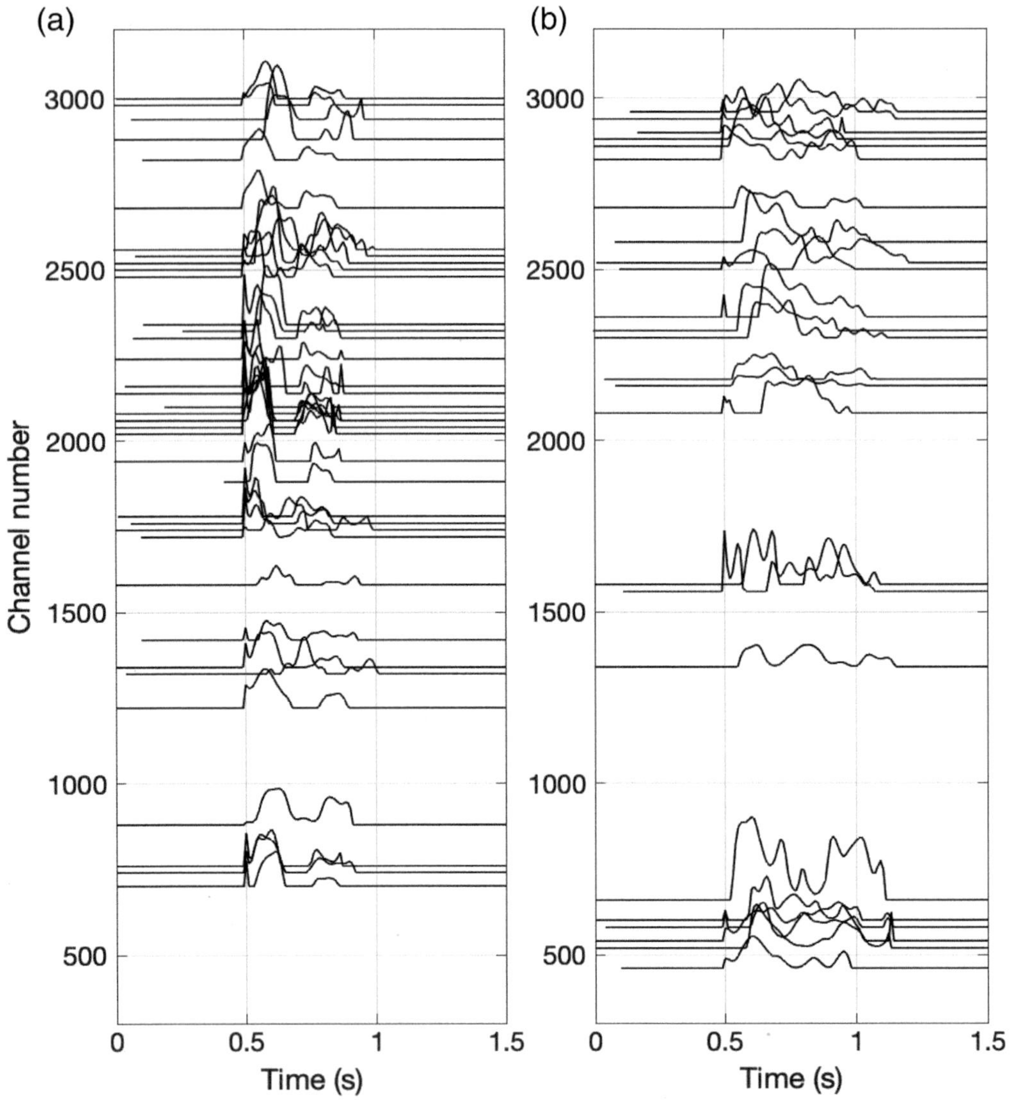

Figure 7. ASTFs for the M 4.8 (a) and M 4.7 (b) *P* waves estimated on binned channel stacks of DAS strain data. All ASTFs for a given earthquake have been normalized in the same way, but the normalization between the two panels is different owing to the significant difference in the mainshock to EGF moment ratios in the two cases (see Fig. S9). The time axes on this figure are defined such that the ASTF starts at 0.5 s regardless of the duration of the pre-*P*-wave seismogram used in the deconvolution.

mainshock, we separately correlate each remaining channel within the bin with all the other remaining channels. We then select the channel with the highest number of correlation coefficients >0.6 as the master channel to define the timing. The remaining channels within the bin are shifted to the alignment that maximizes their correlation with the master channel and stacked. The resulting stacks are normalized by the number of channels in each. No other corrections are made for amplitude variations between channels. Stacks usually range from 2 to 10 channels.

In this process, a few adjustable parameters allow some customization for a given dataset: bin size, filter corners, and the two cross-correlation significance cutoffs. They comprise an effective means to separate the near-adjacent channels with high-quality recordings of ground motion in an automated way. See Figure S8 for an example of the waveforms that were included from a *P*-wave stack for a bin in the southern end of the cable.

Given the stacked mainshock and EGF DAS waveforms for a given channel bin, we apply the same deconvolution procedure that worked well for BSM data (Fig. 6, Figs. S6 and S7). This procedure requires high-resolution picks of the wave arrival times, which specifies the time window in which to fit the mainshock waveforms, and the duration of the apparent moment-rate function (McGuire, 2004). Some studies have used an automated picking procedure for high-quality seismic data (Meng *et al.*, 2020), but in this study picks were done by hand to ensure consistency and minimize potential sources of error. In some cases, the resulting ASTFs for channel bins show 70% or higher variance reductions in mainshock waveform fits and easily pickable durations of the ASTF (Fig. 7). (Many bins do not produce a high variance reduction in the deconvolution procedure and hence do not produce a reliable ASTF; these are not shown.) The DAS-based ASTFs are significantly longer for *P* waves from the M 4.7 earthquake than the M 4.8 earthquake. This relative difference is consistent with the results from nearby seismic stations (Fig. 8) and reflects differences between the directivity and stress drop of the two earthquakes (Guo *et al.*, 2024).

To quantify the reliability of the ASTFs, we plot the relative moment ratio between the mainshock and EGF and the apparent duration of the ASTF as a function of channel bin: the apparent duration measurements are consistently higher (~0.3 versus 0.2 s) for the M 4.7 earthquake than the M 4.8

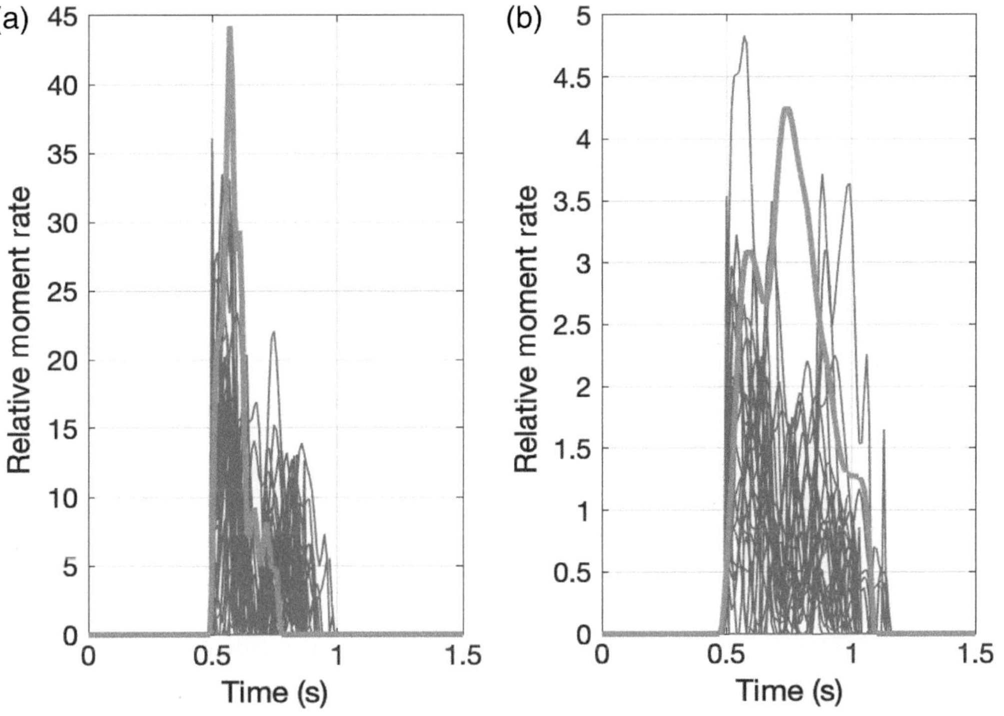

Figure 8. Comparison of the *P*-wave ASTFs derived from the DAS channel stacks in Figure 7 with the results from nearby broadband seismometer BK.JCC.HHZ for the M 4.8 (panel a) and the M 4.7 (panel b) mainshocks. The BK.JCC results are from Guo *et al.* (2024). All ASTFs are aligned with their initiation time. The BK.JCC ASTFs are shown in orange thick lines and the DAS channels in gray thin lines. The relative moment-rate ratio is between the mainshock and EGF. The DAS *P*-wave deconvolutions accurately capture the true amplitude of the relative moment rate as determined by traditional inertial data. The color version of this figure is available only in the electronic edition.

earthquake (Fig. S9). In contrast, the relative moment ratios are consistently higher (~200 versus 50) for the M 4.8 earthquake than the M 4.7 earthquake; this difference in relative moment reflects the relative magnitudes of the mainshocks and EGFs. Collectively, these results demonstrate that the fundamental source properties of earthquakes, such as the shape and amplitude of the moment-rate functions, are systematically retrievable from the first few seconds of the *P*-wave recordings on telecom DAS systems. Recovering this information requires careful identification of the most reliable channels, but the procedure is otherwise no different from working with noisy seismic stations. The high reliability of earthquake source information from the GorDAS system suggests that other applications that require estimating the magnitude from the first few seconds of DAS *P* waves can succeed up to at least the M 5.0 level.

DISCUSSION

A growing collection of case studies indicates that DAS-based magnitudes are accurate compared with a reference catalog and show similar repeatability between comparable methods. In some deployments, DAS-based estimates of moment magnitude are comparable to independent estimates from nearby or colocated seismic data, including induced microseismicity at a hydraulic fracturing experiment and a local earthquake at the Salton Sea geothermal field (Nayak *et al.*, 2024); two moderate-magnitude events in Ridgecrest and Long Valley, California (Yin *et al.*, 2023); local seismicity near the Irpinia near-fault observatory in Italy and an offshore array in the Chilean subduction zone (Strumia *et al.*, 2024); and from an offshore array in central California (Gou *et al.*, 2025). In this compilation, the DAS-based estimates are in remarkably close agreement with seismic-based estimates of earthquake magnitude. Comparing the GorDAS Arcata results with the results from California, Chile, and Italy shows a similarly close agreement across the range of magnitude results regardless of whether the array is offshore or onshore, in a borehole or at the surface. The standard deviation of the differences between magnitudes is relatively low (~0.23; Fig. 9), and applying corrections for additional source and path effects (e.g., Fig. 4) would likely reduce this variability further.

As discussed earlier, removing the site response along the DAS cable is critical for obtaining accurate strain–amplitude-based magnitude estimates. We compared the ratios of characteristic strain attenuation for both DAS to BSM and DAS to DAS from the United States and Japan (Fig. 10) using the scaling relationships from Barbour *et al.* (2021) for BSM and Yin *et al.* (2023) and Baba *et al.* (2024) for DAS. Strain attenuation differs between regions as do displacement attenuation functions used for the M_L and M_{JMA} scales (Katsumata, 1996; Uhrhammer *et al.*, 2011), and these have the strongest impact at near-source distances (Fig. 10aA). These differences translate directly to magnitude estimates (e.g., equation 8); however, they are relatively subtle compared with the magnitude and variability in the site terms S_i (Fig. 10b). Projecting the attenuation curves onto quantiles of S_i indicates that beyond ~21 km from an earthquake source, the effects of localized amplification and attenuation along the fiber strongly affect amplitude-based magnitude estimates if they are not corrected for, and beyond ~48 km, the same effects would most

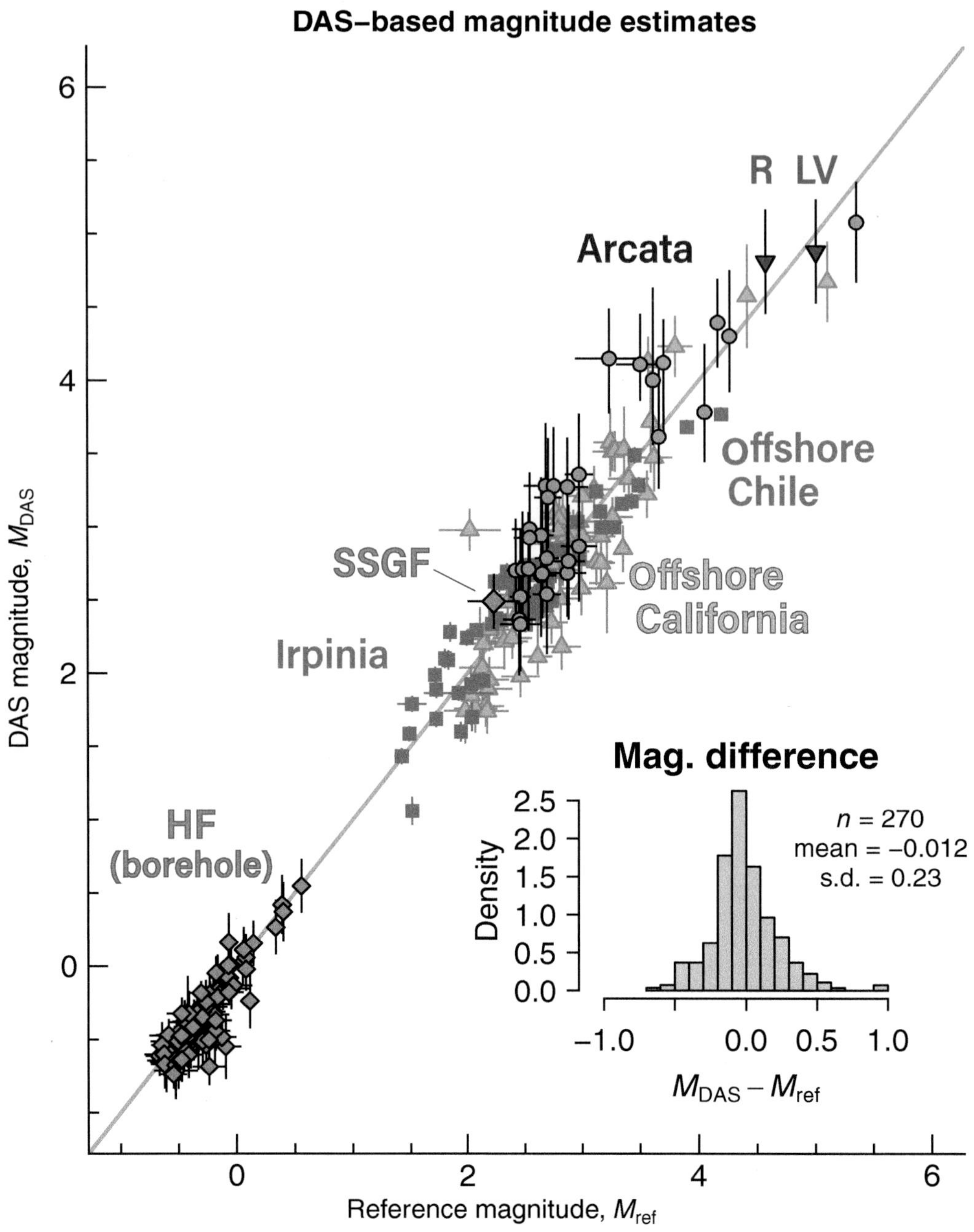

Figure 9. Compilation of DAS-based magnitude estimates in various locations across the world. DAS-estimated source magnitudes are plotted against their reference magnitudes from seismic data (primarily moment magnitudes). The diagonal line shows perfect agreement. For GorDAS Arcata (this study, circles), Ridgecrest and Long Valley ("R" and "LV"; Yin *et al.*, 2023, inverted triangles), and offshore California (Gou *et al.*, 2025, triangles), the reference is the Advanced National Seismic System (ANSS) ComCat catalog (see Data and Resources). The other datasets are from a hydraulic fracturing site ("HF," Nayak *et al.*, 2024, small diamonds); the Salton Sea geothermal field ("SSGF," Nayak *et al.*, 2024, large diamond); Irpinia, Italy (Strumia *et al.*, 2024, blue squares); and offshore Chile (Strumia *et al.*, 2024, red squares). The inset shows a normalized (density) histogram of residual magnitude differences; the standard deviation for all 270 estimates in this compilation is 0.23. Linear regression of DAS-estimated magnitude against reference magnitude indicates a near-unity scaling of 1.004 ± 0.006 from $-0.7 < M < 5.4$. The color version of this figure is available only in the electronic edition.

likely dominate estimates (Fig. 10c). Again, this emphasizes the need for an accurate assessment of variability in strain amplitude response on the fiber on a channel-by-channel basis.

Origin of site-response profile along fiber

The site response along the GorDAS fiber is highly variable, as with other DAS arrays (e.g., Yin *et al.*, 2023; Baba *et al.*, 2024). In some locations, the GorDAS S_i change from being strongly attenuative to strongly amplifying over hundreds of meters. The partial autocorrelation function of these S_i^S indicates that the response at a particular channel is correlated to its neighboring channels within the gauge length (8 m), as expected based on the principles of DAS. The cross-correlation function between S_i^P and S_i^S shows statistically significant correlations out to ~1100 m on either side of a given channel. The fiber-optic cable is buried ~5 m from the surface along the entire path, and McGuire *et al.* (2025) show that the observed strain variability is reflected in the ground motions measured by colocated nodal seismometers, which implies that amplifications in the DAS data represent near-surface conditions within the spatial resolution of the nodal seismometer spacing rather than being purely related to fiber-to-ground coupling. In addition, the site amplification profiles of S_i^P and S_i^S are nearly equivalent. In other words, at any given location along the fiber, both the *P* and *S* waves will be amplified (or attenuated) by approximately the same factor depending on the location along the fiber. This same consistency is observed in deployments across the world, from both terrestrial and seafloor fibers (e.g., Yin *et al.*, 2023; Baba *et al.*, 2024), with a notable exception in offshore California (i.e., Romanowicz *et al.*, 2023), where the *P*- and

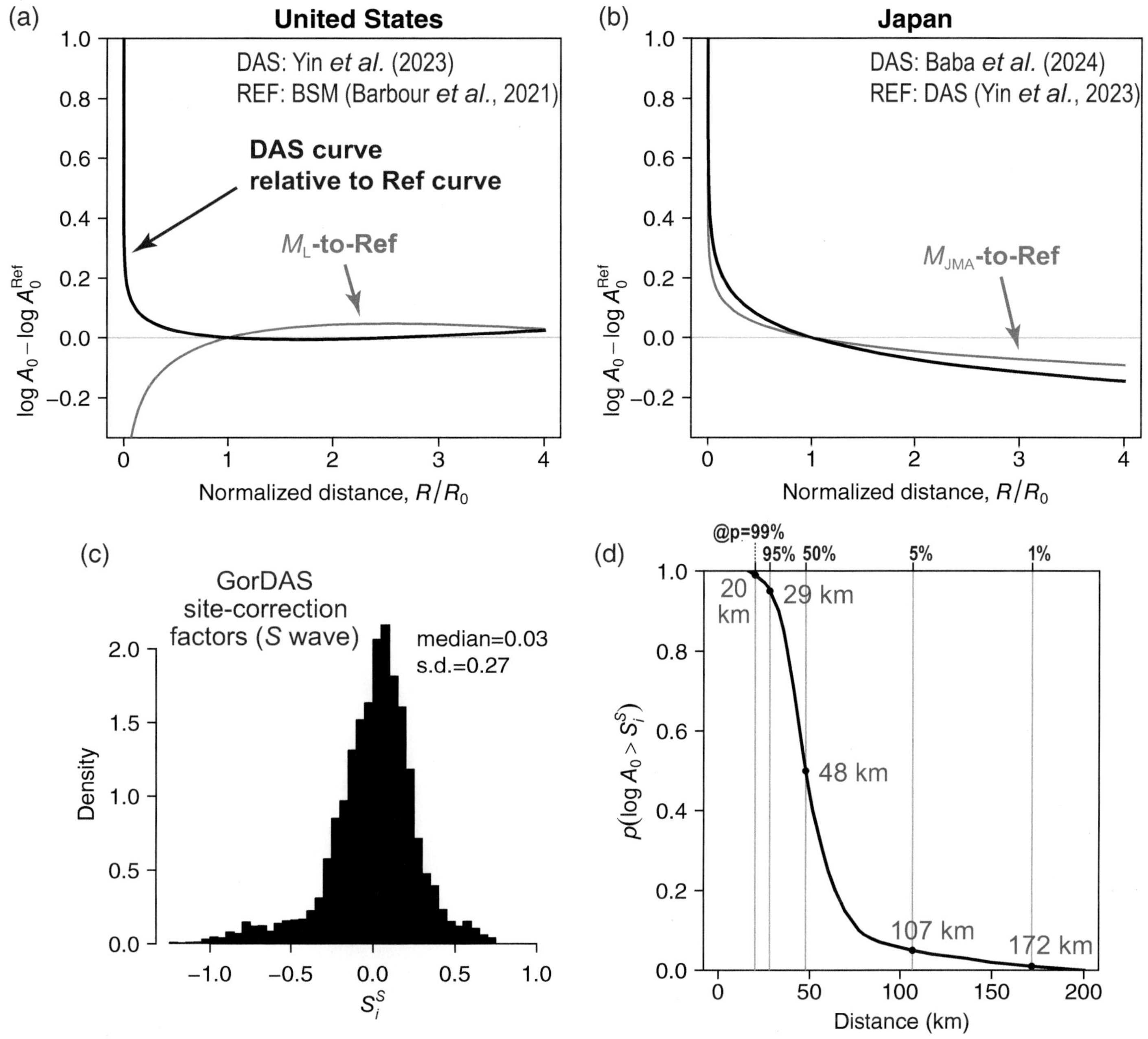

Figure 10. Comparison of characteristic strain attenuation curves ($\log A_0$; e.g., equation 3) and DAS site response S_i^S (equation 6; Fig. 2). (a, b) Difference of log DAS-based strain attenuation and a reference attenuation curve as a function of hypocentral distance (R) normalized by a reference distance ($R_0 = 50$ km). For United States (a,c): DAS-based attenuation from Yin. *et al.* (2023) referenced against BSM-based attenuation from Barbour *et al.* (2021). For additional comparison, the BSM-based attenuation is referenced against the displacement attenuation for the California Integrated Seismic Network (CISN)–M_L scale (Uhrhammer *et al.*, 2011). For Japan (b,d): DAS attenuation from the Tsugaru Strait offshore array (Baba *et al.*, 2024) referenced against the Sanriku offshore array (Yin *et al.*, 2023). The displacement-based attenuation for the Japan Meteorological Agency magnitude (M_{JMA}) scale (Katsumata, 1996) is also shown against the same reference. In both regions, the differences in strain attenuation are strongest for $R \ll R_0/2$. (b) Normalized (density) histogram of GorDAS *S*-wave site-correction factors (S_i^S). (c) Probability that DAS-based strain attenuation exceeds S_i^S; this results from projecting the attenuation curve to quantiles of S_i^S. Without accurate site corrections, peak strains measured on DAS systems located beyond ~20 km from the source will be strongly affected by S_i^S, and beyond ~48 km (the median) peak strains will likely be dominated by S_i^S. The color version of this figure is available only in the electronic edition.

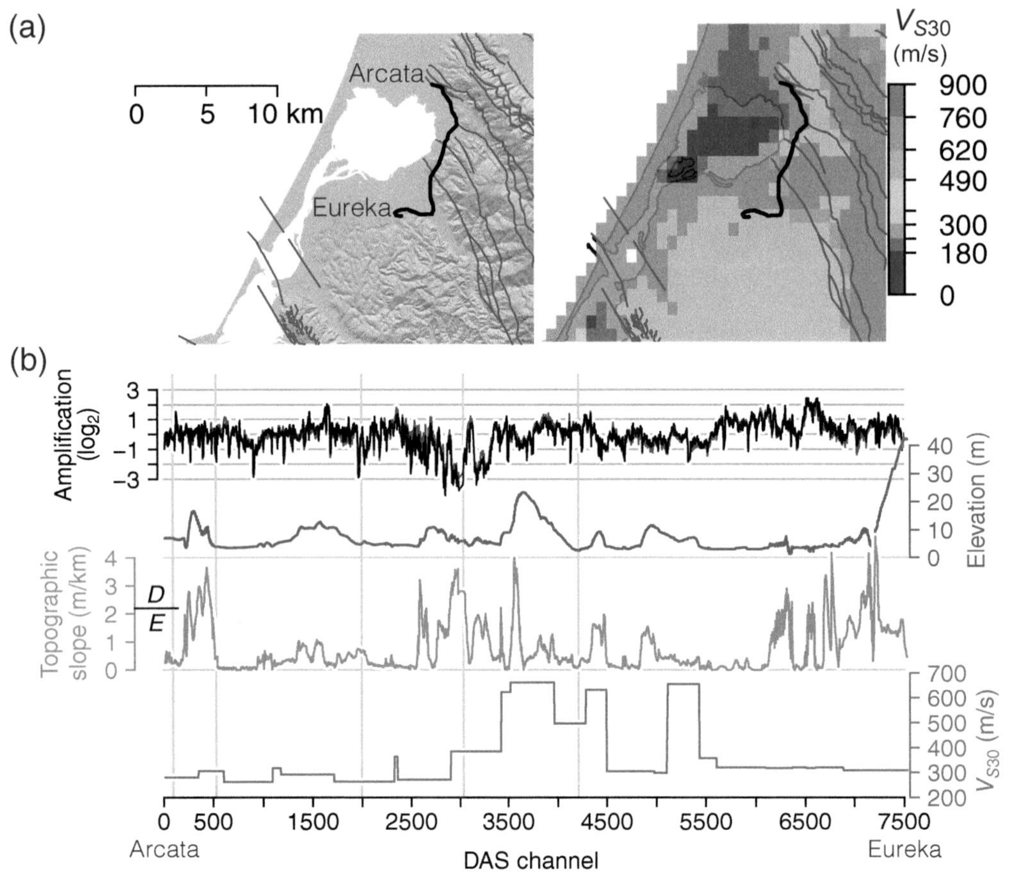

Figure 11. Fiber-optic strain amplification factors, topography, and V_{S30}. (a) Maps of U.S. Geological Survey (USGS) 1/3 arcsec topography, mapped Quaternary faults (brown lines), and the fiber-optic cable path in this study (black line). The right figure shows map of V_{S30} from the USGS Global V_{S30} map, which is derived from 30 s topography (e.g., Allen and Wald, 2007). (b) Variations along the fiber by channel (2 m channel separation). From top to bottom, the figures show DAS *P*-wave and *S*-wave site-response factors S_i^P and S_i^S ($\log_2$ scale, red and black curves, respectively), 1/3 arcsec elevation (meters above sea level [m.a.s.l.], brown curve), and the topographic slope calculated from it (m/km, orange curve, based on the method of Horn, 1981), where the "D/E" marker represents the transition from National Earthquake Hazards Reduction Program (NEHRP) class D–E soils used to convert from slope to V_{S30} in the Global map and V_{S30} from the Global map (m/s, blue curve). The vertical lines show where the fiber-optic cable crosses mapped Quaternary faults. There is little to no apparent relationship between the site-correction factors and either the Global V_{S30} or high-resolution topographic slope, although there is a suggestion of fault-related influences (e.g., around channels 2000). The color version of this figure is available only in the electronic edition.

S-wave amplification factors diverge as the fiber extends to deeper waters off the continental shelf (Gou *et al.*, 2025). Nonetheless, although appealing to variations in cable coupling as the controlling factor is tempting, there are likely geological and geophysical explanations for the patterns in site terms, too.

For an installation like this, where the fiber-optic cable is relatively well coupled to the surrounding materials, expecting some correlation between DAS S_i^P and S_i^S and typical site metrics used in ground-motion modeling is reasonable. We compared the DAS amplification with a profile of V_{S30} along the fiber. V_{S30} is a commonly used metric representing the average shear-wave velocity in the upper 30 m and generally accepted as a first-order estimate of site-response effects in ground-motion recordings. In this region, the main source of V_{S30} comes from a map derived from topographic slope (e.g., Allen and Wald, 2007), specifically slopes calculated from 30 arcsec gridded topography. The observed DAS site response shows weak if not insignificant negative correlation with V_{S30} at −0.024 ($p = 0.05$) at the 30 arcsec database (~0.8 km^2; see Fig. 11). This holds for both *P*- and *S*-wave site-correction factors, S_i^P and S_i^S because they are strongly correlated (0.947, $p \ll 0.0001$; see Fig. 11b).

We also compared the DAS site-response factors to finer spatial resolution from 1/3 arcsec topography (~100 m^2 grid) and its associated topographic slope (Fig. 11b); the correlation with finer topography is insignificant (−0.008, $p = 0.506$), but the correlation with finer topographic slope is weak but statistically significant at −0.162 ($p \ll 0.0001$). This suggests that a stronger correlation with V_{S30} could be observed if derived from either the higher-resolution topographic slope or from a shallow velocity model. Tomographic models would provide additional benefit through alternative metrics such as the depth to $V_S = 1.0$ km/s, which may provide greater insight into compounding influences on the site response, including potential basin effects due to the Mad River and Freshwater fault zones and structures between them. Furthermore, even though the direct correlation with the global V_{S30} data is unclear, there is a suggestion of differences in variability in S_i^P and S_i^S when they are grouped in ranges of V_{S30} based on National Earthquake Hazards Reduction Program (NEHRP) soil classifications (i.e., Allen and Wald, 2007, their table 2). More specifically, the NEHRP groupings suggest that the extremes in S_i^P and S_i^S are more commonly observed at the lower ranges of V_{S30} (e.g., class "D") in slower, softer sediments; however, in the higher ranges of V_{S30} (e.g., class "C" and up), the site-correction factors are more tightly clustered (Fig. S10).

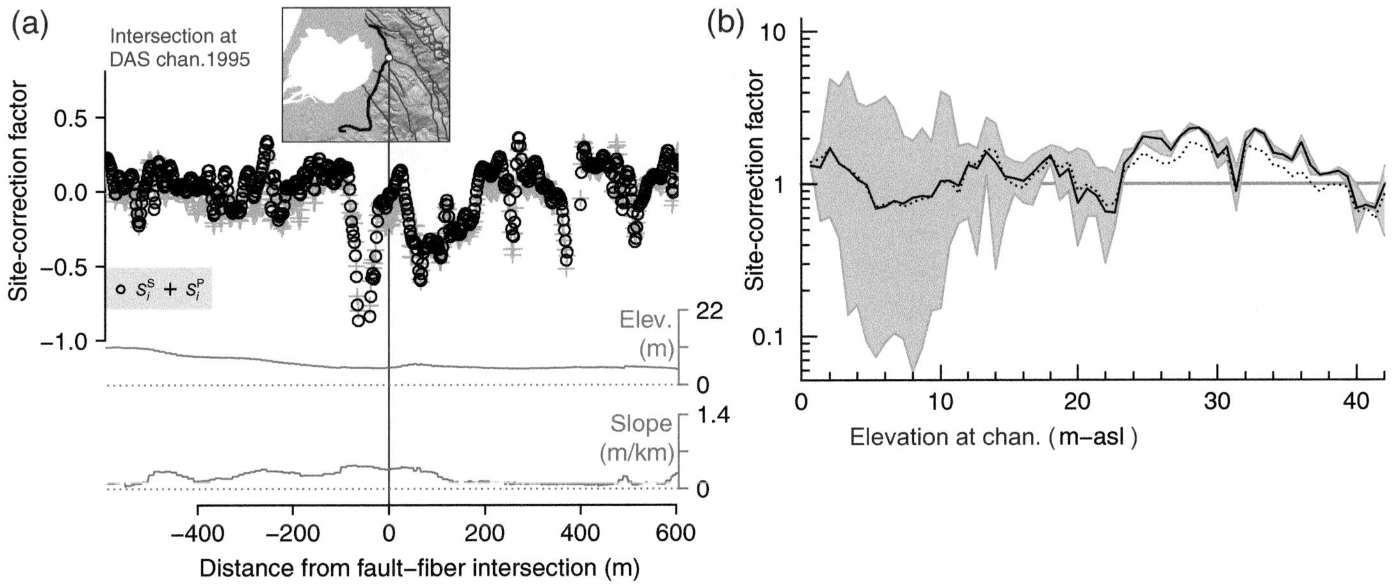

Figure 12. Spatial variability in *S*-wave site-response factors (S_i^S). (a) Factors shown as a function of distance away from a known fault in the Mad River fault zone intersecting the fiber around channel 1995 (see inset map, and Fig. 11). For reference, the *P*-wave factors (S_i^P) are also shown, and the local elevation and topographic slope profiles are shown below. Zones of strong attenuation ∼100–200 m wide are seen on both sides of the mapped fault in a location with relatively small elevation and slope changes.
(b) Distribution of factors by elevation along the fiber at all locations (e.g., Fig. 11b). The gray region shows the range of site-response factors, and the solid line shows the mean response; the dotted line shows the equivalent curve for S_i^P for reference. For fiber sections at lower elevation (<∼22 m), the response is highly variable, showing both attenuation and amplification as in (a); for sections at higher elevations, the response is generally amplified with less variability. The color version of this figure is available only in the electronic edition.

Geological influences on the site-response factors are further suggested by two apparent correlations: one with faults and another with elevation along the fiber (Fig. 12). In some locations where the fiber crosses locations of mapped Quaternary active faults, the DAS site response shows highly localized variations that differ in character from sections of fiber far from known fault crossings (Fig. 12a). Many of the topographic features in this region are due to transpressional slip resulting from locking on the subducting Gorda plate interface (e.g., Materna *et al.*, 2023). The GorDAS cable crosses multiple strands of the Mad River fault zone and Freshwater fault zone, which implies that the intense variability in site response is not only associated with shallow velocity structure owing to sedimentation processes but also potentially by anisotropy associated with fault damage structure and slip history.

The second apparent correlation implicating a geological origin for the response is to elevation along the fiber. Although these elevation changes are relatively small compared with those in the region, the distribution of site-response factors in low-elevation sections (≲22 m a.s.l.) is far more variable than in higher-elevation sections, with fluctuations between amplification and attenuation. In contrast, in sections of fiber above ∼22 m, the site response is generally always amplifying, with little variability (Fig. 12b). Because the fiber-optic cable is buried at approximately the same depth along the full path, this elevation-based correlation is most likely a reflection of the fiber passing through geologic units with differing material properties, such as Quaternary alluvium and terrace deposits at lower elevations and Franciscan melange at higher elevations. In addition, the fiber fault crossings are in low elevation regions, at slope toes (Fig. 11b), which implies that material property contrasts associated with fault core and damage zones contribute to the site-response variability in lower elevations; this phenomenon has been seen before around known fault crossings (e.g., Ma *et al.*, 2024). Our interpretation is complicated by the presence of high levels of fluid saturation (e.g., Arcata Bay) that may enhance fluid–rock coupling effects and increase attenuation. But to disentangle these various contributions to the site response along the fiber, additional in situ testing of site conditions (e.g., cone penetration testing) along the fiber may be needed; using the same DAS deployment to image shallow structure at a resolution warranted by the site-response profiles is also possible (e.g., Atterholt *et al.*, 2022).

CONCLUSIONS

We evaluated the reliability of both amplitude-based magnitudes and spectral ratios for STFs using dynamic strain records from a dark-fiber DAS system. In both applications, magnitudes and realistic source properties are recovered with high accuracy with respect to values from earthquake catalogs and prior studies determined using seismic data. The accuracies of these results hinge on a few key steps, including the removal of site response along the fiber to reduce uncertainty in amplitude-based magnitudes and the use of strain or integrated strain, rather than strain rate, to stabilize spectral-ratio inversions. The site response along the fiber-optic cable is a result of multiple, commonly accepted factors in DAS deployments, including fiber-to-ground coupling and shallow velocity structure, but we also observe persistent zones of body-to-surface-wave scattering around active faults that influence site response. Our results show that DAS waveforms from well-coupled telecom fiber networks faithfully represent earthquake source complexity and confirm fine-scale details in ground-motion amplification suggested by the colocated seismic data (McGuire *et al.*, 2025).

DATA AND RESOURCES

All distributed acoustic sensing (DAS) and nodal data used in this study can be found in the U.S. Geological Survey (USGS) Science Base repository (https://sciencebase.gov) via the official data releases for this experiment by McGuire, Barbour, Karrenbach, *et al.* (2022), McGuire, Barbour, McPherson, *et al.* (2022), and McGuire, *et al.* (2023, 2024). The seismic data for station JCC are from the BK network (BDSN, doi: 10.7932/BDSN) operated by the UC Berkeley Seismological Laboratory, which is archived at the Northern California Earthquake Data Center (NCEDC, doi: 10.7932/NCEDC). Borehole strainmeter (BSM) data are from the Network of the Americas (NOTA) strainmeter network, which is based on services provided by the National Science Foundation (NSF) GAGE Facility, operated by EarthScope Consortium, with support from the NSF, the National Aeronautics and Space Administration, and the U.S. Geological Survey (USGS) under NSF Cooperative Agreement EAR-1724794. BSM data can be obtained from the EarthScope Data Management Center (https://www.earthscope.org/data). Catalog earthquakes used in this study are from the USGS Advanced National Seismic System (ANSS) Comprehensive Earthquake Catalog (ComCat) (doi: 10.5066/F7MS3QZH). The global V_{S30} database is available from the U.S. Geological Survey (USGS) (https://earthquake.usgs.gov/data/vs30). The Quaternary fault database is available from the USGS (doi: 10.5066/P9BCVRCK). The 1/3 arcsec topography comes from the USGS 3D Elevation Program; the relevant tile for this region is "n41w125" (https://www.sciencebase.gov/catalog/item/5f7784f782ce1d74e7d6cbbc). All websites were last accessed in September 2025.

The supplemental material contains figures to help demonstrate details of the analyses above including a comparison of *S*-wave and *P*-wave site amplification by V_{S30} categories, *P*- and *S*-wave DAS data picks from two key earthquakes and their amplitude spectra, a comparison of *S*-wave spectral ratios between two earthquakes, DAS *P*-wave strain time series used for spectral-ratio calculation, empirical Green's function (EGF) deconvolutions using borehole strainmeter data, seismic stations for a few earthquakes with duration estimates, DAS waveform fits of stacked strain records, and a summary of the duration and relative moments derived from EGF deconvolutions. The supplemental material also includes a table of events used for EGF analyses (Table S1), a table of the *S*-wave and *P*-wave site amplification factors (Table S2), and the observed peak dynamic strain (PDS) values and associated magnitudes (Table S3).

DECLARATION OF COMPETING INTERESTS

The authors acknowledge that there are no conflicts of interest recorded.

ACKNOWLEDGMENTS

Their ability to perform this study hinged critically on assistance from Josh Nelson at Vero Networks, the Arcata Police Department, for graciously letting us store the interrogator unit for the duration of the experiment, and Dillon Savage at the City of Arcata for facilitating interrogator access and security. The authors are further indebted to Paul Bodin at the University of Washington; Kari Stockdale, Amanda Admire, Otto Berndt, and Emily Shiver at Cal Poly Humboldt; and Jay Patton at the California Geological Survey for their assistance in the field. The authors thank Yuancong Gou, Avinash Nayak, and Claudio Strumia for assistance with their prior results; Clara Yoon, Theresa Sawi, and Jimmy Atterholt for numerous related discussions; and Victor Yartsev for his unwavering patience and support. The authors are grateful to Associate Editor Cezar Trifu, an anonymous reviewer, and Nate Lindsey for providing thorough reviews that ultimately led to significant improvements in this article. Any use of trade, firm, or product names is for descriptive purposes only and does not imply endorsement by the U.S. government.

REFERENCES

Agnew, D. C., and F. K. Wyatt (2014). Dynamic strains at regional and teleseismic distances, *Bull. Seismol. Soc. Am.* **104,** no. 4, 1846–1859, doi: 10.1785/0120140007.

Ajo-Franklin, J., V. Rodríguez Tribaldos, A. Nayak, F. Cheng, R. Mellors, B. Chi, T. Wood, M. Robertson, C. Rotermund, E. Matzel, *et al.* (2022). The Imperial Valley dark fiber project: Toward seismic studies using DAS and telecom infrastructure for geothermal applications, *Bull. Seismol. Soc. Am.* **93,** no. 5, 2906–2919, doi: 10.1785/0220220072.

Aki, K., and P. G. Richards (2002). *Quantitative Seismology*, University Science Books, Mill Valley, California.

Allen, T. I., and D. J. Wald (2007). Topographic slope as a proxy for seismic site-conditions (VS30) and amplification around the globe, *U.S. Geol. Surv. Open-File Rept. 2007-1357*, 69 pp., doi: 10.3133/ofr20071357.

Ammon, C. J., A. A. Velasco, and T. Lay (1993). Rapid estimation of rupture directivity: Application to the 1992 Landers (Ms = 7.4) and Cape Mendocino (Ms = 7.2) California earthquakes, *Geophys Res. Lett.* **20,** 97–100, doi: 10.1029/92GL03032.

Atterholt, J., Z. Zhan, and Y. Yang (2022). Fault zone imaging with distributed acoustic sensing: Body-to-surface wave scattering, *J. Geophys. Res.* **127,** e2022JB025052, doi: 10.1029/2022JB025052.

Baba, S., E. Araki, T. Yokobiki, K. Kawamata, K. Uchiyama, and T. Yoshizuka (2024). Seismic observation using distributed acoustic sensing around the Tsugaru Strait at the Japan and Kuril trenches, northeastern Japan, *Earth Planets Space* **76,** no. 28, doi: 10.1186/s40623-024-01975-z.

Barbour, A. J., and B. W. Crowell (2017). Dynamic strains for earthquake source characterization, *Seismol. Res. Lett.* **88,** no. 2A, 354–370, doi: 10.1785/0220160155.

Barbour, A. J., J. O. Langbein, and N. S. Farghal (2021). Earthquake magnitudes from dynamic strain, *Bull. Seismol. Soc. Am.* **111,** no. 3, 1325–1346, doi: 10.1785/0120200360.

Benioff, H. (1935). A linear strain seismograph, *Bull. Seismol. Soc. Am.* **25,** no. 4, 283–309, doi: 10.1785/BSSA0250040283.

Benioff, H., F. Press, and S. W. Smith (1961). Excitation of the free oscillations of the earth by earthquakes, *J. Geophys. Res.* **66,** 605–619, doi: 10.1029/JZ066i002p00605.

Boatwright, J. (1980). A spectral theory for circular seismic sources; simple estimates of source dimension, dynamic stress drop, and radiated seismic energy, *Bull. Seismol. Soc. Am.* **70,** no. 1, 1–27.

Brune, J. N. (1970). Tectonic stress and the spectra of seismic shear waves from earthquakes, *J. Geophys. Res.* **75,** no. 26, 4997–5009, doi: 10.1029/JB075i026p04997.

Canitano, A., Y. J. Hsu, H. M. Lee, A. T. Linde, and S. Sacks (2017). A first modeling of dynamic and static crustal strain field from near-field dilatation measurements: Example of the 2013 M_w 6.2 Ruisui earthquake, Taiwan, *J. Geodyn.* **91,** no. 1, 1–8.

Cao, Y., G. P. Mavroeidis, and M. Ashoory (2018). Comparison of observed and synthetic near-fault dynamic ground strains and rotations from the 2004 M_w 6.0 Parkfield, California, earthquake, *Bull. Seismol. Soc. Am.* **108,** no. 3A, 1240–1256, doi: 10.1785/0120170227.

Chen, X. (2023). Source parameter analysis using distributed acoustic sensing–An example with the PoroTomo array, *Geophys. J. Int.* **233,** no. 3, 2208–2214, doi: 10.1093/gji/ggad061.

Deichmann, N. (2017). Theoretical basis for the observed break in M_L/M_w scaling between small and large earthquakes, *Bull. Seismol. Soc. Am.* **107,** no. 2, 505–520, doi: 10.1785/0120160318.

Fan, W., and J. J. McGuire (2018). Investigating microearthquake finite source attributes with IRIS Community Wavefield Demonstration Experiment in Oklahoma, *Geophys. J. Int.* **214,** no. 2, 1072–1087, doi: 10.1093/gji/ggy203.

Gladwin, M. T. (1984). High-precision multicomponent borehole deformation monitoring, *Rev. Sci. Instrum.* **55,** no. 12, 2011–2016, doi: 10.1063/1.1137704.

Gou, Y., R. M. Allen, W. Zhu, T. Taira, and L.-W. Chen (2025). Leveraging submarine DAS arrays for offshore earthquake early warning: A case study in Monterey Bay, California, *Bull. Seismol. Soc. Am.* **115,** no. 2, 516–532, doi: 10.1785/0120240234.

Guo, H., J. W. Atterholt, J. J. McGuire, and C. Thurber (2024). Evidence for low effective stress within the crust of the subducted Gorda plate from the 2022 December M_w 6.4 Ferndale earthquake sequence, *Seismol. Res. Lett.* doi: 10.1785/0220240078.

Hanks, T. C., and H. Kanamori (1979). A moment magnitude scale, *J. Geophys. Res.* **84,** no. B5, 2348–2350, doi: 10.1029/JB084iB05p02348.

Hartog, A. H. (2017). *An Introduction to Distributed Optical Fibre Sensors*, CRC Press, Boca Raton, Florida.

Hirakawa, E., and A. J. Barbour (2020). Kinematic rupture and 3D wave propagation simulations of the 2019 M 7.1 Ridgecrest, California, earthquake, *Bull. Seismol. Soc. Am.* **110,** no. 4, 1644–1659, doi: 10.1785/0120200031.

Horn, B. K. P. (1981). Hill shading and the reflectance map, *Proc. IEEE* **69,** no. 1, 14–47, doi: 10.1109/PROC.1981.11918.

Hough, S. E., and D. S. Dreger (1995). Source parameters of the 23 April 1992 M 6.1 Joshua Tree, California, earthquake and its aftershocks: Empirical Green's function analysis of GEOS and TERRAscope data, *Bull. Seismol. Soc. Am.* **85,** no. 6, 1576–1590.

Ide, S., and G. C. Beroza (2001). Does apparent stress vary with earthquake size? *Geophys. Res. Lett.* **28,** no. 17, 3349–3352, doi: 10.1029/2001GL013106.

Kaneko, Y., and P. M. Shearer (2015). Variability of seismic source spectra, estimated stress drop, and radiated energy, derived from cohesive-zone models of symmetrical and asymmetrical circular and elliptical ruptures, *J. Geophys. Res.* **120,** no. 2, 1053–1079, doi: 10.1002/2014JB011642.

Katsumata, A. (1996). Comparison of magnitudes estimated by the Japan Meteorological Agency with moment magnitudes for intermediate and deep earthquakes, *Bull. Seismol. Soc. Am.* **86,** no. 3, 832–842, doi: 10.1785/BSSA0860030832.

Lanza, V., D. Spallarossa, M. Cattaneo, D. Bindi, and P. Augliera (1999). Source parameters of small events using constrained deconvolution with empirical Green's functions, *Geophys. J. Int.* **137,** no. 3, 651–662.

Lecoulant, J., Y. Ma, J. Dettmer, and D. Eaton (2023). Strain-based forward modeling and inversion of seismic moment tensors using distributed acoustic sensing (DAS) observations, *Front. Earth Sci.* **11,** 1,176,921, doi: 10.3389/feart.2023.1176921.

Li, J., K. Taeho, N. Lapusta, E. Biondi, and Z. Zhan (2023). The break of earthquake asperities imaged by distributed acoustic sensing, *Nature* **620,** no. 7975, 800–806, doi: 10.1038/s41586-023-06227-w.

Li, J., W. Zhu, E. Biondi, and Z. Zhan (2023). Earthquake focal mechanisms with distributed acoustic sensing, *Nat. Commun.* **14,** no. 1, 4181, doi: 10.1038/s41467-023-39639-3.

Lindsey, N. J., and E. R. Martin (2021). Fiber-optic seismology, *Annu. Rev. Earth Planet. Sci.* **49,** 309–336, doi: 10.1146/annurev-earth-072420-065213.

Lindsey, N. J., T. C. Dawe, and J. B. Ajo-Franklin (2019). Illuminating seafloor faults and ocean dynamics with dark fiber distributed acoustic sensing, *Science* **366,** no. 6469, 1103–1107, doi: 10.1126/science.aay5881.

Lindsey, N. J., S. Yuan, A. Lellouch, L. Gualtieri, T. Lecocq, and B. Biondi (2020). City-scale dark fiber DAS measurements of infrastructure use during the COVID-19 pandemic, *Geophys. Res. Lett.* **47,** e2020GL089931, doi: 10.1029/2020GL089931.

Lior, I. (2024). Accurate magnitude and stress drop using the spectral ratios method applied to distributed acoustic sensing, *Geophys. Res. Lett.* **51,** e2023GL105153, doi: 10.1029/2023GL105153.

Lior, I., D. Rivet, J. P. Ampuero, A. Sladen, S. Barrientos, R. Sánchez-Olavarría, G. A. Villarroel Opazo, and J. A. Bustamante Prado (2023). Magnitude estimation and ground motion prediction to harness fiber optic distributed acoustic sensing for earthquake early warning, *Sci. Rep.* **13,** 424, doi: 10.1038/s41598-023-27444-3.

Luo, B., G. Jin, and F. Stanek (2021). Near-field strain in distributed acoustic sensing-based microseismic observation, *Geophysics* **86,** no. 5, 49–60, doi: 10.1190/geo2021-0031.1.

Ma, K. F., S. von Specht, L. W. Kuo, H. H. Huang, C. R. Lin, C. J. Lin, C. S. Ku, E. S. Wu, C. Y. Wang, W. Y. Chang, *et al.* (2024). Broadband strain amplification in an asymmetric fault zone observed from borehole optical fiber and core, *Commun. Earth Environ.* **5,** no. 1, 402, doi: 10.1038/s43247-024-01558-6.

Madariaga, R. (1976). Dynamics of an expanding circular fault, *Bull. Seismol. Soc. Am.* **66,** no. 3, 639–666, doi: 10.1785/BSSA0660030639.

Materna, K., J. R. Murray, F. Pollitz, and J. R. Patton (2023). Slip deficit rates on southern Cascadia faults resolved with viscoelastic earthquake cycle modeling of geodetic deformation, *Bull. Seismol. Soc. Am.* **113,** no. 6, 2505–2518, doi: 10.1785/0120230007.

McGuire, J. J. (2004). Estimating finite source properties of small earthquake ruptures, *Bull. Seismol. Soc. Am.* **94,** no. 2, 377–393, doi: 10.1785/0120030091.

McGuire, J. J., A. J. Barbour, M. Karrenbach, C. Stewart, V. Yartsev, L. Rongrong, and M. Hemphill-Haley (2022). Spring 2022 Arcata to Eureka California, distributed acoustic sensing (DAS) experiment, *U.S. Geol. Surv. Data Release*, doi: 10.5066/P9NYAT5Z.

McGuire, J. J., A. J. Barbour, R. McPherson, M. Hemphill-Haley, A. R. Admire, K. Stockdale, E. A. Shiver, O. Berndt, C. Stewart, and M. Karrenbach (2022). Spring 2022 Arcata to Eureka, California, distributed acoustic sensing (DAS) experiment: Nodal seismometer data, *U.S. Geol. Surv. Data Release*, doi: 10.5066/P9XLMDOL.

McGuire, J. J., A. J. Barbour, R. McPherson, M. Hemphill-Haley, K. Stockdale, J. Patton, and C. Stewart (2023). Winter 2023 Arcata to Eureka, California, deployment of nodal seismometers, *U.S. Geol. Surv. Data Release*, doi: 10.5066/P9CNC1BE.

McGuire, J. J., A. J. Barbour, C. Stewart, V. Yartsev, M. Hemphill-Haley, R. C. McPherson, T. Sawi, and C. Yoon (2024). 2022-2023 Arcata, California, distributed acoustic sensing (DAS) experiment: 2022 M 6.4 Ferndale aftershock sequence, *U.S. Geol. Surv. Data Release*, doi: 10.5066/P1V7CKGA.

McGuire, J. J., A. J. Barbour, C. Stewart, V. Yartsev, M. Karrenbach, M. Hemphill-Haley, R. C. McPherson, K. Stockdale, C. Yoon, and T. Sawi (2025). The GorDAS distributed acoustic sensing experiment above the Cascadia locked zone and subducted Gorda slab, *Seismol. Res. Lett.* **96,** no. 4, doi: 10.1785/0220240415.

Meng, H., J. J. McGuire, and Y. Ben-Zion (2020). Semiautomated estimates of directivity and related source properties of small to moderate southern California earthquakes using second seismic moments, *J. Geophys. Res.* **125,** e2019JB018566, doi: 10.1029/2019JB018566.

Nayak, A., J. Correa, and J. Ajo-Franklin (2024). Seismic magnitude estimation using low-frequency strain amplitudes recorded by DAS arrays at far-field distances, *Bull. Seismol. Soc. Am.* **114,** no. 4, 1818–1838, doi: 10.1785/0120230318.

Richter, C. F. (1935). An instrumental earthquake magnitude scale, *Bull. Seismol. Soc. Am.* **25,** no. 1, 1–32, doi: 10.1785/BSSA0250010001.

Romanowicz, B., R. Allen, K. Brekke, L. W. Chen, Y. Gou, I. Henson, J. Marty, D. Neuhauser, B. Pardini, T. A. Taira, *et al.* (2023). SeaFOAM: A year-long DAS deployment in Monterey Bay, California, *Seismol. Res. Lett.* **94,** no. 5, 2348–2359, doi: 10.1785/0220230047.

Shearer, P. M., R. E. Abercrombie, D. T. Trugman, and W. Wang (2019). Comparing EGF methods for estimating corner frequency and stress drop from P wave spectra, *J. Geophys. Res.* **124,** no. 4, 3966–3986, doi: 10.1029/2018JB016957.

Shelly, D. R., D. E. Goldberg, K. Z. Materna, R. J. Skoumal, J. L. Hardebeck, C. E. Yoon, W. L. Yeck, and P. S. Earle (2024). Subduction intraslab-interface fault interactions in the 2022 M_w 6.4 Ferndale, California, earthquake sequence, *Sci. Adv.* **10,** eadl1226, doi: 10.1785/0320230053.

Strumia, C., A. Trabattoni, M. Supino, M. Baillet, D. Rivet, and G. Festa (2024). Sensing optical fibers for earthquake source characterization using raw DAS records, *J. Geophys. Res.* **129,** no. 1, e2023JB027860, doi: 10.1029/2023JB027860.

Uhrhammer, R. A., M. Hellweg, K. Hutton, P. Lombard, A. W. Walters, E. Hauksson, and D. Oppenheimer (2011). California integrated seismic network (CISN) local magnitude determination in California and vicinity, *Bull. Seismol. Soc. Am.* **101,** no. 6, 2685–2693, doi: 10.1785/0120100106.

Vallée, M., J. Charléty, A. M. Ferreira, B. Delouis, and J. Vergoz (2011). SCARDEC: A new technique for the rapid determination of seismic moment magnitude, focal mechanism and source time functions for large earthquakes using body-wave deconvolution, *Geophys. J. Int.* **184,** no. 1, 338–358, doi: 10.1111/j.1365-246X.2010.04836.x.

Vera Rodriguez, I., and A. Wuestefeld (2020). Strain microseismics: Radiation patterns, synthetics, and moment tensor resolvability with distributed acoustic sensing in isotropic media, *Geophysics* **85,** no. 3, 101–114, doi: 10.1190/geo2019-0373.1.

Viens, L., L. F. Bonilla, Z. J. Spica, K. Nishida, T. Yamada, and M. Shinohara (2022). Nonlinear earthquake response of marine sediments with distributed acoustic sensing, *Geophys. Res. Lett.* **49,** e2022GL100122, doi: 10.1029/2022GL100122.

Yin, J., W. Zhu, J. Li, E. Biondi, Y. Miao, Z. J. Spica, L. Viens, M. Shinohara, S. Ide, K. Mochizuki, *et al.* (2023). Earthquake magnitude with DAS: A transferable data-based scaling relation, *Geophys. Res. Lett.* **50,** e2023GL103045, doi: 10.1029/2023GL103045.

Zhan, Z. (2020). Distributed acoustic sensing turns fiber-optic cables into sensitive seismic antennas, *Seismol. Res. Lett.* **91,** no. 1, 1–15, doi: 10.1785/0220190112.

Manuscript received 21 March 2025
Published online 1 October 2025

High-Precision Earthquake Catalog for Minto Flats Fault Zone, Central Alaska, Reveals Complex and Conjugate Faulting

Nealey E. Sims*[1], Carl Tape[1], Natalia A. Ruppert[2], and Michael E. West[3]

ABSTRACT

The Minto Flats fault zone (MFFZ) in central Alaska is a left-lateral strike-slip fault system situated between the continental-scale right-lateral Denali and Kaltag-Tintina faults. The MFFZ has the potential to generate magnitude 7 earthquakes, and it hosted a magnitude 6 earthquake in 1995. It has also produced exotic events, such as very-low-frequency earthquakes and nucleation signals. We use network-matched filtering and relative earthquake relocation techniques to derive a detailed catalog of earthquake locations for the MFFZ. The catalog spans from August 2014 to December 2019, a time period including 13 temporary seismic stations in the region. Our results provide the most complete catalog for the MFFZ and include deeper events, clusters of shallow seismicity, and a complex and segmented fault structure not observed in the original regional catalog. We document right-lateral strike-slip faulting, conjugate to the main northeast-striking left-lateral faults of the MFFZ. Below Nenana basin, the relocated seismicity reveals northwest-dipping left-lateral faults, supporting the inference that deep crustal active faulting is associated with recent basin deformation.

KEY POINTS

- We establish an enhanced seismicity catalog in the Minto Flats fault zone.
- The catalog reveals a segmented fault system, including faults conjugate to the main strike-slip system.
- The relocated catalog and interpreted faults provide a foundation to understand the tectonic setting.

Supplemental Material

INTRODUCTION

Accurate catalogs of earthquake locations, magnitudes, and origin times provide a foundation for the study of fault dynamics, brittle–ductile transition zones, earthquake migration, and structural seismology. Despite its prolific production of crustal and intraslab seismicity, Alaska has been featured in few relocation studies over the past three decades. Examples from temporary deployments include Li *et al.* (2013) and Daly *et al.* (2021); regional-scale examples include Ratchkovski and Hansen (2002b), Fuis *et al.* (2008), and Zanjani and Lin (2022).

Relative relocation involves exploiting the fact that two nearby events will have very similar ray paths to the same recording station. Using differential travel times (rather than absolute arrival times), the hypocenters can be more precisely determined (Waldhauser and Schaff, 2008; Trugman and Shearer, 2017). Network-matched filtering involves cross-correlating waveforms across a seismic network and enables detection of low-magnitude and otherwise missed earthquakes, leading to more complete catalogs (Gibbons and Ringdal, 2006; Shelly *et al.*, 2007). The relative relocation of earthquakes—combined with network-matched filtering—refines earthquake hypocenter locations, improving seismic catalogs and providing greater insight into fault structures and tectonic processes. Such high-precision catalogs have been used to identify active faults (Rubin *et al.*, 1991; Hauksson *et al.*, 2012), define fault geometries (Matoza *et al.*, 2013; Ross *et al.*, 2017; White *et al.*, 2019; Shelly, 2020), refine the details in seismic sequences (Skoumal *et al.*, 2014; Gibbons *et al.*, 2020), and study spatial and temporal patterns of seismicity (Hotovec-Ellis *et al.*, 2018; Chang and Ide, 2021). In this study, we apply network-matched filtering and relative relocation to Minto Flats fault zone (MFFZ; Fig. 1), a strike-slip fault system in central Alaska that plays an important role in regional

1. Geophysical Institute and College of Natural Sciences, University of Alaska Fairbanks, Fairbanks, Alaska, U.S.A., https://orcid.org/0009-0006-0772-7896 (NES); https://orcid.org/0000-0003-2804-7137 (CT); 2. U.S. Geological Survey Earthquake Science Center, Seattle, Washington, U.S.A., https://orcid.org/0000-0003-0589-1159 (NAR); 3. Alaska Earthquake Center, University of Alaska Fairbanks, Fairbanks, Alaska, U.S.A.

*Corresponding author: nesims@alaska.edu

Cite this article as Sims, N. E., C. Tape, N. A. Ruppert, and M. E. West (2025). High-Precision Earthquake Catalog for Minto Flats Fault Zone, Central Alaska, Reveals Complex and Conjugate Faulting, *Bull. Seismol. Soc. Am.* **116**, 375–396, doi: 10.1785/0120250177

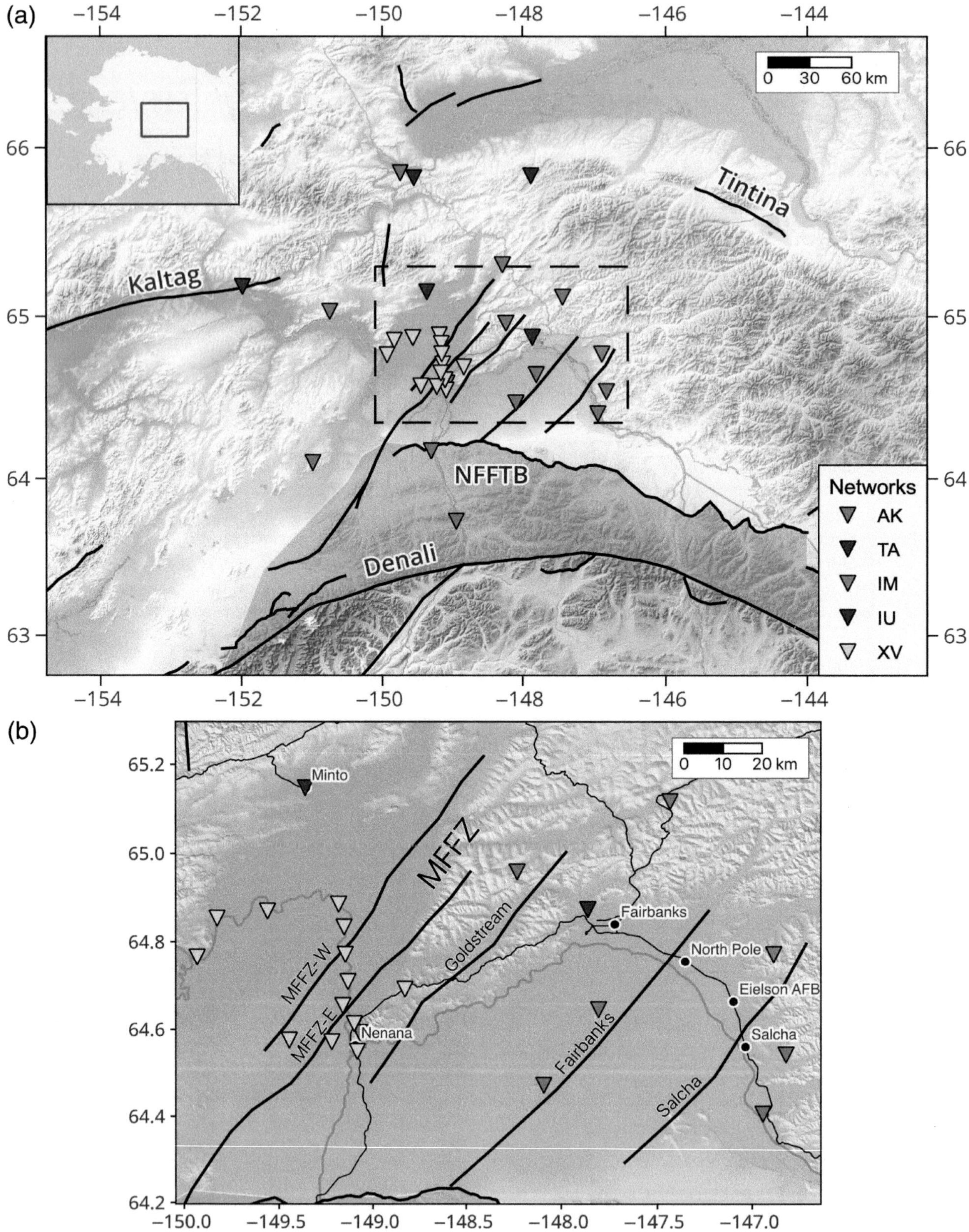

Figure 1. (a) Map of central Alaska, displaying topography, active faults (Koehler *et al.*, 2012; Haeussler *et al.*, 2025), and the 31 seismic stations used in this study. Inset map of Alaska shows a box highlighting the expanded region. (b) The region within the dashed-line box in the upper plot. MFFZ, Minto Flats fault zone (Tape *et al.*, 2015); NFFTB, Northern Foothills fold-and-thrust belt (Bemis and Wallace, 2007). The Fault Locations and Alaska Tectonics from Seismicity (FLATS) network (XV) of 13 stations (2014–2019) is displayed in yellow. The color version of this figure is available only in the electronic edition.

tectonics (Cross and Freymueller, 2008) and generates seismic events with unusual source characteristics (Tape *et al.*, 2018).

Mainland Alaska is a broad region of intraplate crustal faulting influenced by subduction and collision of the Yakutat block—an oceanic plateau attached to the Pacific plate (Bird, 2003; Eberhart-Phillips *et al.*, 2006; Christeson *et al.*, 2010)—that started at ~30 Ma (Brueseke *et al.*, 2019). Interior Alaska is the physiographic region between the Brooks Range and the Alaska Range. Within this region, our focus is on the area bounded by two right-lateral strike-slip fault systems: Kaltag-Tintina in the north and Denali in the south (Fig. 1). The Denali fault system expresses geological and seismological activity, exhibiting 480 km of displacement since 52 Ma (Waldien *et al.*, 2021), including rupturing a 341 km segment during the 2002 M_w 7.9 earthquake (Eberhart-Phillips *et al.*, 2003; Haeussler *et al.*, 2004). The Kaltag and Tintina faults do not record any recent activity in the form of large earthquakes or Holocene fault scarps. The Kaltag fault offsets Cretaceous sedimentary units by at least 60 km (Patton and Hoare, 1968), though no scarps have been identified (Koehler and Carver, 2018). The largest recorded earthquake (3 February 2000 M_w 5.5) is consistent with right-lateral motion (Tape *et al.*, 2017). The Tintina fault exhibits >400 km of right-lateral displacement (Gabrielse *et al.*, 2006; Saltus, 2007) and has produced earthquakes that have mechanisms consistent with expected motion: 28 November 1972 M_s 5.0 (Coffman and von Hake, 1984; Estabrook *et al.*, 1988) and 11 June 2023 M_w 4.7. These events are confined to a short segment that is classified as active (Haeussler *et al.*, 2025).

Between the Kaltag-Tintina and Denali right-lateral faults are two active faulting domains. The first is the Northern Foothills fold-and-thrust belt, a large set of east–west-trending thrust faults north of the Denali fault that accommodates a portion of the convergence between the Pacific and North America plates (Bemis and Wallace, 2007; Bemis *et al.*, 2012; Koehler and Carver, 2018). The second faulting domain is a set of northeast-striking left-lateral faults that have been labeled as the seismic zones of Minto Flats (Gedney *et al.*, 1972; Pulpan, 1988), Fairbanks (Gedney *et al.*, 1980), and Salcha (Biswas and Tytgat, 1988). These seismic zones appear in the 2023 National Seismic Hazard Model (NSHM) compilation as five faults, from west to east: Minto Flats (north), Minto Flats (south), Goldstream, Fairbanks, and Salcha (Powers *et al.*, 2024; Haeussler *et al.*, 2025). These are displayed in Figure 1b; we adopt the labels MFFZ-W and MFFZ-E instead of "Minto Flats (north)" and "Minto Flats (south)." Page *et al.* (1995) interpreted the setting as classical "bookshelf faulting," with the shelves of Kaltag-Tintina and Denali shearing the "books" of Minto Flats, Fairbanks, and Salcha toward the right; as the books tilt to the right, the relative motion between the books is left lateral. Notable historical earthquakes within these fault zones include 1937 M_s 7.3 Salcha, 1967 M_s 5.7 Fairbanks, and 1995 M_w 6.0 Minto Flats. The 1967 Fairbanks sequence included four M_w > 5 events and caused "considerable minor damage … due to broken windows and bottled goods" (Neumann, 1940, p. 24).

The focus of this study is the Minto Flats seismic zone, the westernmost of the left-lateral strike-slip fault zones (Fig. 1). The labeling of these northwest-striking features as seismic zones or fault zones—as well as the number of these features—is debatable. They are seismic zones in the sense that the seismicity forms lineaments, and there is no geological evidence of offset Quaternary units. The 2023 fault database includes Goldstream, Fairbanks, and Salcha, with additional labels to denote that these faults are determined from seismicity.

The Minto Flats seismic zone was labeled by Tape *et al.* (2015) as a fault zone on the basis of strike-slip source mechanisms aligned with two seismic lineaments (MFFZ-W and MFFZ-E in Fig. 1b). The lineaments approximately coincide with the eastern and western margins of Nenana basin, suggesting that the current tectonic setting in Minto Flats is one of the local transtension within a regional field of north–south compression (Tape *et al.*, 2015).

The MFFZ is possibly a significant tectonic boundary within Alaska. Mainland Alaska has been identified as a broad region of diffuse deformation (Page *et al.*, 1991; Bird, 2003). Mackey *et al.* (1997) defined a Bering block (or plate) on the basis of source mechanisms and seismicity. They did not describe the eastern boundary, though it appears to approximately coincide with the MFFZ. The extrusion model of Redfield *et al.* (2007) emphasizes a broader deformation region ("North Pacific Rim orogenic stream") that spans from eastern Alaska westward into the Bering Sea, without identifying the MFFZ as a major boundary. With the benefit of years of Global Positioning System measurements in the Aleutians and western Alaska, Cross and Freymueller (2008) proposed the MFFZ as the eastern boundary for the Bering plate.

In addition to having regional tectonic significance and the ability to produce M_w > 6 earthquakes, MFFZ hosted an unusual earthquake on 11 April 2012. The M_w 3.8 earthquake was triggered by centimeter-scale Love waves that originated from the M_w 8.6 earthquake in the Indian Ocean (Tape *et al.*, 2013). The triggered earthquake exhibited a high-frequency nucleation signal lasting 24 s.

To better characterize the seismicity defining the MFFZ and to explore the different types of events in the MFFZ, the Fault Locations and Alaska Tectonics from Seismicity (FLATS) seismic network was deployed beginning in 2014. The deployment of 13 stations coincided with a M_w 5.0 earthquake that produced thousands of aftershocks. In this study, we use seismic data from the FLATS experiment to produce a new higher resolution catalog of earthquake locations for the region marked by the dashed black rectangle in Figure 1. In the following sections, we describe the data collection and processing methods, including matched-filter detection and relative relocation, in detail. We then present and interpret the resulting earthquake catalog and highlight several seismogenic features and fault structures. In comparison with the transtensional setting proposed by Tape *et al.* (2015), we find that the higher resolution view enabled by our study reveals a more fragmented fault zone, including significant right-lateral conjugate faulting, as well as northwest-dipping left-lateral faults deep below Nenana basin. Future work is needed to elucidate if these structures are responsible for the range of exotic events within the MFFZ region (Tape *et al.*, 2018).

METHODS

Data

With the objective of identifying microseismicity within the MFFZ region, we use continuous seismic data from 2014 to 2019, corresponding to the period of the highest density of seismic station deployment in the region, including 13 FLATS (network XV) stations. We used seismic waveform data from 34 stations: 13 AK, 13 XV, 5 TA, 2 IM, and 1 IU networks (Fig. 1; see Data and Resources for details).

Our data selection begins with the Alaska Earthquake Center (AEC) catalog of events. Within our designated region between longitudes −150.1° to −148.2° and latitudes 64.4° to 65.3°, there are 9621 events, all reviewed by AEC data analysis and containing both automatically detected and manually picked seismic arrivals. We use all waveform data from all stations having a minimum sampling rate of 40 samples per second. We set a threshold of 40 samples per second because small earthquakes primarily contain high-frequency content that is lost at lower sampling rates. All waveform data with higher sampling rates are downsampled to 40 samples per second. The final dataset contains continuous waveform data from 56 stations with 24,837 *P*-wave arrival picks and 12,837 *S*-wave arrival picks.

Network-matched filtering

The network-matched filter earthquake detection method refers to the technique of cross correlating a known seismic signal's waveforms with continuous seismic data to identify analogous signals; see Figures S1–S4, available in the supplemental material to this article, for a visual representation of this process. Network-matched filtering is particularly effective in regions characterized by elevated noise levels, for which analysts may struggle to discern wave arrivals based solely on amplitudes (Shelly *et al.*, 2007). The MFFZ is an ideal candidate for the network-matched filter method because of its apparently diffuse seismicity and its high levels of noise caused by the presence of Nenana basin (Smith *et al.*, 2023) and the Tanana River (Smith and Tape, 2019). To address the detection challenges posed by noise, we use a network-matched filter approach based on Gibbons and Ringdal (2006) with the open-source Python package EQcorrscan (Chamberlain *et al.*, 2017) to detect seismic events in the MFFZ.

The 9621 events extracted from the AEC catalog serve as candidate template events for this investigation. Waveforms of both the templates and continuous seismic data are filtered 2.0–8.0 Hz after visually confirming that it results in the highest signal-to-noise ratio (SNR) in this region. Each template is 2 s long, beginning 0.15 s prior to the *P* pick or *S* pick on each channel for which a pick is available in the AEC catalog. Both *P* and *S* picks are incorporated in this study to optimize the number of channels in regions with sparse coverage. To prevent *S*-wave energy contamination in the *P*-wave templates, we enforce a minimum event-station distance of 25 km for a station channel to be included in a template (Fig. S5). This minimum distance enables us to select a single template length for the entire region without necessitating knowledge of the *S*-wave arrival time for each station. A maximum distance of 90 km is imposed to ensure that the template waveform includes a sufficient portion of the *P* coda. Automatic quality control measures are implemented to limit the inclusion of low-quality templates. Each template must contain a minimum of six channels and exhibit an SNR of at least 2.0 for eligibility in the network-matched filter process. After these checks, we retain a total of 8714 template events for use within this study (Fig. 2). Table 1 and the supplemental material provide more information about our parameter selection and testing.

To identify new detections, we cross correlate the templates with the resampled continuous waveform data. By summing the cross-correlation coefficients for each channel at each sample, we obtain a cross-correlation coefficient sum (cccsum). A detection is deemed significant if its cccsum value exceeds a predefined threshold. In this study, the threshold is set as the median absolute deviation (MAD) of the cccsum multiplied by a set value, as used by Shelly *et al.* (2007). Common thresholds typically range between 8 and 15 times the MAD (Kato and Nakagawa, 2014; Huang *et al.*, 2017; Ross *et al.*, 2017; Shelly, 2020). We adopt a value of 9.0 times the MAD in our analysis to minimize the occurrence of false detections. To eliminate duplicate detections that occur within a 4 s interval, we retain only the detection with the highest cccsum value.

Relative relocation

Precise earthquake locations are important for a number of seismic studies, including earthquake migration and triggering, fault-zone identification and resolution of structure, and improving seismic hazard assessment. Perhaps the most widely used earthquake relocation technique, the double-difference (DD) method (Waldhauser and Ellsworth, 2000) sets up a linear set of equations as a function of the 1D velocity model and differential arrival times and then applies a matrix inversion. However, in recent years, there has been an increase in the use of cluster analysis in earthquake relocation instead of the traditional DD approach. Growclust (Trugman and Shearer, 2017) uses a clustering algorithm based on differential times and cross-correlation values of event pairs at common stations.

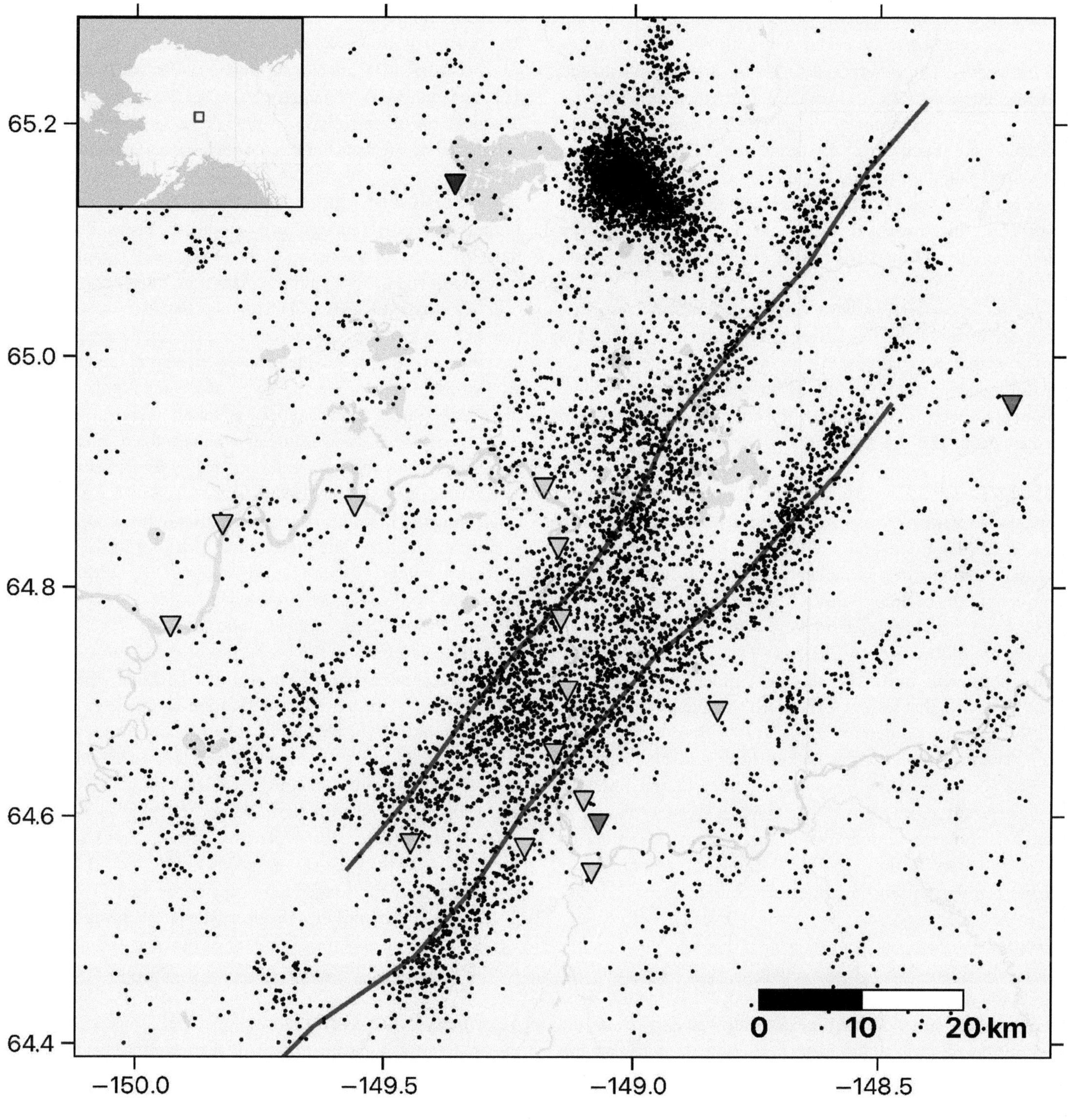

Events are clustered based on waveform similarity, and then each event is relocated relative to its cluster.

In this study, each new detection is initially assigned the location of the template with which it matched. Because the detected events are highly correlated with the template events, they most likely occur in a similar location. Differential travel times from cross correlation for pairs of earthquakes are then obtained using EQcorrscan's waveform cross-correlation library. Traces for each event are band-pass filtered between 2 and 8 Hz and windowed around the associated arrival times.

Figure 2. Events from the Alaska Earthquake Center (AEC) catalog that meet the criteria to become a template for this study. There are 8714 events spanning 1 August 2014 to 31 December 2019 and between longitudes −150.1° and −148.2° and latitudes 64.4° and 65.3°. Seismicity-inferred faults (MFFZ-W, MFFZ-E) are plotted in red, from Figure 1b; our study provides a revised catalog and a revised interpretation of faults. Inset map of Alaska shows the expanded region. The color version of this figure is available only in the electronic edition.

We use a 1.5 s window starting 0.15 s before the associated phase picks and correlate each event with all other events in a 5 km radius. The differential times are then input into the DD relocation algorithm GrowClust (Trugman and Shearer, 2017), where a minimum of six differential times is required to relocate the event. Only relocations that contain at least two differential pairs are retained in the relocated catalog. For all other parameters, we use the default values from the example provided in the GrowClust source code. We use the 1D Alaska velocity model tactmod (Beaudoin *et al.*, 1992; Ratchkovski and Hansen, 2002a).

We use EQcorrscan's relative magnitude function to estimate the magnitudes of the newly detected events. This method is similar to that of Schaff and Richards (2014, their eq. 10), calculating relative magnitudes based on relative amplitude measurements, which are weighted by the cross correlation between the new event and the template used for its detection.

RESULTS

Here, we present our relocated seismicity catalog using two approaches. First, we examine how the seismicity relates to Nenana basin, namely, whether events are inside the main boundary of the basin or outside. The basin boundary is determined from the 2 km depth contour of the basement model of Petrotechnical Resources of Alaska (PRA) (2017), extrapolated to the southwest using the basement model of Dixit *et al.* (2017). We find that seismicity beneath Nenana basin is deeper and less varied with depth than seismicity outside of Nenana basin. The depths are 18.1 ± 2.6 km inside and 11.7 ± 3.3 km outside, with supporting figures in Figures S13 and S14.

Our second approach is to determine a set of 17 fault segments via the process described in the Discussion section. By assigning letters to these seismic lineaments, we can readily discuss features within the relocated catalog.

Catalog

Our analysis provides a new catalog of 41,518 events in the MFFZ for the period between 2014 and 2019. Among these events, 32,420 are relocated successfully via Growclust and are considered high-quality detections (Fig. 3). Most magnitudes are between −0.1 (5th percentile) and 1.1 (95th percentile), with a median value of 0.3.

The catalog contains 258,185 *P*-wave arrival times and 66,652 *S*-wave arrival times. About 41% of the retained events occurred within 5 km of an M_w 5.0 earthquake on 31 August 2014.

Relative relocation uncertainties in the MFFZ vary spatially, with the highest uncertainties observed in the middle of the basin and in the vicinity of the 2014 mainshock sequence. The median horizontal uncertainty for the region is 0.422 km, and the median vertical uncertainty is 0.492 km (Fig. S15).

Figure 4 provides a temporal view of the relocated catalog alongside the catalog of templates. The y axis is controlled by the large number of events following the 31 August 2014 M_w 5.0 earthquake. Most temporal spikes in the seismicity are associated with aftershock sequences for $M_L \geq 3.5$ events. The earthquake on 14 January 2016 M_w 3.7 is the only event that does not seem to have an aftershock sequence; this event has special significance in terms of nucleation (Tape *et al.*, 2018).

Identification of fault segments

From the relocated catalog (Fig. 3), we create a probability density function $p(x,y)$ for the region of interest, using the gaussian_kde function in the SciPy Python package (the integration of $p(x,y)$ over our domain is exactly 1) The map (Fig. S16) served as the primary guide for visually determining the fault segments. Each coauthor provided an independent assessment of fault segments, and we collectively arrived at the set of 17 fault segments shown in Figures 5 and 6. Many alternative "solutions" are possible, and it is expected that these segments will be refined in the future, especially as new regions are illuminated by future activity (such as the case of event a, in 1990).

Among the 17 fault segments, we observe two main patterns in fault orientation. The predominant faulting in the region is northeast–southwest with strike of ~40°. A second set of segments are those which are perpendicular or oblique to the first set; these include N, O, Q, and R.

Table 2 summarizes the properties of the 17 fault segments. Generally speaking, the fault segments outside of the basin (Fig. 7) have seismicity depths that are shallower than faults inside the basin. The shallowest depths occur on the northern segments O, N, and H; segments A and I—outside the basin—exhibit slightly more shallow seismicity than the segments extending south into the basin (B and J; Table 2).

Within the basin, the western segments (J and K) exhibit greater depths than the eastern segments (B and C), a pattern identified with the longer-term catalog as well (Tape *et al.*, 2015). Fault segment L has the deepest overall average seismicity at 23.1 km; it hits the boundary of our domain, and therefore its length in Table 2 is an underestimate (Tape *et al.*, 2015).

Seismicity cross sections

Cross sections of seismicity provide the most informative views of the catalog. A complete set of cross sections is provided by Sims *et al.* (2025). Cross sections in Figure 8 are approximately parallel to the strike of the MFFZ, whereas cross sections in Figure 9 are perpendicular to the MFFZ. These cross sections support our previous inferences. For example, Figure 8a follows the MFFZ-E (Fig. 1b)—spanned by fault segments A-B-C—and it reveals shallower and more depth-varying seismicity outside the basin, to the north. In between the two main lineaments (A-B-C and I-J-K), the seismicity underlies the basin at a depth of about 20 km, with minimal seismicity north of the basin and between MFFZ-E and MFFZ-W (Fig. 8b). MFFZ-W (Fig. 8c) reveals a clear southwestward decrease in the depth of seismicity, quantified by the median values for

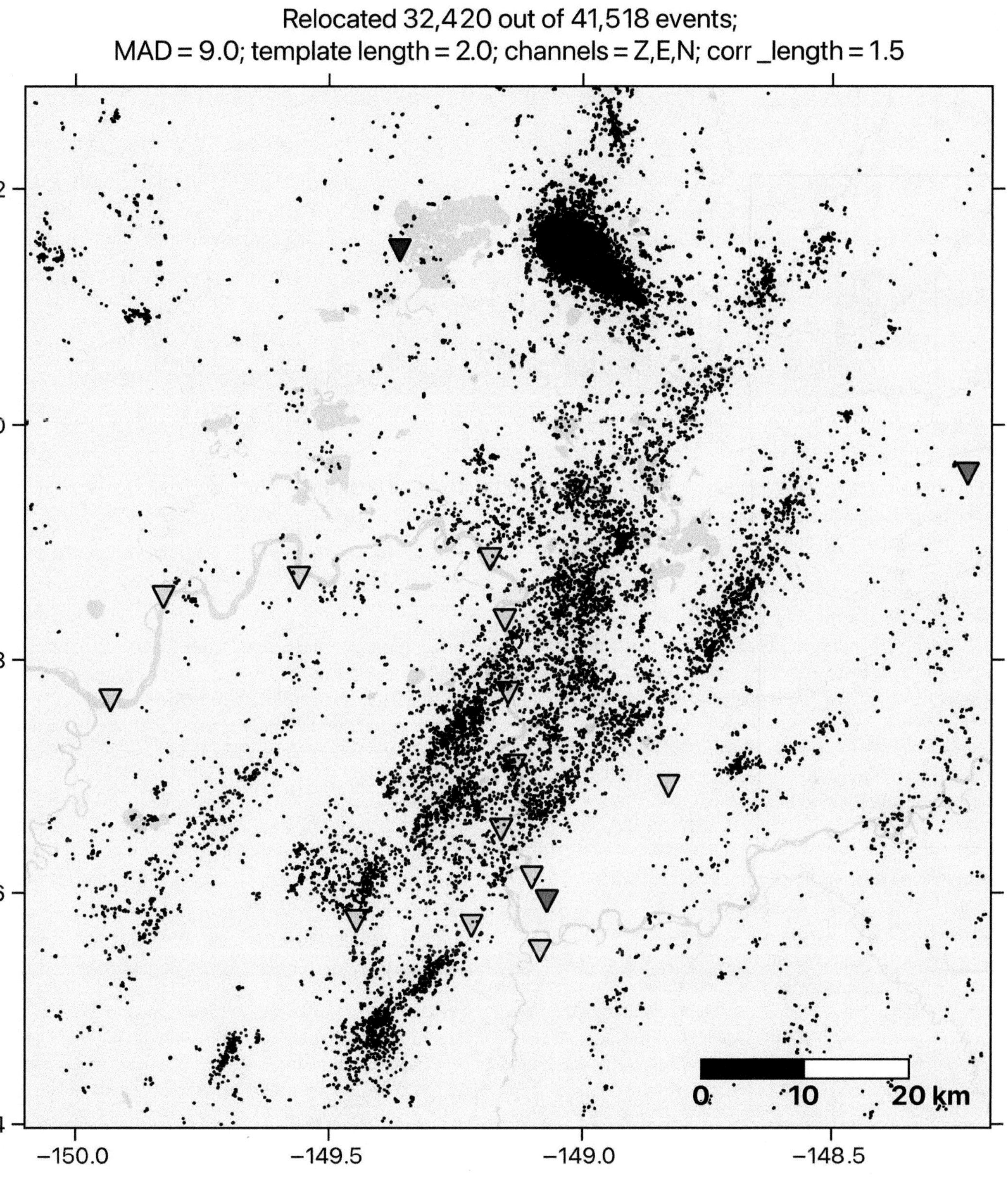

H (8.3 km), I (15.4 km), J (19.6 km), K (22.7 km), and L (23.1 km). Furthermore the variance in depth is much larger north of the basin than below the basin. Beneath the basin, seismicity appears to extend to ~25 km depth and is only 5 km from the underlying Moho (Fig. 8c).

Cross sections perpendicular to the MFFZ (Fig. 9) show that the fault zone is not simply composed of two parallel vertically

Figure 3. Final detected and relocated catalog for the MFFZ, containing 32,420 events. The catalog represents a subset of the 41,518 detections derived from the 8714 template events shown in Figure 2. MAD, median absolute deviation. The header includes various settings, including the detection threshold of 9.0 times the median absolute deviation (MAD). The color version of this figure is available only in the electronic edition.

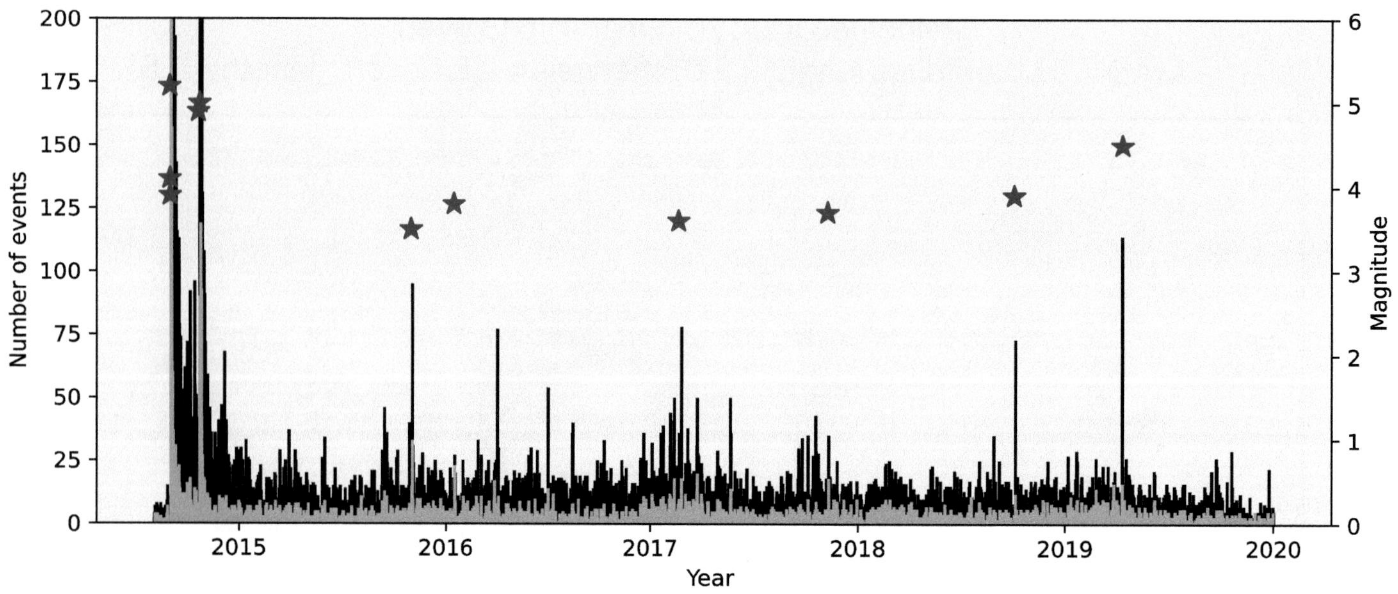

Figure 4. Events within the MFFZ in one-week bins for the AEC catalog (cyan: 9621) and the updated catalog of newly detected events presented in this study (black: 32,420). Events with magnitude $M_L \geq 3.5$ are plotted as red stars with the magnitude axis on the right. The color version of this figure is available only in the electronic edition.

dipping strike-slip faults, as implied by Tape *et al.* (2015). In the south, the seismicity suggests that the possibility of structures dipping to the northwest by ~45° (Fig. 9a,b). These views reveal the challenge of distilling a dipping fault to a segment in map view, as in Figure 6. Shifting to the north (Fig. 9c,d), we see the "emergence" of the two semivertical faults: B and J beneath the basin, then A and I north of the basin. The seismicity structures northwest of MFFZ-W are complex and appear to include structures perpendicular to the MFFZ, such as segment Q, which is aligned northwest–southeast and is shown in Figure 9d. In the Discussion section, we interpret these cross sections in more detail, alongside the reference source mechanisms.

DISCUSSION

Interpretation of fault segments

We have distilled the relocated catalog into a set of 17 fault segments, and now we discuss what types of source mechanisms might be expected on these faults. We are guided by a set of 25 high-quality source mechanisms from previous studies (Fig. 7). These studies considered variations in source depth, magnitude, and mechanism while fitting seismic waveforms of body waves (P) and surface waves (Rayleigh and Love). Among the set of 25 events, there are 11 from Tape *et al.* (2015) and Silwal (2015), 6 from Tape *et al.* (2018) and Silwal (2018), 6 from Smith *et al.* (2023) and Smith (2020), 1 from the AEC fault-plane catalog, and 1 from the Global Centroid Moment Tensor (Global CMT) catalog (Ekström *et al.*, 2012). Given the number of stations and waveforms (body and surface waves) used to estimate the source mechanisms, we expect their uncertainties to be less than ~20° in (Kagan) rotation angle, making this set of mechanisms ideal for pursuing interpretations linking mechanisms to possible faults. The source parameters for the mechanisms are listed in Tables 3 and 4; the events are labeled a–y in order of their origin times, starting with 6 October 1995 M_w 6.0 and finishing with 11 April 2019 M_w 4.15.

The 25 earthquakes do not provide a simple interpretation in the context of the newly inferred fault segments. Questions guiding the interpretation are as follows:

1. Is the mechanism on or near a fault segment?
2. Is one of the two fault planes of the source mechanism aligned with a fault segment?
3. What is the sense of slip implied for each possible fault plane? Is it consistent with the prevailing stress regime of north–south compression and east–west extension (Ratchkovski and Hansen, 2002a)?

There are 23 strike-slip mechanisms among the 25 reference events, and all of these are consistent with the prevailing north–south compression and east–west extension (Fig. 7). One event (o) is a normal fault mechanism. Event w is either a dip-slip fault on a near-vertical plane or a near-horizontal fault plane; for this event, we do not see a link between the mechanism and any interpreted fault.

Next, we will attempt to interpret the mechanisms in the context of our newly identified fault segments. We ascribe 17 events to left-lateral strike-slip faulting on northeast-striking faults and 6 events to right-lateral, conjugate strike-slip faulting (Table 4). Within the set of 17 left-lateral events, there is some ambiguity with 5 events. Two events (d, v) are interpreted to be on a strike-slip fault plane but having a nonhorizontal slip vector; see event d in Figure 8c and event v in

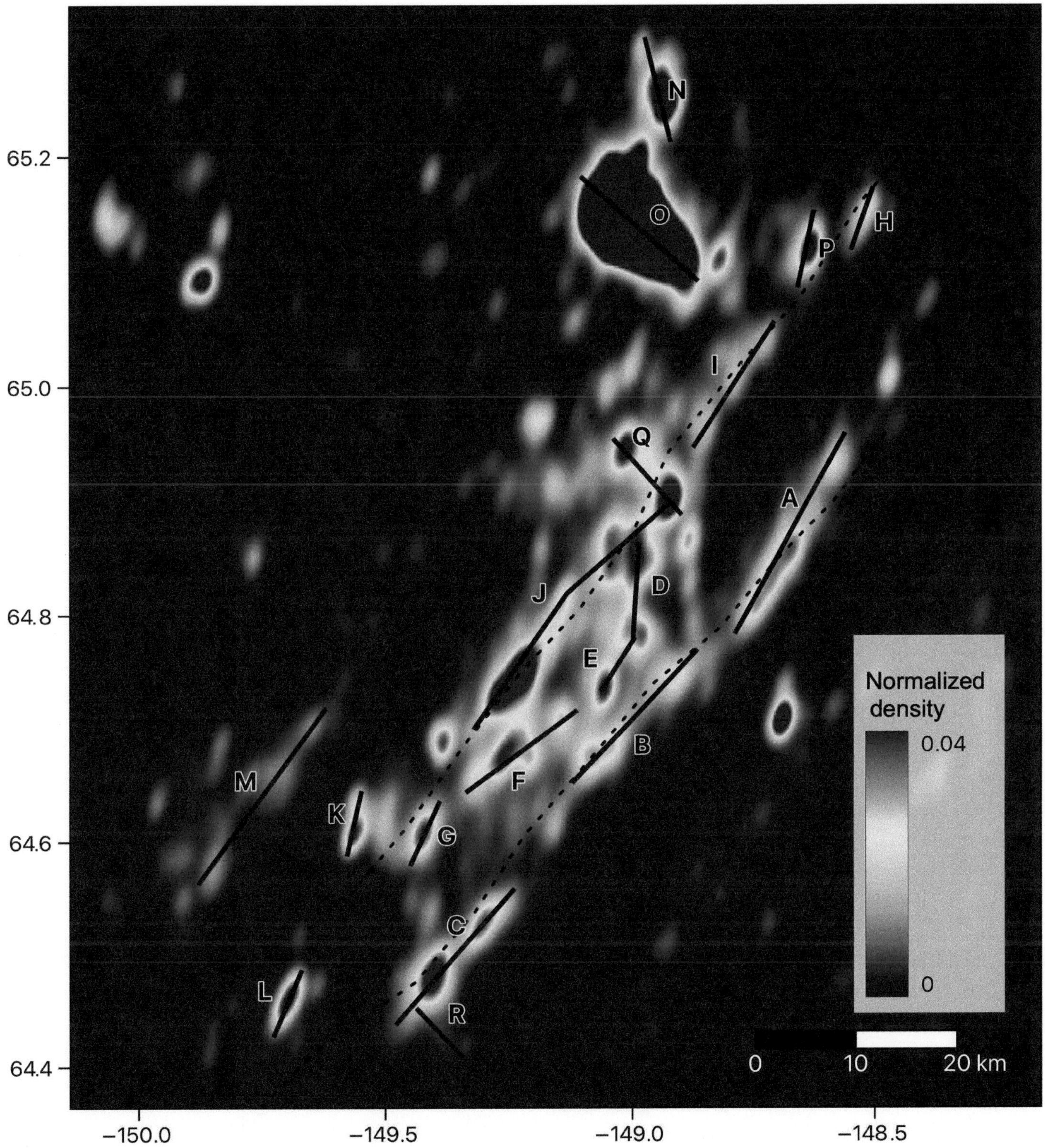

Figure 8a. Event x lies within a complex region of seismicity, and we have a slight preference toward the northeast–southwest-striking plane. Two events (f and p) have the same magnitude (M_w 3.8) and similar mechanisms, and they are both atypical earthquakes. Event f (11 April 2012) was triggered by teleseismic surface waves (Tape *et al.*, 2013) and was interpreted as a very-low-frequency earthquake (Tape *et al.*, 2018). Event p is also a very-low-frequency earthquake (Tape *et al.*,

Figure 5. Probability density function for seismicity, computed using the Python SciPy function gaussian_kde. The interpreted fault segments are plotted as solid lines (Table 2); the larger-scale faults MFFZ-W and MFFZ-E are plotted as dashed lines. The color version of this figure is available only in the electronic edition.

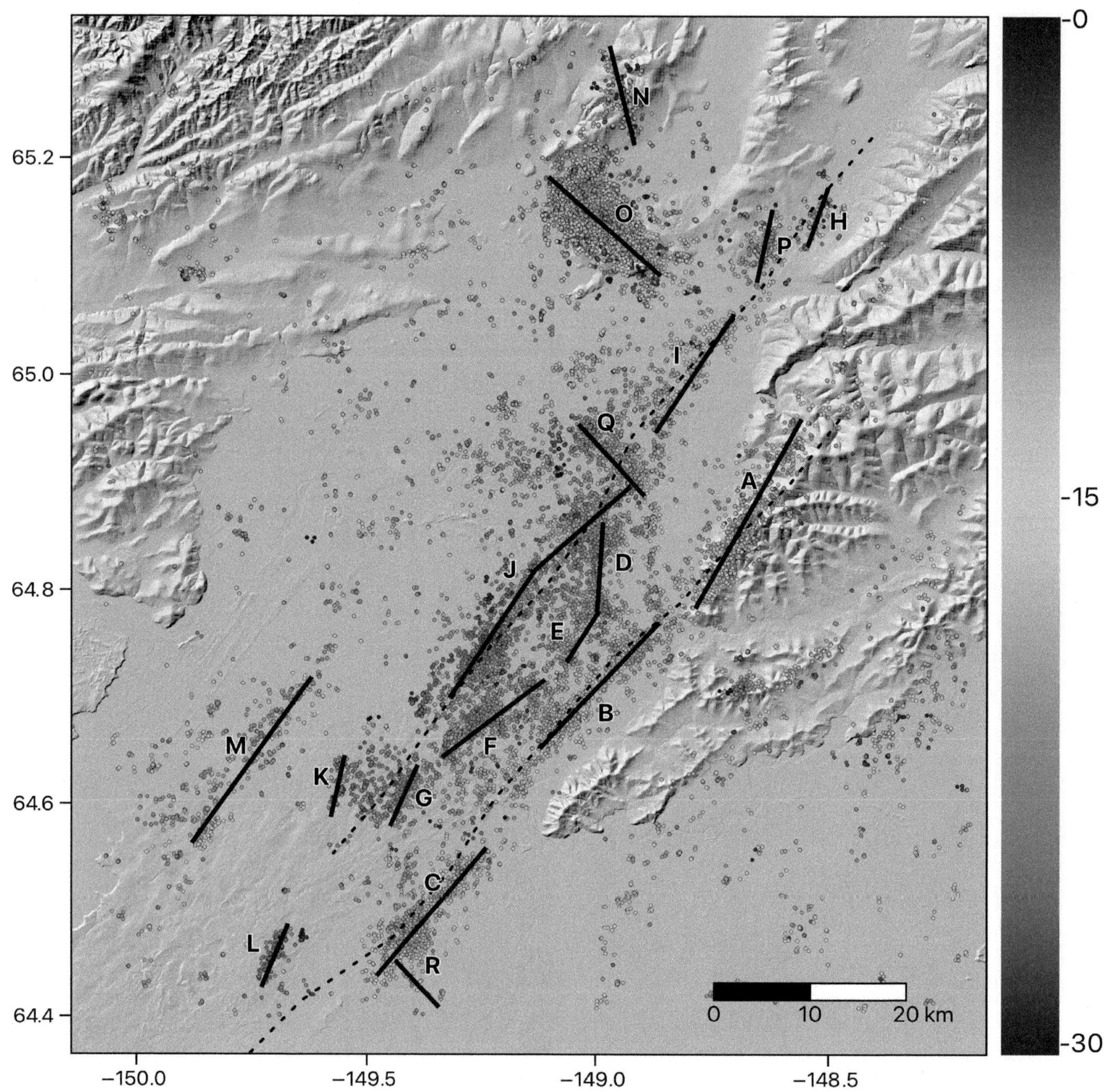

Figure 6. Interpretation of fault segments in the MFFZ, based on our relocated catalog (Fig. 3). See also Table 2. The two dashed lines are MFFZ-W and MFFZ-E. The color version of this figure is available only in the electronic edition.

2018). Given the tectonic setting and the relocated seismicity catalog, it is inconclusive which of the two focal planes was the true fault plane. Both events f and p were previously interpreted as rupturing MFFZ-W on a plane dipping to the northwest. Our new evidence raises the possibility of northwest–southeast right-lateral conjugate faulting, with fault segment Q (event f) or an unmarked fault parallel to fault segment O (event p).

Our data set is limited in the sense that it spans a five-year period (1 August 2014 to 31 December 2019), and therefore the fault segments we identify (Fig. 6) are only the ones that have experienced activity during this time period. By including more data—from an era of lower quality station coverage and waveforms—we would see a more complete, yet fuzzier, view of the fault zone, leading to the two dashed lines in Figure 7 that define the MFFZ and are consistent with the predominance of strike-slip faulting in the region (Ratchkovski and Hansen, 2002a). These two MFFZ faults were first delineated by Tape *et al.* (2013) using smoothed log-scaled seismicity rate (1990–2015), and they remain visible using 10 more years of seismicity.

TABLE 1
Parameters Impacting Waveform Cross Correlation and Relocation

Parameter	Impact and Considerations	Related Parameters	Values Tested
Template configuration			
T_{dur} (s)	Longer P coda may overlap S onset; can be increased if R_{min} is increased	R_{min}	**2.0**, 2.5, 1.5, 1.0
Chans	Z only: $K = N_{stat}$; Z, E, N: $K \geq N_{stat}$	K	**Z, E, N**, Z
K	Higher value leads to fewer templates; increases computation time	–	**6**, 4, 12
Station distance thresholds			
R_{min}	Closer stations increase risk of P window overlapping S onset	T_{dur}	**25**, 0
R_{max}	Distant stations lead to longer P–S time; longer T_{dur} required	T_{dur}	**90**, 150, all
Detection and correlation			
f	High values yield fewer, more reliable events; low values may result in false detections	Requires sufficient K	**9.0**, 8.5, 10
T_{corr} (s)	If too long, P-pick window may include S-wave energy	$T_{corr} \leq T_{dur}$	**1.5**, 1.0, 2.0

See additional parameters in Table S1. Bold text indicates values used in our study.

The 7 January 1990 M_L 5.0 earthquake (event a) is not associated with any fault segment in our 2014–2019 study (Fig. 7). Yet its aftershock sequence in the AEC catalog shows clear delineation of a northwest–southwest fault consistent with right-lateral faulting (Fig. 10). Had it occurred during our time period of enhanced station coverage, it would have resulted in an identified fault segment.

Discussion of features

Northwest-dipping strike-slip faulting: the five years of relocated seismicity in our study, as well as the 35-yr AEC catalog (1990–2025) reveal diffuse seismicity beneath Nenana basin. Upon inspection of the cross sections, much of this apparent diffuseness may be due to dipping faults, as shown in Figure 9 and other cross sections (see Sims *et al.*, 2025).

The seismicity between segments B and J dips to the northwest, represented by three fault segments (D, E, F). These dipping seismicity features are well aligned with one of the two fault planes of the source mechanisms for seven events: c, s, t, q, y, h, and u, with five of these events featured in Figure 9a,b. The cross section in Figure 9b spans fault segments J, E, and B, and there is potentially a fourth fault—farther to the east—whose existence is implied by event h (12 March 2013), which is a very-low-frequency earthquake (Tape *et al.*, 2018). An alternative explanation is that the true depth of event h is 15–20 km rather than the estimated depth of 23 km; this would place the event on MFFZ-E, close to event u.

Event x (3 October 2018 M_w 4.0) is potentially a more extreme case of northeast-dipping strike-slip faulting, in that the dip of the source mechanism (38°) is less than the mechanisms of events to the south. Alternatively, if the plane of Figure 9d is the fault plane (segment Q), then the mechanism would represent southwest-side-up motion.

Shallow faulting north of the MFFZ: this region represents the most seismically active portion of the MFFZ during our study period, accounting for 41% of the recorded events. The seismicity from the AEC catalog, as shown in our set of template events (Fig. 2), reveals elongation in the northwest–southeast direction. The relocated aftershocks form the basis of our assignment of fault segment O to the predominant 2014 seismicity (Fig. 11). The mainshock mechanism (Tape *et al.*, 2015) is consistent with right-lateral faulting on segment O. Both the mainshock depth and the aftershock seismicity are shallower than events within the main MFFZ, as shown in Table 2. A vertical cross section of 2014 seismicity, viewed toward the northeast direction, forms an L shape, with seismicity extending to the southwest in the depth range of 10–15 km and above the mainshock all the way to the surface.

TABLE 2
Seismicity Properties of Fault Segments in the Minto Flats Fault Zone (See Fig. 6)

Segment	Length (km)	Depth (Median, km)	Depth (MAD, km)	Number of Events
A	22.0	14.2	2.5	1,024
B	17.5	15.6	1.2	938
C	17.3	15.3	1.4	937
D	8.9	18.5	1.7	1,105
E	5.8	18.1	1.5	693
F	13.0	18.6	1.6	987
G	6.6	20.4	1.3	406
H	6.0	8.3	3.8	203
I	14.2	15.4	3.1	522
J	28.7	19.6	2.1	2,648
K	6.2	22.7	0.4	334
L	6.7	23.1	0.7	296
M	20.9	18.2	2.5	442
N	10.0	8.6	1.7	791
O	14.8	10.4	2.3	14,830
P	7.2	16.7	2.6	392
Q	9.6	17.3	1.9	1,051
R	6.3	14.9	1.8	260

The calculation of median depth uses events having epicenters within 3 km of each segment. MAD, median absolute deviation.

Although the 2014 mechanism and aftershock seismicity provide evidence for northwest–southeast right-lateral

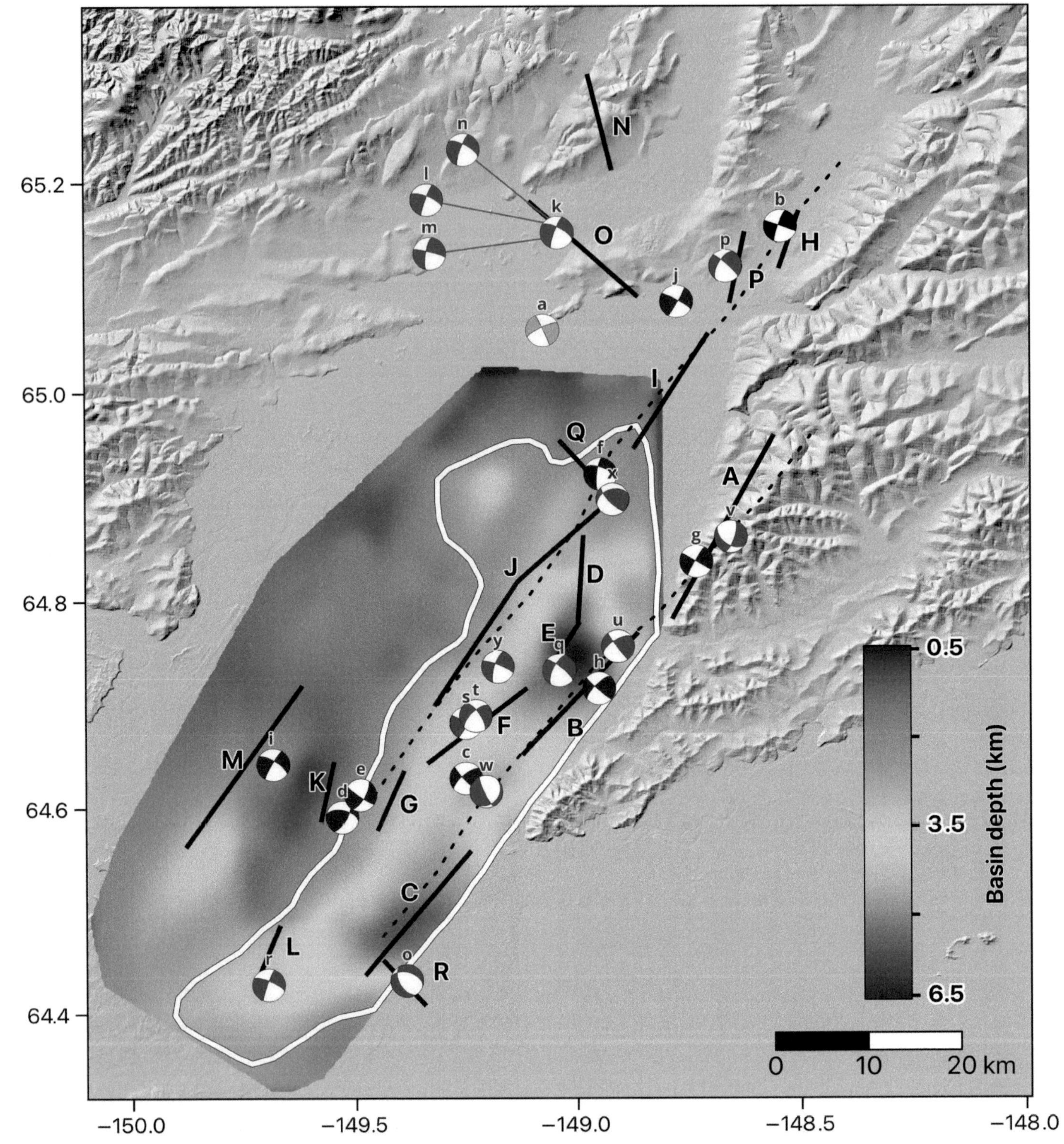

Figure 7. Tectonic elements used to provide context for interpretations of the fault segments (labeled A–R) identified in this study (Fig. 6 and Table 2). The map includes topography, the basement surface for Nenana basin, the features MFFZ-W and MFFZ-E (dashed lines), and a set of beachball source mechanisms for 25 reference events labeled a–y (Tables 3 and 4). The mechanisms are colored red if they occurred during the time period of the seismicity study (1 August 2014 to 31 December 2019) and blue otherwise, with two events colored separately: green for 7 January 1990 M_w 5.0 and black for 6 October 1995 M_w 6.0. These same mechanisms are displayed in the vertical cross sections of seismicity. The color version of this figure is available only in the electronic edition.

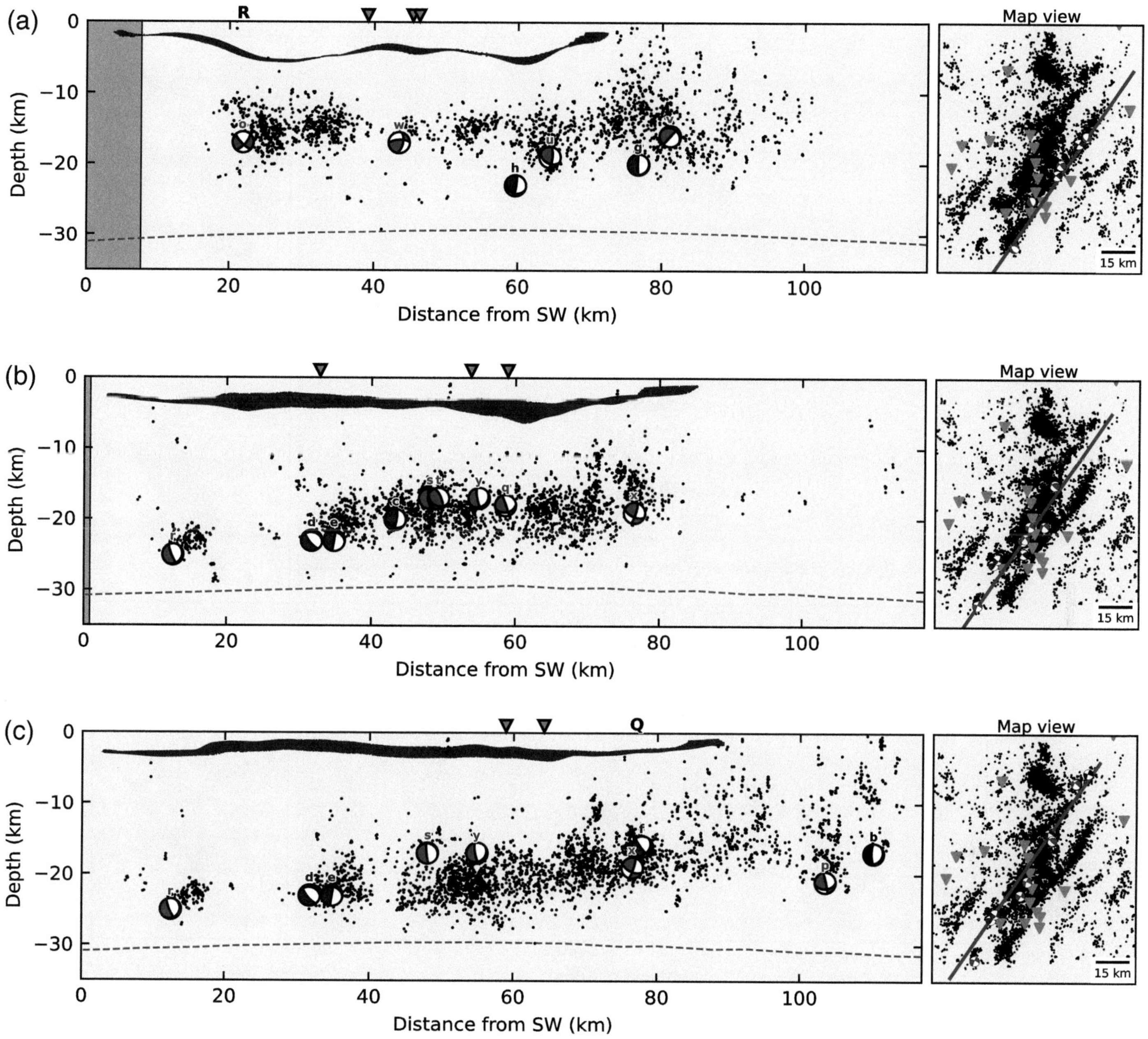

Figure 8. Vertical cross sections of seismicity parallel to the MFFZ, from southeast (a) to northeast (c). Each cross section contains all events within 3 km of a vertical plane depicted by the red solid line in the map view at right. The red-dashed line depicts the Moho (Miller and Moresi, 2018); the blue-shaded region depicts the variation of the base of Nenana basin (PRA, 2017) over the width of the corridor. Seismic stations and source mechanisms for reference events (Fig. 7) are plotted if they are within 5 km of the cross section. Source mechanisms are displayed as back-hemisphere projections, analogous to the lower-hemisphere convention in map view. The color version of this figure is available only in the electronic edition.

faulting, the seismicity alignment remains diffuse (Fig. 11). We examined the aftershock seismicity following a 21 October 2014 M_w 4.7 event (event m). The seismicity is aligned northwest–southeast (Fig. S17), in general agreement with the mechanism obtained from recorded waveforms (Tape *et al.*, 2015). Furthermore, the $M_L \geq 2$ relocated seismicity shows northwest–southeast alignment.

North of the 2014 activity is a newly defined fault segment N, which exhibits the shallowest seismicity, extending from 10 km to the surface (Fig. 12). This feature is unclear from the set of template events (Fig. 2), and our catalog enhancement reveals a clear north–south structure (Fig. 12), whose tectonic origin is unknown. The existence of segment N, combined with segment O, suggests a different (shallower) faulting regime from the segments in the main MFFZ.

Event j (12 July 2013 M_w 3.6) is not directly on any assigned fault segment. But it is close in time and space to the 2014 sequence, as shown in Figure 11 (see also Fig. 10). We interpret event j as occurring on fault segment O and possibly influencing the origin of the 2014 sequence one year later.

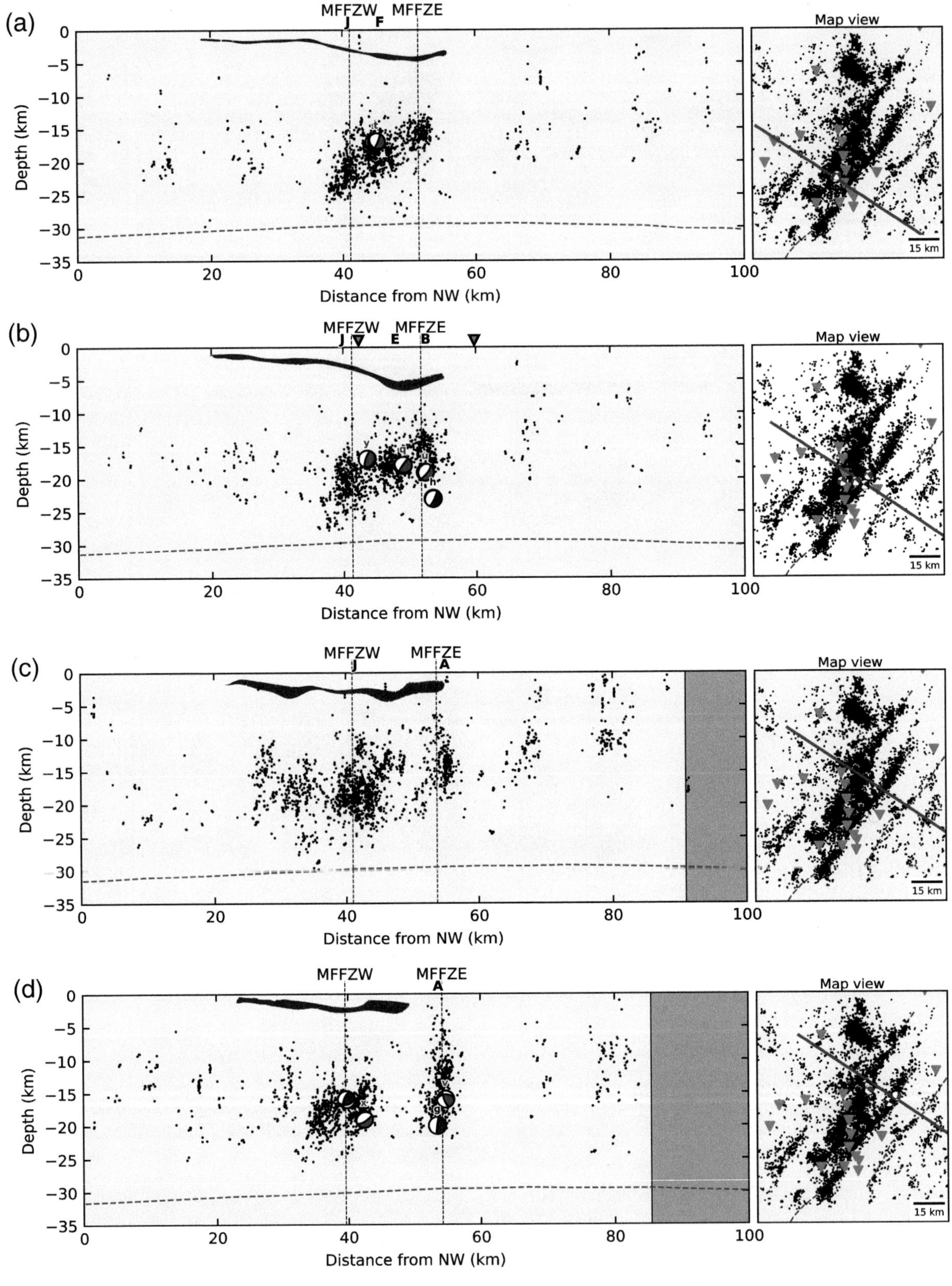

Figure 9. Vertical cross sections of seismicity perpendicular to the MFFZ, from south (a) to north (d). Each cross section contains all events within 4 km of a vertical plane depicted by the solid red line in the map view at the right. See Figure 8 for additional plotting details. The color version of this figure is available only in the electronic edition.

Complex faulting in the northernmost MFFZ: the 6 October 1995 M_w 6.0 earthquake appears to have occurred on the northern end of MFFZ-W, as indicated by its position on the dashed line in Figure 7. Tape *et al.* (2015) performed a finite-source inversion of this event, considering both the northeast-striking (fault) plane and the northwest-striking

TABLE 3
Source Parameters for the 25 Reference Events Displayed in Figure 7

ID	Reference	Origin Time (yyyy/mm/dd hh:mm:ss)	Longitude (°)	Latitude (°)	Depth (km)	M_w
a	AECfp	1990/01/07 11:01:48	−149.0727	65.0597	20	5.00
b	GCMT	1995/10/06 05:23:18	−148.5422	65.1586	17	5.96
c	silwal2015	2001/03/25 11:34:50	−149.2484	64.6291	20	4.40
d	silwal2015	2008/07/16 10:12:00	−149.5299	64.5917	23	3.90
e	silwal2015	2009/07/28 12:13:15	−149.4882	64.6132	23	3.80
f	silwal2018	2012/04/11 09:21:57	−148.9461	64.9222	16	3.80
g	silwal2015	2013/03/05 21:55:58	−148.7323	64.8382	20	3.40
h	silwal2018	2013/03/12 07:39:50	−148.9505	64.7161	23	3.50
i	silwal2015	2013/06/05 18:58:23	−149.6848	64.6426	10	3.90
j	silwal2015	2013/07/12 07:59:17	−148.7745	65.0870	16	3.60
k	silwal2015	2014/08/31 03:06:57	−149.0398	65.1526	12	5.00
l	silwal2015	2014/08/31 12:24:58	−149.0523	65.1611	16	4.10
m	silwal2015	2014/10/21 00:36:58	−149.0413	65.1489	13	4.70
n	silwal2015	2014/10/23 16:30:23	−149.0523	65.1644	13	4.80
o	silwal2015	2014/12/13 15:47:31	−149.3840	64.4325	17	3.40
p	silwal2018	2015/09/12 03:25:12	−148.6646	65.1207	21	3.80
q	silwal2018	2015/10/22 13:16:15	−149.0388	64.7334	18	2.60
r	silwal2018	2015/10/31 02:56:35	−149.6969	64.4285	25	3.40
s	silwal2018	2016/01/14 19:04:10	−149.2479	64.6827	17	3.70
t	smith2020	2017/05/27 16:33:05	−149.2261	64.6896	17	3.20
u	smith2020	2017/06/28 12:58:51	−148.9082	64.7566	19	3.30
v	smith2020	2017/11/08 06:49:11	−148.6552	64.8620	16	3.55
w	smith2020	2018/08/25 18:15:51	−149.2033	64.6164	17	3.20
x	smith2020	2018/10/03 03:29:37	−148.9191	64.8979	19	4.00
y	smith2020	2019/04/11 10:42:45	−149.1761	64.7370	17	4.15

See Table 4 for the parameters describing the mechanisms. AECfp, Ratchkovski and Hansen (2002a); Global Centroid Moment Tensor (GCMT), Ekström *et al.* (2012); silwal2015, Tape *et al.* (2015); silwal2018, Tape *et al.* (2018); smith2020, Smith *et al.* (2023).

(auxiliary) plane. The improved waveform fits for the northeast-striking plane provided the strongest evidence that the 1995 earthquake ruptured this plane. Relocated aftershocks (Ratchkovski and Hansen, 2002a) were also aligned with the northeast-striking plane.

In the region of the 1995 M_s 6.0 earthquake, there is a short segment of seismicity (2014–2019) that we use as the basis to assign fault segment H. The seismicity is aligned with the mainshock fault plane and the relocated 1995 aftershocks of Ratchkovski and Hansen (2002a). The depth of the 2014–2019 seismicity (8.3 km) is shallower than the 1995 aftershocks and the main slip of the 1995 mainshock (17 km: Tape *et al.*, 2015). The region of the 1995 earthquake is complex. While the three reference events (b, p, and j) have similarities (Fig. 7), their hosting structures may all be different (segments H, P, and O), which is our current interpretation. The 1995 event b is likely left-lateral strike-slip faulting on segment H (MFFZ-W). Event j is likely right-lateral strike-slip faulting on fault segment O and may have been a foreshock to the 2014 sequence. The relocated seismicity near event p suggests a short fault structure (segment P) that is offset and misaligned from MFFZ-W. With this interpretation, event p represents left-lateral strike-slip faulting on a plane dipping 50°. It occurred at 21 km near the base of mostly vertically aligned seismicity (see Sims *et al.*, 2025).

Extension of the MFFZ to the south: the structure at the southern end of Nenana basin is unclear. In particular, we do not know if fault segment L is associated with MFFZ-W, MFFZ-E, or something else. Event r (31 October 2015 M_w 3.4) occurred at an anomalous depth of 25 km. The seismicity of fault segment L has a median depth of 23.1 ± 0.7 km. Given these depths, we are inclined to interpret L as a southern extension of MFFZ-W (and segment J-K), rather than a southern extension of the eastern MFFZ fault (and segment C), as suggested by the proximity of the reference event to the MFFZ-E dashed line in Figure 7. However, if L is connected with K, then there is a significant gap in seismicity between the two segments, with very little activity in our time period of analysis, as well as in a wider time period (1990–2025). Figure 8c shows the gap within our relocated catalog.

Event o (13 December 2014 M_w 3.4) is a normal-fault mechanism that occurs at the southern end of fault segment C and on the southeast side of it. In Figure 6, and in the seismicity density map (Fig. 5), there is a hint of seismicity perpendicular to segment C that we interpret to be associated with a northwest-striking normal fault. The cross section perpendicular to MFFZ-E (Sims *et al.*, 2025) does not show a sharp feature that would be expected for MFFZ-E but instead shows a spread of seismicity, suggestive of a fault perpendicular to MFFZ-E. Guided by the faint seismicity as well as the

TABLE 4
Source Parameters for the 25 Reference Events Listed in Table 3 and Displayed in Figure 7

ID	Fault Plane 1			Fault Plane 2			Pick	Slip Vector		Fault Type
	Strike (°)	Dip (°)	Slip (°)	Strike (°)	Dip (°)	Slip (°)		Azimuth	Plunge	
a	244	73	−4	335	86	−163	2	154	17	RL
b	199	77	−1	289	89	−167	1	199	1	LL
c	230	68	10	136	81	158	1	46	9	LL
d	30	68	40	283	53	153	1	193	37	LL*
e	30	68	−10	124	81	−158	1	34	9	LL
f	187	71	−39	292	53	−156	1	202	37	LL?
g	210	83	0	120	90	173	1	30	0	LL
h	225	65	9	131	82	155	1	41	8	LL
i	210	83	−20	303	70	−172	1	213	20	LL
j	30	83	10	299	80	173	1	209	10	RL
k	200	76	−30	298	61	−164	2	110	14	RL
l	200	83	−20	293	70	−172	2	110	7	RL
m	190	68	−10	284	81	−158	2	100	22	RL
n	200	76	−30	298	61	−164	2	110	14	RL
o	150	52	−60	287	47	−123	2	60	38	N
p	211	50	−16	311	78	−139	1	221	12	LL?
q	206	56	−23	309	71	−144	1	219	19	LL
r	200	82	−22	293	68	−171	1	203	22	LL
s	29	81	6	298	84	171	1	208	6	LL
t	227	66	−23	326	69	−155	1	236	21	LL
u	238	54	8	143	84	144	1	53	6	LL
v	18	71	−45	126	48	−154	1	36	42	LL*
w	40	24	−26	155	80	−112	0	–	–	–
x	250	38	30	136	72	124	1	46	18	LL?
y	198	72	−11	292	79	−162	1	202	11	LL

Three angles are listed for each of the two possible fault planes represented by the source mechanisms. The column "pick" indicates which of the two fault planes we think is the true fault plane. The slip vector angles are chosen based on the fault plane on the convention of a positive plunge angle. LL? indicates that there is uncertainty in the choice and LL* indicates that the slip vector has a significant nonhorizontal component (see plunge angle).

location and mechanism of event o, we identified fault segment R, recognizing that it would not have been chosen based on seismicity alone. Fault segment R may designate the termination of fault segment C and in turn MFFZ-E (Fig. 8a). Dixit and Hanks (2021) suggested that event o provided evidence of active basin formation. As shown in Figure 7, it is situated below the southern main depocenter of the basin.

Strike-slip faulting west of MFFZ-W: fault segment M corresponds to the weak lineament documented by Tape *et al.* (2015) as the southwest subregion. The relocated seismicity on segment M (19.6 km) is shallower than on fault segments J (19.6), K (22.7), and L (23.1), which are part of MFFZ-W. Event i (5 June 2013 M_w 3.9) appears to have occurred at a depth (10 km) that is shallower than the relocated seismicity; mechanisms at depths between 8 and 14 km provide best-fitting waveforms (Fig. S18).

A fragmented fault zone with conjugate strike-slip faulting

Our enhanced seismicity catalog (2014–2019) helps illuminate a new perspective of the MFFZ. First, the fault zone is more fragmented than the two-fault view of Tape *et al.* (2013, 2015), represented by the dashed lines in Figure 7. With the benefit of many more small earthquakes—and relocating these earthquakes—we see that the seismicity underneath the basin does not collapse onto the two main faults. Fault segments D–G are interpreted as a new fault system between MFFZ-W and MFFZ-E, and there is still more seismicity without any assigned segment (Fig. 6).

In addition to the fault zone being more fragmented, it contains conjugate faults that are perpendicular or oblique to the MFFZ. Two definitive examples are for the 1990 and 2014 earthquakes, both of which produced northwest–southeast-aligned aftershocks. A third example is fault segment Q, which may have hosted two reference events (f and x): 2012-04-11 M_w 3.8 (Tape *et al.*, 2013, 2018) and 2018-10-03 M_w 4.0 (Smith *et al.*, 2023). The 2012 event was assumed to have occurred on MFFZ-W, triggered by high-amplitude Love waves from the M_w 8.6 Indian Ocean earthquake. The existence of fault segment Q raises the possibility that the triggered earthquake occurred on a northwest–southeast fault plane instead.

Association between faulting and basin

Common to other sedimentary basins, faulting has played an important role in the formation of Nenana basin. However, it is unclear how the modern seismicity is related to the continuing

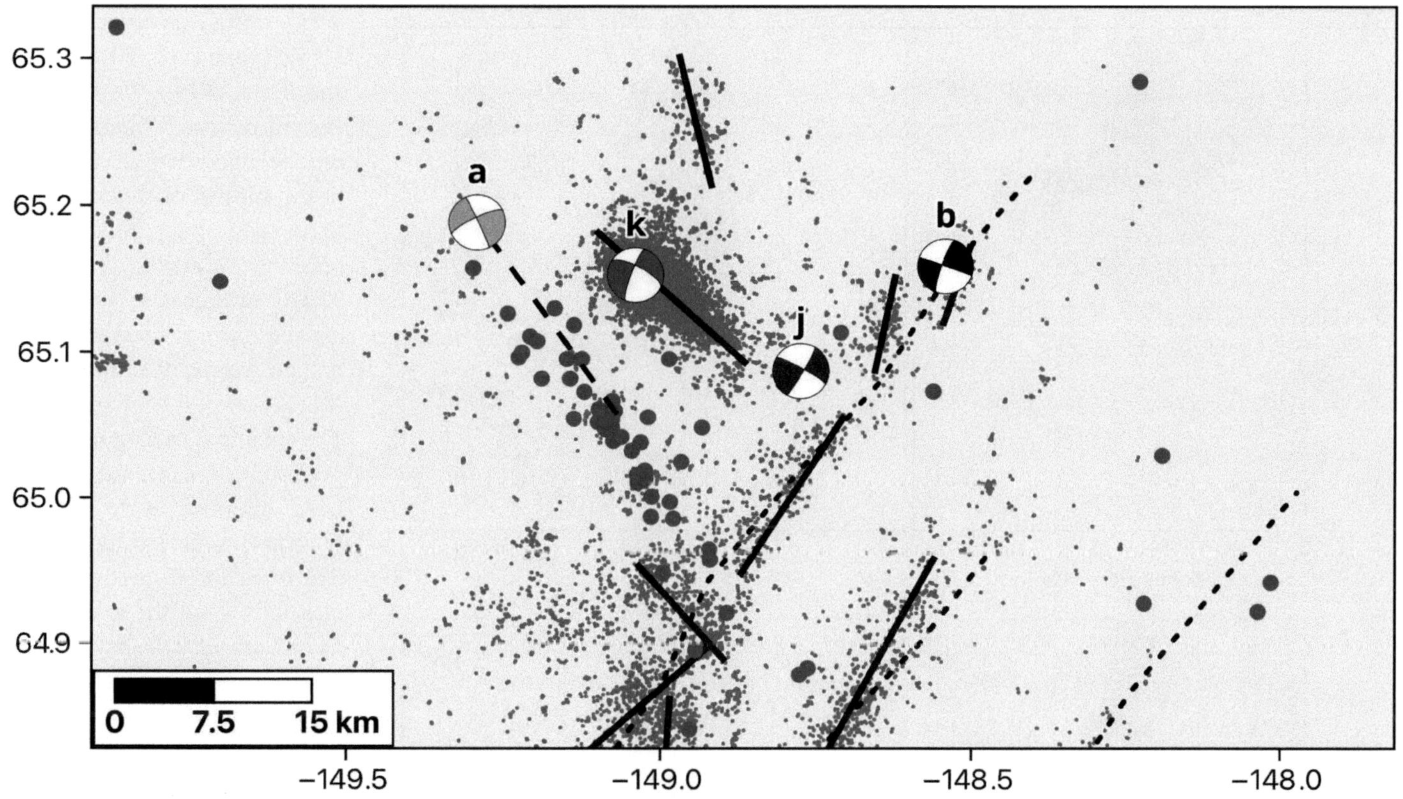

Figure 10. Aftershock seismicity (large red dots) from the AEC catalog for 50 days after event "a" (7 January 1990 M_L 5.0). The seismicity is aligned northwest–southeast, similar to the strike of the mainshock mechanism. The mechanisms for 31 August 2014 M_w 5.0 (event k), 6 October 1995 M_w 6.0 (event b), and 12 July 2015 M_w 3.6 (event j) are also displayed. The color version of this figure is available only in the electronic edition.

development of the basin today or over the past few million years. It is identified as a half-graben basin, with a steep fault on its eastern margin (Van Kooten *et al.*, 2012; Dixit *et al.*, 2017). As discussed by Tape *et al.* (2015), the current seismic regime is more consistent with a transtensional setting, with extension promoted on the overlapping region between MFFZ-W and MFFZ-E.

It is important to point out that there are no geologically identified active faults in the Minto Flats region. While fault exposures would be expected to be poor in the drainage region of the Tanana River, there are sections of the seismically identified fault system that extend into surface bedrock (e.g., fault segment A). What was once suggested as a Minto fault (Péwé *et al.*, 1966; Gedney *et al.*, 1972) was not confirmed after a dedicated field study (Koehler *et al.*, 2015). Active-source seismic data, gravity data, and magnetic data have been used to identify faulting in the deeper sections of the basin and extending into the basement rock (Van Kooten *et al.*, 2012; Tape *et al.*, 2015; Dixit *et al.*, 2017). However, these inferred faults—at depths of 5–10 km—do not seem to be responsible for most of the seismicity in the region, which is at 15–25 km.

There is a vertical gap of 10–15 km between the bottom of Nenana basin and the start of the seismicity, which can best be seen in the cross sections parallel to the MFFZ (Fig. 8). Under MFFZ-E, at the eastern margin of Nenana basin, the basin is deepest (especially in geological models, such as that discussed by Dixit *et al.*, 2017), and the seismicity is at 13–18 km depth (fault segments B and C in Table 2). Under MFFZ-W, at the western margin of Nenana basin, the basin is shallower, and the seismicity is at 20–23 km depth (fault segments J and K in Table 2). The question is: what kind of deformation—if any—is currently occurring above the seismicity? In the extreme example of deep sub-basin seismicity, do the strike-slip faults below 20 km depth extend down to the base of the Moho, at ~30 km (Fig. 8)? Do they extend all the way up to the base of Nenana basin? Do they influence active subsidence of the basin?

Both the seismicity in the MFFZ and the depth in the Nenana basin are anomalous compared with the surrounding region. A few authors have proposed the MFFZ as a major tectonic feature. Cross and Freymueller (2008) suggested that the fault zone marks the eastern boundary of a Bering Sea plate, though their focus was not on Nenana basin or sub-basin seismicity. Dixit and Hanks (2021) integrated the transtensional model of Tape *et al.* (2015) with the Bering plate model of Cross and Freymueller (2008), emphasizing the fundamentally different structure of Nenana basin from the Tanana basin to the east. The geological cross sections in Dixit and Hanks (2021) contain abundant faults to explain the basin structures, but we emphasize that there is essentially no seismic activity on such structures. The largest known earthquake in the MFFZ (6 October 1995 M_w 6.0) ruptured a compact fault patch at 17 km

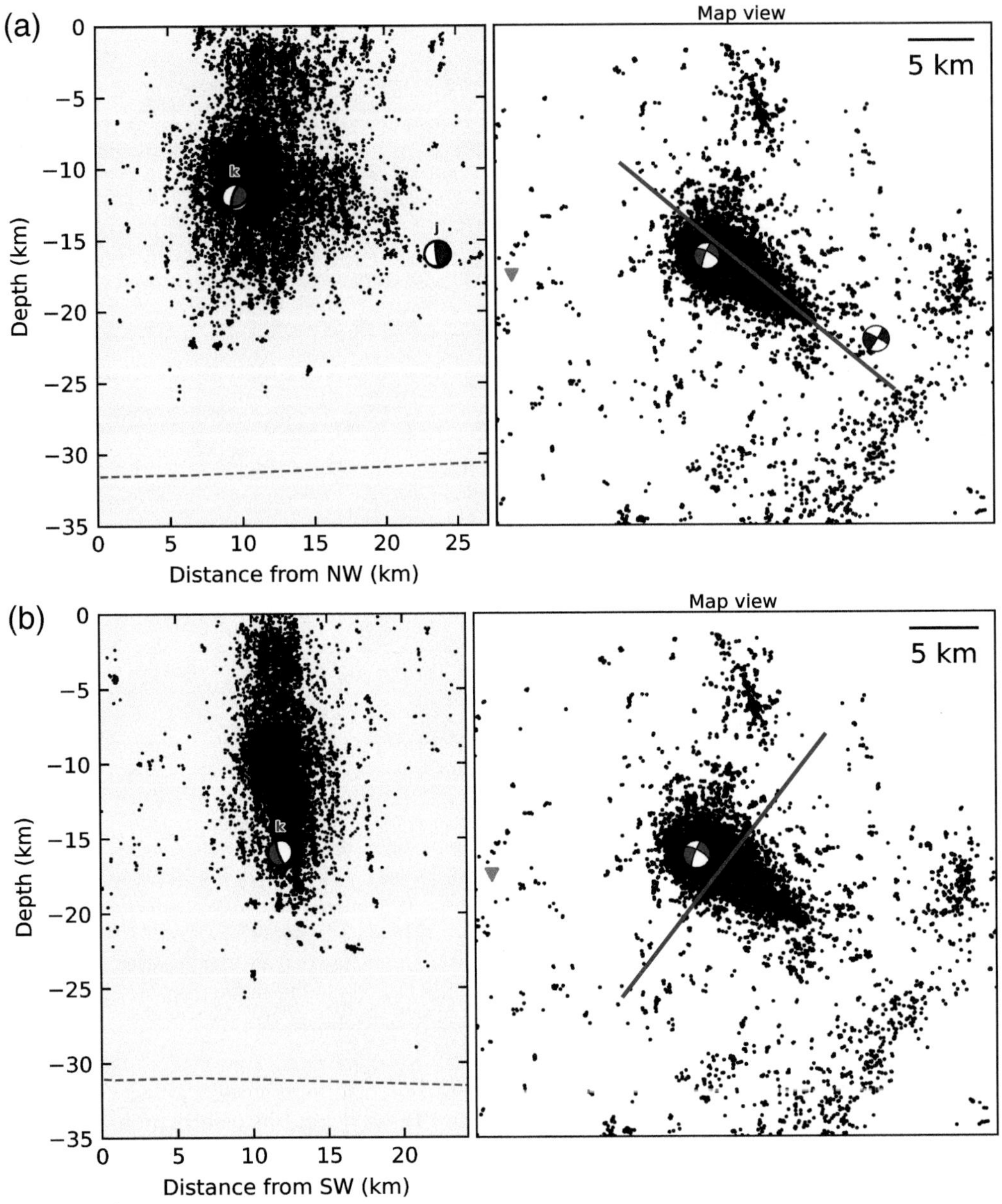

Figure 11. Cross sections of seismicity, featuring the hypocenter region of the 31 August 2014 M_w 5.0 earthquake (event k in Table 3). Also shown is the 12 July 2013 M_w 3.6 earthquake (event j in Table 3), which may have been a foreshock. Source mechanisms in the vertical cross sections, at left, are displayed as back-hemisphere projections. Each vertical cross section contains all events within 4 km of a vertical plane depicted by the red-solid line in the map view at right. (a) Cross section aligned with fault segment O (Fig. 6). The seismicity forms an L shape, with the mainshock mechanism at the corner of the L. (b) Cross section perpendicular to the one in panel (a). The color version of this figure is available only in the electronic edition.

depth, with minimal slip above 6 km (Tape *et al.*, 2015). The link between sub-basin seismicity and basin formation remains an open question, with our new results providing context for the geometry of faulting and the style of faulting at great crustal depths.

CONCLUSION

We compile and analyze five years of seismic waveform data (2014–2019) in central Alaska, focusing on a time period of dense station coverage of the MFFZ (Tape *et al.*, 2018; Smith and Tape, 2019). We use networked-matched filtering and relative relocation to derive a new catalog of earthquake locations and magnitudes. The resulting catalog includes 32,420 earthquakes, representing the most detailed information on seismicity located in the MFFZ between 2014 and 2019. The enhanced catalog improves precision of earthquake locations, allowing us to identify previously unresolved fault structures and to motivate new questions about the spatial variations in fault behavior and mechanical properties throughout the fault zone.

Our relocated catalog leads to three main findings. First, the MFFZ is more fragmented than previously known, suggesting gaps, continuous segments, and multiple fault segments in addition to the two main faults (MFFZ-W and MFFZ-E: Fig. 1b) identified in Tape *et al.* (2013, 2015). The two-fault perspective of the MFFZ is a matter of time scale and resolution: over long time periods, we would expect many of the gaps between fault segments to fill in (e.g., fig. S1 of Tape *et al.*, 2015), as evidenced for the 1990 and 1995 sequences, whose regions are seismically quiet during the time period of our catalog. Our approach of catalog enhancement via smaller event detection and relocation would be needed to achieve the higher resolution view of additional fault segments, yet no other time period besides 2014–2019 has the same or better station coverage than we have exploited in this study.

Our second finding is that conjugate strike-slip faults are prevalent in (or near) the MFFZ, which exhibits northeast-striking, left-lateral faulting. To the north, fault segment Q, then the 1990 event, then the 2014 event (fault segment O) are conjugate, right-lateral strike-slip faults. This raises

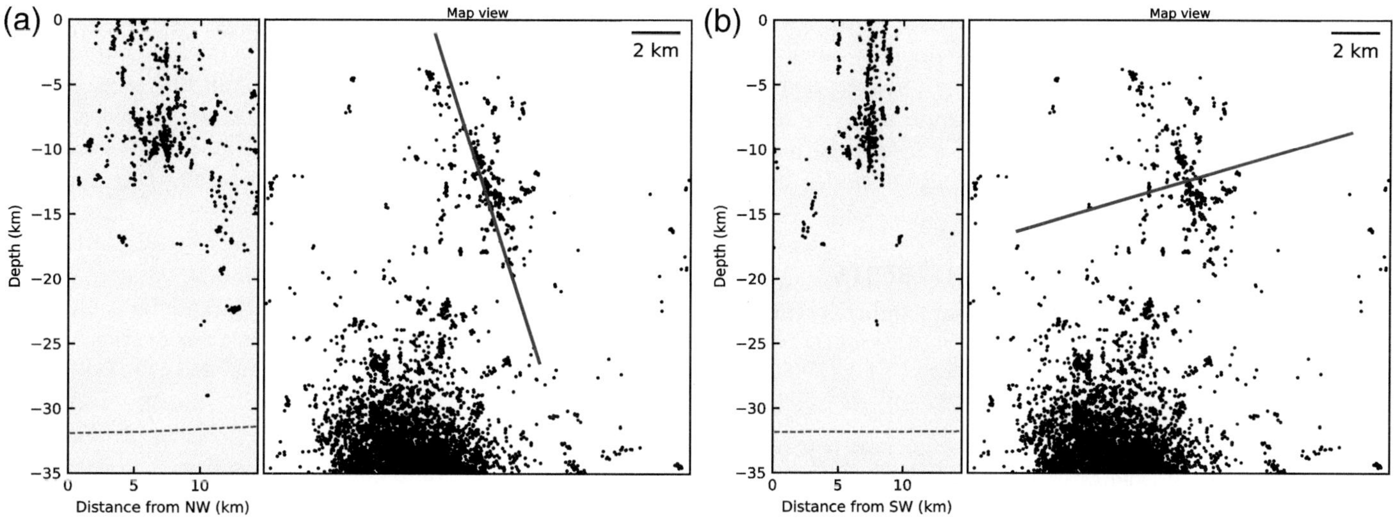

Figure 12. Cross sections of seismicity, featuring the hypocenter region of fault segment N, just north of the dense cloud of 2014 seismicity (Fig. 6). Each vertical cross section contains all events within 4 km of a vertical plane depicted by the red-solid line in the map view at right. (a) North–south cross section aligned with segment N. (b) West–east cross section. The color version of this figure is available only in the electronic edition.

additional questions regarding the structures hosting the strike-slip mechanisms recorded over the past 25 yr (Fig. 7).

Our third finding is that in map view, the persistently diffuse seismicity beneath Nenana basin is caused by vertical-to-northwest-dipping, left-lateral strike-slip faults. Two of these are associated with MFFZ-W (segments H-I-J-K-L) and MFFZ-E (segments A-B-C), and between these two we have interpreted D-E-F-G. In a profile perpendicular to the MFFZ (Fig. 9b), these northwest-dipping faults get progressively deeper from east to west.

A major question remains regarding which fault segments might be active in the next $M_w \geq 6$ earthquake. The 1995 M_w 6.0 earthquake ruptured a small portion of the northern end of the western MFFZ (Fig. 7). What stopped this rupture? Could the projected conjugate fault segment O impede a future rupture? Or the 1990 conjugate structure (Fig. 10) or the proposed conjugate fault Q (Fig. 7)? Large strike-slip earthquake ruptures have illuminated fragmented fault systems, such as the 1992 M_w 7.2 Landers earthquake (Sieh *et al.*, 1993), the 2010 M_w 7.2 El Mayor–Cucapah earthquake (Oskin *et al.*, 2012), and the 2016 M_w 7.8 Kaikōura earthquake (Hamling *et al.*, 2017). A compilation of field observations enabled Wesnousky (2006) to infer the conditions for halting ruptures. At a broader scale—such as the one adopted in compiling the 2023 NSHM—the MFFZ contains two faults (MFFZ-W and MFFZ-E), and each one is long enough to host a $M_w > 7$ earthquake (Tape *et al.*, 2015; Haeussler *et al.*, 2025).

Future efforts to understand the tectonic setting and seismic hazard of the MFFZ can make advances in different realms. Seismologically, the catalogs can be improved via the implementation of machine learning workflows to detect more *S* waves and therefore more events (Zhu and Beroza, 2019; Mousavi *et al.*, 2020). Our study is built on events and picks from the AEC catalog and contains >250,000 *P*-wave arrival picks but only <70,000 *S*-wave arrival picks. Furthermore, advanced relocation methods could take into account the extremely heterogeneous 3D structure of the region, including the Nenana basin, to improve the relocated catalog. The estimation of source mechanisms using waveform data, as well as first-motion data, should enable expansion of the set 25 reference events (Fig. 7). Uncertainties in these mechanisms (Thurin *et al.*, 2025) could be formally integrated into interpretations of faulting. Geophysical (Dixit *et al.*, 2017), geodetic (Cross and Freymueller, 2008), and seismological findings provide a foundation for pursuing a computational model of the deformation occurring in the MFFZ. Such an approach could focus on either the long-term evolution of the basin, to reach its current structure, or the active state of deformation, involving conjugate strike-slip faulting and deep sub-basin seismicity.

DATA AND RESOURCES

The relocated seismicity catalog is available from Sims *et al.* (2025), which also includes a complete set of cross sections, including those in Figures 8 and 9. All waveforms used in this study are accessible from the EarthScope Data Management Center (DMC). We accessed the waveforms from the local databases at the Alaska Earthquake Center (AEC). We used a subset of stations from the following seismic networks (Fig. 1): AK (doi: 10.7914/SN/AK), XV (Tape *et al.*, 2018; doi: 10.7914/SN/XV_2014), TA (Busby and Aderhold, 2020; doi: 10.7914/SN/TA), IU (Ringler *et al.*, 2020; doi: 10.7914/SN/IU), and the ILAR array (generic network code IM) operated by Eielson Air Force Base. All websites were last accessed in October 2025. We used several open-source software packages, including QGIS (QGIS Development Team, 2025), EQcorrscan (Chamberlain *et al.*, 2017), GrowClust (Trugman and Shearer, 2017), and Pyrocko (Heimann *et al.*, 2019), to plot moment tensor beachballs in cross sections. The reference source mechanisms (Fig. 7) were estimated in previous studies using CAP and MTUQ (Zhu and Helmberger, 1996; Silwal and Tape, 2016; Thurin *et al.*, 2025). Figures 2 and 3 were created in QGIS using ArcGIS basemaps by Esri. For more information about Esri software, please visit www.esri.com. Figure 1 was prepared using OpenTopoMap basemaps (OpenStreetMap contributors, Shuttle Radar Topography Mission [SRTM]). The supplemental material contains figures pertaining to the relocated seismicity catalog, including parameter testing.

DECLARATION OF COMPETING INTERESTS

The authors acknowledge that there are no conflicts of interest recorded.

ACKNOWLEDGMENTS

The authors are grateful for detailed manuscript reviews by Adam Ringler, Steven Gibbons, and David Shelly. This study was supported by Grants EAR-1352668 (Fault Locations and Alaska Tectonics from Seismicity [FLATS] project), EAR-1645313, and OAC 2104052 (SCOPED project) from the National Science Foundation (NSF). Seismic data recorded by the Alaska Earthquake Center (AEC) are made possible by support from U.S. Geological Survey (USGS) Advanced National Seismic System (ANSS) program cooperative agreement G25AC00133. The FLATS project was supported in the field by Kyle Smith; its telemetry was enabled by AEC. Matt Gardine provided support in accessing waveforms from the AEC. Stephen Holtkamp, Yoshihiro Kaneko, and Elisabeth Nadin provided helpful discussions. Any use of trade, firm, or product names is for descriptive purposes only and does not imply endorsement by the U.S. Government.

REFERENCES

Beaudoin, B. C., G. S. Fuis, W. D. Mooney, W. J. Nokleberg, and N. I. Christensen (1992). Thin, low-velocity crust beneath the southern Yukon-Tanana terrane, east central Alaska: Results from Trans-Alaska Crustal Transect refraction/wide-angle reflection data, *J. Geophys. Res.* **97,** no. B2, 1921–1942.

Bemis, S. P., and W. K. Wallace (2007). Neotectonic framework of the north-central Alaska Range foothills, in *Tectonic Growth of a Collisional Continental Margin: Crustal Evolution of Southern Alaska*, K. D. Ridgway, J. M. Trop, J. M. G. Glen, and J. M. O'Neill (Editors), Geol. Soc. Am. Special Paper 431, Boulder, Colorado, 549–572.

Bemis, S. P., G. A. Carver, and R. D. Koehler (2012). The Quaternary thrust system of the northern Alaska Range, *Geosphere* **8,** no. 1, 1–10.

Bird, P. (2003). An updated digital model of plate boundaries, *Geochem. Geophy. Geosys.* **4,** 1–52.

Biswas, N. N., and G. Tytgat (1988). Intraplate seismicity in Alaska, *Seismol. Res. Lett.* **59,** no. 4, 227–233.

Brueseke, M. E., J. A. Benowitz, J. M. Trop, K. N. Davis, S. E. Berkelhammer, P. W. Layer, and B. K. Morter (2019). The Alaska Wrangell Arc: ~30 Ma of subduction-related magmatism along a still active arc-transform junction, *Terra Nova* **31,** 59–66.

Busby, R. W., and K. Aderhold (2020). The Alaska Transportable Array: As built, *Seismol. Res. Lett.* **91,** no. 6, 3017–3027.

Chamberlain, C. J., C. J. Hopp, C. M. Boese, E. Warren-Smith, D. Chambers, S. X. Chu, K. Michailos, and J. Townend (2017). EQcorrscan: Repeating and near-repeating earthquake detection and analysis in Python, *Seismol. Res. Lett.* **89,** 173–181.

Chang, T.-W., and S. Ide (2021). Hypocenter hotspots illuminated using a new cross-correlation-based hypocenter and centroid relocation method, *J. Geophys. Res.: Solid Earth* **126,** 1–26.

Christeson, G. L., S. P. S. Gulick, H. J. A. van Avendonk, L. L. Worthington, R. S. Reece, and T. L. Pavlis (2010). The Yakutat terrane: Dramatic change in crustal thickness across the Transition fault, Alaska, *Geology* **38,** no. 10, 895–898.

Coffman, J. L., and C. A. von Hake (1984). United States Earthquakes, 1972, *U.S. Geol. Surv. Open-File Rept. 84-972.*

Cross, R. S., and J. T. Freymueller (2008). Evidence for and implications of a Bering plate based on geodetic measurements from the Aleutians and western Alaska, *J. Geophys. Res.* **113,** 1–19.

Daly, K. A., G. A. Abers, M. E. Mann, S. Roecker, and D. H. Christensen (2021). Subduction of an oceanic plateau across southcentral Alaska: High-resolution seismicity, *J. Geophys. Res.: Solid Earth* **126,** 1–18.

Dixit, N., and C. Hanks (2021). Basement structure and styles of active tectonic deformation in central Interior Alaska, *Geosciences* **11,** no. 3, 1–25.

Dixit, N., C. Hanks, A. Rizzo, P. McCarthy, and B. Coakley (2017). Cenozoic tectonic and thermal history of the Nenana basin, central interior Alaska: New constraints from seismic reflection data, fracture history, and apatite fission-track analyses, *Can. J. Earth Sci.* **54,** 766–784.

Eberhart-Phillips, D., D. H. Christensen, T. M. Brocher, R. Hansen, N. A. Ruppert, P. J. Haeussler, and G. A. Abers (2006). Imaging the transition from Aleutian subduction to Yakutat collision in central Alaska, with local earthquakes and active source data, *J. Geophys. Res.* **111,** 1–31.

Eberhart-Phillips, D., P. J. Haeussler, J. T. Freymueller, A. D. Frankel, C. M. Rubin, P. Craw, N. A. Ratchkovski, G. Anderson, G. A. Carver, A. J. Crone, *et al.* (2003). The 2002 Denali fault earthquake, Alaska: A large magnitude, slip-partitioned event, *Science* **300,** 1113–1118.

Ekström, G., M. Nettles, and A. M. Dziewoński (2012). The global GCMT project 2004–2010: Centroid-moment tensors for 13,017 earthquakes, *Phys. Earth Planet. In.* **200-201,** 1–9.

Estabrook, C. H., D. B. Stone, and J. N. Davies (1988). Seismotectonics of northern Alaska, *J. Geophys. Res.* **93,** no. B10, 12,026–12,040.

Fuis, G. S., T. E. Moore, G. Plafker, T. M. Brocher, M. A. Fisher, W. D. Mooney, W. J. Nokleberg, R. A. Page, B. C. Beaudoin, N. I. Christensen, *et al.* (2008). Trans-Alaska Crustal Transect and continental evolution involving subduction underplating and synchronous foreland thrusting, *Geology* **36,** no. 3, 267–270.

Gabrielse, H., D. C. Murphy, and J. K. Mortensen (2006). Cretaceous and Cenozoic dextral orogen-parallel displacements, magmatism, and paleogeography, north-central Canadian Cordillera, in *Paleogeography of the North American Cordillera: Evidence For and Against Large-Scale Displacements*, J. W. Haggart, R. J. Enkin, and J. W. H. Monger (Editors), Geological Association of Canada, Special Paper 46, 255–276.

Gedney, L., S. Estes, and N. Biswas (1980). Earthquake migration in the Fairbanks, Alaska seismic zone, *Bull. Seismol. Soc. Am.* **70,** no. 1, 223–241.

Gedney, L., L. Shapiro, and D. VanWormer (1972). Correlation of epicenters with mapped Faults, East-Central Alaska, 1968–1971, *U.S. Geol. Surv. Open-File Rept. 72-128*, 7 pp., 1 map.

Gibbons, S. J., and F. Ringdal (2006). The detection of low magnitude seismic events using array-based waveform correlation, *Geophys. J. Int.* **165,** 149–166.

Gibbons, S. J., N. A. Ruppert, E. Karasözen, K. Aderhold, and I. Dickson (2020). Resolving northern Alaska earthquake sequences using the transportable array and probabilistic location methods, *Seismol. Res. Lett.* **91,** no. 6, 3028–3038.

Haeussler, P. J., A. M. Bender, P. M. Powers, R. D. Koehler, and D. S. Brothers (2025). Updating the crustal fault model for the 2023 National Seismic Hazard Model for Alaska, in *Tectonics and Seismic Structure of Alaska and Northwestern Canada: EarthScope and Beyond*, N. A. Ruppert, M. A. Jadamec, and J. T. Freymueller (Editors), Vol. 290, Geophysical Monograph, American Geophysical Union, Washington, D.C., 85–127.

Haeussler, P. J., D. P. Schwartz, T. E. Dawson, H. D. Stenner, J. J. Lienkaemper, B. Sherrod, F. R. Cinti, P. Montone, P. A. Craw, A. J. Crone, *et al.* (2004). Surface rupture and slip distribution of the Denali and Totschunda faults in the 3 November 2002 **M** 7.9 earthquake, Alaska, *Bull. Seismol. Soc. Am.* **94,** no. 6B, S23–S52.

Hamling, I. J., S. Hreinsdóttir, K. Clark, J. Elliott, C. Liang, E. Fielding, N. Litchfield, P. Villamor, L. Wallace, T. J. Wright, *et al.* (2017). Complex multifault rupture during the 2016 M_w 7.8 Kaikōura earthquake, New Zealand, *Science* **154,** 1–10.

Hauksson, E., W. Yang, and P. M. Shearer (2012). Waveform relocated earthquake catalog for southern California (1981 to June 2011), *Bull. Seismol. Soc. Am.* **102,** no. 5, 2239–2244.

Heimann, S., H. Vasyura-Bathke, H. Sudhaus, M. P. Isken, M. Kriegerowski, A. Steinberg, and T. Dahm (2019). A Python framework for efficient use of pre-computed Green's functions in seismological and other physical forward and inverse source problems, *Solid Earth* **10,** 1921–1935.

Hotovec-Ellis, A. J., D. R. Shelly, D. P. Hill, A. M. Pitt, P. B. Dawson, and B. A. Chouet (2018). Deep fluid pathways beneath Mammoth Mountain, California, illuminated by migrating earthquake swarms, *Sci. Adv.* **4,** 1–7.

Huang, H., L. Meng, M. Plasencia, Y. Wang, L. Wang, and M. Xu (2017). Matched-filter detection of the missing pre-mainshock events and aftershocks in the 2015 Gorkha, Nepal earthquake sequence, *Tectonophysics* **714–715,** 71–81.

Kato, A., and S. Nakagawa (2014). Multiple slow-slip events during a foreshock sequence of the 2014 Iquique, Chile M_w 8.1 earthquake, *Geophys. Res. Lett.* **41,** 5420–5427.

Koehler, R. D., and G. A. Carver (2018). Active faults and seismic hazards in Alaska, *Alaska Div. Geol. Geophys. Surv., Misc. Publ. 160*, 59 pp., doi: 10.14509/29705.

Koehler, R. D., R.-E. Farrell, P. A. C. Burns, and R. A. Combellick (2012). Quaternary faults and folds in Alaska: A digital database, *Alaska Div. Geol. Geophys. Surv. Misc. Publ. 141*, 31 pp., 1 sheet, scale 1:3,700,000.

Koehler, R. D., R. D. Reger, E. R. Spangler, and A. I. Gould (2015). Investigation of potentially active tectonic faults along the route of the proposed Alaska Stand Alone Pipeline, Livengood to Cook Inlet, *Alaska. Alaska Div. Geol. Geophys. Surv., Report of Investigation 2015-4*, 71 pp.

Li, J., G. A. Abers, Y. Kim, and D. Christensen (2013). Alaska megathrust 1: Seismicity 43 years after the great 1964 Alaska megathrust earthquake, *J. Geophys. Res.: Solid Earth* **118,** 4861–4871.

Mackey, K. G., K. Fujita, L. V. Gunbina, V. N. Kovalev, V. S. Imaev, B. M. Koz'min, and L. P. Imaeva (1997). Seismicity of the Bering Strait region: Evidence for a Bering block, *Geology* **25,** no. 11, 979–982.

Matoza, R. S., P. M. Shearer, G. Lin, C. J. Wolfe, and P. G. Okubo (2013). Systematic relocation of seismicity on Hawaii Island from 1992 to 2009 using waveform cross correlation and cluster analysis, *J. Geophys. Res.: Solid Earth* **118,** 2275–2288.

Miller, M. S., and L. Moresi (2018). Mapping the Alaska Moho, *Seismol. Res. Lett.* **89,** no. 6, 2430–2436.

Mousavi, S. M., W. L. Ellsworth, W. Zhu, L. Y. Chuang, and G. C. Beroza (2020). Earthquake transformer—An attentive deep-learning model for simultaneous earthquake detection and phase picking, *Nat. Commun.* **2,** 1–12.

Neumann, F. (1940). United States Earthquakes 1937, U.S. Department of Commerce.

Oskin, M. E., J. R. Arrowsmith, A. H. Corona, A. J. Elliott, J. M. Fletcher, E. J. Fielding, P. O. Gold, J. J. G. Garcia, K. W. Hudnut, J. Liu-Zeng, *et al.* (2012). Near-field deformation from the El Mayor–Cucapah earthquake revealed by differential LIDAR, *Science* **335,** 702–705.

Page, R. A., N. N. Biswas, J. C. Lahr, and H. Pulpan (1991). Seismicity of continental Alaska, in *Neotectonics of North America*, D. B. Slemmons, E. R. Engdahl, M. D. Zoback, and D. D. Blackwell (Editors), Vol. 1, The Geology of North America, Chapter 4, Geol. Soc. Am. Decade Map, Boulder, Colorado, 47–68.

Page, R. A., G. Plafker, and H. Pulpan (1995). Block rotation in east-central Alaska: A framework for evaluating earthquake potential? *Geology* **23,** no. 7, 629–632.

Patton, W. W., Jr., and J. M. Hoare (1968). The Kaltag fault, west-central Alaska, in *Geological Survey Research 1968*, U.S. Government Printing Office, Washington, D.C., Professional Paper 600-D, D147–D153.

Péwé, T. L., C. Wahrhaftig, and F. R. Weber (1966). Geologic Map of the Fairbanks Quadrangle, *U.S. Geol. Surv. Misc. Investig. Series I-455.*

Powers, P. M., J. M. Altekruse, A. L. Llenos, A. J. Michael, K. L. Haynie, P. J. Haeussler, A. M. Bender, S. Rezaeian, M. P. Moschetti, J. A. Smith, *et al.* (2024). The 2023 Alaska National Seismic Hazard Model, *Earthq. Spectra* **40,** no. 4, 2545–2597.

Petrotechnical Resources of Alaska (PRA) (2017). Depth to Basement Map of Nenana Basin, Alaska, Petrotechnical Resources of Alaska.

Pulpan, H. (1988). Seismic-hazard analysis of the Nenana agricultural development area, Central Alaska, *Alaska Div. Geol. Geophys. Surv. Report of Investigations 88-1.*

QGIS Development Team (2025). QGIS geographic information system, *Open Source Geospatial Foundation Project*, available at http://qgis.org.

Ratchkovski, N. A., and R. A. Hansen (2002a). New constraints on tectonics of interior Alaska: Earthquake locations, source mechanisms, and stress regime, *Bull. Seismol. Soc. Am.* **92,** no. 3, 998–1014.

Ratchkovski, N. A., and R. A. Hansen (2002b). New evidence for segmentation of the Alaska subduction zone, *Bull. Seismol. Soc. Am.* **92,** no. 5, 1754–1765.

Redfield, T. F., D. W. Scholl, P. G. Fitzgerald, and M. E. Beck Jr. (2007). Escape tectonics and the extrusion of Alaska: Past, present, and future, *Geology* **35,** no. 11, 1039–1042.

Ringler, A. T., J. Steim, D. C. Wilson, R. Widmer-Schnidrig, and R. E. Anthony (2020). Improvements in seismic resolution and current

limitations in the Global Seismographic Network, *Geophys. J. Int.* **220,** 508–521.
Ross, Z. E., E. Hauksson, and Y. Ben-Zion (2017). Abundant off-fault seismicity and orthogonal structures in the San Jacinto fault zone, *Sci. Adv.* **3,** 1–8.
Rubin, A. M., D. Gillard, and J.-L. Got (1991). Streaks of microearthquakes along creeping faults, *Nature* **400,** 635–641.
Saltus, R. W. (2007). Matching magnetic trends and patterns across the Tintina fault, Alaska and Canada—Evidence for offset of about 490 kilometers, in *Recent U.S. Geological Survey Studies in the Tintina Gold Province, Alaska, United States, and Yukon, Canada—Results of a 5-Year Project*, L. P. Gough and W. C. Day (Editors), *U.S. Geol. Survey Sci. Investig. Report 2007-5289-C*, C1–C7.
Schaff, D. P., and P. G. Richards (2014). Improvements in magnitude precision, using the statistics of relative amplitudes measured by cross correlation, *Geophys. J. Int.* **197,** 335–350.
Shelly, D. R. (2020). A high-resolution seismic catalog for the initial 2019 Ridgecrest earthquake sequence: Foreshocks, aftershocks, and faulting complexity, *Seismol. Res. Lett.* **91,** no. 4, 1971–1978.
Shelly, D. R., G. C. Beroza, and S. Ide (2007). Non-volcanic tremor and low-frequency earthquake swarms, *Nature* **446,** 305–307.
Sieh, K., L. Jones, E. Hauksson, K. Hudnut, D. Eberhart-Phillips, T. Heaton, S. Hough, K. Hutton, H. Kanamori, A. Lilje, *et al.* (1993). Near-field investigations of the Landers earthquake sequence, April to July 1992, *Science* **260,** 171–176.
Silwal, V. (2015). Seismic moment tensor catalog for Minto Flats fault zone (2000–2014), *ScholarWorks@UA*, available at http://hdl.handle.net/11122/6267 (last accessed January 2016): descriptor file, text file of catalog, composite figures of waveform fits and depth searches.
Silwal, V. (2018). Seismic moment tensors for six events in the Minto Flats fault zone, 2012–2016, *ScholarWorks@UA*, available at http://hdl.handle.net/11122/8253 (last accessed October 2025): descriptor file, text file of catalog, figures with waveform fits, and input weight files.
Silwal, V., and C. Tape (2016). Seismic moment tensors and estimated uncertainties in southern Alaska, *J. Geophys. Res.: Solid Earth* **121,** 2772–2797.
Sims, N., C. Tape, N. Ruppert, and M. West (2025). Earthquake catalog and seismicity cross sections for "High precision earthquake catalog for Minto Flats fault zone, central Alaska, reveals complex and conjugate faulting" [Data set], *Zenodo*, doi: 10.5281/zenodo.16278806.
Skoumal, R. J., M. R. Brudzinski, B. S. Currie, and J. Levy (2014). Optimizing multi-station earthquake template matching through re-examination of the Youngstown, Ohio, sequence, *Earth Planet. Sci. Lett.* **405,** 274–280.
Smith, K. (2020). Seismic moment tensor catalog for local and regional earthquakes recorded in Nenana basin, central Alaska, *ScholarWorks@UA*, available at http://hdl.handle.net/11122/10984 (last accessed April 2020): descriptor file, text file of catalog, figures with waveform fits, and input weight files.
Smith, K., and C. Tape (2019). Seismic noise in central Alaska and influences from rivers, wind, and sedimentary basins, *J. Geophys. Res.: Solid Earth* **124,** 11,678–11,704.
Smith, K., C. Tape, and V. C. Tsai (2023). Seismic response of Nenana sedimentary basin, central Alaska, *Bull. Seismol. Soc. Am.* **113,** no. 2, 762–781.
Tape, C., S. Holtkamp, V. Silwal, J. Hawthorne, Y. Kaneko, J. P. Ampuero, C. Ji, N. Ruppert, K. Smith, and M. E. West (2018). Earthquake nucleation and fault slip complexity in the lower crust of central Alaska, *Nature Geosci.* **11,** 536–541.
Tape, C., A. Lomax, V. Silwal, J. D. Agnew, and B. Brettschneider (2017). The 1904 M_s 7.3 earthquake in central Alaska, *Bull. Seismol. Soc. Am.* **107,** no. 3, 1147–1174.
Tape, C., V. Silwal, C. Ji, L. Keyson, M. E. West, and N. Ruppert (2015). Transtensional tectonics of the Minto Flats fault zone and Nenana basin, central Alaska, *Bull. Seismol. Soc. Am.* **105,** no. 4, 2081–2100.
Tape, C., M. West, V. Silwal, and N. Ruppert (2013). Earthquake nucleation and triggering on an optimally oriented fault, *Earth Planet. Sci. Lett.* **363,** 231–241.
Thurin, J., R. Modrak, C. Tape, A. McPherson, F. R. Rodríguez-Cardozo, J. Kintner, L. Ding, Q. Liu, and J. Braunmiller (2025). MTUQ: A framework for estimating moment tensors, point forces, and their uncertainties, *Geophys. J. Int.* **241,** 1373–1390.
Trugman, D. T., and P. M. Shearer (2017). GrowClust: A hierarchical clustering algorithm for relative earthquake relocation, with application to the Spanish Springs and Sheldon, Nevada, earthquake sequences, *Seismol. Res. Lett.* **88,** 379–391.
Van Kooten, G. K., M. Richter, and P. A. Zippi (2012). Alaska's Interior rift basins: A new frontier for discovery, *Oil Gas J.* **110,** no. 1a, 48–57.
Waldhauser, F., and W. L. Ellsworth (2000). A double-difference earthquake location algorithm: Method and application to the Northern Hayward fault, California, *Bull. Seismol. Soc. Am.* **90,** no. 6, 1353–1368.
Waldhauser, F., and D. P. Schaff (2008). Large-scale relocation of two decades of Northern California seismicity using cross-correlation and double-difference methods, *J. Geophys. Res.* **113,** 1–12.
Waldien, T. S., S. M. Roeske, and J. A. Benowitz (2021). Tectonic underplating and dismemberment of the Maclaren-Kluane schist records Late Cretaceous terrane accretion polarity and ~480 km of post-52 Ma dextral displacement on the Denali fault, *Tectonics* **40,** 1–35.
Wesnousky, S. G. (2006). Predicting the endpoints of earthquake ruptures, *Nature* **444,** 358–360.
White, M. C. A., Y. Ben-Zion, and F. L. Vernon (2019). A detailed earthquake catalog for the San Jacinto fault-zone region in southern California, *J. Geophys. Res.: Solid Earth* **124,** 6908–6930.
Zanjani, F. A., and G. Lin (2022). Double seismic zones along the Eastern Aleutian-Alaska subduction zone revealed by a high-precision earthquake relocation catalog, *Seismol. Res. Lett.* **93,** no. 5, 2753–2769.
Zhu, L., and D. Helmberger (1996). Advancement in source estimation techniques using broadband regional seismograms, *Bull. Seismol. Soc. Am.* **86,** no. 5, 1634–1641.
Zhu, W., and G. C. Beroza (2019). PhaseNet: A deep-neural-network-based seismic arrival-time picking method, *Geophys. J. Int.* **216,** 261–273.

Manuscript received 25 July 2025
Published online 4 November 2025

Spatiotemporal Variation in Ambient Seismic Noise and Its Effect on the Microearthquake Monitoring Capability of the Pohang Community Seismograph Network (PCSN), South Korea

Yujin Sohn[1], Kwang-Hee Kim[*1], Tae-Seob Kang[2], Byung Seok Ahn[2], Dabeen Heo[3,4], and Hyungjin Jeon[5]

ABSTRACT

Ambient seismic noise from human activities, site conditions, meteorology, and instrument self-noise limits earthquake monitoring. We characterize noise in the Pohang Community Seismograph Network (PCSN), deployed after the 2017 M_w 5.5 Pohang earthquake, using power spectral density (PSD) estimates. The PCSN stations were categorized into four groups based on their location and depth: rural, urban, coastal, and borehole array. We compared PSDs across different period ranges. At very short periods (< 0.03 s), we could occasionally identify elevated noise levels caused by everyday weather conditions. The seismic signature of rainfall was clearly recorded at surface stations, but barely recorded at 500 m depth. At short periods (0.02–1.00 s), anthropogenic noise was predominant. The noise levels were highest in urban areas, followed by coastal areas, and lowest in rural areas. At long periods (1–10 s), we investigated the effect of typhoons and ocean waves. As typhoons Hinnamnor and Nanmadol approached the Korean Peninsula, the background noise level increased and reached a peak as it passed the Pohang region. The geological setting affected the ambient seismic noise: the PSDs of the horizontal component are higher than those of the vertical component in areas with thick sediments. The detection thresholds map in the Pohang region shows the smallest magnitude in the middle of the network in regions surrounded by stations with low-ambient noise levels. The recently compiled PCSN earthquake catalog demonstrates the effect of background noise on earthquake detection capability. The number of detected earthquakes under the magnitude of completeness (0.34) was 53 at night and 5 during the day. These findings underscore the importance of reducing ambient noise levels by relocating or installing seismic stations at depth on bedrock for effective microearthquake observations in a densely populated metropolitan area.

KEY POINTS

- Analyzing ambient noise is important in establishing seismograph networks for microearthquake monitoring.
- We analyze the effect of ambient noise on the Pohang Community Seismograph Network using power spectral density estimates.
- Ambient noise, caused by various factors in different period ranges, is greatly reduced at depth.

Supplemental Material

INTRODUCTION

The earthquake in Pohang, Korea, on 15 November 2017 had a moment magnitude (M_w) of 5.5 and was triggered by industrial activity during unsuccessful attempts to establish an

1. Department of Geological Sciences, Pusan National University, Busan, Republic of Korea, https://orcid.org/0000-0002-9944-9849 (YS); https://orcid.org/0000-0001-9931-7996 (K-HK); 2. Division of Earth Environmental System Science, Pukyong National University, Busan, Republic of Korea, https://orcid.org/0000-0002-0894-1468 (T-SK); https://orcid.org/0000-0002-7482-6273 (BSA); 3. The Institute of Basic Science, Korea University, Seoul, Republic of Korea, https://orcid.org/0000-0003-4086-8042 (DH); 4. Institute of Environmental Geoscience, Pukyong National University, Busan, Republic of Korea; 5. TerraEG, Seoul, Republic of Korea, https://orcid.org/0009-0002-0117-7791 (HJ)

*Corresponding author: kwanghee@pusan.ac.kr

Cite this article as Sohn, Y., K.-H. Kim, T.-S. Kang, B. S. Ahn, D. Heo, and H. Jeon (2025). Spatiotemporal Variation in Ambient Seismic Noise and Its Effect on the Microearthquake Monitoring Capability of the Pohang Community Seismograph Network (PCSN), South Korea, *Bull. Seismol. Soc. Am.* **116**, 397–414, doi: 10.1785/0120250107 underground geothermal reservoir (Grigoli *et al.*, 2018; Kim *et al.*, 2018; Ellsworth *et al.*, 2019; Korean Government Commission on the Cause of the Pohang Earthquake, 2019; Lee *et al.*, 2019; Woo *et al.*, 2019). The earthquake was the most damaging since the start of instrumental seismic observations in Korea in 1905 (Ministry of Interior and Safety [MOIS], 2018). The damage was unprecedented because the epicentral area had not experienced a damaging earthquake in historical times. Establishing a reliable earthquake monitoring system in the Pohang area is one of the main efforts to establish and enforce earthquake safety and risk policies. Although the frequency and magnitude of earthquakes in the area have decreased steadily, continued small, shallow seismicity remains a serious concern for local government and the community, who still suffer from post-traumatic stress disorder stemming from their experiences during the mainshock and aftershocks (Seo and Lee, 2020; Joe *et al.*, 2023). For example, a small earthquake with a local magnitude of 2.3 on the night of 26 September 2019 was felt by local residents and caused distress. Local site conditions that amplify earthquake ground motion and shallow focal depths (mostly 2–6 km) also make residents in the area sensitive to small earthquakes. Repeated small earthquakes and widespread concern forced seismic network operators to target microearthquakes when establishing the monitoring system. Moreover, the monitoring area is not limited to the vicinity of the mainshock epicenter. Studies have shown that rupturing buried faults grow laterally with time (Kim *et al.*, 2020; Son *et al.*, 2020; Woo *et al.*, 2020; Ree *et al.*, 2021; Heo *et al.*, 2024). In addition to the earthquake distribution, felt reports during the mainshock and aftershocks indicate that the decrease in intensity with distance from the epicenter was far from uniform (MOIS, 2024a). These observations mean that the seismic monitoring network must encompass a wide area to provide shaking intensity information to administrators and residents who experienced strong shaking during the 2017–2018 events. In addition, the monitoring system should be able to deal with diverse surface and subsurface settings, including residential areas with population densities of up to 15,748 people/km^2, business districts, industrial parks, farmland, and heavily forested mountain regions. The monitoring area is also on the coast, which experiences steady or fluctuating ocean waves, thereby reducing the microearthquake monitoring capability. All these issues require continuous monitoring and characterization of the background noise to evaluate network capability and achieve the goals of the monitoring project.

Seismometers record both earthquake waveforms and background noise. Ambient seismic noise can be generated through diverse mechanisms. Previous studies have investigated the causes of background noise at various frequencies or periods. At a period of <1 s, anthropogenic noise is the most common source, including factories, trains, and road traffic (e.g., McNamara and Buland, 2004; Vassallo *et al.*, 2012; Anthony *et al.*, 2015, 2022; Lecocq *et al.*, 2020; Uthaman *et al.*, 2022). At periods of 3–10 s, ocean waves contribute to the background noise. For example, large oceanic storms (e.g., typhoons) generate seismic background noise through the superposition of ocean waves of equal period traveling in opposite directions (Longuet-Higgins, 1950); consequently, the approach of the storm to the station is recorded by an increase in the ambient noise level (Sheen *et al.*, 2009; Chi, Chen, *et al.*, 2010; Chi, Chen, and Kuo, 2010; Lee *et al.*, 2012; Park *et al.*, 2016). In addition to extreme weather, the seismic effects of everyday weather, including rainfall, have been evaluated, revealing the seismic signature of rain is prominent at frequencies of >80 Hz (Dean, 2017) or 60–500 Hz (Rindraharisaona *et al.*, 2022).

The ability of seismologists to detect and accurately distinguish earthquakes and other signals of interest is frequently constrained by background seismic noise levels (Sheen and Shin, 2010; Bormann and Wielandt, 2013; Demuth *et al.*, 2016). The lower the background noise level, the higher the expected quality of the data. Microearthquakes in particular are difficult to identify due to their low amplitude and low signal-to-noise ratios (SNRs), and are often overwhelmed by background noise. Therefore, it is important to consider background noise levels at the seismic stations in the Pohang region to monitor microearthquakes effectively. To analyze the seismic background noise recorded in this study, we used the methodology of McNamara and Buland (2004) implemented in the ObsPy Python package (Krischer *et al.*, 2015). This methodology uses a statistical approach to compute the power spectral density (PSD) and characterizes the probability density function (PDF) of the ambient noise.

We characterized the ambient noise levels of the Pohang Community Seismograph Network (PCSN) to study the main features of the background noise, and we discuss spatial and temporal variations, variations with sensor depth, the effects of weather conditions, and the influence of the geological setting in four different period ranges. Finally, we evaluate the earthquake monitoring capability of the PCSN in the 2017 Pohang earthquake region through analysis of the earthquake catalog, detection thresholds, and SNRs. In particular, the utility of borehole sensors is discussed in the context of ambient seismic noise.

DATA AND METHODS

For the long-term monitoring of seismicity in the Pohang region, the Korean government established the PCSN. The PCSN comprises 20 broadband posthole seismic stations at the surface in the Pohang earthquake region and a borehole array at the enhanced geothermal system (EGS) site (Fig. 1; Heo *et al.*, 2024). The borehole array consisted initially of four broadband seismometers at depths of 2.5, 500, 780, and 1400 m; however, the seismometer at 780 m depth failed 35 days after installation, and data recording at 1400 m depth was unsuccessful. Each seismic station at the surface is equipped

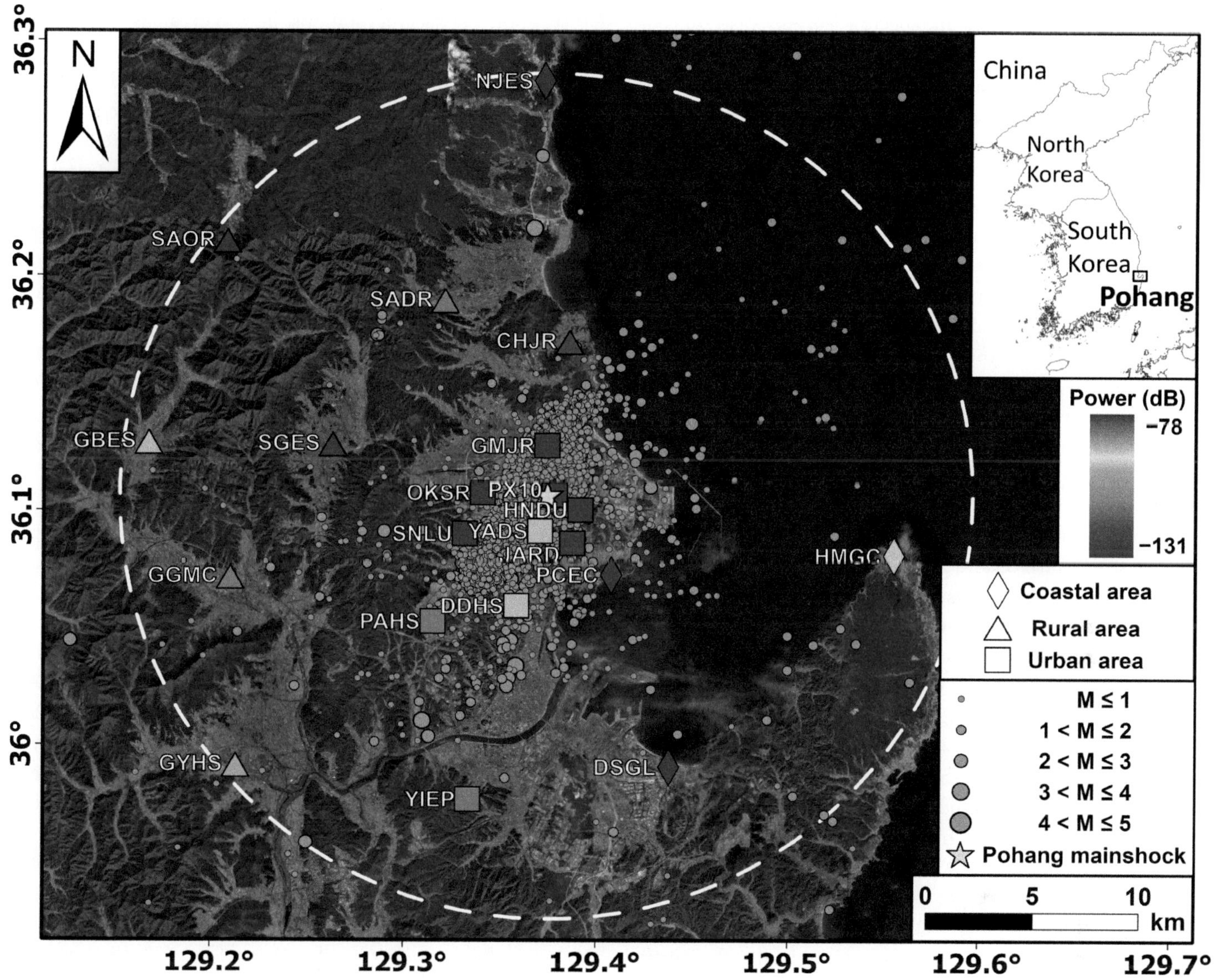

Figure 1. Pohang Community Seismograph Network (PCSN) in the 2017 Pohang earthquake epicenter region. The inset shows the location of the Pohang region on the Korean Peninsula. The white dashed circle represents a 20 km radius around the epicenter of the Pohang earthquake. The symbol color represents the mode of the power spectral density (PSD) values for the vertical component at 0.1 s. Events of the Pohang earthquake sequence between 14 November 2017 and 31 May 2023 (Heo *et al.*, 2024) are shown as circles, and the 2017 M_L 5.4 Pohang earthquake is represented by a yellow star. The color version of this figure is available only in the electronic edition.

with a three-component Nanometrics Trillium Compact Posthole broadband seismic sensor (Nanometrics, 2020) and a Nanometrics Centaur 24-bit digitizer (Nanometrics, 2019). The borehole array contains a Güralp CMG-3T seismometer (Güralp, 2023) at 2.5 m depth and Güralp CMG-3TB seismometers (Güralp, 2019) at greater depths. A Güralp Minimus+ (24 bit; Güralp, 2021) was used as the recorder for the whole borehole array. The stations have been recording data continuously at a rate of 500 samples per second since their installation in May 2021. We examined two years of data, between May 2021 and May 2023, from 20 posthole broadband seismic stations, and 1 year of data (14 May 2022 to May 2023) from two sensors in the borehole array, as they were installed in May 2022.

To estimate the PSD of the ambient noise, we used one-day continuous seismograms over 2 yr, each with a sampling rate of 500 samples per second. For the calculation, continuous time series for each station component were parsed into 1 hr segments that overlapped by 50% and were distributed continuously in time (Cooley and Tukey, 1965). To reduce the variance in the estimated PSD, each 1 hr segment was divided into 13 segments that overlapped by 75%. To speed up the fast Fourier transform (FFT), the number of samples in each of the 13 time-series segments was truncated to a power of 2. The data were transformed to a zero-mean value to minimize the effect of contamination on long-period trends. After applying a 10% cosine taper to the ends of each truncated and detrended time-series segment, spectral leakage was reduced, and the spectrum of each segment was computed by the FFT algorithm. Finally, the instrument response was removed, and the PSD estimate was converted into decibels with respect to an acceleration of 1 $(m/s^2)^2/Hz$ for direct comparison with the new noise models of Peterson (1993). We constructed the PDF of the PSD estimates to investigate the noise level at a given station. The individual PSDs were smoothed using a centered moving mean with a width of 1/8 of an octave. The spectral powers for every 1 hr were binned in 1 dB bins for each period. The probability of occurrence of a given power at a particular period can then be estimated (McNamara and Buland, 2004). The PSD values discussed subsequently are the mode for the vertical component at each station for a given period band.

RESULTS

We analyzed the ambient noise from 20 broadband seismic stations on the surface and 2 sensors in the borehole array. Below, we present the results of the PSD analysis, focusing on spatial and depth considerations. The PCSN has been divided into four categories: rural, urban, coastal, and the borehole array (Fig. 1). The ambient noise with the greatest effect on the earthquake monitoring capability of the seismic network is anthropogenic noise. In addition, given the proximity of the study area to the coast, the ocean could influence the seismic noise level; therefore, the stations were classified as rural, urban, or coastal stations. In addition, despite the borehole array sensors being situated in urban areas, they have been classified separately to analyze variations in ambient noise with depth. Representative PSD PDFs for the east–west, north–south, and vertical components of stations in the PCSN are shown in Figure 2, and the other results are shown in Figures S1–S3, available in the supplemental material to this article, grouped into rural, urban, and coastal areas.

Background noise levels generally increase from rural (Fig. 2a) to urban (Fig. 2b) and finally coastal areas (Fig. 2c), and the seismometer near the surface (Fig. 2d) has a higher background noise level than the sensor installed at greater depth (Fig. 2e). Overall, the horizontal components have noise levels ~20 dB higher than the vertical components, regardless of station siting, at periods of >20 s. From the 22 PCSN stations, we selected five representative stations (SAOR, JARD, PCEC, PX10, and PX11) to examine background noise levels in the relevant period bands.

Seismic stations in rural areas (triangles in Fig. 1) are located near rice fields or forested mountains, for which ambient noise levels caused by human activity are expected to be very low. SAOR station, which is in the middle of the forested mountain area (Figs. 2a, 3a), was selected as representative of rural areas. Most PDFs for rural stations plot between the new low-noise model (NLNM) and the new high-noise model (NHNM) of Peterson (1993) in all period bands.

In contrast, seismic stations in urban areas (squares in Fig. 1) are situated within or near densely populated residential, industrial, or commercial areas and are exposed to various sources of anthropogenic noise. JARD station was chosen as a representative of urban areas because it is situated in the middle of a residential area close to a soccer field and a middle school (Figs. 2b, 3b). Most urban stations have high noise levels at periods of <2 s, higher than the NHNM in all three components.

Seismic stations located in coastal areas (diamonds in Fig. 1) are expected to be more susceptible to noise from sea waves than those in other areas. PCEC station was chosen as a representative of coastal areas because it is the station located closest to the coast (Figs. 2c, 3c). For stations located in coastal areas, the horizontal components mostly exceed the NHNM, whereas the vertical-component plots are between the NLNM and NHNM at periods of >2 s.

The stations installed at the EGS site in a posthole at a depth of 2.5 m (PX10) and in a borehole at a depth of 500 m (PX11) were selected to observe the effect of depth on background noise (Figs. 2d–e, 3d). PX10 has a high noise level, exceeding NHNM at periods of <3 s (Fig. 2d); however, PX11 plots between the NLNM and NHNM for periods of <20 s (Fig. 2e). A problem due to water leakage has been identified as the cause of the increase in moisture levels observed at PX11; therefore, the data for PX11 were restricted to periods of <20 s, thereby limiting the scope and reliability of our interpretations. The lower background noise level is evident in the PSD PDF for PX11, especially at periods of <1 s. At a period of 0.1 s, the PSD was −94.5 dB at a depth of 2.5 m and −127.5 dB at a depth of 500 m. The effect of highway traffic near the EGS site was high at a depth of 2.5 m and decreased by ~33 dB at a depth of 500 m.

To compare with other nationwide seismic networks in South Korea, we chose four seismic stations from the networks of the Korea Meteorological Administration (KMA) and the Korea Institute of Geoscience and Mineral Resources (KIGAM). Figure 4a shows the location and classification of each representative station. We selected the CHS station as a representative of rural areas (Fig. 4b). This rural station has lower ambient noise levels in all period ranges than the rural station of the PCSN (SAOR), and lower levels than the NLNM (Fig. 5). The other stations (GKP2, POHB, and GDDB) are installed in boreholes at a depth of 100 m. We chose the GKP2 and POHB stations as representatives of urban areas. GKP2 is located in similar surroundings to the JARD station, with roads and schools adjacent to the station (Fig. 4c). POHB is located near the borehole array (PX10, PX11) of the PCSN, with a highway passing nearby (Fig. 4d). We selected GDDB as representative of coastal areas because it is 150 m from the coastline (Fig. 4e). However, despite their classification as either urban or coastal stations, their installation at a depth of 100 m reduces the

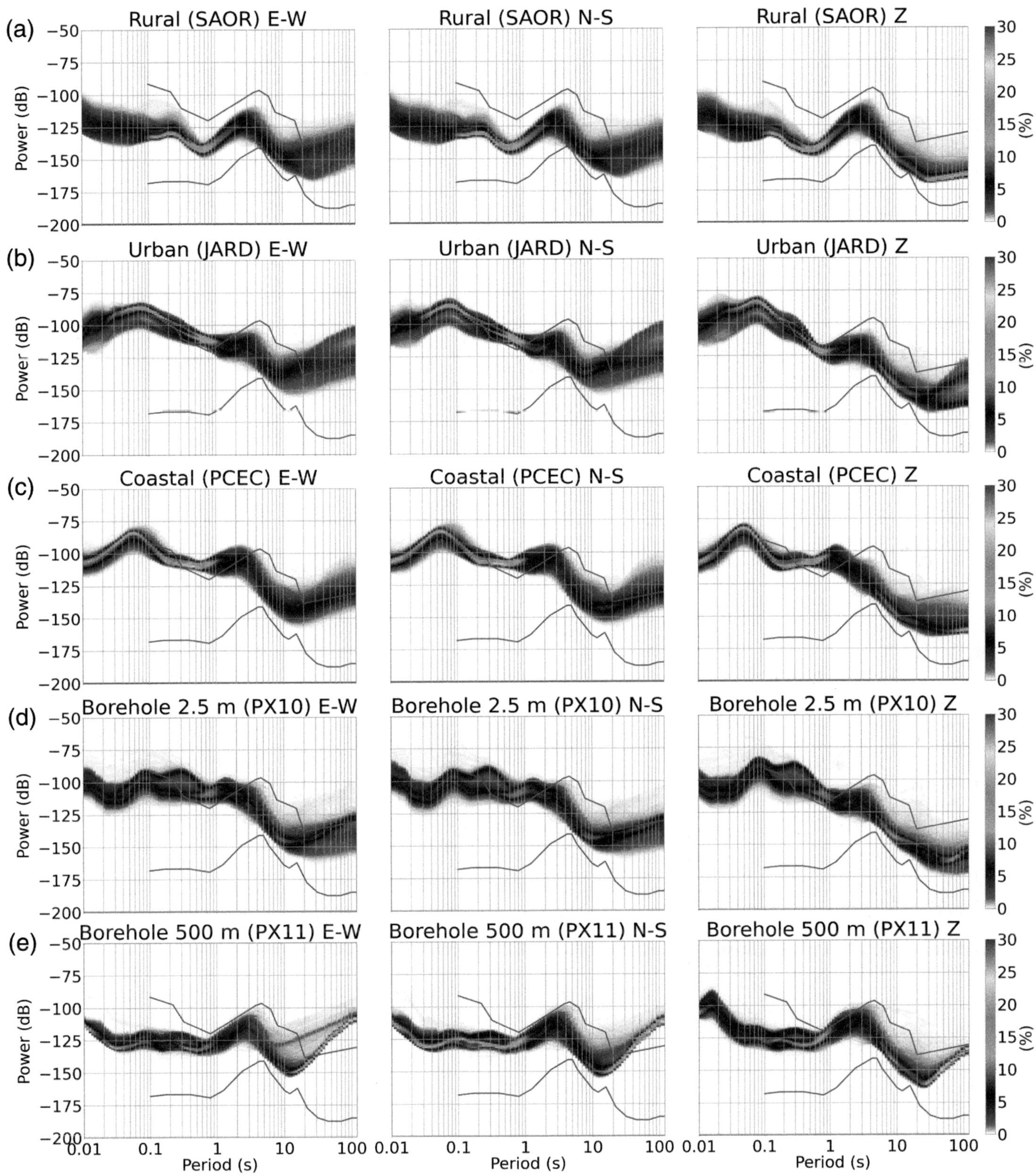

Figure 2. Two-year (May 2021 to May 2023) PSD probability density functions (PDFs) for the three components of representative seismic stations. (a) Rural, (b) urban, and (c) coastal areas, and sensors at (d) 2.5 and (e) 500 m depth in a borehole array. The color represents the probability of noise level at a given period, and the power (dB) on the *y* axis is relative to an acceleration of 1 $(m/s^2)^2/Hz$. The upper and lower gray lines are the new high- and low-noise models (NHNM and NLNM) of Peterson (1993). At all stations, long-period noise levels are higher in the horizontal component than in the vertical component. The color version of this figure is available only in the electronic edition.

Figure 3. Satellite images (left) and site photographs (right) of representative stations in rural, urban, and coastal areas, and the enhanced geothermal system (EGS) site. The symbol for each station on the satellite map corresponds to that in Figure 1. (a) SAOR station, in a rural area, located in the middle of a heavily forested mountain. (b) JARD station, in an urban area, is located between a middle school and a playground. (c) PCEC station, in a coastal area, is the closest station to the coast, which is ~85 m away. (d) The borehole seismic array at the EGS site. A highway with heavy traffic passes close to the array. The color version of this figure is available only in the electronic edition.

background noise levels recorded at these locations to levels that are consistent with the established limits of the NLNM and NHNM.

DISCUSSION

We investigated the variations in ambient seismic noise across different period bands. The influence of anthropogenic noise was examined at short periods (0.02–1.00 s). The seismic signature of weather, specifically precipitation and typhoons, was analyzed in the very short-period (<0.03 s) and long-period (3–10 s) bands, respectively. We also discuss the differences in the PSD between the horizontal and vertical components in relation to the geological setting of the study area. The utility of borehole seismometers was assessed by comparing their ambient seismic noise levels and SNRs with those of posthole seismometers. Finally, the earthquake monitoring capabilities of the PCSN were evaluated spatially and temporally using detection thresholds and earthquake catalog data.

Anthropogenic noise

At short periods (0.02–1.00 s), which are useful for analyzing the dominant effect of anthropogenic noise, background noise originated mostly from human activity. The noise propagates mainly as high-frequency waves that attenuate within several kilometers of the source (Peterson, 1993; McNamara and Buland, 2004). Figure 1 shows the noise levels of the vertical components of stations in PCSN at a period of 0.1 s. Most stations with high noise levels are located in urban areas. The representative station JARD has the highest noise level (−83 dB) in urban areas. As well as the stations in urban areas, the NJES (−78 dB), SGES (−98 dB), and DSGL (−90 dB) stations have high-ambient noise levels. The NJES and SGES stations are located at elementary schools with <60 students. However, the

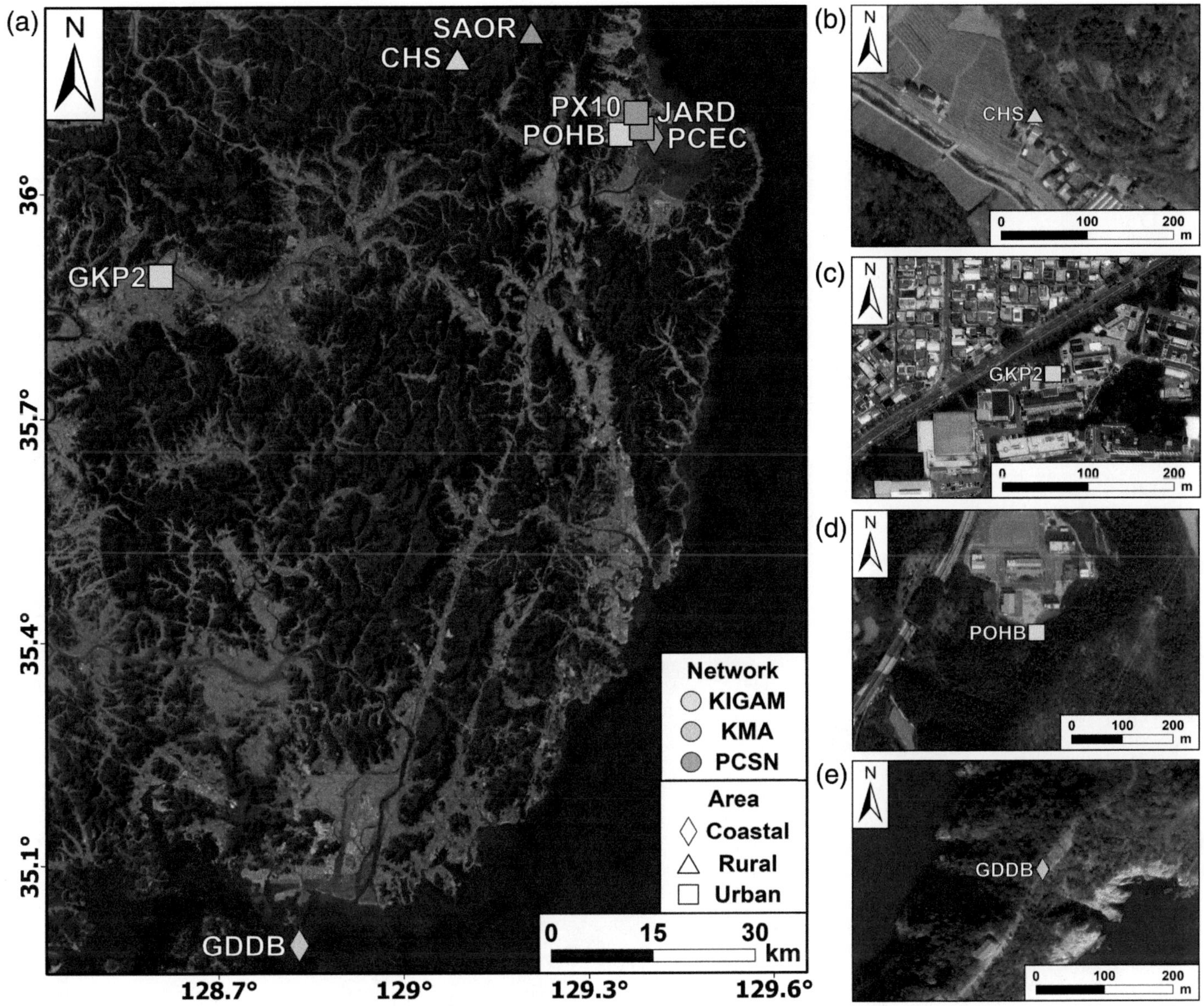

Figure 4. (a) Locations and (b–d) satellite images of representative stations of the network of the Korea Meteorological Administration (KMA) and the Korea Institute of Geoscience and Mineral Resources (KIGAM). The station symbols on the satellite map correspond to those in Figure 1. (b) CHS station, in a rural area, located near the rice fields. (c) GKP2 station, in an urban area, is situated at Kyungpook National University. (d) POHB station, in an urban area, is in close vicinity to the EGS site, with the highway passing by. (e) GDDB station, in a coastal area, is located on an island. The color version of this figure is available only in the electronic edition.

NJES station is installed beside a playground and the SGES station is installed in a parking lot. The DGSL station is located near the highway, within 1 km of Pohang Gyeongju airport. Even though these stations are not located in densely populated areas, their site conditions generate anthropogenic noise and affect the background noise level at short periods.

These high levels of anthropogenic noise can be reduced at a depth of 100 m. The stations of the KMA and KIGAM networks located in urban areas show greatly reduced noise levels at a period of 0.1 s. GKP2 and POHB yield noise levels of −123 and −115 dB, respectively (Fig. 5b–c), whereas JARD and PX10 yield noise levels of up to −83 and −90 dB, respectively.

Figures 6 and 7 show the diurnal and weekly variations at periods of <1 s. The urban and coastal areas have a wider range of noise levels (−110 to −70 dB) than rural areas (−135 to −110 dB). Anthropogenic noise shows strong diurnal variations at all seismic stations. The variation between day and night is greater in stations located in urban areas (~30 dB). Consistent with the results of McNamara and Buland (2004) and Sheen *et al.* (2009), the borehole station (PX11) shows weaker (~15 dB) diurnal variations in the anthropogenic noise band, similar to rural stations. This suggests that much of the ambient noise generated at the surface did not propagate to depth. The difference between weekdays and weekends was difficult to identify at the selected stations; however, the station installed at Pohang Art High School (PAHS) shows clear

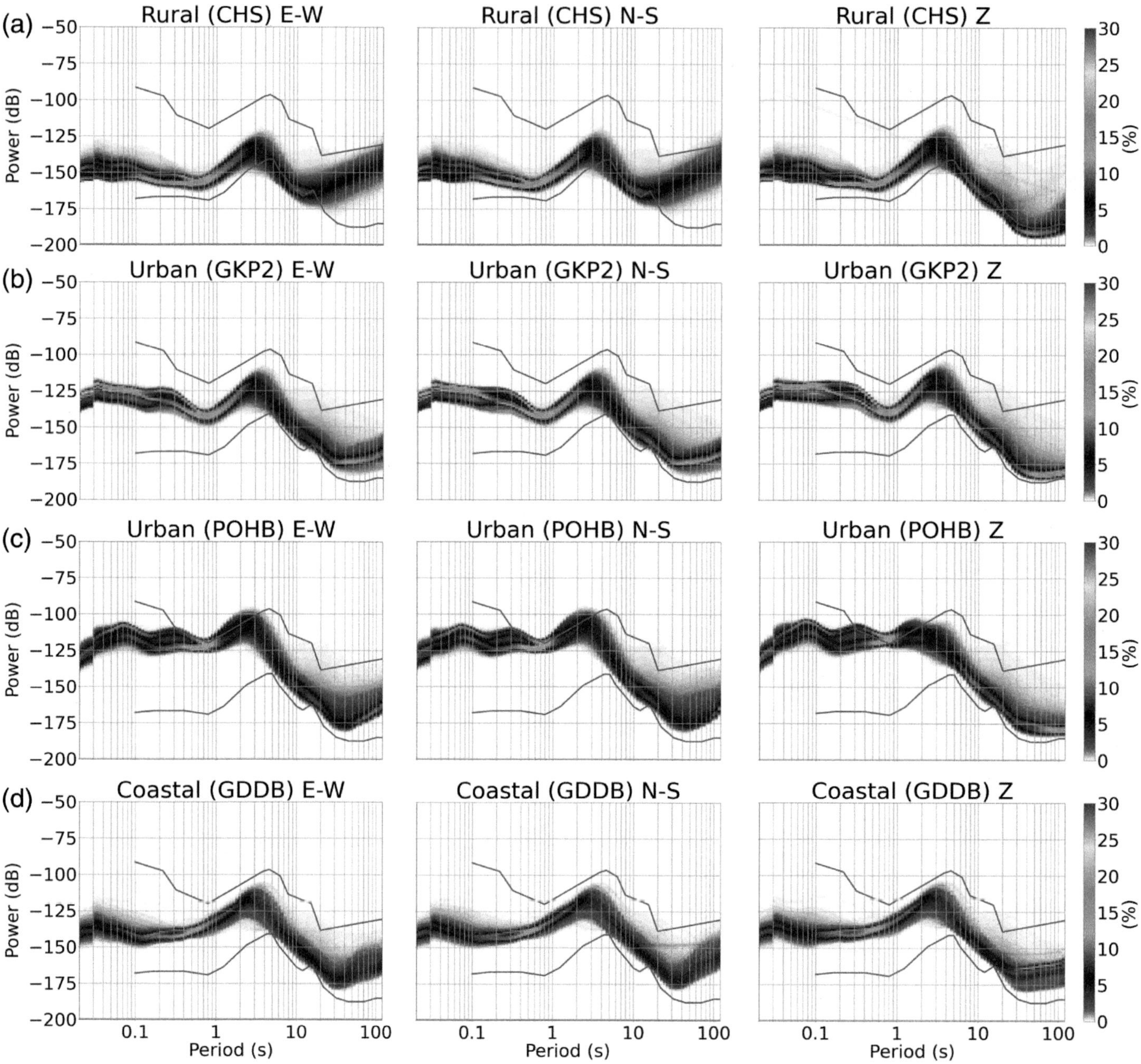

Figure 5. Two-year (May 2021 to May 2023) PSD PDFs for the three components of representative seismic stations from the KMA and KIGAM networks. (a) Rural, (b,c) urban, and (d) coastal areas. The color represents the probability of a noise level at a given period, and the power (dB) on the *y* axis is relative to an acceleration of 1 $(m/s^2)^2/Hz$. The upper and lower gray lines are the new high- and low-noise models (NHNM and NLNM) of Peterson (1993). The color version of this figure is available only in the electronic edition.

weekly variations (Fig. 7) because students and teachers are not at school on Saturday afternoons and Sundays. During weekdays, the background noise level increases to about −93 dB, whereas the noise level starts to decrease on Saturdays and remains low (−103 dB) on Sundays. Interestingly, on 6 June (Fig. 7b), which was a Monday and a national holiday (Memorial Day), noise remained at a relatively low level (−100 dB). This suggests that human activity is the main cause of the diurnal and weekly variations.

Seismic signature of rainfall

We compared background noise levels with precipitation using data provided by the KMA (Korea Meteorological Administration [KMA], 2023a). On 23 June, 34.8 mm of rainfall was recorded over a period of 4 hr (5–9 p.m. UTC; Fig. 8a), and on 22 November, cumulative rainfall of ~64.7 mm was recorded over a period of about 18 hr (6 a.m.–9 p.m.) although there were intermittent breaks in the rainfall (Fig. 8b). On a PSD spectrogram (Fig. 8c,d), elevated background noise levels at very short

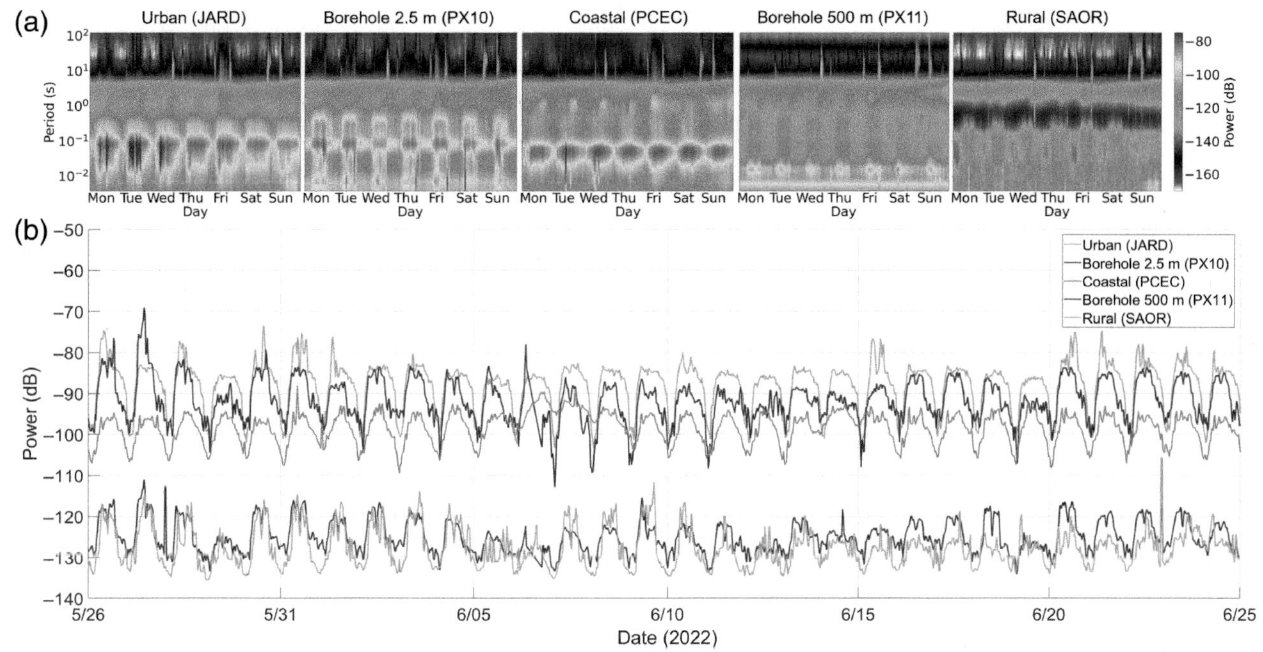

Figure 6. (a) PSD spectrogram of the background noise in the vertical component at representative stations between 30 May (Monday) and 5 June (Sunday) in local time (KST). Diurnal variations can be seen in the ambient noise at a period of 0.01–1.00 s, generated mostly by anthropogenic noise. (b) Temporal PSD variation at a period of 0.1 ± 0.03 s over 1 month (26 May to 25 June 2022). Although there are differences in power, the diurnal variations are observed at all stations. A rural station (SAOR) and the sensor at a depth of 500 m (PX11) have a low noise level (−140 to −115 dB), whereas the urban (JARD) and coastal (PCEC) stations and the seismometer at the surface (PX10) have a high noise level (−110 to −70 dB). The color version of this figure is available only in the electronic edition.

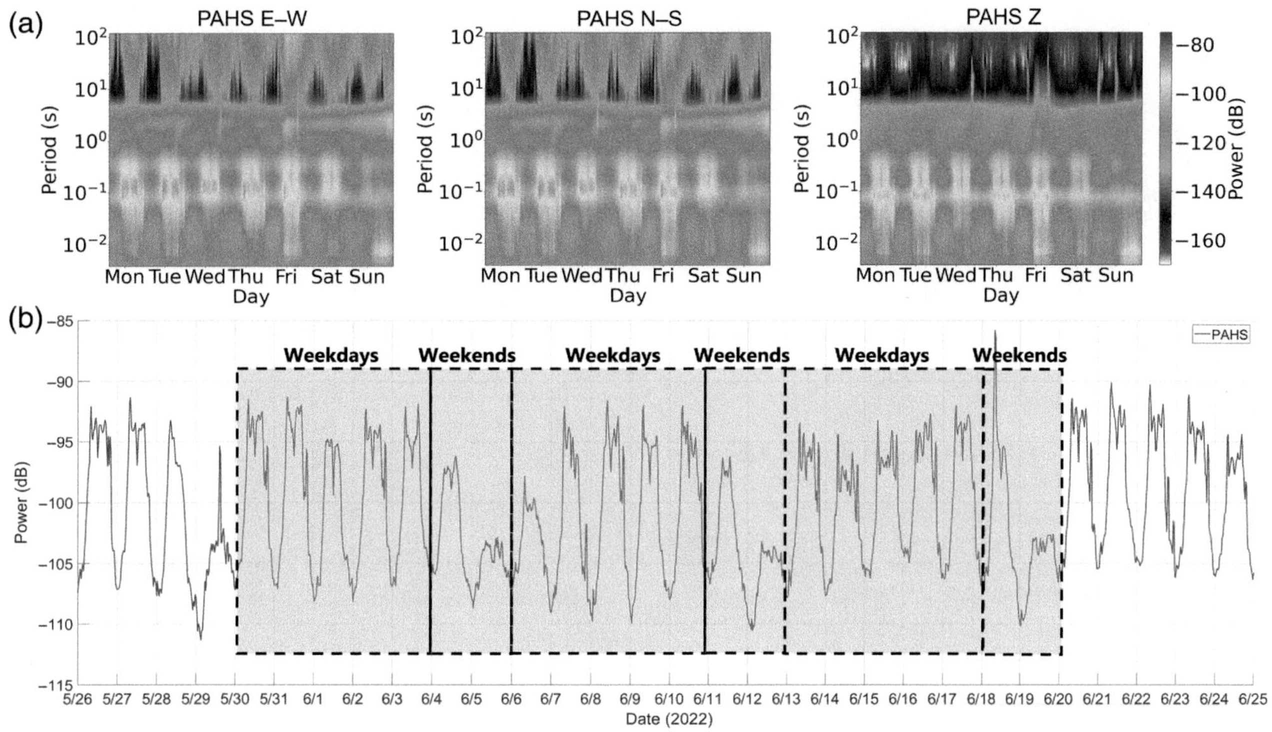

Figure 7. (a) PSD spectrograms of background noise at the PAHS station over the same duration as in Figure 6a. As well as diurnal variations, weekly variations are apparent. (b) Temporal PSD variation at a period of 0.1 ± 0.03 s over 1 month (26 May to 25 June 2022). The pale tan and pale green areas represent weekdays and weekends, respectively. On weekends, the PSD is lower and the fluctuations between day and night are small. On 6 June, the ambient noise level was lower than usual due to a national holiday. The color version of this figure is available only in the electronic edition.

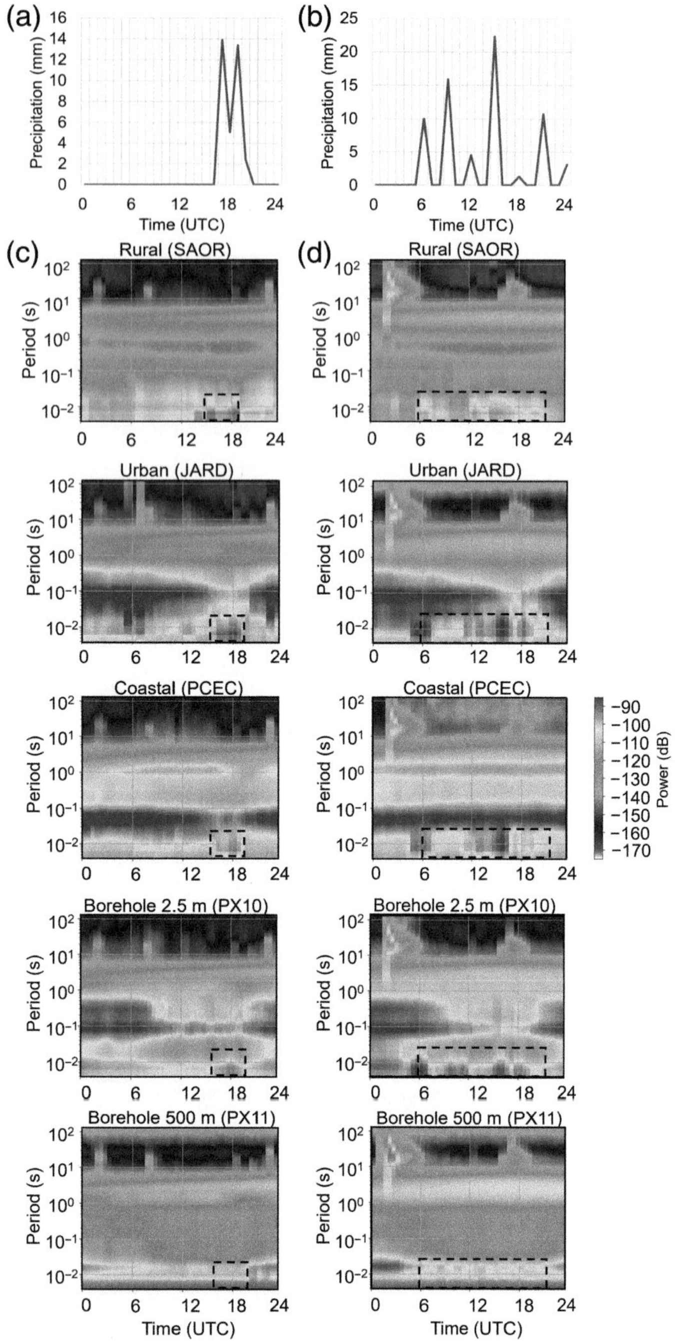

Figure 8. Variations in ambient noise caused by everyday weather conditions (rainfall) on (a) 23 June and (b) 22 November 2022. There were 34.8 mm of continuous precipitation on 23 June over 4 hr (17:00–21:00 UTC) and 64.7 mm of intermittent rain on 22 November (06:00–24:00 UTC; KMA, 2023a). PSD spectra of the vertical component of representative seismic stations on (c) 23 June and (d) 22 November 2022. The black-dashed rectangles represent the periods (<0.03 s) that coincide with a change in precipitation. The color version of this figure is available only in the electronic edition.

periods (<0.03 s) are occasionally observed, coinciding with these rainfall events. These results are consistent with previous studies of the relationship between seismic noise power and precipitation (Dean, 2017; Bakker *et al.*, 2022; Rindraharisaona *et al.*, 2022; Diaz *et al.*, 2023). The intensity of rainfall, even for intensities as low as 1 mm/hr, and raindrops larger than 3 mm have been shown to increase the seismic power (Bakker *et al.*, 2022). Raindrops with a diameter exceeding 3.5 mm do not increase seismic amplitudes, suggesting the threshold for the raindrop size (Diaz *et al.*, 2023). The period associated with precipitation, as observed in this study, is longer than in previous studies (Dean, 2017; Rindraharisaona *et al.*, 2022); however, it corresponds to the background noise observed in the temporary seismic array deployed in Haenam, South Korea, in 2020 (Han *et al.*, 2021). As the sampling rate of PCSN is high (500 samples per second), the signal from precipitation in Pohang was observed in very short period bands (0.004–0.030 s), below the Nyquist frequency. Most of the stations installed near the surface show increased levels of ambient noise at very short-period bands with increasing precipitation, whereas the station at 500 m depth shows little variation in ambient noise with increasing precipitation. This indicates that ~10–20 dB of the seismic noise generated by rainfall was attenuated at 500 m depth and did not affect the ambient seismic noise level.

Seismic signatures of typhoons and ocean waves

Typhoon Hinnamnor made landfall in Pohang during the study period, resulting in >10 fatalities and >26 injured individuals, with >8000 people affected (MOIS, 2024b). The typhoon formed on 28 August 2022, approached the Pohang region on 5 September at 10–11 p.m. (UTC), and dissipated on 6 September 2022 (Fig. 9a; KMA, 2023b). The duration of an earthquake is typically measured in seconds, whereas the lifespan of a typhoon is more than one week. Therefore, we performed spectral analyses of the long-period (3–10 s) ambient noise from 30 August to 8 September (10 days). Figure 10 shows the effect of the typhoon and temporal variations in the ambient noise level of the borehole array sensor. The center of the typhoon was far offshore on 30 August, seven days before it made landfall in Pohang. The background noise level (Fig. 10b,c) increased gradually as the typhoon approached the Korean Peninsula, reaching a peak when it was very close to Pohang. After the typhoon passed and dissipated, the PSD at long periods began to decrease and stabilized at the level observed before the typhoon formed. This trend in the background noise level was also observed at other stations and can be interpreted as the effect of wave–wave interactions generated by the oceanic storm (Longuet-Higgins, 1950; Chi, Chen, *et al.*, 2010; Chi, Chen, and Kuo, 2010). During the study period, two additional typhoons approached or passed close to Pohang: Typhoon Omais in 2021 and Typhoon Nanmadol in 2022 (Fig. S4). Typhoon Nanmadol yielded similar patterns to Typhoon Hinnamnor, showing an increase in the seismic background noise as it approached Pohang, with the noise then decreasing to the same level as before the typhoon formed (Figs. 9b, 10d). Typhoons Hinnamnor and Nanmadol had a large radius with windspeeds of >25 m/s (up to 180 km; Fig. 9). However, Typhoon Omais had a small radius (~145 km)

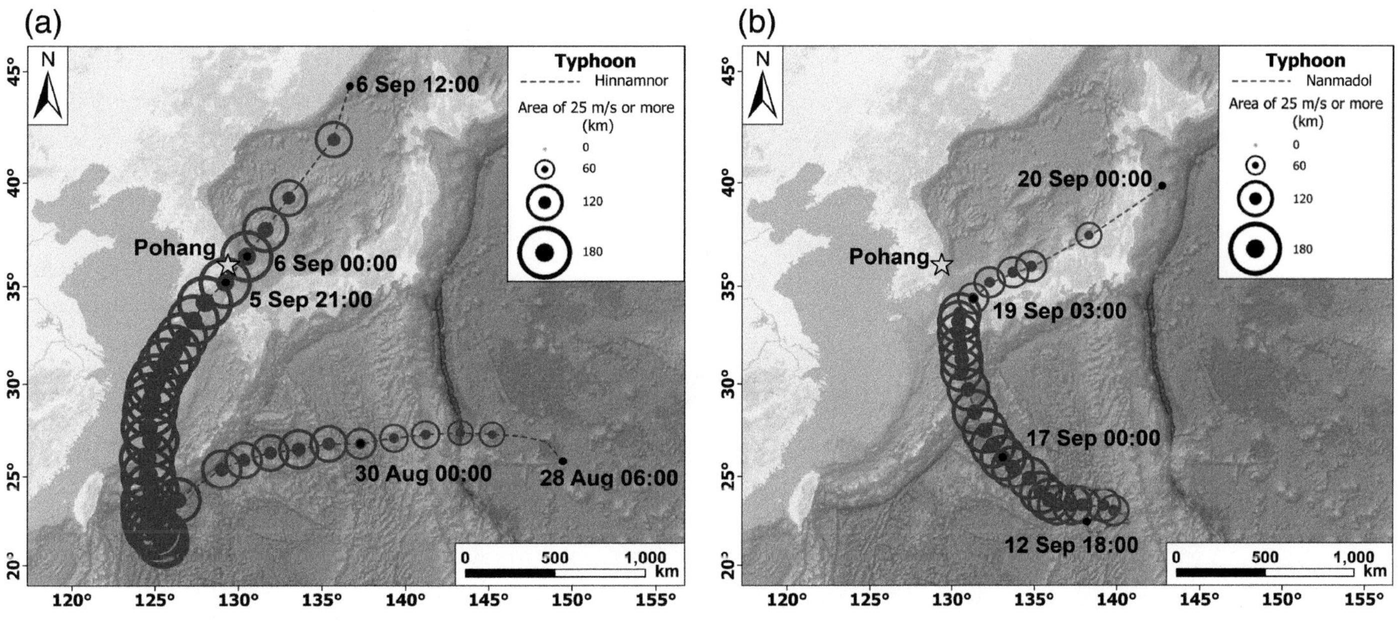

Figure 9. Path of typhoons (a) Hinnamnor and (b) Nanmadol in 2022 (KMA, 2023b). (a) Typhoon Hinnamnor developed on 28 August 2022, approached close to the Pohang region on 5 September at 10–11 p.m. (UTC), and dissipated on 6 September 2022. (b) Typhoon Nanmadol developed on 12 September 2022 and dissipated on 20 September 2022. The typhoon location and radius data were released by the KMA (KMA, 2023b) every 3 or 6 hr. Each circle represents the area that experienced wind speeds of >25 m/s. The color version of this figure is available only in the electronic edition.

with windspeeds of >15 m/s, almost one-third of the radius of the other two typhoons (~430 km; Fig. S4). Therefore, the seismic signal from Typhoon Omais could not be distinguished from seismic background noise.

As indicated by these results and previous studies (Cho *et al.*, 2009; Lee *et al.*, 2012; Park *et al.*, 2016; Shin *et al.*, 2019), secondary microseism peaks tend to be shifted toward relatively short periods (2–3 s). This is explained by the Korean observation stations being located closer to the sea, or on islands, compared with the stations used by Peterson (1993), resulting in weaker attenuation of high-frequency noise originating from ocean waves. Local wave winds and typhoon effects have also been mentioned. In accordance with the hypothesis that a secondary microseism peak is generated at half the primary microseism period (Longuet-Higgins, 1950), and considering that the dominant primary microseism in the East Sea is observed at a period of 5–6 s (Dolgikh *et al.*, 2021), it can be deduced that a secondary microseism peak would appear at 2.5–3.0 s. In addition, the effects of local winds, typhoons, and reflections from shallow continental shelves are thought to be combined. Gualtieri *et al.* (2013, 2015) demonstrated that interactions with the continental shelf and slope can modulate secondary microseism energy. This suggests that short-period secondary microseism peak intensification is possible in regions with an extensive shallow continental shelf, such as the Yellow Sea and the Southern Sea of Korea. As demonstrated by Sheen *et al.* (2009), the source region of the secondary microseism peak is located in the Southeastern Sea of Korea.

During Typhoon Hinnamnor, two other signals can be seen in Figure 10. The background noise at 2.5 m depth was elevated on 9 September. Station PX10 has noise levels of up to −70 dB on 5 September at 00 am (UTC; 9 a.m. in KST); however, elevated noise was not recorded at 500 m depth (black-dashed rectangle in Fig. 10b). This phenomenon coincides with reinforcement work (Geological Society of Korea [GSK], 2023) to prevent damage from Typhoon Hinnamnor, which employed heavy equipment, including forklifts, and generated anthropogenic noise. In addition, there is a spike in the long-period band (Fig. 10c) generated by a teleseismic earthquake of magnitude (M_{ww}) 6.6 in Sichuan, China (Incorporated Research Institutions for Seismology [IRIS], 2024), ~2620 km from the PCSN but observed clearly at all stations (Fig. S5).

In addition to the effects of typhoons, we also examined background noise variations at periods of 2–4 s in relation to changes in ocean wave height observed offshore of Pohang (Fig. 11). We used significant wave height data, which is the mean height of the highest 33% of ocean waves. These data are recorded by a wave buoy installed close to shore to observe wave heights that vary locally due to the effect of complex topography on coastal waves (KMA, 2023a). The significant wave height data are sampled every one hour, whereas the background noise is calculated every 30 min. Therefore, we resampled the noise level at the same times of significant wave heights. At a period of 3 s, the ambient noise levels correlate well with significant wave height; however, there is little difference between locations. Coastal stations show background noise levels ~2 dB higher than rural or urban stations that are located far from the coast (Fig. 11). We quantified the correlation between

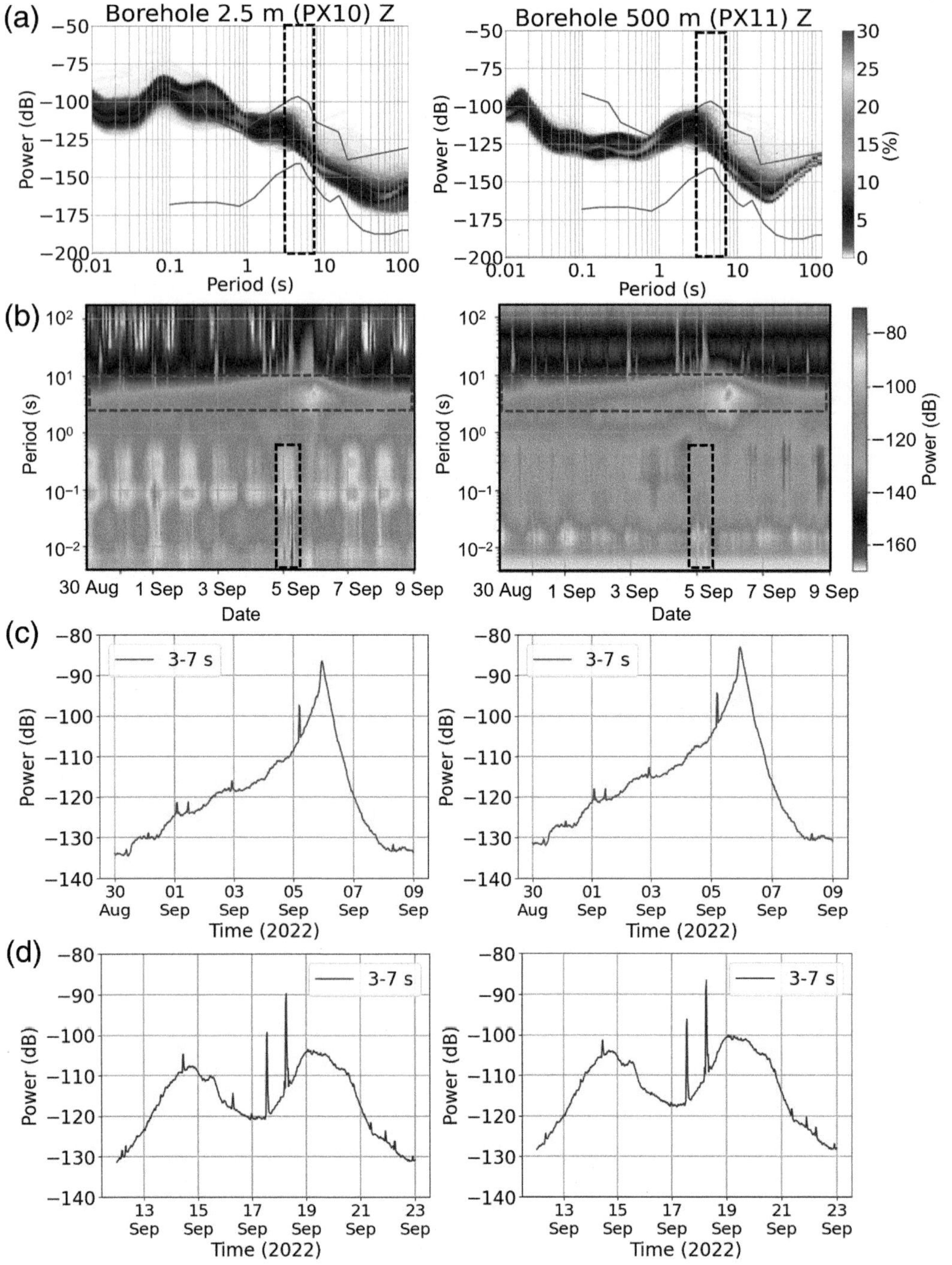

Figure 10. Variations in long-period ambient seismic noise during the passing of typhoon (b,c) Hinnamnor and (d) Nanmadol in 2022. (a) PSD PDFs for the vertical component of seismometers in the borehole array at depths of 2.5 and 500 m. A double peak is observed at periods of 3–7 s, indicated by black dashed rectangles. (b) The effect of typhoon Hinnamnor is apparent in the area indicated by red dashed rectangles. The low-period (0.01–0.100 s) signal on 5 September (black-dashed rectangles) at PX10 coincides with the reinforcement work before Typhoon Hinnamnor, which is not seen at 500 m depth. (c,d) PSD at a period of 3–7 s, which increased as the typhoon passed the Okinawa trench and approached the Korean Peninsula, reaching a peak when it was closest to the Pohang region, then decreasing to the same level as before the typhoon formed. The color version of this figure is available only in the electronic edition.

significant wave height and background noise amplitude using Pearson correlation coefficients (Pearson, 1909). During the period of Figure 11, the correlation coefficients of coastal, urban, and rural stations are 0.871, 0.866, and 0.858, respectively. In general, a strong correlation was observed between significant wave height and background noise level, particularly in instances of significant wave height variation. The coastal station yielded a particularly strong correlation compared with urban and rural stations.

Difference between horizontal and vertical components

There is a difference between horizontal and vertical components in two period ranges. At very long periods (>20 s), all seismic stations have higher noise levels in the horizontal components than in the vertical components (Fig. 2). The longer the period, the greater the difference. The large difference in ambient noise levels between these components at very long periods suggests that the horizontal components are influenced by pressure-field-induced surface tilt (Stutzmann *et al.*, 2000; De Angelis and Bodin, 2012). The geological setting of seismic stations also affects the background noise level. The Pohang basin, where the PCSN is situated, is an early Miocene sedimentary basin (Son *et al.*, 2015) that contains thick unconsolidated and poorly consolidated sediments (Hwang *et al.*, 2021). Kang (2024) measured the resonance frequency of ambient seismic noise in the Pohang region using the horizontal-to-vertical spectral ratio (Nakamura, 1989, 2019). The resonance frequency of each station was used to estimate the thickness of sediments overlying the bedrock, and the resonance frequency at the boundary of the Pohang basin was determined to be 0.32–0.67 Hz (Kang, 2024). A low-resonance frequency indicates the presence of thick sedimentary layers.

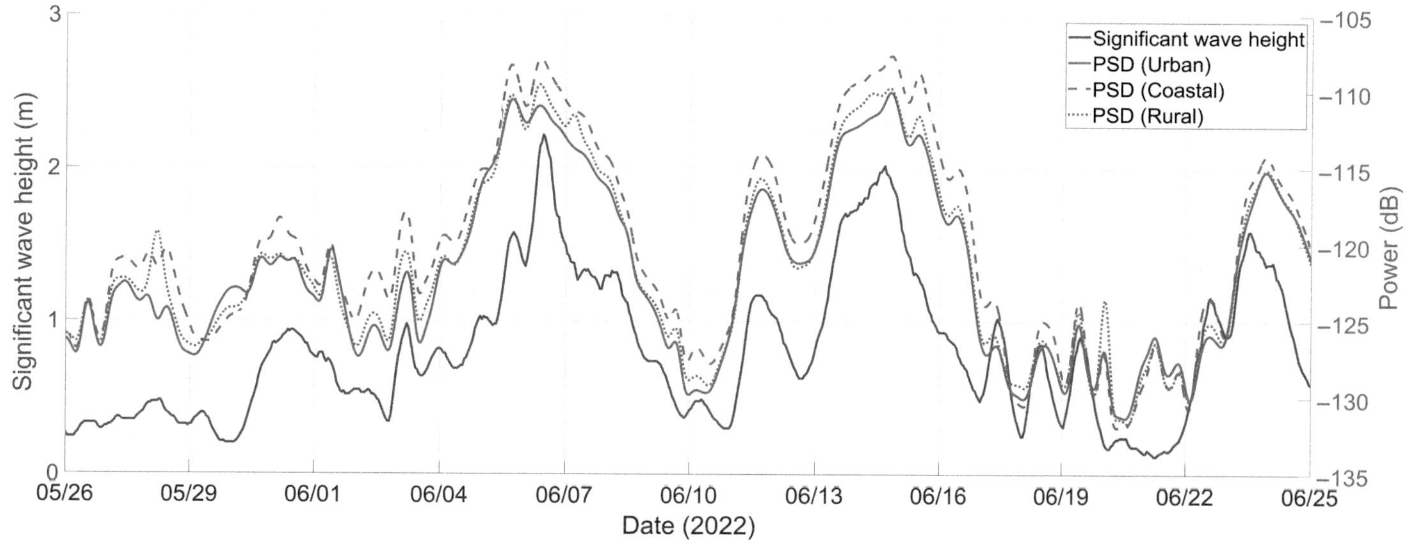

Figure 11. Correlation between the ambient noise level of representative stations at periods of 2–4 s and the significant wave height offshore of Pohang. Significant wave height is the mean height of the highest 33% of ocean waves. The Pearson correlation coefficients of coastal, urban, and rural stations are 0.871, 0.866, and 0.858, respectively. The color version of this figure is available only in the electronic edition.

In the present study, the difference in ambient noise between the horizontal and vertical components was analyzed at periods of 1.5–3.0 s. Stations located on bedrock had similar noise levels in both the horizontal and vertical components (Fig. 12a); however, the PSD of stations in regions with thick sediments has horizontal components with noise levels ~10 dB higher than those of the vertical components (Fig. 12b). This suggests that the seismic waves were amplified in thick sediment layers due to local site effects. The amplification was especially strong in the horizontal direction and less so in the vertical direction. The sediment layer at the 2017 Pohang epicenter is ~300 m thick, and the effect of the sediment layer is shown by the results from the borehole sensors. The maximum difference between the horizontal and vertical components at PX10 is ~10 dB, decreasing to ~5 dB at a depth of 500 m (Fig. 12c).

To improve the monitoring capability of the PCSN in accordance with the geology, we recommend relocating certain stations or modifying their installation. In particular, in areas with a thick sediment layer and within urban or coastal regions, we recommend that stations be relocated to a hard-rock site or installed in a deep borehole. Based on the sediment thickness in the Pohang basin estimated by Kang (2024), we suggest that the DSGL, PCEC, OKSR, SNLU, and PAHS stations be relocated to alternative sites or installed at greater depths. The DSGL and PCEC stations are located close to the coastline and within a sediment layer that is >800 m thick. The OKSR, SNLU, and PAHS stations are located in urban areas within thick sediment layers and yield high levels of anthropogenic noise.

Reduced ambient noise in seismometers installed at depth

At periods that are particularly relevant for microearthquake monitoring (0.07–0.20 s; Lee and Stewart, 1981; Demuth *et al.*, 2016), the PX10 posthole sensor at a depth of 2.5 m has a PSD of −94.5 dB, whereas the PX11 borehole sensor at a depth of 500 m has a PSD of −127.5 dB (Fig. 2d,e). The installation of sensors in a borehole has been shown to reduce background noise substantially in areas where anthropogenic noise is high, especially during the day. The background noise in the borehole array was reduced by ~33 dB at a depth of 500 m. Similar results were reported by Cocco *et al.* (2001) and Yun *et al.* (2013), who found that installing seismometers in a borehole reduced the background noise level by ~40 dB.

We measured the reduction in ambient noise using the SNR of a microearthquake. Waveforms from an M_L 0.41 microearthquake that occurred in the study area are shown in Figure 13, recorded by both sensors in the borehole array. The PX11 sensor successfully detected the event, whereas the PX10 barely detected it. The SNR of the M_L 0.41 earthquake at a depth of 500 m was 11.46 dB, 11 times greater than that at a depth of 2.5 m (1.01 dB). This indicates that the installation of seismometers at a depth of 500 m can lead to a substantial reduction in ambient noise levels and an improvement in the earthquake monitoring capabilities of the seismometer, even in high-traffic urban environments.

Earthquake monitoring capability of the PCSN

All the variations in background noise level discussed earlier affect the earthquake monitoring capability of the seismic network. Our analysis of the earthquake monitoring capability of PCSN has been conducted spatial and temporal variation using the station noise level of PCSN and the Pohang earthquake catalog from 14 November 2017 to 31 May 2023 (circles in Fig. 1; Heo *et al.*, 2024). First, a detection threshold map was determined for the study area by following the method of

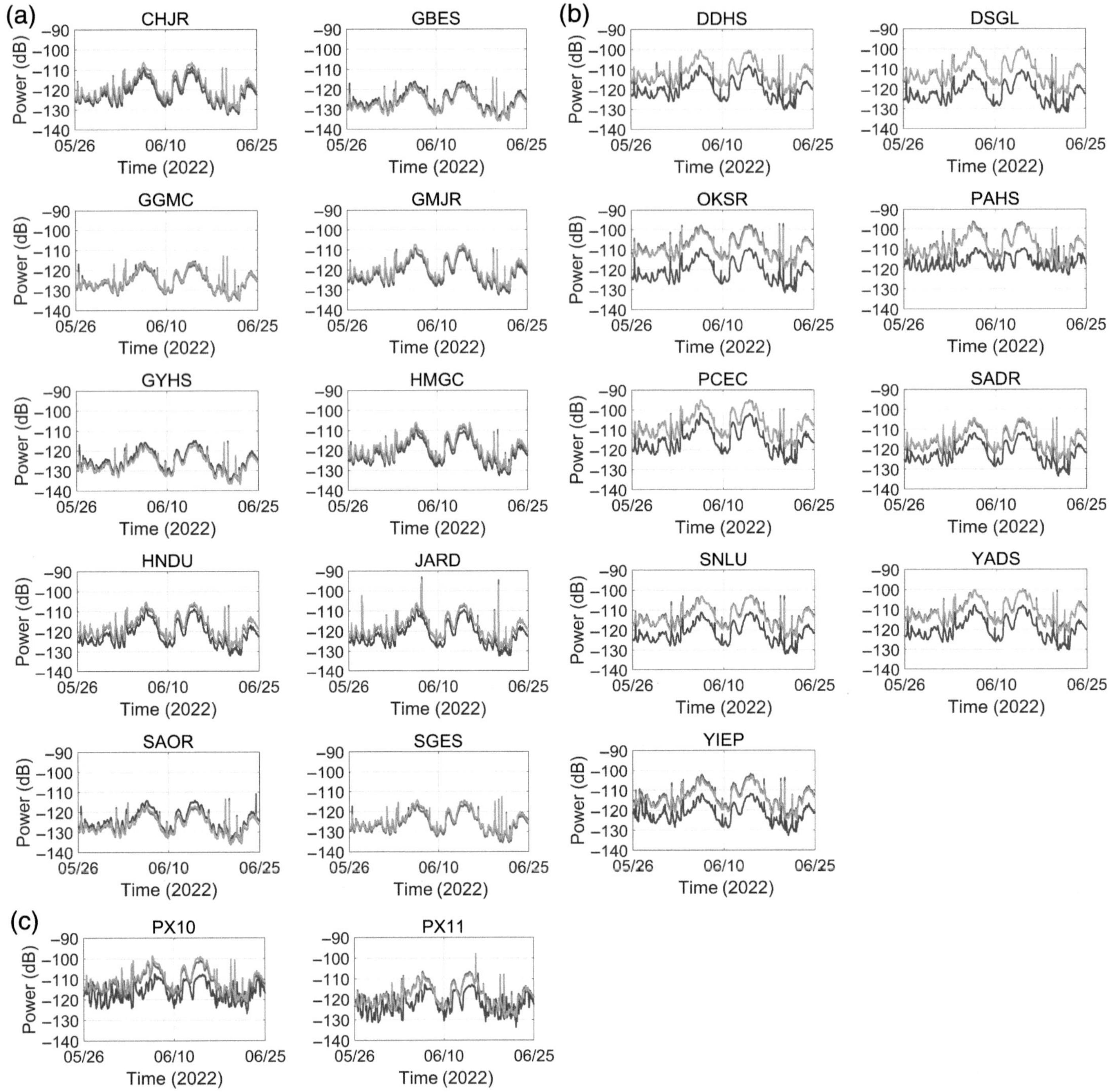

Figure 12. Differences between the PSD of the horizontal and vertical components (periods of 1.5–3.0 s) for instruments installed (a) on bedrock, (b) on a thick sediment layer, and (c) in a borehole array. The vertical component (Z) is shown as a blue line, and the horizontal components (N and E) are shown as orange and yellow lines, respectively. The background noise levels of the horizontal components of seismometers on a thick sediment layer are ~10 dB higher than those of the vertical components. The color version of this figure is available only in the electronic edition.

Wilson *et al.* (2021; Fig. 14). The detection threshold was computed using the background noise in the period band of 0.07–0.20 s (Lee and Stewart, 1981; Demuth *et al.*, 2016), which is relevant for microearthquake monitoring, using waveforms of PCSN on the day of 5 June 2022. Detection thresholds lower than the magnitude of 1.1 occur in the central region of the network, and higher thresholds at the network periphery. The northwest region of the network shows relatively low magnitude due to the distribution of rural stations with low background noise level, whereas the thresholds are bit higher in the southeast due to the proximity of the coastline and urban stations.

Second, we have used a total of 162 earthquakes that were detected within 20 km of the epicenter of the Pohang earthquake between 28 May 2021 and 30 April 2023 (GSK, 2023;

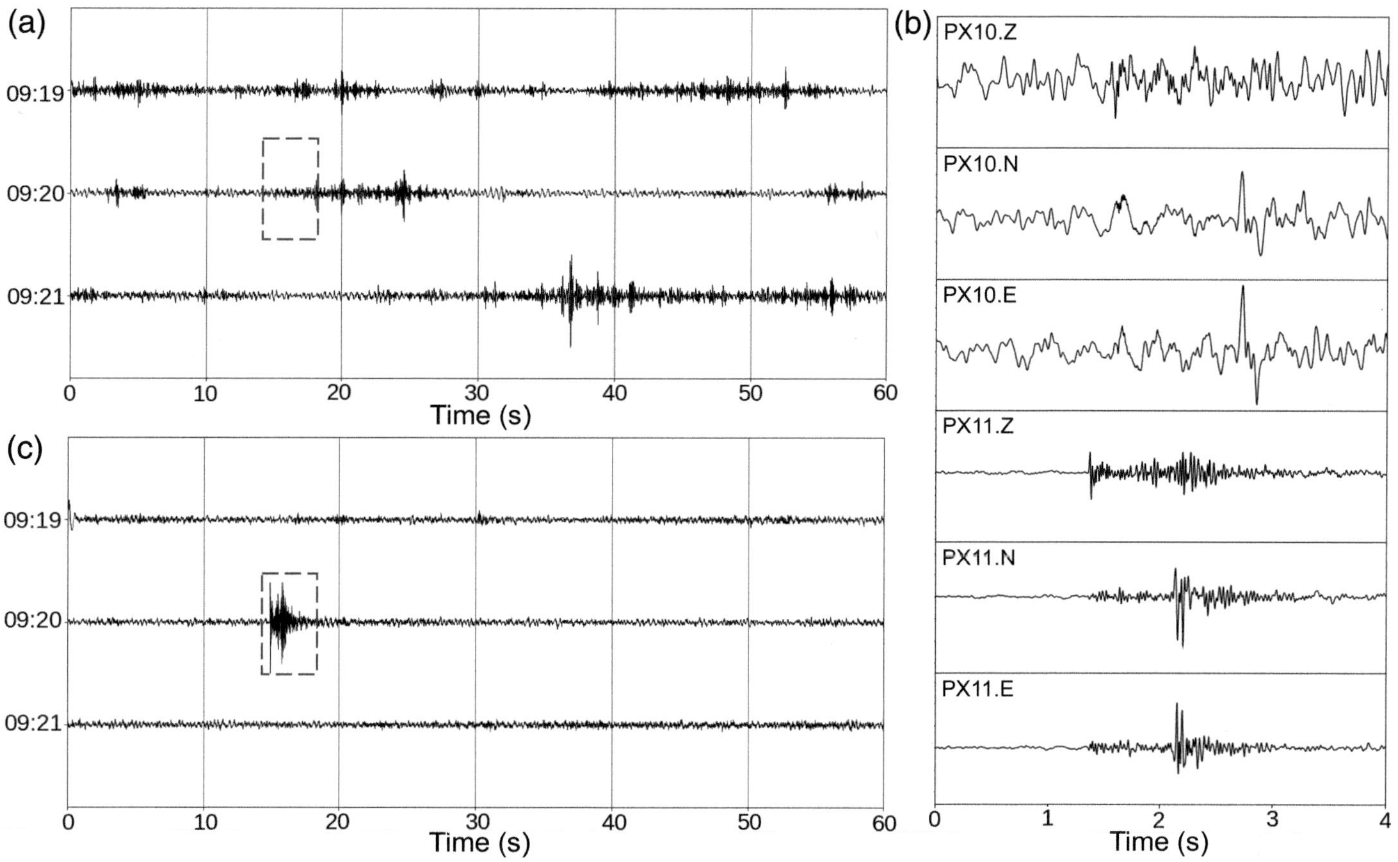

Figure 13. (a,c) Vertical component of waveforms over 5 min (09:18–09:23 UTC) on 29 May 2022. The M_L 0.41 Pohang earthquake is evident at panel (c) 500 m in the borehole array (PX11), whereas it is difficult to identify at (a) 2.5 m depth (PX10). (b) Three-component waveforms of the M_L 0.41 Pohang earthquake recorded at PX10 and PX11. A 2–40 Hz band-pass filter has been applied. The color version of this figure is available only in the electronic edition.

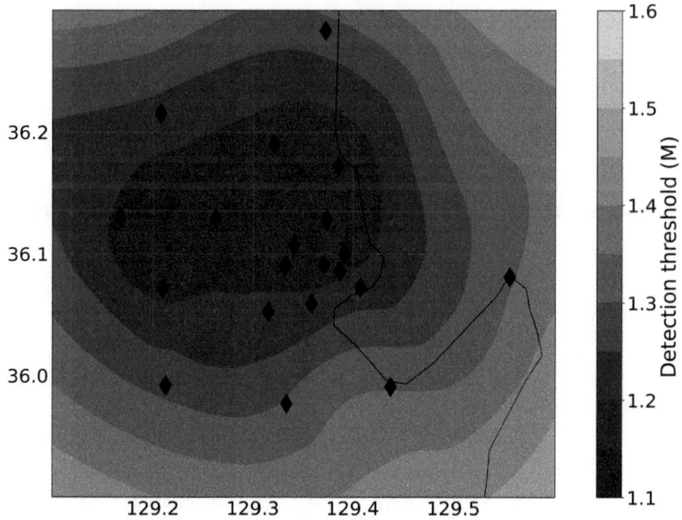

Figure 14. Network detection threshold map for Pohang was determined by following the method of Wilson *et al.* (2021). The station noise level was computed using waveforms of PCSN on the day of 5 June 2022. Black diamonds and lines represent the station of PCSN and the coastline of South Korea, respectively. In areas exhibiting low-background noise levels, the detection threshold demonstrates a similar tendency toward low magnitude. The color version of this figure is available only in the electronic edition.

Heo *et al.*, 2024). There were clear differences in the ambient noise of the PCSN during the day and night, and the improved earthquake monitoring capability of the network during the night, as a result of the lower background noise, is clear in the PCSN catalog. Among the 162 earthquakes, 50 were detected during the day (07:00–19:00 KST) and 112 during the night (19:00–07:00 KST; Fig. 15). To evaluate the micro-earthquake detection capability of the PCSN, we examined the number of earthquakes smaller than the magnitude of completeness (M_c) on a histogram (Fig. 15). Heo *et al.* (2024) estimated that the M_c of the PCSN earthquake catalog (14 November 2017 to 31 May 2023) was 0.34 using the Gutenberg–Richter law and the goodness of fit (Wiemer and Wyss, 2000). A total of 53 earthquakes below the M_c were detected during the night, whereas only 5 were detected during the day.

CONCLUSIONS

The establishment of the PCSN was necessitated by increasing concern over seismic safety in the Pohang region. The network comprises 20 broadband posthole stations and a borehole array at the EGS site. The seismic background noise recorded by the

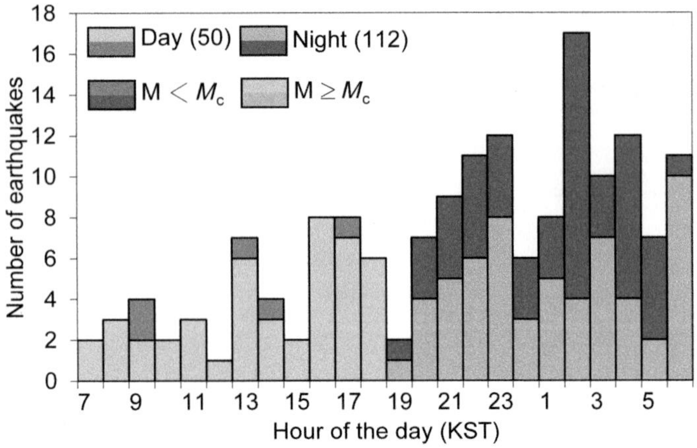

Figure 15. Number of earthquakes in each hour of the day. The time is local time (KST), which is UTC + 9. A total of 162 earthquakes were detected between 28 May 2021 and 30 April 2023. Day and night are shown in orange and blue, respectively. Dark colors represent earthquakes with magnitudes below the magnitude of completeness ($M_c = 0.34$; GSK, 2023; Heo *et al.*, 2024), and light colors represent earthquakes with magnitudes above M_c. Twice as many microearthquakes were detected at night (112) as during the day (50). Most of the earthquakes below M_c were detected at night. The color version of this figure is available only in the electronic edition.

PCSN at different periods varied through time and with location, installation depth, weather conditions, and geological setting. The level of high-frequency seismic noise, generated by rainfall or human activity, is high at stations installed near the surface; however, the noise levels of a seismometer at 500 m depth were low, despite its proximity to a highway, with similar or lower noise levels to those observed in rural areas. At long periods, the seismic noise level was correlated with the path of typhoons Hinnamnor and Nanmadol in 2022 and variations in significant wave height at all stations. In the region with thick sediments, a difference of ~10 dB was observed between the ambient noise in the horizontal and vertical components, attributable to local site effects. We identified the influence of these variations in ambient seismic noise on the microearthquake monitoring capability of the network, using a detection threshold map to investigate the spatial variation and the difference between day and night to investigate the temporal variation. The SNR for microearthquakes was approximately tenfold higher at a depth of 500 m compared with the surface. These results indicate that the deployment of seismometers at a minimum depth of 100 m could lead to a substantial decrease in ambient noise levels within the frequency band of anthropogenic noise. Furthermore, by analyzing the effect of the background noise level, criteria for establishing seismic networks can be established, and the theoretical performance of microearthquake monitoring can be improved.

DATA AND RESOURCES

The data from the Pohang Community Seismograph Network (PCSN) used in this study can be obtained from the Ministry of Trade, Industry, and Energy of South Korea upon request. The seismic waveforms and metadata used in this study were collected by the Geological Society of Korea as part of the project titled "Monitoring and analyses of earthquakes, groundwater, and surface deformation for securing stability of the Pohang EGS project site" (GSK, 2023). The data from the Korea Meteorological Administration (KMA) used in this study can be downloaded from https://necis.kma.go.kr. Data from the Korea Institute of Geoscience and Mineral Resources (KIGAM) used in this study can be downloaded from https://data.kigam.re.kr/quake/. Both websites were last accessed in September 2025. The supplemental material for this article includes five figures. Figures S1–S3 show the power spectral density (PSD) probability density functions (PDFs) of the PCSN in rural, urban, and coastal areas, respectively. Figure S4 shows the path of three typhoons (Omais, Hinnamnor, and Nanmadol) with a radius defined by windspeeds of >15 m/s. Figure S5 shows the waveforms of a teleseismic earthquake that occurred in Sichuan, China, on 5 September 2022.

DECLARATION OF COMPETING INTERESTS

The authors acknowledge that there are no conflicts of interest recorded.

Acknowledgments

The authors would like to thank Associate Editor Cezar I. Trifu and the two anonymous reviewers for their detailed comments, which helped improve this article. This study was supported by the Korea Meteorological Administration (KMA) Research Development Program (RS-2022-KM220610) and the Korea Institute of Energy Technology Evaluation and Planning (KETEP) and the Ministry of Trade, Industry & Energy (MOTIE) (Grand Number 20208310100020).

REFERENCES

Anthony, R. E., R. C. Aster, D. Wiens, A. Nyblade, S. Anandakrishnan, A. Huerta, J. P. Winberry, T. Wilson, and C. Rowe (2015). The seismic noise environment of Antarctica, *Seismol. Res. Lett.* **86,** no. 1, 89–100, doi: 10.1785/0220140109.

Anthony, R. E., A. T. Ringler, and D. C. Wilson (2022). Seismic background noise levels across the continental United States from USArray Transportable Array: The influence of geology and geography, *Bull. Seismol. Soc. Am.* **112,** no. 2, 646–668.

Bakker, M., C. Legout, F. Gimbert, G. Nord, B. Boudevillain, and C. Freche (2022). Seismic modelling and observations of rainfall, *J. Hydrol.* **610,** 127812, doi: 10.1016/j.jhydrol.2022.127812.

Bormann, P., and E. Wielandt (2013). Seismic signals and noise, in *New Manual of Seismological Observatory Practice 2 (NMSOP2)*, P. Bormann (Editor), Deutsches GeoForschungsZentrum GGZ, Potsdam, 62, doi: 10.2312/GFZ.NMSOP-2_ch4.

Chi, W.-C., W.-J. Chen, D. Dolenc, B.-Y. Kuo, C. Lin, and J. Collins (2010). Seismological report on the 2006 Typhoon Shanshan that lit up seismic stations along its way, *Seismol. Res. Lett.* **81,** no. 4, 592–596, doi: 10.1785/gssrl.81.4.592.

Chi, W.-C., W.-J. Chen, and B.-Y. Kuo (2010). Seismic monitoring of western Pacific typhoons, *Mar. Geophys. Res.* **31,** no. 4, 239–251, doi: 10.1007/s11001-010-9105-x.

Cho, B.-J., D.-H. Sheen, B.-G. Jo, S.-C. Park, and E.-H. Hwang (2009). Development of a standard background noise model for broadband seismic stations of KMA, *J. Geol. Soc. Korea* **45,** no. 2, 127–141 (in Korean with English abstract).

Cocco, M., F. Ardizzoni, R. M. Azzara, L. Dall'Olio, A. Delladio, M. D. Bona, L. Malagnini, L. Margheriti, and A. Nardi (2001). Broadband waveforms and site effects at a borehole seismometer in the Po alluvial basin (Italy), *Ann. Geophys.* **44,** no. 1, 137–154, doi: 10.4401/ag-3611.

Cooley, J. W., and J. W. Tukey (1965). An algorithm for the machine calculation of complex Fourier series, *Math. Comput.* **19,** no. 90, 297–301, doi: 10.2307/2003354.

De Angelis, S., and P. Bodin (2012). Watching the wind: Seismic data contamination at long periods due to atmospheric pressure-field-induced tilting, *Bull. Seismol. Soc. Am.* **102,** no. 3, 1255–1265, doi: 10.1785/0120110186.

Dean, T. (2017). The seismic signature of rain, *Geophysics* **82,** no. 5, P53–P60, doi: 10.1190/geo2016-0421.1.

Demuth, A., L. Ottemöller, and H. Keers (2016). Ambient noise levels and detection threshold in Norway, *J. Seismol.* **20,** no. 3, 889–904, doi: 10.1007/s10950-016-9566-8.

Diaz, J., M. Ruiz, M. Udina, F. Polls, D. Marti, and J. Bech (2023). Monitoring storm evolution using a high-density seismic network, *Sci. Rep.* **13,** 1853.

Dolgikh, G. I., O. S. Gromasheva, S. G. Dolgikh, and A. A. Plotnikov (2021). Dynamics and transformation of sea surface gravity waves at the shelf of decreasing depth, *J. Mar. Sci. Eng.* **9,** 861.

Ellsworth, W. L., D. Giardini, J. Townend, S. Ge, and T. Shimamoto (2019). Triggering of the Pohang, Korea, earthquake (M_W 5.5) by enhanced geothermal system stimulation, *Seismol. Res. Lett.* **90,** 1844–1858, doi: 10.1785/0220190102.

Geological Society of Korea (GSK) (2023). Monitoring and analyses of earthquake, groundwater, and surface deformation for securing stability of the Pohang EGS Project Site Report, 96 pp.

Grigoli, F., S. Cesca, A. P. Rinaldi, A. Manconi, J. A. López-Comino, J. F. Clinton, R. Westaway, C. Cauzzi, T. Dahm, and S. Wiemer (2018). The November 2017 M_W 5.5 Pohang earthquake: A possible case of induced seismicity in South Korea, *Science* **360,** 1003–1006, doi: 10.1126/science.aat2010.

Gualtieri, L., E. Stutzmann, Y. Capdeville, F. Ardhuin, M. Schimmel, A. Mangeney, and A. Morelli (2013). Modelling secondary microseismic noise by normal mode summation, *Geophys. J. Int.* **193,** no. 3, 1732–1745.

Gualtieri, L., E. Stutzmann, Y. Capdeville, V. Farra, A. Mangeney, and A. Morelli (2015). On the shaping factors of the secondary microseismic wavefield, *J. Geophys. Res.* **120,** 6241–6262.

Güralp (2019). *Güralp 3TB Operator's Guide*, Güralp Systems Ltd., Reading, United Kingdom.

Güralp (2021). *Güralp Minimus and Minumus+ Technical Manual*, Güralp Systems Ltd., Reading, United Kingdom.

Güralp (2023). *Güralp 3T Operator's Guide*, Güralp Systems Ltd., Reading, United Kingdom.

Han, J., W. Seo, H.-J. Kim, W.-Y. Kim, D. Won, J.-I. Chung, and K.-H. Kim (2021). Monitoring a short-lived earthquake swarm during April–May 2020 in Haenam, Korea, and its preliminary results, *Geosci. J.* **25,** 43–57, doi: 10.1007/s12303-020-0046-3.

Heo, D., B. S. Ahn, K.-H. Kim, J. Rhie, Y. Sohn, and T.-S. Kang (2024). Spatial and temporal evolutions of aftershocks between 2017 and 2023 at the Pohang EGS site and its vicinity, *Episodes* **47,** no. 3, 611–623, doi: 10.18814/epiiugs/2024/02403s07.

Hwang, I. G., J. Son, and S. Cho (2021). Event stratigraphy of Yeonil Group, Pohang Basin: based on correlation of 21 deep cores and outcrop sections, *J. Geol. Soc. Korea* **57,** no. 5, 649–678, doi: 10.14770/jgsk.2021.57.5.649 (in Korean with English abstract).

Incorporated Research Institutions for Seismology (IRIS) (2024). IRIS event page, available at https://ds.iris.edu/ds/nodes/dmc/tools/event/11595065/ (last accessed September 2024).

Joe, S., J. Lee, F. Klaus, H. X. Ng, L. T. Eyler, and Y. Lee (2023). Prolonged unmet mental health needs of the 2017 Pohang earthquake survivors, *Psychiatry Investig.* **20,** no. 6, 541–549.

Kang, S. Y. (2024). Mapping bedrock topography and detecting blind faults using the fundamental resonance of microtremor: A case study of the Pohang Basin, southeastern Korea, *Geophys J. Int.* **238,** 806–819, doi: 10.1093/gji/ggae194.

Kim, K.-H., J.-H. Ree, Y. Kim, S. Kim, S. Y. Kang, and W. Seo (2018). Assessing whether the 2017 M_W 5.4 Pohang earthquake in South Korea was an induced event, *Science* **360,** 1007–1009, doi: 10.1126/science.aat6081.

Kim, K.-H., W. Seo, J. Han, J. Kwon, S. Y. Kang, J.-H. Ree, S. Kim, and K. Liu (2020). The 2017 M_L 5.4 Pohang earthquake sequence, Korea, recorded by a dense seismic network, *Tectonophysics* **774,** 228306, doi: 10.1016/j.tecto.2019.228306.

Korea Meteorological Administration (KMA) (2023a). Weather data open portal, available at https://data.kma.go.kr/cmmn/main.do (last accessed August 2023).

Korea Meteorological Administration (KMA) (2023b). Weather Nuri typhoon information, available at https://www.weather.go.kr/w/typhoon/typ-history.do (last accessed March 2023).

Korean Government Commission on the Cause of the Pohang Earthquake (2019). *Final Report of the Korean Government Commission on Relations Between the 2017 Pohang Earthquake and EGS Project*, Geological Society of Korea, doi: 10.22719/KETEP-2019043001.

Krischer, L., T. Megies, R. Barsch, M. Beyreuther, T. Lecocq, C. Caudron, and J. Wassermann (2015). ObsPy: A bridge for seismology into the scientific Python ecosystem, *Comput. Sci. Disc.* **8,** 014003, doi: 10.1088/1749-4699/8/1/014003.

Lecocq, T., S. P. Hicks, K. Van Noten, K. van Wijk, P. Koelemeijer, R. S. M. De Plaen, F. Massin, G. Hillers, R. E. Anthony, M. T. Apoloner, *et al.* (2020). Global quieting of high-frequency seismic noise due to COVID-19 pandemic lockdown measures, *Science* **369,** 1338–1343, doi: 10.1126/science.aax1878.

Lee, K.-K., W. L. Ellsworth, D. Giardini, J. Townend, S. Ge, T. Shimamoto, I.-W. Yeo, T.-S. Kang, J. Rhie, D.-H. Sheen, *et al.* (2019). Managing injection-induced seismic risks, *Science* **364,** 730–732, doi: 10.1126/science.aax1878.

Lee, W. H. K., and S. W. Stewart (1981). *Principles and Applications of Microearthquake Networks*, Academic Press, New York, New York.

Lee, W.-D., B.-G. Jo, F. Schwab, and S.-B. Jung (2012). Typhoon-generated microseisms observed from the short-period KSRS array, *Geosci. J.* **16,** no. 4, 447–454.

Longuet-Higgins, M. S. (1950). A theory of the origin of microseisms, *Phil. Trans. Roy. Soc. London* **243,** no. 857, 1–35, doi: 10.1098/rsta.1950.0012.

McNamara, D. E., and R. P. Buland (2004). Ambient noise levels in the continental United States, *Bull. Seismol. Soc. Am.* **94,** no. 4, 1517–1527, doi: 10.1785/012003001.

Ministry of Interior and Safety (MOIS) (2018). 2017 Pohang Earthquake Whitepaper, National Disaster and Safety Status Control Center (in Korean).

MOIS (2024a). Safety management daily status report, available at https://www.mois.go.kr/frt/bbs/type001/commonSelectBoardList.do?bbsId=BBSMSTR_000000000336 (last accessed October 2024).

MOIS (2024b). National disaster and safety portal, available at https://www.safekorea.go.kr/idsiSFK/neo/sfk/cs/sfc/tot/toteaiList.jsp?emgPage=Y&menuSeq=111 (last accessed April 2024).

Nakamura, Y. (1989). A method for dynamic characteristics estimation of subsurface using microtremor on the ground surface, *Q. Rep. Railway Tech. Res.* **30,** 25–33.

Nakamura, Y. (2019). What is the Nakamura method? *Seismol. Res. Lett.* **90,** no. 4, 1437–1443. doi: 10.1785/0220180376.

Nanometrics (2019). *Centaur User Guide*, Nanometrics Inc., Ottawa, Canada.

Nanometrics (2020). *Trillium Compact User Guide*, Nanometrics Inc., Ottawa, Canada.

Park, I., K. Y. Kim, and J. Byun (2016). Characteristics of low-frequency ambient seismic noise in South Korea, *Geophys. Geophys. Explor.* **19,** no. 2, 67–75.

Pearson, K. (1909). Determination of the coefficient of correlation, *Science* **30,** no. 757, 23–25.

Peterson, J. R. (1993). Observation and modeling of seismic background noise, *U.S. Geol. Surv. Open-File Rept. 93-222*, doi: 10.3133/ofr93322.

Ree, J.-H., K.-H. Kim, H. Lim, W. Seo, S. Kim, X. An, and Y. Kim (2021). Fault reactivation and propagation during the 2017 Pohang earthquake sequence, *Geothermics* **92,** 102048, doi: 10.1016/j.geothermics.2021.102048.

Rindraharisaona, E. J., A. Réchou, F. R. Fontaine, G. Barruol, P. Stamenoff, B. Boudevillain, F. Rigaud-Louise, and E. Delcher (2022). Seismic signature of rain and wind inferred from seismic data, *Earth Space Sci.* **9,** no. 10, 1–16, doi: 10.1029/2022EA002328.

Seo, H., and O. Lee (2020). Mediating role of post-traumatic stress disorder in post-traumatic growth in adults who experienced the 2017 Pohang earthquake, *J. Affect. Disord.* **263,** 246–251.

Sheen, D.-H., and J. S. Shin (2010). Earthquake detection thresholds of broadband seismic networks in South Korea considering background seismic noise levels, *J. Geol. Soc. Korea* **46,** no. 1, 31–38.

Sheen, D.-H., J. S. Shin, and T.-S. Kang (2009). Seismic noise level variations in South Korea, *Geosci. J.* **13,** 183–190, doi: 10.1007/s12303-009-0018-0.

Shin, J. S., Y.-J. Seong, and M. Son (2019). Characterizing the performance of new seismic stations in southeastern region, Korea using seismic noise levels, *J. Earthq. Eng. Soc. Korea* **23,** no. 6, 321–327 (in Korean with English abstract).

Son, M., C. S. Cho, H. K. Lee, M. Han, J. S. Shin, K. Kim, and S. Kim (2020). Partitioned fault movement and aftershock triggering: Evidence for fault interactions during the 2017 M_W 5.4 Pohang earthquake, South Korea, *J. Geophys. Res.* **125,** e2020JB020005, doi: 10.1029/2020JB020005.

Son, M., C. W. Song, M.-C. Kim, Y. Cheon, H. Cho, and Y. K. Shon (2015). Miocene tectonic evolution of the basins and fault systems, SE Korea: Dextral, simple shear during the East Sea (Sea of Japan) opening, *J. Geol. Soc.* **172,** no. 5, 604–680, doi: 10.1144/jgs2014-079.

Stutzmann, E., G. Roult, and L. Astiz (2000). GEOSCOPE station noise levels, *Bull. Seismol. Soc. Am.* **90,** no. 3, 690–701.

Uthaman, M., C. Singh, A. Singh, N. Jana, A. K. Dubey, S. Sarkar, and A. K. Tiwari (2022). Spatial and temporal variation of the ambient noise environment of the Sikkim Himalaya, *Sci. Rep.* **12,** no. 1, 274, doi: 10.1038/s41598-021-04183-x.

Vassallo, M., G. Festa, and A. Bobbio (2012). Seismic ambient noise analysis in southern Italy, *Bull. Seismol. Soc. Am.* **102,** no. 2, 574–586, doi: 10.1785/0120110018.

Wiemer, S., and M. Wyss (2000). Minimum magnitude of completeness in earthquake catalogs: Examples from Alaska, the western United States, and Japan, *Bull. Seismol. Soc. Am.* **90,** 859–869, doi: 10.1785/01199901114.

Wilson, D. C., E. Wolin, W. L. Yeck, R. E. Anthony, and A. T. Ringler (2021). Modeling seismic network detection threshold using production picking algorithms, *Seismol. Res. Lett.* **93,** no. 1, 149–160.

Woo, J.-U., M. Kim, J. Rhie, and T.-S. Kang (2020). Aftershock sequence and statistics of the 2017 M_W 5.5 Pohang, South Korea, earthquake: Implications of fault heterogeneity and postseismic relaxation, *Bull. Seismol. Soc. Am.* **110,** 2031–2046, doi: 10.1785/0120200059.

Woo, J.-U., M. Kim, D.-H. Sheen, T.-S. Kang, J. Rhie, F. Grigoli, W. L. Ellsworth, and D. Giardini (2019). An in-depth seismological analysis revealing a causal link between the 2017 M_W 5.5 Pohang earthquake and EGS project, *J. Geophys. Res.* **124,** 13,060–13,078, doi: 10.1029/2019JB018368.

Yun, W. Y., S.-C. Park, and K. Y. Kim (2013). Comparison of background noise characteristics between surface and borehole station of Hwacheon, *Geophys. Geophys. Expl.* **16,** no. 4, 203–210, doi: 10.7582/GGE.2013.16.4.203 (in Korean with English Abstract).

Manuscript received 11 May 2025
Published online 29 October 2025

Scaling and Variability of Broadband Earthquake Source Spectra in Japan

Shota Shimmoto*[1]

ABSTRACT

OPEN ACCESS

Accurate evaluation of the scaling and variability of earthquake source spectra is essential for reliable ground-motion prediction. This study presents a comprehensive analysis of the broadband source spectral characteristics of crustal, interplate, and intraslab earthquakes in Japan (2004–2024, $M_w \le 7.5$), aiming to improve the predictability of the scaling and variability of ground motions. A multistage spectral ratio method was applied to estimate source spectra and source parameters, such as the apparent stress and the stress parameter, which represents a form of spectral stress drop that characterizes the high-frequency level. This method enables the estimation of double-corner-frequency (DCF) spectra in contrast to the standard approach that assumes single-corner-frequency (SCF) spectra. A systematic transition from SCF to DCF spectra with increasing magnitude was observed across all earthquake types, suggesting a fundamental difference in rupture characteristics between small and large earthquakes. The variability of the stress parameter is consistent with the between-event variability of peak ground acceleration (PGA), suggesting that the long-standing variability discrepancy between spectral stress drop and PGA has been resolved for all earthquake types. Moreover, PGAs for crustal earthquakes were successfully predicted from the estimated spectral parameters, as indicated by their strong correlation with observations. These findings highlight the effectiveness of the DCF model for improving ground-motion predictions. The study also offers broader implications for source parameter estimation, scaling relations, rupture dynamics, and ground-motion prediction. In conclusion, greater attention to the potential of DCF spectra may yield deeper insights into earthquake rupture physics and contribute to more accurate and robust ground-motion prediction.

KEY POINTS

- The variability discrepancy between peak ground acceleration (PGA) and stress drop is resolved for crustal and subduction zone events.
- The source spectrum evolves from single- to double-corner-frequency (DCF) spectra as magnitude increases.
- Accounting for DCF spectra can be crucial for predicting ground motions over a broad frequency band.

Supplemental Material

INTRODUCTION

Accurate evaluation of the scaling and variability of ground motion is critical for seismic hazard assessment. However, significant discrepancies remain between empirical ground-motion models and theoretical or numerical predictions, particularly regarding ground-motion variability. For instance, Cotton *et al.* (2013) identified that the variability of stress drop estimated from corner frequency (spectral stress drop) is significantly larger than expected from the between-event variability of peak ground acceleration (PGA).

This problem suggests that the variability in the high-frequency level of the acceleration source spectrum is inconsistent with that of PGA. Shimmoto and Miyake (2024) resolved the variability discrepancy between PGA and spectral stress drop for crustal earthquakes with $M_w > 5$ using a new spectral ratio method that enables estimation of double-corner-frequency (DCF) spectra. In addressing this issue, they demonstrated that the omega-square model (Aki, 1967; Brune, 1970), which has a single corner frequency (SCF), is not always adequate for evaluating the high-frequency level because the source spectrum can be more complicated than the spectral shape described by the SCF model. Shimmoto and Miyake (2024) showed that the source spectra of large events are typically better characterized

1. Earthquake Research Institute, The University of Tokyo, Tokyo, Japan, https://orcid.org/0000-0002-6043-1561 (SS)

*Corresponding author: shimmoto@eri.u-tokyo.ac.jp

Cite this article as Shimmoto, S. (2025). Scaling and Variability of Broadband Earthquake Source Spectra in Japan, *Bull. Seismol. Soc. Am.* **116**, 415–435, doi: 10.1785/0120250116 by a DCF model, in particular, the additive DCF (ADCF) model (e.g., Atkinson, 1993; Boore *et al.*, 2014). Therefore, a DCF model is necessary for accurately predicting ground-motion variability.

The necessity of a DCF (or similar) model has been suggested by previous studies of relatively large earthquakes (e.g., Aki, 1972; Gusev, 1983; Papageorgiou and Aki, 1985; Smith *et al.*, 1991; Atkinson, 1993; Boore *et al.*, 2014; Archuleta and Ji, 2016; Shimmoto and Miyake, 2024, and references therein). However, data on the spectral parameters that define a DCF model are scarce, and their scaling and variability are still poorly understood (Gusev, 2013). In particular, robust evaluation of spectral variability requires numerous reliable DCF parameter estimates. Moreover, data covering a wide magnitude range are necessary to determine the scaling law of the source spectrum.

Spectrum estimation for large earthquakes typically relies on teleseismic measurements (e.g., Ye *et al.*, 2016a,b), where the frequency bandwidth is usually limited to below 1.0 Hz. This limited bandwidth is insufficient for reliably evaluating the high-frequency level of the source spectrum. To address this issue, this study estimates the broadband source spectra (up to 20 Hz) for crustal, interplate, and intraslab earthquakes in Japan and conducts a comprehensive analysis.

In particular, this study investigates the scaling relations and variability of source spectra and associated source parameters, such as the stress parameter and apparent stress, across different earthquake types. Shimmoto (2024b) observed a transition from SCF to DCF spectra with increasing magnitude for crustal earthquakes, indicating differences in the underlying physics between small and large earthquakes. This study develops average source spectrum models and shows that the SCF-to-DCF transition generally holds across different earthquake types. Because the issue of the variability discrepancy has already been resolved for crustal earthquakes with $M_w \geq 3.6$ (Shimmoto, 2024b; Shimmoto and Miyake, 2024), this study aims to extend the investigation to interplate and intraslab earthquakes. Furthermore, this study demonstrates that the PGAs predicted from the estimated source spectra successfully reproduce the observed PGA scaling and variability for crustal earthquakes with $M_w \geq 3.6$.

This study further aims to provide insight into earthquake source physics and ground-motion prediction using new source spectral and parameter results from the ADCF model. By combining results from this and previous studies, several important topics are addressed in detail, including some not covered in earlier work. These include the possible origin of the discrepancy in radiated energy estimates between regional and teleseismic studies (e.g., Singh and Ordaz, 1994), the physical mechanisms underlying the scaling relations of source spectra and parameters, and implications from the comparison of observed and predicted PGAs. Finally, this study revisits the use of the term "stress drop" in ground-motion prediction (Atkinson and Beresnev, 1997), considering both DCF spectra and the assumptions underlying stress-drop calculation.

DATA

In this study, source spectra were estimated for 75 crustal, 303 interplate, and 57 intraslab earthquakes that occurred in Japan during 2004–2024 (Fig. 1a, Tables S1 and S2, available in the supplemental material to this article). The moment magnitudes of these events range from M_w 4.7 to 7.5. To investigate the scaling and variability of source spectra and associated source parameters, the new results were combined with previously published source spectral estimates for crustal earthquakes with $M_w \geq 3.6$ (Shimmoto, 2024b; Shimmoto and Miyake, 2024). Several events from Shimmoto and Miyake (2024) were reanalyzed. Table S3 lists the spectral parameters adopted from Shimmoto and Miyake (2024).

Three-component velocity waveforms recorded at Hi-net borehole stations and acceleration waveforms from Kiban–Kyoshin network (KiK-net) borehole stations were used for spectral analysis (National Research Institute for Earth Science and Disaster Resilience, 2019a,b). Hypocenter locations were provided by the Japan Meteorological Agency (JMA), and seismic moment values were taken from F-net (National Research Institute for Earth Science and Disaster Resilience, 2019c). Figure 1b shows hypocenter depths plotted against magnitude. The velocity structure model used for source parameter estimation was constructed by linear interpolation of the layered structure model employed by F-net (Kubo *et al.*, 2002; Fig. 1c).

PGA data were taken from the flat-file database of strong-motion records from Kyoshin net (K-NET) and KiK-net, compiled by Morikawa *et al.* (2024). This dataset includes PGA records only up to the end of 2023. The RotD50 metric (Boore, 2010) was adopted for the PGA analysis. Earthquake types (crustal, interplate, and intraslab) provided in the flat file were primarily used. For events lacking predefined classifications, earthquake types were inferred based on spatial proximity and similarity in focal mechanism to nearby classified events.

METHOD

Overview

This study applied a multistage spectral ratio analysis— an extension of the two-stage method proposed by Shimmoto and Miyake (2024). The motivation behind the two-stage approach is described in detail by Shimmoto and Miyake (2024).

The two-stage approach is briefly summarized subsequently. Consider a target event and two nearby events. Among the two nearby events, the one with the larger magnitude is referred to as the first-stage event, and the smaller one as the sub-nearby event. In the first-stage analysis, the standard spectral ratio analysis is conducted, and the corner frequency of the first-stage event, f_{c1}, is obtained by fitting the following model:

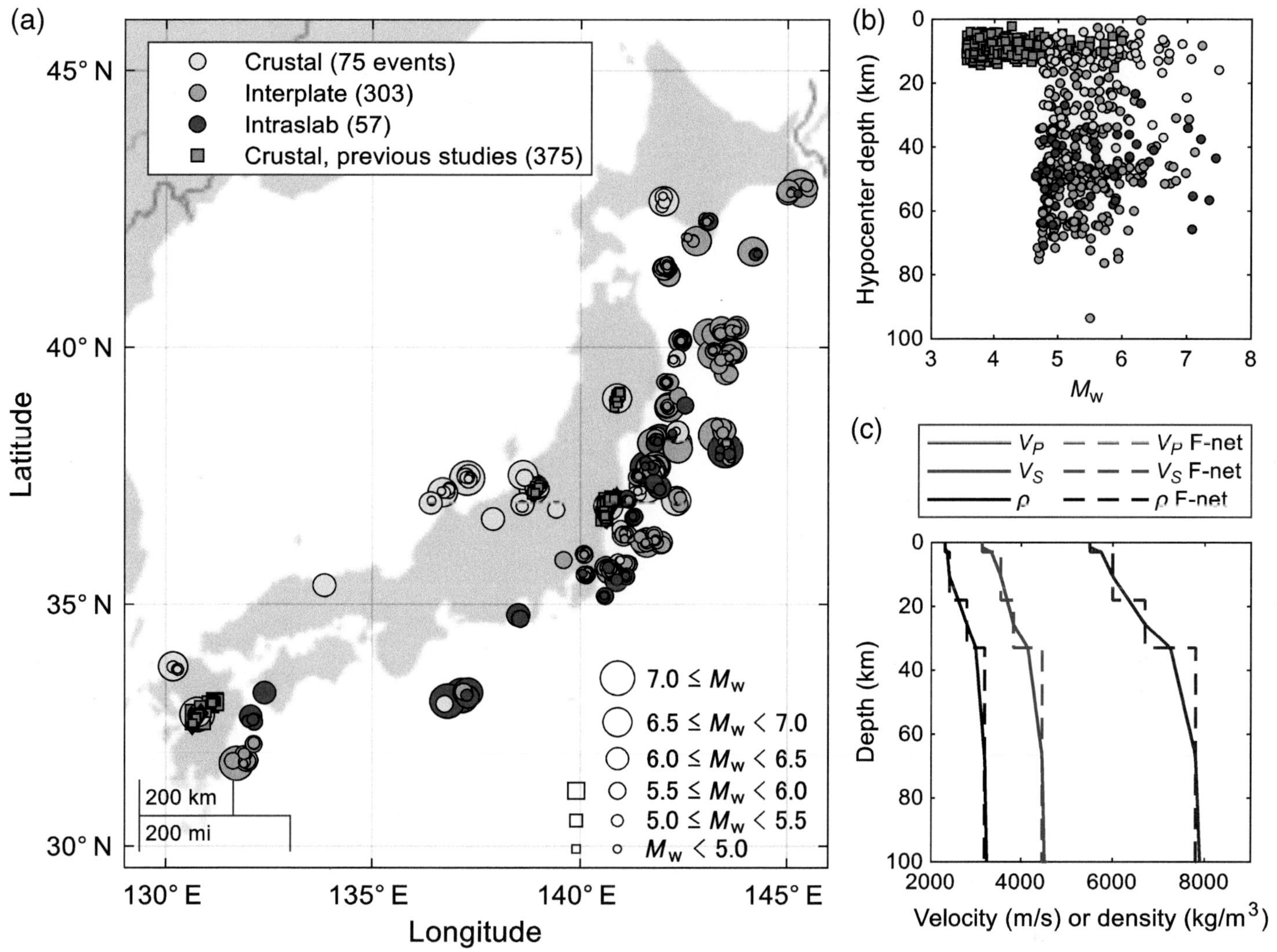

Figure 1. (a) Epicenters of earthquakes analyzed in this and previous studies (Shimmoto, 2024b; Shimmoto and Miyake, 2024). (b) Hypocenter depth versus moment magnitude M_w for the analyzed earthquakes. (c) Depth profiles of P-wave velocity, S-wave velocity, and density. The dashed lines indicate the velocity structure model from Kubo *et al.* (2002). The color version of this figure is available only in the electronic edition.

$$\mathrm{SR}_m(f) = C\frac{1+\left(\frac{f}{f_{csn}}\right)^2}{1+\left(\frac{f}{f_{c1}}\right)^2}, \quad (1)$$

in which f_{csn} is the corner frequency of the sub-nearby event, and C is a constant.

In the second-stage analysis, the source spectrum of the target event, $S_{ot2}(f)$, is estimated as follows:

$$S_{ot2}(f) = \frac{U(f)}{u(f)}\frac{1}{1+\left(\frac{f}{f_{c1}}\right)^2}, \quad (2)$$

in which $U(f)/u(f)$ is the spectral ratio of the target event and the first-stage event. Although the source spectrum of the first-stage event is assumed to follow the SCF model, $S_{ot2}(f)$ is not restricted to any particular spectral model. In this study, the standard spectral ratio analysis is applied only to earthquakes with $M_w \le 4.7$ (or 4.6, depending on data availability).

First-stage analysis

The S waves and the pre-P-wave signals were extracted using a 9-s time window. The pre-P-wave signal was used to compute the noise spectra. Waveform segments were extracted based on the phase arrival times and the travel-time table provided by the JMA. The S wave and noise spectra were computed using the multi-taper method (Thomson, 1982). The spectra were resampled so that the frequency components were equally spaced in the logarithmic frequency domain.

Corner frequencies were estimated from S-wave spectral ratios computed at each station. For each site, the spectral ratios of first-stage events were stacked using multiple sub-nearby events to improve stability. The magnitudes of first-stage events

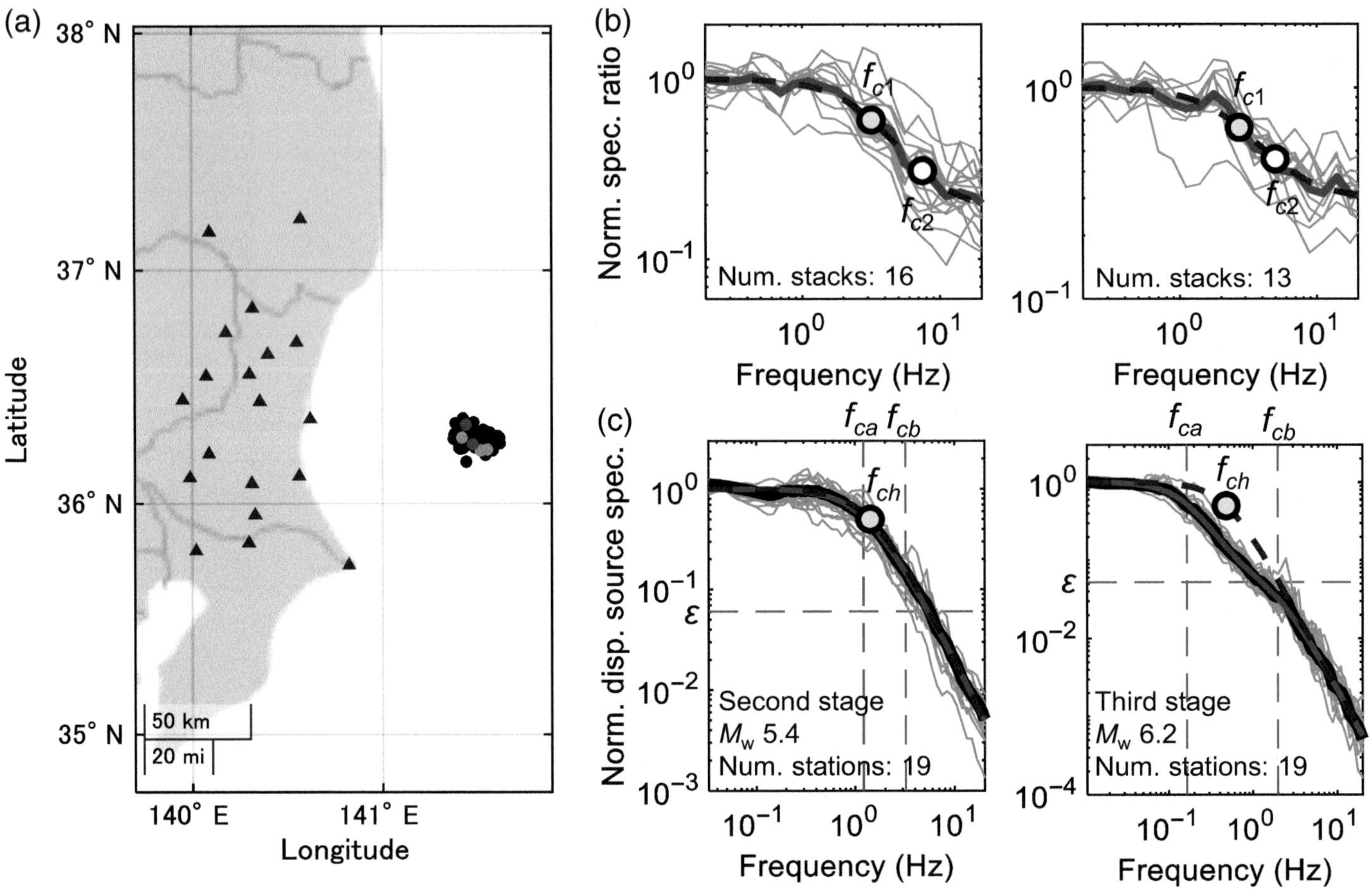

Figure 2. An illustrative example of the three-stage spectral ratio analysis. (a) Map showing stations (blue triangles) and epicenters (dots). The black dots indicate subnearby events, green dots represent first-stage events, and red dots show target events. (b) Spectral ratio fitting for a first-stage event at two different sites. The gray curves show observed spectral ratios for each subnearby event; the red curve is their average, and the blue-dashed curve indicates the best-fit model, $SR_m^{ij}(f)$. (c) Normalized displacement source spectra of the target events. The black curves show observed spectra, equation (7), red curves represent best-fit additive double-corner-frequency (ADCF) models, equation (8), and blue-dashed curves are reference single-corner-frequency (SCF) models calculated with the high-frequency fitted corner frequency, f_{ch}. The color version of this figure is available only in the electronic edition.

ranged from M_w 3.9 to 4.7, and those of the sub-nearby events were 0.5 to 2.0 magnitude units lower in JMA magnitude.

Earthquake clusters were selected based on several criteria, including the number of available events and the source-to-station distance. Figure S1 shows the epicentral locations and stations associated with each cluster. Figure 2a illustrates an example. The selection criteria for depth difference and interevent horizontal distance between sub-nearby and first-stage events were not strictly fixed but typically followed these guidelines: a depth difference of less than 2 km for shallow crustal events and 5–10 km for other types, and an interevent horizontal distance of less than 5 km for shallow crustal events and 10–15 km for the others.

Several criteria were applied for each component, and only spectral ratios that satisfied all criteria were used for stacking. The signal-to-noise ratio (SNR) of the extracted S-wave spectra was required to be at least 2.5. The variance reduction was required to be at least 70%. For the other criteria, refer to Shimmoto (2022, 2024b).

The observed average spectral ratio was fitted to the spectral ratio model to estimate the corner frequency of a first-stage event i at site j, f_{c1}^{ij} (Fig. 2b):

$$\mathrm{SR}_m^{ij}(f) = C\frac{1+\left(\frac{f}{f_{csn}^{j}}\right)^2}{1+\left(\frac{f}{f_{c1}^{ij}}\right)^2}, \quad (3)$$

in which C is a constant, and f_{csn}^{j} is the corner frequency of the stacked spectra for the sub-nearby events.

Source spectrum estimation

The source spectrum of a target event was obtained by stacking, as described subsequently. The same SNR criterion as in the first-stage analysis was applied. No lower limit was imposed on the number of stacked spectral ratios. The spectral ratio analysis was typically conducted using the Hi-net records. Hi-net velocity waveforms were used only when the peak ground velocity was less than 1.0 cm/s for all components, to mitigate spectral distortion caused by significant waveform saturation, based on

Shiomi *et al.* (2005). For some events, the KiK-net records were used to obtain source spectra. Although KiK-net records are not affected by saturation, the duration of the available records is limited. Waveforms and spectral ratios showing clear saturation or other anomalies were visually inspected and excluded from the analysis.

The time-window length was determined by trial and error, considering both the number of events used for stacking and the resolution of the low-frequency spectral level. The minimum time window length was calculated as follows:

$$t_{\min} = 1.8(10^{-14}M_0)^{1/3}, \quad (4)$$

in which M_0 is the seismic moment of a target event. This $t_{\min}$ is approximately eight times the expected average source duration (Shimmoto, 2022). When using the KiK-net records, this minimum time window length was not always applied.

In the second-stage analysis, the displacement source spectra of a target event were obtained for each first-stage event at each station, as follows:

$$S^{ij}_{ot2}(f) = \mathrm{SR}^{ij}_{ot2t1}(f)\frac{1}{1+\left(\frac{f}{f^{ij}_{cn}}\right)^2}, \quad (5)$$

in which $\mathrm{SR}^{ij}_{ot2t1}(f)$ is the observed spectral ratio between a second-stage event and a first-stage event i at site j. Then, the average source spectrum at site j, $S^{j}_{ot2}(f)$, was calculated by averaging $S^{ij}_{ot2}(f)$ over-selected first-stage events:

$$S^{j}_{ot2}(f) = \left(\prod_{i=1}^{N_j} S^{ij}_{ot2}(f)\right)^{\frac{1}{N_j}}, \quad (6)$$

in which N_j is the number of first-stage events at site j. Finally, the source spectrum was averaged over the sites,

$$S_{ot2}(f) = \left(\prod_{j=1}^{N_s} S^{j}_{ot2}(f)\right)^{\frac{1}{N_s}}, \quad (7)$$

in which N_s is the number of sites (Fig. 2c).

The displacement ADCF model is represented as $M_0 S_{\mathrm{AD}}(f)$, in which M_0 is the seismic moment, and $S_{\mathrm{AD}}(f)$ is defined as follows:

$$S_{\mathrm{AD}}(f) = \left\{\frac{1-\varepsilon}{1+(f/f_{ca})^2} + \frac{\varepsilon}{1+(f/f_{cb})^2}\right\}, \quad (8)$$

in which f_{ca} and f_{cb} are the corner frequencies with $f_{ca} \le f_{cb}$, and ε is a weighting parameter that satisfies $0 \le \varepsilon \le 1.0$. The parameters f_{ca}, f_{cb}, ε, and C were estimated by fitting $CS_{\mathrm{AD}}(f)$ to $S_{ot2}(f)$ (Fig. 2c).

From the third-stage analysis onward, the SCF model in equation (5) is replaced by the ADCF model. For instance, in the third-stage analysis, the site-specific source spectrum of a target event, $S^{ij}_{ot3}(f)$, was calculated as follows:

$$S^{ij}_{ot3}(f) = \mathrm{SR}^{ij}_{ot3t2}(f)\left\{\frac{1-\varepsilon^{ij}}{1+(f/f^{ij}_{ca})^2} + \frac{\varepsilon^{ij}}{1+(f/f^{ij}_{cb})^2}\right\}, \quad (9)$$

in which $\mathrm{SR}^{ij}_{ot3t2}(f)$ is the observed spectral ratio of the third-stage event to a second-stage event i at site j, and f^{ij}_{ca}, f^{ij}_{cb}, and ε^{ij} are the parameters estimated by fitting $CS_{\mathrm{AD}}(f)$ to $S^{ij}_{ot2}(f)$, which is the site-specific source spectrum of the second-stage event i. The subsequent procedure follows that of the second-stage analysis.

For two M_w 7.5 events, an additional assumption was made to estimate their source spectra (ID51 and ID95 of Fig. S1). For simplicity, these events are referred to as third-stage events. Because of their large source areas, it was preferable to use records from distant stations. However, the number of available stations was significantly limited by the SNRs of sub-nearby events used in the first-stage analysis. To overcome this limitation, it was assumed that the ADCF model estimated for the station-averaged source spectrum of the second-stage event, $S_{mt2}(f)$, remains valid for a new set of stations. In this case, the source spectrum of a target event, $S_{ot3}(f)$, can be computed as follows:

$$S_{ot3}(f) = \left(\prod_{j=1}^{N} \mathrm{SR}^{j}_{ot3t2}(f)\right)^{\frac{1}{N}} S_{mt2}(f), \quad (10)$$

in which $\mathrm{SR}^{j}_{ot3t2}(f)$ is the observed spectral ratio of the target event to a second-stage event at site j. Equation (10) can be readily extended to the case where multiple second-stage events are used.

SCALING LAW OF SEISMIC SOURCE SPECTRA

The estimated source spectra are shown in Figure S1. The source spectral shapes are diverse, exhibiting both SCF- and DCF-like spectra. It was found that the ADCF model effectively explains the observed spectra, whereas the SCF model often failed to provide a sufficient fit (Fig. S1).

This study first developed empirical models for the spectral parameters and then used them to predict the average scaling behavior of the source spectra. The following models were fitted to the observed spectral parameters for each earthquake type (Fig. 3a–c):

$$f^{\mathrm{ave}}_{ca} = 10^{-a_1 M_w + a_2}, \quad (11)$$

$$f^{\mathrm{ave}}_{cb} = b_1 + 3^{-(M_w - b_2)}, \quad (12)$$

$$\varepsilon^{\mathrm{ave}} = \frac{c_1}{1+10^{(M_w - c_2)}}. \quad (13)$$

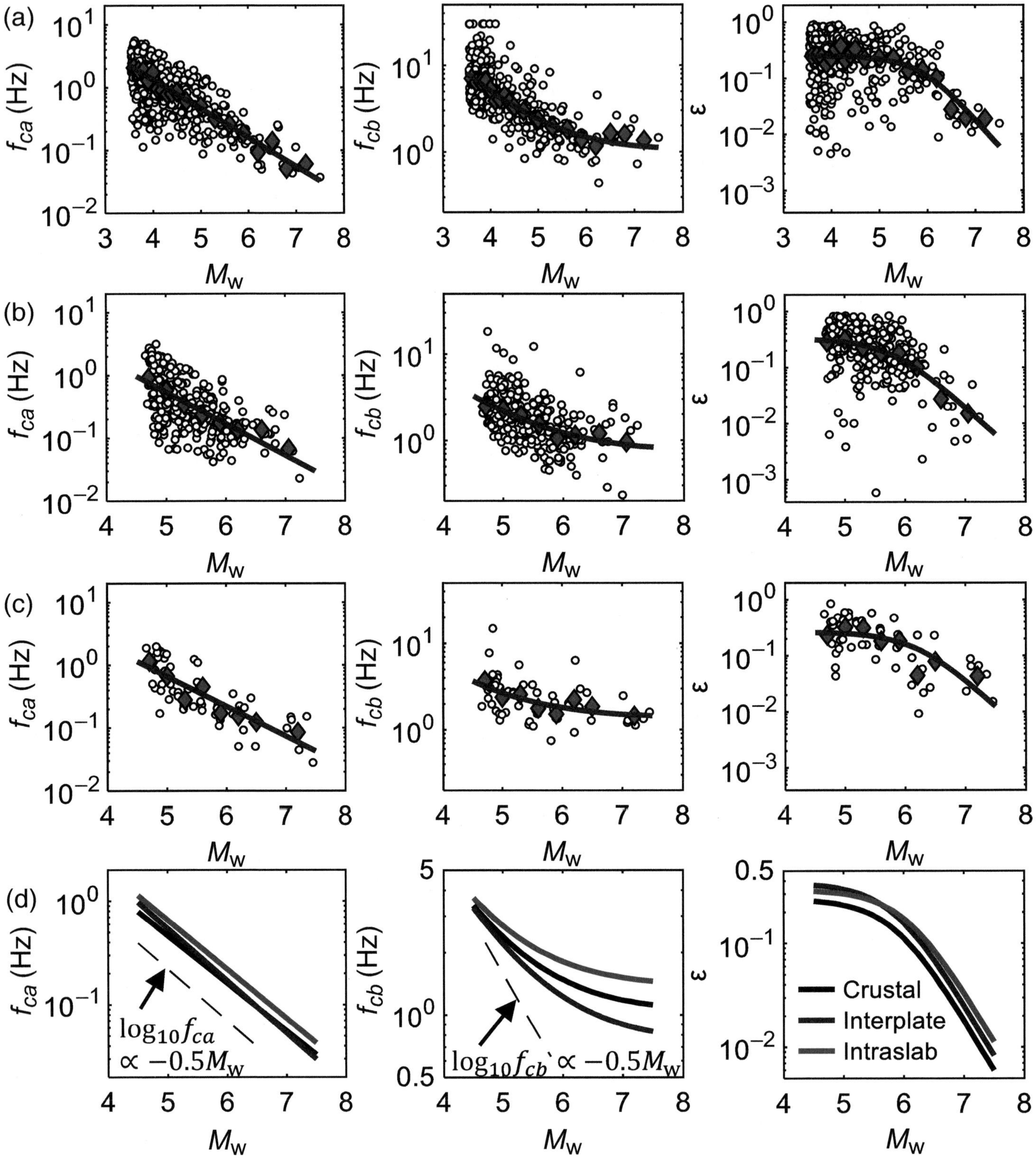

Figure 3. Magnitude dependence of spectral parameters, f_{ca} (left), f_{cb} (middle), and ε (right) for (a) crustal, (b) interplate, and (c) intraslab earthquakes in Japan. The white circles represent individual observations, and the red diamonds indicate their geometric means calculated for each magnitude bin. The blue curves show the regression results. ε is not plotted where $f_{ca} = f_{cb}$. (d) Comparison of the magnitude dependence of average spectral parameters between crustal (black), interplate (blue), and intraslab (red) earthquakes. The color version of this figure is available only in the electronic edition.

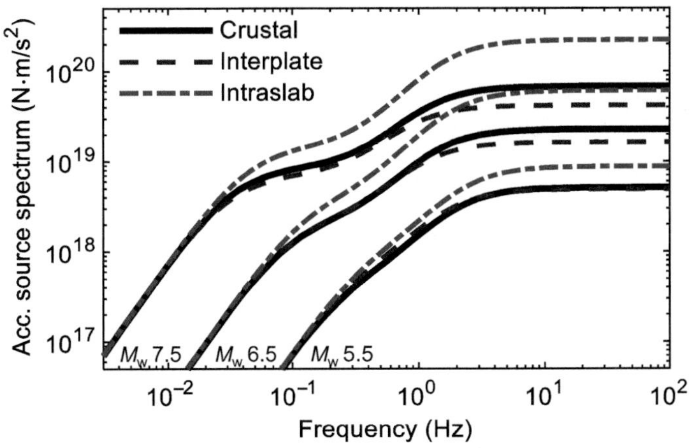

Figure 4. Comparison of the model-predicted acceleration source spectra, $(2\pi f)^2 M_0 S_{AD}(f)$, for crustal, interplate, and intraslab earthquakes at M_w 5.5, 6.5, and 7.5. The color version of this figure is available only in the electronic edition.

The functional forms were determined by trial and error. In cases where $f_{ca} = f_{cb}$, ε becomes undefined and is therefore excluded from the regression. The estimated coefficients are listed in Table 1.

The f_{ca} scaling is approximately consistent with the self-similar scaling, that is, $\log_{10} f_{ca} \propto -0.5M_w$ (Table 1, Fig. 3d). In contrast, f_{cb} decreases with magnitude more slowly than f_{ca} (Fig. 3b) and becomes relatively constant at large magnitudes, with asymptotic values of 1.0, 0.74, and 1.37 Hz for crustal, interplate, and intraslab earthquakes, respectively (Table 1). For crustal and interplate earthquakes, f_{ca} is similar, and f_{ca} of intraslab kes is consistently higher than the others (Fig. 3d).

Figure 4 compares the acceleration source spectra predicted by equations (11)–(13) for each earthquake type for M_w 5.5, 6.5, and 7.5. The spectrum of intraslab earthquakes shows the highest level in the high-frequency range. The high-frequency spectral level of crustal earthquakes is slightly higher than that of interplate earthquakes. The transition from SCF to DCF spectra is consistently observed for all earthquake types. Figure 5 emphasizes this transition by illustrating the scaling law of the source spectrum for M_w 3.5–7.5.

SCALING AND VARIABILITY OF STRESS PARAMETER AND APPARENT STRESS

High-frequency-fitted corner frequency and stress parameter

The stress parameter is often used to characterize the high-frequency level of the acceleration source spectrum in engineering seismology (Boore, 1983; Atkinson and Beresnev, 1997; Boore *et al.*, 2014). The high-frequency-fitted corner frequency f_{ch} is defined as (Boore *et al.*, 2014)

$$f_{ch} = \sqrt{(1-\varepsilon) f_{ca}^2 + \varepsilon f_{cb}^2}. \tag{14}$$

TABLE 1
Parameter Coefficients of the Regression Models for f_{ca}, f_{cb}, and ε

EQ Type	a_1	a_2	b_1	b_2	c_1	c_2
Crustal	0.460	1.967	1.031	5.279	0.266	5.863
Interplate	0.505	2.261	0.737	5.352	0.380	5.850
Intraslab	0.475	2.193	1.368	5.264	0.327	6.054

EQ, earthquake.

The stress parameter can be calculated from the following equation:

$$\Delta\sigma_{fch} = \frac{7}{16} M_0 \left(\frac{f_{ch}}{kV_S}\right)^3, \tag{15}$$

in which M_0 is the seismic moment, V_S is the S-wave velocity in the source region, and k is a constant, which is assumed to be $k = 2.34/(2\pi)$ in this study (Brune, 1970, 1971). The velocity model is used to determine V_S. In this study, hypocenter depth is used instead of centroid depth because centroid depth is sometimes anomalously shallow compared with hypocenter depth, even for small-to-moderate-magnitude events.

Radiated energy and radiated-energy-based corner frequency

The radiated energy, E_R, can be calculated assumingz a double-couple radiation pattern (e.g., Venkataraman and Kanamori, 2004):

$$E_R = \left(\frac{8\pi}{15\rho V_P^5} + \frac{8\pi}{10\rho V_S^5}\right) \int_0^\infty f^2 |S(f)|^2 df, \tag{16}$$

in which ρ and V_P are the density and the P-wave velocity in the source region, and |S(f)| is the displacement source spectral amplitude. From the radiated energy, the apparent stress is given by (e.g., Aki, 1966; Kanamori and Rivera, 2006)

$$\sigma_a = \mu \frac{E_R}{M_0}, \tag{17}$$

in which μ is the shear rigidity.

If we assume $|S(f)| = M_0 S_{AD}(f)$, the radiated energy can be expressed as follows:

$$E_R^{DCF} = \left(\frac{2\pi^2 M_0^2}{15\rho V_P^5} + \frac{\pi^2 M_0^2}{5\rho V_S^5}\right) \left\{(1-\varepsilon)^2 f_{ca}^3 + \varepsilon^2 f_{cb}^3 + \frac{4\varepsilon(1-\varepsilon) f_{ca}^2 f_{cb}^2}{f_{ca} + f_{cb}}\right\}. \tag{18}$$

In this study, the radiated energy was calculated from this equation. Alternatively, when we assume the SCF model by Brune (1970), the radiated energy is expressed as

$$E_R^{SCF} = \left(\frac{2\pi^2 M_0^2}{15\rho V_P^5} + \frac{\pi^2 M_0^2}{5\rho V_S^5}\right) f_c^3. \tag{19}$$

By comparing E_R^{DCF} and E_R^{SCF}, we can define a radiated energy-based corner frequency, f_{cER}, as follows:

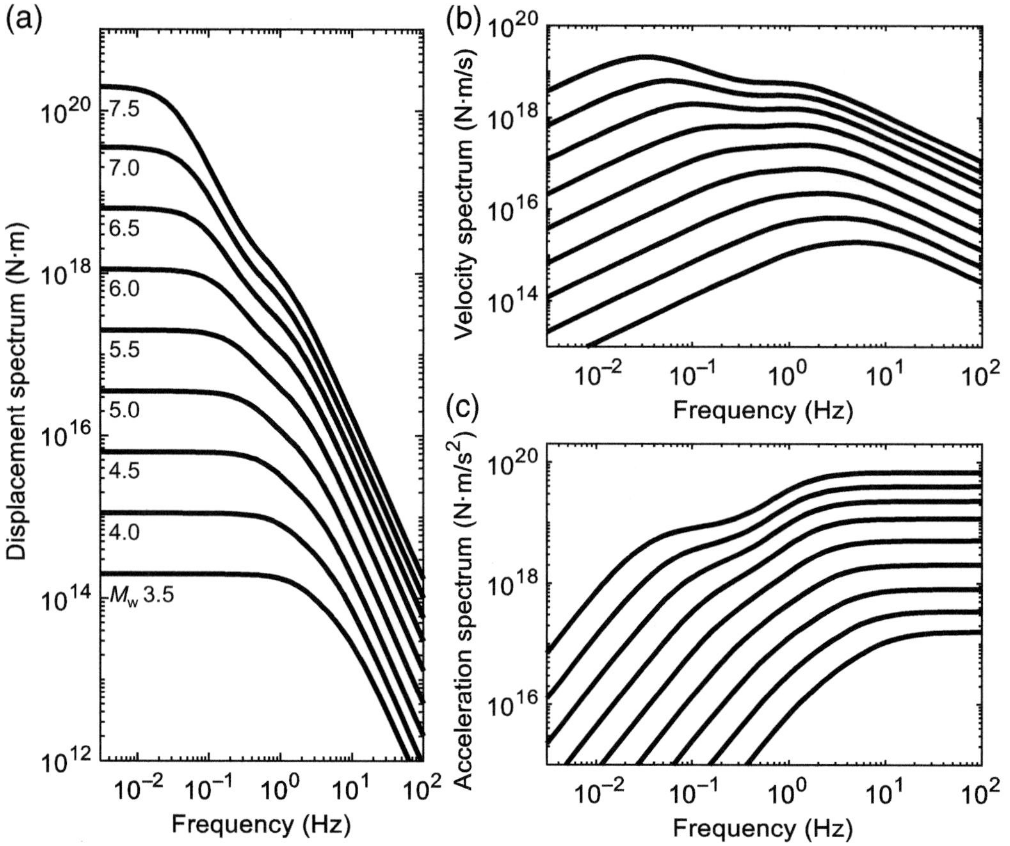

Figure 5. Scaling of seismic source spectra for crustal earthquakes in Japan: (a) displacement spectra, $M_0 S_{AD}(f)$; (b) velocity spectra, $2\pi f M_0 S_{AD}(f)$; and (c) acceleration spectra, $(2\pi f)^2 M_0 S_{AD}(f)$. Spectra are shown for magnitudes ranging from 3.5 to 7.5 in increments of 0.5.

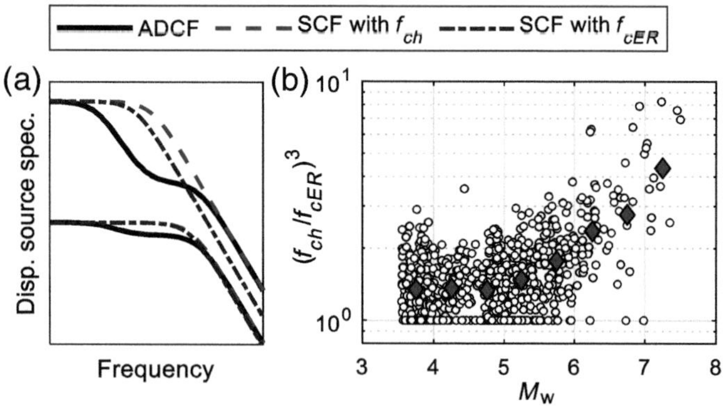

Figure 6. Comparison between the high-frequency-fitted corner frequency f_{ch} and radiated energy-based corner frequency f_{cER}. (a) Examples of SCF models calculated using f_{ch} and f_{cER}. (b) Magnitude dependence of $(f_{ch}/f_{cER})^3$. The red diamonds represent geometric means calculated for each magnitude bin. The color version of this figure is available only in the electronic edition.

$$f_{cER} = \left\{(1-\varepsilon)^2 f_{ca}^3 + \varepsilon^2 f_{cb}^3 + \frac{4\varepsilon(1-\varepsilon) f_{ca}^2 f_{cb}^2}{f_{ca} + f_{cb}}\right\}^{\frac{1}{3}}. \quad (20)$$

Using f_{cER}, we can define a radiated energy-based stress parameter as

$$\Delta\sigma_{fcER} = \frac{7}{16} M_0 \left(\frac{f_{cER}}{kV_S}\right)^3. \quad (21)$$

For a reference, Andrews (1986) defined another corner frequency, corresponding to the predominant frequency in random vibration theory (Cartwright and Longuet-Higgins, 1956; Boore, 1983), which may be expressed in terms of the ADCF model parameters as follows:

$$f_{cRVT} = \sqrt{\frac{f_{cER}^3}{f_{cD}}}, \quad (22)$$

$$f_{cD} = (1-\varepsilon)^2 f_{ca} + \varepsilon^2 f_{cb} + \frac{4\varepsilon(1-\varepsilon) f_{ca} f_{cb}}{f_{ca} + f_{cb}}, \quad (23)$$

in which f_{cD} is another possible definition of corner frequency based on the integration of the square of displacement spectrum, $\int_0^\infty |S(f)|^2 df$. When $f_{ca} = f_{cb}$, $\varepsilon = 0$, or $\varepsilon = 1$, all the corner frequencies, f_{ch}, f_{cER}, f_{cRVT}, and f_{cD}, coincide and reduce to an SCF, $f_c = f_{ca}$ or $f_c = f_{cb}$.

Magnitude dependence of source parameters

Figure 6 shows the comparison between f_{ch} and f_{cER}. Figure 6a illustrates that increasing differences between f_{cER} and f_{ch} are associated with larger deviations from the SCF model. Thus, the difference between f_{cER} and f_{ch} can be used as an indicator of deviation from the SCF model. Figure 6b shows the magnitude dependence of $(f_{ch}/f_{cER})^3$, which is equivalent to $\Delta\sigma_{fch}/\Delta\sigma_{fcER}$. For $M_w < 5$, the average value of $(f_{ch}/f_{cER})^3$ is nearly constant at about 1.35. Subsequently, it increases with increasing magnitudes. The magnitude dependence of $(f_{ch}/f_{cER})^3$ well describes the evolution from SCF to DCF spectra shown in Figures 4 and 5. Figure 6 also suggests that even for large earthquakes, some events have a spectral shape similar to the SCF model, which is indicated by $(f_{ch}/f_{cER})^3 \approx 1.0$.

Figure 7 shows the magnitude dependence of $\Delta\sigma_{fch}$, σ_a, and E_R/M_0. Regression models were fitted for $\Delta\sigma_{fch}$ and σ_a. For crustal earthquakes, the following model was applied:

$$\log_{10} Y = \begin{cases} a_1 M_w + a_2, & M_w < a_3 \\ a_4 M_w + a_1 a_3 - a_3 a_4 - a_2, & M_w \geq a_3 \end{cases}. \quad (24)$$

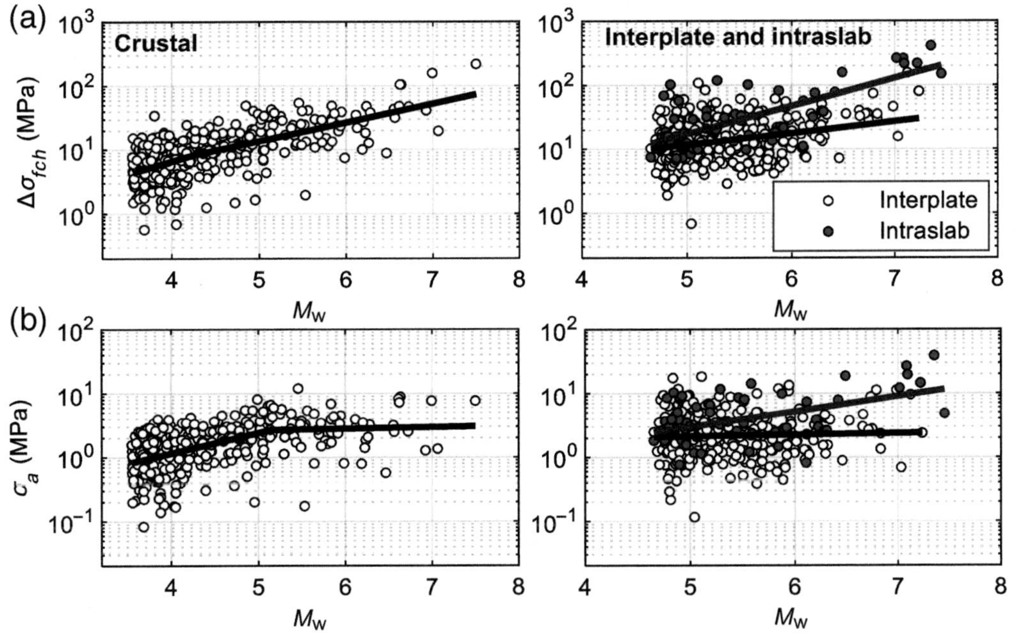

Figure 7. Magnitude dependence of source parameters: (a) $\Delta\sigma_{fch}$ and (b) σ_a. The black and blue lines show the regression results. In the right panels, the black and blue lines indicate the regression results for interplate and intraslab earthquakes, respectively. The color version of this figure is available only in the electronic edition.

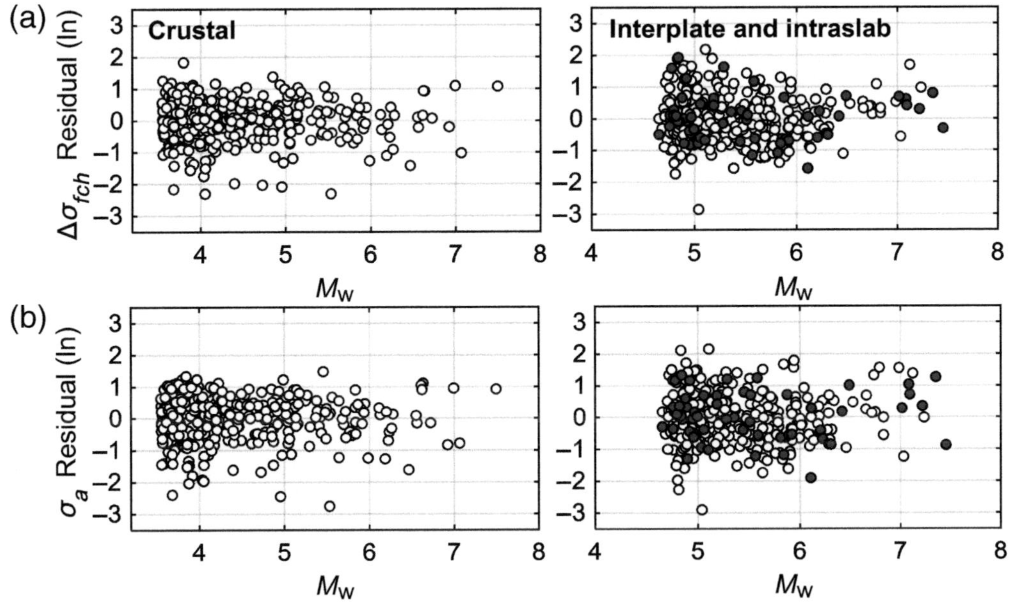

Figure 8. Magnitude versus the residuals (ln units): (a) $\Delta\sigma_{fch}$ and (b) σ_a. Residuals were calculated using the regression results shown in Figure 7. The left panels show the results for crustal earthquakes, and the right panels show results for interplate (white circles) and intraslab (red circles) earthquakes. The color version of this figure is available only in the electronic edition.

For interplate and intraslab earthquakes, the following simple model was used to ensure stability:

$$\log_{10} Y = a_1 M_w + a_2. \quad (25)$$

The coefficient values are listed in Table S4.

The stress parameter $\Delta\sigma_{fch}$ tends to increase with magnitude (Fig. 7a). The geometric average of $\Delta\sigma_{fch}$ for $M_w > 4.7$ is 17.7 MPa for crustal, 13.7 MPa for interplate, and 30.0 MPa for intraslab earthquakes. The apparent stress σ_a for crustal earthquakes exhibits a clear break in the scaling relation (Fig. 7b): it increases with magnitude for $M_w < 5.1$ and then becomes approximately constant for larger magnitudes. In contrast, σ_a of interplate earthquakes remains nearly constant in the studied magnitude range ($M_w > 4.7$), whereas that of intraslab earthquakes shows a mild increase. The geometric average of σ_a for $M_w > 5.1$ is 2.8 MPa (crustal), 2.1 MPa (interplate), and 5.2 MPa (intraslab). Similarly, the geometric average of E_R/M_0 for $M_w > 5.1$ is 8.2×10^{-5} for crustal, 4.1×10^{-5} for interplate, and 9.6×10^{-5} for intraslab earthquakes.

Variability of stress parameter and apparent stress

Figure 8 shows the relationship between M_w and the logarithmic residuals of $\Delta\sigma_{fch}$ and σ_a. The residuals were calculated from

$$\delta = \ln x - \ln x_{\mathrm{model}}, \quad (26)$$

in which x is an observed parameter, and x_{model} is the parameter value predicted by a regression model.

The standard deviation of δ (the residual standard deviation) of $\Delta\sigma_{fch}$ is 0.68, 0.75, and 0.71 (ln unit) for crustal, interplate, and intraslab earthquakes for $M_w > 4.7$. The residual standard deviation of $\Delta\sigma_{fch}$ is 0.61 for crustal earthquakes with $M_w > 3.6$. If we assume the relationship PGA $\propto \Delta\sigma_{fch}^{0.8}$, these residual standard deviations are consistent with the between-event variability of PGA observed in Japan

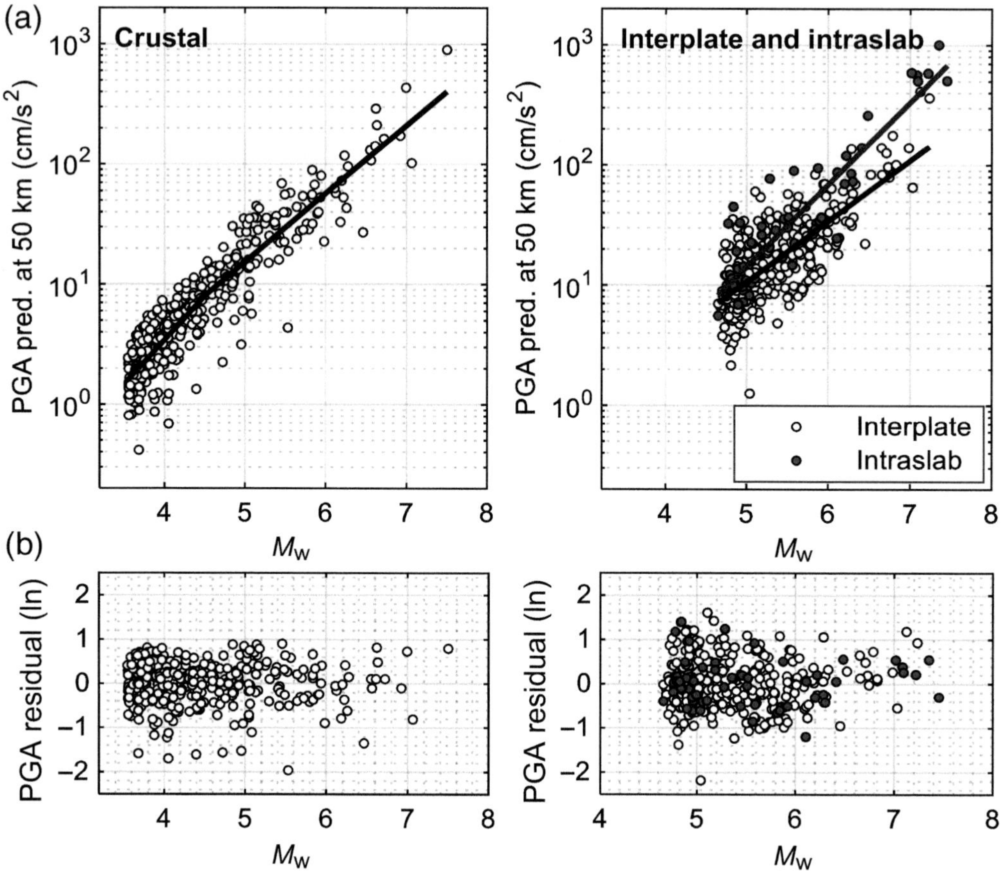

Figure 9. (a) Magnitude dependence of peak ground acceleration (PGA) at 50 km predicted by equation (27). (b) Magnitude versus the residuals of model-predicted PGAs. The solid lines show the regression results. In the right figure, the black and blue lines indicate the regression results for interplate and intraslab earthquakes. The color version of this figure is available only in the electronic edition.

(e.g., Rodriguez-Marek *et al.*, 2011; Oth *et al.*, 2017; Abrahamson and Gulerce, 2022; Si *et al.*, 2022; Sung *et al.*, 2024). The residual standard deviation of σ_a is 0.72, 0.80, and 0.75 for crustal, interplate, and intraslab earthquakes with $M_w > 4.7$. The residual standard deviation of σ_a is 0.66 for crustal earthquakes with $M_w > 3.6$. No clear dependence on hypocenter depth is observed in the residuals of $\Delta\sigma_{fch}$ and σ_a (Fig. S2).

SCALING AND VARIABILITY OF SPECTRUM-PREDICTED PGA

Simple model for predicting PGA

This study aims to show that the observed source spectra are indeed consistent with PGAs by predicting PGAs using the formula proposed by Hanks and McGuire (1981)

$$\mathrm{PGA_{pred}} = \frac{0.85(2\pi)^2\Delta\sigma_{fch}}{\rho R}\sqrt{\frac{f_{\max}}{f_{ch}}}\sqrt{2\ln\left(\frac{2f_{\max}}{f_{ch}}\right)}, \quad (27)$$

in which ρ is the density, and R is the source-to-site distance. PGAs were calculated at $R = 50$ km. By referring to the representation of $f_{\max}$ and an attenuation model (e.g., Hanks and McGuire, 1981; Boore, 2003), this study calculated $f_{\max}$ from

$$f_{\max} = \frac{1}{\pi\kappa_0 + \frac{\pi R}{QV_S}}, \quad (28)$$

in which Q is a quality factor, and κ_0 is interpreted as near-surface attenuation (Anderson and Hough, 1984). In this study, Q was set to 700 based on a typical Q model at high frequencies (e.g., Boore, 2003), and κ_0 was set to 0.033 (Van Houtte *et al.*, 2011). At $R = 50$ km, the effect of κ_0 is dominant.

Equation (27) was derived under several assumptions. One of the most significant limitations may be that equation (27) assumes the SCF model with f_{ch}, which, as previously discussed, is not appropriate for large events. Nevertheless, this formulation provides a direct connection to the paradox highlighted by Cotton *et al.* (2013), who originally pointed out the inconsistency between PGAs and stress drops within this SCF model-based framework. Moreover, to evaluate the consistency between the variability of the observed PGAs and the variability inferred from the estimated source spectra, it is more straightforward and appropriate to investigate the scaling behavior and variability of PGA predicted by equation (27), rather than the variability of $\Delta\sigma_{fch}$. A more detailed prediction of ground motions using the ADCF model is left for future work.

Magnitude dependence and variability of spectrum-predicted PGAs

Figure 9 shows the magnitude scaling and residuals of the PGAs predicted by equation (27). The rate at which PGA increases with magnitude appears to be higher for intraslab earthquakes ($a_1 = 0.684$) than for interplate earthquakes ($a_1 = 0.545$) (Fig. 9a, Table S4). A qualitatively similar trend was reported by Abrahamson and Gulerce (2022).

The residuals were calculated using the regression model (Fig. 9b). The coefficients of the regression models are listed in Table S4. For $M_w > 4.7$, the residual standard deviations of the PGAs predicted by equation (27) are 0.54 for crustal, 0.58 for interplate, and 0.53 for intraslab earthquakes. These standard deviations are consistent with the between-event variability of PGA for moderate-to-large earthquakes in Japan, which is ~0.5–0.6 (e.g., Abrahamson and Gulerce, 2022; Si *et al.*, 2022; Sung *et al.*, 2024). For $M_w > 3.6$, the residual standard deviation of the predicted PGAs for crustal earthquakes is 0.43, consistent with the between-event variability of PGA for small-to-large crustal earthquakes in Japan, for example, 0.43 (Oth *et al.*, 2017) and 0.49 (Rodriguez-Marek *et al.*, 2011). Therefore, the between-event variability of PGAs reported in the previous ground-motion model studies is well reproduced by the estimated source spectra for crustal, interplate, and intraslab earthquakes.

Comparison between the observed and predicted PGAs for crustal earthquakes

For crustal earthquakes, the PGAs at 50 km recorded at surface stations of K-NET and KiK-net were compared with those predicted by equation (27). The main purpose of this comparison is to provide more direct and robust evidence that the estimated source spectra are consistent with observed PGAs. The selection of $R = 50$ km is based on the following considerations. If the distance is too short, PGAs may be strongly affected by finite-fault effects, where they are controlled by rupture on a limited portion of the fault and tend to saturate for large events (e.g., Baltay and Hanks, 2014). At larger distances, the combined effects of Q and geometric spreading become more complex.

Interplate and intraslab earthquakes are not investigated in this study for two main reasons: (1) records are typically absent at $R = 50$ km (often $R > 100$ km), and (2) the depth differences between events are significantly large, which can lead to complex differences in attenuation effects among events. The comparison of PGAs for individual events for these earthquake types is left for future work.

The PGAs at 50 km were obtained by fitting the following attenuation model:

$$\ln \mathrm{PGA} = C_0 + \{C_1 + 0.4271(M_w - 5.6)\}\ln R - 0.0140(R - 1.0), \tag{29}$$

$$R = \sqrt{R_{\mathrm{rup}}^2 + 1.85}, \tag{30}$$

in which R_{rup} is the rupture distance provided by the flat file. The coefficients C_0 and C_1 were determined for each event by fitting the attenuation model to PGA data at distances up to $R =$ 200 km. All other coefficients were adopted from Rodriguez-Marek *et al.* (2011). The constraint range for C_1 was set between 1.8– and −1.0. Events with fewer than five PGA records within the 30–70 km range were excluded from the analysis.

Figure 10 shows the comparison between the observed and predicted PGAs. In this figure, the PGAs were predicted using f_{ch} values determined by Shimmoto (2024b), who estimated them by fitting the SCF model to the high-frequency level, instead of using equation (14). This is because equation (14) sometimes overestimates the high-frequency level within the considered frequency bandwidth due to a high f_{cb} value (for example, refer to fig. S2 of Shimmoto, 2024b).

The magnitude scaling of the predicted PGAs, when scaled by a factor of 1.4, approximately reproduces that of the observed PGAs (Fig. 10a). This scaling coefficient is used to adjust the systematic underestimation in the predicted PGAs and may be attributed to the effects that are not incorporated in equation (27), such as an average site amplification. Figure 10b compares the scaling relations between $\Delta\sigma_{fch}$ and the observed PGAs. Figure 10a,b suggests that the PGAs predicted by equation (27) explain the scaling relation of the observed PGAs more effectively than $\Delta\sigma_{fch}$ does.

A strong positive correlation was found between the observed and predicted PGAs on a logarithmic scale, with a correlation coefficient of 0.92 (Fig. 10c). The correlation coefficient between the observed PGAs and $\Delta\sigma_{fch}$ is 0.80, which is lower than 0.92 but may still be considered strong (Fig. 10d). Figure 10e shows the residuals between the observed and predicted PGAs. The residual standard deviation is 0.45 (ln unit). For $M_w > 6.5$, the predicted PGAs (multiplied by 1.4) are systematically higher than the observed values (Fig. 10a). This bias may be partly attributed to the assumptions of the SCF model with f_{ch} for the large events because the source spectra of large events often have spectral sag at an intermediate-frequency range (Fig. 4). Other influential factors include nonlinear site response under strong ground motion.

DISCUSSION

Limitations

A key assumption is the use of the SCF model in the first-stage analysis. Shimmoto (2024b) applied the two-stage method to earthquakes with M_w 3.6–4.9 using the events of about magnitude 3–3.5 in the first-stage analysis and demonstrated that the SCF model is appropriate for $M_w < 5$. The present study further confirms the validity of the SCF model assumption for $M_w < 5$ (Fig. 4). Thus, the SCF assumption in the first-stage analysis is considered valid. However, the possibility of systematic regional differences in spectral characteristics, such as fall-off rate, cannot be completely ruled out.

The measurement errors in source spectra and source parameters are essentially unavoidable. For instance, an uncertainty of about a factor of two, which is typical in seismological observations, is not unusual for the stress parameter $\Delta\sigma_{fch}$ based on the comparison with the observed PGAs (Fig. 10). There are many factors contributing to spectrum measurement errors, including station coverage, frequency bandwidth, and the selection of nearby events when taking spectral ratios. It is generally difficult and impractical to rigorously quantify all possible error sources in individual spectral estimates, and this difficulty is well recognized in seismological studies. Under these inevitable uncertainties, it is important to carefully select topics that can be reliably discussed based on the data. Therefore, this study instead focuses on the statistical characteristics of source spectra and source

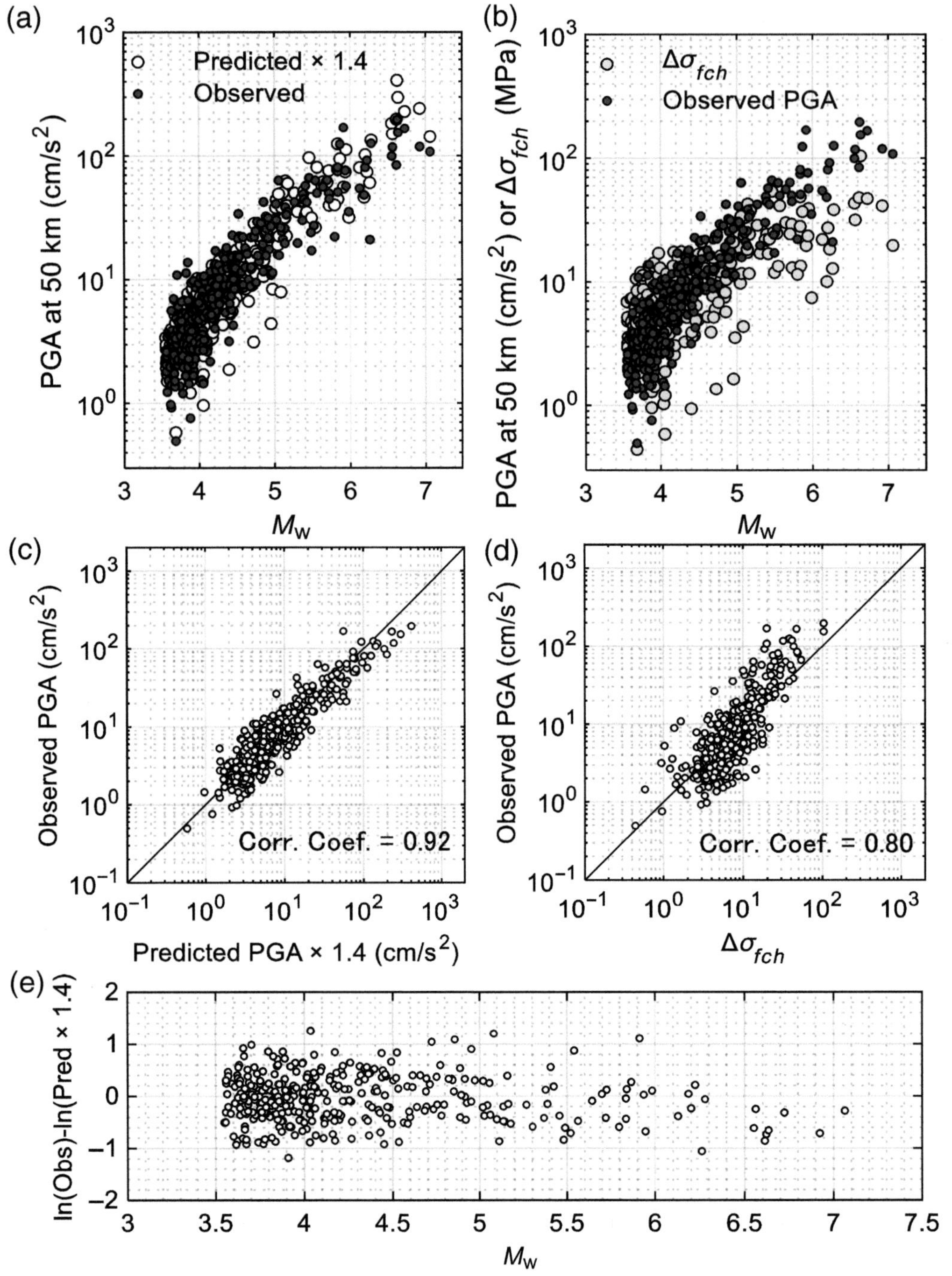

Figure 10. (a) Moment magnitude M_w versus observed and predicted PGAs. Predicted PGA is scaled by multiplying by a factor of 1.4. (b) M_w versus observed PGAs and M_w versus $\Delta\sigma_{fch}$. (c) Correlation between observed and predicted PGAs. (d) Correlation between observed PGAs and $\Delta\sigma_{fch}$. (e) Residuals between observed and predicted PGAs (ln units). The color version of this figure is available only in the electronic edition.

parameters, which are considered relatively robust and less sensitive to individual measurement uncertainties.

Regional versus teleseismic estimates of radiated energy

The radiated energies, E_R, estimated from teleseismic and regional measurements often exhibit systematic differences (e.g., Singh and Ordaz, 1994). The average σ_a value obtained in this study for interplate earthquakes is 2.1 MPa, which is significantly higher than 0.56 MPa reported by Ye *et al.* (2016a). Because Ye *et al.* (2016a) evaluated the radiated energies only up to 1.0 Hz, Figure 11a compares E_R calculated from equation (18) to that computed up to 1.0 Hz using the average spectrum model for interplate earthquakes. The average spectrum models were computed using the ADCF model with the parameters predicted by equations (11)–(13) using the coefficients listed in Table 1. The E_R value computed up to 1.0 Hz underestimates the total energy by a factor of 2.4 for M_w 7 and 1.5 for M_w 8. This underestimation partly explains the discrepancy between teleseismic and regional measurements.

Figure 11b shows the magnitude dependence of σ_a obtained using the average source spectrum model with $V_P = 6600$ m/s, $V_S = 3800$ m/s, and $\rho = 2700$ kg/m^3. If E_R is computed only up to 1.0 Hz, σ_a remains nearly constant at ~0.38 MPa, roughly consistent with Ye *et al.* (2016a). In contrast, when E_R is calculated using equation (18), σ_a is predicted to decrease with increasing M_w, and its average value is 2.2 MPa for $M_w < 7$ and 0.45 MPa for $M_w > 7$.

Figure 11c shows examples of the source spectra predicted from the average source spectrum models up to 2.0 Hz for M_w 7.7, 8.2, and 9.1. These M_w values correspond to three interplate earthquakes in Japan studied by Ye *et al.* (2016a,b). Upon visual comparison, I found that the source spectra in Figure 11c resemble the spectra of the corresponding earthquakes reported by Ye *et al.* (2016b). For comparison, refer to the supporting material of Ye *et al.* (2016b). Furthermore, many other spectra reported

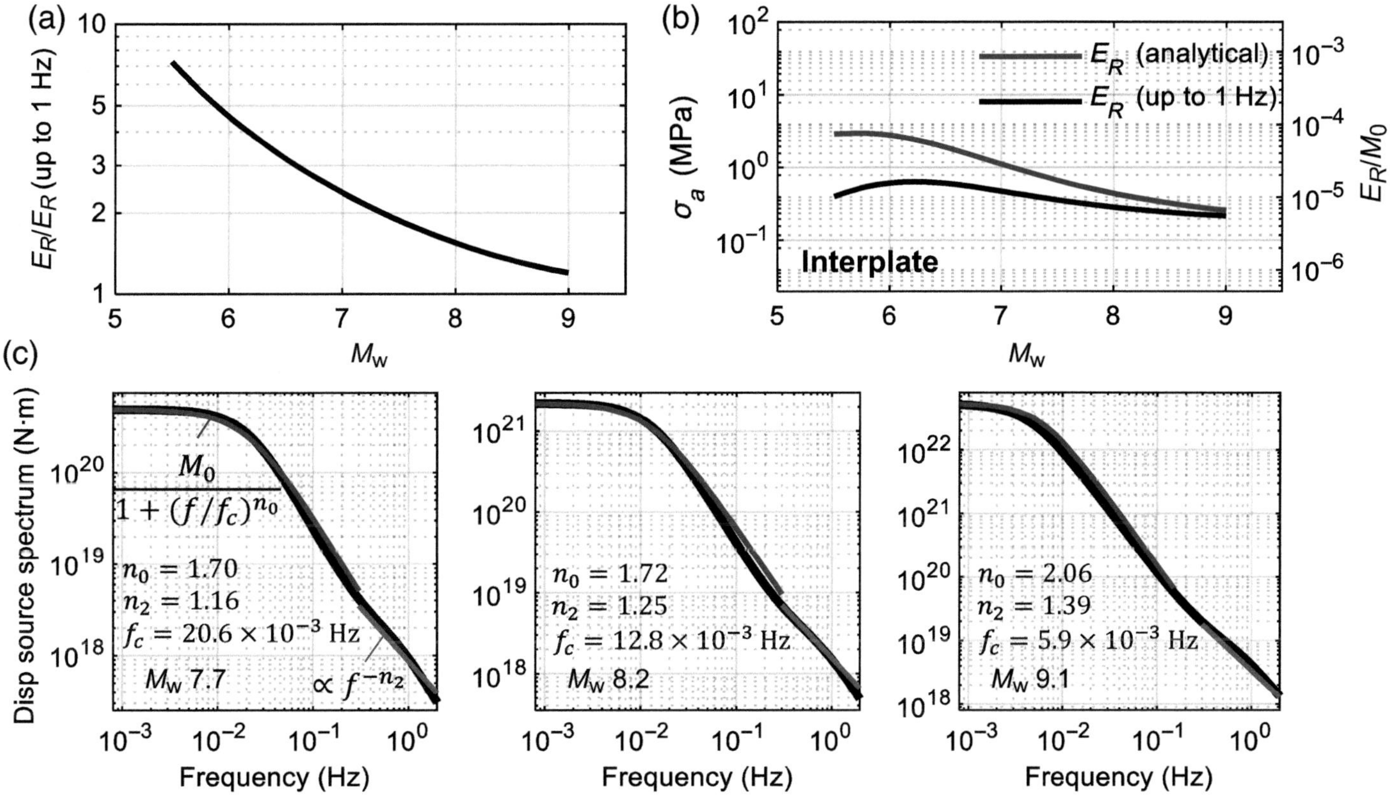

Figure 11. (a) Ratio of E_R calculated from equation (18) to that computed up to 1.0 Hz using the average source spectrum model for interplate earthquakes. (b) Magnitude dependence of σ_a and E_R. (c) Average displacement source spectra predicted from the average source spectrum model for interplate earthquakes with M_w 7.7, 8.2, and 9.1 (the black curves). The red curves and magenta lines are the results of Ye *et al.* (2016a,b). The red curves are the SCF models with a fall-off rate n_0, expressed as $M_0/(1+(f/f_c)^{n_0})$. The magenta lines show the fall-off rate, n_2, estimated in the range of 0.3–2.0 Hz, and were normalized using values visually extracted from the supporting figures of Ye *et al.* (2016a,b). The color version of this figure is available only in the electronic edition.

by Ye *et al.* (2016a,b) appear to be consistent with the average source spectrum model. Taken together, these observations suggest that the average source spectrum models for $M_w > 7.5$ are consistent with the teleseismically observed spectra of large earthquakes.

Scaling relation of source parameters

The average static stress drop is a fundamental parameter for understanding the earthquake energy budget, in addition to σ_a. It is commonly calculated from the seismic moment M_0 and the source area S as follows (e.g., Kanamori and Anderson, 1975):

$$\Delta\sigma_{SM} = \frac{7M_0}{16(S/\pi)^{\frac{3}{2}}}. \tag{31}$$

Figure 12a shows the magnitude dependence of $\Delta\sigma_{SM}$ for crustal earthquakes, adopted from Shimmoto (2022, 2024a). Shimmoto (2022, 2024a) estimated $\Delta\sigma_{SM}$ by the finite-source analysis of observed spectral ratios using the source spectrum model developed by Shimmoto (2020). A regression model incorporating a break in scaling was used:

$$\log_{10} Y = \begin{cases} a_1 M_w + a_2, & M_w < a_3 \\ a_4, & M_w \geq a_3 \end{cases}. \tag{32}$$

The coefficient values are listed in Table S4.

An alternative way to compute the average static stress drop is to take a weighted average of local stress drops using corresponding local slips (or local seismic moments), $\Delta\sigma_{SE}$ (e.g., Madariaga, 1979; Kanamori and Heaton, 2000; Noda *et al.*, 2013). Noda *et al.* (2013) showed that $\Delta\sigma_{SE}$ is suitable for examining earthquake energy partitioning. In the following discussion, $\Delta\sigma_{SE}$ is approximated as $\Delta\sigma_{SE} \cong 2.4\Delta\sigma_{SM}$ based on the single asperity model proposed by Shimmoto (2024a).

Figure 12b shows the magnitude dependence of $\Delta\sigma_{fcER}$, and Figure 12c compares the regression results for $\Delta\sigma_{fcER}$, $\Delta\sigma_{SM}$, and σ_a. For $M_w < 5.1$, the difference between $\Delta\sigma_{fcER}$ and $\Delta\sigma_{SM}$ is small, but $\Delta\sigma_{fcER}$ is higher than $\Delta\sigma_{SM}$ at larger magnitudes, suggesting that $\Delta\sigma_{fcER}$ may not be interpreted as $\Delta\sigma_{SM}$ for large earthquakes.

The radiation efficiency, η_R, is helpful for understanding the difference between $\Delta\sigma_{fcER}$ and $\Delta\sigma_{SM}$. Assuming a simple stress relaxation model with no stress undershoot or overshoot, η_R is given by (e.g., Savage and Wood, 1971; Husseini and Randall, 1976; Kanamori and Rivera, 2006):

$$\eta_R = 2\frac{\sigma_a}{\Delta\sigma_s}, \tag{33}$$

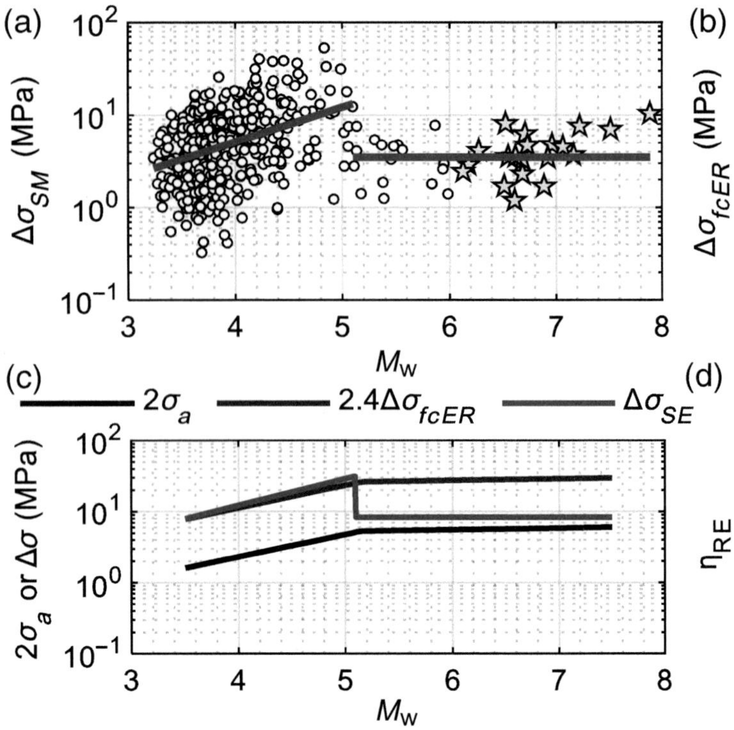

Figure 12. Scaling relation of source parameters. (a) Scaling relation of $\Delta\sigma_{SM}$. The white circles are $\Delta\sigma_{SM}$ estimated by Shimmoto (2022, 2024a), and yellow stars are $\Delta\sigma_{SM}$ for large crustal earthquakes summarized in Shimmoto (2024a). (b) Scaling relation of $\Delta\sigma_{fcER}$. (c) Comparison of the magnitude dependence of $\Delta\sigma_{SE}$, $2.4\Delta\sigma_{fcER}$, and $2\sigma_a$. Each line is based on the corresponding regression models. (d) Comparison of the magnitude dependence of radiation efficiency calculated using $2.4\Delta\sigma_{fcER}$ and $\Delta\sigma_{SE}$. The color version of this figure is available only in the electronic edition.

in which $\Delta\sigma_s$ is an average static stress drop. Substituting $\Delta\sigma_{fcER}$ into $\Delta\sigma$, the following expression is obtained:

$$\eta_R^{fc} = 2\frac{\sigma_a}{\Delta\sigma_{fcER}} = \frac{32\pi^2 k^3}{35}\left(\frac{2V_S^5}{3V_P^5} + 1\right). \quad (34)$$

Neglecting the (V_S^5/V_P^5) term, η_R^{fc} yields a constant value of 0.466 for $k = 2.34/(2\pi)$ (e.g., Singh and Ordaz, 1994), consistent with Brune (1970, 1971). Thus, $\Delta\sigma_{fcER}$ is an extension of Brune's stress drop based on the constant radiation efficiency concept.

Assuming $\Delta\sigma = 2.4\Delta\sigma_{fcER}$, η_R remains approximately constant across magnitudes. In contrast, when $\Delta\sigma = 2.4\Delta\sigma_{SM}$ is assumed, η_R increases beyond M_w 5.1 (Fig. 12d). This difference likely reflects the transition from SCF to DCF spectra around $M_w \sim 5$. For $M_w < 5.1$, source spectra conform to the SCF model, and $\Delta\sigma_{SM}$ and $\Delta\sigma_{fcER}$ are similar. In contrast, for $M_w > 5.1$, earthquake source spectra tend to have two corner frequencies. For such DCF-type spectra, the spectral behavior around f_{ca} reflects $\Delta\sigma_{SM}$, whereas f_{cER} is strongly influenced by f_{cb} (Fig. 6a). Figure 12d suggests that the spectral stress drop calculated assuming the equivalence with apparent stress (e.g., Snoke, 1987) can deviate significantly from $\Delta\sigma_{SM}$ when spectra are inconsistent with the SCF model.

The radiation efficiency defined in equation (33) provides insight into earthquake rupture dynamics. Lambert *et al.* (2021) showed that crack-like rupture yields $\eta_R < 1.0$, whereas self-healing pulse-like ruptures (Heaton, 1990) often result in $\eta_R > 1.0$. Figure 12d supports the interpretation that crustal earthquakes are energetically consistent with crack-like rupture. A similar conclusion was also reached for large interplate earthquakes (Lambert *et al.*, 2021).

Figure 12 and Shimmoto (2024a) suggest that σ_a and $\Delta\sigma_{SE}$ increase with magnitude up to $M_w \sim 5$ and become nearly constant beyond that threshold. Although Figure 11 indicates a possibility that σ_a decreases with increasing magnitude at large magnitudes, the present discussion adopts the scaling trend in Figure 12. Thermal pressurization of pore fluids (e.g., Sibson, 1973; Rice, 2006, and references therein) is a possible mechanism to explain such scaling behavior (Shimmoto, 2024a). Figure 13 illustrates the slip-weakening behavior predicted by the thermal pressurization model.

The fracture energy G is another fundamental parameter for understanding earthquake energy partitioning (Fig. 13). The fracture energy is often derived from observed stress drop and apparent stress, which is denoted as G' (Abercrombie and Rice, 2005). The thermal pressurization model effectively explains the observed trend of G', that is, the increase of G' with increasing slip (e.g., Rice, 2006; Viesca and Garagash, 2015; Perry *et al.*, 2020; Shimmoto, 2024a).

Gabriel *et al.* (2024) proposed a novel scaling relation for G. According to their results, G remains nearly constant ($\sim 10^4$ J/m^2) for small slips ($D < 10^{-2}$ m). For such small slips, their G values are significantly larger than previous G'

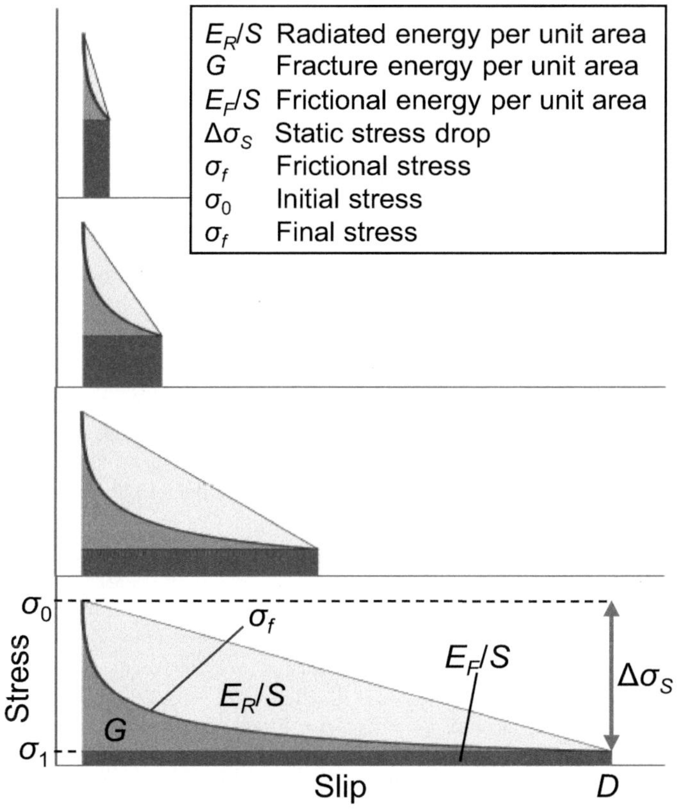

Figure 13. Schematic illustration of slip-weakening behavior based on the thermal pressurization model by Rice (2006). Panels (from top to bottom) show stress relaxation histories for increasing slip magnitudes. The frictional stress σ_f (the red curves) progressively decreases with increasing slip, indicating enhanced dynamic weakening. The static stress drop, $\Delta\sigma_s = \sigma_0 - \sigma_1$, increases with increasing slip up to a characteristic slip length and becomes relatively constant at large slips. The scaling relation of the apparent stress, $\sigma_a = E_R/(SD)$ (D, slip, S, source area), is roughly similar to $\Delta\sigma_s$. The radiation efficiency, $\eta_R = 2\sigma_a/\Delta\sigma_s$, is constant for sufficiently small slips. It increases with increasing slip at large slips and approaches 1.0 asymptotically. For more details, refer to Shimmoto (2024a). The color version of this figure is available only in the electronic edition.

estimates because of a physics-based correction to G' using a flash-heating model. This discrepancy (i.e., $G \gg G'$) is attributed to the presence of dynamic stress undershoot (e.g., Abercrombie and Rice, 2005).

The average σ_a value corresponding to slip magnitudes $D = 10^{-4}$–10^{-2} m in their dataset is estimated to be ~0.1 MPa, based on visual interpretation of Gabriel *et al.* (2024) and figure S2 of Viesca and Garagash (2015). Consequently, the radiated energy per unit area E_R/S for $D = 10^{-4}$–10^{-2} m is 10–1000 J/m^2, which is 1–3 orders of magnitude smaller than $G \sim 10^4$ J/m^2. This substantial deviation appears inconsistent with the stress undershoot model, which is expected to produce E_R/S values comparable to or greater than G (e.g., Lambert *et al.*, 2021). Such internal inconsistency is difficult to reconcile without invoking ad hoc assumptions (e.g., a large strength excess) or reconsidering the stress undershoot hypothesis.

Addressing only the scaling relation of G is insufficient, but a unified explanation of the scaling relations of σ_a, $\Delta\sigma_{SE}$, η_R, and G is necessary. Shimmoto (2024a) demonstrated that enhanced dynamic weakening due to thermal pressurization (Fig. 13) has the potential to consistently explain the scaling of σ_a, $\Delta\sigma_{SE}$, η_R, and G' using the slip-on-plane model by Rice (2006).

Transition in source spectral scaling and source parameter scaling

The transition in source spectral shapes may be relevant to the observed change in the scaling of source parameters because both occur around M_w 5 (e.g., Figs. 7 and 12). Possible contributing mechanisms to such a scaling transition include enhanced dynamic weakening due to thermal pressurization (see Shimmoto, 2024a, for details) and the transition from crack-like to pulse-like ruptures (Meier *et al.*, 2016).

Brune (1970) derived the SCF model based on a simple stress relaxation model by Orowan (1960), in which the effective stress (or dynamic stress drop) equals the static stress drop (Fig. 14a). Brune (1970) also proposed a DCF-like model, known as the partial stress-drop model that incorporates stress healing (Fig. 14b). These models suggest that the SCF-to-DCF spectral transition may correspond to a shift from simple crack-like (no significant undershoot or overshoot) to self-healing pulse-like ruptures (stress undershoot). However, the stress undershoot appears inconsistent with the observations of $\eta_R < 1$ for large earthquakes, according to Figure 12d and previous studies (Lambert *et al.*, 2021; Shimmoto, 2024a). Furthermore, the spectrum of the partial stress drop model has f^{-1} fall-off at intermediate frequencies, but this does not match the observed source spectra (Figs. 4, 5, and 11c).

Another noteworthy idea is the barrier interval hypothesis proposed by Aki *et al.* (1977), which postulates strong barriers spaced at intervals corresponding to ~1 Hz corner frequencies. This frequency range aligns with corner frequencies for $M_w \sim 5$ (Shimmoto, 2022, 2024a) and the asymptotic value of f_b (Table 1). The high stress drops around M_w 5 (Fig. 12a) may reflect the presence of such a barrier. The low stress drops and the increase in η_R for $M_w > 5$ (Fig. 12a,d) may be interpreted as indicating that ruptures can efficiently propagate over a large area, including the regions with low initial stress, once the strength barrier is broken.

The barrier interval is similarly defined as the slip pulse width, which is characterized by rise time (Aki *et al.*, 1977; Gusev, 2014). Gusev (2014) suggested that $1/f_{cb}$ is proportional to the rise time, and this suggests that f_{cb} follows self-similar scaling (Gusev and Chebrov, 2019). Papageorgiou and Aki (1985) also showed that f_{cb} follows the self-similar scaling. However, these predictions are inconsistent with the f_{cb} scaling in this study. Thus, the slip pulse width or barrier interval hypothesis is tentatively not supported (Gusev and Chebrov, 2019). Nevertheless, finite-fault studies generally lack sufficient bandwidth to resolve the link between an equivalent slip pulse width and f_{cb}

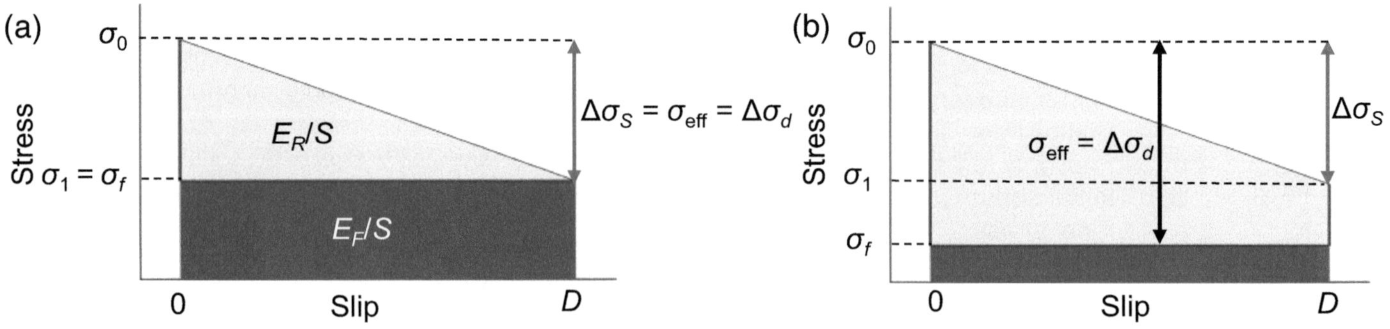

Figure 14. Stress release models based on Brune (1970). (a) The Orowan model. Red lines show stress relaxation history. The effective stress $\sigma_{\rm eff}$ by Brune (1970) is defined as $\sigma_{\rm eff} = \sigma_0 - \sigma_f$ (σ_0, initial stress, σ_f, frictional stress) and is equivalent to the so-called dynamic stress drop $\Delta\sigma_d = \sigma_0 - \sigma_f$. The static stress drop $\Delta\sigma_s$ is defined as $\Delta\sigma_s = \sigma_0 - \sigma_1$ (σ_1, final stress). In this model, $\Delta\sigma_s = \sigma_{\rm eff} = \Delta\sigma_d$. The radiated energy per unit area is given by $E_R/S = \sigma_a D = 0.5(\sigma_0 - \sigma_1)D$ (σ_a, apparent stress). The radiation efficiency $\eta_R = 2\sigma_a/\Delta\sigma_s$ is equal to 1.0 in this model. The frictional energy is defined as $E_F/S = \sigma_f D$. (b) The partial stress drop (stress undershoot) model. In this model, $\sigma_1 > \sigma_f$, $\Delta\sigma_s < \sigma_{\rm eff} = \Delta\sigma_d$, and $E_R/S = \sigma_a D = 0.5(\sigma_0 - \sigma_1)D + (\sigma_1 - \sigma_f)D$. Because $\Delta\sigma_s = \sigma_0 - \sigma_1$, $\eta_R = 1.0 + 2(\sigma_1 - \sigma_f)/(\sigma_0 - \sigma_1) > 1.0$. Note that the definition of $\eta_R = 2\sigma_a/\Delta\sigma_s$ is only appropriate for the case without overshoot or undershoot. The radiation efficiency is properly defined as $E_R/(E_R + E_G)$ (E_G, fracture energy) (e.g., Venkataraman and Kanamori, 2004). In this definition, the radiation efficiency yields 1.0 for both models because $E_G = 0$. The color version of this figure is available only in the electronic edition.

($\gtrsim$1.0 Hz). Thus, testing the hypothesized proportionality between $1/f_{cb}$ and the slip pulse width requires more detailed analysis. The physical basis of the f_{cb} scaling is still unclear.

Stochastic versus deterministic model for high-frequency ground-motion prediction

Based on the observed scaling and variability of PGAs, a stochastic model is more appropriate than a deterministic model for predicting high-frequency ground motions. The difference in PGA scaling behavior between stochastic and deterministic models was noted by Gusev (1983). Brune (1970) derived the omega-square model within a deterministic framework. In contrast, Hanks (1979) treated the acceleration time history as bandlimited white noise and derived the root mean square acceleration based on the flatness of the high-frequency spectrum in Brune's spectrum model, thus implicitly introducing a stochastic model (Gusev, 2014).

From a deterministic perspective, PGA is expected to be proportional to $\Delta\sigma_{fch}$ (Gusev, 1983). However, the scaling relation of the PGA predicted by equation (27) more effectively explains the observed PGA scaling than that of $\Delta\sigma_{fch}$. Moreover, if PGA $\propto \Delta\sigma_{fch}$, the between-event variability of PGA and the variability of $\Delta\sigma_{fch}$ should be comparable, following the discussion by Cotton *et al.* (2013). This expectation, however, is not supported by observations. In contrast, the PGAs predicted using the stochastic model align better with the observed variability and scaling.

The omega-square fall-off rate is generally difficult to reproduce using a simple crack or kinematic model (e.g., Madariaga, 1977). In Brune's source model, the flatness of the acceleration spectrum at high frequencies can be attributed to the presence of a Dirac delta function in the second derivative of the source time function. In many kinematic source models, the Dirac delta function is incorporated into the slip velocity function to produce an f^{-2} fall-off (e.g., Irikura, 1986; Heaton and Hartzell, 1989; Bernard and Herrero, 1994; Shimmoto, 2020). Although the use of the Dirac delta function simplifies model development, it may be physically implausible.

Alternatively, incorporating source heterogeneity provides an alternative explanation for f^{-2} fall-off behavior (Andrews, 1981; Frankel, 1991; Gusev, 2014). In this case, the flatness of the acceleration spectrum is caused by the acceleration time history behaving like white noise at high frequencies. Regardless of whether SCF or DCF spectra are considered, earthquake sources are inherently complex and cannot be represented by a simple circular source.

Spectral behavior around f_{ca} is expected to be dominated by coherent rupture. Spectral amplitudes near f_{ca} are controlled by rupture in the localized regions with large slips (e.g., Miyake *et al.*, 2003; Shimmoto, 2022, 2024a). Shimmoto (2022, 2024a) demonstrated that the spectral rupture directivity effect at low frequencies is successfully reproduced using a simple kinematic source model with a smooth slip distribution developed by Shimmoto (2020). In contrast, Gusev (2014) demonstrated that the directivity effect diminishes at high frequencies, which may not be effectively reproduced by the source model by Shimmoto (2020). According to the result of Gusev (2014), incoherent rupture components are influential to the spectral behavior higher than f_{cb}.

On the use of stress drop for ground-motion predictions

This section revisits and builds upon the critique by Atkinson and Beresnev (1997), titled *Don't Call it Stress Drop*. Although stress drop is considered as a key parameter in predicting ground motions, its definition varies across different methodologies and is often inconsistent. For clarity, this study categorizes stress drop into two types. One is estimated using the corner-frequency method (spectral stress drop $\Delta\sigma_{fc}$, e.g., $\Delta\sigma_{fch}$ or $\Delta\sigma_{fcER}$), and the other is inferred from a finite-fault analysis (average static stress drop, $\Delta\sigma_{SM}$ or $\Delta\sigma_{SE}$). This discussion focuses on spectral stress drop $\Delta\sigma_{fc}$ and $\Delta\sigma_{SM}$. A key difference between $\Delta\sigma_{fc}$ and $\Delta\sigma_{SM}$ lies in the treatment of the coefficient k. We can interpret that $\Delta\sigma_{fc}$ calculations assume a constant k value, whereas the $\Delta\sigma_{SM}$ calculations allow k to vary depending on rupture characteristics.

The spectral stress drop is particularly useful for the (point source) stochastic ground-motion simulation proposed by Boore (1983, 2003), which directly models the source spectrum without relying on kinematic or dynamic source models. In this method, the stress parameter $\Delta\sigma_{fch}$ is often used to characterize the intensity of high-frequency radiation (e.g., Atkinson and Beresnev, 1997; Boore *et al.*, 2014) (Fig. 15a). However, corner frequencies estimated by fitting the SCF model to observed spectra may not accurately capture the high-frequency level because real earthquake source spectra often deviate from the SCF model (Shimmoto and Miyake, 2024) (Fig. 15b). Differently defined corner frequencies can provide inconsistent spectral stress-drop estimates for the spectra deviating from the SCF model (Fig. 15a). Thus, it is important to recognize that unless the definition and estimation procedure for corner frequency are explicitly specified, spectral stress-drop estimates cannot be considered reliable for use in ground-motion prediction.

In contrast, $\Delta\sigma_{SM}$ is essential for physics-based ground-motion prediction, which relies on kinematic or dynamic source models. For example, physics-based seismic hazard assessment using a kinematic source model requires the joint probability distribution of key input parameters, such as $\Delta\sigma_{SM}$ and rupture velocity. The spectral stress drop is unsuitable for this purpose because it is estimated by assuming a constant source model.

Notably, an inverse correlation between $\Delta\sigma_{SM}$ and rupture velocity V_r has been identified in studies employing kinematic models (Tan and Helmberger, 2010; Causse and Song, 2015; Chounet *et al.*, 2018; Shimmoto, 2022, 2024a). This observation implies that a higher $\Delta\sigma_{SM}$ value does not necessarily correspond to a higher corner frequency because the associated reduction in V_r may compensate for or even offset the expected increase in corner frequency (Fig. 16a). By contrast, the spectral stress drop $\Delta\sigma_{fc}$ is always proportional to the cube of the corner frequency. Therefore, $\Delta\sigma_{fc}$ cannot necessarily be regarded as a reliable proxy for $\Delta\sigma_{SM}$ (Fig. 16a), even when source spectra are consistent with the SCF model (Shimmoto, 2022, 2024a). This result also suggests that geophysical conclusions based on $\Delta\sigma_{fc}$ may lack robustness, depending on how $\Delta\sigma_{fc}$ is used.

It is noteworthy that $\Delta\sigma_{SM}$ is more closely associated with f_{ca} rather than f_{ch} or f_{cb} when source spectra significantly deviate from the SCF model. Figure 16b demonstrates that $\Delta\sigma_{SM}$ shows poor agreement with $\Delta\sigma_{fch}$ for large earthquakes. The $\Delta\sigma_{fch}$ values for large magnitudes are generally comparable to or higher than 10 MPa for $M_w > 5$. Similar observations of the

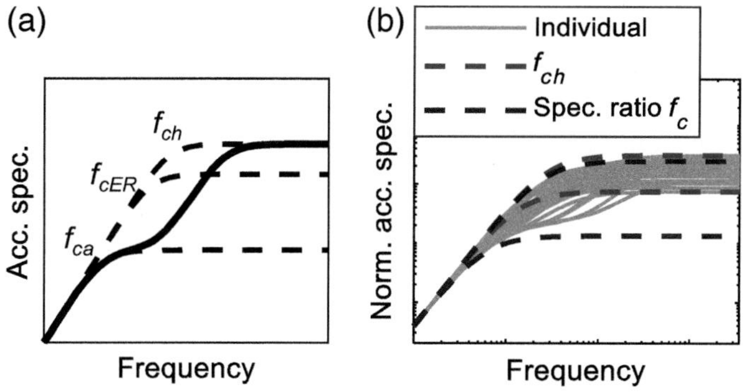

Figure 15. Illustrative examples of ambiguity in the definition and measurement of corner frequencies. (a) Example of inconsistency between differently defined corner frequencies. Only f_{ch} characterizes the high-frequency level and is suitable for comparison with PGA. For DCF spectra, f_{ca} and f_{cER} may be particularly influential for peak ground displacement and velocity, respectively, rather than for PGA. (b) Comparison of corner frequencies estimated by different methods based on the results by Shimmoto and Miyake (2024). The red and blue curves represent the upper and lower bounds. The variability of corner frequency estimated by the standard spectral ratio analysis is significantly larger than the variability of f_{ch}. The color version of this figure is available only in the electronic edition.

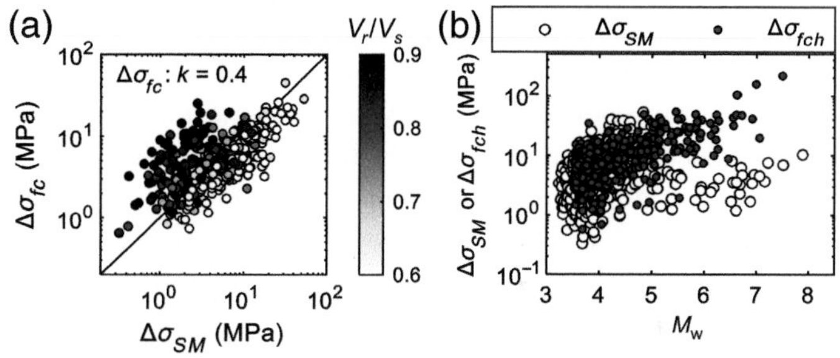

Figure 16. Comparison of static and spectral stress drops. (a) Static stress drop, $\Delta\sigma_{SM}$, versus spectral stress drop, $\Delta\sigma_{fc}$, calculated from the corner frequency estimated by the standard spectral ratio approach (Shimmoto, 2022, 2024a). Here, $\Delta\sigma_{fc}$ can be interpreted as approximately corresponding to $\Delta\sigma_{fch}$ (Shimmoto, 2024b). The color bar represents rupture velocity V_r normalized by S-wave velocity. For instance, a high $\Delta\sigma_{fc}$ estimate often corresponds to a low $\Delta\sigma_{SM}$ estimate with a high rupture velocity. (b) Stress parameter $\Delta\sigma_{fch}$ versus $\Delta\sigma_{SM}$ based on Figures 7a and 12a. For $M_w >$ ~5, the deviation of $\Delta\sigma_{SM}$ from $\Delta\sigma_{fch}$ becomes larger, which corresponds to the SCF-to-DCF spectral transition. The color version of this figure is available only in the electronic edition.

$\Delta\sigma_{fch}$ values are supported by many studies (e.g., Hanks and McGuire, 1981; Atkinson, 1993; García *et al.*, 2004; Boore *et al.*, 2014; Luco, 1985; Ji and Archuleta, 2020). The $\Delta\sigma_{fch}$ values are significantly higher than typical $\Delta\sigma_{SM}$ values for large earthquakes, which range from 1 to 10 MPa (e.g., Kanamori and Anderson, 1975; Shimmoto, 2024a).

Additional observational evidence further supports the potential discrepancy between $\Delta\sigma_{fch}$ and $\Delta\sigma_{SM}$. Kakehi and Irikura (1996) reported that the high-frequency radiation was strong in areas where slip was relatively small during the 1993 Kushiro-Oki, Japan, earthquake (M_w 7.6). This observation highlights that the regions of large slip (i.e., high stress drop) do not necessarily generate high-frequency radiation.

In summary, the static stress drop $\Delta\sigma_{SM}$ may, by itself, be less informative for the high-frequency level, in contrast to $\Delta\sigma_{fch}$. Although $\Delta\sigma_{SM}$ can contribute to some extent at the high-frequency level, the influence of $\Delta\sigma_{SM}$ to high-frequency ground motions remains unclear because the high-frequency level is determined by the combined effect of rupture parameters.

CONCLUSIONS

This study presented a comprehensive analysis of the scaling and variability of broadband source spectra for crustal, interplate, and intraslab earthquakes in Japan. The results reveal that the source spectra are often more complex than can be captured by the SCF model and are more accurately represented by the ADCF model. The source spectra show the transition from SCF to DCF spectra around M_w 5 with increasing magnitude. This result supports a fundamental difference between small and large earthquakes. Notably, even for large earthquakes, earthquake similarity may break down when spectra are evaluated over a broad frequency range, whereas the f_{ca} scaling supports earthquake similarity at low frequencies.

This SCF-to-DCF spectral transition is observed similarly for all earthquake types. Furthermore, in the average source spectrum model developed in this study, the same functional forms, equations (11)–(13), are adequate for representing the scaling relations of f_{ca}, f_{cb}, and ε across these earthquake types. These results suggest the existence of a common physical mechanism controlling the SCF-to-DCF spectral transition for crustal, interplate, and intraslab earthquakes. On the other hand, the difference between these earthquake types emerges in the values of the source and spectral parameters. For instance, intraslab events show systematically higher apparent stress σ_a and stress parameter $\Delta\sigma_{fch}$ than the other earthquake types.

The discrepancy between teleseismic and regional measurements of σ_a was addressed by comparing the teleseismic results obtained by Ye *et al.* (2016a,b). Although the σ_a estimates differ by about a factor of 4, the radiated energy calculated up to 1 Hz, based on the average source spectrum model developed in this study (regional measurements), reproduces the teleseismic measurements of σ_a for large earthquakes studied by Ye *et al.* (2016a,b). The discrepancy is mainly attributed to the limited frequency band in the teleseismic study. Another contributing factor may be differences in the magnitude ranges analyzed in this study and Ye *et al.* (2016a,b), due to the possibility that σ_a decreases with increasing M_w for large magnitudes (Fig. 11b). However, further studies estimating broadband source spectra for large-magnitude events are needed to draw a firm conclusion.

The discrepancy in variability between the spectral stress drop and PGA was effectively resolved across all earthquake types. Furthermore, the PGAs predicted from the estimated source spectra accurately reproduce the variability and scaling of the observed PGAs for crustal earthquakes. The correlation between the observed and predicted PGAs is strong, a correlation coefficient of 0.92. The results suggest that a stochastic source model is more appropriate than deterministic model for explaining high-frequency seismic radiations. Furthermore, the consistency between the observed and predicted PGAs serves as a unique and direct validation of the relative estimates of the high-frequency spectral level across events, a level of verification that has not been achieved in previous spectral studies.

It was shown that the scaling relation of the source parameters changes around M_w 5. The SCF-to-DCF spectral transition and the changes in source parameter scaling appear to occur concurrently around M_w 5, but their physical connection remains unclear. A unified explanation of the physics of the source spectral scaling and source parameter scaling is left for future work. Thermal pressurization has the potential to explain the trend of the source parameter scaling relations consistently. However, considering the stochastic nature of high-frequency ground motions, source heterogeneity should also play the key role for explaining the SCF-to-DCF spectral transition, especially for the scaling relation of f_{cb}.

The concept of stress drop needs to be carefully considered when it is applied to ground-motion predictions. The spectral stress drop is suitable for a method that directly models source spectrum, whereas the static stress drop $\Delta\sigma_{SM}$ can be important for physics-based ground-motion prediction. In the former approach, the stress parameter $\Delta\sigma_{fch}$ is a suitable parameter for characterizing the strength of high-frequency radiation. However, $\Delta\sigma_{fch}$ is not sufficient to characterize overall spectral shape. For accurately predicting ground motions over a broad frequency range, modeling DCF spectral shape is necessary (Luco, 1985; Boore *et al.*, 2014). For predicting high-frequency radiations with physics-based approach, it should be essential to account for the combined effect of source parameters, such as $\Delta\sigma_{SM}$, V_r, and the parameters representing source heterogeneity (e.g., Irikura and Miyake, 2011; Graves and Pitarka, 2015; Gallovič and Valentová, 2023).

In conclusion, estimating broadband source spectra is essential for advancing both the understanding of the earthquake source physics and ground-motion prediction. Although the SCF model is widely used due to its simplicity and effectiveness, greater attention to the potential of DCF spectra may yield deeper insights into earthquake rupture physics and contribute to more accurate and robust ground-motion prediction in the future.

DATA AND RESOURCES

The seismic waveforms were provided by the National Research Institute for Earth Science and Disaster Resilience (NIED; NIED, 2019a,b) and are available from the Hi-net and Kiban–Kyoshin network

(KiK-net) websites (https://www.hinet.bosai.go.jp/?LANG=en and https://www.kyoshin.bosai.go.jp, last accessed May 2025). The 2023 version of the strong-motion flat file (Morikawa *et al.*, 2024) is available from the J-SHIS website (https://www.j-shis.bosai.go.jp/en/labs/ground-motion-flatfile, last accessed May 2025). The seismic moments are provided by NIED (2019c) and are publicly available from the F-net website (https://www.fnet.bosai.go.jp/top.php?LANG=en, last accessed April 2025). The unified earthquake catalog, seismic phase data, and travel-time tables are available on the Japan Meteorological Agency (JMA) website (https://www.jma.go.jp/jma/indexe.html, last accessed May 2025). The supplemental materials contain Figures S1 and S2 and Tables S1–S4. Figure S1 shows the estimated source spectra and the maps of epicenters and stations. Figure S2 provides the depth dependence of the source parameter residuals. Tables S1–S4 provide the source parameters and the coefficients of the regression models.

DECLARATION OF COMPETING INTERESTS

The author acknowledges that there are no conflicts of interest, and there has been no significant financial support for this work that could have influenced its outcome.

ACKNOWLEDGMENTS

The author thanks National Research Institute for Earth Science and Disaster Resilience (NIED) and Japan Meteorological Agency (JMA) for providing data. The author is grateful to Adrien Oth and the reviewers for their comments, which helped improve the article. This work was supported by the Grant-in-Aid for JSPS Fellows Grant Number 23KJ0335.

REFERENCES

Abercrombie, R. E., and J. R. Rice (2005). Can observations of earthquake scaling constrain slip weakening?, *Geophys. J. Int.* **162,** no. 2, 406–424, doi: 10.1111/j.1365-246X.2005.02579.x.

Abrahamson, N. A., and Z. Gulerce (2022). Summary of the Abrahamson and Gulerce NGA-SUB ground-motion model for subduction earthquakes, *Earthq. Spectra* **38,** no. 4, 2638–2681, doi: 10.1177/87552930221114374.

Aki, K. (1966). Generation and propagation of G waves from the Niigata earthquake of June 16, 1964. Part 2. Estimation of earthquake moment, from the G wave spectrum, *Bull. Earthq. Res. Inst. Tokyo Univ.* **44,** 73–88.

Aki, K. (1967). Scaling law of seismic spectrum, *J. Geophys. Res.* **72,** no. 4, 1217–1231, doi: 10.1029/JZ072i004p01217.

Aki, K. (1972). Scaling law of earthquake source time-function, *Geophys. J. Roy. Astron. Soc.* **31,** 3–25, doi: 10.1111/j.1365-246X.1972.tb02356.x.

Aki, K., M. Bouchon, B. Chouet, and S. Das (1977). Quantitative prediction of strong motion for a potential earthquake fault, *Ann. Geofis.* **30,** 341–368.

Anderson, J. G., and S. E. Hough (1984). A model for the shape of the Fourier amplitude spectrum of acceleration at high frequencies, *Bull. Seismol. Soc. Am.* **74,** no. 5, 1969–1993, doi: 10.1785/BSSA0740051969.

Andrews, D. J. (1981). A stochastic fault model: 2. Time-dependent case, *J. Geophys. Res.* **86,** no. B11, 10,821–10,834, doi: 10.1029/JB086iB11p10821.

Andrews, D. J. (1986). Objective determination of source parameters and similarity of earthquakes of different size, in *Earthquake Source Mechanics*, S. Das, J. Boatwright, and C. H. Scholz (Editors), Vol. 37, 259–267, doi: 10.1029/GM037p0259.

Archuleta, R. J., and C. Ji (2016). Moment rate scaling for earthquakes $3.3 \le M \le 5.3$ with implications for stress drop, *Geophys. Res. Lett.* **43,** 12,004–12,011, doi: 10.1002/2016GL071433.

Atkinson, G. M. (1993). Earthquake source spectra in eastern North America, *Bull. Seismol. Soc. Am.* **83,** no. 6, 1778–1798, doi: 10.1785/BSSA0830061778.

Atkinson, G. M., and I. Beresnev (1997). Don't call it stress drop, *Seismol. Res. Lett.* **68,** no. 1, 3–4, doi: 10.1785/gssrl.68.1.3.

Baltay, A. S., and T. C. Hanks (2014). Understanding the magnitude dependence of PGA and PGV in NGA-West 2 data, *Bull. Seismol. Soc. Am.* **104,** no. 6, 2851–2865, doi: 10.1785/0120130283.

Bernard, P., and A. Herrero (1994). Slip heterogeneity, body-wave spectra, and directivity of earthquake ruptures, *Ann. Geofis.* **37,** no. 6, 1679–1690.

Boore, D. M. (1983). Stochastic simulation of high-frequency ground motions based on seismological models of the radiated spectra, *Bull. Seismol. Soc. Am.* **73,** no. 6A, 1865–1894, doi: 10.1785/BSSA07306A1865.

Boore, D. M. (2003). Simulation of ground motion using the stochastic method, *Pure Appl. Geophys.* **160,** 635–676, doi: 10.1007/PL00012553.

Boore, D. M. (2010). Orientation-independent, nongeometric-mean measures of seismic intensity from two horizontal components of motion, *Bull. Seismol. Soc. Am.* **100,** no. 4, 1830–1835, doi: 10.1785/0120090400.

Boore, D. M., C. Alessandro, and N. A. Abrahamson (2014). A generalization of the double-corner-frequency source spectral model and its use in the SCEC BBP validation exercise, *Bull. Seismol. Soc. Am.* **104,** no. 5, 2387–2398, doi: 10.1785/0120140138.

Brune, J. N. (1970). Tectonic stress and the spectra of seismic shear waves from earthquakes, *J. Geophys. Res.* **75,** no. 26, 4997–5009, doi: 10.1029/JB075i026p04997.

Brune, J. N. (1971). Correction to "Tectonic stress and the spectra, of seismic shear waves from earthquakes", *J. Geophys. Res.* **76,** no. 20, 5002–5002, doi: 10.1029/JB076i020p05002.

Cartwright, D. E., and M. S. Longuet-Higgins (1956). The statistical distribution of the maxima of a random function, *Proc. Math. Phys. Sci.* **237,** 212–232.

Causse, M., and S. G. Song (2015). Are stress drop and rupture velocity of earthquakes independent? Insight from observed ground motion variability, *Geophys. Res. Lett.* **42,** 7383–7389, doi: 10.1002/2015GL064793.

Chounet, A., M. Vallée, M. Causse, and F. Courboulex (2018). Global catalog of earthquake rupture velocities shows anticorrelation between stress drop and rupture velocity, *Tectonophysics* **733,** 148–158, doi: 10.1016/j.tecto.2017.11.005.

Cotton, F., R. Archuleta, and M. Causse (2013). What is sigma of the stress drop? *Seismol. Res. Lett.* **84,** no. 1, 42–48, doi: 10.1785/0220120087.

Frankel, A. (1991). High-frequency spectral falloff of earthquakes, fractal dimension of complex rupture, b value, and the scaling of strength on faults, *J. Geophys. Res.* **96,** no. B4, 6291–6302, doi: 10.1029/91JB00237.

Gallovič, F., and Ľ. Valentová (2023). Broadband strong ground motion modeling using planar dynamic rupture with fractal parameters, *J. Geophys. Res.* **128,** e2023JB026506, doi: 10.1029/2023JB026506.

Gabriel, A. A., D. I. Garagash, K. H. Palgunadi, and P. M. Mai (2024). Fault size–dependent fracture energy explains multiscale seismicity and cascading earthquakes, *Science* **385,** eadj9587, doi: 10.1126/science.adj9587.

García, D., S. K. Singh, M. Herraíz, J. F. Pacheco, and M. Ordaz (2004). Inslab earthquakes of Central Mexico: Q, source spectra, and stress drop, *Bull. Seismol. Soc. Am.* **94,** no. 3, 789–802, doi: 10.1785/0120030125.

Graves, R., and A. Pitarka (2015). Refinements to the Graves and Pitarka (2010) broadband ground-motion simulation method, *Seismol. Res. Lett.* **86,** no. 1, 75–80, doi: 10.1785/0220140101.

Gusev, A. A. (1983). Descriptive statistical model of earthquake source radiation and its application to an estimation of short-period strong motion, *Geophys. J. Int.* **74,** no. 3, 787–808, doi: 10.1111/j.1365-246X.1983.tb01904.x.

Gusev, A. A. (2013). High-frequency radiation from an earthquake fault: A review and a hypothesis of fractal rupture front geometry, *Pure Appl. Geophys.* **170,** 65–93, doi: 10.1007/s00024-012-0455-y.

Gusev, A. A. (2014). Doubly stochastic earthquake source model: "Omega-square" spectrum and low high-frequency directivity revealed by numerical experiments, *Pure Appl. Geophys.* **171,** 2581–2599, doi: 10.1007/s00024-013-0764-9.

Gusev, A. A., and D. Chebrov (2019). On scaling of earthquake rise-time estimates, *Bull. Seismol. Soc. Am.* **109,** no. 6, 2741–2745, doi: 10.1785/0120180214.

Hanks, T. C. (1979). b values and ω–γ seismic source models: Implications for tectonic stress variations along active crustal fault zones and the estimation of high-frequency strong ground motion, *J. Geophys. Res.* **84,** no. B5, 2235–2242, doi: 10.1029/JB084iB05p02235.

Hanks, T. C., and R. K. McGuire (1981). The character of high-frequency strong ground motion, *Bull. Seismol. Soc. Am.* **71,** no. 6, 2071–2095, doi: 10.1785/BSSA0710062071.

Heaton, T. H. (1990). Evidence for and implications of self-healing pulses of slip in earthquake rupture, *Phys. Earth Planet. Int.* **64,** 1–20, doi: 10.1016/0031-9201(90)90002-F.

Heaton, T. H., and S. H. Hartzell (1989). Estimation of strong ground motions from hypothetical earthquakes on the Cascadia subduction zone, Pacific Northwest, *Pure Appl. Geophys.* **129,** 131–201, doi: 10.1007/BF00874626.

Husseini, M. I., and M. Randall (1976). Rupture velocity and radiation efficiency, *Bull. Seismol. Soc. Am.* **66,** 1173–1187, doi: 10.1785/BSSA0660041173.

Irikura, K. (1986). Prediction of strong acceleration motion using empirical Green's function, *Proc. 7th Japan Earthquake Engineering Symposium*, Tokyo, Japan, 151–156.

Irikura, K., and H. Miyake (2011). Recipe for predicting strong ground motion from crustal earthquake scenarios, *Pure Appl. Geophys.* **168,** 85–104, doi: 10.1007/s00024-010-0150-9.

Ji, C., and R. J. Archuleta (2020). Two empirical double-corner-frequency source spectra and their physical implications, *Bull. Seismol. Soc. Am.* **111,** no. 2, 737–761, doi: 10.1785/0120200238.

Kakehi, Y., and K. Irikura (1996). Estimation of high-frequency wave radiation areas on the fault plane by the envelope inversion of acceleration seismograms, *Geophys. J. Int.* **125,** no. 3, 892–900, doi: 10.1111/j.1365-246X.1996.tb06032.x.

Kanamori, H., and D. L. Anderson (1975). Theoretical basis of some empirical relations in seismology, *Bull. Seismol. Soc. Am.* **65,** no. 5, 1073–1095, doi: 10.1785/BSSA0650051073.

Kanamori, H., and T. H. Heaton (2000). Microscopic and macroscopic physics of earthquakes, in *Earthquakes: Geocomplexity and the Physics of Earthquakes*, J. B. Rundle, D. L. Turcotte, and W. Klein (Editors), 147–163, doi: 10.1029/GM120p0147.

Kanamori, H., and L. Rivera (2006). Energy partitioning during an earthquake, in *Earthquakes: Radiated Energy and the Physics of Faulting*, R. Abercrombie, A. McGarr, G. Di Toro, and H. Kanamori (Editors), 3–13, doi: 10.1029/170GM03.

Kubo, A., E. Fukuyama, H. Kawai, and K. Nonomura (2002). NIED seismic moment tensor catalogue for regional earthquakes around Japan: Quality test and application, *Tectonophysics* **356,** 23–48, doi: 10.1016/S0040-1951(02)00375-X.

Lambert, V., N. Lapusta, and S. Perry (2021). Propagation of large earthquakes as self-healing pulses or mild cracks, *Nature* **591,** 252–258, doi: 10.1038/s41586-021-03248-1.

Luco, J. E. (1985). On strong ground motion estimates based on models of the radiated spectrum, *Bull. Seismol. Soc. Am.* **75,** no. 3, 641–649, doi: 10.1785/BSSA0750030641.

Madariaga, R. (1977). High-frequency radiation from crack (stress drop) models of earthquake faulting, *Geophys. J. Int.* **51,** no. 3, 625–651, doi: 10.1111/j.1365-246X.1977.tb04211.x.

Madariaga, R. (1979). On the relation between seismic moment and stress drop in the presence of stress and strength heterogeneity, *J. Geophys. Res.* **84,** no. B5, 2243–2250, doi: 10.1029/JB084iB05p02243.

Meier, M.-A., T. H. Heaton, and J. Clinton (2016). Evidence for universal earthquake rupture initiation behavior, *Geophys. Res. Lett.* **43,** 7991–7996, doi: 10.1002/2016GL070081.

Miyake, H., T. Iwata, and K. Irikura (2003). Source characterization for broadband ground-motion simulation: Kinematic heterogeneous source model and strong motion generation area, *Bull. Seismol. Soc. Am.* **93,** no. 6, 2531–2545, doi: 10.1785/0120020183.

Morikawa, N., A. Iwaki, H. Fujiwara, S. Akiyama, T. Maeda, H. Kubo, S. Aoi, T. Hayakawa, M. Takahashi, K. Kato, *et al.* (2024). Flat file of K-NET and KiK-net strong-motion records, *Proc. of the 18th World Conf. on Earthquake Engineering*, Milan, Italy, 5 July 2024.

National Research Institute for Earth Science and Disaster Resilience (2019a). NIED Hi-net [Dataset], National Research Institute for Earth Science and Disaster Resilience, doi: 10.17598/NIED.0003.

National Research Institute for Earth Science and Disaster Resilience (2019b). NIED K-NET, KiK-net [Dataset], National Research Institute for Earth Science and Disaster Resilience, doi: 10.17598/NIED.0004.

National Research Institute for Earth Science and Disaster Resilience (2019c). NIED F-net [Dataset], National Research Institute for Earth Science and Disaster Resilience, doi: 10.17598/NIED.0005.

Noda, H., N. Lapusta, and H. Kanamori (2013). Comparison of average stress drop measures for ruptures with heterogeneous stress change and implications for earthquake physics, *Geophys. J. Int.* **193,** no. 3, 1691–1712, doi: 10.1093/gji/ggt074.

Orowan, E. (1960). Mechanism of seismic faulting in rock deformation, *Geol. Soc. Am. Mem.* **79,** 323–345.

Oth, A., H. Miyake, and D. Bindi (2017). On the relation of earthquake stress drop and ground motion variability, *J. Geophys. Res.* **122,** 5474–5492, doi: 10.1002/2017JB014026.

Papageorgiou, A. S., and K. Aki (1985). Scaling law of far-field spectra based on observed parameters of the specific barrier model, *Pure Appl. Geophys.* **123,** 353–374, doi: 10.1007/BF00880736.

Perry, S. M., V. Lambert, and N. Lapusta (2020). Nearly magnitude-invariant stress drops in simulated crack-like earthquake sequences on rate-and-state faults with thermal pressurization of pore fluids, *J. Geophys. Res.* **125,** e2019JB018597, doi: 10.1029/2019JB018597.

Rice, J. R. (2006). Heating and weakening of faults during earthquake slip, *J. Geophys. Res.* **111,** B05311, doi: 10.1029/2005JB004006.

Rodriguez-Marek, A., G. A. Montalva, F. Cotton, and F. Bonilla (2011). Analysis of single-station standard deviation using the KiK-net data, *Bull. Seismol. Soc. Am.* **101,** no. 3, 1242–1258, doi: 10.1785/0120100252.

Savage, J. C., and M. D. Wood (1971). The relation between apparent stress and stress drop, *Bull. Seismol. Soc. Am.* **61,** no. 5, 1381–1388, doi: 10.1785/BSSA0610051381.

Shimmoto, S. (2020). An earthquake source spectrum model considering rupture directivity and its application for obtaining Green's functions, *Bull. Seismol. Soc. Am.* **110,** no. 6, 2711–2727, doi: 10.1785/0120200061.

Shimmoto, S. (2022). Stress drop estimates for small to moderate earthquakes in Tohoku, Japan considering rupture geometry, speed, and directivity, *J. Geophys. Res.* **127,** e2022JB025157, doi: 10.1029/2022JB025157.

Shimmoto, S. (2024a). Source parameter scaling relations for shallow crustal earthquakes: Exploration with the single asperity model, *J. Geophys. Res.* **129,** e2023JB027690, doi: 10.1029/2023JB027690.

Shimmoto, S. (2024b). A resolution of the variability discrepancy between peak ground acceleration and spectral stress drop, *Seism. Rec.* **4,** no. 4, 268–278, doi: 10.1785/0320240029.

Shimmoto, S., and H. Miyake (2024). Resolving the variability discrepancy between peak ground acceleration and spectral stress drop: Insight from double-corner-frequency spectra, *Bull. Seismol. Soc. Am.* **115,** no. 3, 1162–1176, doi: 10.1785/0120240038.

Shiomi, K., K. Obara, and K. Kasahara (2005). Amplitude saturation of the NIED Hi-net waveforms and simple criteria for recognition, *Zisin (J. Seismol. Soc. Japan), 2nd Ser.* **57,** no. 4, 451–461, doi: 10.4294/zisin1948.57.4_451.

Sibson, R. H. (1973). Interactions between temperature and pore-fluid pressure during earthquake faulting and a mechanism for partial or total stress relief, *Nature* **243,** 66–68, doi: 10.1038/physci243066a0.

Singh, S. K., and M. Ordaz (1994). Seismic energy release in Mexican subduction zone earthquakes, *Bull. Seismol. Soc. Am.* **84,** no. 5, 1553–1550, doi: 10.1785/BSSA0840051533.

Smith, K. D., J. N. Brune, and K. F. Priestley (1991). The seismic spectrum, radiated energy, and the Savage and Wood inequality for complex earthquakes, *Tectonophysics* **188,** 303–320, doi: 10.1016/0040-1951(91)90461-Z.

Snoke, J. A. (1987). Stable determination of (Brune) stress drops, *Bull. Seismol. Soc. Am.* **77,** no. 2, 530–538, doi: 10.1785/BSSA0770020530.

Sung, C.-H., H. Miyake, N. Abrahamson, and N. Morikawa (2024). Nonergodic ground-motion models for subduction zone and crustal earthquakes in Japan, *Bull. Seismol. Soc. Am.* **114,** no. 3, 1717–1738, doi: 10.1785/0120230258.

Si, H., S. Midorikawa, and T. Kishida (2022). Development of NGA-Sub ground-motion prediction equation of 5%-damped pseudo-spectral acceleration based on database of subduction earthquakes in Japan, *Earthq. Spectra* **38,** no. 4, 2682–2706, doi: 10.1177/87552930221090326.

Tan, Y., and D. Helmberger (2010). Rupture directivity characteristics of the 2003 Big Bear Sequence, *Bull. Seismol. Soc. Am.* **100,** no. 3, 1089–1106, doi: 10.1785/0120090074.

Thomson, D. J. (1982). Spectrum estimation and harmonic analysis, *Proc. IEEE* **70,** no. 9, 1055–1096, doi: 10.1109/PROC.1982.12433.

Van Houtte, C., S. Drouet, and F. Cotton (2011). Analysis of the origins of κ (kappa) to compute hard rock to rock adjustment factors for GMPEs, *Bull. Seismol. Soc. Am.* **101,** no. 6, 2926–2941, doi: 10.1785/0120100345.

Venkataraman, A., and H. Kanamori (2004). Observational constraints on the fracture energy of subduction zone earthquakes, *J. Geophys. Res.* **109,** B05302, doi: 10.1029/2003JB002549.

Viesca, R., and D. Garagash (2015). Ubiquitous weakening of faults due to thermal pressurization, *Nature Geosci.* **8,** 875–879, doi: 10.1038/ngeo2554.

Ye, L., T. Lay, H. Kanamori, and L. Rivera (2016a). Rupture characteristics of major and great ($M_w \geq 7.0$) megathrust earthquakes from 1990 to 2015: 1. Source parameter scaling relations, *J. Geophys. Res.* **121,** 826–844, doi: 10.1002/2015JB012426.

Ye, L., T. Lay, H. Kanamori, and L. Rivera (2016b). Rupture characteristics of major and great ($M_w \geq 7.0$) megathrust earthquakes from 1990 to 2015: 2. Depth dependence, *J. Geophys. Res. Solid Earth* **121,** 845–863, doi: 10.1002/2015JB012427.

Manuscript received 15 May 2025
Published online 18 November 2025

Distinguishing Tapered and Non-Tapered Gutenberg–Richter Distributions

Linxuan Li*[1] and Jean-Philippe Avouac[1]

ABSTRACT

The magnitude–frequency distribution (MFD), which quantifies the relative frequency of large versus small earthquakes, is commonly used in seismic hazard assessment studies and is thought to characterize earthquake dynamics. The classic Gutenberg–Richter (GR) model posits that earthquake frequency decays exponentially with magnitude. The tapered Gutenberg–Richter (TGR) model is a variant that assumes a further reduced frequency of larger earthquakes. Distinguishing which of these two distributions better fits observations is important not only for a better understanding of earthquake physics but also for robust forecasting of earthquake magnitudes. Therefore, we evaluate methods used to differentiate these two distributions and their statistical significance given a set of observations. We find the likelihood-ratio test to be the most effective approach. It rarely misclassifies a GR distribution as a TGR distribution, whereas a TGR distribution can be misclassified as GR when the tail of the MFD is insufficiently sampled. We demonstrate that the probability of correctly identifying a TGR model exceeds 90% when the corner magnitude is one unit smaller than the maximum magnitude predicted by the GR distribution. Furthermore, we introduce an objective framework aimed at detecting potential temporal shifts between the two distributions. We apply this framework to global seismicity and two observational cases of induced seismicity. The MFD of global seismicity shows transitions between GR and TGR distributions over time, which might be explained by either inherent temporal variation in behavior or by the random sampling of a bilinear GR model with a larger *b* value for M > 7.6. Regarding the induced seismicity cases, we demonstrate significant and persistent TGR distributions in seismicity induced by geothermal well stimulations at Otaniemi, Finland. Furthermore, we find that earthquakes in the Coso geothermal field (California) exhibit TGR behavior during a specific period, likely influenced by the type of magnitude scale used.

KEY POINTS

- We evaluate methods to distinguish tapered and non-tapered Gutenberg–Richter distributions.
- The likelihood-ratio test is most effective, with a framework for analyzing temporal evolution proposed.
- Different distributions exist in real-world cases, some of which may arise due to observational artifacts.

Supplemental Material

INTRODUCTION

The magnitude–frequency distribution (MFD) describes how the occurrence rate ("frequency") of earthquakes in a seismicity catalog depends on their magnitudes. Earthquake hazard studies and forecasting methods generally assume idealized models. The most common MFD model is the Gutenberg–Richter (GR) distribution (Gutenberg and Richter, 1944), which assumes an exponential decay of the frequency of earthquakes with magnitudes, or equivalently, a power law decay with moment. The GR distribution with a *b* value typically around 1 is known to apply approximately at the global scale, as well as at the local scale, or even in laboratory experiments (e.g., Mogi, 1963; Schorlemmer *et al.*, 2005; Goebel *et al.*, 2013; El-Isa and Eaton, 2014; Scholz, 2015; Peng *et al.*, 2021; Carlino *et al.*, 2022; Taroni and Carafa, 2023). Whatever the scale considered, the GR model must fail at large magnitudes, given the physical limit that earthquake magnitudes cannot be infinitely large due to finite-fault size and that the strain released by earthquakes is bounded by the elastic strain resulting from tectonic loading (Sornette and Sornette, 1999; Utsu, 1999; Kagan and Schoenberg, 2001; Kagan, 2002). Although it is widely

1. Division of Geological and Planetary Sciences, California Institute of Technology (Caltech), Pasadena, California, U.S.A., https://orcid.org/0000-0001-6831-8363 (LL); https://orcid.org/0000-0002-3060-8442 (J-PA)

*Corresponding author: lxli@caltech.edu

Cite this article as Li, L., and J.-P. Avouac (2025). Distinguishing Tapered and Non-Tapered Gutenberg–Richter Distributions, *Bull. Seismol. Soc. Am.* **116**, 436–466, doi: 10.1785/0120250130 admitted that earthquake magnitudes must be bounded, existing seismicity catalogs are generally insufficient to statistically prove the existence of a (hard) upper bound (e.g., Holschneider *et al.*, 2011; van der Elst *et al.*, 2016; Schultz, 2024). Another common view is that larger magnitude events tend to be less frequent than predicted by the GR model, resulting in a tapering of the tail of the MFD, such as in the tapered GR (TGR) model (Vere-Jones *et al.*, 2001; Kagan, 2002). Numerous observational studies suggest that the TGR model better fits both global and regional tectonic earthquake catalogs (Bell *et al.*, 2013; Kagan and Jackson, 2016; Rodríguez-Pérez *et al.*, 2020; Neely and Stein, 2021; Spassiani and Marzocchi, 2021), and induced seismicity (Bachmann *et al.*, 2011; Huang and Beroza, 2015; Bourne and Oates, 2020; Minetto *et al.*, 2023). Therefore, TGR model is commonly used in probabilistic seismic hazard analysis (e.g., Rong *et al.*, 2014; Park *et al.*, 2017; Dutfoy and Senfaute, 2022). However, the validity of the TGR model is not warranted because it has been argued by some studies that the tapering could be due to incomplete sampling of an underlying GR distribution (e.g., Zöller, 2013; Corral and Serra, 2019).

There are, nonetheless, good reasons to think that the MFD of both tectonic and induced earthquakes should be tapered. For example, tapering could be linked to the existence of a (hard) upper limit on magnitude. Marsan and Tan (2020) demonstrated that if one assumes the maximum possible magnitude at any given time is limited by the elastic strain energy available, the MFD will exhibit tapering over long timescales. Tapering can also occur independently of an upper bound on magnitude. It has been proposed that earthquakes large enough to rupture the entire depth range of seismogenic zone (typically $M_w > 7$) are less frequent than expected from the GR distribution of smaller events (Romanowicz and Rundle, 1993). Tapering of the MFD could also emerge in the context of earthquakes induced by human activities (i.e., induced seismicity). For example, Shapiro *et al.* (2011) suggested that if the rupture sizes are constrained by the fluid-perturbed rock volume, the resulting MFD would also exhibit TGR-like behavior with the taper shifting to larger magnitudes with increased volume of injected fluids. Distinguishing whether the GR or TGR model is more appropriate, and whether the distribution is stationary over time, are thus important questions for both earthquake physics and hazard assessment: assuming a TGR model could lead to an underestimate of seismic hazard; on the other hand assuming a GR distribution could lead to substantially overestimate seismic hazard (e.g., Kaveh *et al.*, 2024). Although tapering may seem obvious visually in some instances, we aim to use statistical methods to rigorously assess whether apparent deviations from an unbounded GR distribution are significant, and to determine under what conditions the GR and TGR models can be distinguished from each other. In this study, we therefore test various methods to distinguish the GR and TGR models using synthetic and real-world seismicity catalogs.

This article is structured as follows: the MFD models and parameter estimation section reviews methods for estimating MFD parameters and discusses biases introduced by assuming an inappropriate model, whether GR or TGR. The MFD under the random sampling section discusses the confidence intervals of the MFDs and the distribution of maximum magnitudes. The Determine if a given catalog is GR or TGR section focuses on strategies for determining the appropriate MFD model for a given catalog. The Analyzing temporal variations of MFD section discusses methods to assess the nonstationarity of the MDF model. The Application to observational cases section presents application examples. The Discussion section discusses factors that make MFD deviate from a standard GR distribution. The methodology used to generate random synthetic catalogs is outlined in Text S1, available in the supplemental material to this article. In testing synthetic catalogs, we assume for convenience $m_c = 0$, except in the Effect of magnitude incompleteness section, for which we study the impact of catalog incompleteness. This study aims to compare the GR and TGR models. Because GR is simpler, it serves as the null hypothesis. Rejecting GR does not necessarily mean accepting TGR. However, for ease of exposition, throughout the article we will informally refer to cases for which GR is rejected as following TGR.

MFD MODELS AND PARAMETER ESTIMATION

In this section, we recall the expressions of the GR and TGR distributions and review established methods for estimating the parameters. We then elucidate the biases that result from assuming an incorrect model.

Parametric expression of the GR and TGR distributions

GR distribution (Gutenberg and Richter, 1944) states that the probability of an earthquake with a magnitude greater than or equal to m is

$$P(\geq m) = 10^{-b(m-m_c)}, m_c \leq m, \tag{1a}$$

in which b is the b value, describes the relative number of large and small earthquakes, and m_c is the magnitude of completeness of the seismicity catalog. The GR distribution can also be expressed in terms of seismic moment M, which relates to the moment magnitude m according to $m = \frac{2}{3}\log_{10} M - 6.07$, with M in $N \cdot m$ (Hanks and Kanamori, 1979). It is expressed as

$$P(\geq M) = \left(\frac{M_c}{M}\right)^{\beta}, M_c \leq M, \tag{1b}$$

in which $\beta = \frac{2}{3}b$ and M_c is the moment corresponding to the magnitude of completeness m_c. The b value is typically around 1 (e.g., Mogi, 1963; Schorlemmer *et al.*, 2005; Goebel *et al.*, 2013; El-Isa and Eaton, 2014; Scholz, 2015; Peng *et al.*, 2021; Carlino *et al.*, 2022; Taroni and Carafa, 2023).

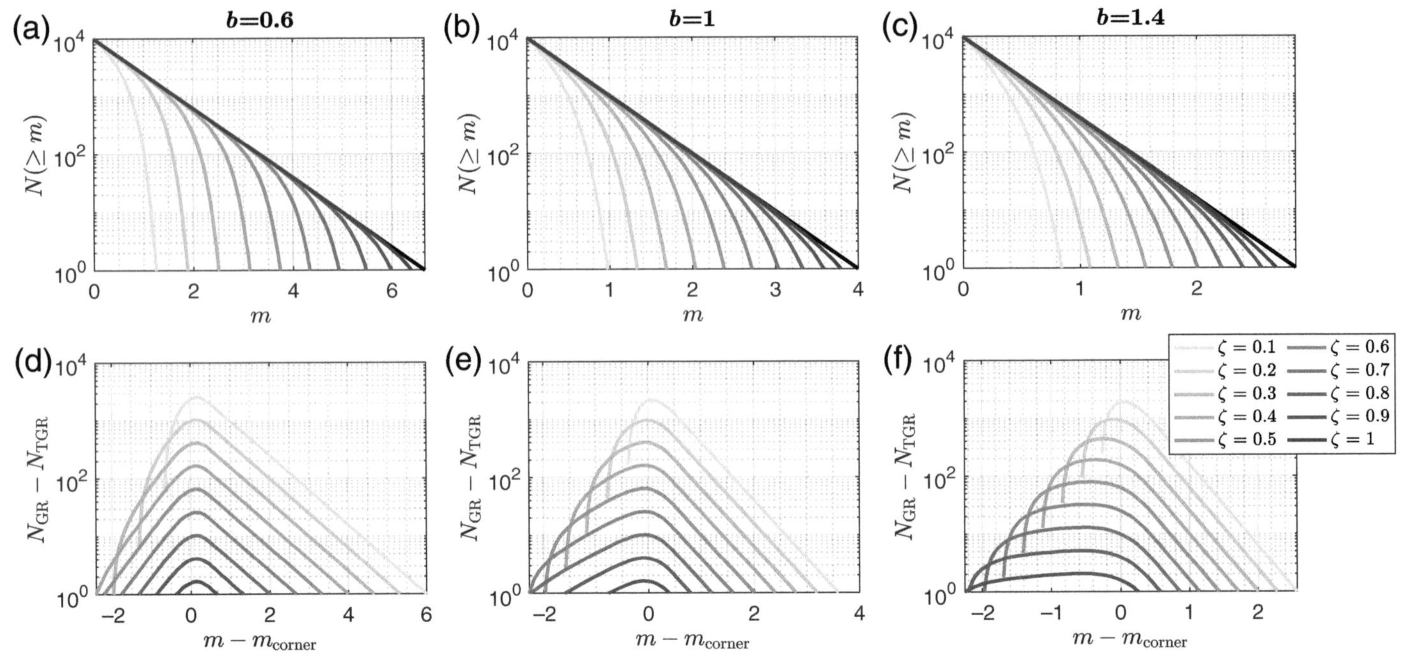

Figure 1. Comparison between Gutenberg–Richter (GR) and tapered GR (TGR) models. (a–c) Cumulative number of earthquakes for GR models (black lines) and TGR models (colored curves) and the (d–f) differences between the GR and the TGR models. In all cases, we assume $m_c = 0$. The color version of this figure is available only in the electronic edition.

One of the most widely used MDF models that introduces a tapering at large magnitudes is the TGR distribution (Vere-Jones *et al.*, 2001; Kagan, 2002), which incorporates an exponential decay into equation (1b),

$$P(\geq M) = \left(\frac{M_c}{M}\right)^{\beta} \exp\left(\frac{M_c - M}{M_{corner}}\right), M_c \leq M, \quad (2)$$

in which M_{corner} is the corner moment, controlling the taper of the distribution, with its magnitude equivalence m_{corner} referred to as the corner magnitude. For convenience, we define

$$\zeta = \frac{m_{corner} - m_c}{\frac{a}{b} - m_c}, \quad (3)$$

in which the a value is the base-10 logarithm of the total number of earthquakes with magnitudes greater than or equal to 0, and the ratio a/b corresponds to the magnitude above which only one earthquake is expected for a non-tapered GR distribution, as predicted by equation (1). Thus, the parameter ζ represents the relative position of m_{corner} within the magnitude (or dynamic) range of a given sequence. A smaller ζ indicates that the taper occurs at relatively lower magnitudes, whereas a larger ζ implies the taper occurs at higher magnitudes. The differences between equations (1) and (2) are shown in Figure 1.

Estimation of the parameters of the GR distribution

Assuming a GR distribution, the maximum-likelihood estimation (MLE) is the most widely used method to estimate the b value. Assuming independent and identically distributed (IID) moment samples, the logarithm of the likelihood function for the GR distribution is (Kagan, 2002)

$$\log L = n[\beta \log(M_c) + \log \beta] - (1 + \beta) \sum_{i=1}^{n} \log M_i, \quad (4)$$

in which n is the number of events with moments not less than M_c. The maximum-likelihood estimate of β is then obtained by (Kagan, 2002)

$$\hat{\beta} = \frac{n}{\sum_{i=1}^{n} \log \frac{M_i}{M_c}}. \quad (5a)$$

Equation (5a) is the moment form of the MLE solution of Aki (1965):

$$\hat{b} = \frac{n}{\log 10 \sum_{i=1}^{n} (m_i - m_c)}. \quad (5b)$$

Because of the effect of finite size, Equations (5a) and (5b) should be multiplied by a coefficient of $(n-1)/n$ to obtain unbiased estimates (Ogata and Yamashina, 1986; Marzocchi *et al.*, 2020). However, this effect is very minor considering the catalog size often analyzed (Marzocchi *et al.*, 2020; Li and Luo, 2024), and therefore, it is disregarded in this article. The standard deviation under a specific catalog size n is given by $\sigma = b/\sqrt{n}$ (Aki, 1965). In addition, for catalogs with a discretization level of Δm (due to magnitude binning or rounding), m_c needs to be replaced by $m_c^{corr} = m_c - \Delta m/2$ in equation (5b; Bender, 1983) and M_c should be replaced by $M_c^{corr} = 10^{1.5[(m_c - \Delta m/2 + 6.07]}$ in equation (5a).

Recently, several alternative methods have been proposed to estimate b values (van der Elst, 2021; Li *et al.*, 2023; Lippiello and Petrillo, 2024). van der Elst (2021) proposed the b-positive method, which uses the positive magnitude difference of two successive events. He suggests that focusing on positive differences can mitigate the effects of temporal variations in m_c, enhancing reliability amid short-term aftershock incompleteness (STAI). Lippiello and Petrillo (2024) expanded this approach by considering positive differences in magnitude, not only between consecutive earthquakes but also between various pairs of earthquakes. Another study by Li *et al.* (2023) shows that the ratio between the *K–M* slope (KMS, a parameter from topological analysis), and the *b* value, remains constant for a specific catalog size. Consequently, the KMS can be employed to calculate the *b* value. The KMS method is less sensitive to magnitude incompleteness than MLE, and although it is less effective than the *b*-positive method under temporal variations in m_c, it does not fail due to spatial variations in m_c (Li *et al.*, 2023; Li and Luo, 2024).

Throughout most of this article, we exclusively present results obtained with the MLE method, except in the Estimation of the parameters of the GR distribution section, in which we explore the performance of these methods when a catalog sampled from a truly TGR distribution is incorrectly treated as sampled from a GR distribution; and in the Can the distribution of (positive) magnitude differences be helpful? section, where we investigate whether positive magnitude differences can help differentiate between GR and TGR distribution.

Estimation of the parameters of the TGR distribution

Assuming IID moment samples, the logarithm of the likelihood function for the TGR distribution is (Kagan and Schoenberg, 2001)

$$\log L = n\beta\log(M_c) + \frac{1}{M_{\text{corner}}}(nM_c - \sum_{i=1}^{n} M_i) - \beta\sum_{i=1}^{n}\log M_i + \sum_{i=1}^{n}\log\left(\frac{\beta}{M_i} + \frac{1}{M_{\text{corner}}}\right). \quad (6)$$

The maximum-likelihood estimate of the model parameters is obtained by numerically solving

$$\begin{cases} \hat{\beta}A + \hat{\eta}B = 1 \\ \frac{1}{n}\sum_{i=1}^{n}\frac{1}{1-\hat{\eta}(B-AM_i)} = 1 \end{cases}, \quad (7)$$

in which $A = \frac{1}{n}\sum_{i=1}^{n}\log(\frac{M_i}{M_c})$, $B = \frac{\sum_{i=1}^{n}(M_i - M_c)}{n}$, and $\eta = \frac{1}{M_{\text{corner}}}$. One can also find the MLE solution using a grid-search method based on equation (6). In this study, we estimate the parameters of the TGR distribution mainly by solving equation (7) numerically using the Newton–Raphson method. However, in the Analyzing temporal variations of MFD and the Application to observational cases sections, we employ the grid-search method for computational efficiency. The bias due to magnitude discretization can be corrected using the same approach as for the GR distribution.

To ensure accurate estimation of both the *b* value and m_{corner}, a sufficient number of earthquakes both below and above m_{corner} is necessary. The estimation becomes biased with a small sample size, as noted by Kagan (2002), although this bias is often overlooked due to its insignificance. Standard errors of the estimate can be derived by inverting the second derivative matrix of the log-likelihood (equations A19 and A21 in Kagan, 2002), or can be obtained from contour lines of the log-likelihood map based on the asymptotic theory (Kagan and Schoenberg, 2001). It is important that the likelihood function in the moment scale exhibits asymmetry, typically favoring larger m_{corner} values (Kagan, 2002).

Potential pitfall: Assuming the wrong distribution

As Kagan (2002) pointed out, the estimates of *b* value and m_{corner} are correlated; that is, either a larger *b* value or a smaller m_{corner} leads to fewer large earthquakes. This implies that if a truly GR distribution is assumed TGR, or vice versa, the estimation of the *b* value could be significantly biased. In this section, we examine the effects of assuming a GR distribution when analyzing a catalog actually sampled from a TGR distribution (assuming the finite m_{corner} to be infinite), and vice versa. Geffers *et al.* (2022) have already shown that the MLE method will overestimate the *b* value if a TGR catalog is treated as GR. They demonstrate the need for a sufficiently large number of earthquakes and a magnitude range to derive reliable results. Here, we revisit their tests with a broader parameter space. Furthermore, we apply the three *b* value estimation methods when assuming a GR model for a TGR catalog. Compared to the findings of Geffers *et al.* (2022), we highlight that: (1) fitting the TGR model to GR data is also biased, especially with small sample sizes and/or large *b* values; and (2) when the GR model is applied to TGR data, the m_{corner}, *b* value, and catalog size all influence the estimation.

We first examine the misapplication of the TGR model to GR samples. We generate a substantial number of random catalogs drawn from a GR distribution (based on the method in Text S1), varying both the catalog size *n* (ranging from 50 to 800) and *b* value (from 0.6 to 1.4). For each catalog, we solve for the optimal parameters using the TGR model. The estimated *b* value is systematically underestimated for smaller sample sizes, as shown in Figure 2a. We further find that, the deviation from the true *b* value can be approximated by the empirical formula (curves in Fig. 2a):

$$\frac{b_{\text{TGR}}}{b} = 1 - \frac{3.32b - 1.17}{n}. \quad (8)$$

The standard deviation of the *b* value estimation conforms to the theoretical estimate for the MLE method ($\sigma = b/\sqrt{n}$) given by Aki (1965; Fig. 2b). In addition, the estimated m_{corner} is close to the maximum magnitude predicted by the GR distribution (*a*/*b*) (Fig. 2c), even though the true m_{corner} is infinite. This highlights an important limitation: the TGR model should

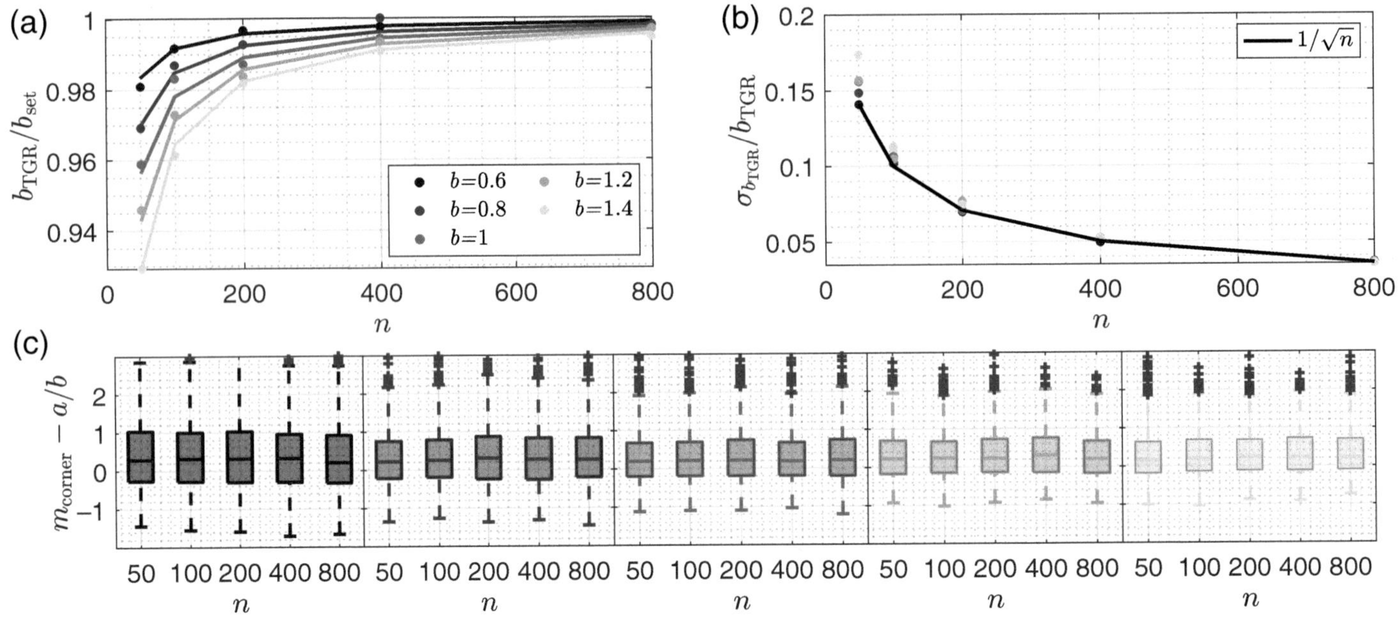

Figure 2. Bias introduced by fitting the TGR model to truly GR catalogs. The distribution of estimated b value is symmetric and is shown by the (a) mean value (with the fitting curves given by equation 8) and (b) standard deviation. The distribution of estimated m_{corner} is asymmetric and is represented (c) by its median value (line within the box) and interquartile range (box extent), which is the distance between the first quartile (lower edge of the box) and third quartile (upper edge of the box). Whiskers extend to the most extreme data points within 1.5 times the interquartile range from the quartiles. Individual red points beyond the whiskers are considered outliers. For each catalog size n (50–800) and b value (0.6–1.4, represented by different colors), we generate 1000 random catalogs. The color version of this figure is available only in the electronic edition.

only be applied when the GR distribution can be statistically rejected (as discussed in the following sections). Given the current data, the TGR model will generally fit the observed data at least as well as the GR model. If the catalog follows the GR distribution, with the catalog size increase, the estimated m_{corner} will increase. Thus, using the TGR model with the estimated m_{corner} based on current data will underestimate the probability of future large earthquakes.

Next, we explore the scenario for which the GR model is applied to truly TGR data. We apply three methods of b value estimation (MLE, b-positive, and KMS) on synthetic catalogs (generated by the method in Text S1) varying in size n (from 50 to 800), b value (0.6, 1, and 1.4), and m_{corner} (ζ ranging from 0.1 to 0.9). As expected, the b value is consistently overestimated, with the degree of overestimation strongly influenced by the value of ζ (Fig. 3). For any specific ζ, the estimated b value tends to converge toward a level consistently higher than the true b value as the catalog size increases. Among the methods tested, the MLE approach not only displays the smallest standard deviation but also provides estimates closest to the actual b value, while still showing significant deviations.

MFD UNDER RANDOM SAMPLING

Figure 1 depicts the mode of the distributions of the number of earthquakes larger than or equal to a specific magnitude for the GR and TGR models. Assuming that magnitudes are randomly sampled, deviations from the mode values will occur, and the GR and TGR distributions may not be as easily distinguishable as Figure 1 suggests. In this section, we first present the confidence intervals for MFDs and subsequently discuss the distribution of the maximum magnitudes as a specific scenario.

One can define two types of confidence intervals associated with the MFD: (1) confidence interval of n for a given magnitude m, and (2) confidence interval of m for a given number n. We will only discuss the latter one, which is more practical in seismological studies. Subsequently, we derive the theoretical formula for the confidence intervals. the confidence intervals can also be estimated numerically by generating a large number of random catalogs (Fig. S1), as done in many previous studies (e.g., Naylor *et al.*, 2009; Eaton *et al.*, 2014; Igonin *et al.*, 2018; Kaveh *et al.*, 2024).

For a given magnitude m_r, the possibility that there are n earthquakes with magnitudes greater than or equal to m_r can be written from the binomial distribution as follows:

$$P(N(\geq m_r) = n | m_r) = C^n_{N_{total}} \prod_{i=1}^{n} P(\geq m_r) \prod_{i=1}^{N_{total}-n} P(< m_r), \quad (9)$$

in which N_{total} is the total number of events, $P(\geq m_r)$ is obtained from equation (1) or (2). Given a number n, the possibility that the minimum magnitude of the n largest events in the catalog is smaller than or equal to m_n can be written as follows:

$$P(m \leq m_n | n) = \frac{\int_0^{m_n} P(N(\geq m_r) = n) \mathrm{d}m_r}{\int_0^{+\infty} P(N(\geq m_r) = n) \mathrm{d}m_r}. \quad (10)$$

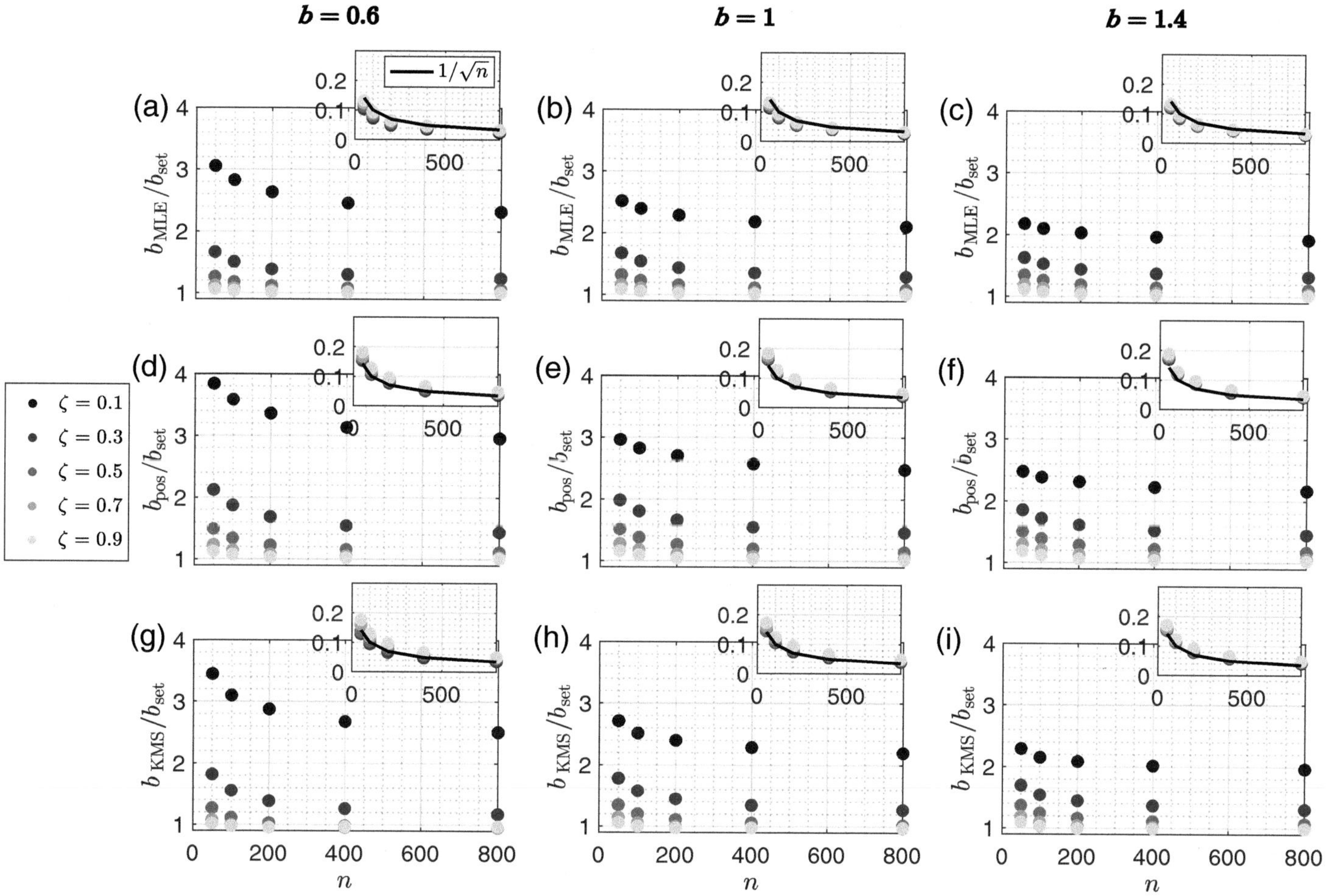

Figure 3. Bias introduced by fitting the GR model to truly TGR catalogs. Assuming the data are drawn from a GR distribution, the mean b value, and corresponding standard deviation (normalized by the estimated mean value, shown in the inset) are obtained using the (a–c) maximum-likelihood estimation (MLE), (d–f) b-positive, and (g–i) K–M slope methods, respectively. For each catalog size n (50–800), b value (0.6, 1, and 1.4), and ζ (0.1–0.9), we generate 1000 random catalogs. KMS, K–M slope. The color version of this figure is available only in the electronic edition.

For a significance level α (e.g., 0.05 or 0.1), the confidence interval $[m_{\frac{\alpha}{2}}, m_{1-\frac{\alpha}{2}}]$, the interval within which a fraction $1-\alpha$ (e.g., 95% or 90%) of the randomly generated magnitudes should lie, is obtained by solving $P(m \le m_{\frac{\alpha}{2}}|n) = \frac{\alpha}{2}$ and $P(m \le m_{1-\frac{\alpha}{2}}|n) = 1 - \frac{\alpha}{2}$. We show examples for both GR and TGR distributions in Figure 4a,b.

Given the relatively wide range of the confidence interval of the GR distribution, a key question that this article attempts to address is how we can discern whether the tapering observed in the MDF of a particular catalog genuinely reflects a TGR distribution, or if it is merely an accidental bias caused by random sampling. We would like to clarify that the confidence interval depicted in Figure 4 is pointwise. This means that there is a 5% chance that any given point of MFD curve will fall outside the lower boundary of the 95% confidence interval. However, the probability that the MFD of an observational catalog lies entirely outside this lower boundary is significantly less than 5%. To rigorously assess whether a catalog conforms to a specific distribution based on confidence intervals, a functional confidence interval would be required. Transitioning from a pointwise to a functional confidence interval is a nontrivial task, though.

A related topic is the distribution of maximum magnitudes, which can be interpreted as the region bounded by the x-intercepts of the confidence intervals in Figure 4. Alternatively, one can directly derive the probability distribution of maximum magnitudes under a given MFD model by considering the probability that all earthquakes in the catalog fall below a certain magnitude, using the binomial distribution—as described by van der Elst *et al.* (2016; see also Appendix A for details). Here, we examine how the distribution of maximum magnitudes for the GR and TGR models evolves with catalog size. We obtain the mode and the 90% confidence interval by generating a large number of synthetic catalogs, and the results are shown in Figure 5. As expected, the unbounded GR distribution can yield extremely large events as the catalog size increases. In contrast, the TGR distribution, while allowing for increasing maximum magnitudes with catalog size, shows only minimal growth. This suggests that even if there is a true truncated magnitude for the TGR model, the catalog size required to test such a hypothesis might be extremely large. Compared to the truncated GR model, for which truncated magnitude has already been shown to be nearly

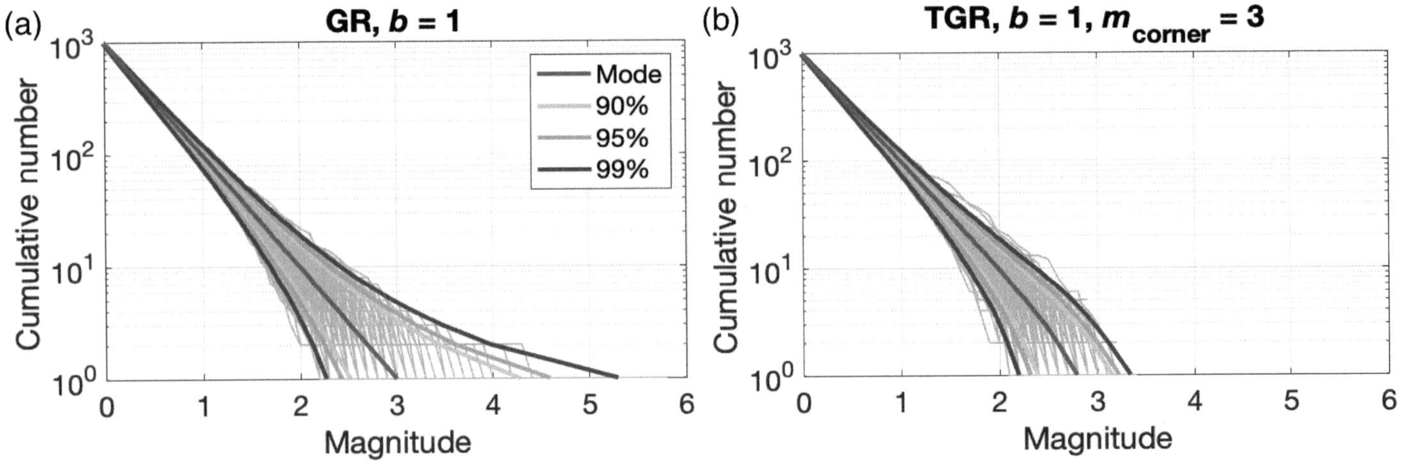

impossible to constrain given the size of real observed catalogs (e.g., Holschneider *et al.*, 2011; van der Elst *et al.*, 2016; Schultz, 2024), the return period of the maximum magnitude for the truncated TGR model would be even longer. Therefore, in this study, we will simply discuss whether we can distinguish between the unbounded GR and TGR models, and if so, which better describes the observations.

DETERMINE IF A GIVEN CATALOG IS GR OR TGR

In this section, we first review methodologies previously employed in the literature to distinguish between GR and TGR distributions. Subsequently, we evaluate their efficacy using synthetic catalogs. We also evaluate the merit of using the distribution of positive magnitude difference, a recently popular approach for *b* value estimation.

Methods used for distinguishing two distributions

The proposed methods for assessing the merits of the two distributions based on observations can be divided into two categories: (1) methods comparing two distributions: Akaike information criterion (AIC), Bayesian information criterion (BIC), and likelihood-ratio (LR) test; and (2) methods aimed at rejecting the GR distribution, such as coefficient of variation (CV) criterion, curve curvature test, Kolmogorov–Smirnov (KS) test, linearity test, and maximum magnitude criterion (introduced in the previous section). Both an excess and a deficit in the number of large earthquakes compared to the prediction by the GR distribution will lead the curve curvature test, KS test, and linearity test to reject the GR distribution. In contrast, the other tests will reject the GR distribution only when the number of large events is lower than expected under the GR distribution. In this study, we reject the null hypothesis (GR distribution) when $p < 0.05$ for the method that gives probability (all except AIC, BIC, and linearity test).

AIC (e.g., Huang and Beroza, 2015; Trugman *et al.*, 2016; Muntendam-Bos and Grobbe, 2022): the AIC relates to the maximum of the log-likelihood values $\log L$ (defined by equations 4 and 6) according to (Akaike, 1974),

Figure 4. Confidence intervals of magnitude–frequency distributions (MFDs), for (a) GR distribution with a catalog size of 1000, and a *b* value of 1, and (b) TGR distribution with a catalog size of 1000, a *b* value of 1, and an m_{corner} of 3. Gray curves show 1000 random catalogs for reference. The color version of this figure is available only in the electronic edition.

$$\mathrm{AIC} = -2\log L + 2k, \tag{11}$$

in which *k* is the number of parameters in the model. The model with the lower AIC is, in principle, preferred. Some studies reject GR distribution only when the AIC of TGR is smaller than that of GR by more than a certain threshold value (e.g., Huang and Beroza, 2015); here, we use the basic version with no threshold.

BIC (e.g., Bell *et al.*, 2013, Geffers *et al.*, 2022): similarly, with the maximum of the log-likelihood values $\log L$, the BIC is calculated by (Leonard and Hsu, 1999)

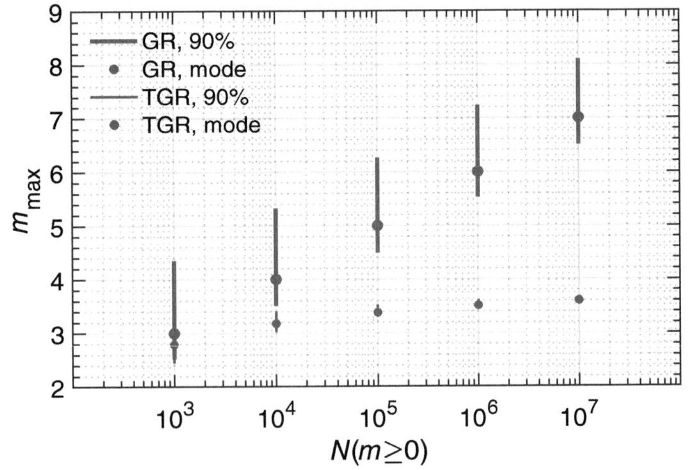

Figure 5. Distribution of maximum magnitudes under different catalog sizes, for GR distribution with a *b* value of 1 and TGR distribution with a *b* value of 1 and an m_{corner} of 3. The circle represents the mode values, whereas the lines represent the 90% confidence intervals. The results are from 1000 random synthetic catalogs. The color version of this figure is available only in the electronic edition.

$$\mathrm{BIC} = -2 \log L + k \log n, \quad (12)$$

in which n is the sample size. The preferred model has a lower BIC. Compared to AIC, BIC penalizes model complexity more heavily, especially as sample size increases.

LR test (Kagan, 2002; Geist and Parsons, 2014; Serra and Corral, 2017): the log-likelihood ratio for two probability distributions A and B, with A nested within B (A has few parameters), is expressed as follows (Kagan, 2002):

$$\mathrm{LR} = \log L_{\mathrm{B}} - \log L_{\mathrm{A}}. \quad (13)$$

Under the null hypothesis that the data originates from the simpler model (A), the probability distribution of the statistic 2LR follows a chi-squared distribution—assuming the sample size is sufficiently large—with degrees of freedom equal to the difference in the number of parameters, $k_{\mathrm{B}} - k_{\mathrm{A}}$. For a specified risk α, the null hypothesis can be rejected if $2\mathrm{LR} > \chi^2_\alpha(k_{\mathrm{B}} - k_{\mathrm{A}})$.

CV criterion (Kagan, 2002): if the estimated corner magnitude is close to infinity (η is close to zero), the catalog should be regarded as GR distribution. This might be reflected as an open confidence region for the estimated m_{corner}. Kagan (2002) suggests that this can be represented by the CV of $\eta = 1/M_{\mathrm{corner}}$,

$$\mathrm{CV} = \frac{\sigma_{\hat{\eta}}}{\hat{\eta}}, \quad (14)$$

in which $\hat{\eta}$ is the estimated value and $\sigma_{\hat{\eta}}$ is the standard deviation of the estimation. Kagan (2002) suggests that the 97.5% confidence interval corresponds to a CV of 0.5. However, as demonstrated in Figure S2, the distribution of CV is also dependent on catalog size. Consequently, the suggested strategy cannot be employed to distinguish between the two distributions. Therefore, this method is not discussed further in the remainder of this article.

Curve curvature test (Dempsey *et al.*, 2016): we fit the MFD using a quadratic function and subsequently calculate the mean curvature of the curve. Simultaneously, we generate a large number of random catalogs based on the optimal GR models and compute the mean curvatures of these catalogs. The risk of rejecting the GR distribution is assessed by comparing the curvature of the target catalog with those of the random catalogs.

KS test (Kamer and Hiemer, 2015): the KS distance is defined as follows:

$$D_{\mathrm{KS}} = \max_x |F_n(x) - F(x)|, \quad (15)$$

in which $F_n(x)$ and $F(x)$ are the empirical cumulative distribution function (CDF) of the target catalog and the CDF of the optimal GR model, respectively. We obtain the D_{KS} for the target catalog, and also for multiple random catalogs generated from the optimal GR model, to evaluate the risk of rejecting the GR distribution.

Linearity test (Tormann*et al.*, 2014): this method assesses the stability of the b value estimation for the given catalog. A series of b values are calculated using different cutoff magnitudes, starting from m_c and extending up to m_{cut50}, which is the highest magnitude no less than which there are still 50 earthquakes. The nonlinearity index (NLIndex) is then defined as follows:

$$\mathrm{NLIndex} = \frac{\mathrm{std}(b)}{b_{m_{\mathrm{cut50}}}/\sqrt{50}}, \quad (16)$$

in which std(b) is the standard deviation of the calculated b values at different cutoff magnitudes, $b_{m_{\mathrm{cut50}}}/\sqrt{50}$ represents the theoretical standard deviation for the error in the b value estimated under m_{cut50}. If NLIndex ≤ 1, the underlying MFD is considered linear, in other words, follows the GR distribution (Tormann *et al.*, 2014).

Maximum magnitude criterion (Corral and Serra, 2019): we generate multiple synthetic earthquake catalogs based on the optimal GR model and compare the maximum magnitude in the observed catalog with those in the simulated ones. This approach allows us to evaluate the probability of rejecting the GR distribution. The standard practice is to conduct the analysis on the total number of events in the catalog. van der Elst *et al.* (2016) proposed an alternative strategy that considers only the number of events occurring prior to the largest event. We examine the implications of these two approaches in the Appendix A. Our analysis shows that considering the total number of earthquakes produces a narrower distribution of maximum magnitudes, making it a more powerful test of the MFD model. Nevertheless, if there is compelling evidence that the catalog is stationary up to the time of the largest event and nonstationarity begins afterward, then considering the number of events before the maximum may be more appropriate. In this study, we refer to the approach based on the total number of events as the "maximum magnitude criterion." Cases of nonstationarity are addressed using the methods described in the Analyzing temporal variations of MFD section.

Performances of different methods

We generate random earthquake catalogs from both GR and TGR distributions and employ the various methods aforementioned to determine the most likely distribution from which they have been drawn. By comparing the results with the known truth, we can evaluate the effectiveness of different methods.

Effect of catalog size. We generate random catalogs of different sizes n (50–2000) and b values (0.6, 1, and 1.4) that obey the GR distribution (Fig. 6a–c). We then use the MLE to determine the parameters of the best-fitting GR and TGR distributions. The methods introduced earlier are used to determine whether a catalog conforms to the GR or TGR distribution (Fig. 6d–f). We find that, except for the AIC, all methods

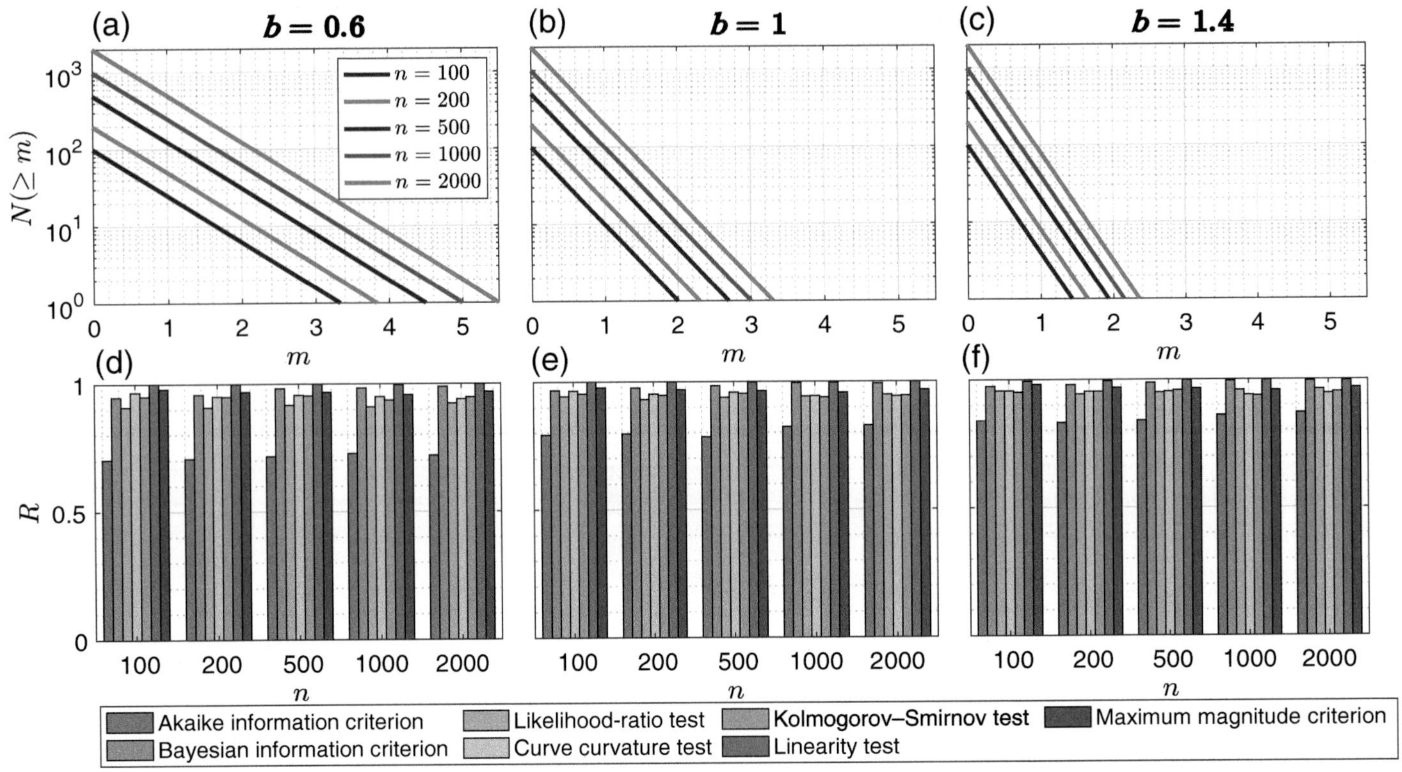

Figure 6. Performance of the different methods tested in this study, applied to GR catalogs. (a–c) Theoretical distributions of the earthquake catalogs used for testing. (d–f) The accuracy R of different methods. For each catalog size n (100–2000) and b value (0.6, 1, and 1.4), we generate 1000 catalogs. The color version of this figure is available only in the electronic edition.

exhibit similarly high accuracy. We set a threshold of 0.05 for methods that provide a p value, which is defined as one minus the accuracy assuming that the true model parameters are known. The results thus further suggest that the influence of parameter estimation uncertainty is minimal because most methods exhibit an accuracy of about 95% (Fig. 6) in close agreement with the selected p value threshold of 5%. The discrepancy is larger when the b value is smaller. For example, for $b = 0.6$, the accuracy of the LR test approximates 90%, marginally below the expected accuracy based on the set p value threshold. However, this accuracy is still adequately high.

We then generate random earthquake catalogs drawn from TGR distributions (Fig. 7a–c), use MLE to estimate the parameters, and employ various methods to determine the underlying distribution. We observe that the capability to identify TGR catalogs is less effective than in the case of GR catalogs. The accuracy diminishes with an increase in the b value, a reduction in catalog size, and an increase in ζ (Fig. 7d–o). Among the methods tested, the AIC, LR test, and maximum magnitude criterion methods exhibit the highest accuracy. However, it is noteworthy that the AIC often misclassifies GR catalogs as TGR (Fig. 6), and appears less reliable for differentiating between the two distributions than the other methods. In addition, we find that catalogs correctly identified by the maximum magnitude criterion are also accurately classified by the LR test, but the converse is not observed (Fig. S3). Consequently, we suggest the LR test to be the most effective method among those evaluated.

We further systematically evaluate the ability of the LR test to identify TGR distributions (Fig. 8). We find that the probability of the LR test making accurate judgments is controlled by the difference between m_{corner} and the predicted maximum magnitude of the GR distribution (a/b). This new parameter combines the effects of catalog size, b value, and ζ (or m_{corner}). Our findings indicate that the TGR distribution can generally be effectively distinguished from the GR distribution when $a/b - m_{corner} > 1$, with a missing rate of less than 10%. If the criterion is not satisfied, a larger catalog size can increase the possibility of identifying TGR catalogs. We also observe that distinguishing the two models becomes more challenging when the catalog size is smaller (<200) or the b value is too low (<0.8; Fig. 8). The condition ($a/b - m_{corner} > 1$) aligns with the results obtained when estimating TGR parameters for the GR catalog (see the Potential pitfall: Assuming the wrong distribution section). Specifically, the estimated m_{corner} frequently falls within the interval a/b − 1 to a/b (Fig. 2c), and the GR and TGR models can then be indistinguishable. In certain cases, one might prefer to treat the TGR model as the null hypothesis for physical reasons (e.g., when earthquakes are observed to be confined within a specific layer). To support this approach, we provide the distribution of p values for different TGR models in Figures S4 and S5, which outline the risk

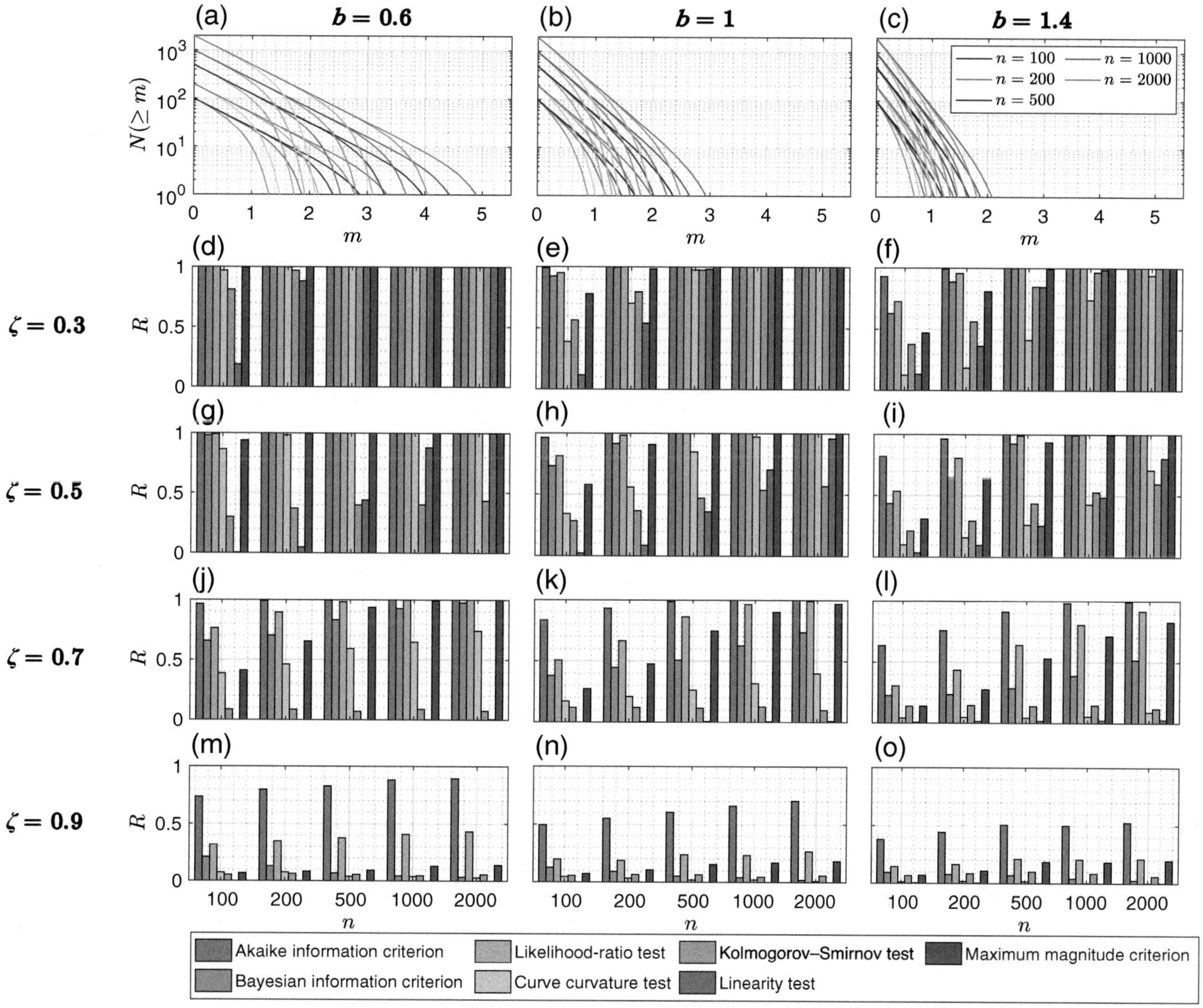

Figure 7. Performance of the different methods tested in this study, applied to TGR catalogs. (a–c) Theoretical distributions of the earthquake catalogs used for testing. Darker colors represent distributions with larger ζ. (d–o) The accuracy of different methods. For each catalog size (100–2000), b value (0.6, 1, and 1.4), and ζ (0.3–0.9), we generate 1000 catalogs. The color version of this figure is available only in the electronic edition.

associated with rejecting the TGR distribution at specific p values obtained by the LR test.

In summary, we find the LR test to be the most robust method for distinguishing between GR and TGR distributions. It inherently accounts for uncertainties in the estimation of MFD parameters. This test rarely misclassifies a GR distribution as a TGR distribution, with the false positive rate closely aligned with the selected p value threshold. However, it may fail to reject the GR hypothesis when the true distribution is TGR, if the catalog is small and the upper tail of the MFD is poorly sampled. Our results show that the ability of the LR test to correctly identify a TGR distribution improves with increasing values of $a/b - m_{\mathrm{corner}}$. Nonetheless, even when $a/b - m_{\mathrm{corner}}$ is relatively small, there remains a probability that the LR test can still detect the TGR distribution. In other words, $a/b - m_{\mathrm{corner}}$ provides a conservative estimate of how large the catalog size (as captured by a) must be to robustly reject the possibility that a given dataset is drawn from a TGR distribution.

Effect of magnitude incompleteness. The detection capability for earthquakes is magnitude dependent, and the detection rate of earthquakes with a magnitude of m is commonly described by (Ogata and Katsura, 2006)

$$q(m|\mu,\sigma) = \int_{-\infty}^{m} \frac{1}{\sqrt{2\pi}\sigma} e^{-\frac{(x-\mu)^2}{2\sigma}} \mathrm{d}x, \tag{17}$$

in which μ represents the magnitude with a missing rate of 50%, and σ is the standard deviation of normal distribution, describing the detection ability near the magnitude μ. For

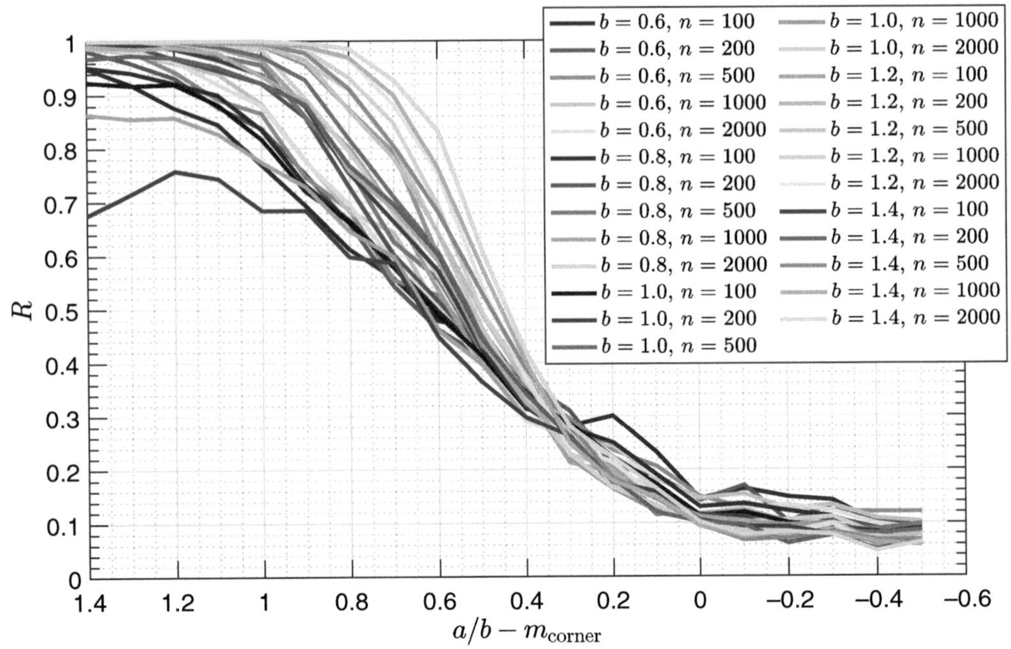

Figure 8. Accuracy R of likelihood-ratio (LR) test on the TGR catalogs as a function of the difference between the maximum magnitude predicted by GR distribution (a/b) and m_{corner}. For each catalog size (100–2000), b value (0.6–1.4), and $a/b - m_{corner}$ (−0.5 to 1.4), we generate 1000 catalogs. The color version of this figure is available only in the electronic edition.

earthquakes with magnitudes of $[\mu + \sigma, \mu + 2\sigma, \mu + 3\sigma]$, the detection rates are approximately [84%, 98%, 100%]. In practice, m_c should be at least $\mu + \sigma$ for an unbiased b value estimation (Li *et al.*, 2023). The typical value of σ for modern catalogs is 0.2 (van der Elst, 2021). Here, we address how magnitude incompleteness affects the discrimination of GR and TGR distributions.

We generate catalogs from GR and TGR distributions with sufficiently large numbers (each containing 10,000 earthquakes), a b value of 1, and a ζ of 0.5 (for TGR catalogs only). This setup ensures that, given a complete catalog, the two distributions can be well distinguished (Figs. 6–8). We apply equation (17) to screen these complete earthquake catalogs (assuming $\mu = 0.8$ and two values of σ, 0.2 and 0.4 to represent different qualities of the catalog), to produce incomplete catalogs (Fig. 9a–d; see Text S1 for implementation details). We select various m_c values, excluding earthquakes below the selected m_c, estimate the model parameters, and then employ different methods to judge the classification of the catalogs. When a lower m_c is selected, GR catalogs might be misclassified as TGR distributions (Fig. 9e, f). Instead, choosing a smaller m_c does not impact the accuracy of identifying TGR catalogs (Fig. 9g,h). But when an extremely large m_c is selected, the number of events may become insufficient to identify TGR distributions (Fig. 9h).

The most intuitive reason why selecting a lower m_c may bias results toward a TGR distribution when the true distribution is GR, is that a lower m_C leads to a lower estimated b value. This, in turn, implies a higher predicted frequency of large earthquakes, which can result in an apparent deficit of large earthquakes. In addition, several tests, including the curve curvature test, KS test, and linearity test, are not specifically designed to emphasize fit at the larger magnitudes, Therefore, they may falsely reject the GR distribution because small-magnitude earthquakes (below the true m_c) tend to deviate from the GR behavior.

Can the distribution of (positive) magnitude differences be helpful?

The b-positive method (van der Elst, 2021) is based on the fact that if a catalog follows the GR distribution, the magnitude differences between two consecutive earthquakes follow a Laplace (or double exponential) distribution with the same parameter (b value; Abramowitz and Stegun, 1968). The b-positive method uses only the positive magnitude differences to estimate the b value, thereby overcoming the STAI, under the assumption that a subsequent earthquake is detected if a preceding smaller earthquake is detected (van der Elst, 2021). This method has become a popular approach for b value estimation (e.g., Zhai *et al.*, 2021; Garza-Girón *et al.*, 2023; Yoshida *et al.*, 2023). In this context, we discuss whether the distribution of positive magnitude differences can aid in distinguishing between the two distributions.

Deriving the Laplace distribution of sequence differences from the GR distribution is straightforward. However, for sequences originating from the TGR distribution, the distribution of their differences does not have an analytical solution. Hence, we generate random catalogs to obtain the distribution of positive magnitude differences for both GR and TGR catalogs, including the confidence intervals (Fig. B1). We find that, unlike the positive magnitude difference sampled from GR distribution, those sampled from TGR distribution exhibit tapering behavior. We use the TGR formulation (equation 2) to fit positive magnitude differences of the TGR distribution, yielding a good fit with the same b value but a smaller m_{corner} (Fig. B2).

Only the second kind of methods in the Methods Used for Distinguishing Two Distributions section is directly applicable to positive magnitude differences because there is no analytical solution for the positive magnitude difference of TGR

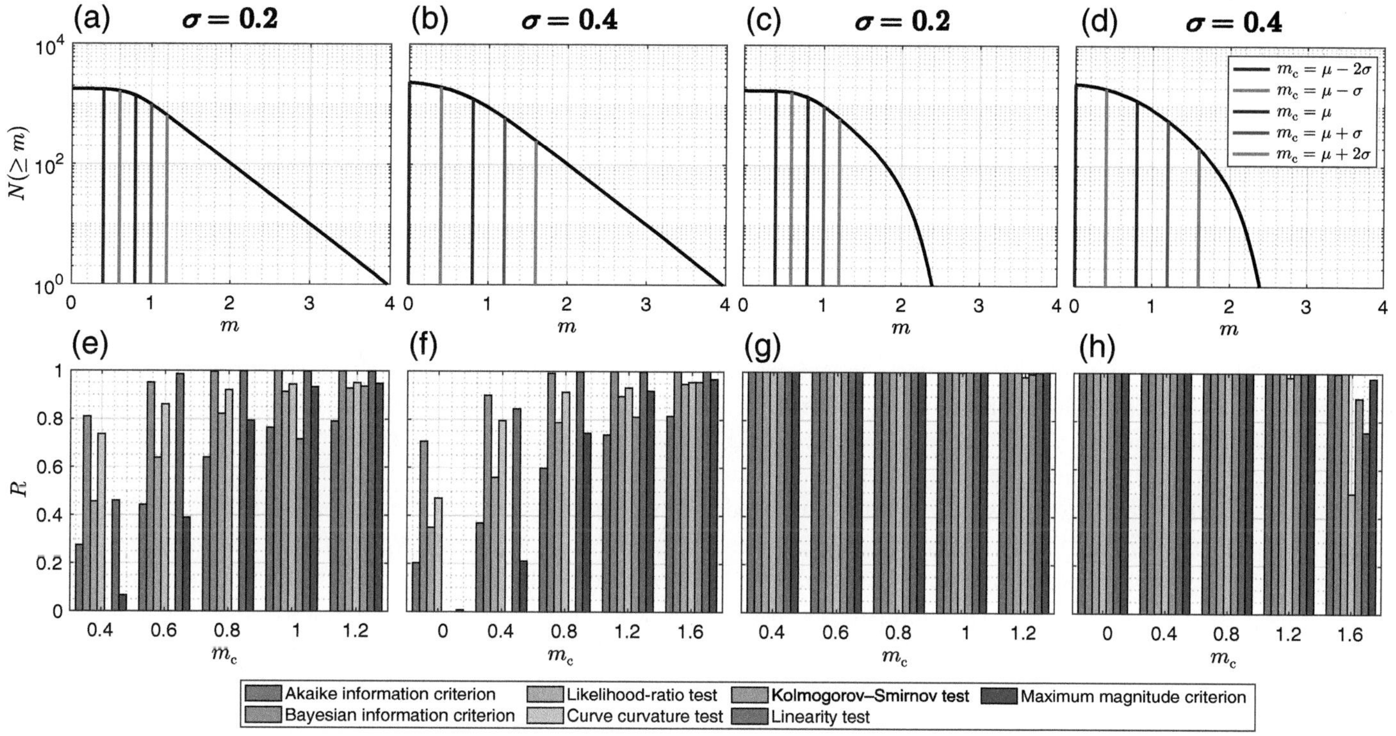

Figure 9. Performance of the different methods tested in this study, applied to incomplete catalogs. (a–d) Theoretical distributions of the earthquake catalogs used for testing ($\mu = 0.8$, $b = 1$), with panels (a,b) representing the GR distributions, and panels (c,d) representing the TGR distributions ($\zeta = 0.5$). Vertical lines represent the selected m_c. The earthquakes with magnitudes of [$\mu - 2\sigma$, $\mu - \sigma$, $\mu + \sigma$, $\mu + 2\sigma$] have missing rates of [~98%, ~84%, ~16%, ~2%], respectively. (e–h) The accuracy R of different methods. For each , we generate 1000 catalogs. The color version of this figure is available only in the electronic edition.

distribution. As a result, we only need to test whether maximum magnitude difference (similar to the maximum magnitude criterion) can outperform the LR test which is based on the magnitude samples. We find that, like the maximum magnitude criterion, those catalogs that can be distinguished by the maximum magnitude difference criterion are essentially distinguishable by the LR test (Fig. S6). Therefore, we conclude that if the catalog is complete, positive magnitude differences do not provide additional useful information for distinguishing if a catalog is GR or TGR. Similarly, the b-positive method does not help b value estimation in cases of uniform incompleteness (Li and Luo, 2024). Therefore, we do not expect positive magnitude distribution to help recognize TGR distribution in this case. However, as we will discuss in the Discussion section, temporal variations of m_c can cause the MFD to resemble a TGR distribution. In such cases, the positive magnitude differences can be used to identify this false TGR distribution because it will not exhibit any tapering characteristics.

ANALYZING TEMPORAL VARIATIONS OF MFD

In this section, we explore the potential of a nonstationary MFD model, which may be either GR or TGR with temporal variations of model parameters, or a transition between GR and TGR. Although our focus primarily lies on temporal variations, these findings are equally applicable to spatial variations.

We first consider the effects of temporal variability in the MFD on parameter estimation. We recall that when using equations (5) or (7) to estimate model parameters, we assume the magnitudes are IID. This assumption is violated in case of temporal evolution of the MFD unless we assume the catalog undergoes only step changes and the windows used for parameter estimation align precisely with the changepoint. We discuss this issue in detail in the Appendix C. We find that for GR catalogs, variations in the b value within the catalog do not significantly bias the estimates, at least when the internal b value deviations are less than 0.4; in other words, the results closely match the "true" mean b value of the catalog, For TGR catalogs, if the change in the m_{corner} is small, such as a variation of less than 0.5 across hundreds of earthquakes, the estimation bias is also negligible. However, in catalogs of similar size, if m_{corner} changes by 1 within 100 events for example, the bias could be substantial. In this case, both the b value and m_{corner} tend to be overestimated.

We now discuss how to detect the evolution of MFD over time, regardless of the potential bias discussed earlier. In some previous studies, an expanding window—referring to a dynamic window that begins at a fixed point and progressively includes additional data points over time—has been applied (e.g., Bell *et al.*, 2013; Serra and Corral, 2017). However, employing expanding windows to study MFD variations can be inappropriate due to the dilution effect of earlier data on the signal from more recent data. Other studies have used time-moving windows of fixed time length (e.g., one month or several years; Huang and Beroza, 2015; Trugman *et al.*, 2016). However, catalog size has an impact on the estimation of the model parameters and on the identification of TGR distribution.

To tackle the issue, we begin by reviewing the estimation of the temporal evolution of the b value, which has been extensively studied in the literature due to its potential physical implications (e.g., Wiemer *et al.*, 1998; Gulia *et al.*, 2016; Peng *et al.*, 2021; Carlino *et al.*, 2022). A well-known factor significantly affecting the reliability of estimating the temporal evolution of b value is the selection of time windows. Choosing a smaller time window not only implies a larger uncertainty but also a higher time resolution. Ensuring that the estimated b value changes are real rather than artifacts is a complex issue, and there have been an increasing number of studies devoted to developing techniques for objectively/automatically selecting spatiotemporal windows. These methods are of three types: the first type uses all available earthquakes but assigns larger weights to earthquakes closer to the time or space nodes (Tormann *et al.*, 2014; Taroni, Zhuang, and Marzocchi, 2021; Taroni, Vocalelli, and de Polis, 2021); the second type employs Bayesian methods, assuming that the underlying distribution of b value changes is known (e.g., step functions) and inverts the parameters of the distribution (Fiedler *et al.*, 2018; Morales-Yáñez *et al.*, 2022; Iwata and Nanjo, 2024; Laporte *et al.*, 2025); and the third type is based on the "ensemble wisdom" of a large number of randomly partitioned windows (Kamer and Hiemer, 2015; Roberts *et al.*, 2016; García-Hernández *et al.*, 2021; Muntendam-Bos and Grobbe, 2022; Yin and Jiang, 2024).

We draw inspiration from the third approach to discern transitions between GR and TGR distributions in a given catalog. We first randomly partition the catalog with a size of N_{total} into w nonoverlapping subcatalogs, ensuring that each subcatalog has a minimum size $N_{\min}$ and a maximum size $N_{\max}$. For each subcatalog, we fit the GR and TGR models separately, then calculate the p value of the LR test and assign it to each earthquake within the subcatalog. We repeat the aforementioned procedure x times (set as 100 here), and then determine the median of these x results as the determined p value evolution for specific w. We choose the median rather than the minimum to avoid the risk of multiple testing (Kato, 2019). Next, we change the value of w, repeat the aforementioned procedure, and obtain the evolution of p values for each w. A final conclusion can be drawn by considering the results across different values of w. The possible value of w ranges from $\lfloor N_{\text{total}}/N_{\max} \rfloor + 1$ to $\lceil N_{\text{total}}/N_{\min} \rceil - 1$, in which $\lfloor y \rfloor$ and $\lceil y \rceil$ mean rounding y down and up to the nearest integer, respectively. If the number of TGR earthquakes is small but the $a/b - m_{\text{corner}}$ is large, only a small window (usually implying a large w) is needed to identify them. If a large window is used, there is a risk of missing them. Conversely, if the number of TGR earthquakes is large but $a/b - m_{\text{corner}}$ is small, using a larger window (smaller w) makes identification easier. Thus, a meticulous analysis of specific instances may necessitate subjective judgments when integrating the results across various w values, particularly if we aim to acquire highly detailed insights about the sequence. For this reason, our approach does not output any quantitative uncertainty. Instead, this approach gives us a way to roughly detect where the MFD changes, allowing us to know how to divide it into subcatalogs for detailed assessment (as we do in the Application to observational cases section). In the subsequent synthetic test, as well as the analysis of observational cases in the Application to observational cases section, we simply designate the median of the results under w from $\lfloor N_{\text{total}}/N_{\max} \rfloor + 1$ to $\min\{\lceil N_{\text{total}}/N_{\min} \rceil - 1, \lfloor N_{\text{total}}/N_{\max} \rfloor + 5\}$ as the temporal evolution of the MFD for the catalog. In other words, we analyze at most five different values of w, which entails implementing 500 random partitioning strategies for the catalog. Our settings are designed to examine the first-order characteristics of the sequence, which may not capture short-period variations. However, this limitation helps reduce the influence of random noise at smaller time scales. We set $N_{\max}$ to 1000 to avoid potential interference in parameter estimation from mixed distributions in the catalog (Appendix C), and $N_{\min}$ to 100 to ensure the ability to identify the TGR distribution (Fig. 8).

We generate synthetic catalogs to test the effectiveness of this framework. We consider two scenarios: the first involves a TGR catalog between two different GR catalogs, and the second involves two different TGR catalogs between two different GR catalogs. For each scenario, we generate 100 random catalogs and use the framework to assess whether transitions between TGR and GR distributions exist. The result is shown in Figure 10, for which the gray curves are the obtained temporal evolution of each catalog and the black curves represent the average of the results for 100 random catalogs. The p value is relatively high and low for periods following GR and TGR distributions, respectively. We show the analysis of one random catalog in Figure D1 for reference. Hence, we demonstrate that the proposed framework can effectively identify transitions in the MFD.

In addition to analyzing the transition between GR and TGR distributions, our framework can also be used to analyze the temporal evolution of the parameters. In fact, this is the premise for analyzing MFD transitions. If the underlying distribution is known, the adjustment lies only in the target of each subcatalog, which is not the p value but rather the b value or/and m_{corner}. Testing on synthetic catalogs is shown in Figures D2 and D3. We acknowledge that uncertainty plays an important role in parameter estimation. However, our methods cannot provide a measure of it. There are two kinds of uncertainties involved in temporal parameter estimation: first, the uncertainty when estimating each subcatalog, and second, the uncertainty caused by dividing the catalog into

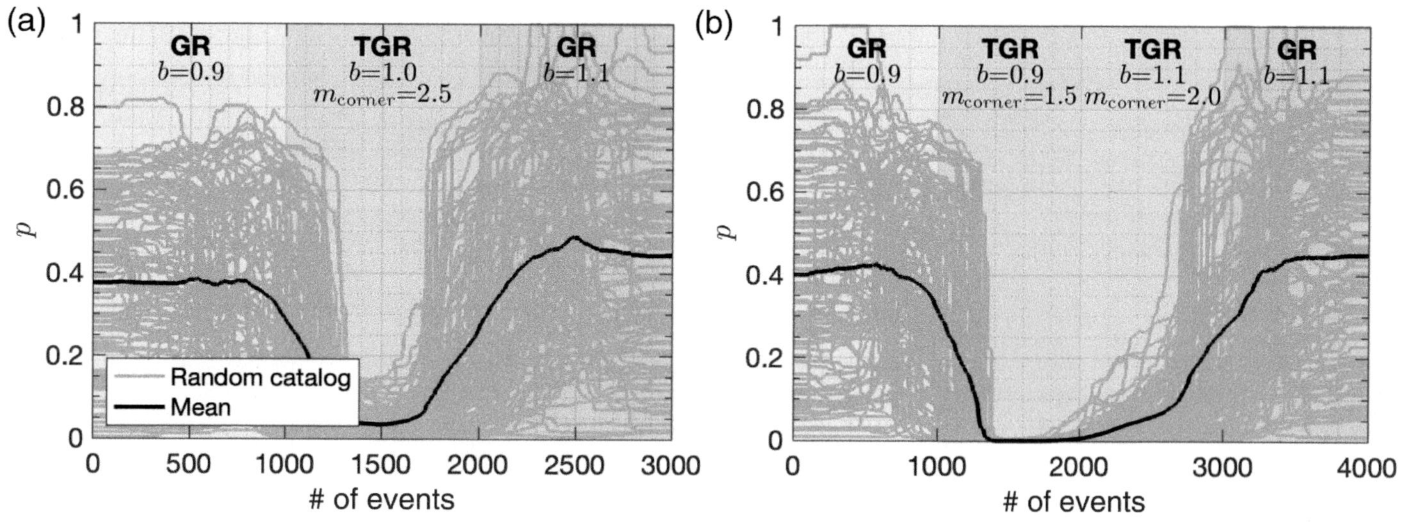

Figure 10. Identifying transitions between GR and TGR distributions over time. (a) A TGR distribution is sandwiched by two GR distributions. (b) Two TGR distributions are sandwiched by two GR distributions. The vertical axis represents the p value given by the LR test, for which lower p values favor TGR distribution. The horizontal axis represents the earthquake index arranged in chronological order. For each scenario, we generate 100 random catalogs. Each gray curve represents the result of a random catalog, and the black curve represents the average of these gray curves. The color version of this figure is available only in the electronic edition.

subcatalogs. The first type of uncertainty is well defined and can be obtained either through the bootstrap method or analytical solutions. However, the second type of uncertainty is more complex to estimate. One potential way to measure this is by analyzing the temporal evolution derived from different random segmentations of the catalog. However, it is not easily achieved, as we define the range of w artificially, and altering this range will unavoidably influence the estimated uncertainty range. We suggest that our method serves primarily to segment the catalog into subcatalogs, which can be used for more detailed analysis using standard methods to determine parameters and their uncertainties.

APPLICATION TO OBSERVATIONAL CASES

With the insights obtained earlier, we now revisit the MFD observed in case examples of natural and induced seismicity.

The first step is to determine the magnitude of completeness (m_c) for each catalog, a task that remains challenging. Although numerous methods have been proposed (Woessner and Wiemer, 2005; Amorese, 2007; Herrmann and Marzocchi, 2021; Lombardi, 2021; Taroni, 2023; Godano *et al.*, 2024), there is no clear consensus on which is best, and the optimal choice is likely case dependent (Zhou *et al.*, 2018; Gong *et al.*, 2024; Wang *et al.*, 2025). In this study, m_c is defined as the maximum among three values: (1) the value obtained from the maximum curvature method with a correction factor of +0.2 (Woessner and Wiemer, 2005), (2) the value from the m_c by b value stability (MBS) method (Cao and Gao, 2002; Woessner and Wiemer, 2005), and (3) the value reported by the data source. The two methods we apply have been widely used and demonstrated to be effective in various benchmark tests (Zhou *et al.*, 2018; Gong *et al.*, 2024; Wang *et al.*, 2025). In particular, the MBS method is relatively conservative, typically yielding higher m_c values (Lombardi, 2021). This is desirable for our purposes, as discussed in the Effect of magnitude incompleteness section: selecting a lower m_c tends to bias the results toward a TGR distribution. Following Zhuang *et al.* (2017), we also plot magnitude versus incremental event count (Fig. S7) to verify that no significant STAI exists above the selected m_c. We assign a constant m_c over time for each catalog, rather than allowing it to vary temporally. This is required by the method we use to analyze the temporal evolution of the MFD, as described in the Analyzing temporal variations of MFD section. Designing tools for distinguishing two distributions under time-varying m_c would be a meaningful direction for future research.

After filtering each catalog using the selected m_c, we first evaluate the property of the entire catalog by providing the optimal GR and TGR models, as well as the p value obtained by the LR test. These results are summarized in Table 1. Subsequently, we use the framework proposed in the Analyzing temporal variations of MFD section to analyze the temporal evolution of the MFD type. We also present the analysis of temporal evolution in MFD parameters, and further, albeit subjectively, segment the catalog into multiple subcatalogs for individual MFD analysis. The analysis of these subcatalogs is also presented in Table 1. We do not discuss the MFD parameters in detail because our study is focused on identifying eventual tapering of the MDF. We convert all magnitudes to moment magnitude based on the relationship between moment magnitude and moment (Hanks and Kanamori, 1979), although some catalogs are presented in other magnitude scales, as it remains unclear which magnitude scale follows the GR distribution (Staudenmaier *et al.*, 2018).

TABLE 1

Summary of the Magnitude–Frequency Distribution for Observational Cases

Catalog	m_c	$N(m \geq m_c)$	b_{GR}	$[b_{GR}^{5\%}, b_{GR}^{95\%}]$	b_{TGR}	$[b_{TGR}^{5\%}, b_{TGR}^{95\%}]$	m_{corner}	$[m_{corner}^{5\%}, m_{corner}^{95\%}]$	p
Global earthquakes (as a whole)	6.5	3603	1.02	[0.99, 1.05]	1.00	[1.00, 1.05]	9.3	[8.6, 9.6]	0.18
Global earthquakes (1920–1940)		650	0.98	[0.93, 1.04]	0.95	[0.85, 1.00]	8.2	[8.0, 8.4]	0.00
Global earthquakes (1940–1970)		983	1.00	[0.96, 1.06]	1.00	[0.95, 1.05]	9.6	[8.6, 9.8]	0.40
Global earthquakes (1970–2000)		1133	1.09	[1.05, 1.14]	1.00	[0.95, 1.05]	8.0	[7.9, 8.1]	0.00
Global earthquakes (2000–2020)		837	0.97	[0.91, 1.03]	0.95	[0.90, 1.00]	9.2	[8.4, 9.5]	0.28
Otaniemi (as a whole)	0.4	675	1.39	[1.30, 1.57]	1.30	[1.20, 1.45]	1.7	[1.5, 1.8]	0.00
Otaniemi (stage 1)		113	1.55	[1.35, 1.80]	1.40	[1.00, 1.65]	1.4	[1.1, 1.7]	0.12
Otaniemi (stages 2–4)		421	1.48	[1.38, 1.60]	1.40	[1.30, 1.55]	1.8	[1.5, 1.9]	0.06
Otaniemi (stage 5)		141	1.09	[0.98, 1.24]	0.95	[0.75, 1.10]	1.6	[1.3, 1.7]	0.00
Coso (as a whole)	1.5	1235	1.15	[1.09, 1.21]	1.15	[1.10, 1.20]	4.4	[3.8, 4.6]	0.44
Coso (1982–1998)		463	1.30	[1.21, 1.41]	1.25	[1.10, 1.35]	3.0	[2.8, 3.1]	0.02
Coso (1998–2022)		772	1.08	[1.01, 1.15]	1.10	[1.00, 1.15]	4.4	[3.8, 4.6]	0.54

Confidence intervals for the parameters are determined using the bootstrap method. As discussed in the Determine if a given catalog is GR or TGR section, note that we do not need to consider the uncertainty in parameter estimation when analyzing the results of likelihood-ratio (LR) test. In the grid-search setup for fitting tapered Gutenberg–Richter (TGR) models, we set the potential candidates for m_{corner} between the m_c and the maximum observed magnitude plus 1, with an interval of 0.05, and control the search range for the b value between 0.4 and 1.9, with an interval of 0.05.

Application to global seismicity

Although the TGR distribution was initially proposed to describe global seismicity (Kagan, 2002), debate continues on whether it describes observational data better than the GR distribution (e.g., Bell *et al.*, 2013; Zöller, 2013; Corral and González, 2019; Corral and Serra, 2019). Furthermore, the question of whether the occurrence patterns of large earthquakes change over time remains a hot topic of discussion (e.g., Shearer and Stark, 2012; Lay, 2015; Zaliapin and Kreemer, 2017), which can be tested by the method presented in the Analyzing temporal variations of MFD section.

We use data covering the period 1920–2019 from version 10.0 of the International Seismological Centre-Global Earthquake Model Global Instrumental Earthquake, ignoring the pre-1920 data due to their high incompleteness (Di Giacomo *et al.*, 2018). The magnitude of completeness generally decreases with time, and never exceeds 6.5 during the time period we analyze (Di Giacomo *et al.*, 2018). To be conservative, we use this value, which is higher than the values determined by the methods we apply.

The LR test indicates that the entire catalog considered as a whole conforms to the GR model; however, visual inspection reveals that neither distribution matches well the tail of the MFD (Fig. 11a and Table 1). We then examine the temporal variations of the MFD (Fig. 11b–e), finding that the catalog can be divided into four stages, each fitting better either the TGR or GR distributions (Fig. 11b,f–i and Table 1). For the period between 2000 and 2020, it appears that the GR model does not provide a perfect fit to the data, although the data points do fall within the 90% confidence interval of the optimal GR model. We find that this period can be further divided into two subperiods: before 2013 and after, with the earlier and later periods aligning with GR and TGR behavior, respectively (Fig. S8). The reason the post-2013 period does not show a significantly low p value in Figure 11b is that our method only explores five different relatively small w values, aiming to capture first-order behavior. The largest earthquakes occurred during the two stages, more consistent with a GR distribution. Given that the MFD parameters and p values before the occurrence of these large earthquakes are calculated over a time window that actually encompasses them, the analysis does not indicate that the transition from TGR to GR occurred before the large earthquakes or that b value variations might precede large earthquakes.

Although there are good reasons to expect that the MFD of global earthquakes should show tapering because of the moment conservation principle, it seems like a simple TGR with a unique b value and constant corner magnitude is not adequate. Therefore, our results might support the idea that the pattern of global large earthquakes changes over time, with some periods having fewer large earthquakes than others. As an alternative, we explore another explanation for the observed behavior. Because very large earthquakes are limited in their depth extent and forced to develop a large aspect ratio, it has been suggested that the MFD of global earthquakes might actually be better described by a bilinear GR distribution ("bilinear" refers here to a piecewise linear function with two intervals; Romanowicz and Rundle, 1993). In support of that view, Yoder *et al.* (2012) found **M** < 7.6 earthquakes to have a b value of 1, whereas **M** > 7.6 larger earthquakes have a b value of 1.5. We suggest that this theory could cause the MFD to appear as either a GR or TGR distribution at different times. Considering the sampling of the largest few earthquakes from $b = 1.5$, if they are relatively small (e.g., following a mode MFD), the entire catalog may appear TGR. From Figure 11, we see that the periods when the TGR distribution is preferred do not include earthquakes larger than **M** ~8.5. By contrast, if several larger (**M** > 8.5) earthquakes are sampled, the entire catalog appears more consistent with the GR model (with $b \approx 1$). We have confirmed this hypothesis by generating synthetic catalogs drawn from such a bilinear distribution with a divide at M 7.6 as

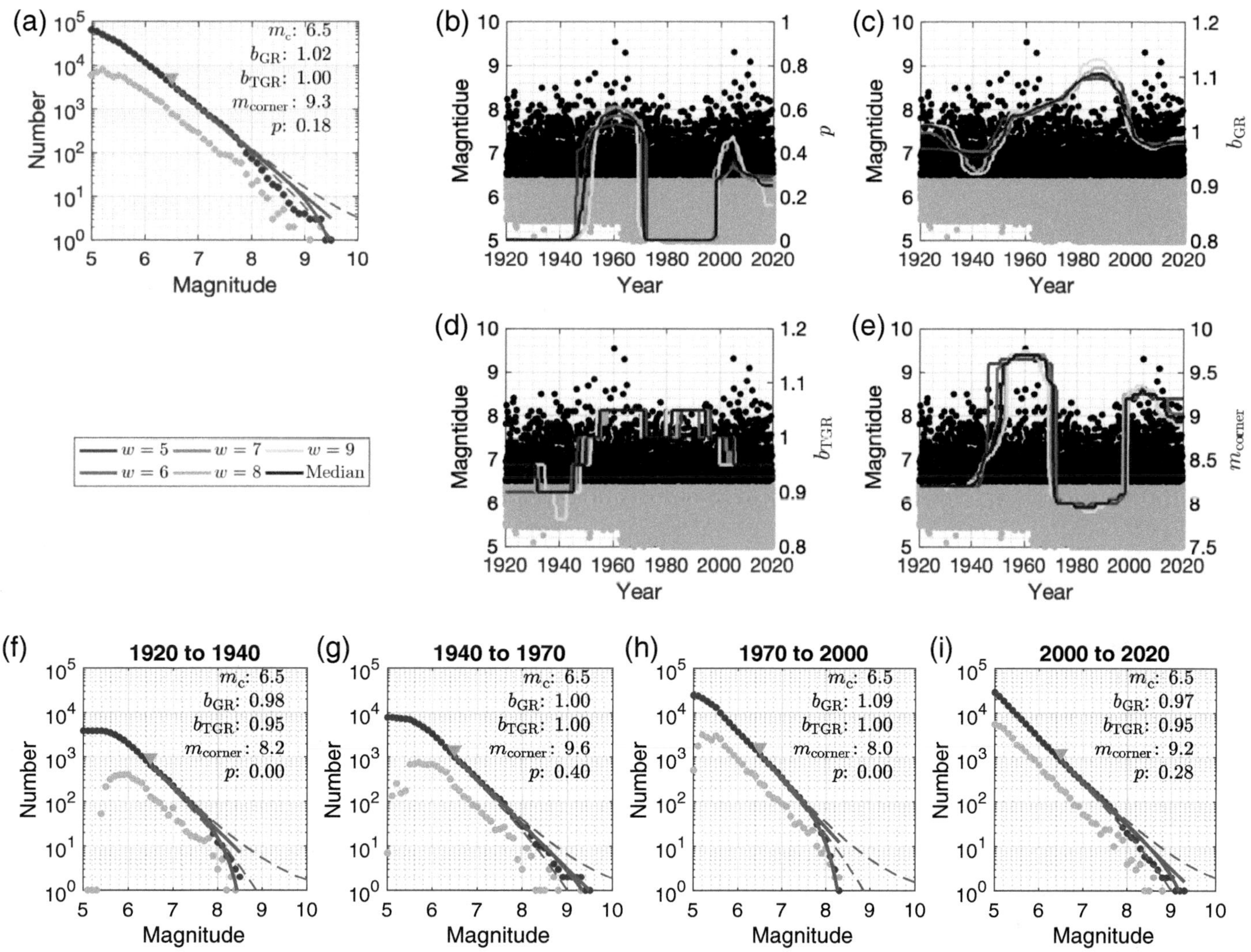

Figure 11. Analysis of global seismicity (Di Giacomo *et al.*, 2018). (a) MFD for all events. The gray circles represent the noncumulative distribution (for magnitude bins of 0.1), whereas the black circles denote the number of samples no less than a specific magnitude (cumulative distribution). The red-solid line represents the best-fitting GR distribution determined using the MLE (equations 5a and 5b), with the 90% confidence interval indicated by the red-dashed curves). The blue curve shows the best-fitting TGR distribution determined using the MLE (equation 7). (b–e) Temporal evolution of the LR test p value, GR and TGR parameters under different number of nonoverlapping windows (w). The magnitude and time of each event is denoted by black (above the magnitude of completeness) and gray (below the magnitude of completeness) circles. (f–i) MFD and best-fitting models for different time periods. The color version of this figure is available only in the electronic edition.

suggested by Yoder *et al.* (2012; Fig. 12). Therefore, we suggest that the bilinear model might actually be a good representation of the MDF of global earthquakes. As a result, the MFD of global earthquakes does not appear to be consistently GR or TGR, depending on how the tail of the distribution is sampled over the period considered. This analysis also shows that, from a statistical point of view, the TGR model is not a good approximation of a bilinear GR model. Describing accurately the MFD of global earthquakes might, in fact, require an even more complicated model. For instance, even if the b value increases for $\mathbf{M} > 7.6$, the tail of the MFD should still be truncated at larger magnitudes. This is because the bilinear GR distribution allows the occurrence of infinitely large magnitudes. Meanwhile, the magnitude at which the b value transition occurs may vary depending on the tectonic context. However, such characteristics may be undetectable given the limited number of large earthquakes.

Application to injection-induced seismicity

It has been proposed that injection-induced seismicity should conform to the TGR model because the extent of earthquake ruptures is limited by the stimulated rock volume (e.g., Shapiro *et al.*, 2011, 2013). Similarly, if the magnitude of "driven" earthquakes (induced earthquakes that do not run away) is limited by the injected volume (McGarr, 2014; Galis *et al.*, 2017), injection-induced earthquakes should, in principle, be tapered. This tapering is expected because the truncation due to moment conservation, combined with a realistic inter-event time distribution, results in a distribution consistent with the TGR model (Marsan and Tan, 2020). The distribution

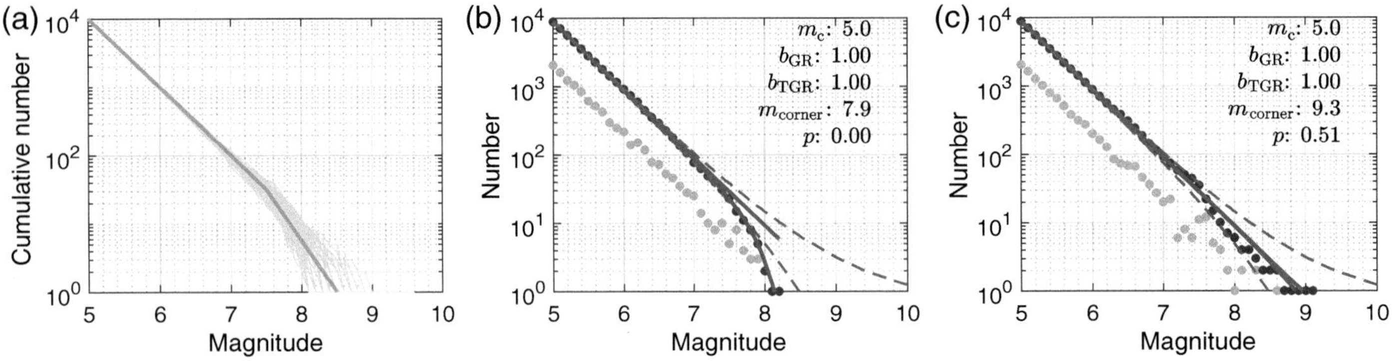

Figure 12. Randomly sampled bilinear MFD. (a) Dark-orange curve represents the bilinear distribution, for which earthquakes below and above M 7.6 follow GR distributions with b values of 1.0 and 1.5, respectively. The light-orange curves show 100 randomly generated catalogs. (b,c) Examples of a random catalog sampled from the bilinear distribution, illustrating the characteristics of TGR and non-tapered GR distributions, respectively. The color version of this figure is available only in the electronic edition.

should also be truncated at sufficiently large magnitudes, but detecting truncation in real data has been a challenge, as we discussed earlier. Tapering might not be detectable either if the sample size is not large enough to constrain the tail of the distribution. Several studies on injection-induced seismicity have reported TGR distributions (e.g., Bachmann *et al.*, 2011; Huang and Beroza, 2015; Minetto *et al.*, 2023). On the other hand, van der Elst *et al.* (2016) analyzed 22 cases of induced earthquakes and found that the observed maximum magnitudes align statistically with the predictions of the GR model. Similarly, Schultz (2024) analyzed 13 cases of induced seismicity and demonstrated that all of them are adequately explained by an unbounded GR distribution. In this section, we examine Otaniemi and Coso geothermal sites with the methods described earlier.

Otaniemi geothermal site. Between June and July 2018, approximately 18,160 m^3 of water was injected at a depth of 5.7–6.1 km within the crystalline basement as part of a geothermal well stimulation project near the Aalto University campus in Otaniemi, Finland—a region lacking natural earthquakes (Kwiatek *et al.*, 2019; Ader *et al.*, 2020; Leonhardt *et al.*, 2020; Kim and Avouac, 2023). The stimulation was conducted in five successive stages (colored in Fig. 13c), each lasting between 2 and 14 days, and moved progressively upward from the bottom of the well at a depth of 6.1–5.7 km. Flow rates varied between 400 and 800 L/min, and well-head pressure between 60 and 90 MPa. Seismicity was detected as early as three hours after injection commenced. Throughout the stimulation period, no significant lag was observed between changes in injection pressure, flow rates, and earthquake occurrences (Kwiatek *et al.*, 2019). A rapid Omori-type decay of the seismicity rate was observed after each shut-in (Kim and Avouac, 2023). Importantly, no red alert was triggered by the Traffic Light System throughout the operation (Kwiatek *et al.*, 2019; Ader *et al.*, 2020).

To assess the MFD of induced seismicity at this site, we use the moment magnitudes from the relocated catalog of Leonhardt *et al.* (2020; Fig. 13a). The catalog consists of 1986 events with magnitudes ranging from M_w − 0.49 to 1.87. The magnitude of completeness was not reported for the relocated catalog previously (Leonhardt *et al.*, 2020). Using local magnitudes from the same source does not affect our conclusions but results in systematically lower b values due to the scale-dependent difference between local and moment magnitudes.

The catalog predominantly follows a TGR distribution with a b value of 1.30 (90% confidence interval: 1.20–1.45) and an m_{corner} of 1.7 (90% confidence interval: 1.5–1.8; Table 1 and Fig. 13b). Thus, the absence of $M_w > 2$ earthquakes (red-alert threshold in the Traffic Light System; Ader *et al.*, 2020), despite the fact that some would have been expected based on the GR distribution, might be attributed to the tapering of the MFD. The LR test indicates relatively low p values throughout the sequence, though some higher values appear when dividing the data into multiple subcatalogs (Fig. 13d). We attribute this to the limitations imposed by small catalog sizes and suggest that the catalog consistently aligns with a TGR distribution (Fig. 13h–j). Notably, a significant decrease in the b value is observed during stage 5 (Fig. 13e,f,h–j). Although m_{corner} shows some temporal variations, the trend is less clear (Fig. 13g,h–j and Table 1).

Coso geothermal field. The Coso geothermal field (Fig. 14a) is located east of the Sierra Nevada Mountains in eastern California (Walter and Weaver, 1980). The geothermal power plants have been in operation since 1987, reaching peak production and injection rates in the early 1990s (Fig. 14d). The earthquakes in this area can result from loading by tectonic and magmatic processes (Hauksson and Unruh, 2007), geothermal power production (Schoenball *et al.*, 2015; Trugman *et al.*, 2016), Earth tides (Wang *et al.*, 2022), and passing seismic waves (Aiken and Peng, 2014; Alfaro-Diaz *et al.*, 2020). We use the waveform-relocated catalog of Southern California from 1981 to 2021 (Hauksson *et al.*, 2012),

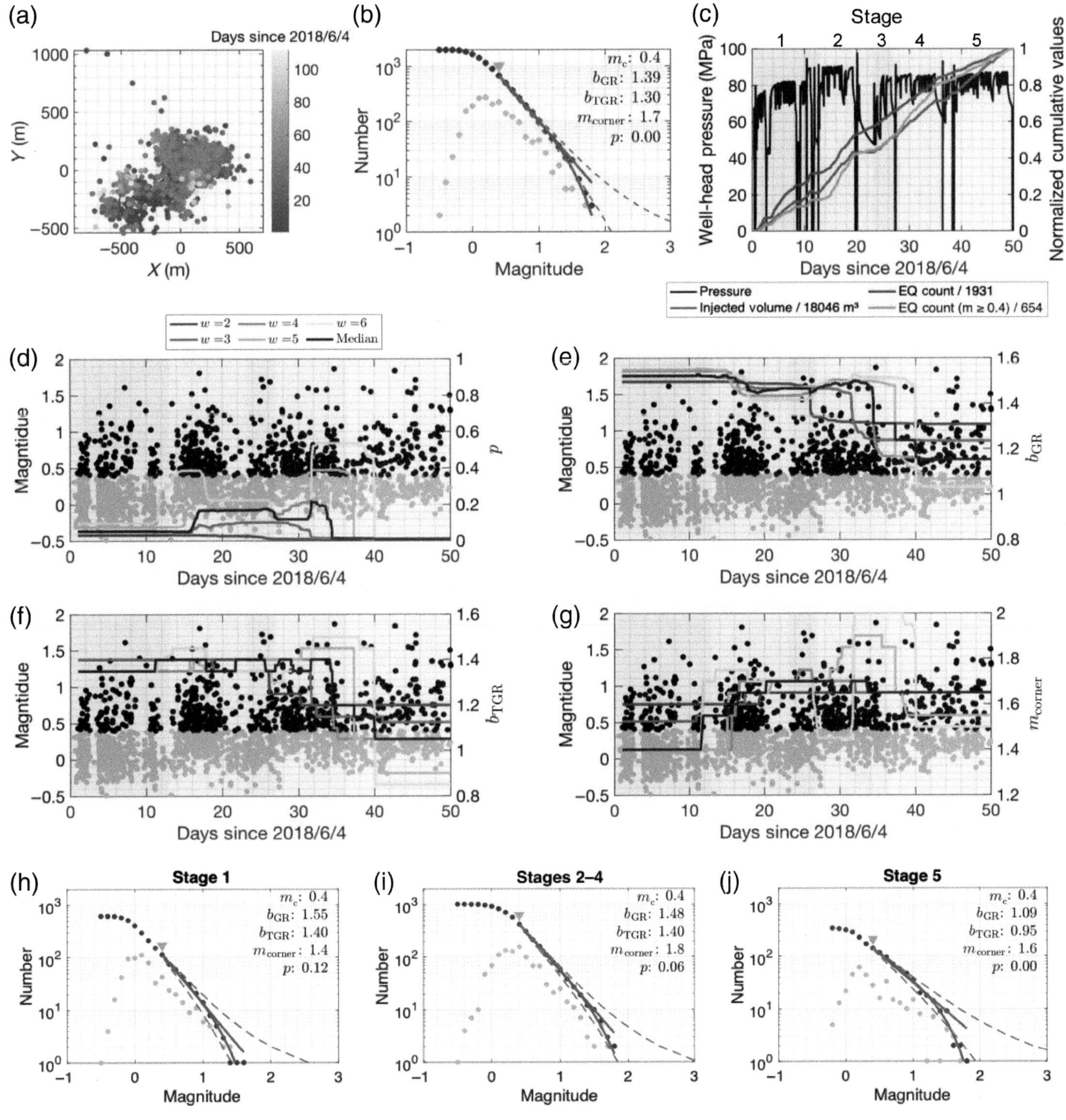

Figure 13. Analysis of induced seismicity at the Otaniemi Geothermal Site (Leonhardt *et al.*, 2020). (a) Spatial distribution of earthquakes. (b) MFD for all events. (c) Comparison between well-head pressure, injection fluid volumes, and the cumulative number of earthquakes. (d–g) Temporal evolution of the LR test p value, GR, and TGR parameters. (h–j) MFD and best-fitting models for different stages. The color version of this figure is available only in the electronic edition.

with refined locations determined with GrowClust (Trugman and Shearer, 2017). Magnitudes for each earthquake are reported in different magnitude scales and range from −0.51 to 4.33 (Fig. 14c). In a previous study, the m_c for the region was estimated to 1.5 (Trugman *et al.*, 2016).

Overall, the catalog is classified as GR distribution with a b value of 1.15 (90% confidence interval: 1.09–1.21; Table 1 and Fig. 14b). However, a careful examination reveals that the MFD varies over time (Fig. 14e). Based on the evolution of the

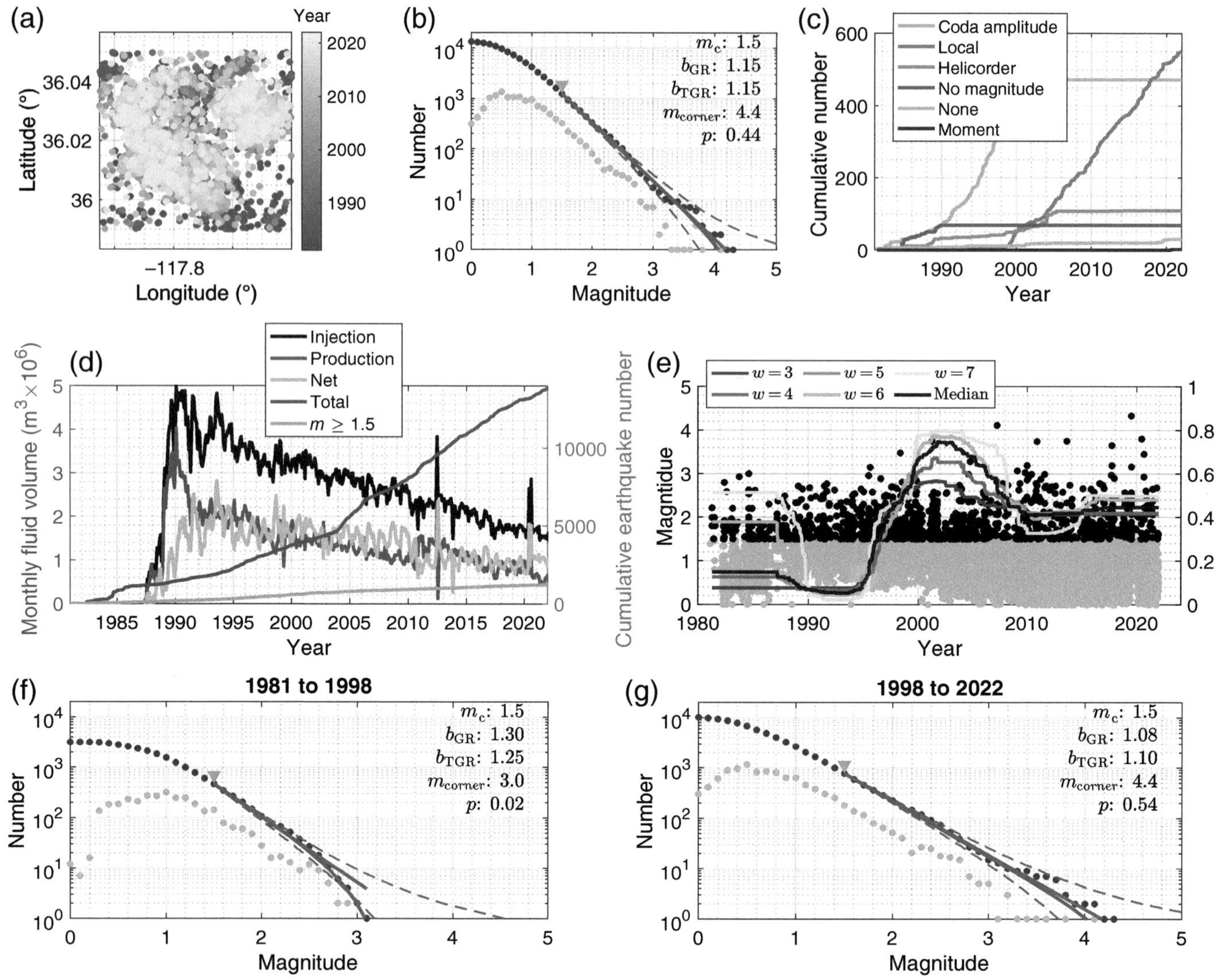

p value, we segment the catalog into two distinct periods (Fig. 14f,g). The seismicity prior to 1998 is TGR and subsequently transitions to GR. The TGR behavior is not due to the induced earthquakes because it is observed before the start of the geothermal operations. We note that our catalog includes multiple magnitude types; prior to 1998, magnitudes were primarily coda amplitude-based, shifting later to include more Helicorder and local magnitudes (Fig. 14c). We also note that for the same source, the catalog for the 1992 Landers sequence shows a downward bending characteristic (predominance of smaller earthquakes) in magnitudes up to 3 (Herrmann and Marzocchi, 2021), aligning with our observed magnitude range for TGR. Thus, we suggest that the observed shift in MFD around 1998 could be due to changes in magnitude types.

Figure 14. Analysis of the earthquakes in the Coso geothermal field (Southern California Earthquake Data Center; see Data and Resources). (a) Spatial distribution of the earthquakes. (b) MFD for all events. (c) Cumulative number of events with magnitudes larger than the magnitude of completeness with a particular magnitude type over time. (d) Comparison between monthly fluid volumes of production, injection, and net production and the cumulative number of earthquakes. (e) Temporal evolution of the LR test p value. (f,g) MFDs and best-fitting models for different time periods. The color version of this figure is available only in the electronic edition.

DISCUSSION

In this study, we present a strategy to assess whether a seismicity catalog is consistent with the GR model or shows significant tapering (TGR). We find that tapering is statistically significant in some observational catalogs and might then warrant a physical explanation. We find that, in some of these cases, the MFD is highly nonstationary, with switches between TGR and GR distributions and variable b values and corner magnitudes. Although we have observed the TGR distribution seems more adequate in at least one stage of each sequence analyzed earlier, we note that most observed earthquake catalogs fit the GR distribution rather well. Furthermore, even though in some cases the MFD might show a meaningful temporal evolution, pointing to possible physical mechanisms, we have encountered cases where the procedure used to produce the earthquake catalogs posed challenges (Coso), or where a nonstationary MFD model might indicate that neither the GR nor the TGR model is fully adequate (global large earthquakes). Several factors can cause deviations from the GR model, as summarized subsequently, and some deviations may be related to physical processes, whereas others are more likely artifacts.

Mixture of different *b* values: if a sequence comprises GR sequences with multiple *b* values, we expect an upward deviation in the tail of the MFD (Fig. C1), indicating a prevalence of larger earthquakes. This pattern emerges because sequences with higher *b* values exhibit a narrower magnitude range, resulting in an MFD that is influenced predominantly by lower *b* values at larger magnitudes. Such an effect has been documented in previous studies (e.g., Igonin *et al.*, 2018). However, it does not necessarily apply when sequences with different *b* values cover varying magnitude ranges, with one example being the proposed bilinear GR distribution for global earthquakes (Yoder *et al.*, 2012). In such a case, the MDF deviates from the standard GR model but may also not be well approximated by a stationary TGR model, as demonstrated by our analysis of the MDF of global seismicity (Figs. 11, 12).

Mixture of different possible maximum magnitudes: assume that each earthquake adheres to the truncated GR distribution, for which all earthquakes are limited by a specific (hard) cutoff magnitude, possibly resulting from the moment conservation principle. This cutoff magnitude might be dynamically determined by the current seismic moment deficit, and therefore, it would vary over time (Marsan and Tan, 2020). On extensive temporal scales, which necessitate multiple recordings of maximal earthquakes, the entire earthquake sequence displays a smooth upper cutoff, a distinctive feature of the TGR distribution (Marsan and Tan, 2020).

Distribution of rupture areas: earthquake magnitudes are thought to scale with rupture dimensions, and physical constraints on rupture dimensions may cause deviations from the GR distribution. This could result from lithological layering (Eaton *et al.*, 2014; Boitz *et al.*, 2024), the limited depth extent of the seismogenic zone (Romanowicz and Rundle, 1993), or the limited size of the anthropogenic stress perturbation in the case of induced seismicity (Shapiro *et al.*, 2011, 2013; McGarr, 2014; Galis *et al.*, 2017). Such constraints usually limit the occurrence of large earthquakes and could lead to different MFDs, including TGR, truncated GR, or multilinear GR distributions.

Mixture of different m_c: The magnitude of completeness m_c in real earthquake catalogs is likely nonuniform neither spatially nor temporally. If equation (17) is still used to describe the detection rate of earthquakes, σ could be large enough for the MFD exhibiting a downward bending above μ, which may be mistakenly identified as the typical tapering of the TGR model. This situation, if related to STAI, can be identified by observing the distribution of positive magnitude differences (van der Elst, 2021).

Different magnitude types: different magnitude scales, such as duration magnitude, local magnitude, and moment magnitude, have been developed to describe the size of earthquakes. The conversion relationships between these scales may vary depending on the magnitude range (e.g., Deichmann, 2017). This variation implies that earthquakes conforming to the GR distribution under one scale might not exhibit the same behavior under a different scale, as demonstrated in the observations made in Parkfield, California (Staudenmaier *et al.*, 2018). More broadly, when an earthquake sequence encompasses diverse magnitude types, the resulting MFD can display complex characteristics, including abrupt changes, upward bending, or downward bending (Herrmann and Marzocchi, 2021).

Magnitude uncertainties: uniform magnitude uncertainties do not affect GR distribution and *b* value estimation (Marzocchi and Sandri, 2003). If magnitude uncertainty is piecewise, the MFD exhibits a hump (Taroni, 2022); if uncertainty decreases with increasing magnitude gradually, the MFD shows a deficit of larger earthquakes (Kagan, 2010); if uncertainty increases with magnitude gradually, the MFD shows an excess of larger earthquakes (Rhoades and Dowrick, 2000). For realistic catalogs, a bimodal relationship between magnitude errors and magnitude may exist (Kamer and Hiemer, 2015).

CONCLUSIONS

The GR model of the MFD of earthquakes is one of the most classical laws in seismology. Based on theoretical considerations and empirical observations, large earthquakes might actually be less frequent than estimated by extrapolating the rate of smaller earthquakes using the GR model, a feature described by the TGR model. Detecting tapering of the MFD at large magnitudes and identifying the physical origins of tapering is important to inform earthquake physics and seismic hazards. These considerations led us to explore methods for distinguishing GR and TGR distributions. We acknowledge that other MFD models could be tested in future studies. The key findings of our study are as follows.

1. When estimating TGR parameters for data that follow a GR distribution, the estimated m_{corner} tends to approach the value a/b. This introduces a risk of underestimating the hazard when using a TGR model inferred from current data without confirming whether the true distribution is GR or TGR. Conversely, fitting a GR model to data that follow a TGR distribution can result in significantly overestimated *b* values.
2. We derive the semianalytical confidence intervals for the MFDs. The intervals for the GR distribution are relatively wide compared to those for the TGR distribution. In addition, we demonstrate that the TGR model is highly effective in suppressing the probability of large magnitudes.
3. The LR test appears to be the most effective method for distinguishing between tapered and non-tapered MFDs. This method inherently accounts for uncertainties in parameter estimation. When applied, the LR test yields a very low

probability of misclassifying a GR distribution as TGR, close to the predefined p value threshold. However, TGR distributions may sometimes be misclassified as GR if $a/b - m_{corner} < 1$. This criterion informs us of the amount of data required to reliably reject a specific TGR distribution.

4. When assessing temporal variations in the MFD, the assumption of IID samples is violated. If the catalog follows a GR distribution, the estimated b values typically show only minor deviations from the true window-averaged values when the b value varies moderately within the window. A similar behavior is observed when considering changes in m_{corner} for the TGR distribution: small changes in m_{corner} result in negligible bias. However, if m_{corner} varies rapidly, for example, by one magnitude unit over 100 events, both the estimated m_{corner} and b value can be significantly overestimated relative to their true value.
5. We propose an objective framework to analyze the first-order characteristics of temporal evolution of the catalog's MFD, focusing specifically on identifying potential transitions between the GR and TGR distributions.
6. We analyze the MFDs of several observational sequences, including global earthquakes and induced seismicity. We observe both GR and TGR distributions, with transitions between these two distributions over time. Although the diverse behaviors of the MFD may indicate interesting physical processes, it is crucial to take into account possible artifacts related to the catalogs.

DATA AND RESOURCES

The global earthquake catalog is sourced from the International Seismological Centre (ISC) and can be accessed at https://www.isc.ac.uk/iscgem. The catalog for the Otaniemi Geothermal Site is from Leonhardt *et al.* (2020) and is available at https://gfzpublic.gfz-potsdam.de/pubman/item/item_5005600. The catalog for the Coso geothermal field is sourced from the Southern California Earthquake Data Center (SCEDC) and is available at https://scedc.caltech.edu (last accessed July 2024). The production history at Coso is obtained from California Department of Conservation and can be accessed at https://www.conservation.ca.gov (last accessed July 2024). Some figures are plotted by Scientific Color Maps (Crameri *et al.*, 2020). The code used to reproduce the results of this study is available at https://github.com/lxli0/Scripts_for_papers/tree/main/LiandAvouac_GRvsTGR_script (last accessed September 2025). The supplemental material for this article includes one text explaining the generation of random synthetic catalogs and eight figures supporting the analysis in the main article.

DECLARATION OF COMPETING INTERESTS

The authors acknowledge that they have no known competing financial interests or personal relationships that could have appeared to influence the work reported in this article.

ACKNOWLEDGMENTS

This study was supported by the National Science Foundation (NSF; Award Number 1822214) via the Industry-University Cooperative Research (ICUR) Center for Geomechanics and Mitigation of Geohazards. The authors thank Editor-in-Chief P. Martin Mai, Associate Editor Matthew C. Gerstenberger, and the two reviewers (Matteo Taroni and an anonymous) for their comments. Linxuan Li contributes conceptualization, methodology, validation, formal analysis, writing—original draft, writing—review and editing, and visualization. Jean-Philippe Avouac contributes conceptualization, methodology, validation, formal analysis, writing—review and editing, supervision, and funding acquisition.

REFERENCES

Abramowitz, M., and I. A. Stegun (1968). *Handbook of Mathematical Functions with Formulas, Graphs, and Mathematical Tables*, US Government Printing Office, Washington, D.C.

Ader, T., M. Chendorain, M. Free, T. Saarno, P. Heikkinen, P. E. Malin, P. Leary, G. Kwiatek, G. Dresen, and F. Bluemle (2020). Design and implementation of a traffic light system for deep geothermal well stimulation in Finland, *J. Seismol.* **24,** 991–1014.

Aiken, C., and Z. Peng (2014). Dynamic triggering of microearthquakes in three geothermal/volcanic regions of California, *J. Geophys. Res.* **119,** 6992–7009.

Akaike, H. (1974). A new look at the statistical model identification, *IEEE Trans. Autom. Control* **19,** 716–723.

Aki, K. (1965). Maximum likelihood estimate of b in the formula logN= a–bM and its confidence limits, *Bull. Earthq. Res. Inst.* **43,** 237–239.

Alfaro-Diaz, R., A. A. Velasco, K. L. Pankow, and D. Kilb (2020). Optimally oriented remote triggering in the Coso geothermal region, *J. Geophys. Res.* **125,** e2019JB019131, doi: 10.1029/2019JB019131.

Amorese, D. (2007). Applying a change-point detection method on frequency-magnitude distributions, *Bull. Seismol. Soc. Am.* **97,** 1742–1749.

Bachmann, C. E., S. Wiemer, J. Woessner, and S. Hainzl (2011). Statistical analysis of the induced Basel 2006 earthquake sequence: Introducing a probability-based monitoring approach for enhanced geothermal systems, *Geophys. J. Int.* **186,** 793–807.

Bell, A. F., M. Naylor, and I. G. Main (2013). Convergence of the frequency-size distribution of global earthquakes, *Geophys. Res. Lett.* **40,** 2585–2589.

Bender, B. (1983). Maximum likelihood estimation of b values for magnitude grouped data, *Bull. Seismol. Soc. Am.* **73,** 831–851.

Boitz, N., C. Langenbruch, and S. A. Shapiro (2024). Production-induced seismicity indicates a low risk of strong earthquakes in the Groningen gas field, *Nat. Commun.* **15,** 329.

Bourne, S. J., and S. J. Oates (2020). Stress-dependent magnitudes of induced earthquakes in the Groningen gas field, *J. Geophys. Res.* **125,** e2020JB020013, doi: 10.1029/2020JB020013.

Cao, A. M., and S. S. Gao (2002). Temporal variation of seismic b-values beneath northeastern Japan island arc, *Geophys. Res. Lett.* **29,** 48.1–48.3.

Carlino, M. F., L. Scarfì, F. Cannavo, G. Barberi, D. Patane, and M. Coltelli (2022). Frequency-magnitude distribution of earthquakes at Etna volcano unravels critical stress changes along magma pathways, *Commun. Earth Environ.* **3,** 68.

Corral, Á., and Á. González (2019). Power law size distributions in geoscience revisited, *Earth Space Sci.* **6,** 673–697.

Corral, Á., and I. Serra (2019). Time window to constrain the corner value of the global seismic-moment distribution, *PLoS ONE* **14,** e0220237, doi: 10.1371/journal.pone.0220237.

Crameri, F., G. E. Shephard, and P. J. Heron (2020). The misuse of colour in science communication, *Nat. Commun.* **11,** 5444.

Deichmann, N. (2017). Theoretical basis for the observed break in ML/Mw scaling between small and large earthquakes, *Bull. Seismol. Soc. Am.* **107,** 505–520.

Dempsey, D., J. Suckale, and Y. Huang (2016). Collective properties of injection-induced earthquake sequences: 2. Spatiotemporal evolution and magnitude frequency distributions, *J. Geophys. Res.* **121,** 3638–3665.

Di Giacomo, D., E. R. Engdahl, and D. A. Storchak (2018). The ISC-GEM earthquake catalogue (1904–2014): status after the extension project, *Earth Syst. Sci. Data* **10,** 1877–1899.

Dutfoy, A., and G. Senfaute (2022). The randomized Gutenberg–Richter model: A recurrence model based on extreme value theory—Impacts on probabilistic seismic hazard analyses and comparison with the standard approach, *Bull. Earthq. Eng.* **20,** 6349–6376.

Eaton, D. W., J. Davidsen, P. K. Pedersen, and N. Boroumand (2014). Breakdown of the Gutenberg-Richter relation for microearthquakes induced by hydraulic fracturing: Influence of stratabound fractures, *Geophys. Prospect.* **62,** 806–818.

El-Isa, Z. H., and D. W. Eaton (2014). Spatiotemporal variations in the b-value of earthquake magnitude-frequency distributions: Classification and causes, *Tectonophysics* **615,** 1–11.

Fiedler, B., S. Hainzl, G. Zöller, and M. Holschneider (2018). Detection of Gutenberg–Richter b-value changes in earthquake time series, *Bull. Seismol. Soc. Am.* **108,** 2778–2787.

Galis, M., J. P. Ampuero, P. M. Mai, and F. Cappa (2017). Induced seismicity provides insight into why earthquake ruptures stop, *Sci. Adv.* **3,** eaap7528, doi: 10.1126/sciadv.aap7528.

García-Hernández, R., L. D'auria, J. Barrancos, G. D. Padilla, and N. M. Pérez (2021). Multiscale temporal and spatial estimation of the b-value, *Seismol. Res. Lett.* **92,** 3712–3724.

Garza-Girón, R., E. E. Brodsky, Z. J. Spica, M. M. Haney, and P. W. Webley (2023). Earthquakes record cycles of opening and closing in the enhanced seismic catalog of the 2008 Okmok Volcano, Alaska, eruption, *J. Geophys. Res.* **128,** e2023JB026893, doi: 10.1029/2023JB026893.

Geffers, G. M., I. G. Main, and M. Naylor (2022). Biases in estimating b-values from small earthquake catalogues: How high are high b-values? *Geophys. J. Int.* **229,** 1840–1855.

Geist, E. L., and T. Parsons (2014). Undersampling power-law size distributions: Effect on the assessment of extreme natural hazards, *Nat. Hazards* **72,** 565–595.

Godano, C., G. Petrillo, and E. Lippiello (2024). Evaluating the incompleteness magnitude using an unbiased estimate of the b value, *Geophys. J. Int.* **236,** 994–1001.

Goebel, T. H. W., D. Schorlemmer, T. W. Becker, G. Dresen, and C. G. Sammis (2013). Acoustic emissions document stress changes over many seismic cycles in stick-slip experiments, *Geophys. Res. Lett.* **40,** 2049–2054.

Gong, W., H. Chen, Y. Gao, Q. Li, and Y. Sun (2024). A test on methods for Mc estimation and spatial-temporal distribution of b-value in the eastern Tibetan Plateau, *Front. Earth Sci.* **12,** 1335938.

Gulia, L., T. Tormann, S. Wiemer, M. Herrmann, and S. Seif (2016). Short-term probabilistic earthquake risk assessment considering time-dependent b values, *Geophys. Res. Lett.* **43,** 1100–1108.

Gutenberg, B., and C. F. Richter (1944). Frequency of earthquakes in California, *Bull. Seismol. Soc. Am.* **34,** 185–188.

Hanks, T. C., and H. Kanamori (1979). A moment magnitude scale, *J. Geophys. Res.* **84,** 2348–2350.

Hauksson, E., and J. Unruh (2007). Regional tectonics of the Coso geothermal area along the intracontinental plate boundary in central eastern California: Three-dimensional Vp and Vp/Vs models, spatial-temporal seismicity patterns, and seismogenic deformation, *J. Geophys. Res.* 112, 10.1029/2006JB004721.

Hauksson, E., W. Yang, and P. M. Shearer (2012). Waveform relocated earthquake catalog for southern California (1981 to June 2011), *Bull. Seismol. Soc. Am.* **102,** 2239–2244.

Herrmann, M., and W. Marzocchi (2021). Inconsistencies and Lurking pitfalls in the magnitude-frequency distribution of high-resolution earthquake catalogs, *Seismol. Res. Lett.* **92,** 909–922.

Holschneider, M., G. Zöller, and S. Hainzl (2011). Estimation of the maximum possible magnitude in the framework of a doubly truncated Gutenberg–Richter model, *Bull. Seismol. Soc. Am.* **101,** 1649–1659.

Huang, Y., and G. C. Beroza (2015). Temporal variation in the magnitude-frequency distribution during the Guy-Greenbrier earthquake sequence, *Geophys. Res. Lett.* **42,** 6639–6646.

Igonin, N., M. Zecevic, and D. W. Eaton (2018). Bilinear magnitude-frequency distributions and characteristic earthquakes during hydraulic fracturing, *Geophys. Res. Lett.* **45,** 12,866–12,874.

Iwata, D., and K. Z. Nanjo (2024). Adaptive estimation of the Gutenberg–Richter b value using a state space model and particle filtering, *Sci. Rep.* **14,** 4630.

Kagan, Y. Y. (2002). Seismic moment distribution revisited: I. Statistical results, *Geophys. J. Int.* **148,** 520–541.

Kagan, Y. Y. (2010). Earthquake size distribution: Power-law with exponent $\beta \equiv 12$? *Tectonophysics* **490,** 103–114.

Kagan, Y. Y., and D. D. Jackson (2016). Earthquake rate and magnitude distributions of great earthquakes for use in global forecasts, *Geophys. J. Int.* **206,** 630–643.

Kagan, Y. Y., and F. Schoenberg (2001). Estimation of the upper cutoff parameter for the tapered Pareto distribution, *J. Appl. Probab.* **38,** 158–175.

Kamer, Y., and S. Hiemer (2015). Data-driven spatial b value estimation with applications to California seismicity: To b or not to b, *J. Geophys. Res.* **120,** 5191–5214.

Kato, M. (2019). On the apparently inappropriate use of multiple hypothesis testing in earthquake prediction studies, *Seismol. Res. Lett.* **90,** 1330–1334.

Kaveh, H., P. Batlle, M. Acosta, P. Kulkarni, S. J. Bourne, and J. P. Avouac (2024). Induced seismicity forecasting with uncertainty quantification: Application to the Groningen gas field, *Seismol. Res. Lett.* **95,** 773–790.

Kim, T., and J.-P. Avouac (2023). Stress-based and convolutional forecasting of injection-induced seismicity: Application to the Otaniemi geothermal reservoir stimulation, *J. Geophys. Res.* **128,** e2022JB024960, doi: 10.1029/2022JB024960.

Kwiatek, G., T. Saarno, T. Ader, F. Bluemle, M. Bohnhoff, M. Chendorain, G. Dresen, P. Heikkinen, I. Kukkonen, and P. Leary (2019). Controlling fluid-induced seismicity during a 6.1-km-deep geothermal stimulation in Finland, *Sci. Adv.* **5,** eaav7224, doi: 10.1126/sciadv.aav7224.

Laporte, M., S. Durand, T. Bodin, B. Gardonio, and D. Marsan (2025). b-Bayesian: The full probabilistic estimate of b-value temporal variations for non-truncated catalogs, *J. Geophys. Res.* **130,** e2024JB029973, doi: 10.1029/2024JB029973.

Lay, T. (2015). The surge of great earthquakes from 2004 to 2014, *Earth Planet. Sci. Lett.* **409,** 133–146.

Leonard, T., and J. S. Hsu (1999). *Bayesian Methods*, Vol. 1, Cambridge series in statistical and probabilistic mathematics, Cambridge University Press, Cambridge, United Kingdom.

Leonhardt, M., G. Kwiatek, P. Martínez-Garzón, M. Bohnhoff, T. Saarno, P. Heikkinen, and G. Dresen (2020). Seismicity during and after stimulation of a 6.1 km deep enhanced geothermal system in Helsinki, Finland, *Solid Earth Discuss.* **2020,** 1–29.

Li, L., and G. Luo (2024). Can we obtain reliable seismic b-values for real-time catalogues? *Geophys. J. Int.* **237,** 1554–1566.

Li, L., G. Luo, and M. Liu (2023). The K– M slope: A potential supplement for b-value, *Seismol. Res. Lett.* **94,** 1892–1899.

Lippiello, E., and G. Petrillo (2024). b-more-incomplete and b-more-positive: Insights on a robust estimator of magnitude distribution, *J. Geophys. Res.* **129,** e2023JB027849, doi: 10.1029/2023JB027849.

Lombardi, A. M. (2021). A Normalized distance test for co-determining the completeness magnitude and b-value of earthquake catalogs, *J. Geophys. Res.* **126,** e2020JB021242, doi: 10.1029/2020JB021242.

Marsan, D., and Y. J. Tan (2020). Maximum earthquake size and seismicity rate from an ETAS model with slip budget, *Bull. Seismol. Soc. Am.* **110,** 874–885.

Marzocchi, W., and L. Sandri (2003). A review and new insights on the estimation of the b-value and its uncertainty, *Ann. Geophys.* **46,** 1271–1282.

Marzocchi, W., I. Spassiani, A. Stallone, and M. Taroni (2020). How to be fooled searching for significant variations of the b-value, *Geophys. J. Int.* **220,** 1845–1856.

McGarr, A. (2014). Maximum magnitude earthquakes induced by fluid injection, *J. Geophys. Res.* **119,** 1008–1019.

Minetto, R., A. Helmstetter, B. Edwards, and P. Guéguen (2023). How injection history can affect hydraulic fracturing-induced seismicity: Insights from downhole monitoring at Preston New Road, UK, *Bull. Seismol. Soc. Am.* **114,** no. 2, 924–941, doi: 10.1785/0120230147

Mogi, K. (1963). Some discussions on aftershocks, foreshocks and earthquake swarms: The fracture of a semi-infinite body caused by an inner stress origin and its relation to the earthquake phenomena (third paper), *Bull. Earthq. Res. Inst.* **41,** 615–658.

Morales-Yáñez, C., L. Bustamante, R. Benavente, C. Sippl, and M. Moreno (2022). B-value variations in the Central Chile seismic gap assessed by a Bayesian transdimensional approach, *Sci. Rep.* **12,** 21,710.

Muntendam-Bos, A., and N. Grobbe (2022). Data-driven spatiotemporal assessment of the event-size distribution of the Groningen extraction-induced seismicity catalogue, *Sci. Rep.* **12,** 10,119.

Naylor, M., J. Greenhough, J. Mccloskey, A. Bell, and I. G. Main (2009). Statistical evaluation of characteristic earthquakes in the frequency-magnitude distributions of Sumatra and other subduction zone regions, *Geophys. Res. Lett.* **36,** doi: 10.1029/2009GL040460.

Neely, J. S., and S. Stein (2021). Why do continental normal fault earthquakes have smaller maximum magnitudes? *Tectonophysics* **809,** 228,854.

Ogata, Y., and K. Katsura (2006). Immediate and updated forecasting of aftershock hazard, *Geophys. Res. Lett.* **33,** L10305, doi: 10.1029/2006GL025888.

Ogata, Y., and K. I. Yamashina (1986). Unbiased estimate for b-value of magnitude frequency, *J. Phys. Earth* **34,** 187–194.

Park, H., D. T. Cox, M. S. Alam, and A. R. Barbosa (2017). Probabilistic seismic and tsunami hazard analysis conditioned on a megathrust rupture of the Cascadia subduction zone, *Front. Built Environ.* **3,** 32.

Peng, G. L., X. L. Lei, G. M. Wang, and F. R. Jiang (2021). Precursory tidal triggering and b value variation before the 2011 M-w 5.1 and 5.0 Tengchong, China earthquakes, *Earth Planet. Sci. Lett.* **574,** 117,167.

Rhoades, D. A., and D. J. Dowrick (2000). Effects of magnitude uncertainties on seismic hazard estimates, *Proc. of the 12th World Conference on Earthquake Engineering*, Auckland, New Zealand, 30 January–4 February.

Roberts, N. S., A. F. Bell, and I. G. Main (2016). Mode switching in volcanic seismicity: El Hierro 2011–2013, *Geophys. Res. Lett.* **43,** 4288–4296.

Rodríguez-Pérez, Q., V. Márquez-Ramírez, and F. Zúñiga (2020). Seismicity characterization of oceanic earthquakes in the Mexican territory, *Solid Earth* **11,** 791–806.

Romanowicz, B., and J. B. Rundle (1993). On scaling relations for large earthquakes, *Bull. Seismol. Soc. Am.* **83,** 1294–1297.

Rong, Y., D. D. Jackson, H. Magistrale, and C. Goldfinger (2014). Magnitude limits of subduction zone earthquakes, *Bull. Seismol. Soc. Am.* **104,** 2359–2377.

Schoenball, M., N. C. Davatzes, and J. M. G. Glen (2015). Differentiating induced and natural seismicity using space-time-magnitude statistics applied to the Coso Geothermal field, *Geophys. Res. Lett.* **42,** 6221–6228.

Scholz, C. H. (2015). On the stress dependence of the earthquake b value, *Geophys. Res. Lett.* **42,** 1399–1402.

Schorlemmer, D., S. Wiemer, and M. Wyss (2005). Variations in earthquake-size distribution across different stress regimes, *Nature* **437,** 539–542.

Schultz, R. (2024). Inferring maximum magnitudes from the ordered sequence of large earthquakes, *Phil. Trans. Roy. Soc. Lond. A* **382,** 20230185, doi: 10.1098/rsta.2023.0185.

Serra, I., and Á. Corral (2017). Deviation from power law of the global seismic moment distribution, *Sci. Rep.* **7,** 40,045.

Shapiro, S. A., O. S. Krüger, and C. Dinske (2013). Probability of inducing given-magnitude earthquakes by perturbing finite volumes of rocks, *J. Geophys. Res.* **118,** 3557–3575.

Shapiro, S. A., O. S. Krüger, C. Dinske, and C. Langenbruch (2011). Magnitudes of induced earthquakes and geometric scales of fluid-stimulated rock volumes, *Geophysics* **76,** WC55–WC63.

Shearer, P. M., and P. B. Stark (2012). Global risk of big earthquakes has not recently increased, *Proc. Natl. Acad. Sci. Unit. States Am.* **109,** 717–721.

Sornette, D., and A. Sornette (1999). General theory of the modified Gutenberg-Richter law for large seismic moments, *Bull. Seismol. Soc. Am.* **89,** 1121–1130.

Spassiani, I., and W. Marzocchi (2021). An energy-dependent earthquake moment–frequency distribution, *Bull. Seismol. Soc. Am.* **111,** 762–774.

Staudenmaier, N., T. Tormann, B. Edwards, N. Deichmann, and S. Wiemer (2018). Bilinearity in the Gutenberg-Richter relation based on ML for magnitudes above and below 2, from systematic

magnitude assessments in Parkfield (California), *Geophys. Res. Lett.* **45,** 6887–6897.
Taroni, M. (2022). The effect of magnitude uncertainty on the Gutenberg-Richter b-value estimation and the magnitude-frequency distribution: 'what hump?', *Geophys. J. Int.* **231,** 907–911.
Taroni, M. (2023). Estimating the magnitude of completeness of earthquake catalogs using a simple random variable transformation, *Seism. Record* **3,** 194–199.
Taroni, M., and M. M. C. Carafa (2023). Earthquake size distributions are slightly different in compression vs extension, *Commun. Earth Environ.* **4,** 398.
Taroni, M., G. Vocalelli, and A. de Polis (2021). Gutenberg–Richter B-value time series forecasting: a weighted likelihood approach, *Forecasting* **3,** 561–569.
Taroni, M., J. Zhuang, and W. Marzocchi (2021). High-definition mapping of the Gutenberg–Richter b-value and its relevance: A case study in Italy, *Seismol. Res. Lett.* **92,** 3778–3784.
Tormann, T., S. Wiemer, and A. Mignan (2014). Systematic survey of high-resolution b value imaging along Californian faults: Inference on asperities, *J. Geophys. Res.* **119,** 2029–2054.
Trugman, D. T., and P. M. Shearer (2017). GrowClust: A hierarchical clustering algorithm for relative earthquake relocation, with application to the Spanish Springs and Sheldon, Nevada, earthquake sequences, *Seismol. Res. Lett.* **88,** 379–391.
Trugman, D. T., P. M. Shearer, A. A. Borsa, and Y. Fialko (2016). A comparison of long-term changes in seismicity at The Geysers, Salton Sea, and Coso geothermal fields, *J. Geophys. Res.* **121,** 225–247.
Utsu, T. (1999). Representation and analysis of the earthquake size distribution: A historical review and some new approaches, *Pure Appl. Geophys.* **155,** 509–535.
van der Elst, N. J. (2021). B-positive: A robust estimator of aftershock magnitude distribution in transiently incomplete catalogs, *J. Geophys. Res.* **126,** e2020JB021027, doi: 10.1029/2020JB021027.
Van Der Elst, N. J., M. T. Page, D. A. Weiser, T. H. Goebel, and S. M. Hosseini (2016). Induced earthquake magnitudes are as large as (statistically) expected, *J. Geophys. Res.* **121,** 4575–4590.
Vere-Jones, D., R. Robinson, and W. Yang (2001). Remarks on the accelerated moment release model: Problems of model formulation, simulation and estimation, *Geophys. J. Int.* **144,** 517–531.
Walter, A. W., and C. S. Weaver (1980). Seismicity of the Coso range, California, *J. Geophys. Res.* **85,** 2441–2458.
Wang, W., P. M. Shearer, J. E. Vidale, X. Xu, D. T. Trugman, and Y. Fialko (2022). Tidal modulation of seismicity at the Coso geothermal field, *Earth Planet. Sci. Lett.* **579,** 117,335.
Wang, X., J. Li, A. Feng, and D. Sornette (2025). Estimating magnitude completeness in earthquake catalogs: A comparative study of catalog-based methods, *J. Geophys. Res.* **130,** e2025JB031441, doi: 10.1029/2025JB031441.
Wiemer, S., S. R. Mcnutt, and M. Wyss (1998). Temporal and three-dimensional spatial analyses of the frequency–magnitude distribution near Long Valley Caldera, California, *Geophys. J. Int.* **134,** 409–421.
Woessner, J., and S. Wiemer (2005). Assessing the quality of earthquake catalogues: Estimating the magnitude of completeness and its uncertainty, *Bull. Seismol. Soc. Am.* **95,** 684–698.
Yin, F., and C. Jiang (2024). Enhanced b-value time-series calculation method using data-driven approach, *Geophys. J. Int.* **236,** 78–87.
Yoder, M. R., J. R. Holliday, D. L. Turcotte, and J. B. Rundle (2012). A geometric frequency–magnitude scaling transition: Measuring b = 1.5 for large earthquakes, *Tectonophysics* **532,** 167–174.
Yoshida, K., M. Uno, T. Matsuzawa, Y. Yukutake, Y. Mukuhira, H. Sato, and T. Yoshida (2023). Upward earthquake swarm migration in the northeastern Noto Peninsula, Japan, initiated from a deep ring-shaped cluster: Possibility of fluid leakage from a hidden magma system, *J. Geophys. Res.* **128,** e2022JB026047, doi: 10.1029/2022JB026047.
Zaliapin, I., and C. Kreemer (2017). Systematic fluctuations in the global seismic moment release, *Geophys. Res. Lett.* **44,** 4820–4828.
Zhai, Q., Z. Peng, L. Y. Chuang, Y. M. Wu, Y. J. Hsu, and S. Wdowinski (2021). Investigating the impacts of a wet typhoon on microseismicity: A case study of the 2009 typhoon Morakot in Taiwan based on a template matching catalog, *J. Geophys. Res.* **126,** e2021JB023026, doi: 10.1029/2021JB023026.
Zhou, Y., S. Zhou, and J. Zhuang (2018). A test on methods for MC estimation based on earthquake catalog, *Earth Planet. Phys.* **2,** 150–162.
Zhuang, J., Y. Ogata, and T. Wang (2017). Data completeness of the Kumamoto earthquake sequence in the JMA catalog and its influence on the estimation of the ETAS parameters, *Earth Planets Space* **69,** 1–12.
Zöller, G. (2013). Convergence of the frequency-magnitude distribution of global earthquakes: Maybe in 200 years, *Geophys. Res. Lett.* **40,** 3873–3877.

APPENDIX A

Distribution of the maximum magnitude

We recall that equations (1) and (2) define the survival function of the Gutenberg–Richter (GR) and tapered GR (TGR) distributions, that is, the complement of the cumulative distribution function (CDF). The probability density function (PDF) of the magnitude is obtained from the derivative of the CDF with respect to magnitude. The PDF of the maximum magnitude $m_{\max}$ is derived by considering that all the magnitudes in the catalog are smaller than $m_{\max}$ (van der Elst *et al.*, 2016), leading to

$$f_{m_{\max}}(m|N_{\text{total}}) = N_{\text{total}} f F^{N_{\text{total}}-1}, \qquad \text{(A1)}$$

in which $N_{\text{total}} = N(\geq 0) = 10^a$. F and f are the CDF and PDF of magnitudes derived from equation (1) or (2), respectively. This is equivalent to determining the interval formed by the intersection points of the confidence interval of the magnitude–frequency distribution (MFD) with $N(\geq 0) = 1$.

As discussed subsequently, a series of analytical expressions for the GR distribution can be obtained, and this will be our main focus. However, analytical solutions generally do not exist for the TGR distribution, not even for the most probable maximum magnitude. For comparison, we will provide the empirical results for the TGR distribution, obtained by generating a large number of random catalogs.

Equation (A1) implies that the most probable maximum magnitude for a given GR catalog of size N_{total} is $\hat{m}_{\max} = a/b$

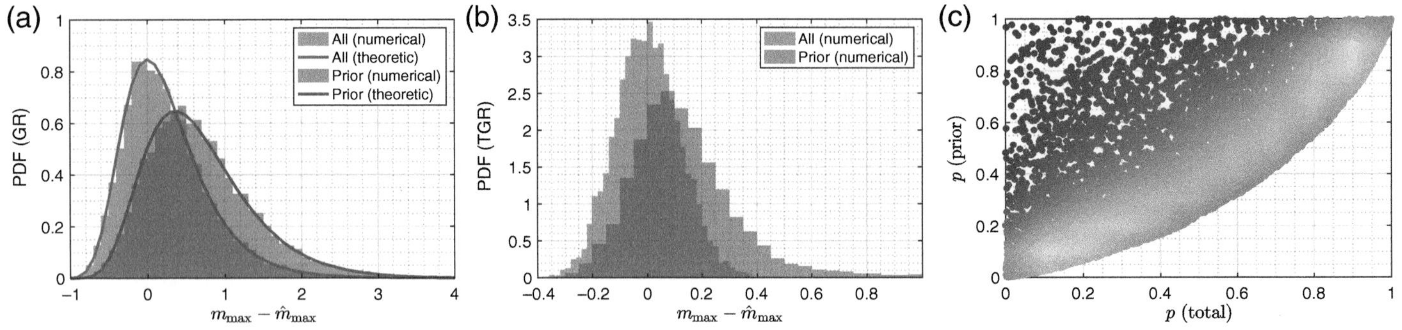

Figure A1. Distribution of maximum magnitudes. (a,b) Probability density functions (PDFs) of the maximum magnitudes for catalogs drawn from (a) GR (with a b value of 1 and a catalogs size of 1000) and (b) TGR (with a b value of 1, a catalogs size of 1000, and an m_{corner} of 2 distributions. Purple and brown show the results considering the total number of events and the number of events before the largest event, respectively. Empirical results from random synthetic catalogs (histograms) are displayed for both GR and TGR distributions, whereas theoretical solutions (the purple curve from equation A1 and the brown curve from equation A3 are only displayed for the GR distribution. (c) A comparison of p values (cumulative density function values) for the same GR catalog, derived from two strategies (considering the total number of earthquakes and considering only the number of earthquakes before the largest one). Each point represents the result from a random catalog, with colors indicating the density of points (yellow denotes higher density). The color version of this figure is available only in the electronic edition.

(van der Elst *et al.*, 2016). The theoretical distribution of equation (A1), as well as the validation via a numerical test, is shown in purple in Figure A1a. A notable point is that the median of the maximum magnitude is greater than $\hat{m}_{max}$. This means that contrary to common intuition, undersampling will lead to larger maximum earthquakes than predicted. In this study, we reject the GR distribution if $F_{m_{max}}(m|N_{total}) < 0.05$. On the other hand, the distribution of m_{max} for the TGR distribution shows a much less significant tail (i.e., it is more symmetric), and its range is also smaller (purple in Fig. 1b).

In addition to equation (A1), van der Elst *et al.* (2016) derived the equations describing the distribution of the maximum magnitude considering only the number of events prior to the largest event (N_{prior}). This consideration was introduced to deal with induced seismicity sequences for which operations were halted at the occurrence time of a large event. Considering that N_{prior} is a uniform random variable from $[1, N_{total}]$, the bias-corrected estimate of the most likely maximum magnitude is (van der Elst *et al.*, 2016)

$$\widehat{m'}_{max} = \frac{1}{b}\log_{10} N_{prior} + \langle \Delta m_{max} \rangle, \quad \text{(A2)}$$

in which $\langle \Delta m_{max} \rangle = \frac{1}{b}[\log_{10} N_{total} - \frac{1}{N_{total}} \sum_{N=1}^{N_{total}} \log_{10} N]$ is the mode value of Δm_{max}, for which distribution follows (van der Elst *et al.*, 2016):

$$f_{\Delta m_{max}}(\Delta m|N_{total}) = b \ln 10 \times 10^{-b\Delta m} \sum_{N=10^{-b\Delta m}}^{N_{total}} \frac{1}{N}\left[1 - \frac{1}{N}10^{-b\Delta m}\right]^{N_{total}-1}. \quad \text{(A3)}$$

In the limit of large N_{total} (>25), the bias-corrected term $\langle \Delta m_{max} \rangle = \log_{10} e \approx 0.4$ (van der Elst *et al.*, 2016). The distribution of the difference between the observed maximum magnitude and the predicted maximum magnitude, considering only the events before the maximum magnitude, is shown in brown in Figure A1a. The distribution with similar consideration for the TGR catalog is shown in brown in Figure A1b.

We now compare the performance of testing whether a catalog belongs to a (stationary) GR distribution using these two considerations: (1) considering the entire catalog size (N_{total}) or (2) considering only the number of earthquakes that occurred before the largest event (N_{prior}). We compare the obtained p values using these two strategies for the same stationary GR catalog. The p value represents the probability that, under the assumption of a GR distribution, the observed maximum magnitude or a smaller value could occur. The p value approaches 0 when the observed maximum magnitude is significantly lower than expected under the GR distribution. Thus, a low p value provides a high likelihood of rejecting the GR distribution. The results are shown in Figure A1c. The two p values are strongly correlated but are not equivalent. When p (total) is large, p (prior) will not be small. Intuitively, this is because a large p (total) indicates that even when considering the total number of earthquakes, the actual maximum magnitude is large compared to the expected maximum magnitude. Then, if only the number of events before the largest earthquake is considered, the expected magnitude should be even smaller (even with the ~0.4 correction term added), and the p (prior) should be large. Using the total number of earthquakes yields a tighter distribution of the maximum magnitudes (N_{total}, Fig. A1a), meaning that it is easier to test the MFD model. If there is clear evidence that the catalog remains stationary until the maximum magnitude occurs, and stationarity is then disrupted due to operations being halted, the distribution based on N_{prior} might be more appropriate for testing whether the induced stationary earthquakes follow a GR distribution. However, this distribution is

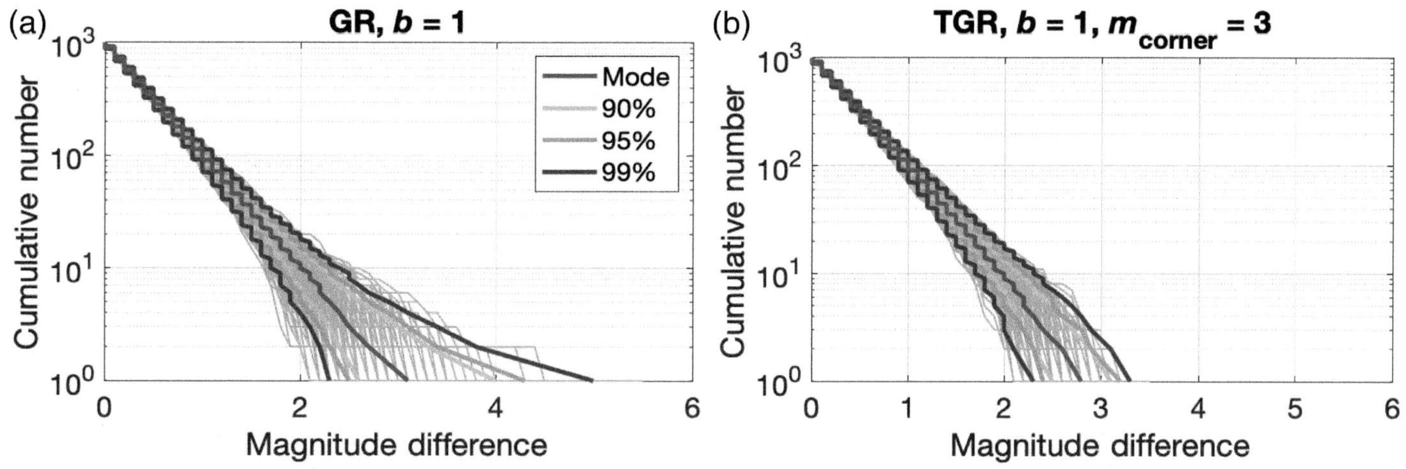

Figure B1. Confidence intervals of positive MFDs, for (a) GR distribution and (b) TGR distribution. The catalog size is ~2000 to get 1000 positive magnitude differences; all other parameters are as in Figure 4. Gray curves show 1000 random catalogs for reference. Confidence intervals are derived from 100,000 synthetic catalogs. The color version of this figure is available only in the electronic edition.

broader (Fig. A1a), making the test less discriminative. Later in this study, we will refer to the maximum magnitude criterion as the first strategy—that is, considering the total number of events—because we aim to characterize the overall properties of the given catalog. Any nonstationarity will be addressed using the methods described in the Analyzing temporal variations of MFD section.

APPENDIX B

Distribution of positive magnitude differences

We present the empirical distribution of positive magnitude differences and their confidence intervals in Figure B1, and show the fitting of equation (2) to the distribution of positive magnitude differences under the TGR model in Figure B2.

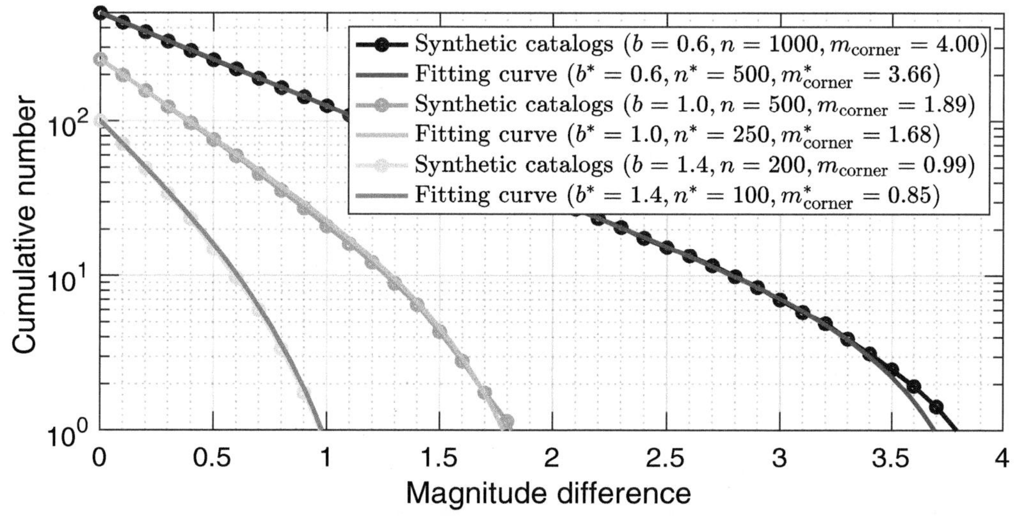

Figure B2. Distribution of positive magnitude differences of randomly generated TGR catalogs (dark blue, cyan, and yellow, with the legend indicating the model parameters) and the fitting curve assuming the distribution can be described by equation (2) (light blue, green, and orange, with the legend indicating the best-fitting parameters). For each case, we present the superposition of 1000 random catalogs and the fitting curves corresponding to the average parameter estimates derived from these 1000 catalogs. The color version of this figure is available only in the electronic edition.

APPENDIX C

Feasibility of parameter estimation for nonstationary catalogs

We begin by providing an analytical analysis of mixture GR distributions to develop intuition regarding this issue.

Consider a catalog with samples generated from two different b values: we assume there are n_1 samples with b_1, and n_2 samples with b_2 (both have an $m_C = 0$). Let $n_1 + n_2 = n$ and $n_2 = \beta n_1$, so that $n_1 = \frac{1}{1+\beta} n = \gamma n (0 \le \gamma \le 1)$. Then, the survival function of the composite distribution can be expressed as follows:

$$P(\geq m) = \gamma 10^{-b_1 m} + (1-\gamma) 10^{-b_2 m}. \quad (C1)$$

The illustration of this equation is shown in Figure C1a (with $b_1 = 0.6$, $b_2 = 1.4$, and varying γ). When γ is not very close to 0 or 1, the mixed catalog significantly deviates from a GR distribution (with any single b value), displaying an upward bending. In most observational catalogs, this upward trend is not obvious, suggesting that most-observed seismic catalogs

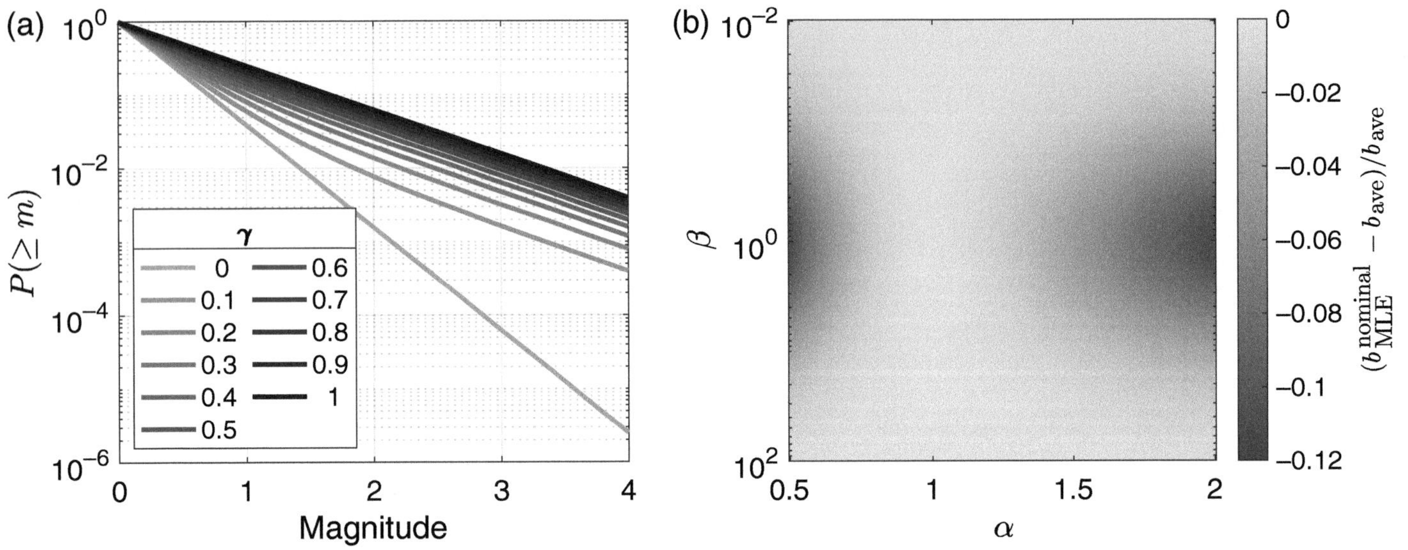

Figure C1. Distribution of a mixed catalog containing two distinct b values. (a) Survival function for a catalog composed of earthquakes with b values of 0.6 and 1.4. The parameter γ represents the proportion of events with $-a$ value of 0.6. (b) Difference between the estimated b value using MLE and the naïve average b value of the catalog. The parameters α and β denote the b value ratio and the catalog size ratio, respectively, between the two subgroups with distinct b values. The color version of this figure is available only in the electronic edition.

are dominated by one particular b value. In other words, if any samples deviate from the dominant b value, they likely constitute only a small proportion of the catalog.

We now consider the results obtained when using the maximum-likelihood estimation (MLE) method (equation 5) to estimate the nominal b value of the mixed catalog described earlier. The MLE estimation relies only on the mean magnitudes, given by $\bar{m} = \frac{n_1\overline{m_1}+n_2\overline{m_2}}{n_1+n_2}$, in which $\overline{m_i} = \frac{1}{\log 10 b_i}$ $(i = 1,2)$. This leads to the estimation $b_{\mathrm{MLE}}^{\mathrm{nominal}} = \frac{b_1 b_2(n_1+n_2)}{n_1 b_2+n_2 b_1}$. We compare this with a naïve weighted average b value $b_{\mathrm{ave}} = \frac{n_1 b_1+n_2 b_2}{n_1+n_2}$, and obtain the following relative difference:

$$\frac{b_{\mathrm{MLE}}^{\mathrm{nominal}} - b_{\mathrm{ave}}}{b_{\mathrm{ave}}} = -\frac{n_1 n_2 (b_1-b_2)^2}{(n_1 b_2 + n_2 b_1)(n_1+n_2)} = -\frac{\beta(1-\alpha)^2}{(\alpha+\beta)(1+\alpha\beta)}, \tag{C2}$$

in which we further assume $b_2 = \alpha b_1$. We note that $b_{\mathrm{MLE}}^{\mathrm{nominal}}$ is always smaller than b_{ave}. Figure C1b shows this difference for various α and β values. The deviation is significant when b_1 and b_2 differ substantially and when n_1 is comparable to n_2. The deviation can reach 10%, indicating that this issue may not always be negligible when these conditions are met.

Subsequently, we conduct additional synthetic tests to further explore this issue and examine the case for TGR catalogs.

For catalogs following the GR distribution, we consider two scenarios (Fig. C2): in the first scenario, the b value gradually increases, with the b value of the ith event being expressed by $b(i) = 1 + \alpha\frac{2i-n-1}{2(n-1)}$, in which n is the catalog size, α describes the magnitude of the b value variations; in the second scenario, the change in b value is step-like, represented as $b(i) = \begin{cases} 1-\frac{\alpha}{2}, i \leq \frac{n}{2} \\ 1+\frac{\alpha}{2}, i > \frac{n}{2} \end{cases}$. In both scenarios, the means of the catalogs' b values are set to 1. We generate 1000 random catalogs for each α value (ranging from 0.05 to 0.4) and catalog size n (ranging from 50 to 1000). We estimate the apparent b values of these catalogs using equation (5). The results are depicted in Figure C2c–f. For reference, we also estimate the b values for catalogs with a uniform b value of 1 for different catalog sizes (Fig. C3). We find that all estimated b values are close to the mean. Interestingly, we do not observe a significant correlation between the bias and the catalog size. We note that the overestimation observed for small catalog sizes is also observed in a uniform catalog, which is related to the inherent bias of equation (5), in which a corrected coefficient $(n-1)$ / n should be added (Ogata and Yamashina, 1986, Marzocchi *et al.*, 2020). The maximum bias occurs when $\alpha = 0.4$ and earthquakes are sampled from two discontinuous b values. However, even this bias can be considered negligible within the commonly accepted accuracy of b value estimation. We acknowledge that a 0.4 change in b values is already substantial; thus, we expect that for practical applications, we can directly use equation (5) to obtain the average b value of the catalog.

Next, we discuss the case of the TGR distribution. Although studies of possible variations in b values are common, studies considering possible time-varying TGR parameters are less common. Therefore, we lack understanding of how the TGR distributions might evolve in reality, if at all. For convenience, we assume that b values remain constant, with only m_{corner} varying. We consider three scenarios (Fig. C4): (1) m_{corner} is always smaller than the maximum magnitude predicted from the GR distirbution for the current earthquake catalog size by a specific value, with the ith earthquake follows $m_{\mathrm{corner}}(i) = \frac{\log_{10} i}{b} - \beta$; (2)

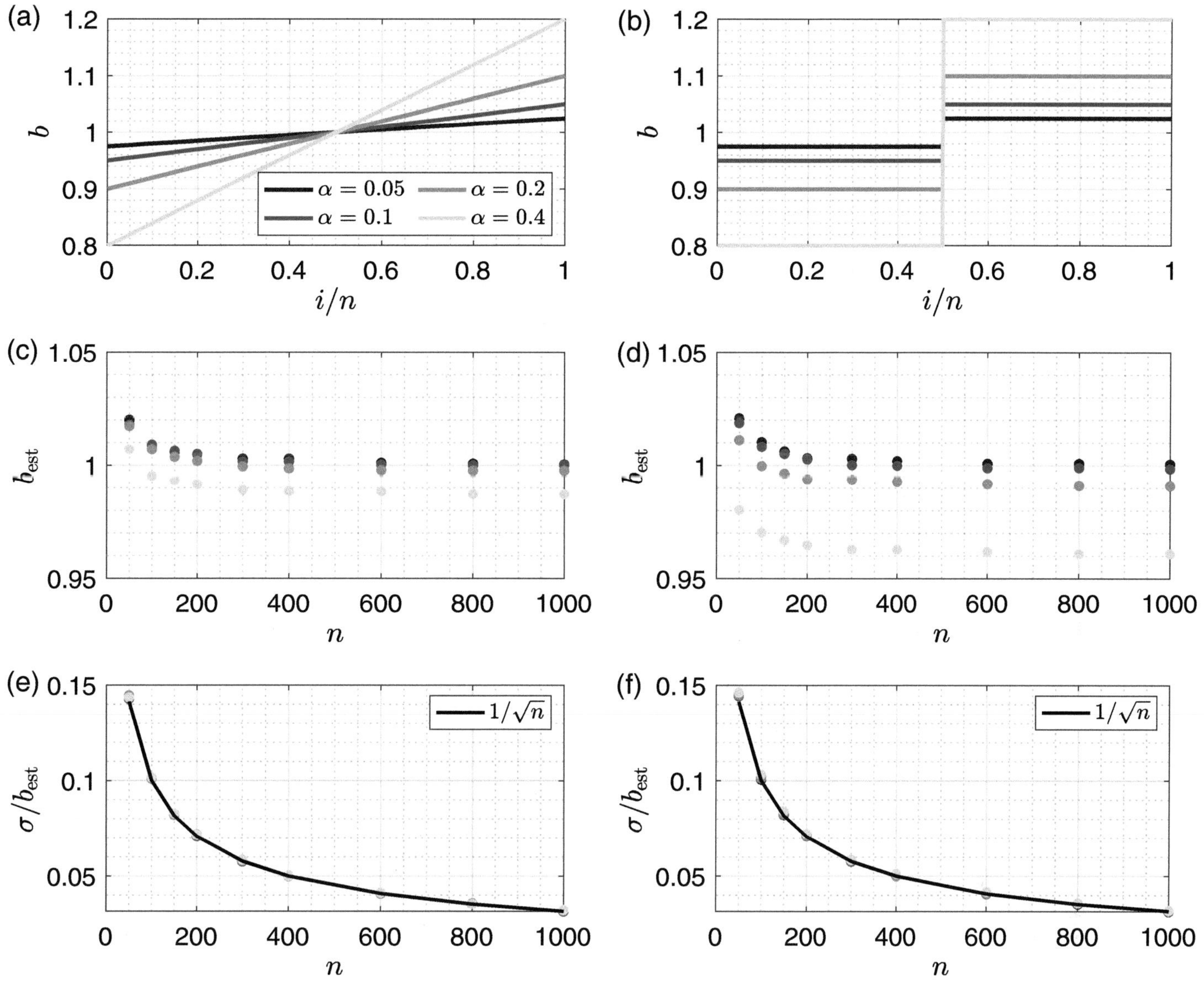

Figure C2. Influence of changes in b values within GR catalogs on the estimation of the overall b value. (a) Evolution of b value, in which i denotes the earthquake index and n represents the total number of earthquakes (catalog size). (c) The estimated overall b value of the catalog for the scenario in panel (a). (e) The standard deviation of the estimated overall b value of the catalog for the scenario in panel (a). Panels (b,d,f) are equivalent to (a,c,e), respectively, but correspond to catalogs sampled from distinct b values. The color version of this figure is available only in the electronic edition.

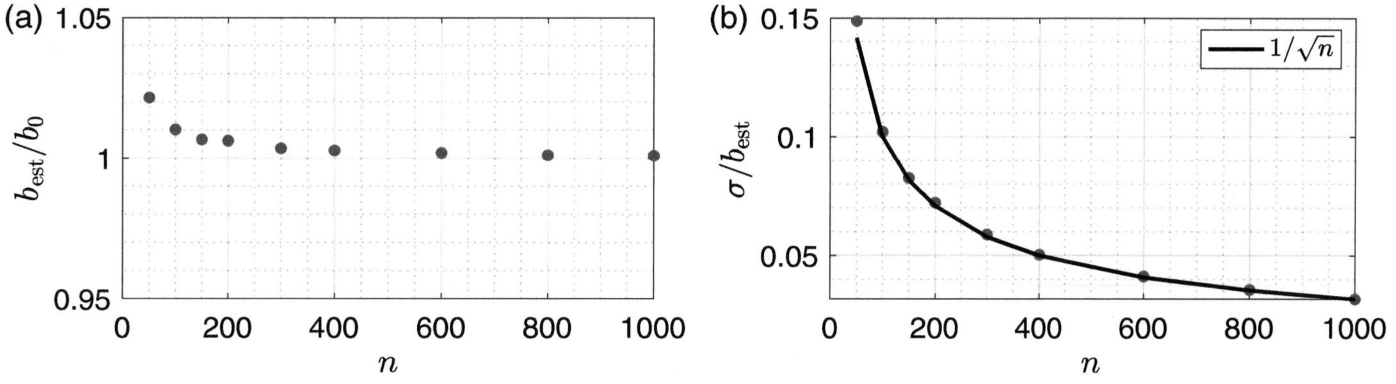

Figure C3. Estimated b values for catalogs generated from GR distribution, with a b value of 1, which is equal to the mean values of those catalogs in Figure C2. (a) The estimated b value and (b) the standard deviation. The color version of this figure is available only in the electronic edition.

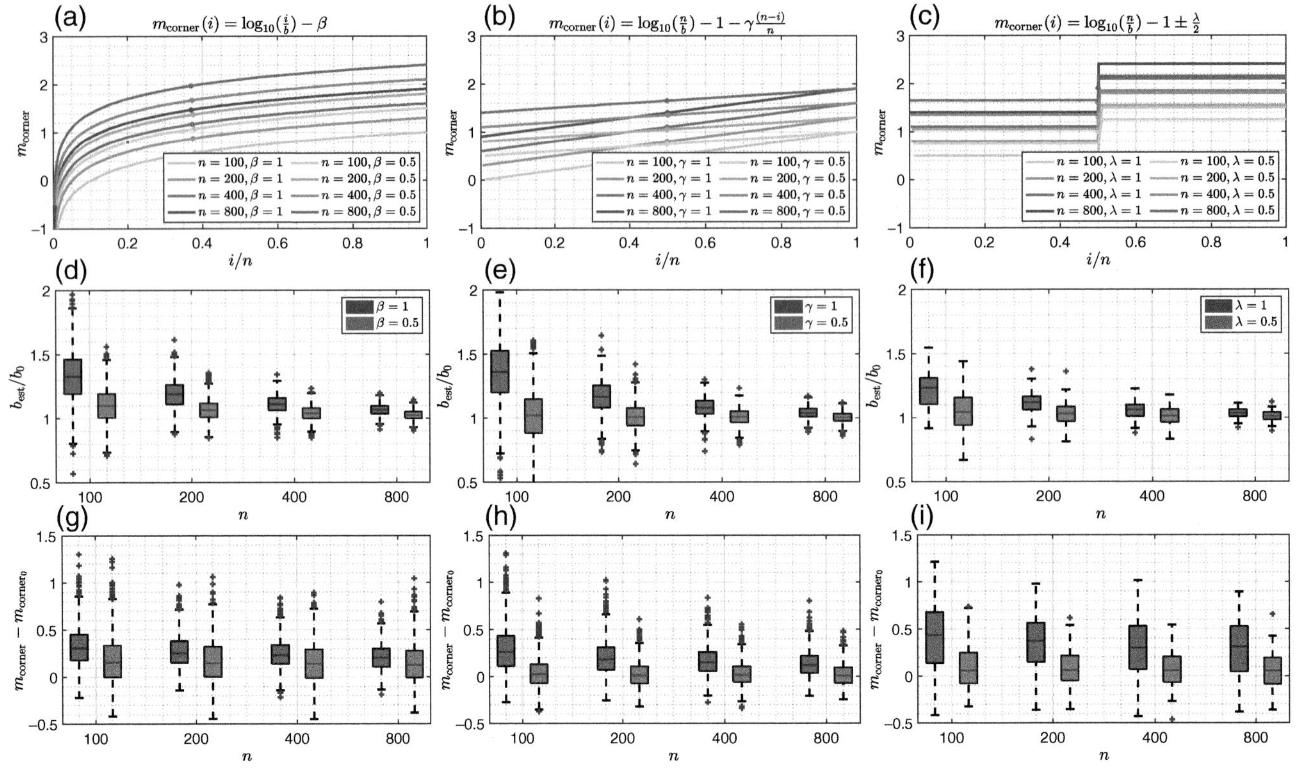

Figure C4. Influence of changes in m_{corner} within the catalog on the overall TGR parameter estimation (b value and m_{corner}). (a) The set evolution of m_{corner}, in which i denotes the earthquake index and n represents the total number of earthquakes (catalog size). The dots represent the mean m_{corner} value. (d,g) The estimated overall b values and m_{corner} of the catalogs with scenario in panel (a). The line within the box represents the median, with the distance between the first quartile (lower edge of the box) and third quartile (upper edge of the box) defining the interquartile range. Whiskers extend to the most extreme data points within 1.5 times the interquartile range from the quartiles, whereas individual points beyond the whiskers are considered outliers. Panels (b,e,h) and (c,f,i) are similar to (a,d,g), but correspond to different changes in m_{corner} within the catalog. The color version of this figure is available only in the electronic edition.

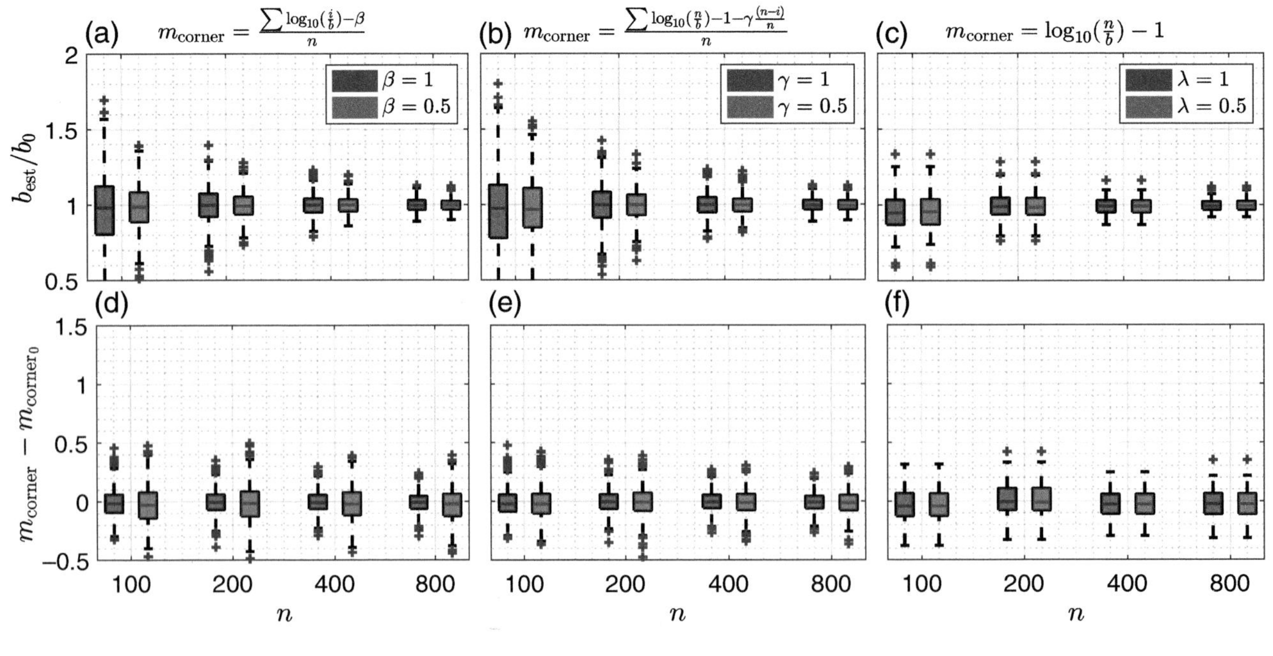

Figure C5. Estimated b values and m_{corner} for catalogs generated from TGR distribution, with a b value of 1, and m_{corner} values equal to the mean values of those catalogs in Figure C4. (a–c) The estimated b value and (d–f) the estimated corner magnitude. The color version of this figure is available only in the electronic edition.

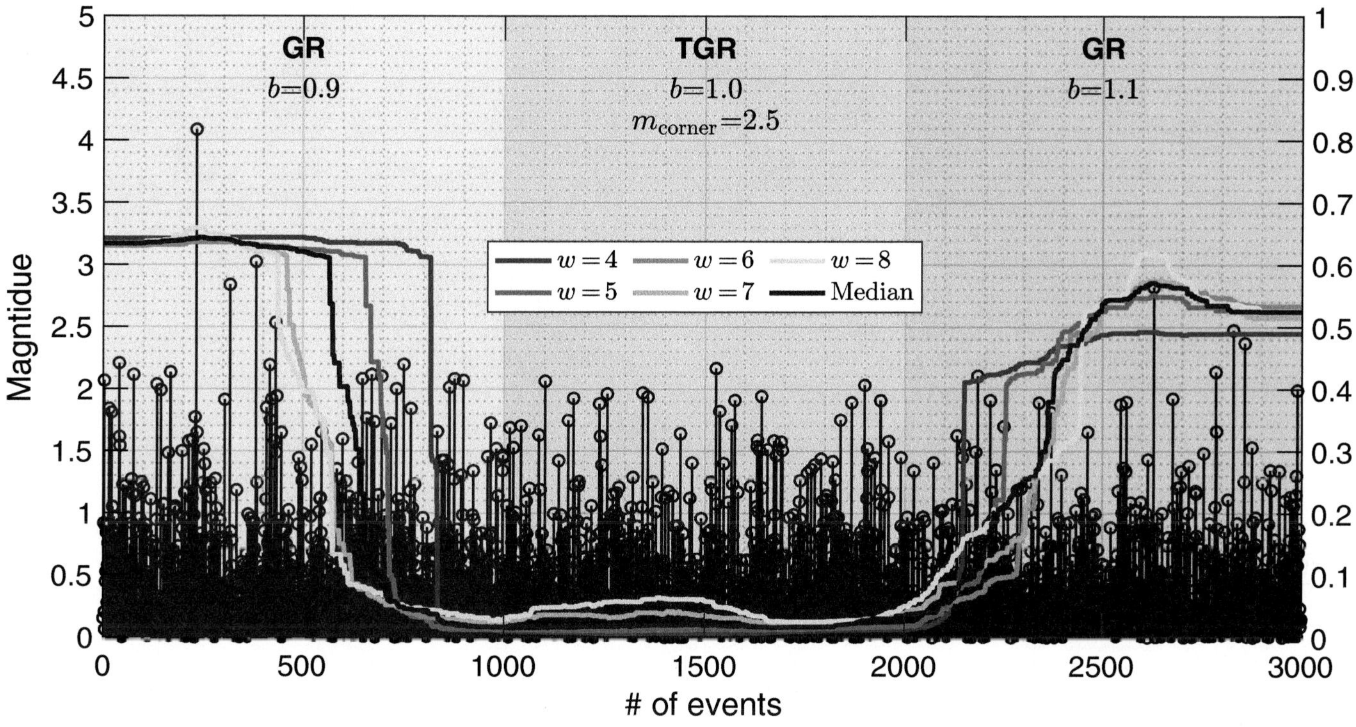

Figure D1. Temporal evolution of the p value obtained by the LR test under different number of nonoverlapping windows (w) for a random catalog. For $w = 7,8$, we observe some oscillations between the 1000th and 1500th events, which likely represent random noise at small timescales. Such noise is almost inevitable. Therefore, we recommend focusing only on the first-order characteristics. This is why, in the Analyzing temporal variations of MFD section, we suggest evaluating the results for at most five different w. The color version of this figure is available only in the electronic edition.

m_{corner} gradually increases as $m_{corner}(i) = \frac{\log_{10} n}{b} - 1 - \gamma \frac{n-i}{n}$; and (3) the change in m_{corner} is step-like, represented as $m_{corner}(i) = \begin{cases} \frac{\log_{10} n}{b} - 1 - \frac{\lambda}{2}, i \le \frac{n}{2} \\ \frac{\log_{10} n}{b} - 1 + \frac{\lambda}{2}, i > \frac{n}{2} \end{cases}$. We set all catalogs to have $b = 1$. For each configuration (varying parameters β,γ, λ, and catalog sizes), we generate 1000 random catalogs and employing equation (7) to estimate the b value and m_{corner} of each catalog. We also estimate the parameters for catalogs with uniformly distributed m_{corner}, equal to the mean depicted in each case, as shown in Figure C5. For these catalogs with nonuniform m_{corner}, we observe a systematic overestimation in both b values and m_{corner}. The greater the change in m_{corner} within the catalog and the smaller the catalog size, the more pronounced the estimation deviation. If the change in m_{corner} is not significant, the estimated deviation may be negligible. Considering that we set a constant b value, the deviation of the estimated b value indicates the interdependence between the b value and the m_{corner} estimate.

APPENDIX D

Temporal evolution of MFDs

In Figure D1, we show a case example of the analyzed temporal evolution of p-value for a synthetic catalog. In Figures D2 and D3, we present the retrieval of temporal evolution of GR and TGR parameters.

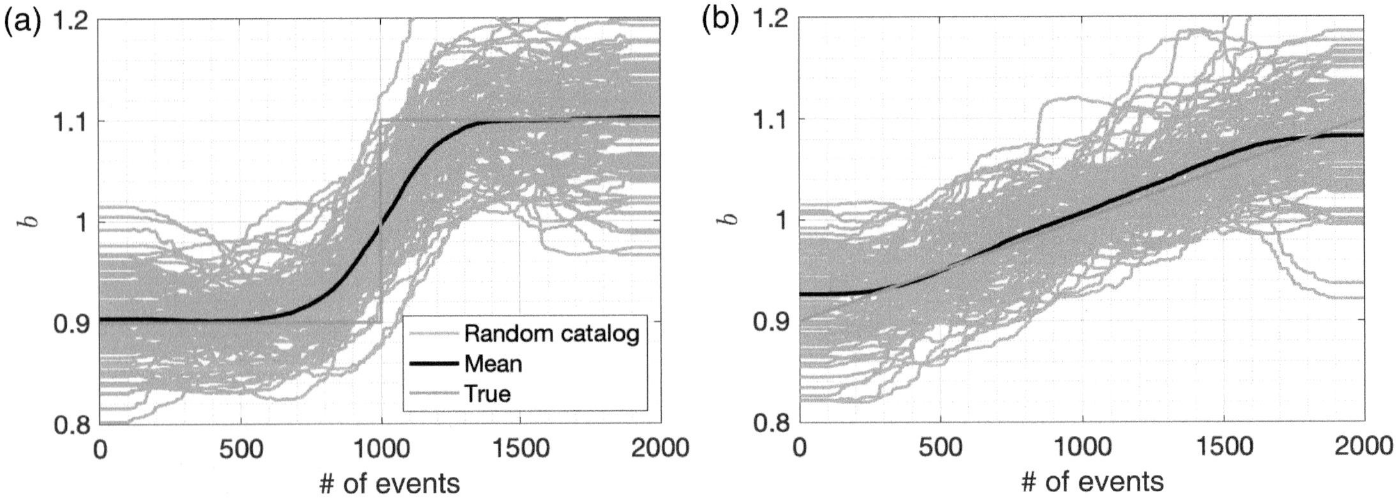

Figure D2. Validation of model parameters estimation for a temporally varying GR model. The true models are represented by orange curves assuming (a) a step change or (b) a gradual linear increase of *b* value. The color version of this figure is available only in the electronic edition.

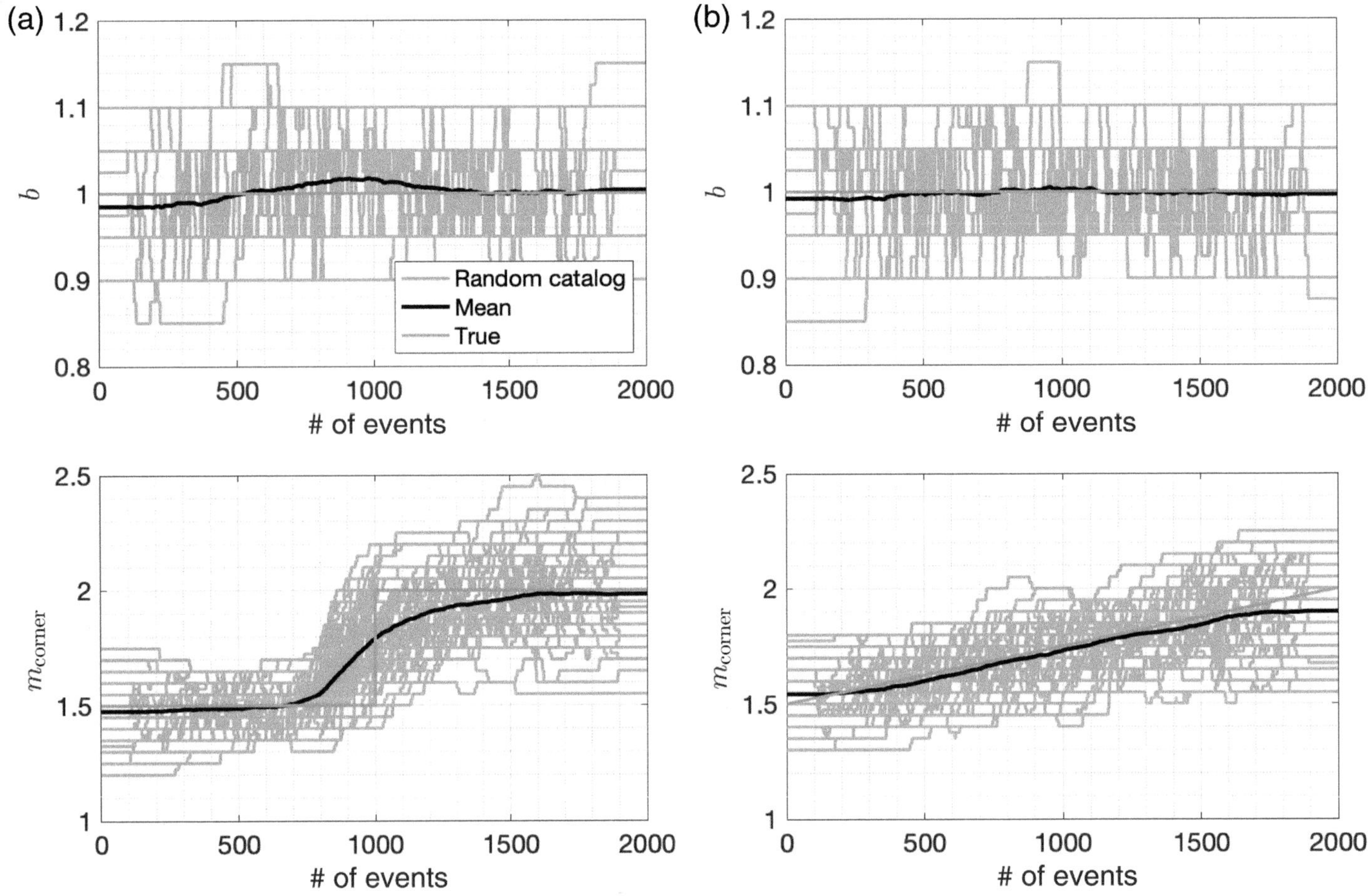

Figure D3. Validation of model parameters estimation for a temporally varying TGR model. The true models are represented by orange curves assuming (a) a step change or (b) a gradual linear increase of m_{corner}. We only change m_{corner}, but both *b* value and m_{corner} are estimated. The color version of this figure is available only in the electronic edition.

Manuscript received 27 May 2025
Published online 17 October 2025

Near-Fault Amplification and Ground-Motion Variability During the 2019 Ridgecrest, California, Sequence

Elizabeth S. Cochran*[1], Grace A. Parker[2], Sarah E. Minson[2], and Annemarie S. Baltay[2]

ABSTRACT

We estimate ground-motion variability near the 2019 M 7.1 Ridgecrest earthquake sequence. Accurate seismic hazard estimation requires understanding ground-motion spatial correlations, yet many studies lack the dense station coverage needed to resolve small-scale variability. The 2019 M 7.1 Ridgecrest earthquake sequence presents a unique opportunity to examine ground motions and their spatial correlations at a range of interstation distances. The permanent seismic network was augmented with hundreds of temporary stations including several fault-crossing nodal arrays. We compute the event (δE_i) and within-event (δW_{ij}) residuals from the observed peak ground velocity and peak ground acceleration data to isolate potential sources of ground-motion variability. We then compare δW_{ij} between station pairs that record an event to understand the semivariance of the ground motion versus interstation distance. By fitting an exponential model to the semivariances, we determine a correlation range of 25 km for the Ridgecrest region. Although the exponential model fits the broad-scale increase of semivariance with interstation distance, we also observe smaller-scale trends. We find that ground motions are less correlated for station pairs that are near or across faults that ruptured during the 2019 Ridgecrest sequence. We also find large, positive median δW_{ij} with relative values 2–3 times larger than nearby stations for individual stations' near-fault traces. Near-fault amplification and greater ground-motion variability can delineate fault zones and may locally increase the seismic hazard.

OPEN ACCESS

KEY POINTS

- Dense seismic data are used to study ground-motion variability near the 2019 Ridgecrest sequence.
- We find a correlation range of 25 km, with significant small-scale variability near-fault surface traces.
- Amplification and greater ground-motion variability close to fault traces may highlight fault zones.

Supplemental Material

INTRODUCTION

Earthquake hazard and loss modeling rely on ground-motion models (GMMs) to predict, for a given site, the median expected ground motions and their variability. Ergodic GMMs, which average over many events and sites provide generalized ground-motion predictions for a region (e.g., Bozorgnia *et al.*, 2014; Douglas *et al.*, 2014). They are often used due to limited recordings across the full range of potential source properties and site conditions. GMMs predict median shaking from an earthquake using parameters such as magnitude, source–station distance, path attenuation, and site effects. However, ground motions are known to be highly variable, even over short distances, and that variability is generally not captured by GMMs. For example, McCann and Boore (1983) found variability up to a factor of 1.3 over distances of less than 0.5 km. Similarly, Karabulut and Bouchon (2007) reported peak accelerations ranging from 0.3g to 1.0g at stations separated by just 1.5 km during the 1999 Düzce earthquake. The standard deviation of the residuals between the observed ground motions and GMM predictions, reported to be 0.2–0.4 log (base 10) units (e.g., Atkinson and Boore, 2003;

1. U.S. Geological Survey, Earthquake Science Center, Pasadena, California, U.S.A., https://orcid.org/0000-0003-2485-4484 (ESC); 2. U.S. Geological Survey, Earthquake Science Center, Moffett Field, California, U.S.A., https://orcid.org/0000-0002-9445-2571 (GAP); https://orcid.org/0000-0001-5869-3477 (SEM); https://orcid.org/0000-0002-6514-852X (ASB)

*Corresponding author: ecochran@usgs.gov

Cite this article as Cochran, E. S., G. A. Parker, S. E. Minson, and A. S. Baltay (2025). Near-Fault Amplification and Ground-Motion Variability During the 2019 Ridgecrest, California, Sequence, *Bull. Seismol. Soc. Am.* **116**, 467–481, doi: 10.1785/0120250160

Strasser *et al.*, 2009; Atkinson, 2015), can introduce large uncertainties in hazard and loss estimates (Bommer and Crowley, 2006). Although residuals are difficult to attribute to specific physical processes (Strasser *et al.*, 2008), studies have reported correlations with various properties including magnitude (Abrahamson, 1988), stress drop (Baltay *et al.*, 2017), source directivity (Iwaki *et al.*, 2017; Parker *et al.*, 2025), source-to-site path or azimuth (Sokolov *et al.*, 2012; Sung and Lee, 2016; Baltay *et al.*, 2017; Iwaki *et al.*, 2017), and site effects (Chen *et al.*, 2021).

Estimating the hazard for spatially distributed systems—such as pipelines, transportation networks, or urban infrastructure—requires understanding how ground motions are spatially correlated (Wesson and Perkins, 2001). Ground motions at sites near to each other tend to be more similar than the ground motions at widely separated sites, even after accounting for attenuation and site effects (e.g., Boore *et al.*, 2003; Goda and Hong, 2008; Bodenmann *et al.*, 2023). Several studies have quantified this variability. Niazi (1985) observed up to a 40% variation in peak ground accelerations (PGAs) within a seismic array spanning just 214 m. Kawakami and Mogi (2003) analyzed arrays in Japan and Taiwan with interstation distances from 5 to 100 km, showing that stations separated by ≤40 m had PGA differences of ≤40% for 95% of cases, whereas differences increased to 400% for stations ≥70 km apart. Boore *et al.* (2003) analyzed PGAs recorded during the 1994 **M** 6.7 Northridge earthquake and proposed a model for the decay of spatial correlation with distance.

These studies used varying approaches, but consistent methods are needed to compare spatial correlations across regions (Jayaram and Baker, 2009). Spatial correlations are typically assessed by comparing residuals between observed ground motions and GMM predictions (Baker and Jayaram, 2008; Jayaram and Baker, 2009; Baker and Chen, 2020). Residuals are split into between- and within-event terms; between-event (δE_i) residuals describe overall differences in the ground motions between earthquakes, whereas within-event residuals (δW_{ij}) capture site-to-site variation for a single event, typically after accounting for site conditions (Boore *et al.*, 2014). Because GMMs provide variances but not correlations in ground motions (Jayaram and Baker, 2009), the difference in δW_{ij} between station pairs for a given earthquake are used to estimate spatial correlation as a function of interstation distance. Assuming isotropy and stationarity, δW_{ij} values from multiple events and pairs can be combined to model the spatial correlation for a region (Baker and Jayaram, 2008).

However, many data sets lack observations at closely spaced station pairs, limiting our ability to quantify fine-scale variability. The well-recorded 2019 Ridgecrest, California, earthquake sequence offers a unique opportunity to study spatial correlations from 100 m to 100 km for magnitude (**M**) 3.3–5.0 earthquakes. Hundreds of temporary stations (Catchings *et al.*, 2020; Cochran *et al.*, 2020), deployed after the **M** 7.1 mainshock, supplemented the permanent network (Hauksson *et al.*, 2020). Existing GMMs match the median observations well for this sequence (McNamara *et al.*, 2020; Parker *et al.*, 2020), allowing us to accurately isolate δW_{ij}. In this study, we use a large set of δW_{ij} to quantify spatial correlations assuming isotropy and stationarity. We then assess deviations from these assumptions by analyzing subsets of the data to understand additional factors that may influence ground-motion variability.

2019 RIDGECREST GROUND-MOTION DATA

The 2019 Ridgecrest, California, aftershock sequence was recorded by permanent seismic network stations (Hauksson *et al.*, 2020), as well as temporary seismic instruments that were installed after the **M** 7.1 mainshock (Catchings *et al.*, 2020; Cochran *et al.*, 2020) (Fig. 1). The permanent seismic network stations included both velocity and accelerometer instrumentation from the BK (University of California, Berkeley, 1980), CE (California Geological Survey, 1972), CI (California Institute of Technology and U. S. Geological Survey [USGS] Pasadena, 1926), NP (USGS, 1931), and SN (University of Nevada, Reno, 1992) networks, providing a backbone of networks spaced ~10–30 km apart.

Several types of temporary arrays were installed, including more traditional rapid aftershock deployment kits with velocity, and/or accelerometer sensors (network codes: ZY and GS) (Cochran *et al.*, 2020), as well as nodal arrays that use 4 Hz geophone sensors (network code 3J) (Catchings *et al.*, 2020). The nodal deployment included 585 individual recording sites that operated for ~30 days, with a maximum of 261 nodes operating at a single time. The nodes were installed on grids covering broad regions near the Ridgecrest and Garlock faults at nominal station spacing of 5–10 km (Catchings *et al.*, 2020). In addition, dense linear arrays were installed in several locations. Here, we focus on five arrays that include a dense fault-crossing array deployed across the **M** 6.4 foreshock fault from 6 July 2019 to 4 August 2019 (array A1) and four fault-crossing arrays installed across the **M** 7.1 mainshock fault from 12 July 2019 to 8 August 2019 (arrays B1-4). These fault-crossing nodal arrays had stations spaced at ~100 m (Catchings *et al.*, 2020). The fault-crossing nodal arrays are located in areas with limited topographic relief and overall similar site conditions, with the exception of disturbed ground near the surface traces.

We examine ground motions recorded by seismic stations within 1° of the **M** 7.1 mainshock that are publicly available for download from the International Federation of Digital Seismograph Networks (FDSN) webservices (International Federation of Digital Seismograph Networks, 2025). We combine data from Rekoske *et al.* (2020), which include ground motions recorded on permanent network stations and aftershock deployments, with nodal seismic data that we processed. We included records of earthquakes of **M** 3.3 and greater that

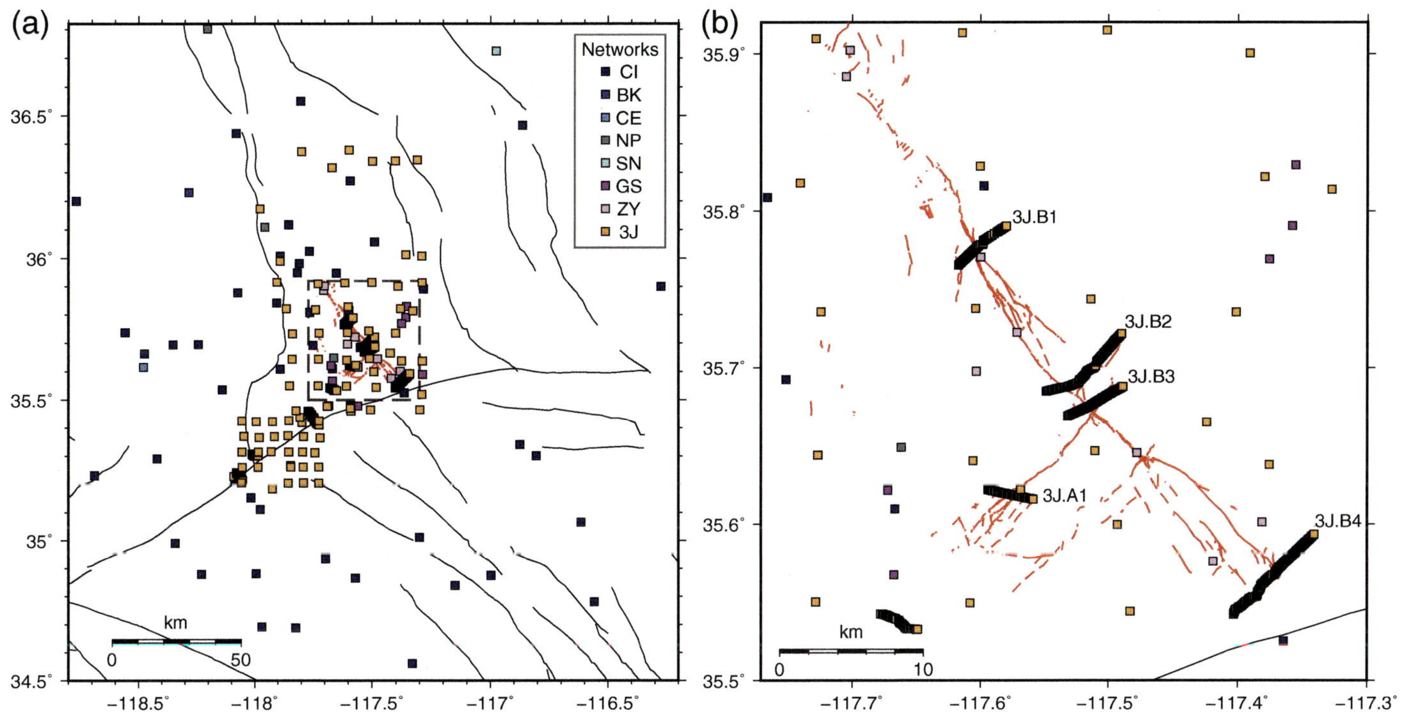

Figure 1. Map of permanent and temporary seismic stations colored by network code near the 2019 Ridgecrest earthquake sequence. Networks include permanent networks: BK, CE, CI, NP, and SN (University of California, Berkeley, 1980; California Institute of Technology and U.S. Geological Survey [USGS] Pasadena, 1926; California Geological Survey, 1972; USGS, 1931; University of Nevada, Reno, 1992) and temporary networks: GS, ZY, and 3J (Catchings *et al.*, 2020; Cochran *et al.*, 2020). (a) Map of the full study area and (b) larger-scale map near the **M** 6.4 and 7.1 rupture traces. Fault-crossing arrays from network 3J that are referred to in the main text are labeled. The black lines show mapped fault traces from USGS and California Geological Survey (2025), with the Ridgecrest surface rupture traces from Ponti *et al.* (2020) shown in red. The **M** 6.4 foreshock was a left-lateral strike-slip fault that primarily ruptured the west-southwest–east-northeast-striking faults, and the **M** 7.1 mainshock was a right-lateral strike-slip rupture that primarily occurred on the northwest–southeast-striking faults.

occurred between 7 July 2019 and 8 September 2019 to align with the duration of the nodal deployment; we only include events down to **M** 3.3 as the GMM used in the analysis was not developed for smaller events. In total, we selected data from 120 earthquakes with magnitudes ranging from **M** 3.3 to 5.0 (Fig. 2a).

To processes the time series and derive peak ground-motion estimates from the nodal records, we follow the approach of Rekoske *et al.* (2020) and Parker *et al.* (2020), although here we focus on records at shorter source-station distances. Nodal time-series processing included baseline removal, and high- and low-pass filtering (0.3–100 Hz). We require a signal-to-noise of at least three and a minimum sampling rate of 40 Hz. Station sample rates were typically >100 Hz. We use gmprocess (Thompson *et al.*, 20204a,b) to determine PGA and peak ground velocity (PGV) values. Nodal data had not previously been processed using the gmprocess software, so we modified the code to allow for removing instrument response from DP (nodal geophone) channels, and to differentiate the recorded velocity from those channels to accelerations for processing. Qualitative comparisons were made to ensure consistency with more traditional broadband and strong-motion sensor data for earthquakes that were recorded on both sensor types. In total, we had 16,416 ground-motion records from 120 earthquakes with magnitudes ranging from **M** 3.3 to 5.0 recorded by 646 unique stations within 1° of the Ridgecrest sequence.

The location and magnitude information for all earthquakes was downloaded from the Advanced National Seismic System Comprehensive Earthquake Catalog (ComCat) (U.S. Geological Survey, Earthquake Hazards Program, 2025). We used event origin information to compute the Joyner–Boore distance (R_{JB}), which is defined as the closest distance between a station and the surface projection of a fault rupture (Joyner and Boore, 1981). In the absence of a finite-fault solution in ComCat, R_{JB} is estimated using the magnitude-dependent model of Thompson and Worden (2018). The source-station pairs cover a range of R_{JB} and M (Fig. 2b), including multiple earthquakes recorded with R_{JB} shorter than 1 km. To define the site conditions, we used the measured time-averaged shear-wave velocity in the top 30 m (V_{S30}) from the Next Generation Attenuation-West2 Project (NGA-West2) database (Ancheta *et al.*, 2014), where available for a station. V_{S30} was otherwise estimated using proxy-based models (Thompson *et al.*, 2014; Wills *et al.*, 2015); values at each station were provided by Rekoske *et al.* (2020) or Thompson (2022).

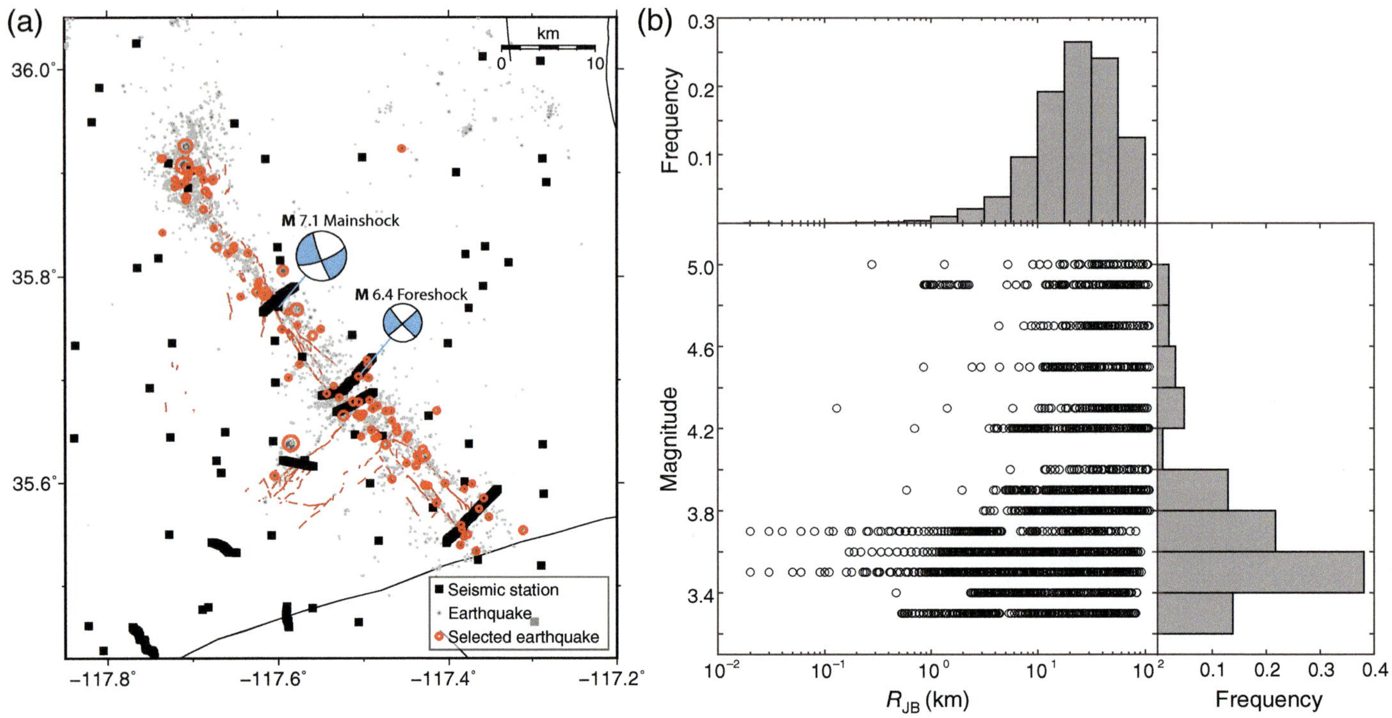

Figure 2. (a) Map of earthquakes during the 2019 Ridgecrest earthquake sequence (M > 2) that occurred between 7 July 2019 and 8 September 2019 (gray dots) (USGS, Earthquake Hazards Program, 2025); the earthquakes used in the analysis are outlined in red. Stations shown as black squares and faults are as in Figure 1. Also shown are the focal mechanisms of the **M** 6.4 foreshock and **M** 7.1 mainshock (USGS, Earthquake Hazards Program, 2025). (b) Distribution of R_{JB} versus magnitudes of the seismic records used in the analyses.

RESIDUAL ANALYSIS

Observed ground motions are the result of a complex combination of source, path, and site effects. GMMs are generally effective in predicting the median expected ground motions for a given magnitude, distance, and site condition (such as V_{S30}). However, observed ground motions often exhibit significant variability due to effects not fully captured by the models. As a result, observed ground motions can differ from model predictions by up to a factor of approximately two (Strasser *et al.*, 2009). In this study, we focus on measuring and understanding thc spatial variability of thc rcsiduals.

The total residual (R_T) of the ground motion of an earthquake i recorded at station j is defined as the difference between the observed ground motion (Y_{ij}) and the median ground motion predicted by the model (u_{ij}), such that

$$R_{T,ij} = \ln(Y_{ij}) - \ln(u_{ij}). \quad (1)$$

Here, we use the GMM of Boore *et al.* (2014) (hereafter referred to as BSSA14), which was shown to be generally consistent with the Ridgecrest aftershock ground motions (McNamara *et al.*, 2020; Parker *et al.*, 2020). R_T can be separated into between-event (δE_i) and within-event residuals (δW_{ij}) by fitting a linear mixed-effects model in which between-event residuals are estimated as random effects (Abrahamson and Youngs, 1992; Atik *et al.*, 2010; Bates *et al.*, 2015; Baltay *et al.*, 2017):

$$R_{T,ij} = \delta E_i + \delta W_{ij}. \quad (2)$$

δE_i is the event term, representing the unmodeled effects associated with the earthquake source (such as stress drop) that affect the ground motions of all stations that record an earthquake. δW_{ij} is the within-event residual, reflecting the unmodeled difference between the GMM prediction and the observed ground motion at a particular station for a given earthquake, including site response and path-to-path variations. δE_i and δW_{ij} are assumed to be independent and normally distributed with standard deviations τ and ϕ, respectively (e.g., Boore *et al.*, 2014). In BSSA14, τ depends only on M, whereas ϕ depends on M, R_{JB}, and V_{S30} (Boore *et al.*, 2014). Here, we wish to compare δW_{ij} across the set of recorded events, so we standardize or normalize δW_{ij} by dividing by ϕ, ensuring a known sample standard deviation (Baker and Chen, 2020). For the remainder of this work, we use normalized δW_{ij} values.

SPATIAL VARIABILITY ANALYSIS

To describe how ground motions vary in space, we compare δW_{ij} between station pairs that record an earthquake. Specifically, we use a semivariogram that describes how similar or dissimilar the ground motions are for station pairs separated by different distances (Jayaram and Baker, 2010; Baker and Chen, 2020; Shao *et al.*, 2024). By assuming that the ground-motion observations are stationary and isotropic, that is, the variance between observations is constant through time and independent of the station locations, all locations separated by a

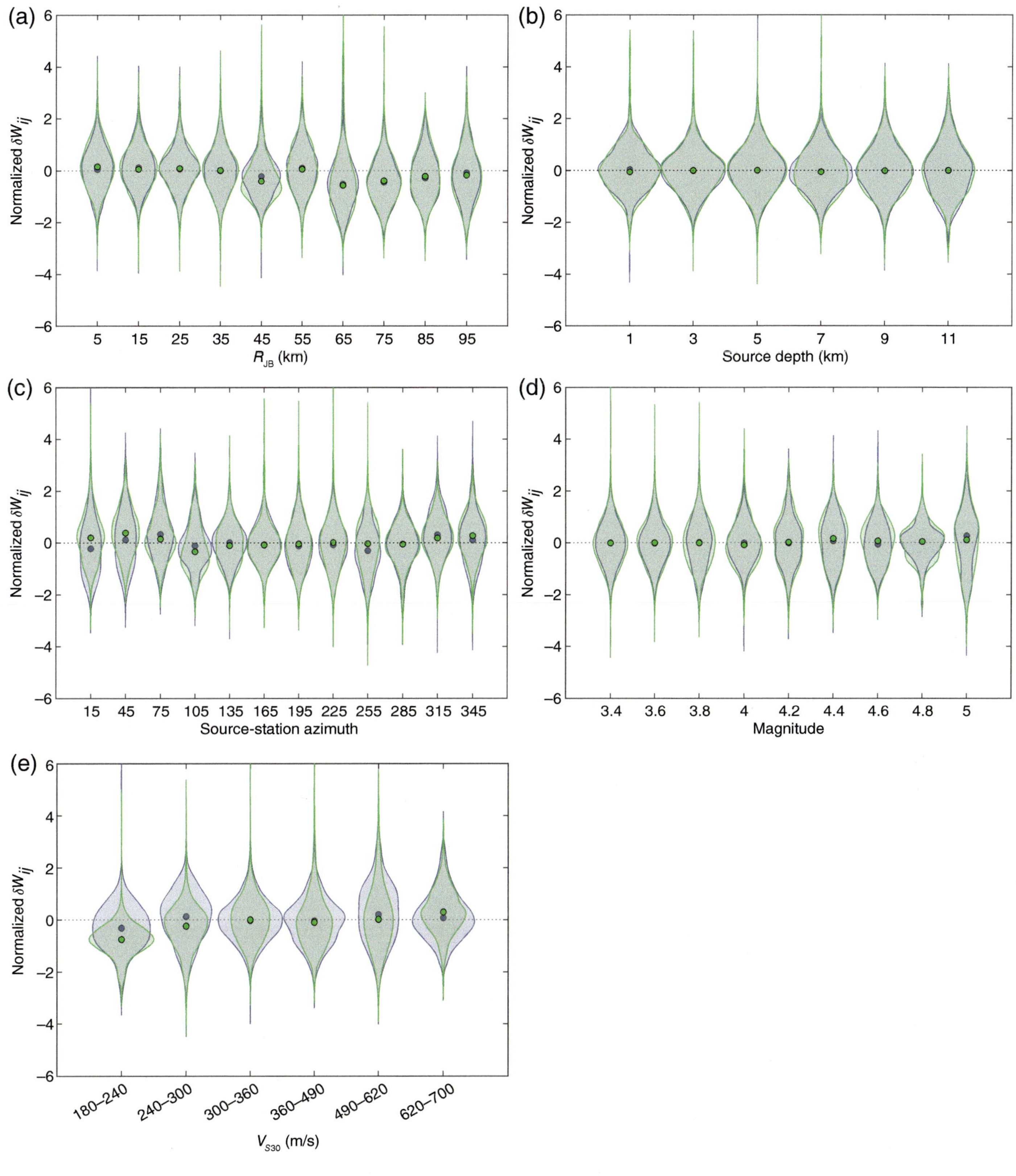

Figure 3. Distribution of normalized δW_{ij} versus (a) R_{JB}, (b) source depth, (c) source-station azimuth, (d) magnitude, and (e) V_{S30} for both peak ground acceleration (PGA) (green) and peak ground velocity (PGV) (blue). The dots give the median value in each bin, and the shaded polygons show the distribution of δW_{ij} values in each bin.

distance h have the same semivariance (Baker and Chen, 2020). Thus, as described in Baker and Chen (2020), the semivariance ($\hat{\gamma}(h)$) for n observations separated by distance h is

$$\hat{\gamma}(h) = \frac{1}{2N(h)} \sum_{i} \sum_{d(j,k)=h} (\delta W_{ij} - \delta W_{ik})^2, \tag{3}$$

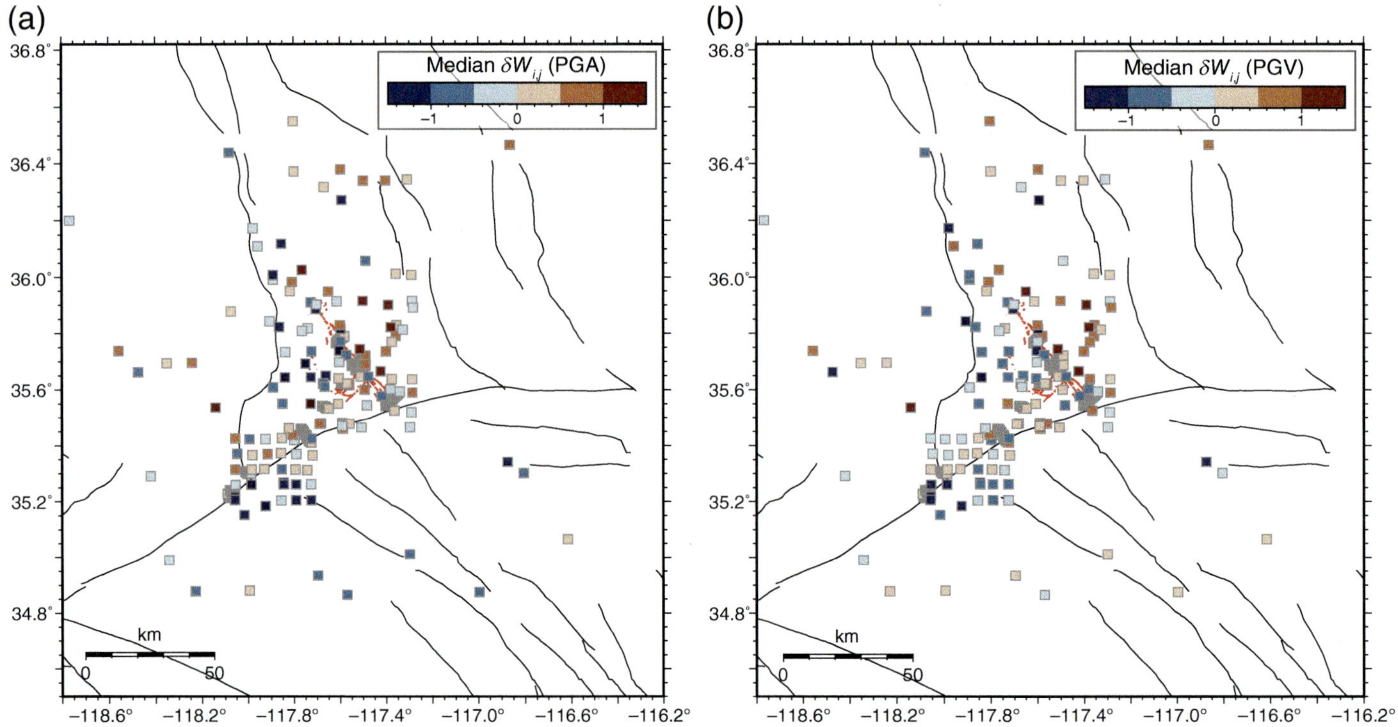

Figure 4. Median normalized within-event residuals (δW_{ij}) at each station with at least five δW_{ij} measurements within the study area for (a) PGA and (b) PGV. Other symbols are as in Figure 1.

in which $d(j,k)$ is the distance between sites j and k, and the sum is taken over all pairs separated by h (within some tolerance), and $N(h)$ is the number of stations separated by h. Because we standardize δW_{ij} by dividing by ϕ we ensure a known sample standard deviation (Baker and Chen, 2020). Normalizing δW_{ij} gives a semivariance of 0 for perfectly correlated ground motions and a semivariance of 1 when the ground motions are uncorrelated.

Using many station pairs at different interstation spacing, we can develop an understanding of how ground-motions variability changes with interstation distance. It has been shown previously that the δW_{ij} values between closely spaced stations (small h) are more similar (have lower semivariance, $\gamma(h)_{j,k}$) than stations separated by a greater distance (e.g., Baker and Jayaram, 2008; Baker and Chen, 2020; Wen *et al.*, 2024). Here, we fit an exponential model to $\hat{\gamma}(h)$ values across a range of h to estimate a correlation range (r) following the method of Baker and Chen (2020):

$$\hat{\gamma}(h) = s\left[1 - \exp\left(\frac{-3h}{r}\right)\right], \quad (4)$$

in which s and r are fitted parameters representing the sill and correlation range, respectively. Given that the data are normalized, the sill (s) is equal to 1. However, if a nugget (n) is included to allow for nonzero semivariance at zero interstation distance; in that case, the sill becomes $1-n$. In this formulation of the model, r is the distance at which $\hat{\gamma}(h)$ equals 0.95 (Schiappapietra and Douglas, 2020).

RESULTS

We compute within-event residuals (δW_{ij}) for 118 earthquakes recorded by 646 unique stations. Stations record between 1 and 55 earthquakes each, with a median of 30 earthquakes. Individual earthquakes are recorded by between 1 and 456 stations, with a median of 106 stations. In total, we use 16,279 within-event residuals from 100 earthquakes on 625 unique stations. The normalized δW_{ij} have a mean of 0 and a standard deviation of 0.895 for PGA with corresponding values of 0.002 and 0.877 for PGV. Note that although we normalized δW_{ij} by ϕ from BSSA14, the mean standard deviations are somewhat less than 1, which may be expected due to the smaller area and magnitude range examined here.

If the GMM is suitable for the region, we should not expect to observe a trend in δW_{ij} with various source, path, and site parameters (Fig. 3). Specifically, we look for any trends δW_{ij} with R_{JB}, source depth, source-station azimuth, magnitude, and V_{S30}. We divide the V_{S30} values into the following bins 180–240 m/s, 240–300 m/s, 300–360 m/s, 360–490 m/s, 490–620 m/s, and 620–760 m/s, corresponding to National Earthquake Hazards Reduction Program (NEHRP) site classes B3, B2, B1, C3, C2, and C1. We do not observe significant trends in δW_{ij} with any of the parameters (Fig. 3); however, we find a weakly positive trend between V_{S30} and δW_{ij} in the PGA (but not PGV) δW_{ij} data.

We examine the median δW_{ij} by station location across the broad study area (Fig. 4). In general, we observe scattered δW_{ij} values with consistent distributions observed in the PGA and PGV data. For stations within about 30 km of the northwest-

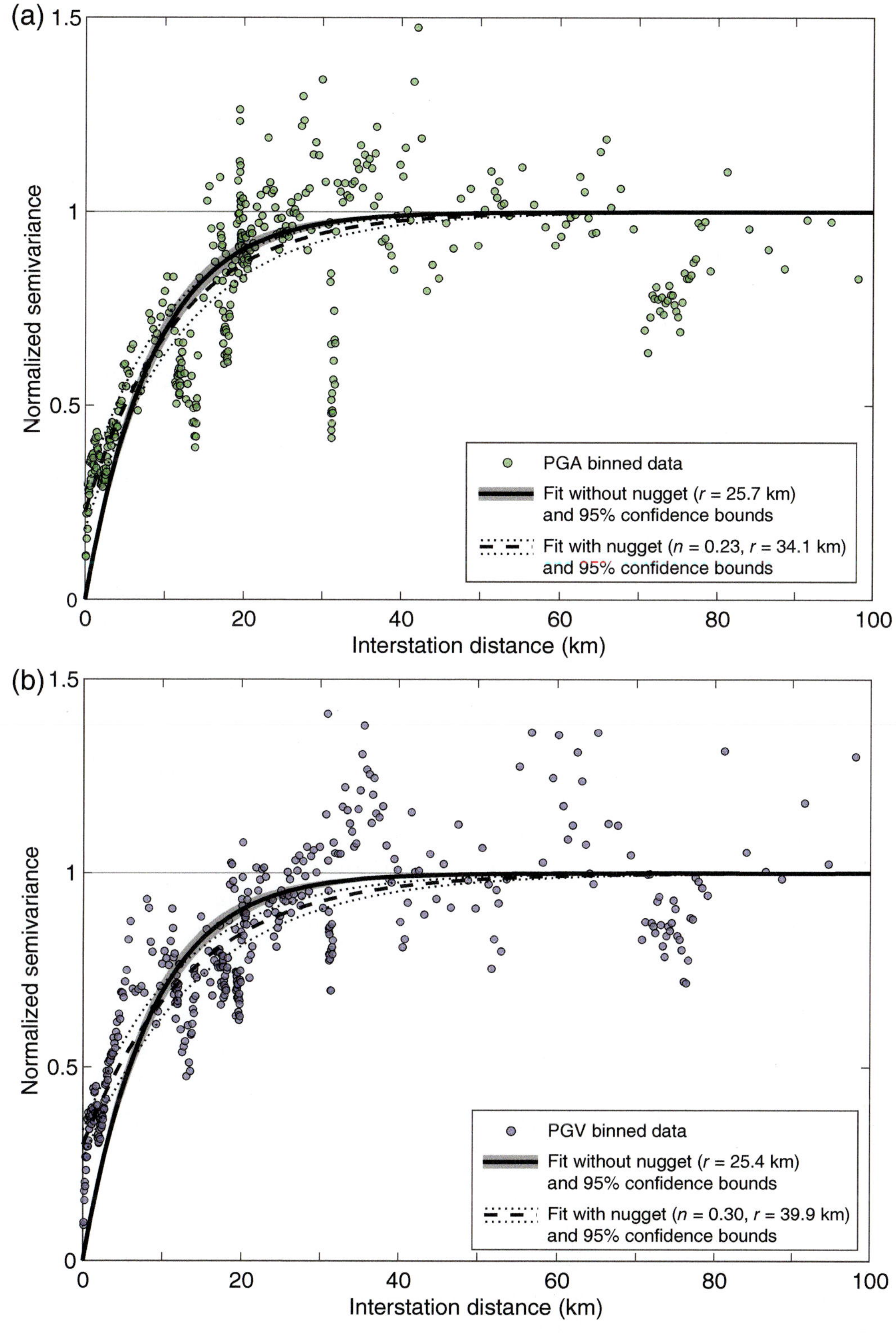

Figure 5. (a) Empirical semivariogram of PGA data; the points are normalized semivariance ($\hat{\gamma}(h)$) versus interstation distance (h). $\hat{\gamma}(h)$ is determined in 400 bins between 0 and 100 km, with equal numbers of data points in each bin. Two exponential models are fit to the data, either with (dashed line) or without (solid line) a nugget (n), to estimate correlation ranges (r). The preferred values for n and r are given in the legend with confidence bounds on the r shown by the dotted lines and shaded area for the models with and without a nugget, respectively. (b) Same as (a), except showing results for PGV data.

oriented mainshock fault, δW_{ij} are somewhat higher on the eastern side of the fault than on the western side. Furthermore, the data suggest that the values of δW_{ij} tend to be positive along the **M** 7.1 and 6.4 rupture planes, and perhaps near the Garlock fault. We will examine the values of the near-fault δW_{ij} in more detail subsequently.

Next, we examine the semivariance of the ground motions under the assumption that the ground motions are stationary and isotropic (see equation 3). We assume that the semivariance of ground motions should be the same for any pair of stations separated by a distance h, independent of the station pair location. We consider only earthquakes recorded by at least 10 stations, stations that record at least five earthquakes, and interstations distances of 100 km or less. In total, we consider 2,095,654 station pairs. We compute $\hat{\gamma}(h)$ following equation (3), using normalized δW_{ij}. We use 400 equal-data bins between 0 and 100 km with ~5170 station pairs per bin. We plot the empirical semivariance (i.e., $\hat{\gamma}(h)$ values versus h) in Figure 5. The general trend in the $\hat{\gamma}(h)$ values is as expected, ranging from near zero at small h to near 1 at interstation distances beyond ~40 km for both the PGA and PGV data. Because we have a data set with many short interstation distance measurements, we have a unique opportunity to examine the semivariance for closely spaced stations. We find $\hat{\gamma}(h)$ values are 0.1 for interstation distances ~100 m for both the PGA and PGV data.

Furthermore, we see that in the first 3 km the $\hat{\gamma}(h)$ values increase rapidly from 0.1 to 0.4.

$\hat{\gamma}(h)$ values do not increase monotonically with increasing distance between stations; some shorter wavelength trends in the data are apparent and consistent across the PGA and PGV plots (Fig. 5). The $\hat{\gamma}(h)$ values for similar interstation distances sometimes vary significantly, even when averaged across many measurements (~5170) in a single bin. This variability suggests that, although the results are generally consistent with our assumption that the ground motions are stationary and isotropic, other unmodeled factors control some of the shorter-wavelength variability in the empirical semivariance.

We fit the exponential function (equation 4) to the $\hat{\gamma}(h)$ values using the Matlab (see Data and Resources) nonlinear least-squares fitting function, allowing r to vary between 0 and 100 km with a starting value of 20 km; tests of different starting values for r gave the same best-fit r value. Because we used bins of $\hat{\gamma}(h)$ with equal numbers of input data, we did not apply a weighting criterion to the data. Figure 5 shows the semivariograms model fits, considering both n equal to zero (no nugget) and allowing for a nugget n. Without a nugget, the PGA data have a correlation range (r) of 25.7 km (23.5–28.0 km, 95% confidence bounds) and the PGV data have a similar correlation range of 25.4 km (23.3–28.0 km). The data show significant scatter around the model fits, and at short interstation distances the observed $\hat{\gamma}(h)$ show higher variances than suggested by the model. This is in part due to the model assumption of zero variance for collocated stations, whereas, as we reported earlier, the observed $\hat{\gamma}(h)$ are never smaller than 0.1. Because of the misfit between the data and model at zero distance, we also solve for the best-fit model allowing for a nugget (n). The best fit to the PGA data has $n = 0.23$ (0.18–0.27) and $r = 34.1$ km (30.6 37.5 km), whereas the PGV data has $n = 0.30$ (0.26–0.33) and $r = 39.9$ km (36.2–43.7 km). By including n, the best-fit r values are larger by about 10 km, suggesting ground motions may correlate to greater distances. However, the modeled nugget n (0.23–0.3) is larger than the observed $\hat{\gamma}$ (0.1) for the shortest interstation distance bins; thus, neither model fully captures the behavior at short interstation distances. Overall, the models that do not include a nugget have r values with narrower confidence bounds, providing a better fit to the data.

The shorter wavelength structure observed in the empirical semivariogram superimposed on the broader trend of increasing $\hat{\gamma}(h)$ with h may suggest that the ground-motion variability is not fully consistent with our assumption that the ground motions are isotropic and stationary. We surmise that event and/or station location may contribute nonrandom variability to the ground motions, and the following sections explore potential contributions.

We start by considering how the semivariograms vary by event by examining four well-recorded earthquakes within our 2019 Ridgecrest aftershock sequence, each with at least 10,000 station pairs: ci38561839 (M_l 3.5 13 July 2019 22:58:40 UTC), ci38574407 (M_l 3.6 15 July 2019 15:43:36 UTC), ci38578567 (M_l 3.6 6 July 2019 05:26:52 UTC), and ci38605023 (M_l 3.5 19 July 2019 UTC) (Fig. 6). As was done for the entire data set above, we fit an exponential model to the data and determined the correlation ranges (r); here, we only consider models without a nugget for ease of comparison. Across these four earthquakes, we find r ranges between ~10 and 45 km. Differences in the semivariances across events could include effects due to changes in both the distribution of stations, source locations, or source properties not modeled by the event term such as directivity. Unfortunately, we lack a sufficient number of earthquakes with well-resolved r values to systematically search for the influence of source location on the correlation range. We also divide the data into two subsets based on earthquake location on the east or west side of the **M** 7.1 mainshock rupture; however, we do not observe a significant difference in the semivariograms by source locations. Similarly, binning data by source-station azimuth did not show significant differences across the resulting semivariograms.

Next, we examine how station location may affect the spatial variability of ground motions. We focus on the longest fault crossing array, consisting of 83 nodal stations B401-B483 (B4 array in network 3J). Figure 7a shows a zoomed map of the median normalized PGA δW_{ij} values in the array. We observe that even over the short distance of the array (8 km) there are significant changes in median δW_{ij} values. In particular, we observe that there is greater variability in δW_{ij} on the western side of the array, whereas the eastern side has more similar median δW_{ij} values. In addition, we observe that the WEIR values tend to be positive, and sometimes strongly positive, where the array crosses fault traces. The δW_{ij} values near the surface traces can be greater than 1; thus, the median observed ground motions are more than one standard deviation above the median ground motions of the data set.

To explore how the spatial correlations change for different sets of station pairs, we show the empirical semivariograms considering only station pairs within array B4. There are a total of 118,386 pairs with h ranging from 43.6 m to 8.01 km. Here, to aid comparison of the empirical semivariogram for the B4 array, we use 100 m bins rather than equal-data bins. The empirical semivariogram for PGV data collected by all station pairs in the B4 array is shown in Figure 7b and compared to the results for the entire data set. The empirical semivariogram for the B4 array is nearly identical to the results of the full data set, both in the overall trend of increasing variance with h and the observed shorter wavelength variability.

Next, we consider the western (stations B401–B448) and eastern (stations B449–B483) sides of the array separately. The stations were divided specifically to compare a set of stations with relatively similar δW_{ij} values (east) to another set of stations with more variable δW_{ij} values (west). The western part of the array has 37,302 pairs at a range of h from 43 m to 4.32 km, and the eastern portion of the array has

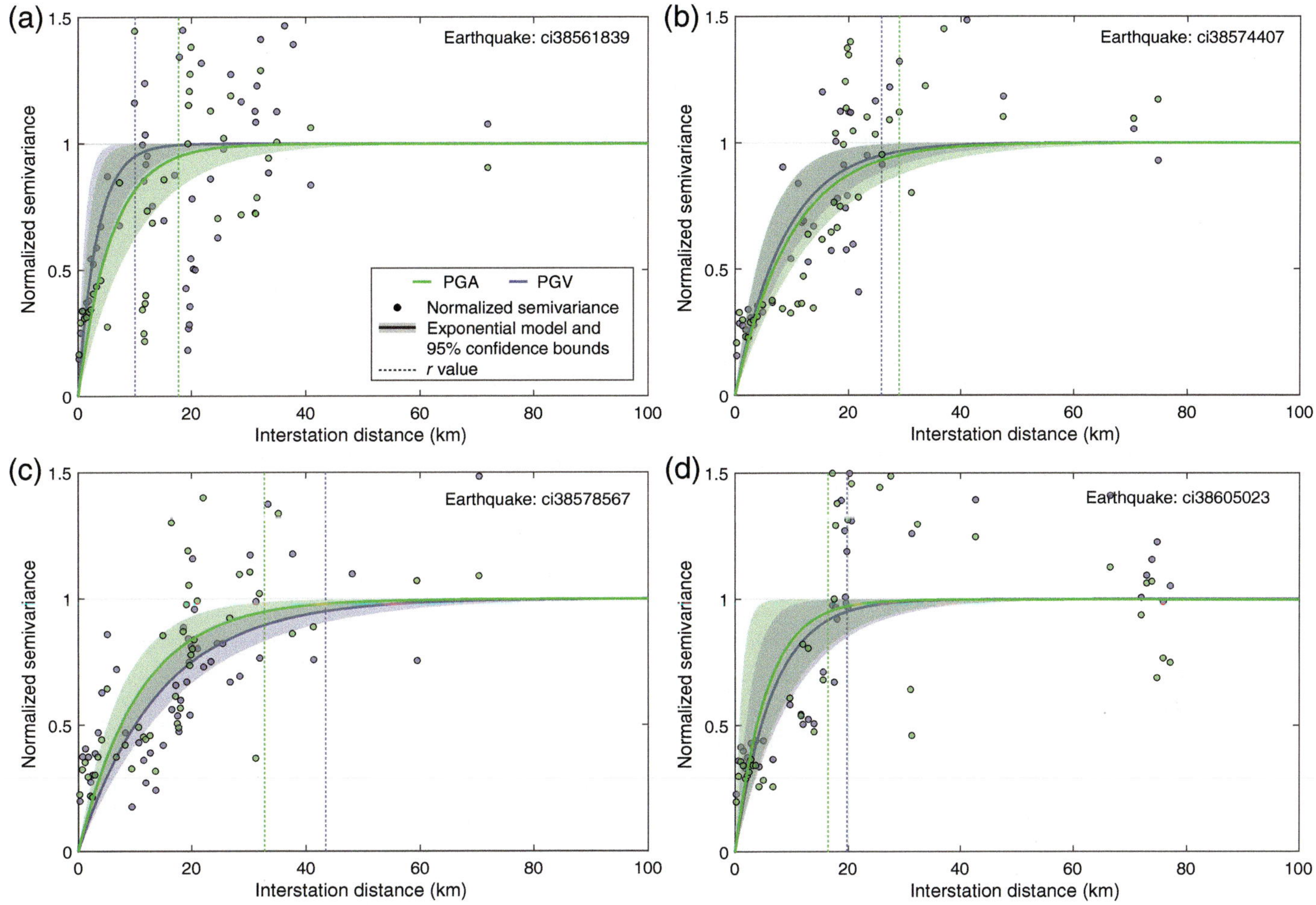

Figure 6. Semivariograms for events: (a) ci38561839 (M_l 3.5 13 July 2019 22:58:40 UTC), (b) ci38574407 (M_l 3.6 15 July 2019 15:43:36 UTC), (c) ci38578567 (M_l 3.6 6 July 2019 05:26:52 UTC), and (d) ci38605023 (M_l 3.5 19 July 2019 UTC). Exponential model fits (solid lines, 95% confidence shown by shaded area) to PGA (green) and PGV (blue) data. Data are given in evenly spaced bins. The correlation ranges (r) are shown by vertical dotted lines.

22,443 pairs with h from 89 m to 3.6 km. The empirical semivariograms for the two partial arrays are compared to the empirical semivariogram for the entire array and the full data set in Figure 7.

We observe that $\hat{\gamma}(h)$ values for the eastern station pairs are significantly lower (the ground motions are more correlated) compared to the whole B4 array as well as the entire data set (Fig. 7b). In fact, for h between 0 and 3 km, the $\hat{\gamma}(h)$ values only range between ~0.1 and 0.2, whereas $\hat{\gamma}(h)$ rapidly increases from 0.1 to 0.4 for the same range of h for the entire B4 array or all stations in the study. Despite the overall lower $\hat{\gamma}(h)$ values, we still observe that the minimum $\hat{\gamma}(h)$ is 0. 06 for the h bin spanning 0–100 m, with a clear offset from the expected value of zero at $h = 0$. In contrast, the western station pairs show overall higher $\hat{\gamma}(h)$ values, reflecting the large variability in δW_{ij} values over short h. $\hat{\gamma}(h)$ values as high as 0.6 within 3 km are observed for the western station pairs. This is significantly higher than the values of 0.2 observed for the eastern station pairs and 0.4 for the other data sets. This result indicates that the western stations have higher ground-motion variability than is typical for the data set as a whole.

The highest δW_{ij} values in Figure 7a appear to roughly correlate with the location of two strands of the **M** 7.1 Ridgecrest surface rupture. We examine this further by mapping the PGV-based δW_{ij} values at the other dense arrays that cross the **M** 6.4 foreshock and **M** 7.1 mainshock surface ruptures (Fig. 8). This includes the four nodal arrays that cross the mainshock rupture (B1, B2, B3, and B4 arrays in network 3J) as well as the array that crosses the foreshock rupture (A1 array in network 3J). Again, we observe that close to the surface traces the δW_{ij} values tend to be higher than the values at other stations in the arrays.

We plot profiles of the mean-removed δW_{ij} values for the five fault-crossing arrays in Figure 9. Here, we show results for both PGA and PGV to highlight the consistency in the relative differences in δW_{ij} for each profile. The locations of the mapped surface traces are indicated, and may suggest the median δW_{ij} values are elevated at stations close to the fault traces. Array B1 shows somewhat elevated δW_{ij} values between

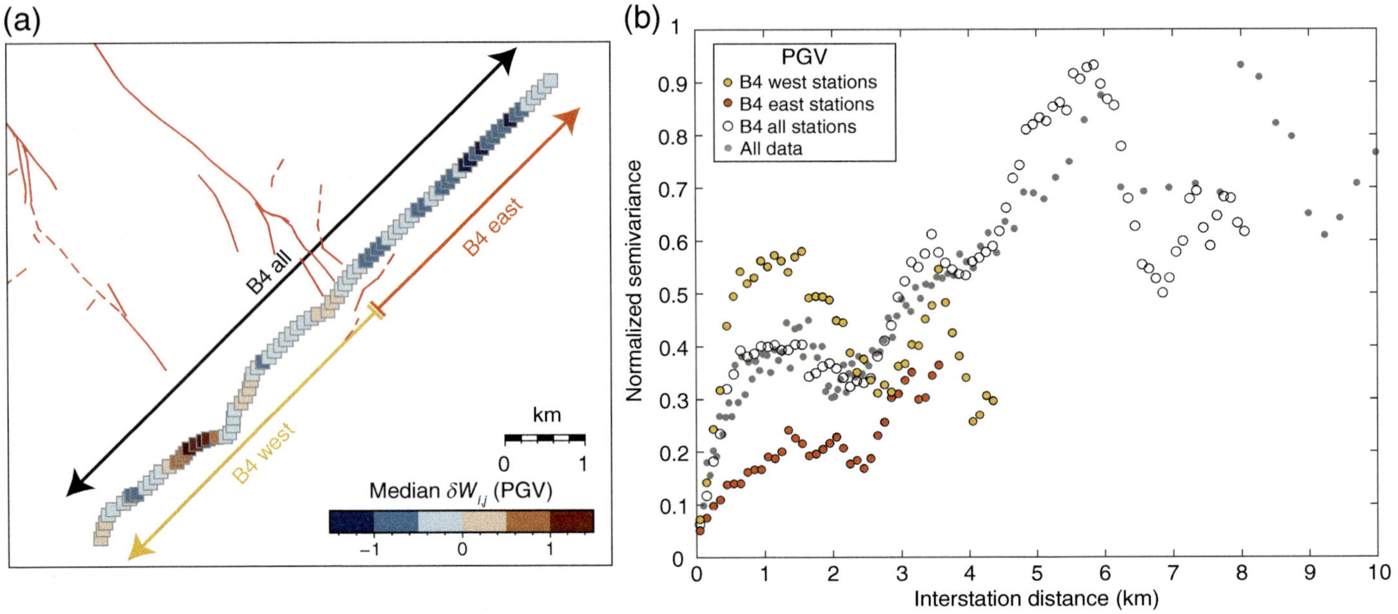

Figure 7. (a) Median normalized δW_{ij} at each station in array 3J.B4 that is located across the southern portion of the **M** 7.1 mainshock rupture. Arrows and labels indicate the entire array (B4 all, black), the set of stations on the western side of the array (B4 west, yellow), and eastern side (B4 east, orange). (b) Corresponding normalized semivariances ($\hat{\gamma}(h)$) for the different sets of stations pairs, including B4 west (yellow), B4 east (orange), B4 all (open black symbols). Also shown are the data from the entire study area (gray-filled dots) from Figure 5b.

the main fault trace and some minor fault strands located ~2 km to the west. The array is located immediately north of where the fault bifurcates from a single primary strand in the north into two branches separated by 1–2 km to the south. In array B2, the mapped fault strand lies on the eastern side of an ~1 km zone of strongly elevated median δW_{ij} values that are 2 times higher near the fault trace compared to stations at greater distance from the fault. Array B3 is located 2 km south of array B2 and shows a smaller peak in a 300-m-wide zone near the main fault strand. Array B4 shows two strong peaks associated with the two primary fault branches with values elevated over 1–2 km near the fault. The largest overall signal is associated with the western fault branch in array B4 with median δW_{ij} up to ~3 times higher than δW_{ij} values farther from the fault trace. The signal associated with the **M** 6.4 foreshock fault traces on array A1 are more muted with perhaps a single station showing elevated δW_{ij} values at the main fault branch. However, the array A1 profile includes multiple closely spaced fault strands that cover more than half of the profile length, so it may be difficult to identify patterns in δW_{ij} in this complex zone of faulting.

DISCUSSION

We used dense recordings of the 2019 Ridgecrest, California, earthquake sequence to examine the spatial correlation of ground motion and explore factors that influence ground-motion variability. As expected, we observed that δW_{ij} are generally more similar for station pairs with smaller separation distances. Fitting an exponential model to the empirical semivariograms, we found correlation ranges of ~25 km (23–28 km, 95% confidence bounds) for both PGA and PGV. These results are broadly consistent with prior studies using similar exponential models. For example, Baker and Chen (2020) reported correlation ranges of 20–30 km for 1 s spectral amplitudes for the 2010 El Mayor–Cucapah, Baja California, and 2002 M 4.3 Yorba Linda earthquakes in southern California. A study in a Central Italy sequence found a somewhat shorter correlation range of 15 km using PGA data (Schiappapietra and Douglas, 2020).

Correlation ranges varied among individual earthquakes, although our analysis did not control for the sets of station pairs that were included across events. We observed no systematic differences in correlation ranges based on whether earthquake source location or source-station azimuth. However, station pairs located near or crossing mapped surface traces showed significantly higher semivariances compared to station pairs with similar interstation distances but located away from the Ridgecrest surface traces. We interpret this variability in semivariance for similar interstation distance bins (Fig. 5) as reflecting strong near-fault effects. For example, consider if one station located 20 km from the Ridgecrest rupture were paired with each of the stations in the B4 array; the interstation distances would be similar for the station pairs (~20 km), yet the semivariances would vary strongly depending on whether the station is near the fault trace.

Previous studies have shown that fault traces can amplify ground motions. Kurzon *et al.* (2014) observed amplification within 1 km of the San Jacinto fault, and found that including fault zone amplification in GMMs reduced uncertainties more

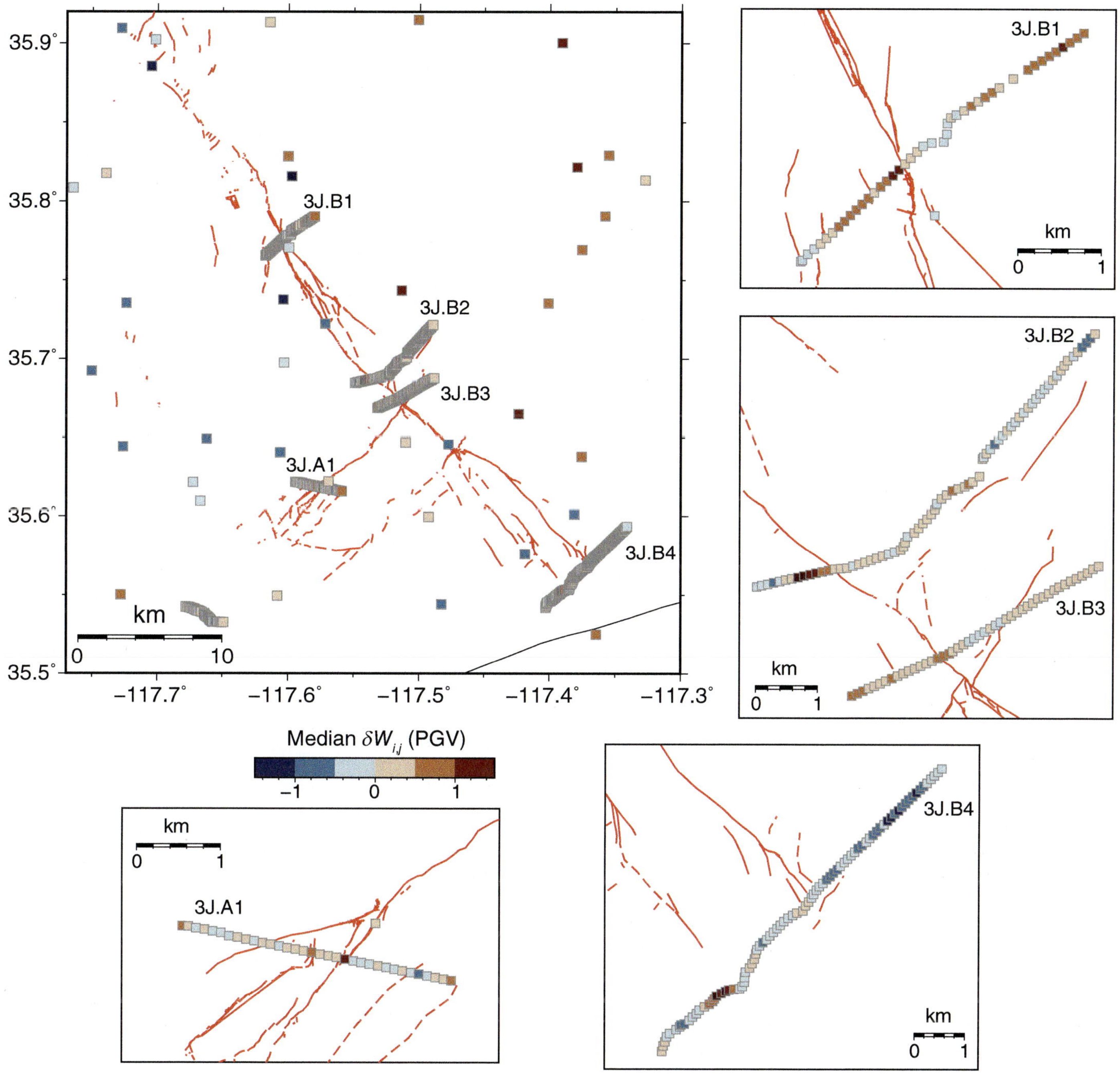

Figure 8. Detailed maps of the nodal arrays that cross the surface rupture of the **M** 6.4 and 7.1 2019 Ridgecrst earthquakes. Arrays B1–B4 (network code: 3J) are located across the **M** 7.1 rupture traces, and array A1 (network code: 3J) is located across the **M** 6.4 rupture trace.

effectively than using V_{S30} to correct for site effects. Similarly, Avallone *et al.* (2014) observed amplified motions at a Global Navigation Satellite Systemsstation within the fault zone during the 2009 **M** 6.1 L'Aquila earthquake, which required a 650-m-wide low-velocity zone (with 50% velocity reduction) to reproduce the observations. We observe a similar phenomenon in Ridgecrest, where large positive median δW_{ij} values occur near faults, with relative values 2–3 times larger than nearby stations. Thus, ground motions are amplified in 100-m to 2-km-wide zones close to faults. We attribute higher δW_{ij} values to the presence of a fault damage zone causing amplification of ground motions due to lower velocities and/or increased scattering.

Fault damage zones have been consistently observed after large earthquakes (e.g., Li *et al.*, 2004; Li *et al.*, 2016). At Ridgecrest, several studies have constrained the fault zone properties using imagery, seismic, and geodetic data. Antoine *et al.* (2021) used optical imagery to estimate individual fault widths ranging from a few meters to a few hundred meters, and broader deformation zones up to 2 km wide. Geodetic analysis suggested fault widths of ~250 m (Xu *et al.*, 2023). Ambient noise

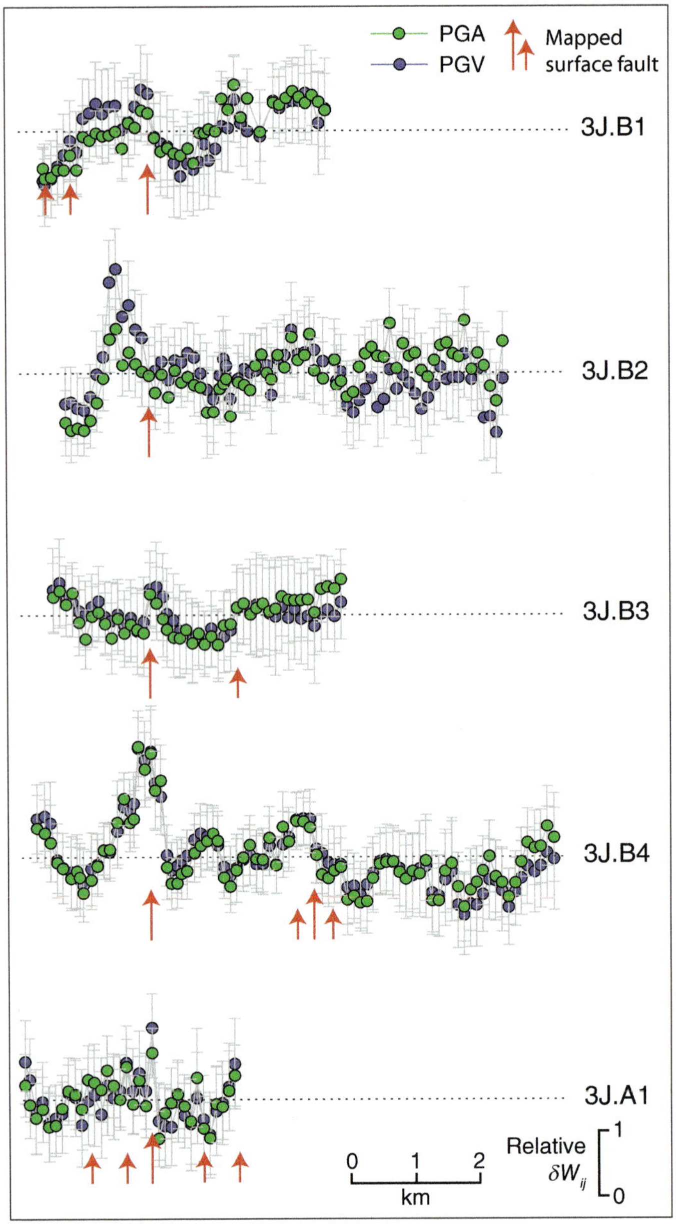

Figure 9. Profiles of relative median station δW_{ij} (PGA and PGV) for the nodal arrays that cross the Ridgecrest mainshock and foreshock surface rupture. The mean δW_{ij} of the array is removed to determine the relative median station δW_{ij} values. Arrays B1, B2, B3, and B4 (network 3J) cross the **M** 7.1 mainshock surface trace, and array A1 (network 3J) extends across the surface trace of the **M** 6.4 foreshock. The arrows indicate the location of throughgoing (larger arrows) and secondary (smaller arrows) fault traces. Note that for array B4, we mark the approximate location of the along-strike extension of the western fault strand (left arrow) as well as the three eastern traces (right arrows). The location of the fault traces are based on the mapped structures of Ponti *et al.* (2020).

tomography suggested broad low-velocity zones with widths up to 5 km (Zhou *et al.*, 2022). Qiu *et al.* (2021) used fault trapped waves to estimate the fault damage zone widths across the same fault crossing nodal arrays that we considered here. They found 1–2-km-wide low-velocity zones at arrays B1 and B4, consistent with the distances over which we observe elevated δW_{ij}. Among the five arrays we examined, array B4 shows the clearest signal associated with the fault zone. Although Qiu *et al.* (2021) could not determine reliable fault widths at arrays B2 and B3, we observe a 300-m-wide zone of higher-than-average δW_{ij} at array B3, and a broader zone extending 1 km southwest from the fault trace at array B2.

Our results only capture ground-motion characteristics in the early postseismic period, and the strong influence of the fault zone on ground motions may become more tempered over time as the fault damage zone heals. However, damage zones have been shown to persist across the seismic cycle (e.g., Cochran *et al.*, 2009; Faulkner *et al.*, 2011). In the Ridgecrest area, Atterholt *et al.* (2022) showed peaks in seismic scattering in DAS data that align with previously mapped, but not recently ruptured, faults. Thus, we might expect that near most fault zones, ground motions may be more likely to be amplified and show greater spatial variability.

CONCLUSIONS

Our analysis of data collected near the 2019 Ridgecrest, California, earthquake sequence suggests that fault zones strongly influence peak ground motions. Overall, we find an exponential model with no nugget and correlation ranges of ~25 km (23–28 km, 95% confidence bounds) fits the empirical δW_{ij} data for both PGA and PGV, broadly consistent with other similar studies. However, close to surface ruptures we find ground motions are amplified, with median values more than one standard deviation above the median for the data set. We also find that near-fault peak ground motions are more spatially variable, with rapid increases in $\hat{\gamma}$ observed within 1 km of the fault. Our results suggest that it may be important to consider the role of fault zones when assessing seismic hazard near faults and in the development of nonergodic GMMs. Ground-motion amplification within fault zones could potentially be modeled as a systematic path or site effect at specific locations and more complex spatial correlations that are not stationary and isotropic, as currently assumed, could be considered.

DATA AND RESOURCES

Seismic data included waveforms recorded by networks such as CI (California Institute of Technology and U.S. Geological Survey [USGS] Pasadena (1926), GS (Albuquerque Seismological Laboratory ASL/USGS, 1980), NN (University of Nevada, Reno, 1971), NP (USGS, 1931), PB (UNAVCO, 2004), SN (University of Nevada, Reno, 1992), ZY (Cochran *et al.*, 2020), and 3J (Catchings *et al.*, 2020). All the waveform data and metadata referenced herein are publicly available and accessed from the Southern California Earthquake Data Center (Southern California Earthquake Data Center [SCEDC], 2013), Earthscope Consortium (Earthscope Consortium, 2024), and Northern California Earthquake Data Center (Northern California Earthquake Data Center [NCEDC], 2014). Matlab can be accessed from The MathWorks Inc. MATLAB R204b (https://www.mathworks.com, last accessed September 2025). The supplemental material includes tables of the calculated residuals.

DECLARATION OF COMPETING INTERESTS

The authors acknowledge that there are no conflicts of interest recorded.

ACKNOWLEDGMENTS

The authors thank Eric Thompson (U.S. Geological Survey [USGS] internal reviewer), Jack Baker, and an anonymous reviewer (*BSSA* journal reviewers) for careful and constructive review of the article. Any use of trade, firm, or product names is for descriptive purposes only and does not imply endorsement by the U.S. Government.

REFERENCES

Abrahamson, N. A. (1988). Statistical properties of peak ground accelerations recorded by the SMART 1 array, *Bull. Seismol. Soc. Am.* **78,** no. 1, 26–41.

Abrahamson, N. A., and R. R. Youngs (1992). A stable algorithm for regression analyses using the random effects model, *Bull. Seismol. Soc. Am.* **82,** no. 1, 505–510.

Albuquerque Seismological Laboratory (ASL)/U.S. Geological Survey (USGS) (1980). US Geological Survey Networks, *International Federation of Digital Seismograph Networks.*

Ancheta, T. D., R. B. Darragh, J. P. Stewart, E. Seyhan, W. J. Silva, B. S.-J. Chiou, K. E. Wooddell, R. W. Graves, A. R. Kottke, D. M. Boore, *et al.* (2014). NGA-West2 database, *Earthq. Spectra* **30,** no. 3, 989–1005.

Antoine, S. L., Y. Klinger, A. Delorme, K. Wang, R. Bürgmann, and R. D. Gold (2021). Diffuse deformation and surface faulting distribution from submetric image correlation along the 2019 Ridgecrest, California, ruptures, *Bull. Seismol. Soc. Am.* **111,** no. 5, 2275–2302.

Atik, L. A., N. Abrahamson, J. J. Bommer, F. Scherbaum, F. Cotton, and N. Kuehn (2010). The variability of ground-motion prediction models and its components, *Seismol. Res. Lett.* **81,** no. 5, 794–801.

Atkinson, G. M. (2015). Ground-motion prediction equation for small-to-moderate events at short hypocentral distances, with application to induced-seismicity hazards, *Bull. Seismol. Soc. Am.* **105,** no. 2A, 981–992.

Atkinson, G. M., and D. M. Boore (2003). Empirical ground-motion relations for subduction-zone earthquakes and their application to Cascadia and other regions, *Bull. Seismol. Soc. Am.* **93,** no. 4, 1703–1729.

Atterholt, J., Z. Zhan, and Y. Yang (2022). Fault zone imaging with distributed acoustic sensing: Body-to-surface wave scattering, *J. Geophys. Res.* **127,** no. 11, e2022JB025052, doi: 10.1029/2022JB024329.

Avallone, A., A. Rovelli, G. Di Giulio, L. Improta, Y. Ben-Zion, G. Milana, and F. Cara (2014). Waveguide effects in very high rate GPS record of the 6 April 2009, M_w 6.1 L'Aquila, central Italy earthquake, *J. Geophys. Res.* **119,** no. 1, 490–501.

Baker, J. W., and Y. Chen (2020). Ground motion spatial correlation fitting methods and estimation uncertainty, *Earthq. Eng. Struct. Dynam.* **49,** no. 15, 1662–1681.

Baker, J. W., and N. Jayaram (2008). Correlation of spectral acceleration values from NGA ground motion models, *Earthq. Spectra* **24,** no. 1, 299–317.

Baltay, A. S., T. C. Hanks, and N. A. Abrahamson (2017). Uncertainty, variability, and earthquake physics in ground-motion prediction equations, *Bull. Seismol. Soc. Am.* **107,** no. 4, 1754–1772.

Bates, D., M. Mächler, B. Bolker, and S. Walker (2015). Fitting linear mixed-effects models using lme4, *J Stat Software* **67,** 1–48.

Bodenmann, L., J. W. Baker, and B. Stojadinović (2023). Accounting for path and site effects in spatial ground-motion correlation models using Bayesian inference, *Nat. Hazards Earth Syst. Sci.* **23,** no. 7, 2387–2402.

Bommer, J. J., and H. Crowley (2006). The influence of ground-motion variability in earthquake loss modelling, *Bull. Earthq. Eng.* **4,** no. 3, 231–248.

Boore, D. M., J. F. Gibbs, W. B. Joyner, J. C. Tinsley, and D. J. Ponti (2003). Estimated ground motion from the 1994 Northridge, California, earthquake at the site of the Interstate 10 and La Cienega Boulevard bridge collapse, West Los Angeles, California, *Bull. Seismol. Soc. Am.* **93,** no. 6, 2737–2751.

Boore, D. M., J. P. Stewart, E. Seyhan, and G. M. Atkinson (2014). NGA-West2 equations for predicting PGA, PGV, and 5% damped PSA for shallow crustal earthquakes, *Earthq. Spectra* **30,** no. 3, 1057–1085.

Bozorgnia, Y., N. A. Abrahamson, L. A. Atik, T. D. Ancheta, G. M. Atkinson, J. W. Baker, A. Baltay, D. M. Boore, K. W. Campbell, B. S.-J. Chiou, *et al.* (2014). NGA-West2 research project, *Earthq. Spectra* **30,** no. 3, 973–987.

California Geological Survey (1972). California Strong Motion Instrumentation Program [Data set], International Federation of Digital Seismograph Networks, doi: 10.7914/b34q-bb70.

California Institute of Technology and USGS Pasadena (1926). Southern California Seismic Network [Data set], International Federation of Digital Seismograph Networks, doi: 10.7914/SN/CI.

Catchings, R. D., M. R. Goldman, J. H. Steidl, J. H. Chan, A. A. Allam, C. J. Criley, Z. Ma, D. S. Langermann, G. J. Huddleston, A. T. McEvilly, *et al.* (2020). Nodal seismograph recordings of the 2019 Ridgecrest earthquake sequence, *Seismol. Res. Lett.* **91,** no. 6, 3622–3633.

Chen, Y., B. A. Bradley, and J. W. Baker (2021). Nonstationary spatial correlation in New Zealand strong ground-motion data, *Earthq. Eng. Struct. Dynam.* **50,** no. 13, 3421–3440.

Cochran, E. S., Y.-G. Li, P. M. Shearer, S. Barbot, Y. Fialko, and J. E. Vidale (2009). Seismic and geodetic evidence for extensive, long-lived fault damage zones, *Geology* **37,** no. 4, 315–318.

Cochran, E. S., E. Wolin, D. E. McNamara, A. Yong, D. Wilson, M. Alvarez, N. van der Elst, A. McClain, and J. Steidl (2020). The U.S. Geological Survey's rapid seismic array deployment for the 2019 Ridgecrest earthquake sequence, *Seismol. Res. Lett.* **91,** no. 4, 1952–1960.

Earthscope Consortium (2024). EarthScope consortium web services, available at https://www.earthscope.org/ (last accessed September 2025).

Douglas, J., S. Akkar, G. Ameri, P.-Y. Bard, D. Bindi, J. J. Bommer, S. S. Bora, F. Cotton, B. Derras, M. Hermkes, *et al.* (2014). Comparisons among the five ground-motion models developed using RESORCE for the prediction of response spectral accelerations due to earthquakes in Europe and the Middle East, *Bull. Earthq. Eng.* **12,** no. 1, 341–358.

Faulkner, D. R., T. M. Mitchell, E. Jensen, and J. Cembrano (2011). Scaling of fault damage zones with displacement and the implications for fault growth processes, *J. Geophys. Res.* **116,** no. B5, doi: 10.1029/2010JB007788.

Goda, K., and H. P. Hong (2008). Spatial correlation of peak ground motions and response spectra. *Bull. Seismol. Soc. Am.* **98,** no. 1, 354–365.

Hauksson, E., C. Yoon, E. Yu, J. R. Andrews, M. Alvarez, R. Bhadha, and V. Thomas (2020). Caltech/USGS Southern California Seismic Network (SCSN) and Southern California Earthquake Data Center (SCEDC): Data Availability for the 2019 Ridgecrest Sequence, *Seismol. Res. Lett.* **91,** no. 4, 1961–1970.

International Federation of Digital Seismograph Networks (2025). FDSN: FDSN web services, available at https://www.fdsn.org/webservices/ (last accessed September 2025).

Iwaki, A., N. Morikawa, T. Maeda, and H. Fujiwara (2017). Spatial distribution of ground-motion variability in broadband ground-motion simulations, *Bull. Seismol. Soc. Am.* **107,** no. 6, 2963–2979.

Jayaram, N., and J. W. Baker (2009). Correlation model for spatially distributed ground-motion intensities, *Earthq. Eng. Struct. Dynam.* **38,** no. 15, 1687–1708.

Jayaram, N., and J. W. Baker (2010). Considering spatial correlation in mixed-effects regression and the impact on ground-motion models, *Bull. Seismol. Soc. Am.* **100,** no. 6, 3295–3303.

Joyner, W. B., and D. M. Boore (1981). Peak horizontal acceleration and velocity from strong-motion records including records from the 1979 Imperial Valley, California, earthquake, *Bull. Seismol. Soc. Am.* **71,** no. 6, 2011–2038.

Karabulut, H., and M. Bouchon (2007). Spatial variability and non-linearity of strong ground motion near a fault, *Geophys. J. Int.* **170,** no. 1, 262–274.

Kawakami, H., and H. Mogi (2003). Analyzing spatial intraevent variability of peak ground accelerations as a function of separation distance, *Bull. Seismol. Soc. Am.* **93,** no. 3, 1079–1090.

Kurzon, I., F. L. Vernon, Y. Ben-Zion, and G. Atkinson (2014). Ground motion prediction equations in the San Jacinto fault zone: Significant effects of rupture directivity and fault zone amplification, *Pure Appl. Geophys.* **171,** no. 11, 3045–3081.

Li, Y., R. D. Catchings, and M. R. Goldman (2016). Subsurface fault damage zone of the 2014 M_w 6.0 South Napa, California, earthquake viewed from fault-zone trapped waves, *Bull. Seismol. Soc. Am.* **106,** no. 6, 2747–2763.

Li, Y.-G., J. E. Vidale, and E. S. Cochran (2004). Low-velocity damaged structure of the San Andreas fault at Parkfield from fault zone trapped waves, *Geophys. Res. Lett.* **31,** L12S06, doi: 10.1029/2003GL019044.

McCann, M. W., Jr., and D. M. Boore (1983). Variability in ground motions: Root mean square acceleration and peak acceleration for the 1971 San Fernando, California, earthquake, *Bull. Seismol. Soc. Am.* **73,** no. 2, 615–632.

McNamara, D. E., E. L. G. Wolin, M. P. Moschetti, E. M. Thompson, P. M. Powers, A. M. Shumway, M. D. Petersen, D. C. Wilson, and H. M. Benz (2020). Evaluation of ground-motion models for USGS seismic hazard models using near-source instrumental ground-motion recordings of the Ridgecrest, California, earthquake sequence, *Bull. Seismol. Soc. Am.* **110,** no. 4, 1517–1529.

Northern California Earthquake Data Center (NCEDC) (2014). Northern California earthquake data center [Data set]. Northern California Earthquake Data Center, doi: 10.7932/NCEDC.

Niazi, M. (1985). Spatial coherence of the ground motion produced by the 1979 Imperial Valley earthquake across El Centro Differential Array, *Phys. Earth Planet. In.* **38,** no. 2, 162–173.

Parker, G. A., A. S. Baltay, and E. T. Hirakawa (2025). An empirical Green's function approach for isolating directivity effects in earthquake ground-motion amplitudes, *Bull. Seismol. Soc. Am.* **115,** 2336–2354.

Parker, G. A., A. S. Baltay, J. Rekoske, and E. M. Thompson (2020). Repeatable source, path, and site effects from the 2019 M 7.1 Ridgecrest earthquake sequence, *Bull. Seismol. Soc. Am.* **110,** no. 4, 1530–1548.

Ponti, D. J., J. L. Blair, C. M. Rosa, K. Thomas, A. J. Pickering, S. Akciz, S. Angster, J. Avouac, J. Bachhuber, S. Bacon, *et al.* (2020). Documentation of surface fault rupture and ground-deformation features produced by the 4 and 5 July 2019 M_w 6.4 and M_w 7.1 Ridgecrest earthquake sequence, *Seismol. Res. Lett.* **91,** no. 5, 2942–2959.

Qiu, H., Y. Ben-Zion, R. Catchings, M. R. Goldman, A. A. Allam, and J. Steidl (2021). Seismic imaging of the M_w 7.1 Ridgecrest earthquake rupture zone from data recorded by dense linear arrays, *J. Geophys. Res.* **126,** no. 7, e2021JB022043, doi: 10.1029/2021JB022043.

Rekoske, J. M., E. M. Thompson, M. P. Moschetti, M. G. Hearne, B. T. Aagaard, and G. A. Parker (2020). The 2019 Ridgecrest, California, earthquake sequence ground motions: Processed records and derived intensity metrics, *Seismol. Res. Lett.* **91,** no. 4, 2010–2023.

Southern California Earthquake Data Center (SCEDC) (2013). Southern California earthquake data center [Data set], doi: 10.7909/C3WD3xH1.

Schiappapietra, E., and J. Douglas (2020). Modelling the spatial correlation of earthquake ground motion: Insights from the literature, data from the 2016–2017 Central Italy earthquake sequence and ground-motion simulations, *Earth Sci. Rev.* **203,** 103,139.

Shao, G., R. Wen, H. Wang, Y. Ren, and B. Zhou (2024). Spatial correlations in ground motion intensity measuring from the 2023 Türkiye earthquake, *Earthq. Res. Adv.* **4,** no. 1, 100,231.

Sokolov, V., F. Wenzel, K.-L. Wen, and W.-Y. Jean (2012). On the influence of site conditions and earthquake magnitude on ground-motion within-earthquake correlation: Analysis of PGA data from TSMIP (Taiwan) network, *Bull. Earthq. Eng.* **10,** no. 5, 1401–1429.

Strasser, F. O., N. A. Abrahamson, and J. J. Bommer (2009). Sigma: Issues, insights, and challenges. *Seismol. Res. Lett.* **80,** no. 1, 40–56.

Strasser, F. O., J. J. Bommer, and N. A. Abrahamson (2008). Truncation of the distribution of ground-motion residuals, *J. Seismol.* **12,** no. 1, 79–105.

Sung, C., and C. Lee (2016). A new methodology for quantification of the systematic path effects on ground-motion variability, *Bull. Seismol. Soc. Am.* **106,** no. 6, 2796–2810.

Thompson, E., D. J. Wald, and C. Worden (2014). A VS30 map for California with geologic and topographic constraints, *Bull. Seismol. Soc. Am.* **104,** no. 5, 2313–2321.

Thompson, E. M. (2022). An updated Vs30 map for California with geologic and topographic constraints, *U.S. Geol. Surv.*

Thompson, E. M., M. Hearne, B. T. Aagaard, J. M. Rekoske, C. B. Worden, M. P. Moschetti, H. E. Hunsinger, G. C. Ferragut, G. A. Parker, J. A. Smith, *et al.* (2024a). Automated, near real-time ground-motion processing at the U.S. Geological Survey, *Seismol. Res. Lett.* **96,** no. 1, 538–553.

Thompson, E. M., M. Hearne, B. T. Aagaard, J. M. Rekoske, C. B. Worden, M. P. Moschetti, H. E. Hunsinger, G. C. Ferragut, G. A. Parker, J. A. Smith, *et al.* (2024b). USGS automated ground motion processing Software Version 2, *U.S. Geol. Surv. Software Release*, doi: 10.5066/P13HMKFJ.

Thompson, E. M., and C. B. Worden (2018). Estimating rupture distances without a rupture, *Bull. Seismol. Soc. Am.* **108,** no. 1, 371–379.

UNAVCO (2004). Plate boundary observatory borehole seismic network (PBO), available at https://www.fdsn.org/networks/detail/PB/ (last accessed September 2025).

University of California, Berkeley (1980). Berkeley Digital Seismograph Network (BDSN) [Data set], Northern California Earthquake Data Center, doi: 10.7932/BDSN

University of Nevada, Reno (1971). Nevada seismic network [Data set], International Federation of Digital Seismograph Networks, doi: 10.7914/SN/NN.

University of Nevada, Reno (1992). Southern Great Basin Network [Data set], International Federation of Digital Seismograph Networks, doi: 10.7914/SN/SN.

U.S. Geological Survey (1931). United States National strong-motion network [Data set], International Federation of Digital Seismograph Networks, doi: 10.7914/SN/NP.

U.S. Geological Survey, Earthquake Hazards Program (2025). Advanced National Seismic System (ANSS) Comprehensive Catalog of Earthquake Events and Products: Various, doi: 10.5066/F7MS3QZH.

USGS and California Geological Survey (2025). Digital database of quaternary and younger faults, available at https://www.usgs.gov/natural-hazards/earthquake-hazards/faults (last accessed September 2025).

Wen, P., B. Zhou, and G. Shao (2024). A new spatial variation model for ground-motion intensities combined with correlation and coherency, *Seismol. Res. Lett.* **95,** no. 4, 2239–2250.

Wesson, R. L., and D. M. Perkins (2001). Spatial correlation of probabilistic earthquake ground motion and loss, *Bull. Seismol. Soc. Am.* **91,** no. 6, 1498–1515.

Wills, C., C. Gutierrez, F. Perez, and D. Branum (2015). A next generation VS30 map for California based on geology and topography, *Bull. Seismol. Soc. Am.* **105,** no. 6, 3083–3091.

Xu, X., D. Liu, and L. Lavier (2023). Constraining fault damage zone properties from geodesy: A case study near the 2019 Ridgecrest earthquake sequence, *Geophys. Res. Lett.* **50,** no. 5, e2022GL101692, doi: 10.1029/2022GL101692.

Zhou, Z., M. Bianco, P. Gerstoft, and K. Olsen (2022). High-resolution imaging of complex shallow fault zones along the July 2019 Ridgecrest ruptures, *Geophys. Res. Lett.* **49,** no. 1, e2021GL095024, doi: 10.1029/2021GL095024.

Manuscript received 1 July 2025
Published online 10 November 2025

A Nonergodic Ground-Motion Model for Türkiye

Chenying Liu[1], Jorge Macedo[*1], Norman Abrahamson[2], and Albert Kottke[3]

ABSTRACT

Existing ground-motion models (GMMs) for Türkiye have primarily relied on ergodic or partially nonergodic frameworks, which are limited in capturing systematic ground-motion characteristics and the trade-off between aleatory and epistemic uncertainties. This study uses a comprehensive Turkish database of over 35,000 shallow crustal ground-motion recordings spanning 1983–2023 to develop a fully nonergodic GMM that accounts for systematic source, site, and path effects. The backbone of the nonergodic model is a regionalized ergodic GMM developed as part of this study, which incorporates an event-specific attenuation term. The nonergodic systematic effects are modeled using Gaussian processes (GPs) based on the residuals of the ergodic backbone GMM. GP parameters are constrained through a variogram-based approach, which is shown to provide advantages compared to a direct GP fitting. Path effects are evaluated using cell-specific attenuation and spatially correlated GPs, accounting for variations in the quality factor and velocity structure. The evaluated source, site, and path terms exhibit different spatial patterns and correlation lengths across spectral periods. Potential factors influencing the patterns are discussed. In particular, we find that the correlation lengths of kappa and the site term at short periods are comparable, suggesting dominating kappa effects at short periods. In addition, we observe parallels between the estimated path effects and available quality factor maps for Türkiye. The spatial distribution of short-period source effects and regional stress drop in western Türkiye also share similarities. The developed nonergodic model reduces aleatory variability by 35%–50% depending on the spectral period. This reduction, once considered in the context of epistemic uncertainties, is key for seismic hazard quantification and performance-based earthquake engineering applications in Türkiye.

KEY POINTS

- A nonergodic ground-motion model for Turkiye that incorporates 3D velocity structure in path effects is developed.
- Incorporating 3D velocity structure is key to reducing aleatory variability in ground motion models
- Nonergodic-based systematic effects are discussed in terms of potential physical interpretations.

Supplemental Material

INTRODUCTION

Türkiye is located in one of the most seismically active regions in the world, mainly due to its proximity to several major fault systems, most notably the North Anatolian fault zone and the East Anatolian fault (EAF) (Emre *et al.*, 2018a). Türkiye's active seismicity underscores the need for adequate seismic hazard quantification, which is commonly conducted through probabilistic seismic hazard assessments (PSHA).

Ground-motion models (GMMs) are a key component of PSHA because they estimate ground-motion intensity measures (IMs) at a site based on the earthquake's magnitude, distance metrics, and local site conditions. Traditionally, GMMs have been developed using the ergodic assumption (Anderson and Brune, 1999), which aggregates global strong-motion data sets, combining data from different regions within the same tectonic environment to provide global estimates for the median IM and its standard deviation. The ergodic assumption results in a large aleatory variability because of the inherent simplifications in modeling physical effects. This large aleatory variability is particularly relevant when designing infrastructure with stringent safety requirements. As empirical data sets have grown, it has become evident that local differences in ground motion exist within specific regions, prompting a shift from ergodic to nonergodic approaches (Lavrentiadis *et al.*, 2022). Nonergodic models account for spatially varying systematic effects, such as local site conditions, source-site path characteristics, and regional

1. Georgia Institute of Technology, Atlanta, Georgia, U.S.A., https://orcid.org/0000-0001-5183-4265 (CL); https://orcid.org/0000-0002-0457-4824 (JM); 2. University of California, Berkeley, California, U.S.A., https://orcid.org/0000-0001-7900-6023 (NA); 3. Pacific Gas & Electric Company, San Francisco, California, U.S.A., https://orcid.org/0000-0002-1861-5682 (AK)

*Corresponding author: jorge.macedo@ce.gatech.edu

Cite this article as Liu, C., J. Macedo, N. Abrahamson, and A. Kottke (2025). A Nonergodic Ground-Motion Model for Türkiye, *Bull. Seismol. Soc. Am.* **116**, 482–497, doi: 10.1785/0120250142 source characteristics. In this context, they include more physical effects to achieve a more appropriate balance between epistemic uncertainty and aleatory variability. Over the last decade, many GMMs have incorporated region-specific adjustments (e.g., Next Generation Attenuation [NGA]-West2, Bozorgnia *et al.*, 2014; NGA-Subduction, Bozorgnia and Stewart, 2020) or have been regionalized using local data sets (e.g., Gülerce *et al.*, 2016). These partially nonergodic models, although still applying the ergodic assumption within a broad region, make adjustments for local differences in distance scaling, site amplification, and other factors. More recent efforts move beyond region-specific adjustments and have focused on incorporating site, source, and path repeatable effects that vary spatially (e.g., Lavrentiadis *et al.*, 2022; Macedo and Liu, 2022). These recent efforts have shown that nonergodic models provide a better balance between aleatory and epistemic uncertainties and more robust median estimates. This has direct implications for PSHA, which in turn affects the design ground motions used in the design of critical infrastructure.

Regarding previous studies in Türkiye, several efforts have been made in developing GMMs. For instance, Boore *et al.* (2014) developed an ergodic GMM using the NGA-West2 database (Bozorgnia *et al.*, 2014), with regional adjustment terms specific to Türkiye. Akkar and Çağnan (2010) developed a GMM based on a Turkish ground-motion database, noting differences in ground-motion scaling compared to global GMMs (NGA-West1 GMMs, Power *et al.*, 2008) at small magnitudes. Kale *et al.* (2015) developed a GMM using ground-motion data from Türkiye and Iran, finding that the scaling for these two countries differs from global GMMs. Sandıkkaya *et al.* (2023) developed simulation-based GMMs for western and eastern Türkiye, respectively, accounting for regional variations in stress drop, geometrical spreading, anelastic attenuation, and site amplification. These previous efforts have been focused on ergodic or partially ergodic GMMs that do not account for systematic site, source, and path effects. Önder (2022) investigated site, source, and path effects in Türkiye by analyzing the residuals of ergodic GMMs. However, their assessments were not in the context of nonergodic GMMs.

This study develops a nonergodic pseudospectral acceleration (PSA) GMM for Türkiye, utilizing a comprehensive database of over 35,000 ground-motion recordings spanning from 1983 to 2023. The model covers spectral periods from 0.02 to 5 s, and it is built upon an ergodic backbone model, which includes an event-specific attenuation term. Residuals from the backbone model are used to estimate nonergodic systematic source, site, and path effects. After presenting an overview of the ground-motion database, we describe the development of the ergodic GMM. We then detail the development of the nonergodic GMM, emphasizing the considerations used to constrain systematic effects. The constrained parameters provide insights into the variability and correlation lengths of systematic source, path, and site effects across different spectral periods. Finally, we quantify the reduction in standard deviation achieved through the nonergodic formulation.

DATABASE

The ground-motion database used in this study considers ground-motion recordings from 1983 to 2023. These recordings, along with associated event and station metadata, were sourced from the Türkiye Disaster and Emergency Management Authority (also abbreviated as AFAD). The ground-motion time histories were processed and the IMs calculated using the GMprocess tool (Thompson *et al.*, 2025), following the procedures established by the Pacific Earthquake Engineering Research Center (Ancheta *et al.*, 2012). For large-magnitude events (moment magnitude, $M_w > 6$), the earthquake metadata was based on case-by-case analysis conducted by Önder (2022) complemented by analyses in this study for the data after 2022. These analyses use available information from various agencies and scientific literature to estimate the rupture plane dimensions and source parameters, which are used to calculate distance metrics. The distance metrics for events with $M_w < 6$ were calculated by Önder (2022) using the Kaklamanos *et al.* (2011) guidelines. Moreover, source parameters, including magnitude, depth, and faulting style, for $M_w < 6$, were based on information compiled by AFAD for data after 2022.

Only events with M_w of at least 3.5, a maximum depth (Z_{tor}) of 30 km, and a minimum of five recordings within 200 km rupture distances (R_{rup}) were considered for developing GMMs. After selection, the final database included 37,438 recordings from 1397 shallow crustal earthquakes across 876 stations. For developing GMMs for PSA at different spectral periods (from 0.02 to 5 s), further selection was performed based on maximum usable frequencies (a function of high-pass filtering frequencies), following the recommendations of Abrahamson *et al.* (2014). Figure 1 shows the number of usable recordings as a function of spectral period, highlighting a significant decline for periods exceeding 1 s. This reduction is primarily attributed to the processing of ground-motion recordings.

Figure 2 illustrates the spatial distribution of earthquakes and strong-motion stations included in the database. The majority of recorded earthquakes are concentrated in the Aegean region and along the EAF. The spatial density of seismic stations varies across Türkiye, with notably high concentrations in the Marmara and Aegean regions, particularly following the 1999 earthquakes, and the EAF. Figure 3 presents the characteristics of the ground-motion database, revealing that ~80% of the events are small-magnitude earthquakes ($M_w < 5$), with a significant portion having magnitudes between 4 and 5. Furthermore, most ground-motion recordings have an R_{rup} between 10 and 200 km, and the V_{S30} (time-averaged shear-wave velocity in the top 30 m) for recording stations predominantly ranges from 280 to 760 m/s.

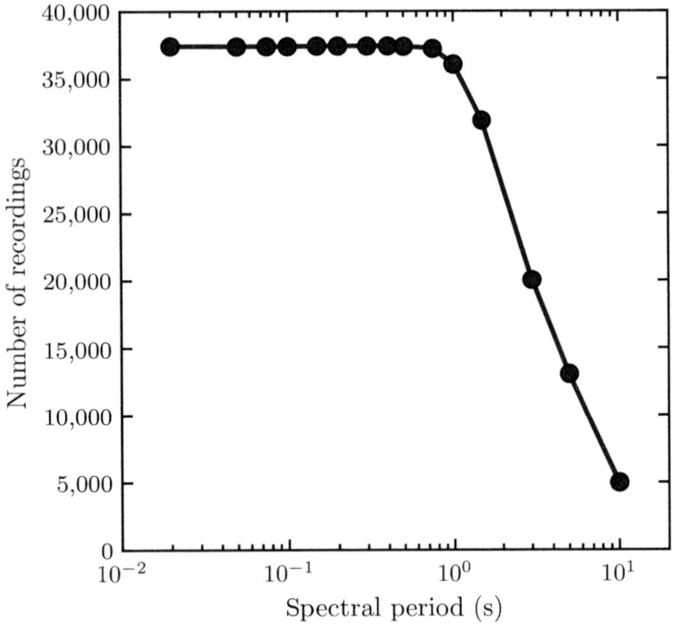

Figure 1. Number of recordings as a function of spectral period. The number of recordings starts to decrease beyond 1 s due to the applied high-pass filter. The color version of this figure is available only in the electronic edition.

DEVELOPMENT OF THE ERGODIC GMM

The functional form of an ergodic GMM is typically expressed as in the following equation:

$$\ln Y_{ij} = f_{\text{ergodic}}(M_w, R_{\text{rup}}, V_{S30}, Z_{\text{tor}}) + \delta B_i + \delta W_{ij}, \quad (1)$$

in which Y_{ij} represents the IM of interest (PSA in the context of this study) for the ith earthquake and jth station, f_{ergodic} constrains the average global IM scaling, often including terms for the magnitude (M_w) scaling, geometrical spreading, anelastic attenuation (e.g., in terms of the rupture distance, R_{rup}), site conditions (e.g., V_{S30}), and source-depth scaling (e.g., Z_{tor}). f_{ergodic} provides a median estimate for the IM of interest, and δB_i and δW_{ij} are the between-event and within-event residuals (often computed using random-effects regression), with zero means and standard deviations of τ and ϕ, respectively. δW_{ij} is further decomposed into δW_{ij}^1 and δW_{ij}^2 according to the following equation:

$$\delta B_i + \delta W_{ij} = \delta B_i + \delta W_{ij}^1 + \delta W_{ij}^2, \quad (2)$$

$$\delta W_{ij}^1 = k_i \frac{R_{\text{rup}}}{100}, \quad (3)$$

in which k_i is an event-specific anelastic attenuation coefficient. δW_{ij}^1 represents the event-specific (anelastic attenuation) path effects, and δW_{ij}^2 represents site and remaining path effects. $\frac{R_{\text{rup}}}{100}$ accommodates a comparable scale between k_i and δB_i. The motivation for using an event-specific k_i is to reduce potential trade-offs between path and source effects before the subsequent development of the nonergodic GMM. These terms can be estimated using mixed-effects regression in libraries such as lme4 (Bates *et al.*, 2007).

The ergodic GMM is developed based on the functional form of ASK14 GMM (Abrahamson *et al.*, 2014) as in the following equation:

$$f_{\text{ergodic}} = a_1 + f_m + a_{17} R_{\text{rup}} + a_{15} \min(Z_{\text{tor}}, 20)/20 + F_n f_n + F_{rv} f_{rv} + f_{\text{site}}, \quad (4)$$

in which Z_{tor} is the depth to the top of the rupture, F_n and F_{rv} are flags with values of 1 for normal- and reverse-fault mechanisms, respectively. f_m, f_{site}, f_{rv}, and f_n represent the magnitude, site amplification, and style of fault scaling as defined subsequently:

$$f_m = \begin{cases} a_5(M_w - M_1) + a_8(8.5 - M_w)^2 + (a_2 + a_3(M_w - M_1)) \ln R, & \text{if } M_w > M_1 \\ a_4(M_w - M_1) + a_8(8.5 - M_w)^2 + (a_2 + a_3(M_w - M_1)) \ln R, & \text{if } M_2 \le M_w \le M_1 \\ a_4(M_2 - M_1) + a_8(8.5 - M_2)^2 + a_6(M_w - M_2) + a_7(M_w - M_2)^2 + (a_2 + a_3(M_2 - M_1)) \ln R, & \text{if } M_w < M_2 \end{cases}, \quad (5)$$

$$R = \sqrt{R_{\text{rup}}^2 + c_4^2}, \quad (6)$$

$$c4 = \begin{cases} c_4, & \text{if } M_w > 5 \\ c_4 - (c_4 - 1)(5 - M), & \text{if } 4 \le M_w \le 5 \\ 1 & \text{if } M_w < 4 \end{cases}, \quad (7)$$

$$f_{\text{site}} = \begin{cases} (a_{10} + bn) \ln \frac{V_{S30}^*}{V_{\text{lin}}}, & \text{if } V_{S30} > V_{\text{lin}} \\ a_{10} \ln \frac{V_{S30}^*}{V_{\text{lin}}} - b \ln(\text{SA}_{1180} + c) + b \ln\left(\text{SA}_{1180} + c\left(\frac{V_{S30}^*}{V_{\text{lin}}}\right)^n\right), & \text{if } V_{S30} \le V_{\text{lin}} \end{cases}, \quad (8)$$

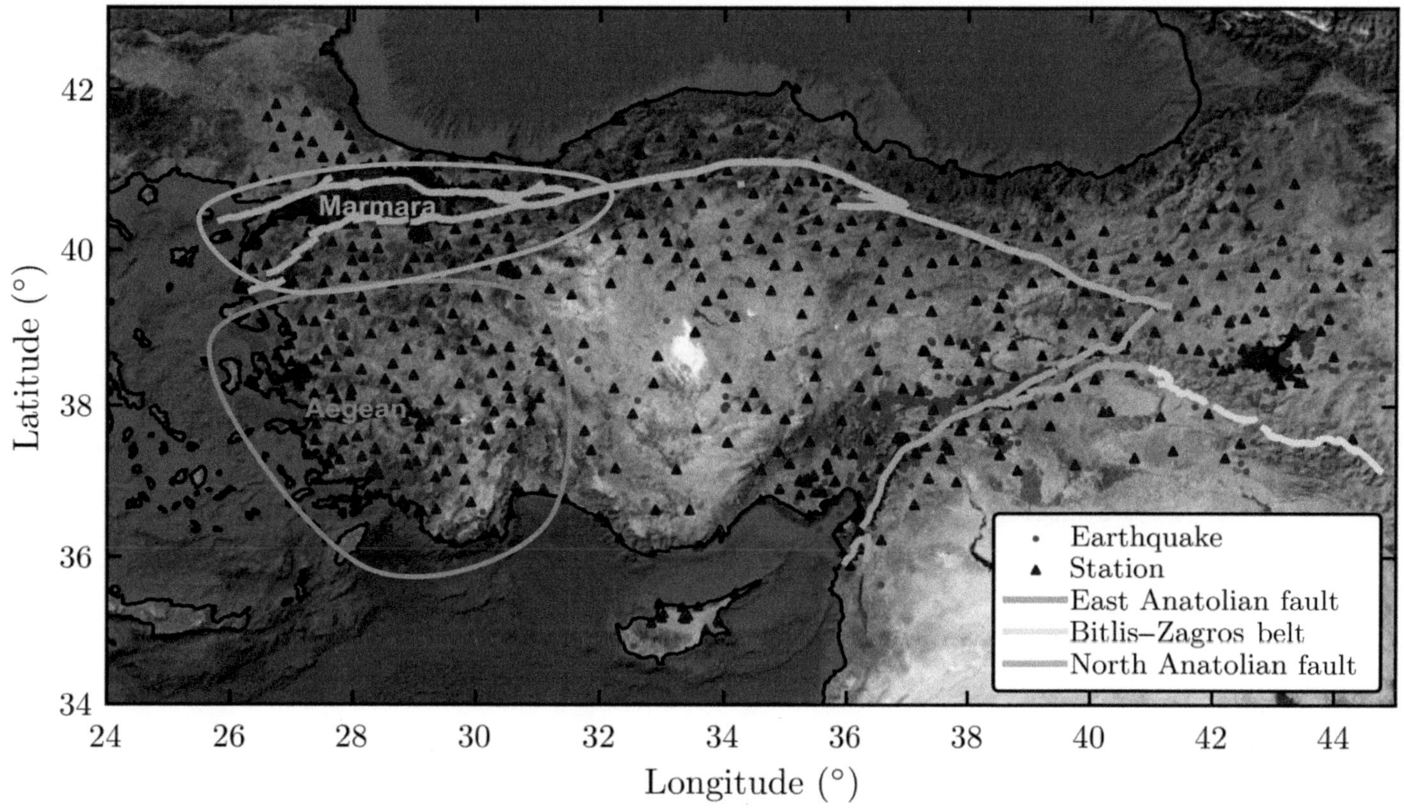

Figure 2. Spatial distribution of stations and earthquake epicenters in the Turkish ground-motion database. Major faults (Emre *et al.*, 2018b) in Türkiye are shown as line segments. The Marmara and Aegean regions are highlighted as regions with high density of seismic stations. The color version of this figure is available only in the electronic edition.

$$V^*_{S30} = \min(V_{S30}, V_1), \quad (9)$$

$$f_{rv} = \begin{cases} a_{11}, & \text{if } M_w > 5 \\ a_{11}(M_w - 4), & \text{if } 4 \le M_w \le 5, \\ 0 & \text{if } M_w < 4 \end{cases} \quad (10)$$

$$f_n = \begin{cases} a_{12}, & \text{if } M_w > 5 \\ a_{12}(M_w - 4), & \text{if } 4 \le M_w \le 5, \\ 0 & \text{if } M_w < 4 \end{cases} \quad (11)$$

in which a_1 to a_{15} are coefficients of the GMM to be estimated, c_4 is the fictitious depth, SA_{1180} is the spectral acceleration at $V_{S30} = 1180$ m/s, and V_{lin} is the V_{S30} threshold that distinguishes nonlinear and linear site response. b, n, and c are coefficients that are derived from numerical site-response analyses. An initial evaluation of the ASK14 GMM using the Turkish ground-motion database reveals a different magnitude (M_w) scaling for small magnitudes, as well as distinct scaling with respect to the depth to the top of rupture (Z_{tor}). To account for these regional differences, we re-estimated the coefficients a_{15}, a_4, and a_6, while retaining the remaining coefficients from the original ASK14 model. We do not modify the large-magnitude scaling or geometric spreading term due to the limited data available at these ranges. The regionalized model preserves the physical constraints and scaling behavior of the ASK14 model for large magnitudes and short distances, while incorporating region-specific modifications for small-magnitude and Z_{tor} scaling, as indicated in the later residuals plots.

Figure 4 shows the residuals of the developed ergodic GMMs. For brevity, we present only the residuals for spectral acceleration (denoted as SA) at 0.02 and 1 s because the residuals for other periods exhibit similar patterns. No apparent trends are observed in the residuals, which is considered satisfactory. The residual plots for other spectral periods and the ergodic GMM coefficients are included in the appendix, available in the supplemental material to this article.

DEVELOPMENT OF THE NONERGODIC GMM

Model functional form

Consistent with Abrahamson *et al.* (2019) and Lavrentiadis *et al.* (2022), the functional form of the nonergodic GMM consists of an ergodic base GMM (equations 1–11) and several adjustment terms to capture repeatable and systematic effects:

$$\ln Y_{ij} = f_{\text{ergodic}} + \delta S2S(x_s) + \delta L2L(x_e) + \delta P2P(x_{cls}, x_s) + \delta B_i^0 + \delta WS_{ij}^0. \quad (12)$$

In equation (12), $\delta S2S(x_s)$, $\delta L2L(x_e)$, and $\delta P2P(x_{cls}, x_s)$ represent the systematic site, source, and path effects that are

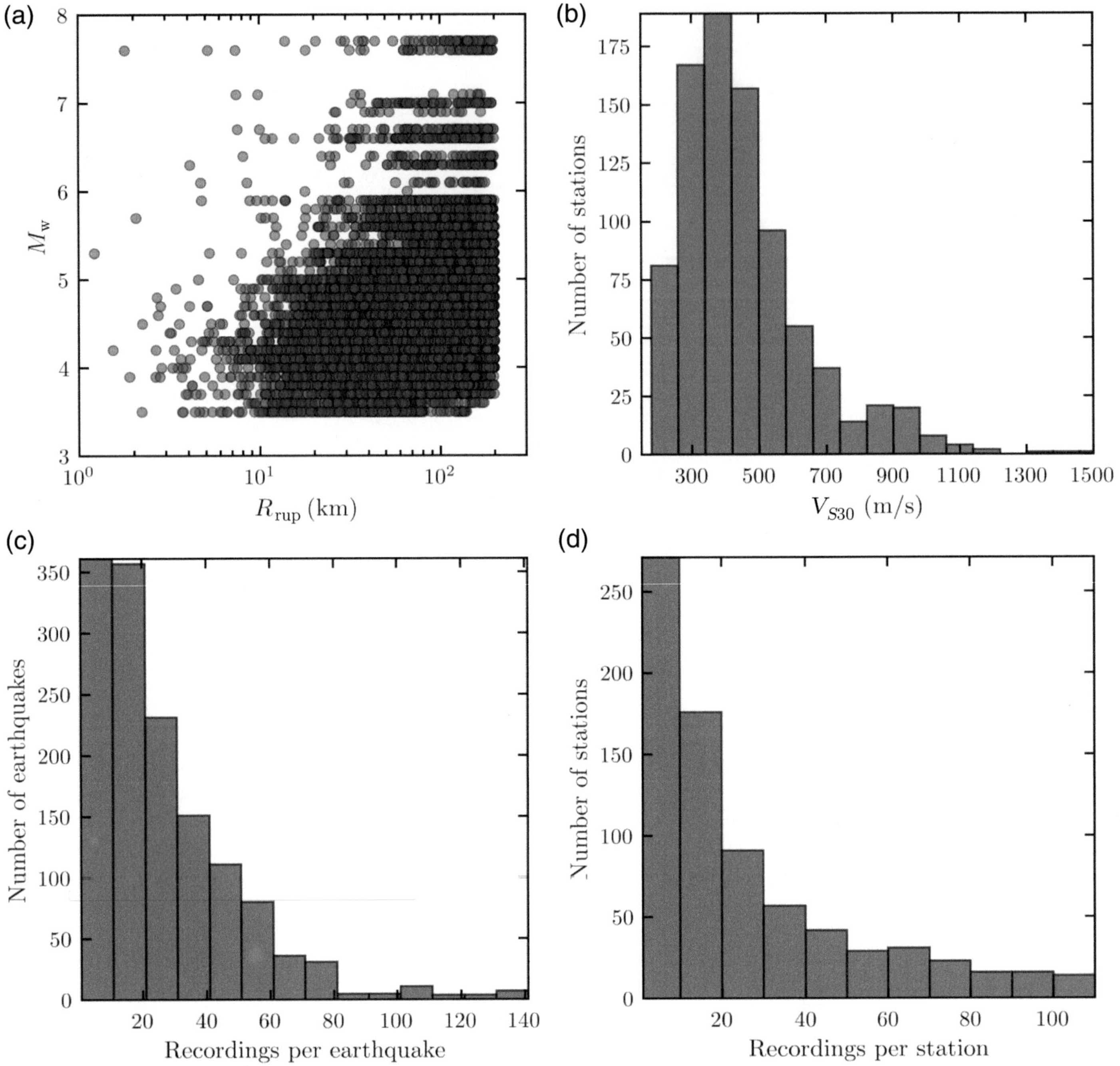

Figure 3. Characteristics of the ground-motion database utilized in this study. (a) Magnitude–distance distribution. (b) Histogram of V_{S30} values. (c) Number of recordings per earthquake. (d) Number of recordings per station. The color version of this figure is available only in the electronic edition.

not captured by the ergodic base GMM, which have standard deviations of ϕ_{S2S}, τ_{L2L}, and ϕ_{P2P}, respectively. These effects are location dependent and modeled as functions of x_s, x_e, and x_{cls}, which are the coordinates of the site, the earthquake epicenter, and the closest point on the rupture to the site, respectively. δB_i^0 and δWS_{ij}^0 represent the aleatory between-event and within-event residuals of the nonergodic GMM with standard deviations of τ^0 and ϕ^0, respectively. Following the approach in Kuehn and Abrahamson (2020) and Abrahamson *et al.* (2019), we model systematic source and site effects as Gaussian processes (GPs):

$$\delta L2L(x_e) \sim \mathrm{GP}(0,k(x_e,x_e')), \tag{13}$$

$$\delta S2S(x_s) = \delta a(x_s) + \delta b(x_s), \tag{14}$$

$$\delta a(x_s) \sim \mathrm{GP}(0,k(x_s,x_s')). \tag{15}$$

As discussed by Lavrentiadis *et al.* (2022, 2023), the site term $\delta S2S(x_s)$ is broken into an underlying continuous and spatially

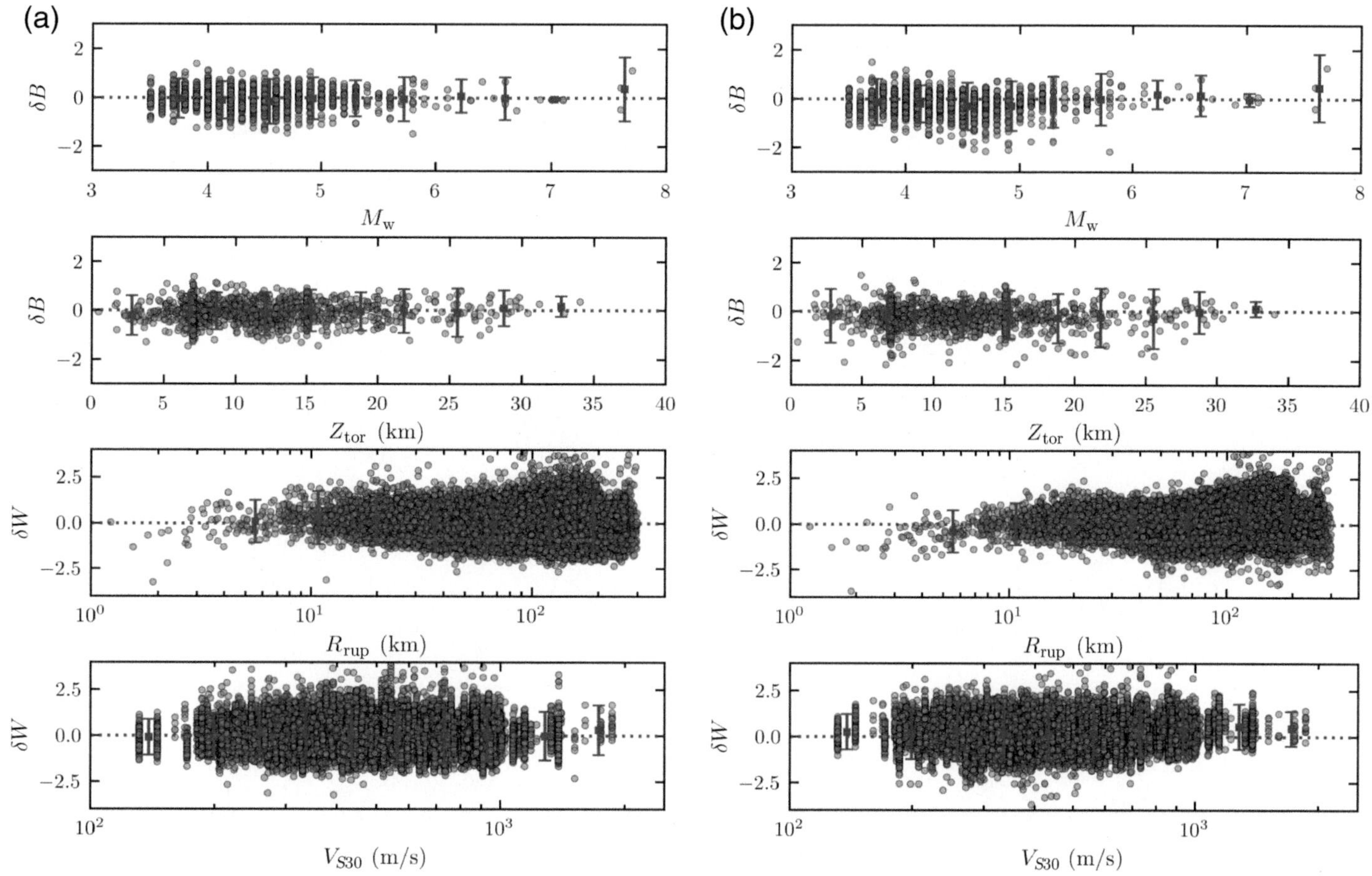

Figure 4. Residuals of the developed ergodic ground-motion model (GMM) for Türkiye for (a) SA (0.02 s) and (b) SA (1 s). ("SA" stands for spectral acceleration). The black circles represent the residuals, and the red bars represent ±2 standard deviation. The color version of this figure is available only in the electronic edition.

correlated adjustment (i.e., $\delta a(x_s)$ with a relatively long correlation length) and a remaining (spatially uncorrelated) site-specific adjustment (i.e., $\delta b(x_s)$ with a very short correlation length). $k(x,x')$ is a covariance function that estimates the correlation between locations x and x', as shown in the following equation:

$$k(x,x') = \theta^2 \exp\left(-\frac{||x - x'||}{\rho}\right), \quad (16)$$

in which θ and ρ are the hyperparameters (i.e., scale and correlation length) of the Gaussian process kernel functions. x and x' are the corresponding coordinates of two earthquakes (equation 13) or two sites (equation 15). Hence, the kernel functions imply that the correlation of ground-motion recordings at two locations (x and x') weakens because the distance between them increases. By assuming $\rho = 0$ (consistent with Lavrentiadis *et al.*, 2022, 2023), $\delta b(x_s)$ can be estimated by subtracting $\delta a(x_s)$ from $\delta S2S$.

The path effects $\delta P2P$ can be further separated into a component related to the variation of the Q (quality factor) structure ($\delta P2P_Q$) and a component related to the variation of the 3D velocity structure ($\delta P2P_V$),

$$\delta P2P(x_{\text{cls}},x_s) = \delta P2P_Q(x_{\text{cls}},x_s) + \delta P2P_V(x_{\text{cls}},x_s), \quad (17)$$

$\delta P2P_Q$ represents the Q spatial variability, which is particularly noticeable in short-period SA at long distances (Sung *et al.*, 2023; Liu *et al.*, 2025). In contrast, $\delta P2P_V$ represents the spatial variability of 3D velocity structure (Sung *et al.*, 2023; Liu *et al.*, 2024a).

The prevalent method for modeling $\delta P2P_Q$ is the cell-specific attenuation approach proposed by Dawood and Rodriguez-Marek (2013) and used in recent efforts (e.g., Abrahamson *et al.*, 2019; Liu *et al.*, 2022; Lavrentiadis *et al.*, 2023). In this methodology, the study region is discretized into rectangular cells, each assigned an attenuation coefficient. For every recording within the data set, the length of the ray path that traverses each cell is computed. The nonergodic path effect is then determined as the cumulative sum of the products of the length of the ray in each cell and the corresponding attenuation coefficient,

$$\delta P2P_Q(x_{\text{cls}},x_s) = -a_{17} R_{\text{rup}} + \sum_{i=1}^{n_{\text{cell}}} c_i R_i, \quad (18)$$

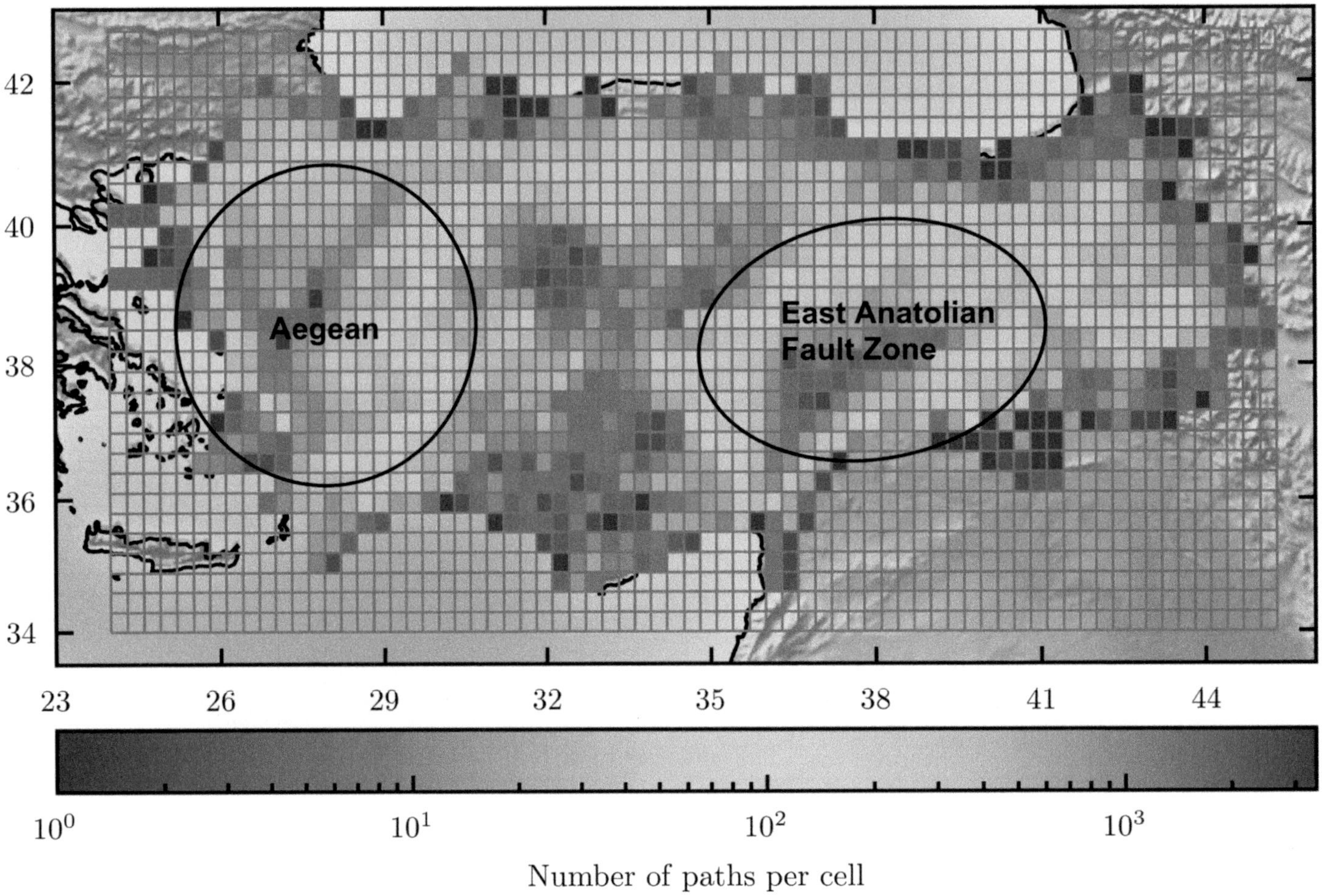

Figure 5. Illustration of the cell-specific attenuation approach. The Turkish territory is divided into multiple cells, and the number of paths within each cell (for pseudospectral acceleration, PSA (0.02 s)) is shown. The color version of this figure is available only in the electronic edition.

in which c_i represents the attenuation coefficient at cell i, R_i (in units of km) is the fraction of the path within that cell, and n_{cell} is the total number of cells in the grid. The term $-a_{17}R_{\text{rup}}$ removes the anelastic attenuation term in the ergodic GMM as the cell-specific attenuation already accounts for it. The Turkish territory is divided into a grid with 30 km by 30 km cells to implement the cell-specific approach. We use the efficient clipping algorithm proposed in Liu *et al.* (2022) to estimate R_i. Figure 5 shows the number of paths within each cell. Consistent with the density of the strong-motion network and epicenter locations in Figure 2, the number of paths is significant in the Aegean region and along the EAF zone.

The $\delta P2P_V$ term is estimated using the spatial correlation model proposed by Lacour *et al.* (2025), which is a physically constrained and computationally robust GP model. In this model, a ray path is conceptualized as a vector defined by its origin, direction, and length. Specifically, the origin is modeled as the site location, the direction as the azimuthal angle, and the length as the site-source rupture distance. The mathematical form of their model is presented subsequently:

$$k((x_{\text{cls}},x_s),(x'_{\text{cls}},x_s)) = \theta^2 \exp\left(-\frac{SS'}{\rho_S}\right)\exp\left(-\frac{\Delta_\theta}{\rho_\theta}\right)\exp\left(-\frac{\Delta R_{\text{rup}}}{\rho_R}\right), \quad (19)$$

in which SS' is the distance between two stations (x_s and x'_s), $\Delta\theta$ is the difference between the azimuthal angles (in degrees) of two paths, and ΔR_{rup} is the difference between the rupture distances of two paths. θ, ρ_S, ρ_θ, and ρ_R are the parameters of the kernel function. The kernel function is based on the principle that the correlation of two paths decreases as SS', $\Delta\theta$, and ΔR_{rup} of two paths increase. More details of the correlation model can be found in Lacour *et al.* (2025) and Liu *et al.* (2025).

Parameter estimation

The systematic source, site, and path effects are estimated from the residuals of the ergodic GMM (i.e., δB, δW^1, and δW^2). More specifically, $\delta L2L$ is first estimated by fitting equation (13) to δB. Then, $\delta S2S$ is estimated from δW^2, and the difference $\delta W^2 - \delta S2S$ is calculated. Finally, $\delta P2P_Q$ is estimated from $\delta W^1 + \delta W^2 - \delta S2S$, following which $\delta P2P_V$ is then estimated. These steps are consistent with the recommendations from Liu

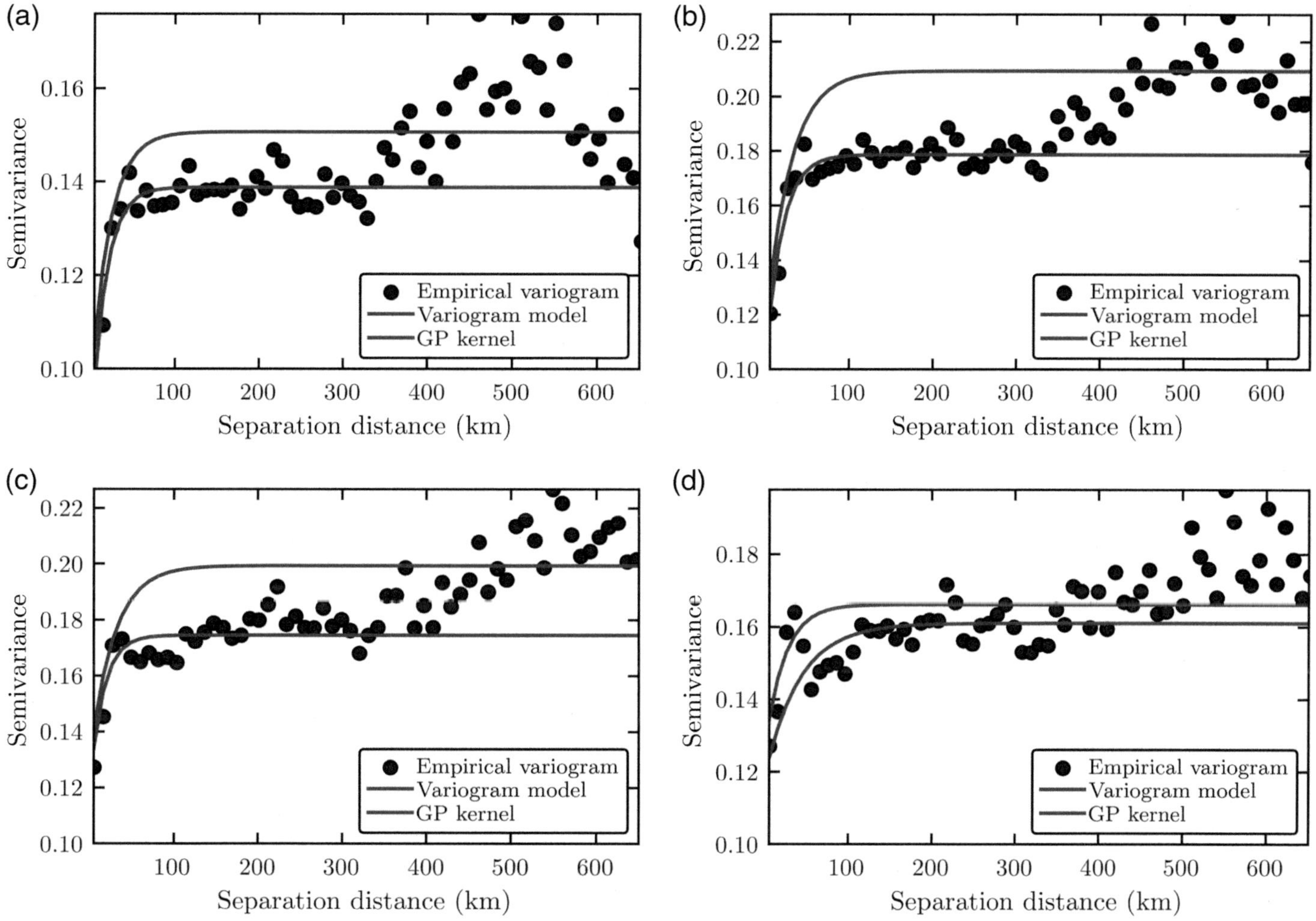

Figure 6. Comparison of Gaussian process (GP) kernel fitting and variogram model fitting for modeling the spatial correlation of $\delta S2S$ for different spectral periods. (a) SA (0.05 s). (b) SA (0.1 s). (c) SA (0.2 s). (d) SA (0.3 s). The color version of this figure is available only in the electronic edition.

et al. (2024b), Kuehn and Abrahamson (2020), and Abrahamson *et al.* (2019) to develop nonergodic GMMs.

The estimation of kernel parameters in GPs is typically performed by maximizing the marginal likelihood of a multivariate Gaussian distribution, as seen in standard packages like GPflow (Matthews *et al.*, 2017) or GPyTorch (Gardner *et al.*, 2018). However, this data-driven approach has limitations. Specifically, directly fitting a GP requires constructing a covariance matrix that accounts for data pairs across all separation distances. A single GP kernel, as described in equation (15), may not adequately capture such correlation structures, particularly when considering point pairs with large separation distances. An alternative method for estimating parameters in a GP involves using a variogram model. In this method, a variogram model is fitted to an empirical semivariogram to constrain the corresponding parameters of a GP kernel. An advantage of fitting a variogram model rather than directly fitting a GP is that variogram models allow for estimation using only a subset of the data. This prevents the estimated parameters from being overly influenced by the data at large separation distances. For example, Figure 6 illustrates the empirical semivariogram used to estimate $\delta S2S$ at four different spectral periods, along with the fitted GP kernel and variogram model. The variogram model is fitted to the semivariogram using separation distances of up to 300 km, whereas the GP kernel is fitted to the entire data set (residuals) by maximizing the marginal likelihood. It is observed that the GP kernel is shifted upward compared to the variogram model because it attempts to account for fluctuations in the empirical semivariogram at large separation distances (>300 km). However, in this case, a single GP kernel fails to capture the complex shape of the empirical semivariogram across the full range of separation distances, leading to significant differences in the estimated spatial correlation parameters. The intricate pattern of the empirical variogram at large distances (>300 km) suggests the need for more sophisticated GP kernels or variogram models to accurately represent the spatial correlation structure. For practical applications, the estimation of nonergodic systematic effects at new locations primarily depends on nearby recordings (<200 km). Therefore, fitting a variogram model to a selected subset with limited separation

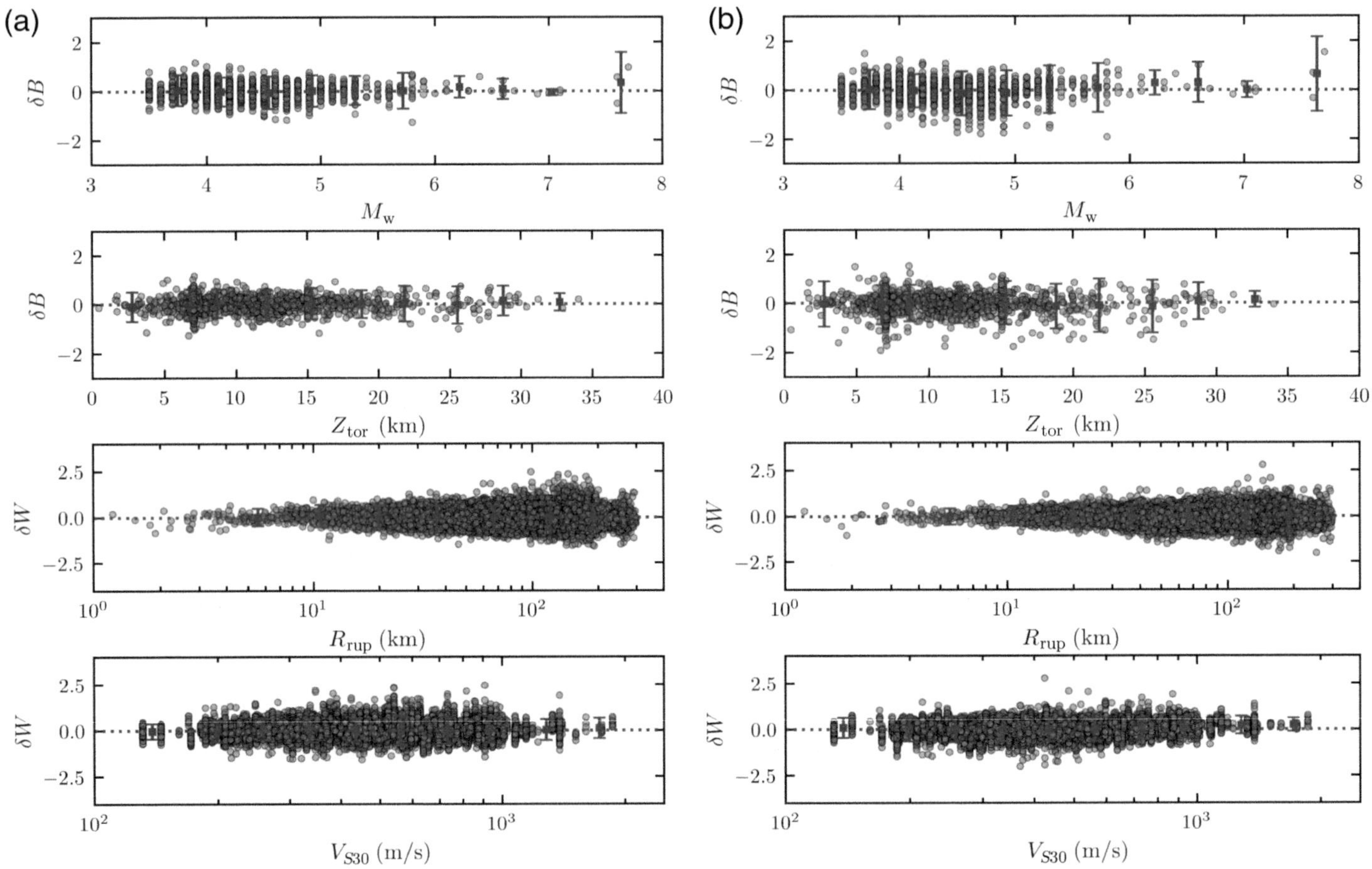

Figure 7. Residuals of the developed nonergodic GMM for Türkiye for (a) SA (0.02 s) and (b) SA (1 s). ("SA" stands for spectral acceleration). The black circles represent the residuals, and the red bars represent ±2 standard deviation. The color version of this figure is available only in the electronic edition.

distances is considered more appropriate than directly fitting a GP to the entire data set.

We employ Bayesian regression and variogram models to estimate the parameters in the GP and cell-specific attenuation terms for all spectral periods (0.02–5 s) considered in the development of the nonergodic GMM. The use of Bayesian regression offers the advantage of incorporating physical constraints on the parameters of the nonergodic GMM. For example, the cell-specific attenuation coefficient c_i must be negative for all cells. This constraint is incorporated by specifying a prior distribution over c_i within the Bayesian framework. Interested readers can find more detailed information on Bayesian regression in Gelman *et al.* (1995). Figure 7 displays the residuals of the nonergodic GMMs for SA (0.02 s) and SA (1 s) against M_w, R_{rup}, Z_{tor}, and V_{S30}. Residuals for other periods exhibit similar patterns and are presented in the supplemental appendix. The nonergodic GMM residuals show reduced variability compared to those from the ergodic GMMs (see Fig. 4). In particular, the residual dispersion across all distances (R_{rup}) is significantly reduced by accounting for path effects associated with the quality factor and 3D velocity structure.

INSIGHTS FROM THE DEVELOPED NONERGODIC GMM AND DISCUSSIONS

Systematic source, path, and site effects

This section presents insights gained from the developed nonergodic GMM, with a focus on the spatial variation of estimated source, site, and path effects. Results are shown for SA (0.02 s) and SA (1 s) as representative short- and long-period SAs. Other periods are omitted for brevity because they exhibit similar spatial patterns and trends.

Figure 8a,b presents the mean values of the estimated source effects ($\delta L2L$) for SA (0.02 s) and SA (1 s), respectively. Figure 8c,d shows the corresponding epistemic standard deviations. A clear spatial pattern is observed: in regions without ground-motion recordings, the source effects exhibit zero means and large standard deviations, consistent with the lack of data to constrain the source effects. In contrast, regions with ground-motion recordings show nonzero means and reduced standard deviations. In addition, the spatial variation of source effects differs between the two periods. This variation is attributed to different source parameters influencing source effects depending on the spectral period. For short-period PSA, the source effects are primarily controlled by stress drop, which influences corner frequencies of source spectra and, consequently, high-frequency ground motion. In contrast, for long-period PSA, variations in source effects are more likely governed by the overall rupture process and fault geometry, rather than specific stress release

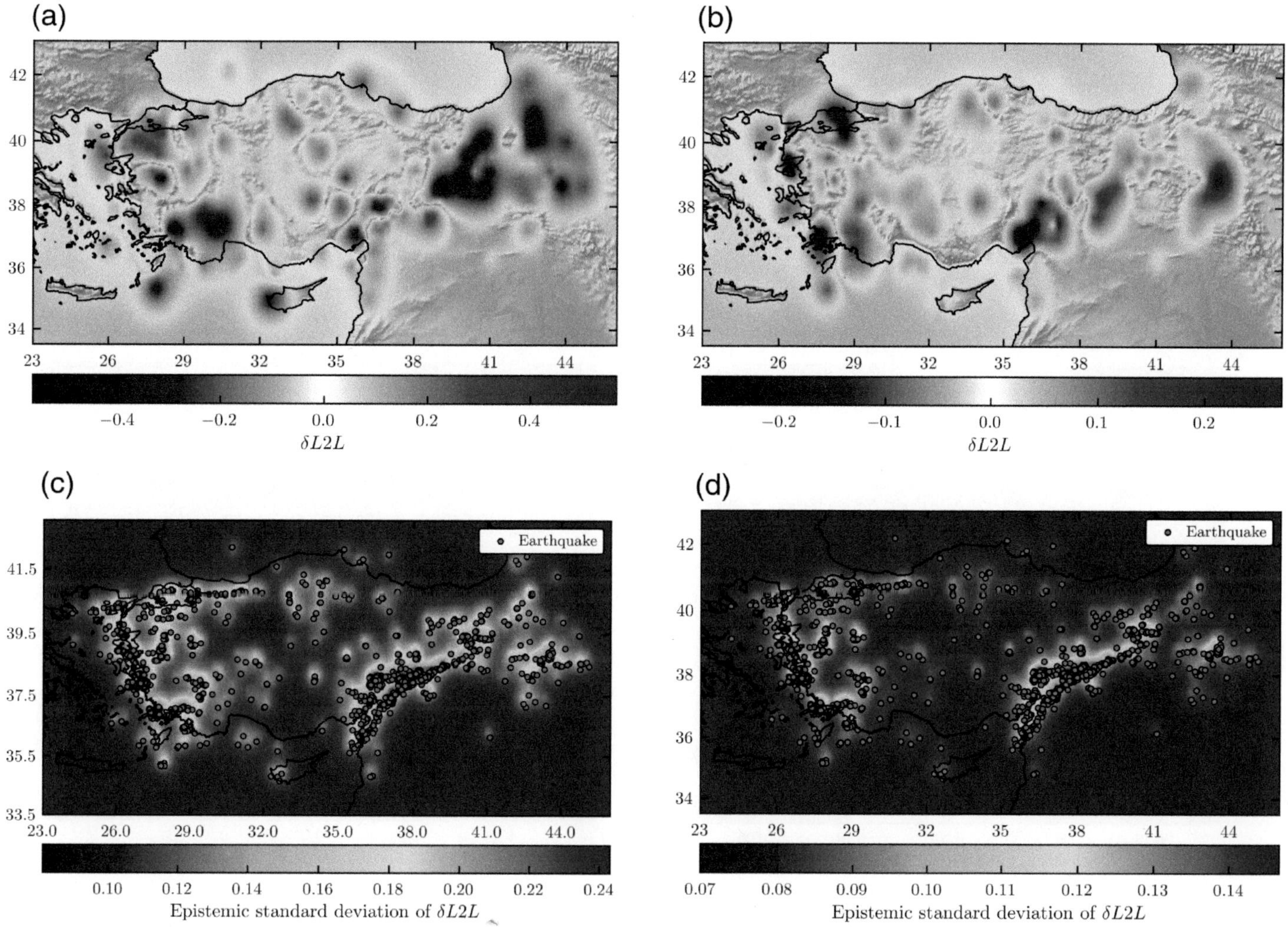

Figure 8. Systematic source effects estimated from the nonergodic GMM. (a,b) Mean values of $\delta L2L$ for SA (0.02 s) and SA (1 s), respectively. (c,d) Epistemic standard deviation of $\delta L2L$ for SA (0.02 s) and SA (1 s), respectively. The color version of this figure is available only in the electronic edition.

characteristics, as also noted in previous studies (Parker *et al.*, 2020; Bindi *et al.*, 2021; Brunelli *et al.*, 2023). Furthermore, in terms of variations in western Türkiye, the differences in the source terms for the Marmara and Aegean regions in Figure 8a are also consistent with the different stress drops highlighted for these regions by Sandıkkaya *et al.* (2023).

Similar plots for site effects (δa) are shown in Figure 9 for SA (0.02 s) and SA (1 s). As with the source effects, site effects exhibit zero means and large standard deviations in regions without recordings, whereas regions with ground-motion recordings show nonzero mean values and reduced standard deviations. The spatial variation in site effects differs across periods, which can be attributed to the influence of different factors. For instance, at short periods, site effects are expected to be influenced by kappa (κ), which reflects the spatial variation of near-surface geology (Cabas *et al.*, 2017). In contrast, for long-period PSA, site effects are likely influenced by deeper geological structures, such as deep basin structures, sediment thickness, and impedance contrast between deep bedrock and overlying sediments (Liu *et al.*, 2022). This leads to different spatial variation patterns for different PSAs.

We further investigate the role of κ by computing $T_{\mathrm{amp1.5}}$, a proxy for κ (Carlton and Abrahamson, 2014), defined as the period at which the response spectrum exceeds 1.5 times the peak ground acceleration. Figure 10a presents the $T_{\mathrm{amp1.5}}$ histogram for the Turkish ground-motion database. We use the estimated values to develop a GMM for $T_{\mathrm{amp1.5}}$. After evaluating several options, we adopt $\ln T_{\mathrm{amp1.5}} = -3.78 + 0.21M_{\mathrm{w}}$, which shows no residual trends (residuals are provided in the supplemental appendix). We fit a variogram to the station-averaged residuals, as shown in Figure 10b, and estimate a correlation length of 30 km. This value aligns with the 29–35 km correlation length of PSA site effects in the 0.02–0.1 s period range, reinforcing the concept that κ governs site-effect correlation at short periods for the developed nonergodic GMM.

Figure 11 presents the mean attenuation coefficients for each cell in the cell-specific attenuation approach for SA (0.02 s) and SA (1 s). Notably, the attenuation coefficients for SA (1 s) exhibit significantly less variation and are generally

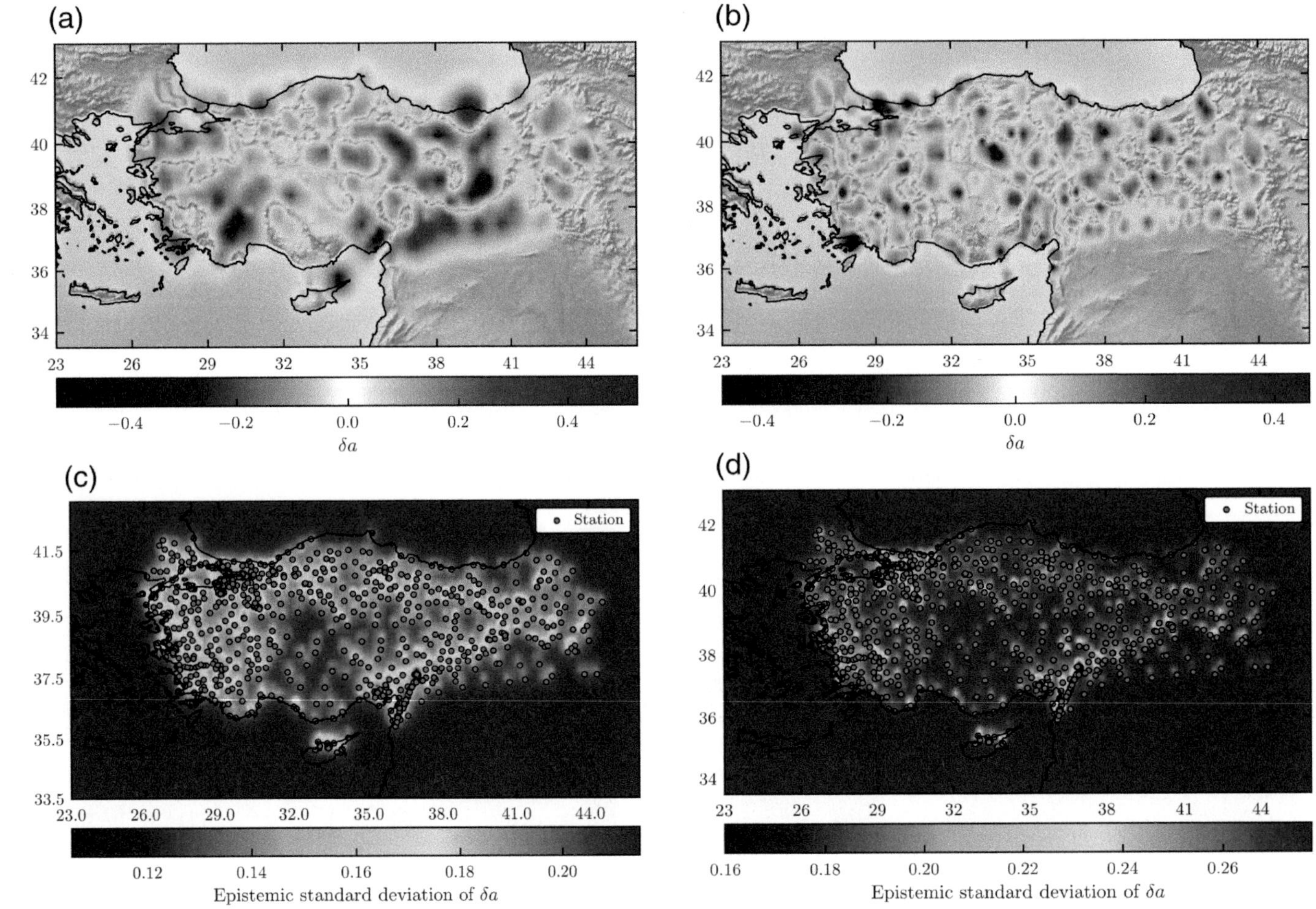

Figure 9. Systematic site effects estimated from the nonergodic GMM. (a,b) Mean values of δa for SA (0.02 s) and SA (1 s), respectively. (c,d) Epistemic standard deviation of δa for SA (0.02 s) and SA (1 s), respectively. The color version of this figure is available only in the electronic edition.

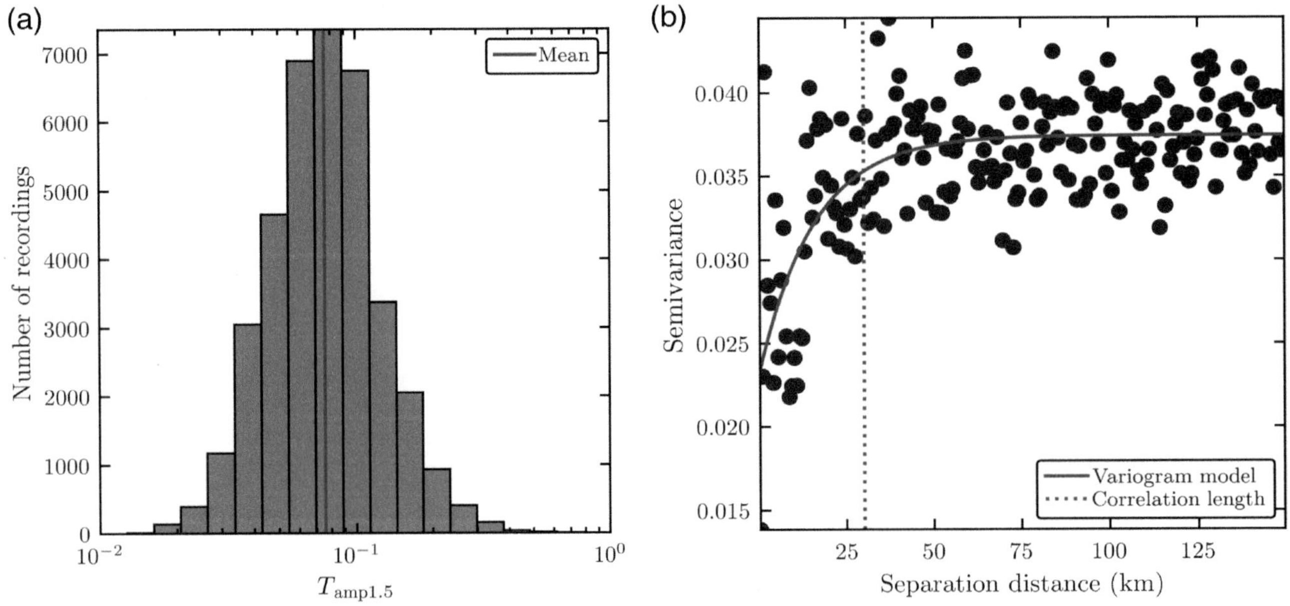

Figure 10. (a) Histogram of $T_{amp1.5}$ in the Turkish database. (b) Empirical variogram and fitted model for the residuals of the $T_{amp1.5}$ GMM. The color version of this figure is available only in the electronic edition.

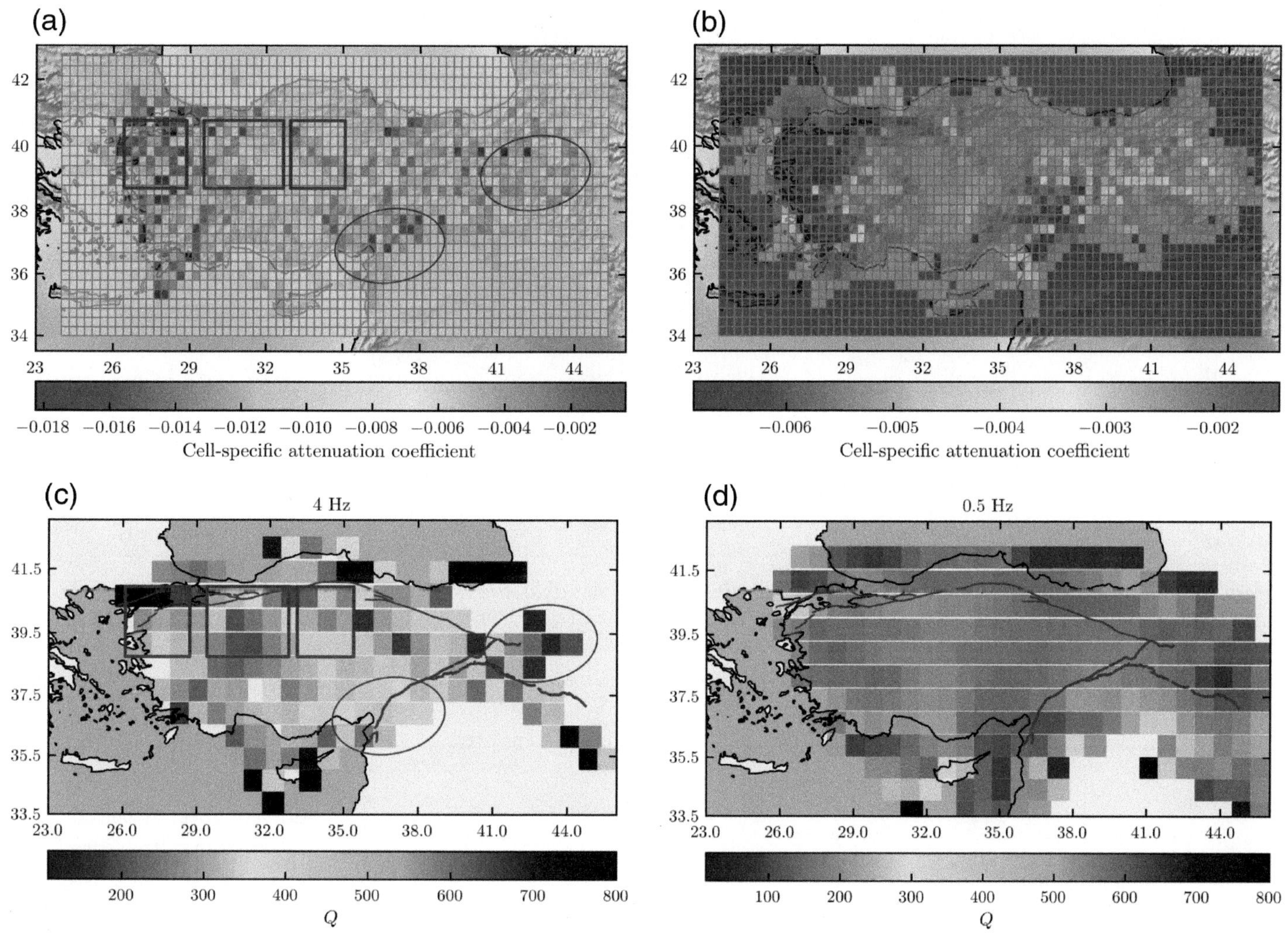

Figure 11. (a) Cell-specific attenuation coefficients for SA (0.02 s). (b) Cell-specific attenuation coefficients for SA (1 s). (c) Q of Türkiye considering a frequency of 4 Hz. (d) Q of Türkiye considering a frequency of 0.5 Hz (Q of Türkiye is taken from Kaviani *et al.*, 2022, and fault traces are marked as purple lines). The purple boxes and ellipses are used to facilitate the comparison of the spatial variation of cell coefficients between Figure 11a,c. The color version of this figure is available only in the electronic edition.

weaker in magnitude compared to SA (0.02 s). This is because anelastic attenuation (a_{17}) is weaker at longer periods than at shorter periods. Similar patterns are observed in the Q maps estimated by Kaviani *et al.* (2022) for Türkiye through tomographic inversions. For example, Figure 11c,d displays Q variations at frequencies of 4 and 0.5 Hz, as reported by Kaviani *et al.* (2022). The Q variation is notably greater at the higher frequency (4 Hz) than at the lower frequency (0.5 Hz), mirroring the greater variability seen in the SA (0.02 s) attenuation coefficients compared to SA (1 s). Because Q is correlated with geometrical spreading and is typically computed by assuming a fixed geometrical spreading rate (e.g., −1.0 or −0.5), the Q values do not need to match the cell-specific attenuation coefficients. However, some qualitative similarities can still be drawn. For instance, Q at 4 Hz decreases from around 500 to 200 and then increases to ~400 when moving from the western to the central part of Türkiye (denoted by purple rectangles). This trend is mirrored by a corresponding increase in the SA (0.02 s) cell coefficients (in absolute value), followed by a decrease (in absolute value) in the same regions. This trend is also consistent with the higher anelastic attenuation coefficients in the Aegean region compared to the Marmara region found by Sandıkkaya *et al.* (2023). Furthermore, along the EAF (denoted by purple ellipses), relatively high Q values (around 450–550) are observed in the western segment, whereas lower values (down to 250) appear in the eastern section. A similar qualitative pattern can be seen in the attenuation coefficients, with lower (absolute) values in the western portion of the fault transitioning to higher (absolute) values in the eastern section.

A region in southeast Türkiye with significant recordings and a site within this region are selected to illustrate the $\delta P2P_V$ spatial variation patterns. A grid of hypothetical earthquake locations (black grid in Fig. 12) is considered for estimating $\delta P2P_V$. Figure 12 illustrates the resulting spatial variation of $\delta P2P_V$ for SA (0.02 s). A notable feature is the circular $\delta P2P_V$ pattern that emerges around the evaluated site. This

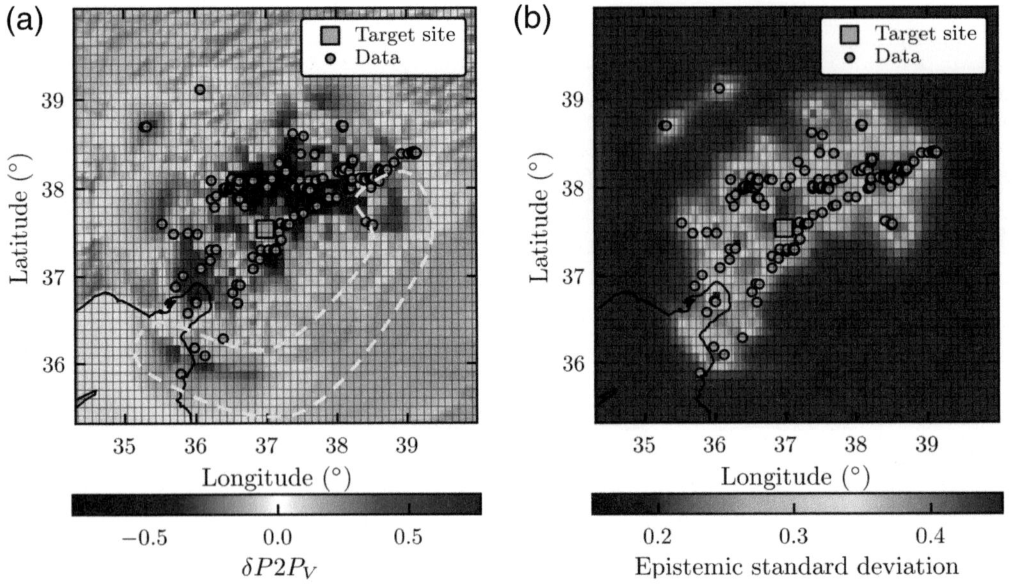

Figure 12. (a) Predicted mean $\delta P2P_V$. (b) Epistemic uncertainty of $\delta P2P_V$. The prediction is generated for a uniform grid of earthquake locations with respect to the target site. The yellow contour illustrates a region with transition of path effects. The color version of this figure is available only in the electronic edition.

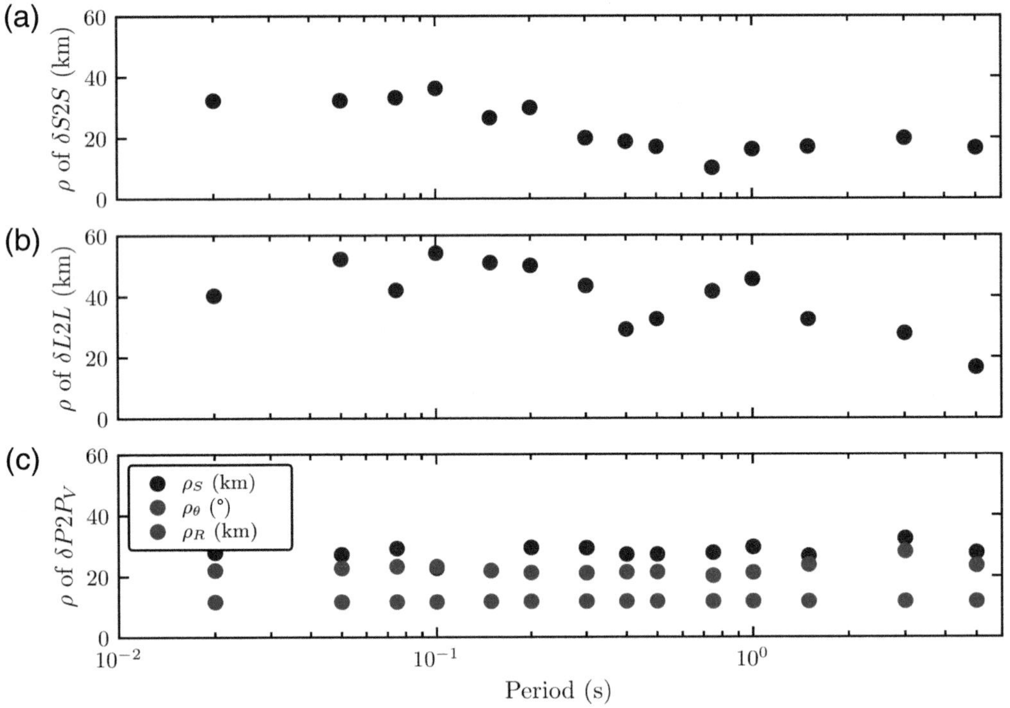

Figure 13. Comparison of correlation length of (a) site, (b) source, and (c) path effects. The blue, red, and green dots represent the correlation length of the three terms in equation (19). The color version of this figure is available only in the electronic edition.

is controlled by ρ_θ. This is illustrated in the lower-right part of Figure 12 (highlighted by the yellow contour), where the $\delta P2P_V$ spatial transition from positive to zero and then to negative values is controlled by the estimated $\rho_\theta = 11°$. For larger ρ_θ, the transition would be smoother, and the opposite would occur for smaller ρ_θ. Figure 12 also presents the estimated epistemic uncertainty, which is significantly lower in regions where data exist, an observation consistent with previous discussions.

Correlation lengths and standard deviation

Figure 13 presents the estimated spatial correlation lengths of the systematic site, source, and path effects across different spectral periods. It is observed that the correlation length of site effects is greater at short periods than at longer periods. The longer spatial correlation length of short-period site effects is likely due to a smooth regional variation of near-surface damping (i.e., κ), whereas long-period motions are influenced by deeper crustal structures that may introduce transitions over shorter distances due to changes in geology. A similar pattern is observed for source effects, where short-period motions exhibit longer correlation lengths. This could be linked to the role of stress drop at short periods, a parameter that is often spatially coherent within a given tectonic regime, as also highlighted by Sandıkkaya *et al.* (2023) for the Marmara, Aegean, and eastern Türkiye regions. Conversely, long-period source effects are influenced by more complex and variable characteristics of the rupture process, such as fault geometry, rupture extent, slip

pattern arises due to the incorporation of the azimuthal angle into the $\delta P2P_V$ GP kernel function, which enhances its ability to reflect the anisotropic nature of seismic wave propagation for different directions. The extrapolation of the $\delta P2P_V$ model

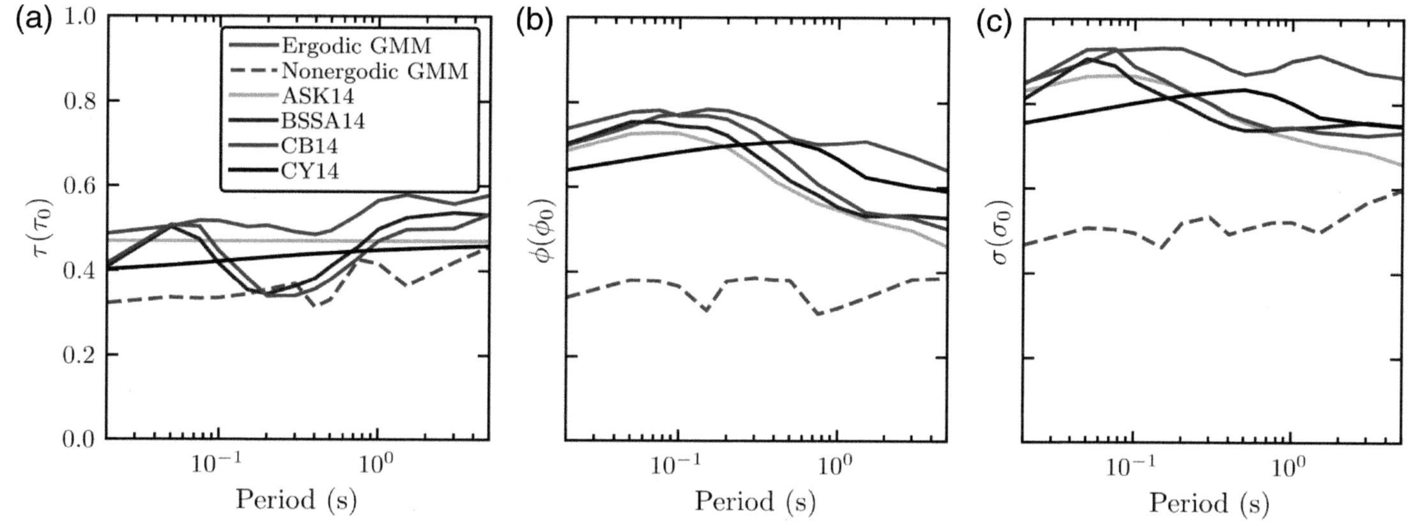

Figure 14. Comparison of standard deviations of the ergodic and nonergodic GMMs developed in this study with the Next Generation Attenuation (NGA)-West2 GMMs (a: τ; b: ϕ; c: σ). The color version of this figure is available only in the electronic edition.

distribution, and directivity. These features can vary significantly across events, even within the same region, resulting in shorter spatial correlation lengths. For $\delta P2P_V$ path effects, the correlation length remains relatively consistent across periods. This may reflect the influence of large-scale crustal velocity structures along typical ray paths. Alternatively, it may indicate limitations in the spatial resolution of the data set, which may not be sufficient to capture the finer-scale, frequency-dependent variations in wave propagation effects, given the complexity of the path-effect GP model.

Figure 14 illustrates the standard deviation of various GMMs as a function of spectral periods. Because the standard deviations of some NGA-West2 GMMs are dependent on magnitude or distance, we use M_w 4.5, $R_{rup} = 100$ km, and $V_{S30} = 500$ m/s for these GMMs to facilitate comparisons. It can be seen that the standard deviations for the ergodic GMM developed in this study are higher than but comparable to those of the NGA-West2 GMMs. This may be attributed to the larger number of ground-motion recordings used in this study. In contrast, the standard deviations for the nonergodic GMM are significantly lower—by up to 50%—compared to those of the NGA-West2 GMMs. This reduction is primarily attributed to the modeling of systematic site and path effects, as reflected by a substantial decrease in ϕ. Table 1 presents the standard deviations of different residual components across various periods. The reduction in ϕ is mainly driven by the modeling of the $\delta P2P_V$ term, which accounts for up to 45% of the variability in ϕ, whereas $\delta S2S$ and $\delta P2P_Q$ contribute ~35% and 20%, respectively. This reduction in standard deviation has important implications for performance-based earthquake engineering applications in Türkiye.

TABLE 1
Summary of Variability Components Across Periods

Period (s)	τ	τ_0	ϕ	ϕ_{S2S}	$\phi_{S2S,P2P_Q}$	$\phi_{S2S,P2P_Q,P2P_V}$
0.020	0.487	0.322	0.698	0.579	0.520	0.338
0.050	0.504	0.336	0.744	0.621	0.550	0.380
0.075	0.518	0.333	0.768	0.622	0.571	0.378
0.100	0.517	0.335	0.772	0.619	0.574	0.366
0.150	0.503	0.344	0.784	0.628	0.581	0.309
0.200	0.506	0.355	0.781	0.635	0.595	0.378
0.300	0.491	0.369	0.761	0.628	0.587	0.386
0.400	0.485	0.313	0.737	0.600	0.557	0.381
0.500	0.494	0.331	0.716	0.574	0.499	0.380
0.750	0.533	0.426	0.701	0.552	0.493	0.301
1.000	0.499	0.417	0.706	0.546	0.481	0.314
1.500	0.579	0.364	0.708	0.528	0.483	0.338
3.000	0.558	0.420	0.672	0.513	0.471	0.373
5.000	0.579	0.456	0.640	0.501	0.472	0.377

Here, ϕ_{S2S} denotes the standard deviation of $\delta W - \delta S2S$; $\phi_{S2S,P2P_Q}$ corresponds to $\delta W - \delta S2S - \delta P2P_Q$; and $\phi_{S2S,P2P_Q,P2P_V}$ to $\delta W - \delta S2S - \delta P2P_Q - \delta P2P_V$. The standard deviations are in the unit of ln g.

CONCLUSIONS

In this study, we developed both ergodic and nonergodic GMMs for shallow crustal earthquakes in Türkiye, leveraging a uniformly processed and comprehensive ground-motion database. The nonergodic GMM is built upon an ergodic GMM, incorporating regional adjustment to align with the specific scaling observed in Turkish ground-motion data. Notably, we introduce an event-specific attenuation parameter into the ergodic GMM to mitigate trade-offs between source and path effects before the quantification of systematic effects in the nonergodic GMM. The residuals of the ergodic model are evaluated, and they do not exhibit apparent trends for the considered spectral periods between 0.02 and 5 s. The ergodic model can be considered in engineering applications in Türkiye, where ergodic approaches are deemed sufficient. In the development of the nonergodic GMMs, we model systematic and repeatable sources, paths, and site effects based on the residuals derived from the ergodic GMM. Specifically, for path effects, we explicitly model components induced by variations in the quality factor and 3D velocity structures, utilizing the cell-specific attenuation approach and Gaussian processes, respectively. This is crucial, because the cell-specific attenuation method is designed to capture quality factor-induced path effects, which are only significant for short-period ground motions at large distances.

The developed nonergodic GMM shows a reduced (up to 50%) aleatory standard deviation compared to the ergodic GMMs from previous studies, primarily due to the explicit modeling of systematic site and path effects. This reduction, largely driven by the $\delta P2P_V$ component, has important implications for probabilistic seismic hazard analysis. Our nonergodic GMM not only offers improved aleatory variability but also quantifies the additional epistemic uncertainty associated with repeatable effects consistent with the data distribution. In regions with limited data, the epistemic uncertainty in repeatable effects is elevated, whereas this uncertainty diminishes in data-rich areas. Furthermore, our investigation reveals significant spatial variations in source, site, and path effects across Türkiye. These spatial variations are period dependent because systematic effects at different periods are controlled by distinct site, source, and path parameters. For instance, we find that the correlation lengths of kappa and the site term at short periods are comparable, suggesting dominating kappa effects at short periods, overtaken by deep geological properties as the spectral period increases. In addition, there are qualitative parallels between the estimated cell coefficients associated with anelastic attenuation and quality factor patterns for Türkiye. Finally, the spatial variation of short-period source effects in some regions seems to be related to stress-drop variations, which is, for example, observed in the Marmara and Aegean in western Türkiye regions.

DATA AND RESOURCES

The Turkish ground-motion database used in this study can be accessed through https://en.afad.gov.tr/. Python (https://www.python.org/, last accessed December 2021), and R software (http://www.R-project.org/, last accessed October 2019) is used to perform the regressions. The regression for the ergodic ground-motion model (GMM) is performed using the lme4 (Bates *et al.*, 2007) and Pymc (Salvatier *et al.*, 2016) packages. The regression for the nonergodic GMM is performed using the GPytorch (Gardner *et al.*, 2018) package. The supplemental material contains residual plots of the ergodic and nonergodic GMMs for all spectral periods.

DECLARATION OF COMPETING INTERESTS

The authors acknowledge that there are no conflicts of interest recorded.

ACKNOWLEDGMENTS

This work was financially supported by a generous gift from Pacific Gas and Electric. The authors also thank Zeynep Gulerce for the continuous discussions on seismic hazard applications for Türkiye.

REFERENCES

Abrahamson, N. A., N. M. Kuehn, M. Walling, and N. Landwehr (2019). Probabilistic seismic hazard analysis in California using nonergodic ground-motion models, *Bull. Seismol. Soc. Am.* **109,** no. 4, 1235–1249.

Abrahamson, N. A., W. J. Silva, and R. Kamai (2014). Summary of the ASK14 ground motion relation for active crustal regions, *Earthq. Spectra* **30,** no. 3, 1025–1055.

Akkar, S., and Z. Çağnan (2010). A local ground-motion predictive model for Turkey, and its comparison with other regional and global ground-motion models, *Bull. Seismol. Soc. Am.* **100,** no. 6, 2978–2995.

Ancheta, T., Y. Bozorgnia, R. Darragh, W. J. Silva, B. Chiou, J. P. Stewart, D. M. Boore, R. Graves, N. A. Abrahamson, K. W. Campbell, *et al.* (2012). Peer NGA-West2 database: A database of ground motions recorded in shallow crustal earthquakes in active tectonic regions, *Proc. 15th World Conf. on Earthquake Engineering*, 24–28.

Anderson, J. G., and J. N. Brune (1999). Probabilistic seismic hazard analysis without the ergodic assumption, *Seismol. Res. Lett.* **70,** no. 1, 19–28.

Bates, D., D. Sarkar, M. D. Bates, and L. Matrix (2007). The lme4 package R package version, Vol. 2, 74, available at https://cran.r-project.org/web/packages/lme4/index.html (last accessed August 2023).

Bindi, D., R. Zaccarelli, and S. R. Kotha (2021). Local and moment magnitude analysis in the Ridgecrest region, California: Impact on interevent ground-motion variability, *Bull. Seismol. Soc. Am.* **111,** no. 1, 339–355.

Boore, D. M., J. P. Stewart, E. Seyhan, and G. M. Atkinson (2014). NGA-West2 equations for predicting PGA, PGV, and 5% damped PSA for shallow crustal earthquakes, *Earthq. Spectra* **30,** no. 3, 1057–1085.

Bozorgnia, Y., and J. P. Stewart (2020). Data resources for NGA-subduction project, *Technical Rept. PEER Rept. 2020/02*, Pacific Earthquake Engineering Research Center, University of California, Berkeley, California.

Bozorgnia, Y., N. A. Abrahamson, L. A. Atik, T. D. Ancheta, G. M. Atkinson, J. W. Baker, A. Baltay, D. M. Boore, K. W. Campbell, B. S. J. Chiou, *et al.* (2014). NGA-West2 research project, *Earthq. Spectra* **30,** no. 3, 973–987.

Brunelli, G., G. Lanzano, S. Sgobba, and L. Luzi (2023). Spatial variability of non-ergodic GMM residuals related to source and path effects in Italy, *Bull. Geoph. Ocean* **64,** 417–432.

Cabas, A., A. Rodriguez-Marek, and L. F. Bonilla (2017). Estimation of site-specific kappa (κ 0)-consistent damping values at KiK-net sites to assess the discrepancy between laboratory-based damping models and observed attenuation (of seismic waves) in the field, *Bull. Seismol. Soc. Am.* **107,** no. 5, 2258–2271.

Carlton, B., and N. Abrahamson (2014). Issues and approaches for implementing conditional mean spectra in practice, *Bull. Seismol. Soc. Am.* **104,** no. 1, 503–512.

Dawood, H. M., and A. Rodriguez-Marek (2013). A method for including path effects in ground-motion prediction equations: An example using the M_w 9.0 Tohoku earthquake aftershocks, *Bull. Seismol. Soc. Am.* **103,** no. 2B, 1360–1372.

Emre, Ö., T. Y. Duman, S. Özalp, F. Şaroğlu, Ş. Olgun, H. Elmacı, and T. Çan (2018a). Active fault database of Turkey, *Bull. Earthq. Eng.* **16,** no. 8, 3229–3275.

Emre, Ö., T. Y. Duman, S. Özalp, F. Şaroğlu, Ş. Olgun, H. Elmacı, and T. Çan (2018b). Active fault database of Turkey, *Bull. Earthq. Eng.* **16,** no. 8, 3229–3275.

Gardner, J., G. Pleiss, K. Q. Weinberger, D. Bindel, and A. G. Wilson (2018). Gpytorch: Blackbox matrix-matrix Gaussian process inference with GPU acceleration, *Advances in Neural Information Processing Systems 31.*

Gelman, A., J. B. Carlin, H. S. Stern, and D. B. Rubin (1995). *Bayesian Data Analysis*, Chapman and Hall/CRC, New York, New York.

Gülerce, Z., B. Kargoıġlu, and N. A. Abrahamson (2016). Turkey-adjusted NGA-W1 horizontal ground motion prediction models, *Earthq. Spectra* **32,** no. 1, 75–100.

Kaklamanos, J., L. G. Baise, and D. M. Boore (2011). Estimating unknown input parameters when implementing the NGA ground-motion prediction equations in engineering practice, *Earthq. Spectra* **27,** no. 4, 1219–1235.

Kale, Ö., S. Akkar, A. Ansari, and H. Hamzehloo (2015). A ground-motion predictive model for Iran and Turkey for horizontal PGA, PGV, and 5% damped response spectrum: Investigation of possible regional effects, *Bull. Seismol. Soc. Am.* **105,** no. 2A, 963–980.

Kaviani, A., E. Sandvol, W. Ku, S. L. Beck, N. Türkelli, A. A. Özacar, and J. R. Delph (2022). Seismic attenuation tomography of the SN phase beneath the Turkish-Iranian plateau and the Zagros mountain belt, *Geosphere* **18,** no. 4, 1377–1393.

Kuehn, N. M., and N. A. Abrahamson (2020). Spatial correlations of ground motion for non-ergodic seismic hazard analysis, *Earthq. Eng. Struct. Dynam.* **49,** no. 1, 4–23.

Lacour, M., N. Abrahamson, and C. Sung (2025). New approach to nonergodic path effects in ground-motion models, *Bull. Seismol. Soc. Am.* **115,** no. 4, 1839–1851.

Lavrentiadis, G., N. A. Abrahamson, and N. M. Kuehn (2023). A non-ergodic effective amplitude ground-motion model for California, *Bull. Earthq. Eng.* **21,** no. 11, 5233–5264.

Lavrentiadis, G., N. A. Abrahamson, K. M. Nicolas, Y. Bozorgnia, C. A. Goulet, A. Babič, J. Macedo, M. Dolšek, N. Gregor, A. R. Kottke, *et al.* (2022). Overview and introduction to development of non-ergodic earthquake ground-motion models, *Bull. Earthq. Eng.* **21,** 5121–5150.

Liu, C., J. Macedo, N. Abrahamson, M. Lacour, Z. Gulerce, A. Kottke, and A. Arda Ozacar (2025). Modeling path effects due to 3d velocity structure for nonergodic ground-motion models: A case study using Turkish ground-motion data, *Bull. Seismol. Soc. Am.* **115,** no. 2, 602–618.

Liu, C., J. Macedo, Z. Gulerce, N. Abrahamson, A. Kottke, B. Akbas, F. M. Onder, and A. Arda Ozacar (2024a). Estimating systematic source, site, and path effects in nonergodic ground-motion models: Insights from the Turkish ground-motion database, *Bull. Seismol. Soc. Am.* **114,** no. 6, 3024–3040.

Liu, C., J. Macedo, Z. Gulerce, N. Abrahamson, A. Kottke, B. Akbas, F. M. Onder, and A. Arda Ozacar (2024b). Estimating systematic source, site, and path effects in nonergodic ground-motion models: Insights from the Turkish ground-motion database, *Bull. Seismol. Soc. Am.* **114,** no. 6, 3024–3040.

Liu, C., J. Macedo, and A. R. Kottke (2022). Evaluating the performance of nonergodic ground motion models in the Ridgecrest area, *Bull. Earthq. Eng.* **21,** 5347.

Macedo, J., and C. Liu (2022). A nonergodic ground motion model for Chile, *Bull. Seismol. Soc. Am.* **112,** no. 5, 2542–2561.

Matthews, A. G. D. G., M. Van Der Wilk, T. Nickson, K. Fujii, A. Boukouvalas, P. León-Villagrá, Z. Ghahramani, and J. Hensman (2017). GPflow: A Gaussian process library using TensorFlow, *J. Machine Learn. Res.* **18,** no. 40, 1–6.

Önder, F. M. (2022). Towards the non-ergodic ground motion models of Turkey: Assessment of systematic site, source and path effects, *Master's Thesis*, Middle East Technical University.

Parker, G. A., A. S. Baltay, J. Rekoske, and E. M. Thompson (2020). Repeatable source, path, and site effects from the 2019 m 7.1 Ridgecrest earthquake sequence, *Bull. Seismol. Soc. Am.* **110,** no. 4, 1530–1548.

Power, M., B. Chiou, N. Abrahamson, Y. Bozorgnia, T. Shantz, and C. Roblee (2008). An overview of the NGA project, *Earthq. Spectra* **24,** no. 1, 3–21.

Salvatier, J., T. V. Wiecki, and C. Fonnesbeck (2016). Probabilistic programming in python using pymc3, *PeerJ Comput. Sci.* **2,** e55.

Sandıkkaya, M. A., S. Akkar, Ö. Kale, and E. Yenier (2023). A simulation-based regional ground-motion model for western Turkiye, *Bull. Earthq. Eng.* **21,** no. 7, 3221–3249.

Sung, C. H., N. Abrahamson, and M. Lacour (2023). Methodology for including path effects due to 3d velocity structure in nonergodic ground-motion models, *Bull. Seismol. Soc. Am.* **113,** no. 5, 2144–2163.

Thompson, E. M., M. Hearne, B. T. Aagaard, J. M. Rekoske, C. B. Worden, M. P. Moschetti, H. E. Hunsinger, G. C. Ferragut, G. A. Parker, J. A. Smith, *et al.* (2025). Automated, near real-time ground-motion processing at the U.S. geological survey, *Seismol. Res. Lett.* **96,** no. 1, 538–553.

Manuscript received 6 June 2025
Published online 8 October 2025

Nonergodic Probabilistic Fault-Displacement Hazard Analysis

Irene Liou[*1,2] and Norman A. Abrahamson[1]

ABSTRACT

A nonergodic probabilistic fault-displacement hazard analysis (PFDHA) framework is developed using paleoseismic displacement data sets with multiple events at each site. The current earthquake-based and displacement-based approaches can be fit into a general framework of ergodic, partially nonergodic, and nonergodic approaches. The paleoseismic data sets do not include the metadata (magnitude and location along strike) typically used for developing a nonergodic fault-displacement model (FDM). We present an approach for estimating the nonergodic standard deviation without the metadata. We show example hazard calculations for ergodic and nonergodic PFDHAs for three cases: (1) without displacement data for the fault, (2) with displacement data at the site, and (3) with displacement data observed on the fault but located down strike from the site. With no displacement data at the site, the 5th–95th epistemic fractiles of hazard based on the nonergodic FDMs can lead to a displacement range of a factor of 20 for high slip-rate faults at typical return periods between 1000 and 10,000 yr used for design, whereas the ergodic fractiles span a range of a factor of ≤ 2. This large difference in the epistemic range shows the strong effects of the nonergodic FDM on the fault-displacement hazard. The very large epistemic uncertainty for nonergodic FDMs without data may motivate using an ergodic approach with much smaller epistemic uncertainty; however, the large uncertainty in nonergodic models more accurately reflects the epistemic range that captures the true hazard at the site. The considerable epistemic uncertainty in nonergodic estimations can be significantly reduced with just a few additional fault-specific displacement observations.

KEY POINTS

- Probabilistic fault displacement hazard lacks the organizational structure for nonergodic analyses.
- The proposed nonergodic framework overcomes the missing magnitudes and locations in paleoseismic data sets.
- Separation of aleatory and epistemic components shows where scientific uncertainty is reducible with more data.

Supplemental Material

INTRODUCTION

Traditionally, ground-motion models (GMMs) used in probabilistic seismic hazard analysis (PSHA) have been based on the ergodic assumption, combining data from similar tectonic regions into a single model to have enough data to constrain the scaling in the GMM. The median and variability of the ground motion for a given magnitude, distance, and site condition are assumed to apply to all sites within the broad region. This corresponds to the ergodic assumption that the median and variability of the ground motion over time at a given location are the same as the median and variability of the ground motion over space for the broad region. The ergodic assumption simplifies the development of the GMM, but by ignoring the systematic differences in the median ground motion for specific source–site pairs, the ergodic assumption leads to large variability in the ground motion for a given scenario and reduced spatial resolution of the differences in the hazard within the region.

To address the limitation of ergodic GMMs, the focus of GMM research has shifted from developing simple ergodic GMMs to developing nonergodic GMMs that include more physical behaviors (e.g., Rodriguez-Marek *et al.*, 2014; Landwehr *et al.*, 2016; Abrahamson *et al.*, 2019; Lavrentiadis, Abrahamson, *et al.*, 2023; Sung *et al.*, 2023). The nonergodic GMMs include adjustments to the ergodic GMM for a given source–site pair. Using nonergodic GMMs to account for the systematic effects of the median source, path, and site effects for a specific source–site pair reduces the apparent aleatory variability of the GMM by up

1. Department of Civil and Environmental Engineering, University of California, Davis, California, U.S.A., https://orcid.org/0009-0003-7106-4909 (IL); https://orcid.org/0000-0001-7900-6023 (NAA); 2. GFZ Helmholtz Centre for Geosciences, Potsdam, Germany

*Corresponding author: ireneliou0@gmail.com

Cite this article as Liou, I., and N. A. Abrahamson (2025). Nonergodic Probabilistic Fault-Displacement Hazard Analysis, *Bull. Seismol. Soc. Am.* **116**, 498–514, doi: 10.1785/0120250064

to a factor of 2 (Lin *et al.*, 2011). Including more physical behaviors in the model improves the overall accuracy of the hazard estimation.

Probabilistic fault-displacement hazard analysis (PFDHA) follows a similar approach to PSHA but uses fault-displacement models (FDMs) in place of the GMMs. Most FDMs have been developed based on global data sets corresponding to an ergodic assumption (e.g., Wells and Coppersmith, 1994; Moss and Ross, 2011; Petersen *et al.*, 2011; Lavrentiadis and Abrahamson, 2023). These ergodic FDMs have the same key limitations regarding accuracy as the ergodic GMMs. To improve the accuracy of PFDHA, the FDMs need to move from ergodic to nonergodic approaches. The concepts for developing nonergodic FDMs for use in PFDHA are similar to those for developing nonergodic GMMs for use in PSHA.

In this article, we address principal displacement hazard and show how the current earthquake-based approach and displacement-based approach described by Youngs *et al.* (2003) fit into a general nonergodic framework for FDMs. In particular, we show how the aleatory variability and epistemic uncertainty framework developed by Liou and Abrahamson (2024) for ergodic, partially nonergodic, and nonergodic GMMs can be applied to ergodic, partially nonergodic, and nonergodic FDMs for principal rupture.

Finally, we show examples of PFDHA calculations using ergodic and nonergodic FDMs for three cases: (1) sites without any observed displacement data for the fault, (2) sites with displacement observations at the site, and (3) sites with displacements observed on the fault of interest but located down strike from the site.

APPROACHES FOR PROBABILISTIC FAULT-DISPLACEMENT HAZARD

A major PDFHA was conducted for the Yucca Mountain, Nevada, project, which investigated the geologic and seismotectonic setting of the site for its potential as a high-level waste repository (Stepp *et al.*, 2001). The PFDHA for the Yucca Mountain Project used earthquake-based and displacement-based approaches as described by Youngs *et al.* (2003).

Earthquake-based approach

In the earthquake-based approach, the probabilistic fault-displacement hazard for principal fault rupture, $\mathrm{Haz}(D > d)$, is computed similar to the ground-motion hazard but with only a single fault considered:

$$\begin{gathered}\mathrm{Haz}(D>d)=N(M>M_{\min})\\ \int_M\int_L\int_{\mathrm{Loc}_R} f_m(M) f_L(L,M,\mathrm{SOF}) f_{\mathrm{Loc}_R}(\mathrm{Loc}_R,L,L_F)\\ P(\mathrm{Surf\,Rup}|M,\mathrm{SOF})P(\mathrm{Surf\,Rup\,past\,site}|L,X_F,L_F)\\ (1-P(\mathrm{Gap}|M,\mathrm{SOF}))P(D>d|M,X/L,\mathrm{SOF})d\mathrm{Loc}_R dL,dM\end{gathered}, \quad (1)$$

in which $N(M > M_{\min})$ is the annual rate of earthquakes on the fault with magnitudes above the minimum magnitude of engineering relevance. The three probability density functions (PDFs), f_m, f_L, and f_{Loc_R}, describe the distribution of magnitude (M), surface rupture length (L), and the location of the end of the surface rupture relative to the end of the fault (Loc_R), respectively. SOF is the style of faulting, and L_F is the length of the fault. The $P(\mathrm{Surf\,Rup}|M,\mathrm{SOF})$ term is the conditional probability of an event's having surface rupture (Surf Rup) anywhere along the fault for a given M and SOF. The $P(\mathrm{Surf\,Rup\,past\,site}|L,X_F,L_F)$ term is the conditional probability that the surface rupture goes past the site (i.e., the site is located between the two ends of the surface rupture) given L and L_F, and the distance from the site to the end of the fault (X_F). The final term, $P(D > d|M,X/L,\mathrm{SOF})$, is the conditional probability of the principal displacement D exceeding displacement level d given M, X/L, and SOF, in which X is the distance from the site to the end of the rupture. The rupture and fault geometry terms are shown in Figure 1.

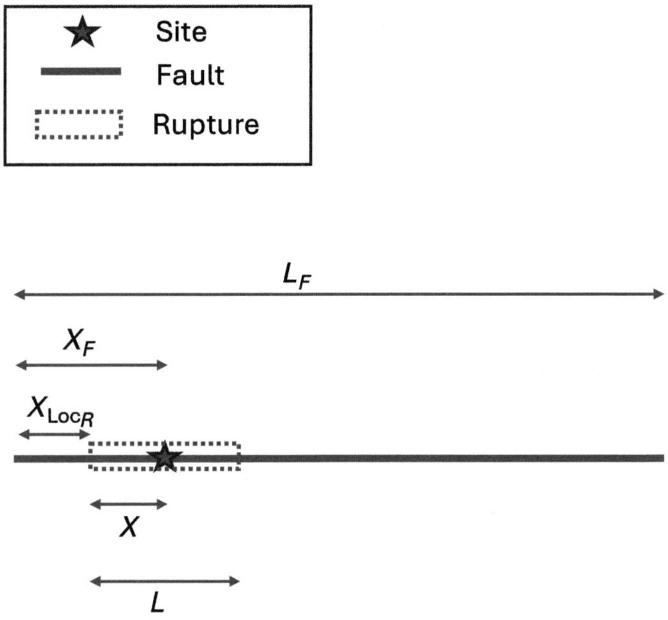

Figure 1. Example of the notation used for the locations of the rupture and site. X_F is the distance from the site to the end of the fault, L_F is the length of the fault, X is the distance from the site to the end of the rupture, L is the rupture length, and Loc_R is the location of the end of the rupture from the end of the fault. The color version of this figure is available only in the electronic edition.

There is a chance of zero displacement at the site, even if the site is located between the two ends of the rupture, because of spatial gaps in the surface rupture along the total rupture length. The effect of gaps in the surface rupture on the $P(\mathrm{Surf\,Rup\,past\,site}|L,X_F,L_F)$ term can be captured by scaling the conditional probability of exceedance by $1 - P(\mathrm{Gap}|M,\mathrm{SOF})$, in which $P(\mathrm{Gap}|M,\mathrm{SOF})$ is the probability that the site is located in a gap with zero displacement. This approach, used by Lavrentiadis and Abrahamson (2023), simplifies the statistical modeling of the distribution of the displacements for the FDM.

The $P(D > d|M,X/L,\text{SOF})$ term is computed based on the FDM. Recent FDMs were developed as part of the fault-displacement hazard initiative (FDHI) project based on a database of 75 historical surface-rupturing earthquakes from shallow crustal tectonic environments (Sarmiento *et al.*, 2021). The FDMs developed as part of the FDHI are summarized in Sarmiento *et al.* (2024).

The $P(\text{Surf Rup}|M,\text{SOF})$ term can be obtained using empirical relations based on global data, such as Wells and Coppersmith (1993), Moss *et al.* (2013), and Pizza *et al.* (2023). Models based on earthquakes from specific regions can also be used, such as Pezzopane and Dawson (1996) and Youngs *et al.* (2003) for the western United States Basin and Range, Takao *et al.* (2013) for Japan, and Yang *et al.* (2021) for Australia. The use of empirical models for $P(\text{Surf Rup}|M,\text{SOF})$ is appropriate if the fault of interest has similar characteristics (down-dip width and depth distribution of hypocenters) as the data used to develop the empirical model. Alternatively, the $P(\text{Surf Rup}|M,\text{SOF})$ term can be calculated based on the fault-specific dimensions and depth distribution of hypocenters (Mammarella *et al.*, 2025).

The location of the rupture along strike is typically modeled by a uniform distribution. For a uniform distribution of the location of the surface rupture along the fault strike, the probability of the rupture going past the site given a surface rupture length L is given by

$$P(\text{Surf Rup past site}|L,X_F,L_F) = 1 - (P_1 + P_2), \qquad (2)$$

in which

$$P_1 = \begin{cases} \frac{X_F-L}{L_F-L} & \text{for } L < X_F \\ 0 & \text{for } L \geq X_F \end{cases}, \qquad (3)$$

and

$$P_2 = \begin{cases} \frac{L_F-L-X_F}{L_F-L} & \text{for } L < L_F - X_F \\ 0 & \text{for } L \geq L_F - X_F \end{cases}. \qquad (4)$$

Displacement-based approach

In the displacement-based approach, observations of the displacement at the site or along the fault of interest are used directly to estimate the probability of exceedance given surface rupture at the site in place of the FDM, and the integrals over M, L, and Loc_R are not needed. The fault-displacement hazard using the displacement-based approach is given by

$$\text{Haz}(D > d) = \lambda_{\text{Surf Rup}} P(D > d|\text{Local disp data}), \qquad (5)$$

in which $\lambda_{\text{Surf Rup}}$ is the rate of events that cause surface rupture at the site and $P(D > d|\text{Local disp data})$ is the empirical estimate of the conditional probability of exceedance based on observed surface ruptures at the site or on the fault of interest.

The $P(D > d|\text{Local disp data})$ term is computed from the distribution of the available paleoseismic displacement data for the fault of interest. At each site, the displacements are normalized by the mean displacement at the site. The site normalized displacement is given by $D_{es}/\overline{D_s}$, in which D_{es} is the displacement from earthquake e at site s and $\overline{D_s}$ is the arithmetic mean displacement at site s.

Data sets with multiple displacements at each site were used by Youngs *et al.* (2003) and Hecker *et al.* (2013), denoted YEA03 and HEA13, respectively. The YEA03 data set is a regional data set that includes multiple displacements at 17 locations on faults in the Yucca Mountain region described in Wong and Stepp (1998). Youngs *et al.* (2003) fit the pooled distribution of the $D_{es}/\overline{D_s}$ values to a gamma distribution. The HEA13 data set is a global data set of multiple displacement observations at a point at 171 sites. Hecker *et al.* (2013) parameterized the pooled distribution of $D_{es}/\overline{D_s}$ by the coefficient of variation (CV). The CV given by Hecker *et al.* (2013) is a global estimate of the variability of slip at a point, and the gamma distribution given by Youngs *et al.* (2003) is a region-specific estimate of the variability of slip at a point.

Differences between earthquake-based and displacement-based approaches

Two key differences exist between the earthquake-based and displacement-based approaches of equations (1) and (5), respectively. First, in the earthquake-based approach, $N(M > M_{\min})$ is the rate of all earthquakes on the fault, including both events that cause surface rupture at the site and events that do not cause surface rupture at the site. In contrast, the $\lambda_{\text{Surf Rup}}$ used in the displacement-based approach only includes the events that cause surface rupture at the site. In the earthquake-based approach, the $P(\text{Surf Rup}|M,\text{SOF})$ scales the earthquake rate to only include surface-rupturing events. Second, the earthquake-based approach uses an FDM to compute the $P(D > d|M,X/L,\text{SOF})$ term, whereas the displacement-based approach uses region-specific or fault-specific observations of the displacement to compute the $P(D > d|\text{Local disp data})$ term.

ERGODIC FDMS

An ergodic model assumes that the distribution of a random variable at a location is equivalent to the distribution at all locations (Anderson and Brune, 1999). The term "ergodic" is used to describe a model based on a global data set of earthquakes from similar tectonic environments. Most FDMs are empirical models developed from global data sets, corresponding to ergodic models.

The displacement parameters used in FDMs are listed in Table 1. Various statistical models have been used for different components of the FDMs. For example, Wells and Coppersmith (1994) used a lognormal distribution for the average displacement along strike for a single event (AD_e); Petersen *et al.* (2011) used a lognormal distribution for the displacement at a site normalized by the average displacement for a single earthquake (D_{es}/AD_e); Moss and Ross (2011) used a gamma distribution for the displacement normalized by the maximum displacement for a single event (D_{es}/MD_e); and Hecker *et al.* (2013) used a

TABLE 1
Notation Used for Displacements

Notation	Definition
D_{es}	Displacement at site s from earthquake e
AD_e	Arithmetic mean displacement averaged along strike for earthquake e
$\overline{D_s}$	Arithmetic mean displacement averaged over all earthquakes at site s
$\overline{D_s^{0.3}}$	Mean transformed displacement averaged over all earthquakes at site s

normal distribution for the displacement normalized by the mean displacement at each site, $D_{es}/\overline{D}_s$. Lavrentiadis and Abrahamson (2023) showed that the variability of the residuals of the unnormalized fault-displacement data from a random-effects regression was consistent with a power-normal distribution, D^θ with $\theta = 0.3$. A power-normal distribution with θ between 0 and 1 has skewness between a normal distribution and a lognormal distribution. The power-normal distribution can provide a good approximation to the shape of the gamma distribution used for variability of the fault-displacement along strike. For example, for the YEA03 data set, a power-normal distribution with a standard deviation of 0.18 in $m^{0.3}$ units provides a good fit to the gamma distribution used by Youngs *et al.* (2003), as shown in Figure 2.

In this study, we use the FDM developed by Lavrentiadis and Abrahamson (2023), denoted LA23, because it uses a statistical model in which the different components of the variability are normally distributed. Using a transformation that leads to normally distributed residuals greatly simplifies the statistical modeling and comparisons of the different components of the aleatory variability. Therefore, we use the power-normal transformation to present the framework for FDMs; however, the overall framework can be applied to other distributions.

The LA23 ergodic FDM used the following statistical model:

$$D_{es}^{0.3} = \mu_{\text{Erg}}(M_e, \text{SOF}, X/L) + \delta B_e + \delta W_{es}, \quad (6)$$

in which $\mu_{\text{Erg}}(M_e, \text{SOF}, X/L)$ is the median displacement in the transformed $m^{0.3}$ units, δB_e is the between-event residual for earthquake e, and δW_{es} is the within-event residual for site s and earthquake e.

To facilitate the move to the nonergodic framework for FDMs, we added a subscript f for the fault in addition to the earthquake index e so that δB_e becomes δB_{fe}. The δB_{fe} term can separated into two terms:

$$\delta B_{fe} = \delta F2F_f + \delta B_{fe}^0, \quad (7)$$

in which $\delta F2F_f$ is the median fault-specific shift in the displacement for fault f relative to the ergodic median displacement for all faults and δB_{fe}^0 is the remaining aleatory variability for the event term.

The δW_{es} term can separated into three terms:

$$\delta W_{fes} = \delta S2S_s + \delta AF_{fes} + \delta_{0,es}, \quad (8)$$

in which $\delta S2S_s$ is the median site-specific shift in displacement, δAF_{es} is the variation of the site-specific displacement, and $\delta_{0,es}$ is the remaining residual due to effects that are not possible to model.

Following the approach used by Liou and Abrahamson (2024) for GMMs, the residuals can be categorized into unmodeled and modeled behaviors, which helps define what is treated as aleatory variability. The unmodeled effects are separated into three classes of aleatory variability: class 1 effects are practical to model, and class 2 effects have physical causes but are currently not practical to model. Class 1 and class 2 effects appear as apparent aleatory variability because the unmodeled behavior is treated as randomness in the context of the simplified model; however, they have a physical basis and are not truly random. The class 3 effects represent aleatory variability from genuinely random effects from a chaotic and quantum level and therefore are impossible to model.

For an ergodic FDM, we can rewrite equation (6) by combining equations (7) and (8):

$$D_{fes}^{0.3} = \underbrace{\mu_{\text{Erg}}(M_e, \text{SOF}, X/L) +}_{\text{Modeled effects}} \underbrace{\underbrace{\delta F2F_f + \delta S2S_s +}_{\text{Class 1}} \underbrace{\delta B_{fe}^0 + \delta AF_{fes} +}_{\text{Class 2}} \underbrace{\delta_{0,es}}_{\text{Class 3}}}_{\text{Unmodeled effects}}, \quad (9)$$

In an ergodic FDM, the $\delta F2F_f$ and $\delta S2S_s$ terms are a part of class 1 apparent aleatory variability because the apparent randomness is due to average effects that are currently practical to model but which are left unmodeled. The variations about the fault and site terms (δB_{fe}^0 and δAF_{fes}, respectively) are a part of class 2 aleatory variability because these are due to physical effects that are currently impractical to model. The $\delta_{0,es}$ is part of the class 3 aleatory variability because the behavior is impossible to model.

In the regression, the δAF and δ_0 terms cannot be separated and are combined into a within-site residual, δWS_{es}:

$$D_{fes}^{0.3} = \underbrace{\mu_{\text{Erg}}(M_e, \text{SOF}, X/L) +}_{\text{Modeled effects}} \underbrace{\delta F2F_f + \delta S2S_s + \delta B_{fe}^0 + \delta WS_{es}}_{\text{Unmodeled effects}}. \quad (10)$$

The standard deviation of the apparent aleatory variability for an ergodic FDM is given by

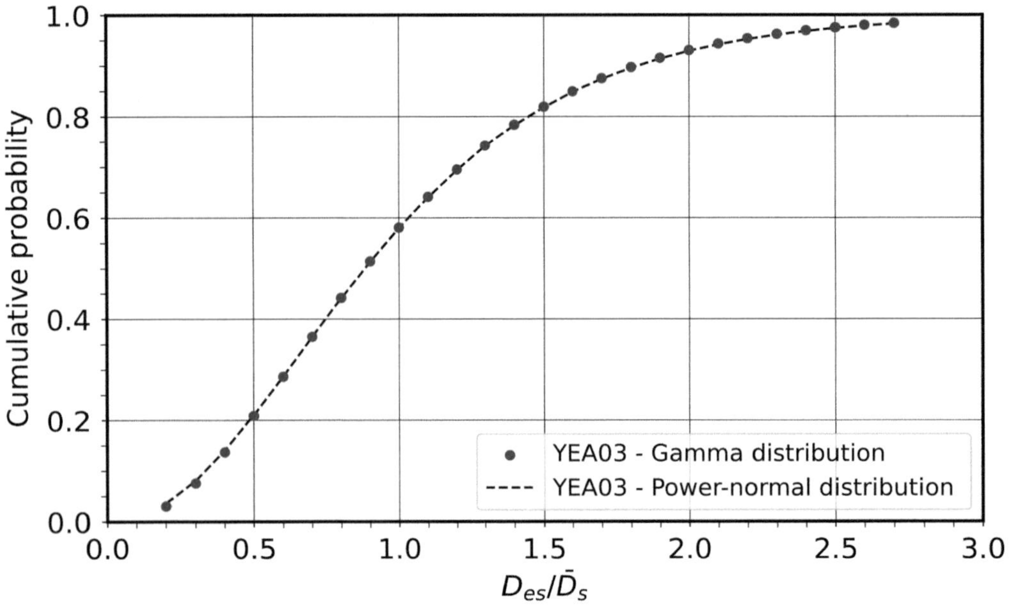

Figure 2. Comparison of the cumulative probability distribution for a power-normal distribution with $\sigma = 0.18$ and the gamma distribution for $(D_{es}/\bar{D}_s)$ given by Youngs *et al.* (2003) ($a = 2.71$, $b = 0.369$) for a small region around Yucca Mountain. The color version of this figure is available only in the electronic edition.

$$\sigma_{\text{Erg}} = \sqrt{\tau_{F2F}^2 + \phi_{S2S}^2 + \tau_0^2 + \phi_{SS}^2}, \tag{11}$$

in which each standard deviation term corresponds to one of the four unmodeled effects in equation (10). The notation for the residuals and corresponding standard deviations is summarized in Table 2.

TABLE 2
Notation Used for Residuals and Standard Deviations for Fault-Displacement Models (FDMs)

Notation	Term	Definition
δB_e	Between-event residual	$\delta F2F_f + \delta B_{fe}^0$
δW_{fes}	Within-event residual	$\delta S2S_s + \delta WS_{fes}$
$\delta F2F_f$	Median fault term	
δB_{fe}^0	Between-event residual	
$\delta S2S_s$	Median site term	
δWS_{fes}	Within-site residual	$\delta AF_s + \delta_{0,es}$
τ	Standard deviation of δB_e	
τ_{F2F}	Standard deviation of $F2F_f$	
ϕ_{S2S}	Standard deviation of $\delta S2S_s$	
τ_0	Standard deviation of δB_{fe}^0	
ϕ_{AF}	Standard deviation of δAF_s	
σ_0	Standard deviation of $\delta_{0,es}$	
ϕ_{SS}	Standard deviation of δWS_{fes}	$\sqrt{\phi_{AF}^2 + \phi_0^2}$
σ_{Erg}	Ergodic standard deviation	$\sqrt{\tau_{F2F}^2 + \phi_{S2S}^2 + \tau_0^2 + \phi_{SS}^2}$
σ_{PN}	Partially nonergodic standard deviation	$\sqrt{\phi_{S2S}^2 + \tau_0^2 + \phi_{SS}^2}$
σ_{NE}	Total nonergodic standard deviation	$\sqrt{\tau_0^2 + \phi_{SS}^2}$

PARTIALLY NONERGODIC APPROACH

A partially nonergodic FDM includes one of the two systematic terms not modeled in the ergodic FDM ($\delta F2F_f$ or $\delta S2S_s$) as part of the model for the median displacement. Partially nonergodic models can differ in terms of which physical effects are modeled. For GMMs, the site term is often included in a partially nonergodic model; however, for FDMs, it is more likely to have displacement data on a specific fault than to have displacement data at a specific site. Therefore, we include the systematic fault term $\delta F2F_f$ in the partially nonergodic FDM rather than including the site term without the fault term.

The partially nonergodic FDM is given by

$$D_{fes}^{0.3} = \underbrace{\mu_{\text{Erg}}(M_e, S_s, X/L) + \delta F2F_f}_{\text{Modeled effects}} + \underbrace{\delta S2S_s + \delta B_{fe}^0 + \delta WS_{fes}}_{\text{Unmodeled effects}}, \tag{12}$$

in which the fault-specific term is part of the modeled effects for the median displacement. With the additional modeled effect, the size of the apparent aleatory variability is reduced in comparison with the ergodic FDM. The standard deviation of the partially nonergodic FDMs is

$$\sigma_{PN} = \sqrt{\phi_{S2S}^2 + \tau_0^2 + \phi_{SS}^2}. \tag{13}$$

FULLY NONERGODIC APPROACH

Fully nonergodic models include all the average (class 1) physical effects. Including both the average fault-specific and site-specific terms as modeled effects leads to a nonergodic FDM:

$$D_{fes}^{0.3} = \underbrace{\mu_{\text{Erg}}(M_e, S_s, X/L) + \delta F2F_f + \delta S2S_s}_{\text{Modeled effects}} + \underbrace{\delta B_{fe}^0 + \delta WS_{fes}}_{\text{Unmodeled effects}}, \tag{14}$$

in which both the median fault-specific and median site-specific terms are modeled. The standard deviation of the nonergodic FDMs, σ_{NE} is given by

$$\sigma_{NE} = \sqrt{\tau_0^2 + \phi_{SS}^2}. \tag{15}$$

EARTHQUAKE-BASED AND DISPLACEMENT-BASED APPROACHES

In general, the earthquake-based and displacement-based approaches do not define ergodic and nonergodic approaches. The earthquake-based approach can be used with ergodic, partially nonergodic, or nonergodic FDMs, whereas the displacement-based approach corresponds to either a partially nonergodic or a nonergodic approach because the conditional probability of exceedance is estimated from pooled local observations, which acts as an FDM with the effect of M and X/L variability.

Estimation of the nonergodic standard deviation

To use the nonergodic framework in a PFDHA, we need an estimate of the nonergodic standard deviation, σ_{NE}. For nonergodic GMMs, the residuals are used to estimate the nonergodic standard deviation terms; however, this approach will not work for the fault-displacement data set because we do not have the metadata (M and X/L) for the paleoseismic events to compute the residuals; however, the empirical distributions of the variability of slip at a point from the YEA03 and HEA13 data sets can be used to estimate σ_{NE}.

We assume that the data sets of YEA03 and HEA13 represent coseismic slip and that the offsets have been accurately assessed temporally (e.g., linking a larger displacement to one event as opposed to multiple smaller events). Using the power-normal transformed displacement data from the YEA03 and HEA13 data sets, we obtain an empirical displacement residual for earthquake e and site s calculated by

$$\delta D_{es} = D_{es}^{0.3} - \overline{D_s^{0.3}}, \tag{16}$$

in which $D^{0.3}$ is the transformed displacement observation and $\overline{D_s^{0.3}}$ is the mean of the transformed observed displacements at site s, which can be written as

$$\overline{D_s^{0.3}} = \mu_{\text{Erg}}(M_e, S_s, X/L) + \delta F2F_f + \delta S2S_s. \tag{17}$$

Similar to equation (14), the transformed displacement observation can be written as

$$D_{es}^{0.3} = \underbrace{\overline{D_s^{0.3}}}_{\text{Modeled effects}} \underbrace{+\delta M + \delta X + \delta B_{fe}^0 + \delta WS_{fes}}_{\text{Unmodeled effects}}, \tag{18}$$

in which δM and δX are the changes in displacement due to deviations from the average magnitude and average X/L for events causing surface rupture at the site.

There are two key differences between equation (18) for the traditional nonergodic residual and equation (14) for the slip at a point nonergodic residual. First, equation (18) uses the mean displacement observation at site s instead of a prediction from the nonergodic median in equation (14). Second, equation (18) includes the effect of variability of different M and X/L values in the observed displacement data at the site.

We denote the standard deviation of the pooled δD_{es} as $\sigma_{NE,MX}$ to explicitly indicate that it includes the variability of the median displacement at the site because of the variability of the M and X/L for the scenarios that caused surface rupture at the site in additional to the variability about the median for a given M and X/L. The $\sigma_{NE,MX}$ is given by the combination of σ_{NE} and σ_{MX}:

$$\sigma_{NE,MX} = \sqrt{\sigma_{NE}^2 + \sigma_{MX}^2}, \tag{19}$$

in which σ_{MX} is the standard deviation of the median displacement due only to the aleatory variability of M and X/L. Estimating the nonergodic standard deviation requires estimates of both the $\sigma_{NE,MX}$ and σ_{MX} terms:

$$\sigma_{NE} = \sqrt{\sigma_{NE,MX}^2 - \sigma_{MX}^2}. \tag{20}$$

Estimation of $\sigma_{NE,MX}$

Using the observed displacement data, the $\sigma_{NE,MX}$ is estimated by

$$\sigma_{NE,MX} = \sqrt{\frac{\sum_{s=1}^{NS}\sum_{e=1}^{N_s}(\delta D_{es})^2}{\left(\sum_{s=1}^{NS} N_s\right) - NS}}, \tag{21}$$

in which NS is the number of sites and N_s is the number of events observed at site s. The denominator includes the loss of degrees of freedom due to estimating the $\overline{D_s^{0.3}}$ (in δD_{es}) at each site.

The number of sites, number of events, and mean displacement for the YEA03 and HEA13 data sets are listed in Table 3. The HEA13 data set is a global data set that consists of displacements from 505 events at 171 sites with between 2 and 9 events per site. The mean displacements at the 171 sites range from 0.08 to 16.4 m. The YEA03 data set consists of 72 displacements at 17 sites from the faults near Yucca Mountain, with 3–8 events per site. The mean displacements at the 17 sites range from 0.18 to 2.9 m.

The $\sigma_{NE,MX}$ values are computed using equation (21) and are listed in Table 3. For the YEA03 data set, only a single estimate of the displacement is given for each event, whereas for the HEA13 data set, the preferred, minimum, and maximum displacements are given. The preferred, minimum, and maximum displacements are assumed to represent the 50th, 10th, and 90th percentiles of the displacement, respectively. This uncertainty range is sampled 100 times, and the average value of $\sigma_{NE,MX}$ for the 100 samples is computed.

Hecker *et al.* (2013) separated the paleoseismic displacement data set into two subsets: sites with a mean displacement 1≥ m and sites with a mean displacement >1 m. They found that the CV was larger for the sites with the smaller mean displacement. We are using the standard deviation of the power-normal distribution rather than the CV of the arithmetic displacements. We evaluated the dependence of the standard deviation of $D^{0.3}$ on the mean displacement. The $\sigma_{NE,MX}$

values for different bins of the mean displacement at the site $\overline{D_s}$ are listed in Table 3 and are plotted in Figure 3.

Using multiple smaller bins provided a better resolution of the displacement dependence of the $\sigma_{NE,MX}$ than the two large bins (≤1 m and >1 m) used by Hecker *et al.* (2013). The $\sigma_{NE,MX}$ values for the YEA03 and HEA13 data sets are consistent. The $\sigma_{NE,MX}$ values are approximately constant for mean displacements <1.5 m and increase for larger values of $\overline{D_s}$. The increase in the $\sigma_{NE,MX}$ with $\overline{D_s}$ as compared with the decrease in the CV with $\overline{D_s}$ found by Hecker *et al.* (2013) is due to the difference between the power-normal and the normal distributions. A comparison of the CV and the power-normal standard deviation is shown in Section S4, available in the supplemental material to this article.

We developed a smooth $\sigma_{NE,MX}$ model based on the combined YEA03 and HEA13 data sets. The standard deviation for mean displacements <1 m is 0.17 $m^{0.3}$. We fixed the $\sigma_{NE,MX}$ for small displacements to a constant of 0.17 $m^{0.3}$. The increase in the standard deviation for larger displacements is modeled by a quadratic term so that the first derivative is continuous. The transition displacement was estimated as part of the regression. The resulting model for $\sigma_{NE,MX}$ is given by

$$\sigma_{NE,MX} = \begin{cases} 0.17 & \text{for } \overline{D_s} \le 1.44 \text{ m} \\ 0.17 + 0.0325(\ln(\overline{D_s}/1.44))^2 & \text{for } \overline{D_s} > 1.44 \text{ m} \end{cases}, \quad (22)$$

in which $\overline{D_s}$ is the arithmetic mean displacement at the site.

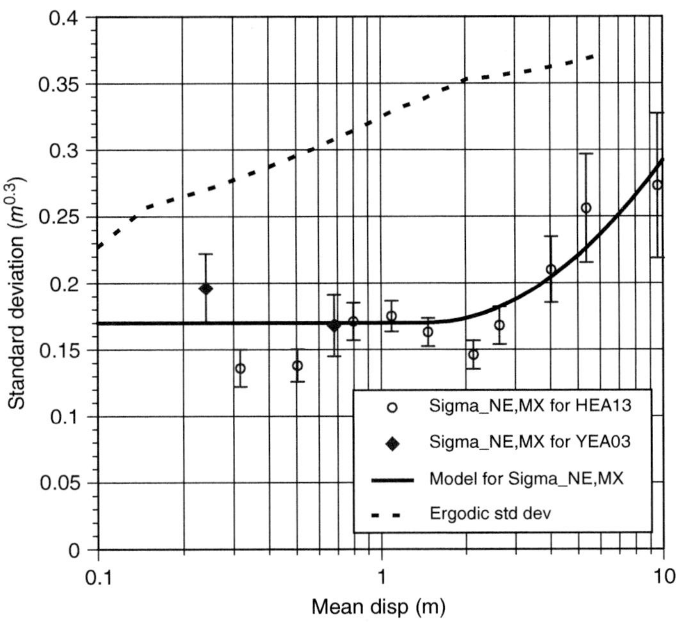

Figure 3. Standard deviation of the transformed displacement-at-a-point data from the global data set of Hecker *et al.* (2013) and the Yucca Mountain data set of Youngs *et al.* (2003). The ergodic standard deviation is from Lavrentiadis and Abrahamson (2023). The standard deviation $\sigma_{NE,MX}$ includes the effect of variability of magnitude and *X/L* in addition to the nonergodic standard deviation. The error bars show ±1 standard error of the standard deviation. The color version of this figure is available only in the electronic edition.

Estimation of σ_{MX}

The σ_{MX} term is the standard deviation of the mean displacement at a site due only to the aleatory variability of the *M* and *X/L*. To estimate the σ_{MX} term, the fault-displacement hazard is computed using the earthquake-based approach with the aleatory variability of the FDM set to zero to isolate the effect of the aleatory variability of *M* and *X/L* from the σ_{NE}.

The cumulative distribution function (CDF) of the displacement is computed from the normalized hazard:

$$\text{CDF}(d) = 1 - \frac{\text{Haz}(D > d|\sigma_{NE} = 0)}{\text{Haz}(D > 0|\sigma_{NE} = 0)}. \quad (23)$$

TABLE 3
Statistics of the Hecker *et al.* (2013) (HEA13) Data Set and the Youngs *et al.* (2003) (YEA03) Data Set Used to Calculate $\sigma_{NE,MX}$

Data Set	D_s Range (m)	N_s	N_{site}	Mean Displacement (m)	$\sigma_{NE,MX}$ ($m^{0.3}$)	Standard Error ($m^{0.3}$)
HEA13	0–0.5	70	22	0.317	0.136	0.014
	0.25–0.75	86	26	0.504	0.138	0.012
	0.5–2.0	107	33	0.797	0.171	0.014
	0.75–2.5	158	49	1.089	0.175	0.012
	1.0–2.0	154	51	1.469	0.163	0.011
	1.5–3.0	160	61	2.13	0.146	0.011
	2.0–4.0	142	53	2.633	0.168	0.014
	3.0–6.0	77	26	4.032	0.210	0.025
	4.0–8.0	38	14	5.37	0.256	0.041
	>6.0	20	9	9.587	0.273	0.054
	All data	505	171	2.0	0.172	0.005
YEA03	0–0.4	9	37	0.24	0.196	0.026
	0.4–3.0	8	35	0.68	0.268	0.023
	All data	72	17	0.54	0.183	0.017

The $\sigma_{NE,MX}$ includes the effect of variability of *M* and *X/L* in addition to the variability of the nonergodic terms.

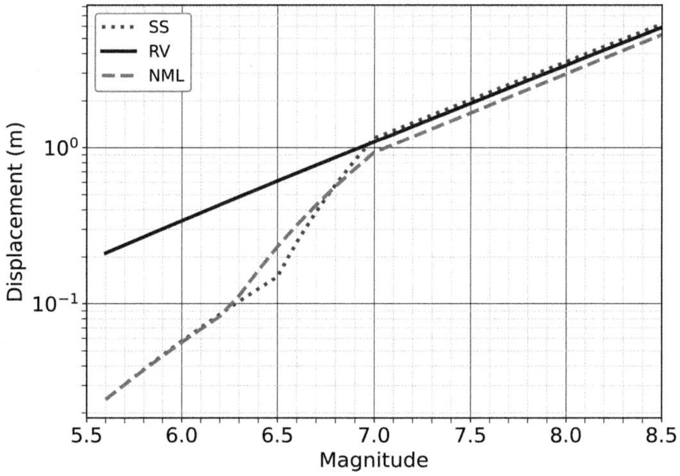

Figure 4. Magnitude scaling of the median displacement of the Lavrentiadis and Abrahamson (2023) fault-displacement model (FDM) for strike-slip (SS), reverse (RV), and normal (NML) earthquakes for $X/L = 0.25$. For strike-slip and normal earthquakes, there is a break in the scaling at **M** 7 with a much steeper slope below **M** 7; for reverse earthquakes, the slope is constant. The change in slope affects the contribution of the magnitude variability to the σ_{MX}. The color version of this figure is available only in the electronic edition.

The σ_{MX} is the standard deviation calculated from the CDF given in equation (23).

We used the LA23 FDM for the hazard calculation to estimate σ_{MX}. Similar to other recent FDMs, the LA23 FDM has a break in the magnitude scaling near **M** 7 for strike-slip and normal events, as shown in Figure 4. The steeper slope between **M** 6.5 and 7 leads to greater variability in the displacement at the site due to the aleatory variability of the magnitudes that cause surface rupture at the site (larger σ_{MX}) for normal (NML) and strike-slip (SS) earthquakes in this magnitude range. As a result, the σ_{MX} can depend on the characteristic magnitude used in the hazard calculation.

In the fault-displacement calculation to estimate σ_{MX}, we used a normal distribution from a pure characteristic model centered on the mean characteristic earthquake with standard deviation values of 0.1 and 0.15 magnitude units for the magnitude PDF. The standard deviations of 0.1 and 0.15 are smaller than the standard deviation of the magnitude–area relations of 0.24 from the global data set of Wells and Coppersmith (1994). We used a smaller standard deviation to account for possible measurement errors in earthquake magnitudes (0.15 magnitude units) and in rupture areas (30%) in the data set used by Wells and Coppersmith (1994) data set. This reduces the standard deviation of the magnitude from 0.24 to 0.15. In addition, there may be regional differences in the median $M(A)$ relation that would not apply to a single fault. If regional differences account for half of the variance, the standard deviation reduces to 0.1 magnitude units. A smaller value of the standard deviation of the magnitude PDF removes less of the aleatory variability

TABLE 4
Source Parameters Used to Calculate σ_{MX}

Parameter or Data Set	SS	NML	RV
Seismothickness (km)	15	15	15
Fault dip (°)	90	50	45
Fault area	Leonard (2010)		
Surface rupture length	Lavrentiadis, Wang, *et al.* (2023)		
HEA13	33%	55%	12%
YEA03	0%	100%	0%
Weights for σ_{MX}	0.289	0.606	0.105

SS, strike-slip earthquake; NML, normal earthquake; RV, reverse earthquake.

from the $\sigma_{NE,MX}$, resulting in a larger estimate of σ_{NE}. An evaluation of σ_{NE} based on other models for the magnitude PDF is given in Section S1 in the supplemental material.

We computed σ_{MX} for mean characteristic magnitudes between 6.0 and 8.0. For each characteristic magnitude, the area of the fault was set to the median area based on the magnitude–area relation, and the seismogenic thickness was set to 15 km. We considered three alternative magnitude–area relations: those of Leonard (2010), Thingbaijam *et al.* (2017), and Hanks and Bakun (2002). The rupture length used the Lavrentiadis, Wang, *et al.* (2023) relation for surface rupture. For each magnitude, five equally weighted site locations were used: $X_F/L_F = 0.05$, 0.15, 0.25, 0.35, and 0.45.

The scaling of the median displacement depends on the style of faulting, as shown in Figure 4. To account for this dependence, the hazard was computed separately for each SOF. The hazard inputs used for computing σ_{MX} are listed in Table 4. The σ_{MX} values for the two values of standard deviations for the magnitude PDF (0.1 and 0.15) are shown in Figure 5 for NML, SS, and reverse (RV) events. The σ_{MX} is largest for NML and SS events in the **M** 6.5–7.0 range because of the steeper slope of magnitude scaling for this magnitude range, as shown in Figure 4. The dependence of σ_{MX} on the selected magnitude–area relation is shown in Figure 6 for the case with $\sigma_M = 0.10$. There is a weak dependence on the magnitude–area relation: the different magnitude–area relations have less of an effect than the two different values of σ_M for the magnitude PDF. For the remaining study, we used the σ_{MX} based on the Leonard (2010) magnitude–area relation.

Whereas the $\sigma_{NE,MX}$ model is a function of the displacement, the σ_{MX} is a function of magnitude. To be able to remove the σ_{MX} from $\sigma_{NE,MX}$, we converted the magnitude dependence of the σ_{MX} to a displacement dependence based on the magnitude scaling of the mean displacement given by the LA23 FDM.

We computed the weighted average of the variances, σ_{MX}^2, as a function of the displacement for the NML, SS, and RV events using weights based on the fraction of events for each SOF for the combined YEA03 and HEA13 data sets. The resulting σ_{MX} values and the smooth model fit to the data are shown in Figure 7. The form of the σ_{MX} model is given by

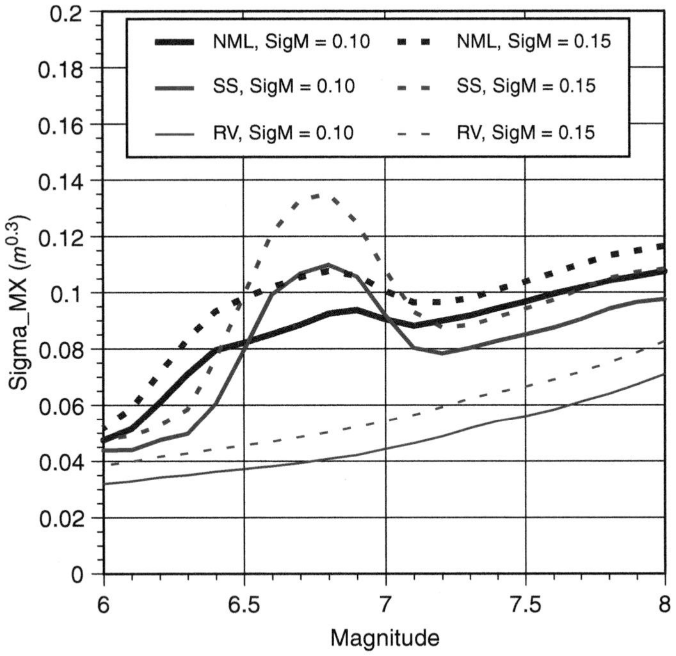

Figure 5. Magnitude dependence of σ_{MX} for NML, SS, and RV events for standard deviations of 0.10 and 0.15 magnitude units for the magnitude probability density function (PDF). The color version of this figure is available only in the electronic edition.

$$\sigma_{MX} = \begin{cases} a_0 & \text{for } \overline{D}_S \geq d_1 \\ a_0 + a_1(\ln(\overline{D}_S/d_1))^2 & \text{for } \overline{D}_S < d_1 \end{cases}. \tag{24}$$

The coefficients for the two magnitude PDFs with $\sigma_M = 0.10$ and $\sigma_M = 0.15$ are listed in Table 5.

Estimation of σ_{NE}

Using the estimates of $\sigma_{NE,MX}$ and σ_{MX}, the σ_{NE} term is computed using equation (20). The model for the σ_{NE} is compared with the ergodic standard deviation and $\sigma_{NE,MX}$ in Figure 8.

PFDHA EXAMPLE

An example PFDHA is conducted using the source characteristics in Table 6 that are representative of a high-slip rate strike-slip fault with a mean characteristic magnitude of 7. We show a logic tree for ergodic and nonergodic calculations in Figure 9. The technical basis for the values and weights of the logic-tree branches is given in Section S2 in the supplemental material.

In the ergodic model, the logic tree includes nodes for the scaled-backbone constants and the value of the σ_{Erg}. We use a scaled-backbone approach with the LA23 FDM as the backbone model, described in Section S2.1, to capture the range of the median displacement from other FDMs. The ergodic model has the largest aleatory variability because it has the most unmodeled behaviors, and it has the smallest epistemic uncertainty range for both the median and the aleatory variability because it is based on the largest (global) data set and has fewer parameters that need to be estimated from the data.

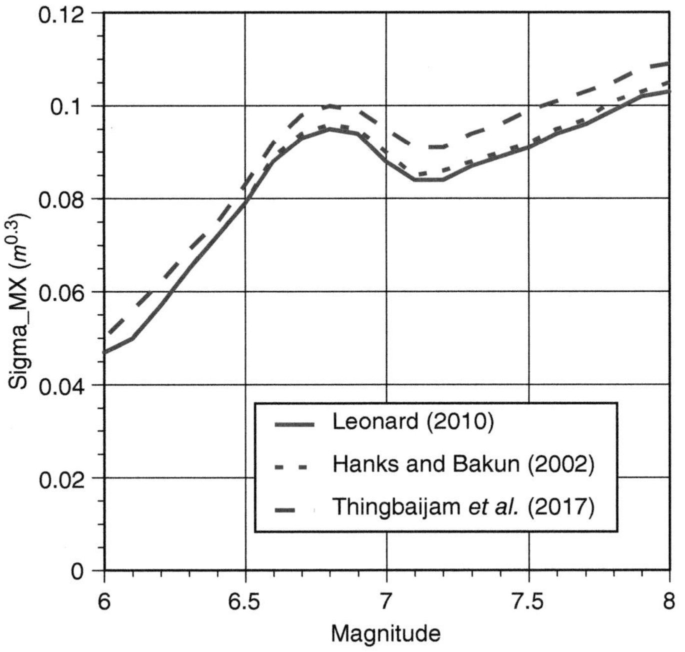

Figure 6. Sensitivity of the magnitude dependence of σ_{MX} to the magnitude–area relation for the case with $\sigma_m = 0.10$ magnitude units for the magnitude PDF. The color version of this figure is available only in the electronic edition.

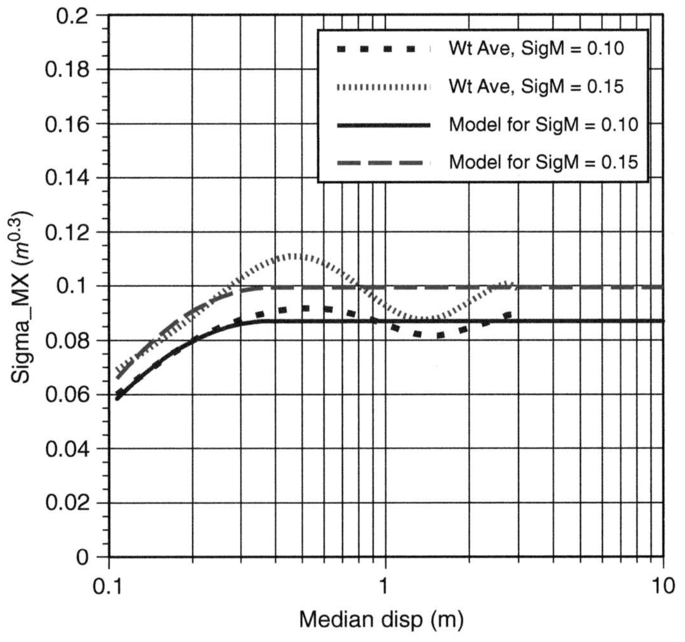

Figure 7. Smoothed model for σ_{MX} converted to a function of displacement. The color version of this figure is available only in the electronic edition.

For the nonergodic models, there is a large reduction in the aleatory variability compared with the ergodic models (0.146 versus 0.33). The aleatory variability for nonergodic models remains the same with or without local data because additional data only systematically reduce epistemic uncertainty in the nonergodic terms $\delta S2S$ and $\delta F2F$.

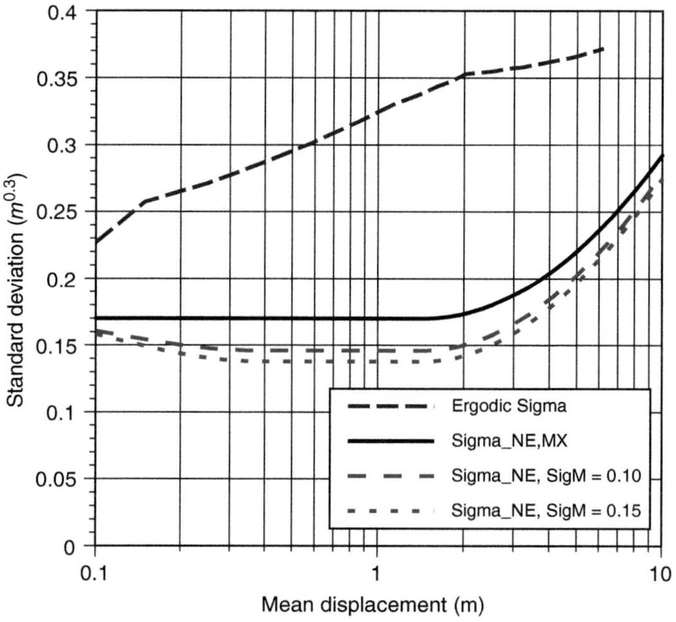

Figure 8. Comparisons of the models for the ergodic standard deviation $\sigma_{NE,MX}$ and σ_{NE}. The color version of this figure is available only in the electronic edition.

Partitioning into aleatory and epistemic

The partitioning of the aleatory and epistemic terms for the cases with and without data is shown in Figure 10. For the case without data, moving from ergodic to nonergodic models directly shifts the aleatory variability into epistemic uncertainty such that the combined aleatory and epistemic variance is unchanged; however, for the case in which there is local data, there can be a significant reduction of the variance of the combined aleatory and epistemic terms, as shown in Figure 10 for a case with five observations of displacements from past events.

For comparison, the relative sizes of the aleatory and epistemic terms for ergodic and nonergodic GMMs are shown in Figure 11. The nonergodic aleatory variance for the GMMs is a larger fraction of the ergodic aleatory variance than for the nonergodic FDMs, indicating that the surface slip at a point is less variable than the ground motion for a specific source-site combination.

TABLE 5
Nonergodic Aleatory Variability That Includes the Variability of *M* and *X*/*L* ($\sigma_{NE,MX}$), the Aleatory Variability of the Combined Effect of *M* and *X*/*L* (σ_{MX}), and the Remaining Nonergodic Aleatory Variability Without the Variability of *M* and *X*/*L* (σ_{NE}) for the Data Sets of Youngs *et al.* (2003) (YEA03) and Hecker *et al.* (2013) (HEA13)

Parameter	$\sigma_M = 0.10$	$\sigma_M = 0.15$
$d_1(m)$	0.380	0.383
a_0	0.087	0.0994
a_1	−0.0178	−0.0206

As a fraction of the ergodic variance, the net reduction of the combined aleatory and epistemic uncertainty for the nonergodic GMMs is less than the net reduction for the nonergodic FDMs.

Data for the example

We generated two data sets, each with five observed displacements listed in Table 7. From the hazard calculation with zero aleatory variability of the FDM, the median displacement is 1.014 $m^{0.3}$. The two data sets have arithmetic mean displacements of 0.590 m and 1.582 m (transformed mean displacements of 0.822 $m^{0.3}$ and 1.122 $m^{0.3}$, respectively). Using equation (20), the σ_{NE} is 0.146 for both cases based on $\sigma_M = 0.1$ for the magnitude pdf.

Nonergodic term without data at the site

For a site without displacement data, we compute the hazard using the ergodic and the nonergodic FDMs. For the ergodic FDM, the standard deviation from the LA23 ergodic FDM for **M** 7 is 0.331 $m^{0.3}$ units. For the nonergodic FDM without data at the site, the mean displacement for an **M** 7 strike-slip event is 1.27 m, leading to a σ_{NE} of 0.146 $m^{0.3}$ units based on $\sigma_M = 0.1$.

The net nonergodic adjustment δNE_{fs} is given by

$$\delta NE_{fs} = \delta F2F_f + \delta S2S_s. \quad (25)$$

If there are no earthquakes with surface displacement at the site ($N_s = 0$), the central estimate of δNE_{fs} is 0, and the epistemic uncertainty of δNE_{fs} is computed from the difference in the variances of the ergodic and nonergodic FDMs given by the following equation:

$$\sigma_{\text{epi},NE}(N_s = 0) = \sqrt{\sigma^2_{\text{Erg}}(M) - \sigma^2_{NE}(D_{\text{mean}})}. \quad (26)$$

TABLE 6
Source Characterization for the Example Hazard Calculations

Parameter	Value or Model
Mean characteristic magnitude	$M_{\text{char}} = 7.0$
Style of faulting	Strike slip
Dip	90°
Fault length	$L_F = 80$ km
Seismogenic thickness (km)	12 km
Down-dip fault width	$W_F = 12$ km
Magnitude PDF	YC85 composite model Youngs and Coppersmith (1985)
Slip rate and weights	7 mm/yr (0.2) 9 mm/yr (0.6) 11 mm/yr (0.2)
Surface rupture length	Lavrentiadis, Wang, *et al.* (2023)
Probability of surface rupture	Wells and Coppersmith (1993) for all SOF
Rupture location along strike	Uniform distribution

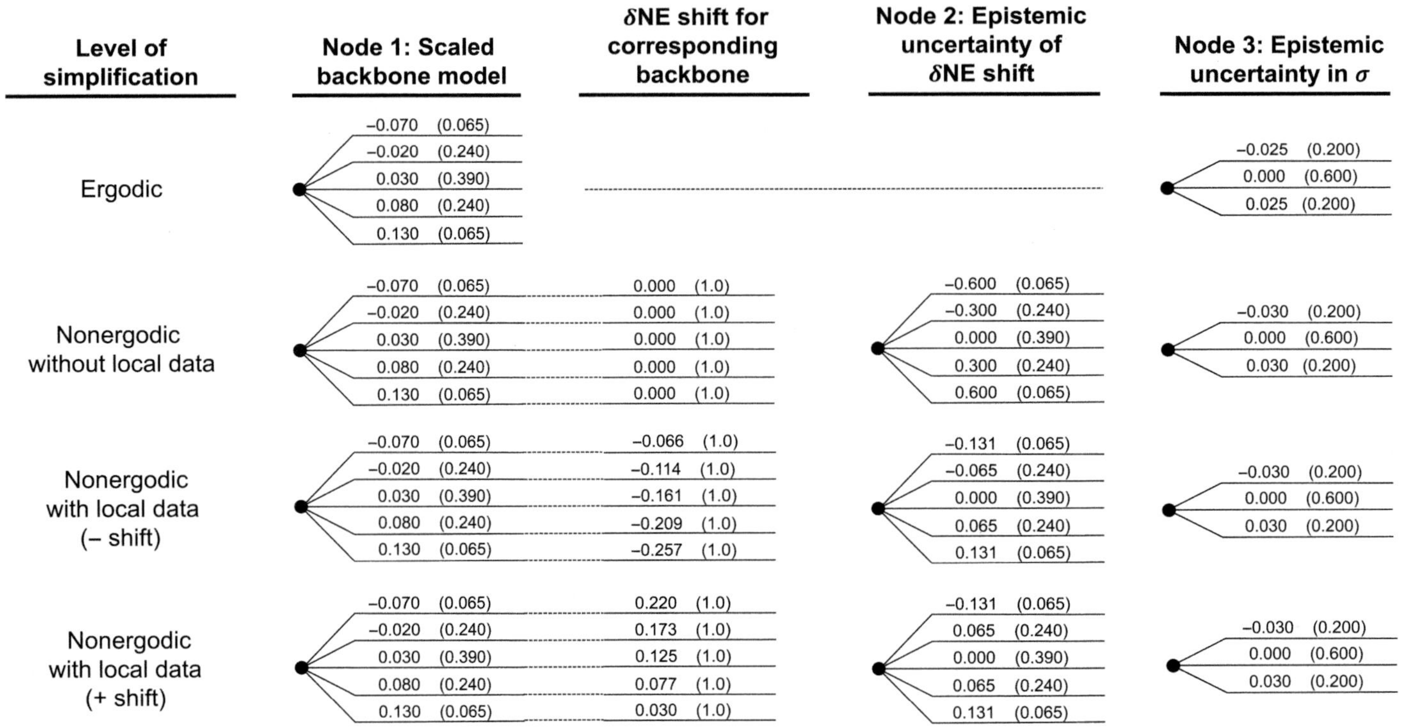

Figure 9. Logic tree used for the hazard calculations shown in Figures 12–14.

The hazard calculation uses the magnitude, but the σ_{NE} model is a function of the mean displacement. For the case without data, the mean displacement for a given magnitude is computed from the FDM. For **M** 7 without data, $\sigma_{\text{epi},NE} = 0.297\ m^{0.3}$ (see Table 8).

The hazard curves for the ergodic FDM and the nonergodic FDM without data are shown in Figure 12. Without data, the epistemic fractiles for the nonergodic approach are very wide. The total combined aleatory variability and epistemic uncertainty remain the same because, without data, the variances of the aleatory variability and epistemic uncertainty have a one-to-one exchange. This results in the same mean hazard. The difference in the mean hazard at long return periods shown in Figure 12 is due to the five-point sampling of the epistemic uncertainty of the δNE_{fs} ($\sigma_{\text{epi},NE}$). If finer sampling was used, then the mean hazard curves would be the same.

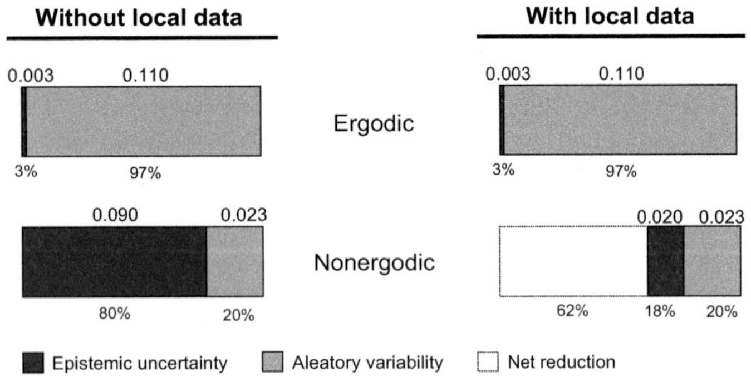

Figure 10. Visual representation of variances for fault-displacement hazard examples. The variances are shown in $m^{0.6}$ units. The nonergodic case without data applies to the hazard curves shown in Figure 12. The nonergodic case with data applies to the hazard curves shown in Figures 13 and 14. For the ergodic FDM, almost all the combined variance is treated as aleatory, whereas for the nonergodic FDM without data, ~80% of the combined variance is epistemic. With some data, there is a large reduction in the epistemic uncertainty, and the combined variance is ~40% of the combined variance without data. The color version of this figure is available only in the electronic edition.

Nonergodic term with data at the site

Using the observed displacement with the nonergodic FDM approach requires an estimate of the mean residual at the site; however, the metadata (magnitude and *X/L*) are generally not available for paleoseismic observations. To estimate the mean

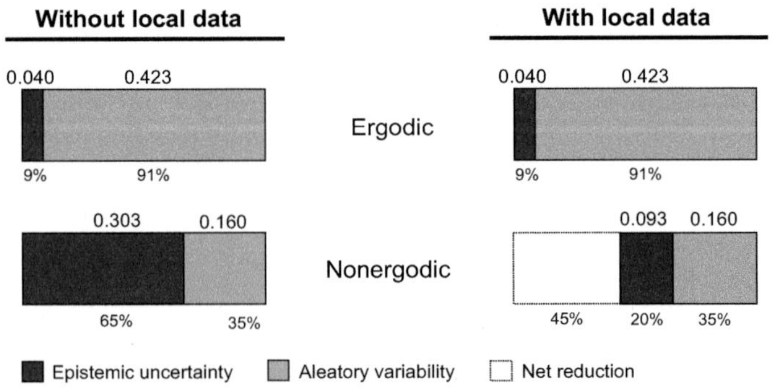

Figure 11. Visual representation of variances for a ground-motion hazard example. The variances are shown in LN^2 units. Compared with the fractional reduction of the variances for displacement ground-motion model (GMM) shown in Figure 10, the aleatory variability for the nonergodic GMM is not reduced by as large a percentage as for the nonergodic FDMs. The color version of this figure is available only in the electronic edition.

TABLE 7

Assumed Data Sets of Observed Displacements for the Example Hazard Calculation

	Displacement (m)	
	Case 1	Case 2
Event or Displacement Parameter	Negative Shift	Positive Shift
Event 1	0.55	2.79
Event 2	0.75	1.29
Event 3	0.11	1.26
Event 4	0.61	1.90
Event 5	0.93	0.67
$\overline{D}_{s,\text{Obs}}$ (m)	0.590	1.582
$\overline{D}^{0.3}_{s,\text{Obs}}(m^{0.3})$	0.822	1.122

$\overline{D}_{s,\text{Obs}}$ is the arithmetic mean of the observed displacements, and the $\overline{D}^{0.3}_{s,\text{Obs}}$ is the mean of the $D^{0.3}_s$.

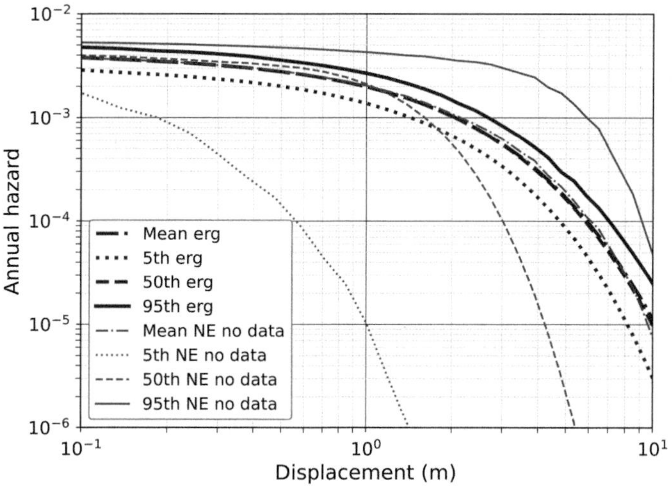

Figure 12. Mean and fractiles of the ergodic and nonergodic hazards for the case with no data. The mean hazard curves are the same, but the fractiles are much wider for the nonergodic hazard because there are no data available to constrain the nonergodic term. The color version of this figure is available only in the electronic edition.

transformed displacement ($\overline{D^{0.3}_s}$) for the site, we use the hazard for the site computed for the nonergodic standard deviation σ_{NE} with a zero nonergodic term ($\delta NE_{fs} = 0$). The mean displacement is calculated using the CDF from the hazard given by equation (23).

The mean residual at site $\overline{\delta_s}$ is estimated by the difference in the mean transformed observed displacement ($\overline{D}^{0.3}_{s,\text{Obs}}$) and the mean transformed displacement from the nonergodic hazard with $\delta NE_{fs} = 0$ ($\overline{D}^{0.3}_{s,\text{Haz}}$):

$$\overline{\delta_s} = \overline{D}^{0.3}_{s,\text{Obs}} - \overline{D}^{0.3}_{s,\text{Haz}}. \tag{27}$$

The residuals include contributions from the nonergodic terms $\delta S2S$ and $\delta F2F$ and from the between-event and within-site residuals. Therefore, the mean residual is not the best estimate of the net nonergodic term by itself. The residuals can be separated into the net nonergodic term ($\delta F2F + \delta S2S$) and the aleatory term ($\delta WS + \delta B^0$) using the maximum-likelihood estimate for the random effects as described by Abrahamson and Youngs (1992). The maximum-likelihood estimate of the nonergodic term is given by

$$\delta NE_{fs} = b\overline{\delta_s} + \delta F2F_f, \tag{28}$$

in which

$$b = \frac{N_s}{N_s + \frac{\sigma^2_{NE}}{(\sigma^2_{\text{epi},\delta NE}(N_s=0))}}, \tag{29}$$

and $\delta F2F_f$ is the mean residual from the observed displacements at all sites along the fault.

The partitioning of mean residual into the systematic nonergodic term and the aleatory variability term depends on the $\sigma^2_{NE}/\sigma^2_{\text{epi},\delta NE}$ ratio. As the number of earthquakes at the site

TABLE 8

Parameter Values Used for the Example Hazard Calculations for Ergodic, Nonergodic Without Data, Nonergodic with $N_s = 5$ and Negative Shift (Case 1), and Nonergodic with $N_s = 5$ and a Positive Shift (Case 2)

			Nonergodic		
Parameter	Reference	Ergodic	No Data	Case 1	Case 2
σ_{Erg} ($m^{0.3}$)	LA23	0.331	–	–	–
Epistemic uncertainty of scaled backbone FDM ($m^{0.3}$)		0.050	0.050	–	–
σ_{NE} ($m^{0.3}$) (for **M** 7)		–	0.146	0.146	0.146
N_s		–	0	5	5
$\overline{D}^{0.3}_{s,\text{Obs}}$ ($m^{0.3}$)	Table 7	–	0	0.822	1.122
$\overline{D}^{0.3}_{s,\text{Haz}}$ ($m^{0.3}$)	Hazard calculation	–	–	0.991	0.991
$\overline{\delta}_s$ ($m^{0.3}$)	Equation (27)	–	–	−0.169	0.131
$\delta NE_{\text{obs}}(m^{0.3})$	Equation (28)	–	0.0	−0.161	0.125
$\sigma_{\text{epi}-\delta NE}$ ($m^{0.3}$)	Equations (26) and (30)	–	0.297	0.065	0.065

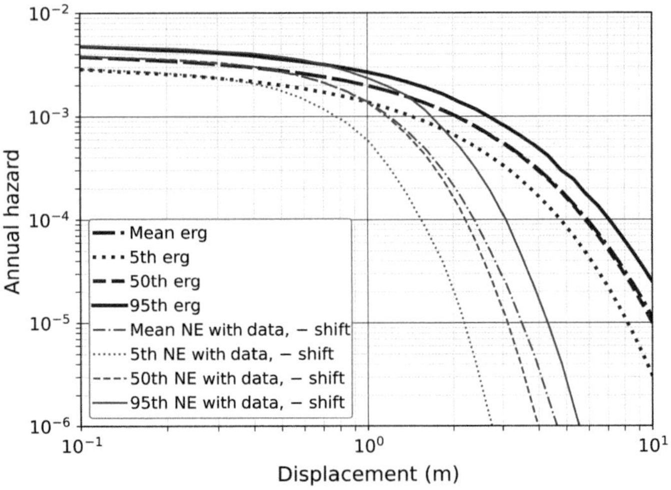

Figure 13. Example of the hazard fractiles based on ergodic and nonergodic FDMs for case 1: a site with data that has a negative mean δNE based on observed displacements from five events listed in Table 7. The color version of this figure is available only in the electronic edition.

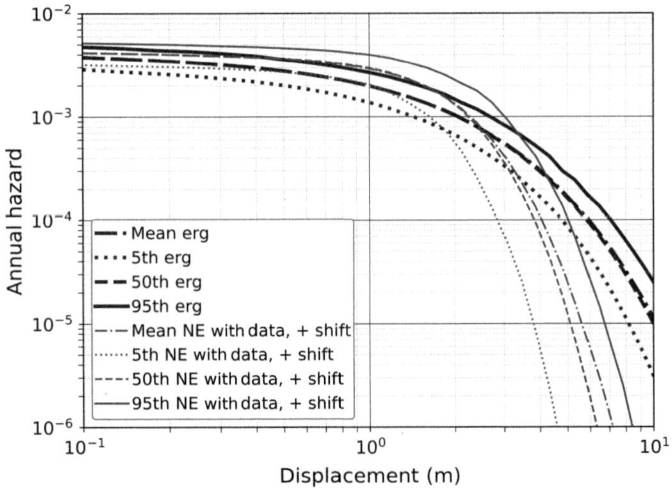

Figure 14. Hazard fractiles based on ergodic and nonergodic FDMs for case 2: a site with data that has a positive mean δNE based on observed displacements from five events listed in Table 7. The color version of this figure is available only in the electronic edition.

becomes large, the δNE_s approaches $\overline{\delta_s}$. The epistemic uncertainty of the δNE_{fs} is given by the standard error of the mean residual:

$$\sigma_{\text{epi},\delta NE}(N_s > 0) = \frac{\sigma_{NE}}{\sqrt{N_s}}. \tag{30}$$

With these estimates of the median and epistemic uncertainty of the nonergodic term, the nonergodic hazard can be computed. The mean and epistemic fractiles of the hazard curves are shown in Figures 13 and 14 for the cases with positive and negative shifts in the nonergodic terms, respectively. Having

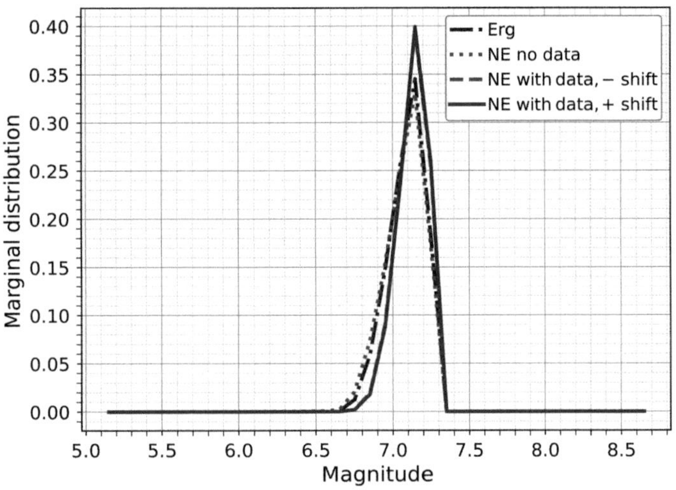

Figure 15. Marginal distribution for magnitude from the disaggregation for a return period of 2500 yr. The color version of this figure is available only in the electronic edition.

data at the site (here, $N_s = 5$) can have a large effect on the fault-displacement hazard and greatly reduce the epistemic uncertainty in the hazard compared with the case with no data. The hazard curves for both the positive and negative nonergodic adjustment terms have steeper slopes than the ergodic hazard because of the reduced aleatory standard deviation. The hazard curves for the positive nonergodic term are shifted above the ergodic hazard at short return periods but cross the ergodic hazard at long return periods. In contrast, for a negative shift in the displacement at the site, the median displacement is smaller than the ergodic median, and the hazard curve is steeper. As a result, the 5th–95th fractiles of the hazard curves for the negative nonergodic terms remain lower than the ergodic hazard fractiles.

Marginal distributions

The marginal distributions for M, X/L, and ϵ from the disaggregation for a 2500 yr return period are shown in Figures 15–17. The range of M and X/L values are similar for the ergodic and nonergodic approaches, but the range of ϵ values changes significantly. For the nonergodic approach with no data, the large epistemic uncertainty in the nonergodic terms leads to models with a large range of median displacements, which in turn leads to a wide range of ϵ values compared with the ergodic case. The ϵ values for the nonergodic approach without data range from −3 to 2, with a mean of −0.46. In contrast, the ϵ values for the ergodic approach range from 0.4 to 2 with a mean of 1.0.

There is little change in the M and X/L distributions compared with the ergodic case, but there is a large change in the ϵ distribution: the mean of the ϵ distribution for the nonergodic case with data is centered at $\epsilon = 1$, similar to mean ϵ for the ergodic case.

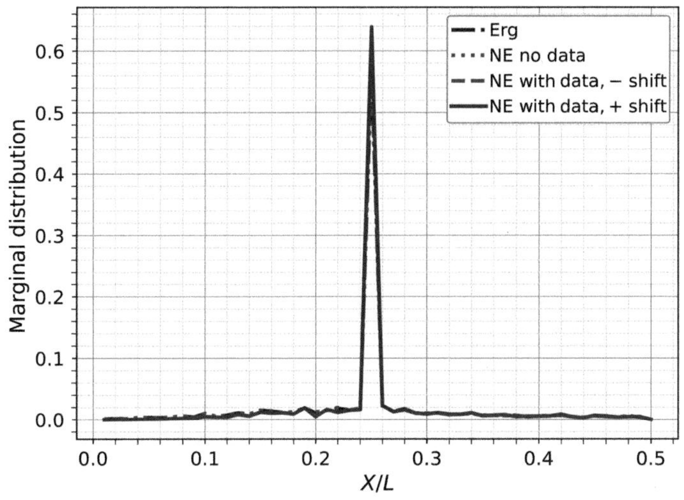

Figure 16. Marginal distribution for X/L from the disaggregation for a return period of 2500 yr. The color version of this figure is available only in the electronic edition.

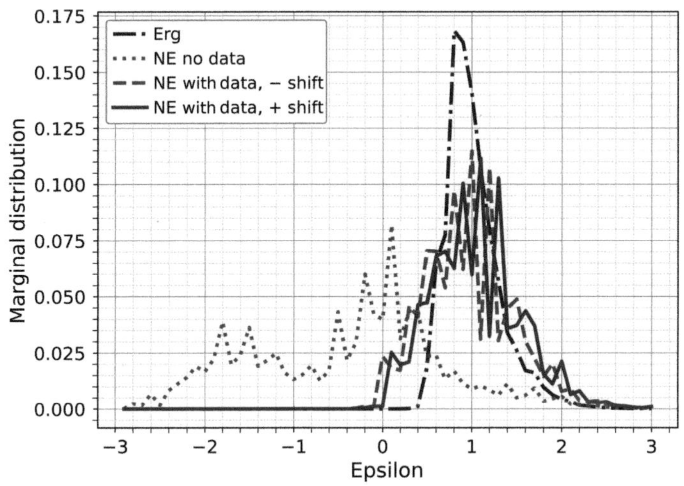

Figure 17. Marginal distribution for ϵ from the disaggregation for a return period of 2500 yr. The color version of this figure is available only in the electronic edition.

Nonergodic term for data located down strike

If the displacement observations are located on the fault but down strike from the site, the nonergodic term for the site will depend on the spatial correlation of the displacement residuals. Lavrentiadis and Abrahamson (2023) developed a model for the spatial correlation of the displacement residuals that is a function of the distance between locations divided by the segment length. To adapt this spatial correlation model to our application, we converted the spatial correlation to be a function of the separation distance and the mean displacement (see Section S3 in the supplemental material). The resulting correlation model $\rho(\Delta X,\overline{D}_{\text{obs}})$ is shown in Figure 18 in which

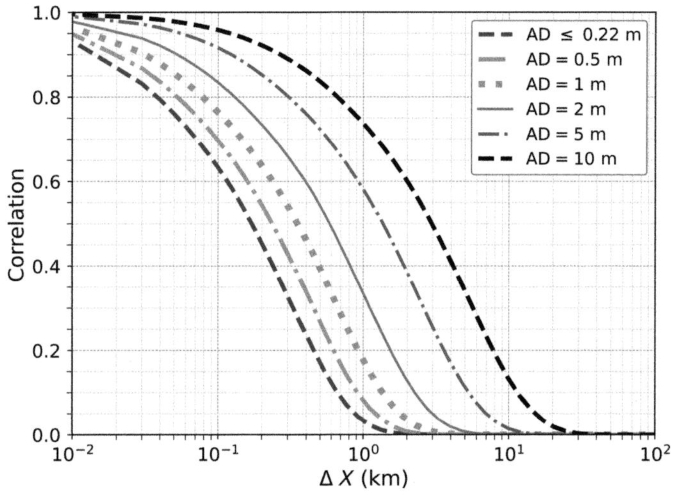

Figure 18. Correlation of the displacement residuals as a function of ΔX for different values of the average displacement (AD). The ΔX measures how farther away the observation is from the project site (both the observation and project site are on the same fault). The color version of this figure is available only in the electronic edition.

ΔX is the distance in kilometers between sites measured along strike. The derivation of the equations for computing the mean and epistemic uncertainty of δNE at the site is given in Section S3. The final equations are summarized here.

If the closest site with observed displacements is located ΔX km from the project site, the mean nonergodic term for the site is computed based on the full correlation of the $\delta F2F$ and partial correlation of the $\delta S2S$:

$$\delta NE_{\text{site}} = \rho(\Delta X,\overline{D}_{\text{obs}})\delta S2S_{\text{obs}} + \delta F2F_{\text{obs}}. \tag{31}$$

If there are multiple observation points along the fault, the estimate of δNE_{site} can be based on the full set of observations, but because the correlation decays rapidly with ΔX, the observations at the closest point will dominate the estimation of δNE_{site}.

The δNE_{site} depends on two variables, $\delta S2S_{\text{obs}}$ and $\delta F2F_{\text{obs}}$. Each of these variables is a function of δNE_{obs}. The epistemic variance of the non-ergodic site term from the observation $\delta S2S_{\text{obs}}$ is given by

$$\phi^2_{\text{epi},\delta S2S,\text{obs}} = (1-c)^2\sigma^2_{\text{epi},\delta NE,\text{obs}} = (1-c)^2\frac{\sigma^2_{NE}}{N_s}, \tag{32}$$

in which $\sigma_{\text{epi},\delta NE,\text{obs}}$ is given by equation (30) and the c term is given by

$$c = \left(1 + \frac{\phi^2_{S2S}}{\tau^2_{F2F}}\right)^{-1}. \tag{33}$$

The variance of $\delta F2F_{\text{obs}}$ is given by

$$\tau^2_{\text{epi},\delta F2F,\text{obs}} = c^2\tau^2_{\text{epi},\delta NE,\text{obs}} = c^2\frac{\sigma^2_{NE}}{N_s}. \tag{34}$$

The epistemic uncertainty in the δ_{NE} at the site is given by

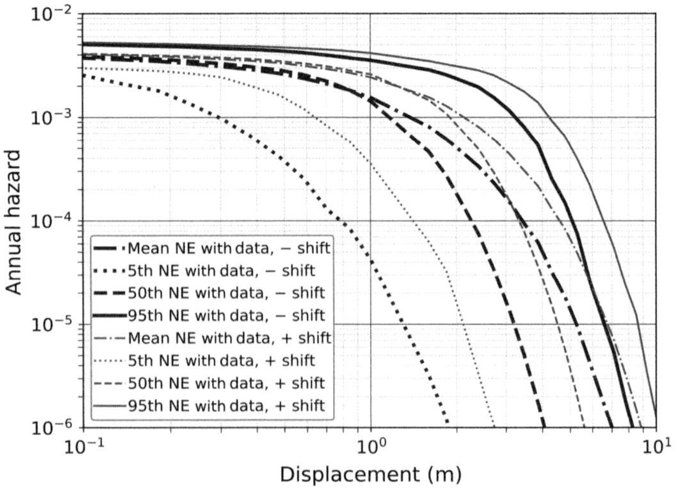

Figure 19. Nonergodic hazard example for $\Delta X = 0.1$ km case 1 (blue) and case 2 (red). The color version of this figure is available only in the electronic edition.

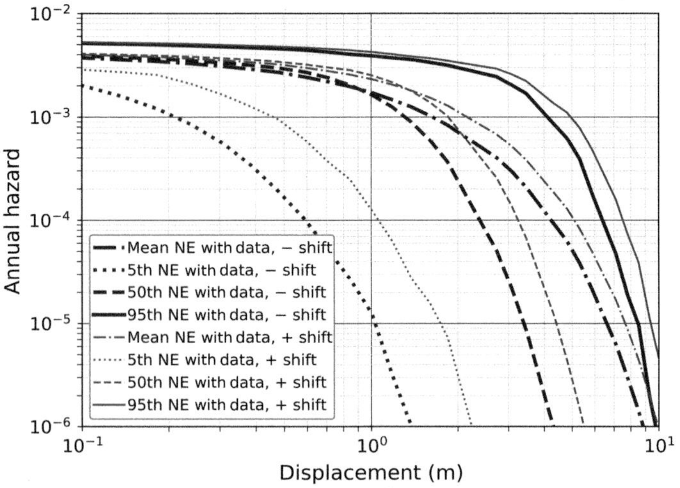

Figure 20. Nonergodic hazard example for $\Delta X = 0.5$ km case 1 (blue) and case 2 (red). The color version of this figure is available only in the electronic edition.

$$\sigma_{\mathrm{epi},\delta NE,\mathrm{site}} = \sqrt{(1-\rho^2(\Delta X))[\sigma^2_{\mathrm{Erg}} - \tau^2_{F2F} - \sigma^2_{NE} - \phi^2_{\mathrm{epi},\delta S2S,\mathrm{obs}}] + \phi^2_{\mathrm{epi},\delta S2S,\mathrm{obs}} + \tau^2_{\mathrm{epi},\delta F2F,\mathrm{obs}}}. \quad (35)$$

We computed the displacement hazard for the observed displacements located ΔX values of 0.1, 0.5, and 2 km down strike from the site using the two cases with positive and negative $\delta_{NE\text{-obs}}$ values shown in Table S1. The intermediate calculations for computing the mean δNE_{fs} and the epistemic uncertainty in the δNE_{fs} are given in Table S1. The values for the median and epistemic uncertainty of the $\delta_{NE\text{-site}}$ terms are summarized in Table 9. As ΔX increases, the mean nonergodic term goes toward zero, and the epistemic uncertainty in the nonergodic term increases toward the epistemic uncertainty for the no-data case.

The mean and fractiles of the hazard curves are shown in Figures 19–21 for ΔX of 0.1, 0.5, and 2 km, respectively. For $\Delta X = 0.1$ km, the hazard curves for the positive $\delta_{NE\text{-obs}}$ case are much higher than the hazard curves for the negative $\delta_{NE\text{-obs}}$ case, indicating that having observations 100 m from the site provides valuable constraints on the hazard. For $\Delta X = 0.5$ km, there is more overlap between the fractiles for the positive and negative $\delta_{NE\text{-obs}}$ cases because of the reduced correlation of the $\delta_{NE\text{-site}}$ and $\delta_{NE\text{-obs}}$ terms compared with the $\Delta X = 0.1$ km case. For $\Delta X = 2$ km, there is only a small difference between the fractiles for the positive and negative $\delta_{NE\text{-obs}}$ cases. This remaining difference is due to the full correlation of the $\delta F2F$ term along strike.

TABLE 9
Comparison of the Nonergodic Terms for Observations at Different Distances from the Site (ΔX) for M 7

	Case 1		Case 2	
ΔX (km)	**$\delta NE_{\mathrm{site}}$ ($m^{0.3}$)**	**$\sigma_{\mathrm{epi},\delta NE,\mathrm{site}}$ ($m^{0.3}$)**	**$\delta NE_{\mathrm{site}}$ ($m^{0.3}$)**	**$\sigma_{\mathrm{epi},\delta NE,\mathrm{site}}$ ($m^{0.3}$)**
0	−0.161	0.065	0.125	0.065
0.1	−0.140	0.155	0.115	0.131
0.5	−0.100	0.230	0.130	0.198
2	−0.042	0.269	0.052	0.259

CONCLUSION

Similar to GMMs used in PSHA, the FDMs used in PFDHA should properly separate the aleatory variability and the epistemic uncertainty components. This separation depends on the level of simplification used in the FDM. Ergodic versus nonergodic models represent fundamentally different levels of simplification. These different levels of simplification should not be included as alternative branches on the logic tree. A consequence of combining two different levels of simplification in a logic tree is a resulting epistemic uncertainty that does not apply to either level of simplification and an unclear definition of what the epistemic uncertainty fractiles represent.

The nonergodic framework for FDMs incorporates the displacement-based approach for computing the conditional probability of exceedance. Rather than an earthquake-based approach versus a displacement-based approach, ergodic, partially nonergodic, and nonergodic approaches clearly define the level of simplification. Using the nonergodic framework

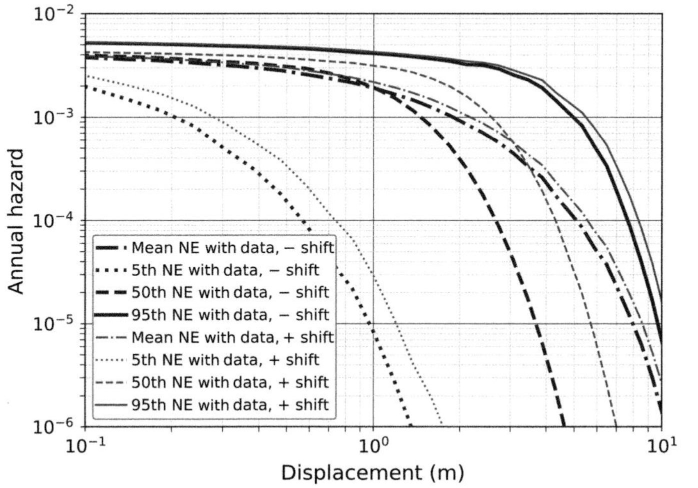

Figure 21. Nonergodic hazard example for $\Delta X = 2$ km case 1 (blue) and case 2 (red). The color version of this figure is available only in the electronic edition.

provided in this article, the earthquake-based approach can be used with a nonergodic FDM.

The observed variability of slip at a point from the YEA03 and HEA13 data sets includes the effect of different magnitudes and *X/L* values in addition to the nonergodic standard deviation of the FDM (σ_{NE}). For a nonergodic FDM, the σ_{NE} needs to be isolated from the effects of different magnitudes and *X/L* values. The proposed methodology overcomes the lack of metadata required to directly compute residuals for estimating σ_{NE} that can be used in a nonergodic FDM.

The nonergodic framework provides a more realistic representation of the hazard than the traditional ergodic approach. Using the current ergodic framework significantly underestimates the epistemic uncertainty for a nonergodic approach, which can provide a false sense of confidence in the PFDHA results. If there is no local data at the site to constrain the nonergodic terms, a common recommendation is to use an ergodic model. This is appropriate if the objective is only the mean hazard, but the fractiles will be much too narrow. For sites without local data, the nonergodic FDM approach can still be used. The mean hazard will be unchanged from the ergodic mean hazard, but the fractiles will be much wider. The large uncertainty in the hazard should be considered as part of the engineering decisions that are made to ensure adequate seismic safety.

DATA AND RESOURCES

The displacement data sets of Hecker *et al.* (2013) and Youngs *et al.* (2003) and the FORTRAN code for the probabilistic fault-displacement hazard analysis (PFDHA) hazard calculation used in this study are available at https://github.com/iyliou/LA25_PFDHA (last accessed September 2025). The supplemental material includes four sections: S1 is an evaluation of the effects of different models for the magnitude probability density function (PDF), S2 gives the technical basis for the values and weights of the logic-tree branches, S3 gives the derivation of the mean and epistemic uncertainty of δNE_{site}, and S4 shows a comparison of the CV and the power-normal standard deviation.

DECLARATION OF COMPETING INTERESTS

The authors acknowledge that there are no conflicts of interest recorded.

ACKNOWLEDGMENTS

The authors thank Alex Sarmiento, Tom Rockwell, and Associate Editor Mark Stirling for their useful comments on the draft article. Partial funding for this study was provided by the PG&E Long-Term Seismic Program.

REFERENCES

Abrahamson, N. A., and R. R. Youngs (1992). A stable algorithm for regression analyses using the random effects model, *Bull. Seismol. Soc. Am.* **82,** no. 1, 505–510.

Abrahamson, N. A., N. M. Kuehn, M. Walling, and N. Landwehr (2019). Probabilistic seismic hazard analysis in California using nonergodic ground-motion models, *Bull. Seismol. Soc. Am.* **109,** no. 4, 1235–1249.

Anderson, J. G., and J. N. Brune (1999). Variability of displacement: Probabilistic seismic hazard analysis without the ergodic assumption, *Seismol. Res. Lett.* **70,** no. 1, 19–28.

Hanks, T. C., and W. Bakun (2002). A bilinear source-scaling model for M–log A observations of continental earthquakes, *Bull. Seismol. Soc. Am.* **92,** no. 5, 1841–1846.

Hecker, S., N. A. Abrahamson, and K. E. Woodell (2013). Variability of displacement: Implications for earthquake size distribution and rupture hazard on faults, *Bull. Seismol. Soc. Am.* **103,** no. 2A, 651–674.

Landwehr, N., N. M. Kuehn, T. Scheffer, and N. A. Abrahamson (2016). A nonergodic ground-motion model for California with spatially varying coefficients, *Bull. Seismol. Soc. Am.* **106,** no. 6, 2574–2583.

Lavrentiadis, G., and N.A. Abrahamson (2023). Fault-displacement models for aggregate and principal displacements, *Earthq. Spectra* **0,** doi: 10.1177/87552930231201531.

Lavrentiadis, G., N. A. Abrahamson, N. M. Kuehn, Y. Bozorgnia, C. A. Goulet, A. Babic, J. Macedo, M. Dolsek, N. Gregor, A. R. Kottke, *et al.* (2023). Overview and introduction to the development of non-ergodic earthquake ground-motion models, *Bull. Earthq. Eng.* **101,** no. 21, 5121–5150.

Lavrentiadis, G., Y. Wang, N. A. Abrahamson, Y. Bozorgnia, and C. A. Goulet (2023). A seismologically consistent surface rupture length model for unbounded and width-limited events, *Earthq. Spectra* 1–21, doi: 10.1177/87552930231205871.

Leonard, M. (2010) Earthquake fault scaling: Self-consistent relating of rupture length, width, average displacement, and moment release, *Bull. Seismol. Soc. Am.* **100,** no. 5A, 1971–1988.

Lin, P.-S., B. Chiou, N. Abrahamson, M. Walling, C.-T. Lee, and C.-T. Cheng (2011). Repeatable source, site, and path effects on the standard deviation for empirical ground-motion prediction models, *Bull. Seismol. Soc. Am.* **101,** no. 5, 2281–2295.

Liou, I. Y., and N. A. Abrahamson (2024). Framework for aleatory variability and epistemic uncertainty for the ground-motion characterization based on the level of simplification, *Bull. Seismol. Soc. Am.* **115,** no. 1, 296–314.

Mammarella, L., F. Visini, P. Boncio, S. Baize, O. Scotti, C. Beauval, B. Pace, and S. Thompson (2025). Conditional probability of surface rupture: A numerical approach for principal faulting, *Earthq. Spectra*, doi: 10.1177/87552930241293570.

Moss, R. E. S., and Z. E. Ross (2011). Probabilistic fault displacement hazard analysis for reverse faults, *Bull. Seismol. Soc. Am.* **101,** no. 4, 1542–1553.

Moss, R. E. S., K. V. Stanton, and M. I. Buelna (2013). The impact of material stiffness on the likelihood of fault rupture propagating to the ground surface, *Seismol. Res. Lett.* **84,** no. 3, 458–488.

Petersen, M., T. Dawson, R. Chen, T. Cao, C. Wills, D. Schwartz, and A. D. Frankel (2011). Fault displacement hazard for strike-slip faults, *Bull. Seismol. Soc. Am.* **101,** no. 2, 805–825.

Pezzopane, S. K., and T. E. Dawson (1996). Fault displacement hazard: A summary of issues and information, in *Seismotectonic Framework and Characterization of Faulting at Yucca Mountain, Nevada*, U.S. Geological Survey Administrative Report, prepared for the U.S. Department of Energy, Yucca Mountain Project MOL. 19970129.0041(9), 160.

Pizza, M., M. F. Ferrario, F. Thomas, G. Tringali, and F. Livio (2023). Likelihood of primary surface faulting: Updating of empirical regressions, *Bull. Seismol. Soc. Am.* **113,** no. 5, 2106–2118.

Rodriguez-Marek, A., E. M. Rathje, J. J. Bommer, F. Scherbaum, and P. J. Stafford (2014). Application of single-station sigma and site-response characterization in a probabilistic seismic-hazard analysis for a new nuclear site, *Bull. Seismol. Soc. Am.* **104,** no. 4, 1601–1619.

Sarmiento, A., G. Lavrentiadis, Y. Bozorgnia, R. Chen, B. Chiou, T. Dawson, A. Kottke, N. Kuehn, C. Madugo, R. Moss, *et al.* (2024). Comparisons of FDHI fault displacement models for principal and aggregate displacement, *Earthq. Spectra*, doi: 10.1177/87552930251327894.

Sarmiento, A., D. Madugo, Y. Bozorgnia, A. Shen, S. Mazzoni, G. Lavrentiadis, T. Dawson, C. Madugo, A. Kottke, S. Thompson, *et al.* (2021). Fault displacement hazard initiative database, report girs-2021-08, *Technical Report*, UCLA Natural Hazards Risk And Resiliency Research Center, Los Angeles, California.

Stepp, J. C., I. Wong, J. Whitney, R. Quittmeyer, N. Abrahamson, G. Toro, R. Youngs, K. Coppersmith, J. Savy, and T. Sullivan (2001). Probabilistic seismic hazard analyses for ground motions and fault displacement at Yucca Mountain, Nevada *Earthq. Spectra* **17,** no. 1, 113–151.

Sung, C. H., N. A. Abrahamson, N. M. Kuehn, P. Traversa, and I. Zentner (2023). A non-ergodic ground-motion model of Fourier amplitude spectra for France, *Bull. Earthq. Eng.* **21,** no. 11, 5293–5317.

Takao, M., J. Tsuchiyama, T. Annaka, and T. Kurita (2013). Application of probabilistic fault displacement hazard analysis in Japan, *J. Jpn. Assoc. Earthq. Eng.* **13**, 17–36.

Thingbaijam, K. K., M. Mai, and K. Goda (2017). New empirical earthquake source-scaling laws, *Bull. Seismol. Soc. Am.* **105,** no. 5, 2225–2246.

Wells, D. L., and K. J. Coppersmith (1993). Likelihood of surface rupture as a function of magnitude, *Seismol. Res. Lett.* **64,** no. 1, 54.

Wells, D. L., and K. J. Coppersmith (1994). New empirical relationships among magnitude, rupture length, rupture width, rupture area, and surface displacement, *Bull. Seismol. Soc. Am.* **84,** 974–1002.

Wong, I. G., and J. C. Stepp (1998). *Probabilistic Seismic Hazard Analyses for Fault Displacement and Vibratory Ground Motion at Yucca Mountain, Nevada*, U.S. Department of Energy DEAC04-94AL85000, Prepared for the U.S. Geological Survey, 23 February, Vol. 3, Oakland, California.

Yang, H., M. Quigley, and T. King (2021). Surface slip distributions and geometric complexity of intraplate reverse-faulting earthquakes, *GSA Bull.* **133,** nos. 9/10, 1909–1929.

Youngs, R. R., and K. J. Coppersmith (1985). Implications of fault slip rates and earthquake recurrence models to probabilistic seismic hazard estimates, *Bull. Seismol. Soc. Am.* **75,** 939–964.

Youngs, R. R., W. J. Arabasz, R. E. Anderson, A. R. Ramelli, J. P. Ake, D. B. Slemmons, J. P. McCalpin, D. I. Doser, C. J. Fridrich, F. H. Swan III, and A. M. Rogers (2003). A methodology for probabilistic fault displacement hazard analysis (PFDHA), *Earthq. Spectra* **19,** no. 1, 191–219.

Manuscript received 24 March 2025
Published online 15 October 2025

Urban Attenuation Lengths in City-Like Environments: Insights from 3D Numerical Simulations of Site–City Interaction

Malcon Celorio*[1,2], Philippe Guéguen[3], Hideo Aochi[1], Florent de Martin[1], and Luis Fabian Bonilla[4]

ABSTRACT

Estimating seismic ground motion in urban environments requires consideration of site–city interaction effects, which involve coupling between incident seismic wavefields and kinematic and inertial interactions with buildings. Although both observational data and numerical simulations have addressed this issue, the attenuation of seismic waves in urban settings remains poorly understood. In this study, we use 3D numerical simulations to examine the evolution of the wavefield in urban-like environments for frequencies up to 12 Hz. The simulations are conducted using the spectral element method. The model consists of a layered half-space with a flat surface, where the shear-wave velocity of the upper layer is 200 m/s and that of the half-space is 650 m/s. The urban configuration includes 30 buildings, each 100 m in height with a footprint of 25 m in both the *x* and *y* directions spaced 100 m apart. The building foundations are modeled as blocks with a depth of 15 m and horizontal dimensions identical to the superstructure. We perform three sets of simulations considering (1) free-field conditions, (2) foundations only, and (3) full buildings. The attenuation of seismic waves with distance is quantified by the amplitude decay of the ballistic wavefield. Our results indicate that at high frequencies (> 5 Hz), seismic wave attenuation is primarily governed by scattering, driven by interactions with the foundations acting as diffractors. At lower frequencies, attenuation is mainly controlled by the buildings' dynamics, leading to energy band gaps at the resonant frequencies of the buildings. Furthermore, the scattering attenuation length is found to be of the same order as the spacing between foundations. Finally, by analyzing the spatial variability of the ground motion within the urban cluster, we observe that the distance at which ground motion becomes uncorrelated is determined by the urban attenuation length, which we introduce as the urban mean free path.

KEY POINTS

- This study addresses how seismic wave attenuation occurs in urban environments through site–city interaction.
- Low-frequency attenuation is controlled by the buildings' motion, whereas foundations control high-frequency attenuation.
- Our results extend the classical attenuation framework by introducing an explicit urban contribution.

Supplemental Material

INTRODUCTION

Since the pioneering works of Jennings (1970), Wirgin and Bard (1996), and Guéguen *et al.* (2002), the significance of site–city interaction effects has been widely acknowledged for the estimation of earthquake ground motions in urban environments. At an individual scale, the interaction between incident ground motion and a building involves two primary mechanisms: (1) the kinematic interaction (Stewart and Fenves, 1998; Kausel, 2010), in which seismic waves are scattered because of the impedance contrast between the soil and the building foundations, and (2) the inertial interaction, which refers to the diffraction of seismic waves back into

1. BRGM: French Geological Survey, Orléans, France, https://orcid.org/0000-0003-1994-993X (MC); https://orcid.org/0000-0001-9405-9596 (HA); https://orcid.org/0000-0003-3746-9067 (FM); 2. Grupo Quimbaya, CEIFI, Observatorio, Sismológico Universidad del Quindío, Armenia, Colombia; 3. ISterre, Université Grenoble Alpes/Université Savoie Mont-Blanc/CNRS/IRD/Université Gustave Eiffel, Grenoble, France, https://orcid.org/0000-0001-6362-0694 (PG); 4. Université Gustave Eiffel, Champs-sur-Marne, France, https://orcid.org/0000-0001-6270-9822 (LFB)

*Corresponding author: malcon0522@hotmail.com

Cite this article as Celorio, M., P. Guéguen, H. Aochi, F. de Martin, and L. F. Bonilla (2025). Urban Attenuation Lengths in City-Like Environments: Insights from 3D Numerical Simulations of Site–City Interaction, *Bull. Seismol. Soc. Am.* **116**, 515–531, doi: 10.1785/0120250139 the ground as a result of the building's vibrating energy (Jennings, 1970; Wirgin and Bard, 1996). In the latter case, direct wave energy may undergo mode conversion (from surface waves to body waves) or experience an increase in ground-motion duration caused by the radiated energy from the buildings (Gueguen *et al.*, 2000).

In the context of ground-motion prediction and earthquake engineering, numerical simulations are commonly used to investigate the interaction between building clusters and incoming wavefields (Guéguen *et al.*, 2002; Kham *et al.*, 2006; Semblat *et al.*, 2008; Taborda and Bielak, 2011; Ichimura *et al.*, 2015; Isbiliroglu *et al.*, 2015; Guéguen and Colombi, 2016). For example, Guéguen *et al.* (2002) numerically assessed the contribution of inertial interaction from a cluster of buildings to seismic ground motion in Mexico City. Their findings highlighted the necessity of incorporating the urban pattern in numerical models to accurately interpret observed ground motions from real data.

Several studies have also investigated site–city interaction effects using experimental data. For instance, Gueguen *et al.* (2000) observed the wavefield generated by a standalone building forced into vibration by a pull-out test. They quantified this phenomenon and the attenuation of seismic waves with distance from the building, noting a conversion from surface waves to body waves. Cornou *et al.* (2004) examined the origin of energy bursts observed in the seismic noise field recorded in the Grenoble basin. Their results indicated that these bursts were linked to interactions between a chimney and the topmost layer resulting from the coincidence of site and structural resonant frequencies. Laurenzano *et al.* (2010) analyzed the effect of vibrating buildings on free-field motion and on adjacent structures, concluding that building vibrations could contaminate free-field motion up to 40% in spectral values at large distances, further supporting the notion of nonlocal effects. Similarly, Bard *et al.* (2025) explored temporal changes in the site response in the Kanto area caused by ongoing urbanization. Their study, based on long-duration strong ground-motion observations, revealed a significant reduction in site amplification for frequencies between 0.2 and 1 Hz, a frequency range corresponding to both site response and the resonance of high-rise buildings.

On the other hand, Guéguen and Colombi (2016) highlighted the complex physics involved in site–city interactions. In their study, numerical simulations demonstrated the coupling between nearby tall buildings, exhibiting typical behaviors associated with metamaterial physics, such as the clustering effects. With the advent of metamaterial physics in various wave phenomena (e.g., electromagnetic and acoustic waves), experimental studies have gained increasing importance in the context of elastic waves and geophysics (Colombi *et al.*, 2016; Roux *et al.*, 2018; Guéguen *et al.*, 2019; Lott *et al.*, 2020; Pilz *et al.*, 2024). In their groundbreaking experiment, Roux *et al.* (2018) used a dense array of seismic receivers installed in a forest. Their initial results revealed the presence of energy band gaps in Rayleigh waves resulting from the interaction between the generated wavefield from active shots and the trees, which acted as resonant elements. In a follow-up study, Lott *et al.* (2020) further investigated the effects of these band gaps on the propagation properties of the medium, including velocity dispersion and attenuation lengths derived from two-point correlations, as well as the intensity ratios between the recorded wavefield inside and outside the forest. Their analysis established a direct link between the vertical resonances of the trees and significant band gaps in frequency-dependent propagation properties, such as attenuation length and phase velocity. Pilz *et al.* (2024) also explored the interaction between seismic wavefields and a cluster of wind turbines. Their study demonstrated the contribution of compressional and flexural vibration modes to surface-wave energy, revealing significant attenuation and variations in phase velocity within a frequency range of engineering interest (a few Hertz).

Despite the extensive body of work on the analysis and characterization of site–city interaction effects, most existing studies have primarily focused on site amplification, ground-motion duration, and building response. However, direct estimations and interpretations of seismic attenuation have yet to be fully addressed. Similarly, in the context of geophysics, although Lott *et al.* (2020) and Pilz *et al.* (2024) estimated attenuation lengths based on coherence analyses, more rigorous characterizations and interpretations of urban-like attenuation mechanisms are needed to better understand their effects on observed ground motion and their implications for variability across urban areas.

In this study, we numerically investigate seismic wave attenuation in an urban environment composed of 30 building-like elements acting as resonators in an area of 600 m × 500 m. Using 3D numerical simulations, we explore site–city interaction effects and separately examine the contributions of different interaction mechanisms (kinematic and inertial) to the amplitude decay of seismic waves. Attenuation measurements are performed by analyzing the direct wave energy component of the radiative transfer equation (RTE) following methodologies previously applied in seismology to quantify scattering and absorption (Fehler *et al.*, 1992; Gaebler *et al.*, 2015; Celorio *et al.*, 2025).

The novelty of this study lies in the perspective it offers on the physical processes underlying site–city interaction. We interpret these effects through the lens of urban attenuation and scattering, modeling buildings, and their foundations as resonant scatterers. To capture this process, we adopt the concept of an urban mean free path, the characteristic distance over which the direct wavefield is significantly scattered by buildings. This framework extends the classical description of seismic attenuation—traditionally expressed in terms of intrinsic absorption (Q_i) and scattering (Q_{sc})—by adding a mechanism specific to urban environments.

The structure of this article is as follows. We begin by presenting the theoretical framework based on energy transport in scattering media along with the numerical settings of the computational domain. We then analyze the effects of building foundations on the incident wavefield, followed by an assessment of the urban attenuation caused by the presence of buildings. Next, we discuss the link between urban attenuation and the spatial variability of ground motion. Finally, we provide the main conclusions of the study.

MATERIALS AND METHODS

Wave propagation and energy transport in scattering media

To investigate the evolution of the ground motion in urban environments, we can initially consider the propagation of a wavefield $\mathbf{u}$ in a 3D viscoelastic medium by the so-known wave equation:

$$\rho(\mathbf{x})\frac{\partial^2\mathbf{u}(t,\mathbf{x})}{\partial t^2} - \nabla\cdot\sigma(t,\mathbf{x}) = f(t,\mathbf{x}), \quad (1)$$

in which ρ and σ are the density and the stress tensor, respectively; t is the lapse time; $\nabla\cdot\sigma$ denotes the divergence of the stress tensor; and $\mathbf{x}$ represents the position vector. The ∇ operator is applied for the divergence of the stress tensor. The external source is given by $f(t,\mathbf{x})$. Note that intrinsic viscoelastic properties such as shear-wave velocity, stiffness modulus, and anelastic attenuation are implicitly included in the stress tensor term. In this work, we can consider that in a highly heterogeneous region, these intrinsic properties can fluctuate in space. Thus, we can express either the shear-wave velocity or the density as

$$\rho(\mathbf{x}) = \rho_0(1+\xi(\mathbf{x})), \quad (2)$$

in which ρ_0 represents the background properties of the medium and ξ denotes the corresponding spatially dependent fluctuations. In the case of an urban-like layer containing several small-scale heterogeneities, such as those introduced by building foundations, fluctuations in the background properties can be as large as 100%, depending on the contrast between the soil and foundation materials. Consequently, perturbative approaches (e.g., mean-field theory, Born approximation; Wu, 1982) used to investigate small-scale inhomogeneities in the crust may not be applicable in this context, especially at high frequency.

Because seismic waves interact with these small-scale heterogeneities, different propagation regimes emerge. The first, known as the ballistic regime, is dominated by primary waves. This regime retains memory of the initial propagation direction and source signatures. The second regime is referred to as single scattering, where waves have been scattered once by the heterogeneities. Finally, the third regime, multiple scattering, involves waves that have interacted multiple times with heterogeneities, leading to a diffusion-like behavior. In this case, the incoherent components of the wavefield dominate over the coherent behavior. Because of the incoherent nature of the scattering process, recorded wave phases tend to become randomized, complicating the use of classical tomography approaches for investigating structural velocities.

To constrain scattering attenuation, most inversion techniques focus on energy transport rather than the waveforms themselves. Here, energy (E) is typically calculated from the square of the envelope of the wavefield $\mathbf{u}$. A common model to simulate the space–time evolution of seismic energy in scattering media is radiative transfer theory (RTT) (e.g., Wu, 1985; Margerin *et al.*, 1998). This model has been widely applied to separate scattering and absorption properties in various geological contexts, such as the crust (Carcole and Sato, 2010) or volcanoes (Hirose *et al.*, 2019; Celorio *et al.*, 2025). Absorption, or intrinsic attenuation, refers to energy dissipation caused by the presence of fluids or internal friction between the particles in the medium. In this work, we focus on the modification of surface waves due to their interaction with foundations and buildings, which are treated as resonating scatterers. Thus, we consider the analytical solution of the RTE for surface waves under the assumption of isotropic scattering (Paasschens, 1997), as follows:

$$E(r,t) = \frac{e^{-ct\ell^{-1}-bt}}{2\pi r}\delta\left(t-\frac{r}{c}\right) + \frac{e^{\ell^{-1}(\sqrt{c^2t^2-r^2}-ct)-bt}}{2\pi\ell\sqrt{c^2t^2-r^2}}H\left(t-\frac{r}{c}\right), \quad (3)$$

in which $E(r,t)$ represents the energy at a propagation distance r and elapsed time t. The parameters ℓ and b are central quantities in RTT and correspond to the mean free path and the absorption parameter, respectively, and c denotes the propagation velocity of the seismic energy. δ and H represent the Dirac delta and Heaviside functions, respectively. The first term on the right side of the equation accounts for the contribution of the direct wavefield, whose attenuation is governed by ℓ and b. The second term describes the backscattered energy that forms the coda, where the amplitude depends on the level of scattering, and the time decay is controlled by absorption. It is important to note that the frequency dependence of $E(r,t)$ is implicitly incorporated into the parameters ℓ and b. In this study, we focus on the ballistic component of the wavefield; therefore, we consider only the first term on the right side of equation (3), which depends on both ℓ and b, that is

$$E(r,t) = \frac{e^{-ct\ell^{-1}-bt}}{2\pi r}\delta\left(t-\frac{r}{c}\right). \quad (4)$$

Now, for $t = r/c$, which corresponds to the travel time of the direct waves, and with $b = c/\ell_a$, equation (4) becomes

$$E(r) \propto \frac{e^{-r(\ell^{-1}+\ell_a^{-1})}}{2\pi r}, \quad (5)$$

in which ℓ_a is the absorption length. In our subsequent analyses, we will assume that the energy decay under free-field

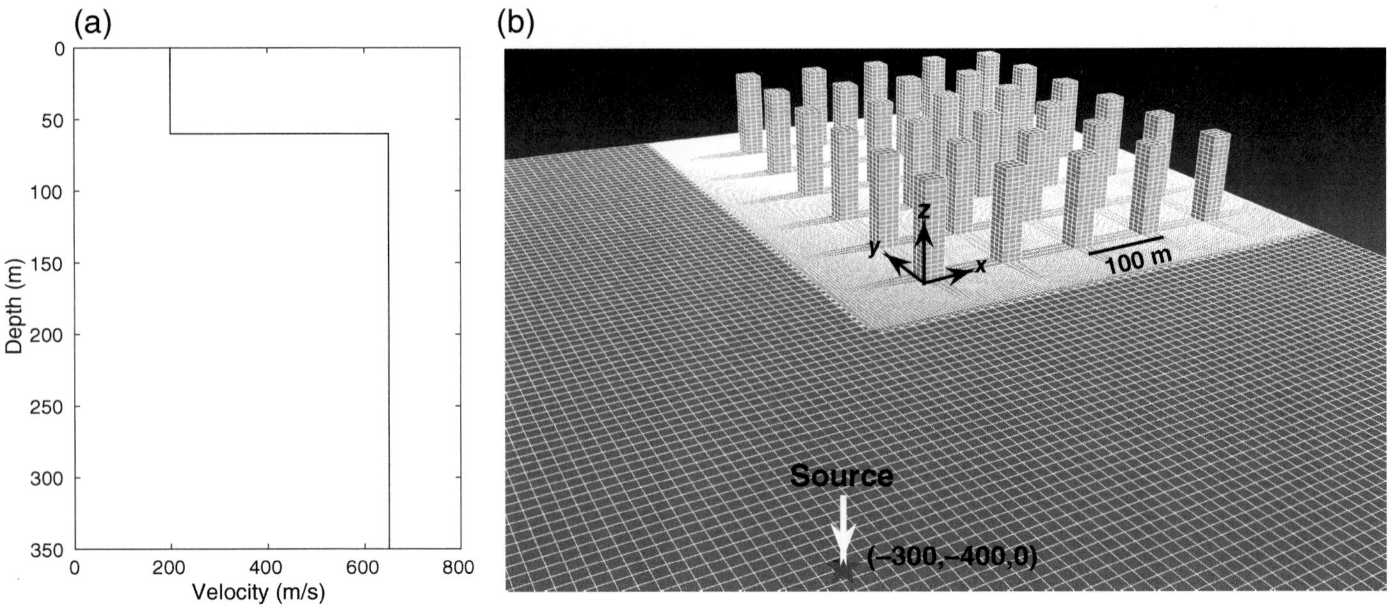

conditions is solely governed by absorption, which, in the numerical model, is represented using the viscoelastic approximation.

For a medium composed of small-scale inhomogeneities, the parameter ℓ can be interpreted as either the scattering mean free path or the transport mean free path. The scattering mean free path represents the typical distance between two consecutive scattering events, whereas the transport mean free path is the length scale required to reach the multiple diffusion regime (e.g., Celorio *et al.*, 2022). Although the isotropic approximation of the RTE does not distinguish between these two quantities, the interpretation of the estimated attenuation length depends on the scattering regime. For example, in the forward scattering regime, Celorio *et al.* (2022) suggest that the energy decay of the ballistic wavefield is controlled by the transport mean free path. Conversely, when the coherent behavior dominates in the wavefield, the energy decay is controlled by the scattering mean free path.

Numerical setting

Numerical simulations of 3D seismic waves in urban environments are carried out using the EFISPEC3D code (De Martin, 2011), which solves the 3D wave equations in viscoelastic media. EFISPEC3D implements the spectral element method (SEM, e.g., Komatitsch and Vilotte, 1998; Chaljub *et al.*, 2007) for spatial discretization, combined with a second-order finite-difference scheme for time integration. SEM simulations has successfully been implemented to study site–city interaction effects in different realistic ground-motion contexts (see Soto *et al.*, 2020; Kato and Wang, 2022). The computational domain is a rectangular volume with dimensions 1000 m in the x direction, 1200 m in the y direction, and 300 m in the z direction. Absorbing boundary conditions (perfectly matched layer) are applied at the lateral and bottom boundaries to minimize artificial reflections, whereas a free-surface boundary condition is applied at the top of the domain.

Figure 1. (a) 1D shear velocity model of the background medium composed by a layer with 200 m/s and the half-space having 650 m/s. (b) 3D numerical mesh with the 30 buildings and the seismic source at ~800 m from the center of the cluster. The color version of this figure is available only in the electronic edition.

To discretize the model, the volume is meshed with hexahedral elements using the CUBIT software. The mesh contains $\sim 4 \times 10^5$ cubic elements with a minimum edge length of 10 m. A fourth-order polynomial basis ($N = 4$) is used to represent the wavefield inside each element, yielding five Gauss–Lobatto–Legendre points per edge. This configuration provides about four or five points per minimum wavelength for the highest frequency considered (12 Hz), given the lowest shear-wave velocity in the model ($V_S = 200$ m/s). Such resolution satisfies the requirements of the SEM and ensures low numerical dispersion. The choice of 12 Hz as maximum frequency is crucial: it guarantees that the model resolves short wavelengths, which are necessary to capture scattering effects produced by the building foundations.

The background medium consists of a 60-m-thick layer overlying a half-space. To model an urban environment incorporating sedimentary fills (site effects) and stiff buildings, the layer has a shear-wave velocity $V_S = 200$ m/s and a quality factor $Q_S = 40$, and the half-space is characterized by $V_S = 650$ m/s and $Q_S = 90$ (see the velocity model in Fig. 1a).

To investigate the influence of buildings on the seismic wavefield, 30 beam-like elements are embedded within the computational domain. Modeling buildings as beam-like viscoelastic elements is a common approach in numerical studies of site–city interaction, particularly when the focus is on the

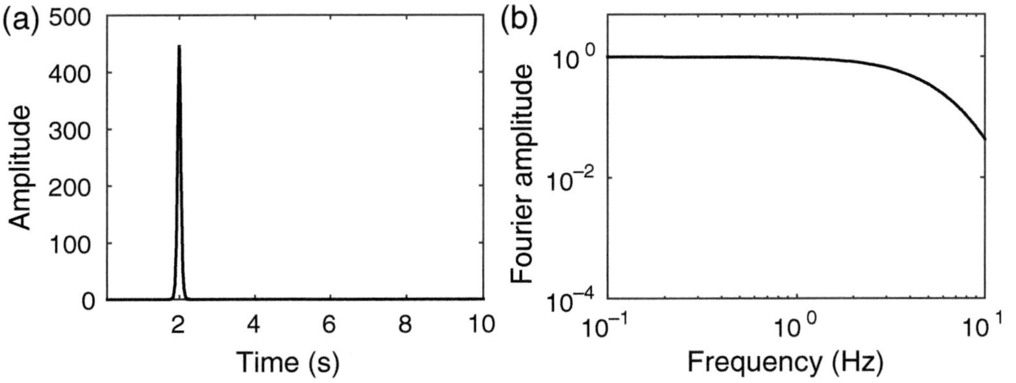

Figure 2. Source time function (a) with its Fourier amplitude spectrum (b) showing energy uniformly distributed between 0.1 and 8 Hz.

dominant dynamic response and its effect on the wavefield (e.g., Taborda and Bielak, 2011; Guéguen and Colombi, 2016). This representation captures the fundamental vibration modes of the structures while keeping the computational cost tractable. In this study, we do not pretend to replicate specific real buildings but rather to model generic resonant elements that contribute actively in the evolution of the seismic wavefield.

Each beam-like element has a height of 100 m and a square cross section with dimensions of 25 m, whereas the buried part (foundation) has a depth of 15 m. The elements are spaced 100 m apart. These buildings are modeled as viscoelastic structures with a shear-wave velocity $V_S = 500$ m/s and a quality factor $Q_S = 20$. Their foundations, in contact with the underground medium, are assigned $V_S = 700$ m/s and $Q_S = 150$, representing stiffer and less absorbing material.

This urban model was designed to provide a controlled configuration in which the fundamental effects of building resonance, spacing, and foundation scattering on seismic energy transport can be isolated and quantified. The regular arrangement facilitates a straightforward physical interpretation of seismic wave attenuation in the urban environment. Although idealized, this configuration serves as a baseline reference for future studies involving more complex and realistic urban settings.

TABLE 1
Viscoelastic Properties of the Materials Composing the 3D Computational Domain

Element	V_S (m/s)	ρ (kg/m^3)	Q_S (ξ in %)
Half-space	650	1800	65 (0.8)
Layer	200	1200	40 (1.25)
Building	500	500	20 (2.5)
Foundation	700	1300	150 (0.33)

Shear-wave velocity and density have units m/s and kg/m^3, respectively. The shear quality Q_S factor is dimensionless. (The corresponding damping value ξ is also shown in percentage.)

The spatial configuration of these elements within the computational domain is shown in Figure 1b. The viscoelastic properties of each element are summarized in Table 1.

In our simulations, both the background medium and the buildings are modeled as linear viscoelastic materials, consistent with the small-strain assumption for soils and structures. Intrinsic attenuation is incorporated through EFISPEC3D's generalized viscoelastic formulation (Day and Minster, 1984; Emmerich and Korn, 1987), which reproduces a target Q over the frequency band of interest. This memory-variable approach is fully integrated into the SEM scheme, ensuring accurate damping without compromising numerical stability (see De Martin, 2011, for details). We acknowledge, however, that nonlinear constitutive models may play a significant role in certain scenarios, particularly under near-fault strong ground motions, where strain-dependent properties and shifting resonant frequencies could influence urban attenuation. Nevertheless, our objective here is to directly analyze and quantify the effects of site–city interaction on wavefield attenuation under controlled and physically interpretable conditions.

To generate the wavefield in the computational domain, we implement a seismic source at the surface as a vertical point force, modeled using the first derivative of a Bouchon pulse with a corner frequency of 8 Hz (see Fig. 2). The source is positioned ~850 m from the center of the building cluster at coordinates $x = -300$ and $y = -400$.

We adopt this simplified source time function to isolate the effects of wave propagation within such a complex medium, minimizing the influence of source-related complexities. This approach allows for a clearer interpretation of site–city interaction phenomena, particularly regarding energy transport and seismic wave attenuation.

After the material properties and seismic source are defined in the numerical model, simulations are conducted for a maximum duration of 30 s. Synthetic waveforms are obtained in the x, y, and z directions from a set of receivers located on the surface of the domain within the building cluster. A total of 117 receivers are placed on the ground, spaced 50 m apart, and 30 receivers are placed at the top of the buildings to capture their modal responses. The following postprocessing steps are applied: (1) seismic traces are downsampled to 100 Hz, and (2) horizontal components (x and y) are rotated into radial and transverse components using the classical transformation matrix, which depends on the source–receiver azimuth. Our

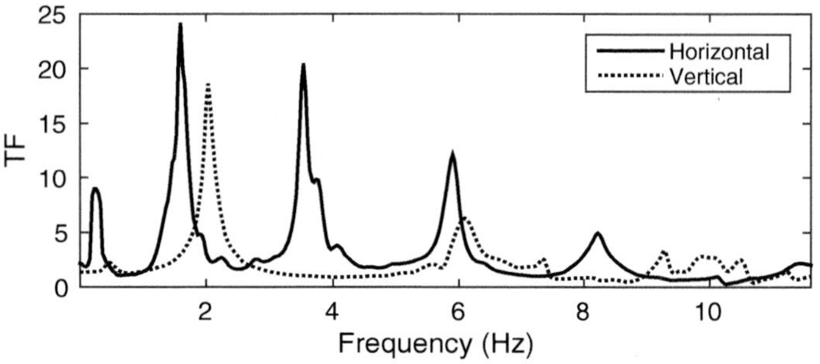

Figure 3. Transfer function of a typical building with height 100 m and with physical properties as those shown in Table 1. The peaks indicate the resonant frequencies for the horizontal (solid line) and vertical (dotted line) components.

study focuses on the Rayleigh-wave behavior, for which we use the vertical and radial components of ground motion.

To supplement the mechanical properties shown in Table 1, we present (Fig. 3) the transfer functions of a stand-alone building with identical viscoelastic properties, as those described in Figure 1. These transfer functions are computed as the spectral ratio between the receiver at the top of the building and that at the bottom. The results are shown for both the horizontal and vertical components of the building's vibration.

For the horizontal component, five vibration modes are identified at ~0.25, 1.5, 4, 6, and 8 Hz. The lowest mode, at 0.25 Hz, corresponds to the roughly expected fundamental frequency of a 100-m-tall fixed-base building and the observed sequence of resonance frequencies is characteristic of a cantilever beam, with fixed-base bending modes following the classical ratios (e.g., 6.3, 17.6, and 34.3). In our study, the wavefield analysis is restricted to the frequency range of 1–12 Hz. Below 1 Hz, the associated wavelengths are too long compared with the spatial extent of the building cluster, and the wavefield lacks a sufficiently developed propagative behavior. Under such conditions, interpreting energy transport and attenuation mechanisms becomes unreliable. For the vertical component, two dominant vibration modes are observed, centered around 2 and 6 Hz.

SCATTERING DUE TO FOUNDATIONS

To separately examine the different processes activated during site–city effects, we first simulate the propagation of seismic waves by considering only the foundations. In this case, the computational domain consists solely of the background medium (layer and half-space) and the buried blocks representing the foundations. Because of the strong impedance contrast between the soil and the foundations (shear-wave velocity contrast of ~200%), seismic scattering is expected, even over short propagation distances. The primary evidences of seismic scattering involve the amplitude decay of direct waves and the emergence of incoherent energy, often referred to as coda waves (Aki and Chouet, 1975). The latter corresponds to the multiple diffusion regime, in which the angular dependence of energy density tends to become uniform over sufficiently long propagation distances. Quantifying these signatures is key to characterizing attenuation properties, either by analyzing energy decay with distance over different time windows (e.g., multiple lapse time-window analyses; Fehler *et al.*, 1992; Carcole and Sato, 2010) or by measuring the energy ratio between ballistic and early diffuse regimes (Celorio *et al.*, 2025). A subsequent area of focus in seismic scattering is understanding the effects of scattering properties on earthquake ground motions (Hartzell *et al.*, 2010; Chaljub *et al.*, 2021; Tchawe *et al.*, 2021). In this context, heterogeneities are typically treated as random and represented by an autocorrelation function describing the spatial variation of elastic properties. In contrast, our medium is considered ordered, with soil variability primarily governed by the separation between foundations.

Energy transport in a foundation cluster

To observe the decay and redistribution of energy caused by the scattering by foundations, we investigate the evolution of the wavefield in terms of the energy envelope of the full waveforms. These observations are performed at different frequencies because the scattering phenomenon depends on wavelength. The simulated waveforms are filtered into different frequency bands with central frequency f_0 ($[5/6f_0 - 7/6f_0]$) using a zero-phase, four-pole Butterworth filter. The energy envelope of the filtered traces $u(t)$ is then computed as

$$E(t) = \frac{1}{2}[\mathcal{H}^2\{u(t)\} + u(t)^2], \quad (6)$$

in which $E(t)$ represents the time-dependent energy and $\mathcal{H}$ is the Hilbert transform operator. To illustrate the effects of foundation scattering, we compare the results from the foundation case with those obtained under the free-field condition (propagation medium without foundations or buildings). Figure 4 displays the synthetic waveforms and the corresponding energy envelopes for a receiver located inside the foundation cluster, at position x = 200 m and y = 450 m, ~986 m from the source. This example is shown for two frequencies, 2 and 6 Hz, representing the low- and high-frequency behavior, respectively.

At low frequencies, there are no significant differences between the foundation case and the free-field condition. The amplitudes remain similar, with only a slight increase in energy at longer lapse times (between 14 and 18 s). This suggests that the interaction between the incident wavefield and the heterogeneities is minimal, first, because the propagation distances are relatively short, and second, because the incident wavelength (~100 m) is much longer than the typical size of the heterogeneities (25 m).

In contrast, at high frequency ($f_0 = 6$), the energy decay of direct waves becomes more pronounced, indicating significant scattering effects. However, the emergence of coda waves is not observed because the multiple diffusion regime is not reached

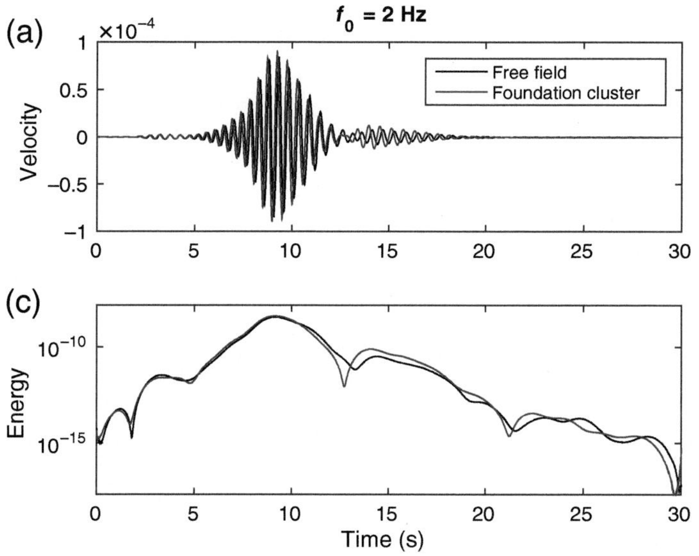

Figure 4. Waveforms and corresponding energy envelopes for central frequencies at 2 (a and c) and 6 Hz (b and d) for a receiver located at 986 m from the source. These examples correspond to the free field (black) and the foundation case (red) for the vertical component of the ground motion. The color version of this figure is available only in the electronic edition.

at these short propagation distances. Achieving this regime would require a greater density of scatterers and longer propagation paths. The absence of a well-developed coda suggests that the recorded wavefield remains predominantly in a ballistic regime, where energy transport is still dominated by direct and singly scattered waves rather than a fully diffusive process. This distinction is important because it implies that the scattering is strong enough to influence the attenuation of direct waves but not sufficient to generate a sustained coda.

To further analyze this, we focus on the amplitude decay of the ballistic energy. Specifically, the ballistic energy is calculated as the integrated energy within a time window of size $2T_0$ (in which $T_0 = 1/f_0$), centered around the peak amplitude. Here, we refer to the ballistic energy in the $2T_0$ window as peak ground energy (PGE). To systematically illustrate the effects of foundations on direct waves, Figure 5 shows the spatial evolution of ballistic energy for different central frequencies, ranging from 1 to 6 Hz. Note that at each central frequency, the ballistic wavefield is normalized by the energy at the receiver nearest to the source. For comparison, the ballistic wavefield under the free-field condition is also included (Fig. 5a–d). Although the ballistic wavefield in the free-field decays almost monotonically with distance, the presence of foundations (Fig. 5e–h) results in a stronger decay (as indicated by the color bars) and introduces significant spatial variability in the ground energy. These effects become more pronounced at higher frequencies as the incident wavelength approaches the size of the heterogeneities.

Ballistic wave attenuation

In this section, we evaluate the amplitude decay resulting from foundation scattering. Scattering attenuation is quantified in terms of the mean free path (ℓ). To achieve this, we use equation (5), in which the energy decay in the foundation case is influenced by both the scattering attenuation length (ℓ) and the absorption length (ℓ_a). In contrast, the energy decay in the free-field condition is governed solely by absorption, as given by $\exp(-r\ell_a^{-1})$.

By assuming that the absorption length remains the same in both cases, we can estimate the scattering attenuation length ℓ^{-1} by considering the difference between the total attenuation α in the foundation case and the absorption length in the free-field condition. This can be expressed as

$$\ell^{-1} = \alpha - \ell_a^{-1}, \tag{7}$$

in which the parameters α and ℓ_a^{-1} are obtained by fitting an exponential regression to the decay of the ballistic wavefield as a function of distance. This fitting procedure is performed for both the foundation case and the free-field condition at each central frequency up to 12 Hz. Subsequently, for a given f_0, the mean free path is estimated from equation (7).

In Figure 6, top, we illustrate the fitting procedure for central frequencies of 2 Hz (panel a) and 6 Hz (panel b). At low frequencies, the decay of the foundation case closely resembles that of the free-field condition, indicating that the energy attenuation is primarily due to absorption mechanisms, with scattering having a negligible effect because the wavefield is not sensitive to the heterogeneities. At 6 Hz, however, the energy decay in the foundation case can be distinctly differentiated from the free-field condition, with this difference being governed by scattering.

The measurements of scattering attenuation lengths (ℓ) for all central frequencies from 1 to 12 Hz are shown in Figure 6c.

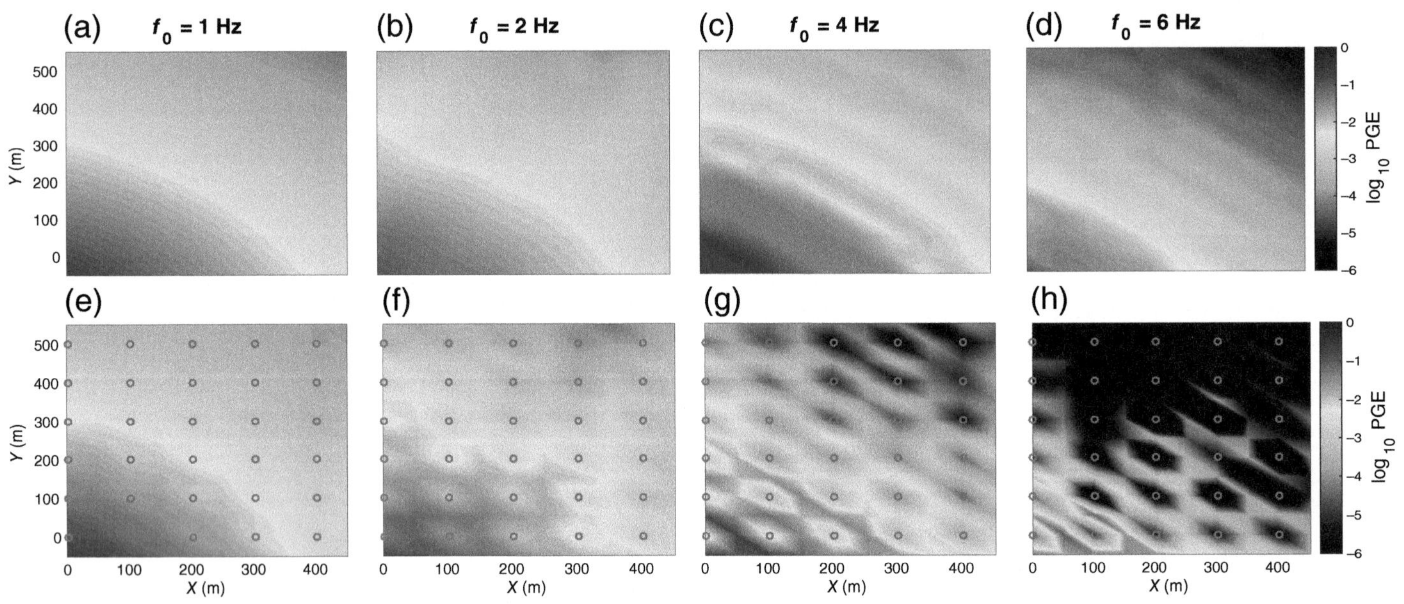

As expected, ℓ is very large at frequencies below 3 Hz. Beyond this frequency, ℓ converges toward the separation distance between the foundations (~141 m).

As discussed before, the interpretation of the estimated scattering attenuation length (ℓ) depends on the propagation regime. From the isotropic solution, it is understood that there is no distinction between the transport mean free path and the scattering mean free path. However, Gaebler *et al.* (2015) suggested, based on real data and Monte Carlo simulations of the RTT, that the estimated ℓ from equation (3) should be interpreted as the transport mean free path when scattering is nonisotropic.

Similarly, Celorio *et al.* (2022), using 2D numerical simulations of *SH* waves in random media, demonstrated that in the forward scattering regime, the decay of the ballistic peak with distance is controlled by the transport mean free path. In our case, the wavefield is unlikely to reach the multiple diffusion regime because the propagation distances are relatively short, and no coda is generated. Therefore, it is expected that our estimates of ℓ are closer to the scattering mean free path for the inhomogeneous medium.

SITE–CITY INTERACTION

In the previous section, we demonstrated how the ballistic wavefield is scattered by the presence of foundations, especially for frequencies where the wavelengths are comparable to the size of the foundations. Although no coda waves were observed, significant attenuation of direct waves was noted at high frequencies. We now expand our analysis to provide a more comprehensive understanding of the site–city interaction phenomenon by examining the wavefield when the full site–foundation–structure system is considered. The objective of this section is to analyze the amplitude decay of ballistic waves within the building cluster, as shown in Figure 1, and

Figure 5. Effect of foundations on seismic energy transport. (a–d) Free-field condition. (e–h) Foundations cluster. The gray circles indicate the location of the foundations. The color bar represents different levels of normalized peak ground energy (PGE) in $\log_{10}$ scale. The color version of this figure is available only in the electronic edition.

to investigate the role of building dynamics in seismic wave attenuation.

Energy transport in an urban cluster

To illustrate the typical effects on the waveforms, Figure 7 presents an example of seismograms and their corresponding energy envelopes at 2 and 6 Hz. This example uses the same receiver as that in the foundation case. As observed in the scattering case, the high-frequency seismogram ($f_0 = 6$ Hz) shows significant attenuation of the direct wave, with a shape that closely resembles the results from the foundation scattering case. In contrast, the low-frequency ($f_0 = 2$ Hz) waveforms exhibit stronger attenuation of the ballistic wave and a marked increase in wave duration. Notably, this central frequency (2 Hz) corresponds to the vertical resonance frequency of the beam-type buildings, as indicated in Figure 3.

The duration elongation observed caused by the presence of buildings has been previously studied for the valley of Mexico City, where exceptional quasi-monochromatic durations of seismic urban ground motion were observed (Wirgin and Bard, 1996; Guéguen *et al.*, 2002).

The evolution of ballistic energy is presented in Figure 8. The evolution of ballistic energy is presented in Figure 8. Panels (a—d) correspond to the free-field case, which is shown as a reference, and panels (e—h) illustrate the wavefield within the building cluster. At 1 Hz, there is no significant modification of the wavefield, with only a slight local amplification

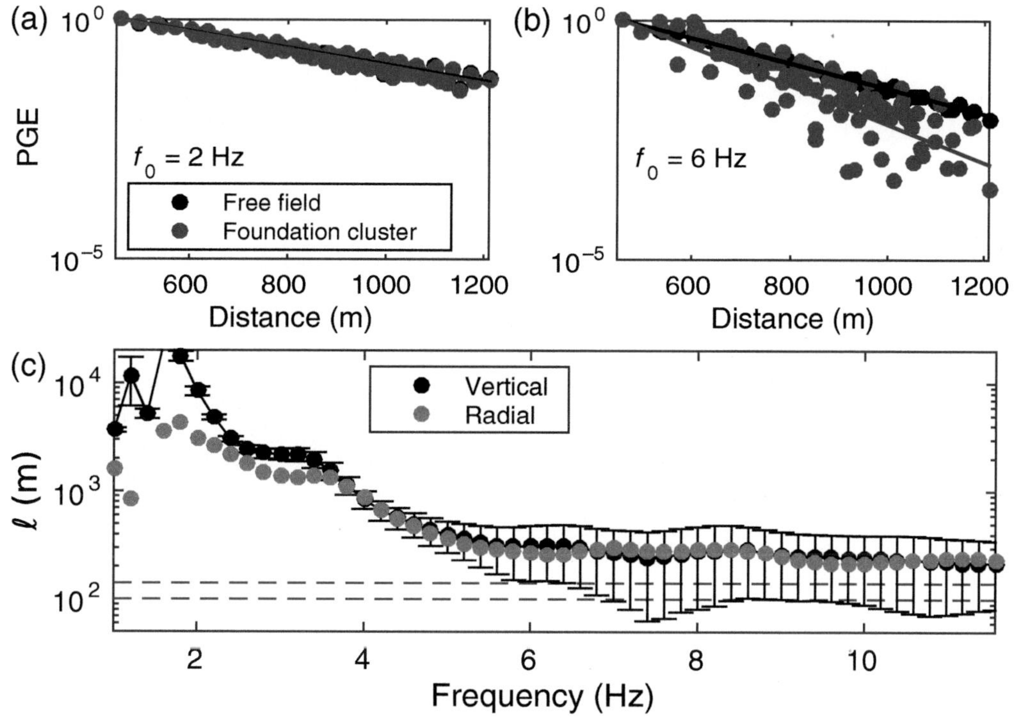

Figure 6. Fitting procedure of scattering attenuation. Top: example of energy decay with distance for the vertical component at low (2 Hz) (a) and high (6 Hz) (b) frequencies (data for the radial component are shown in Fig. S1). An exponential regression (solid line) is fitted to the distance dependence of the ballistic peak (red and black points). Bottom (c): estimated scattering attenuation length (ℓ_{sc}) for frequencies up to 12 Hz. The dashed red lines indicates the distance between successive foundations either in *x/y* direction or diagonal. The color version of this figure is available only in the electronic edition.

observed in the areas in between buildings. The most pronounced amplitude decay occurs at 2 Hz, which corresponds to the vertical resonance frequency of the buildings (as shown in Fig. 3). However, as the frequency increases, the wavefield begins to resemble a scattered field, becoming increasingly similar to the one observed in the foundation scattering case.

Spectral ratios and band gaps

To investigate the relationship between the characteristics of the wavefield in the urban cluster and the modal properties of the buildings, we compute the spectral ratios between the energy in the urban cluster and that in the free-field simulation. These spectral ratios are obtained by dividing the Fourier amplitude spectra of the two cases for each receiver at the same location. Our approach is similar to that of Lott *et al.* (2020), who computed the ratio between the recorded wavefields inside and outside a cluster of resonators (e.g., trees in a forest). The results are shown in Figure 9 for both the radial (panel a) and vertical (panel b) components of the ground motion. These ratios are displayed as data density plots. In addition, we present the average spectral ratios along with the associated standard deviations. Overall, the data become more scattered with frequency, which can be

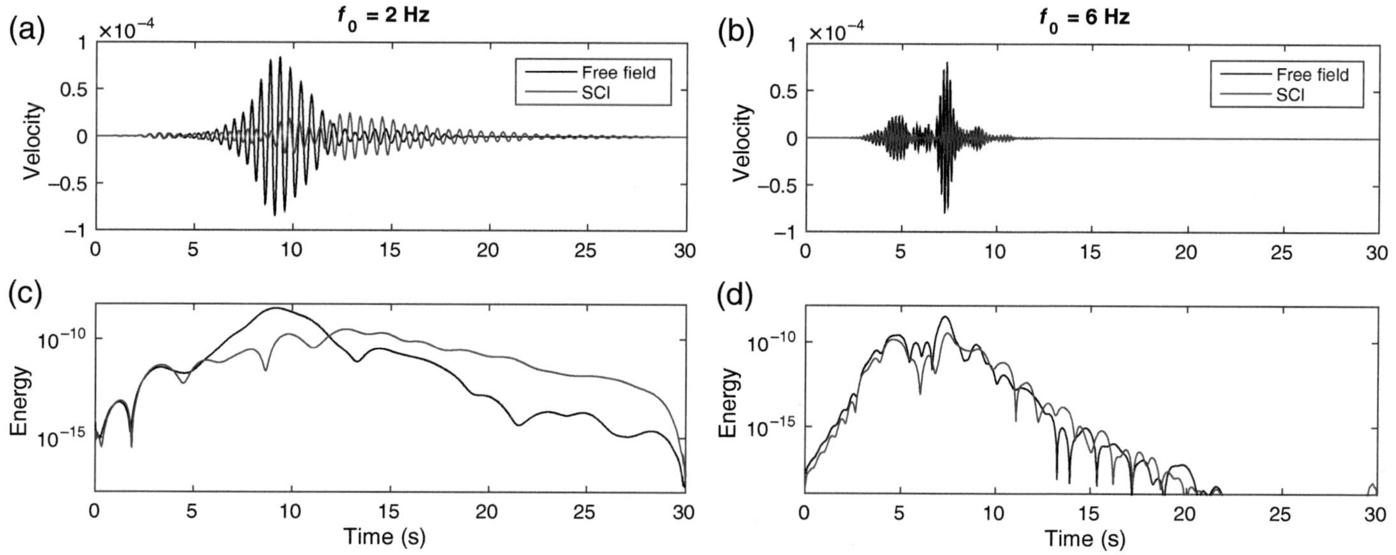

Figure 7. Waveforms and corresponding energy envelopes for central frequencies at 2 (a and c) and 6 Hz (b and d). Examples are shown for the free field (black) and the urban cluster (red). The color version of this figure is available only in the electronic edition.

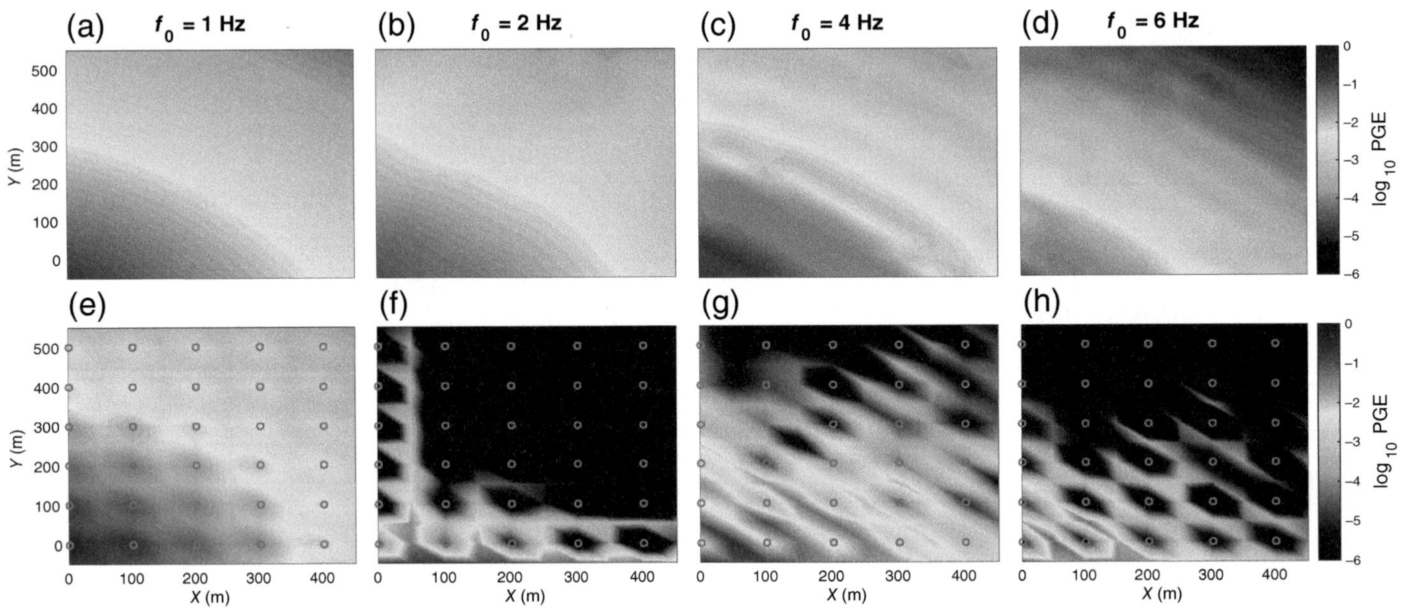

Figure 8. Effect of the building cluster on seismic energy transport. (a–d) Free-field condition. (e–h) Building cluster with gray circles indicating the location of the buildings. The color bar represents different levels of PGE in $\log_{10}$ scale. The color version of this figure is available only in the electronic edition.

attributed to the increased spatial variability of the ground motion at higher frequencies. For reference, we also present the ensemble of transfer functions for all the buildings in Figure 9c for both the radial and vertical components.

The spectral ratios between the urban cluster and the free-field condition show a pronounced energy reduction, particularly around the first radial and vertical resonances of the buildings. This phenomenon, known as a band gap, has been reported in experiments across different scales for meta-materials (Rupin *et al.*, 2014; Colombi *et al.*, 2016; Lott *et al.*, 2020). Notably, there is an amplification just before the first band gap, which corresponds to a typical meta-material behavior at the geophysical scale (Colombi *et al.*, 2016). Smaller band gaps are also observed at higher vibration modes, even around 10 Hz. The uniform energy reduction observed at frequencies between the modal frequencies can be interpreted as seismic attenuation caused by scattering from the foundations. This result highlights that both shear (horizontal) and compressional (vertical) modes can induce significant energy decay in either the vertical and/or radial components of the ground motion. In addition, Figure 9c shows the variable transfer functions of beam-like buildings, all identical in design but whose responses vary depending on their position in the cluster relative to the source. This observation, also reported experimentally by Guéguen and Colombi (2016), even influences the seismic perception of residents during earthquakes, depending on their position within the cluster.

Ballistic wave attenuation in the urban cluster

To quantify the contribution of the structure to the attenuation of ballistic waves, we now measure the energy decay with distance across the entire frequency range (up to 12 Hz). As previously mentioned, we assume that the total attenuation of ballistic energy results from a combination of absorption and scattering. However, we now include the contribution of the building dynamics, which is implicitly represented by the term ℓ_{urb}, referred to here as the urban mean free path. Thus, the evolution of the ballistic wavefield with distance can be expressed as

$$E(r) \propto \frac{e^{-r(\ell_{\mathrm{urb}}^{-1}+\ell_a^{-1})}}{2\pi r}, \tag{8}$$

in which ℓ_{urb} represents the combined contribution of the foundation scattering and the building response. Our approach now involves constraining the term ℓ_{urb} by comparing the total attenuation observed in the urban cluster with that in the free-field condition (in the same way as in equation 7). In Figure 10a,b, we illustrate the procedure used to estimate the urban mean free path for central frequencies of 2 and 6 Hz. A significant amplitude decay is observed at 2 Hz, which is even greater than that at high frequencies. This enhanced attenuation at low frequency is attributed to the coupling between the first vertical and radial resonances of the buildings and the Rayleigh wave.

The entire set of estimations for both the radial and vertical components of the ground motion is presented in Figure 10c. At frequencies below 1.4 Hz, urban attenuation (and consequently, the urban mean free path) is lower (and longer, respectively) because this frequency range is not significantly influenced by the scatterers (foundations) or the vibration modes of the buildings. The strongest attenuation occurs at

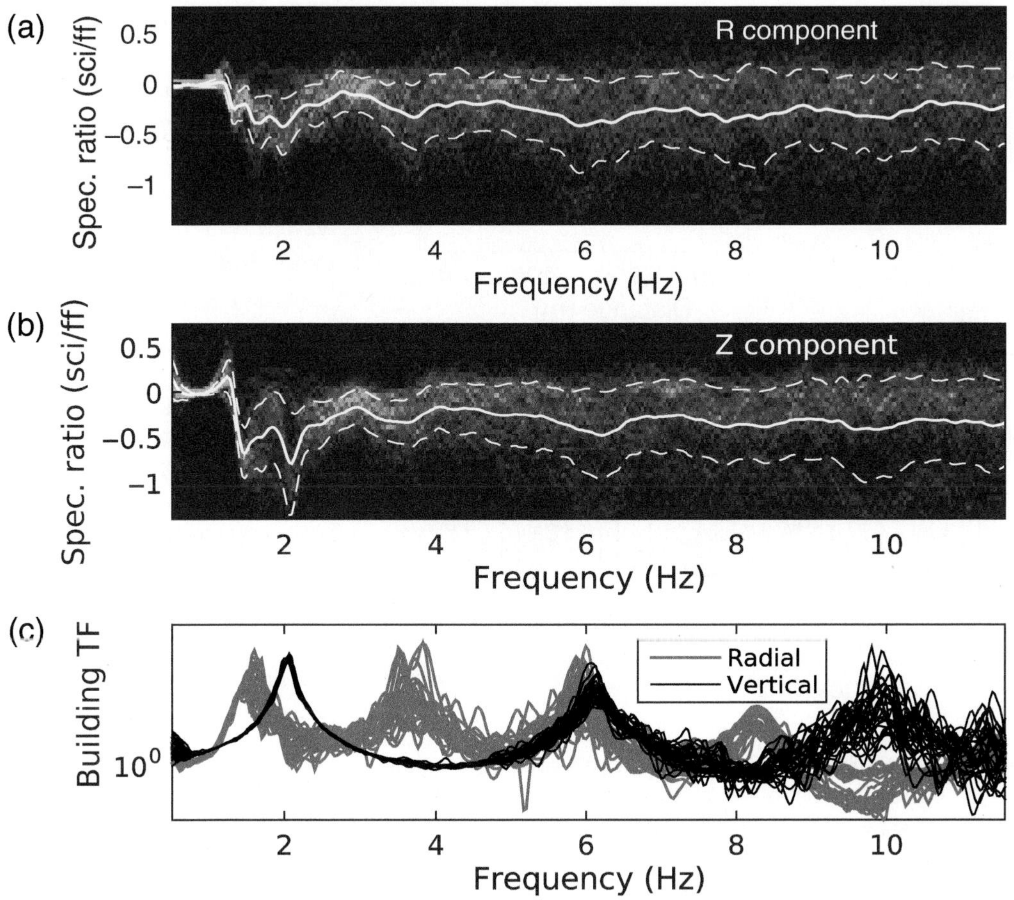

Figure 9. Band gaps and resonant frequencies: spectral ratio between the site–city interaction wavefield and that from the free-field condition for the radial (a) and vertical (b) components of the ground motion. The ensemble of spectral ratios is shown as a 2D density plot. The white solid line represents the mean spectral ratio, and the dashed lines correspond to the standard deviation. (c) Ensemble of transfer functions for all the 30 buildings for the radial (gray lines) and vertical (black lines) components of the building vibration. The color version of this figure is available only in the electronic edition.

the first radial and vertical resonances, around ~1.4 and 2 Hz, respectively. This aligns with the band gaps shown in Figure 9a, b, here represented as blue-shaded rectangles. Because frequency increases, the contribution of higher vibration modes is smaller. On the other hand, there is a noticeable convergence toward the minimum separation distance between buildings, akin to the high-frequency attenuation observed in the foundation case. The associated error bars likely reflect the level of attenuation and the underlying mechanisms. For example, the greatest uncertainty in the estimations arises at the frequencies corresponding to the first two vibration modes (1.4 and 2 Hz), and this uncertainty increases at very high frequencies.

DISCUSSION

Contribution from scattering and building dynamics

Seismic wave attenuation in media composed of resonant elements has been explored in both theoretical and observational studies (Lombaert and Clouteau, 2006; Lott *et al.*, 2020). For example, Lombaert and Clouteau (2006) modeled a city with multiple buildings of varying fundamental frequencies, acting as resonant scatterers. Their theoretical approach, based on the Dyson equation and validated by numerical simulations, provided accurate results for mean free paths and resonant scattering coefficients. However, the estimated scattering parameters in their study only accounted for the contribution of building vibrations, which were idealized as single-degree-of-freedom systems. Similarly, Lott *et al.* (2020) investigated velocity dispersion and attenuation lengths using real data from active shot experiments, examining wavefield coherence through two-point cross correlation. They attributed the loss of coherence to the presence of resonant trees in the environment.

However, attenuation was not the central focus of their work, and they did not distinguish whether the energy decay was due to kinematic or inertial interactions. In contrast, our study shows that these two mechanisms can affect the wavefield in distinct ways.

Figure 11 presents a comparison between the attenuation lengths derived from the foundation-only case and the urban cluster. This comparison clearly reveals two distinct regimes. The first, at low frequencies, shows that urban attenuation (blue) is mainly governed by building vibrations, particularly around 1.4 and 2 Hz. It is noteworthy that the urban mean free path estimations for the radial and vertical components differ slightly. Although both components are strongly influenced by the first shear (1.4 Hz) and compressional (2 Hz) building modes, attenuation is more pronounced in the vertical component. This suggests that the mode conversion from surface to body waves, also known as hybridization, may be more effective in the vertical direction, where the contribution of surface waves is higher than in the radial direction. As the frequency increases, a second regime emerges when the urban mean free path gradually approaches the scattering attenuation length. In this regime, seismic wave attenuation is predominantly controlled by the building foundations.

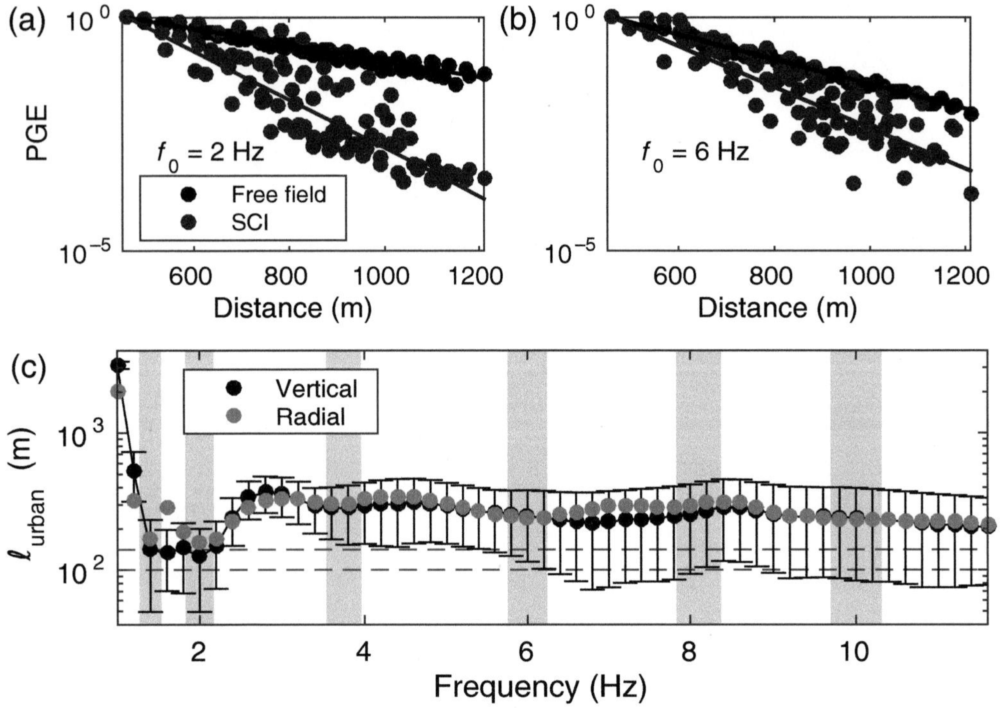

Figure 10. Fitting procedure of urban attenuation. Top: example of energy decay with distance for the vertical component at low (2 Hz) (a) and high (6 Hz) (b) frequencies (data for the radial component are shown in Fig. S2). An exponential regression (solid line) is fitted to the distance dependence of the ballistic peak (blue and black dots). Bottom (c): estimated urban mean free path (ℓ_{urb}) for the radial (gray) and vertical (black) components of the ground motion at frequencies up to 12 Hz. The shaded areas in blue correspond to the vibration modes of the buildings contributing to the urban attenuation. The dashed red lines indicate the distance between successive buildings either in *x/y* direction or diagonal. The color version of this figure is available only in the electronic edition.

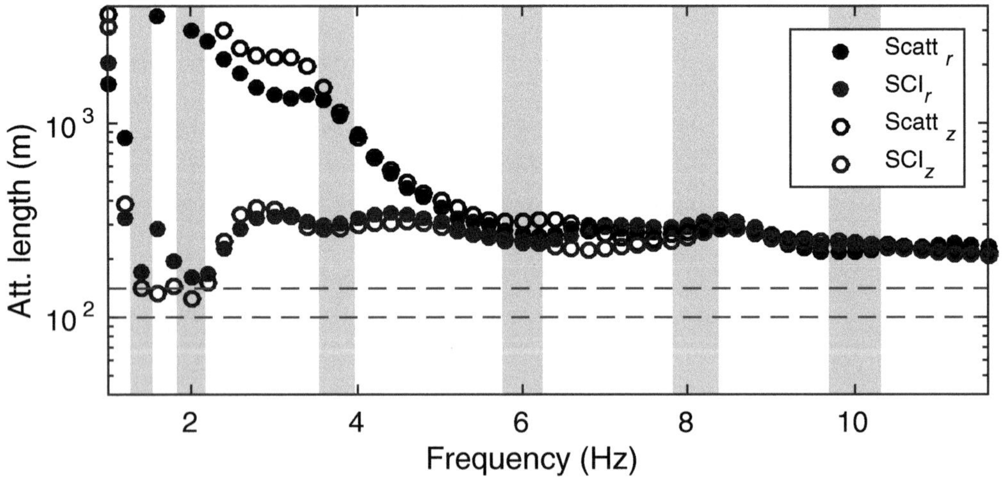

Figure 11. Comparisons of attenuation lengths between the foundation (black dots) and the building (blue dots) clusters. The shaded areas in blue correspond to the vibration modes of the buildings. The dashed red lines represent the building–foundation separations for both *x,y* directions (100 m) and the diagonal direction (141 m). The color version of this figure is available only in the electronic edition.

In highly scattering media, seismic wave attenuation is governed by either the scattering mean free path or the transport mean free path, depending on the propagation regime (Gaebler *et al.*, 2015; Celorio *et al.*, 2022). In this study, the estimated scattering attenuation length in the foundation cluster is interpreted as the scattering mean free path because the wavefield remains predominantly ballistic.

A key finding supporting this interpretation is the convergence of the scattering attenuation length (ℓ) and the urban mean free path (ℓ_{urb}) toward the diagonal separation between successive buildings. Because the incoming wavefield propagates along a diagonal direction relative to the urban cluster (~50°), collisions with buildings are more likely to occur along this diagonal path rather than along the *x*- or *y*-axes. As a result, the high-frequency ℓ_{urb} and ℓ estimations are primarily controlled by this diagonal separation. This suggests that urban mean free path estimates could vary slightly if a different azimuth between the source and the urban cluster is considered. The effects of azimuth on the seismic response of urban clusters have been previously discussed by Guéguen and Colombi (2016) for the three towers of Grenoble.

To further explore this, we simulate different urban configurations with larger separations between buildings (200, 300, and 400 m). It is worth mentioning that for these analyses, we use the same receiver location so that attenuation measurements are performed in the same area. Thus, by increasing the spacing between buildings the number of resonant scatterers is reduced. The resulting urban mean free path estimations are shown in Figure 12 for both the vertical (panel a) and radial (panel b) components (see Figs. S3 and S4, available in the supplemental material to this article, for the energy decay

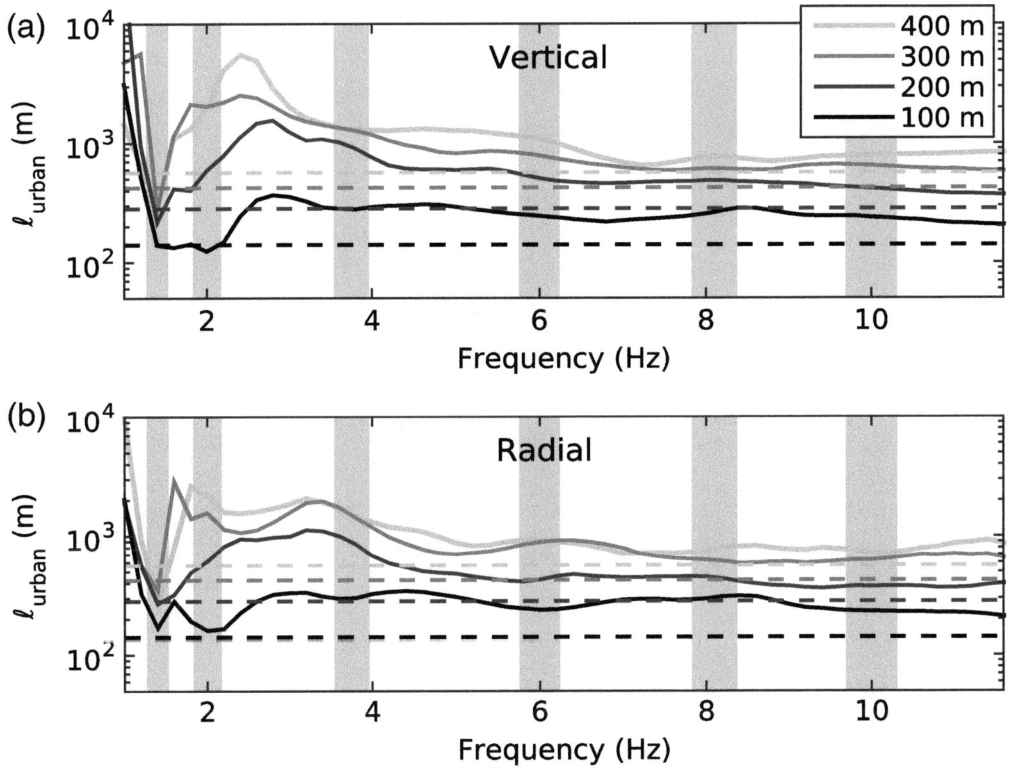

Figure 12. Urban attenuation length for different cases of building separation. The solid lines represent the estimations from the amplitude decay of the ballistic energy with distance. The dashed lines correspond to the diagonal building separation for each case. Vertical (a) and radial components (b). The color version of this figure is available only in the electronic edition.

curves at frequencies 2 and 6 Hz, respectively). For configurations with separation distances of 100, 200, and 300 m, ℓ_{urb} approaches the diagonal separation distance between buildings. This suggests that, in dense urban environments, urban attenuation at high frequencies can be roughly constrained if the typical separation between buildings is known. For the largest separation distance (400 m), attenuation becomes less frequency dependent above 8 Hz.

The low-frequency regime exhibits different behavior. The influence of the first horizontal mode (1.4 Hz) is significant regardless of the building separation. In addition, the impact of the first vertical mode (2 Hz) becomes negligible after 300 m of building separation. This could be because the seismic attenuation associated with the vertical mode is more localized, meaning it is more effective in denser configurations and less so in areas where buildings are more widely spaced. Overall, all the attenuation curves share a similar shape: low-frequency attenuation related to building vibrations and a more stable attenuation behavior at higher frequencies, which converges toward the separation distance between buildings.

Spatial variability of ground motion

Quantifying the spatial variability of earthquake ground motion is crucial for improving seismic hazard and risk assessments, particularly in heterogeneous sites (Yoshimoto *et al.*, 2015) or near-fault regions (Infantino *et al.*, 2021; Schiappapietra and Smerzini, 2021). From a scattering perspective, the level of variability in the ballistic or quasi-ballistic wavefield is closely tied to the propagation regime. It has been shown that a coherent-ballistic regime persists when spatial fluctuations of the wavefield are small. In contrast, because the wavefield fluctuates more significantly in space, the noncoherent and multiple diffusion regimes emerge (Yoshimoto *et al.*, 2015; Emoto and Sato, 2018; Celorio *et al.*, 2022).

In engineering seismology, Infantino *et al.* (2021) assessed spatial variability by analyzing the response spectra of numerically simulated earthquake ground motions in the near field. They used empirical semivariograms of pseudospectral accelerations to quantify the variability. By comparing dissimilarities between receiver pairs at various separation distances, they tested different models—exponential, Gaussian, and spherical—to constrain variability parameters such as the range and sill, with the latter representing the distance at which ground motion becomes uncorrelated.

Yoshimoto *et al.* (2015) studied the effects of a highly heterogeneous crust on wavefield fluctuations for different hypocentral distances. Using numerical simulations, analytical models, and real data, they observed that fluctuations increased significantly as both frequency and propagation distance grew. Like Infantino *et al.* (2021), they found that the variance of dissimilarities between receivers saturated after a certain propagation distance.

In seismic hazard analyses, ground motion at each site is typically modeled as a lognormal variable, reflecting the empirical observation that the logarithm of peak ground-motion amplitudes tends to follow a normal distribution. This behavior is generally associated with a predominantly coherent wavefield, such as direct body waves, in which recorded peak amplitudes at common source–site distances exhibit relatively low variability. However, statistical studies of ballistic waves in random media (Emoto and Sato, 2018; Celorio *et al.*, 2022) have shown that this assumption breaks down beyond certain propagation distances. In these cases, an exponential distribution—characteristic of a noncoherent wavefield—better fits the observed data. These studies reveal the diffusive nature of what may initially appear to be coherent ballistic waves. Furthermore, Celorio *et al.* (2022) demonstrated that the transition from a log-normal to an exponential regime is governed by the scattering mean free path, thereby establishing a clear link between the scattering attenuation properties of heterogeneous media and the spatial variability of ground motion.

In this section, we apply these concepts to evaluate the spatial variability of ground motion generated by site–city interactions, which include building vibrations, foundation scattering, or both. To quantify this variability, we measure the dissimilarity between different receivers (i, j) with common propagation distances (r). These distances are corrected to account for the relative position within the urban cluster region, and we compute dissimilarities as follows:

$$\gamma(r) = \frac{2}{N(r)(N(r)-1)} \sum_{j=1}^{N(r)} \sum_{i=j+1}^{N(r)} \left[\log\left(\frac{E_i(r)}{E_j(r)} \right) \right]^2, \tag{9}$$

in which $N(r)$ is the number of receivers with a common propagation distance r and the ratio $E_i(r)/E_j(r)$ represents the dissimilarity between the ballistic energies $E(r)$ recorded at receivers i and j, both having the same propagation distance. The first term before the sum accounts for the total number of possible receiver combinations at a given distance r. We calculate $\gamma(r)$ in bins of 40 m with an overlap of 20 m. For a wavefield exhibiting a certain level of spatial variability, the first regime is characterized by amplitudes in which variability increases linearly with distance. A second regime typically emerges as a plateau after a certain propagation distance, when the ground motion becomes uncorrelated. Conversely, when spatial variability is negligible, $\gamma(r)$ remains small and does not change systematically with the propagation distance.

After dissimilarities are measured using equation (9), a function (or model) that appropriately fits the data must be selected. For convenience, we use the Gaussian model in this study, as follows:

$$\gamma_g(r) = a[1 - \exp(-3r^2/B^2)], \tag{10}$$

in which a is the range of the random process and B is the sill, which represents the propagation distance after which the variability becomes uncorrelated with distance. To estimate a and B, we perform a least-squares fit over a 2D grid search. The search range for a is between 0.1 and 100, and for B, it extends up to 700 m.

In Figure 13a–c, we present the empirical dissimilarities $\gamma(r)$ as a function of distance r (black dots) for central frequencies of 2, 6, and 11 Hz. The best-fit Gaussian variograms are shown as red solid lines, with the correlation length B marked by the vertical gray line. To illustrate the potential relationship with the attenuation lengths (urban and scattering), we also show ℓ_{scatt} (red dashed) and ℓ_{urb} (blue solid). This example is for the vertical component (see Fig. S5 for the radial component).

At low frequency (2 Hz), which corresponds to the first vertical mode of the buildings, the dissimilarities become nearly independent of distance at shorter propagation distances. In this case, the urban attenuation length is one of the shortest, and it appears to be close to the correlation length B. Similarly, at high frequencies (6 and 11 Hz), the dissimilarities show a more developed shape, transitioning from distance dependent to uncorrelated variability. In both cases, the correlation length closely matches the attenuation lengths.

To more systematically illustrate the proximity between the correlation length and the attenuation lengths, we present (Fig. 13d) the ratio of B to the attenuation lengths ℓ_{urb} (blue circles) and ℓ_{scatt} (red circles). This calculation is performed for both the vertical (circles) and radial (dots) components. We observe that between 1 and 4 Hz, the correlation length remains similar to ℓ_{urb}, whereas at frequencies between 4 and 7 Hz, the similarities with ℓ_{urb} become more pronounced. At higher frequencies, there is no distinction between the scattering and urban lengths. This indicates that (1) at low frequencies, the variability of the ground motion is primarily dominated by the vibrations of the building cluster, and (2) at high frequencies, the variability is primarily driven by foundation scattering.

From the perspective of seismic scattering, the mean free path (ℓ) not only represents the typical distance between two successive scattering events but also plays a crucial role in controlling the attenuation length of the coherent wave. The coherent wave is defined as the portion of the wavefield that retains the memory of the initial propagation direction of the seismic energy. In our study, both ℓ and ℓ_{urb} appear to be close to the point where the wavefield transitions from distance dependent to uncorrelated variability. This transition can be interpreted as a shift in the propagation regime, from coherent to noncoherent wave behavior. This observation aligns with the findings of Celorio *et al.* (2022), who similarly demonstrated that the transition from a lognormal to an exponential distribution of the ballistic wavefield is governed by the scattering mean free path.

CONCLUSIONS

Although various physical processes involved in site–city interaction have been investigated, such as building responses, velocity dispersion, and ground-motion duration, seismic wave attenuation remains, in our view, insufficiently estimated and understood. In this study, we present a numerical simulation-based analysis focusing on the amplitude decay of ballistic waves. The contributions of various site–city interaction mechanisms were quantified and interpreted in terms of attenuation lengths and spatial variability.

We conducted three sets of simulations: (1) free-field conditions, (2) considering only the foundations as scatterers, and

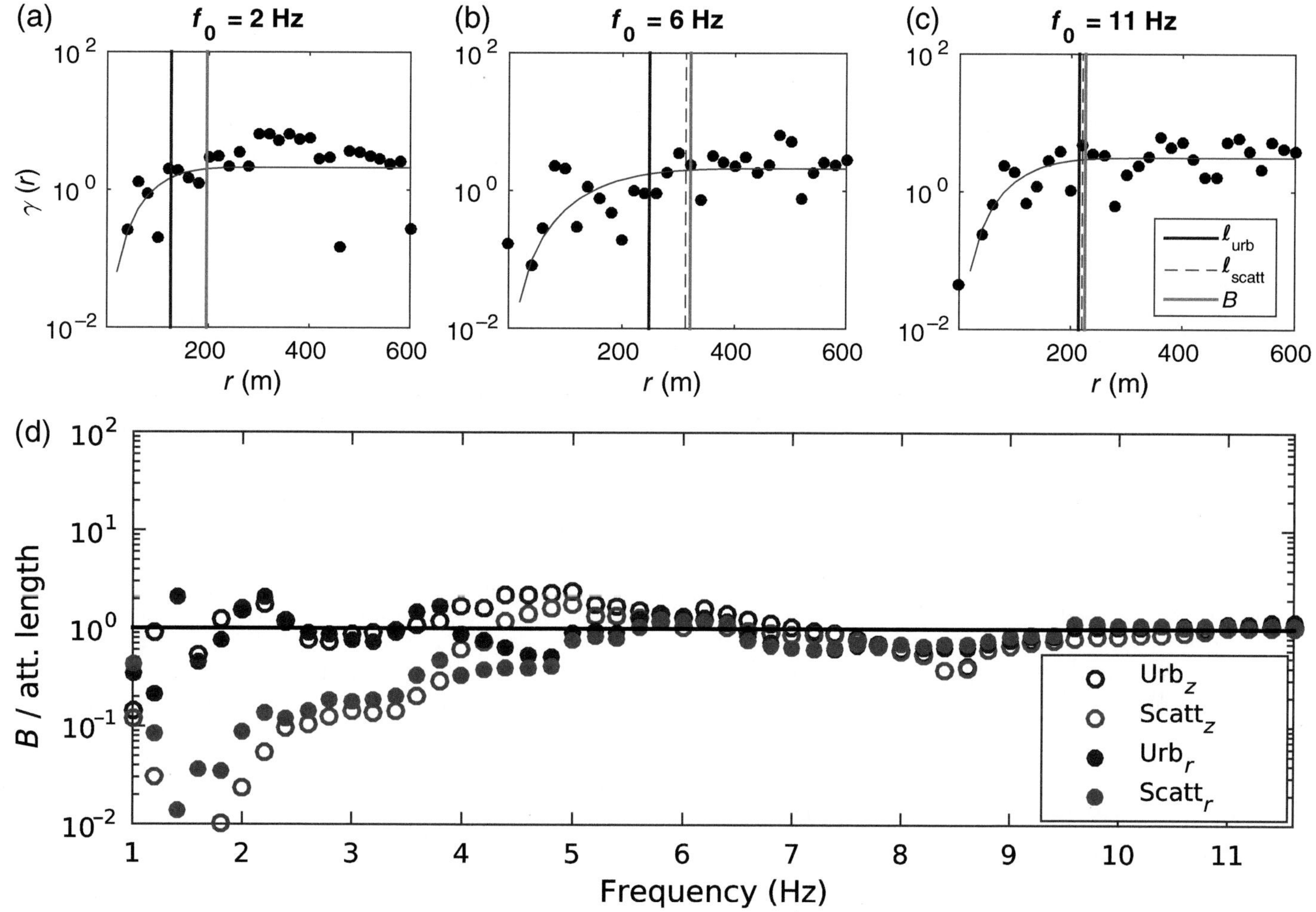

Figure 13. Spatial variability of ground motion. Top: example of empirical dissimilarities (black dots) and Gaussian variograms (red solid line) for the vertical component. (The example for the radial component is shown in Fig. S5.) This is shown for the wavefield at 2 Hz (a), 6 Hz (b), and 11 Hz (c). Vertical lines correspond to different length scales of interest: urban mean free path (blue), scattering mean free path (red dashed) and correlation length (gray). Bottom: (d) ratios between the correlation length and the scattering (red) and the urban (blue) mean free paths. The dots correspond to the radial component, and the circles represent the vertical component of the ground motion. The color version of this figure is available only in the electronic edition.

(3) including the entire system of site–foundation–structure interactions. Our analyses revealed two distinct attenuation regimes across frequencies. At low frequencies, attenuation is governed by the building dynamics, particularly their first vibration modes, leading to band-gap behavior through mode conversion between surface and body waves. At higher frequencies, attenuation is dominated by scattering from foundations, with the attenuation length converging toward the building separation distance, which can be interpreted as the scattering mean free path.

By analyzing the spatial variability of ground motion, we estimated correlation lengths that represent the distance beyond which the ground motion becomes uncorrelated. These estimations suggests that the correlation length is controlled by the urban mean free path, indicating that the loss of coherency in the wavefield arises mainly from interactions with the buildings. This provides a practical approach to quantifying urban attenuation from ground-motion variability, without the need for prior quantification of intrinsic absorption.

Although our simulations were conducted in an idealized, homogeneous urban environment, this approach allowed us to isolate the fundamental mechanisms underlying seismic attenuation in cities. Real urban settings exhibit heterogeneity in building heights, densities, and subsurface conditions, but the main findings—particularly the frequency-dependent attenuation and its link to spatial variability—are expected to be broadly applicable. The framework introduced here can thus guide future studies incorporating more realistic variability to better assess seismic risk in specific cities.

From a broader perspective, this study introduces the concept of urban attenuation, a previously unexplored mechanism of seismic energy loss in cities arising from the collective response of buildings and their foundations. Although intrinsic absorption (Q_i) and scattering (Q_{sc}) have been extensively studied in volcanic and tectonic contexts, urban environments require the inclusion of an additional term. We formalize this extended framework as $Q^{-1} = Q_i^{-1} + Q_{sc}^{-1} + Q_{urb}^{-1}$, in which Q_{urb}^{-1} captures the attenuation associated with site–city interactions. This formulation provides a physically grounded metric for quantifying the decay of ballistic wave energy in urban areas and highlights the role of buildings as active contributors to seismic attenuation. We therefore propose extending the classical framework of seismic attenuation to explicitly account for this urban contribution.

DATA AND RESOURCES

Numerical simulations of seismic waves in urban environments were performed using the EFISPEC3D code (http://efispec.free.fr), and the computational domain was discretized through the CUBIT software package (https://cubit.sandia.gov). Both websites were last accessed in July 2024. Because most of the illustrative examples of ballistic wavefield evolution within the urban and foundation clusters are shown for the vertical component of ground motion, we include in the supplemental material the corresponding results for the radial component, which exhibit similar behavior. Specifically, Figures S1 and S2 show the amplitude decay in the foundation and urban clusters, respectively. Similarly, Figures S3 and S4 present the amplitude decay of the ballistic wavefields for all building separation distances (200, 300, and 400 m). In addition, Figure S5 shows the spatial variability at three central frequencies (2, 6, and 11 Hz) for the radial component.

DECLARATION OF COMPETING INTERESTS

The authors acknowledge that there are no conflicts of interest recorded.

ACKNOWLEDGMENTS

This work was performed within the framework of the ANR project E-City, Grant Number ANR-21-CE22-0020. P. G. thanks LabEx OSUG@2020 (Investissements d'avenir-ANR10LABX56). The authors acknowledge the fruitful discussions with Ssu-Ting Lai, Alessandra Schibuola, and Joseph Grand. The authors also thank the two anonymous reviewers for their constructive comments that helped improve this article.

REFERENCES

Aki, K., and B. Chouet (1975). Origin of coda waves: Source, attenuation, and scattering effects, *J. Geophys. Res.* **80,** no. 23, 3322–3342.

Bard, P.-Y., K. Nakano, E. Ito, J. Sun, Z. Wang, and H. Kawase (2025). From site response to site-city interaction: A case study in the Tokyo area, doi: 10.48550/arXiv.2502.09976.

Carcole, E., and H. Sato (2010). Spatial distribution of scattering loss and intrinsic absorption of short-period waves in the lithosphere of japan on the basis of the multiple lapse time window analysis of hi-net data, *Geophys. J. Int.* **180,** no. 1, 268–290.

Celorio, M., E. Chaljub, L. Margerin, and L. Stehly (2022). Propagation of 2-d SH waves in random media: Insights from ab initio numerical simulations and transport theory, *Front. Earth Sci.* **10,** doi: 10.3389/feart.2022.1033109.

Celorio, M., L. Stehly, and E. Chaljub (2025). A full-envelope based approach to estimate absorption and scattering attenuation from seismic ambient noise, *Geophys. J. Int.* **242,** doi: 10.1093/gji/ggaf209.

Chaljub, E., M. Celorio, C. Cornou, F. De Martin, E. El Haber, L. Margerin, J. Marti, and I. Zentner (2021). Numerical simulation of wave propagation in heterogeneous and random media for site effects assessment in the Grenoble valley, *Sixth IASPEI/IAEE International Symposium on the Effects of Surface Geology on Seismic Motion*, August 2021, Kyoto, Japan.

Chaljub, E., D. Komatitsch, J.-P. Vilotte, Y. Capdeville, B. Valette, and G. Festa (2007). Spectral-element analysis in seismology, in *Advances in Wave Propagation in Heterogenous Earth*, Elsevier, Amsterdam, The Netherlands, 365–419.

Colombi, A., P. Roux, S. Guenneau, P. Gueguen, and R. V. Craster (2016). Forests as a natural seismic metamaterial: Rayleigh wave bandgaps induced by local resonances, *Sci. Rep.* **6,** no. 1, 19,238.

Cornou, C., P. Gueguen, P.-Y. Bard, and E. Haghshenas (2004). Ambient noise energy bursts observation and modeling: Trapping of harmonic structure-soil induced–waves in a topmost sedimentary layer, *J. Seismol.* **8,** 507–524.

Day, S. M., and J. B. Minster (1984). Numerical simulation of attenuated wavefields using a Pade approximant method, *Geophys. J. Int.* **78,** no. 1, 105–118.

De Martin, F. (2011). Verification of a spectral-element method code for the southern California earthquake center loh.3 viscoelastic case, *Bull. Seismol. Soc. Am.* **101,** no. 6, 2855–2865.

Emmerich, H., and M. Korn (1987). Incorporation of attenuation into time-domain computations of seismic wave fields, *Geophysics* **52,** no. 9, 1252–1264.

Emoto, K., and H. Sato (2018). Statistical characteristics of scattered waves in three-dimensional random media: Comparison of the finite difference simulation and statistical methods, *Geophys. J. Int.* **215,** no. 1, 585–599.

Fehler, M., M. Hoshiba, H. Sato, and K. Obara (1992). Separation of scattering and intrinsic attenuation for the Kanto-Tokai region, Japan, using measurements of S-wave energy versus hypocentral distance, *Geophys. J. Int.* **108,** no. 3, 787–800.

Gaebler, P. J., T. Eulenfeld, and U. Wegler (2015). Seismic scattering and absorption parameters in the W-Bohemia/Vogtland region from elastic and acoustic radiative transfer theory, *Geophys. J. Int.* **203,** no. 3, 1471–1481.

Guéguen, P., and A. Colombi (2016). Experimental and numerical evidence of the clustering effect of structures on their response during an earthquake: A case study of three identical towers in the city of Grenoble, France, *Bull. Seismol. Soc. Am.* **106,** no. 6:2855–2864.

Guéguen, P., P.-Y. Bard, and F. J. Chávez-García (2002). Site-city seismic interaction in Mexico city–like environments: An analytical study, *Bull. Seismol. Soc. Am.* **92,** no. 2, 794–811.

Gueguen, P., P.-Y. Bard, and C. S. Oliveira (2000). Experimental and numerical analysis of soil motions caused by free vibrations of a building model, *Bull. Seismol. Soc. Am.* **90,** no. 6, 1464–1479.

Guéguen, P., E. D. Mercerat, J. C. Singaucho, C. Aubert, J. G. Barros, L. F. Bonilla, M. Cripstyani, I. Douste-Bacqué, P. Langlaude, S. Mercier, *et al.* (2019). Metacity-Quito: A semi-dense urban seismic network deployed to analyze the concept of metamaterial for the future design of seismic-proof cities, *Seismol. Res. Lett.* **90,** no. 6, 2318–2326.

Hartzell, S., S. Harmsen, and A. Frankel (2010). Effects of 3D random correlated velocity perturbations on predicted ground motions, *Bull. Seismol. Soc. Am.* **100,** no. 4, 1415–1426.

Hirose, T., H. Nakahara, and T. Nishimura (2019). A passive estimation method of scattering and intrinsic absorption parameters from envelopes of seismic ambient noise cross-correlation functions, *Geophys. Res. Lett.* **46,** no. 7, 3634–3642.

Ichimura, T., K. Fujita, P. E. B. Quinay, L. Maddegedara, M. Hori, S. Tanaka, Y. Shizawa, H. Kobayashi, and K. Minami (2015). Implicit nonlinear wave simulation with 1.08t dof and 0.270t unstructured finite elements to enhance comprehensive earthquake simulation, *Proc. of the International Conf. for High Performance Computing, Networking, Storage and Analysis*, 1–12.

Infantino, M., C. Smerzini, and J. Lin (2021). Spatial correlation of broadband ground motions from physics-based numerical simulations, *Earthq. Eng. Struct. Dynam.* **50,** no. 10.2575–2594.

Isbiliroglu, Y., R. Taborda, and J. Bielak (2015). Coupled soil-structure interaction effects of building clusters during earthquakes, *Earthq. Spectra* **31,** no. 1, 463–500.

Jennings, P. C. (1970). Distant motions from a building vibration test, *Bull. Seismol. Soc. Am.* **60,** no. 6, 2037–2043.

Kato, B., and G. Wang (2022). Seismic site–city interaction analysis of super-tall buildings surrounding an underground station: A case study in Hong Kong, *Bull. Earthq. Eng.* **20,** no. 3, 1431–1454.

Kausel, E. (2010). Early history of soil–structure interaction, *Soil Dynam. Earthq. Eng.* **30,** no. 9, 822–832.

Kham, M., J.-F. Semblat, P.-Y. Bard, and P. Dangla (2006). Seismic site-city interaction: Main governing phenomena through simplified numerical models, *Bull. Seismol. Soc. Am.* **96,** no. 5, 1934–1951.

Komatitsch, D., and J.-P. Vilotte (1998). The spectral element method: An efficient tool to simulate the seismic response of 2D and 3D geological structures, *Bull. Seismol. Soc. Am.* **88,** 368–392.

Laurenzano, G., E. Priolo, M. R. Gallipoli, M. Mucciarelli, and F. C. Ponzo (2010). Effect of vibrating buildings on free-field motion and on adjacent structures: The Bonefro (Italy) case history, *Bull. Seismol. Soc. Am.* **100,** no. 2, 802–818.

Lombaert, G., and D. Clouteau (2006). Resonant multiple wave scattering in the seismic response of a city, *Waves Random Complex Medium* **16,** no. 3, 205–230.

Lott, M., P. Roux, S. Garambois, P. Guéguen, and A. Colombi (2020). Evidence of metamaterial physics at the geophysics scale: The METAFORET experiment, *Geophys. J. Int.* **220,** no. 2, 1330–1339.

Margerin, L., M. Campillo, and B. Tiggelen (1998). Radiative transfer and diffusion of waves in a layered medium: New insight into coda Q, *Geophys. J. Int.* **134,** no. 2, 596–612.

Paasschens, J. (1997). Solution of the time-dependent Boltzmann equation, *Phys. Rev. E* **56,** no. 1, 1135.

Pilz, M., P. Roux, S. A. Mohammed, R. F. Garcia, R. Steinmann, C. Aubert, F. Bernauer, P. Guéguen, M. Ohrnberger, and F. Cotton (2024). Wind turbines as a metamaterial-like urban layer: An experimental investigation using a dense seismic array and complementary sensing technologies, *Front. Earth Sci.* **12,** doi: 10.3389/feart.2024.1352027.

Roux, P., D. Bindi, T. Boxberger, A. Colombi, F. Cotton, I. Douste-Bacque, S. Garambois, P. Gueguen, G. Hillers, D. Hollis, *et al.* (2018). Toward seismic metamaterials: The metaforet project, *Seismol. Res. Lett.* **89,** no. 2A, 582–593.

Rupin, M., F. Lemoult, G. Lerosey, and P. Roux (2014). Experimental demonstration of ordered and disordered multiresonant metamaterials for lamb waves, *Phys. Rev. Lett.* **112,** no. 23, 234,301.

Schiappapietra, E., and C. Smerzini (2021). Spatial correlation of broadband earthquake ground motion in Norcia (central Italy) from physics-based simulations, *Bull. Earthq. Eng.* **19,** no. 12, 4693–4717.

Semblat, J.-F., M. Kham, and P.-Y. Bard (2008). Seismic-wave propagation in alluvial basins and influence of site-city interaction, *Bull. Seismol. Soc. Am.* **98,** no. 6, 2665–2678.

Soto, V., E. Sáez, and C. Magna-Verdugo (2020). Numerical modeling of 3d site-city effects including partially embedded buildings using spectral element methods. Application to the case of Viña del Mar city, Chile, *Eng. Struct.* **223,** 111,188.

Stewart, J. P., and G. L. Fenves (1998). System identification for evaluating soil–structure interaction effects in buildings from strong motion recordings, *Earthq. Eng. Struct. Dynam.* **27,** no. 8, 869–885.

Taborda, R., and J. Bielak (2011). Full 3d integration of site-city effects in regional scale earthquake simulations, *Proc. of the 8th International Conf. on Structural Dynamics*, Leuven Belgium, 511–518.

Tchawe, F. N., C. Gelis, L. F. Bonilla, and F. Lopez-Caballero (2021). Effects of 2-D random velocity perturbations on 2-D SH short-period ground motion simulations in the basin of Nice, France, *Geophys. J. Int.* **226,** no. 2, 847–861.

Wirgin, A., and P.-Y. Bard (1996). Effects of buildings on the duration and amplitude of ground motion in Mexico city, *Bull. Seismol. Soc. Am.* **86,** no. 3, 914–920.

Wu, R.-S. (1982). Mean field attenuation and amplitude attenuation due to wave scattering, *Wave Motion* **4,** no. 3, 305–316.

Wu, R.-S. (1985). Multiple scattering and energy transfer of seismic waves—separation of scattering effect from intrinsic attenuation—I. Theoretical modelling, *Geophys. J. Int.* **82,** no. 1, 57–80.

Yoshimoto, K., S. Takemura, and M. Kobayashi (2015). Application of scattering theory to p-wave amplitude fluctuations in the crust, *Earth Planets Space* **67,** 1–15.

Manuscript received 3 June 2025
Published online 22 October 2025

Erratum to Enhancing V_{S30} Mapping in the Taipei Basin: Integrating New V_S Estimation Functions, Extrapolated V_S Profiles, and Kriging with Varying Local Means

Stefan C. Nicholas[1], Linh Thi Mai Nguyen[1], Chun-Liang Kuo[1], Jia-Cian Gao[1,2,3], Chun-Hsiang Kuo[*2,4,5], Duc-Huy Tran[1], Shih-Jung Wang[1], and Jia-Jyun Dong[1,2,4,6]

There was an oversight in licensing acknowledgment in the caption of figure 2 of the original article (Nicholas *et al.*, 2025). The figure was reused from a previous article (Su *et al.*, 2018), and the license requires that the acknowledgment of reuse be given. A statement is added in the figure caption as an acknowledgment.

The corrected caption of Figure 2 is "(a) Tectonic setting of Taiwan (from Su *et al.*, 2018). (b) Geological provinces within the Taipei basin area (modified from Su *et al.*, 2018). The black line outlines the extent of the Taipei basin. Figure reprinted from Su *et al.* (2018), with permission from Elsevier and International Union for Quaternary Research (INQUA)." Figure 2 itself is not modified in this erratum.

REFERENCES

Nicholas, S. C., L. T. M. Nguyen, C. L. Kuo, J. C. Gao, C. H. Kuo, D. H. Tran, S. J. Wang, and J. J. Dong (2025). Enhancing mapping in the Taipei basin: Integrating new estimation functions, extrapolated profiles, and kriging with varying local means, *Bull. Seismol. Soc. Am.* **115,** 2439–2463, doi: 10.1785/0120250020.

Su, P. J., A. T. S. Lin, J. C. Hu, and L. S. Y. Teng (2018). Tectonic controls on the stratigraphic development of the rifted Taipei Basin: A late quaternary marine-influenced inland half graben, *Quaternary Int.* **482,** 27–45.

1. Graduate Institute of Applied Geology, National Central University, Taoyuan, Taiwan, https://orcid.org/0009-0003-6537-4505 (LTMN); https://orcid.org/0009-0005-6325-7414 (C-LK); https://orcid.org/0000-0001-7870-8496 (D-HT); https://orcid.org/0000-0002-7616-2343 (S-JW); https://orcid.org/0000-0003-4287-7719 (J-JD); 2. Earthquake-Disaster and Risk Evaluation and Management Center, National Central University, Taoyuan, Taiwan, https://orcid.org/0000-0003-4602-385X (C-HK); 3. Graduate College of Sustainability and Green Energy, National Central University, Taoyuan, Taiwan; 4. Department of Earth Sciences, National Central University, Taoyuan, Taiwan; 5. National Center for Research on Earthquake Engineering, Taoyuan, Taiwan; 6. Center for Environmental Studies, National Central University, Taoyuan, Taiwan

*Corresponding author: chkuo@ncu.edu.tw

Cite this erratum as Nicholas, S. C., L. T. M. Nguyen, C.-L. Kuo, J.-C. Gao, C.-H. Kuo, D.-H. Tran, S.-J. Wang, and J.-J. Dong (2025). *Erratum to* Enhancing V_{S30} Mapping in the Taipei Basin: Integrating New V_S Estimation Functions, Extrapolated V_S Profiles, and Kriging with Varying Local Means, *Bull. Seismol. Soc. Am.* **116,** 532–533, doi: 10.1785/0120250224

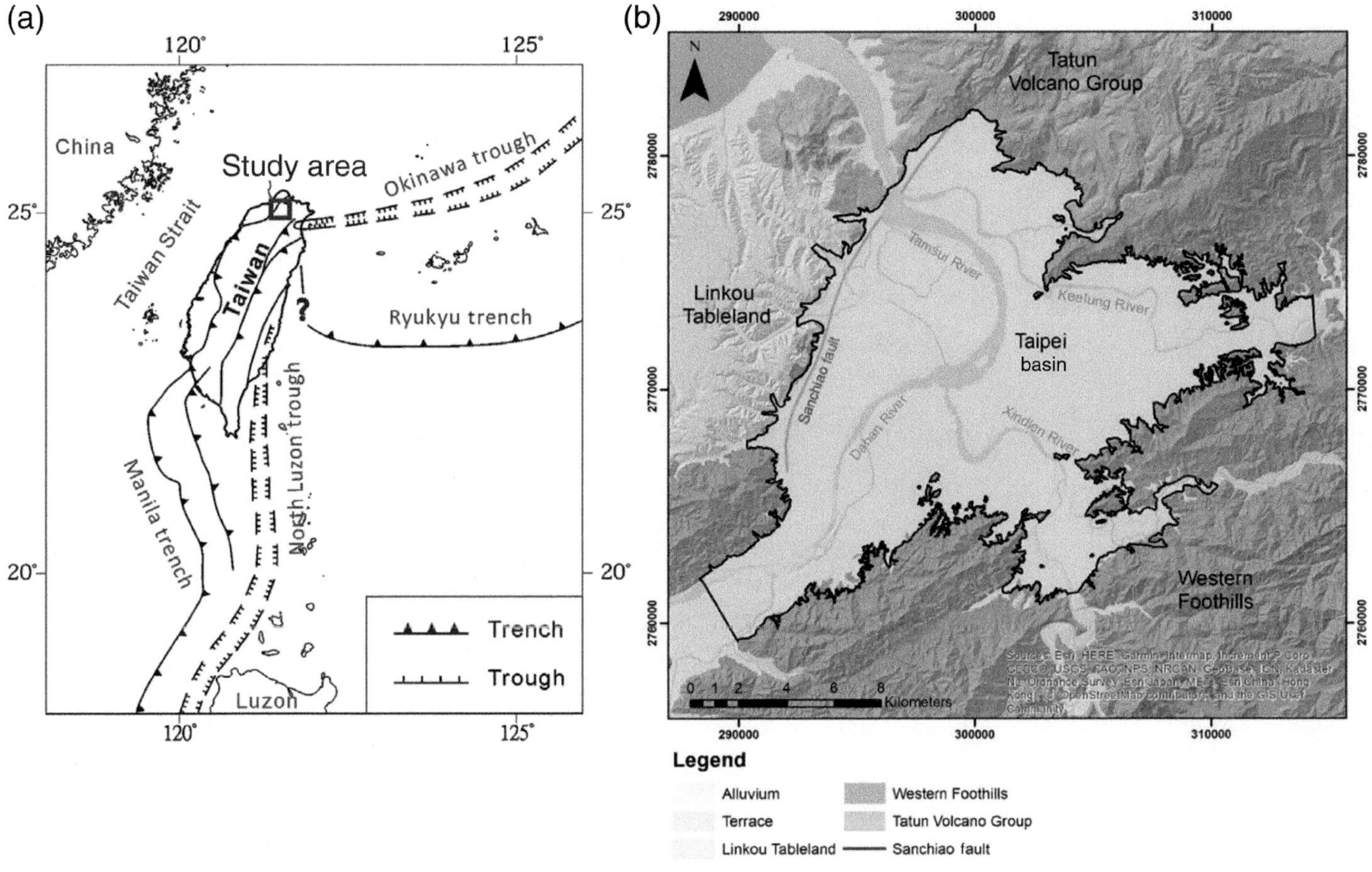

Figure 2. (a) Tectonic setting of Taiwan (from Su *et al.*, 2018). (b) Geological provinces within the Taipei basin area (modified from Su *et al.*, 2018). The black line outlines the extent of the Taipei basin. Figure reprinted from Su *et al.* (2018), with permission from Elsevier and International Union for Quaternary Research (INQUA). The color version of this figure is available only in the electronic edition.

Manuscript received 15 September 2025
Published online 8 October 2025

The Seismological Society of America is an international scientific society devoted to the advancement of seismology and the understanding of earthquakes for the benefit of society.

www.seismosoc.org
www.bssaonline.org

SSA
Seismological Society of America